SRA Open Court Reading

Level 5   Book 1

Cooperation and Competition
•
Back Through the Stars
•
Heritage

Program Authors

Carl Bereiter
Ann Brown
Joe Campione
Iva Carruthers
Robbie Case
Jan Hirshberg
Marilyn Jager Adams
Anne McKeough
Michael Pressley
Marsha Roit
Marlene Scardamalia
Gerald H. Treadway, Jr.

SRA

A Division of The McGraw-Hill Companies

Columbus, Ohio

Acknowledgments

Leonard Baskin: Illustrations from ALBERIC THE WISE AND OTHER JOURNEYS by Norton Juster, illustrated by Leonard Baskin. Reprinted with permission of Leonard Baskin.

Curtis Brown, Ltd.: "The West Side" by Peggy Mann. Copyright © 1972 by Peggy Mann. First appeared in *How Juan Got Home*. Published by Coward-McCann. Reprinted by permission of Curtis Brown, Ltd.

Clarion Books/Houghton Mifflin Company.: "Half Slave and Half Free" from LINCOLN: A Photobiography. Copyright © 1987 by Russell Freedman. Reprinted by permission of Clarion Books/Houghton Mifflin Company. All rights reserved. "So I Became a Soldier," from THE BOYS' WAR by Jim Murphy. Text copyright © 1990 by Jim Murphy. Reprinted by permission of Clarion Books/Houghton Mifflin Company. All rights reserved. VOYAGER TO THE PLANETS by Necia H. Apfel. Copyright © 1991 by Necia H. Apfel. Reprinted by permission of Clarion Books/Houghton Mifflin Company. All rights reserved.

Frances Collin, Literary Agent: "A Meeting in Space" from BARBARY by Vonda N. McIntyre. Reprinted by permission of Frances Collin, Literary Agent. Copyright © 1986 by Vonda N. McIntyre.

Dial Books for Young Readers, a division of Penguin Putnam Inc.: "Emancipation" from TO BE A SLAVE by Julius Lester. Copyright © 1968 by Julius Lester. Used by permission of Dial Books for Young Readers, a division of Penguin Putnam Inc. TANYA'S REUNION by Valerie Flournoy, illustrated by Jerry Pinkney. Copyright © 1995 by Valerie Flournoy, text. Copyright © 1995 by Jerry Pinkney, illustrations. Used by permission of Dial Books for Young Readers, a division of Penguin Putnam Inc.

Dutton Children's Books, a division of Penguin Putnam Inc.: "The Flower-Fed Buffaloes," from GOING TO THE STARS by Vachel Lindsay. Copyright © 1926 by D. Appleton & Co., renewed 1954 by Elizabeth C. Lindsay. A Hawthorn Book. Used by permission of Dutton Children's Books, a division of Penguin Putnam Inc.

Farrar, Straus & Giroux, Inc.: "The Great Dog" and "The Scorpion" from THE HEAVENLY ZOO: LEGENDS AND TALES OF THE STARS by Alison Lurie, pictures by Monika Beisner. Text copyright © 1979 by Alison Lurie. Illustrations copyright © 1979 by Monika Beisner. Reprinted by permission of Farrar, Straus & Giroux, Inc. "When Shlemiel Went to Warsaw" from WHEN SHLEMIEL WENT TO WARSAW AND OTHER STORIES by Isaac Bashevis Singer. Copyright © 1968 by Isaac Bashevis Singer. Reprinted by permission of Farrar, Straus & Giroux, Inc.

Fulcrum Publishing, Inc.: From THE ABACUS CONTEST by Priscilla Wu. Text copyright © 1996 by Priscilla Wu. Reprinted with permission of Fulcrum Publishing, Inc.

Donna Gamache: "Juggling" by Donna Gamache, from Cricket, The Magazine for Children, Vol. 21, No. 10. Copyright © 1994 by Donna Gamache. Reprinted with permission of Donna Gamache.

Greenwillow Books, a division of William Morrow & Company, Inc.: MCBROOM AND THE RAINMAKER from HERE COMES MCBROOM! by Sid Fleischman. Text copyright © 1973 by Sid Fleischman. By permission of Greenwillow Books, a division of William Morrow & Company, Inc..

Harcourt Brace & Company: Text from BILL PICKETT: RODEO RIDIN' COWBOY, copyright © 1996 by Andrea Davis Pinkney, reprinted by permission of Harcourt Brace & Company. "The Marble Champ" from BASEBALL IN APRIL AND OTHER STORIES, copyright © 1990 by Gary Soto, reprinted by permission of Harcourt Brace & Company. "Women" from REVOLUTIONARY PETUNIAS AND OTHER POEMS, copyright © 1970 by Alice Walker, reprinted by permission of Harcourt Brace & Company.

HarperCollins Publishers: "CHINATOWN" from CHILD OF THE OWL by LAURENCE YEP. COPYRIGHT © 1977 BY LAURENCE YEP. Used by permission of HarperCollins Publishers. "HARRIET TUBMAN" from HONEY, I LOVE by ELOISE GREENFIELD. TEXT COPYRIGHT © 1978 BY ELOISE GREENFIELD. Used by permission of HarperCollins Publishers. "OPERA AND KARATE" from THE LAND I LOST by HUYNH QUANG NHUONG. TEXT COPYRIGHT © 1982 BY HUYNH QUANG NHUONG. Used by permission of HarperCollins Publishers. "PARMELE" from CHILDTIMES: A THREE-GENERATION MEMOIR by ELOISE GREENFIELD. COPYRIGHT © 1979 BY ELOISE GREENFIELD AND LESSIE JONES LITTLE. Used by permission of HarperCollins Publishers. "THE SEARCH" from ...AND NOW MIGUEL by JOSEPH KRUMGOLD. COPYRIGHT © 1953 BY JOSEPH KRUMGOLD. Used by permission of HarperCollins Publishers. "STORKS" from THE WHEEL ON THE SCHOOL by MEINDERT DEJONG. TEXT COPYRIGHT © 1954 BY MEINDERT DEJONG. Used by permission of HarperCollins Publishers. "UNDER SEIGE" from VOICES FROM THE CIVIL WAR by MILTON MELTZER. COPYRIGHT © 1989 BY MILTON MELTZER. Used by permission of HarperCollins Publishers.

HarperCollins Publishers, Inc., a division of HarperCollins Publishers: "OLD YELLER AND THE BEAR" from OLD YELLER by FRED GIPSON. Copyright © 1956 by Fred Gipson. Copyright renewed. Reprinted by permission of HarperCollins Publishers, Inc.

HarperCollins Publishers Ltd.: "Roads Go Ever Ever On" from THE HOBBIT by J.R.R. Tolkien. Copyright © 1966 by J.R.R. Tolkien. Reprinted with permission of HarperCollins Publishers Ltd.

John Hawkins & Associates, Inc.: **"Good Sportsmanship"** from **NIGHT WITH ARMOUR** by **Richard Armour.** Copyright © **1958** by **Richard Armour.** Reprinted by permission of John Hawkins & Associates, Inc.

Holiday House, Inc.: Excerpts from BUFFALO HUNT by Russell Freedman. Copyright © 1988 by Russell Freedman. All rights reserved. Reprinted from BUFFALO HUNT by permission of Holiday House, Inc. "Sun" and "Secrets" by Myra Cohn Livingston, illustrations by Leonard Everett Fisher. Illustrations copyright © 1988 by Leonard Everett Fisher. All rights reserved. Reprinted from SPACE SONGS by permission of Holiday House, Inc.

Houghton Mifflin Company: "The Coming of Long Knives," an excerpt from SING DOWN THE MOON. Copyright © 1970 by Scott O'Dell. Reprinted by permission of Houghton Mifflin Company. All rights reserved. Illustrations from THE GETTYSBURG ADDRESS. Illustrations and Afterward copyright © 1995 by Michael McCurdy. Reprinted by permission of Houghton Mifflin Company. All rights reserved. Abridged from IN TWO WORLDS: A Yup'ik Eskimo Family, by Aylette Jenness and Alice Rivers. Text copyright © 1989 by Aylette Jenness and Alice Rivers. Photographs copyright © 1989 by Aylette Jenness. Reprinted by permission of Houghton Mifflin Company. All rights reserved. "Roads Go Ever Ever On," from THE HOBBIT. Copyright © 1966 by J.R.R. Tolkien. Reprinted by permission of Houghton Mifflin Company. All rights reserved. "Telescopes," from THE WAY THINGS WORK by David Macaulay. Compilation copyright © 1988 by Dorling Kindersley, Ltd. Text copyright © 1988 by David Macaulay and Neil Ardley. Illustrations copyright © 1988 by David Macaulay. Reprinted by permission of Houghton Mifflin Company. All rights reserved.

James Houston: "The Whole World is Coming" from SONGS OF THE DREAM PEOPLE: Chants and Images from the Indians and Eskimos of North America. Edited and illustrated by James Houston. Atheneum, New York, copyright © 1972 by James Houston.

Alfred A. Knopf, Inc.: "Carrying the Running-Aways" from THE PEOPLE COULD FLY by Virginia Hamilton, illustrated by Leo and Diane Dillon. Text copyright © 1985 by Virginia Hamilton. Illustrations copyright © 1985 by Leo and Diane Dillon. Reprinted by permission of Alfred A. Knopf, Inc.

Ellen Levine Literary Agency, Inc.: "The Night We Started Dancing" from FREE TO BE A FAMILY by Ann Cameron. **Reprinted by permission of Ellen Levine Literary Agency, Inc. Copyright © 1987 by Ann Cameron.**

Wendy Lipkind Agency: "Alberic the Wise" from ALBERIC THE WISE AND OTHER JOURNEYS by Norton Juster. Copyright © 1965 by Norton Juster. Reprinted with permission of Wendy Lipkind Agency.

Lothrop, Lee & Shepard Books, a division of William Morrow & Company, Inc.: "The Siege of Vicksburg" from THE TAMARACK TREE by Patricia Clapp. Text copyright © 1986 by Patricia Clapp. By permission of Lothrop, Lee & Shepard Books, a division of William Morrow & Company, Inc.. THE STORY OF JUMPING MOUSE. A Native American legend retold and Illustrated by John Steptoe. From SEVEN ARROWS copyright © 1972 by Hymeyohsts Storm. Retold and illustrated for children copyright © 1984 by John Steptoe. By permission of Lothrop, Lee & Shepard Books, a division of William Morrow & Company, Inc., with the approval of the John Steptoe Literary Trust.

Macmillan Library Reference USA, a Simon & Schuster Macmillan Company: "Sacagawea's Journey" by Betty Westrom Skold. Reprinted with permission of Macmillan Library Reference USA, a Simon & Schuster Macmillan Company, from SACAGAWEA by Betty Westrom Skold. Copyright © 1977 by Dillon Press.

Mike Makley: "The New Kid" by Mike Makley, from Cricket, The Magazine for Children, Vol. 2, No. 8. Copyright © 1975 by Mike Makley. Reprinted with permission of Mike Makley.

Elsa Marston: "Circles, Squares, and Daggers: How Native Americans Watched the Skies" by Elsa Marston, from the September 1990 issue of Odyssey magazine. Copyright © 1990 by Elsa Marston. Reprinted with permission of Elsa Marston.

Morrow Junior Books, a division of William Morrow & Company, Inc.: An excerpt from CHARLEY SKEDADDLE by Patricia Beatty. Text copyright © 1987 by Patricia Beatty. By permission of Morrow Junior Books, a division of William Morrow & Company, Inc.. An excerpt from CLASS PRESIDENT by Johanna Hurwitz. Text copyright © 1990 by Johanna Hurwitz. By permission of Morrow Junior Books, a division of William Morrow & Company, Inc.. STARS by Seymour Simon. Text copyright © 1986 by Seymour Simon. By permission of Morrow Junior Books, a division of William Morrow & Company, Inc..

Penguin Books Canada Limited: From ***Underground to Canada*** by Barbara Smucker. Copyright © 1977 by Clarke, Irwin and Company Limited. Illustration by Imre Hofbauer. Copyright © 1978 by Imre Hofbauer. Reprinted by permission of Penguin Books Canada Limited.

Plays, Inc.: "The Book That Saved the Earth" from SPACE AND SCIENCE FICTION PLAYS FOR YOUNG PEOPLE by Claire Boiko. Reprinted with permission of Plays, Inc.

Marian Reiner: "Sun" and "Secrets" from SPACE SONGS by Myra Cohn Livingston. Copyright © 1988 Myra Cohn Livingston. Published by Holiday House. Reprinted by permission of Marian Reiner.

Sand & Sorensen Law Firm: "History of the Tunrit" from SONGS AND STORIES OF THE NETSILIK ESKIMOS, translated by Edward Field from text collected by Knud Rasmussen, illustrated by Pudlo. Reprinted with permission of Sand & Sorensen Law Firm.

Simon & Schuster Books for Young Readers, an imprint of Simon & Schuster Children's Publishing Division: **DEATH OF THE IRON HORSE by Paul Goble.** ***Copyright © 1987, by Paul Goble.*** Reprinted with permission of Simon & Schuster Books for Young Readers, an imprint of Simon & Schuster Children's Publishing Division. All rights reserved. **S.O.R. LOSERS by Avi.** ***Copyright © 1984 by Avi Wortis.*** Reprinted with the permission of Simon & Schuster Books for Young Readers, an imprint of Simon & Schuster Children's Publishing Division.

Steepletop: "Travel" by Edna St. Vincent Millay. From COLLECTED POEMS, HarperCollins. Copyright © 1921, 1948 by Edna St. Vincent Millay. All rights reserved. Reprinted by permission of Elizabeth Barnett, literary executor.

Navin Sullivan: "Galileo" from PIONEER ASTRONOMERS by Navin Sullivan. Copyright © 1964 by Navin Sullivan. Reprinted with permission of Navin Sullivan.

University of Missouri-Kansas City, University Libraries: "Maps" by Dorothy Brown Thompson. Reprinted with permission of University of Missouri-Kansas City, University Libraries.

Laurence S. Untermeyer: "Wander-Thirst" by Gerald Gould from STARS TO STEER by Louis Untermeyer. Copyright © 1941 by Harcourt Brace and Company. Reprinted with permission of Laurence S. Untermeyer.

Viking Children's Books, a division of Penguin Putnam Inc.: From THE NIGHT JOURNEY by Kathryn Lasky, illustrations by Trina Schart Hyman. Copyright © 1981 by Kathryn Lasky, text. Copyright © 1981 by Trina Schart Hyman, illustrations. Used by permission of Viking Children's Books, a division of Penguin Putnam Inc.

Cover Art: Bruce Bowles

SRA/McGraw-Hill

A Division of The ***McGraw·Hill*** *Companies*

Send all inquiries to:
SRA/McGraw-Hill
8787 Orion Place
Columbus, OH 43240-4027

Printed in the United States of America.

ISBN 0-02-830914-6

5 6 7 8 9 WEB 04 03 02 01

Photo Credits

9(tr), ©NASA; **9(br),** ©National Optical Astronomy Observatories; **10,** ©Aylette Jenness; **12(br),** ©CORBIS/Bettman; **12(tr),** ©CORBIS/Bettman; **44,** ©Carolyn Soto; **142,** ©Barbara Adams; **145,** ©Dewey Vanderhoff; **146,** ©Thomas F. Kehoe; **147,** ©Chaokia Mounds State Historic Site; **149,** ©Jerry Jacka; **150,** ©Bob Volpe Infinity Photography; **152,** ©Photographic Services/Paul Riley; **156-171,** ©NASA; **202(t),** ©Gary Benson; **204,** ©Kyle Cudworth, Yerkes Observatory; **205,** ©National Optical Astronomy Ovservatories; **206,** ©NASA/CORBIS; **207(t),** ©U.S. Naval Observatory (PAO)/CORBIS; **207(b),** ©NASA; **208,** ©NASA; **209(t),** ©National Optical Astronomy Observatories; **209(b),** ©NASA; **210,** ©NASA/CORBIS; **211, 213,** ©National Optical Astronomy Observatories; **244, 247,** ©Aylette Jenness; **249,** ©Jesuit Oregon Province Archives, Gonzaga University; **250,** ©Jonathan Jenness; **251-258,** ©Aylette Jenness; **314,** ©K. Yep; **340,** ©Christopher Knight

Unit Opener Acknowledgments

Unit 1 illustration by Brian Lies; **Unit 2** photograph by NASA; **Unit 3** illustration by Tyrone Geter; **Unit 4** painting by Thomas Nast; **Unit 5** illustration by Sandra Speidel; **Unit 6** illustration by Gail Haley.

Classroom Library Acknowledgments

A SEASON OF COMEBACKS by Kathy Mackel. Copyright © Kathy Mackel, 1997. Published by arrangement with Penguin Putnam Books for Young Readers, a division of Penguin Putnam, Inc. From A WRINKLE IN TIME (JACKET COVER ONLY) by Madeleine L'Engle. Copyright © 1962 by Madeleine L'Engle. Used by permission of Random House Children's Books, a division of Random House, Inc. APPALACHIA: THE VOICES OF SLEEPING BIRDS by Cynthia Rylant. Copyright © Cynthia Rylant, 1998. Pulished by Harcourt, Inc. CHILDTIMES: A THREE GENERATION MEMOIR by Eloise Greenfield. Copyright © Eloise Greenfield, 1993. Published by HarperCollins, Inc. COMEBACK! FOUR TRUE STORIES by Jim O'Connor. Copyright © Jim O'Connor, 1992. Published by Random House, Inc. HEADS, I WIN by Patricia Hermes. Copyright © Patricia Hermes, 1989. Published by Simon and Schuster, Inc. IMMIGRANT KIDS by Russell Freedman. Copyright © Russell Freedman, 1980. Published by arrangement with Dutton Children's Books, a division of Penguin Putnam Inc. MY DANIEL by Pam Conrad. Copyright © Pam Conrad, 1991. Published by HarperCollins, Inc.

Classroom Library Acknowledgments continue on Program Appendix 65.

Table *of* Contents

UNIT 3 Heritage

SRA Open Court Reading

Reading in the 21ˢᵗ Century

"Research shows that whether or not kids read adequately at the end of grade one is not just a powerful predictor of how well they'll read later, but also of general school achievement."

—SRA/Open Court Reading Author, Marilyn Jager Adams

About 30% of school-age children have serious reading problems. Children do not outgrow these difficulties. Studies indicate that 74% of the children who are poor readers at the end of third grade will be poor readers in the ninth grade. Adults who cannot read well cannot succeed in today's environment. This is why national and state initiatives are mandating that all children will demonstrate that they can read by the end of third grade.

Reading by 3ʳᵈ Grade Is Not Good Enough

Research in reading has shown that effective classroom instruction in the early grades by well-prepared teachers is the most powerful method for preventing reading and learning problems. Further, the most effective instruction for early reading involves a combination of explicit instruction in word recognition skills and reading comprehension strategies with opportunities to apply and practice these skills in literature.

SRA/Open Court Reading is the only reading program with a history of preparing teachers with the understanding and tools they need to provide the right balance of literature and skills. When provided with this balance, all children can learn to read, become fluent in reading, comprehend what they read, and benefit from reading. It is the only program that is and has been based on a generation of intense empirical research that identifies the factors that lead to success in early reading...with proven results.

This approach to beginning reading instruction has been successful in many thousands of classrooms for more than three decades. Since the first publication of the program in the early 1960s, the approach has recognized that if children are to learn to read with fluency and comprehension, they need explicit, systematic skills instruction *and* rich experiences with authentic literature.

The Goal: Reading in the 1ˢᵗ Grade

In *SRA/Open Court Reading*, explicit phonics and comprehension skills instruction is *balanced* with extensive reading of both decodable texts and quality literature. In addition to explicit skills, from the very beginning, children experience a wide variety of literary forms and genres in a program that emphasizes reading, writing, and learning.

For *SRA/Open Court Reading*, the goal of having all students reading by the end of third grade is not good enough. This program is designed to ensure that by the end of the first half of first grade, all students have the tools they need to begin reading authentic literature on grade level. In addition, from kindergarten through Level 6, the program emphasizes fluency, comprehension, writing, research, and inquiry with the goal of developing students who are truly lifelong learners and readers.

Reading gives children the power to learn and invites them to explore a world of information that is real and useful. Reading also opens the door for students to explore a world of stories, both real and fantasy.

Learning to read empowers children.

This program is designed to ensure that by the end of the first half of Grade 1, all students have the tools they need to begin reading authentic literature on grade level.

Principles

Research-Based Teaching

SRA/Open Court Reading's approach to initial reading instruction relies on the explicit teaching of sounds, on the blending of sounds into words, and on the leverage of using this knowledge for reading and writing. From the beginning *SRA/Open Court Reading* also develops explicit instruction and modeling of comprehension strategies and skills.

The *SRA/Open Court Reading* **Teacher's Edition** provides valuable information about *how, when,* and *why* to use proven effective strategies throughout the program. In addition to information at point of use in the actual lessons, the following issues, as well as others, are addressed specifically with complete instructions in the **Professional Development** section in the back of each *Teacher's Edition:*

The Foundations for Reading

- Reading aloud
- Print awareness
- Phonemic awareness through oral blending and segmentation
- Alphabetic principle
- Explicit systematic phonics and blending
- Fluency using decodable books for initial reading experience
- Comprehension strategies and skills
- Spelling
- Writing

The Goals of Reading

- Authentic literary experiences
- Learning through themes
- Inquiry and research

High Expectations and Support for All Students

SRA/Open Court Reading comes from a long tradition of respecting the intelligence of children and teachers. The program offers the best in reading instruction and expects the best. By making no assumptions about prior knowledge, *SRA/Open Court Reading* ensures that no children fall through the cracks. Phonemic awareness, print awareness, and an understanding of the alphabetic principle are not taken for granted. The program includes:

- Solid foundation for building instruction in decoding, fluency, and comprehension skills.
- Plenty of repetition for students who need help.
- Relevant and efficient practice.
- Daily **Independent Work Time** so that teachers have a chance to focus on specific needs and deficits of individuals. Diverse and individual needs are met by varying the time and intensity of instruction.
- A variety of proven learning experiences that provide for differing language proficiencies and abilities.
- The expectation that all children will be reading on level by the middle of first grade.
- The expectation that children can produce works of genuine research that seeks answers to real questions or solutions to real problems.

Phonemic Awareness
Print Awareness
Explicit Systematic Phonics

Before children can learn the sound/spelling relationships that constitute written language, they need to understand how individual sounds, or phonemes, work together to create spoken language. This awareness of how the system works—*phonemic awareness*—is the first piece of the foundation children need in order to go on to the next step—assigning written symbols to these sounds.

Laying the Foundation

Written English is not perfectly regular, but a more or less predictable association exists between the sounds of the spoken language and the letters in the written language. This *alphabetic principle* that translates spoken sounds into written language permits us to represent thousands of words with just a few symbols. Learning these sound-symbol relationships enables children to decode most of the words in the English language instead of learning each word individually.

Research shows that phonics instruction has to be systematic if it is to work. It cannot start somewhere in the middle or be random or haphazard in approach.

SRA/Open Court Reading does not assume that students can distinguish individual sounds or already know the spellings of these sounds. *SRA/Open Court Reading:*

- Systematically teaches letter knowledge and phonemic awareness in kindergarten.
- Introduces sound/spellings systematically in Level 1.
- Offers direct instruction in blending all of the sounds in words.
- Builds fluency, the key to comprehension through the use of decodable books.
- Connects spelling to phonics through **Dictation and Spelling** activities.

The goal of all of the instruction in phonemic awareness and phonics is to provide children with the tools they need to read with *fluency*. Phonics skills enable children to get beyond the distractions and mechanics of decoding words to focus on the goal of reading—*comprehension*.

Level 5
Teacher's Edition

Fluency

Students need to remain mindful of the ultimate goal of phonics instruction: real reading and writing.

Since the best way to practice reading is to read, *SRA/Open Court Reading* provides a wealth of reading materials at each step along the way. Even after they have learned only a few sounds, there are real books for students to read. These ***Decodable Books*** (Levels K–3) are carefully crafted so that students practice the skills they are learning with connected text and therefore gain confidence in their reading abilities. When all the sound/spellings have been learned, the students continue to develop fluency through authentic reading and writing.

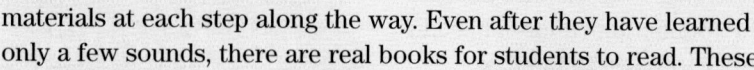

Building on the Foundation

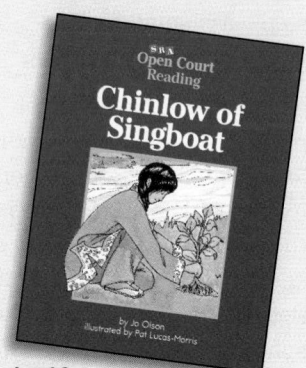

Level 3 Decodable Book

Authentic Literary Experiences

Throughout the program, students participate daily in reading, writing, discussing, researching, and thinking about authentic, high-quality literature in ***Big Books*** (Levels K and 1) and ***Student Anthologies*** (Levels 1–6). Beginning in Kindergarten and continuing through Level 6, students experience a range of text genres, including different forms of fiction and nonfiction. There are also multiple opportunities for writing, allowing students to understand the uses of writing even as they are learning to write. These experiences help to reinforce students' understanding of the structure and conventions of written language.

Level K Big Book

Level 5 Anthology

Integrated Instruction

Learning units are tied to important concepts that call on students to make connections across all areas of the curriculum and to acquire knowledge that can be used beyond a single lesson. Each unit is organized so that a reading selection adds more information or a different perspective to the students' knowledge of a concept. Throughout all units, the focus is on learning *how* to learn through inquiry and research.

Reading, writing, discussion, research, and exploration activities are integrated through lessons that evolve sequentially, becoming increasingly complex and demanding. Through individual, collaborative learning groups, and whole-class activities, students are encouraged to bring their own experiences to the learning situation and, through exploration, to gain deeper understandings. The students' responsibilities are to learn more, and to help classmates discover more about the unit concepts.

Every lesson throughout the program emphasizes the combination of reading skills, comprehension, and learning so that children acquire the tools they need to read and then learn from what they read. The three parts of every ***Teacher's Edition*** lesson provide the lesson plan to teach all of the dimensions of reading.

① Preparing to Read

The first part of every lesson emphasizes the skills of reading, including introduction to sounds and letters, vocabulary, print awareness, and word knowledge.

② Reading and Responding

The second part of every lesson emphasizes comprehension skills and strategies as students read the lesson selection. This part concludes by exploring how the selection adds a perspective to the unit theme.

③ Integrating the Curriculum

The third section of each lesson engages students in the writing process and develops vital language arts skills. **Across the Curriculum** activities extend the selection to other curriculum areas.

Meaningful Comprehension
Inquiry and Research

Throughout the program, students are encouraged to construct meaning by interacting with and responding to outstanding literature. They read widely, write frequently, and listen and speak effectively. The focus is always on building knowledge and deeper understanding. The intent of instruction is to engage students in the kinds of activities that will prepare them for the reading, thinking, and problem solving typical of real-world situations. To participate productively in that world, graduates must know how to go about gaining information, to evaluate it critically, and to adapt it for differing purposes. They must be equipped to deal with a variety of fields, including some that do not even exist today, and to understand and participate in scientific reasoning and problem solving.

Reaching the Goal

Every grade level has specific goals to ensure that children are developing strong, effective reading skills and comprehension.

A Systematic Approach

Kindergarten

The kindergarten level of *SRA/Open Court Reading* has drawn the best available information from research and effective practice to provide maximum flexibility in providing all students with a solid, successful introduction to literacy. The kindergarten program:

- Introduces children to the alphabet and how it works.
- Teaches phonemic awareness.
- Connects sounds with letters.
- Exposes children to how the sounds of the language work together.
- Develops print and book awareness.
- Provides early reading experiences at which children can be successful.
- Helps children focus on the importance of learning and the joy it can bring.
- Explores concepts in science, social studies, literature, and the arts.
- Teaches thinking through story making and participative listening.

Level 1

It is no exaggeration to say that how well children learn to read in first grade profoundly affects how well they do throughout their school years—and their lives. Children who quickly develop the skills necessary to read with fluency and comprehension gain access to all the world's knowledge. They acquire the power to educate themselves and to expand their range of thought and reflection. Level 1 accomplishes the following goals:

- Strengthens the solid foundation in phonemic awareness.
- Introduces children to sound/spelling associations in a systematic manner.
- Teaches the sounds and letters early, intensely, and quickly.
- Launches students into real literature as quickly as possible so that they do not lose sight of the purpose and goal of learning the skills.
- Develops reading fluency.
- Allows students to gain fluency in writing, enabling them to use it as a tool of inquiry as well as communication.
- Gives children responsibility for their own work, their own mental development, and their own paths of inquiry as soon as possible.

Levels 2–6

In Levels 2–6, children continue developing reading fluency, which leads to greater comprehension and enjoyment of reading and the ability to use reading skills and strategies for inquiry and research. Levels 2–6:

- Review the phonetic word knowledge and skill foundation that is developed in Levels K and 1 and provide intervention for students as needed.

- Build fluency in reading.
- Emphasize the presentation of instruction in meaning-based learning units, each of which revolves around compelling concepts from across the curriculum.
- Include many opportunities to read texts that will build comprehension in order to prepare students for the kinds of reading they will encounter in content-area textbooks and in nonacademic texts.
- Lead students to pursue personal and collaborative inquiry through study and research, to identify and access the information they need and to communicate their findings to their classmates.
- Develop writing skills to communicate knowledge.

To thrive in the twenty-first century, students will have to learn how to think about what they read, to put together information from many sources, to communicate effectively in writing and with speech, and to give sustained effort to thinking and problem solving. Becoming this kind of reader, writer, and learner can be a reality for all students. The teacher and student materials of *SRA/Open Court Reading* all focus on developing self-directed, highly motivated students who take primary responsibility for their own learning.

SRA/Open Court Reading is a comprehensive reading, writing, and learning program that:

- Develops confident and fluent readers through print and phonemic awareness activities and explicit, systematic phonics instruction.
- Engages students in constructing meaning through the teaching and application of comprehension skills and strategies and meaningful discussions.
- Incorporates writing as a form of learning and personal communication.
- Creates a classroom environment in which students explore, discuss, and research ideas.
- Develops research and study skills that give students the tools to become independent, self-directed learners.

What does all this mean to teachers, the most important people in students' educational lives? It means that they need to have a thorough understanding of the processes they are teaching so that at each step, they can help their young apprentices thoroughly master the skills they need.

The Teacher Needs to Be the Expert

Children who are thoroughly prepared in kindergarten excel in first grade. Those who sufficiently strengthen their knowledge and skills in first grade shine in second grade. Children who spend second grade honing these skills soar in third grade. In order for this to happen, teachers need the appropriate knowledge and skills to help each and every student build on his or her natural abilities.

SRA/Open Court Reading, gives *you*, the expert, the proven tools and information you need to help your students be the best they can be. If teachers are accountable, this is what they are accountable for.

What Is Reading?

"Skillful reading is not one skill. It is a whole complex system of skills and knowledge. Within this system, the knowledge and activities involved in visually recognizing individual printed words are useless in and of themselves. They are valuable and, in a strong sense, possible only as they are guided and received by complementary knowledge and activities of language comprehension. On the other hand, unless the processes involved in individual word recognition operate properly, nothing else in the system can either."

—*SRA/Open Court Reading*
Author, Marilyn Jager Adams

Reading is defined differently for different ages. Parents take pictures of infants who are holding books looking at pictures and call that "reading." For preschoolers reading may indicate that children can recognize signs and logos or are able to recite the alphabet. Many young children memorize the text of books after repeated readings by parents and that is counted as reading for that age.

All of these events are delightful in young children and announce their interest in and excitement about reading. The same events in older children or adults are signs of reading disability.

Real reading includes:

- Understanding of how phonemes (speech sounds) are connected to print.
- Ability to decode unfamiliar words.
- Ability to read with fluency.
- Knowledge of sufficient background information and vocabulary to foster reading comprehension.
- Ability to use comprehension skills and strategies to get meaning from text.

Many children get by reading poorly in the early grades. It is fourth grade that has been identified as a pivotal year for most readers. In fourth grade much more emphasis is placed on informational reading, and teachers provide much less reading skill instruction. Students are expected to have made the transformation from learning to read to reading to learn. Several states are now mandating that children demonstrate their ability to read at the end of third grade so that they are prepared for this shift in emphasis.

Reading comprehension is an extremely complex behavior. Skillful readers have the ability to recognize letter/sound correspondences automatically, and they interpret sentence structure immediately as they read. The most profound reading problems come from difficulties in recognizing and decoding words and identifying the meanings of individual words. Fluency is also problematic. If a reader does not recognize words quickly enough, the meaning is lost. Even skillful decoders often have difficulty comprehending what has been read. Reading is not the ability to simply decode but also to read with fluency and comprehend text.

Skills in decoding and fluency are necessary but not sufficient to make children successful readers. Comprehension strategies and skills must also be taught in order for students to have the tools they need to understand what they decode.

Reading Instruction in *SRA/Open Court Reading*

In *SRA/Open Court Reading*, reading is a developmental process. Comprehension strategies and skills and writing are emphasized from the very beginning of Level K, even before children can read. At Levels K and 1, decoding skills are developed and combined with **Pre-Decodable** and **Decodable Books** and authentic literary experiences. After Level 1, once decoding skills are in place, emphasis gradually shifts to developing reading fluency and comprehension. In the upper levels reading instruction emphasizes reading to learn, to write, and to gain deeper understanding.

**Level 3
Decodable Book**

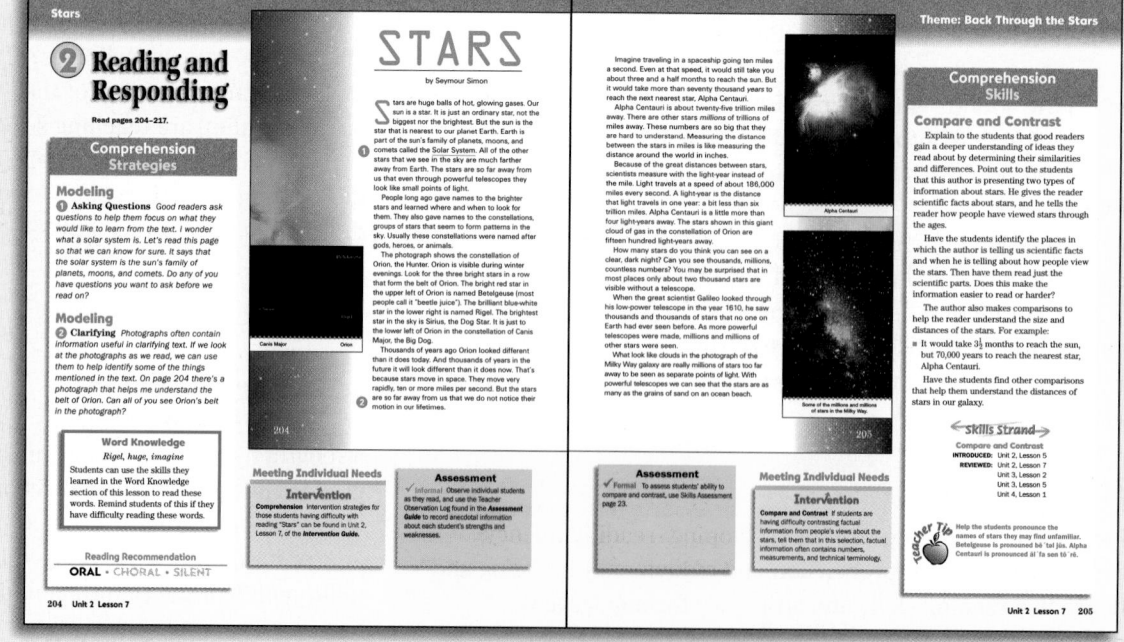

Level 5 Teacher's Edition

Reading Aloud

"It is not just reading to children that makes the difference, it is enjoying the books with them and reflecting on their form and content. It is developing and supporting the children's curiosity about text and the meanings it conveys....And it is showing the children that we value and enjoy reading and we hope that they will too."

—SRA/Open Court Reading
Author, Marilyn Jager Adams

Reading aloud is simply reading out loud to someone else. Teachers, parents, grandparents, and older siblings commonly read aloud to children who may or may not be able to read on their own. It is also a valuable learning technique.

Research has shown that children who are read to by teachers or parents or other adults are more likely than those who do not have this experience to develop the skills they need to read successfully on their own. Reading aloud serves multiple purposes for both readers and nonreaders as it:

- Provokes children's curiosity about text.
- Conveys an awareness that text has meaning.
- Offers both teachers and children the opportunity to model critical reading strategies such as clarifying, predicting, and summarizing—the strategies that children will need in order to become successful readers.
- Demonstrates the various reasons for reading text (for example, to find out about the world around them, to learn useful new information and new skills, or simply for pleasure).
- Exposes children to the "language of literature" which is more complex than the language they ordinarily use and hear.
- Enables good readers to model their own interest in and enjoyment of reading.
- Provides an opportunity to teach the problem-solving strategies that good readers employ.
- Introduces children to a variety of literature.
- Develops vocabulary.
- Builds knowledge.
- Fosters important reading behaviors.
- Provides a natural avenue for discussion.

The importance of reading aloud to children cannot be overemphasized. Reading aloud provides an opportunity to communicate the active nature of reading. As children observe you interacting with the text, expressing your own enthusiasm, and modeling your thinking aloud, they perceive these as valid responses and begin to respond to text in similar ways. They become active listeners and later, when they begin reading on their own, they will begin engaging in the same behaviors.

Reading Aloud in *SRA/Open Court Reading*

Read-Aloud selections in the ***Teacher's Editions*** are directly related to the unit theme. Suggestions in the ***Teacher's Edition*** for stopping to think aloud and to stimulate discussion are included to help teachers focus **Read Aloud** sessions.

Reading aloud is an integral part of the Levels K and 1 lessons. Suggestions for materials that could be read aloud are provided in the ***Teacher's Editions*** for Levels 2–6.

- ✓ Reading aloud
- Print awareness
- Phonemic awareness through oral blending and segmentation
- Alphabetic principle
- Explicit systematic phonics and blending
- Fluency using decodable books for initial reading experience
- Comprehension strategies and skills
- Learning through themes
- Authentic literary experiences
- Spelling
- Writing
- Inquiry and research

References

Adams, M. J. (1990) *Beginning to Read: Thinking and Learning about Print.* Cambridge, MA: M.I.T. Press.

Anderson, R. et al. (1984) *Becoming a Nation of Readers: The Report on the Commission on Reading.* Washington DC: The National Institute of Education, U.S. Department of Education.

Sulzby, E. and Teale, W. (1991) Emergent literacy. In R. Barr, M. L. Kamile, P. B. Mosenthal, and P. D. Pearson (eds.) *Handbook of Reading Research* (pp.727–758). NY: Longmann.

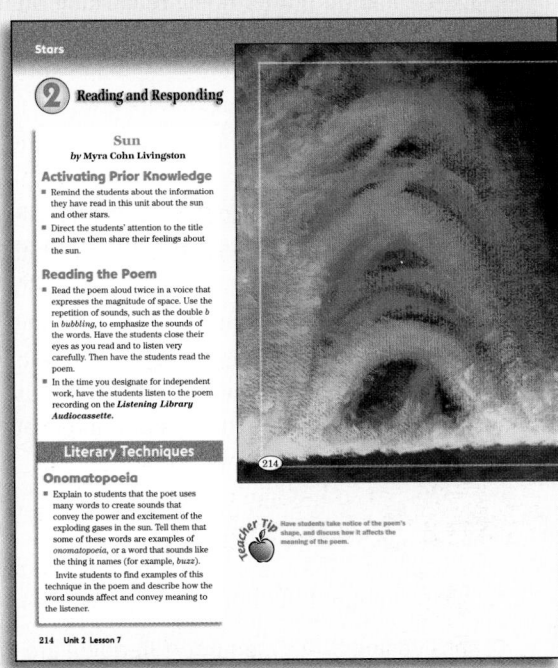

Level 5 Teacher's Edition

Print Awareness

"Print awareness is found to predict future reading achievement and to be strongly correlated with other, more traditional measures of reading readiness and achievement. More than that, analyses of the interdependencies among measures of reading readiness and achievement indicate that basic knowledge about print generally precedes and appears to serve as the very foundation on which orthographic and phonological skills are built."

—SRA/Open Court Reading
Author, Marilyn Jager Adams

Print awareness involves an understanding of the forms, functions, and uses of print. Print awareness is a learner's growing recognition of conventions and characteristics of written language. For early readers this includes such features as the recognition that reading is from left to right, that print corresponds to speech, that white spaces mark boundaries between words, that books progress from front to back, and so on. A child's level of print awareness has been shown to be a key predictor of his or her future reading achievement. Basic knowledge about print precedes and appears to serve as the foundation for the understanding of the written language.

Reading books to children helps engage students in unlocking the selections' messages at the same time it develops print awareness. In school, shared **Big Book** reading experiences invite children to participate in good reading behaviors. The teacher models what a good reader does: remarking on the illustrations and the title, wondering about the content and what might happen, making predictions, and commenting on events. The teacher points to each word as it is read, thus demonstrating that text proceeds from left to right and from top to bottom and helping advance the idea that words are individually spoken and written units. Enjoying the illustrations and connecting them to the text help students learn to explore books for enjoyment and information.

The shared reading experiences offered with **Big Books** (Levels K and 1) invite children to participate in reading behaviors and reading strategies of expert readers: responding to illustrations, thinking about content, predicting what might happen, and making connections between ideas in the story and events in their own lives.

Print Awareness in *SRA/Open Court Reading*

Children using *SRA/Open Court Reading* are given many opportunities, through varied uses of **Big Books,** to become familiar and comfortable with the conventions of print and books. The use of **Big Books** also introduces children to the reading behaviors they will need long before they actually read on their own. In Kindergarten, **Pre-Decodable Books** also help establish print awareness.

Strategies for developing print awareness appear throughout the **Teacher's Edition** in the **Reading and Responding** section of appropriate lessons. These strategies are tools for directing the students' attention to words, letters, and illustrations. They can be used with reading materials from any subject area in addition to the *SRA/Open Court Reading* **Big Books.**

In Kindergarten and Level 1, lessons are centered on the reading of particular **Big Books** that help develop print awareness. By the second half of Level 1, students should have a strong foundation in print awareness but print awareness strategies appear as reteaching and intervention strategies throughout Levels 2-6 for those students who do not have this foundation.

- ✓ Reading aloud
- ✓ Print awareness
- Phonemic awareness through oral blending and segmentation
- Alphabetic principle
- Explicit systematic phonics and blending
- Fluency using decodable books for initial reading experience
- Comprehension strategies and skills
- Learning through themes
- Authentic literary experiences
- Spelling
- Writing
- Inquiry and research

References

Adams, M. J. (1990) *Beginning to Read: Thinking and Learning about Print.* Cambridge, MA: M.I.T. Press.

Clay, M. M. (1979) *What Did I Write? Beginning Writing Behavior.* Portsmouth, NH: Heinemann Educational Books.

Sulzby, E. and Teale, W. (1991) Emergent Literacy. In R. Barr, M. L. Kamile, P. B. Mosenthal, and P. D. Pearson (eds), *Handbook of Reading Research* (pp. 727-758). NY: Longmann.

Level K Big Book

Level K Pre-Decodable Book

Phonemic Awareness

"A lack of appreciation of phonemic awareness is found to be the single most prevalent cause of reading disability. And it's not easy. It does not come naturally from teaching children letter/sound correspondences, from engaging them in reading, or from giving them spelling drill."

—SRA/Open Court Reading
Author, Marilyn Jager Adams

Phonemic awareness is the awareness of the sounds that make up spoken words. While speaking and understanding the English language do not require a conscious reflection on its sounds, reading and writing do. In English, letters represent sounds, or phonemes. In order to learn the correspondences between letters and sounds, a child must have some understanding of the notion that words are made up of phonemes. Poorly developed phonemic awareness is the leading cause of reading failure.

The ability to distinguish individual sounds within words is an essential prerequisite to associating sounds with letters. The students need a strong phonemic awareness in order for phonics instruction to be successful. Frequently, children who have difficulties with phonics do so because they have not developed the prerequisite phonemic awareness. Until children develop an awareness of the component parts of words, they have no tools with which to decode words or put letters together to form words. The basic purpose of providing structured practice in phonemic awareness is to help children hear and understand the sounds from which words are made.

Once children begin reading and writing, this experience with manipulating sounds will help them use what they know about sounds and letters to sound out and spell unfamiliar words. As children progress through different phonemic awareness activities, they will become proficient at listening for and reproducing the sounds they hear.

Oral Blending and Segmentation

Two basic formats are used for teaching phonemic awareness—*oral blending* and *segmentation*. Oral blending helps children understand that words contain component parts—syllables and single sounds—and that these parts can be put together to make words. Segmentation and oral blending complement each other: Oral blending encourages the students to combine sounds to make words. Segmentation, conversely, requires them to isolate sounds from words.

Phonemic Awareness in *SRA/Open Court Reading*

Phonemic awareness activities found primarily at Levels K and 1 provide children with easy practice in discriminating the sounds that make up words. These are brief, teacher-directed exercises that involve some form of word play: words are taken apart in various ways and put back together. With the support of a puppet, children delight in manipulating the sounds of language and playing language games. The activities are carefully sequenced. At the beginning of each series of exercises, the students are given a great deal of support. As students progress, the support is gradually removed, and the exercises become more challenging. From these playful activities, children derive serious knowledge about language. As children gain awareness of how sounds combine to make words, they will be ready to progress to phonics and reading.

Phonemic awareness background information appears in the ***Teacher's Editions*** in Levels 2-6 for reteaching and intervention for those students who have not yet fully developed phonemic awareness.

References
Adams, M. J. (1990) *Beginning to Read: Thinking and Learning about Print.* Cambridge, MA: M.I.T. Press.

Honig, B. (1996) *How Shall We Teach Our Children to Read?* Thousand Oaks, CA: Corwin Press.

Yopp, H. (1992) Developing phonemic awareness in young children. *The Reading Teacher,* 45, 696-703.

- ✓ Reading aloud
- ✓ Print awareness
- ✓ Phonemic awareness through oral blending and segmentation
- Alphabetic principle
- Explicit systematic phonics and blending
- Fluency using decodable books for initial reading experience
- Comprehension strategies and skills
- Learning through themes
- Authentic literary experiences
- Spelling
- Writing
- Inquiry and research

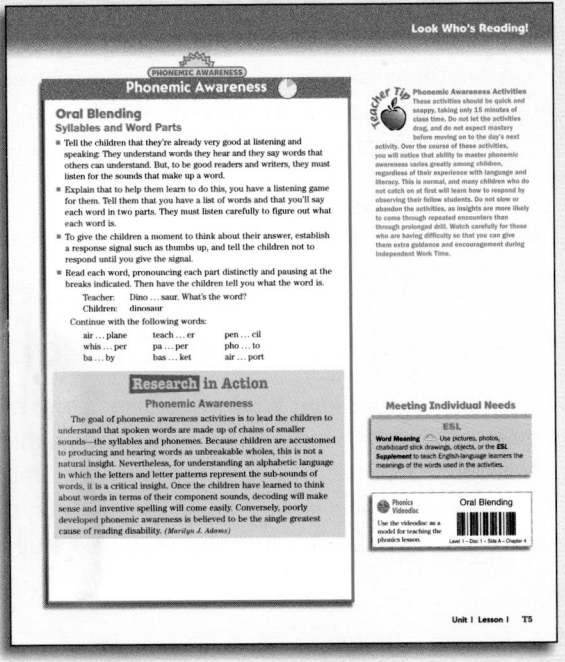

Level 1 Teacher's Edition

Alphabetic Principle: How the Alphabet Works

"In order for children to learn how to read, they have got to break the code. And by teaching them about how the sound structure of their language works, you're only making it that much easier for them to break the code."

**—SRA/Open Court Reading
Author, Jan Hirshberg**

The *alphabetic principle* is simply that there is a fairly predictable association between sounds and the letters that represent them. An understanding of the alphabetic principle extends children's phonemic awareness, that words are made up of sounds to include the notion of how those sounds relate to letters and writing.

The English language has 43 common sounds. Those sounds are represented by 26 letters alone or in some combination. The letters and sounds work together in a systematic way to connect spoken language to written words. Before learning the relationships between sounds and letters, children must learn that such a relationship exists. Like phonemic awareness, for many children the alphabetic principle is not intuitive. To become proficient readers, children must understand the alphabetic principle, that letters represent the sounds of the language.

Key concepts that children need to understand about the alphabetic principle are that

- A limited number of letters combine in different ways to make many different words.
- Words are composed of sounds, and letters represent those sounds.
- Anything that can be pronounced can be spelled.
- Letters and sounds can be used to identify words.
- Meaning can be obtained by using letters and sounds to figure out words.

The Alphabetic Principle
SRA/Open Court Reading

How the Alphabet Works lessons in Level K introduce children to the relationships between sounds and letters through collaborative classroom activities. The activities present a limited set of letters and their corresponding sounds and focus solely on the *concept* of the relationship. With this information and a carefully structured set of

activities, children begin to explore and understand the alphabetic principle in a straightforward and thorough manner. This lays the foundation for explicit systematic phonics instruction. Naturally, keeping children focused on the idea that they are learning about sounds and letters so they can read these books themselves makes the lessons more relevant for children.

The alphabetic principle is reinforced throughout kindergarten as well as in first grade. By the end of Level 1, most students should have established an understanding of the alphabetic principle. Strategies appear throughout the **Teacher's Editions** in all levels for reteaching and intervention for those students who have not yet fully developed an understanding of the alphabetic principle.

References

Beck, I. L. and Juel C. (1995). The role of decoding in learning to read. *American Educator*, 19, 8.

Ehri, L. C. (1994) Development of the ability to read words. In R. Rudell and H. Singer (eds.), *Theoretical Models and Process of Reading*, 4th Edition. (pp. 323-358) Newark, DE: International Reading Association.

Honig, B. (1996) *How Shall We Teach Our Children to Read?* Thousand Oaks, CA: Corwin Press.

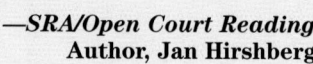

- ✓ Reading aloud
- ✓ Print awareness
- ✓ Phonemic awareness through oral blending and segmentation
- ✓ Alphabetic principle
- Explicit systematic phonics and blending
- Fluency using decodable books for initial reading experience
- Comprehension strategies and skills
- Learning through themes
- Authentic literary experiences
- Spelling
- Writing
- Inquiry and research

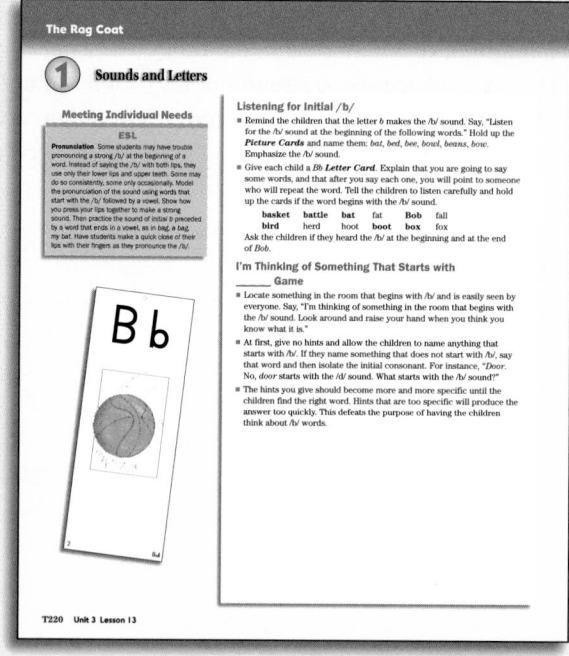

Level K Teacher's Edition

Explicit Systematic Phonics Instruction

"When children are taught about phonics, then phonemic awareness is also increased so the two sort of help one another. Children can learn about phonemic awareness without necessarily having to attach it to spellings, but phonics helps them to see these direct attachments to spellings. Even children who come to school reading can benefit from learning about phonics and the sound system because it can help them with their writing and their spelling."

—SRA/Open Court Reading
Author, Jan Hirshberg

Phonics is a way to teach decoding and spelling that stresses sound/symbol relationships. Explicit systematic phonics is a system of teaching that systematically introduces the spelling of each sound to students, teaches blending directly, and follows up with **Decodable Books** (Levels K–3) for practice so that the reason for learning the sound/symbol relationships is reinforced. **Decodable Books** include words comprised of sounds and spellings that have been taught.

Phonics in *SRA/Open Court Reading*

In *SRA/Open Court Reading,* children learn to relate sounds to letters through a careful series of lessons in the **Teacher's Edition** that incorporates the use of 43 **Sound/Spelling Cards** (Levels 1–6). Each card contains the capital and small letter, and a picture that shows the sound being produced. In Level K the purpose of the **Alphabet/Sound Cards** is to remind children of the sounds of the English language and their letter correspondences. The name of the picture on each card contains the target sound at the beginning of the word for the consonants, and in the middle for the short-vowel sounds. In addition, the picture associates a sound with an action. This action-sound association is introduced through a short, interactive poem found in the **Teacher's Edition** in which the pictured object or character "makes" the sound of the letter. These cards are a resource for children to use to remember sound-letter associations for both reading and spelling.

The **Decodable Books** are used for reading aloud and for class discussion. Repeated reading fosters fluency.

Beginning in kindergarten, children learn the sounds and letters of the alphabet plus the five short vowels. This knowledge forms the foundation for first grade, when children learn the 43 common sounds of the language and the letters or combinations of letters (spellings) that represent those sounds. Second grade begins with a review of these sounds and spellings. Phonetic principles are reviewed throughout each subsequent grade level of the program as reteaching and intervention strategies.

- ✓ Reading aloud
- ✓ Print awareness
- ✓ Phonemic awareness through oral blending and segmentation
- ✓ Alphabetic principle
- ✓ Explicit systematic phonics and blending
- Fluency using decodable books for initial reading experience
- Comprehension strategies and skills
- Learning through themes
- Authentic literary experiences
- Spelling
- Writing
- Inquiry and research

References

Adams, M. J., Treiman, R., and Pressley, M. Reading, writing, and literacy. I. Sigel and A. Renninger (eds.), *Handbook of Child Psychology, Volume 4, Child Psychology and Practice.* New York: John Wiley and Sons.

Anderson, R. et al. (1984) *Becoming a Nation of Readers: The Report of the Commission on Reading.* Washington DC: The National Institute of Education, U.S. Department of Education.

Treiman, R. (1993) *Beginning to Spell.* New York: Oxford University Press.

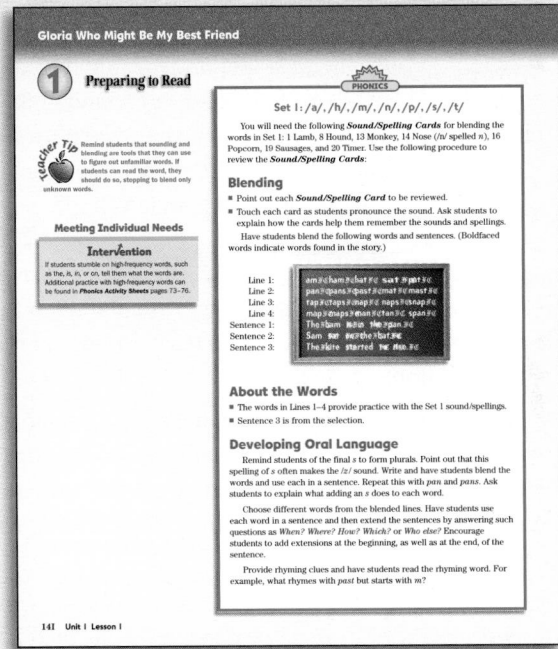

Level 3 Teacher's Edition

Blending

"Deep and thorough knowledge of letters, spelling patterns, and words, and of the phonological translations of all three, are of inescapable importance to both skillful reading and its acquisition. By extension, instruction designed to develop children's sensitivity to spellings and their relations to pronunciations should be of paramount importance in the development of reading skills."

—SRA/Open Court Reading
Author, Marilyn Jager Adams

Blending—learning to put separate spellings for sounds together smoothly to read words—is the heart of phonics instruction. Blending involves combining the sounds represented by letters to pronounce a word. It is the key strategy that children learn in order to apply the alphabetic principle and open up the world of written text.

Blending is not to be confused with *oral blending*, which is a strategy used to develop phonemic awareness. In blending, students are looking at *spellings* that make up words. They first associate individual sounds with print and letters and then blend those sounds into recognizable words. In short, they actually read the words. Oral blending involves just listening and combining *sounds* to make words.

The purpose of blending is to teach children a strategy for figuring out unfamiliar words. Learning the sounds and their spellings is only the first step in learning to read and write. The second step is learning to blend the sounds into words. Initially, children blend sound by sound, then word by word. By blending words sound by sound, children learn the blending process, which allows them to work out for themselves the words they meet in their reading. Blending words into sentences is the logical extension of blending sounds into words. Blending words into sentences helps children move from word fluency to sentence fluency, and the procedure varies greatly from early to later sentences as children's skills develop.

The goal of blending instruction is to have children reading words and stopping to blend only those that are problematic. Ultimately children will sound and blend only those words that they cannot read. Eventually, the blending process will become quick and comfortable for them.

Blending in SRA/Open Court Reading

✓ Reading aloud
✓ Print awareness
✓ Phonemic awareness through oral blending and segmentation
✓ Alphabetic principle
✓ Explicit systematic phonics and blending

Fluency using decodable books for initial reading experience

Comprehension strategies and skills

Learning through themes

Authentic literary experiences

Spelling

Writing

Inquiry and research

In *SRA/Open Court Reading* Levels 1 and 2, blending is a daily routine developed in the first part of the lessons in the **Teacher's Edition.** Children learn to blend sounds and spellings to read words. As the teacher writes the spelling for each sound in a word, students say the sound, relying on the associations fixed by the **Sound/Spelling Cards.** Then they will blend the sounds together into a word. To be sure that they recognize the word in the string of sounds that they have put together, they use the word in a sentence. The connection between the blended words and the word meaning is constantly reinforced, so that students recognize that the sounds they have blended are indeed the word they know from spoken language.

Students use the blending strategy when they read **Decodable Books** and other materials. Initially, children use this strategy for many of the words they read. In time, high-utility words are automatically recognized and the blending strategy is used only for unfamiliar words. The systematic introduction of sounds and spellings coupled with blending develops independent readers in first grade. By second grade, most students may not need to blend words sound by sound and can begin by blending words using the whole-word procedure. Blending is reinforced in reteaching and intervention strategies in Levels 3-6.

Sound/Spelling Cards

References

Adams, M. J. (1990) *Beginning to Read: Thinking and Learning about Print*, Cambridge, MA: M.I.T. Press.

Beck, I. L. and Juel, C. (1995) The role of decoding in learning to read. *American Educator*, 19, 8.

Ehri, L. C. (1992) Reconceptualizing the development of sight word reading and its relationship to recoding. In P. B. Gough. L. C. Ehri, and R. Treiman (eds.). *Reading Acquisition* (pp. 107-144). Hillsdale, NJ: Earlbaum Associates.

Fluency

"The single greatest flaw of reading programs is that they don't give children enough to read and what they do give them gets too hard too fast. The more children read the better they'll read. We want to move them to the point where they like to read but that only happens when they feel that they can read."

—*SRA/Open Court Reading*
Author, **Marilyn Jager Adams**

Decoding is the process of analyzing graphic symbols to determine their intended meaning. To learn to read, a child must learn the code in which something is written in order to decode the written message. *Reading fluency* is the freedom from word-identification problems that hinder reading comprehension.

Gaining reading fluency automatically allows children to use their time and energy to comprehend the whole text rather than using up all their energy in simple word-by-word decoding. Becoming fluent is essential to comprehension. Without fluency there is no comprehension.

The best way for children to gain fluency is to practice reading—even when they have a limited knowledge of sounds and spellings. Practice reading is most effective when the material is decodable with sounds and spellings students already know and sight words they have learned.

Truly decodable books are those in which more than 60% of the words in the book either:

- Contain only sound/spellings that have been explicitly taught.
- Are high-frequency words that have been taught.
- Are nondecodable (irregular) words that have been explicitly taught.

Even high-frequency words such as *and* are considered nondecodable until each and every sound/symbol relationship has been explicitly taught.

Decodable books help children who have learned only a limited number of sounds and spellings practice reading. Most importantly, they help students grasp the idea that learning to use sound/spelling correspondences and a blending strategy unlocks the world of written language.

Applying their growing knowledge of words and phonic elements, children can read these simple, engaging stories themselves and thereby experience early success with reading. As children read and reread these materials, they gain crucial practice in reading and develop fluency, which is the gateway to comprehension.

Fluency in SRA/Open Court Reading

The **Decodable Books** in Levels K–3 of *SRA/Open Court Reading* are designed to help students review and reinforce their expanding knowledge of sound/spelling correspondences. Lessons for use with these books are included in the **Teacher's Edition.** These short, easy stories help students experience success with reading from virtually the beginning of first grade. Each story supports instruction in new phonic elements and incorporates elements and words that have been learned earlier.

Very simple questions are included in the **Teacher's Edition** to check both understanding and attention to words. Since the primary focus for these books is decoding the words and gaining fluency, rather than intensive work on comprehension, the application of strategies is simplified and de-emphasized. Naturally, though, children should understand what they are reading and should feel free to discuss anything in the story that interests them.

The **Decodable Books** are simple, colorfully illustrated stories available to be read again and again. They are also available in consumable and blackline forms that children can decorate and take home to share with their families.

At Level 1, **Decodable Books** help children build fluency and confidence as they apply their growing knowledge of phonics. In Levels 2 and 3, the **Decodable Books** provide further practice and continue to build fluency.

As students acquire fluency, they comprehend better because they are free to concentrate on meaning instead of focusing their attention on decoding words.

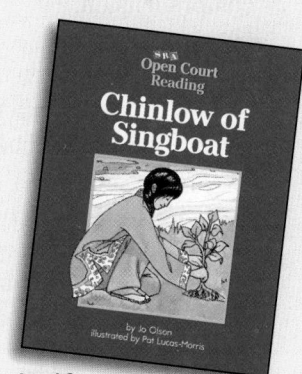

Level 3
Decodable Book

References

Adams, M. J. (1990) *Beginning to Read: Thinking and Learning about Print.* Cambridge, MA: M.I.T. Press.

Anderson, R. et al. (1984) *Becoming a Nation of Readers: The Report of the Commission on Reading.* Washington D.C.: The National Institute of Education, U.S. Department of Education.

Honig, B. (1996) *How Shall We Teach Our Children to Read?* Thousand Oaks, CA: Corwin Press.

✓ Reading aloud
✓ Print awareness
✓ Phonemic awareness through oral blending and segmentation
✓ Alphabetic principle
✓ Explicit systematic phonics and blending
✓ Fluency using decodable books for initial reading experience

Comprehension strategies and skills

Learning through themes

Authentic literary experiences

Spelling

Writing

Inquiry and research

Comprehension Strategies and Skills

"The active construction of meaning is what reading is all about. The focus has shifted away from teaching isolated skills and asking comprehension questions to teaching the comprehension process itself."

—*SRA/Open Court Reading*
Author, Michael Pressley

The primary aim of reading is comprehension. Experienced readers generally understand most of what they read, but just as importantly, they recognize when they do not understand, and they have at their command an assortment of comprehension strategies for monitoring and furthering their understanding.

Research has shown that students don't develop comprehension skills and strategies on their own. These strategies need to be taught and modeled before students begin to use them effectively. These strategies include the following.

Set Reading Goals

Good readers usually know what they want from a text. They:

- **Activate prior knowledge,** considering what they already know about the subject.
- **Browse the text** to get an idea of what to expect from a text.
- **Consider the purpose of reading,** whether it is reading for pleasure or to learn something specific.

Use Comprehension Strategies to Respond to Text

Good readers continually respond to the text they are reading and self check to make sure they're understanding. They

- **Ask questions** about what they are reading to monitor comprehension.
- **Clarify** the meanings of words, phrases, and longer pieces of text. They stop when they don't understand and clarify by rereading, using context, or asking someone else.
- **Make connections** between what they read and what they already know.
- **Make predictions** about what they are reading and then *confirm* or revise those predictions as they read.
- **Summarize** periodically to check their understanding.
- **Visualize,** or picture, what is happening in the text to comprehend descriptions, complex activities, or processes.

Develop Comprehension Skills

Good readers know that they are wasting their time if they don't understand what the author is saying. Good readers have learned to

- Consider the **author's point of view.**
- Understand the **author's purpose.**
- Comprehend **cause-and-effect** relationships.

- **Compare and contrast** items and events.
- **Draw conclusions** from what is read.
- Distinguish **fact from opinion.**
- Identify **main ideas and details.**
- **Make inferences** that help them understand what they are reading.
- Classify information into categories.
- Understand **sequence** of events.

Comprehension Strategies and Skills in *SRA/Open Court Reading*

SRA/Open Court Reading is based on the belief that students learn best when they are actively involved in constructing meaning. Instruction builds and supports the development of critical metacognitive strategies through teacher modeling and by demonstrating behaviors and strategies used by expert readers. The second part of every lesson, **Reading and Responding,** focuses on modeling comprehension strategies while reading **Big Book** and **Anthology** selections. Critical comprehension skills such as *classifying* and *sequencing* help students organize information, while skills such as *inferring* and *drawing conclusions* help students develop a deeper understanding of the author's meaning.

After the teacher models each strategy, gradually the responsibility for using strategies shifts to the students.

References

Anderson, V. and Roit, M. L. (1992) Implementing collaborative reading instruction for delayed readers in grades 6–10. *Elementary School Journal*, 92, 511–554.

Brown, A. L. et al. (1983) Learning, remembering, and understanding. In J. H. Flavell and E. M. Markman (eds.) *Handbook of Child Psychology, Volume 3, Cognitive Development* (pp. 77–166). NY: John Wiley.

Pressley, M. and Woloshyn, V. (1995) *Cognitive Strategy Instruction That Really Improves Children's Academic Performance.* Cambridge, MA: Brookline Books.

✓ Reading aloud
✓ Print awareness
✓ Phonemic awareness through oral blending and segmentation
✓ Alphabetic principle
✓ Explicit systematic phonics and blending
✓ Fluency using decodable books for initial reading experience
✓ Comprehension strategies and skills

Learning through themes

Authentic literary experiences

Spelling

Writing

Inquiry and research

Level 5 Teacher's Edition

Themes

"If schools are going to change in any direction that's relevant to the future, it has to be in helping students work toward deeper knowledge."

—*SRA/Open Court Reading*
Author, Carl Bereiter

There are many ways of organizing collections of literature—by genre, by author, by time period, by geographic area of author or subject matter. Each of these organizational methods has its strengths and is appropriate depending on the desired outcome of the reading.

A theme is another way of organizing literature. Themes are often considered to be topics, such as *animals* or *holidays*, around which literature, subject matter, or art projects are loosely organized. In traditional English literature instruction, themes are familiar as the central or dominating idea in a literary work. In this sense, a theme such as *humans versus nature* is made concrete through the people or action of a work of fiction. Subject areas organize content around themes as well. In the area of science, for example, *patterns of change* and *systems and interactions* are considered themes.

For the purposes of *SRA/Open Court Reading*, a *theme* is a carefully chosen *universal* concept or idea that gives the reader a point of reference from which to think, discuss, and learn.

Themes in *SRA/Open Court Reading*

There are two types of themes in *SRA/Open Court Reading* around which the unit literature is organized. One type of theme is based on *universal topics of interest* such as *Friendship, Perseverance,* and *Courage.* The literature in these units is organized to help students expand their perspectives in familiar areas. As they explore and discuss the unit concepts related to each topic, students are involved in activities that extend their experiences and offer opportunities for reflection.

Other units are organized around *research themes.* In these units, literature has been selected to provide students with a very solid base of information upon which they can build their own inquiry and research. These units delving into such areas as *Fossils* or *Our Country and Its People* invite students to become true researchers by choosing definite areas of interest to research and explore further.

Each unit contains a variety of selections presented as *Big Books* and stories in the *Student Anthologies* that are sequenced in a way that enables students to progressively deepen their insights. Each selection adds more information or a different perspective to

a student's growing body of knowledge. The selections reflect various types of writing, including fiction and nonfiction, all building on the unit theme.

The driving force behind the selection of literature for each unit was its ability to deepen or elaborate upon the theme. Therefore, the *Courage* unit at Level 4 does not just contain a group of stories loosely related to courage. Each selection adds a different insight into what courage is and how different people respond and cope with life challenges that call for courage.

The unit on the *Civil War* at Level 5 broadens students' understanding of what it was like to live through such a period by presenting the war through the eyes of youngsters and adults, soldiers and civilians, and slaves. Through both fiction and nonfiction, students see one event through the perspective of widely varying individuals. From these differing accounts and perspectives, students deepen their understanding of the period, the event, and the people who lived through it.

Themes are the major organizing principle of the literature in *SRA/Open Court Reading* from Levels K–6. The end of the second part of each lesson's selection, **Reading and Responding,** engages students in **Exploring the Theme.** Teaching strategies and suggestions are included in the **Teacher's Edition** in Levels K–6.

References

Brown, A. and Campione, J. (1990) Communities of learning and thinking, or a context by any other name. *Human Development,* 21, 108-125.

Spiro, R. J. et al. (1987) Knowledge acquisition for application: Cognitive flexibility and transfer in complex content domains. In B. K. Britton and S. M. Blynn (eds.), *Executive Control Processes in Reading.* Hillsdale, NJ: Earlbaum.

Willis, S. (1992) Interdisciplinary Learning. *ASCD Curriculum Update,* November, 1-8.

- ✓ Reading aloud
- ✓ Print awareness
- ✓ Phonemic awareness through oral blending and segmentation
- ✓ Alphabetic principle
- ✓ Explicit systematic phonics and blending
- ✓ Fluency using decodable books for initial reading experience
- ✓ Comprehension strategies and skills
- ✓ Learning through themes
- Authentic literary experiences
- Spelling
- Writing
- Inquiry and research

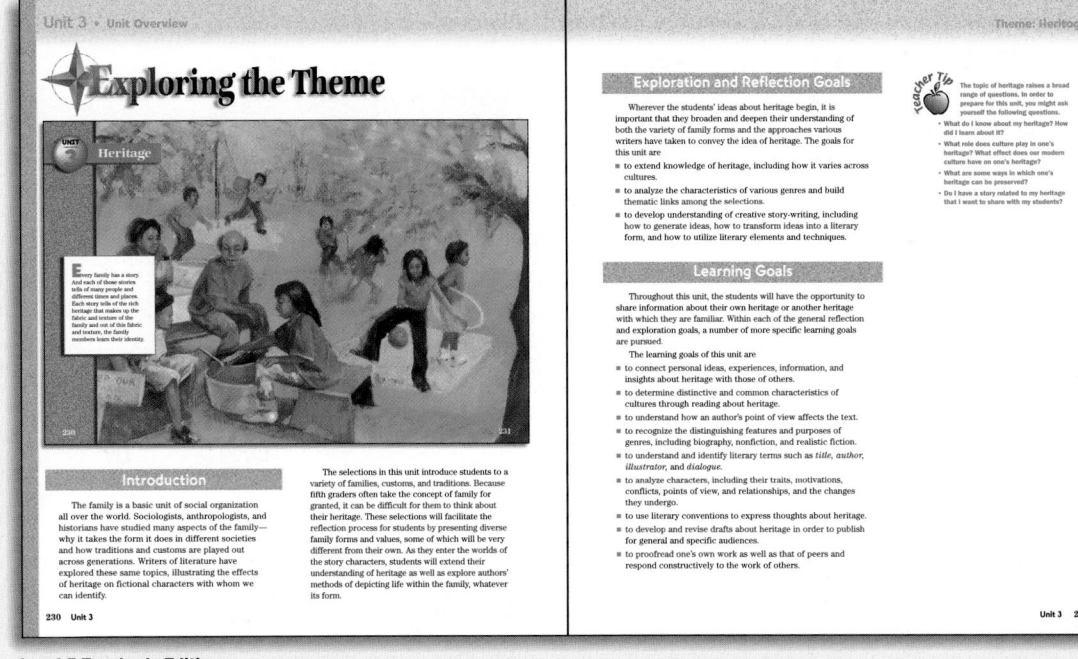

Level 5 Teacher's Edition

Literature

"The notion of bringing students up to fine literature, to history, to sociology, to astronomy instead of bringing the content down to them is critical both to the program and to the spirit students can develop. It's a real "I can do it" spirit, and indeed they can."

—SRA/Open Court Reading
Author, Marlene Scardamalia

Literature is defined as "writing that is regarded as having permanent worth through the very nature of its excellence." Whether the piece of literature is a finely turned short story, a riveting mystery, a moving essay, or a masterful piece of informational writing, literature is defined by its excellence.

Literature is often organized by *genre,* a term used to designate the types or categories of forms of literature. Traditional genres include kinds of literature such as tragedy, comedy, or poetry. Today genre would include novel, short story, essay, drama, mystery, realistic fiction, fantasy, fable, or even television play and informational article.

Classic or great works of literature are those which by common consent have achieved a recognized position in literary history for their superior qualities.

Literature in *SRA/Open Court Reading*

The literature selections in *SRA/Open Court Reading* as well as the approach to teaching the selections represent a long-standing commitment to teachers who are, in turn, committed to teaching children to be competent, independent learners through reading, writing, speaking, and listening. What better way for children to learn to read and grow as readers than through reading and listening to literature that has the stamp of approval of generations of readers?

One of the founding principles of *SRA/Open Court Reading* is that children need to read fine literature. Through fine literature—of every genre—they would and could learn from the best thinkers of every age. They would learn the beauty of the language. They would learn the beauty of an idea. They would and could learn the importance of clarity of thought and word.

Through each level of *SRA/Open Court Reading,* students are given a sampling of fine traditional literature that has withstood the test of time along with contemporary pieces that will someday join the ranks of the classics.

Since the literature pieces form the center core of the instruction, abundant care is taken to present the students with fine, thought-provoking models that they can follow in their own writing and that they

can use as springboards for their thinking, researching, and knowledge building. Students learn from classic and contemporary children's fiction authors such as Don Freeman, Eve Bunting, Patricia MacLachlan, Lloyd Alexander, Lucille Clifton, and Patricia Polacco as well as a growing number of fine writers of nonfiction for children—Milton Meltzer, Barbara Bash, and Ethan Herberman.

Each selection in *SRA/Open Court Reading* from Levels K–6 was chosen specifically because it added a new dimension of thought to the concept of a unit and because it was the best possible example of how different forms of literature can all express a particular theme. These two criteria—deepening of the concept and quality of the literature—formed the basis for all selections found in the program.

Through fine writing, fine minds can be developed.

✓ **Reading aloud**
✓ **Print awareness**
✓ **Phonemic awareness through oral blending and segmentation**
✓ **Alphabetic principle**
✓ **Explicit systematic phonics and blending**
✓ **Fluency using decodable books for initial reading experience**
✓ **Comprehension strategies and skills**
✓ **Learning through themes**
✓ **Authentic literary experiences**
  Spelling
  Writing
  Inquiry and research

References

Brown, A. and Campione, J. (1990) *Communities of learning and thinking, or a context by any other name.* Human Development, 21, 108–125.

International Reading Association. (1997) *More Teachers' Favorite Books for Kids: Teachers' Choices 1994–1996.* Newark, DE: International Reading Association.

Meltzer, Milton. (1994) *Non-Fiction for the Classroom: Milton Meltzer on Writing, History, and Social Responsibility.* Newark, DE: International Reading Association.

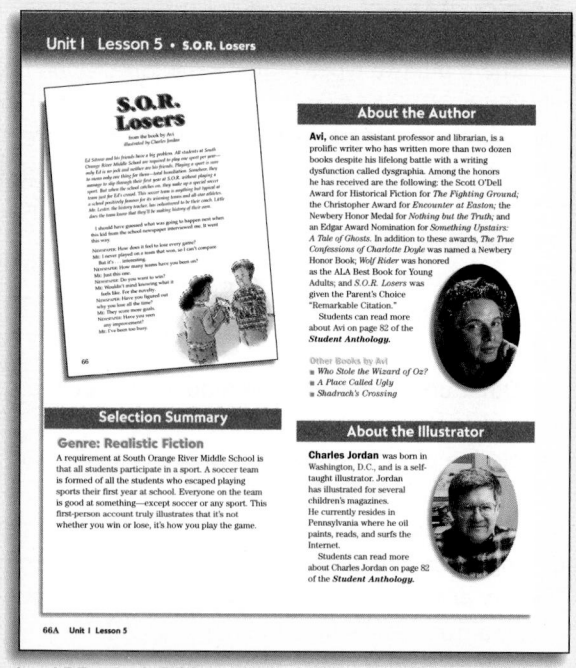

Level 5 Teacher's Edition

Dictation and Spelling

"One of the best ways to improve skill and fluency in decoding (figuring out written words by sounding them out) is encoding (putting spoken words into writing, or spelling)."

—*SRA/Open Court Reading*
Author, Jan Hirshberg

Reading and writing work hand in hand in teaching children how to read. By teaching students to recognize the spellings of the different speech sounds of the language, they learn to read. By teaching them to *listen* to the sounds of the language and assign the appropriate symbols to those sounds, we teach them to write. Reading and writing—these are the goals of all literacy instruction.

Dictation simply means listening carefully as a word or sentence is pronounced and then writing the words. The purpose of dictation is to teach children to write out words based on the sounds and spellings they have already learned. In order to write the words correctly, students must first hear the individual sounds, associate those sounds with specific spelling patterns, and then produce the written symbol that represents the sounds. These constitute a very complex series of abilities and skills.

These first steps in spelling instruction give students a vast advantage over spelling instruction that is based solely on memorization. The students learn quickly that there is no need to memorize most words that they need to spell—they can sound them out to themselves and write the spellings for the sounds they hear. This understanding alone gives students a level of comfort with spelling that cannot be achieved otherwise.

By using dictation as a teaching device rather than an assessment device, students learn the importance of listening carefully without the pressures associated with "testing." Daily dictation sessions enable students to make the connection between *decoding* (reading) and *encoding* (writing) so that they can see and understand the cumulative effects of all that they learn.

Benefits of Sound, Whole Word, and Sentence Dictation

- Increases students' familiarity with sound/spelling correspondences.
- Helps children develop a spelling strategy and integrate reading and writing.
- Introduces proofreading, a critical skill that children will use whenever they write.
- Gives students additional practice in using the conventions of writing, such as capitalization and end punctuation.
- Develops writing fluency as students apply the strategy of reflecting on the sounds they hear to writing unfamiliar words.

Dictation and Spelling in *SRA/Open Court Reading*

Dictation plays an integral part in the students' efforts to learn to read and write in *SRA/Open Court Reading*. From the very first introduction to phonics instruction and decoding, students reinforce their knowledge of sound/symbol relationships through dictation. Initially, they use **Letter Cards** (Levels K and 1) to build words. Soon, they begin writing words the teacher dictates. These activities give students practice writing words based on the sounds and spellings they have learned. After the teacher dictates a word, students identify the individual sounds and spellings in order to write the word. Dictation also includes the writing of sentences, which gives students additional practice using the conventions of writing, such as capitalization and punctuation. Students are at all times aware of the connection between what they hear and what they write.

Throughout the instruction and review of sounds and spellings in Level 1 and through the phonics review lessons in Levels 2 and 3, students are always given the opportunity to exhibit through dictation the sound/spelling knowledge they are acquiring or reviewing.

References

Adams, M. J. (1990) *Beginning to Read: Thinking and Learning about Print*. Cambridge, MA: M.I.T. Press.

Honig, B. (1996) *How Shall We Teach Our Children to Read?* Thousand Oaks, CA: Corwin Press.

Treiman, R. (1993) *Beginning to Spell*. NY: Oxford University Press.

- ✓ Reading aloud
- ✓ Print awareness
- ✓ Phonemic awareness through oral blending and segmentation
- ✓ Alphabetic principle
- ✓ Explicit systematic phonics and blending
- ✓ Fluency using decodable books for initial reading experience
- ✓ Comprehension strategies and skills
- ✓ Learning through themes
- ✓ Authentic literary experiences
- ✓ Spelling
- Writing
- Inquiry and research

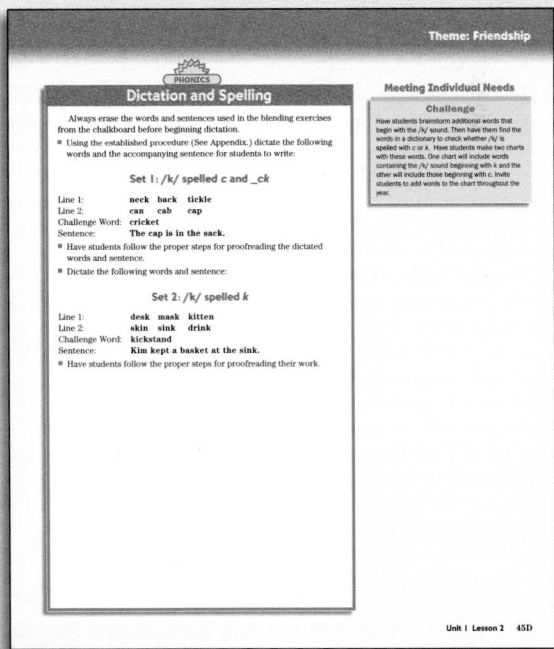

Level 3 Teacher's Edition

Writing

"Our role as teachers of young writers is to coach, encourage, and help children move toward conventional writing."

—*SRA/Open Court Reading*
Author, Marsha Roit

Professional writers go through a process that has implications for students learning to write. Many good writers begin by making notes of writing ideas in journals. They read writing produced by other writers and learn from it. They write for a particular purpose and with a particular audience in mind. They revise their writing until they are satisfied that it achieves its purpose. Often, as they revise, they rethink their original ideas and change their goals for a piece of writing. They may even begin again. They edit their writing to correct errors in spelling, punctuation, and grammar. They seek the advice of editors or other writers. Finally, they publish their work to share it with the audience for whom it is intended.

Writing is a recursive process as authors move back and forth through writing activities, from drafting to revising and back to drafting, to create their final pieces. It is a process of thinking, experimenting, and evaluating.

Children learn to write more effectively if they experience the writing process. Writing is a way of learning. When students work through the phases of the writing process, they gain important insights that promote deeper thinking and reasoning. This is especially true when writing has a clear purpose and is shared with others who respond to it constructively.

The writing process introduces students to the problem-solving and reasoning activities that writers engage in as they form ideas and, finally, communicate them through print. Systematically progressing through the process of prewriting, drafting, revising, proofreading, and sometimes publishing helps students clarify both their thinking and their writing so they can communicate effectively.

An environment with an emphasis on writing provides a multifaceted context for the development of higher-order thinking. Students learn to plan, which allows them to work out ideas in their heads; to set goals, which promotes interest and the ability to monitor progress; and to revise content, which engages them in the reworking and rethinking activities that elevate writing from a craft to a tool for discovery.

Writing in *SRA/Open Court Reading*

In *SRA/Open Court Reading,* writing provides students with a way to explore ideas that interest them and a way to share what they learn with others. Beginning in Level K, children develop their understanding of the writing process through shared writing activities. Opportunities for independent writing are provided as well. Group and individual writing activities conducted in Level 1 lay the foundation for Levels 2-6, when students use writing as a tool for building and sharing knowledge.

In *SRA/Open Court Reading,* critical writing conventions—spelling, punctuation, and grammar—are taught in the natural context of writing and emphasized as aids to communication. Activities like **Sentence Lifting** (Levels 2-6), a proofreading technique, use actual sentences from students' own written works as a vehicle for learning and applying writing skills and for developing proofreading skills.

Writing Seminar (Levels K-6) gives all students—from the most accomplished to the novice—an audience for their writing and a forum for discussing the stages of the writing process with others. As students' writing abilities increase, the kinds of writing they do become more varied, demanding, and challenging.

Throughout the program, from Levels K-6, students write daily. They learn to revise and to ask their peers for feedback. Students are given guidelines for presenting their work and for critiquing the work of their classmates. As students progress, they are expected to write to inform their peers of the research and exploration they are engaged in. Students become comfortable with the idea of revision and review. They learn to ask pertinent questions that help the writer sharpen a piece of writing and become clear and precise in the presentation of his or her ideas.

All of these writing skills work together to help the students become precise, clear thinkers who are capable of presenting their views in a manner that is informative, entertaining, and appropriate to the task and to the audience.

References

Bereiter, C. and Scardamalia, M. (1987) *The Psychology of Written Composition.* Hillsdale, NJ: Lawrence Erlbaum Associates.

Lucas. J. (1993) Teaching writing. *ASCD Curriculum Update,* January, 1-8.

Pressley, M. and Woloshyn, V. (1995) *Cognitive Strategy Instruction That Really Improves Children's Academic Performance.* Cambridge, MA: Brookline Books.

Roit, Marsha. (1992) *Creating a Community of Writers.* Peru, IL: Open Court Publishing Co.

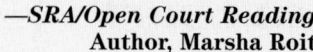

- ✓ Reading aloud
- ✓ Print awareness
- ✓ Phonemic awareness through oral blending and segmentation
- ✓ Alphabetic principle
- ✓ Explicit systematic phonics and blending
- ✓ Fluency using decodable books for initial reading experience
- ✓ Comprehension strategies and skills
- ✓ Learning through themes
- ✓ Authentic literary experiences
- ✓ Spelling
- ✓ Writing
-   Inquiry and research

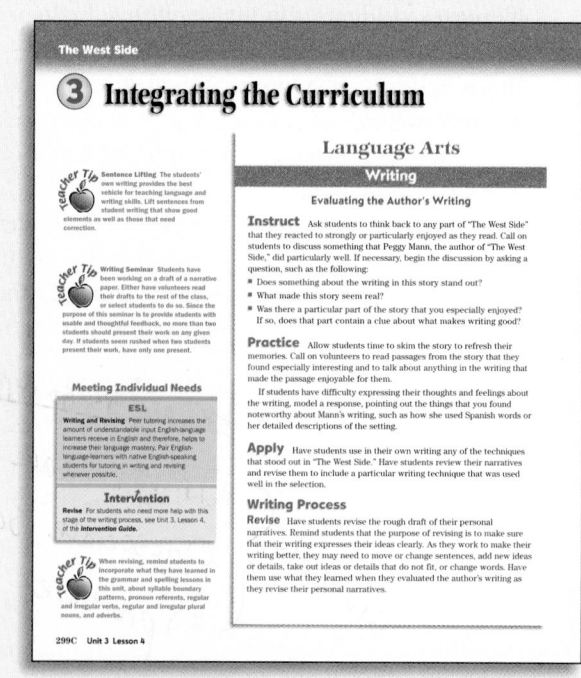

Level 5 Teacher's Edition

Inquiry, Research, and Exploration

"Expertise is acquired through deep and ever-increasing knowledge of a particular subject."

—SRA/Open Court Reading
Author, Carl Bereiter

As they become more fluent readers and writers, students find out that reading and writing give them power: the power to take control of their learning.

Although at times the purpose of reading is the simple pleasure of a good story or a wonderful poem, most adults and all school children spend more time reading to learn specific knowledge than they do reading for pleasure. Students need to be able to read and integrate into their knowledge system such diverse areas of study as American history and biology.

Adult readers research information on topics ranging from tax laws to lawn mower repair and maintenance. The ability to read to find out what you need or want to find out is one of the prime objectives of education.

Helping students learn how to do this—how to research and explore any area in which they are interested or for some reason need to know—is an aspect of education that is often neglected until high school or even college. By that time, it is very hard for many to break away from the simple read-and-report methods of research and exploration most students devise.

True research is a never-ending recursive cycle in which the researcher actively questions, develops ideas, or conjectures about why something is the way it is, and then pursues the answers. The answers for a researcher may never come. What does come is more questions. Developing the questions, pursuing the answers, developing conjectures, revising ideas, and setting off on new avenues of research and exploration are the stuff of which strong, deep knowledge and expertise are made.

Typically, research involves the following steps.

- Decide on a problem or question to research.
- Formulate an idea or conjecture about the research problem.
- Identify needs and make plans.
- Reevaluate the problem or question based on what we have learned so far and the feedback we have received.
- Revise the idea or conjecture.
- Identify new needs and make new plans.
- Informally and formally present findings.
- Develop new questions.

Inquiry, Research, and Exploration in *SRA/Open Court Reading*

Inquiry, research, and exploration form the heart of *SRA/Open Court Reading.* In order to encourage students to understand how reading can enhance their lives and help them to become mature, educated adults, they are asked in each unit to use what they are learning in the unit as the basis for further exploration and research. The unit selections are the base for their explorations.

In *SRA/Open Court Reading,* students model the behavior of expert learners and researchers. Opportunities for students, individually and in groups, to explore, to write about, and to discuss key concepts in a specific area lead to improved critical thinking and reading skills. Students become independent, intentional, self-directed learners.

The idea of research is introduced as early as Kindergarten. Procedures for collaborative research are formalized further in first grade. Beginning in second grade and continuing through sixth grade, students are led, working individually or collaboratively, to pursue problems that interest them in the same manner that an adult would conduct research.

Students use the **Anthology** selections as a knowledge base for further exploration. They read to learn, then share what they learn with each other.

Because each student contributes to the research in a unique way, all students feel the sense of purpose and accomplishment achieved through collaborative research.

References

Brown, A. and Campione, J. (1990) Communities of learning and thinking, or a context by any other name. *Human Development*, 21, 109-125.

Heckman, P. E., et. al. (1994) Planting seeds: Understanding through investigation. *Educational Leadership*, February, 36-39.

Schack, G. D. (1993) Involving students in authentic research. *Educational Leadership*, April, 29-31.

- ✓ Reading aloud
- ✓ Print awareness
- ✓ Phonemic awareness through oral blending and segmentation
- ✓ Alphabetic principle
- ✓ Explicit systematic phonics and blending
- ✓ Fluency using decodable books for initial reading experience
- ✓ Comprehension strategies and skills
- ✓ Learning through themes
- ✓ Authentic literary experiences
- ✓ Spelling
- ✓ Writing
- ✓ Inquiry and research

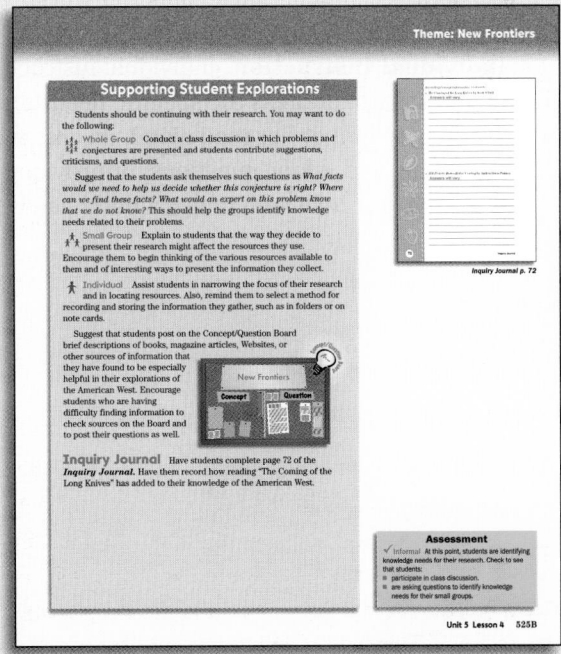

Level 5 Teacher's Edition

Teaching Techniques

> *"We really see a lot of agreement that people want students working on longer-term projects, thinking in depth about things, working collaboratively, and taking responsibility for their own learning. I think that's true of parents, teachers, and administrators."*
>
> —*SRA/Open Court Reading*
> **Author, Joe Campione**

Deciding how you and your students will interact most effectively, how you will best help all of your students learn, how your students can interact with each other to optimize their learning—these are the decisions and considerations all teachers take into account when they decide which teaching techniques will work best. The different techniques include:

- **Whole-Class Instruction.** The understanding that all students in a classroom—the stars as well as those who are faltering—will benefit from the presentation, discussion, and review of all of the subject matter covered is the basis for whole-class instruction. By making whole-class presentations, the student who is struggling gets the benefit of the initial instruction and the discussion and then benefits from the reteaching and reinforcement. He or she is not left out and expected to do and learn less than his or her classmates.

- **Collaborative Learning.** Collaborative learning can take place in whole-class or small-group situations. Collaboration is the process of working with others on classroom instruction as well as on projects. Collaboration occurs in discussions, in research, and in presenting and reviewing another's work.

- **Small-Group Instruction.** Small-group instruction is useful for collaborative research and study, and it is also appropriate for reteaching. Students can strengthen their knowledge and skills and can work with the teacher or their peers to gain the skills and knowledge that they need. In addition, small groups and individuals who are excelling can benefit from the extra encouragement and affirmation that working in small groups or meeting individually with the teacher can afford.

- **Individual Instruction.** Individual instruction provides an opportunity to address the specific needs of a student. It may be listening to him or her read aloud, discussing a piece of writing, answering and asking questions, or providing specific, focused instruction or help with the particular needs of one student.

Teaching Techniques in *SRA/Open Court Reading*

Different teaching techniques have been woven into *SRA/Open Court Reading* to provide for the most effective instruction.

✓ Reading aloud
✓ Print awareness
✓ Phonemic awareness through oral blending and segmentation
✓ Alphabetic principle
✓ Explicit systematic phonics and blending
✓ Fluency using decodable books for initial reading experience
✓ Comprehension strategies and skills
✓ Learning through themes
✓ Authentic literary experiences
✓ Spelling
✓ Writing
✓ Inquiry and research

Whole-Class Instruction. In *SRA/Open Court Reading* rather than breaking the class into "ability groups," the initial instruction is presented to all children. Some will understand it right away, some will understand it as a result of the discussions that take place about the subject, and some won't understand at all. It is only after students have been presented with the material that those who don't understand are singled out for extra help and encouragement.

Collaborative Learning. Discussion plays an integral part in *SRA/Open Court Reading* in whole-class or small-group situations, as students learn to express their opinions, defend their positions, and explain their thoughts. They discover that by working together, they all learn much more than they would have learned individually. Discussion also offers English Language Learners the nonthreatening environment needed for expressing opinions and verifying understandings.

From Level K through Level 6, whole-class discussions of reading selections provide opportunities for students to think, predict, and draw connections between the selection they are reading, other selections, and their own experiences.

Small-Group and Individual Instruction. Once problem areas are identified, small groups or individuals can be given the extra help they need. **Independent Work Time,** built into every day's lesson plan, is the opportune time to administer this extra help. **Independent Work Time** is the regular, established time each day in which students work individually or in small groups, with or without the teacher. Once students become used to **Independent Work Time** and take responsibility for their time and work, the teacher is free to meet individually with students.

References

Aronson, E. (1978) *The Jigsaw Classroom.* Beverly Hills, CA: Sage.

Brown, A. and Campione, J. (1990) Communities of learning and thinking, or a context by any other name. *Human Development,* 21, 108-125.

Willis, S. (1992) Cooperative Learning Shows Staying Power. *ASCD Update,* 34, 1-2.

Technology

"Too often, technology is being used for technology's sake. We always must hold up the standard of why technology becomes a better tool or a better strategy to reach our objectives than some other tool or strategy."

—*SRA/Open Court Reading*
Author, Iva E. Carruthers

At one time, the biggest advance in technology applicable to schools was the invention of the ballpoint pen. The disappearance of inkwells made everyone's life easier and more efficient. Today, the advances in technology and the possible effects these advances may have on schools, teaching, and children is almost mind-boggling. What is technology? How good is it? What can it do for my students and me? When will there be time to learn how to use it all?

Basically, *technology* is applying science to needs. Technology that is applicable to the classroom runs the gamut from overhead projectors to powerful computers. Videocassette players, videodisc players, filmstrip machines, printers, and copiers fall somewhere in between.

Much of this is a boon to the classroom. Movies are now easily accessed and can be shown on television screens—movie projectors are no longer needed. Overhead projectors allow for visual organizers that can be tailored for particular classes. And then there is the computer. There is no doubt that the computer can and does enhance the teaching and learning that goes on in a classroom, but the flood of materials—especially those called educational materials—is overwhelming.

The essential questions to ask about any piece of technology are What can I accomplish with this that I couldn't do without it? and What are the costs and benefits to my students and me?

Technology in *SRA/Open Court Reading*

In *SRA/Open Court Reading,* technology serves very specific purposes. These are

To help expand the students' knowledge of the concepts being presented.

Listening Library Audiocassettes of the selections presented in the program are available to enhance student experience of the selections as well as to help any students who may be having difficulty reading a selection. In addition, students in Levels K–3 will delight in the silly, alliterative stories that help them remember the sounds represented on the **Sound/Spelling Cards.** Each consonant and short vowel is introduced by an engaging character that is the personification of the sound.

To give students multidimensional avenues of review and practice.

Phonics instruction is augmented with an audiocassette of interactive stories to help students hear the sounds they are studying. Along with the audiocassette, students have the opportunity to review and practice their growing phonics skills and increasing fluency by using the **Phonics CD-ROM** (Levels K–3) or accessing these lessons through the **SRA Web Site (www.SRA4kids.com).** These activities offer students an opportunity to interact with animated **Sound/Spelling Cards** as well as review their reading of **Decodable Books** with interactive versions of the stories.

To allow students to learn about information gathering and communication and to use available technology to the best advantage.

Research is an integral part of the *SRA/Open Court Reading* program. Students using the program have access through the **SRA Web Site** to **Internet** sites specifically chosen for their relevance to the concepts the students are working with. Students are able, through the site, to communicate with other students around the country who are using *SRA/Open Court Reading* and can thus extend and deepen their knowledge and insights into the concepts. In addition, the **Research CD-ROM** (Levels 1–6) can help them organize their research and keep track of what they are learning.

- ✓ Reading aloud
- ✓ Print awareness
- ✓ Phonemic awareness through oral blending and segmentation
- ✓ Alphabetic principle
- ✓ Explicit systematic phonics and blending
- ✓ Fluency using decodable books for initial reading experience
- ✓ Comprehension strategies and skills
- ✓ Learning through themes
- ✓ Authentic literary experiences
- ✓ Spelling
- ✓ Writing
- ✓ Inquiry and research

To help the teacher develop the techniques that have been proven effective in teaching children to become strong, competent readers.

Video presentations on videodisc of lessons in Kindergarten through Level 3 help teachers new to *SRA/Open Court Reading* quickly learn the methods and routines found effective in presenting the phonics skills and helping the children become strong, competent readers. These lesson presentations—keyed to specific lessons and lesson parts—can be accessed through a simple swipe of a videodisc barcode. Teachers who do not have access to a videodisc player can view the same material with VCR equipment.

In addition, **Program Videos** are available for training and informational purposes. This video series will give you a full overview of the program, its philosophy, its authors, and very helpful hints and tips on achieving the best results with your class.

To help the teacher manage the lessons and materials.

The **Lesson Planner CD-ROM** can help you manage your teaching schedule, the materials you need to use, and the scores the students attain. You can rearrange your week, make note of what needs to be done on a given day, and print your updated schedules as needed.

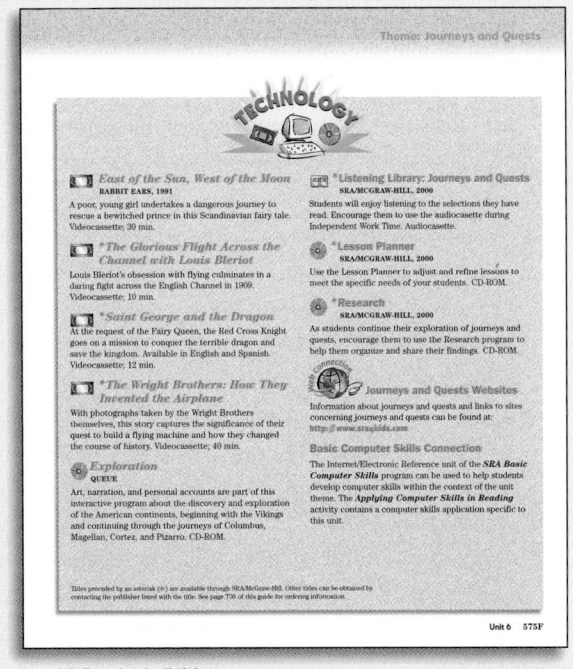

Level 5 Teacher's Edition

Assessment

True assessment is a tool for learning rather than a mere measure of achievement.

—*SRA/Open Court Reading*
Author, Joe Campione

The goal of true assessment is to provide information for instruction. It helps determine what students know and how to change the instruction to help students learn what they need to know.

Assessment in any form is most valuable when it leads to changes in classroom instruction. Assessment tasks should reflect classroom practices and the abilities students are expected to acquire. When the results of assessment suggest that students are having a difficult time mastering a skill, the teacher should implement alternate instructional strategies and materials.

Informal teacher observations, structured assessments, and on-demand reading and writing evaluations provide a comprehensive picture of student growth and progress and avoid the more limited view of performance that results from basing assessment on just one or two measures.

The teacher's professional judgment is the keystone of the evaluation process. The teacher is the person who knows the student best, and teacher observations are the single most important source of information about student growth and potential.

Assessment in *SRA/Open Court Reading*

The assessment components of *SRA/Open Court Reading* reflect the balanced nature of the series itself. The following are principles that guided the development of the assessment components.

- **Ease of use for the teacher.** The assessments are easily administered and scored, feature the same language that is used in the instructional components of the series, and correspond to the sequence of instruction in the series. The assessments are typically short enough to prevent fatigue from affecting student performance yet long enough to provide a dependable measure of student skills and abilities. Assessments are distributed throughout the units of a given grade level so teachers have an opportunity to engage in "continuous assessment," diminishing the likelihood that a student will fall behind without the teacher being aware of it and having an opportunity to intervene.

- **Assessment of critical skills.** The skills that are featured prominently in the series—the skills that are critical to the reading process—are the focus of assessment. These same skills are typically included on standardized tests and in state standards, so the assessments will help teachers respond to the accountability system under which they work.

- **Variety in assessment.** In order to gather evidence of student performance from a range of sources, in addition to the formal and informal assessments described above, *SRA/Open Court Reading* includes

  - **Pre- and Posttests.** Pre- and **Posttests** at each grade level (there is no Pretest for Kindergarten) can be used to guide instruction or for accountability purposes.

- **Unit Tests.** These cover the concepts that were introduced in each unit and give the teacher an opportunity to observe how well students have mastered a range of skills and how they can apply what they have learned in an independent reading situation.

- **Comprehension Assessment.** Selections in the **Anthology** serve as the basis for a comprehension assessment that includes multiple choice, short answer, and extended answer items.

- **Self-Assessment.** The students are continually involved in the process of self-assessment, especially as they meet in **Writing Seminar,** present their findings to their peers and complete the informal end-of-unit wrap-up pages in the **Inquiry Journal** (Levels 2–6).

- **Portfolio Assessment.** The **Inquiry Journal,** an ongoing, cumulative record of the students' explorations and research activities, provides a clear picture of their growth. Throughout the program all student writing is an opportunity for portfolio assessment.

- **Family Evaluation.** A variety of resources promote family involvement and provide the opportunity for home evaluation of a student's progress. Convenient blackline masters of letters, written in English as well as Spanish, explain to families what the students are learning in class. These letters, along with being informative, contain activities that children and their families can complete together.

✓ Reading aloud
✓ Print awareness
✓ Phonemic awareness through oral blending and segmentation
✓ Alphabetic principle
✓ Explicit systematic phonics and blending
✓ Fluency using decodable books for initial reading experience
✓ Comprehension strategies and skills
✓ Learning through themes
✓ Authentic literary experiences
✓ Spelling
✓ Writing
✓ Inquiry and research

References

Hansen, J. (1992) Students' evaluations bring reading and writing together. *The Reading Teacher*, 46, 100-105.

Paris, S. G. et. al. (1992) A framework for authentic literacy assessment. *The Reading Teacher*, 46, 88-98.

Winograd, P. et. al. (1991) Improving the assessment of literacy. *The Reading Teacher*, 45, 108-116.

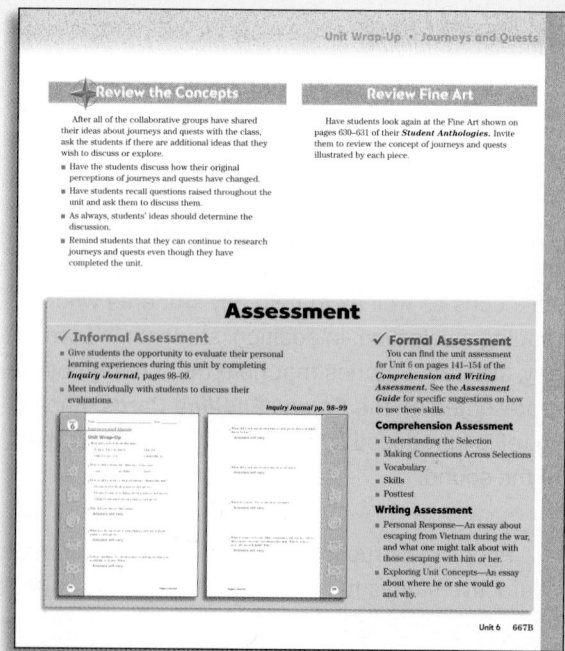

Level 5 Teacher's Edition

SRA Open Court Reading
Program Authors

Well credentialed leaders in their fields of specialization, Open Court's authors are at the forefront of educational research. They are experts on how children learn to read and learn to learn. The instructional components of *SRA/Open Court Reading* provide teachers and students all the advantages that the very best in educational research has to offer to the field of reading instruction.

Marilyn Jager Adams

is a Senior Scientist in the Psychology Department at Bolt Beranek and Newman, Inc., a research and development laboratory in Cambridge, Massachusetts. She has been a Senior Research Scientist at Brown University and has been affiliated with the Center for the Study of Reading at the University of Illinois since 1975. She is the author of *Beginning to Read: Thinking and Learning About Print* (MIT Press, 1990), written on behalf of the U.S. Secretary of Education as mandated by Congress. The book, the most comprehensive study of beginning reading undertaken to date, examines instructional practices from a historical perspective and critiques them in terms of theoretical and empirical research in education, psychology, and linguistics.

Carl Bereiter

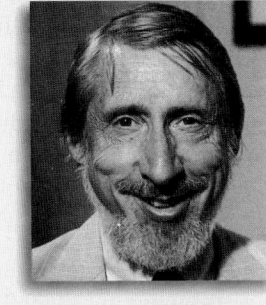

is Professor at the Centre for Applied Cognitive Science at the Ontario Institute for Studies in Education in Toronto. Both he and Open Court author Ann Brown are members of the National Academy of Education. He has co-authored many curriculum projects including SRA/Open Court's reading and mathematics programs. He is the co-author with Marlene Scardamalia of *The Psychology of Written Composition* (1987) *and Surpassing Ourselves: The Nature and Implications of Expertise* (1993) and has published extensively on the nature of teaching and learning.

Ann Brown

is Professor in Math, Science, and Technology in the Graduate School of Education at the University of California at Berkeley. She is Past President of the American Educational Research Association (AERA) and served on the congressional panel to monitor National Assessment of Educational Progress (NAEP) state-by-state assessments. She has received many honors and awards in both the United States and England for her contributions to educational research. At present, Dr. Brown and her husband, Joe Campione, are focusing their classroom research on students as researchers and teachers, a significant aspect of their study of distributed expertise in the classroom.

Joe Campione

is Professor in the School of Education at the University of California at Berkeley. He has long been known for his work in cognitive development, transfer of learning, individual differences, and assessment. He is working with Ann Brown to discover ways to restructure grade-school learning environments to take advantage of distributed expertise in the classroom and to use interactive learning to promote scientific literacy within communities of learners.

Iva Carruthers

is President of Nexus Unlimited, Inc., a human resources development and computer services consulting firm; and Ed Tech, a computer software development company. Formerly Chairperson and Professor of the Sociology Department at Northeastern Illinois University, Dr. Carruthers has also been an elementary school teacher, a high school counselor, and a research-historian. In addition to developing software for teaching African-American history and interdisciplinary subjects, she has produced study guides on African-American and African history used by students to prepare for appearances on the televised academic quiz show, "Know Your Heritage," which she coproduces. She travels worldwide as a consultant and lecturer in both educational technology and matters of multicultural inclusion.

Robbie Case

is Professor of Education at Stanford University and Director of the Laidlaw-Centre at the Institute of Child Study, University of Toronto. He received his Ph.D. from the Ontario Institute for Studies in Education. For the past twenty-five years he has conducted research on the relationship between children's learning and their cognitive development during the elementary school years. His books and scholarly articles on that topic have been translated into many languages.

Jan Hirshberg

holds an Ed.D. in Reading, Language, and Learning Disabilities from Harvard University. She has taught in elementary school classrooms and has also served as a school district reading consultant. At Harvard she was a teaching fellow, research assistant, instructor, and lecturer at the Graduate School of Education. Her reading specialties are in linguistics and early literacy. Her work has focused on how children learn to read and write and the logistics of teaching reading and writing in the early elementary grades. She is an author of the kindergarten and grade 1 levels of Open Court's 1989 reading and writing program as well as *Collections for Young Scholars*, Open Court's 1995 reading, writing, and learning program.

Anne McKeough

is an Associate Professor in the Department of Educational Psychology at the University of Calgary. She holds a Ph.D. in Cognitive Science from the Ontario Institute for Studies in Education, University of Toronto, and has received a number of research awards and grants. She is coeditor of two volumes, *Toward the Practice of Theory Based Instruction: Current Cognitive Theories and Their Educational Promise* (1991) and *Teaching for Transfer: Fostering Generalization in Learning* (1995), and has authored a number of book chapters and articles advocating the benefits of a continued and reflective partnership between teaching practices and child development. Her current research focuses on the cognitive development and developmentally based instruction.

Michael Pressley

is the Director of Masters of Education Program and Programs in Teaching and Leadership, and Professor of Psychology at the University of Notre Dame. Dr. Pressley's wide-ranging research interests have included a mixture of experimental psychology and ethnographic projects. He does both basic laboratory research on cognition and learning and applied work in educational settings. Memory development and reading comprehension strategies have received much of his attention. He is the North American editor of *Applied Cognitive Psychology* and coeditor of the *Journal of Reading Behavior*. He is coeditor of *Promoting Academic Competence and Literacy in School* (1992) and coauthor of *Cognitive Strategy Instruction that Really Improves Children's Academic Performance* (1995).

Marsha Roit

a national consultant on reading, holds a Ph.D. from Harvard University where her studies focused on reading and language development. She spends considerable time in classrooms working with children to develop and demonstrate reading and writing activities and training teachers and administrators. Her work has been published in a variety of education journals, including *Exceptional Children, Journal of Learning Disabilities*, and *The Elementary School Journal*. She has presented her work at national and international conferences.

Marlene Scardamalia

is Professor and Head of the Centre for Applied Cognitive Science at the Ontario Institute for Studies in Education, Toronto. She is a member of editorial and review boards for scholarly journals in areas encompassing research, theory, and application of written communication; learning and instructional sciences; and educational computing. Her published work has focused on developmental and instructional psychology. Dr. Scardamalia is presently engaged in studies of text-based and knowledge-based questioning by children, computer technology for collaborative processes, and collaborative knowledge-building environments for tomorrow's schools.

Gerald H. Treadway, Jr.

is a Professor in the College of Education at San Diego State University. He is responsible for teaching Literacy Training, Bilingual Methods, and Reading Comprehension, Diagnosis, and Assessment. He has been involved with California's Curriculum Development and Supplemental Materials Commission, the California Reading and Literature Project, and the Center for the Improvement of Reading Instruction. He was also chief consultant for Reading Programs in the Dallas Independent School District. He is a frequent speaker at the International Reading Association conference, as well as the California Reading Association conferences.

SRA Open Court Reading
Teacher Reviewers

Raquel Alcocer Grade: 2
Lozano Special Emphasis
Corpus Christi, TX

Janice Baggett Grade: 4
Canopy Oaks Elm
Tallahassee, FL

Martha Berreda Grade: 3
Los Fresnos ISD
Los Fresnos, TX

Stacey Brazzel Grade: 1
Pasadena ISD
Houston, TX

Roberta Carter Grade: 6
Arlington ISD
Arlington, TX

Shirley Castoldi Grade: 5
Canopy Oaks Elm
Tallahassee, FL

Cindy Coffland Grade: K
Rulon M Ellis Elm
Chubbock, ID

Mary Coppage Grade: K
Garden Grove Elm
Garden Grove, FL

Ann Danford Grade: 2
Canopy Oaks Elm
Tallahassee, FL

Emmy Daniel Grade: 1
S Shores Elm
Decatur, IL

Linda English Grade: 3
Pope Elm
Arlington, TX

Pam Everett Grade: 3
Vern Patrick Elm
Redmond, OR

Bobette Finch Grade: 4
Indian Hills Elm
Pocatello, ID

Anne Fowler Grade: K
Smith Elm
Raleigh, NC

Twyla Jo French Grade: 5
New Highland Elm
Elizabethtown, KY

Eva Garcia Grade: K
WB Travis Elm
Corpus Christi, TX

Mandy Garcia-Lopez Grade: 2
Abraham Lincoln Elm
Pomona, CA

Melissa Garza Grade: 2
WB Travis Elm
Corpus Christi, TX

Theresa Gore Grade: 3
Canopy Oaks Elm
Tallahassee, FL

Lupe Guel Grade: 3
WB Travis Elm
Corpus Christi, TX

Kristen Guyon Grade: 3
Edahow Elm
Pocatello, ID

Nancy Hanssen Grade: K
Highland Ranch Elm
San Diego, CA

Maxine Haywood Grade: 5
WB Travis Elm
Corpus Christi, TX

Jennifer Heath Grade: 4
Kelso Elm
Inglewood, CA

Angela Holt Grade: 2
Stephen C. Foster Elm
Indianapolis, IN

Laura Joanos Grade: 1
Canopy Oaks Elm
Tallahassee, FL

Linda Kehe Grade: 1
Tualatin Elm
Tualatin, OR

Nancy Kotkosky Grade: 6
State Street Elm
South Gate, CA

Helen Lee Grade: 1
George R Stuart Elm
Cleveland, TN

Millie Lively Grade: 1
Monclam Elm
Princeton, WV

Mary Massey Grade: K
Schallert Elm
Alice, TX

Pauline McClendon Grade: 4
Odem ISD
Odem, TX

Pauline McClendon Grade: 2
Odem ISD
Odem, TX

Anne McKee Grade: 2
Tualatin Elm.
Tualatin, OR

Lannie McNeese Grade: 1
WB Travis Elm
Corpus Christi, TX

Maxine McPherson Grade: 6
Canopy Oaks Elm
Tallahassee, FL

Patricia Morwood Grade: 2
Marva Collins Prep
Cincinnati, OH

Kristi Mullinix Grade: 5
S Shores Elm
Decatur, IL

Margaret Parker Grade: 5
Hovart Elm
Los Angeles, CA

Marilee Patrick Grade: 4
Vern Patrick Elm
Redmond, OR

Rosa Pope Grade: 3
Camella Elm
Whittier, CA

Laura Powell Grade: 5
Heflen Elm
Houston, TX

Mary Quintal Grade: 1
Hanna Ranch Elm
Hercules, CA

Alice Rabagos Grade: 4
WB Travis Elm
Corpus Christi, TX

Chequetta Roberts Grade: 1
PS 241
Brooklyn, NY

Brenda Scheer Grade: 6
Tendoy Elm
Pocatello, ID

Ruth Ann Schum Grade: 2
S Shores Elm
Decatur, IL

Ana Silva Grade: ESL2
Ysleta ISD
El Paso, TX

Homero Silva Grade: ESL3
Ysleta ISD
El Paso, TX

Cherry Mae Smith Grade: 2
Heyburn Elm
Heyburn, ID

Kathryn Sprinkle Grade: 1
Benito-Martinez Elm
El Paso, TX

Suzanne Stidom Grade: 3
Mary Moore Elm
Arlington, TX

Thelma Strong Grade: 6
Walsh Elm
Chicago, IL

Maryanne Tinker Grade: 1
Robert Lee Frost Elm
Indianapolis, IN

Marsha Van Huss Grade: 1
John F Kennedy Elm
Kingsport, TN

Teresa Vargas Grade: 1
Heyburn Elm
Heyburn, ID

Lorraine Villareal Grade: 1
Los Fresnos ISD
Los Fresnos, TX

Bev Wilker Grade: 5
Tyhee Elm
Pocatello, ID

Getting Started

Preparing to Use

SRA Open Court Reading

This section provides an overview of classroom management issues and introductory activities that explain the function of the **SRA/Open Court Reading** program elements and how to use them.

Organizing Your Classroom

Reading

For students to become more than competent decoders, they must become strategic readers. That is, they must learn how to think about what they read and to use specific reading strategies and behaviors. Teachers help students become strategic readers by modeling the key reading strategies used by expert readers and by providing them with multiple opportunities to read fine literature. First-rate reading selections illustrate for students the best possible use of language and stimulate them to think about, write about, and discuss important ideas and concepts.

Oral Reading

Reading aloud is one of the best ways for students to develop their reading skills. In the course of the daily lessons, students will read orally from the **Student Anthology** selections. To promote students' reading growth, however, you will want multiple opportunities for oral reading. For example, you may:

- ask students to reread in pairs the anthology selections.
- set aside a period of time each day for oral reading of trade books.
- set up a home reading log, asking parents to read with their students.
- have students partner-read content-area texts from other subjects your class is studying.

However you do it, you will find that every minute of oral reading by students pays off in terms of reading growth.

On a regular basis, take time to listen to students as they read favorite stories and books aloud. Listening to students read from an anthology selection provides you with information about their ability to manage the vocabulary and concepts of the text, as well as to gauge their reading fluency. Listening to students read orally allows you to evaluate their developing fluency and to identify particular areas with which they need more work. To complement these activities, you may also want to listen to students read books they have selected for themselves. This will give you insights into their taste in reading materials, their own opinion of their reading ability, as well as their reading progress.

Reading Center

Provide as many books as possible for your classroom Reading Center. During the course of the year the students will be asked to do much reading on specific subjects. Prepare your classroom ahead of time by bringing in books on the concepts or themes the students will be studying. You may choose to order the **Classroom Library** that accompanies the program or you may decide to provide your own library. In either case, you should encourage students to bring in books that they have enjoyed and want to share with their classmates.

Listening Center

Each selection in the **Student Anthology** is recorded on audiotape for use in your classroom. As you read each selection, encourage students to listen to the recording during Independent Work Time. Provide one or two tape recorders that work both with and without earphones. In this way, individual students may listen to selections without disturbing the rest of the class. You will also be able to play the tapes for the whole class if you choose.

You should also encourage students to record their own stories, then share these stories with their classmates.

Writing

Reading and writing are interwoven processes, and each helps build and strengthen the other. Throughout the year, students do a tremendous amount of writing, both independently and collaboratively. They write for an array of purposes and audiences. Extended writing includes stories and various nonfiction pieces such as research reports, biographies, persuasive papers, and letters. In addition, they write daily in the form of note taking, making lists, labeling pictures, and making journal entries.

To assure success in writing, the students will need:

- **A Writing Journal**
  Each student should provide his or her own Writing Journal. This journal can be a three-ring binder with tabbed sections; however, a spiral notebook with sections will work also.

- **A Writing Portfolio**
  An artist's portfolio contains pieces that the artist considers to be the best of his or her work. Help students develop a similar portfolio of their writing. From time to time, hold conferences with individual students so that they can show you the work they have put in their portfolios and explain what they particularly like about the pieces they have chosen to keep.

  You should keep your own portfolio for each student in which you place samples of written work that show the student's progress throughout the year.

- **A Writing-in-Progress Folder**
  Students should be encouraged continually to revise and edit their writing. Each student should have a folder in which to keep this writing-in-progress. Any pocket folder will work for this purpose; however, you may choose to order the **Writing Folders** that accompany the **SRA/Open Court Reading** program. In addition to pockets to hold student writing, these folders contain a list of proofreading marks and tips for revising that students will find useful.

Writing Center

The Writing Center should contain materials students can use to write and illustrate their work, such as pencils, crayons, pens, white paper, colored paper, old magazines they can cut up, scissors, and staplers.

Inquiry, Reflection, and Exploration

In **SRA/Open Court Reading**, lessons are integrated through extensive reading, writing, and discussion. In turn, the lessons are organized into learning units, with each selection in a unit adding more information or a different perspective to the students' growing knowledge of a theme or concept.

The program contains two kinds of units:

- **Reflection** units allow students to expand their perspectives on universal themes such as kindness, courage, perseverance, and friendship by relating what they read to their own experiences.

- **Inquiry** units involve students in the research process, giving them the tools they need to discover and learn on their own and as part of a collaborative group. Inquiry activities provide students with a systematic structure for exploration that is driven by their own interests and conjectures.

Both Reflection and Inquiry units are designed to help students:

- deepen their comprehension by enabling them to apply the skills they are learning to texts and activities of their own choosing.

- synthesize and organize what they are learning in order to present their findings to their classmates.

- determine suitable avenues of inquiry and methods of presentation.

- become more independent and responsible about their time and efforts.

- work efficiently in collaborative groups.

Inquiry Center

The Inquiry Center should contain materials that will facilitate the students' efforts as they work together on unit explorations, including:

- reference books such as dictionaries and encyclopedias.

- computers—preferably with Internet access. The SRA Home Page (see **http://www.sra4kids.com**) includes Internet sites specifically related to the themes the students are studying.

- books on the themes the students are studying. You may choose to order the **Classroom Library** that accompanies the program. In addition, bibliographies of additional related books can be found following each unit in the **Student Anthologies**.

Concept/Question Board

One of the primary goals of *SRA/Open Court Reading* is to help you and your students form a community of learners. To do this, sharing information is essential. The **Concept/Question Board** is a bulletin board or chart. The students can share their growing knowledge about a unit theme or concept by posting on the Board newspaper clippings, magazine articles, information taken from the Internet, photographs, and other items that might be of interest to or help for their classmates. As the class progresses through a unit, the Board serves as the place where common interests become evident. As these interests emerge, the students can use them as the basis for forming collaborative groups to explore ideas in greater depth.

In addition, the Board gives students an outlet for questions that arise as they read on their own. The questions can be written directly on a sheet of paper attached to the Board, or they can be written on separate slips of paper and pinned to it. Self-sticking notepads can also be used. The **Concept/Question Board** lets students know that questions are not problems but a way of learning. Questions thus become a springboard to further exploration. Collaborative groups can be formed around common questions.

The Board should change constantly, reflecting the developing and changing interests of the class. For the **Getting Started** section you can give the Board a title, such as "Reading and Writing."

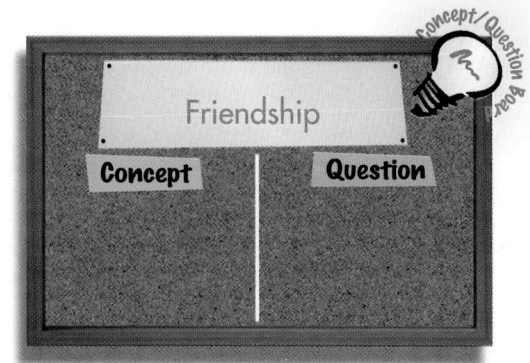

Independent Work Time

Independent Work Time is integral to *SRA/Open Court Reading*. It is during this time, which you designate as a part of each class day, that students gain the experience of managing their own learning process. In Independent Work Time, students work on their own or collaboratively to practice and review material taught in the lessons or to complete projects of their own choosing. As the students gradually take more responsibility for their work, they learn to set learning goals, to make decisions about the use of time and materials, and to collaborate with classmates. Of equal importance, Independent Work Time gives you a designated time each day to work with students one-on-one or in small groups.

During Independent Work Time, your students can:
- read to each other for pleasure and to increase fluency.
- work independently and in small collaborative groups on their exploration projects.
- work on unfinished writing projects.
- work on any unfinished projects or assignments they have.
- assess what projects they have that need work, prioritize their time, and direct their own efforts.

During Independent Work Time, you can:
- work with individuals and small groups who have shown a need for additional instruction.
- listen to individuals read in order to assess informally their progress and help them gain fluency.
- conduct writing conferences with individual students to discuss their progress as writers.

The Reading, Listening, Writing, and Inquiry Centers will be used extensively during Independent Work Time. If possible, equip these areas with furniture that is easy to move and will allow for both independent work and small group work.

Getting Started Checklist

This checklist will help you be prepared for the school year. Look back over the Getting Started section if you have any questions about these program elements.

○ **Organize Student Anthologies and Workbooks**

○ **Set Up Reading Center**

○ **Establish Listening Center**

○ **Plan For Discussions**

○ **Plan for Writing Journal**

○ **Organize Writing Portfolios**

○ **Establish Writing-in-Progress Folder**

○ **Establish Writing Center**

○ **Establish Inquiry Center**

○ **Develop Concept/Question Board**

○ **Plan for Independent Work Time**

Getting Started Introductory Lessons

The major goals of the **Getting Started** introductory lessons are:

- to help students review and restart those skills learned in grade 4.
- to help you obtain a clear picture of your students' strengths, needs, and prior learning.

Why a Special Getting Started Section?

Reading programs are often set up as if the first day of a new school year happens the day after the last day of the previous school year. This approach ignores the fact that students have approximately two months between the end of one school year and the beginning of the next. *SRA/Open Court Reading* recognizes this fact, and the fact that many students do little during those two months to retain and strengthen the skills and knowledge they acquired during the previous school year. This special **Getting Started** section is a quick review of important reading skills that will remind students of previous learning and get them ready for learning in the new school year.

These lessons also introduce key elements of the program, such as Word Wall, Discussion, Writing Seminar, Concept/Question Board, and Writing Center in context.

In addition, the **Getting Started** section offers you an effective way to evaluate what your students already know and what they need to know in order to be successful in your class. This knowledge will allow you to base your reading instruction on fact rather than on assumptions, giving you and the students an opportunity to build on previous learning and to learn new and vital skills.

Most important, the **Getting Started** activities allow students to begin Unit 1 of regular instruction knowing that they possess the necessary skills.

Pacing

Whereas the *SRA/Open Court Reading* Student Anthology lessons are intended to fill three to five days, the five **Getting Started** lessons are presented in a daily lesson format and should be completed in about a week. You may spend more or less time on a specific lesson, depending on the needs of your students. If your students had the *SRA/Open Court Reading* program in grade 4, they should move quickly. These students should soon remember and start using the skills they learned in grade 4.

The atmosphere should be relaxed, and both you and the students should view **Getting Started** as a period of rediscovery before taking on the new challenges of grade 5. Point out to students that the purposes of the lessons are, first, to review quickly what they learned the previous year and, second, to give them a preview of the kind of wonderful stories they will read in grade 5.

Day

Getting Acquainted

Have students introduce themselves to each other. Have students tell which of the other students they have had in their class before. Encourage new students to the school to tell a little about themselves—where they came from, what school they went to, etc.

Reading

Background Knowledge To activate the students' background knowledge, have them discuss what they know about reading. List their comments on the board or on paper.

Encourage students to bring to class their favorite books or stories. Each day, invite a volunteer to read a story. You might want to tell students to practice reading their stories out loud before they read them for the class.

Listeners should be encouraged to politely ask for clarification whenever unfamiliar words or ideas are presented in the reading. Learning to ask promptly and politely for assistance is something that should always be fostered during reading.

Discussion

Discussion is an integral part of learning. Through discussion, students are exposed to different points of view and reactions to text. Also, it is through discussion that students learn to express their thoughts and opinions coherently as well as to respect the ideas and opinions of others.

Listening and responding to each other's ideas and questions is fundamental to learning. Throughout the program students are expected to listen and respond to each other—during Writing Seminar, collaborative activities, exploration of the unit concepts—not just in a discussion about a story. Talk about what a discussion is and what is expected of participants during a discussion. Students must listen to what others are saying and respond to what is being said. Students should:

- not interrupt.
- raise their hands when they want to say something.
- ask questions of each other.
- not talk while others are speaking.
- take turns.
- respond to the question or idea rather than going off on a different or unrelated thought or tangent.

Handing Off Through a process called *handing off*, students learn to take the primary responsibility for holding and controlling a discussion. *Handing off* simply means that each student who responds in a discussion is responsible for drawing another student into the discussion.

During this initial lesson, you may want to begin a discussion by asking a question or making a statement. For example, "I really look forward to the beginning of each new school year. There will be so many new people and experiences. How do you feel at the beginning of a new year?" Have a student respond to your question, ask a question, or make a comment of his or her own, calling on another student to respond or react.

In order for *handing off* to work effectively, a seating arrangement that allows students to see one another is important, just as in a real conversation or discussion. A circle or semicircle is effective.

Concept/Question Board

Encourage students to add to the Concept/Question Board throughout the **Getting Started** lessons. They can write what they know about reading, writing, and learning, find articles and pictures or add information about their favorite books.

Talk about reading and any problems the students had learning to read. Ask about what they read, what they liked, and what they learned. Students should be encouraged to ask questions as well, for example: "Are there many students who don't learn to read?" or "Why do we need to go to school?" Write these ideas and questions on pieces of paper and put them on the Concept/Question Board.

Writing

The writing process will be formally introduced in the first anthology unit. Talking about the process here will help you evaluate your students' understanding of writing. Talk about the idea that one of the most important things that good writers do is take time to think before they write. They think about what they know, what they want to write about, and if they need to get more information about what they want to write about. Have the students talk about reading, problems they have had, favorite stories they have read, and the like. Make a list of possible writing ideas and keep it for tomorrow. Tell the students that they will start to think about these ideas and that tomorrow you will review them and add any more ideas if the students have them.

Day

Getting Acquainted

Have students give their names again. Ask students to pair up and give each student a piece of paper. Then have them write one positive statement about their partner. You may need to model this. For example, *Elizabeth has a lovely smile* or *Laval has deep blue eyes.* The positive statements should be short. Not only will this help students remember something about a fellow student, but making positive comments is also something they will be doing during Writing Seminar and will support effective collaborative group participation.

Reading

Ask students to share some of the stories or books they have brought in. If any of the students are ready, have them read aloud a story to the rest of the class. Start a **Word Wall** with any words the students have difficulty with. Tell students that the **Word Wall** will grow as the year goes on and that in addition to problematic words, they will add words that have to do with particular ideas or concepts and words that they particularly like.

Discussion

Quickly review what good participants do during a discussion.

- They listen to what others are saying.
- They don't interrupt.
- They raise their hands when they want to say something.
- They ask questions of each other.
- They don't talk while others are speaking.
- They take turns.

Remind the students of the discussion they had yesterday and how they led the discussion using *handing off.* Once again, you may have to get the students started with questions or statements such as, "That was interesting. Tell me what you like best about the story." When the first student is finished responding, he or she should select the next student to continue the discussion.

Concept/Question Board Have students place any new questions or comments they have about reading and writing on the Concept/Question Board. Be sure to note any articles, books, or pictures any of the students have brought in and put on the Board.

Writing

Writing Center Discuss with the students the purposes of the Writing Center. Walk the students through the different materials you have in the center: pencils, crayons, markers, pens, white paper, colored paper, old magazines for ideas and illustrations, scissors, staplers, and dictionaries and a thesaurus as reference tools.

Writing Folder Distribute the ***SRA/Open Court Reading* Writing Folder** to the students. Have the students write their names on the folders. Give the students time to look over the folders and comment on them. Tell the students that they will use these folders all year to hold the writing pieces they are working on.

If you didn't order the ***SRA/Open Court Reading* Writing Folder**, have students each bring a pocket folder to use as a Writing Folder.

Drafting Review the ideas for writing that the students generated yesterday and ask if there are new ideas that they would like to add to the list. Explain to the students that after writers think about what they might want to write, they begin writing a first draft. Tell the students that they don't have to worry about this being neat or perfect. Encourage students to leave a line or two between each line they write. This will give them room to make changes later. They will have a chance to rewrite their story after they have read it and made any changes they want. The point of writing in **Getting Started** is for you to get a sense of the students' knowledge of the writing process and writing skills, including spelling, grammar, and mechanics.

Have the students choose a topic from the list or a topic of their own choosing and begin writing. As the students are writing, conference with individual students. Holding conferences with students helps them identify and solve problems. Conferences during this drafting phase help students identify and refine a topic. This is also a good time to observe students as they are writing. Remember, as you are conferencing:

- you don't have to meet with every student every day.
- conferences should be brief.
- don't take ownership of the student's work.
- encourage students to identify what is good and what problems they are having.
- leave students with a positive comment.

At the end of the writing time, have the students put their drafts in their **Writing Folders** and either put their folders in their desks or in a file box in the Writing Center.

Day  3

Getting Acquainted

Have students work with a different partner and write a positive comment about the partner. Then have partners read their comments to each other. As students are working on their comments, circulate around the room and conference with student pairs.

Reading

Give students the grade level **Pretest.** Tell students that this test is a little different from others they have taken; they will not get a grade on this test. This test is to help you know what the students remember from last year. There will be another test like this at the end of the year that will show how much they have learned this year. If the students don't know some of the answers, tell them not to worry. There is a lot to learn about reading and writing and they will be able to meet the challenge and do it by the end of the year.

Writing

Continue Writing Remind students of the Writing Center. During writing today, they can go to the center if they need any materials. Have the students continue the story they began yesterday. Conference with students, noting those that might have something to share during seminar which will be introduced today. Look for students with interesting ideas, creative topics, extended sentences, etc.

Writing Seminar Introduce the students to the idea of Seminar. Seminar is a time when the students will be able to share their work with each other. This is a time when two or three students will share their work with the class and then their classmates will have time to give feedback. Seminar participants must listen carefully and politely, just as they do during discussion and *handing off.* When the author is finished reading, the other students should say something positive about what the author wrote. They can tell what they liked and why; how the author's story made them feel good; what the author's story reminded them of. You may need to model this in the beginning by telling what you liked about the

story and why. Be sure to let students know that over the next few days everyone will have a chance to share their stories.

Independent Work Time

Introduce the idea of Independent Work Time. Independent Work Time is a period of time each day in which the students will work collaboratively or independently to practice and review material taught in the lesson or to complete projects related to the unit theme. Tell the students that every day, there will be a time when they will be working without you, on their own, or in small groups. During that time, they may be working on materials that you assign or they may be partner reading, reading independently, working on writing or a unit project, or meeting with you.

Meet with the students and establish rules for Independent Work Time. These might include:

- be polite.
- share with others.
- use your inside voice (or whisper).
- take only the material you need.
- when you are finished, clean up and put away the materials you used.

You may want to post these rules, review them periodically, and revise them if necessary.

Reading Center

The students have already learned about the Writing Center. Introduce the Reading Center today. In this center, students will find books, magazines, newspapers, and other reading materials. Students should be encouraged to bring in favorite books and share them in the center. Let students know they can come and choose a book any time they have free time, not just during Independent Work Time.

Concept/Question Board

Encourage students to get in the habit of looking over the Concept/Question Board every day to see what has been added, what might have been taken off, and to add their own insights.

Day

Reading

In preparation for beginning the first unit, *Cooperation and Competition*, you might ask the students if they have read any stories about people who have competed with each other for a prize or in a game, or people who have had to really cooperate with each other—teammates perhaps. Encourage the students who have read such stories to retell the stories and tell what they thought of the stories. Gently encourage students to be specific in their comments. Instead of settling for "I liked the story," have the students elaborate on their thoughts by explaining what it was about the story that they liked.

Writing Journal

Throughout the course of the year, your students will be asked to do a tremendous amount of writing. Reading and writing are closely interwoven and each will help build and strengthen the other. In order to assure the best results and success in writing, the students will need a **Writing Journal**. Each student should provide his or her own Writing Journal. This journal can be a three-ring binder with tabbed sections; however, a spiral notebook with sections works also. Use time during **Getting Started** to let the students prepare their Writing Journals. The following sections are suggested:

- **Response Journal** in which students will write a personal response to the literature they read
- **Vocabulary** in which students will record vocabulary or spelling words they need to learn
- **Literary Connection** in which students will record information about literary genre and techniques that they want to remember
- **Writing Ideas** in which students record ideas for future writing they want to do as well as ideas gained during brainstorming sessions
- **Personal Dictionary** in which students record concept-related words or any new word they learn and want to remember

Take time to have students put together their Writing Journals. If some students don't finish, have them complete their journals during Independent Work Time.

Listening Center

Remind the students of the Writing Center and the materials that are there and the fact that students can use them at any time during writing, Independent Work Time, or free time. Today, introduce the Listening Center. Tell students that there will be an audiotape of all the stories in their anthology.

Independent Work Time

Review the rules for Independent Work Time. Tell the students that today they can continue work on their stories or they may want to begin a new story. They can also go to the Reading Center, Listening Center or complete or decorate their Writing Journal. Since this is the first time students are involved in Independent Work Time, you may want to assign students to the different areas. Circulate as students are working.

Concept/Question Board

Give Students a few minutes to add to the Concept/Question Board information about what they learned today or any questions they have. This can be about writing or reading or anything else they want to share.

Day

Reading

If you have a favorite story about people who have either competed with each other or really cooperated with each other, read it to the students. As you and the students read stories about cooperation and competition, encourage discussion about how the stories are alike and how they are different. Stories on the same general topic usually approach the topic differently and help to add new perspectives if the reader is alert to these different perspectives. This ability to see how each new piece of information adds a new perspective will be very important to the students as they progress through their school careers.

Writing

Today you will introduce the students to revision and then proofreading. Have one or two students read their stories as in Seminar. As students are reading their stories, listen for short sentences that could be extended. After students have read their stories, encourage them to extend some of the sentences. Explain that extending sentences makes stories more interesting for the reader. Have students work on revising their stories by extending sentences. Show students how they can do this by putting in a carat (^) and writing their extensions in the blank lines they have left. Conference with individual students or small groups of students as they are revising their stories. At the end, have several students share sentences they have extended.

Proofreading Today, students will also be informally introduced to proofreading. Tell students that when proofreading, if they find a mistake or problem, they should circle the word and write it correctly. Explain to students that they will proofread their stories to be sure the words are spelled correctly, that they have used capitals and punctuation correctly, and have used words correctly.

Sentence Lifting Sentence lifting is an effective and engaging way to model proofreading using sentences taken from the students' writing. Students are expected to identify and correct their own errors. Since you should use both sentences with errors and sentences without errors, the students see examples of correct

writing. The focus is a positive one and helps students understand that all writers make mistakes and need to improve on their writing.

In preparation for sentence lifting, look through the students' writing folders for common errors in capitalization, punctuation, or spelling. Select some sentences that contain errors and others that don't. Copy the sentences on the board or on an overhead transparency.

Read the first sentence with a mistake. Have students identify what needs to be changed. Circle the errors and have the students tell you how to write it correctly. Help the students with spellings they are unsure of. Point out any errors that the students miss.

Give students additional time to proofread their own papers and make changes. Conference with students who need help. You may wish to spend additional time with them during Independent Work Time.

Concept/Question Board

Give the students a few minutes to add to the Concept/Question Board information about what they learned today or any questions they have.

Independent Work Time

Introduce students to the Inquiry Center. Tell students that this area will become very important to them as the year goes on and they do more and more research about the concepts they are studying. Show students what has been supplied for the Inquiry Center and where the supplies are kept. The Inquiry Center should include:

- Reference books such as dictionaries and encyclopedias.
- Computers—preferably with Internet access. The SRA Home Page includes Internet sites specifically related to the themes the students are studying. See **www.http://sra4kids.com.**
- Books on the themes the students are studying. You may choose to buy the Classroom Library that accompanies the program. In addition, bibliographies of additional related books can be found following each unit in the student's anthologies.

By this time, students should be comfortable with the set up of the room, acquainted with you and each other, and ready to move into the anthology.

Exploring the Theme

UNIT 1

Cooperation and Competition

Sometimes we need to cooperate with each other to get things done. Sometimes, though, we find ourselves competing with each other. Sometimes we need to do both at the same time—cooperate with teammates while competing against an opposing team. Cooperation and competition play important roles in our lives and they take on many different faces. How do you see competition and cooperation at work in your life?

18

19

Introduction

Cooperation and competition are part of our daily lives. By the time most students reach the fifth grade, they have spent many hours working together, being part of a team, and helping others. They have also learned a great deal about competition in sports and school, among friends and foes.

This unit is designed to help children develop a deeper understanding of cooperation and competition, their contrasting and complementary natures, and how

they help us reach our goals. Students will encounter story characters who struggle with issues surrounding these themes. Through these characters, they will vicariously experience and reflect upon the many faces of cooperation and competition, and learn to make them positive forces in their lives.

Exploration and Reflection Goals

The goal for this unit is for students to learn about cooperation and competition through literary analysis. With the selections they will be reading, they will:

- learn the motives and specific situations that call for cooperation and competition.
- build thematic links between the selections.
- interpret stories in light of their own personal experiences, and vice versa.

Learning Goals

Throughout this unit, students will engage in guided and independent activities that provide an opportunity for them to speak, read, and write about cooperation and competition. They will learn to identify key concepts and main ideas as communicated through author use of literary devices such as plot, setting, and dialogue. They will also engage in writing independently, in collaboration with classmates, and with the support of the teacher.

The learning goals for this unit are:

- to extend students' knowledge and understanding of the complex natures of cooperation and competition, and the various ways they are expressed.
- to present their ideas through various means including written text, performance, drawing, and oral discussion.
- to learn how to use different writing formats, such as journal entries, storyboards, scripts, and charts, to formulate and express what they have learned about the unit theme.

Teacher Tip The concepts of cooperation and competition raise a wide variety of questions. To stimulate your own thinking, you might ask yourself questions like the following:

- What motivates people to compete and cooperate?
- Which of these traits do I value more, or do I believe they have equal value?
- What were my own experiences related to competition and cooperation when I attended school, took part in extracurricular activities, and interacted with my family?
- What do I want my students to learn about cooperation and competition, and how can they best learn it?

Teacher Tip There are two general types of units included in the Open Court 2000 program at all grade levels. One type of unit is the Inquiry unit, which focuses on reading for information. The other type is the Reflection unit, which focuses on a narrative exploration of some universal theme of relevance to students. We begin the fifth grade program with this latter type of unit. Students are encouraged to reflect on the theme and relate it to their own lives. They are also given a chance to learn about the literature that embodies this theme and how it is constructed. Finally, they are offered an opportunity to apply this knowledge to the task of generating a literary product themselves.

Exploring the Theme

Unit Activities

Unit projects, or activities, are student driven and should emerge from students' interests, encouraged or ignited by their class discussions. Unit activities should involve reading beyond the program material and address both of the conceptual aims of the unit.

Exploration Activities

- The project for this unit is to write and perform a dramatic play. Students will work in small groups to plan the plot line, prepare the first draft using a storyboard format, complete a final draft using a script format, and perform the play. Alternatively, students might transform an existing story into a dramatic script and perform it.

- The intent of this project is to provide an opportunity for students to work independently and in groups to explore the concepts of cooperation and competition. They will learn more about creating story plots and characters, using dialogue to convey a message about cooperation and competition, assuming character roles, and dramatizing events. An overview of how this project might unfold over the course of the unit is offered in the chart below.

	Class President	**The Marble Champ**	**Juggling**
Overview of Selection	■ This realistic fiction selection is about two students who compete in a class election. The story illustrates that altruism can champion over self-interest.	■ This humorous fiction selection is about a girl who practices for a marble championship until her thumb muscle increases in size.	■ This realistic fiction selection is about a boy who has to juggle family and team commitments. When all those affected pull together, he is able to fulfill both of his obligations.
Link to the Theme	■ Cooperative efforts tend to win more friends than competitiveness.	■ Commitment and practice help us succeed in competitions.	■ Demands on our time sometimes conflict, but conflicting needs can often be met through cooperative efforts.
Unit Activities	■ Students discuss personal, family, and literary experiences with cooperation and competition. They work individually and in groups, generating ideas on the theme, plot, and characters for their dramatic play.	■ Students share their ideas in a large group; they receive and give feedback. Small groups revise theme and plot and decide on the setting and characters. They write their play using storyboard format.	■ Students complete the storyboard version of their play and share it with other groups. They give and receive feedback and make revisions to the storyboard version, as they see fit.
Supporting Student Explorations	■ Introduce the unit activity. Schedule a library visit and form unit project groups. Support group discussion and encourage students to use the Concept/Question Board and their Writing Journals.	■ Remind students of appropriate procedure for giving and receiving feedback. Assist them with storyboard technique as necessary.	■ Assist students in making the storyboard as necessary. Schedule group sharing sessions and help students identify issues they might give feedback on, including theme, setting, characters, and dialogue.

Supporting Student Explorations

Students will need ample time to reflect on their own experiences with cooperation and competition. They will also benefit from discussions with their classmates. Teachers can broaden students' conceptions of cooperation and competition by having them discuss and reinterpret their experiences.

Reading fictional accounts of people who have cooperated and competed is another excellent way to deepen students' understanding. Have students read beyond the anthology selections and encourage them to use their personal experiences to interpret the literature they read.

Students will need instruction on how to transform a story line into a dramatic production. Teach them how to plan the dialogue and scenes that express particular ideas about competition and cooperation. In many of the books they have read, a narrator is the prime conveyor of information; characters' voices are typically used only as a secondary source of information. Demonstrate how characters can describe events and how characters' thoughts and feelings can be communicated through words, voice, and actions.

The Abacus Contest	S.O.R. Losers	Storks
■ This realistic fiction selection illustrates the pressures of competition and explores how competition affects individuals differently.	■ This humorous and thoughtful fiction selection questions the assumption that the only goal of a team is to win.	■ This realistic fiction selection tells of a young girl's desire to know why there are no storks in her village by the sea. This selection illustrates the role relationships play in knowledge building.
■ Competition can be both a worry and a stimulating challenge.	■ Cooperation in competitive situations supports individuals.	■ Competition motivates us to learn, but cooperation leads to understanding and solutions.
■ Students write their play in script format, including dialogue and stage directions. They agree on director and actor roles and begin rehearsals.	■ Students complete the final draft of their script, including character list and autobiographical author information, and plan their dress rehearsal.	■ Students complete final dramatic rehearsals and perform their plays. They bind the scripts into a class anthology and prepare a title page and table of contents.
■ Encourage students to make ongoing script revisions as they rehearse. Model how to write meaningful dialogue, and help students to write dialogue by focusing on how competitive and cooperative traits can be communicated.	■ Help students with mechanical corrections to their final drafts. Have them create an author page. Refer them to the author notes as models for their autobiographical author note.	■ Schedule performances and facilitate unit celebration.

Program Resources

Student Materials

Student Anthology
Pages 18–115

Reading and Writing Workbook
Pages 5–46

Inquiry Journal
Pages 5–19

Writing Folder

Teacher Materials

Teacher's Edition, Book 1

Reteach
Pages 5–46

Challenge
Pages 5–25

Home Connection*
Pages 1–14

Skills Assessment
Pages 1–11

Comprehension and Writing Assessment
Pages 1–28

Assessment Guide

ESL Supplement
Unit 1, Lessons 1–6

Overhead Transparencies
Numbers 1–6, 44, 48, 50–51, 53

Intervention Guide
Unit 1, Lessons 1–6

Additional Materials

- Visual Glossary
- Intervention Package
- Teacher's Professional Guides

*Also available in Spanish

Program Resources

Classroom Library*

Comeback! Four True Stories

BY JIM O'CONNOR. RANDOM HOUSE, 1992.

This book contains true stories of four famous athletes who overcame serious injuries or debilitating conditions to become superstars. **(Easy)**

Heads, I Win

BY PATRICIA HERMES. MINSTRAL, 1989. HARCOURT BRACE JOVANOVICH, 1998.

Bailey is tough, independent, and out to become the fifth grade's new president. **(Average)**

A Season of Comebacks

BY KATHY MACKEL. PENGUIN PUTNAM INC., 1998.

Allie and Molly, two competitive sisters, learn that both their lives are better when they work together. **(Average)**

The View from Saturday

BY E.L. KONIGSBURG. ALADDIN, 1998.

A group of offbeat kids come together with their paraplegic teacher to form a champion Academic Bowl team. (Newbery Medal, ALA Notable, SLJ Best) **(Advanced)**

Note: Teachers should preview any trade books and videos for appropriateness in their classrooms before recommending them to students.

* These books, which all support the unit theme Cooperation and Competition, are part of a 24-book Classroom Library available for purchase from SRA/McGraw-Hill.

TECHNOLOGY

*Commodore Perry in the Land of the Shogun

Travel with Matthew Perry on his 1853 expedition to Japan, during which he convinced both Americans and Japanese to overcome their fears of each other's differences. Videocassette; 26 min.

*Jackie Robinson

Find out about the courageous man whose spectacular baseball career paved the way for racial equality in professional sports. Videocassette; 19 min.

*Meet the Caldecott Illustrator: Jerry Pinkney

Learn about the life of this illustrator and how he works in cooperation with authors to create the images that bring text to life. Videocassette; 21 min.

*Philip Hall Likes Me. I Reckon Maybe.

Beth realizes that she's too competitive to let the boy she likes keep outdoing her. Videocassette; 28 min.

Olympic Gold
ZENGER MEDIA

Have students use this interactive program, which uses photos, video clips, narration, articles, and statistics to provide users with an in-depth look at the Olympic Games from their beginning to the present. CD-ROM.

*Listening Library: Cooperation and Competition
SRA/MCGRAW-HILL, 2000

Students will enjoy listening to the selections they have read. Have them use the audiocassette during Independent Work Time. Audiocassette.

*Lesson Planner
SRA/MCGRAW-HILL, 2000

Use the Lesson Planner to adjust and refine lessons to meet the specific needs of your students. CD-ROM.

*Research
SRA/MCGRAW-HILL, 2000

As students continue their exploration of Cooperation and Competition, have them use the Research program to help them organize and share their findings. CD-ROM.

Cooperation and Competition Websites

Have students find information about Cooperation and Competition. Links to sites concerning Cooperation and Competition can be found at: **http://www.sra4kids.com**

*Basic Computer Skills Connection

Have students use the Computer Basics unit of the **SRA Basic Computer Skills** program to help them develop computer skills within the context of the unit theme. The Applying Computer Skills in Reading activity contains a computer skills application specific to this unit.

Titles proceeded by an asterisk (✳) are available through SRA/McGraw-Hill. Other titles can be obtained by contacting the publisher listed with the title. See page 38 of the Program Appendix for ordering information.

Unit Skills Overview

	WORD KNOWLEDGE	COMPREHENSION SKILLS & STRATEGIES	LITERARY ELEMENTS	VOCABULARY & SPELLING
Class President **Genre:** **Realistic Fiction**	■ Word Families ■ Consonant Blends ■ Spellings for /er/	■ Drawing Conclusions ■ Author's Purpose ■ Making Connections ■ Predicting ■ Summarizing	■ Characters	■ Affixes: Suffix –*tion*
The Marble Champ **Genre:** **Realistic Fiction**	■ Synonyms ■ Regular Plurals ■ /n/ spelled *kn*	■ Making Inferences ■ Asking Questions ■ Making Connections ■ Visualizing	■ Recognize and Analyze Story Settings	■ Consonant Before -*le* Syllable Pattern
Juggling **Genre:** **Realistic Fiction**	■ Closed Compound Words ■ Consonant Digraph *th* ■ *s*-family Consonant Blends	■ Author's Point of View ■ Asking Questions ■ Predicting ■ Making Connections	■ Identifying Purpose of Text	■ Spelling -*le* Endings
The Abacus Contest **Genre:** **Realistic Fiction**	■ Content Area Words ■ /ow/ sound *ou* ■ Long e spelled *ea*	■ Sequence ■ Predicting ■ Summarizing ■ Clarifying	■ Recognizing and Analyzing Plot and Problem Resolution	■ Inflectional Endings
S.O.R. Losers **Genre:** **Realistic Fiction**	■ Frequently Misspelled Words ■ Long e spelled *ea* ■ /ch/ spelled *ch*	■ Drawing Conclusions ■ Author's Point of View ■ Visualizing ■ Asking Questions ■ Summarizing	■ Analyzing Characters	■ Words Into Syllables
Storks **Genre:** **Realistic Fiction**	■ Antonyms ■ /ks/ spelled *x* ■ /ch/ spelled *tch*	■ Making Inferences ■ Author's Point of View ■ Cause and Effect ■ Clarifying ■ Summarizing ■ Asking Questions	■ Literary Terms: Title, Author, and Illustrator	■ Inflectional Endings

WRITING	LISTENING/SPEAKING/ VIEWING	GRAMMAR, USAGE, & MECHANICS	STUDY & RESEARCH	ACROSS THE CURRICULUM
■ Introduce the Writing Process ■ Prewrite a Persuasive Paper	■ Persuasive Techniques	■ Prepositions and Prepositional Phrases	■ Parts of the Library	Social Studies ■ Cooperating to Develop Safety Rules Art ■ Cooperation Posters Versus Competion Posters
■ Writing Paragraphs ■ Prewrite	■ Recognize and Distinguish Stories	■ Nouns	■ Organize Information by Making Charts	Drama ■ The Secret of My Success Music ■ Cooperative and Competitive Beats
■ Explaining Topic Sentences ■ Draft	■ Recognizing and Analyzing Story Settings	■ Pronouns	■ Interviewing	Social Studies ■ Money for a Good Cause Physical Education ■ Designing New Games
■ Revise	■ Making Connections with Others	■ Complete Sentences	■ Use Text Organizers	Art ■ Winning Certificates Math ■ Math Competion
■ Analyze the Author's Writing ■ Proofread	■ Asking and Answering Questions	■ Commas in Direct Address	■ Note Taking	Drama ■ Debating Winning and Losing Math ■ An Average Balancing Act
■ Refine Persuasive Paper ■ Publish	■ Illustrations	■ Capitalize titles	■ Using Multiple Sources	Social Studies ■ Olympic Competitions Science ■ Thinking About the Animals

Meeting the Needs of All Children

Meeting Individual Needs

	Reteach	ESL	Challenge
Class President **Genre:** **Realistic Fiction**	**Reading and Responding** ■ Author's Purpose ■ Drawing Conclusions **Integrating the Curriculum** ■ Characters ■ Words with Suffixes: -*tion* ■ Prepositions and Prepositional Phrases	**Preparing to Read** ■ Word Meaning ■ Cultural Context ■ Vocabulary **Reading and Responding** ■ Conversation **Integrating the Curriculum** ■ Listening/Speaking/Viewing	**Reading and Responding** ■ Author's Purpose ■ Drawing Conclusions **Integrating the Curriculum** ■ Characters ■ Words with Suffixes: -*tion* ■ Prepositions and Prepositional Phrases
The Marble Champ **Genre:** **Realistic Fiction**	**Reading and Responding** ■ Making Inferences **Integrating the Curriculum** ■ Setting ■ Spelling -*le* Endings ■ Nouns	**Preparing to Read** ■ Word Meaning ■ Cultural Context ■ Vocabulary **Reading and Responding** ■ Poetry **Integrating the Curriculum** ■ Listening/Speaking/Viewing	**Reading and Responding** ■ Making Inferences **Integrating the Curriculum** ■ Setting ■ Spelling -*le* Endings ■ Nouns
Juggling **Genre:** **Realistic Fiction**	**Reading and Responding** ■ Author's Point of View **Integrating the Curriculum** ■ Identifying Purpose of Text ■ Pronouns	**Preparing to Read** ■ Word Meaning ■ Cultural Context ■ Vocabulary **Reading and Responding** ■ Predicting **Integrating the Curriculum** ■ Peer Tutoring	**Reading and Responding** ■ Author's Point of View **Integrating the Curriculum** ■ Identifying Purpose of Text ■ Spelling -*le* Endings ■ Pronouns
The Abacus Contest **Genre:** **Realistic Fiction**	**Reading and Responding** ■ Sequence **Integrating the Curriculum** ■ Spelling Inflectional Endings ■ Complete Sentences	**Preparing to Read** ■ Word Meaning ■ Vocabulary **Reading and Responding** ■ Summing Up and Asking Questions **Integrating the Curriculum** ■ Conversational Practice	**Reading and Responding** ■ Sequence **Integrating the Curriculum** ■ Spelling Inflectional Endings ■ Complete Sentences
S.O.R. Losers **Genre:** **Realistic Fiction**	**Integrating the Curriculum** ■ Words Into Syllables ■ Commas in Direct Address	**Preparing to Read** ■ Word Meaning ■ Vocabulary ■ Cultural Context **Reading and Responding** ■ Asking Questions ■ Reading **Integrating the Curriculum** ■ Writing Buddies ■ Asking and Answering Questions	**Reading and Responding** ■ Drawing Conclusions **Integrating the Curriculum** ■ Words Into Syllables ■ Commas in Direct Address
Storks **Genre:** **Realistic Fiction**	**Reading and Responding** ■ Cause and Effect ■ Author's Point of View **Integrating the Curriculum** ■ Literary Terms ■ Capitalizing Titles	**Preparing to Read** ■ Word Meaning ■ Vocabulary **Reading and Responding** ■ Making Inferences ■ Cultural Context **Integrating the Curriculum** ■ Expressing Ideas	**Reading and Responding** ■ Cause and Effect ■ Making Inferences ■ Author's Point of View **Integrating the Curriculum** ■ Literary Terms ■ Spelling Inflectional Endings ■ Capitalizing Titles

Assessment

InterVention	✓ Informal	✓ Formal
Preparing to Read ■ Word Knowledge **Reading and Responding** ■ Comprehension ■ Predicting ■ Making Connections ■ Drawing Conclusions ■ Author's Purpose ■ Summarizing **Integrating the Curriculum** ■ Characters ■ Words with Suffixes: *-tion*	**Reading and Writing Workbook** pp. 5–14 **Reteach** pp. 5–14 **Challenge** pp. 5–9 **Teacher Observation Log** **Project Assessment**	**Comprehension and Writing Assessment** pp. 1–8 ■ Pretest ■ "Class President" **Skills Assessment** pp. 1–2 ■ Different Spellings for the /er/ Sound ■ Parts of a Library
Preparing to Read ■ Word Knowledge **Reading and Responding** ■ Comprehension ■ Visualizing ■ Making Connections ■ Making Inferences ■ Asking Questions **Integrating the Curriculum** ■ Prewriting	**Reading and Writing Workbook** pp. 15–22 **Reteach** pp. 15–22 **Challenge** pp. 10–13 **Teacher Observation Log** **Project Assessment**	**Comprehension and Writing Assessment** pp. 9–10 ■ "The Marble Champ" **Skills Assessment** pp. 3–4 ■ Writing Paragraphs ■ Charts
Preparing to Read ■ Consonant Digraphs **Reading and Responding** ■ Comprehension ■ Predicting ■ Author's Point of View **Integrating the Curriculum** ■ Topic Sentences	**Reading and Writing Workbook** pp. 23–28 **Reteach** pp. 23–28 **Challenge** pp. 14–16 **Teacher Observation Log** **Project Assessment**	**Comprehension and Writing Assessment** pp. 11–12 ■ "Juggling" **Skills Assessment** pp. 5–6 ■ Topic Sentences ■ Consonant Before *-le* Syllable
Preparing to Read ■ Word Knowledge **Reading and Responding** ■ Comprehension ■ Sequence ■ Clarifying	**Reading and Writing Workbook** pp. 29–34 **Reteach** pp. 29–34 **Challenge** pp. 17–19 **Teacher Observation Log** **Project Assessment**	**Comprehension and Writing Assessment** pp. 13–14 ■ "The Abacus Contest" **Skills Assessment** p. 7 ■ Plot
Preparing to Read ■ Frequently Misspelled Words **Reading and Responding** ■ Comprehension ■ Asking Questions ■ Summarizing ■ Drawing Conclusions **Integrating the Curriculum** ■ Analyzing Characters ■ Words into Syllables	**Reading and Writing Workbook** pp. 35–38 **Reteach** pp. 35–38 **Challenge** pp. 20–21 **Teacher Observation Log** **Project Assessment**	**Comprehension and Writing Assessment** pp. 15–16 ■ "S.O.R. Losers" **Skills Assessment** pp. 8–9 ■ Drawing Conclusions ■ Author's Point of View
Preparing to Read ■ Antonyms **Reading and Responding** ■ Comprehension ■ Summarizing ■ Asking Questions ■ Cause and Effect ■ Clarifying ■ Making Inferences ■ Author's Point of View	**Reading and Writing Workbook** pp. 39–46 **Reteach** pp. 39–46 **Challenge** pp. 22–25 **Teacher Observation Log** **Project Assessment**	**Comprehension and Writing Assessment** pp. 17–28 ■ "Storks" ■ Unit 1 Review **Skills Assessment** pp. 10–11 ■ Making Inferences ■ Spelling Inflectional Endings

Previewing the Unit

Activating Prior Knowledge

Tell the students the first unit in their anthology centers on the theme Cooperation and Competition. Initiate an open discussion on the topic.

- Invite students to share their encounters with cooperating and competing at the same time (for example, when playing sports).
- Then, ask students to think of situations in which cooperation and competition are mutually exclusive (for example, it's difficult to cooperate with someone with whom you are competing).

Record the students' ideas on the chalkboard. Then encourage students to write about what cooperation and competition means to them in their Writing Journals. (See page 20H for information on the Writing Journal.) Explain that they will reread this entry at the end of the unit to see if and how their understanding has changed and developed.

Home Connection

In our unit, Cooperation and Competition, the students will read stories illustrating the contrasting and complementary natures of these concepts. The students will learn how both cooperation and competition can be positive forces in their lives. An informational letter on cooperation and competition, in both English and Spanish, can be found in the *Home Connection* guide.

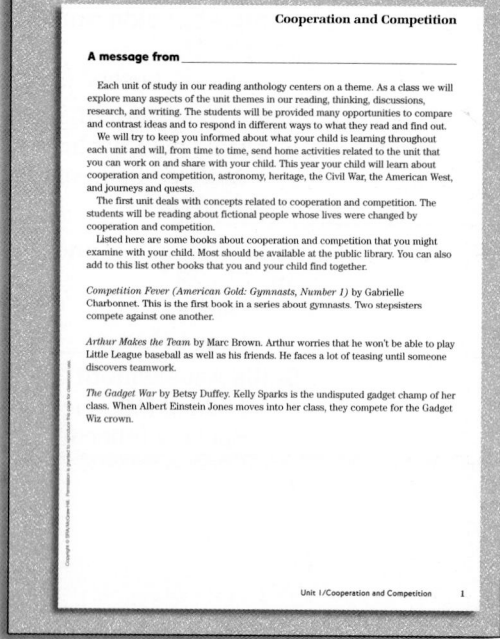

Home Connection page 1

Concept/Question Board

Show students the Concept/Question Board and explain that it is their bulletin board for displaying anything they think and learn about the unit theme. Postings might include ideas, questions, and comments concerning the unit theme and the unit activities. Tell students that by the end of the unit, this Board will be a collage of their ideas, their work, and their cooperative efforts. Throughout the unit, they can refer to this Board for information to use in the activities they will present at the end of the unit. To start the Board:

- Encourage students to create and post semantic maps based on their discussion of the unit theme. In semantic maps, key words related to the unit theme are organized by different concepts.
- Have students brainstorm and post theme-related questions.
- Have students tack up pictures from magazines, demonstrating cooperation and competition, as a springboard for ideas.

Over the course of the unit, have students reread and reflect on the contribution. Encourage them to record in their Writing Journals the contributions that mean the most to them.

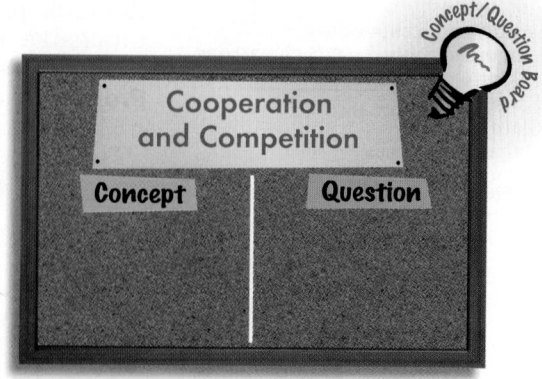

Setting Reading Goals

Have students browse the unit selections independently. Have them make speculations as to what they think the selections will be about and share any similar experiences they have had or heard about.

Remind students that throughout the unit, they will be participating in learning activities that will extend their experiences and deepen and expand their knowledge of cooperation and competition. These reflective activities will include story analysis and writing, drama and art, and discussions and presentations. Explain to students that they will be learning:

- When and why people cooperate or compete.
- The good and bad sides of cooperation and competition.
- The different techniques authors use to make the selections in this unit interesting and entertaining (for example, through realistic and clever characters).

Inquiry Journal

- After students have discussed what they think this unit might be about, have them complete page 5 in their **Inquiry Journals.**
- Have students share ideas about cooperation and competition that they would like to learn more about.

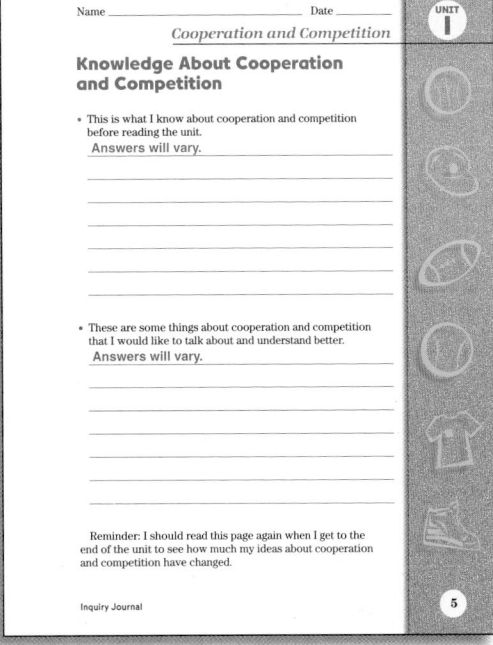

Inquiry Journal page 5

Research in Reading

Michael Pressley on Comprehension Strategy Instruction

Instruction designed to build and support students' metacognitive skills leads to improved reading comprehension. Such instruction is most effective when teachers help students develop the strategies necessary for deep comprehension by modeling and explaining the behaviors and strategies used by expert readers as they tackle a text; by guiding students in using strategies appropriately; by asking students to apply the strategies on their own; and by gradually shifting responsibility to the students for their own learning.

Strategic reading seems to promote the development of comprehension ability most when teachers encourage students to make associations between what they read and their own experiences, to interpret, and to create summaries of what they find important in a text.

Check the Reading link of the **SRA** Web page for information on Research in Reading.
http://www.sra4kids.com

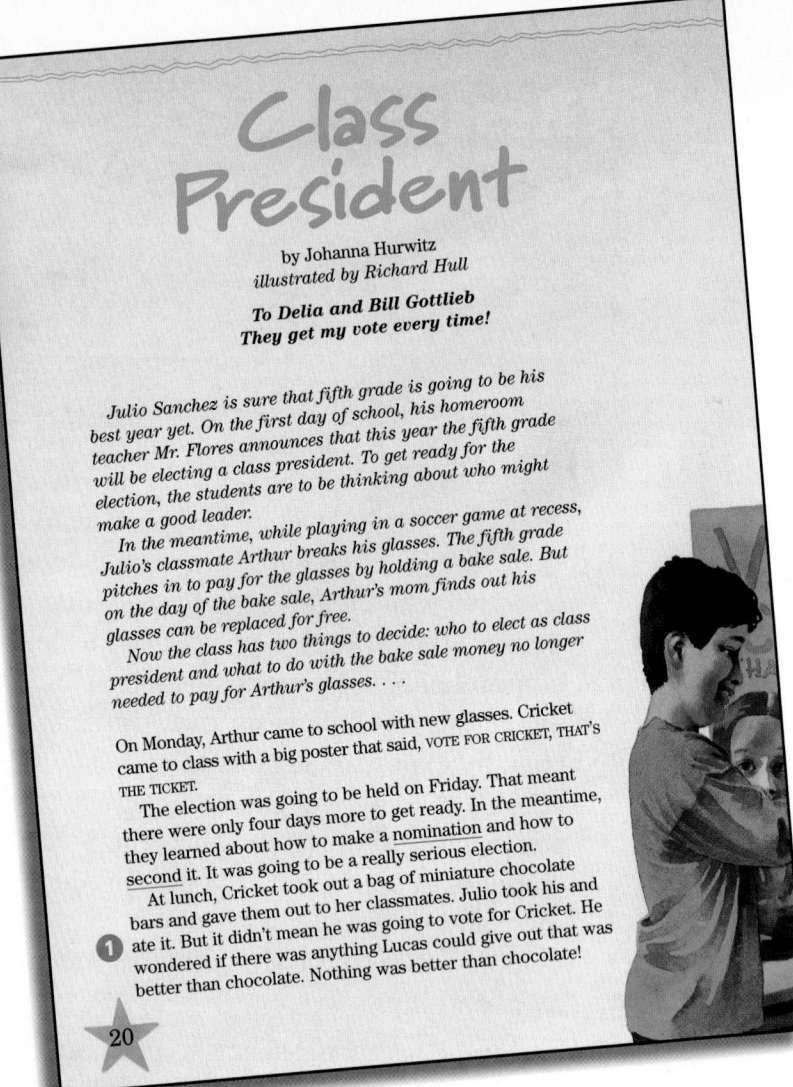

Class
President

by Johanna Hurwitz
illustrated by Richard Hull

To Delia and Bill Gottlieb
They get my vote every time!

Julio Sanchez is sure that fifth grade is going to be his best year yet. On the first day of school, his homeroom teacher Mr. Flores announces that this year the fifth grade will be electing a class president. To get ready for the election, the students are to be thinking about who might make a good leader.

In the meantime, while playing in a soccer game at recess, Julio's classmate Arthur breaks his glasses. The fifth grade pitches in to pay for the glasses by holding a bake sale. But on the day of the bake sale, Arthur's mom finds out his glasses can be replaced for free.

Now the class has two things to decide: who to elect as class president and what to do with the bake sale money no longer needed to pay for Arthur's glasses. . . .

On Monday, Arthur came to school with new glasses. Cricket came to class with a big poster that said, VOTE FOR CRICKET, THAT'S THE TICKET.

The election was going to be held on Friday. That meant there were only four days more to get ready. In the meantime, they learned about how to make a <u>nomination</u> and how to <u>second</u> it. It was going to be a really serious election.

At lunch, Cricket took out a bag of miniature chocolate bars and gave them out to her classmates. Julio took his and ate it. But it didn't mean he was going to vote for Cricket. He wondered if there was anything Lucas could give out that was better than chocolate. Nothing was better than chocolate!

20

Selection Summary

Genre: Realistic Fiction

In this excerpt from the book, *Class President*, the election for class president of the fifth grade shapes up as a two-way race between Cricket and Lucas. Julio is determined to help his friend, Lucas, get elected, but Cricket runs a strong campaign. As the competition heats up, something happens to change the course of events—Mr. Herbertson bans soccer on the playground. Julio suggests that he and the candidates persuade Mr. Herbertson to change his mind. What will the outcome of Julio's leadership be?

About the Author

Johanna Hurwitz has written more than 30 books for children. As an adult, she fulfilled her childhood dream of becoming both a librarian and a writer. *Class Clowns*, which introduced Julio, Cricket, and Lucas, received Kentucky's Bluegrass Award, West Virginia's Children's Book Award, and Mississippi's Children's Book Award.

Students can read more about Johanna Hurwitz on page 34 of the *Student Anthology.*

Other Books by Johanna Hurwitz
- *Aldo Applesauce*
- *Rip-Roaring Russell*
- *The Adventures of Ali Baba Bernstein*
- *The Hot and Cold Summer*

About the Illustrator

Richard Hull teaches illustration at Brigham Young University. He was also an art director and graphic designer with a magazine for fifteen years. He and his wife live in Orem, Utah.

Students can read more about Richard Hull on page 34 of the *Student Anthology.*

Other Books by Richard Hull
- *The Cat & the Fiddle & More*
- *My Sister's Rusty Bike*
- *The Alphabet from Z to A (With Much Confusion on the Way)*

 **Exploring the Theme**

Selection Concepts

"Class President" is realistic fiction that highlights how an "underdog" who is cooperative can achieve more than a vocal, competitive individual. Key concepts to be expored are:

- in many situations, cooperation is more productive than competition.
- focusing on group benefits rather than individual gains is highly desirable in some situations.
- some competition practices, such as campaigning, are fair, while others, such as bribery, are not.
- cooperation and communication are essential for leadership.

Check the Reading link of the **SRA** Web page for links to theme-related Websites.
http:// www.sra4kids.com

Exploration Activity Tips

Before Reading, have students browse through the story and predict how the topics of cooperation and competition will be addressed. Then, have students read the story to identify the message it conveys.

During Reading, have students think about whether they agree or disagree with the story's message. Have them identify the acts of competition and cooperation in the story, and the characters' responses to those acts.

After Reading, have students use their own personal experiences to interpret the story. Ask students what they have learned about the unit theme, and invite them to add information to the Concept/Question Board.

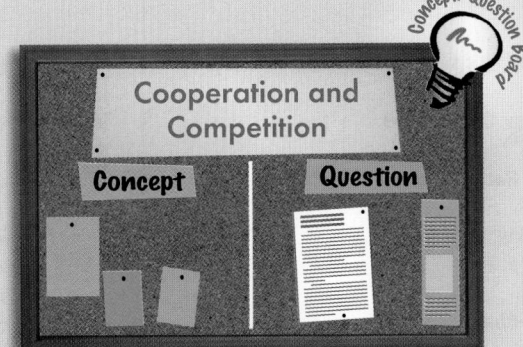

Unit I Exploration Management

Lesson I Class President	**Collaborative Exploration** **Discuss experiences with cooperation and competition. Generate ideas for a dramatic play.** **Supplementary Activity** **Schedule a library visit and form unit activity groups. Support group discussion of unit activities, and encourage use of the Concept/ Question Board.**
Lesson 2	Students give and receive feedback on their unit activity ideas and begin to work in groups on the storyboards for their plays.
Lesson 3	Students complete their storyboards and share them with other groups, then revise the storyboards based on feedback.
Lesson 4	Students begin group work on writing plays in script format. They agree on director and actor roles and begin rehearsals.
Lesson 5	Students complete the final draft of their scripts and plan their dress rehearsals.
Lesson 6	Students complete play rehearsals and perform their plays. They put scripts in a class anthology and prepare a title page and table of contents.

Lesson Planner

Suggested Pacing: 3–5 days	DAY 1	DAY 2
	DAY 1	**DAY 2**
Part 1 Preparing to Read **Materials** ■ Student Anthology, pp. 20–35 ■ Transparencies 1, 44	**Word Knowledge** ✓■ Reading the Words and Sentences, p. 20G ■ Developing Oral Language, p. 20H **Build Background, p. 20H** **Preview and Prepare, p. 20I** **Selection Vocabulary, p. 20J** *election, represent, campaign, candidates, confidence*	**Preview and Prepare, p. 20I** ■ Review Transparency 44
Part 2 Reading and Responding **Materials** ■ Student Anthology, pp. 20–35 ■ Teacher Observation Log ■ Reading and Writing Workbook, pp. 5–8 ■ Inquiry Journal, p. 6 ■ Home Connection, p. 3	**Student Anthology, pp. 20–26** **Comprehension Strategies** ■ Making Connections, pp. 20, 22, 24 ■ Predicting, pp. 20, 22, 24, 26	**Student Anthology, pp. 26–35** **Comprehension Strategies** ■ Making Connections, p. 26 ■ Summarizing, pp. 28, 30 ■ Predicting, pp. 28, 32 **Discussing Strategy Use, p. 32** **Comprehension Skills** ✓■ Discussing the Selection, p. 33 **Exploring the Theme** ■ Selection Vocabulary, p. 35A *election, represent, campaign, candidates, confidence*
Part 3 Integrating the Curriculum **Materials** ■ Student Anthology, pp. 20–35 ■ Reading and Writing Workbook, pp. 9–14 ■ Inquiry Journal, pp. 8–9	**Writing** ■ Introducing the Writing Process, pp. 35C, D **Literary Elements** ✓■ Characters, p. 35E	**Writing Process** ■ Prewrite, p. 35D **Vocabulary** ✓■ Words with Suffixes: *-tion*, p. 35F

| *Independent Work Time*

Materials
■ Reteach, pp. 5–14
■ ESL Supplement
■ Challenge, pp. 5–9
■ Intervention Guide
■ Listening Library Audiocassette | **Writing Process Continued**
Reteach
✓■ Characters, *Reteach*, pp. 9–10
ESL
■ Word Meaning, p. 20G
■ Vocabulary, p. 20J
Challenge
✓■ Characters, *Challenge*, p. 7
Intervention
■ Word Knowledge, p. 20G
■ Predicting, p. 22   ■ Characters, p. 35E | **Writing Process Continued**
Reteach
✓■ Words with Suffixes: *-tion*, *Reteach*, pp. 11–12
ESL
■ Conversation, p. 23
Challenge
✓■ Words with Suffixes: *-tion*, *Challenge*, p. 8
Intervention
■ Comprehension, p. 20
■ Words with Suffixes: *-tion*, p. 35F |

✓ Informal **Assessment Available**   ✓ Formal **Assessment Available**

DAY 2 continued	DAY 3	
DAY 3	**DAY 4**	**DAY 5**
General Review	**General Review**	**Review Word Knowledge**
Student Anthology, pp. 20–35 **Comprehension Skills** ✓ ■ Drawing Conclusions, pp. 21, 23, 25, 31 **Theme Connections** ■ Think About It, p. 35 ■ Make a Poster, p. 35	**Student Anthology, pp. 20–35** **Comprehension Skills** ✓ ■ Author's Purpose, pp. 27, 29 **Exploring the Theme** ■ Reading/Writing Connections, p. 35A ■ Supporting Student Explorations, p. 35B	**Student Anthology, pp. 20–35** ■ Review Selection ■ Complete Discussion ■ Reread Selection in Pairs **Home Connection, p. 35A** ■ Discuss "Class President" ■ Create campaign slogans
Writing Process Continued **Grammar, Usage, and Mechanics** ✓ ■ Prepositions and Prepositional Phrases, p. 35G **Listening/Speaking/Viewing** ■ Persuasive Techniques, p. 35H	**Writing Process Continued** **Study and Research** ✓ ■ Parts of the Library, p. 35I	**Across the Curriculum** **Social Studies** ■ Cooperating to Develop Safety Rules, p. 35J **Art** ■ Cooperation Posters Versus Competition Posters, p. 35J
Writing Process Continued **Reteach** ✓ ■ Drawing Conclusions, *Reteach*, pp. 7–8 **ESL** ■ Listening/Speaking/Viewing, p. 35H **Challenge** ✓ ■ Drawing Conclusions, *Challenge*, p. 6	**Writing Process Continued** **Reteach** ✓ ■ Prepositions and Prepositional Phrases, *Reteach*, pp. 13–14 **Challenge** ✓ ■ Prepositions and Prepositional Phrases, *Challenge*, p. 9 **Unit Project** ■ Discuss Experiences ■ Generate Ideas	**Writing Process Continued** **Reteach** ✓ ■ Author's Purpose, *Reteach*, pp. 5–6 **Challenge** ✓ ■ Author's Purpose, *Challenge*, p. 5 **Unit Project Continued**

Meeting Individual Needs
Independent Work Time

Preparing to Read

Meeting Individual Needs

ESL
- **Word Meaning, p. 20G**
- **Cultural Context, p. 20H**
- **Vocabulary, p. 20J**

Intervention
- **Word Knowledge, p. 20G**

Reading and Responding

Meeting Individual Needs

Reteach
- **Author's Purpose, *Reteach*, pp. 5–6**
- **Drawing Conclusions, *Reteach*, pp. 7–8**

ESL
- **Conversation, p. 23**

Challenge
- **Author's Purpose, *Challenge*, p. 5**
- **Drawing Conclusions, *Challenge*, p. 6**

Intervention
- **Comprehension, p. 20**
- **Predicting, p. 22**
- **Making Connections, p. 24**
- **Drawing Conclusions, p. 25**
- **Author's Purpose, p. 27**
- **Summarizing, p. 28**

Integrating the Curriculum

Meeting Individual Needs

Reteach
- **Characters, *Reteach*, pp. 9–10**
- **Words with Suffixes: *-tion*, *Reteach*, pp. 11–12**
- **Prepositions and Prepositional Phrases, *Reteach*, pp. 13–14**

ESL
- **Listening/Speaking/Viewing, p. 35H**

Challenge
- **Characters, *Challenge*, p. 7**
- **Words with Suffixes: *-tion*, *Challenge*, p. 8**
- **Prepositions and Prepositional Phrases, *Challenge*, p. 9**

Intervention
- **Characters, p. 35E**
- **Words with Suffixes: *-tion*, p. 35F**

Formal Assessment Options

Use these assessment pages along with your informal observations to gauge student progress.

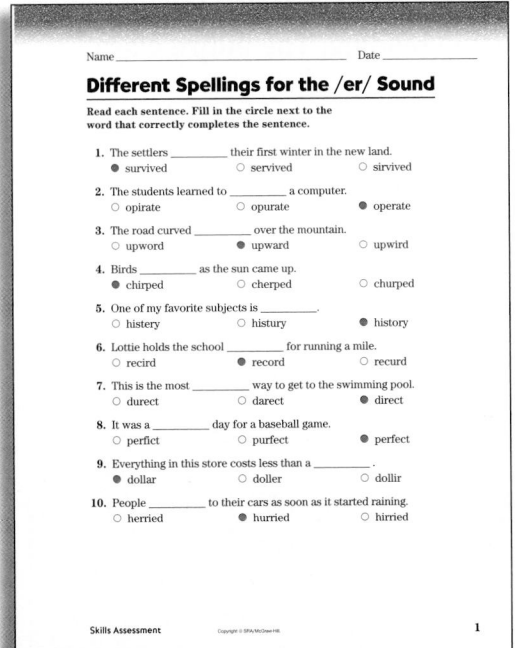

Skills Assessment, p. 1

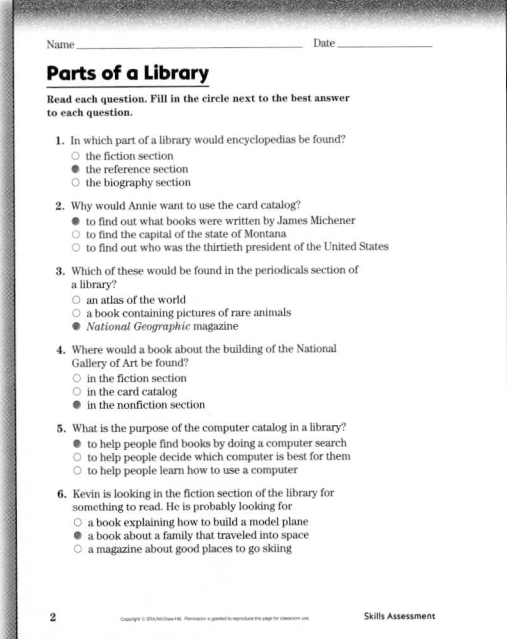

Skills Assessment, p. 2

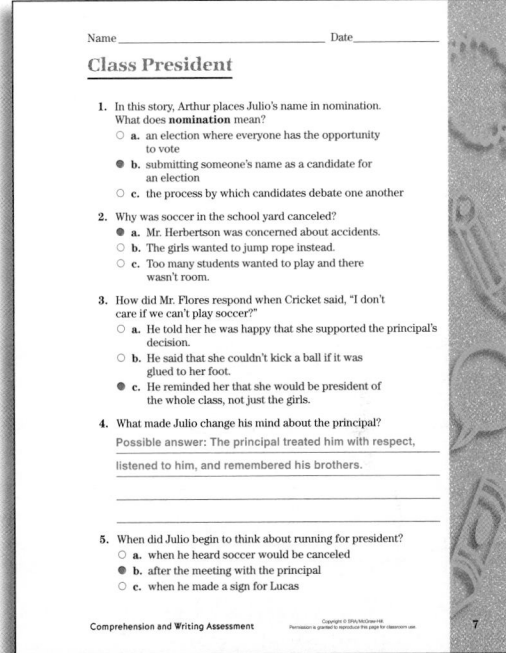

Comprehension and Writing Assessment, p. 7

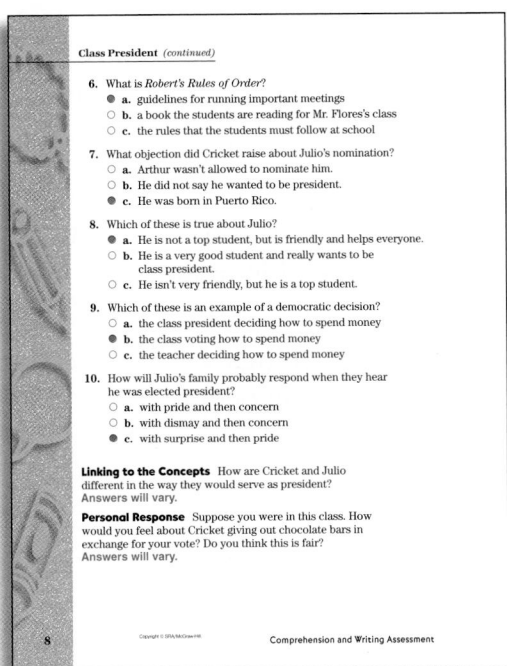

Comprehension and Writing Assessment, p. 8

① Preparing to Read

Teacher Tip Gaining a better understanding of the spellings of sounds and the structure of words will help students as they encounter unfamiliar words in their reading. By this time in grade 5, students should be reading approximately 126 words per minute with fluency and expression.

Meeting Individual Needs

ESL

Word Meaning Make sure English-language learners understand the meanings of the words before they do the exercises. Refer to the *ESL Supplement,* Unit 1, Lesson 1, for specific suggestions.

Intervention

Word Knowledge Have students go through "Class President" and look for word derivatives, *r-* consonant blends, and different endings for the /er/ sound. For students who need more help, see Unit 1, Lesson 1, of *Intervention Guide.*

Assessment

✓ **Formal** To assess students' understanding of different spellings of the /er/sound, have them complete *Skills Assessment,* page 1.

Word Knowledge

Introduction

The Word Knowledge activities show students strategies for figuring out unfamiliar words they encounter while reading. The entire class participates in each of these activities.

Reading the Words and Sentences

Write each word and sentence on the chalkboard. Have students read each word together. After all the words have been read, have students read each sentence in natural phrases or chunks. Use the suggestions in About the Words to discuss the different features of the listed words.

Line 1: compete   competitor   competition
Line 2: broke creature driver Friday green proud tripped writer
Line 3: occur   pressure   painter
Sentence 1: Each competitor was a good writer.
Sentence 2: Some kind of creature broke into the green shed.
Sentence 3: The competition will occur on Friday.

About the Words

- Line 1 contains derivatives that build on the root word *compete.* Have students discuss how the suffixes added to the root word have changed its meaning.

- The words in Line 2 contain blends with the letter *r.* Have students think of other words that have a consonant plus *r* blend at the beginning of a word.

- Line 3 contains words that illustrate different spellings for the /er/ sound. Have volunteers circle where these spellings occur.

Developing Oral Language

To review the words, have students do one or both of the following activities:

- Have students take turns pointing to a word in the lines above to use in a sentence.
- Ask students to choose at least two words from the list and use them in their own sentences. For example, "We felt the *pressure* of the *competition* on *Friday*."

Build Background

Activate Prior Knowledge

Tell students that good readers create links between what they already know and what they are reading. Before reading the selection, have students check the Concept/Question Board to:

- refresh their memories about what they know about cooperation and competition.
- see if there are any questions on the Board that this story might answer.

Background Information

The following information may help students better understand the selection they are about to read.

- "Class President" is an example of realistic fiction. Explain that realistic fiction features believable characters in situations that could happen in real life.
- Explain to students that authors use various techniques to make characters seem real. They help readers understand characters by explaining the thoughts and feelings that motivate their actions. Authors also use dialogue to help readers understand story characters by having characters say certain things that show what they think and believe.
- Toward the end of this selection, the main character, Julio, is nominated to run for class president. One of his potential opponents comments that Julio should not be allowed to run for class president because he is Puerto Rican. This could be a sensitive issue in your classroom and should be discussed before students read the selection.

Meeting Individual Needs

ESL

Cultural Context English-language learners may be unfamiliar with the concept of a class president. Ask English-language learners if they have been in a classroom where there was a president. If so, ask them to say what the president did. If your class does not currently have a president, talk about how the students feel a class president could be helpful.

Teacher Tip Whenever possible, allow students to generate and direct discussion. Allowing them to take control of their learning helps students become active, purposeful learners.

Writing Journal Have students bring in a spiral notebook or binder that they will label Writing Journal. Let them know that their journal will be divided into at least five different sections. These sections include a place for vocabulary words, ideas for writing, personal reactions to stories, notes about genres or techniques, and words for a personal dictionary. Feel free during this year to add other sections that you and your students find useful.

Tell students that they will jot down in their Writing Journals their reactions to the story. Have them be on the lookout for ideas on how to use the process of electing class officers in their dramatic plays.

1 Preparing to Read

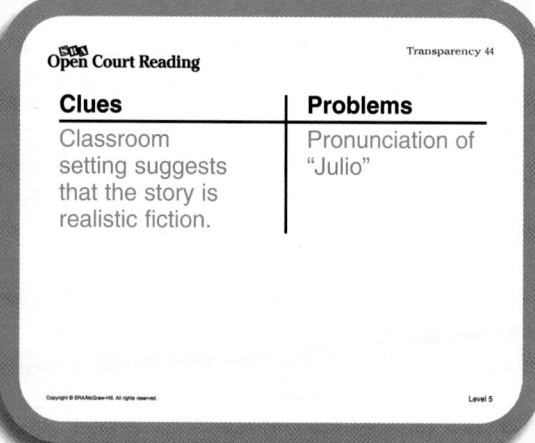

Transparency 44

Preview and Prepare

Browse

Tell the students that before reading each selection, they will *set purposes*, or goals, for their reading and what they want to gain from it. Doing so will give them a sense of the selection and help them to better understand what they read. Explain that before they can set purposes, they will have to *browse* the selection using the *clues and problems* procedure.

Introduce the browsing procedure by having the students quickly look over the first page or two of the selection. From this, have students determine if the selection is fiction or nonfiction. Fiction pieces should not be browsed in their entirety, because browsing might ruin any surprises in the story and the ending of the story.

Display **Transparency 44,** Clues and Problems. Under each heading write in note form the observations that students generate as they browse. For example, students might list the genre of the selection under Clues; they might note any questions that arise during reading and list unfamiliar words under Problems. For a full review of setting reading goals and browsing, see page 4 of the Program Appendix.

■ Have students browse through only the first page or two of the story, so as not to spoil the ending. Discuss with them what they think this story might have to do with cooperation and competition.

■ Have students search for clues that tell them something about the selection, such as the classroom setting with its upcoming election suggests that this is realistic fiction. Have them search for any problems, such as unfamiliar words that they notice while reading. Use **Transparency 44** to record their observations as they browse.

Set Purposes

Have students set and adjust their own purposes for reading. As they read, have students think about which characters learn something about cooperation and competition, what they learn, and how they use that new knowledge.

Also, have students think about how the theme of the story piques their curiosity or connects to their personal interests. Students may also want to look for information that may be useful on the unit projects or activities.

Selection Vocabulary

As students study vocabulary, they will use context clues, word structure, and apposition to clarify these and additional unfamiliar words.

Display **Transparency 1** before reading the selection to introduce the following words and their meanings.

e•lect•ion: how people vote for someone to serve in an office or approve an idea (page 20)

re•pre•sent: to speak for or act for someone else (page 24)

cam•paign: an organized effort to accomplish a purpose (page 23)

can•di•dates: people who are seeking an office, job, or position (page 27)

con•fi•dence: a belief in one's ability to do something (page 27)

Have students read the words in the Word Box on **Transparency 1**. Help students decode multisyllabic words by reading the words syllable by syllable. If the word is not decodable, give the students the pronunciation and mark the non-decodable words. For your convenience, decodable multisyllabic words are divided above.

Have students read the sentences on the transparency to determine the meaning of the underlined words. Model for them how to use *context clues*, *word structure*, and *apposition* to define each of the selection vocabulary words in the sentences (see the Teacher Tip to the right for information on how the words in each sentence can be defined).

■ Tell students that sometimes one can define a word by using *context clues*, or other parts of the sentence that help one figure out the word's meaning.

■ One can also use his or her knowledge of *word structure* (or the word's parts, such as *suffix*, *prefix*, and *root word*).

■ Still yet, sometimes one can easily define the word when the author has used *apposition*, which is when the definition is placed directly before or after the words.

Remind the students to look for context clues, word structure, and apposition whenever they come across an unfamiliar word.

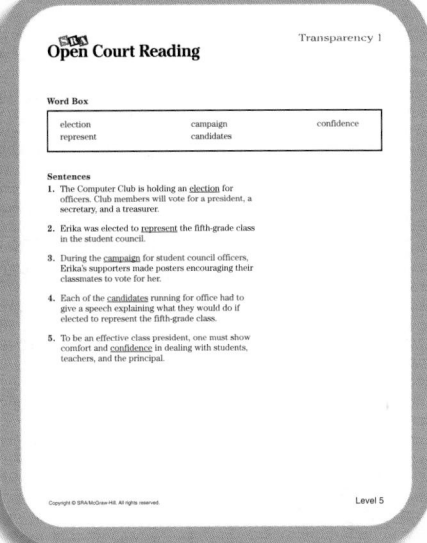

Transparency 1

 To help students decode words, divide them into the syllables shown below. The information following each word tells how students can figure out the meaning of each word in the sentences on **Transparency 1.**

e•lec•tion	context clues, word structure
re•pre•sent	context clues
cam•paign	context clues
can•di•dates	context clues
con•fi•dence	context clues

Meeting Individual Needs

ESL

Vocabulary Check that English-language learners know the meanings of idioms and more difficult vocabulary in the story, including: *election; nomination; how to second [a nomination]; run against; convince; the campaign; good arguments; represent the class; some very good points; a [voting] tie; voted; candidate; out of order; speech; withdraw; ballots.* Explain and show pictures as needed. Model example sentences and help the students make their own sentences. Refer to Unit 1, Lesson 1, of the **ESL Supplement** for teaching suggestions.

Preparing to Read

Teacher Tip Discussing strategy use and evaluating class discussions as a group will help the students understand that they must remain aware of ways that help them make sense of what they read. Encourage each student to participate actively in these discussions.

Reading Recommendations

For each selection, students will use comprehension strategies to develop and monitor their overall understanding of the text, and comprehension skills to enhance their appreciation of its content. The comprehension strategies (located to the left of the reduced student pages in Part 2) should be practiced during an initial reading of the text. The comprehension skills (located to the right of the reduced student pages) should be covered in a second reading of the text, done on another day.

Silent Reading

This story lends itself to silent reading because it is moderate in length and it provides an opportunity to observe students as they read. Have students practice reading on their own for at least five minutes at a time. As they become better readers, students will read silently with increasing ease, over longer periods of time.

Have students make use of the reading strategies listed on page 20 to help them understand the selection. For example, tell them to make as many connections as they can between what they are reading and what they already know; elements in the text that remind them of their own experiences or of the knowledge they already have will help them understand what they are reading. Have students stop reading periodically or wait until they have completed the selection to discuss the reading strategies.

After the students have finished reading the selection, use the "Discussing the Selection" questions to see if they have understood what they have read. If they have not, refer to the *Intervention Guide* for further strategies.

Using Reading Strategies
Modeling and Thinking Aloud

One of the most effective ways to help students use and understand the behaviors practiced by good readers is to make strategic thinking public. Modeling these behaviors and encouraging students to think aloud as they attempt to understand text can demonstrate to everyone in a class how these behaviors are put into practice. Suggestions for models are provided throughout the teacher's edition. The most effective models you can offer, however, will be those that come from your own reading experiences. What kinds of things did you yourself wonder about? What kinds of things surprised you the first time you read a story? What kinds of new information did you learn? What kinds of things were confusing until you reread or read further? Drawing on these questions and on your students' questions and comments as they read will make both the text and the strategic reading process more meaningful to the students.

During the reading of "Class President," you will model the use of the following reading strategies:

- Making Connections
- Predicting
- Summarizing

When modeling, you will think through the reading strategies aloud. Initially, you will model by identifying the strategy, indicating why the strategy is being used at this point, and giving an example of its application. Models are provided in the following pages. As students become more familiar with the strategies, the models will be modified to prompts. The goal of strategy instruction is for students to use strategies independently.

Building Comprehension Skills

Revisiting or rereading a selection allows students to apply skills that give them a more complete understanding of the text. Some follow-up comprehension skills, such as *Main Idea and Details* and *Compare and Contrast*, help students organize information. Others, such as *Author's Purpose, Making Inferences*, and *Drawing Conclusions*, lead to deeper understanding—to "reading between the lines," as mature readers do. In this selection, students will apply the follow-up comprehension skills of *Drawing Conclusions* and *Author's Purpose*. Since two skills are reviewed, you may want to do all of the selection related to one skill before doing the other skill.

Teacher Tip By this time in the fifth grade, good readers should be reading approximately 126 words per minute with fluency and expression. The only way to gain fluency is through practice. As explained in Reading Recommendations, have students reread all or part of the selection to you and to each other during class or Independent Work Time to focus on the comprehension skills and to build fluency.

Teacher Tip Have students who may need extra help reading the contemporary story, "Class President," reread the selection using the *Listening Library Audiocassette* as a proficient, fluent model of oral reading.

② Reading and Responding

Read pages 20–35.

Comprehension Strategies

Modeling

❶ Making Connections *Good readers make connections between what they are reading and what they already know from past experience or previous reading.*

Now is a good time to stop and make a connection with Julio, who appears to be one of the main characters in this selection. Julio ate one of Cricket's chocolate bars, but he decides that doesn't mean he's going to vote for her. I think Julio is right. That reminds me of an election where someone tries to bribe someone with money or gifts.

Have you ever been in a situation like this?

Modeling

❷ Predicting *When reading fiction, good readers constantly make predictions about what they are reading and then confirm these predictions as they go. Predictions are based on what the reader already knows and on clues in the text.*

Now is a good time to think about who seems the most likely to be elected.

Cricket is trying hard to win the election by giving out chocolate bars. But Julio is working hard, too. I think that Lucas will be elected class president. What prediction would you like to make?

Reading Recommendation

ORAL • CHORAL • **SILENT**

Class President

by Johanna Hurwitz
illustrated by Richard Hull

To Delia and Bill Gottlieb
They get my vote every time!

Julio Sanchez is sure that fifth grade is going to be his best year yet. On the first day of school, his homeroom teacher Mr. Flores announces that this year the fifth grade will be electing a class president. To get ready for the election, the students are to be thinking about who might make a good leader.

In the meantime, while playing in a soccer game at recess, Julio's classmate Arthur breaks his glasses. The fifth grade pitches in to pay for the glasses by holding a bake sale. But on the day of the bake sale, Arthur's mom finds out his glasses can be replaced for free.

Now the class has two things to decide: who to elect as class president and what to do with the bake sale money no longer needed to pay for Arthur's glasses. . . .

On Monday, Arthur came to school with new glasses. Cricket came to class with a big poster that said, VOTE FOR CRICKET, THAT'S THE TICKET.

The election was going to be held on Friday. That meant there were only four days more to get ready. In the meantime, they learned about how to make a <u>nomination</u> and how to <u>second</u> it. It was going to be a really serious election.

At lunch, Cricket took out a bag of miniature chocolate bars and gave them out to her classmates. Julio took his and ❶ ate it. But it didn't mean he was going to vote for Cricket. He wondered if there was anything Lucas could give out that was better than chocolate. Nothing was better than chocolate!

★ 20

Meeting Individual Needs

Intervention

Comprehension Intervention strategies for those students having difficulty reading "Class President" can be found in Unit 1, Lesson 1, of the ***Intervention Guide.***

Assessment

✓ **Informal** Observe individual students as they read, and use the Teacher Observation Log, found in the ***Assessment Guide,*** to record anecdotal information about each student's strengths and weaknesses.

"If you're going to run against Cricket, we've got to get to work," Julio told Lucas on their way home. Julio wasn't very good at making posters, as Cricket and Zoe were, but he was determined to help his friend.

The next morning, a new poster appeared in Mr. Flores's classroom. It said, DON'T BUG ME. VOTE FOR LUCAS COTT. Julio had made it.

Before lunch, Mr. Flores read an announcement from the principal. "From now on, there is to be no more soccer playing in the school yard at lunchtime."

"No more soccer playing?" Julio called out. "Why not?"

Mr. Flores looked at Julio. "If you give me a moment, I'll explain. Mr. Herbertson is concerned about accidents. Last week, Arthur broke his glasses. Another time, someone might be injured more seriously."

Julio was about to call out again, but he remembered just in time and raised his hand.

"Yes, Julio," said Mr. Flores.

21

Teacher Tip

On the reduced pages above, words that can be found in the *Student Anthology* glossary are underlined in magenta. These words are underlined in the *Teacher's Edition* only. The magenta-encircled numbers appearing beside the text correspond to the Comprehension Strategies numbered in the column to the left.

Comprehension Skills

Drawing Conclusions

Introduce students to the concept of *drawing conclusions*, which means using pieces of information about a character or story event to make a statement or generalization about that character or story event. For instance, one can figure out quite a bit about a character by making note of how that character looks or behaves. Likewise, one can understand a story's events by paying attention to when and where the story takes place and how the story unfolds.

Have the students read paragraph 3 on page 20. Then ask them these questions:

- What conclusion is Julio drawing about *why* Cricket is handing out the chocolate bars? *(She thinks if they eat the bars, they will vote for her.)*

- What conclusion does Julio draw about *eating* the bar? *(It doesn't mean he has to vote for her.)*

Tell the students to look for additional clues that allow them to draw conclusions about the characters or events in the story.

Skills Strand

Drawing Conclusions
INTRODUCED: Unit 1, Lesson 1
REVIEWED: Unit 1, Lesson 5
Unit 2, Lesson 1
Unit 3, Lesson 4
Unit 3, Lesson 6

Teacher Tip

Julio is pronounced hōō´lē ō. Flores is pronounced flō´rās.

2 Reading and Responding

Comprehension Strategies

Modeling

3 Making Connections *I can connect with how Julio feels. I remember being called into the principal's office when I was a student. I thought I had done something wrong. Do any of you connect with Julio? How?*

Modeling

4 Predicting *This is a good place to stop and predict how we think Julio's appointment with the principal will go. I think it was smart of Julio to invite Cricket along. That way, the principal will know that playing soccer is important to both the boys and girls. I think that Cricket is going to be a big help in talking to the principal, even if she's a bit of a pain the way she is trying to win the election. What do you think will happen, and why?* (This prediction is confirmed on page 24.)

Teacher Tip

Point out that each student may connect to the text in a completely different way. Assure them that this is normal, and that it is impossible to connect to text in a wrong way.

Word Knowledge

cricket, principal, afraid

Students can use the skills they learned in the Word Knowledge section of this lesson to read these words. Remind students of this if they have difficulty reading these words.

"It's not fair to make us stop playing soccer just because someone *might* get hurt. Someone might fall down walking to school, but we still have to come to school every day."

Julio didn't mean to be funny, but everyone started to laugh. Even Mr. Flores smiled.

"There must be other activities to keep you fellows busy at lunchtime," he said. "Is soccer the only thing you can do?"

Lucas raised his hand. "I don't like jumping rope," he said when the teacher called on him.

All the girls giggled at that.

"You could play jacks," suggested Cricket. Everyone knew it wasn't a serious possibility, though.

"Couldn't we tell Mr. Herbertson that we want to play soccer?" asked Julio.

"You could make an appointment to speak to him, if you'd like," said Mr. Flores. "He might change his decision if you convince him that you are right."

"Lucas and I will talk to him," said Julio. "Right, Lucas?"

"Uh, sure," said Lucas, but he didn't look too sure.

3 The principal, Mr. Herbertson, spoke in a loud voice and had eyes that seemed to <u>bore</u> right into your head when he looked at you. Julio had been a little bit afraid of Mr. Herbertson since the very first day of kindergarten. Why had he offered to go to his office and talk to him?

Mr. Flores sent Julio and Lucas down to the principal's office with a note, but the principal was out of the office at a meeting.

"You can talk to him at one o'clock," the secretary said.

★ 22

Meeting Individual Needs

Intervention

Predicting Remind students that predicting helps them think ahead so they will be ready for new information. Reread this section with students having difficulty with predicting. Stop at sentences or paragraphs that signify some change in the action of the story, and work with students to make and revise their predictions.

At lunch, Cricket had more chocolate bars. This time, she had pasted labels on them and printed in tiny letters, *Cricket is the ticket.* She must be spending her whole allowance on the campaign, Julio thought.

After a few more days of free chocolate bars, everyone in the class would be voting for Cricket.

At recess, the girls were jumping rope. You could fall jumping rope, too, Julio thought.

Back in the classroom, Julio wished he could think up some good arguments to tell the principal. He looked over at Lucas. Lucas didn't look very good. Maybe he was coming down with the flu.

Just before one o'clock, Julio had a great idea. Cricket was always saying she wanted to be a lawyer. She always knew what to say in class. Julio figured she'd know just what to do in the principal's office, too. He raised his hand.

"Mr. Flores, can Cricket go down to Mr. Herbertson's office  with Lucas and me? She's running for president, so she should stick up for our class."

"Me?" Cricket said. "I don't care if we can't play soccer."

"Of course," teased Lucas. "You couldn't kick a ball if it was glued to your foot."

23

Comprehension Skills

Drawing Conclusions

Have the students gather pieces of information to help in *drawing conclusions* about characters and events. Ask the students to find places in the text that give information about Julio.

- On page 21, Julio forgets to raise his hand before speaking. What does this say about him? *(Julio is impulsive.)*

- On page 23, Julio suggests that Cricket come speak to the principal, too. What does this tell you about Julio? *(Julio believes in being fair, even to an opponent.)*

Have the students use the information they found to draw conclusions as they continue reading.

Teacher Tip Remind students that information such as the looks and behavior of a character, or the time and place of an event, are helpful when drawing conclusions.

Meeting Individual Needs

ESL

Conversation Provide time for informal conversational practice. Pair English-language learners with each other and with native English-speaking students to discuss their own learning experiences as they relate to the story. What helps them to learn? What is not helpful?

2 Reading and Responding

Comprehension Strategies

Modeling

5 Making Connections *I see that Julio is using a traditional Spanish pronunciation of his first name. This is a good place to stop and make a connection with other words and names spelled with a j pronounced as h. I know that "jalapeño pepper" is spelled with a j but pronounced with an h sound. What connection can you make with the way Julio's name is pronounced?*

Modeling

6 Confirming Predictions *After making a prediction, good readers check as they are reading for information that tells them whether or not their prediction was right. This is called confirming predictions.*

Earlier I predicted that Cricket would be helpful when Julio talked to the principal. Boy, was I wrong! Cricket was no help at all in the principal's office. It was Julio who did all the talking, and now Cricket is even taking credit for getting the principal to allow them to play soccer. I predict the other students will realize who did the persuading, and that Cricket will definitely lose the election. What are your predictions? (This prediction can be checked on page 26.)

Word Knowledge

girls, soccer, returned

Students can use the skills they learned in the Word Knowledge section of this lesson to read these words. Remind students of this if they have difficulty reading these words.

"Cricket," said Mr. Flores, "even if you don't want to play soccer, others in the class do. If you are elected, you will be president of the whole class, not just the girls. I think going to the meeting with Mr. Herbertson will be a good opportunity for you to represent the class."

So that was why at one o'clock Julio, Lucas, and Cricket Kaufman went downstairs to the principal's office.

Mr. Herbertson gestured for them to sit in the chairs facing his desk. Cricket looked as pale as Lucas. Maybe she, too, was coming down with the flu.

Julio waited for the future first woman President of the United States to say something, but Cricket didn't say a word. Neither did Lucas. Julio didn't know what to do. They couldn't just sit here and say nothing.

Julio took a deep breath. If Cricket or Lucas wasn't going to talk, he would have to do it. Julio started right in.

"We came to tell you that it isn't fair that no one can play soccer at recess just because Arthur Lewis broke his eyeglasses. Anybody can have an accident. He could have tripped and broken them getting on the school bus." Julio was amazed that so many words had managed to get out of his mouth. No one else said anything, so he went on. "Besides, a girl could fall jumping rope," said Julio. "But you didn't say that they had to stop jumping rope."

24

Teacher Tip During reading, have students think about whether they agree or disagree with the story's message. Encourage them to identify the acts of competition and cooperation in the story, and the characters' responses to those acts.

Meeting Individual Needs

Intervention

Making Connections For students who are having trouble making connections, remind them that they should try to remember things from their own lives that are similar to events or people in the selection.

"I hadn't thought of that," said Mr. Herbertson.

Cricket looked alarmed. "Can't we jump rope anymore?" she asked.

"I didn't mean that you should make the girls stop jumping rope," Julio went on quickly. He stopped to think of a better example. "Your chair could break while you're sitting on it, Mr. Herbertson," he said.

Mr. Herbertson adjusted himself in his chair. "I certainly hope not," he said, smiling. "What is your name, young man?"

5 "Julio. Julio Sanchez." He pronounced it in the Spanish way with the *J* having an *H* sound.

"You have a couple of brothers who also attended this school, Julio, don't you?" asked the principal. "Nice fellows. I remember them both."

Julio smiled. He didn't know why he had always been afraid of the principal. He was just like any other person.

6 "Julio," Mr. Herbertson went on, "you've got a good head on your shoulders, just like your brothers. You made some very good points this afternoon. I think I can arrange things so that there will be more teachers supervising the yard during recess. Then you fellows can play soccer again tomorrow." He turned to Cricket. "You can jump rope if you'd rather do that," he said.

Cricket smiled. She didn't look so pale anymore.

Julio and Lucas and Cricket returned to Mr. Flores's classroom. "It's all arranged," said Cricket as soon as they walked in the door.

25

Comprehension Skills

Drawing Conclusions

Review with the students that drawing a conclusion means making a statement about a character, thing, or event based on information in the text. Characters in a selection can also draw conclusions based on the facts presented to them.

- Have the students read paragraph 6 on page 22. Is Julio afraid of the principal? *(yes)*

- Have students look carefully at the information about Mr. Herbertson on pages 24–25. What conclusion does Julio draw about Mr. Herbertson on page 25? *(that he is just like any other person)*

- What wrong conclusion had Julio originally drawn about Mr. Herbertson, and on what information did he base it? *(Julio thought Mr. Herbertson was a scary man at first because of his loud voice and stern appearance.)*

Have students find other examples of conclusions that characters in the story have drawn.

Meeting Individual Needs

Intervention

Drawing Conclusions If students are having difficulty with drawing conclusions, review the conclusions drawn above, going back to the selection to find the clues in the text on which they are based.

2 Reading and Responding

Comprehension Strategies

Modeling

7 Confirming Predictions *Here's a good place to check one of our predictions from earlier, and see if perhaps we may want to change it. Julio thinks that all the girls will vote for a girl and all the boys will vote for a boy. I'm not so sure about that. I don't think I would vote for Cricket or Lucas just because they are a boy or a girl. I still think that Cricket is going to lose. What do you think?* (This prediction is confirmed on page 30 of the Teacher's Edition.)

Modeling

8 Making Connections *Here is a good place to stop and make a connection. I see here that they are using* Robert's Rules of Order, *which is a book. I know this from times I've had to attend very formal school meetings. The book tells people how to run a formal meeting, and how to decide who gets to speak first and how long he or she gets to talk.* Robert's Rules of Order *helps keep things fair for everyone. What connections can you make to the way they are running this meeting?*

The class burst into cheers.

"Good work," said Mr. Flores.

Julio was proud that he had stood up to Mr. Herbertson. However, it wasn't fair that Cricket made it seem as if she had done all the work. She had hardly done a thing. For that matter, Lucas hadn't said anything, either. For a moment, Julio wished he hadn't offered to be Lucas's campaign manager. He wished he was the one running for class president. He knew he could be a good leader.

There was bad news on election day. Chris Willard was absent. Since there were twelve girls and twelve boys in Mr. Flores's class, it meant there were more girls than boys to vote in the election. If all the girls voted for Cricket and all the boys voted for Lucas, there would be a tie. Since one boy was absent, Lucas could be in big trouble. Julio hoped it didn't mean that Lucas had lost the election before they even voted.

Then Mr. Flores told the class that the Parent-Teacher Association was going to be holding a book fair in a few weeks. With more than seventeen dollars from the bake sale, the class could buy a good supply of paperbacks for a special classroom library. Cricket seemed to think it was a great idea, but Julio didn't think it was so hot. After all, there was a school library up one flight of stairs. Why did they need extra books, especially books the students had to pay for out of their *own* money?

26

Teacher Tip Have the students think of connections to the story as they are reading. Parts of the selection may remind them of things in their lives— things that they've learned about in other selections, books they've read, or movies or television shows they've seen.

Julio thought that the class should vote on the way the money was spent. Before he had a chance to say anything, it was time for lunch.

Lunch was chicken nuggets, whipped potatoes, string beans, and Jell-O squares. Cricket and Zoe didn't even touch their lunches. Julio knew they were talking about the election. Julio clapped Lucas on the back. "You're going to win, pal," he said. "I just know it." He really wasn't so sure, but he felt it was his job to give his candidate confidence. After all, he had convinced Lucas to run for class president in the first place.

Lucas shrugged, trying to act cool. "Maybe yes, maybe no," he said. But Julio could see that he was too excited to eat much lunch, either. Julio polished off his friend's tuna-fish sandwich and his orange. "I need to keep up my strength to vote for you," he told Lucas.

Cricket had more chocolate bars. "Are you going to vote for me?" she asked everyone.

"Maybe yes, maybe no," said Julio, taking his bar.

When they returned from lunch, Mr. Flores called the class to order. It was time for the election to begin. Mr. Flores reminded ⑧ them about *Robert's Rules of Order*, which was the way school board and other important meetings were conducted.

"You may nominate anyone you choose," he said, "even if your candidate doesn't have a poster up on the wall. Then you

27

Meeting Individual Needs

Intervention

Author's Purpose Point out that many times one can tell a lot about what the author's purpose is for a selection by browsing through the text's illustrations. For example, one can guess that this selection is entertaining because its illustrations are colorful and cartoonlike. Compare this to an informational text in which the illustrations might be charts, graphs, or photographs.

Comprehension Skills

Author's Purpose

Explain to the students that writers always have a *purpose* when they write. That purpose might be to *inform*, to *explain*, to *persuade*, or to *entertain*. Sometimes, a writer has more than one purpose for writing.

Ask students what they think Johanna Hurwitz's purpose might have been in writing "Class President." *(Generally, students should conclude that she is writing to entertain the reader, but some students might also mention informing or explaining about elections.)*

Author's Purpose

2 Reading and Responding

Comprehension Strategies

Modeling

9 Summarizing *To check their understanding, good readers often paraphrase what they have read during as well as after reading a selection. This is helpful when reading a fictional work that has many characters, describes many events, or covers a long period of time.*

There's a lot of interesting information on these pages about how an election works. Let's stop and summarize the information to help us check our understanding. First, a candidate has to be nominated. Someone else has to second the nomination. Once you nominate or second the nomination of a candidate, you can't nominate or second anyone else. Is there anything you would like to add to this summary?

Modeling

10 Predicting *Because there has been a sudden change of events, this is a good time to stop and make a new prediction about who might win the election. I had the feeling that Julio would like to run for president, but I never expected Arthur to nominate him. But with Lucas and Julio both running, half of the boys might vote for Julio and half might vote for Lucas. And if most of the girls vote for Cricket, she might win! On second thought, I don't think all of the girls will vote for Cricket. What do you think? (This prediction is confirmed on page 32.)*

can make a speech in favor of your candidate and try to convince your classmates."

Uh-oh, thought Julio. He was ready to nominate Lucas but he didn't know if he would be able to make a speech. He wasn't good with words, as Cricket and Lucas were.

Zoe Mitchell raised her hand. "I nominate Cricket Kaufman," she said. No surprise there. Julio wondered if Zoe had wanted to run herself.

"Does anyone second the nomination?" Mr. Flores asked.

Julio thought the class election sounded like a TV program, not the way people talked in real life.

Sara Jane seconded the nomination, and Mr. Flores wrote Cricket's name on the chalkboard.

"Are there any other nominations?" he asked.

Sara Jane raised her hand again.

"Do you have a question, Sara Jane?" asked Mr. Flores.

"Now I want to nominate Zoe Mitchell."

28

Meeting Individual Needs

Intervention

Summarizing Remind students that they will better comprehend the text if they use their own words to sum it up. Tell them that the process of putting the information into their own words not only helps good readers remember the text, but also prompts them to evaluate their understanding of the information.

Teacher Tip

Some students might be unfamiliar with the American Territory of Puerto Rico. Encourage them to look in an atlas or encyclopedia for more information.

⑨ "You can't nominate someone when you have already seconded the nomination of someone else," Mr. Flores explained. "That's the way <u>parliamentary procedure</u> works."

Cricket looked relieved. She hadn't been expecting any competition from Zoe.

Julio raised his hand. "I nominate Lucas Cott," he said.

"Does anyone second the nomination?"

"Can I second myself?" asked Lucas.

"I'll second the nomination," said Anne Crosby from the back of the classroom.

"*Ooooh*," giggled one of the girls. "Anne likes Lucas."

"There is no rule that girls can nominate only girls and boys nominate only boys," said Mr. Flores. He wrote Lucas's name on the board. "Are there any other nominations?" he asked.

⑩ Arthur Lewis raised his hand. "I want to nominate Julio Sanchez," he said.

"Julio?" Sara Jane giggled. "He's just a big goof-off."

"Just a minute," said Mr. Flores sharply. "You are quite out of order, Sara Jane. Does anyone wish to second the nomination?"

Julio couldn't believe that Arthur had nominated him. Even though Arthur had said that Julio should run for president, Julio hadn't thought he would come right out and say it in front of everyone.

Cricket raised her hand. "Julio can't run for president," she said. "He was born in Puerto Rico. He isn't an American citizen. You have to be an American citizen to be elected President. We learned that last year in social studies."

"Yeah," Lucas called out. "You also have to be thirty-five years old. You must have been left back a lot of times, Cricket."

⭐ 29

Meeting Individual Needs

Reteach
Author's Purpose Have students who need additional instruction and practice with this concept complete **Reteach,** pages 5–6.

Challenge
Author's Purpose Have students who understand this concept and could benefit from extended practice complete **Challenge,** page 5.

Comprehension Strategies

Author's Purpose

For additional practice on *author's purpose*, have students complete **Reading and Writing Workbook** pages 5–6.

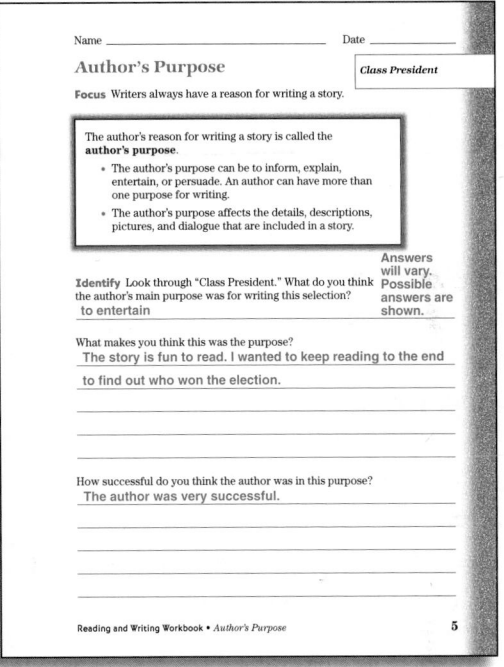

Reading and Writing Workbook pp. 5–6

2 Reading and Responding

Comprehension Strategies

Modeling

⓫ **Summarizing** *Let's summarize again to make sure we understand all of the main ideas. Julio has now been nominated for class president. Lucas has decided not to run and has taken his name off the board. He asks everyone to vote for Julio. So now the race is between Julio and Cricket. This changes things a lot. Is there anything we should add to the summary before we go on?*

Teacher Tip Remind students to make use of their reading strategies to understand the story. Model behaviors good readers use, such as treating problems encountered in the text as interesting learning opportunities rather than something to be avoided or dreaded. Have students ask themselves questions about what they have just read to monitor their own comprehension. If this does not work, have them try to pinpoint exactly what is unclear to them. After the students have read the selection, use the "Discussing the Selection" questions to see if they have read understood what they have read. If they have not, refer to the *Intervention Guide* for further strategies.

Word Knowledge
broke, write, grade
Students can use the skills they learned in the Word Knowledge section of this lesson to read these words. Remind students of this if they have difficulty reading these words.

"Hold on," said Mr. Flores. "Are we electing a President of the United States here, or are we electing a president of this fifth-grade class?"

Cricket looked embarrassed. It wasn't often she was wrong about anything.

Julio stood up without even raising his hand. He didn't care if he was elected president or not, but there was one thing he had to make clear. "I am so an American citizen," he said. "All Puerto Ricans are Americans!"

Julio sat down, and Arthur raised his hand again. Julio figured he was going to say he had changed his mind and didn't want to nominate him after all.

"Arthur?" called Mr. Flores.

Arthur stood up. "It doesn't matter where Julio was born," he said. "He'd make a very good class president. He's fair, and he's always doing nice things for people. When I broke my glasses, he was the one who thought of going to Mr. Herbertson so that we could still play soccer at recess. That shows he would make a good president."

"But Julio is not one of the top students like Zoe or Lucas or me," Cricket said.

"He is tops," said Arthur. "He's tops in my book."

Julio felt his ears getting hot with embarrassment. He had never heard Arthur say so much in all the years that he had known him.

30

"Thank you, Arthur," said Mr. Flores. "That was a very good speech. We still need someone to second the nomination. Do I hear a second?"

Lucas raised his hand.

"I second the nomination of Julio Sanchez," he said.

Mr. Flores turned to write Julio's name on the board. Lucas was still raising his hand.

Mr. Flores turned from the board and called on Lucas again.

"Do you wish to make a campaign speech?" he asked Lucas.

"Yes, I'm going to vote for Julio, and I think everyone else should, too."

"Aren't you even going to vote for yourself?" asked Cricket.

"No," said Lucas. "I want to take my name off the board. Julio is a good leader, like Arthur said. When we went to see Mr. Herbertson, Cricket and I were scared stiff, but Julio just stepped in and did all the talking."

"Are you asking to withdraw your name from nomination, Lucas?" asked Mr. Flores.

"Yes, I am. Everyone who was going to vote for me should vote for Julio."

Julio sat in his seat without moving. He couldn't say a word. He could hardly breathe.

11

31

Meeting Individual Needs

Reteach

Drawing Conclusions Have students who need additional instruction and practice with this concept complete **Reteach,** pages 7–8.

Challenge

Drawing Conclusions Have students who understand this concept and could benefit from extended practice complete **Challenge,** page 6.

Comprehension Skills

Drawing Conclusions

For additional practice with *drawing conclusions*, have students complete ***Reading and Writing Workbook*** pages 7–8.

Name _____ Date _____

Drawing Conclusions

Class President

Focus Good readers know how to draw conclusions about characters or events they read about in a story.

Drawing conclusions means putting information together to make a statement about a character or event in a story. Readers can draw conclusions based on
- how a character behaves or what he or she says.
- when and where a story takes place.

While a conclusion may not be directly stated in the text, it should be supported by examples in the story.

Identify Look through "Class President." What conclusions can you draw about a character or event in the story? Find information in the story that helped you draw your conclusions. Answers will vary. Possible answers are shown.

Page: 24

Conclusion about a character: Julio is a leader.

Information that supports the conclusion: Julio spoke up when he met with the principal.

Page: 32

Conclusion about an event: Julio won the election.

Information that supports the conclusion: Julio got fourteen votes and Cricket got nine.

Reading and Writing Workbook • Drawing Conclusions 7

Drawing Conclusions *(continued)*

Practice and Apply Think of three names of things, such as a computer, a horse, and a soccer ball. Then, write three statements about each thing, without using its name. (Use the word "it" instead.) Answers will vary.

1. _____

2. _____

3. _____

Show your statements to a classmate. See whether your classmate can draw the right conclusions and identify the things you wrote about. Answers will vary.

8 *Drawing Conclusions • Reading and Writing Workbook*

Reading and Writing Workbook pp. 7–8

2 Reading and Responding

Comprehension Strategies

Modeling

12 Confirming Predictions *I was right. Not all the girls voted for Cricket. But Julio was right that all the boys voted for him. I'm glad that Julio was elected class president. I think he'll make a good leader.*

Discussing Strategy Use

After they have read the selection, have students share any problems they encountered and tell what strategies they used to solve them. Then, have them answer the following questions. If they answer "no" to any of the questions, have them reread part of the selection to find the answer.

- Did they summarize in order to help them understand what they have read?
- Were they able to find connections between this story and experiences they have had in their own lives?
- Did they make and confirm predictions about what might happen in the story?

Make sure that students explain how using the strategies helped them understand the selection better and how they read effectively to find answers to the questions they asked as they set purposes.

"Are there any other nominations?" asked Mr. Flores.

Zoe raised her hand. "I <u>move</u> that the nominations be closed."

"I second it," said Lucas.

Then Mr. Flores asked the two candidates if they wanted to say anything to the class.

Cricket stood up. "As you all know," she said, "I'm going to run for President of the United States some day. Being class president will be good practice for me. Besides, I know I will do a much, much better job than Julio." Cricket sat down.

Julio stood. "I might vote for Cricket when she runs for President of the United States," he said. "But right now, I hope you will all vote for me. I think our class should make decisions together, like how we should spend the money that we earned at the bake sale. We should spend the money in a way that everyone likes. Not just the teacher." Julio stopped and looked at Mr. Flores. "That's how I feel," he said.

"If I'm president," said Cricket, "I think the money should go to the Humane Society."

"*You* shouldn't tell us what to do with the money, either," said Julio. "It should be a class decision. We all helped to earn it."

"Julio has made a good point," said Mr. Flores. "I guess we can vote on that in the future."

Mr. Flores passed out the ballots. Julio was sure he knew the results even before the votes were counted. With one boy absent, Cricket would win, twelve to eleven.

12 Julio was right, and he was wrong. All the boys voted for him, but so did some of the girls. When the votes were counted, there were fourteen for Julio Sanchez and nine for Cricket Kaufman. Julio Sanchez was elected president of his fifth-grade class.

⭐ 32

 **Teacher Tip** Reread the selection with students who had difficulty understanding it. Continue modeling and prompting the use of strategies and skills as you reread.

Word Knowledge
teacher, sure, words
Students can use the skills they learned in the Word Knowledge section of this lesson to read these words. Remind students of this if they have difficulty reading these words.

"I think you have made a good choice," said Mr. Flores. "And I know that Cricket will be a very fine vice-president."

Julio beamed. Suddenly he was filled with all sorts of plans for his class.

Mr. Flores took out his guitar. As he had said, they were going to end each week with some singing. Julio thought he had never felt so much like singing in all his life. However, even as he joined the class in the words to the song, he wished it was already time to go home. He could hardly wait to tell his family the news. Wait till he told them who was the fifth-grade class president. Julio, that's who!

At three o'clock, he ran all the way home.

33

Teacher Tip In order for handing off to work effectively, a seating arrangement that allows students to see one another is essential. A circle or a semicircle is effective. In addition, all of the students need to have copies of the materials being discussed. Discussions are described more fully in Program Appendix 28 at the back of the book.

Assessment

✓ **Formal** To assess students' reading comprehension, have them complete *Comprehension and Writing Assessment,* pages 7–8.

Comprehension
Skills

Discussing the Selection

Discussion is an integral part of learning. It is in discussions that students are exposed to points of view different from their own. It is through discussions that they learn how to express their thoughts and opinions coherently.

As the year progresses, the students take more and more responsibility for discussions of the selections and how they progress. This *handing-off process* encourages them to retain complete control of the discussion and to become more actively involved in the learning process. When a student finishes his or her comments, that student should choose (hand off the discussion to) the next speaker. In this way, students maintain a discussion without relying on the teacher to decide who speaks.

Throughout the lessons, discuss the selection and any personal thoughts, reactions, or questions that it raises with the entire class. During this time, have the students return to the clues and problems they noted during browsing and to any questions generated as they set purposes for reading. Have the students determine whether the clues were borne out by the selection, whether and how their problems were solved, and whether questions require additional exploration and discussion. Make sure that students' ideas were not treated as a list to be discussed and eliminated in a linear fashion. Instead, allow the students to decide which items deserve further discussion.

Have students ask each other the kinds of questions that good readers ask themselves about a reading selection: What did I find interesting? What is important here? What was difficult to understand?

2 Reading and Responding

Meet the Author

After the students read the information about Johanna Hurwitz, discuss the following questions with them.

Johanna Hurwitz knew she wanted to be a writer from the time she was ten years old, but she didn't have a book published until she was in her thirties. What does this tell you about her? *(Possible answer: Johanna was determined to be a writer, which made her willing to work hard to achieve her goal.)*

Johanna Hurwitz said, "It seems all my fiction has grown out of real experiences." In what ways could writing from her own experiences have made her writing better? *(Possible answer: Writing about real-life experiences enables her to give vivid details that help the reader feel like the story could really happen.)*

Meet the Illustrator

After the students have finished reading about Richard Hull, discuss the following question with them.

Richard Hull worked as an art director with a magazine before becoming a teacher of illustration. How do you think these different experiences have helped him to illustrate this story? *(Possible answer: He has worked with many different people, and this has helped him illustrate many different personalities.)*

Class President

Meet the Author

Johanna Hurwitz was born in New York, New York. It's not surprising that Ms. Hurwitz knew from the age of ten that she wanted to be a writer. Her parents met in a bookstore. She grew up in a New York City apartment where the walls were lined with books. Her father was a journalist and bookseller, and her mother was a library assistant.

She began her career with books working at the New York City Public Library while still in high school. She then got two degrees in Library Science. She published her first book while in her 30s and has been writing books for children ever since. In one interview she revealed, "It seems as if all my fiction has grown out of real experiences." She has written books about her children's love of baseball, her own childhood and summer vacations, her mother's childhood, and even her cats and their fleas!

Meet the Illustrator

Richard Hull teaches illustration at Brigham Young University. He has also worked as an art director and graphic designer with a magazine for fifteen years. Other books Mr. Hull has illustrated include *The Cat & the Fiddle & More*, *My Sister's Rusty Bike*, and *The Alphabet from Z to A (With Much Confusion on the Way)*. He and his wife currently reside in Orem, Utah.

34

Teacher Tip After reading, have students use their own personal experiences to interpret the story. Ask students what they have learned about the unit theme and invite them to add information to the Concept/Question Board.

Theme Connections

Think About It

With a small group of classmates, discuss what you have learned about cooperation and competition as leadership qualities.

- Which characters in the story acted cooperatively?
- Which characters acted competitively?
- Why did the students want Julio to be their class president?
- What qualities did Julio have that made him a good president?
- Why did students select Julio instead of Cricket?

Check the Concept/Question Board to see if there are any questions that you can answer now. If the selection or your discussions about the selection have raised any new questions about cooperation and competition, put these on the Concept/Question Board. Maybe the next selection will help answer the questions.

Record Ideas

 What have you learned about cooperation and competition? Record your thoughts in your Writing Journal.

Make a Poster

Decide with your group who you want to support for class president—Julio or Cricket. Make a poster that shows why the students should vote for him or her.

35

Theme Connection

Think About It

If necessary, remind the students of the following:

- Julio was motivated to better the playing conditions for all of the students rather than by wanting the title of president.
- Cricket may have been unaware of the group's concerns because she was motivated to gain the title of president.
- Cricket may have been too shy to talk to the principal, which is a role that the class president might need to undertake.

Record Ideas

Consider responding to the students' journal entries, clarifying and extending their thoughts on cooperation and competition through questioning.

Make a Poster

Remind students to highlight the personality traits their candidate has that would make him or her a good class president. Have them display the posters and discuss which of the traits illustrate cooperation and which illustrate competition.

 **Responding**

 # Exploring the Theme

 Some students may choose to conduct a computer search for additional books or information about cooperation and competition. Have them make a list of these books and sources of information to share with classmates and the school librarian. Check the Reading link of the **SRA** Web page for links to theme-related Websites.

http://www.sra4kids.com

 Have students write sentences using the selection vocabulary words. In order to provide additional help in remembering words, students can write synonyms or antonyms for the words if it is appropriate. Some students may even draw something to help them remember the meanings of the words.

Selection Vocabulary

Have students write in their Writing Journals the definitions for words discussed before the reading of the selection and any other interesting words they clarified while reading. Students should be encouraged to refer to these words throughout the unit as they work on student and writing projects. The words from this selection are:

election	**represent**	**candidates**
campaign	**confidence**	

You may create a semantic map on the Concept/Question Board of key words related to the unit theme, Cooperation and Competition, and organize the words' different concepts. Encourage students to find words from other resources, their projects, and family discussions and add them to the map.

Reading/Writing Connections

Discuss with students which of the two main characters they liked best and why. Encourage them to see that the author has created one character with a goal that most readers sympathize with, and the other with a goal that most will agree with less. Explain that authors often use these two character roles—good guy and bad guy—to get readers interested in the story. However, also point out that story characters are seldom all good or all bad, particularly in realistic fiction, because people aren't usually that way.

Have students work together as a large group to create a "character description" chart of the personality traits and character roles of each of the main characters. Have students post their chart on the Concept/Question Board, and refer to it when writing their unit activity.

Home Connection

The class has just finished reading "Class President," a realistic fiction selection about a boy named Julio, whose leadership abilities win him an unexpected nomination for the office of class president. An informational letter on "Class President," in both English and Spanish, can be found in the ***Home Connection*** guide.

"Class President"

A message from _____

Our class has just finished reading *Class President*, a fictional story about a boy who discovers his leadership talents during a class election.

Talk with your child about campaign slogans and how candidates use them to make voters familiar with their names. Tell your child some famous slogans, such as "I Like Ike" and "All the Way with LBJ." Tell your child to think of campaign slogans she or he might use if running for class president. Have your child list the slogans on the lines below, then choose one slogan and design a campaign button or banner in the space at the bottom of the page.

Encourage your child to share the campaign slogans and design with the class.

Unit 1/Cooperation and Competition   3

Home Connection p. 3

Supporting Student Explorations

Tell students that they will learn more about the unit theme by creating and playing the roles of characters that are competitive, cooperative, or both.

To help them think of ideas for their plays, have students think of personal experiences, movies, or stories that deal with competition and cooperation. Have them share these stories explaining what they tell us about competition and cooperation. Discuss with them public personalities, such as athletes, as examples of competitive and cooperative individuals.

Whole Group   Have students select library books that deal with the theme. Have them discuss their books with classmates and use the books as sources for story plots and characters in their unit activities.

Small Group   Have students share their ideas with their group members. Cultivate an atmosphere conducive to open discussions.

Individual   Have students record in their Writing Journals two or three ideas for plot and characters for their plays. Explain that plots should center on the problem or goal of the play's main character and be relevant to the unit theme.

Have students post their plot ideas on the Concept/ Question Board. Have them record new questions, thoughts, and ideas for the unit activity in their Writing Journals. Collect the journals on an ongoing basis and respond to them.

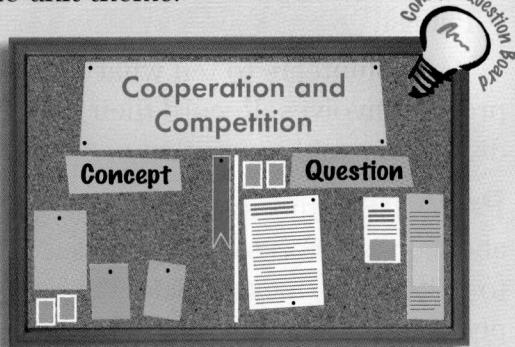

Inquiry Journal

Have the students complete page 6 of the **Inquiry Journal.** Have them record their ideas about how "Class President" added to their knowledge of cooperation and competition.

Teacher Tip   The *Inquiry Journal* is designed for students to record information about unit concepts. The completed pages provide students with a summary of their learning. It gives them a place to respond to each selection, to record questions, to make connections, and to organize research.

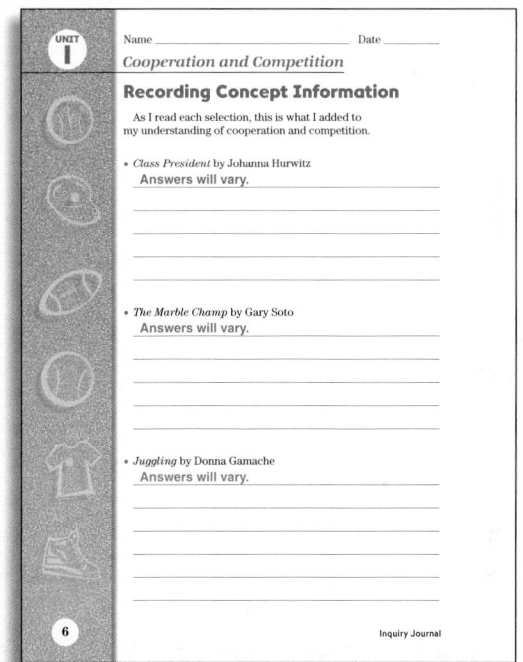

Inquiry Journal p. 6

Assessment

✓ **Informal** Begin anecdotal notes on students' progress and add to them over the course of the Exploration Activity.

③ Integrating the Curriculum

Teacher Tip Tell students that they will be able to use the steps of the writing process for their unit activities, or projects, as well as for their writing assignments.

Language Arts

Writing

Introducing the Writing Process

Instruct Tell students that in this unit, they will each be writing a persuasive paper. Ask students to tell you how they go about writing any kind of paper. Students may mention that first one has to decide what to write about, and then organize the information being used in their papers, so that readers will understand it. Tell students that there is a five-step process they should use whenever they are putting together a piece of writing. Write these steps on the chalkboard and briefly discuss each one:

- Prewrite
- Draft
- Revise
- Proofread
- Publish

Ask volunteers to tell what they understand each phase of this process involves. Record their ideas on the chalkboard. During discussion, make sure that some of the following points are brought out.

Prewrite Students think about and develop an idea they want to write about. In an effort to generate ideas and think through what they are going to write about, they consider their own experiences, they talk with their peers and others, and they explore. This is called brainstorming. During this time, they also define their audience, making sure that the topic they pick will be of interest to this audience. They may also consider their purpose for writing, asking themselves, for example, "Why do I want to write about this topic for this audience?" They should also be encouraged to make their own brief notes on ideas they want to include in their paper and to write a planning statement that briefly describes what they hope to accomplish in this writing, as well as what resources they might need to use.

Draft Explain that when writers are trying to get their ideas down on paper, they write quickly to produce rough drafts. They do not worry about handwriting, spelling, punctuation, or other conventions. As they write, they may use abbreviations, cross out words, leave blanks, or circle things they intend to change later. A writer working on a computer may write several versions of a story and save each one separately.

Revise Be sure students understand that, for authors, revising is probably the most important step in the writing process. Their focus is on improving their writing, not just on mechanical or technical aspects. This is the point at which writers fill in missing details, move sections around, and rewrite sentences to make them work better. They might also use conferences with their classmates to get suggestions.

Proofread At the proofreading stage, writers check for and correct errors in capitalization, punctuation, grammar, and spelling. If they use a computer for writing, they should use the spell checker. However, they should also read carefully for errors, such as omitted or extra words and homophones used incorrectly.

Publish This is the time for sharing with others. Classroom writers make clean, correct copies of their work, illustrate them if they wish, and bind them in some fashion. They then can invite other students to hear them read their work aloud, or place it on the library table for others to read. A writer working on a computer can make more than one copy, autograph each one, and present them to friends or relatives.

Writing Process

Prewrite Have students begin the process of writing a persuasive paper about cooperation and competition by prewriting. At this point in the process, they should be concentrating on brainstorming topics about which they can write convincingly. Tell them that they should start by thinking about what it means to be cooperative or competitive, and whether these qualities are positive or negative. This brainstorming session should involve thinking, talking with peers, and jotting down ideas in the Writing Ideas section of their Writing Journals.

Research in Action
Writing

Reading and writing go hand-in-hand. Students should always be encouraged to notice and comment on outstanding writing as they are reading. Students should be encouraged to use these ideas in their own writing. *(Marlene Scardamalia)*

Teacher Tip For each unit there will be a writing activity. These activities are offered to provide students direct instruction on the writing process. The activities take students through the writing process and give them an opportunity to practice and apply skills such as revising and proofreading. Teachers may choose to do the practice activities here, or they may choose to have students practice the skills as they engage in the Exploration activities or unit project in Part 2 of each lesson. If you opt for the former, students will complete two separate pieces of writing; if you opt for the latter, they will do one. What is essential, though, is that the children be taught these writing process skills.

3 Integrating the Curriculum

Meeting Individual Needs

Traits Reteach

Analyzing Character Traits Have students who need additional instruction and practice with this concept complete *Reteach,* pages 9–10.

Traits Challenge

Analyzing Character Traits Have students who understand this concept and could benefit from extended practice complete *Challenge,* page 7.

Intervention

Analyzing Character Traits Have students jot down the words that come to mind when they think about the character of Cricket. Discuss whether or not they would have voted for her.

Teacher Tip Tell students to keep in mind what they have learned about creating believable characters when working on their dramatic plays.

Literary Elements

Analyzing Character Traits

Instruct Have students think of ways Johanna Hurwitz made the characters in "Class President" seem like real people. Remind students that a character's traits, motivation, conflict, and relationships are depicted through:

- what the character thinks and says.
- what the character does, and why she or he does it.
- what other characters say about the character.

Practice Use the following examples of narrative, action, and dialogue from the selection. Have students tell you how each reveals something about Julio's character. (Possible responses are in parentheses.)

- Page 21: "Julio wasn't very good at making posters, as Cricket and Zoe were, but he was determined to help his friend." *(Trait: He is loyal.)*
- Page 24: "Julio took a deep breath. If Cricket or Lucas wasn't going to talk, he would have to do it." *(Motivation: Julio takes charge of the situation so the problem can be solved.)*
- Page 30: "'He is tops,' said Arthur. 'He's tops in my book.'" *(Relationship: Julio is respected by his classmates.)*

Apply Have students apply the techniques of characterization to their own writing. For additional practice, have students complete *Reading and Writing Workbook,* pages 9–10.

Reading and Writing Workbook pp. 9–10

Name _____ Date _____

Analyzing Character Traits   *Class President*

Focus Writers provide clues to a character's personality by showing how he or she talks and acts, and by what others say about the character.

> **Character traits** can be discovered by paying attention to the character's actions and words and by noticing what others say and think about the character.

Identify Look through "Class President" for examples of ways that the author reveals information about his characters.
Answers will vary. Possible answers are shown.

Page: 22   Character: Lucas
Example: "Uh, sure," said Lucas, but he didn't look too sure.
_____
_____
_____

Page: 22   Character: Cricket
Example: "As you all know," she said, "I'm going to run for President of the United States someday."
_____
_____

Analyzing Character Traits *(continued)*

Practice Write a conversation in which you and your best friend are having an argument. Explain what the argument is about. Include details about how you both feel and how the two of you react to the situation. Answers will vary.
_____
_____
_____
_____
_____
_____
_____
_____

Apply Answer the following questions about the passage you wrote above. Answers will vary.
What does the passage tell the reader about you?
_____
_____
_____

What does the passage tell the reader about your friend?
_____
_____
_____

Reading and Writing Workbook • *Analyzing Character Traits*   9

10   *Analyzing Character Traits* • Reading and Writing Workbook

Vocabulary

Root Words with the Suffix *-tion*

Instruct Have students tell you what they know about affixes. If necessary, remind them that affixes are word parts added to the beginning or ending of a root word to change its meaning. Explain that one kind of affix is a suffix, which is added to the end of a root word. The suffix *-tion* means "an act or state of being." The type of root word to which this suffix is added is always a verb, and the addition of this suffix changes verbs to nouns. For example, a *nomination* is the act of being *nominated*, and *representation* is the act of being *represented*. Point out that knowing the root word can help students recognize how the suffix has affected its meaning.

Practice Have students think of other root words to which the suffix *-tion* can be added (for example, *compete*, *elect*, and *associate*). Write these words on the chalkboard or on an overhead transparency. Then, have students use each word in sentences that demonstrate how the meaning of the word changes with the addition of the suffix. For example, *The people elect a president to office. Tomorrow there will be a presidential election.*

Apply Have students use three of the words from the exercise above to create three more original sentences. Then have them complete *Reading and Writing Workbook* pages 11–12.

Meeting Individual Needs

Reteach

Root Words with the Suffix *-tion* Have students who need additional instruction and practice with this concept complete *Reteach,* pages 11–12.

Challenge

Root Words with the Suffix *-tion* Challenge students to write down as many words with the suffix *-tion* as they can in one minute. Then have them write each base word and suffix as follows: explore + tion = exploration. Have students who understand this concept complete *Challenge,* page 8.

Intervention

Root Words with the Suffix *-tion* Some students may benefit from seeing both forms of the word in sentences and reading both out loud. Examples: *Tom will <u>explain</u> how to do long division. Tom's <u>explanation</u> of long division is helpful.*

Have them find the root word in each affixed form and describe how the word changed when *-tion* was added.

Reading and Writing Workbook pp. 11–12

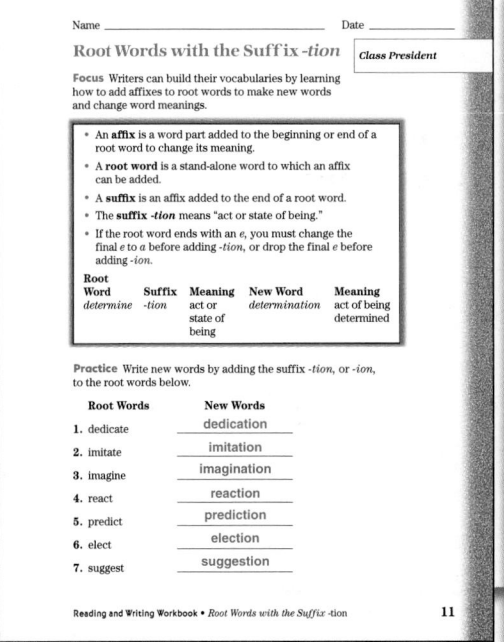

Affixes

INTRODUCED: Unit 1, Lesson 1
REVIEWED: Unit 2, Lesson 5
Unit 6, Lesson 2

Skills Strand

Root Words

INTRODUCED: Unit 1, Lesson 1
REVIEWED: Unit 2, Lesson 4
Unit 4, Lesson 8

Teacher Tip Remind students to check for correct usage of words ending in *-tion* in their writing activities.

 **Integrating the Curriculum**

Meeting Individual Needs

Reteach

Prepositions and Prepositional Phrases Have students who need additional instruction and practice with this concept complete **Reteach,** pages 13–14.

Challenge

Prepositions and Prepositional Phrases Have pairs of students work together. Tell one partner to supply a prepositional phrase for the other partner to use in a sentence. Each partner should take turns thinking of phrases and sentences. Have students who understand this concept complete **Challenge,** page 9.

 Have students evaluate their use of prepositions and prepositional phrases in their own writing by asking themselves the following questions. *Are the phrases placed logically? Do they provide helpful information or important details? Would any sentences be improved by adding one or two phrases?*

Prepositions and Prepositional Phrases

INTRODUCED: Unit 1, Lesson 1
REVIEWED: Unit 4, Lesson 1
Unit 5, Lesson 1

Grammar, Usage, and Mechanics

Prepositions and Prepositional Phrases

Instruct Ask students what they know about prepositions and prepositional phrases. Discuss these guidelines for their use.

- A prepositional phrase begins with a preposition—a connecting word that shows the relation between two words in a sentence—and ends with a noun or a pronoun. Phrases do not contain a subject and predicate.
- Prepositional phrases are used as adjectives or adverbs.
- A noun, or a pronoun and any modifiers, always follows the preposition.
- A prepositional phrase is placed as close as possible to the word it relates to. Give the following examples:

Misleading: *A campaign poster was taped to the wall for Cricket.*
Better: *A campaign poster for Cricket was taped to the wall.*

Practice Have the students find examples of prepositional phrases in "Class President." See the examples below:

- Page 20: "The election was going to be held on Friday."
- Page 23: "Just before one o'clock, Julio had a great idea."
- Page 32: "With one boy absent, Cricket would win, twelve to eleven."

Encourage discussion of what kind of information each phrase gives, and talk about what word the phrase modifies.

Apply For additional practice, have students complete **Reading and Writing Workbook** pages 13–14.

Reading and Writing Workbook pp. 13–14

Name _____ Date _____

Prepositions and Prepositional Phrases

| Class President |

Focus Writers use prepositional phrases to add details to their writing and to make their thoughts clearer.

- A **preposition** shows how one word is related to another word in the sentence.
- Some common prepositions are *at, in, on, to, for, from, with, until, before,* and *after.*
- A **prepositional phrase** always begins with a preposition and is followed by a noun or a pronoun and any of its modifiers.
- Prepositional phrases are used as adjectives and adverbs in a sentence. A prepositional phrase that describes a noun should appear as close to the noun as possible.

Identify Look through "Class President" for examples of prepositional phrases. Write the page number and the complete sentence. Underline each prepositional phrase. *Answers will vary. Possible answers are shown.*

Page: 21

Sentence: Before lunch, Mr. Flores read an announcement from the principal.

Page: 31

Sentence: Everyone who was going to vote for me should vote for Julio.

Page: 32

Sentence: I guess we can vote on that in the future.

Reading and Writing Workbook • *Prepositions and Prepositional Phrases* **13**

Prepositions and Prepositional Phrases *(continued)*

Practice Read the sentences below. Then rewrite each sentence so that the prepositional phrase that describes a noun appears as close as possible to that noun.

1. A woman crossed the street in a raincoat.
   A woman in a raincoat crossed the street.

2. The sweater was lost with blue and white ribbons.
   The sweater with blue and white ribbons was lost.

3. The flowers need some water in the blue vase.
   The flowers in the blue vase need some water.

4. A green car roared down the hill with a white top.
   A green car with a white top roared down the hill.

Apply Choose three of the prepositions shown in the box below. Use each in a sentence as the beginning of a prepositional phrase. Answers will vary.

| near | at | for |
| in | after | with |

1. _____

2. _____

3. _____

14 *Prepositions and Prepositional Phrases* • Reading and Writing Workbook

Listening/Speaking/Viewing

Persuasive Techniques

Tell students that when people speak, they give both verbal and nonverbal messages to their listeners. How a speaker says something is as important as what she or he says. Listeners also must be able to identify and analyze the different kinds of persuasive techniques that a speaker uses, such as promises, dares, and flattery. Talk about how candidates running for office—whether as class president, mayor, or U.S. senator—employ persuasive techniques.

Reading aloud and role-playing sections of "Class President" will give students the opportunity to practice their own persuasive techniques. Have volunteers reenact pages 24–25, where Julio persuades the principal to let students play soccer again, and pages 28–32, the nomination process for class president. Then, discuss with students the various persuasive techniques the characters employed and assess how their language choices affected the tone of what they were saying.

Have each student prepare and give a campaign speech as if he or she were running for class president. Suggest that they practice their speeches in front of someone so they can get feedback on what kinds of nonverbal messages their listeners may be receiving. Do they need to alter their persuasive techniques in any way? Allow time for students to give their speeches to the class.

Teacher Tip Have students think about ways to incorporate persuasive techniques into their dramatic plays.

Meeting Individual Needs

ESL

Listening/Speaking/Viewing Pair English-language learners with native speakers for this exercise. Encourage the students to seek clarification for any words or phrases that are unfamiliar to them.

3 Integrating the Curriculum

Teacher Tip

Handing-off is a useful procedure in research discussions as well as text discussions because it encourages students to talk to one another rather than solely to you.

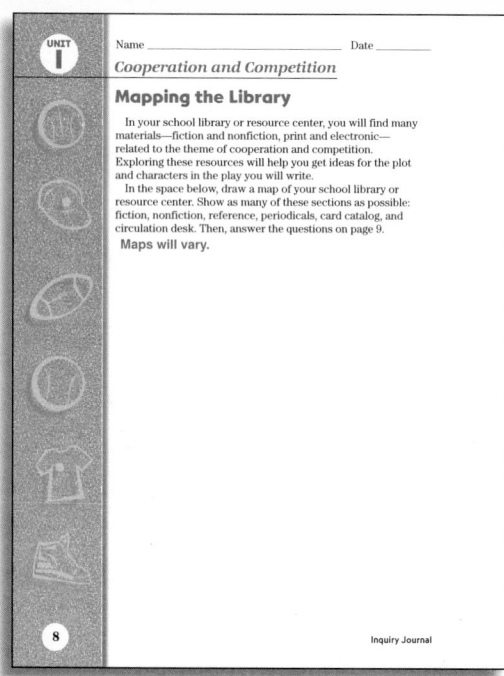

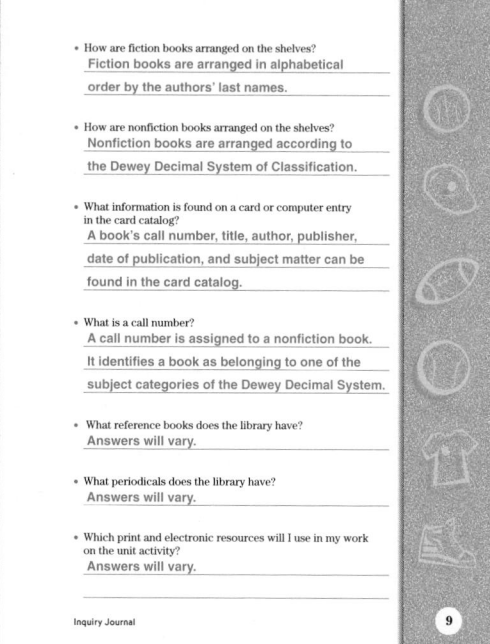

Inquiry Journal pp. 8–9

Study and Research

Parts of the Library

Instruct Have students tell you what they know about the parts of the library and the many kinds of research sources it contains. If necessary, give them the following information:

- Libraries contain print resources such as atlases, almanacs, dictionaries, encyclopedias, books, magazines, and newspapers.
- Atlases, almanacs, dictionaries, and encyclopedias are located in the reference section of the library.
- Magazines and newspapers are usually displayed in a special periodicals area in the library.
- Books are categorized according to subject matter and whether they are fiction or nonfiction.
- Many libraries also provide access to electronic resources such as periodical databases; software for atlases, dictionaries, and encyclopedias; and the Internet.
- Card catalogs list all the books in the library. Some libraries list the books on cards that are filed in small cabinet drawers. Many libraries have computerized their card catalogs.

Practice Have students select a variety of subjects related to "Class President" such as other realistic fiction books set in schools or that have class elections; information about local, state, or federal governments; prominent Puerto Rican Americans; or United States presidents. Let them visit the school or public library to make a list of print and electronic resources available.

Apply Have students write brief reports on their subjects based on the print and electronic resources they found in the library. Also have them describe which parts of the library were most helpful to their research and why.

For additional practice, have students complete *Inquiry Journal* pages 8–9.

Assessment

✔ **Formal** To assess students' understanding of this concept, have them complete *Skills Assessment,* page 2.

Across the Curriculum

 ## Social Studies

Cooperating to Develop Safety Rules

Purpose

To help students develop cooperative skills by working together to create playground safety rules

Procedure

Ask students how fifth-graders could promote safety on the playground without banning any normal activities. To get the discussion started, pose questions such as the following: "What activities should be allowed on the playground? How could you make each of these activities safer?"

- Ask students which activities are especially popular on their playground. Have them describe what measures, if any, have been put in place to make those activities safer.

- Choose one activity and write its name on the chalkboard. Then record students' ideas for making the activity even safer. Encourage students to think of a variety of resources, such as improved equipment, protective gear, and good sportsmanship.

- Finally, using the ideas listed on the chalkboard, have students develop a set of safety rules to use when taking part in the activity on the playground.

 ## Art

Cooperation Posters Versus Competition Posters

Purpose

To show students that art can be used to encourage cooperation or competition

Materials

posterboard, markers, paints

Procedure

Ask students to talk about how they can get information from posters. Start the discussion by asking questions such as the following: "Who puts up posters and why? What kinds of information do posters usually give us?"

- Ask students to think of posters they have seen. Have them describe how the design of the poster caught their eye so that they became interested in reading the text.

- Discuss also how the text was presented (e.g., in brief, bulleted statements, and so on). If necessary, explain that a bullet is a symbol used to indicate a new piece of information.

- Have students brainstorm information that might be communicated by a cooperation poster (for example, posters of class rules). Then have them brainstorm information that might be communicated by a competition poster (for example, posters used in an election).

- Tell students they are going to create a poster that promotes either cooperation or competition. Have them design their poster on scrap paper. Suggest they get feedback from classmates before finalizing their designs on posterboard or drawing paper.

The Marble Champ

from *Baseball in April and Other Stories*
by Gary Soto
illustrated by Maren Scott

Lupe Medrano, a shy girl who spoke in whispers, was the school's spelling bee champion, winner of the reading contest at the public library three summers in a row, blue ribbon awardee in the science fair, the top student at her piano recital, and the playground grand champion in chess. She was a straight-A student and—not counting kindergarten, when she had been stung by a wasp—never missed one day of elementary school. She had received a small trophy for this honor and had been congratulated by the mayor.

But though Lupe had a razor-sharp mind, she could not make her body, no matter how much she tried, run as fast as the other girls'. She begged her body to move faster, but could never beat anyone in the fifty-yard dash.

The truth was that Lupe was no good in sports. She could not catch a pop-up or figure out in which direction to kick the soccer ball. One time she kicked the ball at her own goal and scored a point for the other team. She was no good at baseball or basketball either, and even had a hard time making a hula hoop stay on her hips.

It wasn't until last year, when she was eleven years old, that she learned how to ride a bike. And even then she had to use training wheels. She could walk in the swimming pool but couldn't swim, and chanced roller skating only when her father held her hand.

36

Selection Summary

Genre: Realistic Fiction

Lupe Medrano has won awards for her schoolwork and her nearly perfect attendance, but when it comes to sports, she's a total failure. If only she could excel at a sport, Lupe thinks, "even marbles." Suddenly inspired, Lupe borrows her brother's beautiful glass marbles and begins a routine of thumb-strengthening exercises and shooting practice. Finally, Lupe enters a marble championship and learns about the rewards of competition, hard work, and determination.

About the Author

Gary Soto's life began to turn around when he picked up a poetry anthology and discovered that he, too, wanted to be a writer. From his farm laborer beginnings in Fresno, California, Gary Soto has become an award-winning poet, essayist, and fiction writer for all ages. His short story collection *Baseball in April and Other Stories* was named a Best Book for Young Adults by the American Library Association.

Students can read more about Gary Soto on page 44 of the *Student Anthology.*

Other Books by Gary Soto
- *Crazy Weekend*
- *Boys at Work*
- *Local News*
- *Off and Running*
- *Neighborhood Odes* (poetry)

About the Illustrator

Maren Scott has been drawing since she was a child. Ms. Scott has won awards for both her illustrations and quilt designs. She lives in a small town in Utah with her husband and three sons.

Students can read more about Maren Scott on page 44 of the *Student Anthology.*

Exploring the Theme

Selection Concepts

"The Marble Champ" is a humorous account of a young girl's transformation into a marble champion. Practice makes her thumbs bigger and stronger, and she wins every match. Key concepts to be explored are:

- Competing requires commitment and practice.
- It is important to understand our strengths when competing.

Check the Reading link of the **SRA** Web page for links to theme-related Websites.
http://www.sra4kids.com

Exploration Activity Tips

Before Reading, have students predict how the unit concepts will play into this selection.

During Reading, have students stop frequently to summarize the events and keep notes on these summaries for use in creating a storyboard of the selection after they have finished reading it.

After Reading, have students create storyboards of the selection. Explain that storyboards are like comic strips, and they depict the main events of the story. Each frame of the storyboard should be accompanied by dialogue from the story. Post storyboards on the Concept/Question Board.

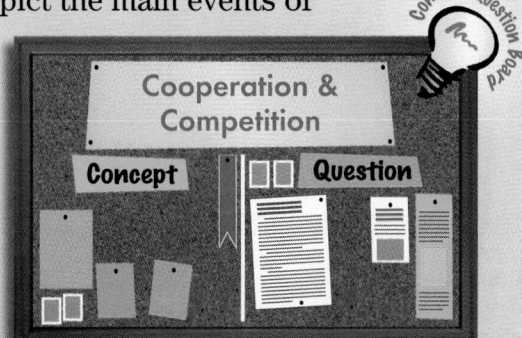

Unit 2 Exploration Management

Lesson 1	Discuss experiences with cooperation and competition. Generate ideas for dramatic play.
Lesson 2 **The Marble Champ**	**Collaborative Exploration** **Students give and receive feedback on their unit activity ideas, and begin to work in groups on the storyboards for their plays.** **Supplementary Activity** **Remind students of appropriate behavior for giving and receiving feedback. Assist them with storyboard techniques as necessary.**
Lesson 3	Students complete their storyboards and share them with other groups, then revise the storyboards based on feedback.
Lesson 4	Students begin group work on writing plays in script format. They agree on director and actor roles and begin rehearsals.
Lesson 5	Students complete the final draft of their scripts and plan their dress rehearsals.
Lesson 6	Students complete play rehearsals and perform their plays. They put scripts in a class anthology and prepare a title page and table of contents.

Lesson Planner

Suggested Pacing: 3–5 days	DAY 1	DAY 2
	DAY 1	DAY 2

Part 1 **Preparing to Read**

Materials
- Student Anthology, pp. 36–45
- Transparencies 2, 44

DAY 1:
Word Knowledge
- Reading the Words and Sentences, p. 36G
- Developing Oral Language, p. 36G

Build Background, p. 36H

Preview and Prepare, p. 36I

Selection Vocabulary, p. 36I
contest, athletic, matches, energy, players, commotion

DAY 2:
Preview and Prepare, p. 36I
- Review Transparency 44

Part 2 **Reading and Responding**

Materials
- Student Anthology, pp. 36–47
- Teacher Observation Log
- Reading and Writing Workbook, pp. 15–16
- Inquiry Journal, p. 6
- Home Connection, p. 5

DAY 1:
Student Anthology, pp. 36–45

Comprehension Strategies
- Asking Questions, pp. 36, 38, 40
- Making Connections, p. 38
- Visualizing, p. 42

Discussing Strategy Use, p. 42

DAY 2:
Student Anthology, pp. 36–45

Comprehension Skills
- ✓ Making Inferences, pp. 37, 39, 41
- ✓ Discussing the Selection, p. 43

Exploring the Theme
- Selection Vocabulary, p. 47A
  contest, athletic, matches, energy, players, commotion

Part 3 **Integrating the Curriculum**

Materials
- Student Anthology, pp. 36–45
- Reading and Writing Workbook, pp. 17–22
- Inquiry Journal, p. 10

DAY 1:
Writing
- ✓ Writing Paragraphs, p. 47C

Literary Elements
- ✓ Recognize and Analyze Story Settings, p. 47E

DAY 2:
Writing Process
- Prewrite, p. 47D

Spelling
- ✓ Consonant Before *-le* Spelling Patterns, p. 47F

Independent Work Time

Materials
- Reteach, pp. 15–22
- ESL Supplement
- Challenge, pp. 10–13
- Intervention Guide
- Research CD-ROM
- Listening Library Audiocassette
- Inquiry Journal, p. 11

DAY 1:
Writing Process Continued
Reteach
- ✓ Setting, *Reteach*, pp. 17–18
ESL
- Word Meaning, p. 36G   ■ Cultural Context, p. 36H
Challenge
- ✓ Setting, *Challenge*, p. 11
Intervention
- Word Knowledge, p. 36G   ■ Comprehension, p. 36
Unit Project
- Give and Receive Feedback   ■ Begin Storyboards

DAY 2:
Writing Process Continued
Reteach
- ✓ Making Inferences, *Reteach*, pp. 15–16
ESL
- Vocabulary, p. 36J
Challenge
- ✓ Making Inferences, *Challenge*, p. 10
Intervention
- Asking Questions, p. 40
- Prewriting, p. 47D
Unit Project Continued

✓ Informal **Assessment Available**   ✓ Formal **Assessment Available**

DAY 2 continued	DAY 3	
DAY 3	DAY 4	DAY 5
General Review	**General Review**	**Review Word Knowledge**
Student Anthology, pp. 36–45 **Theme Connections** ■ Think About It, p. 45 ■ Find a Quotation, p. 45	**Student Anthology, pp. 36–47** **Poetry, pp. 46–47** **Exploring the Theme** ■ Reading/Writing Connections, p. 47A ■ Literature Appreciation, p. 47A ■ Supporting Student Explorations, p. 47B	**Student Anthology, pp. 36–45** ■ Review Selection ■ Complete Discussion ■ Reread Selection in Pairs **Home Connection, p. 47A** ■ Discuss "The Marble Champ" ■ Set a goal and list skills
Writing Process Continued **Grammar, Usage, and Mechanics** ✓■ Nouns, p. 47G **Listening/Speaking/Viewing** ■ Recognize and Distinguish Stories, p. 47H	**Writing Process Continued** **Study and Research** ✓■ Organize Information, p. 47I	**Across the Curriculum** **Drama** ■ The Secret of My Success, p. 47J **Music** ■ Cooperative and Competitive Beats, p. 47J
Writing Process Continued **Reteach** ✓■ Spelling -le Endings, *Reteach*, pp. 19–20 **ESL** ■ Listening/Speaking/Viewing, p. 47H **Challenge** ✓■ Spelling -le Endings, *Challenge*, p. 12 **Unit Project Continued**	**Writing Process Continued** **Reteach** ✓■ Nouns, *Reteach*, pp. 21–22 **ESL** ■ Poetry, p. 47 **Challenge** ✓■ Nouns, *Challenge*, p. 13 **Unit Project Continued**	**Writing Process Continued** **Unit Project Continued**

Meeting Individual Needs
Independent Work Time

Preparing to Read

Meeting Individual Needs

ESL
- Word Meaning, p. 36G
- Cultural Context, p. 36H
- Vocabulary, p. 36J

Intervention
- Word Knowledge, p. 36G

Reading and Responding

Meeting Individual Needs

Reteach
- Making Inferences, *Reteach*, pp. 15–16

ESL
- Poetry, p. 47

Challenge
- Making Inferences, *Challenge*, p. 10

Intervention
- Comprehension, p. 36
- Making Connections, p. 38
- Making Inferences, p. 39
- Asking Questions, p. 40
- Visualizing, p. 42

Integrating the Curriculum

Meeting Individual Needs

Reteach
- Setting, *Reteach*, pp. 17–18
- Spelling -*le* Endings, *Reteach*, pp. 19–20
- Nouns, *Reteach*, pp. 21–22

ESL
- Listening/Speaking/Viewing, p. 47H

Challenge
- Setting, *Challenge*, p. 11
- Spelling -*le* Endings, *Challenge*, p. 12
- Nouns, *Challenge*, p. 13

Intervention
- Prewriting, p. 47D

Formal Assessment Options

Use these assessment pages along with your informal observations to gauge student progress.

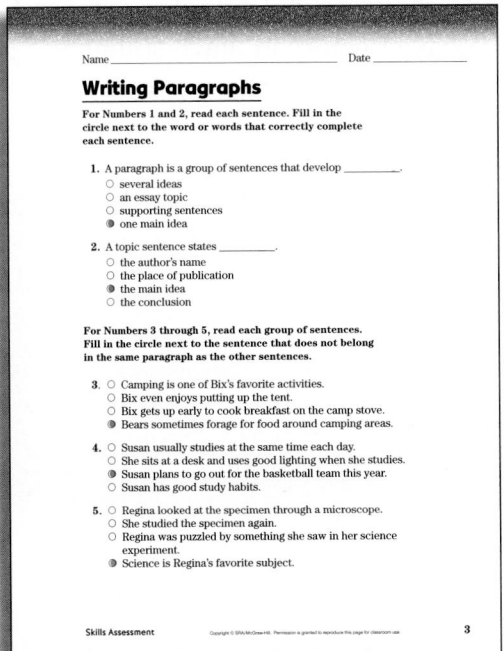

Skills Assessment, p. 3

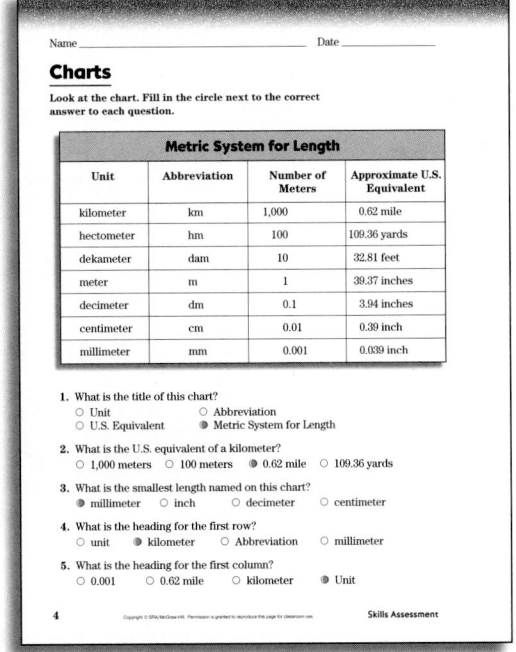

Skills Assessment, p. 4

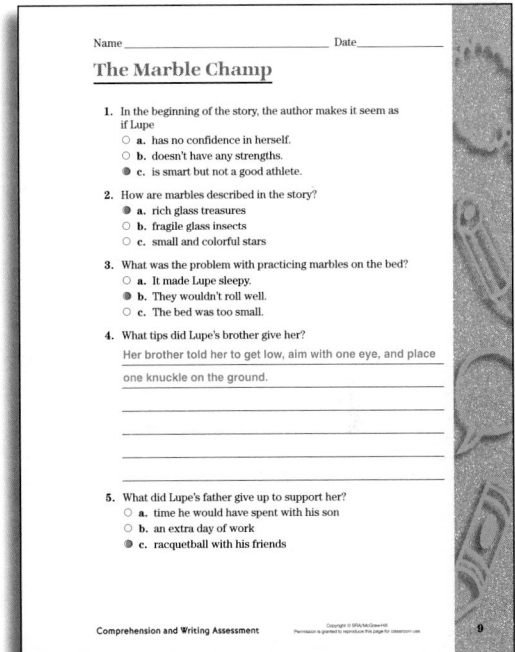

Comprehension and Writing Assessment, p. 9

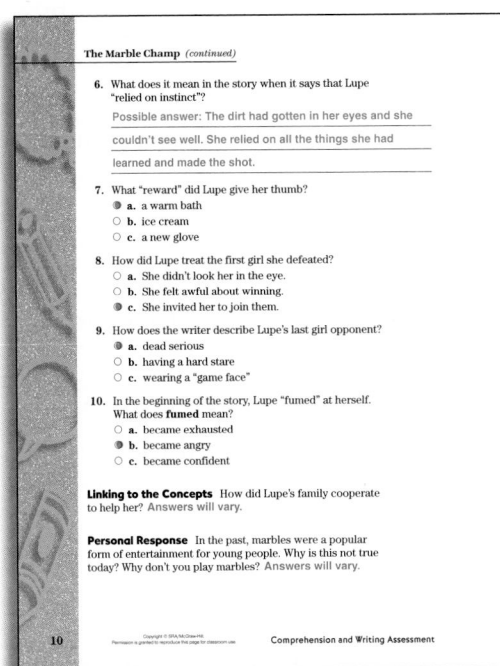

Comprehension and Writing Assessment, p. 10

① Preparing to Read

Teacher Tip When reading the sentences in the Word Knowledge exercise, have students use normal intonation until they come to a word they don't know. Then have them stop to blend the word before rereading the sentence.

Meeting Individual Needs

ESL

Word Meaning Make sure English-language learners understand the meaning of the words before they do the exercises. Refer to Unit 1, Lesson 2, of the **ESL Supplement** for specific suggestions.

Intervention

Word Knowledge For students who need more help with the /n/ sound spelled *kn,* explain that the *k* is silent. Say the words in Line 3 aloud, pointing out that you are pronouncing the words as if the *k* were not there. Write the following list of words on the chalkboard and have students say them aloud:

knight, knife, knockout, doorknob, knead, knell

For students who need more help, see Unit 1, Lesson 2, of the **Intervention Guide.**

Word Knowledge

Reading the Words and Sentences

Write each word and sentence on the chalkboard. Have students read each word together. After all the words have been read, have students read each sentence in natural phrases or chunks. Use the suggestions in About the Words to discuss the different features of the listed words.

Line 1:
Line 2:
Line 3:
Sentence 1:
Sentence 2:
Sentence 3:

> racket disturbance fuss hubbub
> whispers marbles muscles
> knuckle knee knot
> The cheering fans created a racket and a hubbub.
> Playing marbles can strengthen muscles in the hands.
> When I scraped my knees and knuckles, my mom made a fuss.

About the Words

- Line 1 contains words that are synonyms. Synonyms are words that have almost the same meanings. Have students discuss the related meanings.
- The words in Line 2 are regular plurals. Regular plurals are made by simply adding *s* to the end of a word. Have students identify the singular word.
- Line 3 focuses on the /n/ sound spelled *kn.* Invite students to think of other words that begin with the /n/ sound spelled *kn.*

Developing Oral Language

To review the words, have students do one or both of the following activities.

- Write a list of singular words on the chalkboard such as *table, head,* and *competitor.* Ask volunteers to write the regular plural form of the words on the chalkboard. Then have them make up sentences using the plural forms of the words.
- On the chalkboard, write several words from Lines 1–3 that have synonyms. Give a synonym, and have a volunteer say and circle the word for which you gave the synonym. For example, if you say *tie,* a student would circle the word *knot.*

Build Background

Activate Prior Knowledge

Have students check the Concept/Question Board to refresh their memories about cooperation and competition. Discuss the following with students to find out what they may already know about the selection and have already learned about the unit theme. Tell students to use their prior knowledge to help them comprehend the selection they are about to read.

- Have students share what they know about the game of marbles.
- Ask students whether they are familiar with "The Marble Champ," and if so, to tell a little about it.
- Have students share other stories that involve marble games or playing in a championship game.

Background Information

The following information may help students better understand the selection they are about to read.

- If students are not familiar with the game of marbles, tell them it is played with small, hard, round objects that may be made of stone, glass, steel, clay, or plastic. Players shoot a marble at other target marbles placed inside a circle drawn on the ground. Opponents' marbles knocked out of the ring may be kept or scored as points.
- Students might like to know that marble shooters "knuckle down" by placing the knuckle of their first finger on the ground. Then they put the marble in the joint of that finger and use their thumb to snap the marble at their opponents' marbles. Shooters try for accuracy in their aim and distance in their shots.

Meeting Individual Needs

ESL

Cultural Context English-language learners may be unfamiliar with the game of marbles and with the vocabulary connected with it. Stage a few games. Let English-language learners be the players in the first few games and have an English speaker give a running commentary. After a while, give English-language learners the opportunity to give the running commentary.

Writing Journal Tell students that they will jot down in their Writing Journals their reactions to the story. Have them be on the lookout for any ideas they may have for using the topics *Goal, Practice,* and *Competition* in their persuasive papers and unit activities.

1 Preparing to Read

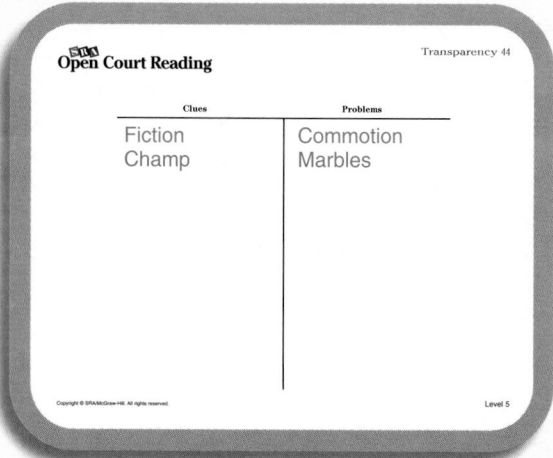

Transparency 44

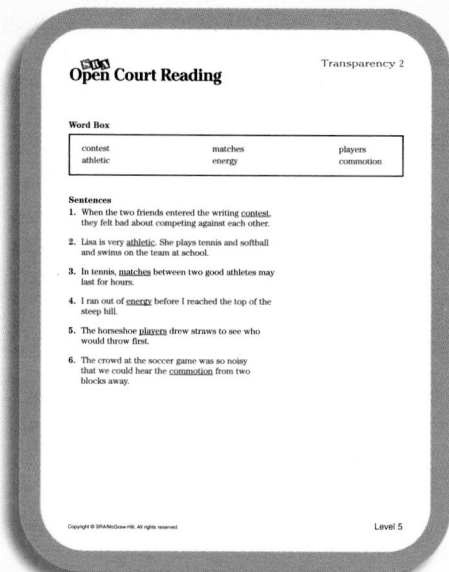

Transparency 2

Teacher Tip

To help students decode words, divide them into the syllables shown below. The information following each word tells how students can figure out the meaning of each word on the transparency.

con·test	context clues
ath·let·ic	context clues, word structure
match·es	context clues
en·er·gy	context clues
play·ers	context clues, word structure
com·mo·tion	context clues

Preview and Prepare

Browse

■ Have a volunteer read the title and author's and illustrator's names aloud. Have students share what they know about fiction.

■ Because this is a fiction piece have the students browse through only the first half of the story. Have them look for words and phrases that connect to what they already know. Record these in the Clues column on **Transparency 44.** Discuss with the students what they think this story might have to do with cooperation and competition.

■ Encourage students to ask questions as they browse. Have them identify any problems they notice while reading in the Problems column.

Set Purposes

As they read, have students think about how setting goals and the support and cooperation of others can lead to successful competition.

Selection Vocabulary

As students study vocabulary, they will use context clues, word structure, and apposition to clarify these and additional unfamiliar words.

Display **Transparency 2** before reading the selection to introduce and discuss the following words and their meanings.

con·test:	a competition (page 36)
ath·let·ic:	having skill and strength in sports and other physical activities (page 38)
match·es:	contests, competitions, or races (page 41)
en·er·gy:	what makes someone active in work and at play (page 42)
play·ers:	people who take part and play against each other in matches (page 42)
com·mo·tion:	noise; excitement; disturbance (page 43)

Have students read the words in the Word Box. Help students decode multisyllabic words by reading them syllable by syllable.

Using the same procedure as in Lesson 1, have students read the sentences on **Transparency 2** to determine the meaning of the underlined words. Remind them to use context clues and structural clues to figure out their meanings. See the teacher tip on the left for information on how the words in each sentence can be defined.

Reading Recommendations

Your first reading of the selection should focus on developing the reading strategies found to the left of the reduced pages. We recommend that the students revisit the selection, rereading sections or the entire selection as a way to enhance their understanding of the text. During rereading, they should focus on the comprehension skills, found to the right of the reduced pages.

Silent Reading

This story lends itself to silent reading because it is an engaging, chronological narrative. Have students practice reading on their own for at least 5 minutes at a time. As they become better readers, students will read silently with increasing ease, over longer periods of time.

Have students make use of the reading strategies listed below to help them understand the selection. Have them stop reading periodically or wait until they have completed the selection to discuss the reading strategies. After the students have finished reading the selection, use the "Discussing the Selection" questions to see if they have understood what they have read. If they have not, refer to the ***Intervention Guide*** for further strategies.

Using Reading Strategies

Reading strategy instruction allows students to become aware of how good readers read. Good readers constantly check their understanding as they are reading and ask themselves questions. In addition, skilled readers recognize when they are having problems and stop to use various reading strategies to help them make sense of what they are reading.

During the reading of "The Marble Champ," you will model the use of the following reading strategies:

- Making Connections
- Asking Questions
- Visualizing

Before reading, have students share how they have used these strategies in the past and any tips they can give each other on their use.

Building Comprehension Skills

Revisiting or rereading a selection allows students to apply skills that give them a more complete understanding of the text. Some follow-up comprehension skills, such as *Main Idea and Details* and *Compare and Contrast*, help students organize information. Others, such as *Author's Purpose*, *Making Inferences*, and *Drawing Conclusions*, lead to deeper understanding—to "reading between the lines," as mature readers do. In this selection, students will apply the follow-up comprehension skill of *Making Inferences*.

Research in Action

Making Connections

Good readers always relate what they read to what they already know. Many elementary-school students may not automatically make such a connection. You can do much to stimulate them to relate new information to prior knowledge by modeling the process out loud for them. *(Jan Hirshberg)*

Meeting Individual Needs

ESL

Vocabulary Check that English-language learners know the meanings of idioms and more difficult vocabulary in the story, including: *awardee, straight-A, razor-sharp, pop-up, budge, let it rip, odd-shaped, flexed, hypnotic, dead serious, quivering, slivers,* and *hard-won.* More information can be found in Unit 1, Lesson 2, of the *ESL Supplement.*

Teacher Tip By this time in the fifth grade, good readers should be reading approximately 126 words per minute with fluency and expression. The only way to gain fluency is through practice. As explained in Reading Recommendations, have students reread all or part of the selection to you and to each other during class or Independent Work Time to focus on the comprehension skills and to build fluency.

Teacher Tip Have students who may need extra help reading "The Marble Champ," reread the selection using the *Listening Library Audiocassette.*

② Reading and Responding

Read pages 36–47.

Comprehension Strategies

Modeling

❶ Asking Questions *Good readers sometimes ask themselves questions to check their understanding as they read. The best questions to ask usually cannot be answered with a simple yes or no; they should begin with Who? What? Why? When? How? or Where?*

Before we start to read, let's ask some questions to help us focus our reading. This story is called "The Marble Champ." Who is the marble champ? Will there be some kind of a contest in this story? What are some of your questions about this story?

Modeling

❷ Answering Questions *As we read on, I see that one of our questions has been answered. Lupe has decided to enter a championship. Have any other questions been answered yet?*

Word Knowledge

whispers, awards, weeks

Students can use the skills they learned in the Word Knowledge section of this lesson to read these words. Remind students of this if they have difficulty reading these words.

Reading Recommendation

ORAL • CHORAL • **SILENT**

The Marble Champ

①

from *Baseball in April and Other Stories*
by Gary Soto
illustrated by Maren Scott

Lupe Medrano, a shy girl who spoke in whispers, was the school's spelling bee champion, winner of the reading contest at the public library three summers in a row, blue ribbon awardee in the science fair, the top student at her piano recital, and the playground grand champion in chess. She was a straight-A student and——not counting kindergarten, when she had been stung by a wasp——never missed one day of elementary school. She had received a small trophy for this honor and had been congratulated by the mayor.

But though Lupe had a razor-sharp mind, she could not make her body, no matter how much she tried, run as fast as the other girls'. She begged her body to move faster, but could never beat anyone in the fifty-yard dash.

The truth was that Lupe was no good in sports. She could not catch a pop-up or figure out in which direction to kick the soccer ball. One time she kicked the ball at her own goal and scored a point for the other team. She was no good at baseball or basketball either, and even had a hard time making a hula hoop stay on her hips.

It wasn't until last year, when she was eleven years old, that she learned how to ride a bike. And even then she had to use training wheels. She could walk in the swimming pool but couldn't swim, and chanced roller skating only when her father held her hand.

36

Meeting Individual Needs

Intervention

Comprehension Intervention strategies for those students having difficulty with reading "The Marble Champ" can be found in Unit 1, Lesson 2, of the *Intervention Guide.*

Assessment

✓ **Informal** Observe individual students as they read, and use the Teacher Observation Log, found in *the Assessment Guide,* to record anecdotal information about each student's strengths and weaknesses.

"I'll never be good at sports," she <u>fumed</u> one rainy day as she lay on her bed gazing at the shelf her father had made to hold her awards. "I wish I could win something, anything, even marbles."

At the word "marbles," she sat up. "That's it. Maybe I could be good at playing marbles." She hopped out of bed and rummaged through the closet until she found a can full of her brother's marbles. She poured the rich glass treasure on her bed and picked five of the most beautiful marbles.

She smoothed her bedspread and practiced shooting, softly at first so that her aim would be accurate. The marble rolled from her thumb and clicked against the targeted marble. But the target wouldn't budge. She tried again and again. Her aim became accurate, but the power from her thumb made the marble move only an inch or two. Then she realized that the bedspread was slowing the marbles. She also had to admit that her thumb was weaker than the neck of a newborn chick.

She looked out the window. The rain was letting up, but the ground was too muddy to play. She sat cross-legged on the bed, rolling her five marbles between her palms. Yes, she thought, I could play marbles, and marbles is a sport. At that moment she realized that she had only two weeks to practice. The playground championship, the same one her brother had entered the previous year, was coming up. She had a lot to do.

Comprehension
Skills

Making Inferences

Introduce students to the comprehension skill *making inferences*. Explain to the students that sometimes writers don't provide all the details in a story. Sometimes authors assume that readers have the same background information and knowledge that he or she does (though this, of course, is not always the case). Other times they are trying to be challenging or funny by making readers "read between the lines." In either case, good readers apply their own understanding of life, based on clues provided by the author, to gain meaning beyond what is written on the page.

Ask the students to make inferences about characters in the story so far. Guide them to see that:

- Lupe is a competitive person. We know this because she has won many scholastic awards and honors. She is unhappy because she hasn't won any sports awards and wants to be good at sports too.

- Lupe's father has built a shelf to hold her awards because he is very proud of her accomplishments.

Teacher Tip Lupe Medrano is pronounced lōō′pā mä drä′nō.

Reading and Responding

Comprehension Strategies

Modeling

3 **Making Connections** *This is a good place to stop and see if I can connect Lupe with someone I know or have read about, because she is the main character in this selection. Wow, Lupe must be serious about marbles if she'd rather practice than do her homework. After all, she's a straight-A student, and she has a whole shelf of awards from school. But I know how it can be when you start doing something new. I once started playing a computer game and I didn't even notice how much time had passed while I was playing! How are you able to connect with Lupe?*

Modeling

4 **Asking Questions** *I am going to stop here and ask a question because I wonder why Lupe isn't telling her parents about her plan. Is she afraid that they'll make her stop practicing? Does she think she's being silly to spend time learning to play marbles? Let's read on and look for the answers to my questions. What questions do you have?* (These questions are answered on page 40.)

Word Knowledge

push-ups, muscles, swirls

Students can use the skills they learned in the Word Knowledge section of this lesson to read these words. Remind students of this if they have difficulty reading these words.

To strengthen her wrists, she decided to do twenty push-ups on her fingertips, five at a time. "One, two, three . . ." she groaned. By the end of the first set she was breathing hard, and her muscles burned from exhaustion. She did one more set and decided that was enough push-ups for the first day.

She squeezed a rubber eraser one hundred times, hoping it would strengthen her thumb. This seemed to work because the next day her thumb was sore. She could hardly hold a marble in her hand, let alone send it flying with power. So Lupe rested that day and listened to her brother, who gave her tips on how to shoot: get low, aim with one eye, and place one knuckle on the ground.

"Think 'eye and thumb'—and let it rip!" he said.

After school the next day she left her homework in her backpack and practiced three hours straight, **3** taking time only to eat a candy bar for energy. With a popsicle stick, she drew an odd-shaped circle and tossed in four marbles. She used her shooter, a milky <u>agate</u> with hypnotic swirls, to blast them. Her thumb *had* become stronger.

After practice, she squeezed the eraser for an hour. **4** She ate dinner with her left hand to spare her shooting hand and said nothing to her parents about her dreams of athletic glory.

Practice, practice, practice. Squeeze, squeeze, squeeze. Lupe got better and beat her brother and Alfonso, a neighbor kid who was supposed to be a champ.

Meeting Individual Needs

Intervention

Making Connections Have the students share a time when they had an experience similar to Lupe's—when they started something new. Did they practice all the time? How did this new experience make them feel? How can they compare and contrast their experiences with Lupe's?

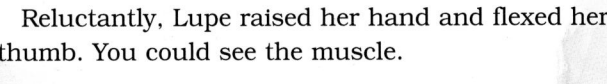

"Man, she's bad!" Alfonso said. "She can beat the other girls for sure. I think."

The weeks passed quickly. Lupe worked so hard that one day, while she was drying dishes, her mother asked why her thumb was swollen.

"It's muscle," Lupe explained. "I've been practicing for the marbles championship."

"You, honey?" Her mother knew Lupe was no good at sports.

"Yeah. I beat Alfonso, and he's pretty good."

That night, over dinner, Mrs. Medrano said, "Honey, you should see Lupe's thumb."

"Huh?" Mr. Medrano said, wiping his mouth and looking at his daughter.

"Show your father."

"Do I have to?" an embarrassed Lupe asked.

"Go on, show your father."

Reluctantly, Lupe raised her hand and flexed her thumb. You could see the muscle.

39

Comprehension
Skills

Making Inferences

Prompt students to tell you what it means to make inferences. If necessary, remind them that it is using information from the text and their own knowledge to form a better understanding of a character, thing, or event in a story.

- We can infer that Lupe did well during practice because she says that her thumb *had* become stronger. (page 38.)

- Based on Lupe's training program, we can infer that she is a very determined person.

Have students share experiences in their own lives that corroborate the inferences made above.

Meeting Individual Needs

Intervention

Making Inferences If students are confused about making inferences, explain that people infer things all the time. For example, if we look out the window and everyone is wearing jackets and other winter gear, we assume it is cold outside. No one tells us this, but we use clues and prior knowledge to make an educated guess. Help students think of other everyday scenarios in which they make inferences.

② Reading and Responding

Comprehension Strategies

Modeling

⑤ Answering Questions *Hmm. This answers my question from earlier. Both Lupe's father and mother seem to want Lupe to win the championship. So, I was wrong when I thought she didn't want to tell them about the championship because they would make her stop practicing or they would think she was being silly. I think she wanted to practice first and see if she was good at marbles before she told anyone. This seems like Lupe because she wants to do everything well.*

Teacher Tip Because questions raised during the story may not always be answered directly, remind students that in some cases they must answer their questions by making inferences.

Word Knowledge

knee, know

Students can use the skills they learned in the Word Knowledge section of this lesson to read these words. Remind students of this if they have difficulty reading these words.

The father put down his fork and asked, "What happened?"

"Dad, I've been working out. I've been squeezing an eraser."

"Why?"

"I'm going to enter the marbles championship."

Her father looked at her mother and then back at his daughter. "When is it, honey?"

"This Saturday. Can you come?"

The father had been planning to play <u>racquetball</u> with a friend Saturday, but he said he would be there.
⑤ He knew his daughter thought she was no good at sports and he wanted to encourage her. He even rigged some lights in the backyard so she could practice after dark. He squatted with one knee on the ground, entranced by the sight of his daughter easily beating her brother.

40

Meeting Individual Needs

Intervention

Asking Questions Have the students work in small groups to ask each other any questions they may have about the story so far. Remind them that some questions can be answered by what they've already read and others will be answered later on in the text.

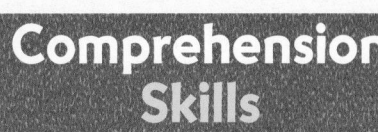

The day of the championship began with a cold blustery sky. The sun was a silvery light behind slate clouds.

"I hope it clears up," her father said, rubbing his hands together as he returned from getting the newspaper. They ate breakfast, paced nervously around the house waiting for 10:00 to arrive, and walked the two blocks to the playground (though Mr. Medrano wanted to drive so Lupe wouldn't get tired). She signed up and was assigned her first match on baseball diamond number three.

Lupe, walking between her brother and her father, shook from the cold, not nerves. She took off her mittens, and everyone stared at her thumb. Someone asked, "How can you play with a broken thumb?" Lupe smiled and said nothing.

She beat her first opponent easily, and felt sorry for the girl because she didn't have anyone to cheer for her. Except for her sack of marbles, she was all alone. Lupe invited the girl, whose name was Rachel, to stay with them. She smiled and said, "OK." The four of them walked to a card table in the middle of the outfield, where Lupe was assigned another opponent.

She also beat this girl, a fifth-grader named Yolanda, and asked her to join their group. They proceeded to more matches and more wins, and soon there was a crowd of people following Lupe to the finals to play a girl in a baseball cap. This girl seemed dead serious. She never even looked at Lupe.

"I don't know, Dad, she looks tough."

41

Meeting Individual Needs

Reteach

Making Inferences Have students who need additional instruction and practice with this concept complete **Reteach,** pages 15–16.

Challenge

Making Inferences Have the students think of a character trait (such as friendliness, meanness, or competitiveness) and then write a paragraph about that trait without actually using the word. Have them share their paragraphs. Have students who understand this concept and could benefit from extended practice complete **Challenge,** page 10.

Comprehension Skills

Making Inferences

For additional practice with *making inferences,* have students complete **Reading and Writing Workbook** pages 15–16.

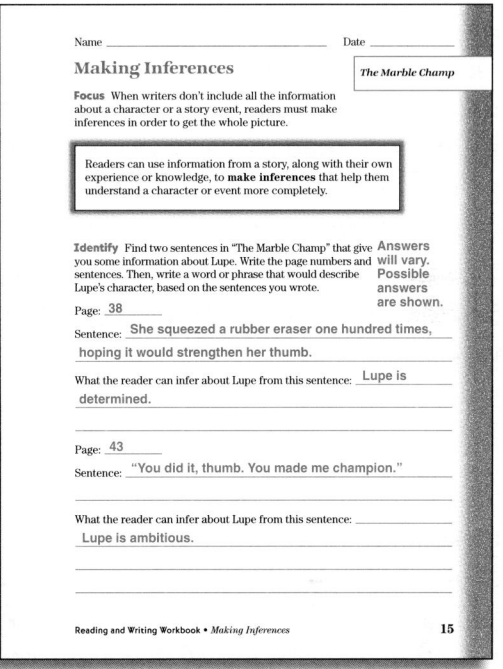

Reading and Writing Workbook pp. 15–16

② Reading and Responding

Comprehension Strategies

Modeling

⑥ Visualizing *As we read about the exciting final match in the marbles championship, how many of you had a mental picture of the action? This is called visualizing. Good readers try to visualize what they are reading as a way of making sure they understand and remember what is happening in the text.*

During the championship, I could visualize Lupe and Miss Baseball's focused faces. What pictures did you see?

Discussing Strategy Use

After they have read the selection, have students share any problems they encountered and tell what strategies they used to solve them. Then, have them answer the following questions. If they answer "no" to any of the questions, have them reread part of the selection to find the answer.

- Did they ask questions and check later to see if their questions were answered?

- Did they visualize story events?

- Did they find connections between the story, their own experiences, and other stories they have read?

Make sure that students explain how using the strategies helped them understand the selection better and how they read effectively to find answers to the questions they asked as they set purposes.

Rachel hugged Lupe and said, "Go get her."

"You can do it," her father encouraged. "Just think of the marbles, not the girl, and let your thumb do the work."

The other girl broke first and earned one marble. She missed her next shot, and Lupe, one eye closed, her thumb <u>quivering</u> with energy, blasted two marbles out of the circle but missed her next shot. Her opponent earned two more before missing. She stamped her foot and said "Shoot!" The score was three to two in favor of Miss Baseball Cap.

The referee stopped the game. "Back up, please, give them room," he shouted. Onlookers had gathered too tightly around the players.

Lupe then earned three marbles and was set to get her fourth when a gust of wind blew dust in her eyes and she missed badly. Her opponent quickly scored two marbles, tying the game, and moved ahead six to five on a lucky shot. Then she missed, and Lupe, whose eyes felt scratchy when she blinked, relied on instinct and thumb muscle to score the tying point. It was now six to six, with only three marbles left. Lupe blew her nose and studied the angles. She dropped to one knee, steadied her hand, and shot so hard she cracked two marbles from the circle. She was the winner!

"I did it!" Lupe said under her breath. She rose from her knees, which hurt from bending all day, and hugged her father. He hugged her back and smiled.

42

Meeting Individual Needs

Intervention

Visualizing Explain to students that when reading, they should be able to picture the setting, characters, and events in the story. If students are having difficulty visualizing the marbles match between Lupe and Miss Baseball, have them think of other competitive events they have attended and how they looked, smelled, sounded, and felt. Then have them compare and contrast their experiences to the one described in "The Marble Champ."

Everyone clapped, except Miss Baseball Cap, who made a face and stared at the ground. Lupe told her she was a great player, and they shook hands. A newspaper photographer took pictures of the two girls standing shoulder-to-shoulder, with Lupe holding the bigger trophy.

Lupe then played the winner of the boys' division, and after a poor start beat him eleven to four. She blasted the marbles, shattering one into sparkling slivers of glass. Her opponent looked on glumly as Lupe did what she did best—win!

The head referee and the President of the Fresno Marble Association stood with Lupe as she displayed her trophies for the newspaper photographer. Lupe shook hands with everyone, including a dog who had come over to see what the commotion was all about.

That night, the family went out for pizza and set the two trophies on the table for everyone in the restaurant to see. People came up to congratulate Lupe, and she felt a little embarrassed, but her father said the trophies belonged there.

Back home, in the privacy of her bedroom, she placed the trophies on her shelf and was happy. She had always earned honors because of her brains, but winning in sports was a new experience. She thanked her tired thumb. "You did it, thumb. You made me champion." As its reward, Lupe went to the bathroom, filled the bathroom sink with warm water, and let her thumb swim and splash as it pleased. Then she climbed into bed and drifted into a hard-won sleep.

Teacher Tip Reread the selection with students who had difficulty understanding it. Continue modeling and prompting the use of strategies and skills as you reread.

Assessment

✓ **Formal** To assess students' reading comprehension, have them complete **Comprehension and Writing Assessment,** pages 9–10.

Comprehension Skills

Discussing the Selection

Following reading, engage the students in a discussion of the selection. Using the *handing-off process* will help the students to take responsibility for the discussion. In addition to the following questions, have them revisit any questions asked when they set purposes before reading. Have students support their responses with text evidence.

- Why was Lupe successful in her competition with the girl in the baseball cap? *(She trained hard for two weeks, exercising her thumb, building a muscle, and practicing hitting the marbles.)*

- Why did the girl in the baseball cap and Rachel respond so differently to losing the competition? *(Answers will vary; students may mention that Rachel lost early in the contest, while the girl in the baseball cap had won many matches.)*

- How has this selection connected with your knowledge of the unit theme? *(Answers will vary—students should compare/contrast examples of cooperation and competition from this selection with their own experiences or past reading and use these connections to make a general statement about the unit theme.)*

During this time, have the students return to the clues and problems that they noted on the transparency before reading. Let the students decide which items deserve further discussion.

When handing off is in place, the teacher's main roles are to occasionally remind students to hand off and to monitor the discussion to ensure that everyone gets a chance to contribute.

 **Reading and Responding**

Meet the Author

After the students read the information about Gary Soto, discuss the following questions with them.

Gary Soto grew up working closely with his parents, grandparents, brothers, and sisters. Lupe, from "The Marble Champ," seems to be close to her family also. Can you think of other things the character of Lupe and the author, Gary Soto, have in common? *(Possible answer: Gary Soto was never interested in school until he found a poem he liked; Lupe was never interested in sports until she started playing marbles.)*

Why do you think that finding a poem he liked changed Gary Soto's feelings about school and learning? *(Possible answer: He found a subject in school that excited him—something that he wanted to know more about. So, learning became something he wanted to do, rather than something he was expected to do.)*

Meet the Illustrator

After the students read the information about Maren Scott, discuss the following question with them.

Maren Scott says that it's okay to make mistakes, and that as you learn from them you get better and better. How is that similar to Lupe's experience with marbles? *(Possible answer: Lupe didn't give up on marbles the first time she tried and failed. She kept practicing until she was so good that she won the championship.)*

The Marble Champ

Meet the Author

Gary Soto was born into a Mexican-American family in Fresno, California. Growing up, he worked alongside his parents, grandparents, brothers and sister, as farm laborers in vineyards, orange groves, and cotton fields around Fresno.

As a young person, Mr. Soto was never very interested in books or schoolwork, but he decided to enroll in college anyway. He discovered he wanted to be a writer at the age of 20. In one of his classes he read a poem called "Unwanted." It had a big effect on him. He started taking poetry classes and writing his own poetry. Mr. Soto continues to write for both adults and children, and he produces short films.

Meet the Illustrator

Maren Scott lives in Utah with her husband and three sons. Besides illustrating, she also enjoys designing quilts. She has won many awards for both her art and her quilts. Ms. Scott advises young people interested in being artists to draw everyday. She says, "Draw what you see and don't be concerned about mistakes. It's okay to make mistakes, just learn from them and you'll get better and better!"

44

Theme Connections

Think About It

With a small group of classmates, discuss some of the experiences you have had when learning a new game.

- How did you learn the game?
- Did you practice to learn it?
- How successful were you at learning it?
- Was cooperation involved in learning it? If so, who cooperated?
- Was competition involved? If so, who did you compete with?

Also, think about this: If you had a marble team, would you want Lupe on it? Why or why not? Would you want to have Lupe as a friend? Why or why not?

Check the Concept/Question Board to see if there are any questions that you can answer now. If the selection or your discussions about the selection have raised any new questions about cooperation and competition, put the questions on the Concept/Question Board. Maybe the next selection will help answer the questions.

Record Ideas

 Record in your Writing Journal any ideas you have thought about or discussed. Highlight or underline anything new you have learned. Try to think of ways you can use what you have learned about cooperation and competition in your dramatic play, and explain them.

Find a Quotation

Look through the story and find a statement made by one of the story characters that shows how he or she feels about competition and cooperation. Write the quote on an index card. Under the quote, write whether or not you agree with the quote. Explain why or why not.

45

Theme Connections

Think About It

Have students examine Lupe's motives for competition. Ask students whether or not they relate to these motives, and why.

Emphasize the effort and practice it takes for anyone to learn a new game. If necessary, point out that when learning a new game, even parents and coaches have to cooperate in the effort. Also, ensure that students understand they can also be in competition with themselves when learning a new game.

Find a Quotation

Have students post their quotations on the Concept/Question Board.

 **Teacher Tip** Use selection vocabulary and other words related to cooperation and competition during discussions with the students to model the utility of these words.

2 Reading and Responding

The New Kid
by Mike Makley

Good Sportsmanship
by Richard Armour

Activating Prior Knowledge

- Discuss with the students how these poems relate to the unit theme. Encourage volunteers to share times when they cooperated with others and times when they didn't.

- Have students share their feelings about baseball and sportsmanship.

Reading the Poem

- Read each poem aloud. Then have volunteers read each stanza aloud. Have them emphasize the rhythm of the language as they read. Other students should listen carefully to the words and focus on the images they bring to mind.

- During Independent Work Time, have students listen to the poems recorded on the *Listening Library Audiocassette*.

Literary Techniques

Rhyme

- Tell students that *rhyme* is the repetition of similiar sounds at the ends of lines in a section of poetry. Discuss with students how *rhyme* contributes to the rhythmic and musical quality of poetry. Then have volunteers pick out rhyming words from the poems on pages 46-47.

The New Kid

by Mike Makley
illustrated by Laurel Aiello

Our baseball team never did very much,
we had me and PeeWee and Earl and Dutch.
And the Oak Street Tigers always got beat
until the new kid moved in on our street.

The kid moved in with a mitt and a bat
and an official New York Yankee hat.
The new kid plays shortstop or second base
and can outrun us all in any race.

The kid never <u>muffs</u> a grounder or fly
no matter how hard it's hit or how high.
And the new kid always acts quite polite,
never yelling or spitting or starting a fight.

We were playing the league champs just last week;
they were trying to break our winning streak.
In the last inning the score was one-one,
when the new kid swung and hit a home run.

A few of the kids and their parents say
they don't believe that the new kid should play.
But she's good as me, Dutch, PeeWee, or Earl,
so we don't care that the new kid's a girl.

46

Tell students that poetry is a special kind of writing in which the sounds and meanings of words are combined to create ideas and feelings. Have students identify these and other elements of poetry:

- Poetry is written in lines and stanzas. Sentences are sometimes broken into parts to create two or more lines. Several lines can be grouped in a poem to form a stanza.
- Some poems have rhythm, or meter. In poetry, a rhythmic pattern of accented and unaccented syllables is called meter. Not all poems have meter.
- Sounds, words, or phrases may be repeated. Alliteration is a form of sound repetition.

Good Sportsmanship

by Richard Armour
illustrated by Laurel Aiello

Good sportsmanship we hail, we sing,
It's always pleasant when you spot it.
There's only one unhappy thing:
You have to lose to prove you've got it.

47

Theme Connection

■ Have the students discuss why cooperation is important to each poem.

■ Have students look for and discuss other themes that connect either or both of these poems with other selections read in this unit. For example, students may mention that sportsmanlike behavior has been a recurring theme and cite examples of how various characters, in "Class President" and "The Marble Champ," were or were not good sports.

Meet the Poet

Richard Armour was a worldwide lecturer and held faculty positions as dean, trustee, and professor of English at universities across the United States. He authored over a dozen children's books, more than 6,000 prose and verse magazine contributions, and over 40 adult nonfiction, poetry, humor, and satire books. ("Good Sportsmanship" appears in his book, *Night with Armour*.) In addition to his many scholarly achievements, the American Film Festival awarded him second prize for his children's educational film, "On Your Marks: A Package of Punctuation," and he was named Author of the Year by PEN, Stanford University, and the Los Angeles Public Library Association. He believed it was his "mission" to make poetry accessible to children. "One thing that keeps me going is their letters, in which they thank me for taking the dullness out of study, [and for] making learning fun."

Teacher Tip

Students might enjoy writing a limerick. A limerick is a short and witty form of verse. The poem contains five short lines. The first, second, and fifth lines rhyme. Lines three and four are shorter and rhyme with each other. The following is an example of a limerick:

There was an Old Man who said, "Do
Tell me *how* I should add two and two?
I think more and more
That it makes about four—
But I fear that is almost too few."
author unknown

Meeting Individual Needs

ESL

Poetry Invite English-language learners to say a poem in their primary language or in English, if they are able, to help them feel more relaxed about using language.

 **Responding**

 Research

As students continue their explorations, have them use the **Research** CD-ROM Program to help organize and share their findings.

 **Teacher Tip**

If you created a semantic map on the Concept/Question Board of key words related to the unit theme Cooperation and Competition, have students find words from other resources, their projects, and family discussions and add them to the appropriate category on the map.

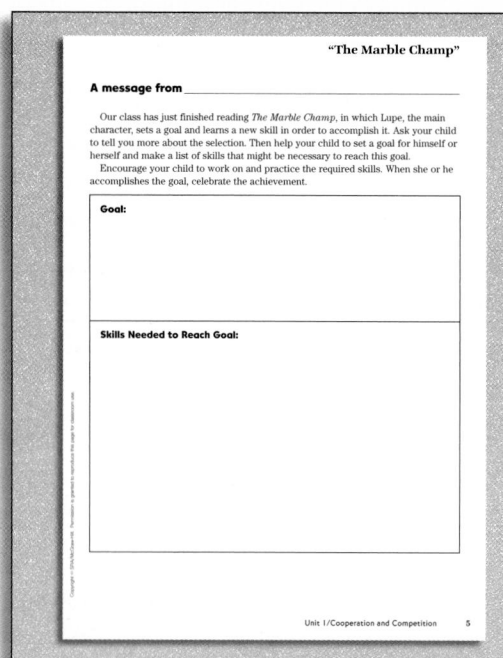

Home Connection p. 5

Exploring the Theme

Selection Vocabulary

Have students write in their Writing Journal the definitions for words discussed before reading the selection and any other interesting words they clarified while reading. Students should be encouraged to refer to these words throughout the unit as they work on student and writing projects. The words from this selection are:

contest	**energy**	**athletic**
matches	**players**	**commotion**

Reading/Writing Connections

Discuss Lupe's goal of becoming a marbles champion. Guide students to understand that although she was good at many things, she was poor at sports and wanted to do some sport well. Explain that Lupe's goal was something that came from inside herself, not from the outside world. Have students describe the goal of the main character and the reason behind it in their plays.

Literature Appreciation

Have students find examples of colorful language they enjoyed while reading "The Marble Champ" that helped them see and know Lupe Medrano. For example, author Gary Soto describes Lupe as a shy girl who "spoke in whispers." Ask students what this description tells them about Lupe in the very first sentence. Help the students find other examples of descriptive language they might wish to discuss.

Home Connection

The class has just finished reading "The Marble Champ," a fictional selection about a girl named Lupe who finds her niche in sports after much practice at the game of marbles. An informational letter on "The Marble Champ," in both English and Spanish, can be found in the **Home Connection** guide.

Supporting Student Explorations

Whole Group Explain to students that in creating characters and writing a play about cooperation and competition they will come to understand these two concepts more fully. Remind them that they will also gain an understanding of cooperation and competition through personal experience, reading stories, and discussing with others.

Have students continue to read their library books. Have them share what the books tell them about the theme and how they can be used as a source for their plays.

Small Group Have members of the small groups respond to the feedback they have received on their play ideas by making any revisions that are necessary. Have them decide on the setting and characters for their play. Tell them to make their characters realistic and remind them that characters' goals and motivations can come from inside themselves or from the outside world. Have them plan settings that they can create in the classroom.

Have groups begin the first draft of their play using a storyboard format. Students can use page 11 of the *Inquiry Journal* to create a storyboard.

As students work in groups, circulate, offering assistance as necessary.

Inquiry Journal
Have the students complete page 6 of the *Inquiry Journal*. Have them record their ideas about how "The Marble Champ" added to their knowledge of cooperation and competition.

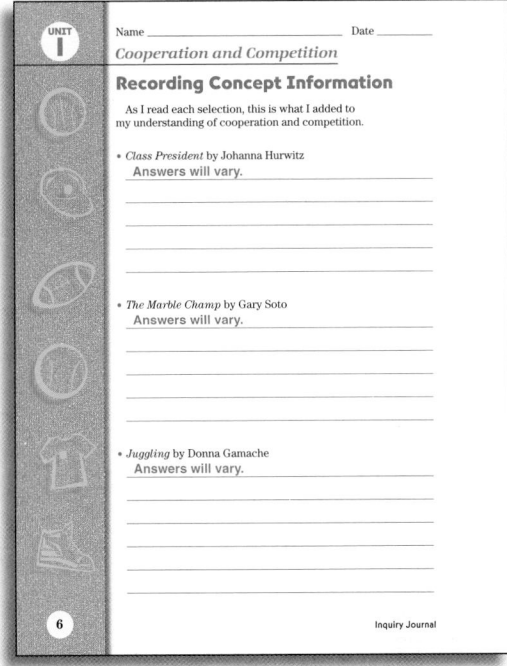

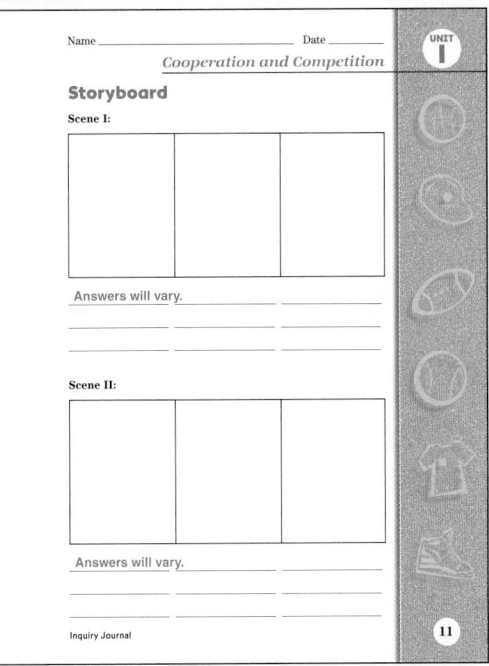

Inquiry Journal pp. 6, 11

Assessment

✓ **Informal** Continue your anecdotal record of students' progress. Note whether students:

- identify relevant thematic contents in their library books.
- use a storyboard to plan elements of their play.

③ Integrating the Curriculum

Language Arts

Writing

Writing Paragraphs

Instruct Lead students to establish that a paragraph is a group of two or more sentences that are related in some way, all telling about the same thing or idea. Sometimes one of the sentences, often the first, provides the main idea of the paragraph. This is usually called a *topic sentence* or a *stated main idea*. Sometimes the main idea is not stated; then it is often called an *implied main idea* because the reader has to infer it. Below are paragraphs from "The Marble Champ" that illustrate how the main idea can be stated or implied.

- Page 36, Paragraph 1: "Lupe Medrano . . . by the mayor.": describes the main character Lupe Medrano. The main idea is implied: Lupe is a shy but very smart girl.

- Page 36, Paragraph 3: "The truth . . . on her hips.": states the idea that Lupe is no good at sports and then lists examples. The topic sentence is the first sentence in the paragraph.

- Page 38, Paragraph 4: "After school . . . become stronger.": explains the series of steps Lupe took when she practiced playing marbles. The main idea is stated in the first sentence.

Practice Have students examine other paragraphs in the selection and tell how their sentences are related, then decide whether the main idea is stated or implied. For example:

- Page 37, Paragraph 3: "She smoothed . . . newborn chick.": describes the related actions of a character. The main idea is stated in the first sentence.

- Page 42, Paragraph 5: "Lupe then earned . . . the winner!": describes one of Lupe's matches. The main idea is implied: Lupe had a close match.

- Page 43, Paragraph 2: "Lupe then played . . . win!" The main idea is stated in the first sentence.

Apply Have students write two or three paragraphs on different aspects of their favorite game or sport. Remind them that all the sentences in a paragraph should support its main idea. Have them try writing the different types of paragraphs discussed above.

Teacher Tip Invite students to share their writing samples with the rest of the class.

Assessment

✓ **Formal** To assess students' understanding of this concept, have them complete **Skills Assessment**, page 3.

Writing Process

Prewrite The phase of the writing process when students think through an idea they want to write about is called *prewriting*. To improve their writing, have students think about their ideas, discuss them, and plan how they want readers to respond. It is important for students to take time before writing to plan ahead so that they can proceed from one phase of the writing process to another without spending unnecessary time making decisions that should have been made earlier. Prewriting is the most time-consuming phase of the process, but it may be the most important.

For students, deciding what to write about may be the most difficult part of the writing process. Let them know that even very good writers sometimes find it difficult to find a topic. However, before writing, good writers ask themselves questions, such as:

- What am I interested in writing about?
- What do I want to say about my topic?
- What do I already know about my topic?
- What do I need to find out?
- Who will read my piece of writing?

Continuing the persuasive writing activity they started in Lesson 1, have students write down and answer the above questions for themselves in their own writing. They may need to continue brainstorming ideas for their topic, keeping in mind that they will have to convince readers to think, feel, or act in a certain way about the topic they choose. Students may find it helpful to brainstorm with a partner or small group to list words and phrases they might use in their writing. Have them list or make a web of related ideas or key words or phrases they want to develop in their papers. For example, if a student wants to write a paper persuading the cafeteria workers to have pizza every Friday, his list might read:

everyone's favorite food	no leftovers
healthy	covers all food groups

Teacher Tip Let students know that not every idea they come up with has to be used in their writing. Tell them not to be afraid to record ideas they are not sure about. They may be able to use them later.

Meeting Individual Needs

Intervention

Prewriting For students who need additional help with prewriting, see Unit 1, Lesson 2, of the *Intervention Guide.*

Assessment

✓ **Informal** Take this opportunity to assess students' progress with the writing process by commenting on the entries in their Writing Journals.

3 Integrating the Curriculum

Teacher Tip Have students think of ways they can incorporate setting into the dramatic plays.

Teacher Tip Explain that it is important for authors to provide vivid settings so readers can visualize what is taking place. Point out that in "The Marble Champ" the author does not describe the story's setting all at once; he drops in details about when and where the action is occurring throughout the selection.

Meeting Individual Needs

Reteach
Setting Have students who need additional instruction and practice with this concept complete **Reteach,** pages 17–18.

Challenge
Setting Have students who understand this concept and could benefit from extended practice complete **Challenge,** page 11.

Literary Elements

Recognize and Analyze Story Setting

Instruct Have students share what they know about the settings of stories. Remind them, if necessary, that *setting* is the time and place in which the events of a story occur.

Have the students identify when and where "The Marble Champ" takes place. Help them establish that the story is set in the present, as shown by details such as the science fair, racquetball, and the attitudes about girls playing sports. Point out that the author also gives general and specific information about where Lupe lives. As an example, share some of the following details:

- Page 37, paragraph 2: "She hopped out of bed and rummaged through the closet."
- Page 41, paragraph 1: "The day of the championship began with a blustery sky."
- Page 41, paragraph 2: "walked the two blocks to the playground"

Practice Have each student find three examples of setting in the selection "Class President" and write them down on a piece of paper. Ask volunteers to share their examples with the class.

Apply For more practice with recognizing and analyzing story settings, have students complete *Reading and Writing Workbook* pages 17–18.

Reading and Writing Workbook pp. 17–18

Name _____ Date _____

Recognize and Analyze Story Setting

The Marble Champ

Focus It is important for writers to provide vivid settings for their stories so that readers can picture where and when the events are taking place.

Setting is the time and place in which the events of a story occur. An author makes the setting more interesting by describing how a place *looks, sounds, smells,* and *feels.* In addition to the general setting of the story, there may be more specific settings where action takes place, such as the character's home or school.

Identify Look through "The Marble Champ." Select a specific setting from the story and list some of the details that the author uses to describe it.

Answers will vary. Possible answers are shown.

Setting	Details That Describe Setting
Lupe's room	shelf her father made to hold awards, bed, bedspread, closet, window
the marble championship games	cold, blustery sky; baseball diamond number three; middle of the outfield

Reading and Writing Workbook • *Recognize and Analyze Story Setting*   17

Recognize and Analyze Story Setting *(continued)*

Practice Think about two or three of your favorite stories. What is the setting for each story? Complete the chart below.

Answers will vary.

THE SETTINGS FOR MY FAVORITE STORIES

Story	Where and When It Takes Place	Details That Describe Setting

Apply Write the first paragraph of a story that takes place in a setting that is familiar to you, such as your house, your room, or your classroom. Include details in your writing that will help readers visualize when and where the story is taking place.

Answers will vary.

_____

_____

_____

_____

_____

18   *Recognize and Analyze Story Setting* • Reading and Writing Workbook

Spelling

Consonant Before -le Syllable Pattern

Instruct Write the following words on the chalkboard and point out that all of the words are found in the selection. Ask students what else the words have in common (the final *-le* spelling and a consonant before the *-le*).

marble (mar•ble)　　　muscle (mus•cle)　　　people (peo•ple)

popsicle (pop•si•cle)　　circle (cir•cle)　　　angle (an•gle)

Point out that the last syllable always begins with the consonant that is before the final *-le*. This makes the final syllable a closed syllable, or one that ends with a consonant sound. Call on volunteers to spell the final syllable in each word and identify the consonant preceding the *-le*.

Practice Have students choose five words from the list above and write a sentence for each word. Have them exchange sentences and check spelling.

Apply Have students think of five words that follow this pattern and then challenge a partner to spell them correctly. Have them check their work in a dictionary.

For additional practice, have students complete ***Reading and Writing Workbook*** pages 19–20.

Remind students that *-le, -el, -al, -il,* and *-ol* are all spellings of the same sound. The *-le* ending is the most common spelling. Remind students to check words with these spellings in a dictionary when writing the scripts for their dramatic plays and their persuasive papers.

Meeting Individual Needs

Reteach

Spelling -le Endings Have students who need additional instruction and practice with this concept complete ***Reteach,*** pages 19–20.

Challenge

Spelling -le Endings Challenge students to think of the other final syllable spellings that have the same pronunciation as *-le;* for example, *-al* as in *final, -ial* as in *special, -il* as in *devil,* and *-el* as in *nickel.* Have them list as many words as they can for each ending. Have them confirm the correct spelling for each word using a dictionary. Have students who can benefit from extended practice of this concept complete ***Challenge,*** page 12.

Reading and Writing Workbook pp. 19–20

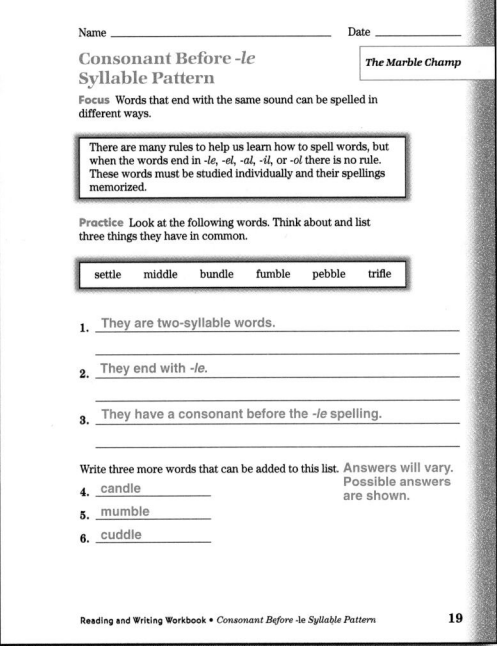

③ Integrating the Curriculum

Teacher Tip Remind students to use what they have learned about nouns as they work on scripts for their dramatic plays and on their persuasive papers.

Meeting Individual Needs

Reteach

Nouns Have students who need additional instruction and practice with this concept complete *Reteach,* pages 21–22.

Challenge

Nouns Have students think of words that can be used as a noun and a verb, for example, the word *muscle.* To establish that the word can be used as both a noun and verb, they should write a sentence showing each part of speech. Have students who can benefit from extended practice of this concept complete *Challenge,* page 13.

Nouns

Grammar, Usage, and Mechanics

Nouns

Instruct Ask students what they know about nouns. If necessary, share that all words can be classified into groups called parts of speech, one of which is nouns. Nouns are words that name people, places, things, or ideas. On the chalkboard, write the following sentence from the selection:

> That night, the family went out for pizza and set the two trophies on the table for everyone in the restaurant to see.

Ask volunteers to underline the nouns in the sentence (*night, family, pizza, trophies, table, restaurant*). Have other students explain whether the nouns name people, places, things, or ideas. Draw a four-column chart on the chalkboard, with the columns labeled *People, Places, Things,* and *Ideas.* Write students' responses in the chart.

Practice Tell the students to select other sentences from "The Marble Champ." After copying the sentences, they should underline each of the nouns, then include them in the chart from the exercise above.

Apply Tell students to select sentences from the previous selection, "Class President." Have them underline the nouns with a colored marker or crayon. Classmates might exchange papers and check each other's work.

For additional practice, have students complete ***Reading and Writing Workbook*** pages 21–22.

Reading and Writing Workbook pp. 21–22

Name _____ Date _____

Nouns *The Marble Champ*

Focus A **noun** is a word that names a person, a place, a thing, or an idea.

Here are some examples of nouns from the story:

- **People:** Alfonso, opponent, President of the Fresno Marble Association
- **Places:** backyard, middle of the outfield, Fresno
- **Things:** sports, thumb, pizza
- **Ideas:** truth, instinct

Identify Read the fourth paragraph on page 41 of "The Marble Champ." On the lines below, list the nouns from this paragraph.

List the nouns that name people: opponent, girl, Lupe, Rachel

List the nouns that name places: outfield

List the nouns that name things: sack, marbles, name

Reading and Writing Workbook • Nouns 21

Nouns *(continued)*

Practice Use the information in the story to fill in the blanks in the following sentences with appropriate nouns.

1. Lupe practiced every night or day until she was ready for the contest or championship

2. Her father or brother was impressed with how hard Lupe could hit the marble

3. Lupe felt embarrassed when all the people in the restaurant came up to congratulate her.

4. They set the trophies on the table in the restaurant for all to see.

Apply Fill in the chart with nouns you can see in your classroom. Write them in the appropriate columns. Answers will vary.

People	Places	Things

22 *Nouns • Reading and Writing Workbook*

Listening/Speaking/Viewing

Recognize and Distinguish Stories

Help students recognize and distinguish different types of stories, their characteristics, and their variants by putting them in a chart. Ask students why it is desirable to present some kinds of information in the form of a chart. Help them to establish that charts can present much information in a small amount of space, and they help to organize information so readers can understand it more easily and quickly.

Have students organize story genres and their characteristics in the chart following these guidelines.

- Write a title that tells what the chart is all about.

- Create row headings and write them down the left side of the page. Row headings are names of the items you will give information about (which, in this case, will be story genres).

- Write short column headings across the top of the chart. These headings tell the kinds of information you will give about the items in the row headings. (In this case there will be only one column heading: Characteristics of Genres.)

- In the blank spaces, write brief information about the items in the row headings. Complete sentences are not needed. For example, if the row heading was *Legend*, one could write in the blank space "passed down through generations, about a heroic character whose deeds have become exaggerated through the story's retellings."

Guide students in distinguishing between the treatment, scope, and organization of different types of stories. Have students brainstorm different story genres to put in their charts. These types include: folktales, fables, myths, legends, tall tales, realistic fiction, historical fiction, fantasy, science fiction, and adventure tales. If possible, have on display examples of each genre for students to peruse, or schedule time for students to research story genres in the library. Have students fill in their charts based on their findings. Focus on distinguishing realistic fiction from other types of story genres.

Teacher Tip Have students use charts to help them organize information they want to use in their persuasive papers and unit activities.

Meeting Individual Needs

ESL

Listening/Speaking/Viewing Have volunteer English-language learners explain characteristics of specific types of stories using the chart.

③ Integrating the Curriculum

Inquiry Journal p. 10

Teacher Tip Allow students to express their ideas without interruption.

Assessment

✓ **Formal** To assess students' understanding of this concept, have them complete *Skills Assessment,* page 4.

Study and Research

Organize Information

Instruct Explain to students that a chart can be useful for organizing information quickly and easily. A chart can display a lot of information in a small space. Remind students that they used a chart in studying about setting (page 47E) and genre (page 47H). Discuss how these charts helped them understand setting.

Practice Create a two-column chart with the headings *Compare* and *Contrast* on an overhead transparency or the chalkboard. Have students compare and contrast the characters of Julio in "Class President" and Lupe in "The Marble Champ." Have volunteers summarize students' responses in the appropriate columns on the chart. After the chart has been completed, discuss the results. Ask students whether Julio and Lupe are more alike than they are different.

Apply Have the students think of one of their favorite books. Then ask them to think about the character or setting in that book. How is the main character alike or different from Lupe in "The Marble Champ"? What similarities and differences do the settings have? Have each create a chart similar to the one in the exercise above for organizing comparisons and contrasts of the two characters and the two settings.

For more practice with organizing information, have students complete *Inquiry Journal* page 10.

Across the Curriculum

Drama

The Secret of My Success

Purpose

To help students gain greater understanding of cooperation and competition

Procedure

Remind students that at the end of the selection, Lupe had her picture taken by a newspaper photographer. Have them pretend that they are newspaper reporters who want to interview Lupe about her success and how she feels about cooperation and competition.

■ Brainstorm with students to generate a series of questions a newspaper reporter might want to ask Lupe about the reasons behind her success and her future plans.

■ Half of the students will play the role of newspaper reporter. The other half of the students will play the role of Lupe. Pair a reporter and a Lupe. The reporters should ask their interview questions. Students playing the role of Lupe should answer the questions, true to character. Have the reporters audiotape or write down the responses.

■ After the interviews, discuss with students which trait Lupe would say was the secret of her success—cooperation or a competitive spirit.

Music

Cooperative and Competitive Beats

Purpose

To develop students' appreciation of the effects of different types of music

Procedure

Play a variety of different types of music for students—jazz, classical, rock and roll, and country. Ask them to jot down whatever thoughts, ideas, and feelings come into their minds as they listen to each type of music. Talk about the impact that the different instruments, the lyrics, and the singers have on the students. Then have students think about what type of music would best demonstrate the themes of cooperation and of competition.

■ Begin by telling students to write the word *Cooperation* at the top of a sheet of paper. Then have them write down words and phrases that they associate with cooperation.

■ Based on the different types of music you played, what type do they think would best illustrate cooperation? They should also describe which instruments they feel would best portray that theme. Some students may suggest specific pieces of music.

■ Ask them to repeat the process with the word *Competition.*

■ Discuss the students' responses, and if possible, play any specific suggestions they had. How do their musical responses to the themes of cooperation and competition compare?

About the Illustrator

Daniel Powers always loved to draw and paint. He studied art history and received an MFA in illustration at Marywood University in Pennsylvania. He currently lives in New Mexico with his wife. They enjoy hiking with their two dogs and, according to Mr. Powers, "exploring the diversity of the universe." The area where they live is near the Native American reservations where Mr. Powers works with the children at the Zuñi Pueblo schools. Other children's books he has illustrated include *Jiro's Pearl*, which was awarded Pick of the List by the American Bestsellers Association; *From the Land of the White Birch*, which received the Original Art Award from the Society of Illustrators; and *Dear Katie, The Volcano Is a Girl*, which earned him an artist-in-residency from the Kalani Honua Institute for Cultural Studies.

Students can read more about Daniel Powers on page 54 of the **Student Anthology.**

Selection Summary

Genre: Realistic Fiction

When Kyle's gym teacher, Mr. Braden, discovers Kyle's talent as a volleyball player, Mr. Braden begins a campaign to recruit Kyle for the school team. But Kyle has another commitment, his paper route, that takes up all of his after-school time. The money Kyle earns from his paper route is very important to his family's income. Kyle's dilemma is this: How can he juggle responsibility to his job and mother and still contribute to his school's team? The solution comes when some teachers and students cooperate to help Kyle juggle his schedule.

# Exploring the Theme

Selection Concepts

"Juggling" is realistic fiction about a young boy who faces the conflicting demands of his family's needs and the needs of his school volleyball team. The key concepts to be explored are:

- Conflicting needs can often be met through cooperative efforts.
- A team effort is effective in both sports and everyday life.
- Cooperation is essential if we are to compete successfully.

 Check the Reading link of the **SRA** Web page for links to theme-related Websites.
http://www.sra4kids.com

Exploration Activity Tips

Before Reading, have students describe the act of juggling. Challenge them to think of the word as a metaphor for the number of things they need and want to do.

During Reading, have students discuss possible solutions to the main character's time conflict. Have students reflect on how various solutions will affect the parties to whom the main character feels responsible.

After Reading, have students discuss the various ways the idea of competition is depicted in the selection. Discuss how cooperation resolved the competition between Kyle's various responsibilities. Have students update the Concept/Question Board.

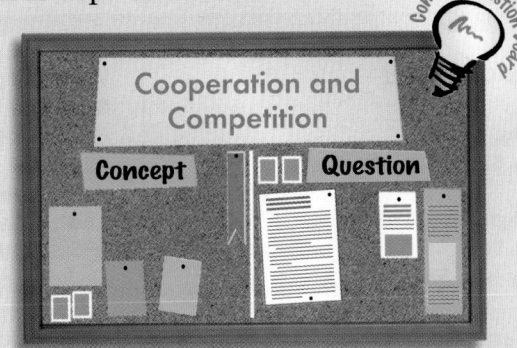

Unit I Exploration Management

Lesson I	Discuss experiences with cooperation and competition. Generate ideas for dramatic play.
Lesson 2	Students give and receive feedback on their unit activity ideas, and begin to work in groups on the storyboards for their plays.
Lesson 3 Juggling	**Collaborative Exploration** **Students complete their storyboards and share them with the other groups, then revise the storyboards based on feedback.** **Supplementary Activity** **Schedule group sharing sessions in which students identify problems they are encountering on their storyboards and possible solutions.**
Lesson 4	Students begin group work on writing plays in script format. They agree on director and actor roles and begin rehearsals.
Lesson 5	Students complete the final draft of their scripts and plan their dress rehearsals.
Lesson 6	Students complete play rehearsals and perform their plays. They put scripts in a class anthology, and prepare a title page and table of contents.

Lesson Planner

Suggested Pacing: 3–5 days	DAY 1	DAY 2	
	DAY 1	DAY 2	

Part 1 — Preparing to Read

Materials
- Student Anthology, pp. 48–55
- Transparencies 3, 44

DAY 1

Word Knowledge
- Reading the Words and Sentences, p. 48G
- Developing Oral Language, p. 48G

Build Background, p. 48H

Preview and Prepare, p. 48I

Selection Vocabulary, p. 48I
serves, juggle, spare, spirit, deliberately

DAY 2

Preview and Prepare, p. 48I
- Review Transparency 44

Part 2 — Reading and Responding

Materials
- Student Anthology, pp. 48–57
- Teacher Observation Log
- Reading and Writing Workbook, pp. 23–24
- Inquiry Journal, p. 6
- Home Connection, p. 7

DAY 1

Student Anthology, pp. 48–55

Comprehension Strategies
- Asking Questions, p. 48
- Predicting, pp. 48, 50, 52
- Making Connections, p. 50

Discussing Strategy Use, p. 52

DAY 2

Student Anthology, pp. 48–55

Comprehension Skills
- ✓ Author's Point of View, pp. 49, 51
- ✓ Discussing the Selection, p. 53

Exploring the Theme
- Selection Vocabulary, p. 57A
  serves, juggle, spare, spirit, deliberately

Part 3 — Integrating the Curriculum

Materials
- Student Anthology, pp. 48–55
- Reading and Writing Workbook, pp. 25–28
- Inquiry Journal, pp. 12–13

DAY 1

Writing
- ✓ Explaining Topic Sentences, p. 57C

Literary Elements
- ✓ Identifying Purpose of Text, p. 57E

DAY 2

Writing Process
- Draft, p. 57D

Spelling
- ✓ Spelling -*le* Endings, p. 57F

Independent Work Time

Materials
- Reteach, pp. 23–28
- ESL Supplement
- Challenge, pp. 14–16
- Intervention Guide
- Listening Library Audiocassette

DAY 1

Writing Process Continued
ESL
- Word Meaning, p. 48G
- Predicting, p. 52

Intervention
- Consonant Digraphs, p. 48G
- Predicting, p. 50
- Topic Sentences, p. 57C

Unit Project
- Complete and Share Storyboards
- Revise Storyboards

DAY 2

Writing Process Continued
Reteach
- ✓ Identifying Purpose of Text, *Reteach*, pp. 25–26
ESL
- Vocabulary, p. 48J
Challenge
- ✓ Identifying Purpose of Text, *Challenge*, p. 15
Intervention
- Comprehension, p. 48
Unit Project Continued

✓ Informal **Assessment Available**   ✓ Formal **Assessment Available**

DAY 2 continued	DAY 3	
DAY 3	**DAY 4**	**DAY 5**
General Review	General Review	Review Word Knowledge
Student Anthology, pp. 48–55 **Theme Connections** ■ Think About It, p. 55 ■ Make a List, p. 55	**Student Anthology, pp. 48–55** **Fine Art, pp. 56–57** **Exploring the Theme** ■ Reading/Writing Connections, p. 57A ■ View Fine Art, p. 57A ■ Supporting Student Explorations, p. 57B	**Student Anthology, pp. 48–55** ■ Review Selection ■ Complete Discussion ■ Reread Selection in Pairs **Home Connection, p. 57A** ■ Discuss "Juggling" ■ Keep track of schedule
Writing Process Continued **Grammar, Usage, and Mechanics** ✓■ Pronouns, p. 57G **Listening/Speaking/Viewing** ■ Recognizing and Analyzing Story Settings, p. 57H	**Writing Process Continued** **Study and Research** ■ Interviewing, p. 57I	**Across the Curriculum** **Social Studies** ■ Money for a Good Cause, p. 57J **Physical Education** ■ Designing New Games, p. 57J
Writing Process Continued **Reteach** ✓■ Author's Point of View, *Reteach*, pp. 23–24 **ESL** ■ Peer Tutoring, p. 57F **Challenge** ✓■ Author's Point of View, *Challenge*, p. 14 ■ Spelling -le Endings, p. 57F **Unit Project Continued**	**Writing Process Continued** **Reteach** ✓■ Pronouns, *Reteach*, pp. 27–28 **Challenge** ✓■ Pronouns, *Challenge*, p. 16 **Unit Project Continued**	**Writing Process Continued** **Unit Project Continued**

Meeting Individual Needs
Independent Work Time

Part 1
Preparing to Read

Meeting Individual Needs

ESL
- Word Meaning, p. 48G
- Cultural Context, p. 48H
- Vocabulary, p. 48J

Intervention
- Consonant Digraphs, p. 48G

Part 2
Reading and Responding

Meeting Individual Needs

Reteach
- Author's Point of View, *Reteach*, pp. 23–24

ESL
- Predicting, p. 52

Challenge
- Author's Point of View, *Challenge*, p. 14

Intervention
- Comprehension, p. 48
- Predicting, p. 50
- Author's Point of View, p. 51

Part 3
Integrating the Curriculum

Meeting Individual Needs

Reteach
- Identifying Purpose of Text, *Reteach*, pp. 25–26
- Pronouns, *Reteach*, pp. 27–28

ESL
- Peer Tutoring, p. 57F

Challenge
- Identifying Purpose of Text, *Challenge*, p. 15
- Spelling -*le* Endings, p. 57F
- Pronouns, *Challenge*, p. 16

Intervention
- Topic Sentences, p. 57C

Formal Assessment Options

Use these assessment pages along with your informal observations to gauge student progress.

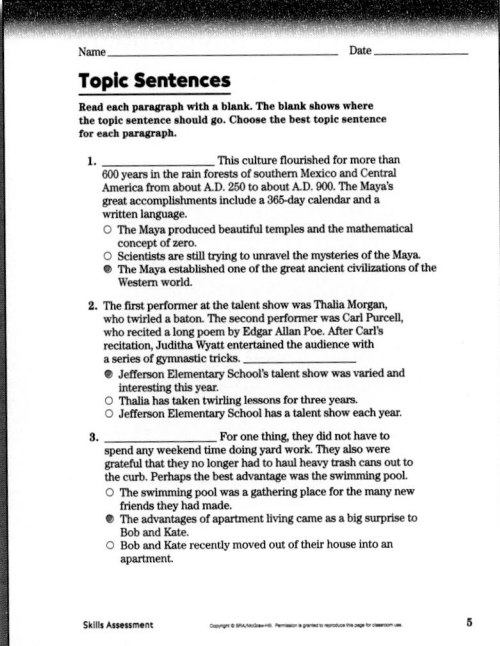

Skills Assessment, p. 5

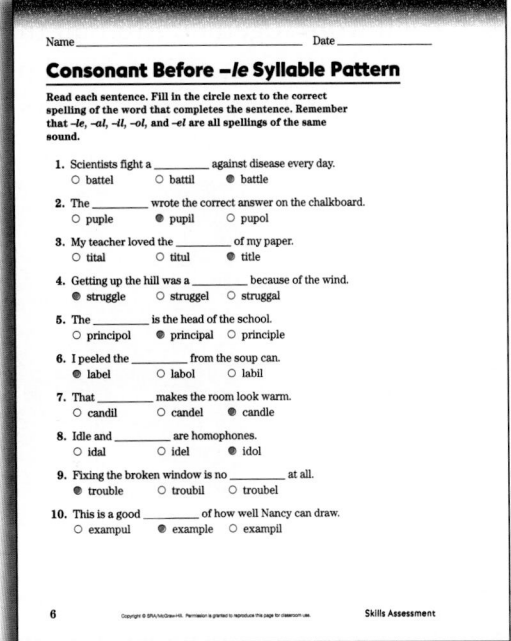

Skills Assessment, p. 6

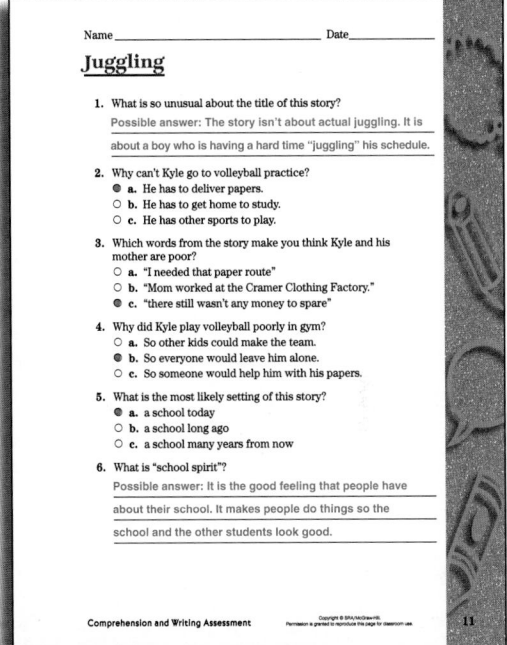

Comprehension and Writing Assessment, p. 11

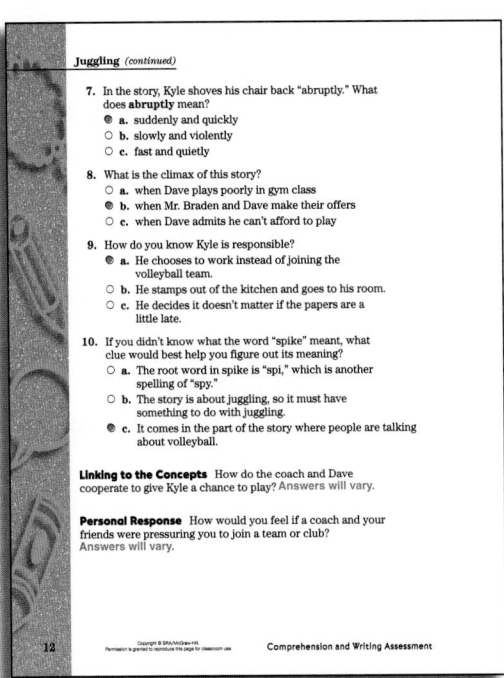

Comprehension and Writing Assessment, p. 12

 # Preparing to Read

Word Knowledge

Reading the Words and Sentences

Write each word and sentence on the chalkboard. Have students read each word together. After all the words have been read, have students read each sentence in natural phrases or chunks. Use the suggestions in About the Words to discuss the different features of the listed words.

Line 1: everyone   volleyball   homework   afternoon
Line 2: then   those   both   truth
Line 3: small   spin   most   scout
Sentence 1: Most students do their homework in the afternoon.
Sentence 2: Everyone saw both sport scouts at the game yesterday.
Sentence 3: The volleyball spins and then skips across the net.

About the Words

- Line 1 contains words that are closed compounds, which are formed by joining together two words. They are considered "closed" because there is no space between the two words.

- The words in Line 2 have the consonant digraph *th*. Digraphs are formed when two letters, placed together, create only one sound.

- Line 3 focuses on *s* consonant blends. Invite students to think of other words that contain these blends.

Developing Oral Language

To review the words, have students do one or both of the following activities:

- Have a student choose two words from one of the lines above and use both words in the same sentence. Then ask volunteers to try using three words and then all four words in the same sentence.

- Ask volunteers to orally alphabetize the four words in each line above.

Meeting Individual Needs

ESL

Word Meaning Make sure the English-language learners understand the meanings of the words before they do the exercises. Refer to Unit 1, Lesson 3, of the **ESL Supplement** for specific suggestions.

Intervention

Consonant Digraphs For students who need more help with the consonant digraph *th,* explain that when the letter *t* and the letter *h* are used together, they make a single sound. Demonstrate the *th* sound as it is pronounced in *then* and *those*. Contrast how *th* sounds when used in *both* and *truth*. Brainstorm with students to generate a list of words that contain the consonant digraph *th*. Have students say each word aloud and use each in a sentence. For students who need more help, see Unit 1, Lesson 3, of the **Intervention Guide.**

Build Background

Activate Prior Knowledge

Have students check the Concept/Question Board to refresh their memories about cooperation and competition. Discuss the following with students to find out what they already know about the selection and the unit theme. Tell students to use their prior knowledge to help them comprehend the selection they are about to read.

- Have students discuss what they know about the art of juggling, as well as what they know about "juggling" activities and time.
- Have students discuss what they know about the game of volleyball.
- If any students are familiar with the story "Juggling," have them tell a little about it.
- Have students share other stories that involve volleyball, juggling, or being part of a team.

Background Information

The following information may help students better understand the selection they are about to read.

- Some students might not be familiar with the concept of a paper route. Tell them that students their own age often do this job, riding their bicycles to deliver the daily newspaper to people's homes.

Research in Action

Intentional Learning

To promote intentional learning, keep students aware of what they are learning and why, rather than letting them focus on the activities. Intentional learning means to turn over—gradually, of course—the responsibility of learning to the children themselves. You should not be forever the one who notices misconceptions and gaps in knowledge, who decides what is learned from an activity, who monitors learning and thinking of remedial actions. Eventually, students must learn to do these things themselves if they are to go out into the world as lifelong learners. *(Carl Bereiter)*

Teacher Tip Remind students that stories often center around a conflict of some sort. The conflict can be *between* the main character and someone or something else, or it can be *within* the main character, as is the case in the present selection.

Meeting Individual Needs

ESL

Cultural Context Ask English-language learners why the writer chose to name this story "Juggling." Encourage them to talk about how they juggle learning English with using their first languages at home.

Writing Journal Tell students that they will be jotting down in their Writing Journals their reactions to the story. Have them be on the lookout for any story ideas they may have about a time when they had to make a choice between responsibility and doing something fun.

1 Preparing to Read

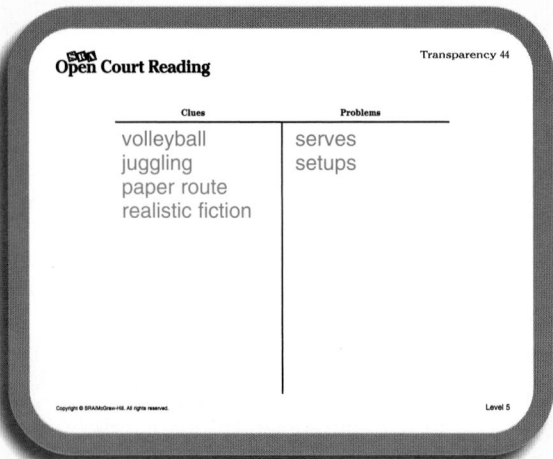

Transparency 44

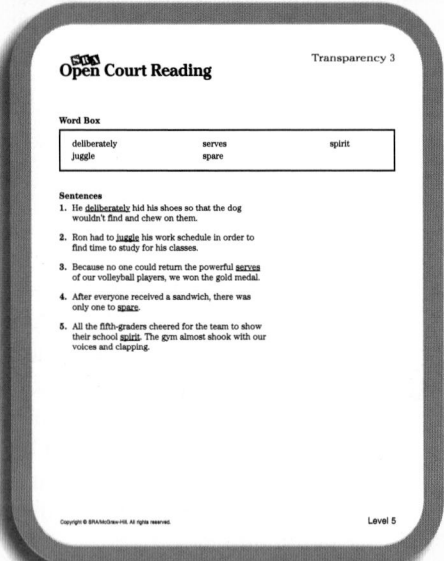

Transparency 3

Preview and Prepare

Browse

- Have a volunteer read the title and the author's and illustrator's names aloud. Have students share what they know about fiction.

- Because this is a fiction selection, have the students browse through only the first half of the story. Have them look for words and phrases that connect to what they already know. Record these in the Clues column on *Transparency 44*. Discuss with the students what they think this story might have to do with cooperation and competition.

- Encourage students to ask questions as they browse. Have them identify any problems they notice while reading, and record them in the Problems column.

Set Purposes

As they read, have students think about what each character learns about cooperation and competition.

Selection Vocabulary

As students study vocabulary, they will use context clues, word structure, and apposition to clarify these and additional unfamiliar words.

Display *Transparency 3* before reading the selection to introduce and discuss the following words and their meanings.

serves: in volleyball and tennis, a way of putting the ball into play by sending it over the net (page 48)

jug·gle: to handle more than one object or activity at one time; perform a clever trick (page 48)

spare: left over; remaining; extra (page 50)

spir·it: enthusiasm; loyalty (page 51)

de·lib·er·ate·ly: when something is done on purpose or intentionally (page 52)

Have students read the words in the Word Box. Help students decode multisyllabic words by reading the words syllable by syllable.

Have students read the sentences on *Transparency 3* to determine the meaning of the underlined words. Remind them to use clues in the sentences and structural clues to figure out the meaning. See the teacher tip on the left for information on how the words in each sentence can be defined.

Reading Recommendations

Your first reading of the selection should focus on developing the reading strategies found to the left of the reduced pages. We recommend that the students revisit the selection, rereading sections or the entire selection as a way to enhance their understanding and appreciation of the text. During rereading, they should focus on the comprehension skills, found to the right of the reduced pages.

Oral Reading

This story lends itself to oral reading because of its reliance on dialogue. As students read aloud, have them read expressively, at an appropriate pace, in natural phrases and chunks. By reading the selection with fluency, students will demonstrate an understanding of the text and an ability to engage the listeners in an effective manner. If students encounter difficulties, have them use the reading strategies below or refer to the Blending Procedure (Program Appendix 15–16).

Using Reading Strategies

Reading strategy instruction allows students to become aware of how good readers read. Good readers constantly check their understanding as they are reading. In addition, skilled readers recognize when they are having problems and stop to use various reading strategies to help them make sense of what they are reading.

During the reading of "Juggling," you will model the use of the following reading strategies:

- Asking Questions
- Predicting
- Making Connections

Before reading, have students share how they have used these strategies in the past and any tips they can give each other on their use.

Building Comprehension Skills

Revisiting or rereading a selection allows students to apply skills that give them a more complete understanding of the text. Some follow-up comprehension skills, such as *Main Idea and Details* and *Compare and Contrast*, help students organize information. Others, such as *Author's Purpose*, *Making Inferences*, and *Drawing Conclusions*, lead to deeper understanding—to "reading between the lines," as mature readers do. In this selection, students will apply the follow-up comprehension skill of *Author's Point of View*.

Teacher Tip
Have students who may need extra help reading "Juggling" reread the selection using the *Listening Library Audiocassette*.

Teacher Tip
During oral reading, have students develop their vocabularies by listening for unfamiliar words as they follow along in the text. Have them quickly jot down the page and paragraph number where each unfamiliar word appears so that they can find it and look it up later. Also, have students jot down pronunciations and text locations for words they would not have recognized had they been reading silently—some difficult words, students will comprehend when they hear them pronounced, even if they cannot identify them by their spellings. After reading, have students work together to clarify and confirm meanings and pronunciations of the words they have listed.

Meeting Individual Needs

ESL

Vocabulary Check that English-language learners know the meanings and idioms and more difficult vocabulary in the story including: *junior, paper route, salary, persuade, spike the ball, shrill, setups, intercom,* and *pestering.* More information can be found in Unit 1, Lesson 3, of the *ESL Supplement.*

Teacher Tip
By this time in the fifth grade, good readers should be reading approximately 126 words per minute with fluency and expression. The only way to gain fluency is through practice. As explained in Reading Recommendations, have students reread all or part of the selection to you and to each other during class or Independent Work Time to focus on the comprehension skills and to build fluency.

② Reading and Responding

Read pages 48–55.

Comprehension Strategies

Modeling

① Asking Questions *This is a good place to stop and ask a question because I have found something I don't understand. Kyle seems to want to play volleyball and Mr. Braden is asking him to join the team. What's wrong with Kyle? Why doesn't he just join the team? Maybe I need to read a bit more carefully.*

Oh, I see. He has a paper route at the same time the practices are being held.

Modeling

② Predicting *Good readers predict what will happen next, and then confirm or revise their predictions as they go. It is important for all predictions to be firmly based on both the text and one's own knowledge and experiences.*

Kyle has a dilemma. From what we have read about him so far, Kyle seems like a very conscientious and level-headed person. Based on that, I predict that he'll just explain his situation to Mr. Braden so that he'll understand why Kyle can't play. (This prediction is confirmed on page 50.)

Reading Recommendation

ORAL · CHORAL · SILENT

Juggling

by Donna Gamache
illustrations by Daniel Powers

In gym class on Monday, we started volleyball, and I hit seven straight serves just over the net, hard and fast. Mr. Braden called me over at the end of the class.

"You've got a good serve, Kyle," he said. "How about coming out for the junior team?"

① "Sorry, Mr. Braden," I said, without looking at him. "I'm busy every afternoon." I knew the practices were three times a week, right after school, and that's when I delivered papers. I'd started a paper route two years ago when I was ten, but this year I'd taken over a second route—a long one, too. I never finished delivering before 5:30.

"Well, think about it," Mr. Braden called as I left for my next class. "We could use a serve like yours. Couldn't you juggle your time a little?"

48

Meeting Individual Needs

Inter✓ention

Comprehension Intervention strategies for those students having difficulty with reading "Juggling" can be found in Unit 1, Lesson 3, of the *Intervention Guide.*

Assessment

✓ **Informal** Observe individual students as they read, and use the Teacher Observation Log, found in the *Assessment Guide,* to record anecdotal information about each student's strengths and weaknesses.`

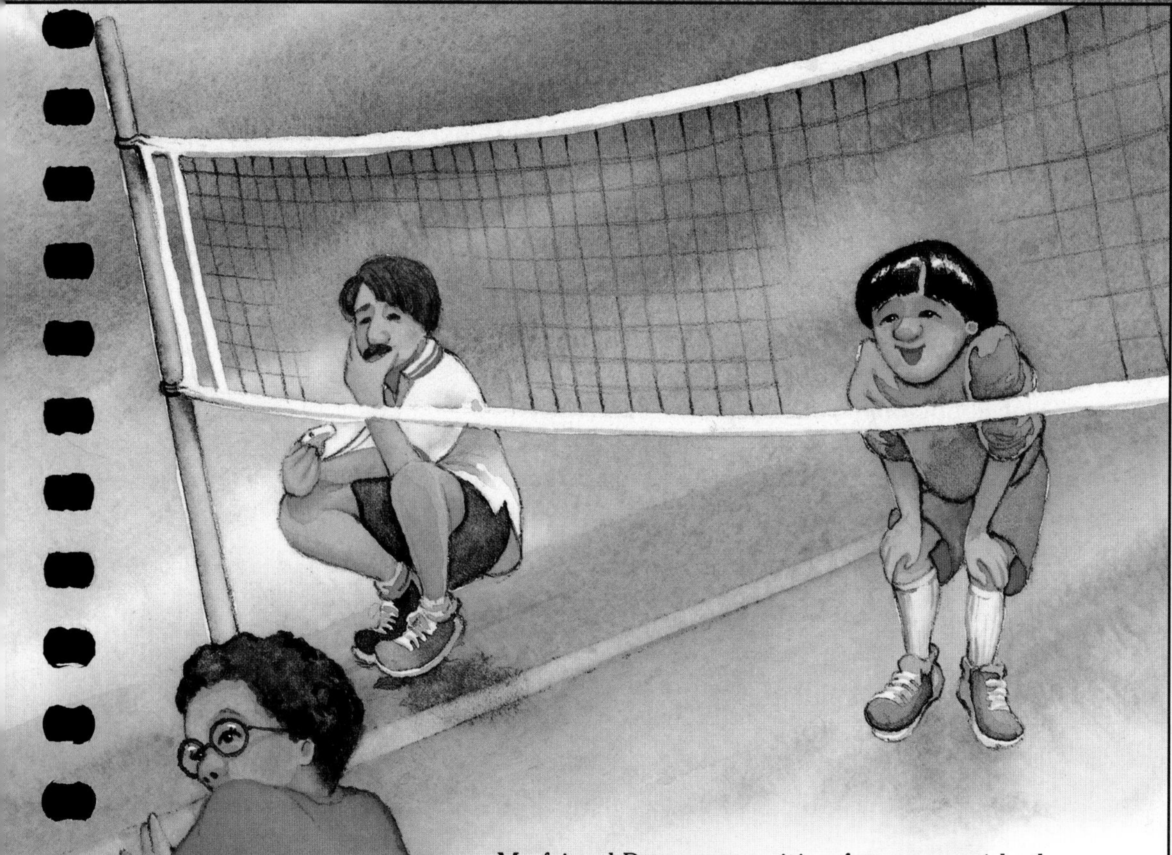

My friend Dave was waiting for me outside the gym door. "Did Mr. Braden ask you to join the team?" he asked.

I nodded. "I told him I was busy."

"You're a lot better than I am," said Dave as we got books from our lockers. "I wish you'd join. We need good servers."

Our next class was math, but it was hard to keep my mind on fractions and percentages. I kept thinking about how good it felt to hit that ball and see it sail over the net. Somehow I managed a spin on the ball that made it hard to hit back.

I'd have loved to say yes to Mr. Braden, but I couldn't afford to. I needed that paper route—or rather, my mom and I *both* needed it. We lived alone in a basement apartment about three blocks from school, and Mom worked at the Cramer Clothing

2

49

Teacher Tip During reading, encourage discussion of possible solutions to the main character's time conflict. Have students reflect on how the solutions will affect the parties to whom the main character feels responsible.

Comprehension Skills

Author's Point of View

Introduce students to the concept of *author's point of view*. Point out that this refers to the kind of narrator that the writer uses to tell the story. In a *first-person narrative*, the story is told by a character in the story. In a *third-person narrative*, the story is told by someone outside of the story.

- "In gym class on Monday, *we* started volleyball, and *I* hit seven straight serves . . ." (page 48)
- "*My* friend Dave was waiting for *me* outside the gym door." (page 49)

Explain that these examples show that this story is being told from a first-person point of view. A third-person point of view would have used the words *he* and *his*, instead of *I* and *my*. Have students find other examples that show this story is being narrated in the first person.

Point out that the reader will learn the most about what Kyle (the narrator) thinks, feels, and does. Knowing whose point of view is being expressed helps the reader understand the story's message.

Author's Point of View

2 Reading and Responding

Comprehension Strategies

Modeling

3 Making Connections *Good readers make connections between what they are reading and what they already know. We should stop and see if we can connect with why Kyle feels so upset. I know just how he feels! There have been times in my life when I've had to give up doing something fun because I'd already promised to do something else. How do you connect with Kyle?*

Modeling

4 Confirming Predictions *Nobody seems to understand why Kyle isn't joining the team. And Kyle hasn't explained things to Mr. Braden yet like I predicted he would. I think that Kyle is going to make everyone so angry at him that they won't want him to join the team at all. What do you think? (This prediction is confirmed on page 52.)*

Factory sewing winter jackets. She didn't earn that much money, and most months her whole salary went for food and rent. Any clothing or school supplies had to come out of what I earned delivering papers. That's why I'd taken on the second route, but there still wasn't any money to spare.

The next day in gym class, Mr. Braden watched me again, and when class ended, he called out loudly, "Think about joining the team, Kyle."

Everyone heard him, and soon several other boys started trying to persuade me. "We haven't got any strong servers," said Jason. "Come on and help us out."

"I bet you could learn to spike the ball," said Billy. "You're tall enough."

They didn't seem to hear me when I mentioned my paper routes.

50

Word Knowledge

started, spike, spirit

Students can use the skills they learned in the Word Knowledge section of this lesson to read these words. Remind students of this if they have difficulty reading these words.

Meeting Individual Needs

Intervention

Predicting Have the students keep a list of the main ideas as they read. Then they can refer to them as they make and revise predictions.

Teacher Tip Tell the students that predicting will help them focus on what they are reading. Remind them to make predictions and to check as they read to see if the predictions come true.

"We finish at 5:15," Jason persisted.

"I'm sorry!" I said. "I can't make the practices." It wouldn't have been so bad if I didn't *want* to play on the team.

"Volleyball season only lasts about two months, you know," said one.

"Where's your school spirit?" asked another.

"Leave me alone!" I finally snapped.

I decided I'd have to see Mr. Braden and tell him the truth—that I couldn't *afford* to play volleyball. But that night I found he'd phoned my mother. I knew right away something was up, but she didn't say anything until we'd finished our spaghetti.

"Your gym teacher called," she said then. "He says he wants you on the volleyball team, but you turned him down."

"Did he tell you the practice times?" I said sharply.

"Yes."

"Then you know why I said no."

Mom sighed. "I told him about the paper routes. He said the practices are over by 5:15."

"My papers have to be delivered by then," I reminded her. "And when there are games, they'll play later than that." I knew my voice was shrill, but I couldn't help it. Everyone was pushing me to do something I already wanted to do, but *couldn't*.

But Mom didn't quit. I guess she knew how much I really wanted to play. "Maybe you could get someone else to deliver the papers on those nights."

51

Meeting Individual Needs

Intervention

Author's Point of View Have students identify sentences, other than dialogue, which show that the story is told from the first-person point of view. Have the students indicate the clue words (*I*, *me*, *our*, and so on). Have the students tell what they have learned about the narrator.

Challenge

Author's Point of View Have students who understand this concept and could benefit from extended practice complete **Challenge,** page 14.

Reteach

Author's Point of View Have students who need additional instruction and practice with this concept complete **Reteach,** pages 23–24.

Comprehension Skills

Author's Point of View

For additional practice with author's viewpoint, ask the students to complete *Reading and Writing Workbook* pages 23–24.

Name _____ Date _____

Author's Point of View

Juggling

Focus Writers must decide from whose **point of view** they will tell a story.

- Stories told through the eyes of a character in the story are in the **first-person** point of view. A first-person narrator uses words such as *I, me, we, us, our,* and *my.*
- Stories told through the eyes of an outside storyteller are in the **third-person** point of view. A third-person narrator uses words such as *he, she, him, her, them, theirs, his,* and *hers.*

Practice and Apply Read each paragraph and write whether it is in the first-person or third-person point of view. Then, rewrite the paragraph, changing the point of view.

1. The room was quiet and empty. As Steven entered, he could not help but feel frightened. However, he was quite curious.

Point of view: third person

New paragraph: Paragraph should be rewritten from the first-person point of view.

Reading and Writing Workbook • *Author's Point of View*   23

Author's Point of View *(continued)*

2. Last week a new girl moved to our block. At first, we didn't like her too much. Then we let us ride her new mountain bike. We changed our minds about her.

Point of view: first person

New paragraph: Paragraph should be written from the third-person point of view.

3. "Never in my wildest dreams did I expect to see you here!" shouted Andy in surprise. I just stood up and smiled. It was good to see Andy after so many months.

Point of view: first person

New paragraph: Paragraph should be written from the third-person point of view.

24   *Author's Point of View* • Reading and Writing Workbook

Reading and Writing Workbook pp. 23–24

② Reading and Responding

Comprehension Strategies

Modeling

❺ Confirming Predictions *I knew that Kyle should explain to Mr. Braden why he couldn't play on the team, but I didn't predict that Mr. Braden would come up with a solution to the problem.*

Discussing Strategy Use

After they have read the selection, have students share any problems they encountered and tell what strategies they used to solve them. Then have them answer the following questions. If they answer "no" to any of the questions, have them reread part of the selection to find the answer.

- Did they ask themselves questions and check whether the answers were in the story?

- Did they make predictions and then check to see if they came true?

- Were they able to find connections between this story and experiences they have had in their own lives?

Make sure that students explain how using the strategies helped them understand the selection better and how they read effectively to find answers to the questions they asked as they set purposes.

Word Knowledge

setups, anything

Students can use the skills they learned in the Word Knowledge section of this lesson to read these words. Remind students of this if they have difficulty reading these words.

"I'd have to pay someone nearly twenty dollars a week to do both routes three times," I said. Abruptly, I shoved my chair back from the table and stamped into my room. I flung myself on the bed and I didn't go out to help Mom with the dishes, either.

The next day in gym class, I <u>deliberately</u> hit all my serves low into the net and I messed up several setups, too. I saw Mr. Braden looking at me in a funny way, but he didn't say anything then. I kept away from Dave all day and ignored the other boys from the team.

At 3:30 I grabbed my homework from my locker and was just heading out the door when my name was called on the intercom. "Kyle Kreerson, please report to Mr. Braden's office."

I thought about ignoring the announcement, but I didn't want to get into trouble. When I reached the office, I saw that Dave was already there. I didn't give Mr. Braden time to speak. I just started right in. "Mr. Braden," I said, "I'm sorry I can't join your team. Will you please stop asking me about it? And ask the other guys to stop <u>pestering</u> me? I'd join if I could. But I *can't!* O.K.?!"

52

Meeting Individual Needs

ESL

Predicting Provide an opportunity for informal conversational practice. Pair English-language learners with native English speakers. Have them compare their predictions with what actually happens in the story.

Teacher Tip Reread the selection with students who had difficulty understanding it. Continue modeling and prompting the use of strategies and skills as you reread.

Nobody spoke for a minute, and then Mr. Braden took a deep breath. His face was red, almost like his hair. "Kyle," he said, "I understand. I'm sorry to <u>pressure</u> you, but I called you here to suggest something. Maybe *I* can do the juggling, instead of you."

"What do you mean?"

"As you know, Miss Foxon coaches the girls' team. Right now, they practice after us, but she's offered to trade practice times. That would start our practices at 5:15."

"I'm not finished with my routes by then," I said sharply.

"If you had some help, you could be, right? Dave is offering to help you."

"I can't afford to pay him," I insisted.

"I don't want to be paid," Dave said.

"Then why do it?"

Dave shrugged. "Because I want to. Because I want you on the team. And because you're my friend."

"Enough reasons?" asked Mr. Braden.

I looked at them both for a moment and I felt good for the first time in four days. "When do we start?" I smiled. **5**

53

Teacher Tip After reading, discuss how cooperation resolved the competition between Kyle's various responsibilities.

Assessment

✓ **Formal** To assess students' reading comprehension, have them complete *Comprehension and Writing Assessment,* pages 11–12.

Comprehension Skills

Discussing the Selection

Following the reading, engage the students in a discussion of the selection. Using the *handing-off process* will help the students take responsibility for the discussion. In addition to the following questions, have them revisit those asked when they set purposes before reading.

■ How did Kyle help his family? (*He made money delivering papers.*)

■ How did the girls' team cooperate so that Kyle could play volleyball? (*They switched practice times with the boys' team.*)

■ Give other examples of how characters in this story worked together. (*Answers will vary but may include that Dave helped out on Kyle's paper route.*)

■ How has this selection connected with your knowledge of the unit theme? (*Answers will vary—students should compare/contrast examples of cooperation and competition from this selection with their own experiences or past reading and use these connections to make a general statement about the unit theme.*)

During this time, have the students return to the clues and problems that they noted on the transparency before reading. Let the students decide which items deserve further discussion.

Having the children "hand off" the discussion to other students instead of the teacher encourages them to retain complete control of the discussion and to become more actively involved in the learning process. When a student finishes his or her comments, that student should choose (hand off the discussion to) the next speaker.

② Reading and Responding

Meet the Illustrator

After the students read the information about Daniel Powers, discuss the following questions with them.

What do you think Daniel Powers teaches the children in the schools of Zuñi Pueblo? *(Possible answer: The book doesn't say what he teaches them, but it probably has to do with art. Maybe he goes into the schools as a special speaker, because he only goes there a couple of times each year.)*

After reading the titles of other books he has illustrated, what do you think are his favorite things to illustrate? *(Possible answer: From the book titles, it sounds as if some of the other stories he has illustrated may have to do with things in nature. It would make sense if he enjoyed doing nature illustrations because one of his favorite hobbies is to go hiking with his wife.)*

Juggling

Meet the Illustrator

Daniel Powers always loved drawing and painting, but he never went to art school until recently. Mr. Powers lives in the high desert country of New Mexico and enjoys hiking there with his wife and two dogs. A couple of times a year he works with children in the schools of the nearby Zuñi Pueblo. He has illustrated many children's books including *Jiro's Pearl*, *From the Land of the White Birch*, and *Dear Katie, The Volcano is a Girl*.

54

Theme Connections

Think About It

With a small group of classmates, discuss what you have learned about how obligations affect one's ability to cooperate and compete. During discussion, address the following questions.

- How did Kyle's feelings change from the beginning of the story to the end?
- Would you want to have a teammate like Kyle? Why or why not?
- Would you want to have a friend like Kyle? Why or why not?
- Why wasn't Kyle pleased to be asked to join the volleyball team?
- Why did Kyle's mother encourage him to join the team, even though they needed the money from his job?

Record Ideas

In your Writing Journal, write what you have learned about cooperation and competition from the class discussions. Also, record any new questions or ideas that may have arisen from discussion.

Make a List

Does your group cooperate when working on your unit activity? Make a list of:

- the ways you cooperate
- the ways cooperating helps you learn
- other things your group could do to learn more cooperatively

55

Think About It

If necessary, remind students that Kyle put his commitment to his customers and his family ahead of his own desires. Help students to see that Kyle was behaving cooperatively.

Have students join in their small groups to discuss the questions. If necessary, remind them of Kyle's conflicting responsibilities and goals.

Record Ideas

Respond to the questions in students' journals and use their questions as a springboard for further discussion on how cooperation and competition can be complementary.

Make a List

Have students post their lists on the Concept/Question Board. Give them time to read and comment on the lists of other students.

Teacher Tip Make note of students who are not participating in discussions. Meet with them in a small group and explicitly model and review answers to discussion questions. If necessary, reread the selection with the students.

Fine Art

Cooperation and Competition

Viewing the Theme Through Fine Art

Students can use the artworks on these pages to explore the unit theme, Cooperation and Competition, in images rather than words. Encourage them to talk about their impressions of the artworks and how each one might relate to the unit theme Cooperation and Competition.

Below is some background information about each of the artworks. Share with students whatever you feel is appropriate for enhancing students' understanding of the unit concept as well as their enjoyment of each artwork. You may also wish to encourage students to find out more about artists and artistic styles that interest them.

Small Roman Abacus

Calculi or *abaculi* were the common names used for the abacus, an instrument used to make arithmetic calculations. There were originally three types of abaci used by the Romans: a table marked for counters, the primitive chalkboard, and a grooved plate with sliding beads, the last to be developed.

Small Roman Abacus is made of a metal plate, possibly bronze, on which the small disks slide. Each disk is assigned a value, which is determined by its position on the plate. The values of ones, tens, and hundreds are most commonly used.

Footballers

Ruskin Spear (1911–   ) was born in London and studied at the Hammersmith School of Art and the Royal College of Art. He is best known for his still lifes, cityscapes, and stocky figures portrayed in a loosely painted technique.

Cooperation and Competition

FINE Art

Small Roman Abacus. Museo Nazionale Romano Delle Terme, Rome, Italy. Photo: SCALA/Art Resource, NY.

Footballers. **Ruskin Spear.** Private collection. Photo: Christie's Images.

56

Artist Pyramid. Josef Hegenbarth. Oil on canvas. Private collection. Photo: Christie's Images.

Catcher on the Line. Robert Riggs. Oil on canvas. Private collection. Photo: Christie's Images.

57

Footballers portrays three young men who are captured in a moment of jubilation, perhaps after a successful play or game. In England, *football* is the name for soccer. These three men depended on the cooperation of their teammates to successfully compete in the game.

Artist Pyramid

Josef Hegenbarth was born in Kamenice, Germany, in 1884. He began his career as a freelance artist creating cartoonlike illustrations for a variety of magazines. From 1946 to 1949, he was a professor at the Akademie der Bildenden Künste.

Artist Pyramid depicts 17 acrobats working together to form a human pyramid. The acrobats appear to completely trust their teammates. Imagine the teamwork and cooperation that must take place for this type of stunt to be successful.

Catcher on the Line

Robert Riggs (1896–1970) was born in Decatur, Illinois. Dramatic scenes such as circus acts, emergency wards, and prize fights were his favorite subject matter. Although he is best known as a skilled lithographer (a printing technique), he also created several dramatic paintings in oils.

Catcher on the Line reveals the quick action play on the sideline near the dugout. The young boys are ready to catch the ball if the player should miss, as his teammates encourage him on the catch. Notice how the action has been stilled and the viewpoint is from a stadium seat to the left of the catcher.

Responding

Exploring the Theme

Selection Vocabulary

Have students write in their Writing Journals the definitions for words discussed before reading the selection and any other interesting words they clarified while reading. Students should be encouraged to refer to these words throughout the unit as they work on student and writing projects. The words from the selection are:

deliberately	**serves**	**spirit**
juggle	**spare**	

Reading/Writing Connections

Remind students that the conflict in this story was conveyed through the main character's thoughts and feelings. Have them record in their Writing Journals what the main characters in their play think and feel about the conflict they experience.

Artist Pyramid.
Josef Hegenbarth.
Oil on canvas.
Private collection.
Photo: Christie's
Images

Student Anthology, p. 57

View Fine Art

Artist Pyramid by **Josef Hegenbarth** is found on page 57 of the *Student Anthology.* This is a picture of a team of acrobats who are working together to form a pyramid. To carry off this balancing act, the acrobats must have complete trust in each other, and work in total cooperation. Have students discuss how acrobats' cooperation is similar to the cooperation that made it possible for Kyle, in "Juggling," to balance his responsibilities.

Home Connection

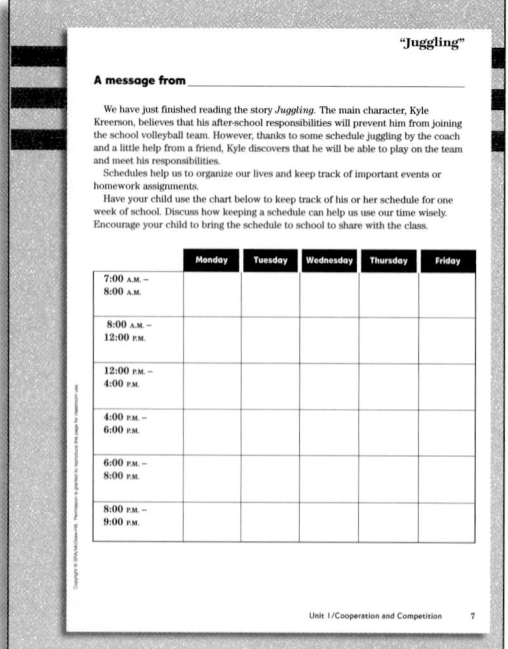

Home Connection p. 7

The class has just finished reading "Juggling," a fiction selection about a boy named Kyle whose teachers and peers cooperate so that he will have time to keep his job and also play on the school volleyball team. An informational letter on "Juggling," in both English and Spanish, can be found in the *Home Connection* guide.

Writing Process

Draft During the *drafting* phase, have students shape their planning notes into a main idea and details. They devote their time and effort to getting words down on paper as quickly and as completely as possible. They will write freely at this phase of the process, organizing sentences into paragraphs. Share these ideas with students before they begin:

- If you don't know how to spell a word, guess at the first letter and leave a space. Later you can look up the spelling in the dictionary.

- Use abbreviations to help you write faster.

- Crossing out is acceptable. It won't interrupt your thoughts the way that erasing will.

- If you can't think of a word or don't know what to say, leave a space. Fill it in later.

- Write on only one side of the page and on every other line so that you will have room to make revisions and so you can see all of your draft at once.

- Keep in mind your purpose and your intended audience.

   Though students should be writing quickly, point out that their finished pieces should be in paragraphs.

Teacher Tip Tell students that this drafting process may be helpful to them in Lesson 4, when they begin writing the scripts for their dramatic plays.

Assessment

✓ **Informal** Take this opportunity to assess students' progress with the writing process by commenting on the entries in their Writing Journals.

Teacher Tip It may help students if you model the drafting process on the chalkboard. Think aloud as you put your ideas into words. Work as fast as you can.
   Leave a blank space in a sentence to show you are having difficulty thinking of the best word. Put parentheses around a word you intend to change. Use abbreviations and invented spelling. Cross out words and sentences, or draw arrows to show where they should be moved.

③ Integrating the Curriculum

Teacher Tip Have students discuss the following questions about the author's purpose in the selection "Juggling."
- If the author's purpose was to inform the reader about the sport of volleyball, how would it be different?
- Would the story have a different main idea?
- Would it have different or more information?
- Would it be written in a different genre or format?

Teacher Tip Have students consider what qualities make texts identifiable as being persuasive. Have them list these qualities and incorporate as many of them as possible into their persuasive writing.

Meeting Individual Needs

Reteach

Identifying Purpose of Text Have students who need additional instruction and practice with this concept complete **Reteach,** pages 25–26.

Challenge

Identifying Purpose of Text Have students who understand this concept and could benefit from extended practice complete **Challenge,** page 15.

Literary Elements

Identifying Purpose of Text

Instruct Provide several copies of daily newspapers for students to examine. Help them identify the purposes of various sections.

- The front page often contains examples of writing to inform. Ask students to find factual information in front-page articles.
- The editorial page probably includes examples of writing to influence or persuade. Have students tell what the writer might feel and what he or she would like the reader to do or think.
- The comics page is an example of writing to entertain. Let students tell why they think people read the comics.

Ask students if they think writing ever combines more than one purpose. For instance, an article on travel could be persuasive as well as informative.

Practice Ask students whether the story "Juggling" informed, persuaded, or entertained them. Could the story have more than one purpose? How would the story differ if the author had a different purpose?

Apply Ask students to select three examples of writing in which each example has a different purpose. Students might search newspapers and magazines for articles, as well as fiction and nonfiction books.

For more practice with identifying the purpose of texts, have students complete **Reading and Writing Workbook** pages 25–26.

Reading and Writing Workbook pp. 25–26

Name _____ Date _____
Identifying Purpose of Text | Juggling

Focus Good readers can identify the **author's purpose**, or reason, for writing a story. Remember, an author can have more than one purpose for writing a story.

> An author may write:
> - **to inform,** or to give an explanation, information, or directions. Textbooks, encyclopedias, and other nonfiction books, such as how-to books, contain informational text.
> - **to entertain,** or to make a reader laugh, feel scared, or otherwise enjoy reading about the characters and situations. Authors write stories, novels, and plays to entertain.
> - **to influence,** or to persuade the reader to do something or think in a certain way. Advertisements and editorials, as well as some nonfiction books, are written to influence or persuade.

Identify If you didn't know anything about the story "Juggling" except its title, what might you think the author's purpose was for writing it? Why?
Answers will vary. Possible answer is shown.
to inform, because it could be about learning how to juggle objects

Reading and Writing Workbook • *Identifying Purpose of Text* 25

Identifying Purpose of Text *(continued)*

Practice Read each passage below. Write the author's purpose and give the reason for your decision.

1. The attic door creaked as Susie opened it. The light was dim, but she could see that cobwebs covered the old furniture and boxes. She approached a large trunk, hoping to find her old doll quickly. All of a sudden—Bang!—the door to the attic slammed shut!
   to entertain; it is a scary story

2. Chop one head of cabbage, two carrots, and a large onion. Place the vegetables in a large pot, cover them with water, and boil them for ten minutes. Reduce the heat and add one can of stewed tomatoes, some salt, pepper, and spices. Simmer for 45 minutes.
   to inform; it tells how to do something

Apply Write a review of "Juggling." Your purpose is to persuade others to read it or not to read it. Answers will vary.

26 *Identifying Purpose of Text* • Reading and Writing Workbook

Spelling

Spelling -*le* Endings

Instruct Have students tell you what they remember about the consonant before the -*le* spelling pattern, taught in Lesson 2. If necessary, remind them that this spelling is found in the unaccented ending syllable of words, such as *article, mumble,* and *staple.* Other spellings of the same sound include -*al,* -*el,* -*il,* and -*ol* (such as in *historical, jewel, pencil,* and *capitol*).

Practice Ask students why the consonant before the -*le* spelling pattern might cause spelling and reading problems. Students may conclude that the words cannot be spelled just by listening to the way they are pronounced. Students may also conclude that this spelling is confusing to readers because it is a closed syllable sound that ends with a vowel instead of a consonant. Have students think of words with the following consonant before -*le* endings: -*ble,* -*dle,* -*gle,* -*ple,* -*tle,* and -*zle* (such as in *paddle, giggle, maple, little,* and *frazzle*).

Apply Have students proofread a few pieces from their **Writing Folders,** looking primarily for spelling errors in words with the -*le,* -*el,* -*al,* -*il,* and -*ol* endings. Suggest that they use a dictionary to double-check their spelling and correct any errors they find. Encourage students to list the words with these endings in their personal dictionaries in their Writing Journals.

 Suggest that students be aware of words with final syllables containing consonants followed by -*le* when they read. They can write down these words, the sentences in which the words appeared, and the texts in the Personal Dictionary section of their Writing Journals.

 Have students look for correct spelling of the consonant before -*le* in their persuasive papers and unit activities.

Meeting Individual Needs

ESL

Peer Tutoring Pair English-language learners with native English speakers to increase the English input they receive. Have the partners work together to brainstorm words that coincide with the spelling lesson.

Challenge

Spelling -*le* Endings Because the final syllable spellings -*le* and -*el* are easily confused, dictate a list of words ending in these letters (-*el* words include *jewel, angel, kernel, shovel, bushel, level,* and *label*).

Let the students see how many they can spell correctly. Have them write the words they misspelled in the Personal Dictionary section of their Writing Journals.

Spelling -*le* Endings
INTRODUCED: Unit 1, Lesson 2
REVIEWED: Unit 1, Lesson 3
Unit 3, Lesson 5

Assessment

✓ **Formal** To assess students' understanding of this concept, have them complete **Skills Assessment** page 6.

3 Integrating the Curriculum

Teacher Tip Remind students to check their persuasive papers and unit activities for correct use of pronouns.

Meeting Individual Needs

Reteach

Pronouns Have students who need additional instruction and practice with this concept complete **Reteach,** pages 27–28.

Challenge

Pronouns Write down sentences containing object pronouns and then scramble the order of the words. Read aloud or write the scrambled sentences on the chalkboard and have students unscramble the sentences and write the words in the correct order. Have students who can benefit from extended practice of this concept complete **Challenge,** page 16.

Skills Strand

Pronouns

INTRODUCED: Unit 1, Lesson 3
REVIEWED: Unit 2, Lesson 2
Unit 4, Lesson 2

Grammar, Usage, and Mechanics

Pronouns

Instruct Prompt students to tell you that the doer of the action in a sentence is the subject. Tell students that when a pronoun is the subject of a sentence, it is in the *nominative case.* Nominative case pronouns include *I, you, he, she, it, we,* and *they.* Help students identify that *He* is the subject or the doer of the action in this sentence: *He plays baseball after school.*

Prompt students to tell you that the direct object of a sentence can be the receiver of the action of the verb, or it can be the noun following the preposition in a prepositional phrase. Tell students that when a pronoun is the direct object, it is in the *objective case.* Objective case pronouns include *me, you, him, her, it, us,* and *them.* Help students identify that *me* is the direct object, or the receiver of the action of the verb in both of these sentences: *Sarah told me about the race. Andy went with me.*

Practice Have students find examples of nominative and objective case pronouns in "Juggling." Tell each student to read aloud a sentence with a nominative or objective case pronoun and explain whether the pronoun is the doer or receiver of the action.

Apply For additional practice, have students complete **Reading and Writing Workbook** pages 27–28.

Reading and Writing Workbook pp. 27–28

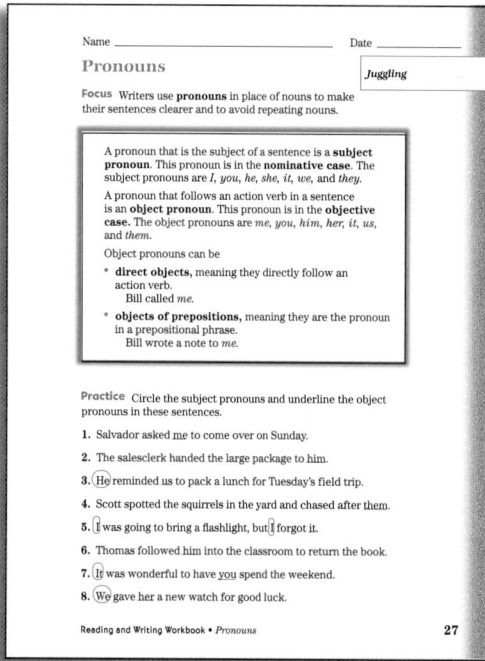

Listening/Speaking/Viewing

Recognizing and Analyzing Story Settings

To help students focus on the images that help to set the time and place of a story, tell them that they are going to do four quick sketches for "*Juggling.*" Give students an opportunity to review the story. Then ask them to close their books and listen while you read these lines containing information about the setting of the story:

- Page 48, paragraph 1: "In gym class on Monday we started volleyball . . . ."

- Page 49, paragraph 1: "My friend Dave was waiting for me outside the gym door."

- Page 49, paragraph 5: "We lived alone in a basement apartment about three blocks from school . . . ."

- Page 53, paragraph 3: "At 3:30 I grabbed my homework from my locker and was just heading out the door . . . ."

After you read each passage, have students open their eyes and make a sketch of the setting that was described. Encourage students to share their sketches. What clues in the drawings help them identify the story settings?

Teacher Tip To encourage class participation by all students, ask the class to help you generate a list of rules that emphasize listening respectfully and asking thoughtful questions (for example, look at the speaker, be quiet when the speaker is talking, etc.).

3 Integrating the Curriculum

Study and Research

Interviewing

Instruct Ask students what they know about interviewing and whether they have ever conducted any interviews. If necessary, tell students that interviewing involves asking a person questions and writing down or tape-recording his or her opinions, information, or personal accounts.

Write these rules for interviewing on the chalkboard and discuss them:

1. Contact the person, ask for permission to conduct an interview, and explain the reason for the interview.
2. Think of questions to ask that will help you get the information you need.
3. Write down your questions in the order you want to ask them.
4. Be polite.
5. Listen carefully.
6. Take notes as the person answers your questions, even if you use a tape recorder.
7. Be polite after the interview, too.
8. Read your notes as soon after the interview as possible.

Practice Have students imagine that they are reporters for the school newspaper who will interview Kyle Kreerson after a winning volleyball season. Tell them to concentrate on the questions they want to ask Kyle, particularly about cooperation and competition. Allow time for students to present their questions and discuss them. After the discussion, ask students whether or not they want to change or add any questions.

Apply Have students conduct interviews with someone they know, such as a family member, a friend, or a schoolmate. Suggest they find out what that person's opinion is about a subject or learn about a feat he or she has accomplished.

For more practice with interviewing, have students complete *Inquiry Journal* pages 12–13.

Inquiry Journal pp. 12–13

Across the Curriculum

 ## Social Studies

Money for a Good Cause

Purpose

To help students learn about the economics of earning and spending money

Procedure

Encourage students to think about different ways they could raise funds for a local charity. Emphasize that everyone in the class must participate in the discussion and they will vote on the charity to which they would like to donate their money.

- Ask the students to think about and then nominate charities in which they have an interest. Encourage them to tell the rest of the class about the charity.

- After everyone has made a nomination, discuss with the students the best way to decide which charity or charities to select. Focus on class cooperation and compromise.

- Then let students brainstorm different fund-raising events. Remind students to consider the potential costs of each event. For instance, holding a car wash would require a location, soap and other cleaners, rags, a supply of water, and workers. They would also have to advertise the event.

- After discussing the pros and cons of all the events, ask the students to work together to decide on the fund-raising event that has the most potential for making money.

- If it's feasible, you may want to let the students adopt a charity and hold a fund-raising event.

 ## Physical Education

Designing New Games

Purpose

To develop students' understanding of cooperation and competition by designing a new game

Procedure

Invite students to create new games based on familiar games. Have students work together in small groups of three to five students.

- Tell the groups to choose a familiar game and create a variation on it by changing the rules or varying the equipment in some way. For instance, they may invent a version of volleyball that is played with the feet and without a net.

- Then the groups should design and illustrate a set of instructions for their new game. Depending on the game, they may also need to design a new game board and game pieces.

- Let the groups recruit "players," who will read the instructions to see if they are clear and give their opinion of the new game.

- The groups may need to refine their games based on the players' feedback.

- When the new games are finished, have groups explain their new games to the class.

- If possible, have students try playing some of the games they have invented.

Selection Summary

Genre: Realistic Fiction

Gao Mai, a young girl living in a small Taiwanese city, is intent on winning a class contest. The author takes us through her perceptions and feelings on the day of the contest. What will Gao Mai do if her best friend wins? What if neither of them wins? Friendships, family, and personal expectations, as well as handling feelings of disappointment, anxiety, and competition, are explored in this thoughtful story.

About the Author

Priscilla Wu's first book is *The Abacus Contest.* She lives in Reno, Nevada, with her family. Wu has been a Montessori teacher and recently completed graduate course work in counseling and marriage therapy at the University of Nevada.

Students can read more about Priscilla Wu on page 64 of the ***Student Anthology.***

About the Illustrator

Yoshi Miyake was born in Tokyo and educated as a scientist. A correspondence course led to her interest in art. Ms. Miyake went on to study at the American Academy of Art in Chicago, where she now lives.

Students can read more about Yoshi Miyake on page 64 of the ***Student Anthology.***

Exploring the Theme

Selection Concepts

"The Abacus Contest" is realistic fiction about a young girl's competitive approach to a contest that she lost the previous year. The key concepts explored are:

- Competition sometimes causes feelings of anxiety.
- Competition can be a stimulating challenge.
- Competitions affect individuals differently.

Check the Reading link of the **SRA** Web page for links to theme-related Websites. **http://www.sra4kids.com**

Exploration Activity Tips

Before Reading, initiate a discussion about how competitions make students feel both mentally and physically. Ask them what kinds of things they want from a competition.

During Reading, have students discuss ways the author allows readers to understand what kind of people the characters are, through their reactions to story events.

After Reading, have students discuss how they act and feel when they are highly anxious. Encourage them to think of ways they can incorporate realistic emotions in their unit activities. Have the students update the Concept/Question Board with their thoughts and ideas.

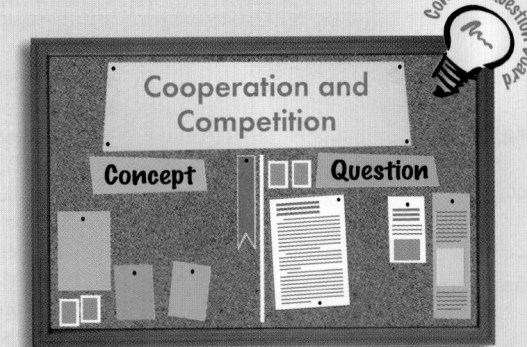

Unit I Exploration Management

Lesson 1	Discuss experiences with cooperation and competition. Generate ideas for dramatic play.
Lesson 2	Students give and receive feedback on their unit activity ideas, and begin to work in groups on the storyboards for their plays.
Lesson 3	Students complete their storyboards and share them with other groups, then revise the storyboards based on feedback.
Lesson 4 **The Abacus Contest**	**Collaborative Exploration** **Students begin group work on writing plays in script format. They agree on director and actor roles and begin rehearsals.** **Supplementary Activity** **Students make ongoing revisions to their scripts as they rehearse. Model and help students compose meaningful dialogue.**
Lesson 5	Students complete the final draft of their scripts and plan their dress rehearsals.
Lesson 6	Students complete play rehearsals and perform their plays. They put scripts in a class anthology and prepare a title page and table of contents.

Lesson Planner

Suggested Pacing: 3–5 days	DAY 1	DAY 2
	DAY 1	DAY 2

Part 1 — Preparing to Read

Materials
- Student Anthology, pp. 58–65
- Transparencies 4, 44

DAY 1

Word Knowledge
- Reading the Words and Sentences, p. 58G
- Developing Oral Language, p. 58G

Build Background, p. 58H

Preview and Prepare, p. 58I

Selection Vocabulary, p. 58I
drills, honored, mischievous, booklets, collided, accuracy

DAY 2

Preview and Prepare, p. 58I
- Review Transparency 44

Part 2 — Reading and Responding

Materials
- Student Anthology, pp. 58–65
- Teacher Observation Log
- Reading and Writing Workbook, pp. 29–30
- Inquiry Journal, p. 7
- Home Connection, p. 9

DAY 1

Student Anthology, pp. 58–65

Comprehension Strategies
- Predicting, pp. 58, 62
- Summarizing, p. 58
- Clarifying, p. 60

Discussing Strategy Use, p. 62

DAY 2

Student Anthology, pp. 58–65

Comprehension Skills
- ✓ Sequence, pp. 59, 61
- ✓ Discussing the Selection, p. 63

Exploring the Theme
- Selection Vocabulary, p. 65A
drills, honored, mischievous, booklets, collided, accuracy

Part 3 — Integrating the Curriculum

Materials
- Student Anthology, pp. 58–65
- Teacher Observation Log
- Reading and Writing Workbook, pp. 31–34
- Transparencies 50, 51
- Inquiry Journal, p. 14

DAY 1

Writing
- Revising a Paper, p. 65C

Literary Elements
- ✓ Recognizing and Analyzing Plot and Problem Resolution, p. 65E

DAY 2

Writing Process
- Revise, p. 65D

Spelling
- ✓ Inflectional Endings, p. 65F

Independent Work Time

Materials
- Reteach, pp. 29–34
- ESL Supplement
- Challenge, pp. 17–19
- Intervention Guide
- Research CD-ROM
- Listening Library Audiocassette

Writing Process Continued
ESL
- Word Meaning, p. 58G

Intervention
- Word Knowledge, p. 58G

Unit Project
- Work on Script
- Begin Rehearsals

Writing Process Continued
Reteach
- ✓ Sequence, *Reteach*, pp. 29–30

ESL
- Vocabulary, p. 58J

Challenge
- ✓ Sequence, *Challenge*, p. 17

Intervention
- Comprehension, p. 58

Unit Project Continued

✓ Informal **Assessment Available**   ✓ Formal **Assessment Available**

DAY 2 continued	DAY 3	
DAY 3	**DAY 4**	**DAY 5**
General Review	**General Review**	**Review Word Knowledge**
Student Anthology, pp. 58–65 **Theme Connections** ■ Think About It, p. 65 ■ Draw a Stick Figure, p. 65	**Student Anthology, pp. 58–65** **Exploring the Theme** ■ Reading/Writing Connections, p. 65A ■ View Fine Art, p. 65A ■ Supporting Student Explorations, p. 65B	**Student Anthology, pp. 58–65** ■ Review Selection ■ Complete Discussion ■ Reread Selection in Pairs **Home Connection, p. 65A** ■ Discuss "The Abacus Contest" ■ Write a paragraph
Writing Process Continued **Grammar, Usage, and Mechanics** ✓■ Complete Sentences, p. 65G **Listening/Speaking/Viewing** ■ Making Connections, p. 65H	**Writing Process Continued** **Study and Research** ■ Using Text Organizers, p. 65I	**Across the Curriculum** **Art** ■ Winning Certificates, p. 65J **Math** ■ Math Competition, p. 65J
Writing Process Continued **Reteach** ✓■ Spelling Inflectional Endings, *Reteach*, pp. 31–32 **ESL** ■ Conversational Practice, p. 65H **Challenge** ✓■ Spelling Inflectional Endings, *Challenge*, p. 18 **Unit Project Continued**	**Writing Process Continued** **Reteach** ✓■ Complete Sentences, *Reteach*, pp. 33–34 **Challenge** ✓■ Complete Sentences, *Challenge*, p. 19 **Unit Project Continued**	**Writing Process Continued** **Unit Project Continued**

Meeting Individual Needs
Independent Work Time

Preparing to Read

Meeting Individual Needs

ESL
- Word Meaning, p. 58G
- Vocabulary, p. 58J

Intervention
- Word Knowledge, p. 58G

Reading and Responding

Meeting Individual Needs

Reteach
- Sequence, *Reteach*, pp. 29–30

ESL
- Summing Up and Asking Questions, p. 62

Challenge
- Sequence, *Challenge*, p. 17

Intervention
- Comprehension, p. 58
- Sequence, p. 59
- Clarifying, p. 60

Integrating the Curriculum

Meeting Individual Needs

Reteach
- Spelling Inflectional Endings, *Reteach*, pp. 31–32
- Complete Sentences, *Reteach*, pp. 33–34

ESL
- Conversational Practice, p. 65H

Challenge
- Spelling Inflectional Endings, *Challenge*, p. 18
- Complete Sentences, *Challenge*, p. 19

Formal Assessment Options

Use these assessment pages along with your informal observations to gauge student progress.

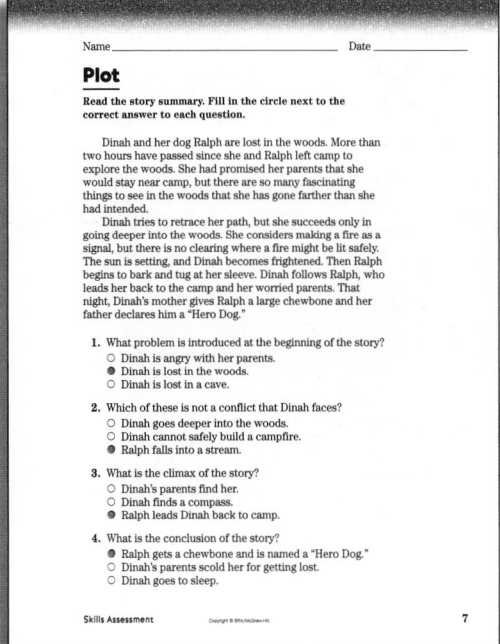

Skills Assessment, p. 7

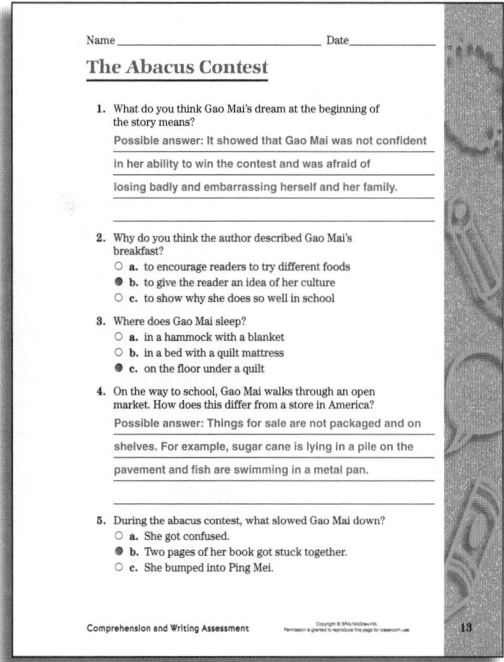

Comprehension and Writing Assessment, p. 13

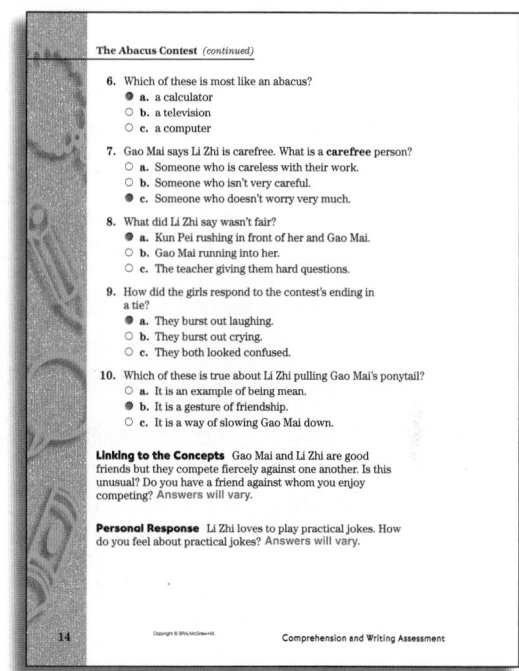

Comprehension and Writing Assessment, p. 14

① Preparing to Read

Meeting Individual Needs

ESL

Word Meaning Make sure the English-language learners understand the meanings of the words before they do the exercises. Refer to Unit 1, Lesson 4, of the **ESL Supplement** for specific suggestions.

Intervention

Word Knowledge Have students go through their mathematics textbooks for more mathematical words. Also ask them to use the index to find references to the mathematical words listed in Line 1. For students who need more help, see Unit 1, Lesson 4, of the **Intervention Guide.**

Word Knowledge

Reading the Words and Sentences

Write each word and sentence on the chalkboard. Have students read each word together. After all the words have been read, have students read each sentence in natural phrases or chunks. Use the suggestions in About the Words to discuss the different features of the listed words.

Line 1:	addition subtraction multiplication division
Line 2:	bounce loud round
Line 3:	teacher bead breathing
Sentence 1:	The teacher showed the students how to do subtraction.
Sentence 2:	The multiplication game is played with a round bead and a game board.
Sentence 3:	The players are breathing hard as they bounce the ball.

About the Words

- Line 1 contains content-area words dealing with mathematics. Point out that each of the words contains a root word that becomes a noun when *-tion* or *-sion* is added.

- The words in Line 2 have the /ow/ sound, as in cow, spelled *ou*. Invite students to think of other words with this spelling of the /ow/ sound.

- In Line 3, the words focus on Long e spelled *ea*. Invite students to think of other words with this spelling of the Long e sound.

Developing Oral Language

To review the words, have students do one or both of the following activities:

- On the chalkboard, list some of the words from Lines 1–3. Create a class paragraph using the words from the list. Start by having a student choose a word and use it in a sentence. Then have another student create a related sentence using another word from the list. Continue the activity to see how many words from the list the students can use to create a cohesive paragraph.

- Write several words from Lines 1–3 on the chalkboard. Invite students to come to the chalkboard and draw a picture clue showing one of the words. The class should then guess which word is being depicted.

Build Background

Activate Prior Knowledge

Have students check the Concept/Question Board to refresh their memories about cooperation and competition. Discuss the following with students to find out what they already know about the selection and have already learned about the unit theme. Tell students to use their prior knowledge to help them comprehend the selection they are about to read.

■ Have students share what they know about using an abacus.

■ Ask students whether they are familiar with the story they are about to read, and if so, to tell a little about it. Remind students, however, not to give away the ending of the selection.

■ Have students share other stories that involve timed contests or intense competition.

Background Information

The following information may help the students better understand the selection they are about to read.

■ An abacus is a device usually made of beads strung on wires. If possible, bring one to class and allow the students to handle it. It is sometimes used in Asian countries such as Taiwan, China, and Japan to add and subtract. Ask volunteers to point out these countries on a world map or globe.

■ Discuss the word *honor*, and talk about the importance of this in regard to family.

■ The game *jian zhi* seems similar to Hacky Sack, a game played with a small leather beanbag in the United States. Have a few students research *jian zhi* to find out the rules and its origin. Have them summarize their findings in a report for the class and then demonstrate how the game is played.

■ Be aware that Gao Mai's motivation to succeed may be a sensitive issue in your classroom. Emphasize that this story is a positive illustration of how people who are in competition with each other can maintain their friendship.

Teacher Tip Remind students that stories typically center on the problem or goal of main characters and that their attempts to solve the problem or achieve the goal are often stymied. By the end of the standard story, however, the main characters typically overcome the blocks and achieve their goal.

Writing Journal Tell students that after reading the selection, they will be jotting down in their Writing Journals their reactions to the story, as well as any ideas they may have for using rivalry in a story.

1 Preparing to Read

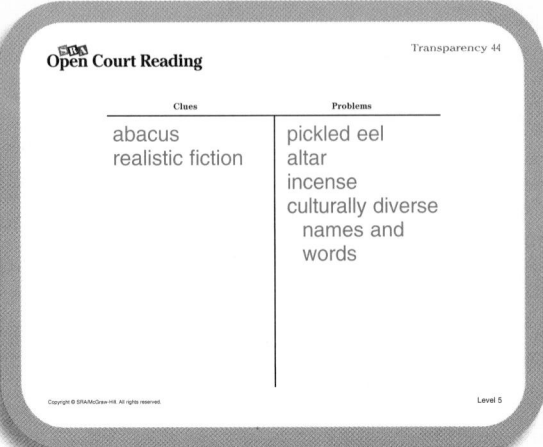

Transparency 44

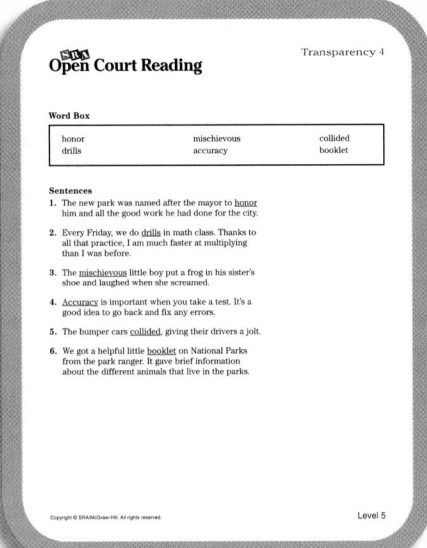

Transparency 4

Preview and Prepare

Browse

■ Have a volunteer read the title and author's and illustrator's names aloud. Have students share what they know about fiction.

■ Because this is a fiction selection, have students browse through the first half of the story. Have them look for words and phrases that connect to what they already know. Record these in the Clues column on **Transparency 44.** Discuss with students what they think this story might have to do with cooperation and competition.

■ Encourage students to ask questions as they browse. Have them identify any problems they notice while reading and record them in the Problems column.

Set Purposes

As they read, have students think about friendship in competitive situations and how this can teach them new lessons.

Selection Vocabulary

As students study vocabulary, they will use context clues, word structure, and apposition to clarify these and additional unfamiliar words.

Display **Transparency 4** before reading the selection to introduce and discuss the following words and their meanings.

drills: exercises to increase your mental or physical skills (page 59)

hon•ored: showed respect (page 59)

mis•chie•vous: full of pranks and teasing fun (page 60)

book•lets: small books, usually with a paper cover (page 60)

col•lid•ed: crashed (page 61)

ac•cur•a•cy: being without mistakes (page 63)

Have students read the words in the Word Box on **Transparency 4.** Help students decode multisyllabic words by reading them syllable by syllable. If the word is not decodable, give the students the pronunciation.

Have students read the sentences on **Transparency 4** to determine the meaning of the underlined words. Remind them to use clues in the sentences and structural clues to figure out the meaning. See the teacher tip on the left for information on how the words in each sentence can be defined.

Reading Recommendations

Your first reading of the selection should focus on developing the reading strategies found to the left of the reduced pages. We recommend that the students revisit the selection, rereading sections or the entire selection as a way to enhance their understanding and appreciation of the text. During rereading, they should focus on the comprehension skills, found to the right of the reduced pages.

Oral Reading

Due to the unfamiliar word pronunciations in this selection, oral reading is recommended. For your convenience, Teacher Tips on the pronunciations of foreign words and names occurring in the selection are featured beside and below the reduced **Student Anthology** pages in the **Teacher's Edition.** As students read aloud, have them read expressively, at an appropriate pace, in natural phrases and chunks. By reading the selection with fluency, students will demonstrate an understanding of the text and an ability to engage the listeners in an effective manner. If students encounter difficulties, have them use the reading strategies below or refer to the Blending Procedure (Program Appendix 15–16).

Using Reading Strategies

Reading strategy instruction allows students to become aware of how good readers read. Good readers constantly check their understanding as they are reading and ask themselves questions. In addition, skilled readers recognize when they are having problems and stop to use various reading strategies to help them make sense of what they are reading.

During the reading of "The Abacus Contest," you will model the use of the following reading strategies:

- Summarizing
- Clarifying
- Predicting

Before reading, have students share how they have used these strategies in the past and any tips they can give each other on their use.

Building Comprehension Skills

Revisiting or rereading a selection allows students to apply skills that give them a more complete understanding of the text. Some follow-up comprehension skills, such as *Main Idea and Details* and *Compare and Contrast*, help students organize information. Others, such as *Author's Purpose*, *Making Inferences*, and *Drawing Conclusions*, lead to deeper understanding—to "reading between the lines," as mature readers do. In this selection, students will apply the comprehension skill *Sequence*.

Teacher Tip Have students who may need extra help reading "The Abacus Contest" reread the selection using the *Listening Library Audiocassette.*

Meeting Individual Needs

ESL

Vocabulary Check that English-language learners know the meanings of idioms and more difficult vocabulary in the story, including *abacus, dried meat, pickled cucumber, incense, burlap, exercises, exchanging, bragged,* and *certificates.* More information can be found in Unit 1, Lesson 4, of the *ESL Supplement.*

Teacher Tip By this time in the fifth grade, good readers should be reading approximately 126 words per minute with fluency and expression. The only way to gain fluency is through practice. As explained in Reading Recommendations, have students reread all or part of the selection to you and to each other during class or Independent Work Time to focus on the comprehension skills and to build fluency.

② Reading and Responding

Read pages 58–65.

Comprehension Strategies

Modeling

❶ Predicting *Good readers make predictions based on their reading and what they know, and confirm or revise their predictions as they go. What a nightmare! Gao Mai must be afraid that Li Zhi will be angry with her for competing against her in the abacus contest. I predict that Li Zhi will not be angry with Gao Mai because they have always been friends. What do you predict? (This prediction is confirmed on page 62.)*

Modeling

❷ Summarizing *Let's stop and summarize what we've just read to help us remember what happened and who everyone is. Let's see, Gao Mai woke up from a bad dream the day of the abacus contest at school. Her father and mother reminded her that she has improved since last year when Gao Mai's best friend, Li Zhi, won. Can anyone add to this summary?*

Word Knowledge

bounced, around, mouth

Students can use the skills they learned in the Word Knowledge section of this lesson to read these words. Remind students of this if they have difficulty reading these words.

Reading Recommendation

ORAL · CHORAL · SILENT

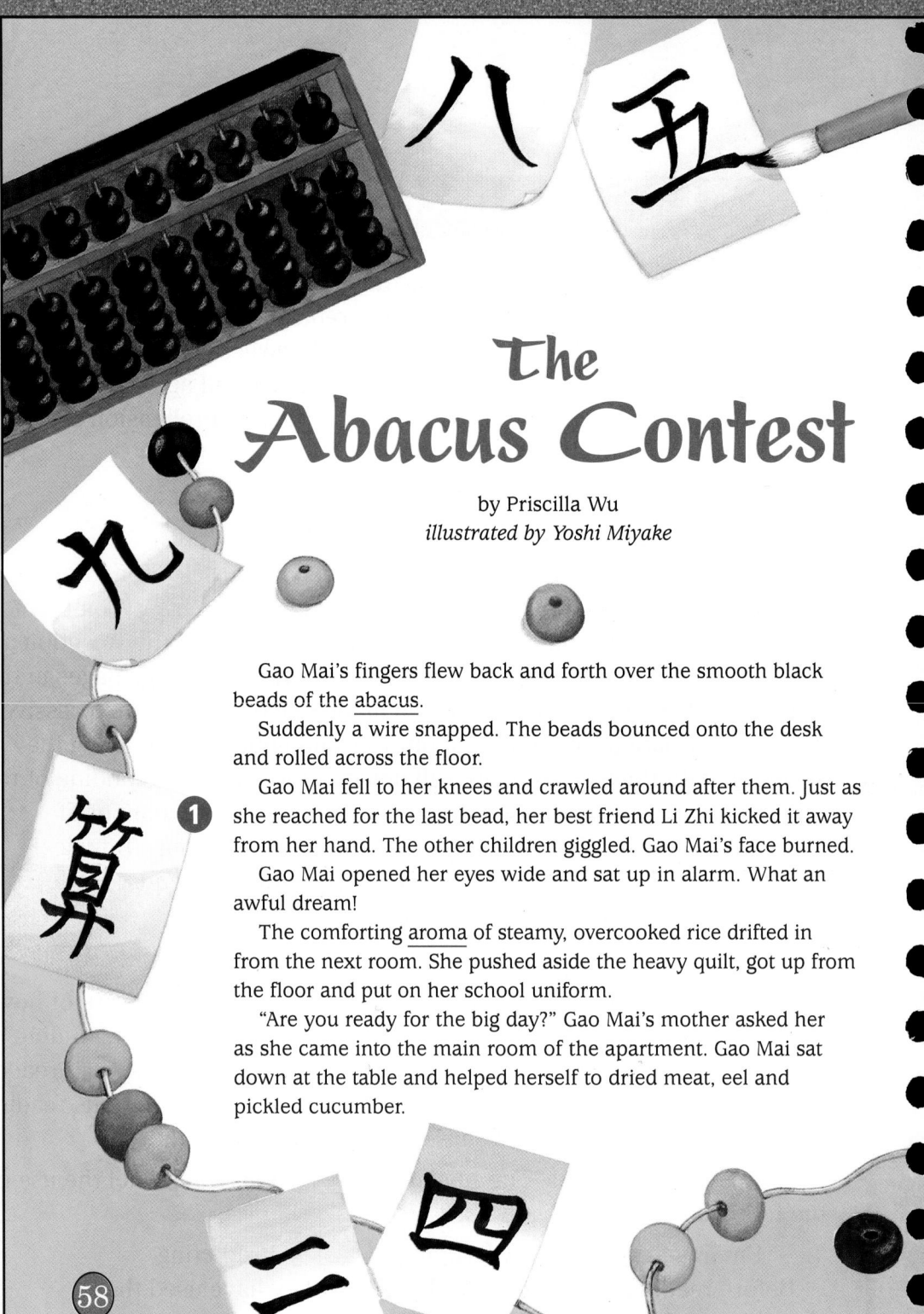

The Abacus Contest

by Priscilla Wu
illustrated by Yoshi Miyake

Gao Mai's fingers flew back and forth over the smooth black beads of the abacus.

Suddenly a wire snapped. The beads bounced onto the desk and rolled across the floor.

Gao Mai fell to her knees and crawled around after them. Just as she reached for the last bead, her best friend Li Zhi kicked it away from her hand. The other children giggled. Gao Mai's face burned.

Gao Mai opened her eyes wide and sat up in alarm. What an awful dream!

The comforting aroma of steamy, overcooked rice drifted in from the next room. She pushed aside the heavy quilt, got up from the floor and put on her school uniform.

"Are you ready for the big day?" Gao Mai's mother asked her as she came into the main room of the apartment. Gao Mai sat down at the table and helped herself to dried meat, eel and pickled cucumber.

58

Meeting Individual Needs

Intervention

Comprehension Intervention strategies for those students having difficulty with reading "The Abacus Contest" can be found in Unit 1, Lesson 4, of the **Intervention Guide.**

Assessment

✓ **Informal** Observe individual students as they read, and use the Teacher Observation Log, found in the **Assessment Guide,** to record anecdotal information about each student's strengths and weaknesses.

The dream was fresh in her mind. "I'm not sure," she said.

"Remember what I told you," said Gao Mai's father. "Imagine the abacus is part of you." He smiled at her. "You did so well when we practiced."

It was true. During a few of her many timed drills she was even faster than her father. And he used the abacus every day at the bank.

"Don't worry," said her mother. "You're one of the best abacus students in your class."

"But what about Li Zhi?" asked Gao Mai. "She's beaten me every year."

"Last time it was only by one second. You've improved so much, I'm sure you'll win. Besides," continued her mother, as she lit the incense on the altar where the family ancestors were honored, "you were born under the lucky sign of the horse. I went to the temple yesterday and said a special prayer for you."

Gao Mai looked at her watch. "I have to go."

"Good luck," said her mother.

2 "Good luck," said her father. "I'll be thinking about you all morning."

Gao Mai ran downstairs to the street and walked quickly through the open market. One farmer had spread a piece of burlap on the pavement and piled it high with cut sugarcane. Her mouth watered as she thought of sucking the sweet juice from the snowy white center. Gao Mai glanced at the fish swimming around in a shallow metal pan. Tonight they would be on someone's plate, maybe even her own.

(59)

Meeting Individual Needs

Intervention

Sequence Have the students quickly reread this part of the story. As they note time-order clues, discuss how each is used. Help students understand that some give broad suggestions for when events take place (last week, last year, and so on). Others relate to the chronological order of events in the story (in a few minutes).

Comprehension Skills

Sequence

Introduce students to the concept of *sequence*. Tell the students that writers often place story events in a certain sequence, or order. This helps the reader locate and recall important events and understand how one event relates to another. Writers often use *time-order words* to help readers follow the sequence.

■ "'Good luck,' said her father. 'I'll be thinking about you all *morning*.'"

■ "*Tonight* they would be on someone's plate, maybe even her own."

Explain to students that these words give clues to tell you what time of day it is. Point out that Gao Mai waking up from a dream is also a clue that it's morning. Remind students to look for sequence clues whenever they read.

Skills Strand

Sequence

INTRODUCED:	Unit 1, Lesson 4
REVIEWED:	Unit 3, Lesson 3
	Unit 4, Lesson 2
	Unit 5, Lesson 7
	Unit 6, Lesson 1

Teacher Tip Some students may be confused because of the culturally diverse names and references in this selection. Tell the students how to pronounce the names properly: **Gao Mai** is pronounced gou mī, and **Li Zhi** is pronounced lē djē. Invite the students to share what they know about Taiwan's culture.

Teacher Tip During reading, have students discuss ways the author allows readers to understand what kind of people the characters are through their reactions to story events.

2 Reading and Responding

Comprehension Strategies

Modeling

3 Clarifying *Good readers know that when they come across an unfamiliar term or idea, it is important to clarify its meaning in order to fully understand the text. Sometimes a word or idea's meaning can be cleared up by reading further into the text.*

I think this is a good time to stop and clarify "jian zhi." Remember, we talked about how this game is played before we began reading the selection. You kick something called a jian zhi into the air, and the more times you can kick it before it hits the ground, the more points you have. I imagine the jian zhi must be like a ball, or maybe a Hacky Sack.

Modeling

4 Clarifying *This is another phrase I don't understand. Ni Hao must be a Taiwanese phrase. Because the teacher is asking a question first thing in the morning, and the class has just stood up to greet him, it might mean, "How is everyone today?"*

What else should be clarified before we go on?

3 She reached the school just as the bell rang. Outside her classroom some boys were playing jian zhi. Her classmate, Kun Pei, scored one point after another by kicking the jian zhi into the air over and over again without letting it hit the ground.

Gao Mai walked into the classroom and Kun Pei yelled: "I won!"

During last year's abacus contest Li Zhi had beaten Kun Pei by four seconds, and Gao Mai had beaten him by three seconds. Today she was hoping to beat both of them.

Gao Mai watched Li Zhi's braids bounce as she tapped everyone on the way to her desk. She knew Li Zhi loved practical jokes and could tell by her <u>mischievous</u> look that she might play one at any moment. Gao Mai smiled while thinking of jokes they had played on their classmates together. Last week they had even played one on Li Zhi's mother. Yesterday Li Zhi had invited her to come over after school today so that they could think of a trick to play on her brother, Da Wei.

"Don't forget who won last year," said Li Zhi, sitting down behind her. She tugged on Gao Mai's ponytail and giggled.

"That was last year." Gao Mai leaned away and said, "If you pull my hair again, I'm not going to your house today."

Li Zhi leaned forward to grab Gao Mai's ponytail but only caught the tip. Gao Mai started to say: That's it, I'm not going to your house today. But the teacher arrived and the class stood up to greet him.

4 "Ni hao?" said Mr. Wang. "While everyone is nice and fresh, we'll begin with the abacus contest." He passed out booklets filled with addition, subtraction, multiplication and division problems.

 60

Word Knowledge

addition, subtraction, multiplication, division

Students can use the skills they learned in the Word Knowledge section of this lesson to read these words. Remind students of this if they have difficulty reading these words.

Meeting Individual Needs

Intervention

Clarifying Have students identify parts of the text that are unclear. Have them find clues in the text and share knowledge with other students to help clarify the parts that are unclear.

Teacher Tip

Kun Pei is pronounced kŏŏn pĭ.
Da Wei is pronounced dä wä.
Jian Zhi is pronounced zhyan djē.
Ni hao is pronounced nē hou.

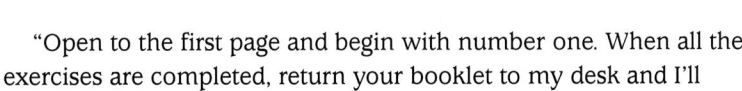

"Open to the first page and begin with number one. When all the exercises are completed, return your booklet to my desk and I'll write the final time. Ready?" He paused. "Begin!"

Gao Mai's left hand moved down the column of numbers rapidly, wrote the answers and turned the test pages. The fingers on her right hand flew back and forth among the smooth, black beads of the abacus.

In a few minutes she was writing the last answer to the addition problems. Gao Mai began subtracting and a moment later heard pages turning. Everyone was right behind her!

She worked carefully. It was easy to make a subtraction mistake, especially when exchanging a higher bead for lesser ones.

After finishing the last subtraction problem she heard Li Zhi's page turn.

Gao Mai <u>frantically</u> turned to the multiplication but two pages were stuck together. She pulled them apart with shaking hands.

Barely breathing, Gao Mai sped through the multiplication and division. Finally she wrote down the last answer, jumped from her seat and collided with Li Zhi.

(61)

Meeting Individual Needs

Reteach

Sequence Have students who need additional instruction and practice with this concept complete **Reteach,** pages 29-30.

Challenge

Sequence Have the students create a list of time-order words, and then use a certain number of them in a paragraph. Have students who understand this concept and could benefit from extended practice complete **Challenge,** page 17.

Comprehension Skills

Sequence

For more practice with sequence, have students complete **Reading and Writing Workbook** pages 29–30.

Name _____ Date _____

Sequence

The Abacus Contest

Focus To help readers make sense of what they read, writers show the **sequence**, or order, of events by using time and order words.

Time and order words provide readers with clues about which events happen before or after others in a story.
* Some words that indicate time are *yesterday, tomorrow, morning, night, moment, minute, suddenly,* and *last year.*
* Some words that indicate order are *first, last, after, next, finally,* and *then.*

Identify Look through "The Abacus Contest." Find examples of words or phrases used by the author to indicate a certain amount of time, a certain time of day, or the order in which events take place.

Answers will vary. Possible answers are shown.

1. Page: _59_   Paragraph: _6_
   Word or phrase: Last time it was only by a second

2. Page: _60_   Paragraph: _4_
   Word or phrase: Yesterday Li Zhi had invited her to come over after school

3. Page: _61_   Paragraph: _5_
   Word or phrase: After finishing the last subtraction problem

Reading and Writing Workbook • *Sequence*   29

Sequence *(continued)*

Practice Read each sentence. Then, fill in the blanks with a word or phrase that indicates time or order.

Answers will vary. Possible answers are shown.

1. We are going to the movies, and _then_ we are going out to dinner.
2. I will call my friend _after_ I do my homework.
3. We waited in line impatiently, but _finally_ they let us in.
4. _Last week_ I went to school, but this week is a vacation.
5. My birthday was _yesterday_.

Apply Write a paragraph about the things you did yesterday. Be sure to include time and order words to help the reader understand when each event took place. Answers will vary.

_____
_____
_____
_____
_____
_____
_____
_____
_____
_____
_____
_____
_____

30   *Sequence* • Reading and Writing Workbook

Reading and Writing Workbook pp. 29–30

② Reading and Responding

Comprehension Strategies

Modeling

 Predicting *It looks as if Gao Mai and Li Zhi are going to lose, just because they ran into each other. I don't think that's fair at all. I predict that the teacher will take that into account. Let's keep reading to find out.*

Modeling

6 **Confirming Predictions** *I see that the teacher looked at how many they got right and their time to decide the winner. It was fair after all.*

I see also that the prediction I made at the beginning of the selection, came true: Li Zhi is not angry with Gao Mai. They're going to spend time together after school.

Discussing Strategy Use

After they have read the selection, have the students share any problems they encountered and tell what strategies they used to solve them. Then, have them answer the following questions. If they answer "no" to any of the questions, have them reread part of the selection to find the answer.

- Did they summarize in order to help them understand what they've read?
- Did they stop to clarify ideas, words, and phrases that they didn't understand?
- Did they make predictions and check them later in the text?

Make sure that students explain how using the strategies helped them understand the selection better and how they read effectively to find answers to the questions they asked as they set purposes.

5 Two desks in front of them, Kun Pei rushed up and dropped his booklet on the teacher's desk.

"Oh, no!" yelled Li Zhi. "It's not fair!" She and Gao Mai dropped their booklets on the desk immediately after him.

"Quiet down, everyone," said the teacher.

Gao Mai returned to her desk and slumped in the seat, unaware of the other students handing in their booklets. Her bad dream had come true.

"Time for recess," said Mr. Wang, "while I check the answers."

Gao Mai was the last to go outside.

"Come on," yelled Ping Mei, wanting her to come and jump rope. But she shook her head. Across the playground, Li Zhi motioned for her to come and play tag with some of their friends. But Gao Mai turned away.

As he kicked the jian zhi into the air, Kun Pei bragged to a group of boys about winning the abacus contest. Gao Mai thought of her father's jian zhi at home on top of the TV. Father! Gao Mai knew he'd be disappointed that she hadn't won. The bell rang and everyone piled back into the classroom.

She heard Li Zhi behind her, laughing. "Hurry up, slowpoke!" she said, pushing past her.

Gao Mai secretly wished she could be carefree, like Li Zhi.

62

Meeting Individual Needs

ESL

Summing Up and Asking Questions
These are valuable tools for English-language learners, and should be used even more often than by other students.

Teacher Tip Reread the selection with students who had difficulty understanding it. Continue modeling and prompting the use of strategies and skills as you reread.

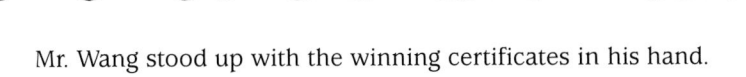

Mr. Wang stood up with the winning certificates in his hand. "Third-place winner of this year's abacus contest is Zong Zong."

The class applauded and a small girl with thick glasses walked quickly to the front of the room and shook hands with the teacher.

"The second-place certificate goes to Kun Pei," Mr. Wang continued.

Kun Pei came forward, looking as if he were about to cry.

"You were first to get your booklet in," Mr. Wang said as he handed him a certificate. "But one answer was wrong."

Gao Mai was confused. She turned around and looked into Li Zhi's bewildered face.

6 "Now," began the teacher, "we have an unusual situation——one that has never happened to me before. First place in speed and accuracy goes to Li Zhi, last year's first-place winner, and also to Gao Mai, last year's second-place winner."

Gao Mai turned and looked at Li Zhi. They burst out laughing and hurried to the front of the room.

"Here's a first-place certificate for both of you," said Mr. Wang.

As Gao Mai shook hands with the teacher, she decided it was a good day to go to Li Zhi's, after all.

63

Teacher Tip

Ping Mei is pronounced ping mā.
Zong Zong is pronounced tsong tsong.

Assessment

✔ **Formal** To assess students' reading comprehension, have them complete *Comprehension and Writing Assessment,* pages 13–14.

Comprehension Skills

Discussing the Selection

Following reading, engage the students in a discussion of the selection. Using the *handing-off process* will help the students take responsibility for the discussion. In addition to the following questions, have them revisit any questions asked when they set purposes before reading.

■ How is Gao Mai like Lupe from "The Marble Champ" and Cricket from "Class President"? How is she different? *(Answers will vary but might include that Gao Mai is driven like the other characters but less ruthless.)*

■ What would have happened to Gao Mai and Li Zhi if Gao Mai had lost again? Would they still be good friends? *(Answers will vary but may include that the girls' humor and mutual respect would protect the friendship.)*

■ How has this selection connected with your knowledge of the unit theme? *(Answers will vary—students should compare/contrast examples of cooperation and competition from this selection with their own experiences or past reading and use these connections to make a general statement about the unit theme.)*

During this time, have the students return to the clues and problems that they noted on the transparency before reading. Let the students decide which items deserve further discussion.

If students want to remember thoughts about or reactions to a selection, suggest that they record these in the Writing Journal. Encourage students to record the thoughts, feelings, or reactions that are elicited by any reading they do.

② Reading and Responding

Meet the Author

After the students read the information about Priscilla Wu, discuss the following questions with them.

Priscilla Wu's father, grandfather, and grandmother were writers. How do you think this influenced her decision to become one? *(Possible answer: Writing has special memories for her, as does sitting around with her family telling stories. She wanted to share her talents with others, especially her children.)*

"Writing is very hard work, but the hard work makes a difference," says Priscilla Wu. Why do you think she believes this? *(Possible answer: She doesn't want others to be discouraged about their writing. The pleasure and pride that come from writing are from all the effort she puts into it.)*

Meet the Illustrator

After the students have read the information about Yoshi Miyake, discuss the following question with them.

Yoshi Miyake didn't study art in college. She studied science. Why do you think she moved to Chicago to study art after college? *(Possible answer: The correspondence class she took made her realize that she wanted to be an artist, so she followed her dream and became one.)*

The Abacus Contest

Meet the Author

Priscilla Wu comes from a family full of writers. Her father and grandfather write books, and her grandmother had some articles published in a newspaper. Says Priscilla, "My dad, I remember him in the basement pounding away on a typewriter. . . . And from my dad's side—he was from the South—there was a tradition of storytelling. I grew up with many stories, or tall tales. . . . And I did the same thing with my own children. We had a lot of storytelling. We used to sit around in the dark at night, and sometimes, rather than read a story, we would tell stories." Priscilla went on to become a writer herself, but not because writing came easily to her. "I wasn't a very good writer in school. I've had to work very hard, and I think it is important to let students know that working hard *does* make a difference."

Meet the Illustrator

Yoshi Miyake was born in Tokyo, Japan. She graduated from the Tokyo Metropolitan University with a degree in chemistry. While in college, she took a correspondence class in art. After graduation, she moved to Chicago to attend the American Academy of Art. She later opened a gallery called American West. Her long-time interest in Native American culture, and her study of the Blackfoot and Sioux languages inspired the theme of this gallery. Yoshi Miyake is the illustrator of more than a dozen children's books.

64

Theme Connections

Think About It

With a small group of classmates, discuss what you have learned about ways that people cooperate and compete. During discussion, address the following questions.

- Why did Gao Mai believe she had to win the contest?
- What might Gao Mai's parents tell her if she told them how nervous she was?
- How did Gao Mai feel about sharing her victory?
- Have you ever wanted to be first in some activity? Why did it matter so much to you?

Record Ideas

 Record what you have learned about the unit theme and the pressures competitors put on themselves. Also, record any new ideas you may have for your unit activity.

Draw a Stick Figure

With a partner from outside your unit activity group, brainstorm the physical feelings people sometimes have before a competition (for example, a queasy stomach or clammy hands). Then, work together to draw a stick person. Identify on it the symptoms you and your partner brainstormed with arrows pointing to parts of the body that are affected.

65

Theme Connections

Think About It

Encourage students to explore the pressures that they can place on themselves. To facilitate the sharing of ideas, form discussion groups that are different from the unit activity groups.

Record Ideas

Respond to the questions in students' Writing Journals, extending their thinking through comments and questions.

Draw a Stick Figure

Have students post their work on the Concept/Question Board, and give them time to view and discuss it with others. Remind students that in their dramatic plays, actors can display some of these symptoms. Invite students to demonstrate how they might do this.

 **Teacher Tip** After reading, have students discuss how they act and feel when they are highly anxious. Encourage them to think of ways they can incorporate realistic emotions in their unit activities.

② Responding

Research

As students continue their explorations, have them use the **Research** CD-ROM Program to help organize and share their findings.

Teacher Tip If you created a semantic map on the Concept/Question Board of key words related to the unit theme, Cooperation and Competition, have students find words from other resources, their projects, and family discussions and add them to the appropriate category on the map.

Small Roman Abacus. Museo Nazionale Romano Delle Terme, Rome, Italy. Photo: SCALA/Art Resource, NY.

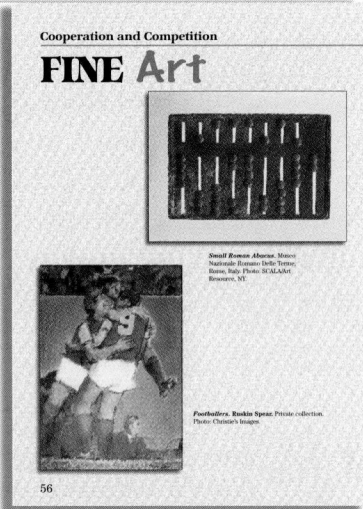

Student Anthology, p. 56

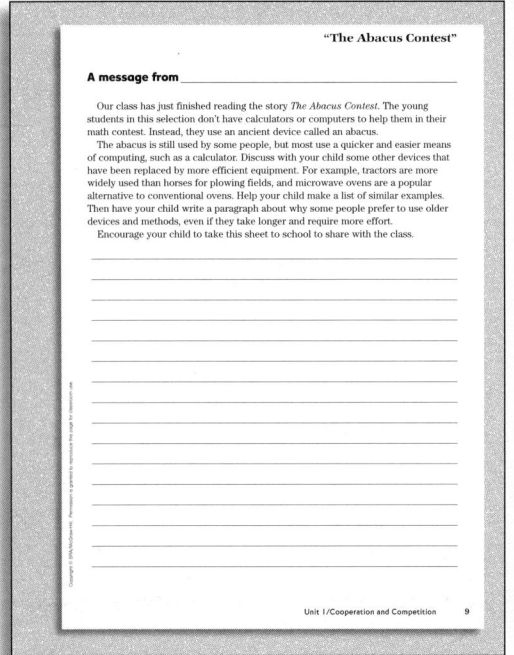

Home Connection p. 9

✦ Exploring the Theme

Selection Vocabulary

Have students write in their Writing Journals the definitions for words discussed before reading the selection and any other interesting words they clarified while reading. Students should be encouraged to refer to these words throughout the unit as they work on student and writing projects. The words from this selection are:

honor	**drills**	**accuracy**
collided	**booklet**	**mischievous**

Reading/Writing Connections

Have students discuss the conflict Gao Mai felt between dreading the competition with her best friend and wanting to win. Have them describe any conflicting feelings the characters in their plays have. Remind students that conflict can happen both within a character and between characters.

View Fine Art

This example of an abacus that was used by early Romans can also be found on page 56. This type of mathematical tool for calculating equations has been used for hundreds of years by a variety of cultures. Have students share their experiences with using or seeing abacuses. Does this abacus look similar to or different from others they have seen?

Home Connection

The class has just finished reading "The Abacus Contest," a fictional selection about a girl named Gao Mai who must compete against her best friend in the class abacus contest. An informational letter on "The Abacus Contest," in both English and Spanish, can be found in the **Home Connection** guide.

Supporting Student Explorations

Whole Group   Discuss with students what they have learned about competition and cooperation so far in the unit. Ask them to explain how this knowledge is expressed in their dramatic plays so far.

Work with the whole group, modeling how to write dialogue that coincides with the first frame or two of each group's storyboard. If necessary, remind students that *dialogue* is the conversation that takes place between the characters in a play. Have students use this model for the rest of their play.

Tell students to assign director and actor roles. Remind them to work cooperatively, putting the success of the play before their personal wants. Tell them they can begin rehearsing each *scene*, or action taking place in a particular moment or location, as the dialogue is completed. Have students make corrections to the dialogue as they practice, when it is necessary.

Small Group   Have students transform their storyboards into script format. Explain to them that they will be writing both dialogue and stage directions for their scripts, and suggest that they use a different color of ink for each.

As they write, have students discuss the plot, asking them how it relates to the unit theme. Review the characters' reasons for acting cooperatively and competitively. Remind students that they can draw on their own experiences and encourage them to share ideas within their group.

Assist students as they create character dialogue. Discuss what kinds of things the characters could say to show their thoughts and feelings. Suggest a few popular television shows as models for their scripts. Point out that the opening scene gets the audience's attention by introducing the problem, or conflict, that will be resolved by the end of the show.

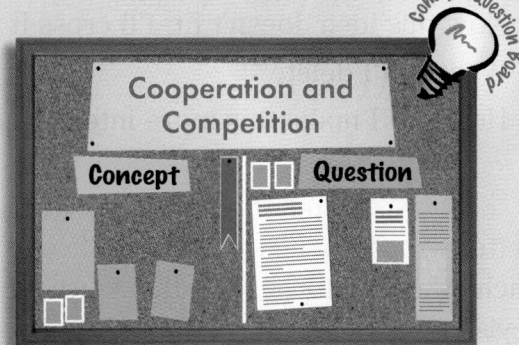

Inquiry Journal

Have the students complete page 7 of the *Inquiry Journal.* Have them record their ideas about how "The Abacus Contest" added to their knowledge of cooperation and competition.

Inquiry Journal p. 7

Assessment

✔ **Informal** Continue to make anecdotal records of students' progress. Note whether students:

- can verbalize what they have learned about competition and cooperation.
- explore the motives underlying characters' competitive and cooperative acts.
- depict the unit theme in the actions and dialogue of the characters in their plays.

③ Integrating the Curriculum

Writing Seminar Students can and should present their writing to their classmates. Students can read pieces in progress in order to:
- make sure that it will be understandable to their audience.
- make sure they have not left out pertinent information.
- gauge the appropriateness of the material for their chosen audience and purpose.
- receive the constructive input to help make their writing clearer.
- learn to listen carefully and offer constructive advice to each other.

Have volunteers read their persuasive paper drafts to the rest of the class or select students to do so. Because the purpose of Seminar is to provide students with usable and thoughtful feedback, no more than two students should present their work on any given day. If students seem rushed when two students present their work, have only one present.

Sentence Lifting Take examples from the students' own work and use them to teach elements such as good grammar, sentence structure, good choice of words, and so on. This should be done as often as possible. On an overhead write two or three sentences from a student draft that contain fairly typical types of errors or errors you notice your class has a tendency to make. In addition, write at least one sentence that is fine the way it is. Have students make suggestions as to how to correct the errors or word the sentence more clearly.

Language Arts

Writing

Revising a Paper

Instruct Ask students what they know about the revising process. Remind them as necessary that the purpose of revising is to make sure that their writing expresses their ideas clearly. As they work to make their writing better, they may need to move or change sentences, add new ideas or details, take out ideas or details that do not fit, or change words.

Model revising for the students. Using a transparency, show your own rough draft of persuasive writing on cooperation or competition. Be sure to include unclear and misplaced passages and incorrect word choices. Work quickly through your rough draft, thinking aloud as you revise. You might model comments such as the following:

- I think I should move this to the end. *(Use arrows to show where to move words or sentences.)*
- I need a better word here. *(Cross out word.)*
- This is good. I'll keep it like it is.
- I should say more about this. I'll add more details to describe this. *(Use an asterisk or number to indicate an insertion.)*
- Now this idea doesn't fit. I'll cross it out. *(Cross out sentence.)*
- What can I delete?
- How can I make this more interesting?

Practice Tell the students that they can help each other become better writers by listening carefully and commenting in a helpful way on each other's writing. Have them critique your writing. Do they agree with revision decisions you've made? What other suggestions do they have?

Apply Have the students work on their own persuasive papers about cooperation and/or competition. During the revising process, encourage them to meet and critique each other's work. Ask the students to share their decision-making processes about whether or not to make the changes.

Writing Process

Revise Tell the students that during the revising process they should focus on ideas and content. Tell students that they should also keep in mind what they have learned in this unit's spelling and grammar lessons about affixes, derivatives, prepositions, prepositional phrases, nouns, pronouns, and spelling words with final syllables ending in the consonant before *-le* syllable pattern. If they notice spelling or grammar mistakes, they can correct the errors; however, final corrections will be made at the next stage of the process.

Stress that once a piece of writing has been critiqued and the writer has had time to think about the suggestions, it is entirely up to the writer to decide whether or not to incorporate those changes. Conduct a Writing Seminar to help students determine what types of changes to their writing they may want to consider. (See the Teacher Tip on page 65C for more information on Writing Seminar.)

 **Teacher Tip** When you have writing conferences with students, do not lead them with content questions. Help them understand how to revise, not what to write.

 **Teacher Tip** Have students use the revising stage of the writing process to refine the content of their scripts for their dramatic plays.

Research in Action
Writing

Many writers claim they need to write in order to understand. For them, writing is a way of transforming knowledge into something useful. Classroom observations suggest that children have little experience with writing as an enjoyable, self-initiated activity that helps them think. Therefore, writing in the classroom needs to be purposeful. Writing for self-expression creates a context for the classroom as a scholarly community, with students setting their own goals and meeting to discuss their text. Beyond this point, growth rests on a foundation of writing as a tool for conveying meaning. *(Marlene Scardamalia)*

Assessment
✓ **Informal** Take this opportunity to assess students' progress with the writing process by commenting on the entries in their Writing Journals.

③ Integrating the Curriculum

Teacher Tip Encourage everyone to participate in the whole-group discussion. Knowing that they will be heard and will receive some response helps build confidence in speaking.

Teacher Tip Have students check their dramatic play scripts to be sure that they contain all the elements of plot and problem resolution.

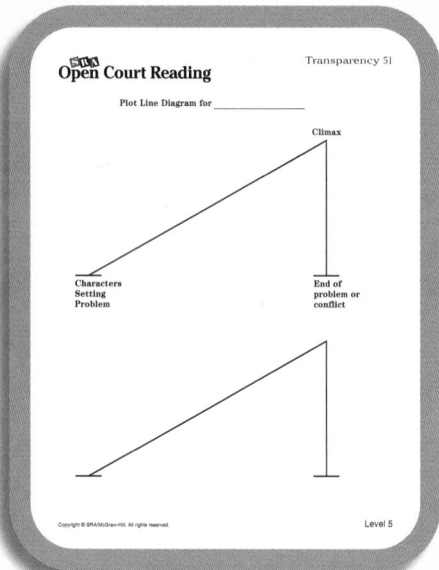

Transparency 51

Assessment

✓ **Formal** To assess students' understanding of this concept, have them complete *Skills Assessment,* page 7.

Literary Elements

Recognizing and Analyzing Plot and Problem Resolution

Instruct Have the students tell you what they know about plot. If necessary, tell them that the sequence of events in a story is called the plot. The plot introduces a problem and follows the characters as they deal with it.

Share the following elements of plot with the students.

- A good plot has a beginning, a middle, and an end.
- A problem that one or more main characters have is usually introduced at the beginning of a story.
- In the middle of the story, the characters go through one or more conflicts as they try to solve the problem. Excitement occurs when the conflicts take place.
- The highest point of interest in the story takes place when the character begins to solve the problem. This is called the climax.
- After the climax, the conclusion occurs. The conclusion tells how the problem was resolved.

Practice Display *Transparency 51,* Plot Line Diagram. Have the students summarize "The Abacus Contest" briefly. Let them tell about the problem Gao Mai had, how she struggled with it, how she solved it, and how the story ended. As the students discuss the story, add their responses to the appropriate spot on the plot line.

Apply Have the students look through the selections they read prior to "The Abacus Contest" in Unit 1. Have them choose one of the selections, and ask them to draw a plot line for that story.

Spelling

Inflections

Instruct Explain to students that you can change the tense of a word by changing the ending. To show that something happened in the past, the inflectional ending *-ed* is added. To show that something is happening right now, the inflectional ending *-ing* is added.

Emphasize the following rules:

- When a word ends in a consonant, simply add the appropriate ending. Example: *add/added*; *subtract/subtracting*.

- If a word ends with a consonant and *y*, change the *y* to *i* when adding *-ed*. Example: *carry/carried*, but *carrying*.

- When adding *-ed* or *-ing* to words that end with *e*, drop the final *e* and add *-ed* or *-ing*. Example: *receive/received/receiving*.

- Adding *-ed* or *-ing* usually does not change the spelling of a word that ends in a consonant; however, sometimes the final consonant is doubled. Example: *plan/planned/planning*.

Practice Tell the students to look through the selection for examples of words ending in *-ing* or *-ed*. Have them tell what the root word is and how each inflectional ending changed its spelling or meaning.

Apply Have the students choose a piece of writing from their Writing Journals. Have them decide whether they have written in the past or present tense. Tell them to edit their work for the correct spelling of the inflectional endings. For more practice, have students complete ***Reading and Writing Workbook*** pages 31–32.

Teacher Tip Have students check their spelling of inflections when working on their persuasive papers and unit activities.

Meeting Individual Needs

Reteach

Inflections For students who need additional instruction and practice with this concept, have them complete ***Reteach,*** pages 31–32.

Challenge

Inflections Have students examine the following words looking for a pattern and then write a grammar rule for the pattern they find. *play/playing/played; destroy/destroying/destroyed*

Have students who could benefit from extended practice of this concept complete ***Challenge,*** page 18.

← Skills Strand →

Spelling Inflectional Endings
INTRODUCED: Unit 1, Lesson 4
REVIEWED: Unit 1, Lesson 6
Unit 6, Lesson 2

Reading and Writing Workbook pp. 31–32

Name _____ Date _____

Inflections

The Abacus Contest

Focus To correctly spell the endings that are added to root words, you must sometimes change the spellings of the root words.

Two common endings that are added to root words are *-ed* and *-ing*. Adding the *-ed* ending to a word shows something that happened in the past. Adding the *-ing* ending to a word shows something that's happening right now.

- When adding the ending *-ed* or *-ing* to a word that ends in a silent *e*, drop the final *e*.
- When adding the ending *-ed* or *-ing* to a word that ends in a *y*, change the *y* to an *i*.
- When adding the ending *-ed* or *-ing* to a word that ends in a consonant, you sometimes have to double the final consonant.

Identify Read through the first page of "The Abacus Contest." List the first eight words you read that end in *-ed*. Then, write the root word for each.

1. snapped — snap
2. bounced — bounce
3. rolled — roll
4. crawled — crawl
5. reached — reach
6. kicked — kick
7. giggled — giggle
8. burned — burn

Reading and Writing Workbook • Inflections — 31

Inflections *(continued)*

Practice Look at the words you just listed. Answer the following questions about the words.

1. For which root words would you drop the final *e* before adding the *-ing* ending? Write the words with the *-ing* ending.

   bouncing, giggling

2. For which root word would you double the final consonant before adding the *-ing* ending? Write that word with the *-ing* ending.

   snapping

3. What change, if any, would you make to the remaining root words before adding the *-ing* ending? Write those words with the *-ing* ending.

   no change; rolling, crawling, reaching, kicking, burning

Apply Write an account of a dream or daydream that you had recently. You may write it in the past or present tense, but be sure to use the correct spellings of the *-ed* and *-ing* endings. Answers will vary.

_____

_____

_____

_____

_____

_____

_____

_____

32 — Inflections • Reading and Writing Workbook

3 Integrating the Curriculum

Teacher Tip Remind students to check for complete sentences in their persuasive papers and unit activities.

Meeting Individual Needs

Reteach

Complete Sentences Have students who need additional instruction and practice with this concept complete **Reteach,** pages 33–34.

Challenge

Complete Sentences Have students look through the first three selections they read for examples of incomplete sentences in the dialogue. Have them identify what parts of the sentences are missing, and then rewrite the sentences, so they are complete. For example, on page 21 of "Class President," a character named Julio says "No more soccer playing?" This sentence could be completed as "There will be no more soccer playing?" Have students who could benefit from extended practice of this concept complete **Challenge,** page 19.

← Skills Strand →

Complete Sentences

Grammar, Usage, and Mechanics

Complete Sentences

Instruct Ask the students what they know about complete sentences. Have them give examples of both complete and incomplete sentences.

If necessary, tell the students that a complete sentence has two parts—a subject and a predicate. The subject tells who or what. The predicate tells what happens or happened.

Practice Write some incomplete sentences, such as the following, on the chalkboard:

- Went to the store.
- Gao Mai and Li Zhi.
- After practice, Tommy.
- Reached for the jar.

Have the students turn the incomplete sentences into complete sentences by adding either a subject or a predicate. Call on volunteers to write their examples on the chalkboard.

Apply Tell the students to look through their own writing to make sure they have used complete sentences. Suggest that they can correct these incomplete sentences by adding either a subject or a predicate.

For additional practice, have students complete **Reading and Writing Workbook** pages 33–34.

Reading and Writing Workbook pp. 33–34

Name _____ Date _____
Complete Sentences   *The Abacus Contest*

Focus Writers use complete sentences so readers can easily understand what the writers want to say.

- A **complete sentence** has a subject and a predicate. A **subject** tells *who* or *what* the sentence is about. A **predicate** tells *what happens* or *has happened.* Our grandfather visits us every summer.
- An **incomplete sentence** is one that is missing a subject or a predicate. Our grandfather. Visits us every summer.

Identify Read the paragraphs below. Underline the incomplete sentences.

Toshi and I walk to school together every morning. Go through the park and across the river. Then we turn left and walk past the post office. Mrs. Rivera, who is in charge of running the post office, always waves to us. At the door to the school, the principal Mr. Hawkins. Out of breath, we run through the door. Just in time for our first class, which is Spanish.

My cat Toby is a real character. Always making me laugh. He loves to play. Chasing his toy mouse around the floor. Toby wakes me up every morning. He jumps on my bed and meows softly. Some mornings, I don't want to get up. Toby meows louder and louder. After breakfast, Toby and I are ready for another great day.

Reading and Writing Workbook • *Complete Sentences*   33

Complete Sentences *(continued)*

Practice Underline the subject in each sentence below.

1. The science fair starts at three o'clock this afternoon.
2. I worked on my science project until ten o'clock this morning.
3. Mrs. Jefferson says that I have a good chance of winning a ribbon for my project.
4. Six teachers will judge the science fair.

Put two lines under the predicate in each sentence below.

5. My best friend worked on the science project with me.
6. Her mother and my father and brother offered to help us with the project.
7. We wanted to do it on our own.
8. They were proud of us for winning second place!

Apply Write a paragraph describing a time when you, or someone you know, competed for a prize or an honor. Make sure you use complete sentences. **Answers will vary.**

_____
_____
_____
_____
_____
_____

34   *Complete Sentences* • Reading and Writing Workbook

Listening/Speaking/Viewing

Making Connections

Remind students that they have used making connections as a reading strategy to help them understand and relate to texts they are reading. Tell them that, likewise, they can make connections that help them understand and relate to other people. Tell them that we make these connections by listening and speaking. While listening, we connect to what the other person is saying by thinking about how it compares or contrasts with our own experiences, information, insights, and ideas. When we respond to what the other person has said, that person has the opportunity to connect with us.

Tell students that each connection we make adds to our store of knowledge. Because conversations and discussions allow for many of these connections, imagine how much they increase our knowledge! Have students engage in a discussion to gain and share knowledge of their own culture in comparison to that of Gao Mai in "The Abacus Contest." Use the following questions as discussion starters.

- What kinds of places did Gao Mai pass on her way to school? What do you see on your way to school, and how is it the same or different?

- What foods were described in the story? How are they similar to or different from foods that you eat?

- What are some games the students played? How are those games similar to or different from the games you and your friends play?

- What kind of calculating tool did Gao Mai and her classmates use? What kinds of calculating tools do you use, and how are they similar to or different from Gao Mai's?

- How does Gao Mai talk to her parents? Her teacher? Her friends? How is this similar to or different from the way you talk to your elders and friends?

As students discuss Gao Mai's culture as opposed to their own, have them also note any differences and similarities they find within their own culture (for instance, most of the students may enjoy playing kickball, but students of different heritages may eat different kinds of food). After the discussion, have volunteers comment on how this discussion changed or enhanced their perceptions of their culture and Gao Mai's.

Meeting Individual Needs

ESL

Conversational Practice Provide opportunities for conversational practice. Pair English-language learners with native English-speaking students. Encourage them to discuss other ways they might be able to connect with Gao Mai and her experiences.

3 Integrating the Curriculum

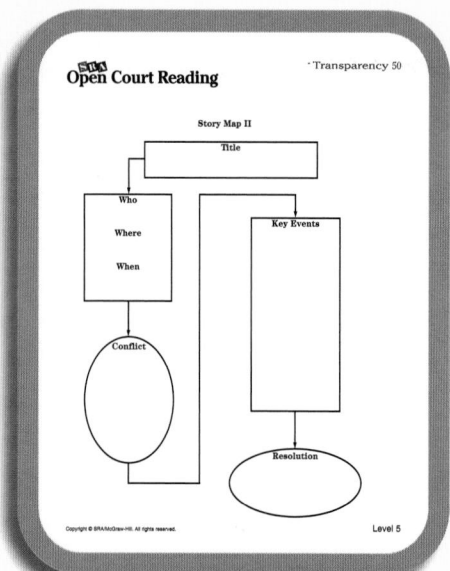

Inquiry Journal p. 14

Transparency 50

Teacher Tip Compare creating a story map to students' creation of storyboards for the unit activity. Tell them that the main difference is they are capturing the main events of the story with words instead of pictures.

Study and Research

Using Text Organizers

Instruct Display Story Map *Transparency 50.* Explain to the students that graphic organizers such as story maps can help them organize and represent information from texts. Walk students through the blank story map. Explain to them that:

- They should write the story's name in the *Title* box.

- In the *Who, What, Where* box, they should include information on the story's characters, the goal they will work toward during the course of the story, and the setting.

- The *Conflict* oval should include problems the characters encounter while trying to reach the goal.

- The *Key Events* box should contain a brief description of turning points in the action of the story that bring the character(s) closer to attaining the goal.

- The *Resolution* oval should state how the characters finally reached their goal.

Explain to students that this map should include brief descriptions only. Students can use story maps to help them remember important information from stories they have already read, or to help them plan stories they want to write.

Practice Review one of the earlier selections in the unit such as "The Marble Champ." Duplicate a copy of the Story Map transparency for each student. As a class, map out "The Marble Champ."

Apply Tell the students to select one of their own stories to map out. You may duplicate a copy of *Transparency 50* for each student or have them draw their own. Consider comparing the types of information recorded in this Story Map to that which was included in the plot line diagrams students created in the Literary Elements lesson for this unit.

For more practice with using text organizers, have students complete *Inquiry Journal* page 14.

Across the Curriculum

 ## Art

Winning Certificates

Purpose

To help students design certificates for winners of cooperative and competitive events

Materials

paper, pencils, pens, crayons, markers

Procedure

Discuss how winners are usually recognized with such things as ribbons, trophies, or certificates. Challenge the students to create their own certificates.

- Have students reread the last page of "The Abacus Contest." Ask them to identify how Mr. Wang rewarded the winners of the contest.

- Tell the students that they are in charge of designing first-, second-, and third-place certificates for both a cooperative and a competitive event.

- Encourage them to use a variety of art materials to create their certificates. Urge them to consider carefully how the certificate for cooperation might differ from the one for competition.

- After students have finished, display the certificates in the classroom.

- Discuss with students how they arrived at the designs for the certificates.

 ## Math

Math Competition

Purpose

To help students become aware of and discuss their feelings about competition and cooperation in relation to learning

Procedure

Have students brainstorm a list of math skills they have been learning this year. Then have the students create and play their own math game.

- On the chalkboard, list the mathematical skills as students recall them.

- Brainstorm some simple rules for a math game that incorporates one or more of the skills. You might ask whether the game should be played in teams or individually.

- Practice the game a few times in an untimed, noncompetitive way.

- Then play the game in a competitive way.

- Compare the students' feelings toward the practice and the actual game, and record these on chart paper. You might use the title *How I Felt* at the top.

S.O.R. Losers

from the book by Avi
illustrated by Charles Jordan

Ed Sitrow and his friends have a big problem. All students at South Orange River Middle School are required to play one sport per year—only Ed is no jock and neither are his friends. Playing a sport is sure to mean only one thing for them—total humiliation. Somehow, they manage to slip through their first year at S.O.R. without playing a sport. But when the school catches on, they make up a special soccer team just for Ed's crowd. This soccer team is anything but typical at a school positively famous for its winning teams and all-star athletes. Mr. Lester, the history teacher, has volunteered to be their coach. Little does the team know that they'll be making history of their own.

I should have guessed what was going to happen next when this kid from the school newspaper interviewed me. It went this way.

NEWSPAPER: How does it feel to lose every game?
ME: I never played on a team that won, so I can't compare. But it's . . . interesting.
NEWSPAPER: How many teams have you been on?
ME: Just this one.
NEWSPAPER: Do you want to win?
ME: Wouldn't mind knowing what it feels like. For the novelty.
NEWSPAPER: Have you figured out why you lose all the time?
ME: They score more goals.
NEWSPAPER: Have you seen any improvement?
ME: I've been too busy.

66

Selection Summary

Genre: Realistic Fiction

A requirement at South Orange River Middle School is that all students participate in a sport. A soccer team is formed of all the students who escaped playing sports their first year at school. Everyone on the team is good at something—except soccer or any sport. This first-person account truly illustrates that it's not whether you win or lose, it's how you play the game.

About the Author

Avi, once an assistant professor and librarian, is a prolific writer who has written more than two dozen books despite his lifelong battle with a writing dysfunction called dysgraphia. Among the honors he has received are the following: the Scott O'Dell Award for Historical Fiction for *The Fighting Ground;* the Christopher Award for *Encounter at Easton;* the Newbery Honor Medal for *Nothing but the Truth;* and an Edgar Award Nomination for *Something Upstairs: A Tale of Ghosts.* In addition to these awards, *The True Confessions of Charlotte Doyle* was named a Newbery Honor Book; *Wolf Rider* was honored as the ALA Best Book for Young Adults; and *S.O.R. Losers* was given the Parent's Choice "Remarkable Citation."

Students can read more about Avi on page 82 of the ***Student Anthology.***

Other Books by Avi
- *Who Stole the Wizard of Oz?*
- *A Place Called Ugly*
- *Shadrach's Crossing*

About the Illustrator

Charles Jordan was born in Washington, D.C., and is a self-taught illustrator. Jordan has illustrated for several children's magazines. He currently resides in Pennsylvania where he oil paints, reads, and surfs the Internet.

Students can read more about Charles Jordan on page 82 of the ***Student Anthology.***

 Exploring the Theme

Selection Concepts

"S.O.R. Losers" is humorous realistic fiction about a group of nonathletic students forced to play soccer and expected to commit to winning. Instead, they decide to be true to their own beliefs and interests. The key concepts are:

- The desire to win is taken as a given in our society.
- Not everyone wants to compete and excel in sports.
- Cooperation within competitive situations facilitates decision making and supports individuals.

 Check the Reading link of the **SRA** Web page for links to theme-related Websites. **http://www.sra4kids.com**

Exploration Activity Tips

Before Reading, have students speculate as to what they think the title of the selection might mean. Encourage them to predict how cooperation and competition will be important in this story.

During Reading, have students reflect upon their own experiences with being forced to compete in activities in which they did not feel proficient. Have them share how they felt about competing under these circumstances.

After Reading, have students revisit the predictions they made before reading the story. Challenge them to think of how the team cooperated, and whether or not they agree with cooperating to achieve this particular end.

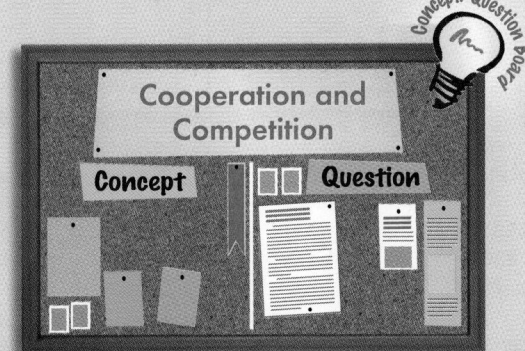

Unit I Exploration Management

Lesson I	Discuss experiences with cooperation and competition. Generate ideas for dramatic play.
Lesson 2	Students give and receive feedback on their unit activity ideas, and begin to work in groups on the storyboards for their plays.
Lesson 3	Students complete their storyboards and share them with other groups, then revise the storyboards based on feedback.
Lesson 4	Students begin group work on writing plays in script format. They agree on director and actor roles and begin rehearsals.
Lesson 5 S.O.R. Losers	**Collaborative Exploration** **Students complete the final drafts of their scripts and plan their dress rehearsals.** **Supplementary Activities** **Help students with mechanical corrections to their final drafts of scripts. Have them make title pages and write author notes.**
Lesson 6	Students complete play rehearsals and perform their plays. They put scripts in a class anthology and prepare a title page and table of contents.

Lesson Planner

Suggested Pacing: 3–5 days	DAY 1	DAY 2
	DAY 1	DAY 2
Part 1 — Preparing to Read **Materials** ■ Student Anthology, pp. 66–83 ■ Transparencies 5, 44	**Word Knowledge** ■ Reading the Words and Sentences, p. 66G ■ Developing Oral Language, p. 66G **Build Background, p. 66H** **Preview and Prepare, p. 66I** **Selection Vocabulary, p. 66I** *interviewed, record, prediction, attitude, ashamed, defeatist*	**Preview and Prepare, p. 66I** ■ Review Transparency 44
Part 2 — Reading and Responding **Materials** ■ Student Anthology, pp. 66–83 ■ Teacher Observation Log ■ Inquiry Journal, p. 7 ■ Home Connection, p. 11	**Student Anthology, pp. 66–74** **Comprehension Strategies** ■ Visualizing, pp. 66, 68, 70, 72 ■ Asking Questions, pp. 68, 72, 74 ■ Summarizing, p. 70	**Student Anthology, pp. 74–83** **Comprehension Strategies** ■ Asking Questions, p. 76 ■ Visualizing, pp. 76, 78 ■ Summarizing, p. 80 **Discussing Strategy Use, p. 80** **Comprehension Skills** ✓ ■ Discussing the Selection, p. 81 **Exploring the Theme** ■ Selection Vocabulary, p. 83A *interviewed, record, prediction, attitude, ashamed, defeatist*
Part 3 — Integrating the Curriculum **Materials** ■ Student Anthology, pp. 66–83 ■ Teacher Observation Log ■ Reading and Writing Workbook, pp. 35–38 ■ Transparencies 5, 53 ■ Inquiry Journal, pp. 15–16	**Writing** ■ Proofread, p. 83C **Literary Elements** ■ Analyzing Characters, p. 83E	**Writing Process** ■ Proofread, p. 83D **Spelling** ✓ ■ Words Into Syllables, p. 83F
Independent Work Time **Materials** ■ Reteach, pp. 35–38 ■ ESL Supplement ■ Challenge, pp. 20–21 ■ Intervention Guide ■ Listening Library Audiocassette	**Writing Process Continued** **ESL** ■ Word Meaning, p. 66G ■ Writing Buddies, p. 83C ■ Asking Questions, p. 74 **Intervention** ■ Frequently Misspelled Words, p. 66G ■ Analyzing Characters, p. 83E **Unit Project** ■ Complete Final Drafts of Scripts ■ Plan Dress Rehearsals	**Writing Process Continued** **ESL** ■ Vocabulary, p. 66J ■ Reading, p. 80 **Intervention** ■ Comprehension, p. 66 ■ Summarizing, p. 70 ■ Words Into Syllables, p. 83F **Unit Project Continued**

✓ Informal Assessment Available   ✓ Formal Assessment Available

DAY 2 continued	DAY 3	
DAY 3	**DAY 4**	**DAY 5**
General Review	General Review	Review Word Knowledge
Student Anthology, pp. 66–83 **Comprehension Skills** ✓ ▪ Drawing Conclusions, pp. 67, 69, 71, 79 **Theme Connections** ▪ Think About It, p. 83 ▪ Create a Comic Strip, p. 83	**Student Anthology, pp. 66–83** **Comprehension Skills** ✓ ▪ Author's Point of View, pp. 73, 75, 77 **Exploring the Theme** ▪ Reading/Writing Connections, p. 83A ▪ Literature Appreciation, p. 83A ▪ Supporting Student Explorations, p. 83B	**Student Anthology, pp. 66–83** ▪ Review Selection ▪ Complete Discussion ▪ Reread Selection in Pairs **Home Connection, p. 83A** ▪ Discuss "S.O.R. Losers" ▪ Compare and Contrast Two Teams
Writing Process Continued **Grammar, Usage, and Mechanics** ✓ ▪ Commas in Direct Address, p. 83G **Listening/Speaking/Viewing** ▪ Asking and Answering Questions, p. 83H	**Writing Process Continued** **Study and Research** ▪ Note Taking, p. 83I	**Across the Curriculum** **Drama** ▪ Debating Winning and Losing, p. 83J **Math** ▪ An Average Balancing Act, p. 83J
Writing Process Continued **Reteach** ✓ ▪ Words Into Syllables, *Reteach*, pp. 35–36 **ESL** ▪ Asking and Answering Questions, p. 83H **Challenge** ✓ ▪ Words Into Syllables, *Challenge*, p. 20 ▪ Drawing Conclusions, p. 69 **Unit Project Continued**	**Writing Process Continued** **Reteach** ✓ ▪ Commas in Direct Address, *Reteach*, pp. 37–38 **Challenge** ✓ ▪ Commas in Direct Address, *Challenge*, p. 21 **Unit Project Continued**	**Writing Process Continued** **Unit Project Continued**

Meeting Individual Needs
Independent Work Time

Preparing to Read

Meeting Individual Needs

ESL
- Word Meaning, p. 66G
- Cultural Context, p. 66H
- Vocabulary, p. 66J

Intervention
- Frequently Misspelled Words, p. 66G

Reading and Responding

Meeting Individual Needs

ESL
- Asking Questions, p. 74
- Reading, p. 80

Challenge
- Drawing Conclusions, p. 69

Intervention
- Comprehension, p. 66
- Summarizing, p. 70
- Drawing Conclusions, p. 71
- Asking Questions, p. 72

Integrating the Curriculum

Meeting Individual Needs

Reteach
- Words Into Syllables, pp. 35–36
- Commas in Direct Address, *Reteach*, pp. 37–38

ESL
- Writing Buddies, p. 83C
- Asking and Answering Questions, p. 83H

Challenge
- Words Into Syllables, *Challenge*, p. 20
- Commas in Direct Address, *Challenge*, p. 21

Intervention
- Analyzing Characters, p. 83E
- Words Into Syllables, p. 83F

Formal Assessment Options

Use these assessment pages along with your informal observations to gauge student progress.

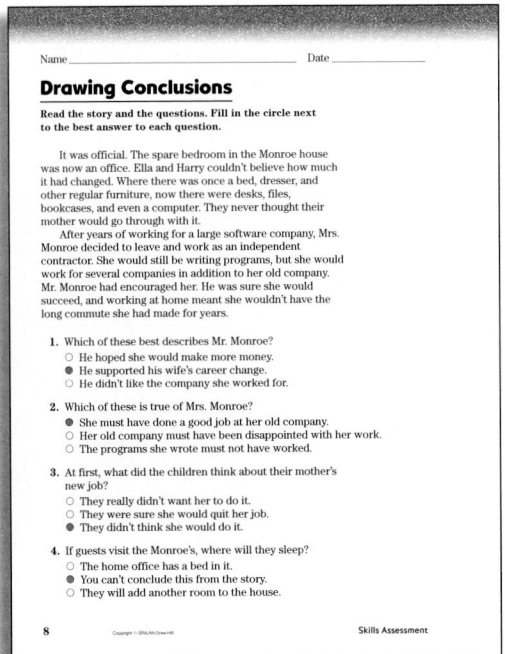

Skills Assessment, p. 8

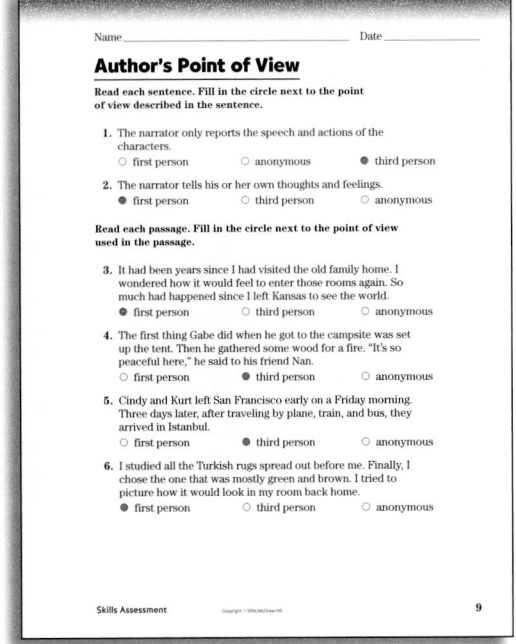

Skills Assessment, p. 9

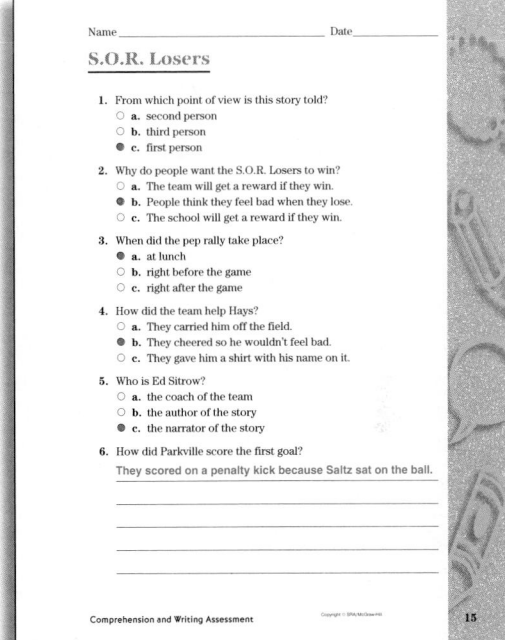

Comprehension and Writing Assessment, p. 15

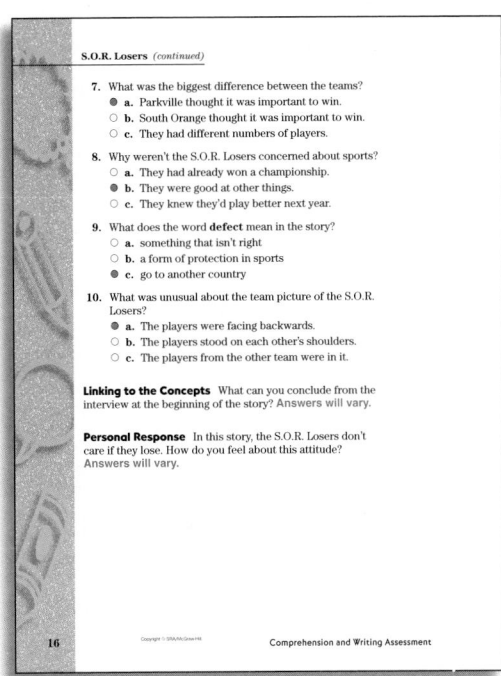

Comprehension and Writing Assessment, p. 16

1 Preparing to Read

Meeting Individual Needs

ESL

Word Meaning Make sure the English-language learners understand the meaning of the words before they do the exercises. Refer to Unit 1, Lesson 5, of the **ESL Supplement** for specific suggestions.

Intervention

Frequently Misspelled Words Make a list of frequently misspelled words. Write them on the chalkboard, and have the students write them down on paper. Then erase the words and ask students to put their lists away. Say each word aloud, and have students write down the words. Continue to work with students on words that they misspell. For students who need more help, see Unit 1, Lesson 5 of the **Intervention Guide.**

Word Knowledge

Reading the Words and Sentences

Write each word and sentence on the chalkboard. Have students read each word together. After all the words have been read, have students read each sentence in natural phrases or chunks. Use the suggestions in About the Words to discuss the different features of the listed words.

Line 1:	loser believe caught through
Line 2:	treason leave defeat
Line 3:	championship cheer chant
Sentence 1:	I believe that I caught you going through the fence.
Sentence 2:	We will defeat your team before you leave the school.
Sentence 3:	At the championship, the students cheered and chanted so loudly that it was difficult to hear anything else.

About the Words

- Line 1 contains words that are frequently misspelled. Review the words and their meanings and spellings with the students.

- In Line 2, the words focus on Long e spelled *ea.* Invite students to think of other words that contain this spelling of the Long e sound.

- The words in Line 3 have the /ch/ sound spelled *ch.* Invite students to think of words that contain this spelling of the /ch/ sound somewhere other than the beginning of the word (for example, *inch, branch,* and *wrench*).

Developing Oral Language

To review the words, have students do one or both of the following activities.

- Challenge students to use as many words as possible from Lines 1–3 in a single sentence. Ask volunteers to read their sentences aloud.

- Give a clue for each of the words in Lines 1–3. For example, for the word *defeat,* you might give the following clue: "What word means *to beat another team* and has the same vowel sound as *weave?*" Have the students identify each word.

Build Background

Activate Prior Knowledge

Have students check the Concept/Question Board to refresh their memories about cooperation and competition. Discuss the following with students to find out what they already know about the unit theme. Tell students to use their prior knowledge to help them comprehend the selection they are about to read.

■ Ask students whether they are familiar with the story they are about to read, and if so, to tell a little about it. Remind students, however, not to give away the ending of the selection.

■ Have students share other stories that involve soccer.

■ Ask students whether they have heard the saying, "It's not important whether you win or lose; it's how you play the game." Have students discuss this saying, focusing on the following questions: *Where have you heard this saying? Do you agree or disagree with its message? How is the American culture, or way of life, reflected in this saying? How is this saying reflective of other cultures?*

Background Information

The following information may help the students better understand the selection they are about to read.

■ Tell students that "S.O.R. Losers" is set in a junior high school.

■ Some students may be unfamiliar with soccer, so allow time for those students who play soccer to give a brief overview of the rules of the game.

Meeting Individual Needs

ESL

Cultural Context Ask English-language learners to talk about what kind of sports are most popular with children in their first culture.

Writing Journal Tell students that after reading they will be jotting down in their Writing Journals their reactions to the story. Have them be on the lookout for any ideas they may have for using a winning or losing team in a story.

1 Preparing to Read

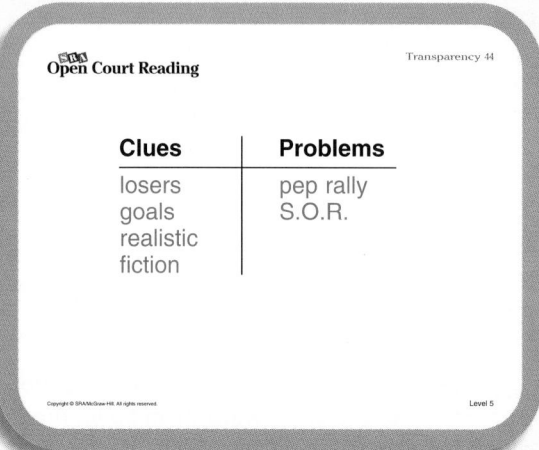

Transparency 44

Teacher Tip To help students decode words, divide them into the syllables shown below. The information following each word tells how students can figure out their meanings on the transparency.

in•ter•viewed	context clues, word structure
rec•ord	context clues
pre•dic•tion	context clues, word structure
at•ti•tude	context clues
a•shamed	context clues, word structure, apposition
de•feat•ist	word structure, apposition

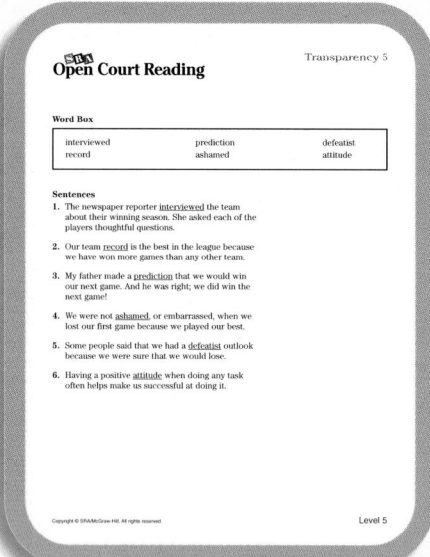

Transparency 5

Preview and Prepare

Browse

- Have a volunteer read the title and author's and illustrator's names aloud. Have students share what they know about realistic fiction.

- Because this is a fiction selection, have the students browse through only the first half of the story. Have them look for words and phrases that connect to what they already know. Record these in the Clues column on **Transparency 44.** Discuss with students what they think this story might have to do with cooperation and competition.

- Encourage students to ask questions as they browse. Have them identify any problems they notice while reading, and record them in the Problems column.

Set Purposes

As they read, have students think about what the characters learn about winning and losing.

Selection Vocabulary

As students study vocabulary, they will use context clues, word structure, and apposition to clarify these and additional unfamiliar words.

Display **Transparency 5** before reading the selection to introduce and discuss the following words and their meanings.

in•ter•viewed: asked questions to find out about a person or what a person thinks (page 66)

rec•ord: a written account of the number of games the team won and lost during the season (page 67)

pre•dic•tion: what someone thinks will happen in the future (page 67)

at•ti•tude: how someone acts or behaves to show his or her feelings or thoughts (page 68)

a•shamed: embarrassed; not proud (page 73)

de•feat•ist: having no confidence to win (page 76)

Have students read the words in the Word Box. Help students decode multisyllabic words by reading them syllable by syllable.

Have students read the sentences on **Transparency 5** to determine the meaning of the underlined words. Remind them to use clues in the sentences and structural clues to figure out the meaning. See the teacher tip to the left for information on how the words in each sentence can be defined.

Reading Recommendations

Your first reading of the selection should focus on developing the reading strategies found to the left of the reduced pages. We recommend that the students revisit the selection, rereading sections or the entire selection as a way to enhance their understanding and appreciation of the text. During reading, they should focus on the comprehension skills, found to the right of the reduced pages.

Oral Reading

This contemporary selection contains a lot of dialogue, so students may enjoy reading it aloud as classmates listen. As students read aloud, have them read expressively, at an appropriate pace, in natural phrases and chunks. By reading the selection with fluency, students will demonstrate an understanding of the text and an ability to engage the listeners in an effective manner. If students encounter difficulties, have them use the reading strategies below or refer to the Blending Procedure (Program Appendix 15–16).

Using Reading Strategies

Reading strategy instruction allows students to become aware of how good readers read. Good readers constantly check their understanding as they are reading and ask themselves questions. In addition, skilled readers recognize when they are having problems and stop to use various reading strategies to help them make sense of what they are reading.

During the reading of "S.O.R. Losers," you will model the use of the following reading strategies:

- Summarizing
- Visualizing
- Asking Questions

Before reading, have students share how they have used these strategies in the past and any tips they can give each other on their use.

Building Comprehension Skills

Revisiting or rereading a selection allows students to apply skills that give them a more complete understanding of the text. Some follow-up comprehension skills, such as *Main Idea and Details* and *Compare and Contrast*, help students organize information. Others, such as *Author's Purpose, Making Inferences*, and *Drawing Conclusions*, lead to deeper understanding—to "reading between the lines," as mature readers do. In this selection, students will apply the follow-up comprehension skills of *Drawing Conclusions* and *Author's Point of View*. Since two skills are reviewed, you may want to do all the sections related to one skill before doing the other skill.

Teacher Tip Have students who may need extra help reading the contemporary story "S.O.R. Losers" reread the selection using the *Listening Library Audiocassette*.

Teacher Tip By this time in the fifth grade, good readers should be reading approximately 126 words per minute with fluency and expression. The only way to gain fluency is through practice. As explained in Reading Recommendations, have students reread all or part of the selection to you and to each other during class or Independent Work Time to focus on the comprehension skills and to build fluency.

Meeting Individual Needs

ESL

Vocabulary Check that English-language learners know the meanings of idioms and more difficult vocabulary in the story, including: *tension; interviewed; to lose every game; prediction; a pep rally; terminal illness; supportive; bribe; blocking; team captain; the school chant; the pits; beneath the pits; disown; a complete vote of no confidence; ironed on press letters; being rejected; final pointers; the ref; we broke up at that; penalty; stolen ball; sore losers.* Explain and show pictures as needed. Model example sentences and help English-speaking students make their own sentences. Refer to Unit 1, Lesson 5, of the *ESL Supplement* for teaching suggestions.

② Reading and Responding

Read pages 66–83.

Comprehension Strategies

Modeling

❶ Visualizing *Because we are just finding out about one of the selection's main characters, we should stop and try to form a mental image of him. The text doesn't seem to say much about the way he looks. I would imagine that he is probably not the burly, athletic type, because he doesn't play sports. He's probably about eleven or twelve. You can tell by the things he says that he is smart and has a sense of humor. Despite the fact that he isn't good at soccer, he seems like a pretty confident person, too. How do you imagine he looks?*

Teacher Tip Some students might be confused by the interview format at the beginning of this story. Show them newspaper or magazine interviews with similar formatting.

Word Knowledge
teacher, coach

Students can use the skills they learned in the Word Knowledge section of this lesson to read these words. Remind students of this if they have difficulty reading these words.

Reading Recommendation

ORAL · CHORAL · SILENT

S.O.R. Losers

from the book by Avi
illustrated by Charles Jordan

Ed Sitrow and his friends have a big problem. All students at South Orange River Middle School are required to play one sport per year— only Ed is no jock and neither are his friends. Playing a sport is sure to mean only one thing for them—total humiliation. Somehow, they manage to slip through their first year at S.O.R. without playing a sport. But when the school catches on, they make up a special soccer team just for Ed's crowd. This soccer team is anything but typical at a school positively famous for its winning teams and all-star athletes. Mr. Lester, the history teacher, has volunteered to be their coach. Little does the team know that they'll be making history of their own.

I should have guessed what was going to happen next when this kid from the school newspaper interviewed me. It went this way.

NEWSPAPER: How does it feel to lose every game?
ME: I never played on a team that won, so I can't compare. But it's . . . interesting.
NEWSPAPER: How many teams have you been on?
ME: Just this one.
NEWSPAPER: Do you want to win?
ME: Wouldn't mind knowing what it feels like. For the novelty.
NEWSPAPER: Have you figured out why you lose all the time?
ME: They score more goals.
NEWSPAPER: Have you seen any improvement?
ME: I've been too busy.

66

Assessment
✔ **Informal** Observe individual students as they read, and use the Teacher Observation Log, found in the **Assessment Guide,** to record anecdotal information about each student's strengths and weaknesses.

Meeting Individual Needs

Intervention

Comprehension Intervention strategies for those students having difficulty with reading "S.O.R. Losers" can be found in Unit 1, Lesson 5, of the **Intervention Guide.**

NEWSPAPER: Busy with what?

ME: Trying to stop their goals. Ha-ha.

NEWSPAPER: From the scores, it doesn't seem like you've been too successful with that.

ME: You can imagine what the scores would have been if I wasn't there. Actually, I'm the tallest.

NEWSPAPER: What's that have to do with it?

ME: Ask Mr. Lester.

NEWSPAPER: No S.O.R. team has ever lost all its games in one season. How do you feel about that record?

ME: I read somewhere that records are made to be broken.

NEWSPAPER: But how will you feel?

ME: Same as I do now.

NEWSPAPER: How's that?

ME: Fine.

NEWSPAPER: Give us a prediction. Will you win or lose your last game?

ME: As captain, I can promise only one thing.

NEWSPAPER: What's that?

1 ME: I don't want to be there to see what happens.

Naturally, they printed all that. Next thing I knew some kids decided to hold a pep rally.

"What for?" asked Radosh.

"To fill us full of pep, I suppose."

"What's pep?"

Hays looked it up. "Dash," he read.

Saltz shook his head.

"What's dash?" asked Porter.

"Sounds like a deodorant soap," said Eliscue.

And then Ms. Appleton called me aside. "Ed," she said, sort of whispering (I guess she was embarrassed to be seen talking to any of us), "people are asking, 'Do they *want* to lose?'"

"Who's asking?"

"It came up at the last teachers' meeting. Mr. Tillman thinks you might be encouraging a defeatist attitude in the school. And Mr. Lester . . ."

"What about him?"

"He doesn't know."

67

Comprehension Skills

Drawing Conclusions

Tell the students that good readers *draw conclusions,* or make generalizations and judgments, about characters or story events based on information in the text.

Point out that the title of this selection, "S.O.R. Losers" is a pun. The "S.O.R." part stands for South Orange River. Because the title of the story is a pun, a reader might draw the conclusion that the rest of the story will be humorous as well.

Have the students draw conclusions about Ed's attitude towards sports in general from clues in the first two pages of the story.

Drawing Conclusions

INTRODUCED: Unit 1, Lesson 1

REVIEWED: Unit 1, Lesson 5

Unit 2, Lesson 1

Unit 3, Lesson 4

Unit 3, Lesson 6

Reading and Responding

Comprehension Strategies

Modeling

2 Visualizing *The idea of a country without sports is an interesting one. I visualize people playing a lot of board games and going to see concerts or plays, instead of sports events. What do you visualize?*

Modeling

3 Asking Questions *Good readers ask questions to help prepare them for what they will learn. Ed seems to be very upset, so we need to ask why he would feel this way. Is he upset because people are bugging him, or is there a part of him that feels bad because he's losing? When we read on, we see that Ed says he feels fine about losing. Is that really true? We should pay close attention to Ed's feelings as we continue to read.* (This question is answered on page 72. See the Teacher Tip on that page.)

Teacher Tip Tell the students that asking questions will help them focus on what they are reading. Remind them to look for the answers to their questions as they read. In some cases, the answer may not be in the text. In such instances, students should infer the answer from the information they do have.

Word Knowledge
beats, peace, eating

Students can use the skills they learned in the Word Knowledge section of this lesson to read these words. Remind students of this if they have difficulty reading these words.

It figured. "Ms. Appleton," I said, "why do people care so much if we win or lose?"

"It's your . . . attitude," she said. "It's so unusual. We're not used to . . . well . . . not winning sometimes. Or . . . not caring if you lose."

"Think there's something the matter with us?" I wanted to know.

"No," she said, but when you say "no" the way she did, slowly, there's lots of time to sneak in a good hint of "yes." "I don't think you *mean* to lose."

"That's not what I asked."

"It's important to win," she said.

"Why? We're good at other things. Why can't we stick with that?"

But all she said was, "Try harder."

I went back to my seat. "I'm getting nervous," I mumbled.

"About time," said Saltz.

"Maybe we should defect."

"Where to?"

2 "There must be some country that doesn't have sports."

Then, of course, when my family sat down for dinner that night it went on.

"In two days you'll have your last game, won't you," my ma said. It was false cheerful, as if I had a terminal illness and she wanted to pretend it was only a head cold.

"Yeah," I said.

"You're going to win," my father announced.

"How do you know?" I snapped.

"I sense it."

"Didn't know you could tell the future."

68

"Don't be so smart," he returned. "I'm trying to be supportive."

"I'm sick of support!" I yelled and left the room.

Twenty minutes later I got a call. Saltz.

"Guess what?" he said.

"I give up."

"Two things. My father offered me a bribe."

"To lose the game?"

"No, to win it. A new bike."

"Wow. What did you say?"

"I told him I was too honest to win a game."

"What was the second thing?"

"I found out that at lunch tomorrow they are doing that pep rally, and worse. They're going to call up the whole team."

I sighed. "Why are they doing all this?" I asked.

"Nobody loves a loser," said Saltz.

"Why?" I asked him, just as I had asked everybody else.

"Beats me. Like everybody else does." He hung up.

I went into my room and flung myself on my bed and stared up at the ceiling. A short time later my father came into the room. "Come on, kid," he said, "I was just trying to be a pal."

"Why can't people let us lose in peace?"

"People think you feel bad."

③ "We feel *fine!*"

"Come on. We won't talk about it any more. Eat your dinner." I went.

Next day, when I walked into the school eating area for lunch there was the usual madhouse. But there was also a big banner across the front part of the room:

Make the Losers Winners
Keep Up the Good Name of
S.O.R.

I wanted to start a food fight right then and there.

69

Comprehension Skills

Drawing Conclusions

Share the following lines from the text: "We're not used to not winning something." "It's important to win." "I found out at lunch tomorrow they are doing that pep rally." "Nobody loves a loser."

What conclusions can the students draw from this information? Guide them to see that the school is ashamed of Ed and his team because they keep losing.

Ask the students what conclusions they can draw about Saltz's and Ed's character traits. Help students note that they are funny—they have a good sense of humor. What clues support this conclusion?

Meeting Individual Needs

Challenge

Drawing Conclusions Have the students work in small groups to write and act out the scene at the pep rally. Have them imagine what Ed's team will say to the rest of the school about why they keep losing and how it's okay with them. Then have students use the conclusions they drew in the exercise to predict how the rest of the school will react to what Ed's team says.

Reading and Responding

Comprehension Strategies

Modeling

4 **Visualizing** *Visualizing the events in a story can help us connect with its characters. They made poor Ed speak in front of everyone without even giving him any warning. From the way he was talking, I imagine he looked pretty nervous. I can visualize him standing up on a stage in front of everyone in the cafeteria and looking very small up there by himself. I would hate it if I were in that position. How do you visualize this part of the story?*

Modeling

5 **Summarizing** *Let's stop and quickly sum up what's happened so far. This will help us check our understanding of the events up to this point. Ed's team has lost all its soccer games this season, but they don't seem to care. The rest of the school really cares. The newspaper prints an article about his team, the teachers bring it up at a meeting, and the students decide to hold a pep rally. That's a lot of pressure on Ed and his team. Can you add anything to this summary?*

I'm not going through the whole bit. But halfway through the lunch period, the president of the School Council, of all people, went to the microphone and called for attention. Then she made a speech.

"We just want to say to the Special Seventh-Grade Soccer Team that we're all behind you."

"It's in front of us where we need people," whispered Saltz. "Blocking."

The president went on. "Would you come up and take a bow." One by one she called our names. Each time one of us went up, looking like <u>cringing</u> but grinning worms, there was some general craziness, hooting, foot stomping, and an occasional milk carton shooting through the air.

The president said: "I'd like the team captain, Ed Sitrow, to say a few words."

What could I do? Trapped, I cleared my throat. Four times. "Ah, well . . . we . . . ah . . . sure . . . hope to get there . . . and . . . you know . . . I suppose . . . play and . . . you know!"

The whole room stood up to cheer. They even began the school chant.

"Give me an S! Give me an O . . . "

After that we went back to our seats. I was madder than ever. And as I sat there, maybe two hundred and fifty kids filed by, thumping me hard on the back, shoulder, neck and head, yelling, "Good luck! Good luck!" They couldn't fool me. I knew what they were doing: beating me.

5 "Saltz," I said when they were gone and I was merely numb, "I'm calling an emergency meeting of the team."

Like thieves, we met behind the school, out of sight. I looked around. I could see everybody was feeling rotten.

"I'm sick and tired of people telling me we have to win," said Root.

"I think my folks are getting ready to <u>disown</u> me," said Hays. "My brother and sister too."

"Why can't they just let us lose?" asked Macht.

"Yeah," said Barish, "because we're not going to win."

70

Meeting Individual Needs

Intervention

Summarizing Review with students that it is a good idea to summarize frequently when reading a story that has many characters or events, or covers a long period of time. Reread this part of the selection with students having difficulty with its main ideas.

"We might," Lifsom offered. "Parkville is supposed to be the pits too."

"Yeah," said Radosh, "but we're beneath the pits."

"Right," agreed Porter.

For a moment it looked like everyone was going to start to cry.

"I'd just like to do my math," said Macht. "I like that."

There it was. Something clicked. "Hays," I said, "you're good at music, right."

"Yeah, well, sure—rock 'n' roll."

"Okay. And Macht, what's the lowest score you've pulled in math so far?"

"A-plus."

"Last year?"

"Same."

71

Comprehension Skills

Drawing Conclusions

Have students continue to draw conclusions about the text.

■ What conclusions can the students draw about why Ed and his team were not good at sports? *(They spend a lot of time doing the things they are good at like math and music, and don't spend time playing sports.)*

Have the students support their answers with examples from the text and their own knowledge.

Teacher Tip Some students might enjoy writing cheers for Ed's team. Encourage them to write cheers expressing Ed's indifference about winning.

Meeting Individual Needs

Intervention

Drawing Conclusions Help students who are having difficulty see that the conclusions are not written in the text, but the author leaves clues that lead to the conclusions. Illustrate these points by giving students examples of conclusions they should not make, based on the text.

2 Reading and Responding

Comprehension Strategies

Modeling

6 **Asking Questions** *That's a good question Radosh is asking. Why are sports so important? Are they more important than painting or writing a poem or doing math? What do you think?*

When I think about what we read, I can see that Ed and his team don't think so. I wonder how Ed and his team can make the rest of the school understand that. Let's keep reading. (The question is answered on page 76.)

Modeling

7 **Visualizing** *The ability to visualize helps readers better understand and enjoy the selection. Right now, I am visualizing the secret meeting, between Ed and his friends, behind the school building. I can imagine how miserable they feel at first, knowing that it means so much to everyone else that they be winners in soccer when they know they never will be. But, I can also picture their growing excitement as they figure out that they don't need to be good at soccer because they are all good at other things.*

"Lifsom," I went on, getting excited, "how's your painting coming?"

"I just finished something real neat and . . . "

"That's it," I cut in, because that kid can go on forever about his painting. "Every one of us is good at something. Right? Maybe more than one thing. The point is, *other* things."

"Sure," said Barish.

"Except," put in Saltz, "sports."

We were quiet for a moment. Then I saw what had been coming to me: "That's *their* problem. I mean, we are good, good at *lots* of things. Why can't we just plain stink in some places? That's got to be normal."

"Let's hear it for normal," chanted Dorman.

"Doesn't bother me to lose at sports," I said. "At least, it didn't bother me until I let other people make me bothered."

"What about the school record?" asked Porter. "You know, no team ever losing for a whole season. Want to be famous for that?"

72

Word Knowledge

real, neat, season

Students can use the skills they learned in the Word Knowledge section of this lesson to read these words. Remind students of this if they have difficulty reading these words.

Meeting Individual Needs

Intervention

Asking Questions Read students small portions of the text, then stop and ask a question about what they have read. Breaking the text into small chunks will help students get used to asking questions.

Teacher Tip

Remind the students to look for the answers to the questions they ask as they read. The answer to the question asked in the strategy exercise on page 68 is answered on line 15 of page 72.

"Listen," I said, "did we want to be on this team?"

"No!" they all shouted.

"I can see some of it," I said. "You know, doing something different. But I don't like sports. I'm not good at it. I don't enjoy it. So I say, so what? I mean if Saltz here writes a stinko poem–and he does all the time–do they yell at him? When was the last time Mr. Tillman came around and said, 'Saltz, I *believe* in your being a poet!'"

"Never," said Saltz.

6 "Yeah," said Radosh. "How come sports is so important?"

"You know," said Dorman, "maybe a loser makes people think of things *they* lost. Like Mr. Tillman not getting into pro football. Us losing makes him remember that."

"Us winning, he forgets," cut in Eliscue.

"Right," I agreed. "He needs us to win for *him*, not for us. Maybe it's the same for others."

"Yeah, but how are you going to convince them of that?" said Barish.

"By not caring if we lose," I said.

"Only one thing," put in Saltz. "They say this Parkville team is pretty bad too. What happens if we, you know, by mistake, win?"

That set us back a moment.

"I think," suggested Hays after a moment, "that if we just go on out there, relax, and do our best, and not worry so much, we'll lose."

7 There was general agreement on that point.

"Do you know what I heard?" said Eliscue.

"What?"

"I didn't want to say it before, but since the game's a home game, they're talking about letting the whole school out to cheer us on to a win."

"You're kidding."

He shook his head.

There was a long, deep silence.

"Probably think," said Saltz, "that we'd be ashamed to lose in front of everybody."

I took a quick count. "You afraid to lose?" I asked Saltz.

73

Comprehension Skills

Author's Point of View

Point out that the *author's point of view* tells what kind of narrator the writer uses to tell the story. In a *first-person narrative*, one of the characters tells the story. In the *third-person narrative*, the story is told by someone outside of the story.

■ "*We* were quiet for a moment. Then *I* saw what had been coming to *me*: 'That's their problem...'" (page 72)

Explain that this example shows that the story is told from a first-person point of view. A third-person point of view would have used the words *he*, *him*, and *their* instead of *I*, *me* and *we*. The story is told in this point of view so that the reader will be allowed to know what the narrator, Ed, is thinking. The story would be quite different from another point of view—readers wouldn't know how the "S.O.R. Losers" felt about "losing." They would only know what an outside narrator thought they felt. This point of view also helps readers really get to know Ed's personality.

Skills Strand

Author's Point of View

INTRODUCED:	Unit 1, Lesson 3
REVIEWED:	Unit 1, Lesson 5
	Unit 1, Lesson 6
	Unit 3, Lesson 1
	Unit 3, Lesson 6

Teacher Tip

Have the students write descriptions of new sporting events that would combine physical activity with the strengths of Ed's teammates. One example might be a bicycle race in which the riders complete both the course and a painting in order to win. Another example could be an obstacle course that required one to solve math equations in order to pass from obstacle to obstacle.

2 Reading and Responding

Comprehension Strategies

Modeling

8 Asking Questions *What is Ed up to here? I'm asking this because first he asks his team mates for money and then he says they'll show the school that they really don't care about winning. Now, he says that he's looking forward to the game! I think he's planning something, but he isn't telling us what that is. Let's keep on reading and see if he tells us.*

Modeling

9 Asking Questions *Now Ed is sneaking into the home ec room so we can't see what he's doing. This still doesn't answer our question about why he wanted the money and what he's doing with the T-shirts. But maybe I'll find out when the game starts. After all, they have to put on those T-shirts sooner or later! (This question is answered on page 76.)*

Teacher Tip

Remind the students to jot down whatever questions they have to help them remember to look for the answers to their questions as they read.

Word Knowledge

treason, really, leaned

Students can use the skills they learned in the Word Knowledge section of this lesson to read these words. Remind students of this if they have difficulty reading these words.

"No way."

"Hays?"

"No."

"Porter?"

"Nope."

And so on. I felt encouraged. It was a complete vote of no confidence.

"Well," I said, "they just might see us lose again. With Parkville so bad I'm not saying it's automatic. But I'm not going to care if we do."

"Right," said Radosh. "It's not like we're committing treason or something. People have a right to be losers."

We considered that for a moment. It was then I had my most brilliant idea. "Who has money?"

"What for?"

"I'm your tall captain, right? Trust me. And bring your soccer T-shirts to me in the morning, early."

I collected about four bucks and we split up. I held Saltz back.

"What's the money all about?" he wanted to know. "And the T-shirts."

8 "Come on," I told him. "Maybe we can show them we really mean it."

When I woke the next morning, I have to admit, I was excited. It wasn't going to be an ordinary day. I looked outside and saw the sun was shining. I thought, "Good."

For the first time I *wanted* a game to happen.

I got to breakfast a little early, actually feeling happy.

"Today's the day," Dad announced.

"Right."

74

Meeting Individual Needs

"Today you'll really win," chipped in my ma.

"Could be."

My father leaned across the table and gave me a tap. "Winning the last game is what matters. Go out with your head high, Ed."

"And my backside up if I lose?" I wanted to know.

"Ed," said my ma, "don't be so hard on yourself. Your father and I are coming to watch."

"Suit yourselves," I said, and beat it to the bus.

As soon as I got to class Saltz and I collected the T-shirts. "What are you going to do with them?" the others kept asking.

"You picked me as captain, didn't you?"

"Mr. Lester did."

"Well, this time, trust *me*."

9 When we got all the shirts, Saltz and I sneaked into the home ec room and did what needed to be done. Putting them into a bag so no one would see, we went back to class.

"Just about over," I said.

"I'm almost sorry," confessed Saltz.

"Me too," I said. "And I can't figure out why."

"Maybe it's—the team that loses together, really stays together."

"Right. Not one fathead on the whole team. Do you think we should have gotten a farewell present for Mr. Lester?"

"Like what?"

"A begging cup."

It was hard getting through the day. And it's impossible to know how many people wished me luck. From all I got it was clear they considered me the unluckiest guy in the whole world. I kept wishing I could have banked it for something important.

75

Comprehension Skills

Author's Point of View

Remind the students that using a first-person point of view limits the author to showing only that character's thoughts and feelings. Point out the following passages from the text:

- "When I woke the next morning, I have to admit, I was excited." (page 74)
- "For the first time I *wanted* a game to happen." (page 74)
- "My father leaned across the table and gave me a tap." (page 75)

Explain that the author is showing story events through Ed's eyes and sharing how Ed feels.

Teacher Tip Explain that two techniques authors use to allow characters to express their thoughts and feelings directly are using dialogue and telling the story from a first-person point of view.

② Reading and Responding

Comprehension Strategies

Modeling

⑩ Answering Questions *That answers two of our questions from earlier. The money was to buy press-on letters to write "Losers" on their shirts. Making their shirts say "S.O.R. Losers" is a funny way to tell people they don't care about winning. Do you have any questions about that?*

Modeling

⑪ Visualizing *I know that happy beads are a kind of necklace made of glass or wooden beads. I think the reason people wear them is so that they can rub the beads together and remind themselves to have a good attitude. Now that I've made that connection, I think that if Mr. Tillman is shaking them furiously, they are not doing him much good. Can you visualize how Mr. Tillman must have looked?*

Word Knowledge

chimed, touch

Students can use the skills they learned in the Word Knowledge section of this lesson to read these words. Remind students of this if they have difficulty reading these words.

But the day got done.

It was down in the locker room, when we got ready, that I passed out the T-shirts.

Barish held his up. It was the regular shirt with "S.O.R." on the back. But under it Saltz and I had ironed on press letters. Now they all read:

⑩   **S.O.R.**
         LOSERS

Barish's reaction was just to stare. That was my only nervous moment. Then he cracked up, laughing like crazy. And the rest, once they saw, joined in. When Mr. Lester came down he brought Mr. Tillman. We all stood up and turned our backs to them.

"Oh, my goodness," moaned Mr. Lester.

"That's sick," said Mr. Tillman. "Sick!" His happy beads ⑪ shook furiously.

"It's honest," I said.

"It's defeatist," he yelled.

"Mr. Tillman," I asked, "is that true, about your trying out for pro football?"

He started to say something, then stopped, his mouth open. "Yeah. I tried to make it with the pros, but couldn't."

"So you lost too, right?"

"Yeah," chimed in Radosh, "everyone loses sometime."

"Listen here, you guys," said Mr. Tillman, "it's no fun being rejected."

76

Research in Action
Strategy Use

Modeling should always be used to get the children started, but it should stop as soon as they think independently at the level you have demonstrated. They show you they can do this by thinking aloud themselves during the reading lesson. Once you have turned the thinking aloud over to the children, your involvement should be limited to tactful shaping of their comments to improve their appropriateness.

(Jan Hirshberg)

"Can't it be okay to lose sometimes? You did. Lots do. You're still alive. And we don't dislike you because of that."

"Right. We got other reasons," I heard a voice say. I think it was Saltz.

Mr. Tillman started to say something, but turned and fled.

Mr. Lester tried to give us a few final pointers, like don't touch the ball with our hands, only use feet, things that we didn't always remember to do.

"Well," he said finally, "I enjoyed this."

"You did?" said Porter, surprised.

"Well, not much," he admitted. "I never coached anything before. To tell the truth, I don't know anything about soccer."

"Now you tell us," said Eliscue. But he was kidding. We sort of guessed that before.

Just as we started out onto the field, Saltz whispered to me, "What if we win?"

"With our luck, we will," I said.

And on we went.

As we ran onto the field we were met with something like a roar. Maybe the whole school wasn't there. But a lot were. And they were chanting, "Win! Win! Win!"

But when they saw the backs of our shirts, they really went wild. Crazy. And you couldn't tell if they were for us or against us. I mean scary . . .

Oh yes, the game . . .

We had been told that Parkville was a team that hadn't won a game either. They looked it. From the way they kicked the ball around—tried to kick the ball around—it was clear this was going to be a true contest between horribles.

77

Comprehension Skills

Author's Point of View

Remind the students that authors choose a specific point of view, first or third person, depending on the kind of information they want to share with readers. In this story, the writer wanted to tell story events through the eyes of the character Ed. Explain that much of the fun comes from Ed's sense of humor as he tells the story.

■ "Mr. Lester tried to give us a few final pointers, like don't touch the ball with our hands, only use feet, things that we didn't always remember to do." (page 77)

Have students look for other examples of Ed's humor in the text.

Teacher Tip Observe students' nonverbal reactions as they read—a puzzled frown, a long pause, a look of surprise, a smile. When you see such reactions, ask students to share their questions and comments.

Assessment
✓ **Formal** To assess students' progress in Author's Point of View, have them complete *Skills Assessment,* page 9.

② Reading and Responding

Comprehension Strategies

Modeling

⑫ Visualizing *Ed and his team have reached the crucial moment, where they will be either winners or losers in this final competition between "horribles." For this reason, I am visualizing what it must be like to be walking out onto the soccer field with them in their "S.O.R. Loser" jerseys, with all those people watching. Ed says that the crowd starts getting a little crazy when it begins to sense that he and his team don't care if they win or lose. I think I would be a little scared of all those victory-obsessed fans myself.*

What do you see in this scene?

Teacher Tip If a new or unexpected idea is generated during discussion, have students comment on it.

Word Knowledge
screams, leading, easy

Students can use the skills they learned in the Word Knowledge section of this lesson to read these words. Remind students of this if they have difficulty reading these words.

The big difference was their faces. Stiff and tight. You could see, they *wanted* to win. Had to win. We were relaxed and fooling around. Having a grand old time.

Not them.

The ref blew his whistle and called captains. I went out, shook hands. The Parkville guy was really tense. He kept squeezing his hands, rubbing his face. The whole bit.

The ref said he wanted the usual, a clean, hard game, and he told us which side we should defend. "May the best team win," he said. A believer!

Anyway, we started.

(I know the way this is supposed to work . . . . There we are, relaxed, having a good time, not caring really what goes on, maybe by this time, not even sweating the outcome. That should make us, in television land—winners. Especially as it becomes very clear that Parkville is frantic about winning. Like crazy. They have a coach who screams himself red-faced all the time. Who knows. Maybe he's going to lose his job if they lose.)

Well . . .

A lot of things happened that game. There was the moment, just like the first game, when their side, dressed in stunning scarlet, came plunging down our way. Mighty Saltz went out to meet them like a battleship. True to form (red face and wild) he gave a mighty kick, and missed. But he added something new. Leave it to my buddy Saltz. He swung so hard he sat down, sat down on the ball. Like he was hatching an egg.

78

We broke up at that. So did everyone else. Except the Parkville coach. He was screaming, "Penalty! Penalty!"

So they got the ball. And, it's true, I was laughing so much they scored an easy goal. It was worth it.

"Least you could have done is hatched it," I yelled at Saltz.

"I think they allow only eleven on a team," he yelled back.

Then there was the moment when Porter, Radosh and Dorman got into a really terrific struggle to get the ball–from each other. Only when they looked up did they realize with whom they were struggling. By that time, of course, it was too late. Stolen ball.

There was the moment when Parkville knocked the ball out of bounds. Macht had to throw it in. He snatched up the ball, held it over his head, got ready to heave it, then–dropped it.

It was a close game though. The closest. By the time it was almost over they were leading by only one. We were actually in the game.

And how did the crowd react? They didn't know what to do. Sometimes they laughed. Sometimes they chanted that "Win! Win!" thing. It was like a party for them.

⑫ Then it happened . . .

Macht took the ball on a pass from Lifsom. Lifsom <u>dribbled</u> down the right side and flipped it toward the middle. Hays got it fairly well, and, still driving, shot a pass back to Radosh, who somehow managed to snap it easy over to Porter, who was right near the side of the goal.

79

Comprehension Skills

Drawing Conclusions

Have students draw conclusions about Ed's plan and how well it has worked. Have them discuss the reactions of the other students in the audience and the difference between Ed's team and the Parkville team. Have students support any statements they make with examples from the text or their own experience.

Assessment

✔ **Formal** To assess students' progress in Drawing Conclusions, have them complete *Skills Assessment,* page 8.

2 Reading and Responding

Comprehension Strategies

Modeling

13 Summarizing *Let's sum up the story. The school wanted the team to win, but Ed and his friends didn't care. They knew they were good at other things and accepted the fact that they were lousy at sports. But when Hays missed an easy shot, he did feel bad. So Ed and the team shouted "S.O.R. Loser" to remind him that it was about having fun and not winning or losing.*

Can anyone tell me why it was a good idea for us to stop and sum up?

Discussing Strategy Use

After they have read the selection, have students share any problems they encountered and tell what strategies they used to solve them. Then, have them answer the following questions. If they answer "no" to any of the questions, have them reread part of the selection to find the answer.

- Did they ask questions and check later to see if their questions were answered in the text?

- Did they visualize scenes in the story?

- Did they summarize in order to help them understand what they've read?

Make sure that students explain how using the strategies helped them understand the selection better and how they read effectively to find answers to the questions they asked as they set purposes.

Porter, not able to shoot, knocked the ball back to Hays, who charged toward the goal–only some Parkville guy managed to get in the way. Hays, screaming, ran right over him, still controlling the ball.

I stood there, astonished. "They've gotten to him," I said to myself. "He's flipped."

I mean, Hays was like a wild man. Not only had he the cleanest shot in the universe, he was desperate.

And so . . . he tripped. Fell flat on his face. Thunk!

Their goalie scooped up the ball, flung it downfield and that was the end of that.

As for Hays, he picked himself up, slowly, too slowly. The crowd grew still.

You could see it all over Hays. Shame. The crowd waited. They were feeling sorry for him. You could feel it. And standing there in the middle of the field—everything had just stopped—everybody was watching Hays—the poor guy began to cry.

That's all you could hear. His sobs. He had failed.

Then I remembered. "SOR LOSER!" I bellowed.

At my yell, our team snapped up their heads and looked around.

"SOR LOSER!" I bellowed again.

The team picked up the words and began to run toward Hays, yelling, cheering, screaming, "SOR LOSER! SOR LOSER! SOR LOSER!"

Hays, stunned, began to get his eyes up.

Meanwhile, the whole team, and I'm not kidding, joined hands and began to run in circles around Hays, still giving the chant.

80

Meeting Individual Needs

ESL

Reading Have English-language learners preread or reread parts of a selection, stopping after each sentence of paragraph to tell in their words what the sentence or paragraph says.

Teacher Tip

Reread the selection with students who had difficulty understanding it. Continue modeling and prompting the use of strategies and skills as you reread.

The watching crowd, trying to figure out what was happening, finally began to understand. And they began to cheer!

13 "SOR LOSER   SOR LOSER   SOR LOSER!"

As for Hays, well, you should have seen his face. It was like a Disney nature-film flower blooming. Slow, but steady. Fantastic! There grew this great grin on his face. Then he lifted his arms in victory and he too began to cheer. He had won—himself.

Right about then the horn blared. The game was over. The season was done. Losers again. Champions of the <u>bloody</u> bottom.

We hugged each other, screamed and hooted like teams do when they win championships. And we were a lot happier than those Parkville guys who had won.

In the locker room we started to take off our uniforms. Mr. Lester broke in.

"Wait a minute," he announced. "Team picture."

We trooped out again, lining up, arm in arm, our *backs* to the camera. We were having fun!

"English test tomorrow," said Saltz as he and I headed for home. "I haven't studied yet. I'll be up half the night."

"Don't worry, I said. "For *that*, I believe in you."

"You know what?" he said. "So do I."

And he did. <u>Aced</u> it. *Our* way.

81

Teacher Tip
After reading the selection, challenge students to think about how the team cooperated, and whether or not they agree with cooperating to achieve this particular end.

Assessment
✓ **Formal** To assess students' reading comprehension, have them complete *Comprehension and Writing Assessment,* pages 15–16.

Comprehension Skills

Discussing the Selection

Following reading, engage the students in a discussion of the selection. Using the *handing-off process* will help the students take responsibility for the discussion. In addition to the following questions, have them revisit any questions asked when they set purposes before reading. Have students support their responses with text evidence.

■ Why was it so important to everyone else that Ed's team win a soccer game? *(They were more competitive than the team.)*

■ What if Ed and his friends had cared about winning? Is it possible they might have won some games then? *(With the team's ability to cooperate, they might have won.)*

■ Would Ed and his friends have cared more about winning if they had been competing for an award in something they did better, such as an art contest or a quiz show? *(Such a competition would have had more meaning for the team.)*

■ How has this selection connected with your knowledge of the unit theme? *(Answers will vary—students should compare/contrast examples of cooperation and competition from this selection with their own experiences or past reading and use these connections to make a general statement about the unit theme.)*

During this time, have students return to the clues and problems that they noted on the transparency before reading. Let the students decide which items deserve further discussion.

Actively encourage this handing-off process by letting students know that they, not you, are in control of the discussion.

② Reading and Responding

Meet the Author

After the students read the information about Avi, discuss the following questions with them.

Why do you suppose Avi loved to read so much when he didn't much care for school otherwise? *(Possible answer: He might have liked to read because it allowed him to escape into new places he had never been before.)*

Why do you think Avi would not allow his dysgraphia to keep him from eventually writing his own children's books? *(Possible answer: His love of reading made him want to be able to tell stories too, so he was willing to work hard to reach his goal.)*

Meet the Illustrator

After the students have read the information about Charles Jordan, discuss the following question with them.

It says here that Charles Jordan is a self-taught artist. What do you think this means? *(Possible answer: He didn't go to school to learn to draw. He learned on his own, by practicing.)*

S.O.R. Losers

Meet the Author

Avi was born in New York City and raised in Brooklyn. His twin sister Emily nicknamed him Avi when they were children. To this day, it is the only name he uses. He was shy, uninterested in sports, and not a very good student. He failed at one school and nearly "flunked out" of another one before anybody realized he suffered from dysgraphia. This learning disability made writing very difficult for Avi. It caused him to reverse letters in words or spell them incorrectly. Reading, however, was not a problem. Though he hated Fridays in school because they were spelling test days, he loved Fridays because they were library days. He read everything he could find and even started his own library of favorite books.

Meet the Illustrator

Charles Jordan is mostly a self-taught artist, though he did take art classes in the public schools he attended while growing up. His love of drawing, along with the support of his parents and teachers, led him to seek a career as an illustrator. Mr. Jordan won an award for his work from the magazine, *Highlights for Children*. He has also won an award for Artist of the Year from the National Science Teachers Association. He currently resides in Pennsylvania with his wife and two children.

82

Theme Connections

Think About It

With a small group of classmates, discuss what you have learned about different people's views on cooperation and competition. During discussion, address the following questions:

- Why did the soccer players choose to cooperate with each other?
- How would the story have been altered if the soccer players had chosen to try to win?
- Would you cooperate with the players if you were on this soccer team? Why or why not?
- If someone decided not to cooperate, would he or she be a bad team member?

Record Ideas

Working with a partner, identify two or three examples of humorous situations in the story. In your Writing Journal, write a short description of the situations and tell why you find each humorous.

Create a Comic Strip

Work with a partner—someone not on your unit project—and create a short comic strip about your favorite segment of the story. Use only dialogue to convey the messages of cooperation or competition. Post your comic strips on the Concept/Question Board.

83

Theme Connections

Think About It

If necessary, remind the students that the soccer players were not talented athletically and they were aware of their limitations. Point out the humor in collaborating against the time-honored tradition of "giving it your all."

Also, have the students consider the elements that made the story humorous. For example, the fans' disbelief of the soccer team's attitude was funny because they were reflecting common beliefs and expectations.

Record Ideas

Consider responding to student entries, clarifying and extending their thinking through comments and questions.

Create a Comic Strip

Have students post their work on the Concept/Question Board, and give them time to view and discuss it with others. Remind students that in their dramatic plays, actors can display some of these feelings. Have students demonstrate how they might do this.

Teacher Tip Wait time is an important factor in getting students to express ideas. Be sure to give them plenty of time to generate ideas. Don't resort immediately to asking questions in order to end a period of silence. Wait time is necessary to foster thinking. Watch how students respond to this period of wait time and encourage them to spend this time reflecting and thinking.

② Responding

Exploring the Theme

Some students may choose to conduct a computer search for additional books or information about cooperation and competition. Invite them to make a list of these books and sources of information to share with classmates and the school librarian. Check the Reading link of the **SRA** Web page for links to theme-related Websites.
http://www.sra4kids.com

Encourage students to write sentences using the selection vocabulary words. In order to provide additional help in remembering words, students can write synonyms or antonyms for the words if it is appropriate. Some students may even draw something to help them remember the meanings of the words.

Selection Vocabulary

Have students write in their Writing Journals the definitions for words discussed before the reading of the selection and any other interesting words they clarified while reading. Students should be encouraged to refer to these words throughout the unit as they work on student and writing projects. The words from this selection are:

interviewed	**record**	**prediction**
ashamed	**defeatist**	**attitude**

Reading/Writing Connections

Discuss how the members of this soccer team are unusual when compared to other athletes. Have students explain why they felt the way they did about competition. Have students also discuss the various conflicts referred to in this selection, both within the characters themselves, and between characters, and how those conflicts were resolved. Have students identify the conflicts experienced by the characters in their own plays.

Literature Appreciation

Have students think of interview questions to ask Ed Sitrow or another player on the S.O.R. soccer team after the final game. Have them review the interview in the first part of the story before they begin. Have them exchange and answer each other's questions as they think Ed might.

Home Connection

The class has just finished reading "S.O.R. Losers," a humorous, realistic fiction selection about an unlikely soccer team that sets out to prove that it's not whether you win or lose, it's how you play the game. An informational letter on "S.O.R. Losers," in both English and Spanish, can be found in the **Home Connection** guide.

Home Connection p. 11

Supporting Student Explorations

Small Group   Have students work in groups to complete the final draft of their scripts. Have them make a title page and include the list of characters. Ensure that they also create an author page, including brief autobiographical notes, which can be modeled after the notes included with each of the unit selections.

Have students continue rehearsing and revising their scripts in preparation for their performances.

Have them plan a dress rehearsal. Explain that this requires that students plan the scenes and settings they need and create costumes for their characters. Remind them that this is an important time to act cooperatively. Invite groups that have completed their final drafts to stage their dress rehearsals.

Individual   Have students use their Writing Journals to record their thoughts, ideas, and questions regarding this process, and respond to their journal entries.

Inquiry Journal   Have the students complete page 7 of the *Inquiry Journal*. Have them record their ideas about how "S.O.R. Losers" added to their knowledge of cooperation and competition.

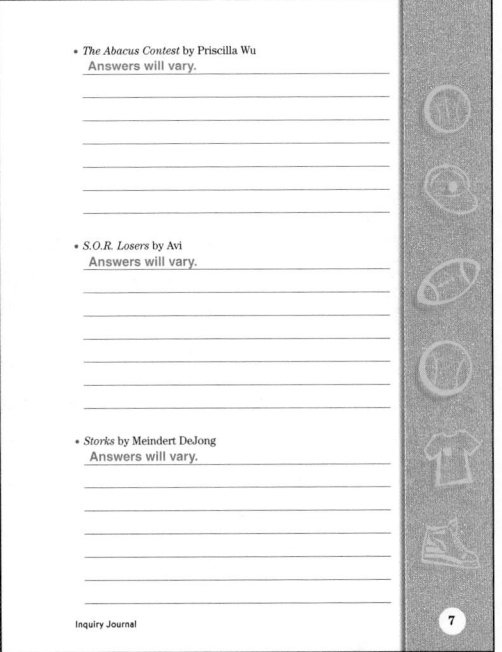

Inquiry Journal p. 7

Assessment

✓ **Informal**   Continue your anecdotal record of students' progress. Check to see that students:
- work cooperatively in small groups.
- effectively plan the dress rehearsal of their plays.

③ Integrating the Curriculum

Teacher Tip Encourage students to keep a list of frequently misspelled or misused words and to refer to it often when they write. If a student notes the same type of mistakes over and over in her or his writing, suggest that the student review the concept and rules related to that problem. If, after this review, the problem no longer appears in the student's writing, recognize this achievement by praising the student individually and/or to the class.

Meeting Individual Needs

ESL

Writing Buddies It can be intimidating for English-language learners to present their creative work to the class. Working in pairs with an English speaker who listens and gives feedback may be more productive. Encourage English-language learners to develop a trusting relationship with a classmate who can be a writing buddy, to help them in their transition to writing in English.

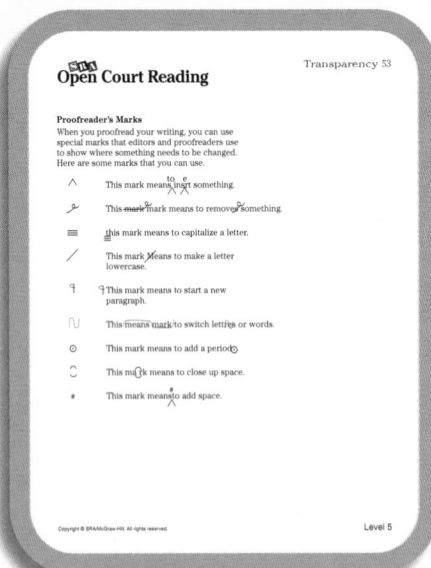

Transparency 53

Language Arts

Writing

Proofread

Instruct Tell students that after they revise a paper for content and style, they must read it carefully to make sure it contains no errors. This is called *proofreading*. Proofreading helps students communicate their ideas more effectively and notice errors they make repeatedly. At this stage, students should be making mechanical changes only. In order to do so, they will need a list of proofreader's marks. Use ***Transparency 53*** to share and discuss each of the marks in the examples listed.

PROOFREADER'S MARKS

Meaning	Mark	Example
Add	∧	Monday wasn't *my* best day.
Delete (take out)	℈	I ran to school in the wet rain.
Make a capital	≡	i raced back for my report.
Make lowercase	/	I didn't know it was a Holiday.
Make a new paragraph	¶	¶ School was closed.
Transpose	∽	I fell almost as I hurried.
Add a period	⊙	I forgot my homework.
Close up space	◡	Put the book case over there.
Add space	#	What a horrible day!

Practice Write the following examples on the chalkboard. Have volunteers correct each sentence or phrase, using proofreader's marks.

1. Every summer sue vacations in Daytona Florida
2. Sam I think you should stu dy for your math test
3. Every Saturday Morning.
4. Our class is having a scating party.
5. Don't forgret to bring your jacket.
6. Do have you a pencil.
7. Mollie just got a puppy. She namedhim jack.

Apply Have students choose a piece of writing from earlier in the unit to edit using proofreader's marks.

Writing Process

Proofread Have students go back to their ***Writing Folders*** and take out the persuasive writing piece they have been working on throughout the unit. Have them use the checklist below to help them proofread their paper. While they should concentrate on the items on the checklist, they should also keep in mind the other skills that they have worked on in this unit, which include correct use of nouns and pronouns, complete sentences, and commas in direct address.

Proofread your writing to make sure that:

_____ each sentence begins with a capital letter and ends with the correct punctuation.

_____ you have not accidentally written an incomplete sentence or a run-on sentence and no words are missing from sentences.

_____ no punctuation marks are missing from sentences.

_____ the subject and verb agree.

_____ the grammar is correct.

_____ you have used words correctly.

_____ no words are misspelled.

_____ each paragraph is indented.

Teacher Tip

Sentence Lifting Lift two or three sentences from a student draft and copy them onto an overhead. The sentences should contain errors fairly typical of those of students in your class. Have students proofread the sentences for errors in spelling, grammar, and language use, covering one element at a time. Discuss any changes that need to be made, and then make the corrections using proofreader's marks. See the sentence lifting activities in the proofreading portion of the appendix.

Assessment

✓ **Informal** Take this opportunity to assess students' progress with the writing process by commenting on the entries in their Writing Journals.

3 Integrating the Curriculum

Teacher Tip Encourage students to identify with the selection by asking whether Ed or any of the other characters reminds them of anyone in their own lives.

Meeting Individual Needs

Intervention

Analyzing Characters Ask students to look back through the stories they have already read in Unit 1. Have them find other examples of stories told from the first-person point of view.

Literary Elements

Analyzing Characters

Instruct Ask students to tell you what they remember about analyzing character traits from Lesson 1 of this unit. If necessary, review with them that a character's traits are his or her distinguishing qualities, such as personality, beliefs, and values. Remind students that often the author does not come out and say exactly what a character's traits are, though one can infer them by analyzing the character's actions and how others react to him or her.

Have students review Ed's interview with the school newspaper on pages 66–67. Ask them what they can infer about Ed's personality, beliefs, and values from reading this interview. Students may comment that Ed is witty, he has a sense of humor, and he seems fairly comfortable with the fact that he does not play for a winning soccer team.

Practice Write the following character traits on the chalkboard. Have students discuss why they agree or disagree that Ed exhibits each of the character traits. Have students use examples from the selection to support their arguments.

- leader
- fun to be with
- smart
- lazy
- selfish
- wants to be like everyone else
- afraid to challenge norms
- supportive

Apply Have each student think of three character traits (for example, *humble, shy, intelligent*). Then have each write a short paragraph about someone who exhibits one of the three traits, without actually naming what the trait is. When they are finished writing, have students exchange their paragraphs with partners, and see if their partners can name the character trait that they have described.

Spelling

Words Into Syllables

Instruct Ask students what they know about breaking words into syllables. Tell students that breaking a word into syllables can sometimes help them pronounce or spell an unfamiliar word. Write the following words from "S.O.R. Losers" on the chalkboard.

in/ter/viewed   cap/tains   rub/bing   un/der/stand

Invite volunteers to come to the chalkboard, say the word, and draw a line between the syllables in each word. Point out that the following guidelines apply to each of the words on the chalkboard.

- The vowel in the first syllable is a short vowel.
- Sometimes words can be broken into syllables between double consonants.

Practice Say the following words from "S.O.R. Losers" aloud: *wor/ry, fan/tas/tic, En/glish, yel/ling.* After you say each word, have the students write the word, drawing a line between each syllable and spelling it correctly. Then have students trade papers with a partner to check their spellings and syllable breaks.

Apply Have students find and write four more words from "S.O.R. Losers" that can be divided into syllables between consonants. For more practice, have them complete **Reading and Writing Workbook** pages 35–36.

Meeting Individual Needs

Reteach

Words Into Syllables Have students who need additional instruction and practice with this concept complete **Reteach,** pages 35–36.

Challenge

Words Into Syllables Challenge students to find words with more than four syllables. Have students write words they find on a class chart, using slash marks to show the syllable breaks. Have students who understand this concept complete **Challenge,** page 20.

Intervention

Words Into Syllables Work with individual students or small groups to clap the syllables in the words on **Transparency 5.**

Skills Strand

Words Into Syllables
INTRODUCED: Unit 1, Lesson 5
REVIEWED: Unit 5, Lesson 2
Unit 5, Lesson 7

Reading and Writing Workbook pp. 35–36

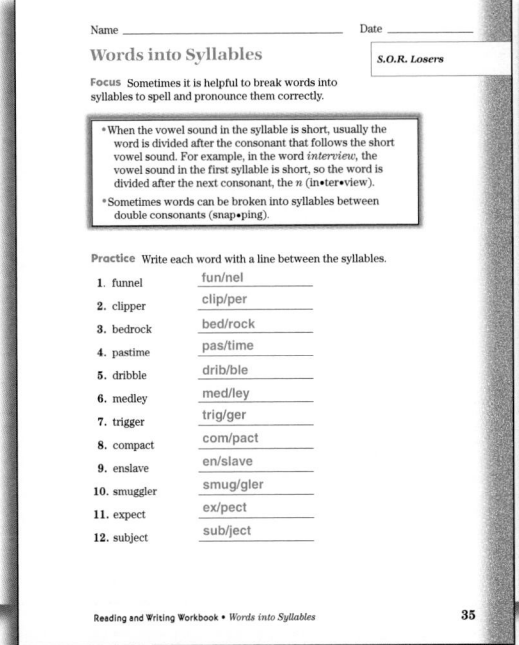

3 Integrating the Curriculum

Teacher Tip Remind students to check for correct use of commas in direct address in their persuasive papers and unit activities.

Meeting Individual Needs

Reteach

Commas in Direct Address Have students who need additional instruction and practice with this concept complete **Reteach,** pages 37–38.

Challenge

Commas in Direct Address Have students look through the selections they have read to find two examples for each rule listed in Instruct. Have students who can benefit from extended practice with this concept complete **Challenge,** page 21.

Commas in Direct Address

INTRODUCED: Unit 1, Lesson 5
REVIEWED: Unit 2, Lesson 7
Unit 4, Lesson 8

Grammar, Usage, and Mechanics

Commas in Direct Address

Instruct Ask students what they know about commas. If necessary, tell them that a comma is used to set apart the name of a person being spoken to or addressed. Give the following rules:

- When the first word in a sentence is the name of the person being addressed, a comma follows the name.
- When the name of the person being addressed is the last word in a sentence, a comma comes before it.
- When the name of the person being addressed is in the middle of a sentence, a comma comes before and after the name.

Have students find examples of commas in direct address in "S.O.R. Losers" and read them aloud, pausing at each comma.

Practice Have students copy the following conversation from "S.O.R Losers," adding the comma of direct address wherever it is needed.

"You're late Ed. Where have you been?" *("You're late, Ed.)*

"Mom I told you I was going to the library with Hays." *("Mom, I . . .)*

"Was that today? I thought that was tomorrow. I'm sorry Eddie." *("I'm sorry, Eddie.)*

Apply Tell students to check a piece of their own writing to make sure they have placed commas appropriately. For additional practice, have students complete **Reading and Writing Workbook** pages 37–38.

Reading and Writing Workbook pp. 37–38

Name _____ Date _____

Commas in Direct Address

S.O.R. Losers

Focus Use commas to set apart words of direct address in sentences. The correct use of commas helps to make writing clear to readers.

> If a speaker addresses someone by name, use a comma to separate the name from the rest of the sentence.
> - If the name is at the beginning of a sentence, a comma comes after it.
>   Ed, don't you want to win?
> - If the name is at the end of a sentence, a comma comes before it.
>   Do you think winning is most important, Mr. Tillman?
> - If the name is in the middle of a sentence, a comma comes before and after it.
>   Listen here, John, I don't care if we lose.

Identify Look through "S.O.R. Losers" for examples of dialogue in which the name of the person who is being spoken to is part of a sentence. Write the page number, the name of the person spoken to, and the sentence. Pay special attention to where the commas are placed.

Answers will vary. Possible answers are shown.

Page: 68   Person's name: Ms. Appleton

Sentence: "Ms. Appleton," I said, "why do people care so much if we win or lose?"

Page: 71   Person's name: Macht

Sentence: "Okay. And Macht, what's the lowest score you've pulled in math so far?"

Reading and Writing Workbook • *Commas in Direct Address*   37

Commas in Direct Address *(continued)*

Practice Read the following dialogue. Some of the sentences are missing commas to set apart the names used in direct address. Insert commas where they belong.

> "Mr. Tillman,isn't it true that you tried out for pro football?"
> "Well, yes,Ed, that is true."
> "So you lost once, too, Mr. Tillman."
> "Yes, Ed,I lost. But we don't have time to talk. We've got a game to play! Okay,team,let's go out there and win this time!"

Apply Write a conversation between you and a classmate, using names in direct address. Pay special attention to where commas are placed. Answers will vary.

38   *Commas in Direct Address* • Reading and Writing Workbook

Listening/Speaking/Viewing

Asking and Answering Questions

Have students reread the beginning of the story to see how the author wrote the interview between the reporter from the school newspaper and the character Ed Sitrow. Discuss the questions the reporter asked, and analyze them to see how many of them were open-ended questions. Let students evaluate whether the reporter gained the information he or she was hoping for.

Tell students that they are going to ask and answer a set of questions regarding factual information and their opinions. First, work with students to choose a subject that they can ask about, perhaps a school issue or event involving cooperation and competition, of which they all have knowledge and an opinion. Next, work with them to write a few questions that they can ask each other about the chosen topic. Be sure they include some questions that ask for factual information and some that ask for an opinion. Write these questions on the chalkboard. Have the students pair up with a partner to take turns asking and answering the questions. Tell them to take notes on their partner's answers.

Suggest that they write up the interviews like the one in "S.O.R. Losers."

Meeting Individual Needs

ESL

Asking and Answering Questions Have English-language learners come up with a set of questions about American culture and have native English-speaking students answer them. Then, have students discuss how connecting their experiences, information, insights, and ideas, through listening and speaking, broadened their knowledge of American culture.

3 Integrating the Curriculum

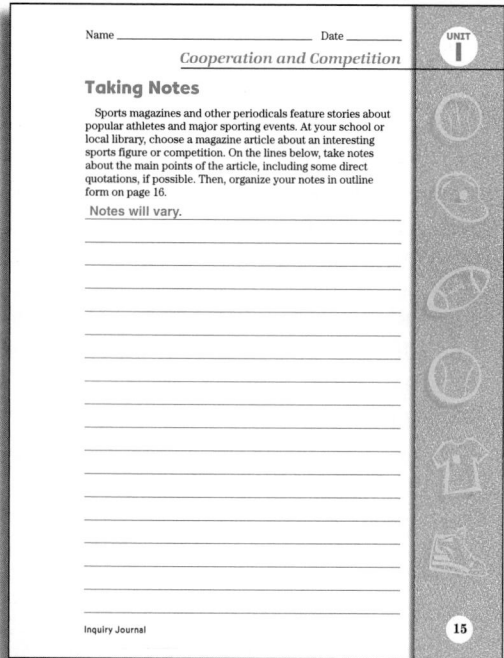

Inquiry Journal pp. 15–16

Teacher Tip You may wish to remind students of the way you have been making notations on the Clues and Problems Transparency when they browse a selection. Point out that, except for very formal papers that require exact quotes or extensive outlines, they should use short, incomplete sentences that convey the thought quickly.

Study and Research

Note Taking

Instruct Tell the students to talk about times when they have taken notes and how the notes have helped them. Emphasize that note taking is an important part of the research process. Researchers find appropriate sources and then read and take notes on the information they need to help them organize and recall it later. They summarize and paraphrase important facts, ideas, or opinions that pertain to their research. Sometimes researchers may include direct quotations from a person to explain an idea or state an opinion. Write the following guidelines on the chalkboard:

1. Organize your notes under subject headings.

2. Write notes in your own words.

3. Summarize the most important information.

4. Keep your notes short. Use abbreviations, key phrases, and short sentences.

5. Put an author's exact words within quotation marks. Include the author's name, the book title (or magazine and article title), and the page number.

6. Write neatly and clearly.

Practice Have the students think about the following research question: How do winning and losing affect a team's attitude? Suggest that students use "S.O.R. Losers" as a source for the research question. Tell them to skim the selection and take notes on facts related to the questions. Tell students to use abbreviations and key phrases and to sum up the information in a sentence or two as researchers do when organizing their ideas on a subject of study.

Apply Have the students write a brief report on the research question. Remind them to base the reports on their notes. For more practice with note taking, have students complete *Inquiry Journal* pages 15–16.

Across the Curriculum

 ## Drama

Debating Winning and Losing

Purpose

To increase students' awareness of the nature of competition.

Procedure

Urge students to think about competition and whether they believe it is better to win or lose. Ask pairs to debate the issue.

- Ask the students if they've ever heard the following phrase: It's not whether you win or lose, it's how you play the game. Do they agree with the phrase? Challenge them to justify their positions.

- Then pair students who hold different positions. Tell them to debate the phrase. They may refer to notes they have made.

- Before the debates begin, set some rules such as the following:

  1. Only one person should speak at a time.

  2. Take turns responding to each other.

  3. No one should interrupt while the other person is speaking.

  4. Listen while the other person is speaking.

  5. Speak clearly and firmly, but not loudly.

- Monitor the debates.

- Ask each pair of students to conclude which of them won the debate. Discuss whether or not their positions changed because of the debate.

 ## Math

An Average Balancing Act

Purpose

To develop students' mathematical skills as they study their coordination.

Procedure

Tell students that they are going to be taking a timed coordination test. Then they will take the average of the scores and find out what the class average is.

- Review how to find the average of a set of test scores. Remind students that they should add the scores and then divide the sum by the total number of scores.

- Challenge the students to see how long they can balance on one foot with their eyes closed. Tell them they must keep their eyes closed while they're balancing.

- Have students time each other using the second hand of a clock or a watch. They will need to have one person watching the clock and one person watching the person balancing. As soon as the raised foot touches the floor at all, they must stop timing.

- Write the scores on the chalkboard.

- Ask the students to find the average. See which student can find the average first.

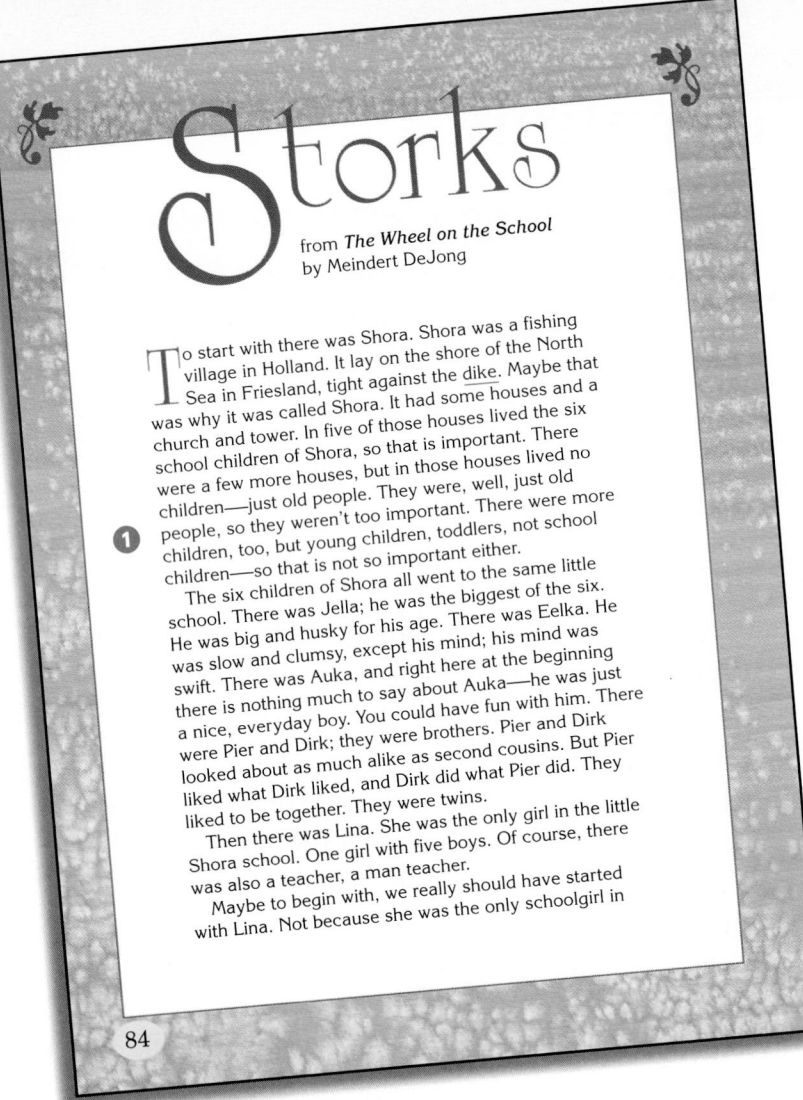

Storks

from *The Wheel on the School*
by Meindert DeJong

To start with there was Shora. Shora was a fishing village in Holland. It lay on the shore of the North Sea in Friesland, tight against the dike. Maybe that was why it was called Shora. It had some houses and a church and tower. In five of those houses lived the six school children of Shora, so that is important. There were a few more houses, but in those houses lived no children—just old people. They were, well, just old people, so they weren't too important. There were more children, too, but young children, toddlers, not school children—so that is not so important either.

The six children of Shora all went to the same little school. There was Jella; he was the biggest of the six. He was big and husky for his age. There was Eelka. He was slow and clumsy, except his mind; his mind was swift. There was Auka, and right here at the beginning there is nothing much to say about Auka—he was just a nice, everyday boy. You could have fun with him. There were Pier and Dirk; they were brothers. Pier and Dirk looked about as much alike as second cousins. But Pier liked what Dirk liked, and Dirk did what Pier did. They liked to be together. They were twins.

Then there was Lina. She was the only girl in the little Shora school. One girl with five boys. Of course, there was also a teacher, a man teacher.

Maybe to begin with, we really should have started with Lina. Not because she was the only schoolgirl in

84

About the Author

Meindert DeJong was born in Weirum, a small village in Holland. He moved to Grand Rapids, Michigan, when he was eight years old. Many of his books for children are based on his childhood memories. He has received many awards, including the Hans Christian Andersen International Children's Book Medal, the National Book Award, and the Newbery Medal for *Wheel on the School*, from which "Storks" is excerpted.

Students can read more about Meindert DeJong on page 112 of the **Student Anthology.**

Other Books by Meindert DeJong
- *Hurry Home, Candy*
- *The House of Sixty Fathers*
- *Journey from Peppermint Street*

Selection Summary

Genre: Realistic Fiction

When Lina, the only girl in the school, writes an essay about storks, she inspires her teacher and classmates to wonder why there are no storks in their village of Shora. Lina discovers that once, a long time ago, there *were* storks in Shora. Can the students and the teacher work together to bring back the storks?

 **Exploring the Theme**

Selection Concepts

"Storks" is realistic fiction that chronicles a young girl's desire for knowledge and illustrates the role that relationships play in our learning. The key concepts are:

- Feeling excluded can give rise to competitiveness.
- Feeling competitive can spur us to learn.
- We can learn a great deal from unexpected sources.
- Cooperative efforts can lead to solutions to problems and deeper understanding.

 Check the Reading link of the **SRA** Web page for links to theme-related Websites.
http://www.sra4kids.com

Exploration Activity Tips

Before Reading, initiate discussion about whether or not it is possible to be cooperative and competitive at the same time, and why someone might choose to be one but not the other.

During Reading, have students record words and phrases that describe each of the main characters.

After Reading, have students review the descriptions they wrote for each of the characters. Ask them how their understanding of each character grew and changed from the beginning of the story to the end.

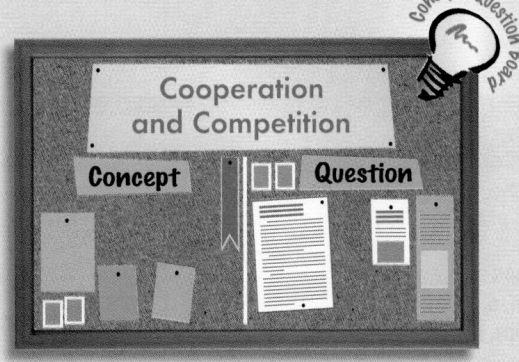

Unit I Exploration Management

Lesson 1	Discuss experiences with cooperation and competition. Generate ideas for dramatic play.
Lesson 2	Students give and receive feedback on their unit activity ideas, and begin to work in groups on the storyboards for their plays.
Lesson 3	Students complete their storyboards and share them with other groups, then revise the storyboards based on feedback.
Lesson 4	Students begin group work on writing plays in script format. They agree on director and actor roles and begin rehearsal.
Lesson 5	Students complete the final drafts of their scripts and plan their dress rehearsals.
Lesson 6 **Storks**	**Collaborative Exploration** **Students complete play rehearsals and perform their plays. They put scripts in a class anthology and prepare a title page and table of contents.** **Supplementary Activity** **Schedule performances and oversee unit celebration.**

Lesson Planner

Suggested Pacing: 3–5 days	DAY 1	DAY 2	
	DAY 1	DAY 2	
Part 1 · Preparing to Read **Materials** ■ Student Anthology, pp. 84–113 ■ Transparencies 6, 44	**Word Knowledge** ■ Reading the Words and Sentences, p. 84G ■ Developing Oral Language, p. 84G **Build Background, p. 84H** **Preview and Prepare, p. 84I** **Selection Vocabulary, p. 84I** *dike, wretchedly, deign, ponder, ramshackle*	**Preview and Prepare, p. 84I** ■ Review Transparency 44	
Part 2 · Reading and Responding **Materials** ■ Student Anthology, pp. 84–113 ■ Teacher Observation Log ■ Reading and Writing Workbook, pp. 39–42 ■ Inquiry Journal, p. 7 ■ Transparency 48 ■ Home Connection, p. 13	**Student Anthology, pp. 84–97** **Comprehension Strategies** ■ Clarifying, pp. 84, 90, 92, 94 ■ Summarizing, p. 86 ■ Asking Questions, pp. 88, 90, 96	**Student Anthology, pp. 98–113** **Comprehension Strategies** ■ Summarizing, pp. 98, 102, 104, 106, 108, 110 ■ Clarifying, p. 100 ■ Asking Questions, pp. 102, 110 **Discussing Strategy Use, p. 110** **Comprehension Skills** ✓ ■ Cause and Effect, pp. 85, 87, 89, 97, 99 ✓ ■ Discussing the Selection, p. 111 **Exploring the Theme** ■ Selection Vocabulary, p. 113A *dike, wretchedly, deign, ponder, ramshackle*	
Part 3 · Integrating the Curriculum **Materials** ■ Student Anthology, pp. 84–113 ■ Reading and Writing Workbook, pp. 43–46 ■ Inquiry Journal, p. 17	**Writing** ■ Publish, pp. 113C, D **Literary Elements** ✓ ■ Literary Terms, p. 113E	**Writing Process** ■ Publish, p. 113D **Spelling** ✓ ■ Inflectional Endings, p. 113F	
Independent Work Time **Materials** ■ Reteach, pp. 39–46 ■ ESL Supplement ■ Challenge, pp. 22–25 ■ Intervention Guide ■ Research CD-ROM ■ Listening Library Audiocassette	**Writing Process Continued** **ESL** ■ Word Meaning, p. 84G **Intervention** ■ Antonyms, p. 84G ■ Comprehension, p. 84 ■ Asking Questions, p. 88 **Unit Project: Perform Plays**	**Writing Process Continued** **Reteach** ✓ ■ Literary Terms, *Reteach*, pp. 43–44 **ESL** ■ Vocabulary, p. 84J **Challenge** ✓ ■ Literary Terms, *Challenge*, p. 24 ■ Spelling Inflectional Endings, p. 113F **Intervention** ■ Clarifying, p. 92 **Unit Project Continued**	

✓ **Informal** Assessment Available   ✓ **Formal** Assessment Available

DAY 2 continued	DAY 3	
DAY 3	**DAY 4**	**DAY 5**

General Review | **General Review** | **Review Word Knowledge**

Student Anthology, pp. 84–113
Comprehension Skills
✓ ■ Making Inferences, pp. 91, 93, 95, 107, 109
Theme Connections
■ Think About It, p. 113
■ Descriptive Writing, p. 113

Student Anthology, pp. 84–113
Comprehension Skills
✓ ■ Author's Point of View, pp. 101, 103, 105
Exploring the Theme
■ Reading/Writing Connections, p. 113A
■ Literature Appreciation, p. 113A
■ Supporting Student Explorations, p. 113B

Student Anthology, pp. 84–113
■ Review Selection
■ Complete Discussion
■ Reread Selection in Pairs
Home Connection, p. 113A
■ Discuss "Storks"
■ Write a plan for developing a habitat

Writing Process Continued
Grammar, Usage, and Mechanics
✓ ■ Capitalizing Titles, p. 113G
Listening/Speaking/Viewing
■ Illustrations, p. 113H

Writing Process Continued
Study and Research
■ Using Multiple Sources, p. 113I

Across the Curriculum
Social Studies
■ Olympic Competitions, p. 113J
Science
■ Thinking About the Animals, p. 113J
Unit I Test

Writing Process Continued
Reteach
✓ ■ Cause and Effect, *Reteach*, pp. 39–40
ESL
■ Making Inferences, p. 93
Challenge
✓ ■ Cause and Effect, *Challenge*, p. 22
■ Making Inferences, p. 95
Intervention
■ Clarifying, p. 94
Unit Project Continued

Writing Process Continued
Reteach
✓ ■ Capitalizing Titles, *Reteach*, pp. 45–46
Challenge
✓ ■ Capitalizing Titles, *Challenge*, p. 25
■ Author's Point of View, p. 103
Unit Project Continued

Complete Writing Process
Reteach
✓ ■ Author's Point of View, *Reteach*, pp. 41–42
Challenge
✓ ■ Author's Point of View, *Challenge*, p. 23
Complete Unit Project

Meeting Individual Needs
Independent Work Time

Part 1
Preparing to Read

Meeting Individual Needs

ESL
- Word Meaning, p. 84G
- Vocabulary, p. 84J

Intervention
- Antonyms, p. 84G

Part 2
Reading and Responding

Meeting Individual Needs

Reteach
- Cause and Effect, *Reteach*, pp. 39–40
- Author's Point of View, *Reteach*, pp. 41–42

ESL
- Making Inferences, p. 93
- Cultural Context, p. 108

Challenge
- Cause and Effect, p. 89
- Making Inferences, p. 95
- Cause and Effect, *Challenge*, p. 22
- Author's Point of View, p. 103
- Author's Point of View, *Challenge*, p. 23

Intervention
- Comprehension, p. 84
- Summarizing, pp. 86, 102
- Asking Questions, p. 88
- Cause and Effect, p. 89
- Clarifying, pp. 92, 94
- Making Inferences, p. 95
- Author's Point of View, p. 101

Part 3
Integrating the Curriculum

Meeting Individual Needs

Reteach
- Literary Terms, *Reteach*, pp. 43–44
- Capitalizing Titles, *Reteach*, pp. 45–46

ESL
- Expressing Ideas, p. 113H

Challenge
- Literary Terms, *Challenge*, p. 24
- Spelling Inflectional Endings, p. 113F
- Capitalizing Titles, *Challenge*, p. 25

Formal Assessment Options

Use these assessment pages along with your informal observations to gauge student progress.

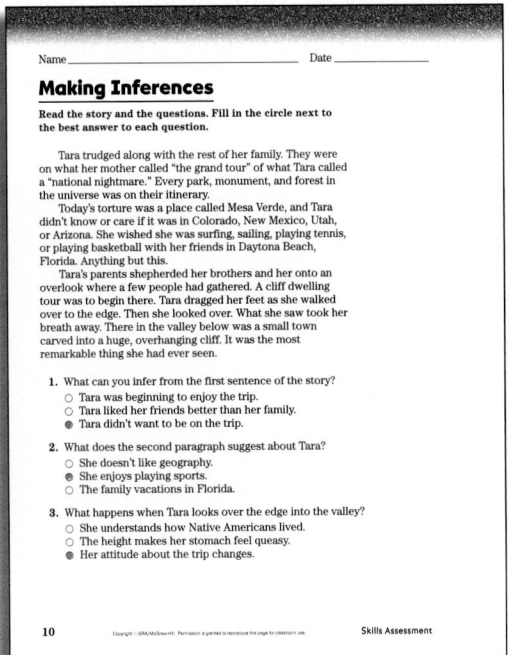

Skills Assessment, p. 10

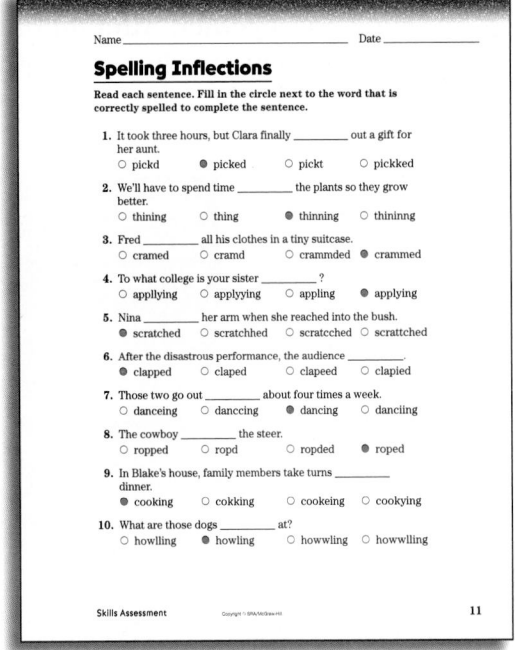

Skills Assessment, p. 11

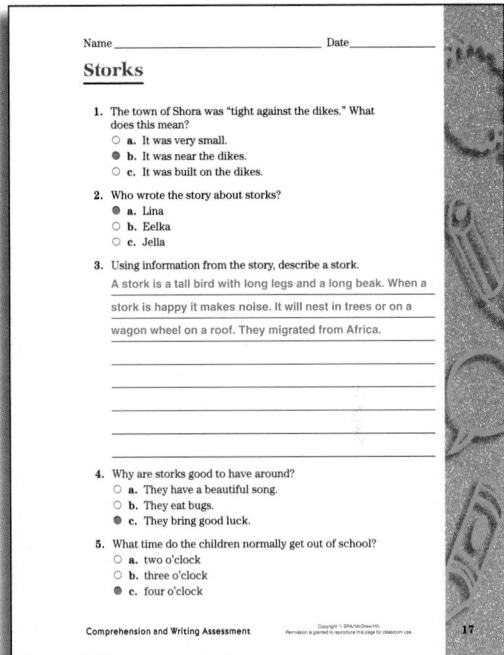

Comprehension and Writing Assessment, p. 17

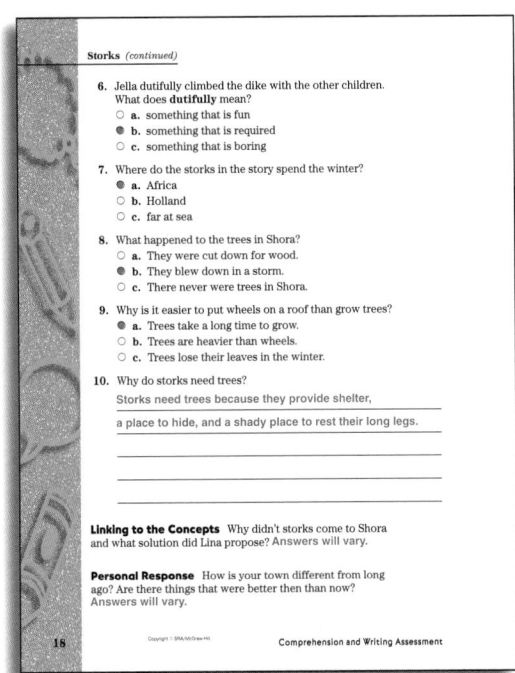

Comprehension and Writing Assessment, p. 18

① Preparing to Read

Meeting Individual Needs

ESL

Word Meaning Make sure the English-language learners understand the meaning of the words before they do the exercises. Refer to Unit 1, Lesson 6 of the *ESL Supplement* for specific suggestions.

Intervention

Antonyms Make a list of words. Next to each word, write an antonym and a synonym. Say the words aloud to students. Ask them to tell you which word is the antonym and how they know. If necessary, remind students that antonyms are words that have opposite meanings. For students who need more help, see Unit 1, Lesson 6 of the *Intervention Guide.*

Reading the Words and Sentences

Write each word and sentence on the chalkboard. Have students read each word together. After all the words have been read, have students read each sentence in natural phrases or chunks. Use the suggestions in About the Words to discuss the different features of the listed words.

Line 1: hurried dawdled neat messy distant close
Line 2: except explanation excite
Line 3: kitchen ditch watch
Sentence 1: She had an explanation for why the kitchen was so messy.
Sentence 2: Except for my cousin Joe, who is very neat, none of my relatives live close to here.
Sentence 3: They hurried after the ball, but they had to watch it roll into the ditch.

About the Words

- The word sets in Line 1 are antonyms. Antonyms are two words that mean the opposite of each other.

- The words in Line 2 have the /ks/ sound spelled *x*. Point out that this spelling of the /ks/ sound is always preceded by a short vowel.

- Line 3 contains words with the /ch/ sound spelled *tch*. Invite students to think of other words that contain this spelling of the /ch/ sound.

Developing Oral Language

To review the words, use one of the following activities.

- Draw students' attention to the second paragraph of the selection where the author gives descriptions of the characters. Point out these descriptions and see if students can give antonyms for them. For example, Eelka is *slow*; an antonym is *fast*. Write these antonym pairs on the chalkboard.

- Have one student point to one of the words on the chalkboard and ask another student to use that word in a sentence.

- Have students read the sentences focusing on fluency and intonation. Both of these are critical prerequisites for comprehension.

Build Background

Activate Prior Knowledge

Have students check the Concept/Question Board to refresh their memories about cooperation and competition. Discuss the following with students to find out what they already know about the selection and have already learned about the unit theme. Tell students to use their prior knowledge to help them comprehend the selection they are about to read.

- Ask students whether they are familiar with the story they are about to read, and if so, to tell a little about it. Remind students, however, not to give away the ending of the selection.
- Have students share any other stories that involve storks or Holland.
- Tell students to review what they have learned about cooperation and competition from the previous selections in this unit or from personal experiences.

Background Information

The following information may help the students better understand the selection they are about to read.

- The fictional village of Shora is on the shore of the North Sea in Friesland, which is in the northeast corner of Holland. Point out these locations on a world map.
- Holland is also called the Netherlands. About half of the Netherlands was once covered by the sea. Since about 1300, the Dutch have been reclaiming land from the sea by building walls of earth or stone called *dikes* and by pumping out seawater from behind the dikes into canals that flow into the North Sea.

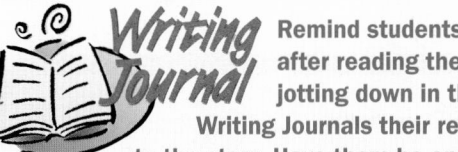
Writing Journal Remind students that after reading they will be jotting down in their Writing Journals their reactions to the story. Have them be on the lookout for any ideas they have for writing a story about a group of people trying to solve a common problem.

Teacher Tip Stories often have a main plot and several related sub-plots. As the story is read, explain that the main plot centers on the children's discovery of why the storks left Shora and how they might be enticed to return. One sub-plot focuses on the girl's interactions with her male classmates and another centers on her relationship with the old woman.

Preparing to Read

Transparency 44

To help students decode words, divide them into the syllables shown below. The information following each word tells how students can figure out the meaning of each word on the transparency.

dike	context clues
wretch·ed·ly	context clues, word structure
deign	context clues
pon·der	context clues
ram·shack·le	context clues

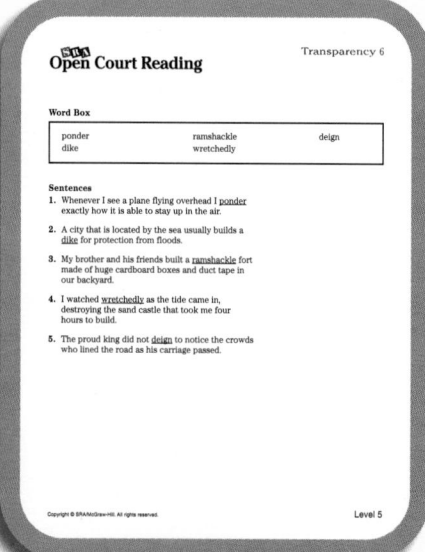

Transparency 6

Preview and Prepare

Browse

- Have a volunteer read the title and author's name aloud. Have students share what they know about realistic fiction.

- Have the students browse through the first half of the story, looking for words and phrases that connect to what they already know. Record these in the Clues column on **Transparency 44.** Discuss with students what they think this story might have to do with cooperation and competition.

- Encourage students to ask questions and identify any problems they notice while reading in the Problems column.

Set Purposes

As they read, have students think about how the teacher gets his students to work cooperatively together on investigating storks.

Selection Vocabulary

As students study vocabulary, they will use context clues, word structure, and apposition to clarify these and additional unfamiliar words.

Display **Transparency 6** before reading the selection to introduce and discuss the following words and their meanings.

dike:	a wall of earth or stone used to confine or control water (page 84)
wretch·ed·ly:	very unhappily (page 91)
deign:	to reluctantly agree to give, offer, or recognize something (page 91)
pon·der:	to think about or reflect on deeply (page 96)
ram·shack·le:	loosely held together (page 101)

Have students read the words in the Word Box. Help students decode multisyllabic words syllable by syllable.

Have students read the sentences on **Transparency 6** to determine the meaning of the underlined words. Remind them to use clues in the sentences and structural clues to figure out the meaning. See the teacher tip to the left for information on how the words in each sentence can be defined.

Reading Recommendations

Your first reading of the selection should focus on developing the reading strategies found to the left of the reduced pages. We recommend that the students revisit the selection, rereading sections or the entire selection as a way to enhance their understanding and appreciation of the text. During rereading, they should focus on the comprehension skills, found to the right of the reduced pages.

Oral Reading

Before having the students listen as classmates read this classic selection aloud, practice as a class the pronunciations of the characters' names. For your convenience, Teacher Tips on the pronunciations of foreign words and names occurring in the selection are featured beside and below the reduced **Student Anthology** pages in the **Teacher's Edition.** As students read aloud, have them read expressively, at an appropriate pace, in natural phrases and chunks. By reading the selection with fluency, students will demonstrate an understanding of the text and an ability to engage the listeners in an effective manner. If students encounter difficulties, have them use the reading strategies below or refer to the Blending Procedure (Program Appendix 15-16).

Using Reading Strategies

Reading strategy instruction allows students to become aware of how good readers read. Good readers constantly check their understanding as they are reading and ask themselves questions. In addition, skilled readers recognize when they are having problems and stop to use various reading strategies to help them make sense of what they are reading.

During the reading of "Storks," you will model the use of the following reading strategies:

- Asking Questions
- Summarizing
- Clarifying

Before reading, have students share how they have used these strategies in the past and any tips they can give each other on their use.

Building Comprehension Skills

Revisiting or rereading a selection allows students to apply skills that give them a more complete understanding of the text. Some follow-up comprehension skills help students organize information. Others lead to deeper understanding—to "reading between the lines," as mature readers do. In this section, students will apply the follow-up comprehension skills of, *Author's Point of View, Cause and Effect,* and *Making Inferences.* Since three skills are reviewed, you may want to do all the sections related to one skill before doing the next skill.

Teacher Tip Have students who may need extra help reading the classic story "Storks" reread the selection using the *Listening Library Audiocassette.*

Teacher Tip By this time in the fifth grade, good readers should be reading approximately 126 words per minute with fluency and expression. The only way to gain fluency is through practice. As explained in Reading Recommendations, have students reread all or part of the selection to you and to each other during class or Independent Work Time to focus on the comprehension skills and to build fluency.

Meeting Individual Needs

ESL

Vocabulary Check that English-language learners know the meanings of idioms and more difficult vocabulary in the story, including *composition, surly, wonderment, ponder, of her own accord, dike, lagged, mystified, inquisitive, deign, portal, woebegone, wheedling, ramshackle,* and *skulk.* For more information, refer to Unit 1, Lesson 6, of the **ESL Supplement.**

② Reading and Responding

Read pages 84–113.

Comprehension Strategies

Modeling

❶ **Clarifying** *Good readers stop to clarify words or ideas that they don't understand. I wonder why the author says that houses without children are not important. Perhaps the text will give us some clues that clarify why the author would say something so unusual. The author also says that young children are not important.*
It seems as if only the six school children are important.

When we continue reading we see that the author keeps talking about them. I'm sure that the story events will have to do with these six children.

Modeling

❷ **Clarifying** *Lina calls her piece of writing a story, and the author says it's really an essay. Let's clarify the difference between a story and an essay. A story has characters in it and tells about something that happened. An essay usually gives information about one topic. Is there anything else that should be clarified before we read on?*

 **Teacher Tip** There are many names in this selection that students will find unfamiliar. Help them to pronounce these. Jella is pronounced ye′iä; Eelka is pronounced āl′kä; Auka is pronounced ō′kä; Pier is pronounced pēr; Dirk is pronounced dėrk; Lina is pronounced lē′na.

Reading Recommendation

ORAL · CHORAL · SILENT

Storks

from *The Wheel on the School*
by Meindert DeJong

To start with there was Shora. Shora was a fishing village in Holland. It lay on the shore of the North Sea in Friesland, tight against the <u>dike</u>. Maybe that was why it was called Shora. It had some houses and a church and tower. In five of those houses lived the six school children of Shora, so that is important. There were a few more houses, but in those houses lived no children—just old people. They were, well, just old ❶ people, so they weren't too important. There were more children, too, but young children, toddlers, not school children—so that is not so important either.

The six children of Shora all went to the same little school. There was Jella; he was the biggest of the six. He was big and husky for his age. There was Eelka. He was slow and clumsy, except his mind; his mind was swift. There was Auka, and right here at the beginning there is nothing much to say about Auka—he was just a nice, everyday boy. You could have fun with him. There were Pier and Dirk; they were brothers. Pier and Dirk looked about as much alike as second cousins. But Pier liked what Dirk liked, and Dirk did what Pier did. They liked to be together. They were twins.

Then there was Lina. She was the only girl in the little Shora school. One girl with five boys. Of course, there was also a teacher, a man teacher.

Maybe to begin with, we really should have started with Lina. Not because she was the only schoolgirl in

84

Meeting Individual Needs

Intervention

Comprehension Intervention strategies for those students having difficulty with reading "Storks" can be found in Unit 1, Lesson 6, of the **Intervention Guide.**

Shora, but because she wrote a story about storks. There were no storks in Shora. Lina had written this story about storks of her own accord—the teacher hadn't asked her to write it. In fact, until Lina read it out loud to the five boys and the teacher, nobody in school had even thought about storks.

But there one day, right in the middle of the arithmetic lesson, Lina raised her hand and asked, "Teacher, may I read a little story about storks? I wrote it all myself, and it's about storks."

2 Lina called it a story, but it was really an essay, a composition. The teacher was so pleased that Lina had written a little piece of her own accord, he stopped the arithmetic lesson right there and let Lina read her story. She began with the title and read on:

Do You Know About Storks?

Do you know about storks? Storks on your roof bring all kinds of good luck. I know this about storks; they are big and white and have long yellow bills and tall yellow legs. They build great big messy nests, sometimes right on your roof. But when they build a nest on the roof of a house, they bring good luck to that house and to the whole village that that house stands in. Storks do not sing. They make a noise like you do when you clap your hands when you feel happy and good. I think storks clap their bills to make the happy sounds when they feel happy and good. They clap their bills almost all the time except when they are in the marshes and ditches hunting

85

Comprehension Skills

Cause and Effect

Introduce students to the concept of *cause and effect*. A *cause* is *why* something happens. The *effect* is *what* happens. Authors use cause and effect to advance the plot. Reasons and causes tell why things happen, why people feel as they do, or why things are the way they are. Have students read paragraph 3 from page 85. Point out that:

■ The teacher was pleased (the effect) *because* Lina had written a story on her own (the cause).

■ *Because* he was so pleased (the cause), he stopped the lesson and let her read the story out loud (the effect).

Point out that causes and effects can be related. (In the examples above, the teacher being pleased is first a cause and then an effect.) Also, tell students that authors sometimes use clue words to indicate cause and effect. For example, the author says we should start with Lina *because* she wrote a story about storks. Display ***Transparency 48.*** Have the students fill in the causes and effects in the table on the transparency using information found in the story.

← **Skills Strand** →

Cause and Effect
INTRODUCED: Unit 1, Lesson 6
REVIEWED: Unit 2, Lesson 6
Unit 4, Lesson 4

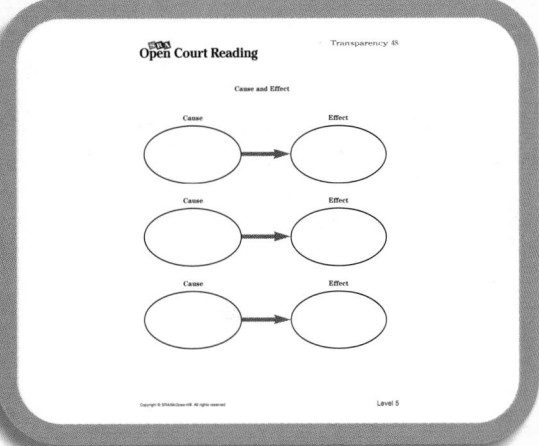

Transparency 48

 **Reading and Responding**

Comprehension Strategies

Modeling

3 **Summarizing** *Good readers stop periodically to paraphrase what they have read to help them recall it. It might be a good time for us to stop here and sum up the information in the essay. Storks are white, with yellow bills and legs. They build nests on roofs. They bring good luck and make happy sounds. They hunt frogs and small fish. There are no storks in Shora.*

Can anyone tell me another reason why it was important for us to sum up the essay? (to check one's understanding of the text)

---

for frogs and little fishes and things. Then they are quiet. But on your roof they are noisy. But it is a happy noise, and I like happy noises.

That is all I know about storks; but my aunt in the village of Nes knows a lot about storks, because every year two big storks come to build their nest right on her roof. But I do not know much about storks, because storks never come to Shora. They go to all the villages all around, but they never come to Shora. That is the most that I know about storks, but if they came to Shora, **3** I would know more about storks.

After Lina had finished reading her story, the room was quiet. The teacher stood there looking proud and pleased. Then he said, "That was a fine story, Lina. A very fine composition, and you know quite a lot about storks!" His eyes were pleased and bright. He turned to big Jella. "Jella," he said, "what do you know about storks?"

"About storks, Teacher?" Jella said slowly. "About storks—nothing." He looked surly and stubborn, because he felt stupid. He thought he ought to explain. "You see," he told the teacher, "I can't bring them down with my slingshot. I've tried and tried, but I just can't seem to do it."

The teacher looked startled. "But why would you want to shoot them down?"

"Oh, I don't know," Jella said. He wriggled a little in his seat. He looked unhappy. "Because they move, I guess."

"Oh," the teacher said. "Pier," he said then, "Dirk, what do you twins know about storks?"

86

Word Knowledge

explain

Students can use the skills they learned in the Word Knowledge section of this lesson to read this word. Remind students of this if they have difficulty reading this word.

Meeting Individual Needs

Intervention

Summarizing Have the students share their own knowledge about storks. Have them summarize what they have learned about storks from the story. Remind the students to reread if they have a hard time remembering what has happened. Have the students discuss some of the things that surprised them in the essay.

"About storks?" Pier asked. "Nothing."

"Dirk," the teacher said.

"Just the same as Pier," Dirk said. "Nothing."

"Pier," the teacher said, "if I had asked Dirk first, what would have been your answer?"

"The same as Dirk's," Pier answered promptly. "Teacher, that's the trouble with being twins—if you don't know something, you don't know it double."

The teacher and the room liked that. It made everybody laugh. "Well, Auka," the teacher said, "how about you?"

Auka was still chuckling and feeling good about what Pier had said, but now he looked serious. "All I know is that if storks make happy noises with their bills like Lina said in her story, then I would like storks, too."

The teacher looked around and said: "Well, Eelka, there in the corner, that leaves only you."

Eelka thought awhile. "I'm like Lina, Teacher; I know little about storks. But if storks would come to Shora, then I think I would learn to know a lot about storks."

"Yes, that is true," the teacher said. "But now what do you think would happen if we all began to think a lot about storks? School's almost out for today, but if, from now until tomorrow morning when you come back to school, you thought and thought about storks, do you think things would begin to happen?"

They all sat still and thought that over. Eelka raised his hand. "But I'm afraid I can't think much about storks when I don't know much about storks. I'd be through in a minute."

87

Comprehension Skills

Cause and Effect

Call the students' attention to the following examples of how cause and effect move along the plot of a story. Have students find the other examples themselves.

- Page 85: "Storks on your roof bring all kinds of good luck." (Storks on the roof is the cause; good luck is the effect.)

- Page 86: Lina says, "I do not know much about storks *because* storks never come to Shora." (Note the use of the clue word *because*.)

- Page 86: Jella looks surly and stubborn *because* he feels stupid. (Note the use of the clue word *because*.)

Have the students find more examples of cause and effect as they continue reading.

Teacher Tip Point out that by identifying the causes of characters' behavior, one can infer a great deal about their personalities and how they react to certain situations.

2 Reading and Responding

Comprehension Strategies

Modeling

 **4 Asking Questions** *Good readers ask questions that prepare them for what they will learn. They answer these questions by reading the text or referring to outside sources to check their understanding of the text and add to their store of knowledge.*

Why is the teacher so eager to have the students wonder about storks? He even lets them out an hour early from school just to wonder! This is such an odd occurrence, I know that it is important for us to question it.

When we reread, we see that he says if they wonder, then something will begin to happen. Let's keep reading to find out what that could be. (This question is answered on page 102.)

Students may wish to share their questions with other students. Can any of them be answered? Remind the students to look for the answers to their questions as they read.

Word Knowledge

ditch

Students can use the skills they learned in the Word Knowledge section of this lesson to read this word. Remind students of this if they have difficulty reading this word.

Everybody laughed, but the teacher's eyes weren't pleased. "True, true," he said. "That's right, Eelka. We can't think much when we don't know much. But we can wonder! From now until tomorrow morning when you come to school again, will you do that? Will you wonder why and wonder why? Will you wonder why storks don't come to Shora to build their nests on the roofs, the way they do in all the villages around? For sometimes when we wonder, we can make things begin to happen.

4 "If you'll do that—then school is out right now!"

There they were out in the schoolyard—free! Jella peered again over the roofs on the houses at the distant tower rising beside the dike. He couldn't believe it. But the big white face of the tower clock spelled out three—a little past three. "Boy," Jella said in wonderment, "he let us out almost a whole hour early, just because of storks." Jella was beginning to appreciate storks. "What'll we do?" he said eagerly to the other boys.

But Lina took charge. Since she had started it with her essay about storks, she felt responsible. It was a wonderful day, the sky was bright and blue, the dike was sunny. "Let's all go and sit on the dike and wonder why, just like the teacher said."

Nobody objected. They all dutifully set out for the dike, still feeling happy because of the hour of freedom that had so suddenly and unexpectedly come to them. Still grateful enough to the storks and Lina to be obedient to her and sit on the dike and think about storks. But Jella lagged behind, and that was unusual. Big Jella was generally in

88

Meeting Individual Needs

Intervention

Asking Questions Have the students keep notes on questions asked and answered about storks in the selection in a fact sheet format. Not only will this help them track their questions and answers, they can also use it to make a summary of the selection once they have finished reading it.

the lead. Going down the village street he stared at every house he passed as if they were something new in the new freedom. But he dutifully climbed the dike and dutifully sat down at the end of the row of boys. Lina sat at the other end.

They sat. Nobody seemed to know just how to begin to wonder without the teacher there to start them off. Jella stared up at the sky. There wasn't a cloud in the sky. There were no storks. There wasn't even a gull. Jella looked at the sea stretching empty before him—there wasn't a ship in the sea.

Jella looked along the quiet row. Everybody was just sitting, hugging his knees. Everybody looked quiet and awkward and uncomfortable. Suddenly Jella had had enough. He looked along the row of boys at Lina. "The teacher didn't say we had to sit in a row on the dike to wonder, did he?"

"No," Lina said, "but I thought, well, he's never given us a whole hour off from school before, and I thought . . ."

"Well, then," Jella said . . . It just didn't feel right to sit when you were free. But the quiet sea and the quiet sky suggested nothing to him. Then fortunately a slow canalboat came pushing around a faraway bend in the canal. The two men on deck lowered the sail and the mast, so the boat could slide under the low bridge. The men picked up poles to push the boat along under the bridge. Jella jumped up. Now he had an idea. "Hey, let's all go get our poles and go ditch jumping!"

89

Comprehension Skills

Cause and Effect

Point out that words such as *because, since,* and *therefore* help indicate a cause-and-effect relationship. Ask the students for examples of main ideas from their reading that are supported by reasons or causes. Point out that sometimes an author gives reasons for events in a story, or for the way characters feel, or the way things are. Other times the author tells what *causes* something to happen or to be the way it is.

Ask the students to reread page 88. Point out that the teacher asks the students to wonder about storks. This request *causes* the rest of the story to happen. If the teacher didn't ask the students to wonder about storks, there would be no story—or at least, it would be a different story completely.

Meeting Individual Needs

Challenge

Cause and Effect Remind students that cause-and-effect relationships are interrelated. Have the students look through the story for chains of causes and effects (for example, cause → effect → cause).

Intervention

Cause and Effect Review the causes and effects discussed so far. Help students understand what the cause and effect are in each situation. Work with the students to find more examples in the story.

2 Reading and Responding

Comprehension Strategies

Modeling

5 Clarifying *I don't know what ditch jumping is. Let me try to clarify. Well, Jella tells the other boys to get their poles, so somehow that is used in ditch jumping. I know that Holland has a lot of canals. Maybe ditch jumping is like pole vaulting. Only instead of jumping over a bar, you put the pole in the water of a canal and jump from one side to the other. Why was it important for us to clarify this part?*

Modeling

6 Asking Questions *Why is Lina so upset with the boys?*

When we keep reading we see that she feels left out. The boys don't want her to jump ditches with them. Being the only girl is hard on Lina. We also read that Jella is worried that Lina will tell the teacher that they jumped ditches instead of wondering. Will she? Let's read on to see if she does. (This question is answered on page 102.)

What questions about this part of the story do you have?

Word Knowledge

catch, wretchedly

Students can use the skills they learned in the Word Knowledge section of this lesson to read these words. Remind students of this if they have difficulty reading these words.

All the boys, with the exception of Eelka, jumped up eagerly. Here was something to do—fun in the freedom.

"You, too, Eelka. Run and get your pole," Jella said. "And tell Auka to get mine, too. I'll wait here."

5 Lina stared at Jella in dismay. Even Eelka had to go. When it came to ditch jumping, Eelka generally was left out—he was too fat and slow and clumsy. "But I thought we were going to wonder why storks don't come to Shora?" Lina said. If even Eelka had to go along, she was going to be left behind all alone.

6 Lina glared down the dike after the running boys. "All right for you, Eelka," she yelled unhappily. She looked darkly at Jella. "Boy, if the teacher finds out that you . . ." She swallowed her words. It was a bitter, lost feeling to be left behind all alone in the surprise free hour.

Lina had a sudden hopeful thought. It must be that Jella wanted them all in on the ditch jumping, so that if the teacher found out, they'd all catch it together. Maybe he'd let her in on it, too! Maybe that was why he had stayed here with her on the dike. "Jella," Lina asked, "can I go, too? Why, if it wasn't for me, you'd be sitting in school right now. And I could get my mother's clothes pole. It's long and smooth and . . ."

"Naw," Jella said immediately. "Girls are no good at jumping. It's a boy's game."

"I'd be just as good as Eelka. Better even," Lina said indignantly.

"Yeah, I guess so. But Eelka doesn't mind getting wet, but girls worry about wet feet and their dresses flying.

90

Tell the students to clarify parts of the text that they find unclear as they read. Clues in the text and sharing knowledge with other students are two ways to clarify unfamiliar words and ideas.

And they squeal and scream, and then they get scared and go giggly."

Jella seemed to have thought a lot about it. Lina could see it was totally no use wheedling or arguing. She drew her wooden shoes primly up under her, hugged her knees, and stared wretchedly out at the sea. "Teacher said we were to wonder why the storks don't come. He even said if we wondered really hard things might begin to happen."

"We'll wonder while we jump ditches," Jella said shortly. He was a bit uneasy. But now the boys were coming back, Auka with two vaulting poles. Jella started to leave. "And we don't care if you do tell the teacher! He didn't say we were supposed to sit like dopes on the dike."

So Jella did care—he was even worried she would tell. She was no tattletale! Lina did not <u>deign</u> to turn around to answer. But she couldn't help looking down the dike when Eelka came dragging his long vaulting pole. "All right, for you, Eelka," she said stormily.

That was the trouble with being the only girl: you got left out of things. And if Eelka didn't also get left out, there was nothing for her to do but sit by herself or play with her little sister Linda and the other little children. What was the fun of that? Well, she'd show them. She'd sit right here and think and wonder really hard. Tomorrow morning when the teacher asked, up would go her hand, but there they'd all sit stupid and with their mouths full of teeth. It did not seem much of a threat. The excited voices of the boys came drifting back to her.

91

Making Inferences

Review with the students that writers don't always provide all the information in a selection. Readers use clues from the text and their own knowledge to better understand a character or event in a story. This is called *making inferences*.

Point out the following information.

- Jella comes up with the idea for the boys to jump the ditches.
- Jella tells Eelka to tell Auka to bring his pole.
- Jella decides that Lina can't jump ditches with the boys and Lina accepts his decision.

What generalizations can the students make about Jella's character, based on the text and their own experiences? Suggest that Jella is a strong, forceful (even if not quite nice) leader. What are other clues that allow them to make an inference about Jella? Does Jella remind them of someone they know or another character they have read about? Point out that inferences are not spelled out, but are supported by clues in the story.

Skills Strand

Making Inferences

2 Reading and Responding

Comprehension Strategies

Modeling

7 Clarifying *I need to get clarification on something. We read that Lina is wearing wooden shoes. I've seen pictures of wooden shoes from Holland. I know that people wore wooden shoes a long time ago. But do they still wear wooden shoes? They may, but they probably also wear sneakers or boots like people do in this country. I think this story was written a long time ago, or else the author has set the story in the past. That would explain why Lina is wearing wooden shoes.*

Teacher Tip Students might enjoy asking their grandparents or older people in the community about changes in the local environment during their lifetimes.

Lina fixed her eyes hard upon a distant hazy swirling far out above the sea, wanting it to be a stork but knowing all the time it was just a sea gull. She wouldn't play with Eelka again for a week! Maybe ten days even, maybe three weeks! Even if in all that time Jella and the rest left Eelka out of every one of their games. She wouldn't bother with Eelka either. She just wouldn't bother!

She stared hard at the gull. It was still a gull; it wasn't a stork. Suppose a whole big flock of storks came flying up out of the sea. The boys, jumping ditches, wouldn't even see them. But Lina had to admit to herself it wouldn't make much difference if they saw the storks or not. The storks wouldn't stay in Shora, and the boys couldn't make them stay, so what was the difference. Lina sighed. It was hard being the only girl in Shora.

7 She took off one of her wooden shoes and sat staring moodily into it. She caught herself doing it. It was a lonely habit. She often sat staring into her shoe. It somehow made her feel better and seemed to help her to think better, but she didn't know why. She often wished she could wear her wooden shoes in the schoolroom instead of just socks. The wooden shoes had to be left out in the portal. Lina was sure it would help no end if she could pull off one of her shoes and stare and dream into it awhile—especially before doing an arithmetic problem. Lina sighed. You couldn't dream with arithmetic. With arithmetic you could only think. It made arithmetic sort of scary. Hard and scary and not very exciting.

92

Word Knowledge

fixed, exciting

Students can use the skills they learned in the Word Knowledge section of this lesson to read these words. Remind students of this if they have difficulty reading these words.

Meeting Individual Needs

Intervention

Clarifying Have the students work in pairs as partners to clarify unfamiliar terms and ideas in the text. Have them model the process for each other. It may sometimes be necessary to ask the students about parts of the text that you think may be confusing and then help them clarify the term or idea.

Storks were exciting! "Wonder why? Wonder why?" Lina said quite hard into her wooden shoe. The words came bouncing back at her out of the hard wooden shell. She whispered it into the shoe; the words came whispering back. She sat dreaming, staring into the shoe. And the sea gull was swirling and sailing far out at sea.

Still thinking and dreaming about storks, she got up in her nice hazy daze and wandered away from the dike, one shoe in her hand. She went slowly down the street, staring intently at the roofs of all the houses as if she'd never seen them before. The village street lay quiet and empty. Lina had it to herself all the way through the village to the little school. The school had the sharpest roof of all, Lina decided. All the roofs were sharp, but the school's was the sharpest.

A thin faraway shout and a shrill laugh came through to her. She turned. In the far, flat distance she could see the boys. Now big Jella, it must be Jella, went sailing high over a ditch. Hard behind him, first sprinting, then sailing high on their poles, came the other three boys. And then there came one more; it must be Eelka. But Eelka disappeared—he must have gone into the ditch. Now there was a lot of shouting and running. Lina caught herself waiting anxiously for Eelka to appear out of the ditch. Then she remembered that she wasn't going to play with Eelka for three weeks. She turned her back to the distant boys. "I hope he went in up to his neck," she heard herself saying half-aloud. It surprised her. For now it didn't matter whether or not Eelka went into the water

93

Comprehension Skills

Making Inferences

Continue to have the students make inferences. Point out the following sentences.

■ "Lina sighed. It was hard being the only girl in Shora." (page 92)

■ "She sat dreaming, staring into the shoe." (page 93)

Have students find more clues from the text to make inferences about Lina. What can the students infer about Lina? Help them see that she appears to be lonely and dreamy, and would like things to be different. Ask students if they remember a time when they felt "left out." How did it make them feel?

Meeting Individual Needs

ESL

Making Inferences Provide time for informal conversational practice. Pair English-language learners with native English-speaking students. Have partners compare inferences they have made about each of the characters, and the basis for those inferences.

2 Reading and Responding

Comprehension Strategies

Modeling

8 Clarifying *I don't understand what she plans to do with the wagon wheel. I need to reread that section for clarification.*

Now I see that they really did put a wagon wheel on the roof so it makes a surface on which the storks can land. If they don't have the wheel, then the storks can't land on the roof because it's too sharp. They can sit on the flat wagon wheel.

Is there anything else that is unclear?

Teacher Tip Remind the students that clarifying is a process. They may be helped by watching as you or another student models how to clarify a confusing word or idea.

---

up to his neck; it didn't matter that the boys were having fun. She knew why the storks didn't come to build their nests in Shora. The roofs were all too sharp! But not only did she know the reason why, she also knew what to do about it! They had to put a wagon wheel on top of one of **8** the roofs—a wagon wheel just like her aunt in Nes had on her roof. Tomorrow morning she would spring it on them in the schoolroom. They'd be surprised!

Lina started to hurry back to the village, almost as if she had to hurry to tell someone. She put her wooden shoe back on to hurry better. There wasn't anyone there, she knew. The boys were playing in the fields; the teacher had gone. She could go home and tell her mother, but she would tell her mother anyway. It just seemed to her there had to be somebody *new* to tell it to—she had that feeling. There wasn't anyone like that. The whole street lay empty. It made her hurrying suddenly seem senseless. Lina slowed herself by staring at a house.

Once more Lina dawdled down the street, once more she stood a dreamy while before each house. Her shoe came off again. She was staring up at the roof of Grandmother Sibble III's house when the old lady came out. It startled Lina.

"I know I'm a nosy old creature," Grandmother Sibble III said, "but there you stand again, staring. I've been watching you wandering from the dike to the school and back again like a little lost sheep."

Lina laughed a polite little laugh. "Oh, I'm not exactly wandering. I'm wondering."

94

Word Knowledge

watching, exactly, explain

Students can use the skills they learned in the Word Knowledge section of this lesson to read these words. Remind students of this if they have difficulty reading these words.

Meeting Individual Needs

Intervention

Clarifying Students may want to make a list of all the confusing ideas and unfamiliar words they encounter in this selection. As they achieve clarification on the items on their lists, have them note each item's definition and how it was obtained. Encourage students to save their lists in the Personal Dictionary section of their Writer's Journals.

"Oh," said the old lady, <u>mystified</u>. "Well, I guess wondering is always better than wandering. It makes more sense." She chuckled a nice little old lady's chuckle.

They looked at each other. And Lina thought how she had never talked much to Grandmother Sibble III except to say a polite "hello" as she walked by. Now she did not know just what to say to her.

The old lady was still looking at her curiously. "Is that why you have your shoe in your hand?" she said gently. "Because you were wondering so hard?"

In surprise Lina glanced down at her hand holding the wooden shoe. She reddened a little and hastily slipped it on her foot. What must Grandmother Sibble think—not that she was her grandmother, she was just the grandmother of the whole village, the oldest old lady. It certainly must have looked silly, her hobbling down the street on one shoe, carrying the other. No wonder Grandmother Sibble III had come out of the house!

"I . . ." Lina said, trying to explain. She giggled a little. "Oh, isn't it silly?" She fished in her mind for some sensible explanation. None would come. But Grandmother Sibble III wasn't standing there grinning in a superior, adult way. She just looked—well, mystified and <u>inquisitive</u>. Lina decided to tell her. "I guess it does look silly and odd, but it somehow helps me think better to look into my shoe. Then when I get to thinking really hard, I forget to put it back on again," she said defensively.

"Why, yes," the old lady said immediately. "Isn't it funny how odd little things like that help? Now I can think

95

Comprehension Skills

Making Inferences

Explain that characters can also make inferences. Direct the students to the last paragraph on page 94. Point out that Lina is using her knowledge to make the inference that storks don't come to Shora because the roofs are too sharp.

See if students can find other examples in the text where characters use their knowledge to make inferences. *(For example, on page 92, Lina makes an inference that arithmetic is not exciting, using her knowledge that with arithmetic you can't dream. You can only think.)*

Warn students that inferences can change as one gets more information. Lina's idea might change, too, as the story goes on.

Meeting Individual Needs

Challenge

Making Inferences Have students make a chart with the following headings: *Character, Clues,* and *Inference.* Have students fill in the chart for the teacher, Jella, Eelka, and other characters as they read the story.

Intervention

Making Inferences Review Lina's inferences about the roofs in Shora. Help the students see that she used clues and her own knowledge to make the inferences. Suggest that this is a good model for them to follow when making their own inferences. Discuss other inferences the students have made about the story events or characters. Again, discuss their reasoning.

2 Reading and Responding

Comprehension Strategies

Modeling

9 Asking Questions *What is Grandmother Sibble getting at here? She doesn't seem to think that the roofs are the only reason the storks aren't nesting in Shora. Maybe Lina's idea wasn't so good after all! Let's keep reading and see what happens.*

Modeling

10 Answering Questions *Here's our answer. Grandmother Sibble thinks that part of the problem might be the roofs, but another part of the problem is that there are no trees in Shora. It wasn't that Lina was wrong exactly— she just didn't have the whole answer. Could there be more to the problem than roofs and trees? Maybe if we keep on reading, we'll find out.*

Encourage students to volunteer their own questions freely. Let them know that they do not have to wait until after you have used Asking Questions as a reading strategy for a particular section.

Word Knowledge

There are many multisyllabic words in this selection. Be sure students are using the skills they learned in the Word Knowledge section of this lesson.

much better by sort of rocking myself and sucking on a piece of candy, and I've done it ever since I was a little girl like you." She carefully settled herself on the top step of her brick stoop. She looked as if she was settling herself for a good, long chat. "Now of course, I've just got to know what it was you were thinking about so hard it made you forget your shoe." She chuckled her little old chuckle again. "And if you don't tell me, I won't sleep all night from trying to guess."

They laughed together. Grandmother Sibble patted the stoop next to her. "Why don't you come and sit down with me and tell me about it."

Lina eagerly sat down—close, exactly where the old lady had patted. Old Grandmother Sibble was nice, she thought to herself. It was a nice surprise. She didn't talk to you as if you were a tiny tot, almost a baby, and miles of years away, the way grownups usually did. She even understood silly girl things like looking into a wooden shoe. She understood it the way a girl friend—if you had a girl friend—would understand. A girl friend who also had silly tricks and secretly told you about them. Aloud Lina said, "I was thinking about storks, Grandmother Sibble. Why storks don't come and build their nests in Shora."

Grandmother Sibble looked thoughtful. "Well, that is a thing to ponder all right. No wonder you had your shoe off. We here in Shora always without storks."

"But I figured out why," Lina told the old lady proudly. "Our roofs are too sharp!"

96

"Well, yes . . . Yes, I guess so," the old lady said carefully, sensing Lina's sharp excitement. "But that could be remedied by putting a wagon wheel on the roof, couldn't it? The way they do in the other villages?"

"Yes, I'd thought of that," Lina said promptly. "My aunt in Nes has a wagon wheel on her roof, and storks nest on it every year."

(9) "Ah, yes," the old lady said, "but doesn't your aunt's house have trees around it, too?"

"Yes, it has," Lina said, looking in surprise at the little old lady. Why, Grandmother Sibble must have been thinking about storks, too. It seemed amazing, the old, old lady thinking about storks. "I guess I never thought about trees. Well, just because there are no trees in Shora—so I didn't think about trees." Lina's voice faded away. Here was a whole new thing to think about.

"Would a stork think about trees?" the old lady wanted to know. "It seems to me a stork would think about trees. And it seems to me that in order to figure out what a stork would want, we should try to think the way a stork would think."

Lina sat bolt upright. What a wonderful thing to say! Lina fumbled for her shoe while she eagerly looked at the old lady.

(10) "You see, if I were a stork, even if I had my nest on a roof, I think I would still like to hide myself in a tree now and then and settle down in the shade and rest my long legs. Not be on the bare peak of a roof for everybody to see me all the time."

97

Cause and Effect

Review with students the concept of *cause and effect*. Explain that writers use *cause and effect* to create drama and excitement in a story. Point out these examples from pages 96–97.

■ Lina's aunt's house has a wagon wheel on its roof *(cause)*, so storks nest in it every year *(effect)*.

■ Lina is excited *(effect)* because Grandma Sibble has also been thinking about storks *(cause)*.

Have the students find other examples of cause and effect.

2 Reading and Responding

Comprehension Strategies

Modeling

11 Summarizing *Well, that was quite a story. There was a lot of information in what Grandmother Sibble said, so I think we ought to stop and sum up what we've just read. Grandmother Sibble's grandmother had a house right where the school is now. There were storks living on the roof and in the willow trees. But a storm blew down some trees and salt spray killed the others. Then the storks left Shora and never came back. Have we left anything out of our summary?*

Teacher Tip Summarizing can be more fun when done as a game. Have students summarize in a round-robin fashion, with one person stating a sentence at a time, followed by the next person, and so on until the summary is complete.

Word Knowledge

There are many multisyllabic words in this selection. Be sure students are using the skills they learned in the Word Knowledge section of this lesson.

Lina pulled her feet up under her and looked down confusedly at her wooden shoes. She really needed her wooden shoe right now. Her thoughts were racing.

"You see, years ago," Grandmother Sibble was explaining, "oh, years and years ago when I was the only girl in Shora, the way you are the only girl now, there were trees in Shora and there were storks! The only trees in Shora grew on my grandmother's place. My grandmother was then the only grandmother of Shora. She was Grandmother Sibble I, just like I am now Grandmother Sibble III and you would someday be Grandmother Sibble IV if your mother had named you Sibble instead of Lina. I asked her to! Oh, I had no business asking—we're not even related—but it just seems there should always be a Grandmother Sibble in Shora. But that's beside the point.

"The point is, my grandmother's little house stood exactly where your school stands now but, oh, so different from your little naked school. Really different! My grandmother's house was roofed with reeds and storks like reeds. And my grandmother's house was hidden in trees. And storks like trees. Weeping willow trees grew around the edge of a deep moat that went all around my grandmother's house. And in the shadowy water under the hanging willows, <u>pickerel</u> swam in the moat. And over the moat there was a little footbridge leading right to my grandmother's door. And in one of the willows there was always a stork nest, and there was another nest on the low reed roof of my grandmother's house. As a little girl I used to stand on the footbridge

98

---

and think that I could almost reach up to the low roof of the little house and touch the storks, so close they seemed."

"Oh, I didn't know. I never knew," Lina said breathlessly.

Grandmother Sibble did not seem to hear. Her eyes were looking far, far back. She shook her head. "A storm came," she said. "As storms so often come to Shora. But this was a real storm. The wind and waves roared up the dike for longer than a week. For a whole week the water pounded and the salt spray flew. The air was full of salt; you even tasted the salt on your bread in your houses. And when it was all done, there were only three willows left at Sibble's Corner—that is what they called my grandmother's house, because everybody gathered there of a warm summer day to sit and chat and rest from work in the only shade in Shora, to talk and to lean their tired backs against the only trees. Then even those three left-over trees sickened and died. I guess their leaves had just taken in too much salt that long week of the storm.

"Later, after Grandmother Sibble I died, they came and tore down her house and chopped out the old rotted stumps of the willows and filled the moat with dirt. Then there was nothing for years and years, until they built your naked little school on the same spot. But the storks never came back."

⑪

Lina sat wide-eyed, hugging her knees, staring straight ahead, drinking it in, dreaming it over—the things the old lady had said—dreaming the picture. It sounded like a faraway tale, and yet it had been! Grandmother Sibble III had seen it! She had thought as a little girl that she

99

Comprehension
Skills

Cause and Effect

For more practice with cause and effect, have students complete *Reading and Writing Workbook* pages 39–40.

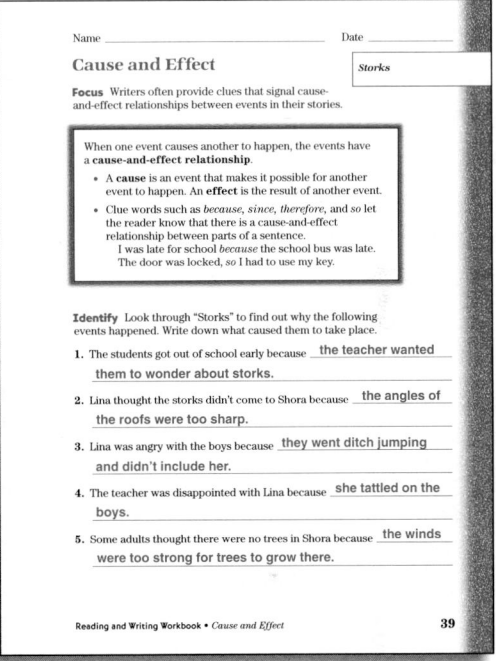

Reading and Writing Workbook pp. 39–40

Meeting Individual Needs

Reteach	**Challenge**
Cause and Effect Have students who need additional instruction and practice with this concept complete *Reteach,* pages 39–40.	**Cause and Effect** Have students who understand this concept and could benefit from extended practice complete *Challenge,* page 22.

Reading and Responding

Comprehension Strategies

Modeling

12 **Clarifying** *Wineballs? I've never heard of wineballs. We need to clarify this. They must be some kind of a candy or treat. Because they are called wineballs, I guess they are round. Grandmother Sibble talks about sucking on them, so they must be hard candy. Maybe they are called wineballs because they are purple, like wine. What do you think?*

It is important for students to recognize that they may understand all the words in a sentence without understanding the sentence. Just as important, they may understand what the sentence as a whole means even if they are unclear about the meaning of a certain word.

Word Knowledge

kitchen

Students can use the skills they learned in the Word Knowledge section of this lesson to read this word. Remind students of this if they have difficulty reading this word.

---

could reach up and touch the storks, it had been so real and so close. Right in Shora!

"I never knew. I never knew," Lina whispered to herself. "And even a little footbridge," she told herself and hugged her knees.

Grandmother Sibble III roused herself. "So you see you mustn't think our sharp roofs is the whole story, must you?" she said softly. "We must think about other things, too. Like our lack of trees, our storms, our salt spray. We must think about everything. And to think it right, we must try to think the way a stork would think!"

Grandmother Sibble said "we"!

"Then have you been thinking about storks, too?" Lina asked in astonishment.

"Ever since I was a little girl. And ever since then I've wanted them back. They're lucky and cozy and friendly and, well, just right. It's never seemed right again—the village without storks. But nobody ever did anything about it."

"Teacher says," Lina told the old lady softly, "that maybe if we wonder and wonder, then things will begin to happen."

"Is that what he said? Ah, but that is so right," the old lady said. "But now you run in the house. There's a little tin on my kitchen shelf and in it there are wineballs. You get us each a wineball out of the tin. Then I'll sit on my stoop and you sit on yours, and we'll think about storks. But we'll think better each on his own stoop, because often thinking gets lost in talking. And maybe your teacher is right—that

100

(12) if we begin to think and wonder, somebody will begin to make things happen. But you go find the candy tin; I can think much better sucking on a wineball. And you take one, too. You watch if it doesn't work much better than looking inside an old wooden shoe."

Lina had never been in Grandmother Sibble III's house before, never in the neat kitchen. There was the shelf, and there was the candy tin. There were storks on the candy tin! Pictures of storks in high sweeping trees were all around the four sides of the candy tin. On the lid was a village, and on every house there was a huge, <u>ramshackle</u> stork nest. In every nest tall storks stood as though making happy noises with their bills up into a happy blue sky.

Lina kept turning the candy tin to see the pictures again and again. Suddenly she woke up to the fact that she was staying in Grandmother Sibble's house a long, long time. Her first time in Grandmother Sibble's house, too! What would she think? She hastily shoved the candy tin back on its shelf and hurried to the stoop.

"Grandmother Sibble, storks on your candy tin! And on every roof a nest! Oh . . ." Suddenly Lina realized she'd forgotten the wineballs. She raced back. It was hard not to look at the storks, but she kept her face partly turned away and picked out two round, red wineballs. Then she ran back. "I forgot all about the wineballs," she apologized.

"Yes, I know," Grandmother Sibble said gently, for she saw that Lina—though looking straight at her while handing her her wineball—was not seeing her at all. Lina had dreams in her eyes. Lina was seeing storks on every

101

Comprehension Skills

Author's Point of View

Tell the students that writers choose a point of view from which to tell stories. In a *first-person narrative*, the story is told by a character in the story. In the *third-person narrative*, the story is told by someone outside of the story. Ask students what the point of view is in this story *(third person)*.

Ask the students to read paragraphs 2 and 3 on page 100. Ask them to point out the clue words that indicate that this story is written in the third person *(she, herself)*.

Ask the students to read paragraph 4 on page 101 and think about the other sections of the story. Point out that the author is showing Lina's thoughts and feelings. Explain that, while the story is told in the third person, it almost always stays with Lina's thoughts and actions, reflecting her point of view. Have students find examples that illustrate this.

Author's Point of View
INTRODUCED: Unit 1, Lesson 3
REVIEWED: Unit 1, Lesson 5
Unit 1, Lesson 6
Unit 3, Lesson 1
Unit 3, Lesson 6

Meeting Individual Needs

Intervention

Author's Point of View Help students find the difference between the first- and third-person narrative by comparing "Storks" to "Juggling" or "S.O.R. Losers." Help students note the clue words that indicate each type of narrator.

Reading and Responding

Comprehension Strategies

Modeling

13 Answering Questions *At the beginning of the story, I asked why the teacher wanted the students to wonder about storks. The teacher said that things might happen just because the children wondered. We just read that something very nice has happened. Now Lina has a friend she can talk to.*

Modeling

14 Summarizing *Because there is a break in the text, this is a good place to stop and summarize the important things that happened so far. Lina wrote about storks, and the teacher told the children to wonder why there were no storks. While the boys played games, Lina wandered the village and decided that the roofs needed wagon wheels for storks to make nests in. Grandmother Sibble told her that storks needed trees, too. Lina made a new friend.*

Why is this summary important?

Modeling

15 Answering Questions *At the beginning of this story, we wondered if Lina would tell the teacher about the boys playing instead of wondering. Well, she has and look what has happened. The boys didn't get in trouble. Instead, they just got angry at Lina and the teacher seems disappointed in her. I know she's sorry she told.*

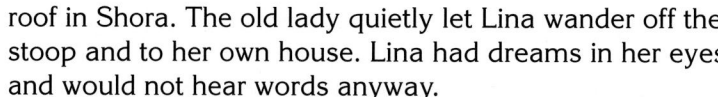

roof in Shora. The old lady quietly let Lina wander off the stoop and to her own house. Lina had dreams in her eyes and would not hear words anyway.

On her own stoop Lina looked back for the first time. There sat Grandmother Sibble III rocking herself a little and sucking on her wineball. But the dream Lina was dreaming was not just about storks—not directly. Later she would think about storks, try to think the way a stork would think, as Grandmother Sibble had said. But now she thought about Grandmother Sibble, who had a candy tin in her house with storks on it and who had known storks and who, when she was a little girl, had imagined she could reach up and almost touch the storks.

But that was not the wonder either, not quite. The real wonder was that, just as the teacher had said, things *had* begun to happen. Begin to wonder why, the teacher had said, and maybe things will begin to happen. And they had! For there sat Grandmother Sibble III on the stoop of her little house, and suddenly she had become important. She wasn't just an old person any more, miles of years away, she was a friend. A friend, like another girl, who **13** also wondered about storks.

Lina looked again at the little old lady, sitting there on the stoop. She marveled; she sat feeling nice and warm about a little old lady who had become a friend. It was a lovely feeling, as sweet as a wineball, as sweet as a dream. Lina took one shoe off and peered into it. Why, storks did bring good luck! The storks had made a friend for her. Why, now when the boys left her out of their games, she could go to Grandmother Sibble, and they

102

Meeting Individual Needs

Intervention

Summarizing Have the students share their ideas about why summarizing is useful. Have them suggest some strategies that would make summarizing easier, such as writing down main ideas as they read.

14 would sit and talk and chat. Lina looked up out of the shoe triumphantly. Why, yes!

In the morning it was school again. There they were in the schoolroom again, the five boys and Lina and the teacher. But this Saturday morning they did not start out by singing the old, old song about the country——"my lovely spot of ground, my fatherland, where once my cradle stood." No, they sat quietly as the teacher stood looking at each one of them in turn. And then he said, "Who wondered why? And where did it lead you?"

Lina's hand shot up. To her amazement every hand shot up with hers, even Jella's and Eelka's. The teacher looked so happy and pleased about it, it made Lina furious. "Why, Teacher, they never did! They went ditch jumping."

She clapped her hand to her mouth, but it was too late. She wasn't a tattletale. It was just that it had come boiling up out of her, because it had made her so furious. They were fooling the teacher, and it was making him happy.

15 The teacher looked at her a short moment. He seemed surprised. He turned away from her to Jella. Jella sat there in the front seat, big and stubborn and angry. He was really angry with her. But the teacher was saying, "Well, Jella, and what did you think was the reason why storks do not come to Shora?"

"Oh, I didn't think," Jella told the teacher honestly. "I asked my mother."

The teacher smiled. "Well, next to thinking, asking is the way to become wise. What did your mother say?"

"She said storks don't come to Shora because they never did. She said storks go back every year to the same

103

Comprehension Skills

Author's Point of View

Remind the students that writers often tell their story through a narrator. A first-person narrator is a character in the story. A third-person narrator is outside of the story. A first-person narrator tells the story through the eyes of one character.

Have the students look at the second paragraph on page 102. Discuss through whose eyes the author is telling the story. Guide the students to see that even though this is a third-person narrative, the story is being told through Lina's eyes. What do we learn about Lina?

Direct the students to Grandmother Sibble III's story within the story. Note that this story is told in the first person, from Grandmother Sibble's point of view.

Teacher Tip Some students might enjoy finding more information about Holland and creating a report for the class or a travel brochure about the country.

Meeting Individual Needs

Challenge

Author's Point of View Have the students rewrite a passage from this story from a first-person point of view, with Lina as the narrator. How might the passage change?

2 Reading and Responding

Comprehension Strategies

Modeling

16 Summarizing *This story has a lot of important information. Let's stop and summarize again so that we can make sense of it all. Back in school, Lina tells on the boys before she can stop herself. She is so excited that she also tells the whole story that Grandmother Sibble told her. She says that she thinks the sharp roofs are a main reason there are no storks. She also tells about Grandmother Sibble's candy box. Is there anything we should add to this summary?*

Teacher Tip Remind students that summarizing will help them be sure that they understand what they are reading. They should summarize in their own words and in the order in which the most important events occurred. Summing up as they read is a good habit whenever the students read long, difficult selections. It is also a good idea to sum up when they read a selection in several sittings.

Word Knowledge

There are many multisyllabic words in this selection. Be sure students are using the skills they learned in the Word Knowledge section of this lesson.

---

nesting spots. So if they never came to Shora, they never will. So there's just nothing to be done about it, she said."

Lina sat in her seat, trembling with eagerness to tell them that storks had once come to Shora, to tell them what Grandmother Sibble had said. She wanted to wave her hand frantically. But all the boys were angry with her, and even the teacher had been surprised and disappointed. It was a woebegone feeling, but still she had to do something. She quivered with eagerness. Then she *was* waving her hand, almost getting up out of her seat, but the teacher didn't take notice. She had to tell them! Lina heard herself saying out loud, "Oh, but storks did once upon a time come to Shora!"

They all turned to her, even the teacher. The next moment Lina was excitedly telling the room the story that Grandmother Sibble had told her about Sibble's Corner and the storks and the willow trees all around and the moat with the footbridge. About storks right here in the exact spot where the school now stood! She even told **16** about the pickerel in the moat.

Jella in the front seat turned right around when he heard about the pickerel. He forgot he was angry with her; he forgot he was in school. He just said right out loud, without permission, "Oh, boy, pickerel! Were they big, Lina?"

All the boys had big excited eyes. They seemed to be much more interested in the pickerel than in the storks. All but Eelka. Eelka raised his hand, and now he was saying in his slow way, "What Lina said about trees. You know, Teacher, that is exactly what I thought when I

104

---

wondered why. Storks don't come to Shora because we have no trees!"

Eelka's desk was next to Lina's. She twisted in her seat to stare at him. How did he dare? He'd wondered why! He'd gone jumping ditches!

It was as if Eelka knew what she was thinking, for he calmly told the teacher, "I don't suppose I would have thought of trees. It was really when I jumped right smack into the middle of a ditch and went under that I thought of it. I really got soaked, and I wished there was a tree to hang my clothes on. But there aren't any trees, so I had to go home dripping wet. Boy, did I catch it from my mother!"

The teacher laughed as long and hard as the class. Even Lina had to laugh.

"Well, Eelka," the teacher said, "even though you had to do your thinking under water, it was still good thinking." His eyes were bright with laughter as he turned to the class. "All right, now. Does everyone agree with Eelka that the number one reason why storks do not come to Shora is because we have no trees?" He turned to the blackboard and wrote in big letters:

The Reasons Why Storks Do Not Come to Shora

Under the words he put a big number one and waited.

"I still think the number one reason is what my mother said," Jella spoke up.

"Ah, but Lina has just told us that storks used to come to Shora. In fact, Jella, Grandmother Sibble III has seen storks nesting above the spot where you are sitting now. Where our school now stands. Imagine it!" said the teacher.

105

Meeting Individual Needs

Reteach
Author's Point of View Have students who need additional instruction and practice with this concept complete *Reteach*, pages 41–42.

Challenge
Author's Point of View Have students who understand this concept and could benefit from extended practice complete *Challenge*, page 23.

Author's Point of View

For more practice with author's point of view, have students complete *Reading and Writing Workbook* pages 41–42.

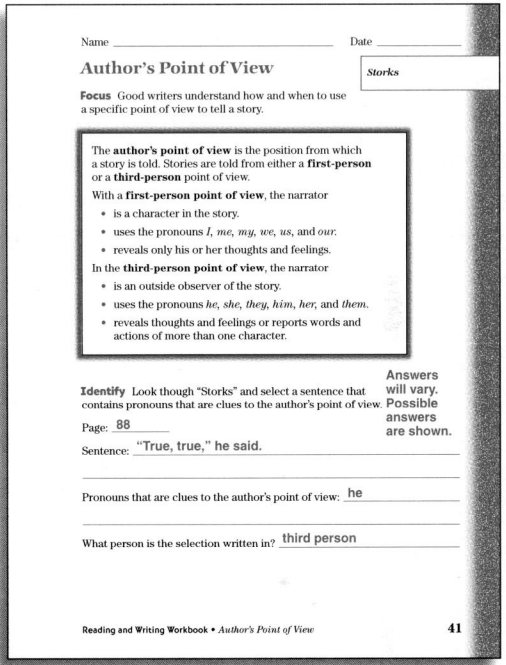

Reading and Writing Workbook pp. 41–42

Reading and Responding

Comprehension Strategies

Modeling

17 **Summarizing** *Let's summarize all the information they've discussed with the teacher. There are two problems with the storks. One is the lack of trees, and the other is the sharp roofs. It's possible to put wheels on the roofs fairly quickly, but the trees would take years to grow. They would have to be protected against the storms and the salt. But it could be done.*

Teacher Tip

Have students make predictions about whether or not they think the storks will come back to Shora, based on the summary above.

Word Knowledge

There are many multisyllabic words in this selection. Be sure students are using the skills they learned in the Word Knowledge section of this lesson.

"I guess maybe my mother was wrong," Jella said slowly. He seemed to hate to have to admit it. He looked up at the ceiling in a troubled way.

Then Auka raised his hand and quietly said, "Then the number one reason is still NO TREES."

"That's what Grandmother Sibble thinks, too," Lina told the class honestly. "She says storks like shelter and trees and hiding and a shady place to rest their long legs. She said she would if she were a stork! And Grandmother Sibble told me the way to find out what a stork would want is to try to think like a stork."

The teacher stood looking at Lina. "Is that what Grandmother Sibble III told you? I think that is wonderful," he said. He turned back to the class. "Well, are we agreed then that the number one reason for no storks in Shora is no trees?" He turned toward the board with his chalk as if to write it down.

Lina frantically waved her hand to stop him. "Not trees—roofs!" she almost shouted when the teacher did not turn. "Teacher," she said desperately to the teacher's back, "even though Grandmother Sibble and everybody thinks it is trees, it has to be roofs. Storks don't just build nests in trees, they build their nests on roofs, too. But our roofs in Shora are too sharp! Oh, it just has to be roofs," she pleaded. "Because we can put wheels on the roofs for storks to build their nests on, but we can't do anything soon about trees." Breathlessly she told the class about Grandmother Sibble's candy tin with the

106

Research in Action

Modeling

Research increasingly shows that the best way to teach children how to read, write, and study is to show them. So modeling—showing—is the best method for teaching strategies, though you must tell the students what you are going to do and why it is important. Unless they know that you expect them to learn how to think as you are thinking, students will not understand the importance of paying attention. *(Michael Pressley)*

picture of a whole village on its lid and stork nests on every roof—because there was a wheel on every roof for the storks to build their nests on!

Pier and Dirk said almost together, "Oh, man, imagine a nest on every roof in Shora!"

"Even on the roof of our school!" Auka shouted.

"But that's just it. That's just it!" Lina all but shouted at them. "There's not a single wheel on any roof in Shora, because, just like Grandmother Sibble, everybody else must have figured it was no trees. So nobody ever put up a wheel. Nobody even tried! But how can we know if we don't try?"

Lina sat back waiting breathlessly, hopefully looking at the teacher. Oh, she had to be right! Teacher had to think it was right.

The teacher liked their excitement. He stood before the blackboard turning the piece of chalk in his hand in no hurry to write anything down. He looked at the boys who were still looking in surprise at Lina. He looked at Lina. "Aha," he said proudly. "Little Lina." And then he wrote on the blackboard Lina's reason in big white letters:

No Wheels on Our Sharp Roofs

He turned back to the class. "Could it be?" he asked. "If we put wheels on our sharp roofs, could there be storks on every roof in Shora, the way Lina saw it in the picture on the candy tin?"

"Aw, that was just a picture," Jella said, scornfully. "You can put anything in a picture. All that is is a dream."

107

Comprehension Skills

Making Inferences

Review *making inferences* with the students. Good readers use information in a text as well as their own knowledge to help form a more complete understanding of a character or event in a story.

Have students read the last paragraph on page 107. Ask, "Why is Jella being scornful about Lina's idea to put wheels on the roofs in Shora?" Possible answer: *Jella is feeling competitive with Lina because he is still angry with her for telling on him.*

Have the students make their own inferences about the stork problem, and the problem of growing trees, based on the text and their own knowledge.

Reading and Responding

Comprehension Strategies

Modeling

18 **Summarizing** *This is a good place to stop and summarize. The children are making plans for making Shora a place where storks would nest. The teacher suggests that they could raise trees that are stronger than willows, or maybe plant some poplar trees to protect the willows. Can someone add to this summary?*

Teacher Tip Have the students think of other ways Lina and her friends could make Shora a good place for storks. Remind them that to accomplish their goal, the children will have to work cooperatively.

Word Knowledge

stretching

Students can use the skills they learned in the Word Knowledge section of this lesson to read this word. Remind students of this if they have difficulty reading this word.

"Ah, yes, that's all it is," the teacher said. "As yet! But there's where things have to start—with a dream. Of course, if you just go on dreaming, then it stays a dream and becomes stale and dead. But first to dream and then to do—isn't that the way to make a dream come true? Now sit for a moment, picture it for a moment: our Shora with trees and storks. Now Shora is bare, but try to see Shora with trees and storks and life. The blue sky above and the blue sea stretching behind the dike and storks flying over Shora. Do you see it?"

"Trees won't grow in Shora," Jella argued stubbornly. "It's the salt spray and the wind storms. There's only one tree in Shora, and that's a small cherry tree in the back yard of legless Janus. But the yard's got a high wall around it, so high you can hardly climb it. The cherry tree grows against the sunny wall of the house, and Janus pets it and guards it. He won't let a bird or a kid get even one cherry. Not one!"

"Well, but doesn't that show us something?" the teacher said. "That to raise trees in Shora we must perhaps protect them. And couldn't we raise trees that could withstand the storms and salt spray—stouter and stronger than willows? There must be trees that grow along the sea. Or maybe we would have to protect the willows with a windbreak of poplar trees. The point is, if trees once grew here, couldn't we make them do it again?"

"Oh, but that would take too long," Dirk said. "That would take years."

"Making dreams become real often takes long," the teacher said. "I don't mean that it should be done at once.

108

Meeting Individual Needs

ESL

Cultural Context Provide an opportunity for English-language learners to share their knowledge and experiences. If applicable, have them talk about school life in the countries where they lived. How is it the same? How is it different?

Our first problem is how to make just one pair of storks come to nest in Shora. That is what we are trying to do right now by first thinking out the reasons why the storks don't nest in Shora. But after that . . . If trees once grew where our school now stands, wouldn't they grow there again? Think of it. Trees all around our school!"

"And a moat with pickerel in it," Jella promptly added. "We boys could even dig it ourselves, and Lina could make hot chocolate milk for the diggers."

"Yes, Jella, now you are getting into the spirit of it. For that matter, we could even plant our own little trees. But first, before we can even start to think of all that, what must we do?"

"Find a wheel to put on a roof," Lina promptly cried.

"Ah, hah," the teacher said. "Now we are getting to something that we can do. Now do you see? We wondered why and we reasoned it out. Now we must do. Now we must find a wagon wheel, and then we must put it up on a roof. But behind doing that lies the long dream—storks on every roof in Shora. Trees! Maybe even a moat around the school. Can you picture our Shora like that?"

Excitement was in his voice; excitement was in the whole room. Lina couldn't sit still. She squirmed and squirmed, and then her hand shot up. "And a footbridge leading right to the door! We'd go over the footbridge to school. Teacher," she pleaded. "Teacher, I could get Grandmother Sibble's candy tin. Then we could all see what Shora would be like with storks and trees."

The teacher nodded. "Run then, Lina."

Grandmother Sibble III had no objections whatever to Lina's taking the candy tin to school. "Oh, no, child, keep

109

Comprehension Skills

Making Inferences

Review that readers *make inferences* from information in the text as well as their own knowledge to help them understand a character or event in a story.

- Remind the students about when Jella told Lina that she couldn't jump ditches with the boys.

- Point out when Jella says, "We boys could even dig [the moat] ourselves, and Lina could make hot chocolate milk for the diggers."

Have the students discuss how girls are viewed by the boys in Shora. Have them support their statements with other examples from the text.

Assessment

✓ **Formal** To assess students' understanding of Making Inferences, have them complete *Skills Assessment,* page 10.

 **Reading and Responding**

Comprehension Strategies

Modeling

19 Asking Questions *Why is the teacher talking about zebras and giraffes?*

Now I see why . . . They are found in Africa, where the stork is from also.

Modeling

20 Summarizing *Let's sum up what we've read. All the students spent time wondering why there were no storks in Shora. Some asked adults about why there were no storks. Then, they shared the information they'd gathered and came up with a way to bring the storks back.*

Discussing Strategy Use

After they have read the selection, have students share any problems they encountered and tell what strategies they used to solve them. Then, have them answer the following questions. If they answer "no" to any of the questions, have them reread part of the selection to find the answer.

- Did they summarize in order to help them understand what they've read?

- Did they ask questions and check later to see if the questions were answered?

- Did they stop to clarify words, phrases, and ideas that they didn't understand?

Make sure the students explain how using the strategies helped them understand the selection better and how they read effectively to find answers to the questions they asked as they set purposes.

it there as long as you like. Keep it until you get real storks in Shora." She opened the tin and took out a wineball. "Why, enough left for a wineball for each of you."

In the schoolroom they passed the candy tin around from hand to hand, and each one looked at all the pictures on the sides and on the lid. Each took out one wineball before reluctantly passing the tin on. The teacher took out the last wineball and then put the candy tin on the top ledge of the blackboard, on its side, so that the village with the trees and the storks on every roof could be seen from every point in the room. And underneath the tin, he wrote on the blackboard in big letters: "COULD IT BE?"

He turned back to the class. "Imagine a zebra in Shora," he said. "Imagine the long necks of two giraffes poking over the top of the dike. Imagine a giraffe running  along our dike."

"Imagine a lion in Shora!" Auka said.

"Yes, Auka, even imagine a lion in Shora," the teacher surprisingly agreed. "A good lion, a gentle lion in our street. But isn't it almost like that with storks? Do you know where our storks come from—where they are when they aren't in Holland? Imagine the heart of Africa. The head of a big river deep in Africa, where it isn't a river any more but little <u>rivulets</u> and reedy swampland and marshes that go to make the beginnings of a big river. That's where our storks are now. Right there among the zebras and the herds of gazelles, among the lions and the buffaloes. Do you see our stork? There's an old rhinoceros right behind him, <u>skulking</u> in the brush. Do you see the stork

110

Teacher Tip Reread this selection with students who had difficulty understanding it. Continue modeling and prompting the use of strategies and skills as you reread.

standing on the banks of the river where the river begins? Just beyond him in the swampy river is a herd of hippopotamuses, snorting and blowing in the deeper water. And the stork lives among them! Until a time comes and the big noble bird spreads his great wings, flaps his big wings, and comes out of the wilds of Africa to live among us. A great wild bird, yet tame and gentle, living among us in a village. Isn't it wonderful? And maybe, just maybe— It's still a dream. We haven't even a wheel as yet; we don't even know what roof we'll put it on."

"Oh, yes, we do! Oh, yes, we do!" the whole class shouted. "It's got to go right on the roof of our school."

"Why, yes," the teacher said. "Why, yes, class! Then who's going to look for a wagon wheel? Look for a wagon wheel where one is and where one isn't; where one could be and where one couldn't possibly be?"

They were all too breathless to say a word. But Jella hastily swallowed his wineball whole, then blurted it out for all of them. "We all are. From the moment school is out until we find one."

The teacher nodded and nodded. "That's how we'll begin to make a dream come true. We'll begin at noon. It's Saturday, and we have our free afternoon before us. We'll have a whole afternoon to try to find a wagon wheel. We'll really work at it, because that is how to start to make a dream come true . . ."

20

111

Teacher Tip After reading, encourage students to identify three subplots *(the challenge issued by the teacher, the girl's interaction with her male classmates, and the girl's relationship with the old woman)*. Discuss how the characters' attitude toward cooperation and competition evolved.

Comprehension Skills

Discussing the Selection

Following reading, engage the students in a discussion of the selection. Using the *handing-off process* will help the students take responsibility for the discussion. In addition to the following questions, have them revisit any questions asked when they set purposes before reading.

- Do you think that wondering is as important as the teacher thinks it is? *(Answers will vary. Students should echo the idea that wondering leads to action. Without wondering, nothing may happen.)*

- Will the students be able to work together and bring the storks back to Shora? *(Answers will vary but may include that the students' enthusiasm will ensure cooperation.)*

- Will Lina remain lonely? *(Answers will vary but may include that cooperation on a class project will provide opportunities for forming friendships.)*

- How has this selection connected with your knowledge of the unit theme? *(Answers will vary—students should compare/contrast examples of cooperation and competition from this selection with their own experiences or past reading, and use these connections to make a general statement about the unit theme.)*

During this time, have the students return to the clues and problems that they noted on the transparency before reading. Let the students decide which items deserve further discussion.

Have students take responsibility for the discussion. The teacher should not be the one to call on the next speaker.

2 Reading and Responding

Meet the Author

After the students read the information about Meindert DeJong, discuss the following questions with them.

Why do you think Meindert DeJong placed the setting of "Storks" in Holland? *(Possible answer: He placed it in Holland because he was writing from his own experiences there as a child.)*

Meindert DeJong writes with the theme of peace and goodwill toward others always in mind. How does the children's goal to bring storks back to Shora fit into this theme? *(Possible answer: The students, as well as the entire community, would have to work together cooperatively if they wanted to be successful.)*

Meet the Author

Meindert DeJong was born in the village of Wierum, Friesland in Holland. When he was eight, his family immigrated to America and settled in Grand Rapids, Michigan. His family was very poor, so he and his brothers had to work to help support them.

He had a strict Calvinist upbringing and attended Calvinist schools all the way through college. He graduated during the Great Depression, so there were no jobs to be found when he finished school. Instead he tried to support himself by tinning, grave digging, and farming. When World War II broke out, he was sent to China as an official historian for the Chinese-American Air Force. After the war, he returned to the U.S. and his wife Hattie in Grand Rapids. He traveled to the Netherlands and Mexico and eventually moved to Chapel Hill, North Carolina.

His books reflect his own personal experiences. He loves and respects animals and humanity and writes with the theme of peace and goodwill towards others always in mind.

112

Theme Connections

Think About It

With a small group of classmates, discuss how people learn through cooperation and competition. During discussion, address the following questions.

- Did Lina change throughout the story? How?
- How did feeling excluded affect Lina's competitiveness?
- Did feeling competitive help Lina learn about storks?
- How did cooperation help the children and the town?

Record Ideas

Answer the following questions in your Writing Journal.

- Why could the old woman help the children find out about the storks?
- Do you think that young people can learn from their elders?
- What have you learned from an older friend or your grandparents?

Descriptive Writing

Working with your unit activity group, review the story and identify passages where its setting is described.

Now work independently. Write a description of the setting for your dramatic play. Use all five senses to describe your setting, modeling it after the setting description in "Storks." Then share your setting with members of your group.

Revise your setting to include any of your partners' suggestions that you liked. Ask yourself: Is it better to work cooperatively or competitively when you are learning?

113

Theme Connections

Think About It

If necessary, prompt students to review Lina's initial enthusiasm and desire to learn more about storks. This could be contrasted with her later mean-spiritedness and competitiveness after feeling rejected by the boys.

Encourage the exchange of ideas by having students form discussion groups different from their activity groups. Ensure that all students have an opportunity to express their ideas.

Record Ideas

Have students reflect on their own experiences with elders. Respond to their thoughts and ideas through comments and questions.

Descriptive Writing

Draw students' attention to the vivid language used by the author to describe the countryside. Ensure that all students have an opportunity to share their setting descriptions. Have them discuss the benefits of working cooperatively.

 Have students locate the Netherlands on a globe, a world map, or a map of Europe.

 **Responding**

✦ Exploring the Theme

 **Research**

As students continue their explorations, have them use the *Research* CD-ROM Program to help organize and share their findings.

 **If you created a semantic map on the Concept/Question Board of key words related to the unit theme, Cooperation and Competition, have students find words from other resources, their projects, and family discussions and add them to the appropriate category on the map.**

Selection Vocabulary

Have students write in their Writing Journals the definitions for words discussed before reading the selection and any other interesting words they clarified while reading. Students should be encouraged to refer to these words throughout the unit as they work on writing and student projects. The words from the selection are:

ponder	dike	ramshackle
wretchedly	deign	

Reading/Writing Connection

Have each student write a journal entry from the perspective of his or her favorite character from "Storks." The entry should explain the main problem of the story from that character's point of view. When entries are finished, have students read them to the class without revealing the name of the character. The other students will try to identify the character.

Literature Appreciation

Remind students that Lina learned about how her village had changed by talking to Grandmother Sibble III. Explain that most places change over time. Have students find out what the place where they live was like 50 years ago. How was it different then? How was it the same? Brainstorm with students a list of ideas on how they might learn about their home and its history. Include talking to long-time residents, calling historical societies, and searching the library for old photos or newspapers.

Home Connection

The class has just finished reading "Storks," a realistic fiction selection about a class that works together to find a way to bring storks back to the village of Shora. An informational letter on "Storks," in both English and Spanish, can be found in the *Home Connection* guide.

"Storks"

A message from _____

Our class has just finished reading *Storks*, in which one girl, Lina, gets her classmates interested in storks. Lina's curiosity leads the students to construct a habitat for storks in hopes that the majestic birds will return to the students' tiny Dutch fishing village.

Talk with your child about an animal that he or she would like to attract to the region in which you live, even if it's improbable. Have your child conduct research about the animal and its natural habitat. This information will be found in books available at the school or local library.

When the research is complete, have your child use the space below to write a plan for converting some area of your community into a habitat for the chosen animal.

Encourage your child to share his or her plan with the class.

Unit I/Cooperation and Competition   13

Home Connection p. 13

Supporting Student Explorations

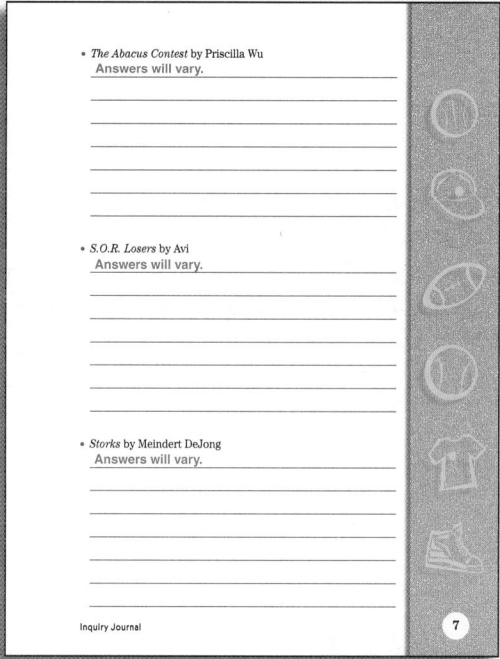

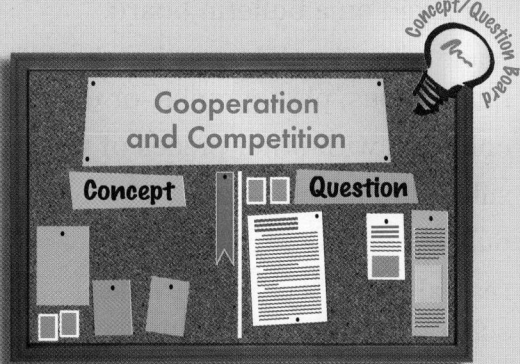 **Small Group** Have students stage their dress rehearsals. Tell them to make any final revisions to their scripts and schedule performance times for their plays. Review appropriate audience behavior. Consider videotaping the performances, if the necessary resources are available.

If time permits, have students illustrate their characters and sets. Have students decide how to bind their plays into a class anthology. Have volunteers prepare a table of contents and title page.

Inquiry Journal
Have the students complete page 7 of the *Inquiry Journal.* Have them record their ideas about how "Storks" added to their knowledge of cooperation and competition.

Teacher Tip Point out to students that performing their dramatic plays and binding the scripts together into a class anthology are ways of publishing their works. Tell them they will learn more about publishing in the next writing lesson.

Assessment
✓ **Informal** In the continuing anecdotal record, note whether students' final dramatic plays explore the unit theme by depicting the actions, thoughts, and feelings of characters.

③ Integrating the Curriculum

Teacher Tip Tell students that they should remember this information on publishing when working on future writing and unit activities.

Language Arts

Writing

Publish

Instruct Remind students that once they have written, revised, proofread, and made final changes to a piece of writing, it may be considered finished. They may want to share the completed work with others by publishing it. Writing can be published in several ways. It can be:

- displayed on a bulletin board.
- made into a book by putting the pages between covers (with illustrations, photographs, or diagrams if appropriate).
- collected with other pieces of writing and published in an anthology.
- submitted for publication to a local newspaper or a national magazine.
- published in a school newspaper.
- read aloud to the class, to other classes, to younger students in the school, or to another group.

Publishing will not always require large blocks of class time. Students will wish to spend more time elaborately presenting their favorite pieces and less time on other works. However, an individual publishing conference may be useful. In the conference each student will discuss what he or she would like to publish, how to prepare the piece for publication, and what form the published work should take. As you read through the piece, tell the student if any corrections still need to be made. Make suggestions about the best way to publish a piece if a student has trouble coming up with an idea. However, leave final decisions about form and design of their work up to the individual students.

Practice Schedule a trip to the library, or bring in samples of some of the publications discussed in the Instruct exercise above. Have students browse these samples, noting the purpose and genre of each piece, how it was illustrated, how its text was organized, and whether or not they think its ideas were communicated clearly and effectively. Have students take notes on what they like and dislike about each sample. Then have students consider which formats or presentations best suit their nonfiction, persuasive papers.

Apply

Have students decide how they want to publish their writing. Encourage them to consider whether or not they want to illustrate their work in some way, either with photographs or illustrations. Remind them to include a title page that contains the title of the work and their names as authors (and illustrators).

Have students use the following checklist to help them as they publish their works. They should note, however, that not every question applies to every form of publishing.

_____ Have I chosen my best piece?

_____ Have I revised it to make it better?

_____ Have I proofread it carefully?

_____ Have I decided upon my illustrations?

_____ Have I recopied my piece carefully and illustrated it?

_____ Have I numbered the pages?

_____ Have I made a cover that tells the title and my name?

Writing Process

Publish In general, if a student has brought a work to the proofreading stage, he or she should publish it. However, the decision to publish is the student's. Give students a quota—perhaps six or seven works for the year. Students may want to publish their persuasive writing pieces that they have been working on throughout the unit. If so, have them decide what form of publication they want to use for their work.

For additional information on publishing, see Program Appendix, page 26.

Teacher Tip Provide materials for a publishing center and explain their use to students. A word processor or typewriter might be located in this center along with other tools for writing and illustrating books and making covers. Also have a variety of books and anthologies in the center for the students to use as models.

Before students decide which piece to publish and make their final corrections to it, have a brief publishing conference with each one. At this time, help the student make any last-minute changes that are necessary before the piece is published.

Assessment

✓ **Informal** Take this opportunity to assess students' progress with the writing process by commenting on the entries in their Writing Journals.

③ Integrating the Curriculum

Have students use the information from this lesson to create a title page for their published persuasive papers.

Meeting Individual Needs

Reteach

Literary Terms Have students who need additional instruction and practice with this concept complete **Reteach**, pages 43–44.

Challenge

Literary Terms Have students who understand this concept and could benefit from extended practice complete **Challenge**, page 24.

Literary Elements

Literary Terms: Title, Author, Illustrator

Instruct Ask students to share the names of some of their favorite stories. As they tell you the names, write them on the chalkboard or overhead projector. Explain if necessary that the name of a story is called the *title*. Also talk about the literary terms *author* and *illustrator*. Have them identify the author and illustrator of "Storks" and other selections in this unit. Then display a book and open it to the title page. Tell students that the title page contains the story's title, the author's name, and the illustrator's name if there is one.

Practice Have students look at some of their books or other stories they have read and write out the title, author, and illustrator of each book or story.

Apply Have students create title pages for some of their own stories.

For more practice with literary terms, have students complete ***Reading and Writing Workbook*** pages 43–44.

Reading and Writing Workbook pp. 43–44

Spelling

Inflectional Endings

Instruct Ask the students what they remember about the inflectional endings *-ed* and *-ing*. Remind students of the rules for writing inflections that change the tense of the root word.

- When a word ends in a consonant, simply add the appropriate ending (*-ed*, *-ing*). Examples: *jump, jumped, jumping.*
- When adding *-ed* to most words ending in a consonant followed by *y*, drop the *y* and add an *i* before the ending. Examples: *apply, applied, applying.*
- When a word has one syllable, one short vowel in the middle, and one consonant at the end, double the final consonant before adding *-ed* or *-ing.* Examples: *hop, hopped, hopping.*
- When a word ends with a Silent e following a consonant, drop the Silent e before adding *-ed* or *-ing.* Examples: *whine, whined, whining.*

Practice Copy the chart below on the chalkboard.

Add *-ing* or *-ed.*	Change the *y to i.* Add *-ed.*	Double the final consonant. Add *-ing* or *-ed.*	Drop the Silent e. Add *-ing* or *-ed.*

Write the following words on the chalkboard and have volunteers add *-ed* or *-ing.* Have them write the words in the appropriate column in the chart.

explore	divide	stay
mix	subtract	finish
hurry	multiply	reply

Apply Have students check a piece of their writing for the correct spelling of inflections.

Teacher Tip Have students check for accurate spelling of inflections in their persuasive papers and unit activities.

Meeting Individual Needs

Challenge

Spelling Inflectional Endings Hold an Inflections spelling bee. Give students words that end in *-ed* and *-ing.* Challenge them to not only spell the words correctly but also give and spell the root word and explain any changes that occurred in the root word. Set a time limit of 15 seconds for each response. Decrease the time with each round.

Assessment

✓ **Formal** To assess students' understanding of this concept, have them complete *Skills Assessment,* page 11.

Skills Strand

Spelling Inflectional Endings
INTRODUCED: Unit 1, Lesson 4
REVIEWED: Unit 1, Lesson 6
Unit 6, Lesson 2

3 Integrating the Curriculum

Meeting Individual Needs

Reteach

Capitalizing Titles Have students who need additional instruction and practice with this concept complete **Reteach,** pages 45–46.

Challenge

Capitalizing Titles Have students create titles such as the following: a title of two or more words with every word capitalized (such as *Big Bad Henry*), with every other word capitalized (such as *Cindy is Going to France in Pigtails*), and a four-word title with the first and last words capitalized (such as *Man on the Moon*). Have students who could benefit from extended practice of this concept complete **Challenge,** page 25.

Capitalizing Titles

INTRODUCED: Unit 1, Lesson 6
REVIEWED: Unit 3, Lesson 6
Unit 5, Lesson 6

Suggest that students make notes for their *Writing Folders* about any errors in capitalization they make. Have them include the rule for capitalizing titles along with some examples of several titles.

Have students check that the titles for their persuasive papers and unit activities are capitalized correctly.

Grammar, Usage, & Mechanics

Capitalizing Titles

Instruct Ask students what they know about capitalization. Then focus their attention on the titles of the selections in the **Student Anthology.** What do they notice about the use of capitalization in the titles? What conclusions can they draw about capitalizing titles? If necessary, tell them that the first word and all important words in a title are capitalized, and small words such as *a, the, in,* and *of* are not. This includes book titles, story titles, and magazine titles. Also point out that titles used with people's names are capitalized, such as *Dr. Burns, Mr. Leyva, Mrs. Teresa Gray,* and *Ms. Hatten.*

Practice Have students share the titles of some of their favorite books, stories, and magazines. Write the titles in lowercase letters on the chalkboard. Have volunteers come to the chalkboard and capitalize the titles. Do the rest of the students agree with what the volunteers did? Repeat the activity with titles associated with people's names.

Apply Tell students to look over the titles in their own writing. Do they notice any errors in capitalization? Is there a pattern in the errors they need to pay attention to?

For additional practice, have students complete **Reading and Writing Workbook** pages 45–46.

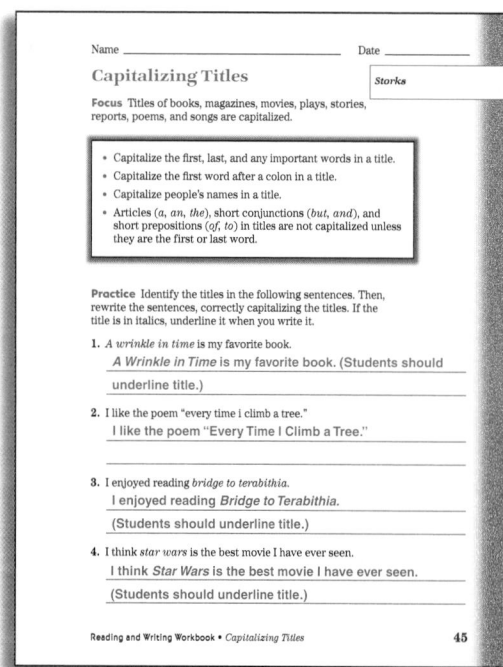

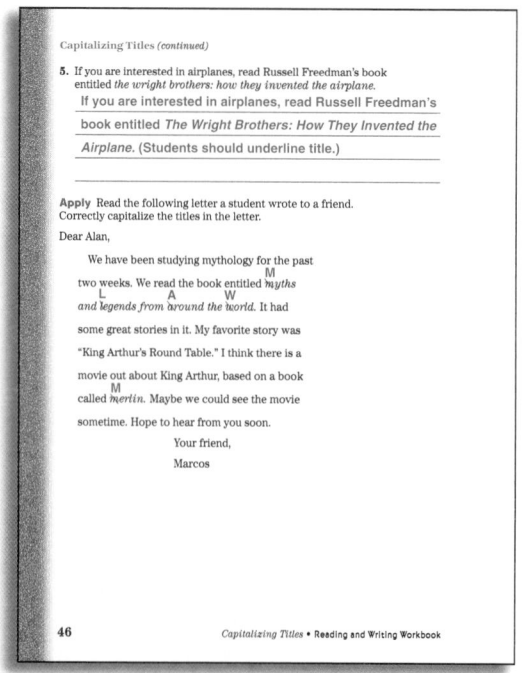

Reading and Writing Workbook pp. 45–46

Listening/Speaking/Viewing

Illustrations

Have students look back at the illustrations for "Class President," "The Marble Champ," "Juggling," "The Abacus Contest," and "S.O.R. Losers." Ask them to use descriptive words to tell about what they see. Discuss the styles of the pictures. Are they unrealistic or realistic? Are the lines definite or soft?

As the students respond, ask how they think the pictures help them understand the story. Do they feel that the pictures represent or go with the story well? Do the pictures help extend the meaning of the story? How do the pictures reflect the mood of the story?

Have each student choose a favorite scene from "Storks" and illustrate it, keeping in mind how he or she wants to reflect the meaning and mood of the story. Ask volunteers to share their completed illustrations with the class and explain why they illustrated their scenes as they did.

Teacher Tip Tell students that they may want to consider illustrating future published works. Point out that they will want to remember what they have learned in this lesson when they are creating those illustrations.

Meeting Individual Needs

ESL

Expressing Ideas Encourage English-language learners to express ideas that are important to them. Have them discuss their ideas as they relate to the stories and illustrations, based on their own knowledge and experiences.

3 Integrating the Curriculum

Teacher Tip *Handing-off* is a useful process in research discussions as well as in text discussions, because it encourages the students to talk to one another rather than to you.

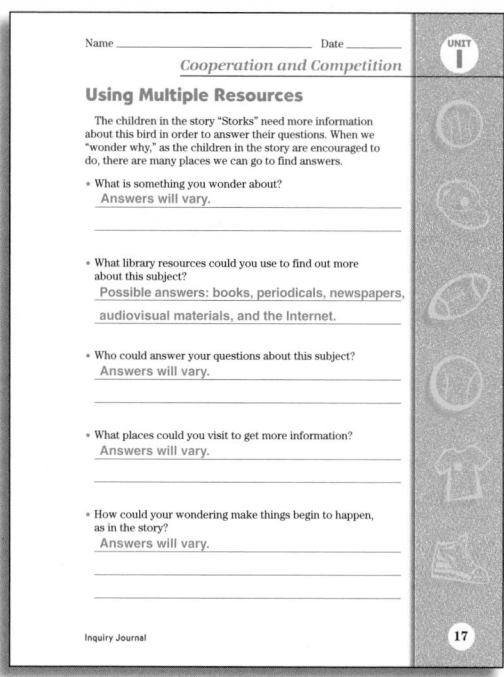

Inquiry Journal p. 17

Study and Research

Using Multiple Sources

Instruct Have students name and discuss the many sources that they have consulted when researching an idea or the answer to a question. What kind of information did they get from these sources, and where did they find the sources? List the different sources that students mention on the chalkboard. Add the following sources if necessary: library sources, including atlases, almanacs, dictionaries, encyclopedias, nonfiction books, magazines and newspapers, videotapes and audiocassettes; Internet access; interviews with experts; museums; pamphlets and brochures from businesses and other organizations; World Wide Web. Call on volunteers to give examples of what kind of information they might gather from each source.

Practice Have students discuss the research questions they are currently pursuing. Write the questions on the chalkboard, and add several research questions about cooperation and competition that you've thought of for students to consider. Which sources would students use to research each question, and why? List their responses on the board beside each question.

Apply Tell students to explore at least two sources for their research questions. Have them evaluate the usefulness of each source. Have students share their evaluations with the rest of the class.

For more practice with using multiple resources, have students complete *Inquiry Journal* page 17.

Across the Curriculum

 ## Social Studies

Olympic Competitions

Purpose

To encourage students to use resource materials for learning more about competition between countries in the Olympics

Procedure

Ask students to tell you what they know about the Olympics. Discuss their favorite Olympic sports and the sports figures from different countries they know about. Tell students to research how some countries fare in Olympic swimming and downhill skiing.

■ Divide students into pairs and let each pair choose a country to research. Encourage the class to select a variety of large and small countries. Have a world map available for them to study.

■ Ask students where they might look to find information on the results of Olympic competitions. Possible answers could be almanacs, the encyclopedia, nonfiction books, sports magazines, or the Internet.

■ Have students compare the medal standings of their countries across the two sports. You may want to have them present the information in charts or graphs.

■ Allow time for them to discuss their findings with the class.

 ## Science

Thinking About the Animals

Purpose

To help students become aware of how animals and people sometimes compete for the same habitat

Materials

poster board, paints, markers

Procedure

Ask students if they know what *habitat* is. Remind them that habitat is what we call the natural environment of an animal or plant. Encourage discussion of animals that lived in the students' area, but now have lost their habitat, or other endangered animals. Then have students express their thoughts on posters.

■ Ask students to consider the following: Could the animals be brought back? Would the community want the animals to come back? If so, what could be done to encourage their return?

■ Tell each student to choose one animal and create a poster, using posterboard and paints or colored markers. Subject matter for the posters might include pictures of the animals and their habitats, reasons why the animals have lost their habitat, whether or not the students would like to see the animals come back to their area, and, if so, what could be done to bring them back.

■ Have students share finished posters with the class.

Bibliography

Extending the Unit Theme

Have students explore other dimensions of cooperation and competition by reading and discussing the books listed on these pages.

Promoting Reading for Pleasure

There are several ways you can promote reading for pleasure.

- Read aloud a variety of selections to your students daily. Include the books from which anthology selections have been excerpted.

- Provide time for silent reading each day. Make sure students have their reading material chosen before beginning. Model good silent reading behaviors for the students.

Using the Bibliography Pages

To get started, have students read each of the book descriptions on pages 114–115. Ask if anyone is familiar with any of the books or authors represented. Encourage students to share what they know about them without giving away important parts of a story.

Tips for Teaching

- Tell students to consider whether they are reading a selection simply for pleasure or to learn something from it.

- As students read their selections, remind them to wonder about characters, events, or information. They should ask themselves questions and be aware of the answers in the text. If their questions are not answered in a nonfiction selection, encourage them to look elsewhere and thus add to their store of knowledge.

- Remind students to sum up what they have read after each chapter or section.

Cooperation and Competition

Bibliography

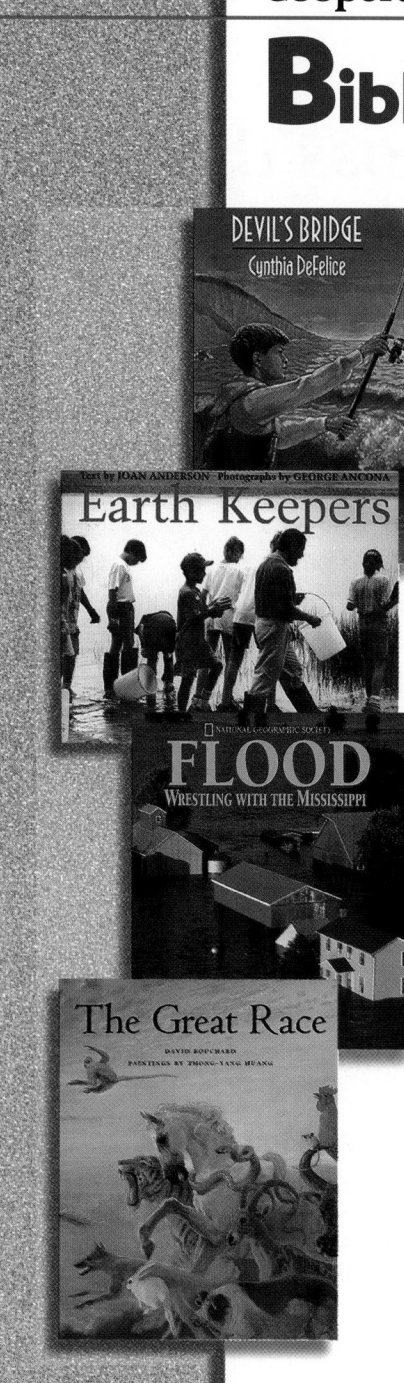

Devil's Bridge

by **Cynthia DeFelice.** Ben Dagget hopes to win the Striped Bass Derby for a number of reasons, but little does he know how the contest will affect his life. Easy

Earth Keepers

by **Joan Anderson and George Ancona.** Read about the people who work together to rescue the earth in the places where it is most needed. Their cooperation is crucial to the earth's life. Average

Flood: Wrestling with the Mississippi

by **Patricia Lauber.** In 1927 and 1993 the mighty Mississippi unleashed all its power in damaging floods. This is the story of those floods and the people who worked together to repair the damage. Average

The Great Race

by **David Bouchard.** Who will win the race and be the first to reach Jade City? Will it be the ox, the rat, the horse, or one of the other creatures in the Chinese zodiac? Average

114

Iditarod Dream: Dusty and His Sled Dogs Compete in Alaska's Jr. Iditarod

by Ted Wood. Travel the 158-mile course of the Junior Iditarod with Dusty and his team of dogs and find out who wins the grueling competition. Average

Philip Hall Likes Me. I Reckon Maybe.

by Bette Greene. A little competition can't hurt a friendship, can it? Average

Ten Mile Day: And the Building of the Transcontinental Railroad

by Mary Ann Fraser. How do you measure your days? In minutes, hours? Working together, these men measured theirs in miles. Average

A World In Our Hands: In Honor of the 50th Anniversary of the United Nations: Young People of the World

by the Young People of the World Staff. Young people from 115 different countries celebrate in prose, poetry and art, the mission of the United Nations. They believe that people can make the world a better place to live. Advanced

115

Discussing the Books

Have each student select one or more of the books for reading and discussion. Use the following questions as discussion starters:

- Did you choose a fiction or expository selection? How do you know? Why did you choose it?
- What questions did you have as you read? Were they answered? Were you satisfied with the answers?
- Did your selection support cooperation or competition? Is one better than the other? Explain.
- What was a significant event or turning point in your selection?

Tips for Discussion

- Remind students that listening attentively and politely is as important in a group discussion as sharing ideas.
- Remind students that not everyone responds to a text in the same way. Each person's reaction to a selection is individual and personal. Encourage them to respect each other's ideas and opinions.

Student Recommendations

Ask two or more students who have read the same book from this bibliography to work together to present reasons others should read the selection. Also, encourage students to recommend and share other books they have read that contain characters or events that focus on cooperation and competition.

Note: Teachers should preview any trade books for appropriateness in their classrooms before recommending them to students.

Exploration Wrap-Up

Whole-Group Discussion

- Initiate a class discussion of the unit selections, focusing on the theme of cooperation and competition.

- Have the students refer to page 5 of their **Inquiry Journals** to remind themselves of what their ideas about cooperation and competition were when the unit began and what they expected to learn from the unit. Have them describe the new ideas they have acquired and the new information they have learned.

- Remind the students to think about their previous discussions of ideas from the Concept/Question Board.

Inquiry Journal page 5

Extending the Discussion

- Have the students conduct an evaluation of the unit selections, identifying those selections they found most interesting and those they found least interesting.

- Have the students conduct an evaluation of the unit activities. Which activities did they find the most enjoyable and the most informative?

- Have the students evaluate the overall unit. How well did the unit cover the topic of cooperation and competition? Did they enjoy the selections? Were they inspired to do any independent reading on the unit theme?

- Invite the students to suggest ideas related to cooperation and competition that are worth further exploration, possibly beginning with any questions left on the Concept/Question Board.

Small-Group Discussion

- Have the students work in small groups to discuss the unit. Encourage group members to refer to the Concept/Question Board, browse the unit selections, and review their **Inquiry Journal** pages for Unit 1 to refresh their memories for important ideas raised in the unit.

- Call on the groups to share with classmates important points and conclusions from their discussions.

Unit Celebration

Encourage the students to suggest how they might celebrate their learning. You might offer ideas such as the following:

- Create a learning mural. In small groups, the students could plan and draw scenes from the selections in the unit, or their dramatic play from their own experiences. Each student should be encouraged to contribute to the mural.

- Invite family members to "tour" the classroom, with the children explaining displayed projects, performing their plays, and discussing the materials on the Concept/Question Board.

Review the Concepts

After the group discussion, encourage students to think about and share how their own understandings of cooperation and competition have changed.

- Invite them to share their thoughts on how useful the unit activities were.
- Ask students if they feel they have learned more about organizing, revising, and presenting information when expressing their ideas.
- Challenge them to explain how writing a play helped them learn about cooperation and competition.
- Encourage them to continue learning about cooperation and competition on their own, and to share anything they learn with the rest of the class, including the teacher.

- As always, students' ideas should determine the discussion.
- Remind students that they can continue to research cooperation and competition even though they have completed the unit.

Review Fine Art

Have students look again at the Fine Art shown on pages 56–57 of their *Student Anthologies*. Have them review the cooperation and competition concept illustrated by each piece.

Assessment

✓ Informal Assessment

- Give the students the opportunity to evaluate their personal learning experiences during this unit by completing *Inquiry Journal* pages 18–19.
- Meet individually with the students to discuss their evaluations.

Inquiry Journal pages 18–19

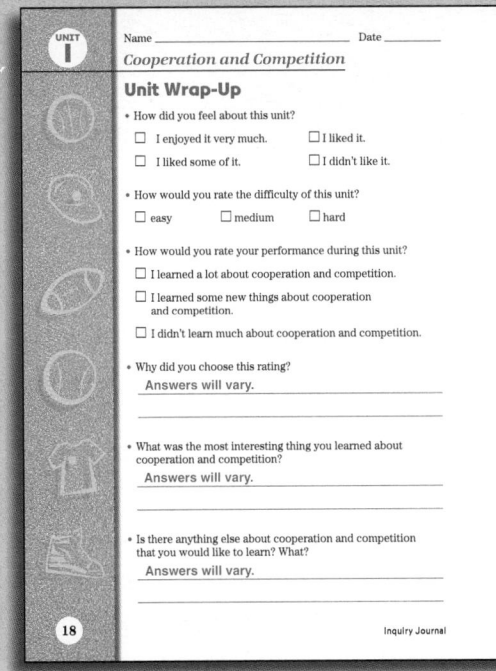

✓ Formal Assessment

You can find the unit assessment for Unit 1 on pages 19–28 of the *Comprehension and Writing Assessment*. See the *Assessment Guide* for specific suggestions on how to use these skills.

Comprehension Assessment

- Understanding the Selection
- Making Connections Across Selections
- Vocabulary
- Skills

Writing Assessment

- Personal Response—Students write an essay about something important they did with a friend and explain why it was important.
- Exploring Unit Concepts—Students write an essay giving their opinions about why Americans seem to compete more in sports than in school subjects.

Exploring the Theme

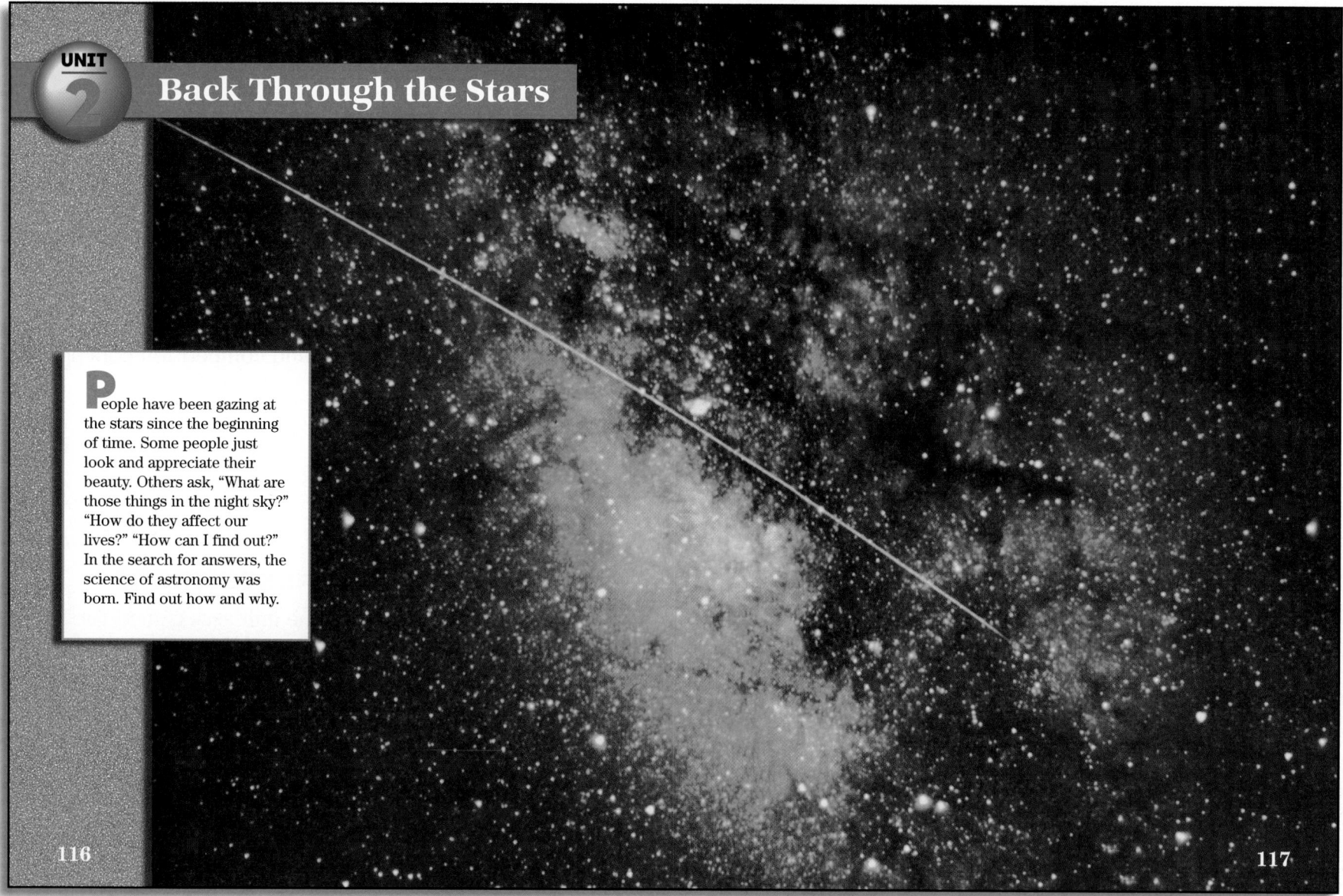

UNIT 2

Back Through the Stars

People have been gazing at the stars since the beginning of time. Some people just look and appreciate their beauty. Others ask, "What are those things in the night sky?" "How do they affect our lives?" "How can I find out?" In the search for answers, the science of astronomy was born. Find out how and why.

116

117

Introduction

Although by fifth grade most students have learned that Earth is round and that it goes around the sun, studies have shown that they are often very unclear about this, and that they harbor serious doubts about the "official" story. In this unit, they will learn that all over the world, and for centuries, people have wondered about many of the same things—how it is that the sun can disappear each night in the west and reappear each morning in the east, why we do not fall off Earth, whether there is an end to time or space, and so on.

Accordingly, the emphasis throughout this unit will be on spelling out what students really do think about Earth, the moon, the sun, and the universe; developing those ideas; and relating them to the different concepts they read about.

This is a research unit in which students can explore astronomy from its most ancient, prehistoric forms to the most up-to-the-minute findings from space probes and telescopes.

Exploration and Inquiry Goals

Space and the vastness of the universe are mysteries to most people. From the earliest times, we have looked to the stars with awe and wonder and a need to know more. The inquiry goals for this unit are:

- to understand what astronomers do and how the study of astronomy began.
- to extend knowledge of the solar system and the stars.
- to get a sense of the vastness and activity of the universe.
- to develop basic concepts of astronomy and an understanding of how astronomers acquire information about the universe.

Learning Goals

The stars have held a fascination for humankind since its inception. Searchers, artists, dreamers, poets, and scientists alike have looked to the stars and formulated notions about their origins, their meaning, and their connection to humans. Because of this, a variety of texts is available to students in their study of stars. Informational articles, myths, fiction, poetry, and a play will help students see the range of knowledge and ideas that have been applied to the study of the universe.

The learning goals of this unit are:

- to form and revise questions for investigations of astronomy.
- to interpret and use graphic sources of information to address research questions about astronomy.
- to represent text information in different ways, such as outlines, time lines, and graphic organizers.
- to use multiple sources to locate information relevant to research questions about astronomy.
- to summarize and organize information from multiple sources by outlining ideas and making charts.
- to present information in various forms using available technology.
- to take notes about astronomy from relevant and authoritative sources.
- to evelute one's own research and raise new questions for further investigation of astronomy.

Teacher Tip

A unit on astronomy raises a broad range of questions. In order to prepare for this unit, you might ask yourself the following questions:

- What has the telescope been able to show us about the universe that we would not have known without it?
- Have ancient myths and stories about the stars and planets lost their value?
- What can ancient sites such as Stonehenge and Bighorn Medicine Wheel tell us about what people long ago knew about the sun and stars?

Exploring the Theme

Unit Activities

Unit activities are student-driven and should emerge from students' interests, encouraged or ignited by their reading and class discussions. Unit activities should involve reading beyond the program material and address both of the conceptual aims of the unit.

Exploration Activities

- Students might want to find out how ancient astronomers developed their theories of the universe.

- Some students might want to write a science fiction story or play. This can be an appropriate way of presenting research findings but should not be a substitute for research.
- Students might compare and contrast the structures and purposes of ancient astronomical landmarks such as Bighorn Medicine Wheel and Stonehenge.
- Some students might explore the *Voyager* space probes and the information scientists have gained from their journeys.

	Galileo	Telescopes	The Heavenly Zoo
Overview of Selection	■ In this biographical selection, Galileo's telescope reveals things about the heavens that eventually put him at odds with church authorities.	■ This nonfiction selection explains how different kinds of telescopes work, including the Hubble space telescope.	■ The origins of three astrological patterns are explained by ancient myths from different cultures.
Link to the Theme	■ Galileo introduced many people to the faraway planets, satellites, and stars studied in astronomy.	■ Telescopes, the basic tools of astronomy since the 1600s, have become more powerful and sophisticated.	■ Lacking scientific knowledge of the stars, ancient peoples created myths to give meaning to these phenomena. ■ Constellation myths helped ancient people remember, locate, and identify stars.
Unit Activities	■ Brainstorm research problems. ■ Form interest-based groups. ■ Develop and discuss initial research plans.	■ Groups finalize plans, allocate tasks, and begin research. ■ Class discusses initial findings and resources.	■ Research continues. ■ Groups consider revision of their activity focus.
Supporting Student Explorations	■ Plot target dates for activities, including start and end dates and interim deadlines. ■ Conduct class discussion of research problems and questions.	■ Use multiple sources to locate relevant information. ■ Use and interpret diagrams to answer research questions. ■ Use the card catalog to locate research materials.	■ Students make conjectures and record them for later use. ■ Take notes from relevant and authoritative sources.

Supporting Student Explorations

Throughout the unit, the students will engage in activities of their own choosing—such as those shown on the chart below—that allow them to explore astronomy more deeply and to use the questions they have raised to do so. These explorations may relate to the selection the students are reading or to a number of selections, but they must revolve around the theme concepts.

As they proceed with their research, students might complete the following steps and activities.

- Discuss research problems and questions.
- Interpret and use diagrams.
- Use the card catalog to locate research materials.

- Make conjectures and record them for later use.
- Present problems and conjectures to the class.
- List knowledge needs and sources of information.
- Organize and summarize information in outlines and charts.
- Make class presentations in the form of mini-debates, problem presentations, or poster sessions and get feedback from peers.

Explain to the students that they may work on their unit activities alone, with partners, or in small groups. Throughout each lesson, monitor student progress and encourage students to report problems they encounter in preparing their activities as the problems arise.

Circles, Squares, and Daggers	Voyager to the Planets	A Meeting in Space	Stars	The Book That Saved the Earth
■ This nonfiction selection illustrates how Native Americans of long ago created structures to mark the cycles of seasons and the passing of time.	■ This nonfiction selection illustrates how astronomers learned a great deal about the solar system from the 12-year journey of the space probe *Voyager 2*.	■ In this science fiction selection, two young girls, zooming through space in search of their lost cat, come upon an alien spaceship.	■ This nonfiction selection provides an introduction to the different kinds of distant objects and systems that modern astronomers investigate.	■ This humorous science fiction play suggests that some aliens may not be as intelligent as we think.
■ Archaeoastronomy is a field of study that combines archaeology and astronomy.	■ Space missions to distant planets have broadened our knowledge of the field of astronomy.	■ The study of astronomy has led many to wonder if human-inhabited space stations and contact with alien life are in our future.	■ Nebulas, supernovas, and quasars are some of the types of stars in the universe that have been discovered through astronomy.	■ The study of astronomy leads some to wonder what alien life-forms would think of our culture if they should discover us first.
■ Research continues. ■ Initial findings are presented.	■ Research continues. ■ Interesting findings or problems are presented.	■ Research continues. ■ Interesting findings or problems are presented.	■ Research findings are organized and presentations are prepared.	■ Activities are presented.
■ Conduct class discussion of problems and conjectures. ■ List knowledge needs and possible sources of information.	■ Conduct class discussions to help identify knowledge needs, to remind groups that they can still change their research problems, and to provide guidance.	■ Research groups present their plans for discussion and possible refinement. ■ Summarize and organize information in an outline.	■ Organize information in a chart. ■ Groups make informal presentations in the form of mini-debates, problem presentations, or poster sessions.	■ Groups present their research activities. ■ Raise new questions for further investigation.

Program Resources

Student Materials

Student Anthology
Pages 116–229

**Reading and
Writing Workbook**
Pages 47–82

Inquiry Journal
Pages 20–39

Writing Folder

Teacher Materials

Teacher's Edition, Book 1

Reteach
Pages 47–82

Challenge
Pages 26–43

Home Connection
Pages 15–32

Skills Assessment
Pages 12–26

Comprehension and Writing Assessment
Pages 29–53

Assessment Guide

ESL Supplement
Unit 2, Lessons 1–8

Overhead Transparencies
Numbers 7–14, 44, 46, 48, 52–53

Intervention Guide
Unit 2, Lessons 1–8

Additional Materials
- **Visual Glossary**
- **Intervention Package**
- **Teacher's Professional Guides**

Program Resources

Classroom Library*

The Planets

BY GAIL GIBBONS. HOLIDAY HOUSE, 1994.

In basic scientific terms, the author describes the characteristics of the nine planets in our solor system and how they orbit. **(Easy)**

Science Fair Projects: Flight, Space and Astronomy

BY BOB BONNET AND DAN KEEN. STERLING PUBLICATIONS, 1998.

This book offers 53 simple experiments and projects focusing on space science. **(Advanced)**

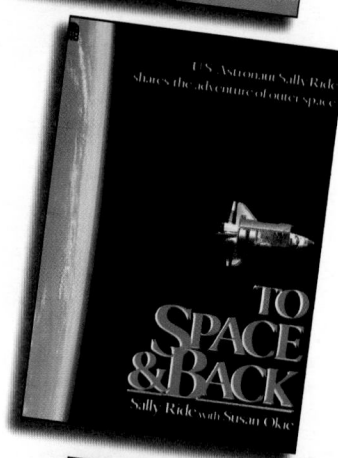

To Space and Back

BY SALLY RIDE WITH SUSAN OKIE. LOTHROP LEE & SHEPARD, 1989.

An astronaut tells what it's like to live on a space shuttle. Great color photographs from NASA files. (Outstanding Science Trade Book) **(Average)**

A Wrinkle in Time

BY MADELEINE L'ENGLE. YEARLING, 1973.

Meg and Charles embark on a perilous journey through space to find their missing father. (Newbery Medal, Sequoyah Children's Book) **(Advanced)**

Note: Teachers should preview any trade books and videos for appropriateness in their classrooms before recommending them to students.

* These books, which all support the unit theme Back Through the Stars, are part of a 24-book *Classroom Library* available for purchase from SRA/McGraw-Hill.

*Follow the Drinking Gourd

A handyman who is a friend to the slaves teaches them a song about following the stars that will lead them to freedom. Videocassette;11 min.

*Liftoff! Space and Astronomy

Explore the exciting world of aviation and space technology in the videos "Reach for the Stars" and "To the Moon." Videocassette; about 20 min. each.

Starting with the Stars
PYRAMID FILM & VIDEO, 1992

This film takes the viewer on a journey to the sun and to the second-nearest star, Alpha Centauri. It also contains a discussion of what we see through telescopes. Videocassette; 14 min.

Skywatching
FOREST TECHNOLOGIES/DISCOVERY CHANNEL

Have students use this CD-ROM which tells what's in the sky and how to find what you're looking for. An interactive map displays the night sky from anywhere on Earth at any time. CD-ROM.

Astronomical Explorations
QUEUE

Have students use this planet-by-planet journey through the solar system which features full-motion video clips from NASA. CD-ROM.

*Listening Library: Back Through the Stars
SRA/MCGRAW-HILL, 2000

Students will enjoy listening to the selections they have read. Have them use the audiocassette during Independent Work Time. Audiocassette.

*Lesson Planner
SRA/MCGRAW-HILL, 2000

Use the Lesson Planner to adjust and refine lessons to meet the specific needs of your students. CD-ROM.

*Research
SRA/MCGRAW-HILL, 2000

As students continue their exploration of astronomy, have them use the Research program to help them organize and share their findings. CD-ROM.

Back Through the Stars Websites

Have students find information about Back Through the Stars and links to sites concerning astronomy at:
http://www.sra4kids.com

*Basic Computer Skills Connection

Have students use the Keyboarding and Word Processing units of the **SRA Basic Computer Skills** program to help them develop computer skills within the context of the unit theme. The Applying Computer Skills in Reading activity contains a computer skills application specific to this unit.

Titles preceded by an asterisk (✳) are available through SRA/McGraw-Hill. Other titles can be obtained by contacting the publisher listed with the title. See page 38 of the Program Appendix for ordering information.

Unit Skills Overview

		WORD KNOWLEDGE	COMPREHENSION SKILLS & STRATEGIES	LITERARY ELEMENTS	VOCABULARY & SPELLING
Galileo Genre: **Biography**		■ Word Families ■ /k/ spelled *c* ■ /s/ spelled *c*	■ Drawing Conclusions ■ Clarifying ■ Asking Questions ■ Summarizing	■ Recognizing a Biography	■ Content-Area Words
Telescopes Genre: **Nonfiction**		■ Closed Compound Words ■ The Prefix *tele-* ■ The Suffix *-ize*	■ Main Idea and Details ■ Summarizing ■ Clarifying ■ Asking Questions	■ Features of Informational Text	■ Content-Area Words
The Heavenly Zoo Genre: **Myth**		■ Hyphenated Compound Words ■ Forming the Superlative with *-est* Ending ■ Inflectional Ending *-ed*	■ Making Inferences ■ Predicting ■ Making Connections ■ Summarizing	■ Recognize and Distinguish Myths	■ Listening Vocabulary
Circles, Squares, and Daggers: How Native, Americans, Watched the Sky Genre: **Nonfiction**		■ Content-Area Words ■ /f/ spelled *ph* ■ Plurals of Words That End in *x*	■ Classifying and Categorizing ■ Main Idea and Details ■ Clarifying ■ Visualizing ■ Making Connections	■ Informational Text	■ Meanings of Derivatives
Voyager to the Planets Genre: **Nonfiction**		■ Hyphenated Compound Words ■ Comparative and Superlative Adjectives ■ *i*-family Consonant Blends	■ Classifying and Categorizing ■ Compare and Contrast ■ Clarifying ■ Asking Questions ■ Summarizing	■ Recognizing Informational Texts	■ Affixes and Meanings
A Meeting in Space Genre: **Science Fiction**		■ Frequently Misspelled Words ■ /kw/ splelled *qu* ■ *r*-family Consonant Blends	■ Cause and Effect ■ Clarifying ■ Summarizing ■ Predicting	■ Title, Author, Illustrator	■ Listening Vocabulary
Stars Genre: **Nonfiction**		■ Antonyms ■ /ow/ spelled *ou* ■ /j/ spelled *ge* or *gi*	■ Classifying and Categorizing ■ Compare and Contrast ■ Asking Questions ■ Clarifying ■ Summarizing	■ Authors Organize Information in Specific Ways	■ Content-Area Words
The Book That Saved the Earth Genre: **Science Fiction Play**		■ Synonyms ■ Consonant Blends ■ The Ending *-ly*	■ Main Idea and Details ■ Clarifying ■ Visualizing ■ Predicting	■ Literary Terms Related to Plays	■ Listening Vocabulary

WRITING	LISTENING/ SPEAKING/VIEWING	GRAMMAR, USAGE, & MECHANICS	STUDY & RESEARCH	ACROSS THE CURRICULUM
■ Expository Writing ■ Prewrite	■ Give Precise Directions and Instructions	■ Nouns	■ Time Lines	Science ■ Spacecraft *Galileo* Social Studies ■ Recent Astronomers
■ Prewrite	■ Listening for Information	■ Pronouns	■ Diagrams	Science ■ Experimenting with Magnifiers Music ■ Appreciating Music Social Studies ■ How Is the Hubble Telescope Doing Now? Math ■ How Much Is 15 Billion?
■ Writing Paragraphs and Topic Sentences ■ Draft		■ Present–Tense Verbs— Regular and Irregular	■ Card and Computer Catalog	Science ■ Finding Our Own Constellations Health ■ Making a Safety Poster
■ Writing Paragraphs ■ Draft	■ Using Media	■ Present–Tense Verbs— Regular and Irregular	■ Outlining	Math ■ Astronomy Word Problems Social Studies ■ Names in Space
■ Revise	■ Interpreting a Graph	■ Complete Sentences	■ Creating a Chart	Math ■ Comparing Planets Art ■ Visualizing the Planets
■ Proofread	■ Dramatizations	■ Subject and Verb agreement	■ Create Diagrams Using Technology	Math ■ Word Problem Invasion Art ■ Alien Creatures Science ■ Drafting a Model Space Station Art ■ Picture Books
■ Evaluating the Author's Writing ■ Students Choose Focus of Writing Process	■ Major Ideas and Supporting Evidence in Speech	■ Commas in Direct Address	■ Note Taking	Science ■ Planets of Our Solar System Social Studies ■ Astronaut Heroes Art ■ Making Star Models Math ■ Measurement
■ Publish	■ Dramatic Interpretation of Poetry	■ Commas in a Series	■ Evaluating Writing by Assessing Research	Art ■ Design an Astronomical Set Social Studies ■ U.S. Space Missions

Meeting the Needs of All Children

Meeting Individual Needs

	Reteach	ESL	Challenge
Galileo Genre: **Biography**	**Reading and Responding** ■ Drawing Conclusions **Integrating the Curriculum** ■ Biography ■ Content-Area Words	**Preparing to Read** ■ Word Meaning ■ Cultural Context ■ Vocabulary **Reading and Responding** ■ Summarizing **Integrating the Curriculum** ■ Giving Directions	**Reading and Responding** ■ Drawing Conclusions **Integrating the Curriculum** ■ Biography ■ Content-Area Words ■ Nouns
Telescopes Genre: **Nonfiction**	**Reading and Responding** ■ Main Idea and Details **Integrating the Curriculum** ■ Informational Text	**Preparing to Read** ■ Word Meaning ■ Vocabulary **Reading and Responding** ■ Discussing the Selection **Integrating the Curriculum** ■ Leadership	**Reading and Responding** ■ Main Idea and Details **Integrating the Curriculum** ■ Informational Text ■ Content-Area Words ■ Pronouns ■ Diagrams
The Heavenly Zoo Genre: **Myth**	**Reading and Responding** ■ Making Inferences **Integrating the Curriculum** ■ Myth ■ Listening Vocabulary ■ Regular and Irregular Verbs	**Preparing to Read** ■ Word Meaning ■ Cultural Context ■ Vocabulary **Reading and Responding** ■ Summarizing **Integrating the Curriculum** ■ Listening Strategies ■ Card and Computer Catalog	**Reading and Responding** ■ Making Inferences **Integrating the Curriculum** ■ Myth ■ Listening Vocabulary ■ Regular and Irregular Verbs
Circles, Squares, and Daggers: How Native Americans Watched the Sky Genre: **Nonfiction**	**Reading and Responding** ■ Classifying and Categorizing	**Preparing to Read** ■ Word Meaning ■ Cultural Context ■ Vocabulary **Reading and Responding** ■ Discussion **Integrating the Curriculum** ■ Derivatives	**Reading and Responding** ■ Main Idea and Details ■ Classifying and Categorizing **Integrating the Curriculum** ■ Derivatives ■ Irregular Verbs
Voyager to the Planets Genre: **Nonfiction**	**Reading and Responding** ■ Compare and Contrast	**Preparing to Read** ■ Word Meaning ■ Vocabulary **Reading and Responding** ■ Discussion ■ Word Meaning **Integrating the Curriculum** ■ Recognizing Informational Texts	**Reading and Responding** ■ Compare and Contrast ■ Classifying and Categorizing **Integrating the Curriculum** ■ Affixes ■ Complete and Incomplete Sentences
A Meeting in Space Genre: **Science Fiction**	**Integrating the Curriculum** ■ Subject and Verb Agreement	**Preparing to Read** ■ Word Meaning **Reading and Responding** ■ Cause and Effect ■ Improvising Endings **Integrating the Curriculum** ■ Proofread ■ Dramatizations	**Reading and Responding** ■ Cause and Effect **Integrating the Curriculum** ■ Title ■ Listening Vocabulary ■ Subject and Verb Agreement
Stars Genre: **Nonfiction**	**Reading and Responding** ■ Classifying and Categorizing **Integrating the Curriculum** ■ Organizing Information ■ Content-Area Words	**Preparing to Read** ■ Word Meaning ■ Vocabulary **Reading and Responding** ■ Public Speaking **Integrating the Curriculum** ■ Picture Story	**Reading and Responding** ■ Classifying and Categorizing **Integrating the Curriculum** ■ Organizing Information ■ Content-Area Words ■ Commas in Direct Address
The Book That Saved the Earth Genre: **Science Fiction Play**	**Reading and Responding** ■ Main Idea and Details **Integrating the Curriculum** ■ Listening Vocabulary ■ Commas in a Series	**Preparing to Read** ■ Word Meaning **Reading and Responding** ■ Participation ■ Choral Reading **Integrating the Curriculum** ■ Commas in a Series	**Reading and Responding** ■ Main Idea and Details **Integrating the Curriculum** ■ Listening Vocabulary ■ Commas in a Series

Assessment

InterVention	✓ Informal	✓ Formal
Preparing to Read ■ Word Knowledge **Reading and Responding** ■ Comprehension ■ Drawing Conclusions ■ Asking Questions ■ Summarizing ■ Clarifying	Reading and Writing Workbook pp. 47–52 Reteach pp. 47–52 Challenge pp. 26–28 Teacher Observation Log Project Assessment	Comprehension and Writing Assessment pp. 29–30 ■ "Galileo" Skills Assessment pp. 12–13 ■ Word Families ■ Nouns
Preparing to Read ■ Word Knowledge ■ Looking at Diagrams **Reading and Responding** ■ Comprehension ■ Asking Questions ■ Main Idea and Details **Integrating the Curriculum** ■ Pronouns ■ Diagrams	Reading and Writing Workbook pp. 53–56 Reteach pp. 53–56 Challenge pp. 29–30 Teacher Observation Log Project Assessment	Comprehension and Writing Assessment pp. 31–32 ■ "Telescopes" Skills Assessment p. 14 ■ Word Meanings Across Curricular Content Areas
Preparing to Read ■ Inflectional Endings **Reading and Responding** ■ Comprehension ■ Predicting ■ Summarizing **Integrating the Curriculum** ■ Draft ■ Myth ■ Listening Vocabulary ■ Card and Computer Catalog	Reading and Writing Workbook pp. 57–64 Reteach pp. 57–64 Challenge pp. 31–34 Teacher Observation Log Project Assessment	Comprehension and Writing Assessment pp. 33–34 ■ "The Heavenly Zoo" Skills Assessment p. 15 ■ Using the Card or Computer Catalog
Preparing to Read ■ Plurals **Reading and Responding** ■ Comprehension ■ Main Idea and Details ■ Classifying and Categorizing ■ Clarifying **Integrating the Curriculum** ■ Draft	Reading and Writing Workbook pp. 65–66 Reteach pp. 65–66 Challenge p. 35 Teacher Observation Log Project Assessment	Comprehension and Writing Assessment pp. 35–36 ■ "Circles, Squares, and Daggers: How Native Americans Watched the Sky" Skills Assessment pp. 16–17 ■ Main Idea and Details ■ Regular and Irregular Verbs
Preparing to Read ■ Adjectives **Reading and Responding** ■ Comprehension ■ Compare and Contrast ■ Summarizing ■ Asking Questions ■ Classifying and Categorizing	Reading and Writing Workbook pp. 67–68 Reteach pp. 67–68 Challenge p. 36 Teacher Observation Log Project Assessment	Comprehension and Writing Assessment pp. 37–38 ■ "Voyager to the Planets" Skills Assessment pp. 18–19 ■ Classifying and Categorizing ■ Complete and Incomplete Sentences
Preparing to Read ■ Word Knowledge **Reading and Responding** ■ Comprehension ■ Cause and Effect ■ Clarifying ■ Predicting ■ Summarizing **Integrating the Curriculum** ■ Proofread	Reading and Writing Workbook pp. 69–70 Reteach pp. 69–70 Challenge p. 37 Teacher Observation Log Project Assessment	Comprehension and Writing Assessment pp. 39–40 ■ "A Meeting in Space" Skills Assessment pp. 20–22 ■ Frequently Misspelled Words ■ Cause and Effect ■ Developing Vocabulary by Listening to Selections Read Aloud
Preparing to Read ■ Antonyms **Reading and Responding** ■ Comprehension ■ Compare and Contrast ■ Summarizing ■ Clarifying ■ Classifying and Categorizing **Integrating the Curriculum** ■ Evaluating Author's Writing	Reading and Writing Workbook pp. 71–76 Reteach pp. 71–76 Challenge pp. 38–40 Teacher Observation Log Project Assessment	Comprehension and Writing Assessment pp. 41–42 ■ "Stars" Skills Assessment pp. 23–25 ■ Compare and Contrast ■ Commas in a Direct Address ■ Note-Taking
Preparing to Read ■ Synonyms **Reading and Responding** ■ Comprehension ■ Clarifying ■ Main Idea and Details ■ Predicting **Integrating the Curriculum** ■ Publishing	Reading and Writing Workbook pp. 77–82 Reteach pp. 77–82 Challenge pp. 41–43 Teacher Observation Log Project Assessment	Comprehension and Writing Assessment pp. 43–53 ■ "The Book That Saved the Earth" ■ Unit 2 Review Skills Assessment p. 26 ■ Consonant Blends and Digraphs

Previewing the Unit

Activating Prior Knowledge

Have the students discuss what they already know about stars, planets, and space exploration. Let the discussion develop naturally, then gradually direct it toward what students wonder about or would like to know about astronomy.

Suggest that students consider the following:

- how the tools of early astronomers have evolved into sophisticated space technology
- what ancient peoples saw in the night sky and how they made sense of it
- the role of the astronaut in gathering information about space and conducting experiments to benefit those on Earth
- what life on a space colony would be like

When students have had some time to compose their thoughts and ideas, call on volunteers to speak. After each student expresses himself or herself, allow a few minutes for questions. You may wish to spread this activity out over several days. As students present their ideas, add them to the Concept/Question Board.

Home Connection

In our unit, Back Through the Stars, the students will read selections that range from nonfiction accounts of discoveries made through astronomy to futuristic stories about space travel and extraterrestrials. An informational letter on Back Through the Stars, in both English and Spanish, can be found in the **Home Connection** guide.

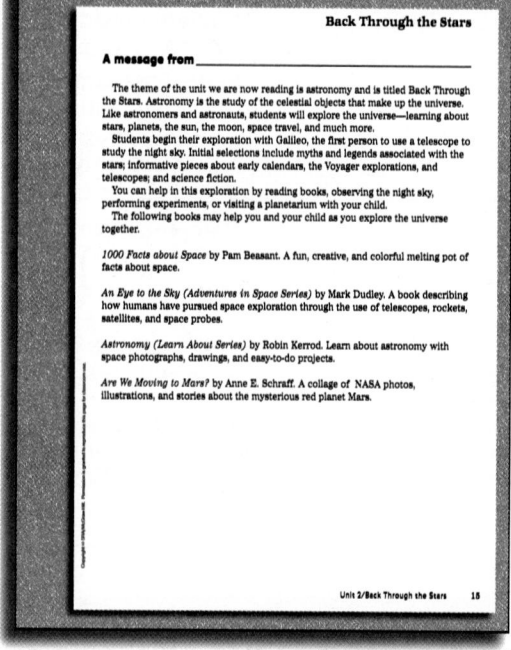

Home Connection p. 15

Using the Concept/Question Board

- Start the Concept/Question Board for this unit.
- Remind the students that the Concept/Question Board is where they are to post new information and ideas about astronomy that they gather as they do their research.
- Record the students' contributions on the Concept/Question Board.
- Have students recall the gist of each student's contribution and note the method he or she used to express his or her ideas.
- Have those students who have chosen not to contribute orally add their ideas to the written record.
- Draw students' attention to the array of content and the various presentation modes.

Over the course of the first week of the unit, have students reread and reflect on the contributions listed on the Concept/Question Board. Have them note in their Writing Journals the contributions that mean the most to them. Suggest that they expand on the original contributions by adding their own thoughts and associated material—stories, articles, pictures, and so on.

Setting Reading Goals

Have the students open their anthologies to the first page of this astronomy unit. Discuss the unit opener illustration on pages 116–117. It may prompt questions about the unit.

- Have the students spend a few minutes browsing the selections in the unit. This initial browsing will provide the students with many research ideas. Ask the students to share what interests them most about the subject. Record their ideas on the Concept/Question Board.

- Have students report and discuss what they have noticed in their browsing, raise any questions they have, and post their questions on the Concept/Question Board.

- If there are different opinions as to what this unit will be about, record these on the chalkboard and keep them for discussion after students have read some of the selections.

- Tell the students that this unit has been designated as a research unit. Astronomy is a subject for which there is abundant factual material and one that might naturally arouse curiosity.

- Point out to students that there are additional research ideas at the end of each selection. Make sure students take the time to notice these in their browsing.

Inquiry Journal

- After the students have discussed what they think this unit might be about, have them complete page 20 in their *Inquiry Journals.*

- Share ideas about astronomy that students would like to learn more about.

Inquiry Journal page 20

Research in Reading

Carl Bereiter and Marlene Scardamalia on the *Inquiry cycle in Elementary School Classrooms*

Ann Brown and Joe Campione have designed inquiry projects that have proven how eagerly students embrace the role of "researcher." Students enjoy seeing their own reading improve and contribute to their skills, particularly if the teacher works at establishing a "community of learners" in which they are active members.

Carl Bereiter and Marlene Scardamalia conducted a project on the consequences of participation in a knowledge-building community. One of the most interesting of these consequences is that students realize that research is a cyclical process. Researchers usually start with one idea or theory about what they will find, but then modify this idea as they gain new information, and go on to conduct another research cycle with this new idea or theory as their guide. This gives students a new slant on reading and writing because these activities are seen as essential—not just for recording knowledge, but for developing that knowledge in the first place.

See the Reading link of the **SRA** Web page for information on Research in Reading:

http://www.sra4kids.com

Galileo

from *Pioneer Astronomers*
by Navin Sullivan
illustrated by Jim Roldan

One May evening in 1609, a carriage rattled briskly through the streets of Padua, in Italy. In it was Galileo Galilei, professor of mathematics, returning from a trip to Venice. While he was there, he had received news from a former pupil named Jacques Badovere—news that had sent him hurrying home.

"A marvelous tube is on sale here," wrote Badovere, who was now living in Paris. "This tube makes distant objects appear close. A man two miles away can be seen distinctly. People call these tubes 'Dutch perspectives' or 'Dutch cylinders.' Some say that they were invented by Hans Lippershey, an obscure maker of eyeglasses in Middleburg, Holland. What is sure is that they employ two lenses, one convex and the other concave."

The carriage turned into the Borgo dei Vignali and stopped outside Galileo's house. Pausing only to glance at his garden, Galileo hurried indoors and went to his study.

"One convex and one concave," he repeated as though in a trance. He drew writing paper toward him, dipped a sharpened quill in the ink, and began to draw.

"Suppose the convex lens is placed in front, to gather the light," he muttered. "Then if the concave lens is placed the right distance behind, it should magnify the gathered light."

118

Selection Summary

Genre: Biography

In this selection, readers will meet a pioneer astronomer whose work opened up amazing new worlds in the field of astronomy. Galileo Galilei (1564–1642) was the first person ever to view the night sky through a telescope, and one of only a few scientists of his time who were willing to defy authority by publicly asserting that Earth is not the center of the universe. Navin Sullivan's friendly, conversational style brings the scholar and his work to life.

About the Author

Navin Sullivan is the award-winning author of "Galileo," which was excerpted from his book *Pioneer Astronomers*. Sullivan has had a lifelong interest in various fields of science. He has written many children's science books, and published numerous fictional stories for children in both English and American magazines.

Students can read more about Navin Sullivan on page 128 of the *Student Anthology.*

Other Books by Navin Sullivan
- *Pioneer Germ Fighters*
- *Progress in the Modern World*
- *Animal Timekeepers*

About the Illustrator

Jim Roldan was born in New York City. He graduated from the Rhode Island School of Design with a degree in illustration. He worked in a graphic design studio in New Hampshire and now owns his own business, illustrating advertisements, magazines, books, and posters. He lives in East Hampstead, New Hampshire, with his wife and two cats.

Students can read more about Jim Roldan on page 128 of the *Student Anthology.*

 Exploring the Theme

Selection Concepts

The events of "Galileo" illustrate the enormous importance of tools and technology in expanding people's knowledge of the universe. Galileo Galilei, the first person ever to view the night sky through a telescope, learned more about our solar system than earlier sky watchers had discerned over thousands of years of observing the heavens with the naked eye. Key concepts explored are:

■ the telescope helped astronomers acquire new information about the workings of the solar system as a whole, as well as about individual bodies within it.

■ Galileo's ideas about the solar system are widely accepted now but caused him serious trouble in his lifetime.

 Check the Reading link of the **SRA** Web page for links to theme-related Websites. **http://www.sra4kids.com**

Exploration Activity Tips

Before Reading, have the students discuss anything they know about using telescopes to observe the night sky. Then have them browse for clues about Galileo's discoveries.

During Reading, have students note evidence of the thought processes that made Galileo a great science scholar.

After Reading, as a class, review Galileo's discoveries about the moon and planets, and discuss how he made these discoveries—reconstructing thought processes is a fundamental part of scientific learning and thinking. Then have students update the Concept/Question Board. Some may want to revise their activity plans based on what they have learned from the selection.

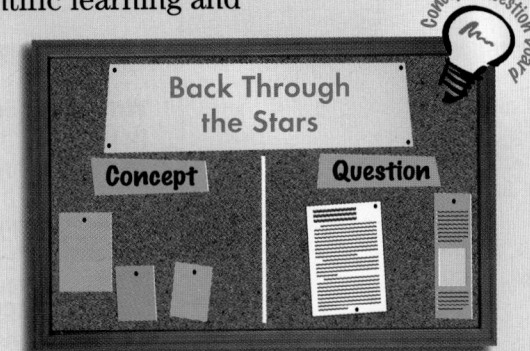

Unit 2 Exploration Management

Lesson 1 Galileo	**Collaborative Exploration** **Brainstorm research problems. Form interest-based groups. Develop and discuss initial research plans.** **Supplementary Activity** **Plot target dates for project and conduct class discussion of research problems and questions.**
Lesson 2	Groups finalize plans, allocate tasks, and begin research. Discuss initial findings and resources.
Lesson 3	Research continues as groups consider revision of their activity focus.
Lesson 4	Students continue with research and present their initial findings.
Lesson 5	Research continues. Students present interesting findings or problems.
Lesson 6	Research continues. Students present interesting findings or problems.
Lesson 7	Students organize research findings and prepare presentations.
Lesson 8	Students present their activities.

Lesson Planner

Suggested Pacing: 3–5 days	DAY 1	DAY 2	
	DAY 1	DAY 2	
Part 1 — Preparing to Read **Materials** ■ Student Anthology, pp. 118–129 ■ Transparencies 7, 44	**Word Knowledge** ■ Reading the Words and Sentences, p. 118G ✓ ■ Developing Oral Language, p. 118G **Build Background, p. 118H** **Preview and Prepare, p. 118I** **Selection Vocabulary, p. 118I** *apparatus, extraordinary, constellation, celestial, interrogation*	**Preview and Prepare, p. 118I** ■ Review Transparency 44	
Part 2 — Reading and Responding **Materials** ■ Student Anthology, pp. 118–129 ■ Teacher Observation Log ■ Reading and Writing Workbook, pp. 47–48 ■ Inquiry Journal, p. 21 ■ Home Connection, p. 17	**Student Anthology, pp. 118–129** **Comprehension Strategies** ■ Clarifying, pp. 118, 126 ■ Asking Questions, p. 120 ■ Summarizing, pp. 122, 124 **Discussing Strategy Use, p. 126**	**Student Anthology, pp. 118–129** **Comprehension Skills** ■ Drawing Conclusions, pp. 119, 121, 123, 125 ✓ ■ Discussing the Selection, p. 127 **Exploring the Theme** ■ Selection Vocabulary, p. 129A *apparatus, extraordinary, constellation, celestial, interrogation*	
Part 3 — Integrating the Curriculum **Materials** ■ Student Anthology, pp. 118–129 ■ Reading and Writing Workbook, pp. 49–52 ■ Transparency 52 ■ Inquiry Journal, p. 25	**Writing** ■ Expository Writing: Providing Specific Facts, p. 129C **Literary Elements** ✓ ■ Recognizing a Biography, p. 129D	**Writing Process** ■ Prewrite, p. 129C **Grammar, Usage, and Mechanics** ✓ ■ Nouns, p. 129F	
Independent Work Time **Materials** ■ Reteach, pp. 47–52 ■ ESL Supplement ■ Challenge, pp. 26–28 ■ Intervention Guide ■ Listening Library Audiocassette ■ Inquiry Journal, p. 24	**Writing Process Continued** **ESL** ■ Word Meaning, p. 118G ■ Summarizing, p. 123 **Intervention** ■ Word Knowledge, p. 118G ■ Asking Questions, p. 120	**Writing Process Continued** **Reteach** ✓ ■ Biography, *Reteach*, pp. 49–50 **ESL** ■ Vocabulary, p. 118J **Challenge** ✓ ■ Biography, *Challenge*, p. 27 ■ Drawing Conclusions, p. 121 ■ Nouns, p. 129F **Intervention** ■ Comprehension, p. 118 ■ Drawing Conclusions, p. 119	

✓ **Informal** Assessment Available   ✓ **Formal** Assessment Available

DAY 2 continued	DAY 3	
DAY 3	DAY 4	DAY 5

General Review	General Review	Review Word Knowledge

Student Anthology, pp. 118–129	**Student Anthology, pp. 118–129**	**Student Anthology, pp. 118–129**
Theme Connections	**Exploring the Theme**	■ Review Selection
■ Think About It, p. 129	■ Reading/Writing Connections, p. 129A	■ Complete Discussion
■ Research Ideas, p. 129	■ Literature Appreciation, p. 129A	■ Reread Selection in Pairs
	■ Supporting Student Explorations, p. 129B	**Home Connection, p. 129A**
		■ Discuss "Galileo"
		■ Illustrate the night sky

Writing Process Continued	**Writing Process Continued**	**Across the Curriculum**
Vocabulary	**Study and Research**	**Science**
✓ ■ Content-Area Words, p. 129E	■ Time Lines, p. 129G	■ Spacecraft *Galileo*, p. 129H
Listening/Speaking/Viewing		**Social Studies**
■ Giving Directions, p. 129F		■ Recent Astronomers, p. 129H

Writing Process Continued	**Writing Process Continued**	**Writing Process Continued**
Reteach	**Reteach**	**Unit Project Continued**
✓ ■ Drawing Conclusions, *Reteach*, pp. 47–48	✓ ■ Content-Area Words, *Reteach*, pp. 51–52	
ESL	**Challenge**	
■ Giving Directions, p. 129F	✓ ■ Content-Area Words, *Challenge*, p. 28	
Challenge	**Intervention**	
✓ ■ Drawing Conclusions, *Challenge*, p. 26	■ Clarifying, p. 124	
Intervention	**Unit Project**	
■ Summarizing, p. 122	■ Brainstorm Research Problems	
	■ Form Groups	
	■ Develop and Discuss Initial Research Plans	

Meeting Individual Needs
Independent Work Time

Preparing to Read

Meeting Individual Needs

ESL
- Word Meaning, p. 118G
- Cultural Context, p. 118H
- Vocabulary, p. 118J

Intervention
- Word Knowledge, p. 118G

Reading and Responding

Meeting Individual Needs

Reteach
- Drawing Conclusions, *Reteach*, pp. 47–48

ESL
- Summarizing, p. 123

Challenge
- Drawing Conclusions, p. 121
- Drawing Conclusions, *Challenge*, p. 26

Intervention
- Comprehension, p. 118
- Drawing Conclusions, p. 119
- Asking Questions, p. 120
- Summarizing, p. 122
- Clarifying, p. 124

Integrating the Curriculum

Meeting Individual Needs

Reteach
- Biography, *Reteach*, pp. 49–50
- Content-Area Words, *Reteach*, pp. 51–52

ESL
- Giving Directions, p. 129F

Challenge
- Biography, *Challenge*, p. 27
- Content-Area Words, *Challenge*, p. 28
- Nouns, p. 129F

Formal Assessment Options

Use these assessment pages along with your informal observations to gauge student progress.

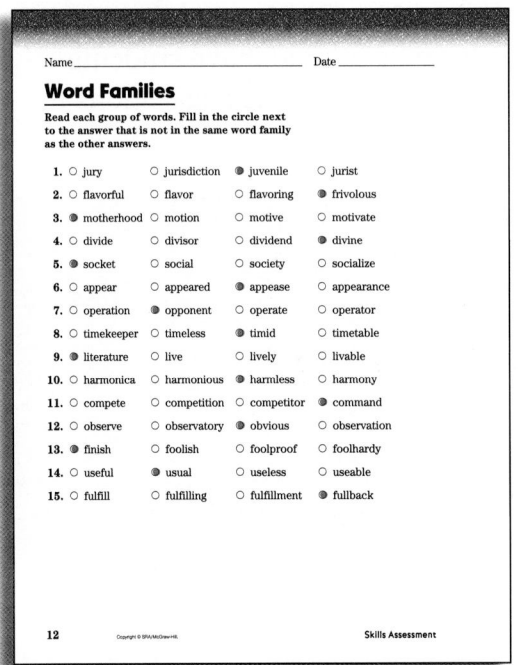

Skills Assessment, p. 12

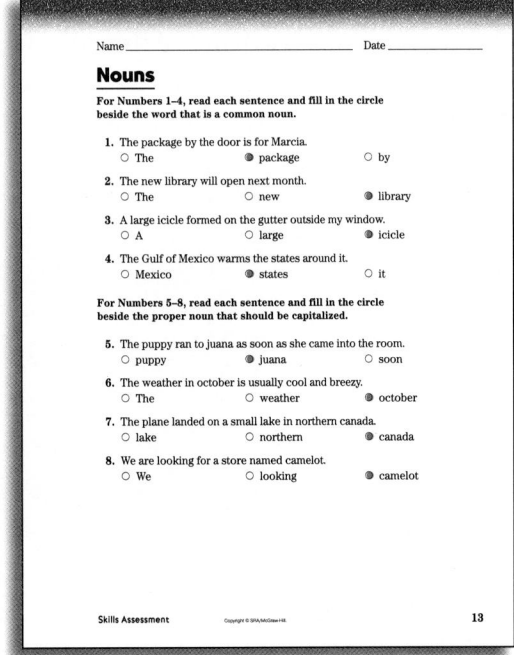

Skills Assessment, p. 13

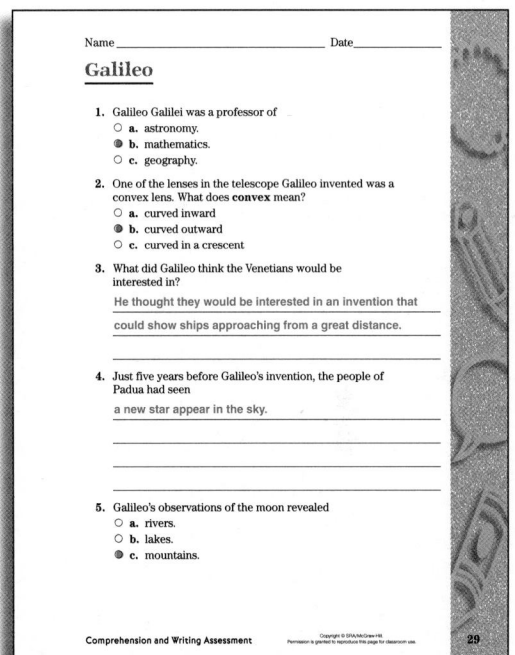

Comprehension and Writing Assessment, p. 29

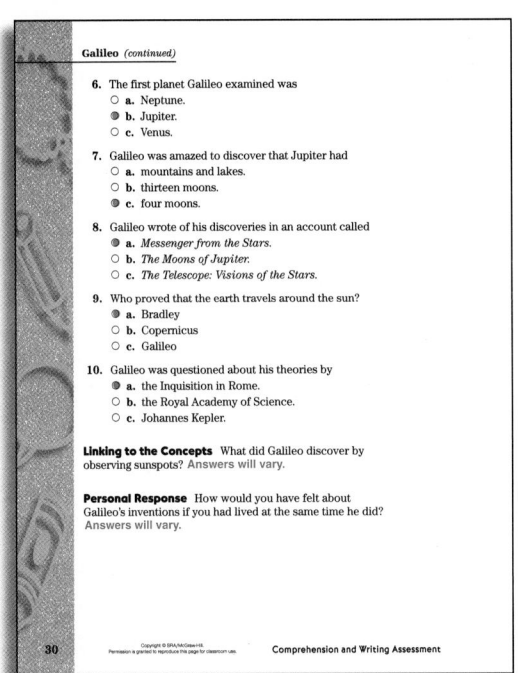

Comprehension and Writing Assessment, p. 30

① Preparing to Read

Meeting Individual Needs

ESL

Word Meaning Make sure the English-language learners understand the meaning of the words before you do the exercises with them. See Unit 2, Lesson 1, of the *ESL Supplement* for specific suggestions for use with the words used in this lesson.

Intervention

Word Knowledge Explain to students who need more help that *c* has the /k/ sound when it comes before *a*, *o*, or *u*. *C* has the /s/ sound when it comes before *i*, *e*, or *y*. Have them brainstorm and list as many words with a *c* as they can (*city, receive, car, concave, carry, center,* and so on.). Then have them separate the words in their list into categories: *c* with the /k/ sound and *c* with the /s/ sound. Have them pronounce the words aloud as they categorize them. For students who need more help, see Unit 2, Lesson 1, of the *Intervention Guide.*

Teacher Tip Gaining a better understanding of the spellings of sounds and the structure of words will help students as they encounter unfamiliar words in their reading. By this time in Grade 5, students should be reading approximately 126 words per minute with fluency and expression.

Assessment
✓ **Formal** To assess students' understanding of word families, have them complete *Skills Assessment,* page 12.

Word Knowledge

Reading the Words and Sentences

Write each word and sentence on the chalkboard. Have students read each word together. After all the words have been read, have students read each sentence in natural phrases or chunks. Use the suggestions in About the Words to discuss the different features of the listed words.

Line 1: observe observatory observation
Line 2: carriage convex concave constellation
Line 3: circle celestial cycle
Sentence 1: The citizens observed the constellations in the sky.
Sentence 2: A telescope has concave and convex lenses.
Sentence 3: The moon is a celestial body that circles Earth.

About the Words

■ The words in Line 1 build on the root word *observe*, meaning *to see.* Have students comment on how the different suffixes change the meaning of the word.

■ Line 2 contains words that illustrate the /k/ sound spelled *c* before *a*, *o*, or *u*. Have students think of other words containing this spelling of the /k/ sound.

■ Line 3 contains words that demonstrate the /s/ sound spelled *c* before *i*, *e*, or *y*. Remind students that *i*, *e*, and *y* signal the sound /s/ for c. Have volunteers use each word in a sentence.

Developing Oral Language

To review the words, have students do one or both of the following activities:

■ Have a student point to one word in the lines above and select a classmate to read the word and use it in a sentence.

■ Write several words from the lines above on the chalkboard. Give a clue for each of the words. For example, for the word *circle*, "Which word is a shape that is round?" Invite a student to come to the chalkboard and erase the correct answer.

Build Background

Activate Prior Knowledge

Discuss the following with students to find out what they may already know about the selection and have already learned about the unit theme. Tell students to use their prior knowledge to help them comprehend the selection they are about to read.

- Ask students whether they are familiar with Galileo. Have them discuss what they know about him.
- Have students share any other stories that have information about astronomy in them.

Background Information

The following information may help the students better understand the selection they are about to read.

- Introduce students to the writing genre, biography. Tell them that a biography is a true story about a real person that is written by another person. This selection is a biography about Galileo, who is famous for his discoveries in the field of astronomy.
- Although Galileo did not invent the refracting telescope, he was the first person to build his own telescopes to study the sky.
- In Galileo's time, the Roman Catholic Church was the highest religious authority and also the political ruler over much of what is now Italy. It was a powerful institution to which many looked for the final word on controversial matters. For this reason, scientific discoveries that contradicted what was already accepted as fact were subject to the Church's scrutiny. The Church, which taught that Earth was the center of the universe, considered Galileo's teachings heresy.
- Aristotle was a philosopher who said Earth was the center of the universe. The Roman Catholic Church believed this theory. In 1543, Copernicus, an astronomer, said that the sun, not Earth, was the center of the universe. The Church denounced Copernicus's theory.

Meeting Individual Needs

ESL

Cultural Context Some English-language learners may be unfamiliar with the Roman Catholic Church. If any English-language learners are Catholic, encourage them to describe a few beliefs and practices. Also, locate Italy on a map of the world, or on a globe, and have English-language learners point to it.

Teacher Tip If any questions about Galileo and the field of astronomy come up while activating prior knowledge, write them down on the chalkboard. Refer back to these questions when they are answered in the selection or through discussion and research.

Writing Journal Tell students that they will be encouraged to jot down in their Writing Journals their reactions to this selection and any ideas they may have for using astronomy in a story.

Preparing to Read

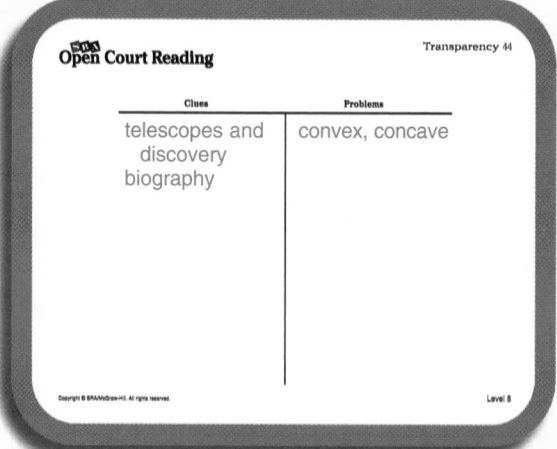

Transparency 44

Teacher Tip To help students decode words, divide them into the syllables shown below. The information following each word tells how students can figure out the meaning of each word from the sentences on the transparencies.

ap·pa·ra·tus	context clues
ex·tra·or·di·na·ry	context clues, word structure
con·stel·la·tion	context clues
ce·les·tial	context clues
in·ter·ro·ga·tion	context clues, word structure

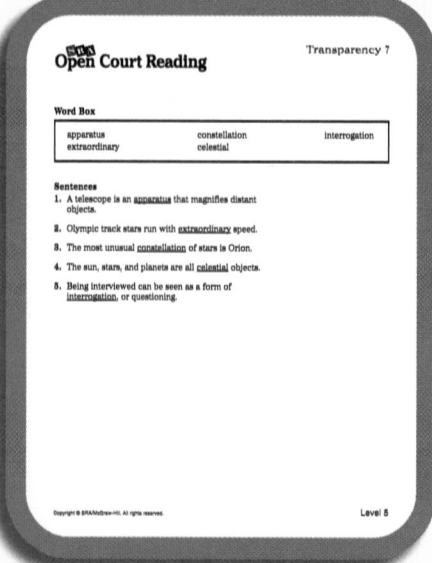

Transparency 7

Preview and Prepare

Browse

- Have a volunteer read the title and author's and illustrator's names aloud. Have students share what they know about biographies.

- Because this is a nonfiction selection, have the students browse the entire selection and look for words and phrases that connect to what they already know. Record these in the Clues column on **Transparency 44.** Discuss with students what they think this selection might have to do with astronomy.

- Encourage students to identify any problems they notice while reading in the Problems column.

Set Purposes

As they read, have students think about the importance of telescopes in expanding our knowledge of astronomy.

Selection Vocabulary

As students study vocabulary, they will use a variety of skills to determine the meaning of a word. These include context clues, word structure, and apposition. Students will apply these same skills while reading to clarify additional unfamiliar words.

Display **Transparency 7** before reading the selection to introduce and discuss the following words and their meanings.

ap·pa·ra·tus:	a piece of equipment that has a particular use (page 119)
ex·tra·or·di·na·ry:	unusual or amazing (page 120)
con·stel·la·tion:	group of stars that form shapes in the sky (page 122)
ce·les·tial:	relating to the sky (page 125)
in·ter·ro·ga·tion:	questioning (page 126)

Have students read the words in the Word Box, stopping to blend any words that they have trouble reading. Help students decode multisyllabic words by breaking the words into syllables and blending the syllables.

Have students read the sentences to determine the meaning of the underlined words. Remind them to use clues in the sentences and structural clues to figure out the meaning. See the teacher tip on the left for information on how words can be defined.

Reading Recommendations

Your first reading of the selection should focus on developing the reading strategies found to the left of the reduced pages. During rereading, they should focus on the comprehension skills, found to the right of the reduced pages.

Oral Reading

Because of the scientific nature and the level of detail of the information presented in this selection, the students may need assistance. Oral reading is recommended. As students read aloud, have them read expressively, at an appropriate pace, in natural phrases and chunks. By reading the selection with fluency, students will demonstrate an understanding of the text and an ability to engage the listeners in an effective manner. If students encounter difficulties, have them use the reading strategies below or refer to the Blending Procedure (Program Appendix 15–16).

As this is a nonfiction selection and students are reading to be informed, allow students more time for reading. Have students adjust their reading rate by reading more slowly or by rereading certain sections of the selection in order to comprehend the information presented.

Using Reading Strategies

Reading-strategy instruction allows students to become aware of how good readers read. Good readers constantly check their understanding as they are reading and ask themselves questions. In addition, skilled readers recognize when they are having problems and stop to use various reading strategies to help them make sense of what they are reading.

During the reading of "Galileo," you will model the use of the following reading strategies:

- Clarifying
- Asking questions
- Summarizing

Before reading, have students explain how they have used these strategies in the past and share any tips they can give each other on their use.

Building Comprehension Skills

Revisiting or rereading a selection allows students to apply skills that give them a more complete understanding of the text. Some follow-up comprehension skills help students organize information. Others lead to deeper understanding—to "reading between the lines," as mature readers do. In this selection, students will apply the comprehension skill, *Drawing Conclusions*.

Teacher Tip Have students who may need extra help reading "Galileo" reread the selection using the *Listening Library Audiocassette.*

Meeting Individual Needs

ESL

Vocabulary Check that English-language learners know the meanings of idioms and more difficult vocabulary in the story, including: *tube, cylinders, lenses, convex, concave, magnify, actual sizes, magnified three times, lens grinding, magnifications, tripod stand, diameter, myriads more than that, pendulum, planet, orbits, satellite moons, celestial object, blemish, axis,* and *defiance.* Explain and show pictures as needed. Model example sentences and help English-speaking students make their own sentences. Refer to Unit 2, Lesson 1, of the *ESL Supplement* for teaching suggestions.

Teacher Tip By this time in the fifth grade, good readers should be reading approximately 126 words per minute with fluency and expression. The only way to gain fluency is through practice. As explained in Reading Recommendations, have students reread all or part of the selection to you and to each other during class or Independent Work Time to focus on the comprehension skills and to build fluency.

② Reading and Responding

Read pages 118–129.

Comprehension Strategies

Modeling

❶ Clarifying *Good readers stop to clarify terms or ideas they do not understand. I have never heard of* Dutch Perspectives. *This is a good time to stop and see if there are any clues in the text that help us clarify what a* Dutch Perspective *is. Badovere wrote that they are tubes that make "distant objects appear close." This sounds like a telescope;* Dutch Perspectives *may have been the first telescopes. As we read on we will probably find out for certain if that is what they are. Are there any other terms you need to have clarified?*

Teacher Tip

Point out that there will be many unfamiliar words in this selection. Help students read these words by providing the following pronunciations. Galileo Galilei is pronounced gä lē lā' ō ga lē lā' ē. Jacques Badovere is pronounced zhäk bā dō vā' rā. Hans Lippershey is pronounced häns lip ərs hā'. Borgo dei Vignali is pronounced bor' gō dā' ē vē nyä' lē.

Word Knowledge

received, concave, convex

Students can use the skills they learned in the Word Knowledge section of this lesson to read these words. Remind students of this if they have difficulty reading these words.

Reading Recommendation

ORAL · CHORAL · SILENT

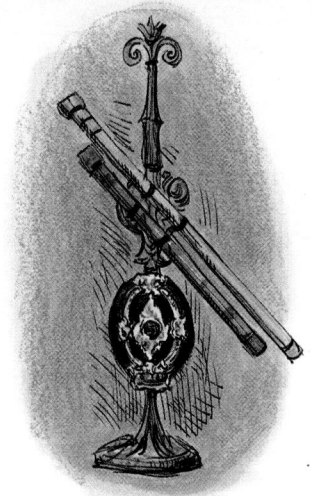

Galileo

from *Pioneer Astronomers*
by Navin Sullivan
illustrated by Jim Roldan

One May evening in 1609, a carriage rattled briskly through the streets of Padua, in Italy. In it was Galileo Galilei, professor of mathematics, returning from a trip to Venice. While he was there, he had received news from a former pupil named Jacques Badovere——news that had sent him hurrying home.

"A marvelous tube is on sale here," wrote Badovere, who was now living in Paris. "This tube makes distant objects appear close. A man two miles away can be seen distinctly. People call these tubes 'Dutch perspectives' or 'Dutch cylinders.' Some say that they were invented by Hans Lippershey, an obscure maker of eyeglasses in Middleburg, Holland. What is sure is that they employ two lenses, one convex and the other concave."

The carriage turned into the Borgo dei Vignali and stopped outside Galileo's house. Pausing only to glance at his garden, Galileo hurried indoors and went to his study.

"One convex and one concave," he repeated as though in a trance. He drew writing paper toward him, dipped a sharpened quill in the ink, and began to draw.

"Suppose the convex lens is placed in front, to gather the light," he muttered. "Then if the concave lens is placed the right distance behind, it should magnify the gathered light."

118

He only had to figure the distance and he would be able to make one of these marvelous "Dutch perspectives" for himself! He had already taken the <u>precaution</u> of bringing a good assortment of eyeglass lenses from Venice.

By the time that Galileo went to bed he felt fairly sure that he had solved the problem. Early the next morning he hurried to his workshop. The place was filled with gadgets he had already invented, including an apparatus for indicating temperature and another for timing the pulse of a patient. Now he would make a tube to <u>demolish</u> distance.

Seizing a handy piece of lead tubing, he cut it down to the length he wanted. Then he took a convex lens and placed it in one end, and placed a concave lens in the other. Excitedly, he held the tube to his eye and peered through. Immediately he gave a cry of delight. It worked! The church tower several streets away might have been just outside.

How much did his tube magnify? Galileo cut different-sized circles of paper and pinned them up on a wall. When he found that his tube made a small circle look the size of a larger one seen with the naked eye, he could figure the <u>magnification</u> by comparing the actual sizes of the circles. In this way he found that his telescope magnified three times.

Proudly he sat down and wrote to his friends in Venice telling them of his success. Then, after getting the lenses mounted in a more imposing tube made of wood, he hurried back to Venice himself. The Venetians were famous as sailors and navigators. This tube would show them ships out at sea long before they could be seen with the naked eye. Surely, thought Galileo, the nobles of Venice would pay well for such a device.

119

Comprehension Skills

Drawing Conclusions

Tell the students that readers can make better sense of the text by *drawing conclusions* about a character or event based on information in the text.

Have the students draw conclusions about why the Venetian Senate would pay so much for a telescope. If necessary, point out the following information in the text that the students can use to help them draw conclusions.

- The author notes that Venetians were excellent sailors.

- Telescopes make distant objects appear closer.

Drawing Conclusions
INTRODUCED: Unit 1, Lesson 1
REVIEWED: Unit 1, Lesson 5
Unit 2, Lesson 1
Unit 3, Lesson 4
Unit 3, Lesson 6

Meeting Individual Needs

Intervention

Drawing Conclusions Walk students who need extra help through drawing conclusions by showing them how to use context clues to make a judgement about a character or event in a story.

2 Reading and Responding

Comprehension Strategies

Modeling

2 Asking Questions *Good readers ask questions to prepare them for what they will learn. The author said that Galileo wanted to make even stronger telescopes. I wonder why he would need them. What would Galileo be looking at that he would need a stronger telescope? When we keep reading, I hope we find these answers.*

As I read on, I see that Galileo was not interested in looking out to sea with his telescope—he wanted to use it to study a new star that had appeared in the sky.

Teacher Tip Help the students form their own questions about the text. Invite them to note where in the text their questions are answered.

Word Knowledge

cathedral, circling, crescent

Students can use the skills they learned in the Word Knowledge section of this lesson to read these words. Remind students of this if they have difficulty reading these words.

His thinking was right. On August 8, 1609, even the aged members of the Venetian Senate <u>clambered</u> painfully up to the very top of the tower of St. Mark's Cathedral, the highest building in Venice. There they gazed out to sea through Galileo's primitive telescope and, to their delight, found that they could see ships sailing toward them a good two hours before they were visible with the naked eye. They promptly doubled Galileo's salary as professor of mathematics which, although he was at the University of Padua, was controlled by them.

2 Galileo returned triumphantly to Padua and disappeared into his workshop. Already he was planning better lenses and longer tubes. He intended to teach himself lens grinding. He dreamed of magnifications of 8, 20, even 30!

And when he had made these telescopes, he was going to use them to look not at the sea but the sky. Five years earlier, all Padua had seen an extraordinary happening: a new star had appeared in the sky. (The astronomer Johannes Kepler had seen it too, and had pointed out that evidently the stars were not unchanging, as people then believed.) Like everyone else, Galileo had been surprised and puzzled by the new star. Now he promised himself that he was going to look more closely at the heavens.

120

Meeting Individual Needs

Intervention

Asking Questions Remind students that asking questions as they read helps keep them involved in what they are reading. Reread the last few pages with small groups and have each student jot down a question. Decide if the question can be answered by rereading or if the student will need to keep reading. Remind students that sometimes they have to infer answers based on what they are reading as well as other knowledge.

It was four days after new moon. Galileo's newest telescope, magnifying 30 times, was resting in its cradle on a <u>tripod</u> stand. He squinted through it at the bright crescent, then drew what he saw by the light of a flickering candle.

The moon was, he knew, lit from one side by the sun. He noticed that the boundary between light and dark on the moon's surface was wavy and uneven. Also, he saw bright spots of light dotted over the dark area. What could they be?

He puzzled over them for a while, and then he made a bold <u>deduction</u>.

"These spots of light are mountain peaks just catching the sunlight," he decided. "And the wavy line at the boundary between light and dark exists because there are mountains there, too. It is sunrise up there and, just as on earth at dawn, the mountain peaks are bathed in sunlight while the valleys are still dark." It seemed incredible. Yet it must be true. There were mountains on the moon, as there were on earth!

Until then no one had seriously supposed that the moon might be something like the earth. People had thought of the moon and planets as heavenly bodies, things quite different in kind from the earth.

How high were the mountains? Galileo could not measure them directly, but he devised a way of comparing them with the diameter of the moon, which was fairly accurately known. When he had worked out the figures, he could hardly believe them. The moon mountains proved to be enormous, much higher than earthly mountains: up to four miles high.

It was a whole new world that Galileo was looking at. But was it full of living creatures or was it dead? He wondered if there was air on it, and shuddered at the idea that it might be cold and silent, a dead world forever circling the earth.

121

Comprehension Skills

Drawing Conclusions

Have students note the following information about Galileo.

- He is able to create a telescope based on only a description. His workshop is filled with gadgets that he invented. He decides that there are mountains on the moon, even though it seems incredible.

Discuss conclusions about Galileo based on these facts. Lead the students to see that Galileo has talent inventing things. He is self-confident and sticks by his beliefs.

Ask them to point out information that supports these conclusions.

 **Teacher Tip** Students should note evidence of Galileo's thought processes that made him a great scholar in the field of science.

Meeting Individual Needs

Challenge

Drawing Conclusions Have students play a game of charades, miming characters, objects, and events from the selection "Galileo." Students will draw conclusions as to what is being mimed, based on their knowledge of the text and their own experiences with communicating ideas.

Reading and Responding

Comprehension Strategies

Modeling

③ **Summarizing** *We know that good readers summarize to make sure that they understand what they are reading. Putting a piece of text in one's own words also helps one to recall it. Let's summarize this selection so far. First, Galileo heard about telescopes from a friend. He made some telescopes, sold a few, and then made a stronger one for himself. Galileo was able to use the stronger telescope to discover stars that no one else had ever seen before.*

Teacher Tip During discussions with the students, use vocabulary words related to explorable concepts in order to model the utility of these words.

Word Knowledge

constellation, observers, course

Students can use the skills they learned in the Word Knowledge section of this lesson to read these words. Remind students of this if they have difficulty reading these words.

Then he began to explore the sky. Night after night he gazed upward, and what he found was a revelation. With the naked eye only about 2,000 stars are visible at any one time. Even with his relatively low-power telescope, Galileo found <u>myriads</u> more than that.

He examined the belt and sword of Orion: instead of the usual nine stars he found 89! The constellation of the Pleiades, in which sharp-eyed observers could only see seven stars, became a swarm of 43. As for the Milky Way—it was impossible to think of counting the stars in it. Wherever Galileo looked, his telescope showed crowded clusters of stars.

③ "Many of them are tolerably large and extremely bright," he noted, "but the number of small ones is quite beyond determination."

On January 7, 1610, while he was gazing at the sky an hour after sunset, he noticed that the planet Jupiter was visible. Immediately he turned his telescope onto it, eager to examine one of the planets for the first time.

He saw that it was a small, round disk that did not sparkle like a star. Peering more closely, he saw something else: three bright little points of light were grouped near it, two to the east of Jupiter, one to the west.

(East)   X   XO   X   (West)

At first he told himself that these bright points must be three fixed stars. But the next night, to his astonishment, they were differently grouped: all three were to the west of Jupiter.

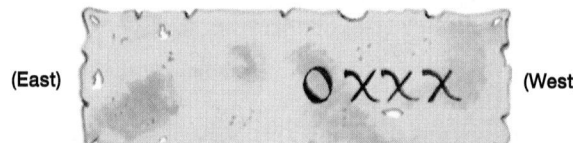
(East)   O XXX   (West)

122

Meeting Individual Needs

Inter**v**ention

Summarizing If students are having difficulty summing up the events, reread this section aloud and have students raise their hands whenever they detect a change in the action of the text.

"Can Jupiter have moved past them?" Galileo asked himself in bewilderment. "If so, it is not traveling the way astronomers have always said it does."

He waited impatiently to look again the next night, but to his disappointment the sky was cloudy. However, the following night was clear. He rushed to his telescope and turned it with trembling hands toward Jupiter. This is what he saw:

(East)   (West)

For a moment he wondered if he were going crazy. Now there were only two points of light, and both were to the east of Jupiter.

"Is Jupiter moving back and forth like a pendulum?" he muttered.

He searched the sky nearby, checking to see if Jupiter had moved in this way against the background of the fixed stars. It had not; it was on the course that astronomers had always charted for it.

"If Jupiter is not swinging to and fro, then the little points of light are," reasoned Galileo. "And since one of them has disappeared tonight, it is probably hidden by Jupiter——it has probably gone behind the planet. It looks as if these points of light are swinging *around* Jupiter!"

123

Comprehension Skills

Drawing Conclusions

Have the students trace Galileo's day-by-day observations about the "points of light."

- Have students draw conclusions about Galileo, based on these studies. Help students conclude that Galileo was a careful and meticulous scientist, who understood the importance of his observations about the sky.

- Based on their own knowledge of the solar system, have students draw conclusions about the impact of Galileo's discoveries on astronomy today. Have students compare their conclusions about the importance of these discoveries with those of Galileo.

Meeting Individual Needs

ESL

Summarizing Pair English-language learners with native English speakers. Have the partners practice summarizing to each other.

2 Reading and Responding

Comprehension Strategies

Prompting

4 Summarizing *Now is a good time to sum up what has happened to Galileo so far. This will let us know if we understand all of the important ideas. We know that first, he started to make telescopes. Then, he used the telescopes to look at the sky. What are some things that happened after this?*

Student Sample

5 Summarizing *Galileo began to discover things in the sky that no one had ever seen before. He saw many more stars than could be seen without a telescope. Finally he discovered that Jupiter had moons, just like Earth.*

Teacher Tip

Call on several volunteers to provide a part of the summary until all of the text has been summarized.

Word Knowledge

discoveries, decided, celestial

Students can use the skills they learned in the Word Knowledge section of this lesson to read these words. Remind students of this if they have difficulty reading these words.

This meant that the points of light could not be stars. To make sure that they were swinging around Jupiter, Galileo began a methodical series of observations.

On the next night, January 11th, he still saw only two of them, but now they had moved farther away from the planet. On the 12th they were closer again, and a third had appeared on the west of the planet. On the 13th, he had **4** another surprise: there were four points of light.

(East)   X O X X X   (West)

He doubted no longer. "These are not fixed stars, but bodies belonging to Jupiter and going around it in various orbits," he decided. "Jupiter has four satellite moons of its **5** own, just as the Earth has one!"

Full of excitement, he settled down to write a short account of all that he had discovered with his telescope. Two months later this was published in Venice, under the title *Messenger from the Stars*. His discoveries amazed the whole of Europe. Soon they were even being discussed in faraway Peking (now Beijing).

Meeting Individual Needs

Intervention

Clarifying Students who have trouble understanding Galileo's discoveries can use pieces of paper or small objects to track the "bright little points of light" as Galileo did.

Galileo had opened up a new vision of the heavens. He had shown that the moon is a rocky, mountainous globe, that the earth is not unique in having a satellite moon, and that millions upon millions of stars exist. Soon he went further and discovered that Venus appears first as a crescent, then full, then dark, as it circles the sun and reflects light at different angles. He even traced the movement of mysterious spots across the face of the sun. The fact that the sun has spots shocked some people, who felt that a celestial object ought to be without blemish. Galileo, however, was very interested, for the movement of the spots, in one direction, indicated that the sun, like the earth, was spinning round on its axis.

To many people this probing of the skies was exciting. They realized that for the first time people had a means of exploring space. But to others it was unsettling, even dangerous. This was because, although they were living 70 years after Copernicus, they still believed that the earth did not move and was the center of the universe. The Church of Rome officially agreed with this belief, although some of its members did not.

Until now Galileo had not dared to defy the Church openly and declare that the earth moved round the sun.

"I would certainly dare to publish my ideas at once if more people like you existed," he had once written to Kepler. "Since they don't, I shall refrain from doing so."

However, his discoveries made Galileo a much more important man. He decided, finally, that the Church would not dare to curb him, and he began to state publicly that the earth circled the sun.

"Let them try to prove me wrong!" he exclaimed.

125

Comprehension Skills

Drawing Conclusions

For additional help with *drawing conclusions*, have students complete ***Reading and Writing Workbook*** pages 47–48.

Name _____ Date _____

Drawing Conclusions | Galileo |

Focus When writers don't include all the information about a character or event in their story, good readers draw conclusions using information in the text.

> **Drawing conclusions** means putting together information from the text to make a statement about a character or event. The conclusion won't be stated directly, but should be supported by information in the text.

Identify Look through "Galileo." What conclusions did you come to about people or events in the selection? Find places in the text that helped you to draw conclusions. Answers will vary. Possible answers are provided below.

Page: 119
Conclusion: Galileo has a talent for building things.
Information that supports the conclusion: His workshop was filled with gadgets.

Page: 125
Conclusion: Galileo's discoveries changed astronomy.
Information that supports the conclusion: "Galileo had opened up a new vision of the heavens."

Reading and Writing Workbook • *Drawing Conclusions*   47

Drawing Conclusions *(continued)*

Practice Think about an important space discovery that you might want a reader to draw a conclusion about. It could be in the past, or it could be a more recent discovery. First, decide what conclusion you want the reader to draw. Then, write some clues that will help the reader come to that conclusion. Answers will vary.

The discovery: _____
Conclusion: _____
Clues: _____

Apply Use the above clues to write a paragraph about the discovery you chose. Read your paragraph to a classmate and have him or her draw a conclusion about the discovery. Discuss what information in the paragraph the conclusion was based on. Answers will vary.

48   *Drawing Conclusions* • Reading and Writing Workbook

Reading and Writing Workbook pp. 47–48

Meeting Individual Needs

Reteach	**Challenge**
Drawing Conclusions Have students who need additional instruction and practice with this concept complete **Reteach,** pages 47–48.	**Drawing Conclusions** Have students who understand this concept complete **Challenge,** page 26.

2 Reading and Responding

Comprehension Strategies

Modeling

6 Clarifying *I wonder what an Inquisition is. Let's look up* Inquisition *in the dictionary and see if that helps us figure out what it is.*

Let's see . . . It says that the Roman Catholic Church used to have a court called a tribunal. This court was set up especially for questioning and testing ideas that contradicted what was commonly accepted as fact. One could be punished for continuing to publish ideas that the Church did not recognize as truth.

Discussing Strategy Use

After they have read the selection, have students share any problems they encountered and tell what strategies they used to solve them. Then, have them answer the following questions. If they answer "no" to any of the questions, have them reread part of the selection to find the answer.

- How did asking questions help students understand the discoveries of Galileo and his world?

- Did students clarify parts of the text that were unusual or hard to understand?

- Did they stop to sum up during the selection to help them understand and remember all the information?

Make sure that students explain how using the strategies helped them understand the selection better and how they read effectively to find answers to the questions they asked as they set purposes.

For some years the Roman Catholic Church let Galileo talk freely, only warning him from time to time, but many high officials of the Church remained unconvinced. And in fact, whatever Galileo said, he could not *prove* that the earth goes round the sun; he could only say, with Copernicus, that it seemed likely. (It was not until 1728 that conclusive proof was given by James Bradley, Third Astronomer Royal of England.)

In 1623 a new Pope was elected and the Church hardened against Galileo. He received more severe warnings than before, but would not give way. In 1632 he published a brilliant argument in favor of his beliefs, entitled *Dialogue on the Great World Systems.*

This was open defiance of the Church, and Galileo was summoned to appear before the Inquisition in Rome. Interrogation began on April 12, 1633. Galileo was asked to declare that he was wrong and that the earth stood still. The questioning continued for a month.

6 The great astronomer was now seventy years old, and he was worn out by fatigue and by fear of the Inquisition. In the end, Galileo did as he was told. Never again did he say in public that the earth moved.

126

Research in Action

Discussing Strategy Use

Remember to discuss with the students difficulties that occurred during reading. While problems that arise during reading should be addressed as they occur, it is important to reflect on the problems and how they were solved. After reading, have students identify the difficulties. Probe with questions that foster metacognition, or thinking about thinking, such as *What did you find difficult here? How did you try to figure it out? Did that work? What else might work? (Michael Pressley)*

127

Comprehension Skills

Discussing the Selection

Following reading, engage the students in a discussion of the selection. Using the *handing-off process* will help the students take responsibility for the discussion. In addition to the following questions, have them revisit any questions asked when they set purposes before reading.

- How was Galileo able to make new discoveries about the moon, the planets, and the stars? (*He made telescopes and used them to magnify objects in the sky.*)

- What did Galileo conclude about Jupiter? (*that the planet is circled by four moons, just as Earth is orbited by one*)

- What did the Inquisition do about Galileo's ideas? (*They warned him against talking freely about the Earth moving.*)

- How has this selection connected with your knowledge of the unit theme? (*Answers will vary—students should compare/contrast examples of astronomy from this selection with their own experiences or past reading and use these connections to make a general statement about the unit theme.*)

During this time, have the students return to the clues and problems that they noted on the transparency before reading to determine whether the clues were borne out by the selection. Let students decide which items deserve further discussion. Encourage students to record the thoughts, feelings, or reactions that are elicited by any reading they do.

Assessment

✓ **Formal** To assess students' reading comprehension, have them complete **Comprehension and Writing Assessment,** page 29-30.

Teacher Tip In order for handing off to work effectively, a seating arrangement that allows students to see one another is essential. A circle or a semicircle is effective. In addition, all of the students need to have copies of the materials being discussed.

Teacher Tip Copernicus is pronounced ko pər' ni kəs.

② Reading and Responding

Meet the Author

After the students read the information about Navin Sullivan discuss the following questions with them.

Why do you think Navin Sullivan is fascinated with scientific discoverers? *(Possible answer: He is fascinated with scientific discoverers because their findings and inventions make it possible for people to do things such as travel in space and cure diseases.)*

Why do you think that Navin Sullivan wrote about Galileo, an inventor who lived more than 300 years ago? *(Possible answer: He wrote about Galileo because his discoveries about planets, stars, and moons still have an impact on scientific study of our universe.)*

Meet the Illustrator

After students have read the information about Jim Roldan, discuss the following question with them.

Jim Roldan says that as a kid, he always drew. How did this love of drawing affect his adult life? *(Possible answer: It made him want to become an illustrator and eventually own his own illustrating business.)*

Galileo

Meet the Author

Navin Sullivan has written and edited science books since he was a young man in his twenties. He is fascinated with people who make discoveries about things like outer space, medicine, and the human body. He calls them "pioneers" because they explore new territories in science. He has made it his goal to teach others about these scientists and their discoveries. He does this by writing books, like *Pioneer Astronomers* and *Pioneer Germ Fighters*. He also writes about these discoverers in short stories, magazines, and radio scripts.

Meet the Illustrator

Jim Roldan's first memorable gift as a child was a box of 64 colored crayons. He drew pictures of cartoon characters, animals, comic book heroes, dinosaurs and spaceships. He went on to earn a degree in Fine Art. After a few years working in a graphic design studio, Mr. Roldan started his own business illustrating ads, magazines, posters, books, and the occasional cartoon character. He currently lives and works in New Hampshire where he shares a house with his wife and their two cats.

128

Theme Connections

Think About It

With a small group of classmates, consider how the telescope made a difference in Galileo's investigations.

- Why did Galileo study the same objects in the sky night after night?
- Would Galileo have made even more discoveries if he could have spoken about his findings publicly?

Check the Concept/Question Board to see if there are any questions there that you can answer now. If the selection or your discussions about the selection have raised any new questions about astronomy, put the questions on the Concept/Question Board. Maybe the next selection will help answer the questions.

Record Ideas

Why was the idea of Earth orbiting the sun controversial in Galileo's time? Record your notes and ideas in your Writing Journal.

Research Ideas

- Study famous astronomers and their discoveries. Find out what tools they used to acquire their information.
- How do you become an astronomer? What different subjects do you have to study?

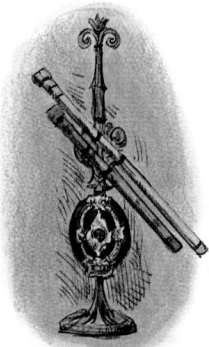

129

Theme Connections

Think About It

- As groups of students discuss what they have learned about Galileo's use of telescopes, circulate and observe the discussions. Note how students relate to each other and how well they allow sharing of opinions and differing ideas.

- Encourage students to note how the telescope changed the field of astronomy.

- Have the students report what they discussed. Encourage them to record on the Concept/Question Board any questions they may have.

Research Ideas

Help the students locate books and articles about Galileo and other famous astronomers, such as Johannes Kepler, Tycho Brache, Nicolaus Copernicus, and Isaac Newton.

Teacher Tip Share your own thoughts and thinking processes with students, and encourage them to do the same.

② Responding

✦Exploring the Theme

Some students may choose to conduct a computer search for additional books or information about astronomy. Have them make a list of these books and sources of information to share with classmates and the school librarian. Check the Reading link of the **SRA** Web page for links to theme-related Websites.

http://www.sra4kids.com

Have students write sentences using the selection vocabulary words. In order to provide additional help in remembering words, students can write synonyms or antonyms for the words if it is appropriate. Some students may even draw something to help them remember the meaning of the words.

Selection Vocabulary

Have students write in their Writing Journal the definitions for words discussed before the reading of the selection and any other interesting words they clarified while reading. Students should be encouraged to refer to these words throughout the unit as they work on student and writing projects. The words from this selection are:

**apparatus   extraordinary   constellation
celestial   interrogation**

You may create a word wall on the Concept/Question Board of key words related to the unit theme, Back Through the Stars, and organize the words by nouns, verbs, and so on. Encourage students to find words from other resources, their activities, and family discussions and add them to the wall.

Reading/Writing Connections

Using additional books from the library or the selection, have students write daily journals as if they were Galileo. Have them include personal feelings and thoughts that Galileo may have had during these times of discovery. Refer them to the dates used in the selection.

Literature Appreciation

Working in small groups, students will choose 10–15 words from the selection that relate to Galileo and astronomy. Have the groups design crossword puzzles using these selected words. Remind students that their definitions must be accurate for the puzzles to be completed by other groups. Have students exchange their puzzles with the other groups and complete them.

Home Connection

The class has just finished reading "Galileo," a biography of the man whose discoveries with the telescope changed the face of astronomy. An informational letter on "Galileo," in both English and Spanish, can be found in the **Home Connection** guide.

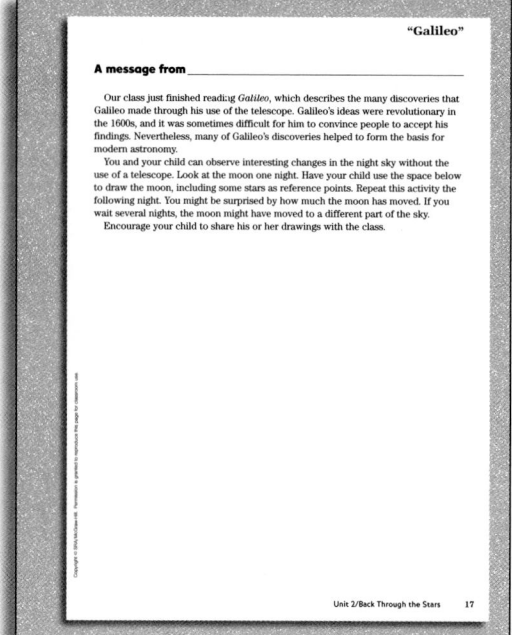

Home Connection p. 17

Supporting Student Explorations

To help students choose a unit activity, you may want to do the following:

Whole Group   Outline the research activity schedule for the students. Explain that the type of research they will conduct will take several weeks and will require them to make important decisions about managing their time.

Small Group   Explain to students that a good research problem or question is one that will be engaging, will generate further questions, will add to the group's knowledge of astronomy, and will require them to consult multiple sources. Conduct a free-floating discussion of problems and questions that interest the students. List ideas on the chalkboard.

Individual   Have students elaborate on their reasons for wanting to research their stated problems. They should go beyond simple expressions of interest or liking and indicate what is puzzling, important, potentially informative, and so forth.

Have students select books, magazines, Websites, and other sources to aid their research. Suggest that students post on the Concept/Question Board brief descriptions of sources of information that they have found to be especially helpful in their exploration of Galileo and astronomy. Encourage students who are having difficulty finding information to check sources on the Concept/Question Board and to post their questions as well.

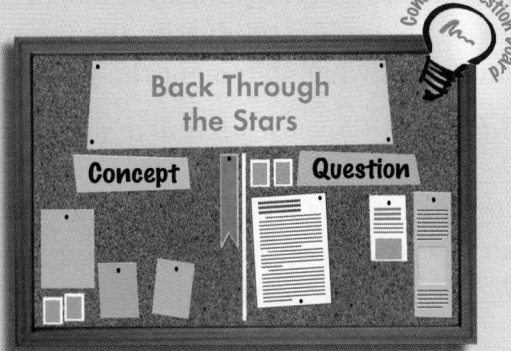

Inquiry Journal   Have students complete page 21 of the *Inquiry Journal.* Have them record their ideas about how "Galileo" added to their knowledge of astronomy.

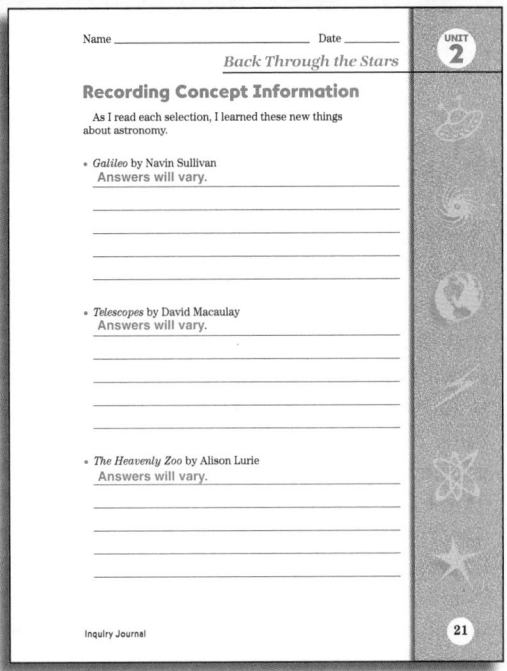

Inquiry Journal p. 21

Assessment

✓ **Informal**   Students are beginning their research project. Check to be sure that students:

- understand the criteria for good topics.
- participate appropriately in discussion.
- generate ideas for research.

③ Integrating the Curriculum

To help students understand the difference between a research topic and a research problem, have them consider the difference between the topic "California" and the problem "Why do so many people move to California?" Explain that if they choose to research the topic "California," *everything* about California would be related in some way to their topic. Tell students that choosing a specific problem, one that particularly interests them, will help to narrow their exploration. Explain that the question "Why do so many people move to California?" is much easier to research. Information to answer that specific question will be much easier to locate, record, and organize.

Assessment

✓ **Informal** Take this opportunity to assess students' progress with the writing process by commenting on the entries in their Writing Journals.

You may choose to make the writing activity a separate piece of writing from that which students will do for their unit research activities. However, you may choose to have students practice their writing skills as they engage in the Exploration Activities suggested in Part 2 of each lesson. What is essential is that students be taught these writing skills.

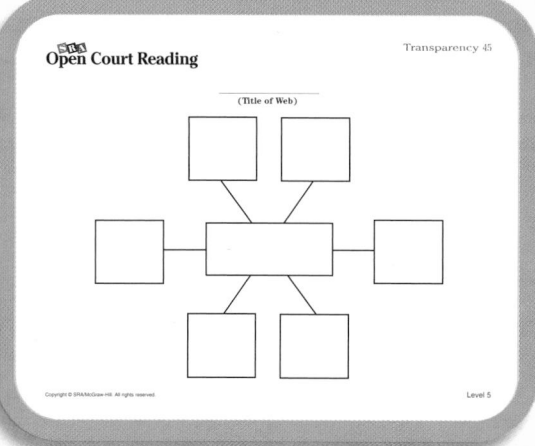

Transparency 45

Language Arts

Writing

Expository Writing: Providing Specific Facts

Instruct Ask students what they know about expository writing. If necessary, explain to them that *expository writing* means writing to explain. Tell them that one way we can explain ourselves is through providing specific facts. Point out that facts make writing clearer, and writers often use important facts in their writing to try to make their ideas more believable. Discuss with students how useful this technique is when writing about nonfiction topics.

Practice Copy the following sentences from "Galileo" on the chalkboard or an overhead transparency, without the underscores. Invite volunteers to identify the important facts (underscored below) and to tell what statement the facts help to support.

Galileo had opened up a new vision of the heavens. He had shown that <u>*the moon is a rocky, mountainous globe*</u>*, that* <u>*the earth is not unique in having a satellite moon*</u>*, and that* <u>*millions of stars exist*</u>*. Soon he went further and discovered that* <u>*Venus appears first as a crescent, then full, then dark, as it circles the sun and reflects light at different angles*</u>*.*

Have students look through the rest of "Galileo" in their **Student Anthologies** for examples of how the author used important facts to explain his writing and support his statements.

Apply Tell students that in Unit 2 they will be doing their own expository writing about a process, problem, or question related to astronomy. To help students think about what they might like to research, conduct a brainstorming session. Model for students how to turn their ideas into good research problems by asking specific questions about broad topics.

Writing Process

Prewrite Brainstorm possible topics, problems, and questions using **Transparency 45.** Encourage students to jot down their ideas on a sheet of paper.

Literary Elements

Recognizing a Biography

Instruct Ask students what a biography is. Have them brainstorm with you a list of elements found in a biography, using "Galileo" as a model. Your list should include the following: *a written history of a real person's life, chronological order, important events*, and *a third-person point of view*. In comparison, an autobiography is a book about the life of its author.

Gather books from the library that show various types of writing, such as fiction, nonfiction, autobiography, and biography. Choose books and topics that are familiar to the students. Have students identify the literary format of each book.

Practice Have students think of someone related to the field of astronomy, about whom they could write a biographical piece. This person could be anyone from an early astronomer to a modern-day astronaut. Then have students make a list of places they might look, or people they might ask, for information on the subject of their biographies. For example, they could find books and articles about their subject at the library or on the Internet; or they could write to NASA requesting information.

Apply For additional practice, have students complete *Reading and Writing Workbook* pages 49–50.

Reading and Writing Workbook pp. 49–50

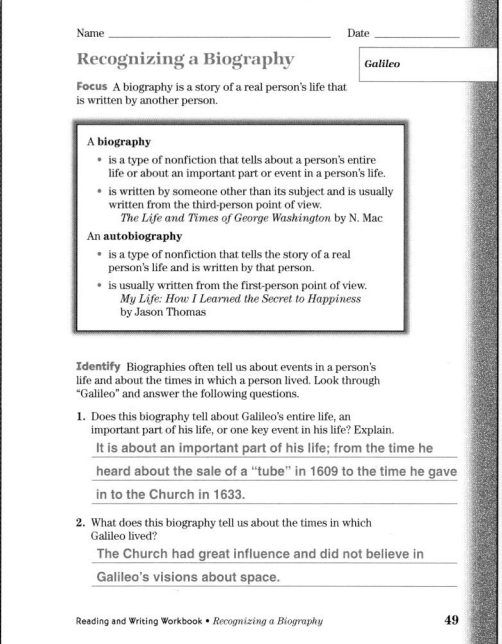

3 Integrating the Curriculum

Meeting Individual Needs

Reteach
Content-Area Words Have students who need additional instruction and practice with this concept complete **Reteach,** pages 51–52.

Challenge
Content-Area Words Challenge students to start an astronomy word web. They may begin by webbing some key words from "Galileo." As they read further into the unit, they can add more key astronomy words from other selections. Have them web from each key word several contexts in which it can be used other than astronomy. Have students who understand this concept complete **Challenge,** page 28.

←Skills Strand→

Content-Area Words
INTRODUCED: Unit 2, Lesson 1
REVIEWED: Unit 2, Lesson 2
Unit 2, Lesson 7

Teacher Tip Tell students to use new terms in various subjects soon after they learn them. Tell students that once they've used a term three times in different contexts, it becomes a part of their vocabulary.

Vocabulary

Content-Area Words

Instruct Write these words from the selection on the chalkboard: *perspective, convex, concave, navigator, deduction, diameter,* and *satellite.* Then, ask students what they know about content-area words. If necessary, tell them that content-area words are terms that relate to a certain subject or field of study.

Have students tell you to what subject or field of study the words on the chalkboard relate *(astronomy)*. Ask students in what other subject besides astronomy they could use the word *perspective (art)*. If necessary, have students look up in the dictionary the definition for *perspective* as it pertains to art. Then, have a volunteer write a sentence on the chalkboard, using *perspective* as an artistic term.

Practice Discuss the other astronomy terms on the chalkboard that can be used in subject areas other than astronomy (*concave* in art and mathematics; *navigator* in history; *deduction* in mathematics; and so on.). Tell students to write a sentence for each of these words, using it to say something about a subject other than astronomy: *diameter, convex, satellite.*

Apply For additional practice, have students complete *Reading and Writing Workbook* pages 51–52.

Reading and Writing Workbook pp. 51–52

Name _____ Date _____
Content-Area Words
Galileo
Focus Good readers know that the meaning of a word may depend on the content area, or subject, in which it is being used.

To understand the meaning of a word with multiple meanings, note
• the subject area in which the word is encountered.
• the context in which the word is being used in a sentence.
For example, the word *volume* has different meanings.

Subject Area	Context Sentence	Meaning
math	What is the *volume* of this box?	amount of space occupied by a three-dimensional object
science	Turn up the *volume* on the radio.	loudness of sound
language arts	What *volume* of the book do you need?	printed sheets bound together to make a book

Identify Read the following sentences from "Galileo." Determine the meaning of the underlined words and write a sentence using each of them in a different context.

Sentences will vary. Possible answers are provided below.

1. "He saw that it was a small round <u>disk</u> that did not sparkle like a star."
Different context: The computer disk fell on the floor.

2. "Galileo had opened up a new <u>vision</u> of the heavens."
Different context: The eye doctor said my vision was perfect.

Reading and Writing Workbook • *Content-Area Words*   51

Content-Area Words *(continued)*

Practice Write a mathematical meaning for each of these words. If you need help, use a dictionary.

1. diameter: a line that passes through the center of a circle or sphere, dividing it in half

2. axis: a line that passes through an object and around which an object turns or seems to turn

3. angle: two rays with the same endpoint; the surface between two lines or surfaces that meet

Apply Write a sentence for each of the following words from "Galileo," but use a meaning that is in a content area other than astronomy. Sentences will vary.

1. boundary: _____

2. distance: _____

3. deduction: _____

52   *Content-Area Words* • Reading and Writing Workbook

Grammar, Usage, & Mechanics

Nouns

Instruct Tell students that in order to express their ideas clearly, they need to know how nouns function in a sentence. Remind them that all words can be classified into groups called *parts of speech*. Remind them also that one group is *nouns*. Encourage students to give you the definition of a noun *(A noun is a person, place, or thing.)*.

Practice Have volunteers write on the chalkboard sentences containing at least one noun. Ask other volunteers to underline the noun or nouns in each sentence.

Apply Tell students to select a piece of writing from their **Writing Folders** and look through it for examples of nouns. Using a colored marker or crayon, have the students underline all of the nouns they find. Classmates might then exchange papers and check each other's work.

Listening/Speaking/Viewing

Giving Directions

Have students look at some examples of texts that contain directions, such as a cookbook, a "how-to" book, or instructions for using or assembling an appliance. Help them realize that the author of each text followed these specific guidelines for organizing the information.

- Include every step in the process or activity.

- Describe the steps in chronological order.

- Number the steps as they occur, or use signal words (such as *first, then, before,* and *finally*) to show the order of events.

Have students read page 119, paragraph 3, of "Galileo." Point out that this is a description of Galileo's process for creating and using a Dutch Perspective. Have students paraphrase this process and rewrite it in the form of directions. For example: *First, cut a piece of lead tubing to the desired length. Next, place a convex lens at one end of the lead tubing. Then, place a concave lens at the other end of the lead tubing. Finally, pick a distant object. Hold the tube up to your eye and view the object through the lenses in the tube.*

Meeting Individual Needs

Challenge

Nouns Challenge students to see how many nouns they can use in one sentence. Challenge other students to see how many nouns they can find in one sentence.

Assessment

✓ **Formal** To assess students' understanding of nouns, have them complete *Skills Assessment*, page 13.

Skills Strand

Nouns
INTRODUCED: Unit 1, Lesson 2
REVIEWED: Unit 2, Lesson 1
　　　　　　　Unit 4, Lesson 2

Encourage students to incorporate directions for a process into their unit projects or writing activities.

Meeting Individual Needs

ESL

Giving Directions Have English-language learners write directions for one of their favorite games from their own cultures. Then have them share their directions with the class and, if possible, engage volunteers in a demonstration of the game.

Galileo

③ Integrating the Curriculum

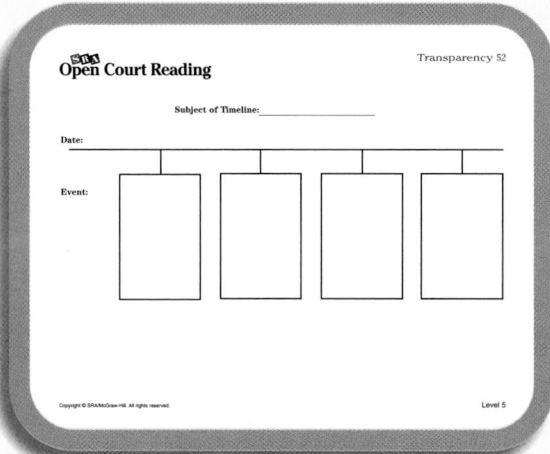

Transparency 52

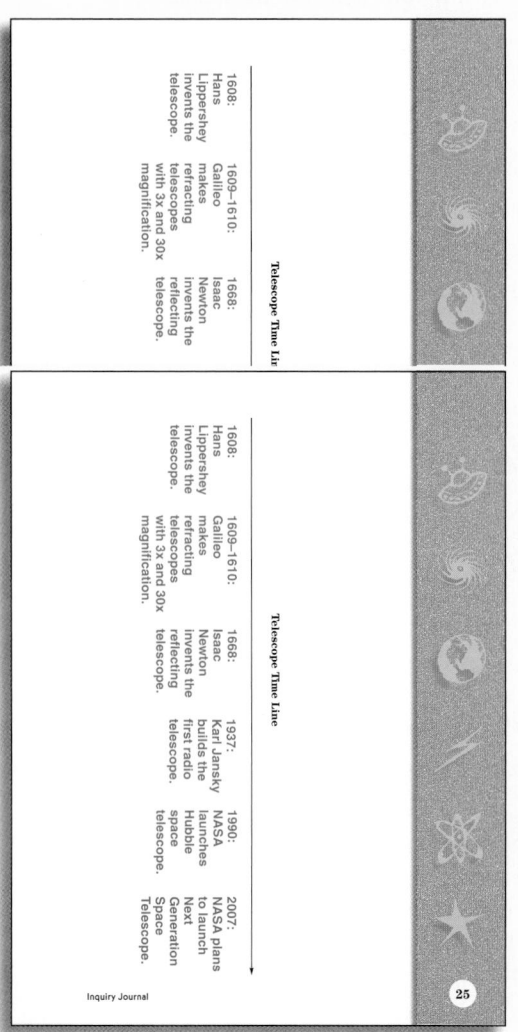

Inquiry Journal pp. 24–25

Study and Research

Time Lines

Instruct Ask students if they have ever seen or created a time line. Discuss what a time line is and how it is used. Tell students that a time line is a way of recording events in chronological order. It is a chart that tells when and in what order things happened in the past.

Practice Show students *Transparency 52* and fill it in together, using the "Galileo" selection. Below are the dates that might appear on your time line. There are other dates noted in the selection that may not be significant.

Tell students that not all of the significant dates appear in the text. They may need to figure out when an event took place by adding months to a date that is given.

May 1609	Galileo learns of the telescope.
August 1609	Members of Senate view the sea through Galileo's telescope.
January 7, 1610	Galileo sees Jupiter.
January 13, 1610	Galileo sees Jupiter's moons.
March 1610	Galileo's findings about the universe are published.
1632	Galileo publishes an article in favor of his beliefs.
April 12, 1633	Galileo is interrogated by the Catholic Church.

Apply Have each student draw a time line based on the transparency. Ask them to choose an interval of time in their lives and create their own time lines.

For more practice, have students complete *Inquiry Journal,* pages 24–25. Students can also search the Internet for time lines on Galileo's life and discoveries.

Across the Curriculum

 ## Science

Spacecraft *Galileo*

Purpose

To learn about the spacecraft *Galileo* and its mission

Procedure

Brainstorm with students some of the space discoveries that have occurred since Galileo made his discovery *(orbiting the moon, walking on the moon, orbiting Mars, and so on)*. Tell students that they are going to research the *Galileo* spacecraft that is now orbiting Jupiter.

- Have each student create a list of questions to answer about this mission. Examples are: Why was the spacecraft named for Galileo? What is the purpose of this mission? When did the spacecraft go into space and when did it reach Jupiter? How long will *Galileo* remain in space?

- If students have Internet access, have them use a search engine to find information from NASA on the *Galileo* spacecraft mission and summarize the information by taking notes to answer their questions. If students do not have computer access, have them find information about the *Galileo* mission in the library.

- Using the answers to these questions, have each student write a news broadcast of the events. Then students may perform their broadcasts for the class.

- You may want to have student pairs or small groups design their own spacecraft for specific missions and make three-dimensional models of their designs.

 ## Social Studies

Recent Astronomers

Purpose

To acquaint students with researching astronomers

Procedure

Either have students find books in the library or search the Internet for information about recent astronomers, such as Carl Sagan. Discuss with students that astronomy is not an old-fashioned profession and there are still astronomers making amazing discoveries (comets, stars, and so on).

- Have each student select an astronomer to research.

- Create a large chart using butcher paper and tape it to the wall. Headings may be: Astronomer's Name, Country, Discovery, and Date of Discovery. Have students fill in the chart by summarizing information from their research. During an oral discussion, have students tell the significance of their astronomer's discovery.

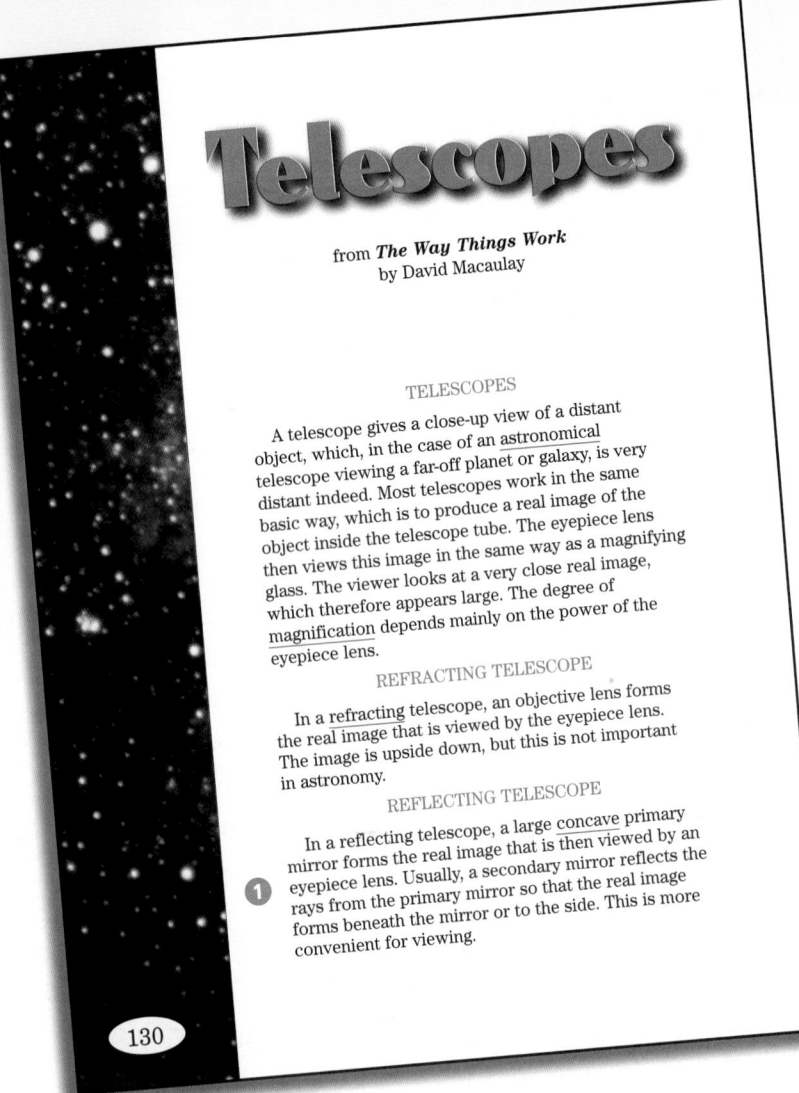

Telescopes

from *The Way Things Work*
by David Macaulay

TELESCOPES

A telescope gives a close-up view of a distant object, which, in the case of an <u>astronomical</u> telescope viewing a far-off planet or galaxy, is very distant indeed. Most telescopes work in the same basic way, which is to produce a real image of the object inside the telescope tube. The eyepiece lens then views this image in the same way as a magnifying glass. The viewer looks at a very close real image, which therefore appears large. The degree of <u>magnification</u> depends mainly on the power of the eyepiece lens.

REFRACTING TELESCOPE

In a refracting telescope, an objective lens forms the real image that is viewed by the eyepiece lens. The image is upside down, but this is not important in astronomy.

REFLECTING TELESCOPE

In a reflecting telescope, a large <u>concave</u> primary mirror forms the real image that is then viewed by an eyepiece lens. Usually, a secondary mirror reflects the rays from the primary mirror so that the real image forms beneath the mirror or to the side. This is more convenient for viewing.

130

About the Author/Illustrator

David Macaulay was born in England and moved to the United States when he was 11 years old. He studied architecture in college but wanted to illustrate and write children's books. He worked for three years researching and making drawings for *The Way Things Work.* In this book he explains and illustrates hundreds of machines and the scientific principles behind them.

Macaulay's books have won many awards including the Caldecott Medal, the *New York Times* Outstanding Children's Book of the Year, Parents' Choice Award for Illustration in Children's Books, and American Institute of Physics Best Science Book of the Year Award.

Students can read more about David Macaulay on page 134 of the **Student Anthology.**

Other Books by David Macaulay
- *Cathedral: The Story of Its Construction*
- *Pyramid*
- *Underground*
- *Unbuilding*
- *Black and White*

Selection Summary

Genre: Nonfiction

In this selection, excerpted from his award-winning book *The Way Things Work*, respected children's nonfiction author David Macaulay uses thoroughly detailed diagrams and clear, concise prose to explain the workings of astronomers' most important tools. Readers will learn how reflecting, refracting, radio, and space telescopes work.

Exploring the Theme

Selection Concepts

The advent of the telescope as an astronomer's tool might be considered the birth of modern astronomy. "Telescopes" explains the basic structure of refracting and reflecting telescopes, the tools used by astronomers since Galileo's time. Two very modern astronomers' tools, the radio telescope and the Hubble space telescope, are also described. Key concepts to be explored are:

■ Diagrams help explain the workings of astronomers' most important tools.

■ Different types of telescopes provide us with different types of information.

Check the Reading link of the **SRA** Web page for links to theme-related Websites.
http://www.sra4kids.com

Exploration Activity Tips

Before Reading, bring a telescope to class if you can, and have the students offer their ideas about how it works. Invite students to tell of their own experiences with, and ideas about, telescopes. Then have students browse the selection for clues about the different types of telescopes.

During Reading, model cause-and-effect reasoning for the students. Tell them that because this selection is an article about how things work, cause-and-effect reasoning is crucial for comprehension.

After Reading, have students work collaboratively to form explanations for parts of the selection that they did not understand. Then have students update the Concept/Question Board. Some may want to revise their activity plans based on what they have learned.

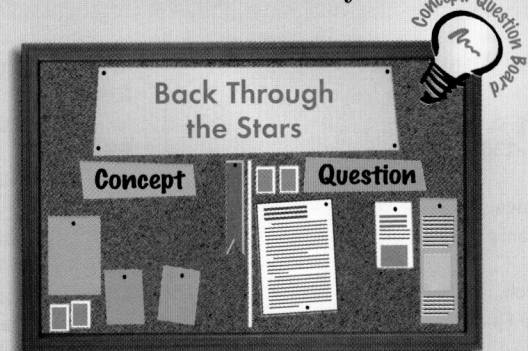

Unit 2 Exploration Management	
Lesson 1	Brainstorm research problems. Form interest-based groups. Develop and discuss initial research plans.
Lesson 2 Telescopes	**Collaborative Exploration** **Groups finalize plans, allocate tasks, and begin research. Discuss initial finding and resources.** **Supplementary Activity** **Use multiple sources to locate information. Interpret and use diagrams. Use the card catalog to locate research materials.**
Lesson 3	Research continues as groups consider revision of their activity focus.
Lesson 4	Students continue with research and present their initial findings.
Lesson 5	Research continues. Students present interesting findings or problems.
Lesson 6	Research continues. Students present interesting findings or problems.
Lesson 7	Students organize research findings and prepare presentations.
Lesson 8	Students present their activities.

Lesson Planner

Suggested Pacing: 3–5 days	DAY 1	DAY 2	
	DAY 1	DAY 2	
Part 1 · Preparing to Read **Materials** ■ Student Anthology, pp. 130–135 ■ Transparencies 8, 44	**Word Knowledge** ■ Reading the Words and Sentences, p. 130G ■ Developing Oral Language, p. 130G **Build Background, p. 130H** **Preview and Prepare, p. 130I** **Selection Vocabulary, p. 130I** *galaxy, universe, bodies, frequency, revolutionize*	**Preview and Prepare, p. 130I** ■ Review Transparency 44	
Part 2 · Reading and Responding **Materials** ■ Student Anthology, pp. 130–135 ■ Teacher Observation Log ■ Reading and Writing Workbook, pp. 53–54 ■ Inquiry Journal, p. 21 ■ Home Connection, p. 19	**Student Anthology, pp. 130–135** **Comprehension Strategies** ■ Summarizing, p. 130 ■ Clarifying, p. 130 ■ Asking Questions, p. 132 **Discussing Strategy Use, p. 132**	**Student Anthology, pp. 130–135** **Comprehension Skills** ✓ ■ Main Idea and Details, p. 131 ✓ ■ Discussing the Selection, p. 133 **Exploring the Theme** ■ Selection Vocabulary, p. 135A *galaxy, universe, bodies, frequency, revolutionize*	
Part 3 · Integrating the Curriculum **Materials** ■ Student Anthology, pp. 130–135 ■ Reading and Writing Workbook, pp. 55–56 ■ Inquiry Journal, p. 29	**Writing** ■ Prewriting, p. 135C **Literary Elements** ✓ ■ Features of Informational Text, p. 135D	**Writing Process** ■ Prewrite, p. 135C **Vocabulary** ✓ ■ Content-Area Words, p. 135E	

| *Independent Work Time*

Materials
■ Reteach, pp. 53–56
■ ESL Supplement
■ Challenge, pp. 29–30
■ Intervention Guide
■ Research CD-ROM
■ Listening Library Audiocassette
■ Inquiry Journal, pp. 26–28 | **Writing Process Continued**
ESL
■ Word Meaning, p. 130G
■ Vocabulary, p. 130J
Intervention
■ Word Knowledge, p. 130G
■ Comprehension, p. 130
Unit Project
■ Begin Research
■ Discuss Initial Findings | **Writing Process Continued**
Reteach
✓ ■ Informational Text, *Reteach*, pp. 55–56
ESL
■ Discussing the Selection, p. 133
Challenge
✓ ■ Informational Text, *Challenge*, p. 30
■ Content-Area Words, p. 135E
Intervention
■ Main Idea and Details, p. 131
Unit Project Continued | |

✓ Informal **Assessment Available**   ✓ Formal **Assessment Available**

DAY 2 continued	DAY 3	
DAY 3	**DAY 4**	**DAY 5**
General Review	**General Review**	**Review Word Knowledge**
Student Anthology, pp. 130–135 **Theme Connections** ■ Think About It, p. 135 ■ Research Ideas, p. 135	**Student Anthology, pp. 130–135** **Exploring the Theme** ■ Reading/Writing Connections, p. 135A ■ Literature Appreciation, p. 135A ■ Supporting Student Explorations, p. 135B	**Student Anthology, pp. 130–135** ■ Review Selection ■ Complete Discussion ■ Reread Selection in Pairs **Home Connection, p. 135A** ■ Discuss "Telescopes" ■ Complete telescopes chart
Writing Process Continued **Grammar, Usage, and Mechanics** ■ Pronouns, p. 135F **Listening/Speaking/Viewing** ■ Listening for Information, p. 135G	**Writing Process Continued** **Study and Research** ■ Diagrams, p. 135H	**Across the Curriculum** **Science** ■ Experimenting with Magnifiers, p. 135I **Music** ■ Appreciating Music, p. 135I **Social Studies** ■ How Is the Hubble Space Telescope Doing Now?, p. 135J **Math** ■ How Much Is 15 Billion?, p. 135J
Writing Process Continued **Reteach** ✓■ Main Idea and Details, *Reteach*, pp. 53–54 **Challenge** ✓■ Main Idea and Details, *Challenge*, p. 29 **Intervention** ■ Pronouns, p. 135F **Unit Project Continued**	**Writing Process Continued** **Challenge** ■ Pronouns, p. 135F **Intervention** ■ Diagrams, p. 135H **Unit Project Continued**	**Writing Process Continued** **Challenge** ■ Diagrams, p. 135H **Unit Project Continued**

Meeting Individual Needs
Independent Work Time

Part 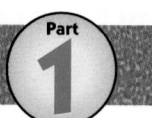 1
Preparing to Read

Meeting Individual Needs

ESL
- Word Meaning, p. 130G
- Vocabulary, p. 130J

Interv̂ention
- Word Knowledge, p. 130G

Part  2
Reading and Responding

Meeting Individual Needs

Reteach
- Main Idea and Details, *Reteach,* pp. 53–54

ESL
- Discussing the Selection, p. 133

Challenge
- Main Idea and Details, *Challenge,* p. 29

Interv̂ention
- Comprehension, p. 130
- Main Idea and Details, p. 131
- Asking Questions, p. 132

Part 3
Integrating the Curriculum

Meeting Individual Needs

Reteach
- Informational Text, *Reteach,* pp. 55–56

ESL
- Leadership, p. 135C

Challenge
- Informational Text, *Challenge,* p. 30
- Content-Area Words, p. 135E
- Pronouns, p. 135F
- Diagrams, p. 135H

Interv̂ention
- Pronouns, p. 135F
- Diagrams, p. 135H

Formal Assessment Options

Use these assessment pages along with your informal observations to gauge student progress.

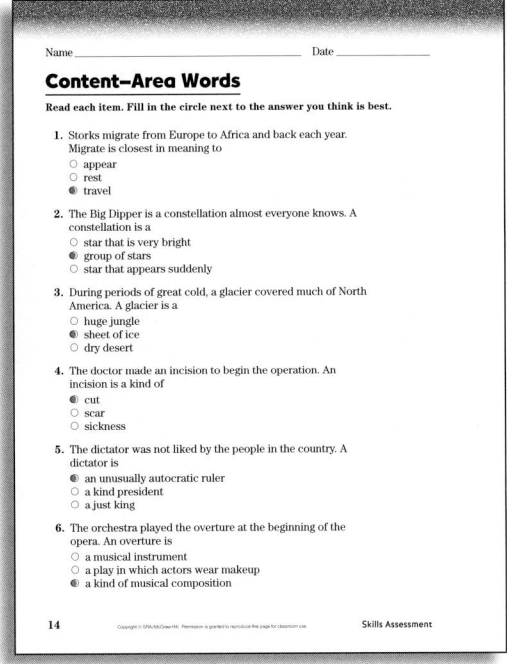

Skills Assessment, p. 14

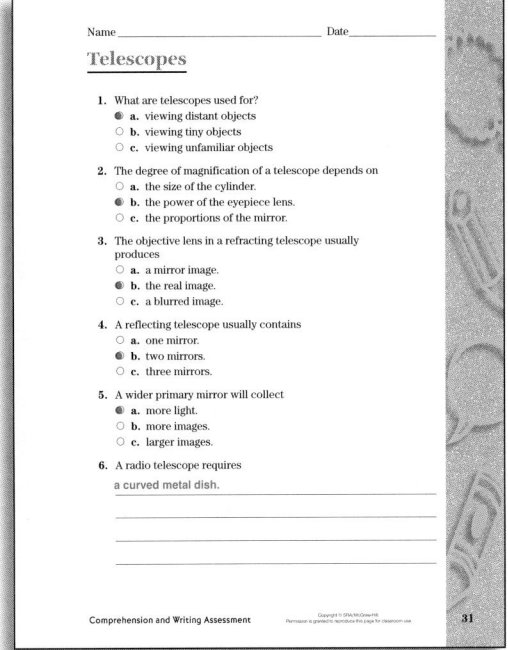

Comprehension and Writing Assessment, p. 31

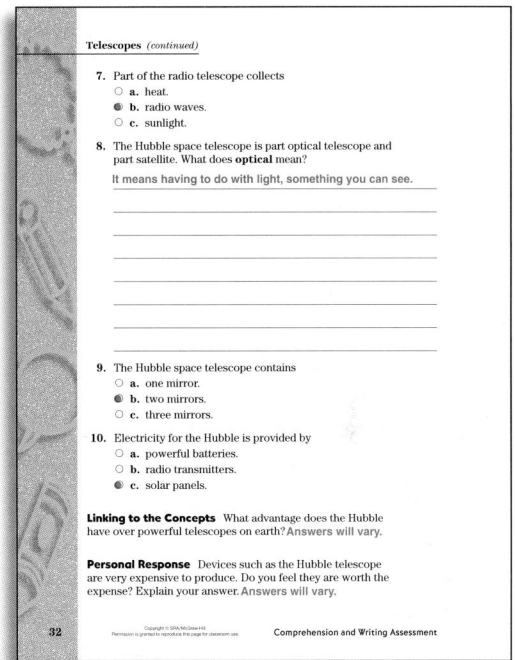

Comprehension and Writing Assessment, p. 32

1 Preparing to Read

Meeting Individual Needs

ESL

Word Meaning Make sure English-language learners understand the meanings of the words before they do the exercises. Refer to Unit 2, Lesson 2, of the *ESL Supplement* for specific suggestions.

Intervention

Word Knowledge Ask students who need more help with the affixes whether they know what each means. If they do not, explain that *tele-* is a prefix that means "far." Explain that *-ize* is a suffix that means "to cause to be" or "to become." Discuss how the affixes affect the meanings of the words. Have students look at other stories they have read to find words with the prefix *tele-* and the suffix *-ize*. For students who need additional help, see Unit 2, Lesson 2, of the *Intervention Guide.*

Word Knowledge

Reading the Words and Sentences

Write each word and sentence on the chalkboard. Have students read each word together. After all the words have been read, have students read each sentence in natural phrases or chunks. Use the suggestions in About the Words to discuss the different features of the listed words.

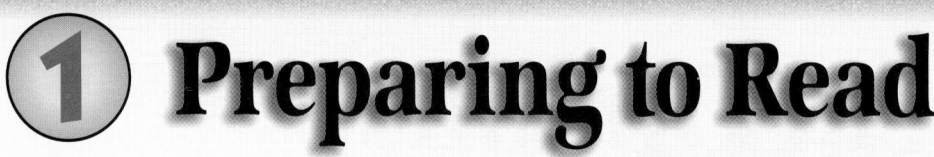

Line 1: eyepiece   eyeglasses   eyeball
Line 2: telescope   telephone   telegraph
Line 3: revolutionize   stabilize   dramatize
Sentence 1: The secretary took off his eyeglasses when answering the telephone.
Sentence 2: The eyepiece was broken when the telescope was knocked over.
Sentence 3: In order to dramatize the functions of a telegraph machine, the teacher brought in a typewriter.

About the Words

- Line 1 contains words that are closed compounds. These words are created when two or more words are put together with no spaces in between.

- In Line 2, the words all begin with the prefix *tele-*. This prefix means "distant."

- The words in Line 3 all have the suffix *-ize*. In these words, the *-ize* suffix means to cause to be or "to become" (for example, *stabilize* means "to become stable"). The suffix *-ize* changes the noun to a verb.

Developing Oral Language

To review the words, have students do one or both of the following activities.

- Have a student point to one word on the chalkboard, and select a classmate to read the word and use it in a sentence.

- Give the students clues or definitions to the words on Lines 1–3. Have them read the word that goes with the clue or definition.

Build Background

Activate Prior Knowledge

Have students check the Concept/Question Board to refresh their memories about astronomy. Discuss the following with students to find out what they know about telescopes and what they have learned about the unit theme. Tell students to use their prior knowledge to help them comprehend the selection they are about to read.

- Students may recall that when Galileo heard about telescopes, he immediately set about making one. Have them discuss how his observations with the telescope changed the way many people thought of the universe.

- Ask students whether they are familiar with the selection they are about to read, and if so, to tell a little bit about it.

- Have students share any other selections that have telescopes or other scientific discoveries in them.

Background Information

The following information may help the students better understand the selection they are about to read.

- Tell students that "Telescopes" is an excerpt from a nonfiction book, *The Way Things Work*.

- Tell students that the selection explains the basic structure of refracting and reflecting telescopes, the tools used by astronomers since Galileo's time. It describes two modern astronomers' tools, the radio telescope and the Hubble space telescope.

- Tell students that mention of the "Big Bang" is made in this selection. This is in reference to the scientific theory that the universe as we know it is the result of an immense cosmic explosion.

 *Writing Journal* Tell students that they will be jotting down in their Writing Journals their reactions to the story. Have them be on the lookout for any ideas they might have for using information about telescopes in a story.

 *Teacher Tip* Have the students share their own experiences with telescopes. Have the students browse the selection for clues about different types of telescopes.

1 Preparing to Read

Transparency 44

Teacher Tip When setting purposes, students may want to think about why the theme of the story piques their curiosity or connects to their personal interests.

Teacher Tip To help students decode words, divide them into the syllables shown below. The information following each word tells how students can figure out the meaning of each word from the sentences on the transparency.

gal·ax·y	context clues
un·i·verse	context clues, word structure
bod·ies	context clues
fre·quen·cy	context clues
rev·o·lu·tion·ize	context clues, word structure

Transparency 8

Preview and Prepare

Browse

- Have a volunteer read the title and author's name aloud. Have students share what they know about nonfiction.
- Have the students browse through the subheads, diagrams, and captions. Discuss ways this selection connects with astronomy.
- Have students search for words and phrases that connect to what they already know. Record these in the Clues column on *Transparency 44.*
- Encourage students to ask questions as they browse. Have them identify any problems that they notice while reading in the Problems column.

Set Purposes

As they read, have students think about how improvements in telescopes have helped the study of astronomy.

Selection Vocabulary

As students study vocabulary, they will use a variety of skills to determine the meaning of a word. These include context clues, word structure, and apposition. Students will apply these same skills while reading to clarify additional unfamiliar words.

Display *Transparency 8* before reading the selection to introduce and discuss the following words and their meanings.

> **gal·ax·y:** a large group of stars, dust, and gas (page 130)
> **un·i·verse:** all things, including stars, planets, and so on (page 132)
> **bod·ies:** objects such as stars and asteroids (page 132)
> **fre·quen·cy:** how often something happens within a set period of time (page 132)
> **rev·o·lu·tion·ize:** to cause dramatic change (page 133)

Have students read the words in the Word Box. Help students decode multisyllabic words by reading them syllable by syllable.

Using the same procedure as in Lesson 1, have students read the sentences on *Transparency 8* to determine the meaning of the underlined words. Remind them to use clues in the sentences and structural clues to figure out the meaning. See the teacher tip on the left for information on how the words in each sentence can be defined.

Reading Recommendations

Your first reading of the selection should focus on developing the reading strategies found to the left of the reduced pages. During rereading, they should focus on the comprehension skills, found to the right of the reduced pages.

Oral Reading

Because this selection is packed with technical information, students may want to read the text and study the diagrams in small groups. As this is a nonfiction selection and students are reading to be informed, allow students more time for reading. Have students adjust their reading rate by reading more slowly or by rereading certain sections of the selection in order to comprehend the information presented.

As students read aloud, have them read expressively, at an appropriate pace, in natural phrases and chunks. By reading the selection with fluency, students will demonstrate an understanding of the text and an ability to engage the listeners in an effective manner. If students encounter difficulties, have them use the reading strategies below or refer to the Blending Procedure (Program Appendix 15–16).

Using Reading Strategies

Reading strategy instruction allows students to become aware of how good readers read. Good readers constantly check their understanding, recognize when they are having problems, and stop to use various reading strategies to help them make sense of what they are reading.

During the reading of "Telescopes," you will model the use of the following reading strategies.

- Summarizing
- Clarifying
- Asking Questions

Before reading, have students share how they have used these strategies in the past and any tips they can give each other on their use.

Building Comprehension Skills

Revisiting or rereading a selection allows students to apply skills that give them a more complete understanding of the text. Some follow-up comprehension skills help students organize information. Others lead to deeper understanding—to "reading between the lines," as mature readers do. In this selection, students will apply the follow-up comprehension skill of *Main Idea and Details*.

Research in Action

Reading Strategy Use

Students can become autonomous in their use of strategies only by being given years of encouragement in choosing appropriate strategies. Thus, you should not tell the students when to predict or when to summarize. Rather, you should prompt the students who are not using strategies to choose a strategy that helps them make sense of what they are reading. *(Jan Hirshberg)*

Meeting Individual Needs

ESL

Vocabulary Check that English-language learners know the meanings of idioms and more difficult vocabulary in the story, including: *close-up, galaxy, magnifying glass, the degree of magnification, convenient, reflects, intercepts, electric signal, detect, previously unknown bodies, scanning,* and *the source.* Explain and show pictures as needed. Model example sentences and help English-speaking students make their own sentences. Refer to Unit 2, Lesson 2, of the *ESL Supplement* for teaching suggestions.

Teacher Tip Have students who may need extra help reading "Telescopes" reread the selection using the *Listening Library Audiocassette.*

Teacher Tip By this time in the fifth grade, good readers should be reading approximately **126 words per minute** with fluency and expression. The only way to gain fluency is through practice. As explained in Reading Recommendations, have students reread all or part of the selection to you and to each other during class or Independent Work Time to focus on the comprehension skills and to build fluency.

② Reading and Responding

Read pages 130–135.

Comprehension Strategies

Modeling

① Summarizing *There is a lot of information about how the different kinds of telescopes work. Summarizing in our own words what we have read might make it clearer. In a refracting telescope, an objective lens forms the real image that is seen by the eyepiece lens. Does anyone want to summarize how the reflecting telescope works?*

Modeling

② Clarifying *Good readers know it is important to stop and clarify terms or ideas that they don't understand. I'm finding it hard to understand how the different kinds of telescopes work. Maybe if we reread this part and study the diagram, it will become clearer.*

Oh, I see. In a refracting telescope, the image of an object is sent directly from the lens to the eyepiece, but it's seen upside down. In a reflecting telescope, the image is reflected off one mirror onto another.

Word Knowledge

There are many multisyllabic words in this selection. Be sure students are using the skills they learned in the Word Knowledge section of this lesson.

Reading Recommendation

ORAL · CHORAL · SILENT

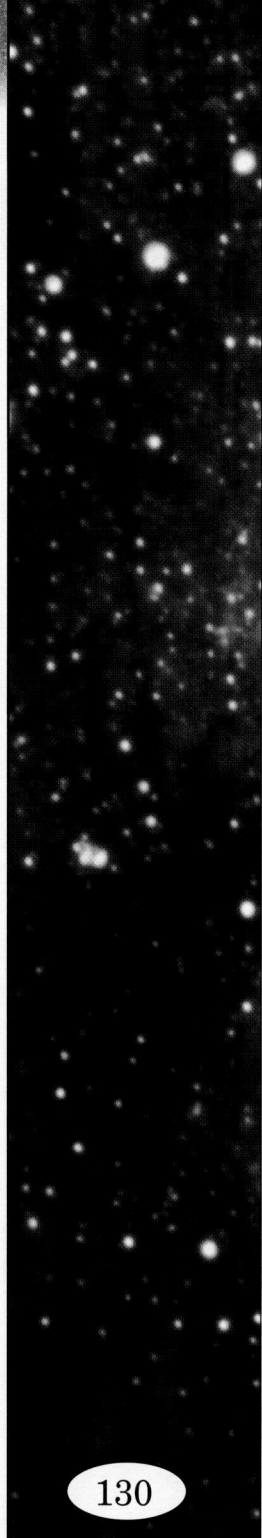

Telescopes

from *The Way Things Work*
by David Macaulay

TELESCOPES

A telescope gives a close-up view of a distant object, which, in the case of an astronomical telescope viewing a far-off planet or galaxy, is very distant indeed. Most telescopes work in the same basic way, which is to produce a real image of the object inside the telescope tube. The eyepiece lens then views this image in the same way as a magnifying glass. The viewer looks at a very close real image, which therefore appears large. The degree of magnification depends mainly on the power of the eyepiece lens.

REFRACTING TELESCOPE

In a refracting telescope, an objective lens forms the real image that is viewed by the eyepiece lens. The image is upside down, but this is not important in astronomy.

REFLECTING TELESCOPE

In a reflecting telescope, a large concave primary mirror forms the real image that is then viewed by an eyepiece lens. Usually, a secondary mirror reflects the rays from the primary mirror so that the real image forms beneath the mirror or to the side. This is more convenient for viewing.

130

Meeting Individual Needs

Intervention

Comprehension Intervention strategies for those students having difficulty with reading "Telescopes" can be found in Unit 2, Lesson 2, of the **Intervention Guide.**

Assessment

✓ **Informal** Observe individual students as they read, and use the Teacher Observation Log, found in the **Assessment Guide** to record anecdotal information about each student's strengths and weaknesses.

Reflecting telescopes are important in astronomy because the primary mirror can be very wide. This enables it to collect a lot of light, making faint objects visible. Collecting light from an object is often more important than magnifying it because distant stars do not appear bigger even when magnified.

Reflecting Telescope

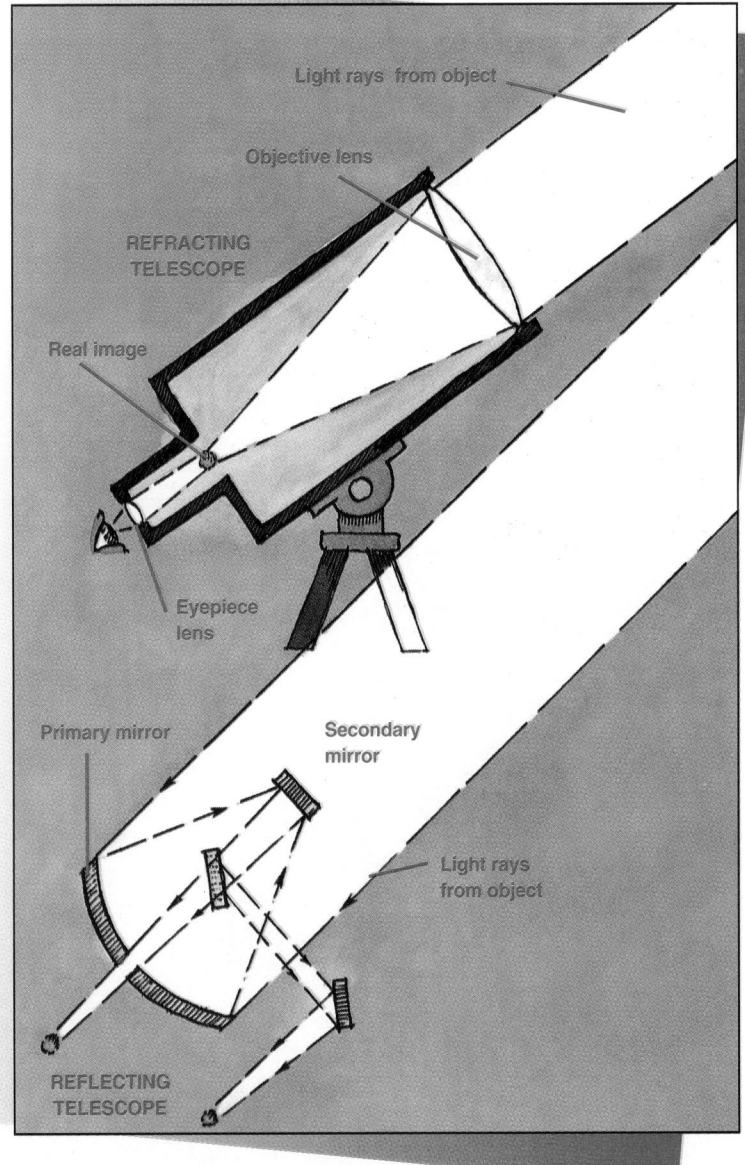

Light rays from object

Objective lens

REFRACTING TELESCOPE

Real image

Eyepiece lens

Primary mirror

Secondary mirror

Light rays from object

REFLECTING TELESCOPE

131

Comprehension Skills

Main Idea and Details

Introduce students to the concept of *main idea*. A *main idea* is what the paragraph is mostly about. Writers often provide a clear topic sentence that states the main idea of a paragraph. The other sentences in the paragraph will give supporting *details*.

Point out to the students that the paragraph on page 131 is an example in which the main idea is stated in the first sentence. Point out that the headings in the text are also main ideas.

For additional help in identifying main idea and details, have the students complete ***Reading and Writing Workbook*** pages 53–54.

Name _____ Date _____

Main Idea and Details   *Telescopes*

Focus Writers make their ideas clear by organizing them into paragraphs.

- The **main idea** is what a paragraph is mostly about. Writers often place the main idea in a topic sentence at the beginning or the end of a paragraph.
- The other sentences in a paragraph provide **details**, or more information, that support the main idea.

Identify Look back at "Telescopes." Identify a paragraph with a main idea stated in a topic sentence. Write the page number, the main idea, and a detail from the paragraph that supports the main idea.

Answers will vary. Possible answers are provided below.

Page: 132   Main idea in topic sentence: Objects in the universe send out radio waves and a radio telescope can pick these up.

Detail that supports the main idea: A curved metal dish collects the radio waves and reflects them to a focus point above the center of the dish.

Reading and Writing Workbook • *Main Idea and Details*   53

Reading and Writing Workbook p. 53

Meeting Individual Needs

Intervention

Main Idea and Details If students are having difficulties identifying the main idea and details, reread the the section with them, encouraging them to point out specific places where unfamiliar terms or ideas may be confusing them.

← Skills Strand →

Main Idea and Details
INTRODUCED: Unit 2, Lesson 2
REVIEWED: Unit 2, Lesson 4
Unit 2, Lesson 8
Unit 3, Lesson 2
Unit 3, Lesson 7

2 Reading and Responding

Comprehension Strategies

Modeling

3 Asking Questions *I have a question about how a radio telescope works. Let's reread the text and see if we can answer this question.*

Now that we read it again, I understand that the metal dish collects radio waves and sends them to the antenna. Then a computer reads them.

Has this selection raised any questions about telescopes that you may want to research?

Discussing Strategy Use

After they have read the selection, have students share any problems they encountered and tell what strategies they used to solve them. Then have them answer the following questions. If they answer "no" to any of the questions, have them reread part of the selection to find the answer.

- Did they use the diagrams to help them clarify the information in this selection?

- Did they summarize to help them understand and remember all the information?

- Did they ask questions to explore the differences between the various telescopes?

Make sure that students explain how using the strategies helped them understand the selection better and how they read effectively to find answers to the questions they asked as they set purposes.

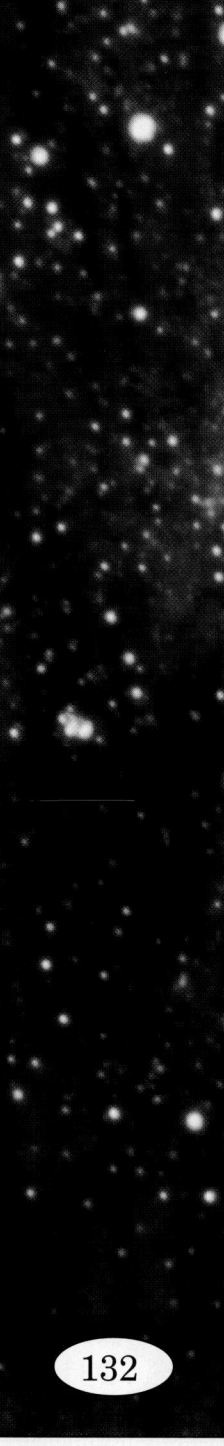

RADIO TELESCOPE

Many objects in the universe send out radio waves, and a radio telescope can be used to detect them. A large curved metal dish collects the radio waves and reflects them to a focus point above the center of the dish, rather as the curved mirror of a reflecting telescope gathers light waves from space. At this point, an antenna intercepts the radio waves and turns them into a weak electric signal. The signal goes to a computer. Radio telescopes detect very weak waves, and can also communicate with spacecraft.

By detecting radio waves coming from galaxies and other objects in space, radio telescopes have discovered the existence of many previously unknown **3** bodies. It is possible to make visible images of radio sources by scanning the telescope or a group of telescopes across the source. This yields a sequence of signals from different parts of the source, which the computer can process to form an image. Differences in frequency of the signals give information about the composition and motion of the radio source.

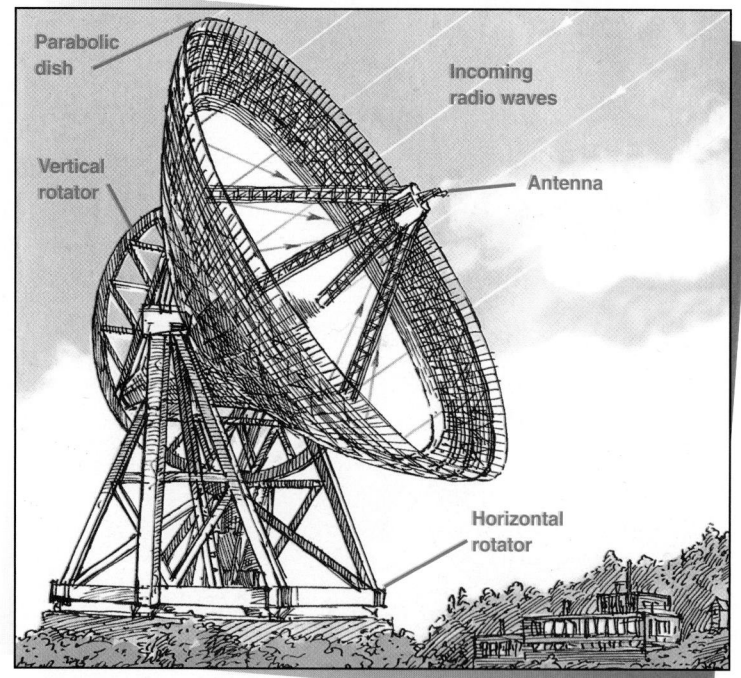

Radio Telescope

Parabolic dish

Incoming radio waves

Vertical rotator

Antenna

Horizontal rotator

132

Meeting Individual Needs

Intervention

Asking Questions Remind students that good readers wonder about the text they're reading as a natural response to being introduced to new words and concepts. Encourage students not to feel constrained only to ask questions they think will be answered in the text.

Teacher Tip Reread the selection with students who had difficulty understanding it. Continue modeling and prompting the use of strategies and skills as you reread. Summarizing frequently may be useful in a technical selection such as this one.

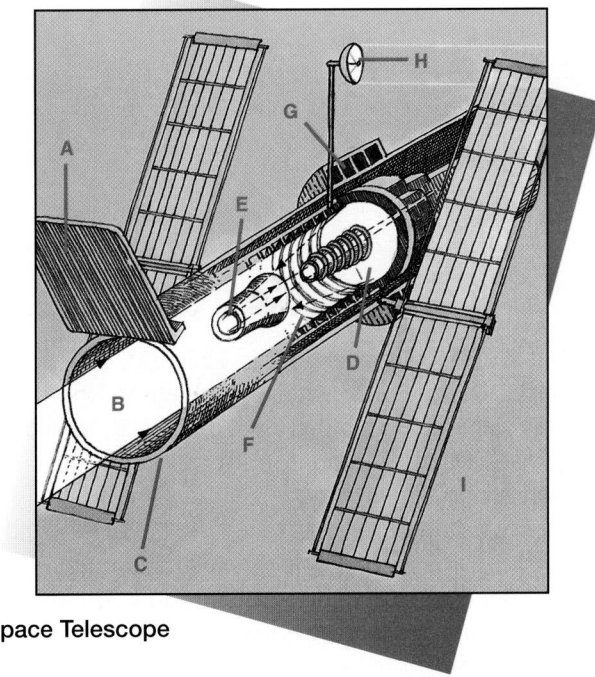

Space Telescope

A. Aperture door. B. Light rays from star or galaxy. C. Telescope tube.
The main body of the telescope is 43 feet long and 14 feet across.
D. Primary mirror. The space telescope is a reflecting telescope with a
main mirror eight feet in diameter. E. Secondary mirror. F. Baffles. These
ridges reduce the reflection of stray light from surfaces in the tube.
G. Equipment section. Light detectors change the visual images produced
by the mirrors into television signals. The space telescope also contains
scientific instruments. H. Radio dish. The dish sends telescope images and
measurements from instruments back by radio to ground stations below.
I. Solar panels. The pair of panels provides electricity to work the
instruments aboard the space telescope.

SPACE TELESCOPE

The Hubble space telescope is part <u>optical</u> telescope
and part satellite. It promises to revolutionize
<u>astronomy</u> because it operates outside the atmosphere,
which hampers any observations made from the
ground. The space telescope orbits the earth, observing
distant stars and galaxies in the total clarity of space.
It can peer seven times further into the universe than
we can see from the ground, and can also detect very
faint objects. The telescope may be able to "see" far
back in time by observing ancient light waves from the
most distant galaxies. Among these may be light waves
produced just after the big bang that blew the universe
into existence some 15 billion years ago.

133

Meeting Individual Needs

Comprehension Skills

Discussing the Selection

Following reading, engage the students in
discussion of the selection. Using the
handing-off process will help the students
take responsibility for the discussion. In
addition to the following questions, have
them revisit any questions asked when they
set purposes before reading.

- What is the purpose of a telescope in
  astronomy? *(to give a close-up view of
  distant objects)*

- What are radio telescopes used for? *(to
  detect radio waves from objects and to
  produce images of the objects)*

- Why is it important that the Hubble
  telescope is outside Earth's atmosphere?
  (The atmosphere hampers observations.)

- How has this selection connected with
  your knowledge of the unit theme?
  *(Answers will vary—students should
  compare/contrast examples of astronomy
  from this selection with their own
  experiences or past reading and use these
  connections to make a general statement
  about the unit theme.)*

During this time, have the students return
to the clues and problems that they noted on
the transparency before reading. Let the
students decide which items deserve further
discussion.

As the year progresses, the students take
more and more responsibility for discussions
of the selections and how they progress.
This *handing-off process* encourages them
to retain complete control of the discussion
and to become more actively involved in
the learning process. When a student finishes
his or her comments, that student should
choose (hand off the discussion to) the
next speaker.

2 Reading and Responding

Meet the Author and Illustrator

After students read the information about David Macaulay, discuss the following questions with them.

Why do you think David Macaulay wrote about how simple machines such as nail clippers work in the same book that he wrote about more complex machines, such as a car's automatic transmission? *(Possible answer: He wrote about both in the same book to show that the basic principles that go into making simple machines work also are used to make complex machines work.)*

Why do you think an architect, such as David Macaulay, might be interested in the way machines work? *(Possible answer: An architect might be interested in the way machines work because of a general interest in putting things together, or building.)*

Students might connect David Macaulay's interest in figuring out how things are put together to that of Galileo.

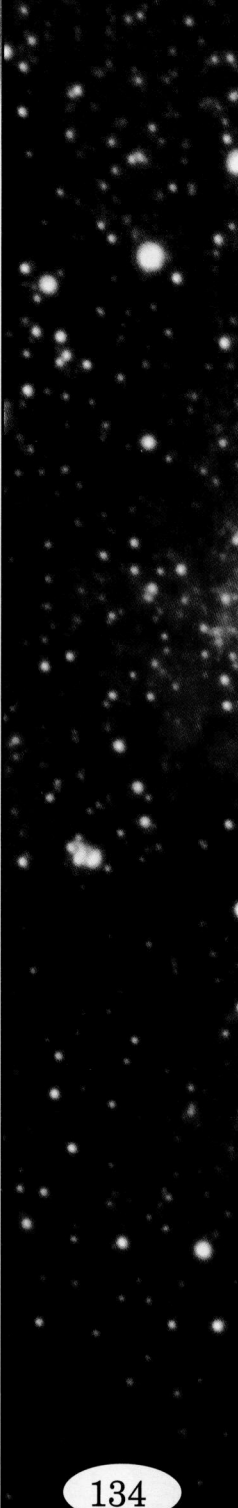

Telescopes

Meet the Author and Illustrator

David Macaulay was born in England, but he moved to America at the age of 11. He went to college in Rhode Island and earned a degree in architecture. Afterward, he worked as a junior high art teacher, and an interior designer. He now writes and illustrates his own books. "Telescopes" was taken from his award-winning book, *The Way Things Work*. In it he explains how telescopes work, along with everything from nail clippers and zippers to a car's automatic transmission. Mr. Macaulay is the author of other fascinating books too, like *Pyramid*, *Black and White*, *Underground*, and *Motel of the Mysteries*.

Anthology Story Mini
Author/Illustrator
Page Number 134

134

Theme Connections

Think About It

With a small group of classmates, discuss the variety of telescopes and their uses.

- What are some types of information we gather with telescopes?
- What makes the Hubble space telescope different from other powerful telescopes?

Check the Concept/Question Board to see if there are any questions that you can answer now. If the selection or your discussions about the selection have raised any new questions about the unit theme, put the questions on the Concept/Question Board. Maybe the next selection will help answer the questions.

Record Ideas

Why is it important for scientists to learn more about how the universe began? Use your Writing Journal to record your notes and ideas.

Research Ideas

- Find out more about the Hubble space telescope and whether it is considered a successful venture.

135

Theme Connections

Think About It

- As students discuss the variety of telescopes and their uses, circulate and observe the discussions. Encourage students to refer to the diagrams in the selection during the course of their discussions.

- Suggest that the students compare Galileo's telescopes with those described in this selection.

- Have the students report what they discussed. Encourage them to record on the Concept/Question Board any questions they may have.

Research Ideas

If there is an astronomical observatory in your area, suggest that the students visit it to view the different telescopes the observatory uses. Students can find more information about telescopes in their school or community library.

② Responding

✦Exploring the Theme

 **Research**

As students continue their explorations, have them use the **Research** CD-ROM Program to help organize and share their findings.

Teacher Tip If you created a word wall on the Concept/Question Board of key words related to the unit theme "Back Through the Stars" have students find words from other resources, their activities, and family discussions and add them the appropriate category on the wall.

Selection Vocabulary

Have students write in their Writing Journals the definitions for words discussed before the reading of the selection and any other interesting words they clarified while reading. Students should be encouraged to refer to these words throughout the unit as they work on student and writing projects. The words from this selection are:

galaxy	**universe**	**bodies**
frequency	**revolutionize**	

Reading/Writing Connections

Remind students that Galileo's student wrote to him and told him about the new invention, a telescope. Have students write a letter to Galileo telling him about the radio telescope or about the space telescope. Then have them pretend to be Galileo and write a letter back.

Literature Appreciation

Have students imagine that they are astronomers using the Hubble space telescope and have just made an exciting discovery. Have them prepare and present a press release to be aired on the evening news.

Home Connection

The class has just finished reading "Telescopes," an expository selection about how various types of telescopes work. An informational letter on "Telescopes," in both English and Spanish, can be found in the *Home Connection* guide.

Home Connection p. 19

"Telescopes"

A message from _____

We have just finished reading the selection *Telescopes*, in which David Macaulay explains the four major types of telescopes that are used in the exploration of space. You can help your child to better understand how these different telescopes work by having him or her fill in the chart below. Have your child list the main characteristics of each telescope or write a description of how each kind of telescope works. When the chart is completed, discuss what makes each type of telescope different from the others.

Encourage your child to share this chart with the class.

Telescope	Characteristics
Refracting	
Reflecting	
Radio	
Space	

Unit 2/Back Through the Stars   19

Supporting Student Explorations

Help students complete their research plans by doing the following:

Whole Group Have students present their proposed problems to the class, allowing open discussion of how promising and interesting various proposed problems are. To aid the formation of groups, have students record their problems on the chalkboard, then draw arrows to link related problems.

Small Group Have each group meet to agree on and state their research problem and what their research will contribute to the rest of the class's knowledge of astronomy. Constant emphasis on group knowledge building will help set a clear purpose for the students' research.

Individual As students begin their research, confirm that they know what they are trying to find out or understand, and that they can articulate what is interesting about the question they are investigating.

Students may wish to post on the Concept/Question Board newspaper clippings, magazine articles, computer Websites, and information about nonfiction books relating to the study of astronomy.

Inquiry Journal Have students complete page 21 of the *Inquiry Journal*. Have them record their ideas about how "Telescopes" added to their knowledge of astronomy. Then have students complete the project planning chart on pages 26–27, and also page 28, for topic exploration.

Inquiry Journal pp. 26, 28

Inquiry Journal p. 21

Assessment

✓ **Informal** At this point in the project students have formed groups and are confirming their research topics. Check to see that students:

- have a clear idea of their research topic.
- work cooperatively to establish their projects.
- understand the range of resources for their research.

 # Integrating the Curriculum

Assessment

✓ **Informal** Take this opportunity to assess students' progress with the writing process by commenting on the entries in their Writing Journals.

Meeting Individual Needs

ESL

Leadership Provide opportunities for English-language learners to be leaders. Encourage them to list the ideas generated during the prewriting session.

Language Arts

Writing

Prewriting

Instruct The phase of the writing process when students think through an idea they want to write about is called *prewriting*. Students should think about their ideas, discuss them, and plan how they want readers to respond. It is important for students to plan ahead so that they can proceed from one phase of the writing process to another without spending unnecessary time making decisions. Prewriting is the most time-consuming phase of the process, but it may be the most important.

Let students know that even very good writers sometimes find it difficult to find a topic to write about. Therefore, they ask themselves questions such as, *"What am I interested in writing about? What do I want to say about my topic? What do I already know about my topic? What do I need to find out? Who will read my piece of writing?"*

Practice Write the above questions on the chalkboard. Have students use the selection "Telescopes," and the author's biography to speculate on how David Macaulay answered the above questions. Students should be able to come up with definitive answers for most of the questions.

Apply Have students repeat the above process using the previous selection, "Galileo."

Writing Process

Prewrite Continuing the expository writing activity they started in Lesson 1, students should write down and answer the above questions for their own writing. Students may find it helpful to brainstorm with a partner or small group to list research topics, problems, and questions they might use in their writing. Have them list or make a web of related ideas, key words, or phrases they want to develop in their papers. For example, if a student wants to research telescopes, the student's list might read:

refracting telescope   *concave mirror*   *radio telescope*
reflecting telescope   *eyepiece lens*

Literary Elements

Features of Informational Text

Instruct Prompt students to tell you that "Telescopes" is a nonfiction selection that is considered *informational text*. The primary purpose of informational text is usually to explain or instruct. Contrast this with other types of nonfiction, such as biography or newspaper articles. Use the selection "Telescopes" for examples of the identifying features in informative texts.

- Discuss how a title, such as "Telescopes" or *The Way Things Work*, often gives a clue that the work is informative.
- Point out the headings dividing the text in "Telescopes" as another indicator of informative text.
- Next, call attention to the diagrams in "Telescopes." The diagrams present the information in a simpler form. Other visual aids used in informational texts include charts and graphs.
- Explain that technical words are often a feature of informational texts.
- Tell students that some informational texts have additional features not found in "Telescopes," such as footnotes and bibliographies.

Practice Have students look through their anthologies and list other examples of informational text, noting the similarities in their treatment, scope, and organization.

Apply For additional practice, have students complete *Reading and Writing Workbook,* pages 55–56.

Meeting Individual Needs

Reteach

Informational Text For those students who need more practice, choose a book or article from the *Classroom Library* and point out the examples of the characteristics of informational text. For additional instruction and practice with this concept, have them complete *Reteach,* pages 55–56.

Challenge

Informational Text Challenge students to find an article or book about astronomy that exhibits all of the features of informational texts. Have students who understand this concept complete *Challenge,* page 30.

Reading and Writing Workbook pp. 55–56.

Name _____ Date _____

Features of Informational Text | Telescopes |

Focus A good writer of informational text presents facts in a way that is informative, interesting, and well organized.

Informational text
- is nonfiction.
- has a main topic.
- contains subtopics that relate to the main topic.
- explains several facts about each subtopic.
- sometimes contains charts, tables, and diagrams.

Identify Look through "Telescopes" and write an *X* next to the features of informational text that it includes.

X	main topic	X	explanation of technical terms
X	subtopics	X	facts about each subtopic
	footnotes		glossary
X	tables, charts, or diagrams		bibliography
	index		table of contents
X	nonfiction		photographs

Reading and Writing Workbook • *Features of Informational Text* 55

Features of Informational Text *(continued)*

Practice Read the following informational text and complete the outline.

Small Moving Objects in Our Solar System

If you study the night sky for a month, you can see planets like Mars and Saturn creep about. Some small objects, such as comets or meteoroids, streak across the sky in a matter of days or even moments.

A comet is a lump of ice and dust that revolves around the sun in a very large orbit. It can be seen from Earth when its orbit comes close to the sun. As it heats up, it releases gas and dust, which are seen as a streak in the sky.

A meteoroid is a chunk of stone or metal that plunges into our atmosphere at high speed. When it enters Earth's atmosphere, it heats up and is seen as a "falling star." A meteoroid that falls to Earth is called a meteorite.

Title: Small Moving Objects in Our Solar System

Main Topic: Objects that move quickly across the sky

A. Subtopic 1: Comets

Fact 1: They are lumps of ice and dust.

Fact 2: They heat up and release gas and dust that streak the sky.

B. Subtopic 2: Meteoroids

Fact 1: They are chunks of stone or metal.

Fact 2: They heat up and fall into Earth's atmosphere as "falling stars."

Apply On a sheet of paper, write informational text that describes how an object, such as a bicycle or camera, works. Remember to include a main topic, subtopics, and facts about each subtopic. You may also choose to include a diagram. Answers will vary.

56 *Features of Informational Text* • Reading and Writing Workbook

3 Integrating the Curriculum

Meeting Individual Needs

Challenge

Content-Area Words Have students list these words on a piece of paper: *court, hearing, trial, sentence.* Point out that these words each have more than one meaning, one of which is associated with the subject *law.* Have students write two sentences for each word—one using it as a *law* content-area word and the other demonstrating one of its other meanings.

Skills Strand

Content-Area Words
INTRODUCED: Unit 2, Lesson 1
REVIEWED: Unit 2, Lesson 2
Unit 2, Lesson 7

Teacher Tip Tell students that many current-events topics have content-area words associated with them. Have students brainstorm a list of current-events topics (for example, *politics, medicine, education,* and *the environment*). Then, have each student browse newspapers and magazines for five unfamiliar words associated with at least one of the current-events topics listed. In the Personal Dictionary section of their Writing Journals, have students list each word they found, along with its correlating current-events topic and a definition based on the word's context and dictionary meaning.

Assessment

✓ **Formal** To assess students' understanding of this concept, have them complete **Skills Assessment,** page 14.

Vocabulary

Content-Area Words

Instruct Have students tell you what they remember about content-area words from Unit 2, Lesson 1. If necessary, remind them that content-area words are terms associated with a particular subject or field of study. Point out that "Telescopes" contains many such terms.

Practice Have students look through the selection "Telescopes" and write as many astronomy content-area words as they can find. Have them look up any unfamiliar terms in the dictionary. Then have them write brief definitions for each, using their own words.

Apply Have students place check marks beside words from the list they created above that they recognize from the selection "Galileo." Encourage students to keep terms with hard-to-remember definitions in the personal dictionary section of their Writing Journals. Tell them that knowing these terms may be useful to them when reading other selections in this unit and when working on their unit activities.

Grammar, Usage, and Mechanics

Pronouns

Instruct Remind students that all words are classified into groups called *parts of speech*. One part of speech is *pronouns*. Ask students what a pronoun does. *(A pronoun takes the place of a noun.)*

Have students tell you what they remember about nominative-case pronouns. *(The pronoun is the doer, or the subject, of the action.)* Ask students to name the nominative-case pronouns *(I, you, he, she, it, we, they)*.

Have students tell you what they remember about objective-case pronouns. *(The pronoun is the receiver, or the direct object, of the action of the verb.)* Have students name the objective-case pronouns *(me, you, him, her, us, it, them)*.

Practice Have students identify examples of correct pronoun usage in "Telescopes." Then, have students write three of their own sentences using nominative-case pronouns and three using objective-case pronouns.

Apply Have students apply the correct use of the pronouns *I*, *me*, *they*, *them*, *we*, and *us* in both their speaking and writing. Write the following sentences on the chalkboard, giving the students a choice of the two pronouns. Tell them that they will supply the correct pronouns.

- Will you sit with _____ at the game? (*I* or <u>*me*</u>)
- _____ would like a cookie. (<u>*I*</u> or *me*)
- Tomorrow, _____ will go back to school. (<u>*they*</u> or *them*)
- Please tell _____ to bring snacks. (*they* or <u>*them*</u>)
- The card is from all of _____. (*we* or <u>*us*</u>)
- Every summer _____ go on vacation. (<u>*we*</u> or *us*)

Teacher Tip Remind students to check for correct usage of pronouns in their expository writing and unit activities.

Meeting Individual Needs

Challenge

Pronouns Have students work in pairs. Each student will write original sentences that each contain at least one noun. Partners will then exchange papers, underline the nouns in their partner's sentences, and change the nouns to pronouns. Remind students to check each other's work.

Intervention

Pronouns Have those students who need more practice look for nouns in selections they have read. Have them read the sentences and then replace the nouns with pronouns.

Skills Strand

Pronouns
INTRODUCED: Unit 1, Lesson 3
REVIEWED: Unit 2, Lesson 2
Unit 4, Lesson 2

③ Integrating the Curriculum

Teacher Tip It may come up in discussion that listening to a radio broadcast for information on astronomy and telescopes could be more difficult than reading about them because unfamiliar technical terms may not be clarified on the spot. For this reason, jotting down notes on the main ideas of the broadcast is a good aid for comprehension.

Listening/ Speaking/ Viewing

Listening for Information

Tell students to pretend that they will be listening to a radio broadcast about telescopes and astronomy later in the day. Discuss with students the kinds of things they can do to make sure that they remember the information they hear (for example, *listen attentively*, *take notes*, and *write down key words*).

Tell students that one way to help focus their attention on the broadcast information is to think of questions that they hope will be answered. Have students write four or five questions about telescopes and astronomy that might be answered in the radio broadcast. Have volunteers share their questions with the class.

Study and Research

Diagrams

Instruct Ask students what kind of pictures were included in "Telescopes" *(diagrams).* Ask volunteers to tell what a diagram is *(a drawing that shows the parts of something).* Discuss with students why David Macaulay chose to include diagrams. *(Diagrams help the reader understand what is being presented.)*

Have the students look at the diagrams of a reflecting and a refracting telescope on page 131 of the **Student Anthology.** Point out that the title of each diagram is in capital letters. Draw students' attention to the labels and to the lines pointing to the various parts of the telescopes.

Work with students to devise a list like the following to explain that diagrams can show:

■ how something is put together.

■ how something is arranged.

■ how something works.

■ where parts are located in relation to other parts.

■ how things are joined together.

■ what parts are larger than others.

■ the names of the parts.

Practice Divide the students into four groups and assign each group one of the diagrams in the selection. Have group members discuss what their diagram shows. Then, using the diagram, have a representative from each group give an oral presentation for classmates on how the telescope works.

Apply Ask students to consider what kinds of diagrams might enhance their own expository papers in this unit. Have them begin work on a diagram to be incorporated into their papers during the publishing step of the writing process in this unit.

For more practice, have students complete **Inquiry Journal** page 29.

Meeting Individual Needs

Challenge

Diagrams Challenge students to draw a diagram of an ordinary, everyday item such as a toaster or an electric pencil sharpener.

Inter√ention

Diagrams For those students who need more practice, choose a different diagram and review the parts. Ask students to explain what the diagram shows.

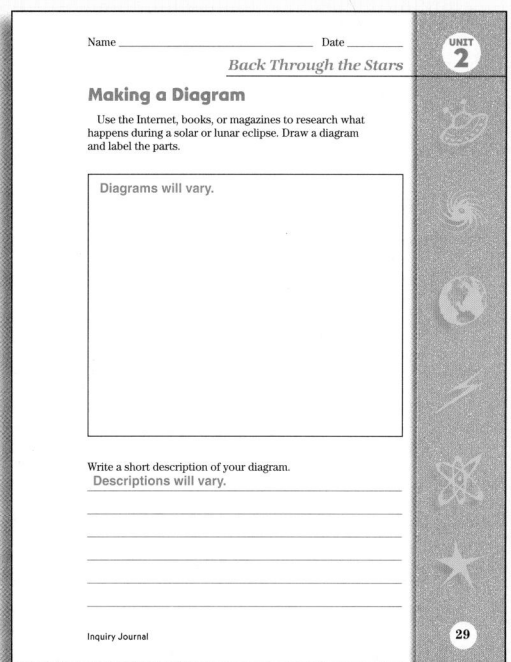

Inquiry Journal p. 29

Across the Curriculum

Science

Experimenting with Magnifiers

Purpose

To help students recognize the effects of magnification

Materials

Various magnifying glasses, jeweler's eyeglasses, microscopes and slides, telescopes, and so on; small piece of dark-colored paper for each student; a sewing needle or pin; and a page with small print such as a newspaper or a magazine.

Procedure

Write directions for making magnifiers as follows.

1. Use the needle or pin to poke a tiny hole through the paper.
2. Hold the paper next to your eye and look through the hole.
3. Hold a printed page and bring it closer to your eye. What do you notice?

Set up a station for each type of magnifying device and a station with the paper, pins, and newspaper for students to make their own magnifiers.

- Remind students that when Galileo made his first telescope, it only magnified objects three times. Finally, he built a telescope that would magnify 30 times. Modern astronomical telescopes magnify many more times.

- Discuss the various types of magnifying devices and their uses. Point out that for some uses such as watch and jewelry repair, a little magnification is all that's needed. Ask students to speculate on the magnification provided by each of the devices.

- Have them prepare a chart to record their observations of the magnification ability of the various devices.

Music

Appreciating Music

Purpose

To help students become aware of and appreciate classical music

Procedure

Obtain a recording of *The Planets* by Gustav Holtz. Students may be interested to note that not all the planets are represented because astronomers had not discovered them all when the music was written.

- Prepare students for listening to excerpts of the music by explaining that the orchestral piece is divided into several movements, each based on one of the planets. Ask students to use what they know about the planets to predict what each movement might be like.

- Have students get comfortable and then begin the music. As students listen, encourage them to let their minds wander and let the sound of the music make an impression on them.

- After listening, elicit students' reactions to the music. Discuss whether Holtz's musical ideas about the planets match the students' ideas and in what ways they differ.

Across the Curriculum

 ## Social Studies

How Is the Hubble Space Telescope Doing Now?

Purpose

To help students research recent events

Procedure

Share the following information with students:

Soon after the Hubble space telescope was launched in 1990, scientists realized that its primary mirror was deformed, making the instrument "nearsighted." Although computer manipulations of the Hubble's images enabled scientists to see many things that could not be seen from Earth, the orbiting telescope's usefulness as a scientific instrument fell far short of expectations. A shuttle repair mission in 1993 provided "eyeglasses" in the form of ten corrective mirrors. It took seven astronauts working for several days to correct Hubble's vision.

■ Have students do research to find more information about the Hubble telescope. Suggest that they concentrate on what has happened to the telescope since the repair mission and what it has shown astronomers. Have students use science magazines, current affairs magazines, recently published books, and the Internet in their research. The Concept/Question Board may also include information they can use.

■ Students may wish to work in small groups to organize their findings. Suggest that they present their findings in oral presentations.

 ## Math

How Much Is 15 Billion?

Purpose

To help students comprehend large numbers

Procedure

Remind students that the closing sentence of "Telescopes" mentions 15 billion years. Explain that the science of astronomy includes many gigantic numbers like this. Tell students that a light-year, used to measure distance to the stars, is the distance that light travels in one year—5,878 trillion miles.

■ Have students work in small groups to determine a way to represent either 15 billion or 6 trillion. If necessary, tell students that a million is a thousand thousand, a billion is a thousand million, and a trillion is a thousand billion.

■ A group may want to draw items, each person representing a part of the total. For example, students might choose to draw cars, each car representing a thousand or ten thousand.

■ Alternatively, groups may want to represent the idea of large numbers by drawing lines in ratio. Each line could be a different length to stand for different numbers. Students may need to use the length of a school hallway or circle the classroom several times.

■ Encourage the groups to be inventive and the participants to think as creatively as possible.

■ Allow time for groups to present their representations. You may wish to invite another class to the presentations.

Selection Summary

Genre: Myth

Thousands of years ago, people gazed at the night sky and saw men, women, and beasts in the stars. They invented engaging and fanciful tales to explain how these creatures came to live in the sky. Readers will enjoy these constellation myths about a loyal prince and a heroic scorpion while learning something about the beliefs and values of the ancient Indian and Greek cultures.

About the Author

Alison Lurie began writing as a child, making up poems and stories to amuse herself and her family. A literary critic, teacher, and author, Lurie won the Pulitzer Prize for fiction for her novel *Foreign Affairs.*

Students can read more about Alison Lurie on page 142 of the **Student Anthology.**

Other Books by Alison Lurie
- *Clever Gretchen and Other Forgotten Folktales*
- *Imaginary Friends, Real People*
- *The War Between the Tates*
- *Fabulous Beasts*

About the Illustrator

Monika Beisner has collaborated on two books with Alison Lurie. She has also written and illustrated several books of her own. She lives in London and Malta.

Students can read more about Monika Beisner on page 142 of the **Student Anthology.**

Other Books Illustrated by Monika Beisner
- *Catch That Cat! A Picture Book of Rhymes and Puzzles*
- *Topsy Turvy, Monika Beisner's Book of Riddles*

Exploring the Theme

Selection Concepts

This pair of myths, one Indian and one Greek, illustrates how early people attempted to make sense of a mysterious universe. By studying star patterns, recognizing familiar objects in the patterns, and creating stories about them, the ancients could attribute meaning to a phenomenon—stars—about which they had no technical knowledge. Key concepts explored are:

- Creating myths such as "The Great Dog" and "The Scorpion" helped ancient peoples make the unknown familiar.

- Constellation myths can tell us something about the beliefs and values of the ancient civilizations from which they originated.

Check the Reading link of the **SRA** Web page for links to theme-related Websites.
http://www.sra4kids.com

Exploration Activity Tips

Before Reading, have the students share any myths they know about the sun, moon, stars, or planets. For instance, they may have heard the Native American legend about the coyote who arranged the stars in the shapes of his animal friends.

During Reading, have the students respond to the text by making predictions as they read "The Heavenly Zoo."

After Reading, have the students make up constellation myths. Have them illustrate their constellation using black paper and white crayons or chalk. Afterward, have students update the Concept/Question Board. Some may want to revise their activity plans based on what they have learned from the selection.

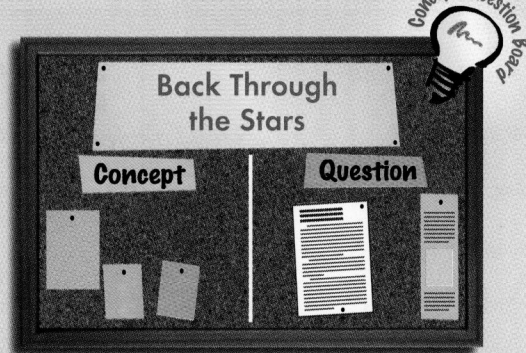

Unit 2 Exploration Management

Lesson 1	Brainstorm research problems. Form interest-based groups. Develop and discuss initial research plans.
Lesson 2	Groups finalize plans, allocate tasks, and begin research. Discuss initial findings and resources.
Lesson 3 **The Heavenly Zoo**	**Collaborative Exploration** **Research continues as groups consider revision of their activity focus.** **Supplementary Activity** **Make conjectures and record them for later use. Take notes from relevant and authoritative sources.**
Lesson 4	Students continue with research and present their initial findings.
Lesson 5	Research continues. Students present interesting findings or problems.
Lesson 6	Research continues. Students present interesting findings or problems.
Lesson 7	Students organize research findings and prepare presentations.
Lesson 8	Students present their activities.

Lesson Planner

Suggested Pacing: 3–5 days	DAY 1	DAY 2	
	DAY 1	DAY 2	
Part 1 — Preparing to Read **Materials** ■ Student Anthology, pp. 136–143 ■ Transparencies 9, 44	**Word Knowledge** ■ Reading the Words and Sentences, p. 136G ■ Developing Oral Language, p. 136G **Build Background, p. 136H** **Preview and Prepare, p. 136I** **Selection Vocabulary, p. 136I** *ancestors, summoning, attendants, heavens, vain*	**Preview and Prepare, p. 136I** ■ Review Transparency 44	
Part 2 — Reading and Responding **Materials** ■ Student Anthology, pp. 136–143 ■ Teacher Observation Log ■ Reading and Writing Workbook, pp. 57–58 ■ Inquiry Journal, p. 21 ■ Transparency 46 ■ Home Connection, p. 21	**Student Anthology, pp. 136–143** **Comprehension Strategies** ■ Predicting, pp. 136, 138 ■ Making Connections, p. 136 ■ Summarizing, pp. 138, 140 **Discussing Strategy Use, p. 140**	**Student Anthology, pp. 136–143** **Comprehension Skills** ✓■ Making Inferences, pp. 137, 139 ✓■ Discussing the Selection, p. 141 **Exploring the Theme** ■ Selection Vocabulary, p. 143A *ancestors, summoning, attendants, heavens, vain*	
Part 3 — Integrating the Curriculum **Materials** ■ Student Anthology, pp. 136–143 ■ Reading and Writing Workbook, pp. 59–64 ■ Inquiry Journal, p. 30	**Writing** ■ Writing Paragraphs and Topic Sentences, p. 143C **Literary Elements** ✓■ Recognize Myths, p. 143D	**Writing Process** ■ Draft, p. 143C **Vocabulary** ✓■ Develop Vocabulary by Listening, p. 143E	
Independent Work Time **Materials** ■ Reteach, pp. 57–64 ■ ESL Supplement ■ Challenge, pp. 31–34 ■ Intervention Guide ■ Listening Library Audiocassette	**Writing Process Continued** **Reteach** ✓■ Myth, *Reteach*, pp. 59–60 **ESL** ■ Word Meaning, p. 136G ■ Vocabulary, p. 136J **Challenge** ✓■ Myth, *Challenge*, p. 32 **Intervention** ■ Inflectional Endings, p. 136G ■ Myth, p. 143E **Unit Project** ■ Continue Research ■ Revise Activity Focus	**Writing Process Continued** **Reteach** ✓■ Making Inferences, *Reteach*, pp. 57–58 **ESL** ■ Listening Strategies, p. 143E **Challenge** ✓■ Making Inferences, *Challenge*, p. 31 **Intervention** ■ Comprehension, p. 136 ■ Draft, p. 143C **Unit Project Continued**	

✓Informal **Assessment Available**   ✓Formal **Assessment Available**

DAY 2 continued	**DAY 3**	
DAY 3	**DAY 4**	**DAY 5**
General Review	**General Review**	**Review Word Knowledge**
Student Anthology, pp. 136–143 **Theme Connections** ■ Think About It, p. 143 ■ Research Ideas, p. 143	**Student Anthology, pp. 136–143** **Exploring the Theme** ■ Reading/Writing Connections, p. 143A ■ Literature Appreciation, p. 143A ■ Supporting Student Explorations, p. 143B	**Student Anthology, pp. 136–143** ■ Review Selection ■ Complete Discussion ■ Reread Selection in Pairs **Home Connection, p. 143A** ■ Discuss "The Heavenly Zoo" ■ Research a star formation
Writing Process Continued **Grammar, Usage, and Mechanics** ✓■ Present-Tense Verbs—Regular and Irregular, p. 143F	**Writing Process Continued** **Study and Research** ✓■ Card and Computer Catalog, p. 143G	**Across the Curriculum** **Science** ■ Finding Our Own Constellations, p. 143H **Health** ■ Making a Safety Poster, p. 143H
Writing Process Continued **Reteach** ✓■ Listening Vocabulary, *Reteach*, pp. 61–62 **Challenge** ■ Making Inferences, p. 141 ✓■ Listening Vocabulary, *Challenge*, p. 33 **Intervention** ■ Listening Vocabulary, p. 143E **Unit Project Continued**	**Writing Process Continued** **Reteach** ✓■ Regular and Irregular Verbs, *Reteach*, pp. 63–64 **ESL** ■ Card and Computer Catalog, p. 143G **Challenge** ✓■ Regular and Irregular Verbs, *Challenge*, p. 34 **Intervention** ■ Card and Computer Catalog, p. 143G **Unit Project Continued**	**Writing Process Continued** **Unit Project Continued**

Meeting Individual Needs
Independent Work Time

Preparing to Read

Meeting Individual Needs

ESL
- Word Meaning, p. 136G
- Cultural Context, p. 136H
- Vocabulary, p. 136J

Intervention
- Inflectional Endings, p. 136G

Reading and Responding

Meeting Individual Needs

Reteach
- Making Inferences, *Reteach*, pp. 57–58

ESL
- Summarizing, p. 140

Challenge
- Making Inferences, *Challenge*, p. 31
- Making Inferences, p. 141

Intervention
- Comprehension, p. 136
- Predicting, p. 138

Integrating the Curriculum

Meeting Individual Needs

Reteach
- Myth, *Reteach*, pp. 59–60
- Listening Vocabulary, *Reteach*, pp. 61–62
- Regular and Irregular Verbs, *Reteach*, pp. 63–64

ESL
- Listening Strategies, p. 143E
- Card and Computer Catalog, p. 143G

Challenge
- Myth, *Challenge*, p. 32
- Listening Vocabulary, *Challenge*, p. 33
- Regular and Irregular Verbs, *Challenge*, p. 34

Intervention
- Draft, p. 143C
- Myth, p. 143D
- Listening Vocabulary, p. 143E
- Card and Computer Catalog, p. 143G

Formal Assessment Options

Use these assessment pages along with your informal observations to gauge student progress.

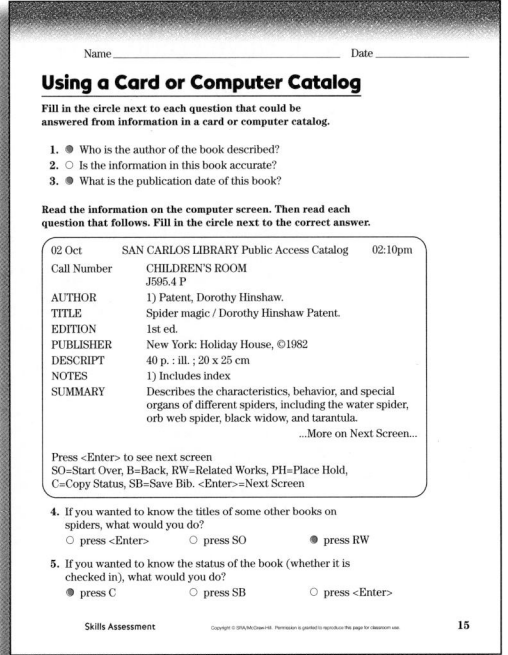

Skills Assessment, p. 15

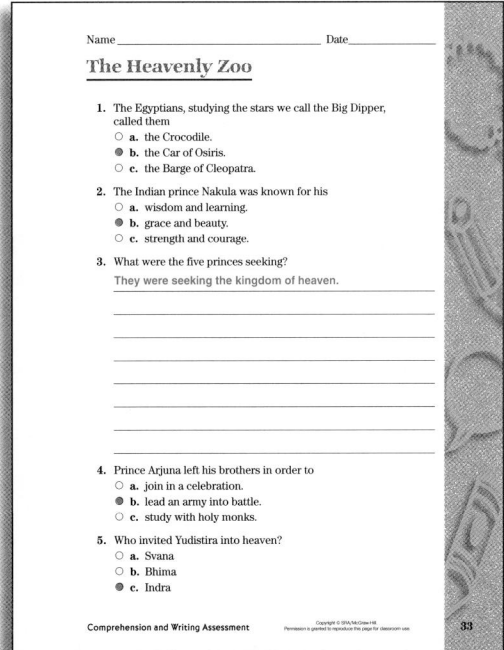

Comprehension and Writing Assessment, p. 33

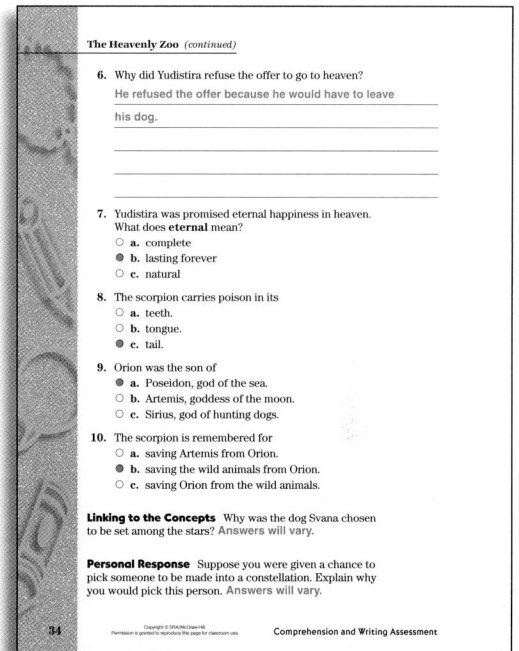

Comprehension and Writing Assessment, p. 34

1 Preparing to Read

Word Knowledge

Reading the Words and Sentences

Write each word and sentence on the chalkboard. Have students read each word together. After all the words have been read, have students read each sentence in natural phrases or chunks. Use the suggestions in About the Words to discuss the different features of the listed words.

Line 1:	all-round	all-star	sword-belt
Line 2:	smallest	fastest	biggest
Line 3:	regretted	journeyed	scared
Sentence 1:	An all-round athlete like Rachel plays volleyball, basketball, and softball.		
Sentence 2:	The smallest kid in the class might also be the fastest.		
Sentence 3:	I don't know about you, but the roller coaster scared me.		

About the Words

- Line 1 contains hyphenated compounds. Have students try to brainstorm other hyphenated compound words.
- The words in Line 2 form the superlative by adding -est. This suffix is added to adjectives to designate the extreme intensity of the word.
- The words in Line 3 all have the inflectional ending -ed. Adding this ending to a verb changes it from present to past tense.

Developing Oral Language

To review the words, have students do one or both of the following activities.

- Have students use various words in sentences and then have them extend their sentences by answering *when, why, where,* or *how* questions.
- Have each student write a riddle for one of the words on the chalkboard in his or her Writing Journal. For example, *Why didn't the chicken cross the road? Because it was scared.* Then have the students take turns asking their riddles.

Meeting Individual Needs

ESL

Word Meaning Make sure the English-language learners understand the meanings of the words before they do the exercises. Refer to Unit 2, Lesson 3, of the *ESL Supplement* for specific suggestions.

InterVention

Inflectional Endings For students who need additional help with the inflectional ending -ed, ask what they notice about the words in the third line. *(They all end with* -ed.) Point out that the final e in *regretted* is voiced, while in the other words, it is silent. Help the students discover that when root words end in d or t, the e in the -ed inflection is voiced. You may also wish to remind students that when a root word ends with a single consonant preceded by a short vowel, the consonant is usually doubled before adding -ed, for example, *regretted, propelled,* and *robbed.* For students who need more help, see Unit 2, Lesson 3, of the *Intervention Guide.*

Build Background

Activate Prior Knowledge

Have students check the Concept/Question Board to refresh their memories about astronomy. Discuss the following with students to find out what they may already know about the selection and have already learned about the unit theme. Tell students to use their prior knowledge to help them comprehend the selection they are about to read.

- Discuss with students what they learned about astronomy in "Galileo" and "Telescopes." Be sure that Galileo is mentioned as a pioneer of modern astronomy who developed telescopes and discovered information about the planets.

- Ask students whether they are familiar with the story they are about to read, and if so, to tell a little about it. Remind students, however, not to give away the ending of the selection.

- Have students share any other stories about the constellations.

Background Information

The following information may help the students better understand the selection they are about to read.

- If necessary, remind students that a myth is a story created to explain events that happen in nature. Tell students that the two stories they are about to read are myths that explain how the two constellations came to be.

- Inform students that "The Great Dog" is an Indian myth written more than 2000 years ago.

- Tell students that "The Scorpion" is a Greek myth.

Teacher Tip "The Great Dog" is an excerpt from the *Mahabharata* (mə hä bä´ rə tə), one of two Classical Sanskrit epics of ancient India. The *Mahabharata* is a legend by definition, but portions of it are mythical. Because "The Great Dog" exhibits some mythical qualities, it is treated as a myth in this lesson.

Writing Journal After reading, have students jot down their reactions to the stories, as well as any ideas they have for using the origin of a constellation in a story.

Preparing to Read

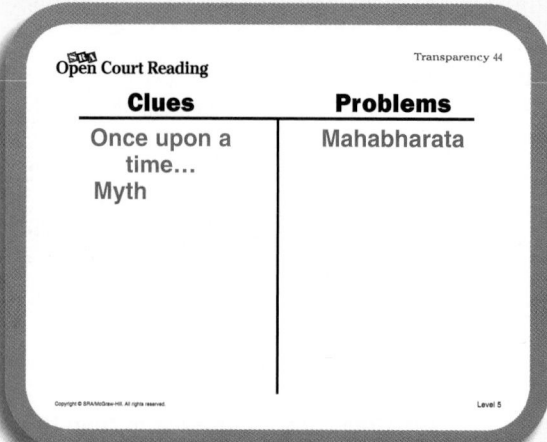

Transparency 44

Teacher Tip To help students decode words, divide them into the syllables shown below. The information following each word tells how students can figure out the meaning of each word from the sentences on the transparency.

an·ces·tors   context clues

sum·mon·ing   context clues, word structure

at·ten·dants   context clues, word structure

heav·ens   context clues

vain   context clues

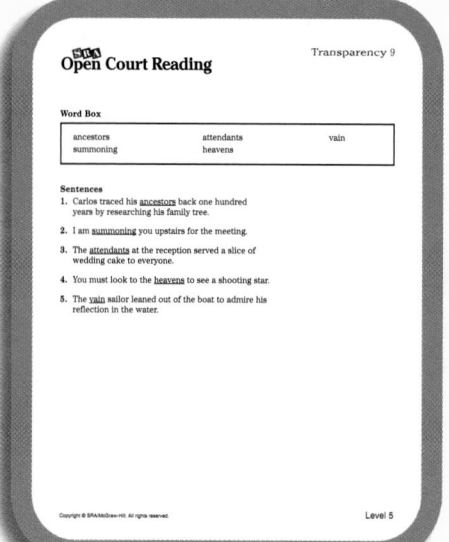

Transparency 9

Preview and Prepare

Browse

- Have a volunteer read the title and author's and illustrator's names aloud. Have students share what they know about myths.

- Have the students browse through the story for words and phrases that connect to what they already know. Record these in the Clues column on **Transparency 44.** Discuss with them what they think the stories in this selection might have to do with astronomy.

- Encourage students to ask questions as they browse. Have them identify any problems they notice and record them in the Problems column.

Set Purposes

As they read, have the students think about how the two myths from ancient times compare to what they know about the night sky.

Selection Vocabulary

Students will use context clues, word structure, and apposition to determine word meaning of vocabulary and other unfamiliar words.

Display **Transparency 9** before reading the selection to introduce and discuss the following words and their meanings.

an·ces·tors: people from whom one is descended (page 136)

sum·mon·ing: asking to come (page 137)

at·ten·dants: people who wait on someone (page 138)

heav·ens: the sky as viewed from Earth (page 139)

vain: conceited (page 140)

Have students read the words in the Word Box. Help students decode multisyllabic words by reading them syllable by syllable.

Have students read the sentences on **Transparency 9** to determine the meaning of the underlined words. Remind them to use clues in the sentences and structural clues to figure out the meaning.

Reading Recommendations

Your first reading of the selection should focus on developing the reading strategies found to the left of the reduced pages. We recommend that the students revisit the selection, rereading sections or the entire selection as a way to enhance their understanding and appreciation of the text. During rereading, they should focus on the comprehension skills, found to the right of the reduced pages.

Oral Reading

Because the terms and ideas in this selection may be unfamiliar to students, oral reading is recommended for this selection. Have students adjust their reading rate by reading more slowly or by rereading certain sections of the selection in order to comprehend the information presented.

As students read aloud, have them read expressively, at an appropriate pace, in natural phrases and chunks. By reading the selection with fluency, students will demonstrate an understanding of the text and an ability to engage the listeners in an effective manner. If students encounter difficulties, have them use the reading strategies below or refer to the Blending Procedure (Program Appendix 15–16).

Using Reading Strategies

Reading strategy instruction allows students to become aware of how good readers read. During the reading of "The Heavenly Zoo," you will model the use of the following reading strategies:

- Making Connections
- Summarizing
- Predicting

Before reading, have students share how they have used these strategies in the past and any tips they can give each other on their use.

Building Comprehension Skills

Revisiting or rereading a selection allows students to apply skills that give them a more complete understanding of the text. Some follow-up comprehension skills, such as *Main Idea and Details* and *Compare and Contrast*, help students organize information. Others, such as *Author's Purpose*, *Making Inferences*, and *Drawing Conclusions*, lead to deeper understanding—to "reading between the lines," as mature readers do. In this selection, students will apply the follow-up comprehension skill of *Making Inferences*.

Teacher Tip The following are goals students may want to keep in mind while they are reading:
- to resolve problems listed in the Clues and Problems transparency
- to identify what interests them about the selection's theme
- to collect information to use in their projects

Meeting Individual Needs

ESL

Vocabulary Check that English-language learners know the meanings of idioms and more difficult vocabulary in the story, including: *great burning globes of gas, constellation, ancestors, legend, temple, prayer, cast off, renounce, devotion, track, oppression,* and *boast.* Explain and show pictures as needed. Model example sentences and help English-speaking students make their own sentences. Refer to Unit 2, Lesson 3, of the *ESL Supplement* for teaching suggestions.

Teacher Tip Have students who may need extra help reading "The Heavenly Zoo" reread the selection using the *Listening Library Audiocassette.*

Teacher Tip By this time in the fifth grade, good readers should be reading approximately 126 words per minute with fluency and expression. The only way to gain fluency is through practice. As explained in Reading Recommendations, have students reread all or part of the selection to you and to each other during class or Independent Work Time to focus on the comprehension skills and to build fluency.

② Reading and Responding

Read pages 136–143.

Comprehension Strategies

Modeling

① Predicting *Good readers make predictions based on the text and their own knowledge, revising and confirming these predictions as they read. The title of this selection is "The Heavenly Zoo." The author writes about people seeing the sky as "full of magical pictures outlined with points of light." "Heavenly" must refer to the stars, and zoos are places with animals. I predict that this selection will be about animal constellations. As we read the rest of the page, I see that my prediction was correct.*

Modeling

② Making Connections *Good readers make connections between what they are reading and what they already know or have read. This gives them a deeper understanding of the text. I have read some myths about how constellations were formed. I wonder if these will be like the ones I already know.*

Word Knowledge

earliest, all-powerful, journeyed

Students can use the skills they learned in the Word Knowledge section of this lesson to read these words. Remind students of this if they have difficulty reading these words.

Reading Recommendation

ORAL · CHORAL · SILENT

The Heavenly Zoo

from *The Heavenly Zoo*
retold by Alison Lurie
illustrated by Monika Beisner

① From the earliest times people have looked at the night sky and tried to understand what they saw there. Long before anyone knew that the stars were great burning globes of gas many millions of miles from the earth and from one another, men and women saw the sky as full of magical pictures outlined with points of light.

What shapes ancient people saw in the sky depended on who and where they were. Thus the group of stars that we call the Big Dipper, which is part of the Great Bear, was known to the Egyptians as the Car of Osiris, to the Norse as Odin's Wagon, and in Britain first as King Arthur's Chariot and later as the Plough. Many of the pictures that we see today are very old. The constellation we call the Great Dog was first known as a dog five thousand years ago in Sumeria; Taurus the Bull was already a bull in Babylon and Egypt.

Our ancestors saw all sorts of things in the stars: men and women, gods and demons, rivers and ships. But what they saw most often were beasts, birds, and fish. And for most of these creatures there was a legend of how they came to be there.

②

136

Meeting Individual Needs

Inter**v**ention

Comprehension Intervention strategies for those students having difficulty with reading "The Heavenly Zoo" can be found in Unit 2, Lesson 3, of the *Intervention Guide.*

THE GREAT DOG

This story is from the Mahabharata, *which was written in India. Parts of this collection of stories were written more than two thousand years ago.*

Once upon a time in India there were five princes who left their kingdom to seek the kingdom of heaven. With them they took only food and drink for the journey; and the prince Yudistira brought his dog Svana.

Now besides Yudistira, who was the eldest, the brothers were Sahadeva the all-wise, who was learned beyond other men; Nakula the all-handsome, famed for his grace and beauty; Arjuna the all-powerful, who had never been defeated in any contest of arms; and Bhima the all-joyful, known far and wide for his good temper and love of pleasure.

So they set forth, and journeyed many days and many nights. Presently they came to a fair, where music was playing and people were drinking and dancing and feasting. Some of them saw Bhima the all-joyful, and called out for him to come and join them. Bhima said to himself, "I will rest here today and be happy, and seek the kingdom of heaven tomorrow." So he entered into the dance. And Yudistira and his brothers Sahadeva and Nakula and Arjuna and his dog Svana went on without him.

They traveled for many days and many nights, till they came to a broad plain where a great army was drawn up in ranks facing the enemy. When the soldiers saw Arjuna the all-powerful they shouted out, summoning him to come and lead them into battle.

137

Comprehension Skills

Making Inferences

Tell the students that readers make inferences by using information from the text along with their own knowledge to help them understand the total picture of a character or story event.

Point out the following information in "The Heavenly Zoo."

■ Bhima would rather dance than find the kingdom of heaven.

■ Arjuna goes to fight with his friends, rather than seek the kingdom of heaven.

Have students think of something they really want to do. Are they excited about it? Is it all they think about? Lead students to infer that, based on their own experiences, the princes are not serious about seeking the kingdom of heaven, because they are easily diverted from their goal.

Skills Strand

Making Inferences
INTRODUCED: Unit 1, Lesson 2
REVIEWED: Unit 1, Lesson 6
          Unit 2, Lesson 3
          Unit 3, Lesson 3
          Unit 4, Lesson 5

Teacher Tip Students may have trouble pronouncing the names in this selection. Osiris is pronounced ō sē′ris. Mahabharata is pronounced mə hä bä′ rə tə. Yudistira is pronounced yōō dis′ti ra. Sahadeva is pronounced sə hä dā′ vä. Nakula is pronounced nä′ku lä. Arjuna is pronounced ar′jōō nä. Bhima is pronounced bē′mä. Svana is pronounced svä′nä.

Research in Action

Comprehension

Comprehension of a selection is affected by what occurs before, during, and after reading. As the students discuss the selection and its relation to the concepts, notice the students who are having difficulties using concept-related terms or making connections between selections. These students may need additional, explicit instruction or modeling in the use of prior knowledge to make sense of new information. Modeling and corrective feedback are powerful tools for improving and refining comprehension skills. *(Michael Pressley)*

2 Reading and Responding

Comprehension Strategies

Prompting

3 Summarizing *Now is a good time to summarize what we have read so far. This will help us remember and understand the story. The story began with five princes seeking the doorway to heaven. One prince, Bhima, stopped searching to dance. Another one, Arjuna, stopped to join the army. Nakula stopped because he fell in love. Does anyone want to continue?*

Student Sample

Summarizing *After Nakula stopped because he fell in love, Sahadeva stopped to pray and study. Yudistira and Svana went on without him.*

Modeling

4 Predicting *Yudistira and Svana get to heaven, and Indra doesn't want to let the dog in. Will Yudistira enter the Kingdom of Heaven? I predict that he has come so far that he will. Let's read on to see.*

After reading, I see that he is loyal and won't leave his dog. That seems to serve him well because he gets into heaven anyway. So my prediction about him getting into Heaven was right.

Word Knowledge

all-handsome, appeared

Students can use the skills they learned in the Word Knowledge section of this lesson to read these words. Remind students of this if they have difficulty reading these words.

Arjuna said to himself, "I will fight today for my country, and seek the kingdom of heaven tomorrow." So he joined the soldiers; and Yudistira and his brothers Sahadeva and Nakula and his dog Svana went on without him.

So they traveled for many days and nights, till they came to a magnificent palace surrounded by a garden full of flowers and fountains; and in this garden a beautiful princess was walking with her attendants. When she saw Nakula the all-handsome she was seized with love and longing, and she cried out for him to come nearer. Nakula too was struck with love, and said to himself, "I will stay with this princess today, and seek the kingdom of heaven tomorrow." So he went into the garden, and Yudistira and his brother Sahadeva and his dog Svana went on without him.

They journeyed on for many weary days and nights, until they came to a great temple. When the holy men who lived there saw Sahadeva the all-wise they ran out, inviting him to come and join them in prayer and study. And Sahadeva said to himself, "I will stay here today, and seek the kingdom of heaven tomorrow." So he went into the temple, and Yudistira and his dog Svana went on without him.

3 At last Yudistira came to Mount Meru, which is the doorway to heaven. And Indra the Lord of Past and Present appeared before him, and invited him to ascend. Yudistira bowed low and replied, "Very willingly I will do so, if I may bring my dog Svana with me."

138

Teacher Tip

Meru is pronounced mā´ro͞o.
Indra is pronounced in´drä.

Meeting Individual Needs

Intervention

Predicting Remind students that their predictions should not be based on wild guesses. Have students summarize what they know about how Yudistira feels about his quest to find heaven and how he feels about Svana, his dog. Then have them base their predictions on that summary.

"That may not be," said Indra. "There is no place in heaven for dogs. Cast off this beast, and enter into <u>eternal</u> happiness."

"I cannot do that," said Yudistira. "I do not wish for any happiness for which I must cast off so dear a companion."

"You traveled on without your four brothers," said Indra. "Why will you not ascend to heaven without this dog?"

"My lord," replied Yudistira, "my brothers left me to follow the desires of their hearts. But Svana has given his heart to me; rather than <u>renounce</u> him I must renounce heaven."

"You have spoken well," said Indra. "Come in, and bring your dog with you." So Yudistira and Svana ascended into paradise; and Indra, in recognition of their devotion to each other, set in the sky the constellation of the *Great Dog,* whose central star Sirius is the brightest of all in the heavens.

4

139

Meeting Individual Needs

Reteach
Making Inferences Have students who need additional instruction and practice with this concept complete **Reteach,** pages 57-58.

Challenge
Making Inferences Have students who understand this concept complete **Challenge,** page 31.

Comprehension Skills

Making Inferences

For additional help in *making inferences,* ask the students to complete **Reading and Writing Workbook** pages 57–58.

Name _____ Date _____

Making Inferences

The Heavenly Zoo

Focus Good readers can make inferences about a character or event in a story.

> Making inferences is using information from the text, along with one's own experiences or knowledge, to
> • get a fuller understanding of story characters.
> • figure out a more complete picture of story events.

Identify Make an inference about each of the following characters from "The Heavenly Zoo." Then, write down the examples from the story that helped you make the inference.

Answers will vary. Possible answers are given below.

Orion: He became vain and boastful of his skills.

Examples: "Orion began to boast that he would soon have killed all the animals in Crete."

Yudistira: He is determined and is the only one of his brothers to complete the trip.

Examples: "My brothers left me to follow the desires of their hearts."

Arjuna: He was strong and powerful. He wants to fight in a battle.

Examples: Arjuna answered the soldiers that he would stay and "fight today for my country."

Reading and Writing Workbook • *Making Inferences*   57

Making Inferences *(continued)*

Practice Prepare to write a paragraph that will leave out information for the reader to infer. First, choose a famous person and write down his or her name. Then, list some characteristics or other information about the person. Answers will vary.

Famous person: _____

Characteristics or other information: _____

Apply Now, use your notes to write a paragraph about the person you chose. Do not use the person's name in your paragraph. Show your paragraph to a classmate to see if he or she can infer from your paragraph who the person is. Answers will vary.

58   *Making Inferences* • Reading and Writing Workbook

Reading and Writing Workbook pp. 57–58

2 Reading and Responding

Comprehension Strategies

Prompting

5 Summarizing *Let's summarize the important facts about the scorpion. Orion was a great hunter. One day, he boasted that he could kill all the wild animals in Crete. The scorpion didn't like this and killed him.*

Student Sample

Summarizing *After the scorpion killed Orion, the gods transported Orion to the sky instead of sending him to the underworld. The gods also raised the scorpion to the sky because he saved the animals of Crete.*

Discussing Strategy Use

After they have read the selection, have students share any problems they encountered and tell what strategies they used to solve them. Then, have them answer the following questions. If they answer "no" to any of the questions, have them reread part of the selection to find the answer.

- Did they make connections in the text to other myths they have read or heard?

- Did they stop to summarize during the selection to help them understand and remember all the information?

- Did they make and check predictions about what would happen?

Make sure that students explain how using the strategies helped them understand the selection better and how they read effectively to find answers to the questions they asked as they set purposes.

THE SCORPION

This story was told in ancient Greece.

Orion was one of the greatest of the Greek giants. Because he was the son of Poseidon, the god of the sea, he was as much at home in the water as on land. When he wished to get from one island to another he walked across on the bottom of the ocean; he was so tall that his head was always above the waves, and so large and broad that his travels caused high tides.

From childhood on Orion was famous for his beauty and his tremendous strength. He grew up to be a great hunter, able to track and slay all kinds of beasts with the help of his giant hound Sirius. When the island of Chios was oppressed and terrified by lions and wolves, Orion came to its assistance. He tracked down and destroyed every one, so that the people and their flocks could live in safety.

By the time Orion came to the large island of Crete, his fame was so great that Artemis, the goddess of the moon, invited him to go hunting with her. All went well until Orion, who had become vain of his skill, began to boast that he would soon have killed all the wild animals in Crete. Now the scorpion, who was listening, said to himself that this must not be. So he lay in wait for Orion, and stung him to death with his poisoned tail.

140

Meeting Individual Needs

ESL

Summarizing Encourage English-language learners to summarize aloud as a way of trying out their dialogue. Gauging an audience response helps develop the capacity to revise as students work toward a more finished version.

Teacher Tip Reread the selection with students who seem to be having trouble understanding the selection and participating in discussion. Continue to model strategies and comprehension skills.

But Orion's spirit did not have to go down to dwell in the Underworld with the souls of ordinary mortals. The gods, who loved him, transported him instead to the sky, where he can be seen in his golden armor and sword-belt, holding up his golden shield, with his faithful dog Sirius at his heel. The scorpion who saved the wild animals of Crete was also raised into the heavens, and became a constellation in the southern sky.

⑤ Every night, as the *Scorpion* rises, Orion fades and vanishes.

141

Meeting Individual Needs

Challenge

Making Inferences Break students into small groups. Review the definition of making inferences, then invite them to discuss what generalizations they can make about ancient Grecian values by reading the section on "The Scorpion."

Assessment

✓ **Formal** To assess students' reading comprehension and have them complete *Comprehension and Writing Assessment,* pages 33–34.

Teacher Tip Sirius is pronounced sir´ē əs. Chios is pronounced kē´ōs.

Comprehension
Skills

Discussing the Selection

Following reading, engage the students in discussion of the selection. Using the *handing-off process* will help the students take responsibility for the discussion. In addition to the following questions, have them revisit any questions asked when they set purposes before reading.

■ What did you learn about constellations? *(There are many stories about how the constellations were formed.)*

■ What do you infer was valued in ancient India? *(loyalty)*

■ What do you infer was not valued in ancient Greece? *(being boastful)*

■ How has this selection connected with your knowledge of the unit theme? *(Answers will vary—students should compare/contrast examples of astronomy from this selection with their own experiences or past reading and use these connections to make a general statement about the unit theme.)*

During this time, have the students return to the clues and problems that they noted on the transparency before reading. Let the students decide which items deserve further discussion.

Often, students who are taking responsibility for controlling a discussion tend to have all "turns" go through the teacher, and the teacher is the one who is expected to call on the next speaker, the result being that the teacher remains the pivotal figure in the discussion. The teacher's main roles should be to occasionally remind students to hand off and to ensure that everyone gets a chance to contribute.

2 Reading and Responding

Meet the Author

After the students read the information about Alison Lurie, discuss the following questions with them.

What does it mean when we say that Alison Lurie reinvented her world through writing? *(Possible answer: It means that Alison Lurie was able to make the wonderful world in her imagination come to life by writing about it.)*

What is an example of how Alison Lurie was able to take something bad that happened to her and turn it into something good? *(Possible answer: Even though she often felt lonely as a child, she spent the time she had by herself developing her imagination, which she used in her writing.)*

Meet the Illustrator

After the students read the information about Monika Beisner, discuss the following questions with them.

Why do you think Monika Beisner likes to imagine living in a world where nothing is as you would expect it to be? *(Possible answer: She likes to imagine places where nothing is as you would expect it to be because she wonders how she would react to the surprising things that would happen to her.)*

What stories does Monika Beisner tell in her illustrations for "The Heavely Zoo?" *(Answers will vary.)*

The Heavenly Zoo

Meet the Author

Alison Lurie always felt like an outcast as a child. Born in 1926, she was deaf in one ear due to an injury at birth. This injury also damaged the muscles in her face, causing her mouth to turn sideways and her smile to look like a sneer. Often ignored by other children, she learned from an early age to entertain herself by making up stories and poems. Through writing, she could reinvent her world. This talent led her to study English in college. Today she lives in New York, and is an author and English professor. *The Heavenly Zoo: Legends and Tales of the Stars* was her first children's book. She went on to also write *Clever Gretchen and Other Forgotten Folktales* and *Fabulous Beasts*.

Meet the Illustrator

Monika Beisner is an author and illustrator who lives in England. She is fascinated with mysterious lands and creatures. One of her favorite things to imagine is what it would be like to live in a world where nothing is as you expect it to be. Reading her stories is like walking into just such a world, with a surprise around every corner. Her illustrations are also full of surprises and hidden meanings. The places she paints are odd, but almost life-like. In ways, her pictures are like beautiful puzzles. People who look at their details long enough, find that she tells as many stories through her paintings, as she does with words.

142

Theme Connections

Think About It

With a small group of classmates, consider what this selection has taught you about the beliefs and values of the ancient Indian and Greek cultures.

- What are some similarities between the two myths presented in this selection?
- Many ancient cultures devised myths about the constellations. Why did people of long ago make up these stories?

Check the Concept/Question Board to see if there are any questions there that you can answer now. If the selection or your discussions about the selection have raised any new questions about astronomy, put the questions on the Concept/Question Board. Maybe the next selection will help answer the questions.

Record Ideas

Why do cultures preserve myths that are no longer taken seriously as explanations for natural phenomena? Record your notes and ideas in your Writing Journal.

Research Ideas

- Investigate constellation myths from a variety of cultures.
- Find out more about the origins of "The Great Dog," which is thought to be based on actual events that took place between 1400 B.C. and 1000 B.C.

143

Theme Connections

Think About It

- As students discuss the ancient Greek and Indian constellation myths, circulate and observe the discussions.

- Have students compare and contrast ancient Greek and Indian cultures based on this selection and previous reading.

- Have the students report what they discussed. Encourage them to record on the Concept/Question Board any questions they may have.

Research Ideas

Students who are interested in reading about the origins of other constellations should look for books in the library. Alison Lurie's *The Heavenly Zoo: Legends and Tales of the Stars* is a good source.

Questions that arise from reading the selections provide good springboards for research ideas. Always ask the students what each selection makes them wonder about. Encourage students to verbalize their inquiries.

2 Responding

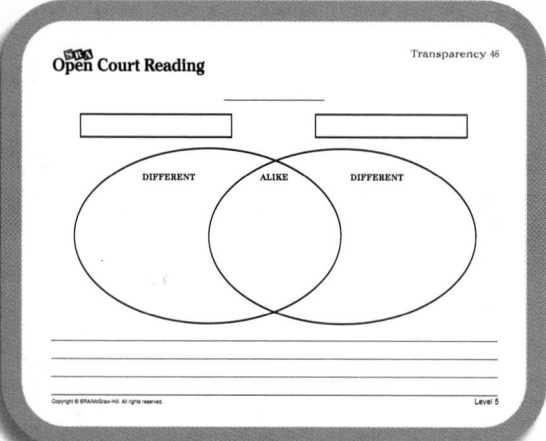

Transparency 46

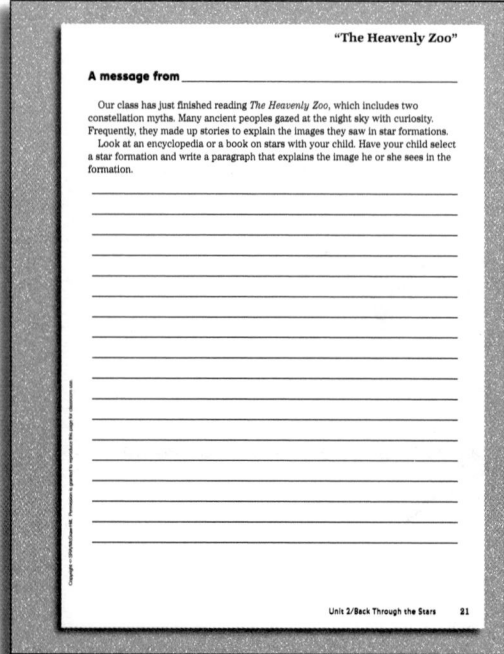

Home Connection p. 21

Exploring the Theme

Selection Vocabulary

Have students write in their Writing Journals the definitions for words discussed before the reading of the selection and any other interesting words they clarified while reading. Students should be encouraged to refer to these words throughout the unit as they work on student and writing projects. The words from this selection are:

ancestors	attendants	summoning
	heavens	vain

Reading/Writing Connections

Divide the class into groups. Have each group prepare a skit based on one of the myths in "The Heavenly Zoo." Have groups create dialogue for their characters. Students may wish to make masks or other costumes for their characters. Allow time for the groups to practice their skits before presenting them to the class.

Literature Appreciation

Have students think about how Galileo and astronomers who have followed him have changed how people think of the universe compared to people's thoughts when the stories in "The Heavenly Zoo" were created. Use the Venn diagram on *Transparency 46* to note the similarities and differences that students suggest.

Home Connection

The class has just finished reading "The Heavenly Zoo," constellation myths about a loyal prince and a heroic scorpion. An informational letter on "The Heavenly Zoo," in both English and Spanish, can be found in the *Home Connection* guide.

Supporting Student Explorations

At this point students should be conducting research. You may want to do the following:

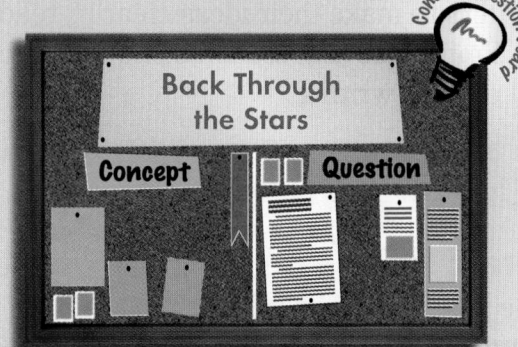

Whole Group Explain to students that to help focus their research, they should make conjectures as to what the answers to their research questions might be. Explain that a *conjecture* is a kind of educated guess based on research and one's own knowledge of how things work, and it attempts to explain something without a great deal of evidence. Model for students how to make a conjecture.

Then, tell students that the purpose of further research should be to prove or disprove the validity of their conjectures. Tell students that a conjecture is considered valid if one can find enough evidence to support it. Through further research, they may find it is necessary to revise their conjectures or even their research questions. Tell students that this is a normal part of research and that sometimes researchers must revise their questions and conjectures many times before coming to a conclusion about their topics.

Small Group Have groups brainstorm conjectures about their unit activity subjects. As you observe the groups discussing their conjectures, encourage them to record each group member's ideas. Have students revise their conjectures and questions as they collect information. Rephrasing the students' conjectures will help you elicit additional information from the groups and will help them clarify and refine their ideas.

Suggest that students post on the Concept/Question Board brief descriptions of books, magazine articles, computer Websites, or other sources of information that they have found to be especially helpful in their explorations of astronomy. Encourage students who are having difficulty finding information to check sources on the Board and to post their questions as well.

Inquiry Journal
Have students complete page 21 of the *Inquiry Journal* as they continue to write ideas and conjectures for their research activity.

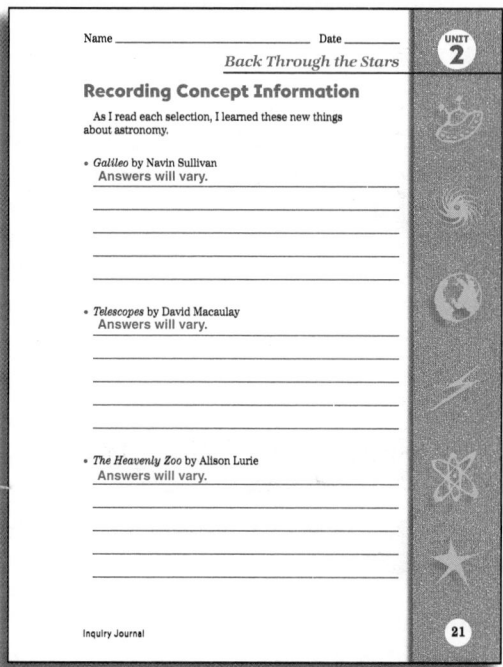

Name _____ Date _____
Back Through the Stars

UNIT 2

Recording Concept Information

As I read each selection, I learned these new things about astronomy.

• *Galileo* by Navin Sullivan
  Answers will vary.

• *Telescopes* by David Macaulay
  Answers will vary.

• *The Heavenly Zoo* by Alison Lurie
  Answers will vary.

Inquiry Journal

21

Inquiry Journal p. 21

Assessment
✓ **Informal** At this point in the project students are doing active research. Check to be sure that students:
■ understand conjecture.
■ record ideas.
■ use varied resources.

③ Integrating the Curriculum

Language Arts

Writing

Writing Paragraphs and Topic Sentences

Instruct Prompt students to explain that a paragraph is a group of two or more sentences that discuss the same main idea. Explain that paragraphs are used to organize information *(an idea with examples illustrating it, a description, a series of steps, or a set of related facts).*

Practice Focus students' attention on the first paragraph of "The Scorpion" from "The Heavenly Zoo." Identify the topic sentence of the paragraph *("Orion was one of the greatest of Greek giants."),* then explain how the other sentences support this main idea. Have students duplicate this process using other paragraphs from this selection.

Apply Using the prewriting exercises students worked on in Lessons 1 and 2, have students start writing about their chosen topic. Explain that each paragraph should be about a new subject or a new part of a larger idea. Remind students that a strong topic sentence is a good way for writers to make their ideas clear to readers.

Emphasize that students should check for good paragraph structure in all of their writing.

Writing Process

Draft During the drafting phase, students quickly shape their notes from the planning and brainstorming session into main ideas and details. Tell students that the main ideas will become topic sentences, and the details will become supporting sentences—the goal is to get their ideas into paragraph form. Remind students to keep in mind their purpose for writing and their intended audience.

Encourage students to write on every other line in order to leave space for revisions. Tell students that proper sentence structure and correct spelling and punctuation can wait. They may use abbreviations, cross out unnecessary words, and leave space when they need to find an exact word. They will revise their drafts and proofread their work, making necessary corrections, later.

 **Teacher Tip** Allow adequate time for writing. Students may not all work at the same pace, or they may not be able to concentrate on their writing for more than fifteen to twenty minutes. Some students may still be thinking while others are writing, muttering to themselves, or reading what they have written. Some may feel stuck during the writing phase and may need to go back and try a different prewriting technique.

 **Teacher Tip** It may help students if you model the drafting process on the chalkboard. Think aloud as you put your ideas into words. Work as fast as you can. Leave a blank space in a sentence to show you are having difficulty thinking of the best word. Put parentheses around a word you intend to change. Use abbreviations and invented spellings. Cross out words and sentences, or draw arrows to show where they should be moved.

Meeting Individual Needs

Intervention

Draft Intervention strategies for students who need more help can be found in Unit 2, Lesson 3, of the *Intervention Guide.*

Literary Elements

Recognizing Myths

Instruct Ask students if they know what a myth is. If necessary, discuss with students that myths:

■ explain imaginatively why something in nature happens or looks the way it does—for example, why lightning occurs, or why frogs live in ponds.

■ explain why people act the way they do—for example, why they like some people and dislike others.

■ are often about gods and goddesses as well as humans.

Practice Have students discuss why both of the stories in "The Heavenly Zoo" meet the criteria for being myths. Students should mention that both explain the natural phenomenon of constellations, and both involve interaction with gods. You may also want to discuss with students that, while they do not explain why people act the way they do, both stories do prescribe how people should act. For example, Yudistira is rewarded for his loyalty when Indra allows him to bring Svana into heaven, and the gods honor both Orion and the Scorpion because in life, both had used their abilities to protect others.

Apply Have students name other stories with the characteristics of myths. For additional practice on myths have students complete *Reading and Writing Workbook,* pages 59–60.

Meeting Individual Needs

Reteach
Recognizing Myths Have students who need additional instruction and practice with this concept complete *Reteach,* pages 59–60.

Challenge
Recognizing Myths Challenge each student to work with a partner to develop a plot outline for a myth to explain something in nature. Remind them to keep in mind the characteristics described in the lesson. Have students who understand this concept complete *Challenge,* page 32.

Intervention
Recognizing Myths Have students who need more help understanding the characteristics of myths select a simple myth and read it aloud, pointing out what the myth explains.

Reading and Writing Workbook pp. 59–60

Name _____ Date _____
Recognizing Myths   *The Heavenly Zoo*

Focus Myths are stories that have been told for centuries in cultures all around the world. Because they were originally told by word of mouth, different versions of myths appear in written form.

> **Myths**
> • often explain something about nature.
> • suggest mystical reasons for why natural events occur.
> • feature main characters who have a special gift or skill.

Identify Look through the two stories in "The Heavenly Zoo." Write down details from each story that indicate the stories are both myths. Details will vary. Possible answers are provided.
Details from "The Great Dog": the five brothers set out to discover the kingdom of heaven; Mount Meru, the doorway to heaven; Indra invited Yudistira to ascend into heaven

Details from "The Scorpion": Orion walked across the bottom of the ocean; he was so tall that his head was always above the waves; he destroyed all lions and wolves on Chios; the gods transported him into the sky

Reading and Writing Workbook • Recognizing Myths   **59**

Recognizing Myths *(continued)*

Practice After each story description, explain why each story is a myth. Answers will vary.

1. Baal, the creator of storms, uses his mace to make thunder. Then, with his lance, he creates lightning, which flashes across the sky.

2. Demeter, the ruler of growing things, is sad when her daughter Persephone goes to live for four months of every year with Hades, ruler of the underworld. As a result, she allows nothing to grow during the time each year that her daughter is gone. This story is an explanation for why there are seasons.

Apply Read a myth that you've checked out from your school or local library. Write the name of the story, then explain why the story is a myth. Answers will vary.

Title of story: _____
Explanation: _____

60   *Recognizing Myths • Reading and Writing Workbook*

 Tell students that many myths have been told and retold for hundreds of years. *Oral tradition,* the passing of stories from generation to generation by word of mouth, has kept these myths alive since long before it was common to read or write books. These stories have had "staying power" because they contain bits and pieces of the history, values, and beliefs of the people who have told them. For this reason, studying the oral tradition within a certain region or culture can reveal much about the people who have occupied it. Ask students what they can infer about the Greek and Indian cultures from the myths in this lesson. Why do they think these stories are still told?

 **Integrating the Curriculum**

Meeting Individual Needs

Reteach

Listening Vocabulary Have students who need additional instruction and practice with this concept complete **Reteach,** pages 61–62.

ESL

Listening Strategies If listening to an entire article about astronomy or mythology read aloud would be too much for English-language learners to absorb, let them hear one or two sentences from an English speaker and use that as a basis for a discussion of listening strategies and vocabulary expansion.

Challenge

Listening Vocabulary Have students begin a list of words that they learned through listening. Have students write an original sentence for each word. Have them share their sentences with classmates. Have students who understand this concept complete **Challenge,** page 33.

Intervention

Listening Vocabulary If students have difficulty dealing with unfamiliar words in spoken material, offer them more practice in the form of sentences and then paragraphs read aloud. As you say each sentence, ask students if there are words they do not understand. Help them recognize the clues to meaning in preceding and following sentences.

Listening Vocabulary

INTRODUCED: Unit 2, Lesson 3
REVIEWED: Unit 2, Lesson 6
Unit 2, Lesson 8

Vocabulary

Developing Vocabulary by Listening

Instruct Ask students to suggest ways that they can learn the meanings of unfamiliar words that they hear *(listen for context clues, read ahead, look at pictures or other visual aids, find the word in a dictionary).*

- Point out that some of the same techniques that are used for reading can be used when listening, too. Discuss the following points:

  Sometimes a definition for a word is given in the same sentence.

  Sometimes the next few sentences suggest enough about the word for the listener to understand the whole concept.

- In a TV show or movie, the action often gives clues to word meaning. Remind students that, unless they are alone watching a movie with a VCR, or listening to a tape or CD, they cannot stop and rewind. Suggest that they jot down any unfamiliar words and look them up in a dictionary later.

Practice Choose a book or article related to astronomy or another myth or legend and read it to students. Tell them to practice the techniques suggested above. After reading, ask students to share the words that were unfamiliar to them and how they have discovered or will discover their meanings.

Apply For additional practice, have students complete *Reading and Writing Workbook,* pages 61–62.

Reading and Writing Workbook pp. 61–62

Name _____ Date _____

Developing Vocabulary by Listening

The Heavenly Zoo

Focus Writers can develop their vocabularies by listening carefully for unfamiliar words.

When you hear an unfamiliar word,
- write the word.
- listen for familiar word parts that could provide clues about the meaning of the word.
- listen for other sentences that include the word to help make the meaning clear.
- think about what the definition might be.
- discuss the word with another person.
- look up the word in a dictionary later.

Practice With a partner, read aloud each sentence below. Discuss the meaning of the underlined word and circle the clue word or words in the sentence that help to explain its meaning.

1. The hero was weary after the long, tiring travel home.
2. Yudistira's brothers were all summoned, or called away, from their journey.
3. Svana was Yudistira's true friend and companion, because he stayed with Yudistira for the entire journey.
4. Orion was asked to live with the gods instead of dwelling in the Underworld.
5. He was seized with love and captured by her beauty.

Reading and Writing Workbook • *Developing Vocabulary by Listening* 61

Developing Vocabulary by Listening *(continued)*

Apply Write a story that explains how the Big Dipper (or the Great Bear) was created. Include some of the vocabulary words you learned from "The Heavenly Zoo." Stories will vary.

62 *Developing Vocabulary by Listening* • Reading and Writing Workbook

Grammar, Usage, & Mechanics

Present-Tense Verbs—Regular and Irregular

Instruct Prompt students to tell you that a present-tense verb names an action that is happening now or that happens repeatedly.

1. If the subject of a sentence is singular, add the -s or -es inflectional ending to a regular verb to form the present tense. If the verb ends with a consonant followed by *y*, change the *y* to *i* before adding -es. For example: *Mom <u>pulls</u> over. A fire truck <u>passes</u> our car and <u>hurries</u> away.*

2. If the subject is *I* or *you*, there is no ending added to a regular verb. For example: *I <u>smell</u> smoke. You <u>cover</u> your nose.*

3. If the subject is plural, do not add an ending to a regular verb. For example: *Firefighters <u>put</u> out the flames. They <u>save</u> people.*

4. Verbs that do not follow the above rules are called irregular verbs. They have special forms to use. Here are some examples:

Verb	Present-Tense Forms
be	I *am.* You *are.* We *are.* They *are.* He *is.* She *is.* It *is.*
do	I *do.* We *do.* You *do.* They *do.* He *does.* She *does.* It *does.*
have	I *have.* We *have.* You *have.* They *have.* He *has.* She *has.* It *has.*

Practice Have volunteers find and read aloud sentences from the ***Student Anthology*** containing regular and irregular present-tense verbs. Then have students identify the verb, whether it is regular or irregular, and how it reflects that the subject is singular or plural.

Apply For additional practice, have students complete ***Reading and Writing Workbook,*** pages 63–64.

Reading and Writing Workbook pp. 63–64

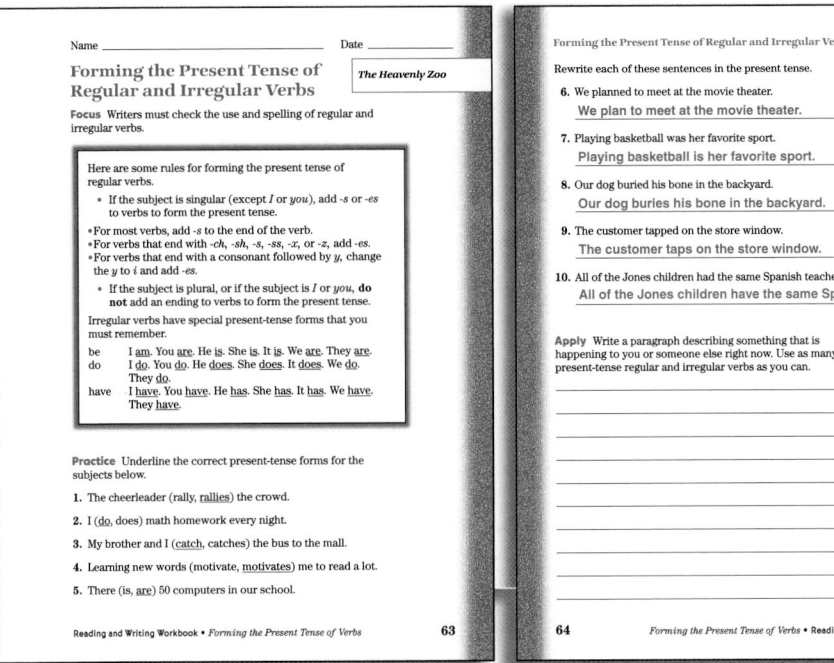

Meeting Individual Needs

Reteach

Regular and Irregular Verbs Have students who need additional instruction and practice with this concept complete ***Reteach,*** pages 63–64.

Challenge

Regular and Irregular Verbs Challenge students to write two original sentences for each of the rules using present-tense verbs. Then, have them trade their sentences with a partner. Ask them to underline the verb in each sentence on their partner's paper and identify which rule it follows. Have partners trade papers again and check each other's work. Have students who understand this concept complete ***Challenge,*** page 34.

Skills Strand

Regular and Irregular Verbs

INTRODUCED:	Unit 2, Lesson 3
REVIEWED:	Unit 2, Lesson 4
	Unit 3, Lesson 2
	Unit 6, Lesson 1

Have students check for correct use and spelling of regular and irregular verbs in their expository papers and unit activities.

3 Integrating the Curriculum

Meeting Individual Needs

ESL

Card and Computer Catalog Have students name a subject that interests them. Encourage students to use the card or computer catalog to find one fiction, two nonfiction, and three reference books about their subject. Tell students to write the titles, authors, and call numbers on index cards to reference during the current or future research projects.

Intervention

Card and Computer Catalog Have each student who needs more practice with a card or computer catalog choose a book from the class library and create a subject card, title card, and author card for his or her book.

Teacher Tip If your school library does not have electronic files, you may wish to plan a trip to a local library that does so that students can explore the computer catalog.

Assessment

✓ **Formal** To assess students' understanding of this concept, have them complete *Skills Assessment,* page 15.

Study and Research

Card and Computer Catalog

Instruct Remind students that most libraries have card catalogs, either with index cards in drawers or on computers. Prompt students to tell you that each book is included three times—by the title of the book, by the author's name, and by the subject of the book.

- Point out that each card contains the same information about the book—title, author, illustrator, subject, publisher, date of publication, number of pages, a summary, and a call number that tells where the book can be found in the library.

- Call on a volunteer to tell where one would look in the card catalog to locate books about the constellations *(under Constellations).*

- Ask where one would look in the card catalog to find other books by Alison Lurie *(in the card catalog under Lurie).* Point out that there will be a card for each book Alison Lurie has written.

Practice Write the following three items on the chalkboard and have students tell how they would find the item in the card catalog:

> *The Way Things Work (by title)*
> astronomy *(by subject)*
> David Macaulay *(by author)*

Apply For additional practice, give students a short list of authors, subjects, and titles. Have them identify on their own how they would find each item in the card catalog.

Remind students that the guidelines they are learning for using a card or computer catalog will be useful to them as they look for resources for their research activities and papers. Then have students complete ***Inquiry Journal,*** page 30.

Inquiry Journal p. 30

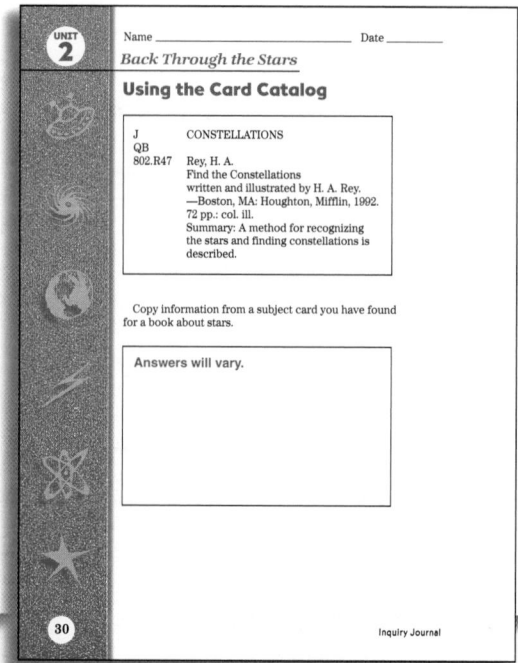

Across the Curriculum

Science

Finding Our Own Constellations

Purpose

To encourage students to examine the stars in a personal way

Materials

Photocopies of an astronomical chart of the stars for everyone in the classroom, markers, lined paper

Procedure

Remind students of Yudistira's devotion to his dog, Svana. Does this remind them of their pets, places, or people that students would like to remember by naming them in the night sky?

■ Encourage students to examine their photocopy of the stars with a partner.

■ Ask students to look carefully at the stars and find their own constellations, perhaps in the shape of a favorite pet. Have students use their markers to connect the stars that form their constellation and then have them name the constellation.

■ Have students work with their partners to write a story about their constellation in one or two paragraphs.

■ Invite volunteers to draw their constellations on the chalkboard and share their significance with the class.

Health

Making a Safety Poster

Purpose

To help students recognize the dangers of the sun

Materials

Large sheets of paper, markers, crayons

Procedure

Remind students that the sun is also a star. It seems bigger than the other stars because it is the closest star to Earth.

■ Discuss the dangers that exposure to the sun can pose, including sunburn, heatstroke, eye damage, and cancer risk. List the students' suggestions on the chalkboard.

■ Ask students to suggest ways to minimize the dangers while enjoying time outside. They may suggest wearing long-sleeved clothing, hats, and sunglasses; the application of sunscreen; avoiding the sun during the midday hours; and limiting exposure time to the sun.

■ Have each student create a poster about dangers and safety tips to make time in the sun enjoyable and safe. Display the completed posters in the classroom or hallway.

Circles, Squares, and Daggers:

How Native Americans Watched the Skies

by Elsa Marston

You have probably heard about stargazers of the past such as the ancient Egyptians, the builders of Stonehenge, and the Mayas. Did you know that Native Americans, too, made astronomical observatories—long before Europeans arrived?

The study of these ancient observatories is called *archaeoastronomy*. By combining astronomy with archaeology, we are beginning to understand how people of the past observed the skies.

Archaeoastronomy is a very new field. The Native American observatories have been discovered—or their purposes understood—only recently. Most of the sites had been abandoned centuries ago, and their original uses had been forgotten.

Let's look at some of the different ways Native Americans devised to follow the movements of the sun and, in certain cases, the stars.

144

About the Author

Elsa Marston's talents lie in both art and literature. To this combination she adds a lifelong interest in history. In 1983, she won the Short Story Award from the Illinois Wesleyan Writers' Conference. Her first book for young adults, *The Cliffs of Cairo*, features a mystery that involves the art and history of medieval Cairo.

Students can read more about Elsa Marston on page 152 of the ***Student Anthology.***

Other Books by Elsa Marston
- *How to Be a Helper*
- *The Dogs of Rue Astarte*
- *Stray Friends of Hercules*

Selection Summary

Genre: Nonfiction

Lacking calendars and clocks, early Native Americans relied on the sun and stars to tell them when to plant crops, prepare for winter, or hold ceremonies. This selection introduces readers to the field of archaeoastronomy as it describes the workings of sophisticated early observatories erected by Native Americans to help them track the passing of time and the changing of the seasons.

Exploring the Theme

Selection Concepts

Even before people knew much about the sun, they were aware of its influence over their lives. The Native American peoples described in "Circles, Squares, and Daggers" had no knowledge about what the sun and other stars were made of or how they came to be, but they could and did observe the movement of the sun and stars over long periods of time. Key concepts to be explored are:

- Early Native Americans relied on the sun and stars to tell them when to plant crops, prepare for winter, and hold ceremonies.
- The field of archaeoastronomy involves the study of ancient observatories and the observation of the skies.

 Check the Reading link of the **SRA** Web page for links to theme-related Websites.
http://www.sra4kids.com

Exploration Activity Tips

Before Reading, ask the students why certain dates are important—what dates are important to them and what dates or times of year would have been important to people long ago. Have the students discuss what they know about how people measured time before clocks and calendars were invented.

During Reading, tell students to use visualization as a strategy for understanding the selection. Have students draw their own diagrams to aid comprehension.

After Reading, have students discuss how the ancient observatories worked. Allow them to draw diagrams on the chalkboard. Then have students update the Concept/Question Board. Some may want to revise their activity plans based on what they have learned from the selection.

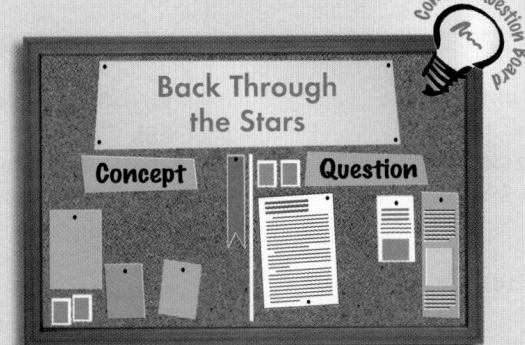

Unit 2 Exploration Management

Lesson 1	Brainstorm research problems. Form interest-based groups. Develop and discuss initial research plans.
Lesson 2	Groups finalize plans, allocate tasks, and begin research. Discuss initial findings and resources.
Lesson 3	Research continues as groups consider revision of their activity focus.
Lesson 4 Circles, Squares, and Daggers	**Collaborative Exploration** **Students continue with research and present their initial findings.** **Supplementary Activity** **Conduct class discussion of problems and conjectures. List knowledge needs and possible sources of information.**
Lesson 5	Research continues. Students present interesting findings or problems.
Lesson 6	Research continues. Students present interesting findings or problems.
Lesson 7	Students organize research findings and prepare presentations.
Lesson 8	Students present their activities.

Lesson Planner

Suggested Pacing: 3–5 days	DAY 1	DAY 2	

Part 1 — Preparing to Read

Materials
- Student Anthology, pp. 144–153
- Transparencies 10, 44

DAY 1:
Word Knowledge
- Reading the Words and Sentences, p. 144G
- Developing Oral Language, p. 144G

Build Background, p. 144H

Preview and Prepare, p. 144I

Selection Vocabulary, p. 144I
astronomical observatories, archaeoastronomy, horizon, carbon dating, petroglyphs

DAY 2:
Preview and Prepare, p. 144I
- Review Transparency 44

Part 2 — Reading and Responding

Materials
- Student Anthology, pp. 144–155
- Teacher Observation Log
- Reading and Writing Workbook, pp. 65–66
- Inquiry Journal, p. 22
- Home Connection, p. 23

DAY 1:
Student Anthology, pp. 144–153

Comprehension Strategies
- Clarifying, pp. 144, 146, 150
- Visualizing, p. 148
- Making Connections, p. 144

Discussing Strategy Use, p. 150

DAY 2:
Student Anthology, pp. 144–153

Comprehension Skills
- ✓ Main Idea and Details, p. 145
- ✓ Discussing the Selection, p. 151

Exploring the Theme
- Selection Vocabulary, p. 155A
astronomical observatories, archaeoastronomy, horizon, carbon dating, petroglyphs

---

Part 3 — Integrating the Curriculum

Materials
- Student Anthology, pp. 144–153
- Inquiry Journal, p. 31

DAY 1:
Writing
- Writing Paragraphs, p. 155C

Literary Elements
- Informational Text, p. 155E

DAY 2:
Writing Process
- Draft, p. 155D

Vocabulary
- Meanings of Derivatives, p. 155F

Independent Work Time

Materials
- Reteach, pp. 65–66
- ESL Supplement
- Challenge, p. 35
- Intervention Guide
- Research CD-ROM
- Listening Library Audiocassette

DAY 1:
Writing Process Continued
ESL
- Word Meaning, p. 144G
- Cultural Context, p. 144H

Intervention
- Plurals, p. 144G
- Comprehension, p. 144

Unit Project
- Continue Research
- Present Initial Findings

DAY 2:
Writing Process Continued
ESL
- Vocabulary, p. 144J
- Derivatives, p. 155F

Challenge
- Derivatives, p. 155F

Intervention
- Main Idea and Details, p. 145
- Draft, p. 155F

Unit Project Continued

✓ Informal **Assessment Available**   ✓ **Formal Assessment Available**

DAY 2 continued	DAY 3	
DAY 3	DAY 4	DAY 5
General Review	**General Review**	**Review Word Knowledge**
Student Anthology, pp. 144–153 **Comprehension Skills** ✓ ■ Classifying and Categorizing, pp. 147, 149 **Theme Connections** ■ Think About It, p. 153 ■ Research Ideas, p. 153	**Student Anthology, pp. 144–153** **Fine Art, pp. 154–155** **Exploring the Theme** ■ Reading/Writing Connections, p. 155A ■ View Fine Art, p. 155A ■ Supporting Student Explorations, p. 155B	**Student Anthology, pp. 144–153** ■ Review Selection ■ Complete Discussion ■ Reread Selection in Pairs **Home Connection, p. 155A** ■ Discuss "Circles, Squares, and Daggers: How Native Americans Watched the Sky" ■ Research a seasonal Native American ritual
Writing Process Continued **Grammar, Usage, and Mechanics** ✓ ■ Present-Tense Verbs—Regular and Irregular, p. 155G **Listening/Speaking/Viewing** ■ Using Media, p. 155H	**Writing Process Continued** **Study and Research** ■ Outlining, p. 155I	**Across the Curriculum** **Math** ■ Astronomy Word Problems, p. 155J **Social Studies** ■ Names in Space, p. 155J
Writing Process Continued **Reteach** ✓ ■ Classifying and Categorizing, *Reteach*, pp. 65–66 **Challenge** ✓ ■ Classifying and Categorizing, *Challenge*, p. 35 **Intervention** ■ Classifying and Categorizing, p. 147 **Unit Project Continued**	**Writing Process Continued** **Challenge** ■ Irregular Verbs, p. 155G **Unit Project Continued**	**Writing Process Continued** **Unit Project Continued**

Meeting Individual Needs
Independent Work Time

Preparing to Read

Meeting Individual Needs

ESL
- Word Meaning, p. 144G
- Cultural Context, p. 144H
- Vocabulary, p. 144J

Intervention
- Plurals, p. 144G

Reading and Responding

Meeting Individual Needs

Reteach
- Classifying and Categorizing, *Reteach*, pp. 65–66

ESL
- Discussion, p. 151

Challenge
- Main Idea and Details, p. 145
- Classifying and Categorizing, *Challenge*, p. 35

Intervention
- Comprehension, p. 144
- Main Idea and Details, p. 145
- Clarifying, p. 146
- Classifying and Categorizing, p. 147

Integrating the Curriculum

Meeting Individual Needs

ESL
- Derivatives, p. 155F

Challenge
- Derivatives, p. 155F
- Irregular Verbs, p. 155G

Intervention
- Draft, p. 155D

Formal Assessment Options

Use these assessment pages along with your informal observations to gauge student progress.

Name _____ **Date** _____

Main Idea and Details

Read the story and the questions. Fill in the circle next to the best answer to each question.

The Inca nation was one of the most highly organized Native American nations. The Inca created a vast, well-organized society in the mountains of South America in the region now known as Peru. They built a vast highway system that improved transportation and communication. The Inca did not have a written language, but they created a unique form of communication called quipu. Runners traversed the highways carrying quipu, which were devices composed of specially knotted strings that were deciphered to relay messages.

The Inca army earned a reputation for efficiency. Once the Inca conquered a village, they allowed the village to join the empire peacefully by allowing the villagers to keep their customs and deities. However, the Inca expected the conquered villages to add Inca customs and deities to their own. The Inca also expected conquered villages to pay tribute to Sappa Inca, the ruler of the empire.

The Sappa Inca was respected as a wise and powerful descendant of the Sun god. Tribute was paid in gold, grain, and labor, and much of it went to build and maintain Inca temples. A portion of the grain tribute was redistributed to the people during emergencies, such as crop failures or earthquakes, so no one in the Inca empire ever went hungry.

1. What is the main idea of this article?
   ○ It is hard to communicate or transport goods in the mountains.
   ● The Inca empire was well organized.
   ○ The Inca army was not as violent as the Aztec army.

2. The Inca army's reputation for efficiency contributed to the growth and order of the empire by:
   ○ continuous fighting
   ○ the punishments it inflicted upon the people it conquered
   ● encouraging villages to join the empire peacefully

3. What does the final sentence in the article suggest?
   ○ The people were forced to pay high tribute, but they still had enough to eat.
   ○ The Inca empire grew more grain than it needed.
   ● The empire's emergency plan benefitted the people.

16   Copyright © SRA/McGraw-Hill   Skills Assessment

Skills Assessment, p. 16

Name _____ **Date** _____

Regular and Irregular Verbs

Read each sentence. Fill in the circle next to the correct form of the verb to complete the sentence.

1. The firefighters _____ the blaze and put it out.
   ○ fighted   ○ fights   ● fought   ○ fighting

2. I should have _____ the floor yesterday.
   ○ sweeped   ○ sweep   ○ sweeping   ● swept

3. My friends and I _____ apples at the orchard.
   ○ picks   ○ picking   ● picked   ○ be picking

4. Your father _____ his coat here.
   ● left   ○ leave   ○ leaving   ○ are leaving

5. The Martins will need help _____ their piano.
   ○ move   ● moving   ○ moved   ○ moves

6. We all _____ bad about losing the game.
   ○ feels   ○ feeling   ○ have feeled   ● felt

7. By tomorrow, we will _____ all the children's stories.
   ● have heard   ○ heard   ○ hearing   ○ hears

8. The family _____ their grandmother at the airport.
   ○ meet   ○ meeting   ● met   ○ have met

9. Marge _____ two baseball bats this week.
   ○ breaks   ○ breaking   ● has broken   ○ break

10. Everyone _____ hard for the Brain Games.
    ○ study   ● studied   ○ studying   ○ is studied

Skills Assessment   Copyright © SRA/McGraw-Hill   17

Skills Assessment, p. 17

Name _____ **Date** _____

Circles, Squares, and Daggers: How Native Americans Watched the Skies

1. The study of how people of the past observed the skies is called
   ○ **a.** astroarchaeology.
   ● **b.** archaeoastronomy.
   ○ **c.** archaeoastrology.

2. The Bighorn Medicine Wheel is found on a plateau high in the mountains of Wyoming. What is a **plateau**?
   It is an area of high, flat land.
   _____
   _____
   _____

3. Early Native Americans' medicine wheels were
   ○ **a.** laboratories.
   ● **b.** observatories.
   ○ **c.** conservatories.

4. The Moose Mountain Medicine Wheel was discovered in
   ● **a.** Saskatchewan, Canada.
   ○ **b.** Cahokia, Illinois.
   ○ **c.** Chaco Canyon, New Mexico.

5. The "sun daggers" are the work of a group of Native Americans called
   ○ **a.** the Poncas.
   ● **b.** the Anasazi.
   ○ **c.** the Apache.

Comprehension and Writing Assessment   Copyright © SRA/McGraw-Hill. Permission is granted to reproduce this page for classroom use.   35

Comprehension and Writing Assessment, p. 35

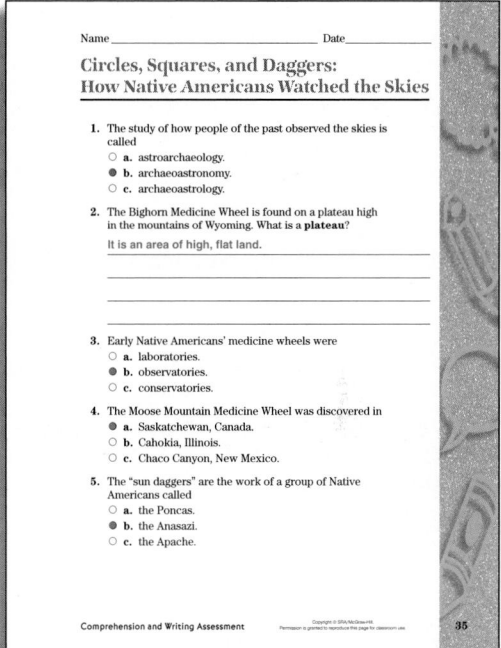

Circles, Squares, and Daggers: How Native Americans Watched the Skies *(continued)*

6. What is attached to Hovenweep Castle?
   ○ **a.** a medicine wheel
   ○ **b.** a sun dial
   ● **c.** a sun room

7. Early Native Americans used the sky as their
   ○ **a.** home.
   ● **b.** calendar.
   ○ **c.** television.

8. Early Native Americans' observatories told them
   when to plant, prepare for winter, or to move on.
   _____
   _____
   _____

9. Knowing how to use the observatories probably added to the power of
   ● **a.** chiefs and religious leaders.
   ○ **b.** animals.
   ○ **c.** astroarchaeologists.

10. For the early Native Americans, astronomy had
    ○ **a.** a playful side.
    ○ **b.** only ceremonial importance.
    ● **c.** deep religious meaning.

Linking to the Concepts Explain the connection between early Native American observatories and important tribal ceremonies. Answers will vary.

Personal Response Calendars today are still used to plan festivities or make decisions. Give two examples of plans or decisions you and your family make based on the calendar. Answers will vary.

36   Copyright © SRA/McGraw-Hill   Permission is granted to reproduce this page for classroom use.   Comprehension and Writing Assessment

Comprehension and Writing Assessment, p. 36

① Preparing to Read

Meeting Individual Needs

ESL

Word Meaning Make sure English-language learners understand the meanings of the words before they do the exercises. Refer to Unit 2, Lesson 4, of the **ESL Supplement** for specific suggestions.

Intervention

Plurals For students who need more help forming the plurals of words that end in *x*, explain the rule: If the noun ends in *sh, ch, s, x,* or *z*, add -es to make it plural. Have students brainstorm a list of words that end in *x*. Then, ask them to make each word on their list plural. Check their work aloud. For students who need more help, see Unit 2, Lesson 4, of the **Intervention Guide.**

Word Knowledge

Reading the Words and Sentences

Write each word and sentence on the chalkboard. Have students read each word together. After all the words have been read, have students read each sentence in natural phrases or chunks. Use the suggestions in About the Words to discuss the different features of the listed words.

Line 1:	telescope	observation	constellations
Line 2:	alphabet	photograph	pharmacy
Line 3:	taxes	mixes	boxes
Sentence 1:	We saw the constellations through a telescope.		
Sentence 2:	The alphabet book used a photograph of cake mixes.		
Sentence 3:	Remove the broken boxes from the pharmacy.		

About the Words

- Line 1 contains words dealing with astronomy. Students may recognize some of these words from other selections in Unit 2.
- The words in Line 2 illustrate the /f/ sound spelled *ph.* The *ph* spelling is often found in words with Greek roots. Have students brainstorm other words containing this spelling of the /f/ sound.
- Line 3 contains plural forms of words that end with *x.* Remind students that all words ending in *x* are made plural by adding *-es.*

Developing Oral Language

To review the words, have students do one or both of the following activities.

- Give a clue for one of the words above. For example, for the word *photograph,* what word begins and ends with the sound you hear at the beginning of the word *film?*
- Have individual students use any two words from the list in one sentence.

Build Background

Activate Prior Knowledge

Have students check the Concept/Question Board to refresh their memories about astronomy. Discuss the following with students to find out what they may already know about the selection and have already learned about the unit theme. Tell students to use their prior knowledge to help them to comprehend the selection they are about to read.

- Remind students that until the time described in "Galileo," the first selection in this unit, people could use only their unaided eyes to make observations.

- Ask students whether they are familiar with the story they are about to read, and if so, to tell a little about it.

- Have students discuss what earlier selections in this unit told them about how people explained the stars.

Background Information

The following information may help the students to better understand the selection they are about to read.

- Lead students to understand that astronomy is an ever-expanding field of knowledge that builds on early ideas. For example, Galileo's ideas were built on what he learned from Copernicus. It was the observation of the heavens by early people that led to the first calendars. The simple telescopes of the sixteenth century eventually led to the radio telescopes of today.

- "Circles, Squares, and Daggers" is an informational piece that asks students to visualize complex sites. Students may find it helpful after reading about each observatory to discuss how it looked and functioned.

- Explain that studies in astronomy are constantly updated as new discoveries are made. Tell students that since the writing of this article, studies of Native American observatories have been ongoing. Discuss with students ways they can obtain up-to-the-minute information on the progress of these studies (for example, via the Internet or by contacting the national parks where these sites are located).

Meeting Individual Needs

ESL

Cultural Context English-language learners may be unfamiliar with the places named in this selection. Help them find the following places on a map of North America: *the Bighorn Mountains, Wyoming; Saskatchewan, Canada; St. Louis, Illinois; Kansas City, Missouri; Chaco Canyon, New Mexico; Tucson* and *Phoenix, Arizona.*

Teacher Tip In the selection, there are many references to the word *observatory*. Although this word usually means "a place designed for astronomers to study the stars," in this selection it means "a calendar-keeping device."

Writing Journal Tell students that after reading, they will be jotting down in their Writing Journals their reactions to the selection. Tell them to be on the lookout for ideas for using the discovery of observatories in a story.

Preparing to Read

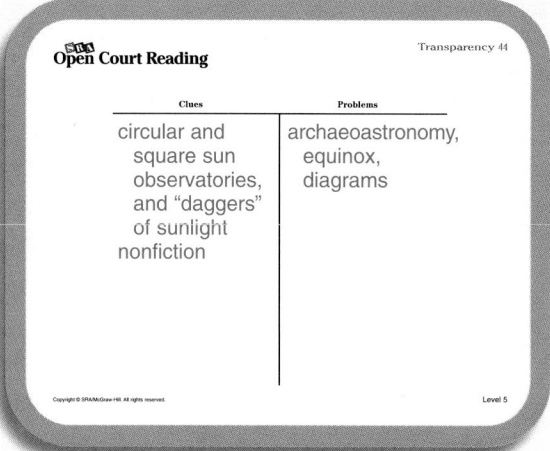

Transparency 44

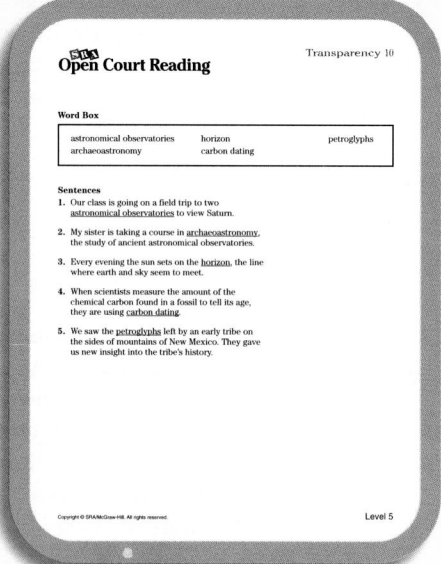

Transparency 10

Teacher Tip To help students decode words, divide them into syllables as shown below. The information following each word tells how students can figure out the meaning of each word from the sentences on the transparency.

as•tro•nom•i•cal ob•ser•va•to•ries	context clues, word structure
ar•chae•o•as•tron•o•my	word structure, apposition
ho•ri•zon	apposition
car•bon dat•ing	word structure, apposition
pet•ro•glyphs	context clues, word structure

Preview and Prepare

Browse

- Have a volunteer read the title and author's name aloud. Have students share what they know about nonfiction.

- Because this is a nonfiction selection, have students browse through the entire selection, reading subheads and looking at diagrams and captions. Discuss with them what they think this story might have to do with astronomy.

- Have students search for words and phrases that connect to what they already know. Record these in the Clues column on **Transparency 44**.

- Have students identify any problems they notice while reading and record them in the Problems column.

Set Purposes

As they read, have students think about how astronomy has changed.

Selection Vocabulary

As students study vocabulary, they will use context clues, word structure, and apposition, as with other unfamiliar words.

Display **Transparency 10,** then introduce and discuss the following.

as•tro•nom•i•cal ob•ser•va•to•ries: places designed to watch the universe beyond Earth, including stars, planets, and galaxies (page 144)

ar•chae•o•as•tron•o•my: the study of ancient astronomical observatories (page 144)

ho•ri•zon: the line where Earth and sky seem to meet (page 146)

car•bon dat•ing: using carbon 14 to find out the age of old material (page 146)

pet•ro•glyphs: drawings or words cut into a rock (page 149)

Have students read the words in the Word Box. Help students decode multisyllabic words by blending them syllable by syllable. If the word is not decodable, give students the pronunciation. (archaeoastronomy)

Have students read the sentences on **Transparency 10** to determine the meaning of the underlined words. Remind them to use clues in the sentences and structural clues to figure out the meaning.

Reading Recommendations

Your first reading of the selection should focus on developing the reading strategies found to the left of the reduced pages. During rereading, they should focus on the comprehension skills, found to the right of the reduced pages.

Oral Reading

Because of the difficult vocabulary and challenging content presented in this selection, students may need assistance. Oral reading is recommended. As this is a nonfiction selection and students are reading to be informed, allow students more time for reading. Have students adjust their reading rate by reading more slowly or by rereading certain sections of the selection in order to comprehend the information presented.

As students read aloud, have them read expressively, at an appropriate pace, in natural phrases and chunks. By reading the selection with fluency, students will demonstrate an understanding of the text and an ability to engage the listeners in an effective manner. If students encounter difficulties, have them use the reading strategies below or refer to the Blending Procedure (Program Appendix 15–16).

Using Reading Strategies

Reading-strategy instruction allows students to become aware of how good readers read. During the reading of "Circles, Squares, and Daggers," you will model the use of the following reading strategies:

- Visualizing - Clarifying - Making Connections

Before reading, have students share how they have used these strategies in the past and any tips they can give each other on their use.

Building Comprehension Skills

Revisiting or rereading a selection allows students to apply skills that give them a more complete understanding of the text. Some follow-up comprehension skills, such as *Main Idea and Details* and *Compare and Contrast*, help students organize information. Others, such as *Author's Purpose, Making Inferences*, and *Drawing Conclusions*, lead to deeper understanding—to "reading between the lines," as mature readers do. In this selection, students will apply the follow-up comprehension skills of *Main Idea and Details* and *Classifying and Categorizing*. Because two skills are reviewed, you may want to do all the sections related to one skill before doing the other.

Meeting Individual Needs

ESL

Vocabulary Check that English-language learners know the meanings of idioms and more difficult vocabulary in the story, including: *Stonehenge, Mayas, astronomical observatories, a very new field, sites, supernatural, alignments, horizon, carbon dating, reconstructed, vertical rock face, a symbol of winter*, and *came up with ingenious ways*. Explain and show pictures as needed. Model example sentences and help English-speaking students make their own sentences. Refer to Unit 2, Lesson 4 of the *ESL Supplement* for teaching suggestions.

Have students who may need extra help reading "Circles, Squares, and Daggers" reread the selection using the *Listening Library Audiocassette*.

By this time in the fifth grade, good readers should be reading approximately 126 words per minute with fluency and expression. The only way to gain fluency is through practice. As explained in Reading Recommendations, have students reread all or part of the selection to you and to each other during class or Independent Work Time to focus on the comprehension skills and to build fluency.

② Reading and Responding

Read pages 144–153.

Comprehension Strategies

Modeling

① Making Connections *Good readers connect what they are reading to things they already know about or have seen. This helps them better understand what they are reading. I've never been to an ancient observatory before, but what we have read about them reminds me of the planetarium I visited. A planetarium is a place where one can go to learn the names and locations of stars and constellations. It is a room with a domed ceiling on which points of light are projected in the same pattern as stars appear in the night sky.*

Modeling

② Clarifying *It is important to stop and clarify anything we don't understand in our reading. I wonder what a "medicine wheel" is. As we read further, maybe we will find the answer to this question. Oh, I see. It says here that "medicine" meant holy or supernatural. The medicine wheel was probably used for something Native Americans considered very important.*

Reading Recommendation

ORAL · CHORAL · SILENT

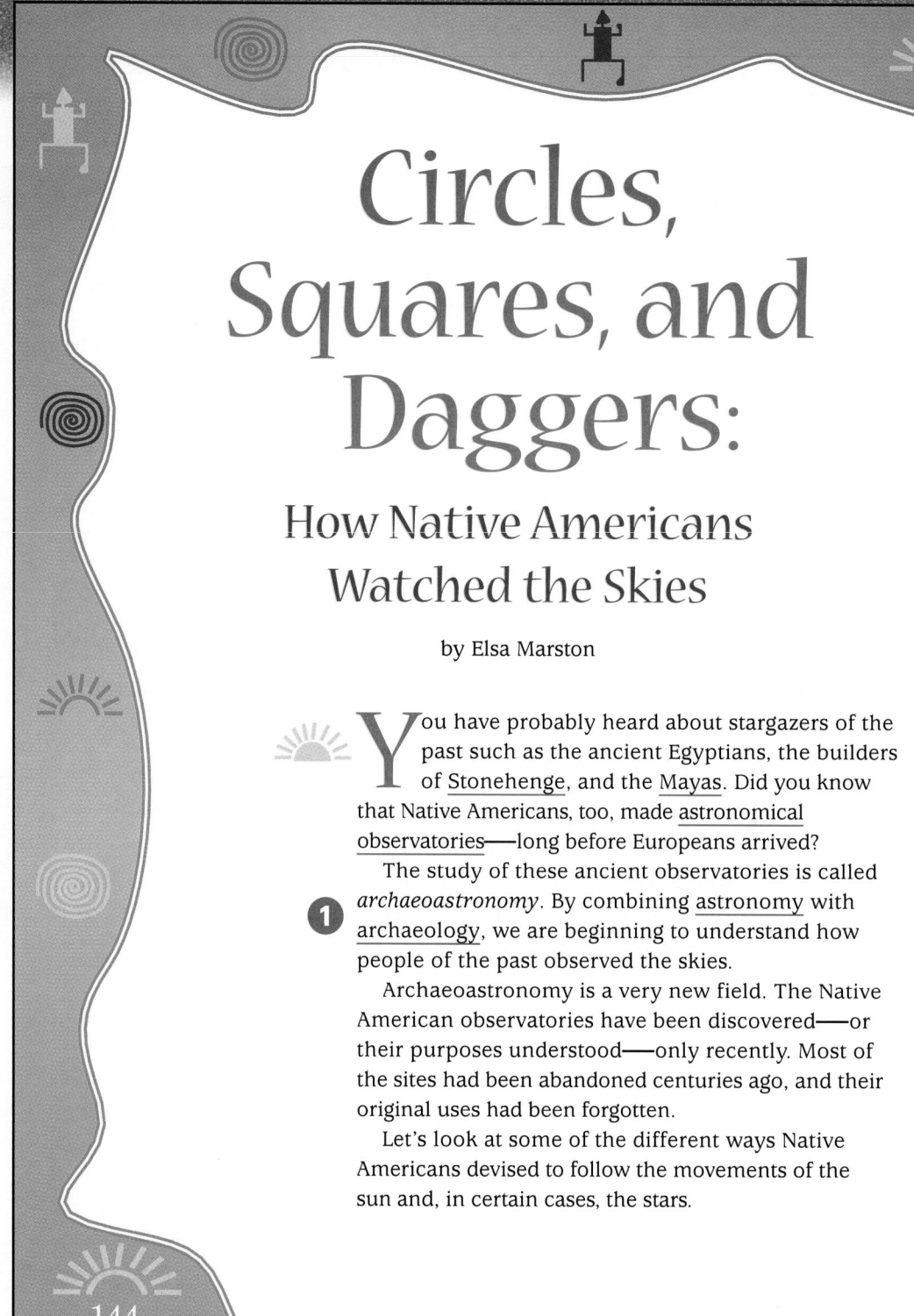

Circles, Squares, and Daggers:

How Native Americans Watched the Skies

by Elsa Marston

You have probably heard about stargazers of the past such as the ancient Egyptians, the builders of Stonehenge, and the Mayas. Did you know that Native Americans, too, made astronomical observatories——long before Europeans arrived?

The study of these ancient observatories is called ① *archaeoastronomy*. By combining astronomy with archaeology, we are beginning to understand how people of the past observed the skies.

Archaeoastronomy is a very new field. The Native American observatories have been discovered——or their purposes understood——only recently. Most of the sites had been abandoned centuries ago, and their original uses had been forgotten.

Let's look at some of the different ways Native Americans devised to follow the movements of the sun and, in certain cases, the stars.

144

Meeting Individual Needs

Intervention

Comprehension Intervention strategies for those students having difficulty with reading "Circles, Squares and Daggers" can be found in Unit 2, Lesson 5, of the *Intervention Guide.*

Assessment

✓ **Informal** Observe individual students as they read, and use the Teacher Observation Log found in the *Assessment Guide* to record anecdotal information about each student's strengths and weaknesses.

Medicine Wheels

One of the most dramatic observatories lies on a windswept <u>plateau</u> high in the Bighorn Mountains of Wyoming. It is simply a circle of stones that looks something like a wheel, 80 feet across. In fact, it's called the Bighorn Medicine Wheel ("medicine" means holy or supernatural).

In the center of the wheel is a large pile of stones called a <u>cairn</u>. Twenty-eight lines of stones lead like spokes from the "hub" to the rim. Just outside the circle stand six smaller cairns.

Though the wheel had been known for about a hundred years, it was not until the early 1970s that its secrets began to come clear. An astronomer, John Eddy, discovered how the wheel "works."

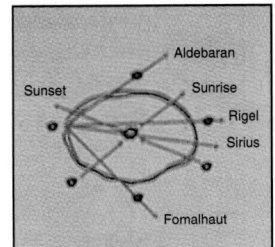

The Bighorn Medicine Wheel. The diagram shows cairns marking sunrise and sunset on the summer solstice and the rising of the bright stars Aldebaran, Rigel, Sirius, and Fomalhaut.

Bighorn Medicine Wheel

145

Comprehension
Skills

Main Idea and Details

Have the students tell what they know about *main idea and details*. Review with the students that a paragraph usually has a main idea that is clearly stated in a topic sentence.

Tell students that a section or passage can also have a main idea. Have the students reread page 144 and look for the main idea of the section. Guide the students to the last sentence of the page. The sentence presents the main idea of the section. The supporting details will follow.

On page 145, call the students' attention to the heading, "Medicine Wheels." Have them explain that this heading tells what the section is mainly about. Have the students list some of the details about medicine wheels.

←Skills Strand→

Main Idea and Details
INTRODUCED: Unit 2, Lesson 2
REVIEWED: Unit 2, Lesson 4
Unit 2, Lesson 8
Unit 3, Lesson 2
Unit 3, Lesson 7

Help students pronounce unfamiliar words such as Maya: mä´ yə.

Explain to students that in the context of this selection and some Native American beliefs, the word *medicine* means "holy or supernatural."

Meeting Individual Needs

Challenge

Main Idea and Details Have students browse the selection "Galileo" and identify its main idea and details.

Intervention

Main Idea and Details Help students list the main idea and details from pages 144–145 in the selection. Point out that the headings can help them identify the main idea.

Assessment

✓ **Formal** To assess students' understanding of Main Idea and Details, have them complete *Skills Assessment*, page 16.

2 Reading and Responding

Comprehension Strategies

Modeling

3 Clarifying *The author doesn't say exactly what the summer solstice is, but there are hints in the text. This paragraph says that the medicine wheel tells when the longest day of the year has arrived. It also says that the sun rises and sets directly over the center cairn at the summer solstice. Putting that information together, I think that the solstice must be the longest day of the year, which is the first day of summer.*

Should anything else be clarified before we read on?

Modeling

4 Clarifying *There is something I don't understand. Why would the Native Americans need the Bighorn Wheel? Let's reread to find the answer.*

When I reread I see that the wheel helped keep track of the days. That makes sense. They probably used it to track the passing days and seasons. What questions do you have about the text so far?

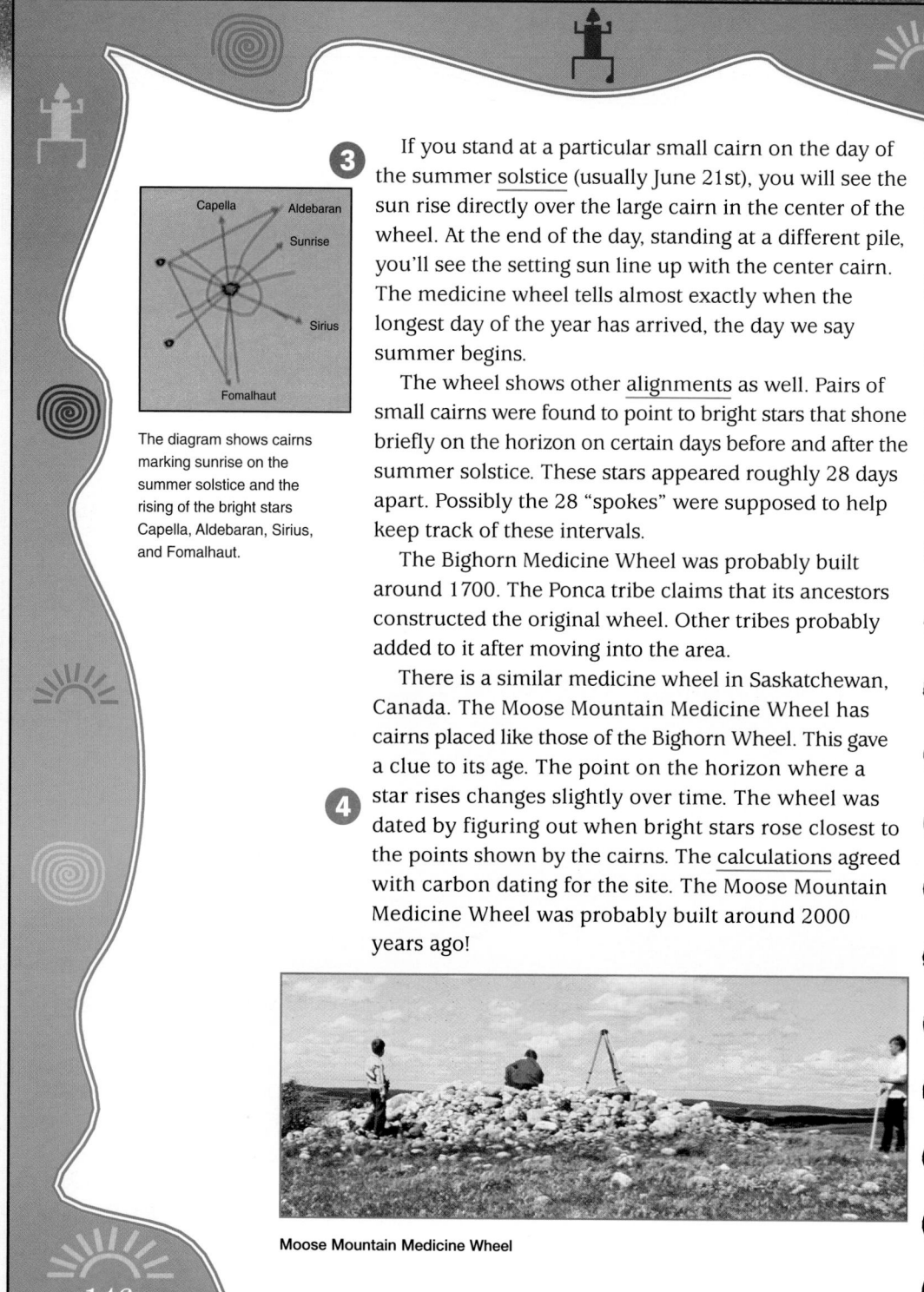

The diagram shows cairns marking sunrise on the summer solstice and the rising of the bright stars Capella, Aldebaran, Sirius, and Fomalhaut.

3 If you stand at a particular small cairn on the day of the summer <u>solstice</u> (usually June 21st), you will see the sun rise directly over the large cairn in the center of the wheel. At the end of the day, standing at a different pile, you'll see the setting sun line up with the center cairn. The medicine wheel tells almost exactly when the longest day of the year has arrived, the day we say summer begins.

The wheel shows other <u>alignments</u> as well. Pairs of small cairns were found to point to bright stars that shone briefly on the horizon on certain days before and after the summer solstice. These stars appeared roughly 28 days apart. Possibly the 28 "spokes" were supposed to help keep track of these intervals.

The Bighorn Medicine Wheel was probably built around 1700. The Ponca tribe claims that its ancestors constructed the original wheel. Other tribes probably added to it after moving into the area.

There is a similar medicine wheel in Saskatchewan, Canada. The Moose Mountain Medicine Wheel has cairns placed like those of the Bighorn Wheel. This gave a clue to its age. The point on the horizon where a **4** star rises changes slightly over time. The wheel was dated by figuring out when bright stars rose closest to the points shown by the cairns. The <u>calculations</u> agreed with carbon dating for the site. The Moose Mountain Medicine Wheel was probably built around 2000 years ago!

Moose Mountain Medicine Wheel

146

Meeting Individual Needs

Circles and Squares

At Cahokia, a major Native American site in western Illinois near St. Louis, archaeologists discovered traces of four large circles of wooden posts. They reconstructed part of one of these circles.

Seen from the center at dawn, the sun lines up with certain posts at the summer solstice and winter solstice (the shortest day of the year, usually December 21st). A third post is <u>aligned</u> with the rising sun at the spring and fall equinoxes (usually March 21st and September 21st, when day and night are of equal length).

Another observatory was discovered near Kansas City, Missouri, in the early 1980s. Again, traces of posts were found, but this time in the shape of a square. About 35 feet long on each side, the square suggested a building such as a fort—except that the corners were open. A triangle of posts had stood in the center, and on the south side of the square was a double row of post marks.

A local astronomy society made a simple reconstruction of the square. They found that on the summer solstice, a person standing a certain distance from the center posts could see the sun rise and set through two of the open corners. The other two corners framed the sunrise and sunset at the winter solstice. On the equinoxes, the sun shone directly between the double lines of posts. Both observatories were made by Native Americans of the Mississippian culture, probably about a thousand years ago.

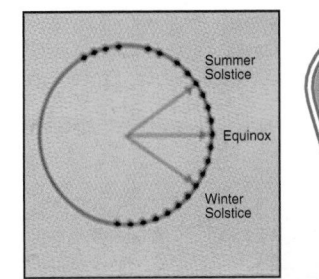

At Cahokia, the sun rises over a post marker at the equinox. The diagram shows posts marking sunrises at the summer and winter solstices.

Cahokia

147

Comprehension Skills

Classifying and Categorizing

Introduce the comprehension skills *classifying and categorizing* to the students. Explain to them that when we classify and categorize, we group things according to what they have in common.

On the chalkboard, write the heading, *Observatories*. Under this heading, in a vertical line, write the categories *medicine wheels*, and *circles and squares*. Have the students create a chart by filling in the names and locations of the observatories found on pages 146–147, as well as the names of the people who built them.

Teacher Tip Tell students that since this article was written, more pole sites have been found at the Cahokia observatory.

Teacher Tip Ponca is pronounced päng′ kə. Cahokia is pronounced kə′ hō′kē ə. Saskatchewan is pronounced sə ska′ chə wən.

Meeting Individual Needs

Intervention

Classifying and Categorizing Review the definition of *classifying and categorizing* with students having difficulty with this concept. Then have students skim pages 146-147 for the approximate age of each observatory, and add that information to the chart created in the "skills" lesson.

2 Reading and Responding

Comprehension Strategies

Modeling

5 Visualizing *Sometimes, forming a mental image of how a process works can help one understand it. I can see how this observatory would work. The sun comes through the spaces between the rocks and looks like a dagger as it falls on the spiral behind the rocks. As the year goes by, the light moves, like hands on a clock. What pictures are you getting in your head as you read?*

Teacher Tip To help students visualize the sunlight on the petroglyphs, use a flashlight and a piece of cardboard with a hole in it to demonstrate how a focused light might move over time.

Teacher Tip Anasazi is pronounced ä nə sä´ zē. Fajada is pronounced fä hä´ dä. Casa Grande is pronounced kä´ sä grän´ dä.

Word Knowledge

petroglyphs, Phoenix

Students can use the skills they learned in the Word Knowledge section of this lesson to read these words. Remind students of this if they have difficulty reading these words.

Sun Daggers

The Anasazi—a name that means simply "ancient ones"—lived in the beautiful but dry country of northern New Mexico, Colorado, Utah, and Arizona around 900 years ago. In Chaco Canyon, New Mexico, they designed an especially clever kind of observatory. It was discovered in 1977 by an artist, Anna Sofaer, who was examining rock carvings.

Near the top of Fajada Butte, a high rock that rises from the canyon floor, three large slabs of stone lean against a vertical rock face. About 9 feet long, they stand on end only a few inches apart, their narrow sides against the rock. On the shadowed rock behind them, two spirals have been cut.

5 At noon on the summer solstice, a tiny shaft of sunlight falls between two of the slabs. It makes a spot that looks like a dagger—cutting right through the middle of the larger spiral.

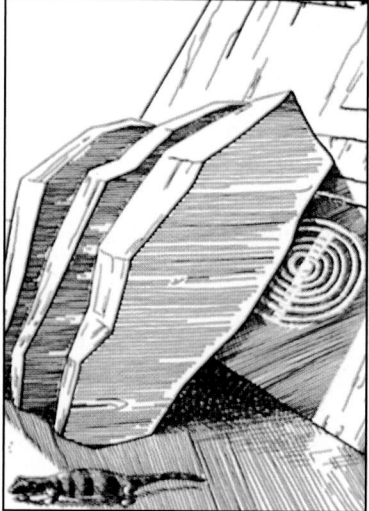

The solar marker in Chaco Canyon at noon on the summer solstice.

Fall equinox.

Winter solstice.

Spring equinox.

As the weeks pass, the "dagger" of sunlight moves to the right. Meanwhile, a second vertical streak of light appears. At the fall equinox, it cuts through the smaller spiral. By the winter solstice, the two "daggers" rest on the edges of the larger spiral. It's as though the spiral, now empty of sunlight, is a symbol of winter when the world is cold. Gradually, then, the sun daggers move to the left until, on the longest day of the year, the first one again strikes the center of the larger spiral.

All over the Southwest there are many such figures, called petroglyphs, cut in the rock. Spirals, crosses, rough outlines of humans, lizards, birds—all had meanings.

At many sites, the petroglyphs are touched by spots of sunlight, usually falling between two large rocks. Astronomer Robert Preston and his wife Ann, an artist, discovered many of these sites in Arizona. Light strikes the rock carving at the solstices, the equinoxes, or, in some cases, a point halfway between the fall equinox and the winter solstice.

"Sun Rooms"

The Anasazi thought of other ways to observe the travels of the sun. Between Tucson and Phoenix, Arizona, rises a three-story adobe building known as Casa Grande ("Great House"). At dawn, a person standing inside this ancient structure will see the sun shining through a small hole high in the east wall. The spot of light strikes the opposite wall, moves toward a small hole in that wall, and disappears into it. The spot of sunlight hits this bull's-eye only on the days close to the spring and fall equinoxes.

Casa Grande a little after dawn, at the time of the spring equinox. Sunlight passes through holes in two different walls, one behind the other.

149

Comprehension Skills

Classifying and Categorizing

For more practice with *classifying and categorizing*, have the students complete ***Reading and Writing Workbook,*** pages 65–66.

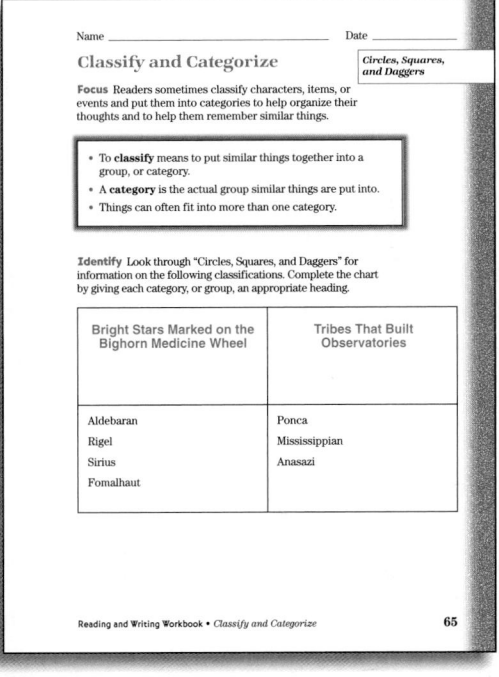

Reading and Writing Workbook pp. 65–66

Meeting Individual Needs

Reteach

Classifying and Categorizing Have students who need additional instruction and practice with this concept complete **Reteach,** pages 65–66.

Challenge

Classifying and Categorizing Have students who understand this concept complete **Challenge,** page 35.

② Reading and Responding

Comprehension Strategies

Modeling

⑥ Clarifying *Why was the solstice important to the Native Americans? The heading in this section is "Why?" Maybe the answer is here.*

Discussing Strategy Use

After they have read the selection, have students share any problems they encountered and tell what strategies they used to solve them. Then, have them answer the following questions. If they answer "no" to any of the questions, have them reread part of the selection to find the answer.

■ What did they do to clarify the unusual terms in this selection?

■ Did they make connections between what they read and what they know?

■ Did they get images in their heads about what was in the selection?

Make sure that students explain how using the strategies helped them understand the selection better and how they read effectively to find answers to the questions they asked as they set purposes.

Word Knowledge

astronomical observatories

Students can use the skills they learned in the Word Knowledge section of this lesson to read these words. Remind students of this if they have difficulty reading these words.

Hovenweep Castle

There is a different type of Anasazi "sun room" at Hovenweep National Monument in Utah. Attached to a large stone structure called Hovenweep Castle is a tower-like room. At sunset on the solstices and equinoxes, the sun's rays enter small holes and a door, shine through the room, and strike doorways in the inside walls. The archaeoastronomer who studied Hovenweep Castle, Ray Williamson, determined that the beams of sunlight could not enter the room in this way merely by chance.

150

Teacher Tip Reread the selection with students who had difficulty understanding it. Continue modeling and prompting the use of strategies as you reread.

Why?

All over this country, Native Americans came up with ingenious ways to observe the skies. But *why* did they study astronomy?

The skies were the Native Americans' calendar. They had no fixed, written calendar as we do today. They relied on what nature would tell them about the changing times of the year. Important solar events such as the solstices and the equinoxes helped them know when to plant their crops, when to start preparing for the winter, when to move from one place to another.

The sun and stars told Native Americans when important ceremonies were supposed to take place. These ceremonies were usually concerned with the "return" of the sun and start of a new year, and with planting, harvesting, and hunting.

Other special occasions might have been for social purposes such as tribal rituals, gatherings of tribes, trade, or payment of tribute. For example, the most likely function of the Bighorn Medicine Wheel was to keep a calendar so large groups could assemble in summer for trading fairs.

It's probable that only special persons knew how to use the observatories and make the announcements awaited by the people. The observatories must have strengthened the power of the chiefs and religious leaders.

There is a deep religious meaning in Native American astronomy. The sun is a vital symbol in the beliefs of many Native American cultures. And something equally important: Native Americans' understanding of the heavens helped them feel in harmony with the universe——for in many Native American religions, human beings are only one small part of the world, living in peace with the rest of nature.

Today we are coming to recognize Native Americans' achievements in astronomical knowledge——and to appreciate the ways in which they used that understanding.

151

Meeting Individual Needs

ESL

Discussion When discussing difficult concepts with English-language learners, provide expansions, restatements, and explanations.

Assessment

✓ **Formal** To assess students' reading comprehension, have them complete *Comprehension and Writing Assessment,* pages 35–36.

Comprehension Skills

Discussing the Selection

Following reading, engage the students in a discussion of the selection. Using the *handing-off process* will help students take responsibility for the discussion. In addition to the following questions, have them revisit any questions asked when the students set purposes before reading. Have students support their responses with text evidence.

■ What was the main idea of this selection? *(to describe ancient observatories created by Native Americans)*

■ What is the meaning of this selection's title? *(It describes, by shapes, the categories of the different kinds of observatories Native Americans used.)*

■ In what ways did the Native Americans use astronomy? *(They used it to mark time and for religious purposes.)*

■ How has this selection connected with your knowledge of the unit theme? *(Answers will vary—students should compare/contrast examples of astronomy from this selection with their own experiences or past reading and use these connections to make a general statement about the unit theme.)*

During this time, have the students return to the clues and problems that they noted on the transparency before reading to determine whether the clues were borne out by the selection. Let the students decide which items deserve further discussion.

When the student finishes his or her comments, that student should hand off the discussion to the next speaker. In this way, students maintain a discussion without relying on the teacher to decide who speaks.

2 Reading and Responding

Meet the Author

After the students read the information about Elsa Marston, discuss the following questions with them.

Why does Elsa Marston think it is important to learn about the cultures of other people? *(Possible answer: She thinks it is important to learn about the cultures of other people because it creates an "awareness of the world beyond here and now.")*

How does "Circles, Squares, and Daggers" teach about the culture of other people? *(Possible answer: The selection teaches about the culture of other people by showing how Native Americans of the past predicted the changing seasons, and that being able to do so was important to them.)*

Circles, Squares, and Daggers:

How Native Americans Watched the Skies

Meet the Author

Elsa Marston was born in Newton, Massachusetts. Although she is a writer and an artist, she has had a wide variety of jobs and interests. She has lived both in Europe and the Middle East. In her lifetime she has taught English, been the head of an art gallery, and organized a jail improvement committee. She is also a nature lover and an active community worker. Her children's books are often based on experiences she has had. She says, "My basic philosophy in writing for young people is that I want to share what is important to me." Her favorite things to write about are the cultures of other people, both in the past and present. With her books, she hopes to "encourage an awareness of the world beyond here and now."

152

Theme Connections

Think About It

With a small group of classmates, discuss what you have learned about observatories built by early Native Americans.

- Why did Native Americans want to track the movements of the sun and stars?
- What can the astronomical records and observatories that remain tell us about what was important to early Native American civilizations and about how they lived?

Check the Concept/Question Board to see if there are any questions there that you can answer now. If the selection or your discussions about the selection have raised any new questions about the unit theme, put the questions on the Concept/Question Board. Maybe the next selection will help answer the questions.

Record Ideas

How does the effectiveness of ancient Native American observatories compare with modern calendars? Use your Writing Journal to record your notes and ideas about the different ways people track time and their reasons for doing so.

Research Ideas

- Compare the sky-watching methods of ancient Native Americans with those of ancient Greeks.
- Find out more about the importance of heavenly bodies in Native American ceremonies and rituals.

153

Theme Connections

Think About It

- As students discuss ancient Native American observatories, circulate and observe the discussions.

- Have students connect, compare, and contrast Native Americans' ideas for astronomy's uses with the other ideas discussed in this unit. For example, students may mention that Native Americans' ideas were similar to those presented in "Galileo" and "Telescopes" because they were practical; however, their ideas served different purposes.

- Have students compare and contrast what they learned about ancient Native American cultures with what they learned about ancient Greek and Indian cultures from the previous selection. What characteristics do these cultures share? How are these cultures different?

- Have the students report what they discussed. Encourage them to record on the Concept/Question Board any questions they may have.

Research Ideas

If the natural history museum in your community features Native American cultures, it may contain information or an exhibit about astronomical observations.

 **Teacher Tip** Students may be interested in researching Native American myths and legends about the sun and the stars, and comparing them to the Indian and Grecian constellation myths read earlier in this unit.

Fine Art

Back Through the Stars

Viewing the Theme Through Fine Art

Students can use the artworks on these pages to explore the unit theme, Back Through the Stars, in images rather than words. Encourage them to talk about their impressions of the artworks and how each one might relate to the unit theme.

Following is some background information about each of the artworks. Share with students whatever you feel is appropriate. For more detailed suggestions on using the art to enhance students' understanding of the unit concept as well as their enjoyment of each artwork, see pages 155A and 217A. You may also wish to encourage students to find out more about artists and artistic styles that interest them.

Pictorial Quilt/detail Falling Stars

Harriet Powers (1837–1911) was born in Athens, Georgia, as a slave. After the emancipation, she and her husband were free and were able to purchase a small farm to raise their family. Although she was not famous for her quilts while alive, Powers' works are considered some of the best examples of African-American quilts today.

Pictorial Quilt/detail *Falling Stars* depicts a scene from local history. On November 13, 1833, a meteor shower took place. This piece portrays the frightened people and animals as the stars shower down upon them. Many people thought this was the end of time.

Back Through the Stars

FINE Art

Pictorial Quilt, detail *Falling Stars*. 1895–98. **Harriet Powers.** Pieced, appliquéd and printed cotton embroidered with cotton and metallic yarns. 69 × 105 in. Bequest of Maxim Karolik. Courtesy, Museum of Fine Arts, Boston.

154

Teacher Tip Students should recall from the selection, "The Heavenly Zoo," that the constellation Orion (ə rī´ ən) is named for a figure in Greek mythology.

Orion in December. 1959.
Charles Burchfield. Watercolor and pencil on paper. $39\frac{7}{8} \times 32\frac{7}{8}$ in. National Museum of American Art, Smithsonian Institution, Washington, DC. Photo: Art Resource, NY.

The Starry Night. 1889. **Vincent van Gogh.** Oil on canvas. $29 \times 36\frac{1}{4}$ in. The Museum of Modern Art, New York. Acquired through the Lillie P. Bliss Bequest. Photograph ©1999 The Museum of Modern Art, New York.

155

Orion in December

Charles Burchfield (1893–1967) was born in Ohio and later moved to Buffalo, New York. His career began as a wallpaper designer, and in 1915, he began painting scenes of small American towns and country life. He is best known for his fantasy landscape paintings, which he created using layered watercolor paints. His work reflects his interests in the beauty of nature, seasonal changes, and the loneliness he saw in Ohio and New York.

Orion in December conveys a winter fantasy landscape and the spectacular constellation Orion the Hunter, who holds a club in his right hand and a shield in his left. The star outlined in red represents one of the largest stars known, Betelgeuse, and marks the right shoulder of Orion. During the winter it can be seen from the northern hemisphere.

The Starry Night

Vincent van Gogh (1853–1890) was born in the small Dutch village of Groot-Zundert. Much of what the world knows of him has been learned through numerous letters he wrote to his best friend and younger brother, Theo. Van Gogh began his life as an artist at the age of 27 after having tried numerous careers, including that of a teacher and missionary. Although his life was short and tragic, he left behind 1600 remarkable drawings and paintings, which reflect the beauty he found in nature and the world around him.

The Starry Night was painted from memory after van Gogh had placed himself in a mental hospital for severe depression. He had previously painted a starry night scene from life, attaching a ring of candles to his hat so that he could see to paint. He was fascinated by the sparkling evening sky and the radiating lights of the stars.

2 Responding

✦Exploring the Theme

Research

As students continue their explorations have them use the **Research** CD-ROM Program to help organize and share their findings.

The Starry Night.
1889. *Vincent van Gogh.* Oil on canvas.
29 x 36 ¼ in. The Museum of Modern Art, New York. Acquired through the Lillie P. Bliss Bequest. Photograph © 1999 The Museum of Modern Art, New York

Student Anthology p. 155

Home Connection p. 23

Selection Vocabulary

Have students write in their Writing Journals the definitions for words discussed before the reading of the selection and any other interesting words they clarified while reading. Students should be encouraged to refer to these words throughout the unit as they work on student and writing projects. The words from this selection are:

astronomical observatories   **archaeoastronomy**
horizon   **carbon dating**   **petroglyphs**

Reading/Writing Connections

Invite each student to select an idea for a nonfiction or fiction piece about a particular place, and create a list of details that conveys everything a reader may need to know about it. Ask each student to then star the details that are most important to the work as a whole. Encourage students to put the lists in their *Writing Folders* for future use.

View Fine Art

Have students look at *The Starry Night* by *Vincent van Gogh* on page 155 of the *Student Anthology.* Tell students that the evening sky and the stars fascinated van Gogh, and that he painted this particular scene from memory. Ask students if they can infer from this painting what it was that van Gogh liked about stars. Have students comment on van Gogh's fascination with the stars as compared and contrasted to that of the Native Americans who built the observatories in "Circles, Squares, and Daggers."

Home Connection

The class has just finished reading "Circles, Squares, and Daggers," which describes the workings of early observatories constructed by Native Americans. An informational letter on "Circles, Squares, and Daggers," in both English and Spanish, can be found in the *Home Connection* guide.

Supporting Student Explorations

Students should be continuing with their research. You may want to do the following:

Whole Group Conduct a class discussion in which problems and conjectures are presented and students contribute suggestions, criticisms, and questions.

Inform students about alternative sources of information, such as interviews, films, and primary source materials. Explain to students that the way they decide to present their research might affect the resources they use. Have the students think of interesting ways to present the information they collect. Presentation ideas may include reports, posters, dioramas, video presentations, plays, or a combination of methods.

Individual Meet with students to discuss their research projects. Assist them in narrowing the focus of their research and in locating resources. As students look at their resources, have them put their ideas and the information they obtain in outline form (student instruction on how to outline information is on p.155I of the *Teacher's Edition*). Tell students that summarizing information in outline form will help them keep it organized which in turn will help them create a presentation that effectively represents what they have learned.

Suggest that students post on the Concept/Question Board brief descriptions of books, magazine articles, computer Websites, or other sources of information that they have found to be especially helpful in their exploration of astronomy. Encourage students who are having difficulty finding information to check sources on the Board and to post their questions as well.

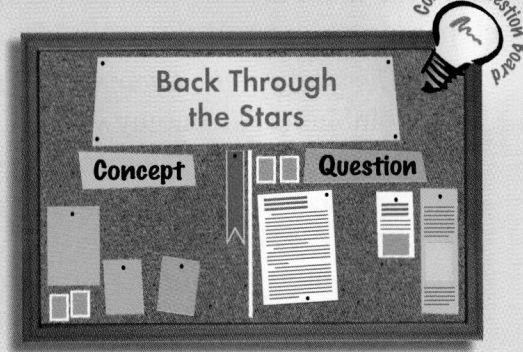

Inquiry Journal Have students complete page 22 of the *Inquiry Journal.* Have them record their ideas about how "Circles, Squares, and Daggers" added to their knowledge about astronomy.

Teacher Tip When meeting with students on an individual basis, focus on any problems they may be having with their unit activities. Help students identify resources to help solve their problems.

Assessment

✓ **Informal** At this point in the activity, students should be using many different sources of information and should be able to summarize the information they have found. They should have a clear understanding of characteristics of astronomy. Check to see that students:

- use a variety of resources to find information.
- summarize information.
- identify characteristics of astronomy.

Recording Concept Information (continued)

• *Circles, Squares, and Daggers: How Native Americans Watched the Skies* by Elsa Marston
  Answers will vary.

• *Voyager to the Planets* by Necia Apfel
  Answers will vary.

• *A Meeting in Space* by Vonda N. McIntyre
  Answers will vary.

22   Inquiry Journal

Inquiry Journal p. 22

 **Integrating the Curriculum**

Language Arts

Writing

Writing Paragraphs

Instruct Prompt students to define *paragraph (a group of at least two sentences that tell about the same thing)*. Review that a topic sentence states the main idea, and supporting sentences provide details in a paragraph. Then give students the following rules for writing paragraphs:

1. Indent the first line of a paragraph.
2. Write about only one main idea in each paragraph.
3. Use a topic sentence to state the main idea of each paragraph.
4. Write other sentences to develop the main idea.
5. Do not write unnecessary sentences that do not fit with the paragraph.

Practice On the chalkboard write the following examples from "Circles, Squares, and Daggers." These examples show indentation, topic sentences, and a new paragraph to develop a new idea. Have volunteers identify the main idea of each paragraph and tell how other sentences in each paragraph support the main idea.

> *The study of the ancient observatories is called* archaeoastronomy. By combining astronomy with archaeology, we are beginning to understand how people of the past observed the skies.
> *Archaeoastronomy is a very new field.* The Native American observatories have been discovered—or their purposes understood—only recently. Most of the sites had been abandoned centuries ago, and their original uses had been forgotten.

Apply Have students select three paragraphs from "Telescopes." Have them write the topic sentence for each paragraph, along with a brief summary of the paragraph's main idea and details.

Assessment

✓ **Informal** Take this opportunity to assess students' progress with the writing process by commenting on the entries in their Writing Journals.

Teacher Tip Sometimes the hardest part of the writing process is getting the first sentence down on paper. It may help a student who feels stuck even before he or she starts writing to begin a story in the middle or to write the word DRAFT in big letters at the top of the page.

Writing Process

Draft Have students take out the piece of expository writing they started in Lesson 3 and continue to draft, keeping in mind the rules about writing paragraphs with topic sentences.

Research in Action
Writing Process

If the students are having trouble thinking of what to write about, this is usually a symptom of other difficulties. This checklist may help you pin down a particular student's problems.

- Is the student trying to write on a different topic every time? Help the student develop personally meaningful and longer pieces that occupy several days.

- Does the student avoid rewriting? Try to get a commitment during Independent Work Time. Prompt group interest in a revised version.

- Does the student treat writing as a chore? Use conferences to express genuine interest in what the student has to say.

- Is the student overly dependent on teacher guidance? Assign a peer helper or a small group to ease the student away from dependence on you.

- Has everything else failed? Suggest topics based on the student's interests and previous writing successes. *(Marsha Roit)*

③ Integrating the Curriculum

Teacher Tip Point out that expository writing, by definition, falls under the category of *Informational Text.*

Literary Elements

Informational Text

Instruct Write on the chalkboard the words *Informational Text* and underline them. Have students tell what they remember about how authors organize informational text from lesson 2 of this unit. If necessary, review with them these distinguishing characteristics:

- It is nonfiction.
- It may include diagrams, photos, charts, or graphs.
- It may include captions, heads, and subheads.
- It may include footnotes and a bibliography.
- Its general purpose is to instruct or explain.

Practice Ask students why these texts are or are not examples of informational text: *a legend, a biography, a newspaper article reporting on a baseball game, a myth, a novel, and a math book.*

Apply Have students consider what topics they would like to read about in an informational text. Then ask them in what parts of the library they might find informational text on their subjects of interest. *(Answers may vary; students may mention the nonfiction, reference, and periodical sections.)*

Vocabulary

Meanings of Derivatives

Instruct On the chalkboard, write the following columns of words and their derivatives:

- Point to pairs of words, and have volunteers read them aloud.

astronomy	astronomical
observe	observatories
nature	natural
calculate	calculations
construct	reconstruction

- Ask students how the word in the right-hand column was derived, or formed, from the word on the left (that is, what prefixes or suffixes were added).

- Have students point out any changes in the spelling of the root word when the prefix or suffix was added.

- Explain that knowing the meaning of the root word can help them figure out the meaning of the derived form. Tell students that sometimes words may take on a different but related meaning. Ask them to explain the meaning of *astronomical* in this sentence:

  Prices in that store are astronomical.

  Explain that because astronomy deals with objects that appear to be high above, the word *astronomical* means "very high."

- If necessary, also point out changes to the root word's part of speech when a suffix or prefix is added (for example, when *nature* becomes *natural*, it changes from a noun to an adjective).

- Tell students that when in doubt, they should use a dictionary to determine a derivative's meaning, pronunciation, and part of speech.

Practice Challenge pairs of students to write sentences that use each pair of words from the list above. For example:

  To research astronomical topics, I looked under the topic "Astronomy."

Apply For additional practice, have students write at least one other derivative for each of the root words written on the chalkboard. Students may come up with words such as *astronomer, observation, naturalist, calculator,* and *constructed.* Have students write a sentence for each word. Then, have volunteers share their sentences, explaining how the derivative they used is related to its root word in meaning.

Meeting Individual Needs

ESL

Derivatives Have those students who have difficulty reading the listed words in isolation work with a partner to read aloud the sentence or paragraph in which they appear. Point out that using knowledge of the root word and the context together will help them understand the derived form.

Challenge

Derivatives Challenge students to come up with as many derivatives as they can for each of the words listed on the board, as well as any other terms that are appropriate to add (*medicine, align, harmony,* and so on).

Skills Strand

Root Words
INTRODUCED: Unit 1, Lesson 1
REVIEWED: Unit 2, Lesson 4
Unit 4, Lesson 8

3 Integrating the Curriculum

Teacher Tip Tell students that when describing a process, as they may do for their expository writing or unit activity, they should use present-tense verbs.

Assessment

✓ **Formal** To assess students' understanding of this concept, have them complete **Skills Assessment,** page 17.

Meeting Individual Needs

Challenge

Irregular Verbs Copy this chart of irregular verbs onto the chalkboard, omitting the present-tense forms. Challenge students to supply the correct verb forms to complete the chart.

Verb	Present-Tense Forms
be	I *am.* You *are.* We *are.* They *are.* He *is.* She *is.* It *is.*
do	I *do.* We *do.* You *do.* They *do.* He *does.* She *does.* It *does.*
have	I *have.* We *have.* You *have.* They *have.* He *has.* She *has.* It *has.*

Regular and Irregular Verbs
INTRODUCED: Unit 2, Lesson 3
REVIEWED: Unit 2, Lesson 4
Unit 3, Lesson 2
Unit 6, Lesson 1

Grammar, Usage, and Mechanics

Present-Tense Verbs—Regular and Irregular

Instruct Prompt students to tell you the four rules for using present-tense, regular, and irregular verbs learned in Lesson 3 of this unit. As they tell you, list the rules on the chalkboard or write them on an overhead:

- If the subject of the verb is singular, add the *-s* or *-es* inflectional ending to the verb.
- If the subject is I or *you*, add no ending to the verb.
- If the subject is plural, do not add an ending to the verb.
- If the verb does not follow the above rules, it is an irregular verb. These verbs include *have*, *do*, and *be* and have special forms to use.

Practice Divide the class into six groups, designating one of the above rules to each group.

Group 1: Rule 1	Group 4: Irregular verb *be*
Group 2: Rule 2	Group 5: Irregular verb *do*
Group 3: Rule 3	Group 6: Irregular verb *have*

Have each group write sample sentences for one of the rules listed on the chalkboard. When all groups have finished writing, have them present their sentences in the class, telling how they used the verb in each.

Apply Remind students that when they write about something that is happening now, they should use the present tense throughout the entire piece. Have them check for this when they proofread their writing.

Listening/Speaking/Viewing

Using Media

Tell students to put themselves in the role of codirectors of a panel discussion on astronomy. Their responsibility is to bring together a group that represents many different approaches to the topic. Have students brainstorm whom they might call on. Examples might include an astronaut, an astronomer, a writer for a science magazine, the host of a children's science program on television, and the editor of a weekly page on science for a local paper.

Have students break into small groups and role-play the professionals listed above. Bring all the groups together to discuss what conclusions they came to about how different media deal with a single topic. For example, a writer for a science magazine would assume a depth of knowledge on the part of the periodical's audience. The host of a children's program, on the other hand, would be presenting relatively simple concepts. Point out that understanding how different media present information should make a difference in which sources writers consult and quote when preparing informational text.

Teacher Tip Remind students to pick appropriate informational sources for use when writing their expository papers or preparing their unit activities.

3 Integrating the Curriculum

Teacher Tip

Continue the outline on "Popular Olympic Sports." Demonstrate for students how to add a second main topic, "Sports on Ice." Then have students brainstorm various subtopics for "Sports on Ice," (for example, "Ice Skating"). Then have them brainstorm details for each subtopic (for example, "Speed skating"). Have volunteers continue the outline on the chalkboard, correctly placing new subtopics and details under the second main topic.

Study and Research

Outlining

Instruct Ask students what they know about outlines. Tell them that when reading, outlines help them summarize important information. Outlines can also be used as a way of organizing one's ideas and research notes when prewriting.

Practice Copy the following outline on the chalkboard. Discuss with students proper outline format, title, main topics, subtopics, and details.

Popular Olympic Winter Sports

I. Sports in snow
    A. Alpine skiing
        1. Downhill racing
        2. Slalom and giant slalom
        3. Freestyle with moguls
    B. Nordic skiing
        1. Cross-country ski racing
        2. Ski jumping

Title: Center the title, and capitalize all important words.

Main Topic: Begin at the left with a Roman numeral (I, II, III, IV, and so on) followed by a period. Capitalize only the first word and any proper nouns. Include at least two main topics in any outline.

Subtopic: Indent as shown. Begin with a capital letter (A, B, C, and so on) followed by a period. Capitalize only the first word and any proper nouns. Include at least two subtopics under a main topic—or none at all.

Details: Indent as shown. Begin with an Arabic numeral (1, 2, 3, and so on) followed by a period. Capitalize only the first word and any proper nouns. Include at least two details under a subtopic—or none at all.

Apply Have students use the format you have discussed to outline "Circles, Squares, and Daggers." Tell students that paraphrasing the selection in outline form will help them recall the selection's main points. Then have students complete *Inquiry Journal*, page 31.

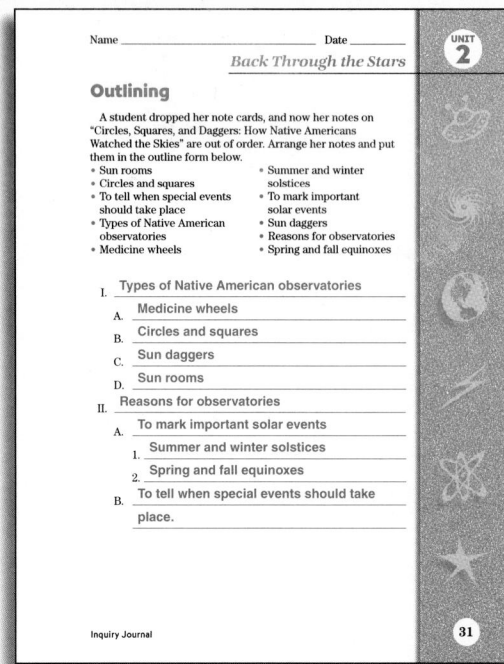

Inquiry Journal p. 31

Across the Curriculum

Math

Astronomy Word Problems

Purpose

To show that good math skills are part of being an astronomer

Procedure

Explain that Native Americans made calculations based on their observation of the sun's movement to create and perfect their calendars, and that modern-day astronomers do the same. Use the following word problems to demonstrate why it is important to incorporate math when making observations about the sun and stars.

■ There are about 365.25 days in one year. How many leap years will there be in the period 1999–2050? Tell students to remember the following rules about leap years: They are those years whose last two digits are divisible by 4, and only those century years divisible by 400. *(There will be 13 leap years between 1999–2050.)*

■ Our calendar would be off by how many days if, for a period of 50 years, we did not count that extra 0.25 day at the end of the year? *(Our calendar would be off by 12.5 days after 50 years.)*

Have students discuss reasons why our calendars would not be as effective if we did not continue to add a day to the calendar every four years. Students may bring up that months would no longer fall predictably into certain seasons. For example, the summer month of July would eventually become a winter month.

Social Studies

Names in Space

Purpose

To help students understand how planets and stars are named

Procedure

Have students speculate on how planets and stars get their names by asking the following questions:

What are the names of the planets?
Where else have you seen those names used?
Why do you think so many planets have names from ancient mythology?

■ Explain that comets and features of the planets and moon are often named after their discoverers, some of whom were amateur astronomers. They are also sometimes named for people who are famous for achievements outside of science.

■ Point out that the names of stars and planets vary from one culture to another. Even the way people have viewed constellations over time could be very different. This is sometimes due to the fact that the shapes of constellations vary over time. Also, the southern and northern hemispheres' views of constellations vary.

■ Have students locate the names of various stars, including those mentioned in "Circles, Squares, and Daggers," and research their origins in field guides and other resource books. Students should find that the stars' names come from various sources. For example, Aldebaran is Arabic, while Sirius is Greek. Capella is Latin.

■ Have students conduct similar research on the names of other stars in such easily identified constellations as the Big Dipper and Orion.

VOYAGER to the PLANETS

from the book by Necia H. Apfel

156

About the Author

Necia Apfel studied astronomy in college and currently both writes about and teaches the subject. She has won many awards including ALA Notable Book, NCTE Outstanding Nonfiction, and Best Science Books for Children.

Students can read more about Necia Apfel on page 172 of the **Student Anthology.**

Other Books by Necia Apfel

- *It's All Relative: Einstein's Theory of Relativity*
- *Stars and Galaxies*
- *The Moon and Its Exploration*
- *Astronomy and Planetology*
- *Astronomy Projects for Young Scientists*

Selection Summary

Genre: Nonfiction

This selection tells the true story of the 12-year journey of the *Voyager 2* space probe from Earth to Neptune. Stunning photographs of the planets and their moons, taken by the *Voyager* spacecraft, help to emphasize how much astronomers have learned as a result of this mission.

Exploring the Theme

Selection Concepts

"Voyager to the Planets" demonstrates the increase in information about the solar system made possible by modern technology. Until rockets and other technologies made space probes possible, the only information astronomers had about the planets and their moons came from observations made on Earth with telescopes. Key concepts explored are:

- *Voyager's* 12-year journey from Earth to Neptune provided astronomers with fascinating facts and an up-close view of faraway planets, rings, and moons.

- Engineers and scientists on Earth must be prepared to troubleshoot and to make precise calculations in order to communicate with space probes and get desired results.

Check the Reading link of **SRA** Web page for links to theme-related Websites.
http://www.sra4kids.com

Exploration Activity Tips

Before Reading, read aloud the italicized introductory text. Have students raise questions about space probes based on this text, then browse the story for clues about which questions will be addressed.

During Reading, have students note any answers to the questions raised before reading and any details they find interesting.

After Reading, have students tell what information from this selection is helpful in their research. Then have students update the Concept/Question Board. Some may want to revise their activity plans based on what they have learned from the selection.

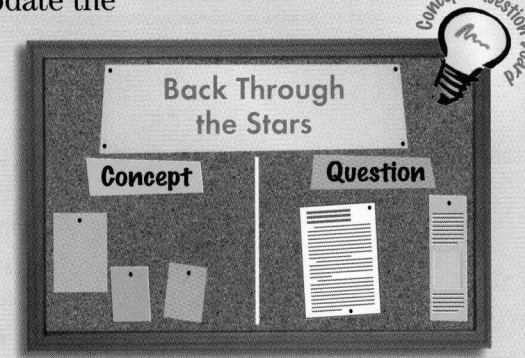

Unit 2 Exploration Management	
Lesson 1	Brainstorm research problems. Form interest-based groups. Develop and discuss initial research plans.
Lesson 2	Groups finalize plans, allocate tasks, and begin research. Discuss initial findings and resources.
Lesson 3	Research continues as groups consider revision of their activity focus.
Lesson 4	Students continue with research and present their initial findings.
Lesson 5 Voyager to the Planets	**Collaborative Exploration** **Research continues. Students present interesting findings or problems.** **Supplementary Activity** **Conduct class discussion to help identification of knowledge needs, to remind groups that they can still change their research problems, and to provide any other needed guidance.**
Lesson 6	Research continues. Students present interesting findings or problems.
Lesson 7	Students organize research findings and prepare presentations.
Lesson 8	Students present their activities.

Lesson Planner

Suggested Pacing: 3–5 days	DAY 1	DAY 2	
	DAY 1	DAY 2	
Part 1 Preparing to Read **Materials** ■ Student Anthology, pp. 156–173 ■ Transparencies 11, 44	**Word Knowledge** ■ Reading the Words and Sentences, p. 156G ■ Developing Oral Language, p. 156G **Build Background,** p. 156H **Preview and Prepare,** p. 156I **Selection Vocabulary,** p. 156I *space probe, shepherd satellites, retrograde, gravitational attraction*	**Preview and Prepare,** p. 156I ■ Review Transparency 44	
Part 2 Reading and Responding **Materials** ■ Student Anthology, pp. 156–173 ■ Teacher Observation Log ■ Reading and Writing Workbook, pp. 67–68 ■ Inquiry Journal, p. 22 ■ Home Connection, p. 25	**Student Anthology,** pp. 156–167 **Comprehension Strategies** ■ Clarifying, pp. 156, 160, 162 ■ Asking Questions, pp. 156, 164, 166 ■ Summarizing, pp. 158, 162, 164, 166	**Student Anthology,** pp. 168–173 **Comprehension Strategies** ■ Summarizing, pp. 168, 170 **Discussing Strategy Use,** p. 170 **Comprehension Skills** ✓■ Discussing the Selection, p. 171 **Exploring the Theme** ■ Selection Vocabulary, p. 173A *space probe, shepherd satellites, retrograde, gravitational attraction*	
Part 3 Integrating the Curriculum **Materials** ■ Student Anthology, pp. 156–173 ■ Inquiry Journal, pp. 32–33	**Writing** ■ Revising Process, p. 173C **Literary Elements** ■ Recognizing Informational Texts, p. 173D	**Writing Process** ■ Revise, p. 173C **Vocabulary** ■ Affixes and Meaning, p. 173E	
Independent Work Time **Materials** ■ Reteach, pp. 67–68 ■ ESL Supplement ■ Challenge, p. 36 ■ Intervention Guide ■ Listening Library Audiocassette	**Writing Process Continued** **ESL** ■ Word Meaning, pp. 156G, 166 ■ Vocabulary, p. 156J **Intervention** ■ Adjectives, p. 156G ■ Asking Questions, p. 164 **Unit Project: Continue Research**	**Writing Process Continued** **ESL** ■ Recognizing Informational Texts, p. 173D **Challenge** ■ Affixes, p. 173E **Intervention** ■ Comprehension, p. 156 **Unit Project Continued**	

✓ Informal **Assessment Available**   ✓ Formal **Assessment Available**

DAY 2 continued	DAY 3	
DAY 3	**DAY 4**	**DAY 5**
General Review	**General Review**	**Review Word Knowledge**

Student Anthology, pp. 156–173 **Comprehension Skills** ✓ ■ Compare and Contrast, pp. 157, 159, 161, 165 **Theme Connections** ■ Think About It, p. 173 ■ Research Ideas, p. 173	**Student Anthology, pp. 156–173** **Comprehension Skills** ✓ ■ Classifying and Categorizing, pp. 163, 167, 169 **Exploring the Theme** ■ Reading/Writing Connections, p. 173A ■ Literature Appreciation, p. 173A ■ Supporting Student Explorations, p. 173B	**Student Anthology, pp. 156–173** ■ Review Selection ■ Complete Discussion ■ Reread Selection in Pairs **Home Connection, p. 173A** ■ Discuss "Voyager to the Planets" ■ List questions or experiments for a special space mission

Writing Process Continued **Grammar, Usage, and Mechanics** ✓ ■ Complete Sentences, p. 173F **Listening/Speaking/Viewing** ■ Interpreting a Graph, p. 173G	**Writing Process Continued** **Study and Research** ■ Creating a Chart, p. 173G	**Across the Curriculum** **Math** ■ Comparing Planets, p. 173H **Art** ■ Visualizing the Planets, p. 173H

Writing Process Continued **Reteach** ✓ ■ Compare and Contrast, *Reteach*, pp. 67–68 **Challenge** ✓ ■ Compare and Contrast, *Challenge*, p. 36 **Intervention** ■ Compare and Contrast, p. 159 **Unit Project Continued**	**Writing Process Continued** **Challenge** ■ Complete and Incomplete Sentences, p. 173F **Intervention** ■ Classifying and Categorizing, p. 167 **Unit Project Continued**	**Writing Process Continued** **Challenge** ■ Classifying and Categorizing, p. 167 **Unit Project Continued**

Meeting Individual Needs
Independent Work Time

Preparing to Read

Meeting Individual Needs

ESL
- Word Meaning, p. 156G
- Vocabulary, p. 156J

Intervention
- Adjectives, p. 156G

Reading and Responding

Meeting Individual Needs

Reteach
- Compare and Contrast, *Reteach*, pp. 67–68

ESL
- Discussion, p. 163
- Word Meaning, p. 166

Challenge
- Compare and Contrast, *Challenge*, p. 36
- Classifying and Categorizing, p. 167

Intervention
- Comprehension, p. 156
- Compare and Contrast, p. 159
- Asking Questions, p. 164
- Classifying and Categorizing, p. 167

Integrating the Curriculum

Meeting Individual Needs

ESL
- Recognizing Informational Texts, p. 173D

Challenge
- Affixes, p. 173E
- Complete and Incomplete Sentences, p. 173F

Formal Assessment Options

Use these assessment pages along with your informal observations to gauge student progress.

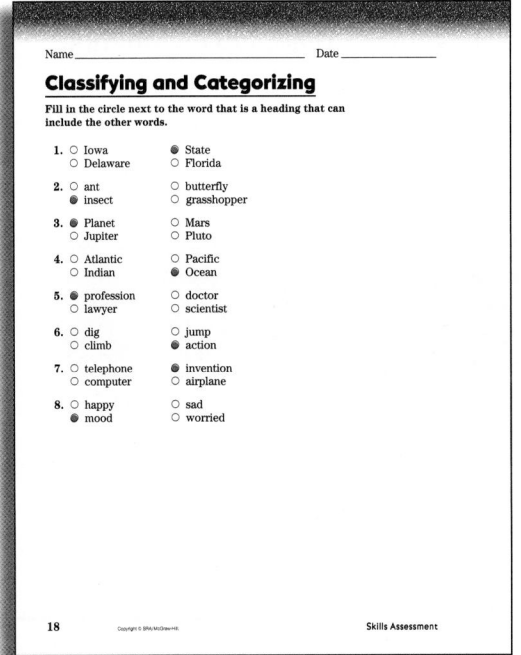

Skills Assessment, p. 18

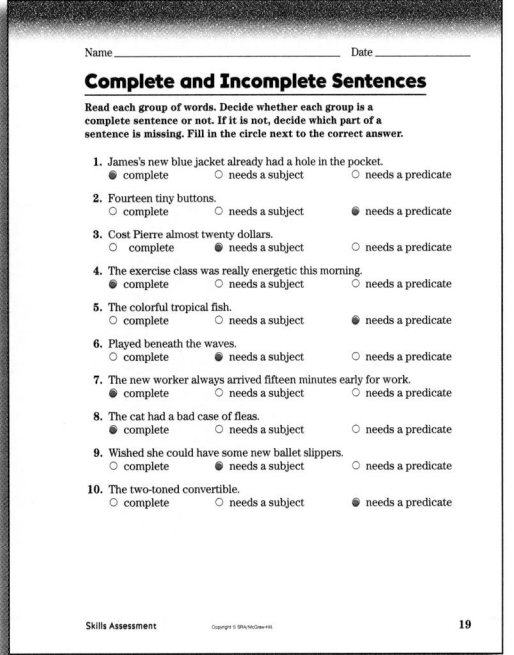

Skills Assessment, p. 19

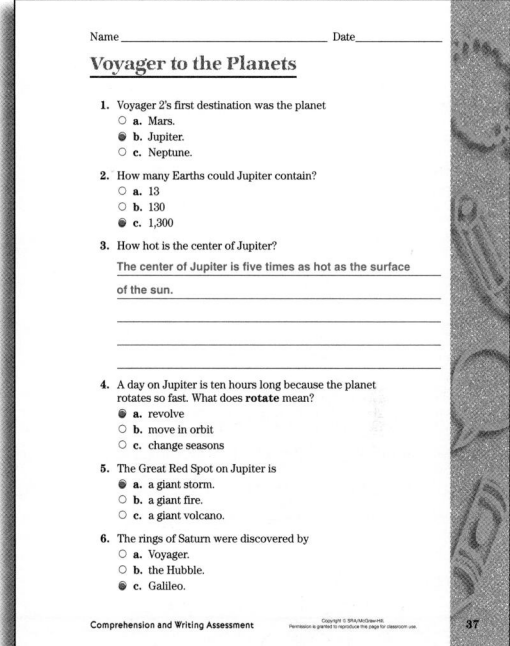

Comprehension and Writing Assessment, p. 37

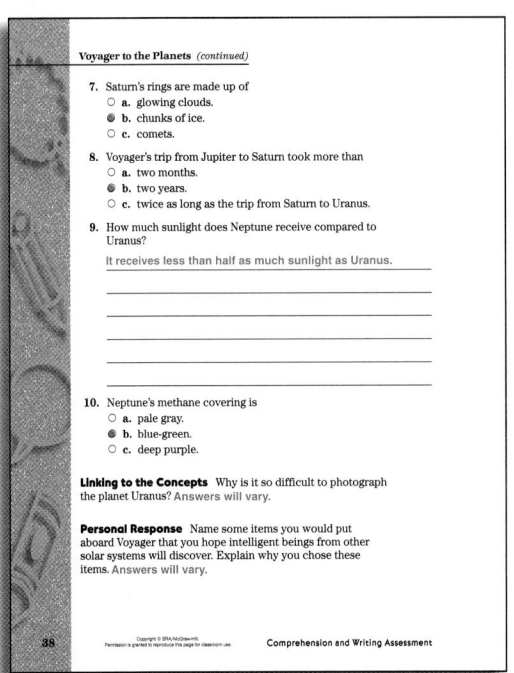

Comprehension and Writing Assessment, p. 38

① Preparing to Read

Meeting Individual Needs

ESL

Word Meaning Make sure the English-language learners understand the meanings of the words before they do the exercises. Refer to Unit 2, Lesson 5, of the *ESL Supplement* for specific suggestions.

Inter**v**ention

Adjectives Remind students who need more help with comparative and superlative forms of adjectives of what adjectives do. Then ask them for examples. Use the words the students have given and show them how to add the *-er* and *-est* endings when making a comparison. For example, you might discuss *tall*, *taller*, and *tallest*. For students who need more help, see Unit 2, Lesson 5, of the *Intervention Guide.*

Word Knowledge

Reading the Words and Sentences

Write each word and sentence on the chalkboard. Have students read each word together. After all the words have been read, have students read each sentence in natural phrases or chunks. Use the suggestions in About the Words to discuss the different features of the listed words.

Line 1:
Line 2:
Line 3:
Sentence 1:
Sentence 2:
Sentence 3:

> umbrella-shaped half-billion blue-green
> smart smarter smartest big bigger biggest
> black cloud slope
> Neptune is a beautiful blue-green color.
> Jupiter is the biggest planet visited by *Voyager 2.*
> Thick clouds cover the planet Uranus.

About the Words

- The words in Line 1 are hyphenated compounds. Have students try to think of other examples of hyphenated words from earlier Word Knowledge lessons.

- Line 2 contains the three forms of adjectives: the adjective, the comparative, and the superlative. Add the suffix *-er* to form comparative adjectives; add the suffix *-est* to form superlative adjectives.

- The words in Line 3 all contain a consonant-*l* blend. Invite students to brainstorm other words containing consonant-*l* blends.

Developing Oral Language

To review the words, have students do one or both of the following activities.

- Have one student point to a word in the lines above and select a classmate to read the word and use it in a sentence.

- After you have explained the three different types of words from Line 2, choose one of the forms and ask a student to find an example of this kind of word in the story. Have the student read the sentence in the story where he or she found the word. Call on another student to use the same word in a new sentence.

Build Background

Activate Prior Knowledge

Have students check the Concept/Question Board to refresh their memories about astronomy. Discuss the following with students to find out what they may already know about space exploration and have already learned about the unit theme. Tell students to use their prior knowledge to help them comprehend the selection they are about to read.

- Remind students of what they learned about the first important discoveries about the solar system in "Galileo."

- Ask students whether they are familiar with the story they are about to read, and if so, to tell a little about it.

- Have students share any other stories that have spacecraft in them.

Background Information

The following information may help students better understand the selection they are about to read.

- In 1976, *Viking I* and *Viking II* actually landed on Mars and sent back information.

- Scientists wanted to find out more about the outer planets, but because of the enormous distance, it would take 30 years or more to reach Neptune.

- By observing asteroids and comets, scientists discovered a way to use Jupiter's gravity to boost the space probe in the right direction and use each planet's gravity in succession to speed the space probe along.

- In 1977, *Voyager 2* made a "grand tour" of Jupiter, Saturn, Uranus, and Neptune.

- Some students may have trouble remembering all the planets in the solar system. If you have a map of the solar system, point out the planets visited by *Voyager 2* as they are mentioned in the text.

Writing Journal Tell students that after reading, they will jot down in their Writing Journals their reactions to this selection. Have them be on the lookout for any ideas they may have for using an unmanned spacecraft in a story.

Teacher Tip Ask students what types of information an unmanned spacecraft might bring back to Earth.

Preparing to Read

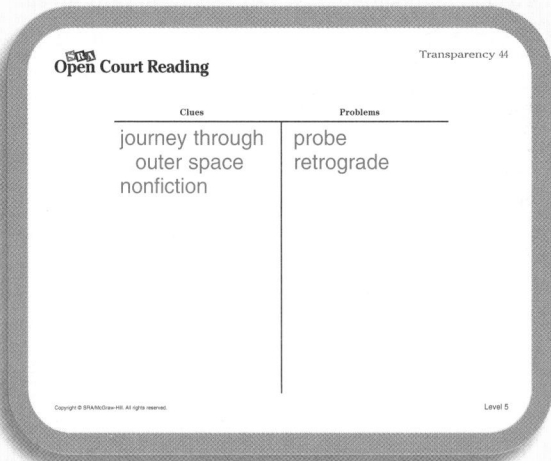

Transparency 44

Teacher Tip

To help students decode words, divide them into the syllables shown below. The information following each word tells how students can figure out the meaning of each word from the sentences on the transparency.

space probe	context clues
shep·herd sat·el·lites	apposition
ret·ro·grade	context clues
grav·i·ta·tion·al at·trac·tion	word structure, context clues

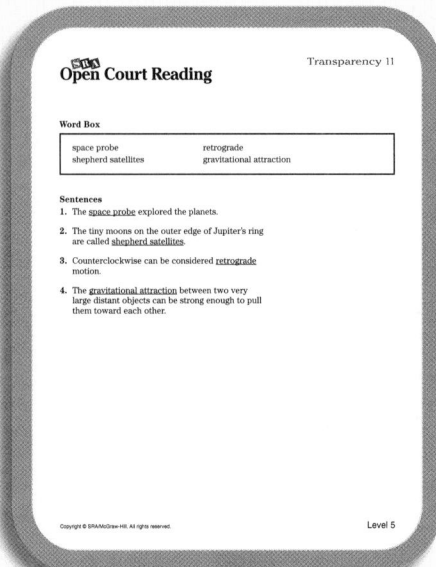

Transparency 11

Preview and Prepare

Browse

- Have a volunteer read the title and author's name aloud. Have students share what they know about nonfiction.

- Because this is nonfiction, have students browse through the entire selection, looking at diagrams, photos, and captions. Discuss with them what they think this story might have to do with astronomy.

- Have students search for words and phrases that connect to what they already know. Record these on *Transparency 44* in the Clues column.

- Encourage students to ask questions as they browse. Have them identify any problems while reading and record them in the Problems column.

Set Purposes

As they read, have students think about space and the planets in our solar system.

Selection Vocabulary

Students will use context clues, word structure, and apposition to clarify these and additional unfamiliar words.

Display *Transparency 11* before reading the selection to introduce and discuss the following words and their meanings.

space probe:	spacecraft sent out to explore other planets (page 157)
shep·herd sat·el·lites:	tiny moons that orbit rapidly around a planet (page 162)
ret·ro·grade:	moving backwards or opposite to the usual direction (page 170)
grav·i·ta·tion·al at·trac·tion:	a force that pulls two free bodies or objects toward each other (page 171)

Have students read the words in the Word Box. Help students decode multisyllabic words by reading them syllable by syllable.

Have students read the sentences on *Transparency 11.* Remind them to use clues in the sentences and structural clues to figure out the meaning of the underlined words. See the teacher tip on the left for information on how the words in each sentence can be defined.

Reading Recommendations

Your first reading of the selection should focus on developing the reading strategies found to the left of the reduced pages. We recommend that the students revisit the selection, rereading sections or the entire selection as a way to enhance their understanding and appreciation of the text. During rereading, they should focus on the comprehension skills, found to the right of the reduced pages.

Oral Reading

Have students read this selection aloud so that they can ask one another questions and help one another clarify the meanings of difficult passages. As this is a nonfiction selection and students are reading to be informed, allow students more time for reading. Have students adjust their reading rate by reading more slowly or by rereading certain sections of the selection in order to comprehend the information presented.

As students read aloud, have them read expressively, at an appropriate pace, in natural phrases and chunks. By reading the selection with fluency, students will demonstrate an understanding of the text and an ability to engage the listeners in an effective manner. If students encounter difficulties, have them use the reading strategies below or refer to the Blending Procedure (Program Appendix 15–16).

Using Reading Strategies

Reading-strategy instruction allows students to become aware of how good readers read. Skilled readers recognize when they are having problems and stop to use various reading strategies to help them make sense of what they are reading.

During the reading of "Voyager to the Planets" you will model the use of the following reading strategies:

- Clarifying
- Asking Questions
- Summarizing

Before reading, have students explain how they have used these strategies in the past and share any tips they can give each other on their use.

Building Comprehension Skills

Revisiting or rereading a selection allows students to apply skills that give them a more complete understanding of the text. Some follow-up comprehension skills help students organize information. Others lead to deeper understanding—to "reading between the lines," as mature readers do. In this selection, students will apply the follow-up comprehension skills of *Compare and Contrast* and *Classifying and Categorizing*.

Meeting Individual Needs

ESL

Vocabulary Check that English-language learners know the meanings of idioms and more difficult vocabulary in the story, including: *data, countdown, engineers, instruments, primary radio system, backup radio receiver, short circuit, programmers, rotates, drifts, equator, miniature solar system, theorizing, following similar orbits, wispy diffusion of tiny particles, the frigid emptiness of space, haze, confined orbits, a gravity-assist change of direction, lubricant, to compensate for this rapid forward motion, a turbulent state, cirrus-like clouds, a retrograde motion,* and *gravitational attraction.* Explain and show pictures as needed. Model example sentences and help English-speaking students make their own sentences. Refer to Unit 2, Lesson 5, of the *ESL Supplement* for teaching suggestions.

 Have students who may need extra help reading "Voyager to the Planets" reread the selection using the *Listening Library Audiocassette.*

 By this time in the fifth grade, good readers should be reading approximately 126 words per minute with fluency and expression. The only way to gain fluency is through practice. As explained in Reading Recommendations, have students reread all or part of the selection to you and to each other during class or Independent Work Time to focus on the comprehension skills and to build fluency.

② Reading and Responding

Read pages 156–173.

Comprehension Strategies

Modeling

❶ Clarifying *Good readers always clarify any terms they do not understand before continuing their reading. I see that Voyager 2 went on a "grand tour" of several planets. I'm not sure what that means. On page 157 there is a diagram. If we look there, it might show us which planets were explored by Voyager 2. Now we see that Voyager 2 went to Jupiter, Saturn, Uranus, and Neptune. That certainly would be a grand tour!*

Modeling

❷ Asking Questions *Asking questions helps readers focus on what they would like to learn from their reading. It looks as if Voyager 2 went by Saturn. I wonder what the rings are made of? Maybe we'll find out later as we read more.* (The answer to this question can be found on page 162 in the Teacher Tip.)

Word Knowledge

explore, flew, strange-looking

Students can use the skills they learned in the Word Knowledge section of this lesson to read these words. Remind students of this if they have difficulty reading these words.

Reading Recommendation

ORAL • CHORAL • SILENT

VOYAGER
to the
PLANETS

from the book by Necia H. Apfel

156

Assessment

✓ **Informal** Observe individual students as they read, and use the Teacher Observation Log found in the Assessment Guide to record anecdotal information about each student's strengths and weaknesses.

Meeting Individual Needs

Intervention

Comprehension Intervention strategies for those students having difficulty with reading "Voyager to the Planets" can be found in Unit 2, Lesson 5, of the *Intervention Guide.*

Voyagers 1 and 2 are space probes, spacecraft sent to explore other planets. Space probes carry instruments that collect information and send photographs and other data back to earth. Before the Voyagers, space probes had been sent to gather information from Mars, Venus, Jupiter, Saturn, and Mercury. Voyager 1 flew by Jupiter and Saturn. Voyager 2, however, was the first space probe to go on a "grand tour" of several planets. This selection follows the long journey of Voyager 2 from the time it left Earth.

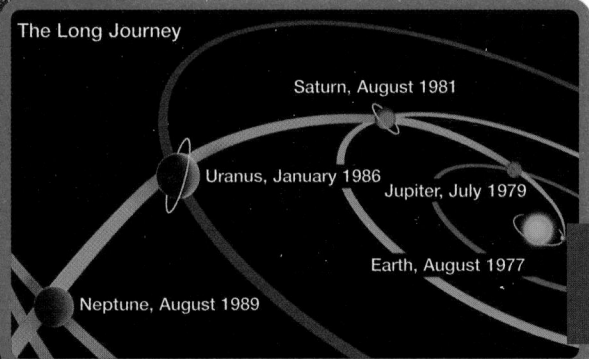

The Long Journey

Saturn, August 1981

Uranus, January 1986

Jupiter, July 1979

Earth, August 1977

Neptune, August 1989

Diagram of Voyager 2's twelve-year journey to Jupiter, Saturn, Uranus, and Neptune.

On August 20, 1977, Voyager 2 was placed atop a Titan 3-E/Centaur rocket at the United States launching site on Cape Canaveral in Florida. The rocket blasted off and rose majestically into the clear blue sky.

All was well. But now the real countdown began. Voyager would take two years to reach its first destination—the giant planet Jupiter.

Voyager is a strange-looking machine with tubes and boxlike structures sticking out all over it. These contain

157

Comprehension
Skills

Compare and Contrast

Introduce the students to *compare and contrast*, which means to identify similarities and differences between two or more elements of a selection. Tell students that this skill will help them understand each element more completely, thus enhancing their understanding of the selection.

To help students understand the concept, have them compare and contrast common things, for example, airplanes and trains or doctors and dentists. Then have the students compare *Voyager 2* with *Voyager 1*.

Tell them that this selection is going to describe the planets visited by *Voyager 2*. Suggest that they set up a chart or table with columns headed by the different planets in the diagram on page 157 (including Earth) to help them compare the planets as they read.

←Skills Strand→

Compare and Contrast
INTRODUCED: Unit 2, Lesson 5
REVIEWED: Unit 2, Lesson 7
Unit 3, Lesson 2
Unit 3, Lesson 5
Unit 4, Lesson 1

Teacher Tip Teach the students the following mnemonic device to help them remember the names of the planets in the solar system: *My Very Educated Mother Just Served Us Nine Pizzas.* The planets are Mercury, Venus, Earth, Mars, Jupiter, Saturn, Uranus, Neptune, and Pluto.

2 Reading and Responding

Comprehension Strategies

Prompting

3 Summarizing *I know that good readers summarize to check their comprehension. Let's sum up what we've read so far. Voyager 2 was the first probe to do a grand tour of the planets. It blasted off on August 20, 1977. It would take Voyager 2 two years to reach its first stop—Jupiter. Who would like to continue the summary?*

Student Sample

Summarizing *Voyager 2 was equipped with instruments for collecting data from the places it would visit. It also had an antenna for receiving directions on where to go and what data to collect. The people who built Voyager 2 tried to think of all the things that might go wrong on its trip.*

Word Knowledge

umbrella-shaped, problems, clouds
Students can use the skills they learned in the Word Knowledge section of this lesson to read these words. Remind students of this if they have difficulty reading these words.

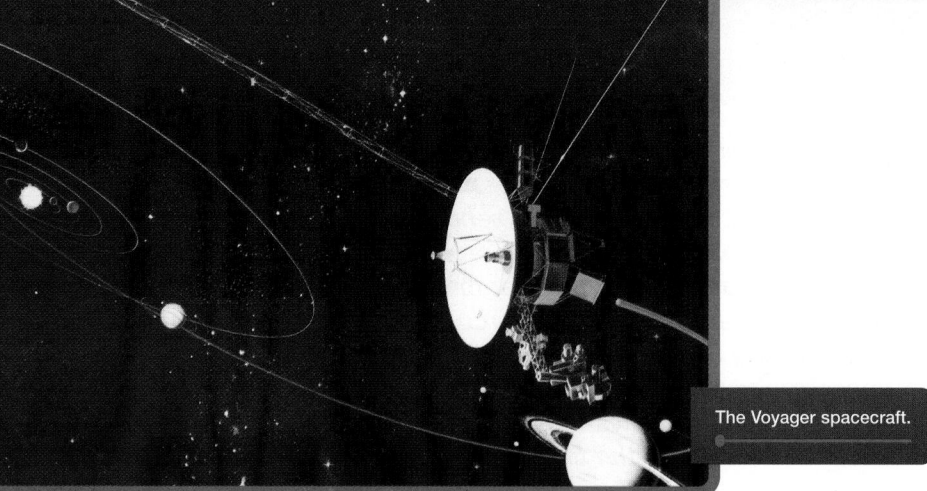

The Voyager spacecraft.

its many instruments, including cameras, radio receivers, and <u>ultraviolet</u> and <u>infrared</u> <u>sensors</u>. The instruments were designed to collect data from places Voyager would visit and to send this information back to Earth, where scientists and engineers were eagerly awaiting the reports.

Sometimes instructions had to be sent from stations on Earth to Voyager, telling it when to change its position, what data to record, or which instruments to use. Voyager was equipped with a big umbrella-shaped antenna to receive these directions.

3 In designing Voyager, the engineers tried very hard to <u>anticipate</u> any problems or emergencies that might arise on its long journey. But the first difficulty occurred much sooner than they expected. Only eight months after Voyager was launched, its <u>primary</u> radio system stopped working and the backup radio receiver developed a short <u>circuit</u>. These <u>defects</u> drastically reduced Voyager's ability to receive instructions from the scientists. New computer programs had to be sent to Voyager so that it could respond to future commands. The scientists could only hope that the defective radio system would last for the entire journey. Otherwise, there would be no way for them to communicate with Voyager.

158

Research in Action

Reading Strategies

Whenever readers summarize or visualize the text, they are interpreting it. That is, it is the reader who decides what should be a summary or visualization of text and, thus, every summary and visualization is a personal perspective on the meaning of a text.
(Michael Pressley)

With its faulty radio operating weakly, Voyager kept sailing farther into space. After two years it finally arrived at the colorfully banded planet Jupiter, passing closest to it on July 9, 1979.

Jupiter is so big that more than 1,300 Earths could fit inside of it. It has more material in it than all the other planets in the solar system combined. It is truly a giant planet.

Following commands from programmers on Earth, Voyager took pictures of Jupiter's clouds, recorded their temperatures and speeds, and analyzed their composition. The spacecraft found that it is very cold out there, a half-billion miles from the sun. Jupiter receives only one twenty-fifth the sunlight we receive on Earth. Its pretty clouds have temperatures of about –230° F. Deep inside Jupiter it is much warmer, and at the planet's center the temperature rises to 54,000° F. That's around five times as hot as the surface of the sun.

This great heat rising from the interior would make Jupiter's cloud tops look like a multicolored bubbling mixture if the planet were not turning around rapidly on its axis. But Jupiter rotates very fast. A day on Jupiter lasts only ten hours. This rapid rotation causes the clouds to be pulled out into a series of colored bands. Different substances in the clouds give them their varied colors.

159

Comprehension Skills

Compare and Contrast

Point out how the author compares Jupiter to Earth.

- Jupiter is so big that more than 1,300 Earths could fit inside it. (page 159)

- Jupiter receives only $\frac{1}{25}$ the sunlight we receive on Earth. (page 159)

Have students discuss how these comparisons help their understanding about Jupiter. They should be able to conclude that Jupiter is very big and very cold on the surface. Remind students to record this information on their comparison chart of the planets.

Teacher Tip To help students compare the size of Jupiter with Earth, ask them to imagine a large gumball machine filled with 1,300 gumballs. Tell them to think of the machine as Jupiter and each gumball as one Earth.

Meeting Individual Needs

Intervention

Compare and Contrast Help students make comparisons by rereading the selection in sections. For example, read about Jupiter and Saturn. Then prompt students to ask themselves, "How are these planets alike? How are they different?"

② Reading and Responding

Comprehension Strategies

Modeling

4 Clarifying *There's a lot of description here about Jupiter. Sometimes it's hard to remember so many facts. If we look at the photograph of Jupiter as we read, it might help. For example, I can see what the Great Red Spot looks like by looking at the photograph.*

Teacher Tip The author mentions Galileo's discovery of the rings of Saturn. Remind the students to connect information from "Galileo" to this selection.

The planet Jupiter. The Great Red Spot is just below the planet's equator.

The bands of clouds circling Jupiter are not smooth or featureless. Within them are huge, <u>turbulent</u> storms, whirlpools, and other disturbances. Weather on this giant planet is extremely violent and forceful. The most noticeable storm is called the Great Red Spot. It is so big that it can be observed through telescopes on Earth and has been seen for at least three hundred years.

4 Long before Voyager was launched, astronomers knew that the Great Red Spot was a giant storm, towering 10 miles above the rest of the clouds that swirl around it. Through their telescopes, they had seen the Red Spot change in size and in brightness, although it never seemed to vanish completely. Voyager's pictures showed the Red Spot to be about the size of Earth, but at other times it was known to be three times the size of Earth. Its color also varied from bright cherry red to very faint reddish <u>hues</u>. Astronomers aren't sure why the Great Red Spot appears red or why it has lasted such a long time.

Although the Great Red Spot drifts around the planet, it is always about the same distance below

160

Word Knowledge

completely, bigger, smaller

Students can use the skills they learned in the Word Knowledge section of this lesson to read these words. Remind students of this if they have difficulty reading these words.

A closeup of the Great Red Spot surrounded by turbulent cloud formations.

Jupiter's equator. As it drifts, it also rotates, taking about six days to turn around once. This rotation and drifting cause the gases around the Red Spot to eddy and swirl, somewhat like the way rocks and other barriers cause a rapidly rushing stream of water to froth and foam into small whirlpools and eddies. The photographs taken by Voyager show these eddies and swirls in great detail.

Jupiter is the center of its own miniature solar system. It has at least sixteen moons, three of which were discovered by Voyager. Four of Jupiter's moons are very large, with diameters of several thousands of miles. The other twelve moons are no bigger than a few hundred miles across, and many are much smaller.

We now know that all four of the planets visited by Voyager have ring systems. Saturn's magnificent ring system was discovered about 1610 by Galileo. In 1977, more than 350 years later, faint rings around the planet Uranus were detected through powerful telescopes. Astronomers started theorizing that perhaps Jupiter and Neptune also had ring systems. Voyager proved them right when it discovered rings around both planets.

161

Comprehension Skills

Compare and Contrast

Have the students identify places in the text where the author compares two different planets. Does the author make comparisons between any other objects in these pages? For example, students might note the differences among Jupiter's moons, as well as the number of moons that Jupiter and Earth have. Discuss the comparisons of the ring systems. Ask if these comparisons are helpful in visualizing or understanding the rings being compared.

Have the students fill in their charts of the planets as they continue to read the selection. For example, students should fill in which planets have ring systems.

Teacher Tip While the students are reading, have them note any answers to the questions raised before reading and any details they find interesting.

Reading and Responding

Comprehension Strategies

Modeling

5 Clarifying *I'm puzzled. How could the rings around Jupiter and Saturn look solid and be made of chunks of ice? Maybe if we imagined things we've seen that spin very quickly, like a top or a figure skater, I'll get a better picture. When they go fast, they start to look blurry. Maybe that's why we can't see the chunks of ice distinctly.*

Modeling

6 Summarizing *If I try to summarize the information I read about Jupiter in my own words, I will be able to figure out what information is most important. Jupiter is a giant planet. Jupiter is very cold because it is so far from the sun. Inside of Jupiter, however, it is even hotter than the sun. Jupiter's clouds contain huge storms, the biggest of which is called the Great Red Spot.*

Teacher Tip Point out to the students that the question asked in Strategy 2 is answered on page 163, line 18, of the *Student Anthology*.

Word Knowledge

farther, half-billion, float

Students can use the skills they learned in the Word Knowledge section of this lesson to read these words. Remind students of this if they have difficulty reading these words.

---

5 From afar, all these ring systems appear solid, but they are actually composed of thousands of individual chunks of ice, all following similar orbits around a planet. Saturn's rings are the most spectacular, but all four ring systems are fascinating in different ways.

Voyager found that Jupiter's ring system is just a single ring consisting of several parts with no gaps between them. The brightest part is the outer edge, but even this section is too faint to be detected from Earth. Just outside this edge Voyager found two very small moons. Both moons race rapidly around Jupiter, taking only about seven hours to complete their orbits. By contrast, our moon takes twenty-nine and one-half days to orbit Earth, which is a much smaller planet.

By moving so quickly, these tiny moons prevent any ring particles from straying beyond the ring's outer edge, farther out into space. Astronomers call such moons shepherd satellites because, like sheep dogs with sheep, they keep ring particles confined within certain regions.

Because no shepherd satellites control the inner particles of Jupiter's ring system, they have spread out very thinly, reaching all the way to Jupiter's cloud tops. Only when Voyager was very close to Jupiter could it **6** detect this faint, wispy <u>diffusion</u> of tiny particles.

Leaving Jupiter, Voyager headed farther into the <u>frigid</u> emptiness of space. For two more years it traveled outward another half-billion miles, reaching the ringed planet Saturn in August 1981.

Saturn's rapid rotation, like Jupiter's, causes its clouds to appear as colorful bands. But Saturn has no giant storms like Jupiter's Great Red Spot. It has much

162

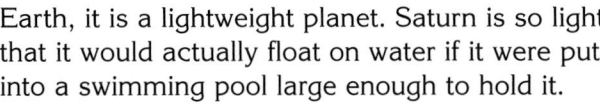
The planet Saturn.

smaller storms that look brown and white in Voyager's photographs.

Saturn also has much less material in it than Jupiter. In fact, although it is the second largest planet and has a diameter ten times that of Earth, it is a lightweight planet. Saturn is so light that it would actually float on water if it were put into a swimming pool large enough to hold it.

A thick layer of haze covers Saturn, making its atmospheric markings look much more muted than Jupiter's. Its clouds appear in different shades of butterscotch rather than bright orange, yellow, and white.

Nothing obscures Saturn's magnificent rings. Billions of icy particles orbit the planet in a flat sheet, extending outward more than 45,000 miles. But the

The many rings of Saturn. Differences in the color of the rings indicate different chemical compositions.

163

Comprehension Skills

Classifying and Categorizing

Introduce the students to *classifying and categorizing*. Tell them that when similar things are placed into one group, they are being classified or categorized. If, for example, apples, pears, oranges, and bananas were placed in one group, the classification or category of that group would be *fruit*.

Tell students that *classifying and categorizing* helps them establish relationships between things they read about, which, in turn, gives them a deeper understanding of the text.

Have students select something from this selection that they can classify or categorize. If they need a suggestion, have them classify the planets that *Voyager* visited. Tell them that the category is *Planets that Voyager Visited* and write this as a heading on the chalkboard. Tell the students to find all of the planets discussed so far in this selection and write those under the heading on the chalkboard.

←**Skills Strand**→

Classifying and Categorizing
INTRODUCED: Unit 2, Lesson 4
REVIEWED: Unit 2, Lesson 5
Unit 2, Lesson 7

Meeting Individual Needs

ESL

Discussion English-language learners, like all other students, should be encouraged to take an active part in the discussions. These discussions will help provide them with the opportunity to use and become more proficient in English.

Teacher Tip Continue to have the students compare and contrast the information presented in this selection.

Reading and Responding

Comprehension Strategies

Modeling

7 Summarizing *We have read a lot about Titan. Let's summarize to see if we got the most important information right. Titan has such a thick atmosphere that its surface can't be seen. The atmosphere is mostly nitrogen. Its surface temperature is incredibly cold.*

Prompting

8 Asking Questions *In this selection, we have learned a lot of interesting things about the planets Jupiter and Saturn. Now that we are getting ready to read about Uranus, what questions can you think of about this planet that might be answered by reading this passage?*

Student Sample

Asking Questions *What is special about Uranus? If I read closely, maybe I can answer this question. (This question is answered on page 166.)*

Word Knowledge

miniature, poster, remembered

Students can use the skills they learned in the Word Knowledge section of this lesson to read these words. Remind students of this if they have difficulty reading these words.

---

thickness of this sheet is only about one hundred yards, the length of a football field. The rings cast shadows on Saturn's clouds but are thin enough for stars to be seen through them, even from Earth. As Voyager had found at Jupiter, shepherd satellites help herd the tiny particles of Saturn's rings into confined orbits.

Saturn, like Jupiter, has its own solar system, with at least eighteen moons. But Saturn has only one large moon, Titan. The rest are quite small. Eight of these have been called "moonlets" or "the Rocks" because they are very tiny, irregular chunks of rocky material. Some of them are shepherd satellites.

Titan, on the other hand, is bigger than the planet Mercury. It is also the only moon in the solar system that has a thick atmosphere. This atmosphere is so thick, in fact, that Voyager couldn't see Titan's surface at all. Titan's atmosphere is mainly nitrogen, much like Earth's atmosphere, which also contains oxygen. Titan lacks oxygen, the element so vital to life on Earth.

Beneath its thick, smoglike clouds, Titan's surface must be a dark, gloomy place, much like the depths of an ocean on Earth. Because of its nitrogen atmosphere, Titan may be the way Earth was billions of years ago. Of course, Titan is much colder than Earth ever was. Its surface temperature is around –296° F.

Voyager had been carefully aimed so that Saturn could give it a gravity-assist change of direction toward Uranus. Before Voyager 2 reached Uranus, however, the engineers found that the spacecraft had lost much of the lubricant needed to keep its scanning platform operating. Without the ability to turn easily, the cameras mounted on this platform could not be aimed properly. Instead, the entire spacecraft would have to be rotated,

164

Meeting Individual Needs

Intervention

Asking Questions Remind students that often their questions are answered further in the selection. Encourage them to write down their questions and then look for answers as they read.

Teacher Tip A solar map might help the students see how unique Uranus's rotation is.

a much more difficult <u>maneuver</u>. Also, Voyager's computer software, especially those commands controlling Voyager's <u>stabilization</u> and photographing instructions, had to be redesigned.

8   The engineers knew that whereas Voyager had been able to spend several days at Jupiter and Saturn, it would have only about six hours at Uranus. And because Uranus is so much farther from the sun than either Jupiter or Saturn, much, much less sunlight reaches it. Taking a picture at Uranus has been compared to photographing a ball park at night by the light of a single candle.

The engineers calculated that Voyager would be moving at about 12 miles per second when it went past Uranus. This meant that in 10 seconds it would move 120 miles. So Voyager's camera had to be moved backward at just the right speed to <u>compensate</u> for this rapid forward motion. All these commands had to be sent to Voyager almost three hours beforehand, because that's how long it takes light or radio waves, traveling at the speed of light, to reach the planet from Earth.

Also, because of the increased distance, Voyager's radio signals back to Earth became much weaker. The engineers had to expand the Deep Space Network that tracked and communicated with Voyager. To do this, they started using powerful radio telescopes, such as the Very Large Array (VLA) in New Mexico and a similar one in Australia. These large series of connected radio telescopes act as one huge telescope, detecting radio waves too faint for a single receiver to pick up. Once again, when Voyager had in effect radioed home for help, the engineers were able to devise new and brilliant solutions. Voyager's engineers were the real heroes of this story.

165

Meeting Individual Needs

Reteach

Compare and Contrast Have students who need additional help and instruction and practice with this concept complete *Reteach,* pages 67–68.

Challenge

Compare and Contrast Review the definition of *compare and contrast.* Have students browse the selection "Telescopes" and make a chart of the three telescopes' differences and similarities. Have students who understand this concept complete *Challenge,* page 36.

Comprehension Skills

Compare and Contrast

For additional help with compare and contrast, have students complete *Reading and Writing Workbook* pages 67–68.

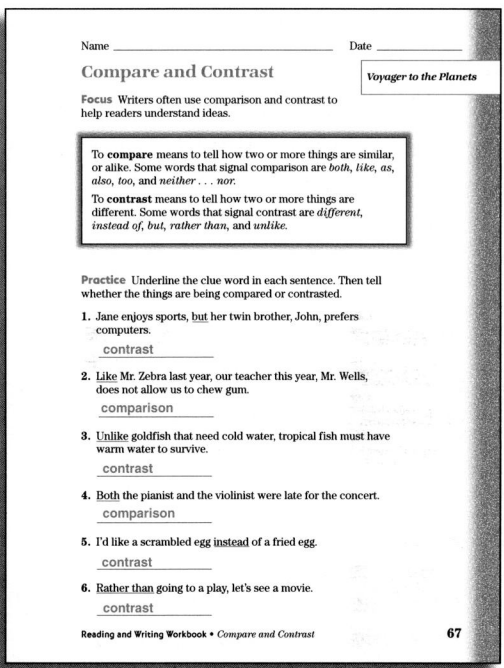

Reading and Writing Workbook pp. 67–68

2 Reading and Responding

Comprehension Strategies

Modeling

9 **Answering Questions** *Remember the question we had about what is special about Uranus? This is our answer: Uranus rolls in its orbit like a top spinning on its side. That's why it has an 84-year orbit that faces the sun only half of the time.*

Modeling

10 **Summarizing** *The section about Uranus is over, and Voyager is about to go to Neptune. This would be a good time to stop and summarize. I read about Uranus's rotation, its number of moons, and its ring system.*

Prompting

11 **Asking Questions** *Now that we have read about Jupiter, Saturn, and Uranus, what questions do you have about Neptune that might be answered when we read the next passage?*

Student Sample

Asking Questions *How big is Neptune? How far away is it?*

I read that Neptune is about the same size as Uranus. It is more than a billion miles farther away from the sun than Uranus.

Word Knowledge

English, blue-green, larger

Students can use the skills they learned in the Word Knowledge section of this lesson to read these words. Remind students of this if they have difficulty reading these words.

All these preparations took place while Voyager silently traveled onward. On January 24, 1986, after four and a half long years, the sturdy spacecraft came within about 50,000 miles of Uranus. It was only 10 miles off the desired point after having traveled 2 billion miles from Earth.

Uranus was discovered during the time of the American Revolutionary War. In 1781, the English astronomer Sir William Herschel realized that what previously had been recorded as a star was actually the seventh planet in our solar system. Many years later, five moons were found orbiting Uranus, and then in 1977 Uranus's ring system was detected.

Uranus's main peculiarity, however, was known long before Voyager's journey. It is not the planet's rings or its moons that are unique. It is the planet itself. Unlike other planets, which rotate in an upright position, **9** Uranus rolls along in its orbit like a top spinning on its side. As a result, during half of its eighty-four-year orbit Uranus's north pole faces the sun, and during the other half its south pole is sunlit. Uranus's moons and rings also follow this strange orientation because they all have orbits directly above Uranus's equator.

Astronomers were disappointed at how few features Voyager was able to detect in Uranus's clouds. Layers of thick haze hang over most of the upper clouds, obscuring any details that may exist below. A small amount of methane gas in the haze and clouds gives the planet its soft blue-green color.

Although Voyager found Uranus almost featureless, the visit was not in vain. Besides discovering ten new Uranian moons and obtaining close-up photographs of the five known ones, Voyager was able to distinguish ten very narrow rings of particles in Uranus's ring system. The rings are widely separated by several shepherd satellites that were among the ten new moons found by Voyager.

166

Meeting Individual Needs

ESL

Word Meaning Review difficult words and technical terms in the selection with English-language learners beforehand to ensure that they know the meanings. Use pictures of objects, chalkboard drawings, or pantomime. Refer to Unit 2, Lesson 5, of the ***ESL Supplement*** for teaching suggestions.

Teacher Tip It is important that summing up not be intrusive. Therefore, it should be done quickly and only a few times in the course of most active readings.

The planet Uranus. One of Uranus's moons, Miranda, is shown in the foreground.

Particles in the rings are made of ice but are covered with sootlike material, which makes them appear very dark. Most of the particles are about the size of a fist or bigger. One would expect to find smaller particles as well, possibly as small as dust. Astronomers theorize that some process must be sweeping the rings clear, leaving only the larger chunks.

10

11 The astronomers would have liked Voyager to linger longer at Uranus. But even as the spacecraft approached Uranus, they were preparing speed and direction commands to be radioed to it. With a gravity-assist from Uranus, Voyager would head toward Neptune.

By the time Voyager arrived at Neptune, the engineers were already jokingly describing the spacecraft as being hard of hearing with a touch of arthritis and a slight loss of memory. Voyager was a very old spacecraft indeed.

167

Comprehension Skills

Classifying and Categorizing

Remind the students that when similar or like objects are placed in the same group, they are being classified or categorized.

This part of the selection deals with what *Voyager* found on the planet Uranus. Write "What *Voyager* Found on Uranus" on the chalkboard and tell the students that this is the name of a category. Tell them to read pages 166 and 167 of the selection and to name what objects *Voyager* found existing on Uranus. Write these under the heading on the chalkboard. *(Answers: ten Uranian moons, ten narrow rings, several shepherd satellites)*

Meeting Individual Needs

Challenge

Classifying and Categorizing Invite students to revisit the selection "Telescopes" and find ways to classify and categorize the information presented there.

Intervention

Classifying and Categorizing If students are having difficulty with this concept, tell students that creating visual aids can help them to keep track of the information they are trying to classify or categorize. Show them how to put the information categorized in the lesson above into chart form.

2 Reading and Responding

Comprehension Strategies

Prompting

⑫ Summarizing *This is a good place to pause and summarize what we have learned about Neptune. Neptune is about the same size as Uranus and is blue-green because of methane gas in its clouds. It has very strong storms in its atmosphere, including the Great Dark Spot, the Great Dark Spot Two, and Scooter. Would anyone else like to add to this summary?*

Student Sample

Summarizing *Neptune also has a ring system. The first two rings are narrow and have shepherd satellites. The third ring is a lot wider. There are also two more rings beyond the third one.*

Word Knowledge

peaceful-looking, slight, faster

Students can use the skills they learned in the Word Knowledge section of this lesson to read these words. Remind students of this if they have difficulty reading these words.

However, Voyager came closer to Neptune than it did to any other object in its long journey. It passed 2,700 miles above the cloud tops over Neptune's north pole. That was on August 25, 1989, twelve years after its launch. Voyager was now $2^3/4$ billion miles from Earth. The spacecraft was so far from the people who sent commands to it that it would have to operate at the very limit of its capability to hear their directions.

Neptune is too far away from us to be seen without a telescope. Sunlight reaching Uranus is very dim, but it is two and a half times as much as the amount of light reaching Neptune. Neptune receives only one-thousandth the amount of light we receive on Earth.

Astronomers thought that Neptune would be featureless like Uranus. They were delightfully surprised. Neptune is about the same size as Uranus and shares the same blue-green color because of a small amount of methane in its clouds. But heat rising from Neptune's hot interior keeps its cloud top temperatures similar to Uranus's temperatures, even though Neptune is more than a billion miles farther away from the sun.

This rising heat drives fierce winds, creating huge storms in Neptune's atmosphere, much like those found on Jupiter. Instead of finding a peaceful-looking planet, Voyager found active cloud structures in a turbulent state.

Neptune's biggest feature is called the Great Dark Spot, which is a huge rotating storm about the size of Earth. Unlike Jupiter's Great Red Spot, the Great Dark Spot is a hole or depression in the clouds. It lets us look deep into Neptune's atmosphere, although all

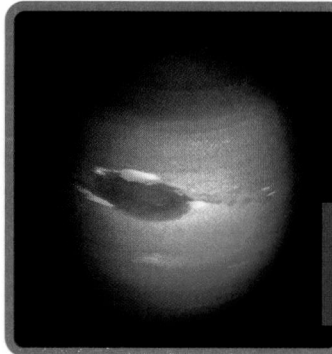

The planet Neptune. The Great Dark Spot is at the equator, just above the white cloud.

168

we see is darker shades of Neptune's blue-green methane covering.

About 30 miles above the atmosphere, white cirruslike clouds form and <u>dissipate</u> around the Great Dark Spot, similar to the way clouds form on mountainsides on Earth. White wispy clouds are also found near a small triangular-shaped storm, which moves around the planet faster than the Great Dark Spot and has therefore been dubbed Scooter. Another storm, Dark Spot Two, is smaller than the Great Dark Spot and is <u>oval</u> in shape. It has a white cloud hovering above its center.

The thick blue-green clouds covering Uranus and Neptune make up only about 10 to 20 percent of the planets' mass. The rest is rock and ice beneath the clouds. Uranus and Neptune are not true gas planets like Jupiter and Saturn. Scientists believe that they may be the <u>accumulation</u> of thousands of huge boulders that crashed together and formed planets early in the solar system's history.

After Voyager confirmed that both Jupiter and Uranus had ring systems, astronomers were fairly sure that Neptune would have one, too. They were, therefore, not surprised when Voyager detected it. When the spacecraft was still far away from Neptune, the pictures it sent back to Earth showed only sections of rings. Not until Voyager was much closer could the rest of the rings be observed. The brighter sections seen at first were found simply to have more material in them, making them more visible. And once again, Voyager detected shepherd satellites confining two of the first three rings it discovered into very narrow areas. The third ring is much more spread out. Later, after studying Voyager's photographs more closely, (12) astronomers discovered a fourth and fifth ring.

169

Assessment

✔ **Formal** To assess students' understanding of this concept, have them complete **Skills Assessment,** page 18.

Comprehension Skills

Classifying and Categorizing

Remind the students that when similar or like objects are placed in the same group they are being classified or categorized.

Have the students review the selections to locate the various storms that *Voyager* discovered. Write "Storms *Voyager* Discovered" on the chalkboard. *(Answers: Great Red Spot, Great Dark Spot, Scooter, and Dark Spot Two)*

Teacher Tip Invite students to tell what information from this selection is helpful in their research. Have students update the Concept/Question Board.

② Reading and Responding

Comprehension Strategies

Modeling

⑬ Summarizing *Because we know that summarizing will help us check our comprehension, this may be a good time for us to sum up what we have learned about Neptune's largest moon, Triton. We know that Triton spins around Neptune in the direction opposite to Neptune's spin. It has snowfalls, volcanoes, and geysers. However, it has few craters, which means that its crust is young and ever-changing.*

Discussing Strategy Use

After they have read the selection, have students share any problems they encountered and tell what strategies they used to solve them. Then, have them answer the following questions. If they answer "no" to any of the questions, have them reread part of the selection to find the answer.

- What questions did they ask before reading about the planets? Did these questions help focus their reading? Were they answered in the selection?

- How did they clarify some of the puzzling information in this selection?

- Did they find it helpful to summarize after every major section?

Make sure that students explain how using the strategies helped them understand the selection better and how they read effectively to find answers to the questions they asked as they set purposes.

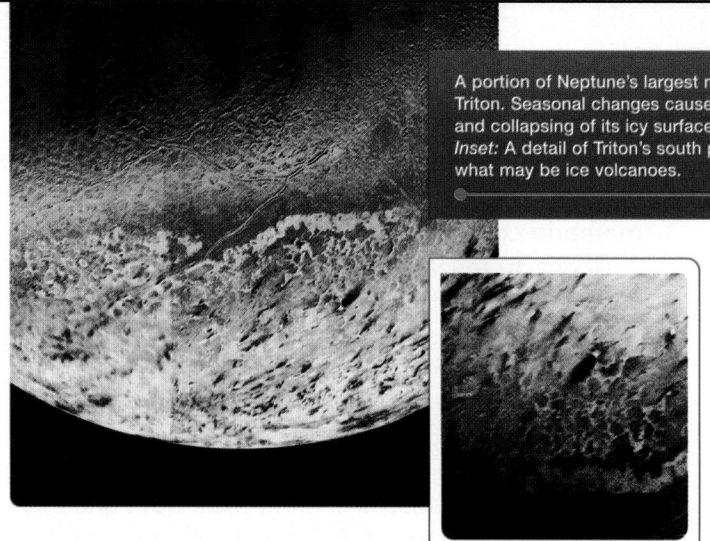

A portion of Neptune's largest moon, Triton. Seasonal changes cause melting and collapsing of its icy surface. *Inset:* A detail of Triton's south pole shows what may be ice volcanoes.

Voyager also found six new moons orbiting Neptune, raising the total number known to eight. But most amazing was what Voyager discovered about Triton, Neptune's largest moon. Although Triton had been observed from Earth many years before, little was known about it other than that it was one of the largest satellites in the solar system. Triton orbits Neptune in a retrograde motion, which means that it goes around Neptune in the direction opposite to Neptune's spin. It is the only major moon in the solar system to have this characteristic, although some of the smaller moons of Jupiter have retrograde motion.

The surface of Triton, as revealed by Voyager, is fascinating. Bright snowfalls only a few decades old contrast with craters billions of years old. In general, however, craters are very scarce on Triton, indicating that its crust is quite young and is constantly changing.

Voyager found several active volcanoes on Triton. The material coming from them is not molten rock like the hot lava that comes out of volcanoes on Earth. Instead, water mixed with other substances is <u>spewed</u> out, making the volcanoes more like <u>geysers</u>.

Voyager also photographed dark plumes of dust-filled nitrogen gas erupting from beneath Triton's surface. The gas rises some 5 miles into the thin

170

Teacher Tip Reread the selection with students who had difficulty understanding it. Continue modeling and prompting the use of strategies and skills as you reread.

(13) atmosphere before being blown more than 150 miles across the moon. The dark plumes are seen as streaks of black on the much lighter landscape.

After Voyager 2 passed Neptune, its program was given a new name—Voyager Interstellar Mission (VIM)—because now it is headed out of the solar system, out to the stars.

Very little will change on Voyager as it sails on through outer space. Eventually its electrical power will be used up and its instruments will cease to function, but there is nothing in space that will stop Voyager from traveling farther and farther from us. Only when it comes close enough to be affected by another star's gravitational attraction will its path be altered. Astronomers have calculated that that won't happen for at least twenty-seven thousand years!

We don't know if there are any intelligent beings elsewhere in the universe, but if there are—and if they find either of the two Voyagers wandering out in space— they will discover, in addition to all the instruments, a very special gold-plated record on the side of each spacecraft. On each record is a recorded greeting from the people on Earth in fifty-five languages as well as many sounds that are common on Earth. These include the roar of a jet plane, the crying of babies, the chirping of crickets, and ninety minutes of a variety of music. Covering this precious record is a diagram showing what Earth people look like and where Earth is in the solar system. The story of Voyager will be an ancient legend before any alien being can possibly find the spacecraft. But maybe, many thousands of years from now . . .

One of Voyager's last pictures of Neptune and Triton.

171

Comprehension Skills

Discussing the Selection

Following reading, engage the students in discussion of the selection. Using the *handing-off process* will help students take responsibility for the discussion. In addition to the following questions, have them revisit any questions asked when they set purposes before reading.

■ Ask students to review the charts of the planets they made. Did they help in comparing the different planets? *(Answers will vary. Students should determine that by comparing and contrasting the planets, they understood and learned more about them.)*

■ How many different types of things did the author compare and contrast in the selection? *(Answers may vary. Remind students that the author compared the planets to Earth and to the sun, as well as comparing the things scientists knew about a planet before and after Voyager 2 visited that planet.)*

■ How has this selection connected with your knowledge of the unit theme? *(Answers will vary—students should compare/contrast examples of astronomy from this selection with their own experiences or past reading, and use these connections to make a general statement about the unit theme.)*

During this time, have the students return to the clues and problems that they noted on the transparency before reading. Let the students decide which items deserve further discussion.

Having the children hand off the discussion to other students instead of the teacher encourages them to retain complete control of the discussion.

Assessment

✔ **Formal** To assess students' reading comprehension, have them complete *Comprehension and Writing Assessment,* pages 37–38.

2 Reading and Responding

Meet the Author

After the students read the information about Necia Apfel, discuss the following questions with them.

Why do you think Necia Apfel studied astronomy, even though people tried to discourage her from doing so?
(Possible answer: Necia Apfel studied astronomy because she loved it. She had been fascinated with the stars and planets since she was a little girl.)

Why do you think Necia Apfel likes to teach astronomy to children?
(Possible answer: Necia Apfel likes to teach astronomy to children because she remembers the questions and excitement she had about astronomy as a child.)

VOYAGER
to the
PLANETS

Meet the Author

Necia H. Apfel thought stars and planets were fascinating, even as a child. However, adults tried to discourage her interest by telling her women did not become astronomers. Despite this, she went on to study astronomy in college. Today, she both teaches and writes about her beloved subject. Children are her favorite students because she says, "they are by far the most exciting and imaginative." She speaks at schools and has given classes to children at the Adler Planetarium, in Chicago. She also writes a monthly column for young readers in *Odyssey* magazine. In it she answers children's questions about astronomy. "Only children can think up the kind of questions I receive," she said. "They are marvelous."

172

Theme Connections

Think About It

This selection included many facts about the planets that Voyager 2 visited. With a small group of classmates, discuss what you found to be the most interesting discovery.

- Why do scientists on Earth want to gather as much information as possible about the other planets?
- Advances in technology have greatly increased our knowledge of the solar system. What will be the next step in exploring the planets?

Check the Concept/Question Board to see if there are any questions there that you can answer now. If the selection or your discussions about the selection have raised any new questions about astronomy, put the questions on the Concept/Question Board. Maybe the next selection will help answer the questions.

Record Ideas

Would you spend 12 years of your life traveling to and exploring other planets? Record your notes and ideas in your Writing Journal.

Research Ideas

- Find out more about the experiments conducted with space probes.
- Investigate the challenges of communicating with a space probe from Earth.

173

Theme Connections

Think About It

- As students discuss the discoveries of *Voyager 2*, circulate and observe the discussions. Encourage students to refer to the selection to check facts during the course of their discussions.

- Suggest that students discuss how the study of astronomy has progressed, based on what they have read in the first five selections of this unit.

- Have the students report what they discussed. Encourage them to record on the Concept/Question Board any questions they may have.

Research Ideas

Students who would like to learn more about the *Voyager* space probes might look at Necia Apfel's book *Voyager to the Planets*, from which this excerpt is taken. Interested students might also use library resources to find further information about the planets and their moons.

Teacher Tip Encourage students to bring their own experiences to familiar themes, and through exploration and research to gain a deeper perspective. Set aside time in class for students to present their findings.

② Responding

✦Exploring the Theme

Some students may choose to conduct a computer search for additional books or information about astronomy. Have them make a list of these books and sources of information to share with classmates and the school librarian. Check the Reading link of the **SRA** Web page for links to theme-related Websites.
http://www.sra4kids.com

Have students write sentences using the selection vocabulary words. In order to provide additional help in remembering words, students can write synonyms or antonyms for the words if it is appropriate. Some students may even draw something to help them remember the meanings of the words.

Selection Vocabulary

In their Writing Journals, have students write the definitions for words discussed before the reading of the selection and any other interesting words they clarified while reading. Students should be encouraged to refer to these words throughout the unit as they work on student and writing projects. The words from this selection are:

space probe   shepherd satellites
retrograde   gravitational attraction

Reading/Writing Connections

Have students think of nonfiction books or articles they have read about the planets Jupiter, Saturn, Uranus, and Neptune, or places to look for that information. Have each student choose one of the four planets to write about using information from "Voyager to the Planets" and the sources discussed above. Have volunteers share conclusions they have drawn from their research with the class or with partners.

Literature Appreciation

Because "Voyager to the Planets" has a lot of information, students may need some help clarifying the meanings of some words. Tell students to scan the selection looking for unfamiliar words. Have them write down words and page numbers. When they have finished, have them practice using context clues to try and decode these words for more complete understanding of the selection.

Home Connection

The class has just finished reading "Voyager to the Planets," the true story of the twelve-year journey of the *Voyager 2* space probe from Earth to Neptune. An informational letter on "Voyager to the Planets," in both English and Spanish, can be found in the ***Home Connection*** guide.

"Voyager to the Planets"

A message from _____

We have just finished reading the selection *Voyager to the Planets*, which is about the discoveries of the *Voyager 2* space probe. In 1977, *Voyager 2* began exploring the outer edges of the solar system and sending back fascinating information to scientists on Earth.

Talk with your child about the variety of ways we gain information about the solar system. Space probes, space shuttles, and space stations have all contributed to our knowledge of the solar system. Work with your child to create a list of questions to be answered or experiments to be conducted on a special space mission.

Encourage your child to share the list of questions or experiments with the rest of the class.

Unit 2/Back Through the Stars   25

Home Connection p. 25

Supporting Student Explorations

Students should be continuing with their research. You may want to do the following:

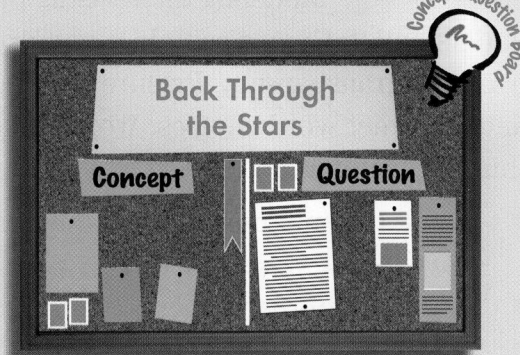 **Whole Group** Conduct a class discussion to help students who are having trouble identifying knowledge needs, to remind groups that they can still change their research problems, and to provide any other needed discussion or guidance before students complete their research plans.

Small Group Have students work together to assign tasks to each group member. As you observe the groups making job assignments, encourage students to take on tasks that are related to their strengths and interests. Tell them that it is important for each student to play a significant role in the group and to provide valuable information to help the group in its investigation.

Have students examine their planning calendars. Assist them in allotting enough time to conduct their research and complete their activities before the end date.

Suggest that students post on the Concept/Question Board brief descriptions of books, magazine articles, computer Websites, or other sources of information that they have found to be especially helpful in their explorations of astronomy. Encourage students who are having difficulty finding information to check sources on the Board and to post their questions as well.

Inquiry Journal Have students complete page 22 of the *Inquiry Journal.* Have them record their ideas about how "Voyager to the Planets" added to their knowledge about astronomy.

Assessment

✓ Informal At this point in the project students are doing active research. Check to be sure that students:
- take on a significant role in the group.
- examine planning calendars.
- post research information.

Recording Concept Information (continued)

• *Circles, Squares, and Daggers: How Native Americans Watched the Skies* by Elsa Marston
Answers will vary.

• *Voyager to the Planets* by Necia Apfel
Answers will vary.

• *A Meeting in Space* by Vonda N. McIntyre
Answers will vary.

22   Inquiry Journal

Inquiry Journal p. 22

③ Integrating the Curriculum

Teacher Tip Remind students to incorporate what they have learned in this unit's grammar and spelling lessons when they are revising. In this unit they have learned about content-area words, nouns, pronouns, regular and irregular present-tense verbs, and word derivatives.

Teacher Tip **Sentence Lifting** The students' own writings provide the best vehicle for teaching language and writing skills. Lift sentences from student writing to show both elements that are very good as well as those things that need change or correction.

Teacher Tip **Writing Seminar** Students have been working on revising their expository paper. Either have volunteers read their work to the rest of the class or select students to do so. Since the purpose of Seminar is to provide students with usable and thoughtful feedback, no more than two students should present their work on any given day. If students seem rushed when two students present their work, have only one present.

Language Arts

Writing

Revising Process

Instruct Tell students that the purpose of *revising* is to make sure that a piece of writing expresses the writer's ideas clearly and completely. Revising is usually thought of as something writers do only between writing the first draft and proofreading. But writers may revise at any time during the writing process. When writers revise, they work on order, content, and clarity. They add or change information, and may experiment with new beginnings and endings.

Practice Modeling the revising process will help students understand it. Copy a sample rough draft for an expository paper onto an overhead transparency. Be sure to include unclear, misplaced passages and incorrect word choices. Work quickly through your rough draft, thinking aloud as you revise. For example:

- I think I should move this to the end. (*Use arrows to show where to move words or sentences.*)
- I need a better word here. (*Cross out word.*)
- This is good. I'll keep it as it is.
- I should say more about this. I'll add more details to describe this. (*Use an asterisk or a number to indicate an insertion.*)
- Now this idea doesn't fit. I'll cross it out. (*Cross out sentence.*)

Encourage students' suggestions for improving your draft. Have students move around or change sentences, add new ideas or details, take out ideas or details that do not fit, and change words.

Apply Have students go back to their ***Writing Folders*** and take out the expository draft they worked on in Lessons 3 and 4. Have them begin revising their papers using the process practiced above.

Writing Process

Revise Have students revise their expository drafts by asking themselves the following questions: *Does this make sense? How can I make it clearer? What can I get rid of? Is this appropriate for my audience?*

Literary Elements

Recognizing Informational Texts

Instruct Call on volunteers to tell the main purpose of the following kinds of writing: a humorous essay *(to entertain)*, a newspaper editorial on why to vote for Issue 5 *(to persuade)*, a mystery novel *(to entertain)*. Now, ask students to tell the main purpose of an article such as "How to Build Model Airplanes" *(to instruct or explain)*. Share with students that a process description is one kind of *informational text.* Discuss the following features of *informational text.*

- Its purpose is to tell the reader about something or someone.
- It is about real events and people.
- It presents facts in a simple, clear way.
- It is composed using clear transitions.
- It may be organized by order of events (as in a process description) or by topic.
- It answers the questions *Who? What? Where? When? Why?* and *How?*

Practice Have students consider the answers to the questions *Who? What? Where? When? Why?* and *How?* in "Voyager to the Planets." Write their responses on the chalkboard.

Apply Have students look back at the informational text "Circles, Squares, and Daggers: How Native Americans Watched the Skies." Have them identify which of the features of informational text, listed above, are demonstrated in that selection.

 **Integrating the Curriculum**

Vocabulary

Affixes and Meaning

Instruct Have students tell you what they have learned about affixes. If necessary, remind them that an affix can be added to the beginning or ending of a word. Suffixes and prefixes are types of affixes.

Have students tell you what they know about the *re-* prefix and how adding it to a word changes its meaning. Students should mention that *re-* means "to do again" (for example, *rewrite* means "to write again").

Then have students tell you what they know about the *-tion* suffix and how adding it to a word changes its meaning. Students should mention that *-tion* means "the act or state of being." This suffix can be added to a verb to change it to a noun (for example, a *creation* is something one *creates*, or something in the act or state of being *created*).

Practice Have students scan "Voyager to the Planets" for examples of words with the *re-* or *-tion* affixes. Write these words on the chalkboard. Then have students try to figure out the word's meanings by first defining the root word and then defining the affix.

Apply Have students check their expository papers for accurate spelling and usage of the affixes *re-* and *-tion*.

Meeting Individual Needs

Challenge

Affixes Have students think of other examples of affixes (such as *-ment, -ful, -al, -ness,* and *im-*). Then challenge students to combine the root words listed below with prefixes or suffixes to form nine new words.

enjoy	patience	mature
approve	form	thought
attach	happy	resource

 **Teacher Tip** Remind students that knowing how affixes change the meanings of root words helps build vocabulary. Encourage them to keep a record of words with affixes in the Personal Dictionary section of their Writing Journals, so that they can reference these words easily when writing.

 **Skills Strand**

Affixes
INTRODUCED: Unit 1, Lesson 1
REVIEWED: Unit 2, Lesson 5
Unit 6, Lesson 2

Grammar, Usage, and Mechanics

Complete Sentences

Instruct Copy the following list of rules for writing complete sentences on the chalkboard and review them aloud.

1. A complete sentence has two parts: a subject and a predicate. The *subject* of a sentence tells *who* or *what.*

   The newspaper story told all about a contest. (What is the subject? The newspaper story.)

   The writer outlines the rules. (Who is the subject? The writer.)

2. The *predicate* of a sentence tells *what happens or happened.*

   A batting contest *was held on Saturday.* (What happened to the batting contest? It was held on Saturday.)

3. A sentence is incomplete if it is missing a subject.

   Showed up at the field. (*Who* or *what* showed up at the field?)

4. A sentence is incomplete if it is missing a predicate.

   Thousands of kids. (*What* happened to the kids?)

Practice On the chalkboard, write five examples of incomplete sentences, each of which should be missing either a subject or a predicate. Read each incomplete sentence to students, asking them if the sentence is missing a subject or predicate. If students are having difficulty identifying why the sentence is incomplete, remind them that the subject of a sentence answers the question "Who or what is the sentence about?" The predicate answers the question "What happened?" Have volunteers suggest a subject or predicate that would make the sentence complete.

Have the students discuss why writers use complete sentences in their writing. If necessary, explain the importance of communicating complete ideas clearly.

Apply Have students look for incomplete sentences in their expository papers. Remind students to check their sentences for a subject.

Meeting Individual Needs

Challenge

Complete Sentences Write examples of complete and incomplete sentences on the chalkboard. Use sentences from students' writing or the *Student Anthology.* Challenge students to identify which sentences are complete and which are incomplete. Then, have them add the missing part to the incomplete sentences, making them complete.

Assessment

✓ **Formal** To assess students' understanding of this concept, have them complete *Skills Assessment,* page 19.

Complete Sentences
INTRODUCED: Unit 1, Lesson 4
REVIEWED: Unit 2, Lesson 5
Unit 4, Lesson 4
Unit 5, Lesson 5
Unit 6, Lesson 6

③ Integrating the Curriculum

Teacher Tip Ask students where they have seen charts used to organize information. Have students share examples of charts and the types of information organized in them from their textbooks for other subjects (for example, math).

Listening/Speaking/Viewing

Interpreting a Graph

Ask students where they have seen graphs used to organize information (for example, in math books). Copy the graph below onto the chalkboard or an overhead transparency. Have students point out the parts of a graph, such as the title and labels. Also, have them demonstrate how to use the points plotted on a graph to locate information about *Voyager's* path.

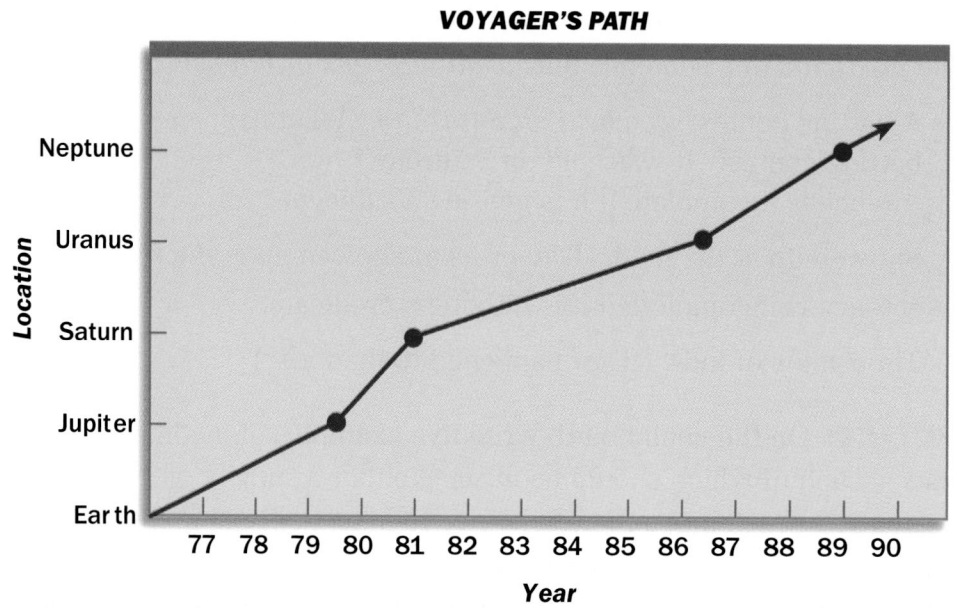

VOYAGER'S PATH

Study and Research

Creating a Chart

Instruct Prompt students to tell you that graphic features help organize information so readers can understand and locate it more easily and quickly. Find an example of a chart or table for students, and have students identify the title, column headings, and row headings.

Practice With the help of students, create a chart on the chalkboard to organize information on the number of rings, moons, and shepherd satellites that *Voyager 2* found on each of the planets it visited. Let students suggest how the chart headings should be set up. Then have them skim the selection for information to add to the chart.

Apply Have students complete *Inquiry Journal,* pages 32–33.

Inquiry Journal p. 32

UNIT 2

Name _____ Date _____

Back Through the Stars

Moons of the Planets

Jupiter, Saturn, Uranus, and Neptune have many moons. One moon of each of these planets is named in the first column of the chart below. Find information about the four moons to complete the chart. **Answers will vary.**

	Size	Atmosphere	Surface
Moon of Jupiter: Io	3630 km in diameter	Sulfur and frozen sulfur dioxide	Flat plains, some mountain ranges
Moon of Saturn: Hyperion	286 km in diameter	Unknown	Uniform surface covered by a layer of dark material
Moon of Uranus: Oberon	1523 km in diameter	Unknown	Heavily cratered and icy
Moon of Neptune: Triton	2700 km in diameter	Nitrogen with small amount of methane	Extensive ridges and valleys in complex patterns

32   Inquiry Journal

Inquiry Journal p. 33

Other Features	Miscellaneous Information
Active volcanoes Iron inner core Orbital period: 1.77 days Orbital speed: 17.34 km/sec	Discovered in 1610 *Voyager* observed 11 active volcanoes
Composed of water, ice, and rock Orbital period: 21.28 days Orbital speed: 5.07 km/sec	Discovered in 1848 The largest highly irregular body in the solar system
Large faults across southern hemisphere Orbital period: 13.46 days Orbital speed: 3.15 km/sec	Outermost of Uranus's known satellites Surface shows little evidence of internal activity
Seasonal changes Ice volcanoes Orbital period: –5.88 days Orbital speed: –4.39 km/sec	The only large moon to orbit backward Colder than any other measured object in the solar system

Inquiry Journal   33

Inquiry Journal pp. 32–33

Across the Curriculum

Math

Comparing Planets

Purpose

To help students synthesize information in a different way using math comparisons

Procedure

Much of the information in "Voyager to the Planets" is given in numbers. Examples of this are temperature and distance from the sun.

- Have students scan the selection for information given in numbers.

- Help students organize this information under chart headings, such as *Temperature, Distance from the Sun,* or *Number of Moons.*

- When information is collected, have each student choose one type of information to compare between the planets, using subtraction.

- Using the differences between the planets, have students write comparative sentences. For example, *Voyager 2* came 47,200 miles closer to Neptune than to Uranus.

Art

Visualizing the Planets

Purpose

To help students visualize what they read through drawing

Materials

paper, crayons, markers, colored pencils, paints

Procedure

Have students find the parts of the selection that describe the physical characteristics of the planets.

- Tell students to look for color words and other adjectives.

- Point out certain characteristics, such as rings and storms on the planets' surfaces, and have students reread these sections.

- After students have found descriptions of the planets, have each student choose one planet to draw and color with crayon, marker, or watercolor.

- Have students practice visualizing before they start drawing.

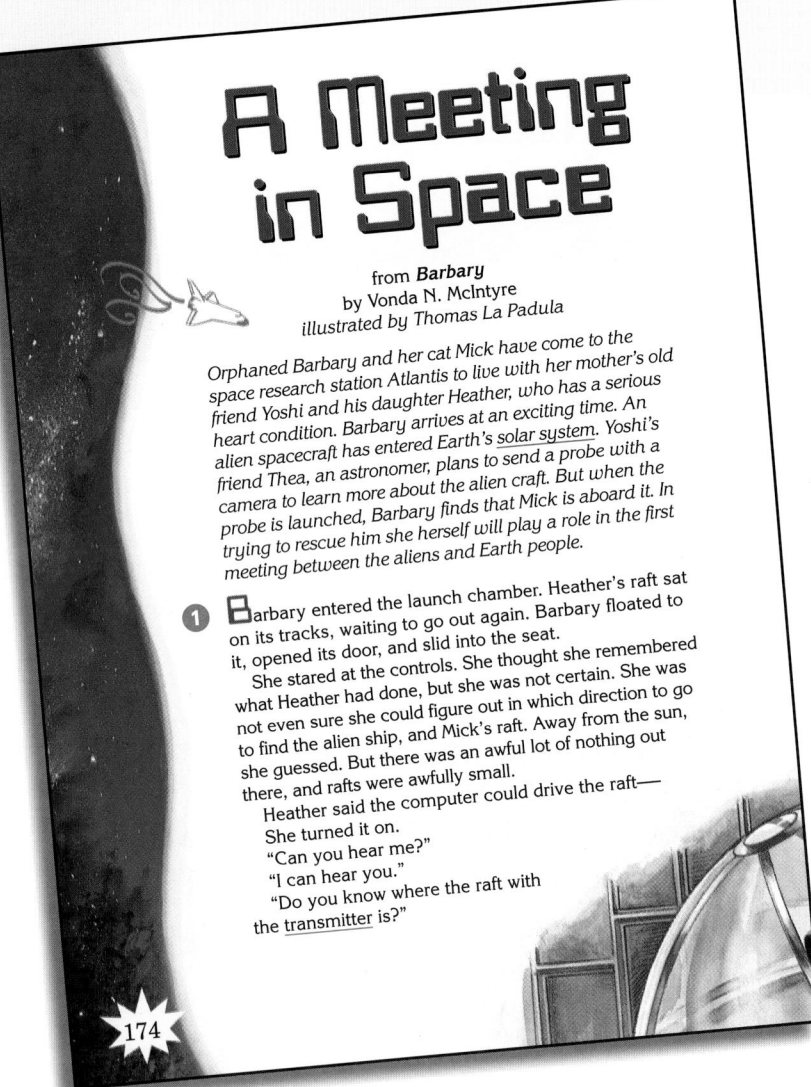

A Meeting in Space

from *Barbary*
by Vonda N. McIntyre
illustrated by Thomas La Padula

Orphaned Barbary and her cat Mick have come to the space research station *Atlantis* to live with her mother's old friend Yoshi and his daughter Heather, who has a serious heart condition. Barbary arrives at an exciting time. An alien spacecraft has entered Earth's <u>solar system</u>. Yoshi's friend Thea, an astronomer, plans to send a probe with a camera to learn more about the alien craft. But when the probe is launched, Barbary finds that Mick is aboard it. In trying to rescue him she herself will play a role in the first meeting between the aliens and Earth people.

1 Barbary entered the launch chamber. Heather's raft sat on its tracks, waiting to go out again. Barbary floated to it, opened its door, and slid into the seat.

She stared at the controls. She thought she remembered what Heather had done, but she was not certain. She was not even sure she could figure out in which direction to go to find the alien ship, and Mick's raft. Away from the sun, she guessed. But there was an awful lot of nothing out there, and rafts were awfully small.

Heather said the computer could drive the raft—

She turned it on.

"Can you hear me?"

"I can hear you."

"Do you know where the raft with the <u>transmitter</u> is?"

174

About the Author

Vonda N. McIntyre is the award-winning, science fiction author of "A Meeting in Space," which was excerpted from her first book for younger readers, *Barbary*. Her novelette *Of Mist, and Grass, and Sand* won the Nebula Award from Science Fiction Writers of America, and her book *Dreamsnake* won the Nebula Award, the Hugo Award from the World Science Fiction Convention, and a nomination for the American Book Award. She wrote the novel versions of the movies for *Star Trek II: The Wrath of Khan; Star Trek III: The Search for Spock;* and *Star Trek IV: The Voyage Home*. She also wrote another novel about *Star Trek* characters, *Enterprise: The First Adventure*.

Students can read more about Vonda N. McIntyre on page 202 of the ***Student Anthology***.

Selection Summary

Genre: Science Fiction

"A Meeting in Space" takes readers on a thrilling ride through space as Barbary and Heather attempt to rescue Barbary's runaway cat while avoiding Heather's worried father and the mysterious alien spaceship that lurks near the space station they call home.

This selection will stimulate readers to wonder about worlds beyond our solar system and the life that may inhabit them.

About the Illustrator

Thomas La Padula has illustrated for magazines, advertising agencies, and publishing houses. He has participated in numerous group shows across the country, including the Norman Rockwell Museum and the Society of Illustrators. His art is also displayed as part of the Johnson and Johnson Corporation's private collection. Students can read more about Thomas La Padula on page 202 of the ***Student Anthology***.

Exploring the Theme

Selection Concepts

In reading "A Meeting in Space," students are encouraged to wonder about how people of the future will learn about the universe. Space-research stations such as Atlantis are likely to add greatly to their knowledge of astronomy. This selection will also stimulate readers to wonder about worlds beyond our solar system and the life that may inhabit them. Key concepts explored are:

- Many of today's astronomers first became interested in learning about the universe through science fiction.
- Predictions made by science fiction writers are usually based on scientific work being conducted at the time the story is written.

Check the Reading link of the **SRA** Web page for links to theme-related Websites.
http:// www.sra4kids.com

Exploration Activity Tips

Before Reading, have students compare science fiction with other kinds of fiction. Encourage them to share what they like or dislike about the science fiction genre. Because this selection is excerpted from a larger story, have students browse for context clues.

During Reading, have students seek clarification on the characters, setting, and plot that have been established before the part of the story they are reading.

After Reading, as a class, discuss whether this story is realistic. Have students compare this selection to factual scientific articles they have read. Then have students update the Concept/Question Board. Some may want to revise their project plans based on what they have learned from the selection.

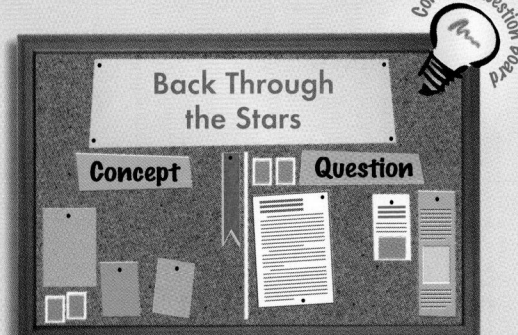

Unit 2 Exploration Management	
Lesson 1	Brainstorm research problems. Form interest-based groups. Develop and discuss initial research plans.
Lesson 2	Groups finalize plans, allocate tasks, and begin research. Discuss initial findings and resources.
Lesson 3	Research continues as groups consider revision of their activity focus.
Lesson 4	Students continue with research and present their initial findings.
Lesson 5	Research continues. Students present interesting findings or problems.
Lesson 6 A Meeting in Space	**Collaborative Exploration** **Research continues. Students present interesting findings or problems.** **Supplementary Activity** **Research groups present their plans for discussion and possible refinement. Summarize and organize information in an outline.**
Lesson 7	Students organize research findings and prepare presentations.
Lesson 8	Students present their activities.

Lesson Planner

Suggested Pacing: 3–5 days	DAY 1 DAY 1	DAY 2 DAY 2	
Part 1 **Preparing to Read** **Materials** ■ Student Anthology, pp. 174–203 ■ Transparencies 12, 44	**Word Knowledge** ■ Reading the Words and Sentences, p. 174G ✓ Developing Oral Language, p. 174G **Build Background, p. 174H** **Preview and Prepare, p. 174I** **Selection Vocabulary, p. 174I** *transparent, contraption, acceleration, three-dimensional, incomprehensible*	**Preview and Prepare, p. 174I** ■ Review Transparency 44	
Part 2 **Reading and Responding** **Materials** ■ Student Anthology, pp. 174–203 ■ Teacher Observation Log ■ Reading and Writing Workbook, pp. 69–70 ■ Inquiry Journal, p. 22 ■ Transparency 48 ■ Home Connection, p. 27	**Student Anthology, pp. 174–188** **Comprehension Strategies** ■ Clarifying, pp. 174, 176, 180, 182, 186 ■ Summarizing, pp. 178, 188 ■ Predicting, pp. 178, 184, 188	**Student Anthology, pp. 189–203** **Comprehension Strategies** ■ Clarifying, pp. 190, 192, 196 ■ Predicting, pp. 194, 198, 200 ■ Summarizing, p. 198 **Discussing Strategy Use, p. 200** **Comprehension Skills** ✓ ■ Discussing the Selection, p. 201 **Exploring the Theme** ■ Selection Vocabulary, p. 203A *transparent, contraption, acceleration, three-dimensional, incomprehensible*	
Part 3 **Integrating the Curriculum** **Materials** ■ Student Anthology, pp. 174–203 ■ Transparency 53 ■ Inquiry Journal, p. 34	**Writing** ■ Proofreading, p. 203C **Literary Elements** ■ Title, Author, Illustrator, p. 203D	**Writing Process** ■ Proofread, p. 203C **Vocabulary** ✓ ■ Listening Vocabulary, p. 203E	
Independent Work Time **Materials** ■ Reteach, pp. 69–70 ■ ESL Supplement ■ Challenge, p. 37 ■ Intervention Guide ■ Research CD-ROM ■ Listening Library Audiocassette	**Writing Process Continued** **ESL** ■ Word Meaning, p. 174G **Challenge** ■ Title, p. 203D **Intervention** ■ Word Knowledge, p. 174G ■ Comprehension, p. 174 **Unit Project: Continue Research**	**Writing Process Continued** **ESL** ■ Proofread, p. 203C **Challenge** ■ Listening Vocabulary, p. 203E **Intervention** ■ Proofread, p. 203C **Unit Project Continued**	

     ✓ Informal **Assessment Available**   ✓ **Formal Assessment Available**

DAY 2 continued	DAY 3	
DAY 3	**DAY 4**	**DAY 5**
General Review	General Review	Review Word Knowledge
Student Anthology, pp. 174–203 **Comprehension Skills** ■ Cause and Effect, pp. 175, 177, 179, 181, 183, 185, 187 **Theme Connections** ■ Think About It, p. 203 ■ Research Ideas, p. 203	**Student Anthology, pp. 174–203** **Comprehension Skills** ✓■ Cause and Effect, pp. 189, 191, 193, 195, 197, 199 **Exploring the Theme** ■ Reading/Writing Connections, p. 203A ■ Literature Appreciation, p. 203A ■ Supporting Student Explorations, p. 203B	**Student Anthology, pp. 174–203** ■ Review Selection ■ Complete Discussion ■ Reread Selection in Pairs **Home Connection, p. 203A** ■ Discuss "A Meeting in Space" ■ Create an ad for a space raft
Writing Process Continued **Grammar, Usage, and Mechanics** ✓■ Subject and Verb Agreement, p. 203F **Listening/Speaking/Viewing** ■ Dramatizations, p. 203G	**Writing Process Continued** **Study and Research** ■ Create Diagrams Using Technology, p. 203H	**Across the Curriculum** **Math** ■ Word Problem Invasion, p. 203I **Art** ■ Alien Creatures, p. 203I ■ Picture Books, p. 203J **Science** ■ Drafting a Model Space Station, p. 203J
Writing Process Continued **ESL** ■ Improvising Endings, p. 203A **Challenge** ■ Cause and Effect, p. 179 **Unit Project Continued**	**Writing Process Continued** **Reteach** ✓■ Subject and Verb Agreement, *Reteach*, pp. 69–70 **Challenge** ✓■ Subject and Verb Agreement, *Challenge*, p. 37 **Unit Project Continued**	**Writing Process Continued** **Unit Project Continued**

Meeting Individual Needs
Independent Work Time

Preparing to Read

Meeting Individual Needs

ESL
- Word Meaning, p. 174G

Intervention
- Word Knowledge, p. 174G

Reading and Responding

Meeting Individual Needs

ESL
- Cause and Effect, p. 175
- Improvising Endings, p. 203A

Challenge
- Cause and Effect, p. 179

Intervention
- Comprehension, p. 174
- Cause and Effect, p. 177
- Clarifying, p. 184
- Predicting, p. 186
- Summarizing, p. 186

Integrating the Curriculum

Meeting Individual Needs

Reteach
- Subject and Verb Agreement, *Reteach*, pp. 69–70

ESL
- Proofread, p. 203C
- Dramatizations, p. 203G

Challenge
- Title, p. 203D
- Listening Vocabulary, p. 203E
- Subject and Verb Agreement, *Challenge*, p. 37

Intervention
- Proofread, p. 203C

Formal Assessment Options

Use these assessment pages along with your informal observations to gauge student progress.

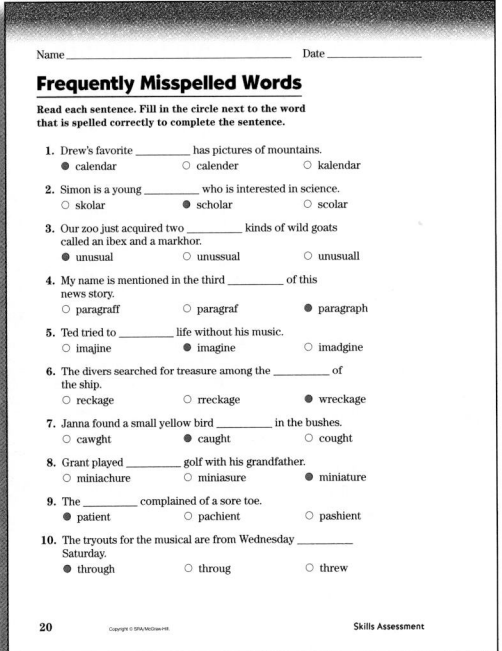

Skills Assessment, p. 20

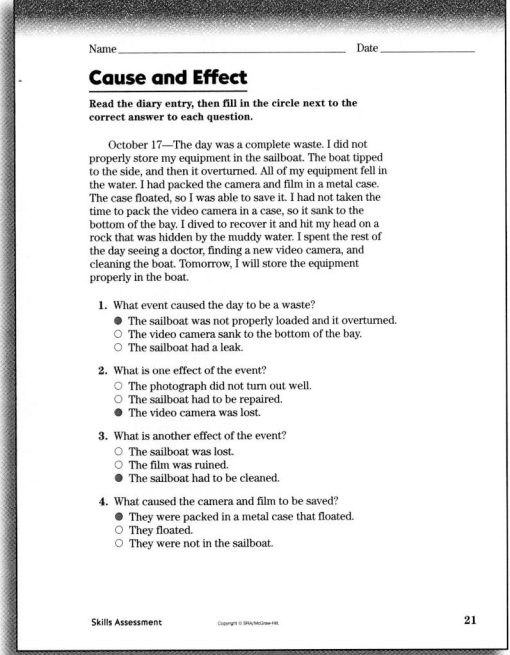

Skills Assessment, p. 21

Skills Assessment, p. 22

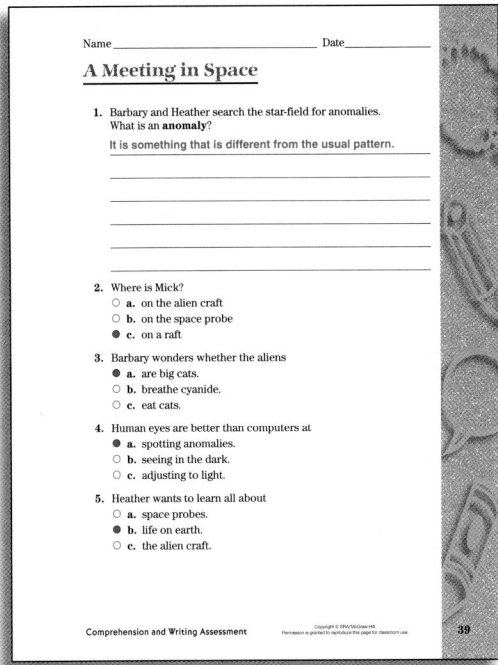

Comprehension and Writing Assessment, p. 39

Comprehension and Writing Assessment, p. 40

1 Preparing to Read

Meeting Individual Needs

ESL

Word Meaning Make sure English-language learners understand the meanings of the words before they do the exercises. Refer to Unit 2, Lesson 6, of the **ESL Supplement** for specific suggestions.

Intervention

Word Knowledge Tell students who need more help with *r* consonant blends that when forming the blend, each consonant maintains its own sound in the order in which it is spelled. Have students brainstorm the other words containing *r* consonant blends. For students who need more help, see Unit 2, Lesson 6, of the **Intervention Guide.**

Assessment

✓ **Formal** To assess students' ability to spell frequently misspelled words, use **Skills Assessment,** page 20.

Word Knowledge

Reading the Words and Sentences

Write each word and sentence on the chalkboard. Have students read each word together. After all the words have been read, have students read each sentence in natural phrases or chunks. Use the suggestions in About the Words to discuss the different features of the listed words.

Line 1: people though friend
Line 2: quick squirm squint
Line 3: transmitter bravado creative growl frown drive
Sentence 1: People expected Heather to squirm at the sight of the worm.
Sentence 2: She frowned and squinted at the bright sun.
Sentence 3: The transmitter sends a quick signal.

About the Words

- Line 1 contains words that are frequently misspelled because they all contain silent letters.
- Line 2 contains words that demonstrate the /kw/ sound spelled *qu*. Invite students to think of other words spelled *qu* with a /kw/ sound.
- The words in Line 3 contain consonant-*r* blends. In consonant blends, both consonants maintain their own sounds.

Developing Oral Language

To review the words, have students do one or both of the following activities:

- Write several words from the lines above on the chalkboard. Give a clue for each of the words. For example, for the word *squeak*, "Which word is a sound that can be made by a floor or a mouse?" Invite students to come to the chalkboard and erase the correct answer.
- Have a student select a word from the lines above and choose another student to use the word in a science fiction sentence.

Build Background

Activate Prior Knowledge

Have students check the Concept/Question Board to refresh their memories about astronomy. Discuss the following with students to find out what they may already know about space travel and have already learned about the unit theme. Tell students to use their prior knowledge to help them comprehend the selection they are about to read.

- Students may recall that in "Circles, Squares, and Daggers: How Native Americans Watched the Skies" they learned how Native Americans studied the skies long ago, illustrating humanity's continuing interest in astronomy.

- Ask students whether they are familiar with the story they are about to read, and if so, to tell a little about it. Remind students, however, not to give away the ending of the selection.

- Have students share any other stories that have space travel in them.

Background Information

The following information may help the students better understand the selection they are about to read.

- Many astronomers working today first became interested in learning about the universe through science fiction.

- Science fiction began in the late nineteenth century with the French writer Jules Verne. Verne used the science of his day to make predictions about the future in such books as *Journey to the Center of the Earth*, *Twenty Thousand Leagues Under the Sea*, and *From the Earth to the Moon*.

- A science fiction story has these elements: technology that is not yet invented, settings in the future, and characters who are creatures or humans from other planets.

- The best science fiction is scientifically accurate. Robert A. Heinlein, a well-known writer of science fiction, says that the author of science fiction must always stick to the truth of "the real world as we know it, including all established facts and natural laws."

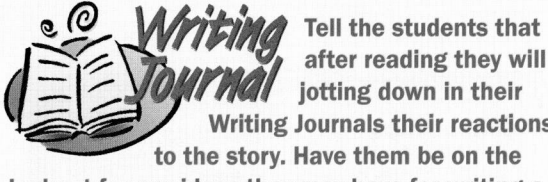

Writing Journal Tell the students that after reading they will be jotting down in their Writing Journals their reactions to the story. Have them be on the lookout for any ideas they may have for writing a science fiction story.

Teacher Tip Encourage the students to compare science fiction with other types of fiction.

1 Preparing to Read

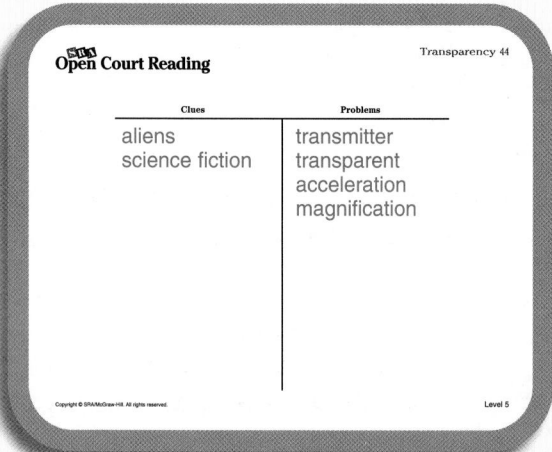

Transparency 44

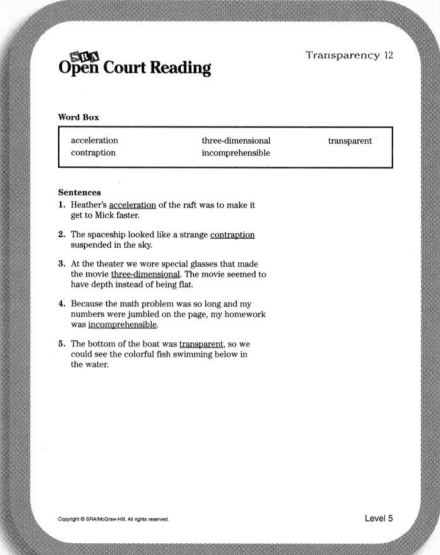

To help students decode words, divide them into the syllables shown below. The information following each word tells how students can figure out the meaning of each word from the sentences on the transparency.

trans·par·ent	context clues
con·trap·tion	context clues
ac·cel·er·ation	context clues
three-di·men·sion·al	word structure, apposition
in·com·pre·hen·si·ble	context clues, word structure

Transparency 12

Preview and Prepare

Browse

- Have a volunteer read the title and author's and illustrator's names aloud. Have students share what they know about science fiction. Discuss how it is different from realistic fiction.

- Because this is fiction, have students browse through the first half of the selection, looking for words and phrases that connect to what they already know. Record these in the Clues column of *Transparency 44.* Discuss with them how this story might connect with the unit theme, Back Through the Stars.

- Encourage students to ask questions as they browse. Have them identify any problems in the Problems column they notice while reading.

Set Purposes

As they read, have students think about the world in the future and what types of life may live beyond Earth and adjust their purposes for reading to achieve clarification on unfamiliar terms and ideas.

Selection Vocabulary

As students study vocabulary, they will use context clues, word structure, and apposition to determine the meaning of these and additional unfamiliar words.

Display *Transparency 12* before reading the selection to introduce and discuss the following words and their meanings.

trans·par·ent:	clear enough to be seen through (page 175)
con·trap·tion:	a device (page 175)
ac·cel·er·ation:	the action of speeding up (page 176)
three-di·men·sion·al:	when a picture or flat image gives the illusion that it has depth (page 176)
in·com·pre·hen·si·ble:	impossible to understand (page 195)

Have students read the words in the Word Box. Help students decode multisyllabic words by reading them syllable by syllable. Students may need help with *transparent.*

Have students read the sentences on *Transparency 12* to determine the meaning of the underlined words. Remind them to use clues in the sentences and structural clues to figure out the meaning. See the teacher tip on the left for information on how the words in each sentence can be defined.

Reading Recommendations

Your first reading of the selection should focus on developing the reading strategies found to the left of the reduced pages. We recommend that the students revisit the selection, rereading sections or the entire selection as a way to enhance their understanding and appreciation of the text. During rereading, they should focus on the comprehension skills, found to the right of the reduced pages.

Silent Reading

Because this contemporary story is full of suspense and excitement, it is recommended that the students read it silently. Have them practice reading on their own for at least 5 minutes at a time. As they become better readers, students will read silently with increasing ease, over longer periods of time. Due to the length of this selection, you may choose to read it in two sessions. If so, be sure to summarize what was read the first day before continuing reading on the second day.

Have students make use of the reading strategies listed below to help them understand the selection. Have them stop reading periodically or wait until they have completed the selection to discuss the reading strategies. After the students have finished reading the selection, use the "Discussing the Selection" questions to see if they have understood what they have read. If they have not, refer to the *Intervention Guide* for further strategies.

Using Reading Strategies

Reading strategy instruction allows students to become aware of how good readers read. During the reading of "A Meeting in Space," you will model the use of the following reading strategies:

■ Clarifying   ■ Summarizing   ■ Predicting

Before reading, have students share how they have used these strategies in the past and any tips they can give each other on their use.

Building Comprehension Skills

Revisiting or rereading a selection allows students to apply skills that give them a more complete understanding of the text. Some follow-up comprehension skills help students organize information. Others lead to deeper understanding—to "reading between the lines," as mature readers do. In this selection, students will apply the follow-up comprehension skill of *Cause and Effect*.

 **Teacher Tip** Have students who may need extra help reading "A Meeting in Space" reread the selection using the *Listening Library Audiocassette*.

 **Teacher Tip** By this time in the fifth grade, good readers should be reading approximately 126 words per minute with fluency and expression. The only way to gain fluency is through practice. As explained in Reading Recommendations, have students reread all or part of the selection to you and to each other during class or Independent Work Time to focus on the comprehension skills and to build fluency.

② Reading and Responding

Read pages 174–203.

Comprehension Strategies

Modeling

❶ Clarifying *In order to clarify a difficult idea, the reader must recognize what about the idea does not make sense and then read on to see if the author clarifies it. For example, the idea of a raft that is not used on water is something I am not familiar with. The author says that the "raft" is in a launch chamber, sitting on tracks, and that Barbary floats to it. It sounds more like some kind of a spaceship to me. Maybe it's called a "raft" because it's not very big or very fast. What are some other things that should be clarified before we read on?*

Modeling

❷ Clarifying *Barbary is saying that Thea's "contraption" is going to be shot. What do you think a "contraption" is? She said that Mick was still inside it, and we know that Mick is inside the probe, so she must be talking about the probe. She is afraid that the probe will be shot with Mick inside it.*

Teacher Tip Remind students that one of the most important behaviors good readers exhibit is stopping when something fails to make sense.

Reading Recommendation

ORAL • CHORAL • **SILENT**

A Meeting in Space

from *Barbary*
by Vonda N. McIntyre
illustrated by Thomas La Padula

Orphaned Barbary and her cat Mick have come to the space research station Atlantis to live with her mother's old friend Yoshi and his daughter Heather, who has a serious heart condition. Barbary arrives at an exciting time. An alien spacecraft has entered Earth's solar system. Yoshi's friend Thea, an astronomer, plans to send a probe with a camera to learn more about the alien craft. But when the probe is launched, Barbary finds that Mick is aboard it. In trying to rescue him she herself will play a role in the first meeting between the aliens and Earth people.

❶ Barbary entered the launch chamber. Heather's raft sat on its tracks, waiting to go out again. Barbary floated to it, opened its door, and slid into the seat.

She stared at the controls. She thought she remembered what Heather had done, but she was not certain. She was not even sure she could figure out in which direction to go to find the alien ship, and Mick's raft. Away from the sun, she guessed. But there was an awful lot of nothing out there, and rafts were awfully small.

Heather said the computer could drive the raft—
She turned it on.
"Can you hear me?"
"I can hear you."
"Do you know where the raft with the transmitter is?"

174

Meeting Individual Needs

Intervention

Comprehension Intervention strategies for students having difficulty reading "A Meeting in Space" can be found in Unit 2, Lesson 6, of the **Intervention Guide.**

Assessment

✓ **Informal** Observe individual students as they read, and use the Teacher Observation Log found in the **Assessment Guide** to record anecdotal information about each student's strengths and weaknesses.

"Yes."

"I want to go there."

"Please wait."

The kaleidoscope patterns appeared. Barbary gritted her teeth. Computers were supposed to know everything instantly.

But if it knew the location of Mick's raft, why was it making her wait? The only reason she could think of was that it was reporting her.

She slapped the switch that turned off the computer. She did not know if that would keep it from reporting her—if that was what it was doing—but it was the only thing she could think of. She would have to find Mick herself. She pulled down the door and sealed it and tried to remember what control Heather had used first.

"Open up!"

Barbary started at the muffled voice and the rap on the transparent roof.

Heather stared in at her. She looked furious.

Barbary opened the hatch.

"Move over!"

"Heather, they're going to shoot Thea's contraption, and Mick's inside it. I have to stop them——"

"Move over!"

Barbary obeyed.

Heather swung in, slammed the hatch shut, and fastened her seat belt.

"Your computer told me part of it, and I figured out the rest." She took over the controls.

"Thea tried to make her camera come back, but it wouldn't."

"Mick probably knocked loose some of the connections." Their raft slid into the airlock. The hatch closed.

175

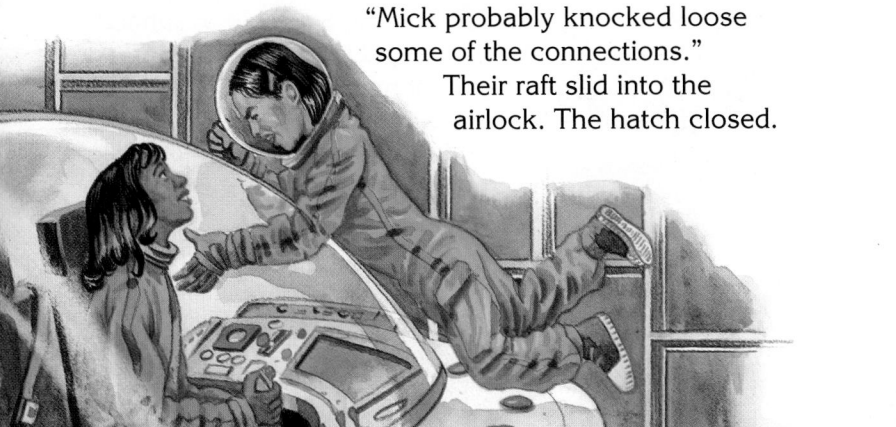

Meeting Individual Needs

ESL

Cause and Effect While the concept may not be difficult for English-language learners in their native language, they may need extra help finding these relationships when reading English text. It may help to restate the cause and effect directly. For example, Barbary tried to fly Heather's raft because she wanted to get Mick.

Comprehension
Skills

Cause and Effect

Remind students of the concept of *cause and effect*. A *cause* is *why* something happens. The *effect* is *what* happens. For example, if a person plants a seedling, a tree will grow. The planting is the *cause*. The tree is the *effect*. Tell students that determining *cause-and-effect* relationships helps them know the reasons behind an event's occurrence and predict that event's impact on what will happen in the future. Help the students think of other *cause-and-effect* relationships.

Have students look for examples of *cause and effect* in the first two pages of "A Meeting in Space." For example:

■ Barbary's fear for Mick causes her to try to fly Heather's raft. Her fear is the cause. Flying the raft is the effect.

■ Barbary's fear of being reported causes her to turn off the computer. Her fear is the cause and turning off the computer is the effect.

■ Barbary tries to sneak off, which causes Heather to be angry. Sneaking off is the cause and being angry is the effect.

←**Skills Strand**→

Cause and Effect
INTRODUCED: Unit 1, Lesson 6
REVIEWED: Unit 2, Lesson 6
Unit 4, Lesson 4

2 Reading and Responding

Comprehension Strategies

Modeling

3 **Clarifying** *I'm not sure what this piece of equipment is. This author doesn't seem to tell us everything. Sometimes we just have to imagine what something in the story is, or try to think of something similar that we already know about. In this case, because it uses a focus knob and Barbary sees the alien ship through it, I'll guess that it's a telescope, or like a telescope.*

Help students learn to make what they read an integral part of their lives by noticing and asking how the text makes them feel.

Word Knowledge

freeze, triumph, squinted

Students can use the skills they learned in the Word Knowledge section of this lesson to read these words. Remind students of this if they have difficulty reading these words.

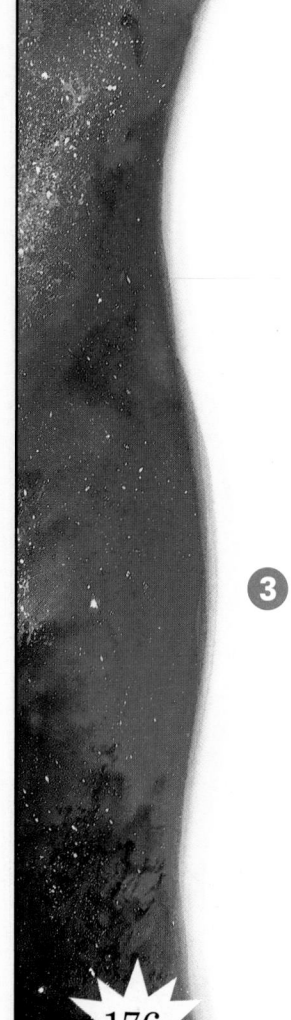

"I just hope I got here soon enough to get us out," Heather said. "I bet they'll freeze all the hatches in about two seconds, if they haven't already—"

The outer door slid open.

Heather made a sound of triumph and slammed on the power. The <u>acceleration</u> pushed them both back into their seats.

With the raft accelerating and the station growing smaller behind them, Heather glared at Barbary.

"Now," she said. "Why didn't you wake me up?"

"There wasn't time," Barbary said.

"Oh." Heather's scowl softened. "That's a good point."

Barbary squinted into starry space. "How do you know where to go?"

"It's not that hard. From where the station is now, and the direction and speed the ship's approaching, it has to be lined up with Betelgeuse, if Atlantis is directly behind us."

Barbary tried to imagine the geometry of the arrangement Heather described, with all the elements moving independently of one another, and came to the conclusion that it *was* hard, even if Heather was so used to it that she didn't know it.

She peered into the blackness, unable to make out anything but the bright multicolored points of stars.

Heather drew a piece of equipment from the control panel. It looked like a face mask attached to a corrugated rubber pipe. Heather fiddled with a control.

"Here," she said, and pushed the mask toward Barbary. **3** "You can focus with this knob if you need to."

The image of the <u>alien</u> ship floated before her, a sharp, clear three-dimensional <u>miniature</u>, a jumble of <u>spheres</u> and cylinders, panels, struts, and irregularities, some with the hard-edged gleam of metal, some with the softer gloss of plastic, some with a rough and <u>organic</u>

176

appearance, like tree bark. But for all Barbary knew, alien plastic looked like tree bark and their trees looked like steel. If they had trees, or plastic, or steel.

"Can you make it show Mick's raft?"

"That's harder," Heather said, "since I don't know what course Thea used. But I'll try." She bent over the mask, fiddling. "Hey, Barbary," she said.

"Yeah?"

"Were you really going to come out here all by yourself?"

"I guess so. I couldn't think of anything else to do."

"That was brave."

"Dumb, though," Barbary said. She never would have remembered the right controls, and she would have headed off in the wrong direction. "I guess you would have had to come out and get me and Mick both."

"Still, it was brave."

"Did you find Mick yet?" Barbary asked, embarrassed.

"Unh-uh, not yet."

"Can we use his transmitter?"

Heather glanced up, frowning.

"We could," she said, "but we can't, if you see what I mean. We'd have to use the computer, and if we turn it on it would probably lock our controls and take us home. But we'll find him, don't worry."

177

Meeting Individual Needs

Intervention

Cause and Effect Some students may better understand cause-and-effect relationships if they are put in the following framework:

(*Effect*) happens because of (*cause*).

Comprehension Skills

Cause and Effect

Point out that stories are often built around causes and effects. Certain events have to take place in a story for the action to move forward. Have the students discuss the following story points and their effects.

■ What would have happened if Heather had not shown up at the raft?

■ What if the outer door to the launch chamber had not opened?

■ What if Heather hadn't been asleep when Barbary learned that Mick was on the space probe?

Discuss the cause-and-effect relationships involved and how the events suggested above would have changed everything. For example:

■ What effect did Heather's showing up at the raft have? (*They were able to get out of the space station because Heather showed up and knew what to do.*)

■ What effect did the opening of the launch chamber have? (*They were able to get out, whereas, otherwise, they may have been trapped.*)

■ What was the effect of Heather being asleep when Barbary learned that Mick was on the space probe? (*Barbary turned on the raft's computer because she didn't know how to drive the raft, and the computer reported her. If Heather were awake, she could have flown the raft without turning on the computer.*)

② Reading and Responding

Comprehension Strategies

Modeling

④ Summarizing *I know that good readers stop occasionally to summarize what has happened in a story to help them understand and recall the events. Because there is a break here, now would be a good time to sum up the events of the story so far. Barbary has realized that her cat is in a raft heading toward the alien ship. She sets off in another raft to rescue him. At the last minute, Heather joins her. Would anyone like to do a summary?*

Modeling

⑤ Predicting *Good readers make predictions, based on their reading and their own experiences, and confirm or revise these predictions as they go. Barbary suggests that the aliens could look like big cats, but Heather doesn't think that's very likely. I predict that Heather is right and that the aliens are going to be very different from human beings. However, Barbary might be right about the death-rays! As I read on, I'll check to see if my predictions are correct. (This prediction is addressed on page 198.)*

Word Knowledge

traveled, bravado, transmission
Students can use the skills they learned in the Word Knowledge section of this lesson to read these words. Remind students of this if they have difficulty reading these words.

"Okay," Barbary said. "How long before we catch up to him, do you think?"

"It sort of depends on how fast the raft went out and how rapidly it was accelerating. Which I don't know. But it couldn't have been too fast, or it would use up all its fuel before it got to the ship. Then it wouldn't be able to maneuver, so it would just fly by very fast. Without much time to take pictures. So it has to be going slowly, instead. Anyway, we ought to catch up within a couple of hours. I don't want *us* to run out of fuel—and I don't want to get going so fast that we go right past without seeing Mick."

The raft hummed through silent space. Barbary kept expecting the stars to change, to appear to grow closer as the raft traveled toward them. But the stars were so distant that she would have to travel for years and years before even a few of them looked any closer or appeared to move, and even then they would still be an enormous distance away.

"Heather . . . "

"Yeah?"

"Thanks for coming with me," she said.

"Hey," Heather said, her cheerfulness touched with bravado. "What are sisters for?"

A red light on the control panel blinked on.

"Uh-oh," Heather said.

"What is it?"

"Radio transmission. Somebody from the station calling us. With orders to come back, probably."

They stared at the light. Heather reached for the radio headset.

Barbary grabbed Heather's hand. "If you answer them, they'll just try to persuade us to turn around."

178

Teacher Tip There are many strange machines and ideas in this story. Have students choose one and draw a diagram, based on information in the story and their own imagination, that shows how the machine works and what it does.

"But we ought to at least tell them that it's us out here," Heather said.

"They probably already know. If they don't, maybe we ought to wait until they figure it out."

"Yoshi will be worried," Heather said sadly, "when he comes home, and he can't find us."

"We're going to have to transmit a message to the aliens anyway," Barbary said. "To tell them we don't mean to bother them, but Mick is in the first raft and we're coming out to rescue him. When we do that, they'll hear us back in Atlantis." **4**

"Uh-huh." Heather gazed into the scanner. "I wonder why they don't want us to come near them? I wonder what they do when somebody does?"

"I guess they could blow us up with death-rays," Barbary said. "But that doesn't seem too civilized."

"And how are we going to explain cats to them? I wonder if they have pets? I wonder what they look like?"

"Maybe they're big cats themselves, like the aliens in *Jenny and the Spaceship,*" Barbary said. "Did you read that?" **5**

"Big *cats?*" Heather said. "That's silly, Barbary. The aliens come from some other star system. They evolved on a whole different planet. They probably don't even have the same chemistry we do. They might breathe cyanide or methane or something. Big *cats?*"

"Okay, okay, forget it," Barbary said. "It was just a book."

The radio light continued to glow. To Barbary, it seemed to be getting brighter and brighter, more and more insistent.

Heather finally put on the headset. When she turned on the radio, she spoke before a transmission from Atlantis could come through.

179

Comprehension
Skills

Cause and Effect

Point out the following causes and effects.

- The girls are afraid to turn on the computer because the space station will make them go back *(cause)*, so they don't know if the aliens are trying to contact them *(effect)*.

- Because the girls don't want to turn back *(cause)*, they don't pick up the radio transmission from the space station *(effect)*.

- Because the girls have to transmit a message to the aliens *(cause)*, the people in Atlantis will know they are okay *(effect)*.

Have the students discuss what might happen to the girls if they continue going toward the alien ship. Point out that knowing what has happened but not knowing what the effect will be creates suspense and excitement in a story.

Teacher Tip

Because Heather mentions that the aliens might breathe cyanide or methane, this is a good place to remind students of the information about the atmospheres of planets they read about in "Voyager to the Planets."

Meeting Individual Needs

Challenge

Cause and Effect The space station in the story is named Atlantis, which was a legendary island that disappeared. Invite students to imagine they are building a space station. Have them draw a plan of all the things they think a space station would need. Have them write a paragraph about why they set up their space station the way they did.

2 Reading and Responding

Comprehension Strategies

Modeling

6 Clarifying *I wonder what an anomaly is. Heather and Barbary are searching the starfield to find anomalies. Let's keep reading to see if we can clarify this. Heather and Barbary first think they see stars, but then see the difference between the anomalies and the stars. An anomaly must be something that is different, irregular, or unusual from other identified objects. They must figure that an unusual-looking object in a sky filled with stars must be the probe.*

Students may need clarification on the characters, setting, and plot that have been established before the part of the story they are reading. Encourage them to ask questions for clarification.

Word Knowledge

trying, pretty

Students can use the skills they learned in the Word Knowledge section of this lesson to read these words. Remind students of this if they have difficulty reading these words.

"Raft to alien ship, raft to alien ship. Um . . . hi. My sister Barbary and I—I'm Heather—are trying to rescue a . . . a sort of friend of ours who got stuck in the first raft by mistake. Now we can't make the raft turn around, so we have to catch up to it to get him." She hesitated. "Please don't be mad or anything. Over and out."

In the instant between the time Heather stopped transmitting and turned off the radio, the receiver burst into noise.

"—do you hear me? You girls get back here right now, or—"

Barbary recognized the voice of the vice president.

Heather clicked off the radio.

"He sounded pretty mad," she said. "I guess now they'll tell Yoshi where we are."

"Heather, what if the aliens try to call us? We won't be able to hear them, if we don't leave the radio turned on."

Heather raised one eyebrow and flicked the switch again.

"—return immediately, and you won't be punished. But if—"

She turned it off.

180

She shrugged cheerfully. "We wouldn't be able to hear the aliens anyway, with Atlantis broadcasting nonstop at us, unless the aliens just blasted through their signal. I'll try later—maybe the vice president will get tired of yelling at us."

"What do we do now?"

"We just wait," Heather said. "I'll keep looking for Mickey's raft. When we find it we'll know better what we need to do and how long it'll take."

"Let me help look," Barbary said.

"Okay."

Heather showed her how to search the star-field for <u>anomalies</u>. At first glance, they looked like stars. But if one looked at an anomaly at two different times, the bright speck would have moved in relation to the real stars. The scanner could save an image and display it alternately with a later view of the same area. An anomaly would blink from one place on the image to another, and the human eye could see the difference. A computer could, too, but it took processing time or a lot of memory, or both, to do what a person could do in an instant.

181

Comprehension
Skills

Cause and Effect

Have volunteers discuss how *cause* and *effect* are related. If necessary, remind them that a cause is *why* something happens. An effect is *what* happens. Have them give a few examples of cause-and-effect relationships.

■ What caused Heather to turn off the radio? *(Atlantis broadcasted signals to them nonstop and they didn't want to hear the signals.)*

■ What is the effect of Barbary scanning for the alien ship? *(She finally finds it and feels pleased with herself.)*

■ What caused Barbary to let Heather have the scanner? *(She knew Heather could find Mick about a hundred times faster than she could.)*

Have the students continue to look for causes and effects on these pages.

Teacher Tip Have students discuss the author's purpose for writing this story. Help the students understand that while the main purpose is to entertain, the author also provides factual information about space.

2 Reading and Responding

Comprehension Strategies

Modeling

7 Clarifying *I see that the author is giving more explanation now about how space travel works in this story. I know that gravity is caused by the spinning of planets and other objects, and I remember that Voyager 2 used the gravity of Uranus to help push it toward Neptune. It seems like the author is trying to make the way people travel in this story as realistic as possible, even if it is science fiction.*

Word Knowledge

quite, question, equipment
Students can use the skills they learned in the Word Knowledge section of this lesson to read these words. Remind students of this if they have difficulty reading these words.

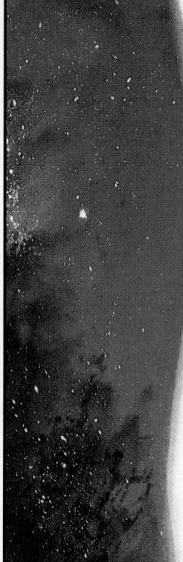

"Astronomers used to discover new planets and comets and things this way," Heather said. "You can also search by turning up the magnification, but that means you can only see a little bit of space at once. So unless you got really lucky, you'd spend days and days trying to find what you were looking for."

Barbary scanned for the alien ship. When she finally found it she felt pleased with herself, until she remembered how easily Heather had done the same thing.

"Shouldn't Mick's raft be right in between us and the alien ship?" Barbary asked.

7 "It could be," Heather said. "But it isn't. Nothing moves in straight lines in space, not when there are gravity fields to affect your course. Besides, I'm sure Thea didn't send her camera on a direct line to where the ship is now. She probably planned to arc around it. I mean, she wouldn't want to run into it. There's no way to tell exactly what course she chose. We could call and ask her——"

"As if she'd tell us——"

"She would. But I don't think the VIPs would let her."

"So we just keep looking?"

"Yeah."

Barbary let Heather have the scanner. She knew Heather could find Mick about a hundred times faster than she could.

"What's it like, back on earth?" Heather said abruptly, without looking up. "What's it like to visit a farm, or camp out in the wilderness?" She waited quite a while, as Barbary tried to figure out how to answer her. Finally Heather said in a small voice, "Never mind. I didn't mean to pry."

"It's okay," Barbary said. "It isn't that. It's just a hard question to answer. There are so many different places and different things to see—only I haven't seen most of them. It's hard to get a permit to go out in the wilderness, and you need a lot of equipment, and that costs money. Nobody I knew ever did it."

182

"What about farms? Did you see cows and horses and stuff?"

"I've never been on a farm, either. There weren't any near where I lived, and they aren't like in movies. They're all <u>automated</u>. Big machines run them. Some of them are covered with plastic to keep the water and the heat in. A couple years ago I snuck off to a zoo. I saw a cow then. It looked kind of bored and dumb. Horses are prettier, but hardly anybody on farms has them anymore. Mostly, rich people keep them to ride."

"How about an ocean?"

"I never saw that, either."

"Oh."

"I wish I could tell you . . ."

"That's all right. I've talked to other people about it, and I've seen pictures and tapes. But I can't figure out what it would be like to see it myself."

"You know, Heather," Barbary said, "an awful lot of people talk about going to the mountains, or going to the ocean, but hardly anybody ever did it. Not anybody I knew, anyway."

183

Comprehension
Skills

Cause and Effect

Note that sometimes authors show the effect of something and leave the cause to the reader's imagination.

Point out the conversation between Barbary and Heather about Earth. It sounds as if Earth has changed from the world we know today. Discuss with students what might have caused Earth to change. Encourage them to support their ideas with information from the text.

Teacher Tip Remind students that making connections with their own experiences and prior knowledge can help them determine cause-and-effect relationships.

2 Reading and Responding

Comprehension Strategies

Prompting

8 Predicting *The girls are having a pretty hard time finding Mick. What do you predict will happen next, and why? Don't forget to check your prediction as you read to see if it comes true.*

Student Sample

Predicting *I predict that the girls will have to turn around and go home before they find Mick because they are tired and low on food. As I read on, though, it looks as if they have found Mick after all.*

One way to visualize how difficult it is to steer one spacecraft toward another is to have the students try to hit a ball with another ball while the first one is moving away from them. Suggest that they try this with balls or marbles.

Word Knowledge

stretched, brought

Students can use the skills they learned in the Word Knowledge section of this lesson to read these words. Remind students of this if they have difficulty reading these words.

"But they could have gone if they wanted."

"Yeah. They could have."

"I usually don't care. But sometimes I wish I could go see the mountains or the ocean, or blue sky."

"Your sky is prettier."

"I bet a blue one would be easier to find a raft in." Heather raised her head from the scanner. She looked exhausted. She had dark circles under her eyes. Barbary felt afraid for her.

"Want me to look?" Barbary asked.

"I'll do it a while longer, then it'll be your turn," Heather said. She stretched, and hunched and relaxed her shoulders a couple of times. "I don't suppose you brought along any sandwiches or anything, did you?"

"No," Barbary said. "I didn't even think of it."

"Oh, well. There are some rations in the survival ball. But they're pretty boring. Probably we should wait till we're really hungry before we use them."

Barbary thought she would get sick if she tried to eat. She felt empty and scared.

Heather bent over the scanner once more. "Hey! Look at this!"

184

Meeting Individual Needs

Intervention

Clarifying Some students may be unfamiliar with degrees and angles. Have them look at a diagram of an angle to see how the lines get further and further apart as they extend outward.

Barbary peered into the scanner.

"I just see stars."

"Keep looking." Heather touched the blink control.

In the center of the picture, one of the bright points jumped.

"Is that Mick?"

"Has to be," Heather said.

Barbary flashed the control again; again the image jumped.

"Now zoom in."

Barbary did so. The raft appeared. The airless distance of space <u>transmitted</u> details sharp and clear, but all she could find was the silver and plastic shape of the raft, and the shadows of Thea's contraption inside. Nothing moved.

"There it is!" she said. She magnified it even more. "I don't see Mick, though."

"Let me look."

Heather teased the scanner controls.

"Can you see him?"

"Umm . . . no," Heather said. "I can't. But there's a lot of stuff in there. He'd practically have to sit on top of it for me to find him."

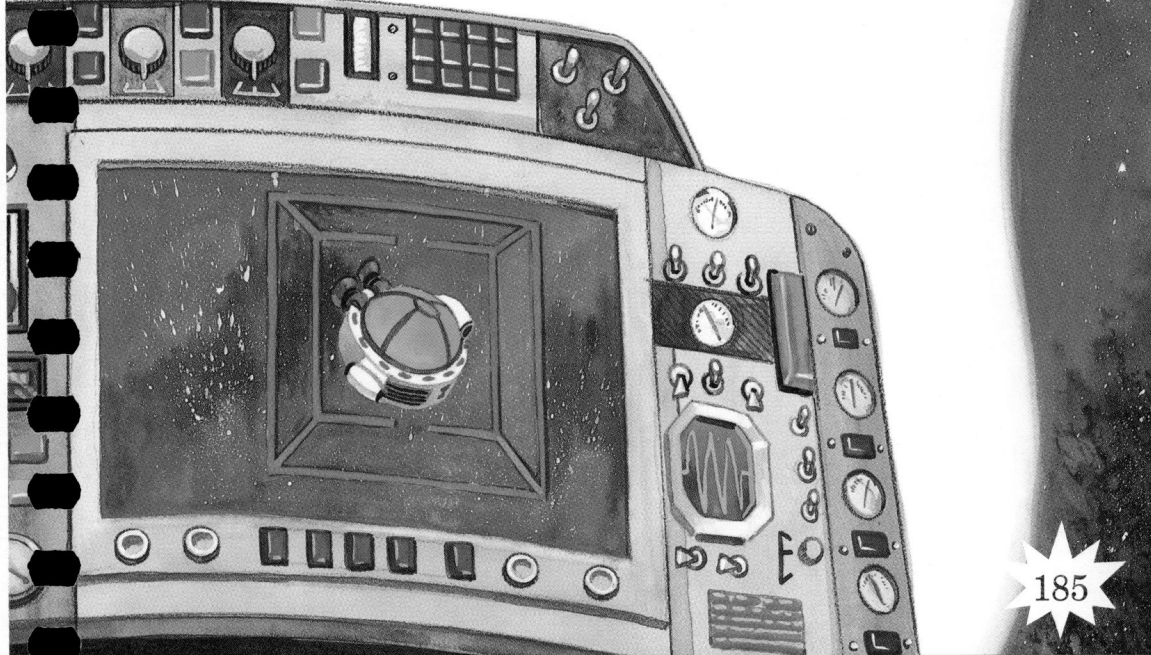

185

Comprehension
Skills

Cause and Effect

Continue to discuss that writers sometimes include an *effect* but leave the *cause* to the reader's imagination.

Have the students discuss the following effect and tell what might have caused it.

■ Barbary says that Mick is probably yowling or growling like a wildcat. *(She knows that he is afraid or wants to get out of the ship and can't.)*

Guide the students to see that Barbary uses her knowledge of Mick to figure out how he must be behaving. Have the students look for other examples in the story where a character uses prior knowledge to say what another character is doing.

Also, have students find other examples of cause and effect on these pages. For example:

■ The girls cannot get Mick onto the raft when they find him *(effect)* because the cat is unable to get into a space suit or survival ball by himself *(cause)*.

Reading and Responding

Comprehension Strategies

Modeling

9 Clarifying *I don't understand why it is so difficult to make a turn or go faster in space. Isn't the raft similar to an airplane?*

When I reread, I see that being in a vacuum—without any air—makes it more difficult.

Teacher Tip Take notes on student predictions so that they can be checked later, during rereading.

Word Knowledge

probably, growling, front
Students can use the skills they learned in the Word Knowledge section of this lesson to read these words. Remind students of this if they have difficulty reading these words.

"He's probably sitting under it," Barbary said. "Yowling. Or growling like a wildcat."

Heather laughed. "I bet you're right."

Barbary felt both overjoyed and terrified. Heather had found Mick—but Barbary would not be able to stop worrying till she saw for herself that he was all right.

"Where is he?" she asked. "Right in front of us?"

"No, he's kind of over to the side." Heather pointed. "Thea must have planned to circle all the way around the alien ship, then follow it as far as she could. I'm going to have to turn us pretty hard. Are you strapped in?"

"Uh-huh. How long will it take to get there?"

"A couple of hours, maybe. I'm just guessing, though."

"How do we get him when we get there?"

"We can't. There's no safe way to open a raft in space unless everybody inside is in a space suit or a survival ball, and Mick couldn't get in one by himself. So we'll stick out our claws and grab his raft and turn us both around, and go back."

"Oh," Barbary said. She had been hoping there was some way of getting from one raft to another. But at least she would be able to look inside and see Mick.

"Hang on."

The raft plunged into free fall as Heather cut the acceleration. Barbary flung her hands out before her, for it really did feel as if she were falling. The steering rocket flared on, the stars swung, and the rocket on the other side counteracted their spin. Now, Barbary knew, they were traveling in the same direction as before, but Heather had turned the raft a few degrees to the left.

Heather applied some thrust to the raft. The new acceleration would add to their previous velocity, changing their direction and speed so they would be heading more nearly toward Mickey.

186

Meeting Individual Needs

Intervention

Predicting Have the students follow up on their summaries by predicting what will happen next. Tell them to remember their predictions and to check them later.

Summarizing Because this is a long selection that may be read over the course of a couple of days, have a volunteer sum up the events that took place during the reading that day. Take notes on the summary and refer to them before reading is continued the next day.

Getting to the right spot in space took a lot of care and **9** calculation. It would have been much easier if they could have flown the raft like an airplane, or like a spaceship in a movie, banking into turns and *swooshing* from place to place. But in a vacuum, without any air, ships could not bank into turns or *swoosh*.

"I don't want to kill any more velocity than I have to," Heather said. "It takes too much fuel. So I'll probably have to correct our course a bunch of times. But for now we're sort of heading for where Mick ought to be when we get there."

Barbary tried to figure out how that worked. It sounded suspiciously like a math word problem, which she had never been very good at. She had never seen the point of figuring out when two trains would pass each other when the only trains left were tourist attractions that she had never ridden anyway. But being able to figure out in her head how to meet another raft in space would be useful. She wished she had paid more attention to word problems in school, and she wondered if it was too late for her to learn how to do what Heather could do.

"Hey, Heather—Heather!"

Heather jerked up from the scanner, blinking and confused.

"Huh? What? I'm awake!" She stopped, abashed.

187

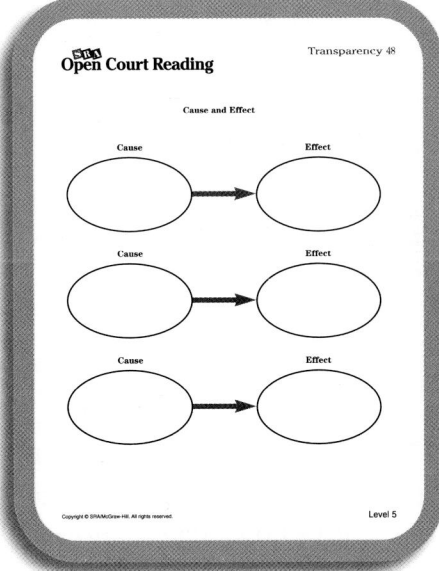

Comprehension Skills

Cause and Effect

Explain to the students that events or actions (a cause) can have an effect on characters in the story. Share these examples with the students.

- Barbary feels guilty because Heather had to come help her and is now tired and ill.
- Heather gets angry when Barbary suggests that they turn back.
- Barbary gets worried because of the alien ship and turns on the radio.

Help students understand cause and effect by setting up a chart. Photocopy **Transparency 48** and give each student a copy. Have students list on the chart three examples of cause and effect from the selection.

Transparency 48

Reading and Responding

Strategies

Modeling

10 Summarizing *Here is another break in the text. This is a good spot for us to sum up the important things that have happened so far. Barbary and Heather went out in their raft to rescue Mick. They've found Mick's raft, but they don't know if Mick is okay or not. They don't know whether or not the aliens will let them rescue Mick. Heather seems very ill and tired. She's gone to sleep, so Barbary has to fly the raft.*

Modeling

11 Predicting *Now that we've summarized what happened so far, it's easy to predict what will happen next. I think that without Heather's help, Barbary will not be able to rescue Mick, even if the aliens do not interfere. (This prediction is addressed on page 192, in the Teacher Tip.)*

Teacher Tip An absence of questions does not necessarily indicate that students understand what they are reading. Be especially alert to students who never seem to ask questions.

Word Knowledge

square, squirmed, quickly
Students can use the skills they learned in the Word Knowledge section of this lesson to read these words. Remind students of this if they have difficulty reading these words.

"No, you're not," Barbary said. "You fell asleep sitting up! Heather . . . look . . . maybe . . ." With a shock, she realized how much danger she and Mick had put Heather in.

"Oh, no!" Heather said. "Don't even say it! We're not turning around and going back like we just came out here to make trouble and then lost our nerve!"

Barbary hunched in her seat. She felt miserable.

"I'm afraid you're going to get sick," she said.

"I'm okay! I'm just a little tired!" Heather snapped. Her expression softened. "Look," she said. "I don't have to do anything for a while. I could take a nap, and you could keep an eye on the scanner. I'll set it so the image of Mick's raft will get closer and closer to the center till we intercept it. If it goes past the center of the focus, wake me up to correct the course." She showed Barbary the faint band of color outlining a square in the center of the scanner. The other raft lay at the left edge of the screen; it moved, almost imperceptibly, centerward.

"That sounds easy enough," Barbary said.

Heather grinned. "It's a lot easier than trying to sleep in a raft, that's for sure." She squirmed around, trying to get comfortable.

"Lie down crosswise and put your head in my lap," Barbary said. "I'll try not to bonk you with the scanner."

10
11
"Okay."

Barbary took off her jacket and tucked it around Heather's shoulders. Heather curled up under it, hiding her eyes from the light of the control panel. Her position still did not look very comfortable, but within a few minutes she was fast asleep.

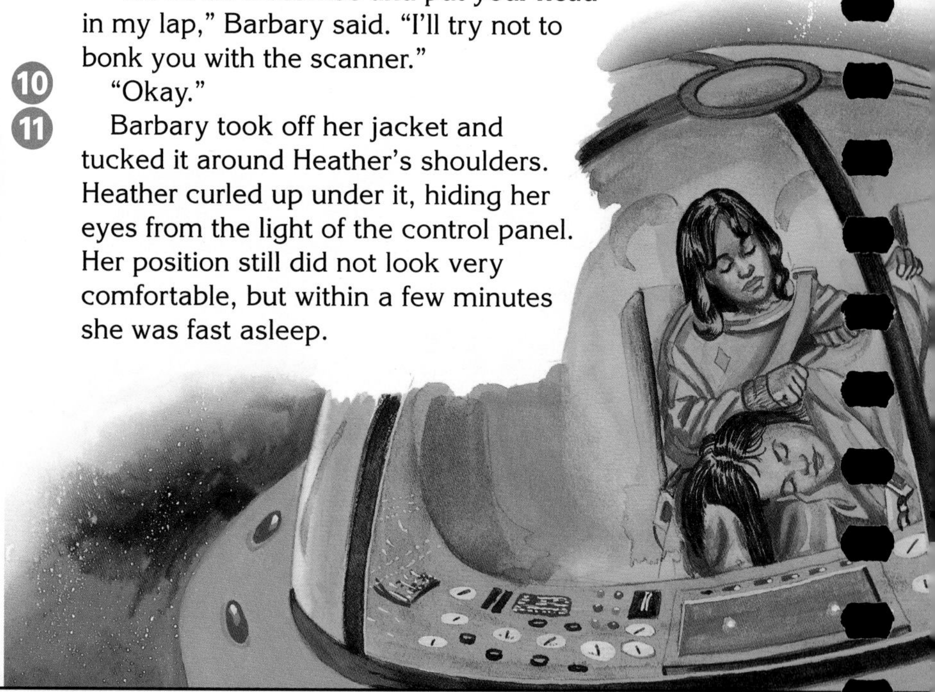

188

Barbary looked around.

Far behind her, spinning, lit from behind, the station grew smaller. The earth and the moon each showed only a slender crescent of light, for Barbary was on their night sides. The raft's automatic shield hid the sun and prevented it from blinding her.

Even in the observation bubble of the transport ship, she had never felt so alone and so remote. Beauty surrounded her, a beauty too distant and too enormous for her ever to reach or comprehend. She gazed out at the stars for a very long time, till she realized how long she had been staring. She quickly grabbed the scanner. To her relief, the other raft still lay within the field, halfway to the center of the focus.

Barbary increased the magnification, but that sent the raft all the way off the screen. If she moved the focus, she might not get it back to the place where Heather had aimed it. That also meant she could not use the scanner to find the alien ship, to see if it was doing anything threatening or even simply different.

Heather slept on. The radio receiver's light never flickered from its brilliant red. Trying to keep her attention on the scanner, Barbary forced herself to remain calm. But worry raced through her mind. She began to wonder if perhaps the aliens, and not the space station, might be trying to call the raft: to tell her they understood, everything was all right; to tell her they did not understand, please try to explain more clearly; or to tell her they understood, but they did not believe her and did not trust her and did not care anyway, and were going to shoot both rafts with death-rays.

189

Comprehension Skills

Cause and Effect

Guide the students to see that causes and effects move the plot along.

- What caused Barbary to turn on the radio and transmitter? *(She was concerned that the alien ship might be trying to reach her.)*
- What caused Barbary to cut the power on the radio? *(The vice president started to yell at her again and she didn't want to get into a fight with him.)*
- What caused Barbary to stay awake? *(She shook her head, yawned, and pinched herself hard.)*
- What caused Barbary's heart to pound with excitement? *(Something glided across the picture.)*

Have the students keep looking for causes and effects as they continue to read.

Teacher Tip Help students state cause-and-effect relationships in the following way: *Effect* happens because of *cause*.

Reading and Responding

Comprehension Strategies

Prompting

12 Clarifying *Yoshi? Who is Yoshi? I know he was mentioned before but I don't remember who he is. He sounds important. Let's reread the introduction and see if he is mentioned.*

Oh, yes. It says that Barbary is staying with him and he is Heather's father.

What other things should be clarified before we read on?

Student Sample

13 Clarifying *I wonder why the author describes the space station as a toy. The paragraph says that the crescents of Earth and the moon are distant. Maybe the station is being compared with a toy because it is so far away that it looks small and toylike.*

As students learn more about reading strategies, class discussion should be more and more student directed and less teacher directed.

Word Knowledge

bright, crescents, quiet

Students can use the skills they learned in the Word Knowledge section of this lesson to read these words. Remind students of this if they have difficulty reading these words.

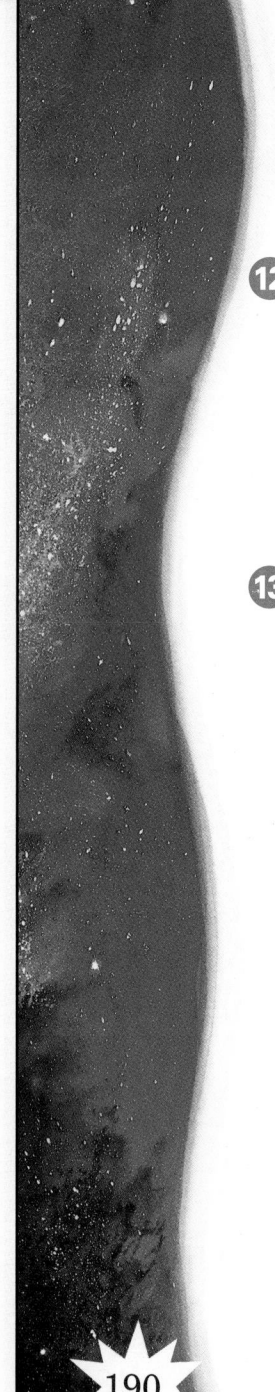

She put on the headset and turned on the radio and the transmitter.

"This is the second raft calling, in case you didn't hear us before." She whispered, trying not to wake Heather. "We're coming out to rescue the first raft so it won't bother you. It's a mistake that it's out here, and we're really sorry. We're trying to fix things."

She turned off the transmitter, leaving the channel open for just a moment.

12 "Barbary!" Yoshi said. "Is Heather all right?"

"You two turn around and——"

The vice president's voice faded as Barbary cut the power to the radio without replying. She would have liked to reassure Yoshi, but she was afraid to get into a fight with any of the adults, especially Yoshi. . . . Yoshi could say things that would make her want to turn around and go back, so he would not be so disappointed with her.

13 She glanced behind the raft. The science station was a bright turning toy, part lit, part shadowed, spinning between the more distant crescents of the earth and the moon.

Before her, space lay beautiful but still. Somehow the stars reminded her of snow early in the morning, before dawn, in a quiet, windless winter. She peered into the scanner to reassure herself that the other raft was still there. She squinted, searching for any sign of Mick. But his raft drifted onward, showing no signs of life.

She yawned, then shook her head to wake herself up. She could not go to sleep, though Heather's steady breathing in the silence of the little ship had a hypnotic effect. She yawned again. She pinched herself, hard.

A glimmer of light on metal caught her gaze.

Off to the left, far away but as clear as a close-up model, Mick's raft crept along. Now that she had found it, Barbary did not understand how she could have failed to see it for so long. She could tell it was in motion; she could tell her own raft was approaching it, slowly and at a tangent. In the scanner, the image had touched the outer edge of the focus square.

190

She started to touch Heather's shoulder, but decided against waking her yet. They still had quite a way to go before their raft intercepted Mick's, and Heather needed the rest.

Still careful not to change the direction of the scanner, Barbary increased the magnification. Now she could see part of the raft in the center of the frame. But the transparent roof had not yet come into view. Barbary stared at the image, willing it to move faster so she could look inside. It crept onto the screen, appearing to move sideways because of its orientation and because she was approaching it from behind and to one side. She wished she could see its front. Often, when Mick had ridden in a car, he crouched up front looking through the windshield. But she supposed he would have trouble crouching on the dashboard of a raft, without any gravity.

Something glided through the picture.

Her heart pounding with excitement, Barbary bent closer over the scanner.

"Mick," she whispered, "hey, come past again, okay?" The portion of the image taken up by transparent raft roof increased. She held her breath.

As if he knew she was coming after him, Mick brought himself up short against the plastic and peered directly at her. He opened his mouth wide. If they had not been

191

Comprehension
Skills

Cause and Effect

Have students continue the flow chart showing how each cause and effect on this page leads to other causes and effects.

- Getting close to Mick's raft causes Barbary to try to wake Heather.
- Because Heather doesn't wake up, Barbary must try to catch the probe herself.
- Catching the probe causes both ships to tumble in a spiral.
- Trying to stop the ship, Barbary turns on the radio.

2 Reading and Responding

Comprehension Strategies

Modeling

14 Clarifying *This is weird. I don't see why the ship keeps spinning for so long. When I think about what we read earlier and what I know, it makes me think it probably has something to do with the lack of gravity and air.*

Teacher Tip Point out to the students that the prediction made in Strategy 11 is addressed on page 193 of the Student Edition.

Word Knowledge

grew, crying, grasps

Students can use the skills they learned in the Word Knowledge section of this lesson to read these words. Remind students of this if they have difficulty reading these words.

separated by the vacuum of space, she would have heard his plaintive yowl.

"Okay," she said, laughing with relief. "I'm coming to get you, you dumb cat."

The scanner grew foggy. She had come so close to crying that she had misted up the mask. She sat up and reached into it to rub away the condensation with her sleeve. She glanced outside to check the position of Mick's raft.

To her shock, it—and Mick, looking at her—lay no more than twenty meters away. She was gaining on it.

"Heather!" she cried.

She pushed the scanner out of the way and pulled her jacket off Heather's shoulders. She shook her, but Heather remained sound asleep.

"Heather, come on!"

Barbary did not intend to come this far and lose Mick. She did not know if they could turn around and come back for him if they passed his raft. She jammed her hands into the grasps of the claw controls. She reached out; the grapples extended from beneath the raft. She opened her fingers and closed them; the claws followed her motion.

The distance between the rafts diminished to ten meters, then to five.

192

Barbary reminded herself again and again that the key to doing anything in space was to do it calmly and smoothly. She did not feel calm. She felt terrified and ignorant. Sweat rolled into her eyes. She could not take her hands from the grasps, and she was afraid to take her gaze off the other raft long enough to lean down and rub her forehead on her sleeve.

"Heather——!"

Even if Heather woke now, there was no time for her to take over the controls. As her raft approached Mick's, so much faster than it had seemed to be moving when they were far away, Barbary grabbed for it.

As she clenched her fingers in the grappler controls, the two rafts came together with a tremendous, wrenching *clang*. Barbary gasped, fearing she had rammed hard enough to breach the hull of Mick's raft or her own. The ships began a slow tumble. Around them, the stars spun. Barbary squeezed her eyes tight shut. That was even worse. She opened her eyes again. The claws kept the two vehicles clamped tight together. She could no longer see Mick, for he was underneath her. But as the reverberations of the crash faded, she heard, transmitted through the hulls, Mick's angry, objecting howl.

193

Comprehension Skills

Cause and Effect

Have students continue to add to their flowcharts as they read. Help them see how one event leads to another. For example:

- Because the rotation slowed, Barbary saw a huge shape slide past the roof.

- Because the rotation stopped, Barbary saw the alien ship through the roof.

- Barbary kept telling herself she was going up because she felt she was falling upside down and in slow motion.

- Barbary blinked because she was trying to figure out if she'd only imagined light outside.

Teacher Tip
Some students may be unfamiliar with the sugar crystal described. If possible, bring in a piece of sugar crystal candy to show them.

② Reading and Responding

Comprehension Strategies

Modeling

15 **Predicting** *I wonder why the radio is silent. It doesn't sound as if Barbary's idea worked. In fact, I predict they might be in a lot of trouble. I predict that the aliens have jammed the radio signals somehow. I can't wait to find out what happens!*

As we read on, it does not appear that the radio has been jammed at all!

Remind students that predictions are not wild guesses; they are based on the reader's prior knowledge and on clues in the text or illustrations.

Word Knowledge

frightened, bring, protect
Students can use the skills they learned in the Word Knowledge section of this lesson to read these words. Remind students of this if they have difficulty reading these words.

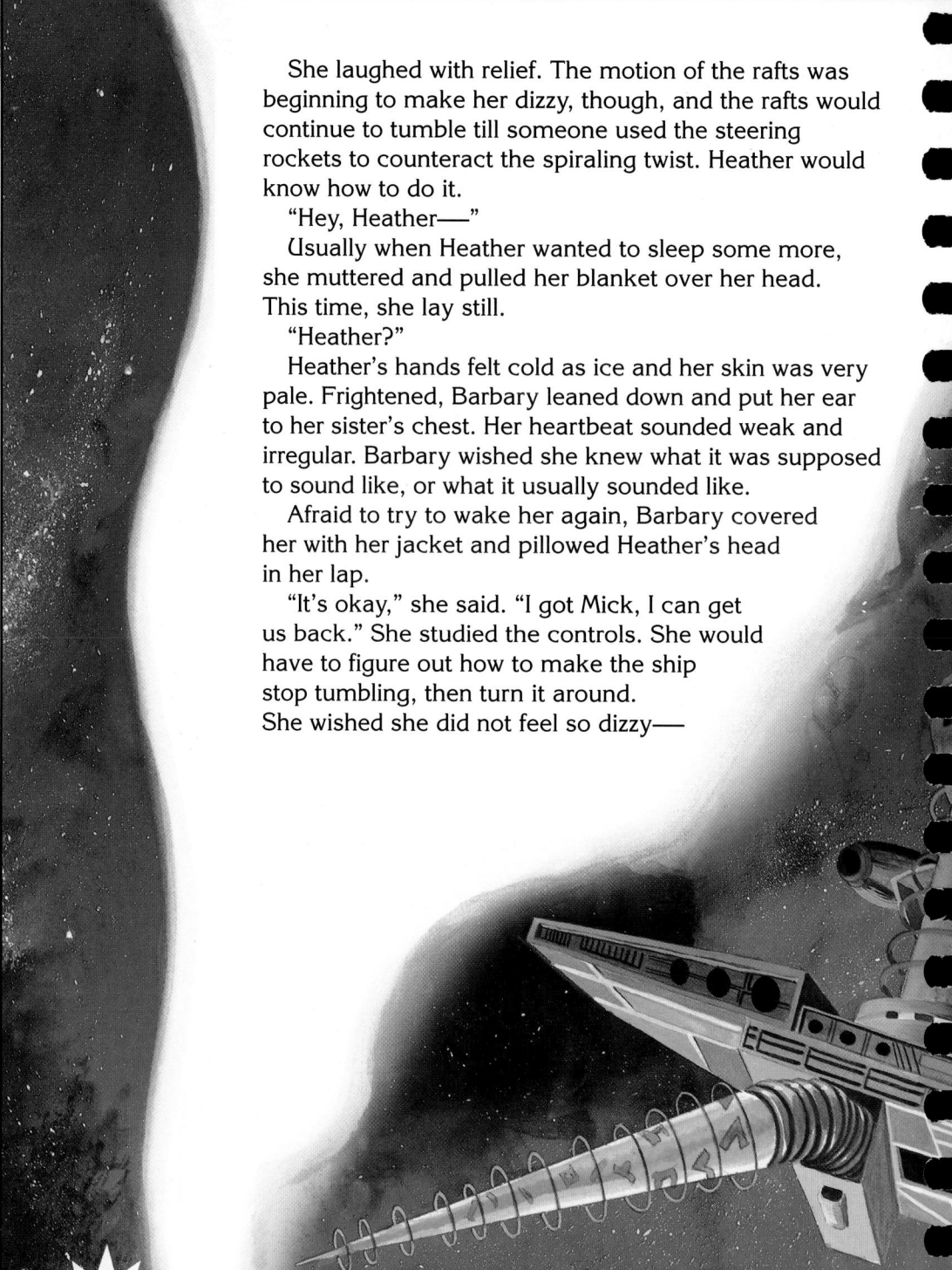

She laughed with relief. The motion of the rafts was beginning to make her dizzy, though, and the rafts would continue to tumble till someone used the steering rockets to counteract the spiraling twist. Heather would know how to do it.

"Hey, Heather——"

Usually when Heather wanted to sleep some more, she muttered and pulled her blanket over her head. This time, she lay still.

"Heather?"

Heather's hands felt cold as ice and her skin was very pale. Frightened, Barbary leaned down and put her ear to her sister's chest. Her heartbeat sounded weak and irregular. Barbary wished she knew what it was supposed to sound like, or what it usually sounded like.

Afraid to try to wake her again, Barbary covered her with her jacket and pillowed Heather's head in her lap.

"It's okay," she said. "I got Mick, I can get us back." She studied the controls. She would have to figure out how to make the ship stop tumbling, then turn it around. She wished she did not feel so dizzy——

194

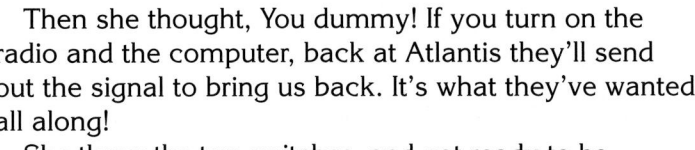

Then she thought, You dummy! If you turn on the radio and the computer, back at Atlantis they'll send out the signal to bring us back. It's what they've wanted all along!

She threw the two switches, and got ready to be bawled out.

The radio remained silent.

As the raft rotated, an enormous shape slid past the roof.

The rotation of the raft slowed, though Barbary felt no vibration from the steering rockets.

The huge shape slid into view again, the rotation stopped, and Barbary found herself gazing through the roof at the looming alien ship.

Barbary put her arms across Heather as if she could protect her.

Slowly, the raft moved toward the irregular, multicolored hull.

The alien ship drew the raft closer, growing larger and larger till its expanse of incomprehensible shapes stretched as far as Barbary could see.

Trembling, she hugged Heather closer. She wrapped her jacket closer around her sister's shoulders,

195

Comprehension
Skills

Cause and Effect

Have students continue to work on their flowcharts to show major causes and effects in the selection.

- Mick gets stuck in the probe, so Barbary and Heather must rescue him.

- Their fear of being stopped causes Barbary and Heather to turn off the computer controls.

- Because Heather gets ill, Barbary must try to catch Mick's raft by herself.

- Because the rafts are out of control, the aliens allow them into their ship.

② Reading and Responding

Comprehension Strategies

Modeling

16 Clarifying *I don't get this paragraph at all. Is the raft going up, down, or sideways? Because Barbary kept telling herself that she was falling up, I guess they were going up. I bet this weird feeling is tied to gravity and weightlessness.*

Modeling

17 Clarifying *I'm confused. Is Barbary concerned about the effect of gravity on Heather? In the introduction it said that Heather had a heart condition. Maybe Heather needs low gravity for her health. Let's read on and see if we can find more clues about Heather's condition, and why Barbary is concerned with the effect of gravity.*

Word Knowledge

strands, crystals, gravity
Students can use the skills they learned in the Word Knowledge section of this lesson to read these words. Remind students of this if they have difficulty reading these words.

trying to keep her warm. The raft slid between two irregular projections from the alien ship's hull: a spire taller than any building on earth, covered with delicate strands and symbols, and a wavy, faceted shape resembling the crystals that form around a string suspended in a supersaturated solution of sugar and water.

16 Roof first, Barbary's raft floated toward a wide black slash in the ship's hull. If she did not keep telling herself she was going "up," she felt as if she were falling, upside down and in slow motion.

Intense darkness closed in around her.

The raft's control panel spread a ghostly light on Heather's pale face and Barbary's hands. She heard the echo of Mick's plaintive miaow, and the feathery whisper of Heather's breath.

A faint chime rang, growing louder and closer. Barbary blinked, trying to figure out if she only imagined light outside the raft, or if she were seeing a glow as gentle as dawn. The ringing reached a pleasant level and remained there, while the light brightened till Barbary could see. She had weight as well, but she had not noticed when the gravity appeared. She felt as if she **17** weighed as much as she did on earth, and this increased her concern for Heather.

196

Her raft hung in a round room whose surface glistened like <u>mother-of-pearl</u>. The columns supporting the ceiling looked like frozen waterfalls or <u>translucent</u> pillars of melted glass. She searched for the opening that had let her in, but it had closed or sealed itself up. From the wind-chime sound transmitted to her through the raft's body, she decided she must be surrounded by an atmosphere, but she did not know if it was oxygen or—as Heather had speculated—methane or cyanide. She had no way to tell whether it was safe to breathe, or poisonous.

Mick miaowed again, louder.

"It's okay, Mick," she said. She swallowed hard, trying to steady her voice. "It's going to be okay."

"Do you hear us?"

The radio spoke with the beautiful voice of the alien's first message to Atlantis.

"Yes," she whispered, her throat dry. "Can you hear me?"

"We sense you. Will you meet us?"

"I want to. I really do," Barbary said. "But I have to get Heather into zero gravity and back to the space

197

Comprehension
Skills

Cause and Effect

Have the students complete their cause-and-effect flowchart with the final events of the story. For example:

- Because the crystalline beings thought Mick was a small person, Barbary could not help but laugh. (page 200)

- Because the gravity was so low, Heather's weight was insignificant when Barbary picked her up. (page 200)

The final sentence of the story offers the cause and effect for the entire story.

- Because Mick jumped on board the probe, Barbary and Heather got into a lot of trouble. (page 201)

Teacher Tip

You may wish to continue the flowchart with more cause-and-effect sequences. For example:
- Because Heather needed low gravity, the aliens adjusted the gravity.
- Because the aliens could fly them to the space station more quickly, the girls decided to stay on board.

2 Reading and Responding

Comprehension Strategies

Modeling

18 Predicting *Where are the aliens? We've read the description of the room, but I don't see anything that looks like an alien to me. Barbary thinks they are hiding behind the tall glass pillars, but they don't sound afraid. I think they'll turn out to be see-through, maybe clouds of gas. Hopefully, I'll find out as I keep reading.*

Oh, I see now. Barbary is seeing them because they are the crystal columns. I was right earlier when I predicted that the aliens would be very different from human beings.

Modeling

19 Summarizing *Let's take a moment to summarize what has just happened. Barbary has figured out that the aliens are the crystal columns. They thought they had figured out the correct gravity for their visitors but did not realize that Heather's gravity needs were different from Barbary's, so they readjusted the levels. The aliens have the appearance of being worried and friendly. This gives me the impression that they will try to help Barbary, Heather, and Mick. Would anyone like to add to my summary?*

Word Knowledge

creatures, friendly, trees
Students can use the skills they learned in the Word Knowledge section of this lesson to read these words. Remind students of this if they have difficulty reading these words.

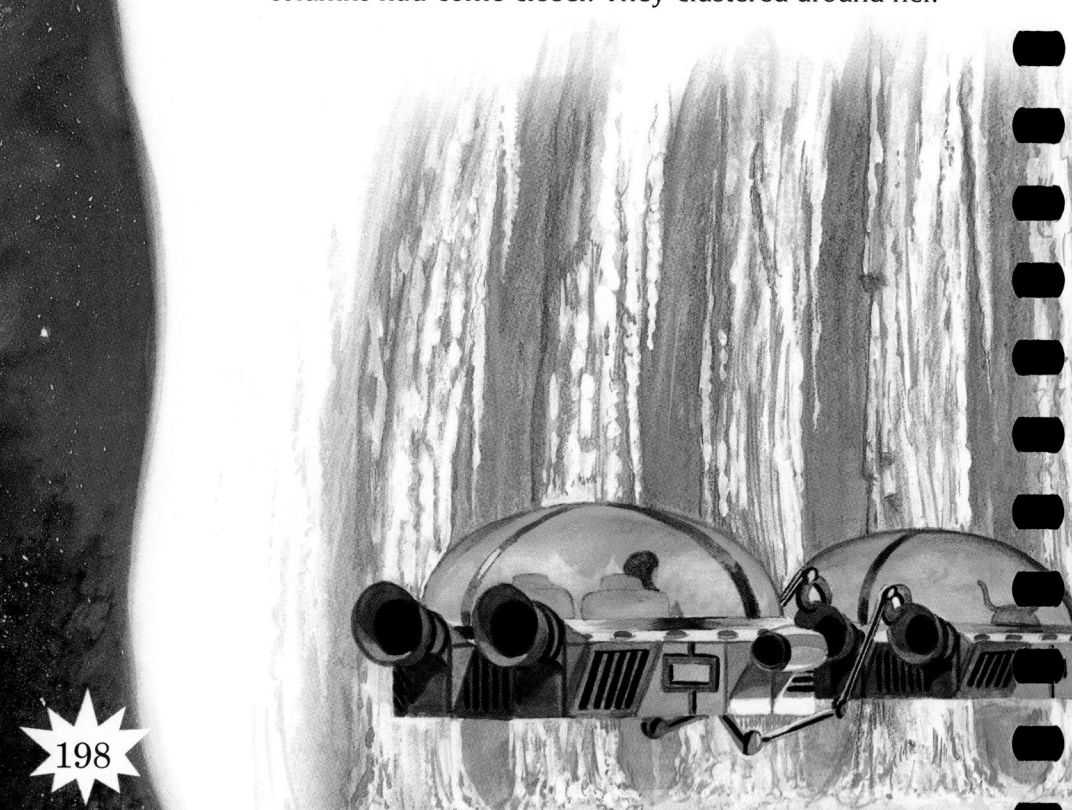

station. She's sick and I can't wake her up. The gravity's too strong for her here. Besides, all the important people are waiting to meet you, and they'll be really angry if I see you first."

"But," the voice said, "you have already seen us."

Barbary stared around the chamber, looking for creatures, great ugly things like the aliens in old movies, or small furry things like the aliens in books. They must be hiding behind the tall glass pillars.

The gravity faded till it was barely enough to give Barbary's surroundings a "down" and an "up."

"Is this gravity more comfortable for you?"

"Yes," Barbary said. "Thanks."

"We believed we <u>calibrated</u> your gravity correctly."

"You did," Barbary said. "At least it felt okay to me. But Heather . . . Heather has to live in lower gravity. Won't you let us go? She's sick! Anyway, I can't see you——" She stopped, amazed.

Though she had not seen them move, the crystal columns had come closer. They clustered around her.

198

Their <u>rigid</u> forms remained upright, yet they gave the impression of bending down like a group of worried aunts or friendly trees. A long row of crystalline fibers grew along the side of each column. The fibers quivered rapidly, vibrating against and stroking the main body of each being, producing the wind-chime voices.

"Oh," she said. "Oh. I *do* see you. You're beautiful!" **19**

"We will loose your craft if you wish," the voice on the radio said. "But our ship will reach your habitat before your vessel could fly to it, and here the gravity can be controlled."

"Can you hurry? I'm really worried about Heather."

"We will hurry."

Barbary listened to Heather's rapid, irregular heartbeat.

"Can't you help her?" she said to the aliens. She remembered all the movies she had seen where people got hurt and aliens healed them. "Can't you make her well? Aliens are supposed to be able to make people well!"

"But we have only just met you," one of the aliens said, perplexed and regretful. "We know little of your physiology. Perhaps in a few decades, if you wish us to study you . . ."

199

Assessment

✓ **Formal** To assess students' understanding of cause and effect, have them complete **Skills Assessment,** page 21.

Comprehension Skills

Cause and Effect

Now that the students have completed their cause-and-effect flowcharts for "A Meeting in Space," have them create a cause-and-effect flowchart for another selection that they have read in this unit. Remind them that the cause-and-effect relationship may exist in all of the genres of writing.

② Reading and Responding

Comprehension Strategies

Modeling

⑳ Confirming Predictions *Now that we've finished the selection, we can check all our predictions and see if they were confirmed. Some were, but I was certainly surprised by the aliens. They weren't at all the way I expected them to be.*

Discussing Strategy Use

After they have read the selection, have students share any problems they encountered and tell what strategies they used to solve them. Then, have them answer the following questions. If they answer "no" to any of the questions, have them reread part of the selection to find the answer.

- What did they do to clarify some of the puzzling parts of this selection?

- Did they make predictions and check to see if they were right?

- Did they find it helpful to stop and summarize occasionally?

Make sure that students explain how using the strategies helped them understand the selection better and how they read effectively to find answers to the questions they asked as they set purposes.

Barbary thought she should have learned by now not to expect anything to work the way it did in books or movies. She leaned over Heather again, willing her to awaken.

Heather's eyelids fluttered.

"Barbary . . . ?"

Heather opened her eyes. She sounded weak, confused, and tired.

"It's okay, Heather. Anyway, I think it is—what about you?"

"I feel kind of awful. What happened?"

"We're on the alien ship."

A spark of excitement brought some of the color back to her sister's cheeks. She struggled to a sitting position.

"Are there aliens?" Heather whispered. She was shivering. Barbary chafed her cold hands and helped her put on the jacket.

"There are other beings," the gentle voice said. "We hope not to be alien, one to the other, for very long. Will you meet us?"

"Can we breathe your air?" Heather hugged the jacket around her.

"It is not our air. We do not use air. It is your air. You should find it life-sustaining, uninfectious, and sufficiently warm to maintain you."

Barbary gingerly cracked the seal of the roof-hatch. Warm, fresh air filled the raft. Heather took a deep breath. Her shivering eased.

"If you join us," a voice said, no longer from the radio but from one of the crystalline beings, "then we may rotate your vehicles and release the small person in the lower craft. It does not respond to our communications in an intelligible fashion, and it appears to be quite perturbed."

Barbary could not help it: she laughed. Heather managed to smile. Barbary picked her up—her weight was insignificant in this gravity—and carried her from the raft. The aliens

200

Teacher Tip Reread the selection with students who had difficulty understanding it. Continue modeling and prompting the use of strategies and skills as you reread.

Word Knowledge

earliest, all-powerful, journeyed

Students can use the skills they learned in the Word Knowledge section of this lesson to read these words. Remind students of this if they have difficulty reading these words.

made a spot among them for her; they slid across the mother-of-pearl floor as if, like starfish, they had thousands of tiny sucker-feet at their bases. The floor gave off a comforting warmth. Barbary laid Heather on the yielding surface.

"I'm okay, I really am," Heather said. She tried to sit up, but she was still weak. Barbary helped her, letting Heather lean back against her. Heather gazed at the aliens. "Holy cow."

Mick's furry form hurtled across the space between the rafts and Barbary. He landed against her with all four feet extended and stopped himself by hooking his claws into her shirt. Somehow he managed to do it without touching her skin with his claws. He burrowed his head against her, and she wrapped her arms around him and laid her cheek against his soft fur.

"Boy, Mick," she whispered, "did you cause a lot of trouble." **20**

201

Assessment

✓ **Formal** To assess students' reading comprehension, have them complete *Comprehension and Writing Assessment,* pages 39–40.

Comprehension
Skills

Discussing the Selection

Following reading, engage the students in a discussion of the selection. Using the *handing-off process* will help the students take responsibility for the discussion. In addition to the following questions, have them revisit any questions asked when they set purposes before reading. Have students support their responses with text evidence.

■ Why was it hard to fly the raft in space? *(There was no gravity and it was a vacuum.)*

■ How was living with Heather different from living on Earth? *(The sky was blue on Earth and there was gravity there. Here the sky was dark and they experienced weightlessness.)*

■ How is Earth in the story different from Earth as we know it? *(There are no animals on the farms and they are all automated. It is not common to go to the zoo, the ocean, or the mountains.)*

■ How has this selection connected with your knowledge of the unit theme? *(Answers will vary—students should compare/contrast examples of astronomy from this selection with their own experiences or past reading and use these connections to make a general statement about the unit theme.)*

During this time, have the students return to the clues and problems that they noted on the transparency before reading. Let the students decide which items deserve further discussion.

When "handing off" is in place, the teacher's main roles are to occasionally remind students to hand off and to monitor the discussion to ensure that everyone gets a chance to contribute.

② Reading and Responding

Meet the Author

After the students read the information about Vonda McIntyre, discuss the following questions with them.

Why does Vonda McIntyre like to write science fiction? *(Possible answer: She likes to write science fiction because it is about things that haven't happened yet but could happen in the future.)*

Why does Vonda McIntyre think it is possible that humans will someday be able to travel at the speed of light? *(Possible answer: She thinks it is possible that humans will someday be able to travel at the speed of light because scientific knowledge is continually advancing.)*

Meet the Illustrator

After the students read the information about Thomas La Padula, discuss the following question with them.

How do you think illustrating for magazines, advertising agencies, and publishing houses would be different? *(Possible answer: Illustrating for magazines might be more factual; illustrating for advertising agencies would involve products; illustrating for publishing houses might be for fictional stories.)*

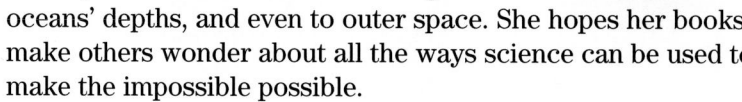

A Meeting in Space

Meet the Author

Vonda N. McIntyre likes to write science fiction because it is about things that haven't happened yet, but could happen in the future. She thinks about what it would be like to live underwater like fish, or be a starship pilot who could travel faster than the speed of light. She believes one day humans will be able to do all of these things. Scientific knowledge already allows them to travel through the oceans' depths, and even to outer space. She hopes her books make others wonder about all the ways science can be used to make the impossible possible.

Meet the Illustrator

Thomas La Padula has been illustrating for magazines, advertising agencies, and publishing houses for the last two decades. He is also a professor at the Pratt Institute where he teaches classes in illustration. Mr. La Padula has participated in numerous group art shows across the country.

202

Theme Connections

Think About It

With a small group of classmates, imagine what it might be like to set off on a dangerous journey through space.

- Do you think this story presents a realistic idea of life in future centuries?
- How did Barbary's preconceived ideas about the aliens compare with what they were really like?

Check the Concept/Question Board to see if there are any questions there that you can answer now. If the selection or your discussions about the selection have raised any new questions about astronomy, put the questions on the Concept/Question Board. Maybe the next selection will help answer the questions.

Record Ideas

Why might people eventually want to live in space? Use your Writing Journal to record notes and ideas about the possibility of neighborhoods in space.

Research Ideas

- Investigate the physical adjustments that astronauts undergo when traveling in space.
- Find out more about the space station Mir—its successes and its failures.

203

Theme Connections

Think About It

- As students discuss space travel, circulate and observe the discussions. Encourage students to use their imaginations.
- Suggest that students compare this science fiction selection with the factual selections they have read in this unit.
- Have the students report what they discussed. Encourage them to record on the Concept/Question Board any questions they may have.

Research Ideas

You might want to invite the school librarian to speak to the class about the variety of science fiction materials available in the library.

Teacher Tip As a class, discuss whether the story is realistic. Have students compare and contrast the scope, treatment, and organization of this selection to the scope, treatment, and organization of factual scientific articles they have read.

② Responding

✦Exploring the Theme

Meeting Individual Needs

ESL

Improvising Endings It may help English-language learners to divide into small groups and improvise their ideas for the ways this selection might end. Allow students to verbalize their ideas and attempt to extend those ideas logically through improvisation.

If you created a word wall on the Concept/Question Board of key words related to the unit theme, *Back Through the Stars,* have students find words from other resources, their projects, and family discussions and add them to the appropriate category on the wall.

Research

As students continue their explorations, have them use the *Research* CD-ROM Program to help organize and share their findings.

"A Meeting in Space"

A message from _____

We have just finished reading the science fiction story *A Meeting in Space,* in which two girls fly toward an alien spaceship in order to rescue their cat.

Discuss with your child how space travel has changed over the past 20 years and how it will continue to evolve. Imagine that people will routinely live in space colonies in the future, and they will need space vehicles to travel from place to place. In the space below, have your child write an advertisement for a new model of space vehicle, such as the raft used in *A Meeting in Space.* Look at car advertisements with your child to help him or her get ideas about what features to include in an advertisement for a space raft. Help your child decide whether to design a sporty, luxury, economy, or family space raft.

Encourage your child to use his or her imagination and to share the advertisement with the class.

Unit 2/Back Through the Stars 27

Home Connection p. 27

Selection Vocabulary

Have students write in their Writing Journals the definitions for words discussed before the reading of the selection and any other interesting words they clarified while reading. Students should be encouraged to refer to these words throughout the unit as they work on student and writing projects. The words from the selection are:

acceleration	contraption	three-dimensional
incomprehensible	transparent	

Reading/Writing Connections

Discuss with students what they think happened to Barbary, Heather, and Mick after they met the aliens. Have students write an ending to the excerpted story and share their endings with the class.

Literature Appreciation

Have students pretend that they are news reporters on Atlantis at the time that Barbary and Heather take their raft to rescue Mick. Have students interpret the story events from a journalist's perspective by writing reports of what they would know as observers of the event. Tell them to concentrate on aspects of the story that would be of particular interest to their audience, the crew of the Atlantis. Students may record and broadcast their story to the class.

Home Connection

The class has just finished reading "A Meeting in Space," a science fiction story that stimulates readers to wonder about worlds beyond our solar system. An informational letter on "A Meeting in Space," in both English and Spanish, can be found in the *Home Connection* guide.

Supporting Student Explorations

Have students continue with their research. You may want to do the following:

Whole Group   Have groups present their research plans for discussion and possible refinement. Tell them that most real thinking and knowledge building occurs during discussions regarding revisions. Explain to students that knowledge does not come simply from the acquisition of new information. Have them reconsider and raise new research questions and conjectures in light of new information they have acquired.

Small Group   Provide guidance to ensure that groups are progressing through the phases of the Research Cycle—obtaining information; revising problems, conjectures, needs, and plans; and proceeding to a further cycle of problem, conjecture, and so forth.

Individual   Have students check the Concept/Question Board for new ideas relating to astronomy. New ideas about their questions might prompt them to explore new resources.

Suggest that students post on the Concept/Question Board brief descriptions of books, magazine articles, computer Web sites, or other sources of information that they have found to be especially helpful in their explorations of astronomy. Encourage students who are having difficulty finding information to check sources on the Board and to post their questions as well.

Inquiry Journal Have students complete page 22 of the ***Inquiry Journal.*** Have them record their ideas about how "A Meeting in Space" added to their knowledge of astronomy.

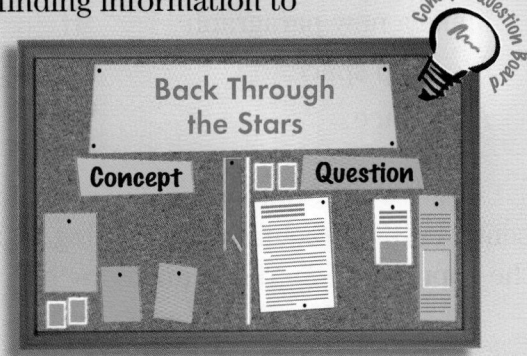

Assessment

✓ **Informal** At this point, students continue with their research. They should be:
- discussing and refining plans.
- progressing through the research cycle.

Recording Concept Information (continued)

- *Circles, Squares, and Daggers: How Native Americans Watched the Skies* by Elsa Marston
  Answers will vary.

- *Voyager to the Planets* by Necia Apfel
  Answers will vary.

- *A Meeting in Space* by Vonda N. McIntyre
  Answers will vary.

22   Inquiry Journal

③ Integrating the Curriculum

Meeting Individual Needs

ESL

Proofread ESL students may have difficulty applying all the items on their proofreading checklist. Explain that catching all the errors in a piece of work is not always quick or easy, even for those proficient in the English language. Review the students' writing and suggest concentrating on one or two items on the checklist that apply to the problems most prevalent in the students' writing,

Intervention

Proofread Work with students who are having difficulty proofreading their work. Suggest that they double-space their work to allow sufficient room for making proofreading marks. Suggest that they read through their work several times, checking for only one or two items from the checklist at a time. Go over the chart of proofreaders' marks and make sure that the students understand their purposes.

Students may find the following checklist helpful when proofreading their papers. Proofread your writing to make sure that:

- each sentence begins with a capital letter
- each sentence ends with the correct punctuation
- there are no incomplete or run-on sentences
- no words are missing from sentences
- no punctuation marks are missing from sentences
- the subject and verb agree
- the grammar is correct
- words are used correctly
- words are spelled correctly
- each new paragraph is indented

Language Arts

Writing

Proofreading

Instruct Tell students that after they revise a paper for content, they must read it carefully, checking for and correcting errors in grammar, spelling, or punctuation. This process is called proofreading and should require mechanical changes only. Display or make copies of Proofreader's Marks **Transparency 53,** and explain how each of the marks is used.

Meaning	Mark	Example
Add	∧	Monday wasn't ∧ best day. *my*
Delete (take out)	ℰ	I ran to school in the ~~wet~~ rain.
Add a period	⊙	I forgot Mr Boyd's homework⊙
Make a capital	≡	i̲ raced back for my report.
Transpose	*tr* ∿	I fell almost as I hurried.
Make a small letter	/	I didn't know it was a /Holiday.
Make a new paragraph	¶	¶School was closed.
Close up space	⌒	Put the book case over there.
Add space	#	What a horrible#day!

Practice Compose and write on the chalkboard nine or ten sentences that require proofreading and correcting. Have volunteers use the appropriate marks to make the corrections.

Apply Tell each student to compose five sentences that need corrections, exchange papers, and use proofreaders' marks to make the necessary corrections. Invite students to share the types of problems they encountered and to tell how they made the corrections.

Writing Process

Proofread Have students proofread and correct the expository writing they have been working on throughout the lessons in this unit.

Literary Elements

Title, Author, Illustrator

Instruct Prompt students to define the literary terms *title*, *author*, and *illustrator*. Then have them look at some of the selections in this unit and notice that on the first page of the selection, the title of a piece is listed first, followed by the name of the author and then the name of the illustrator.

Practice Collect several science fiction books from the library. Select one of the books that you collected, and show students that they will find the book's title, author, and illustrator on the book's cover and on its title page. Also point out that they can find the title, author, and illustrator names listed in the same order as they are found in the ***Student Anthology.*** Pass around the classroom the other books you have collected to demonstrate that students can consistently find this information in the same locations and order as in the first book that they were shown.

Apply Have students make book jackets of their own. Students should come up with original science fiction titles to include on their book jackets and list the author and illustrator names in the correct order (students may want to use their own names as the author and/or illustrator). Have them draw a picture on the cover that represents the main idea of the story.

Meeting Individual Needs

Challenge

Title Reinforce students' understanding of the importance of developing the title for their work. First, browse the school library card catalog and compile a list of several interesting titles. Challenge students to infer from the title what the book is about. Your list should include both fiction and nonfiction. Have students check their inferences by looking up the titles in the card catalog. Invite students to read any of the works that pique their interests.

Explain to students that choosing the title for a text is a very important task. For expository text authors usually try to develop a title that conveys the main idea of the text. For fiction, authors often create titles that tease the reader by only hinting about the contents of the story or book. Fiction titles need to entice people to read the work, but these titles should not give away exciting details or surprise endings.

3 Integrating the Curriculum

Meeting Individual Needs

Challenge

Listening Vocabulary Have students list the following selection vocabulary words on a piece of paper: *contraption, transparent, accelerate, three-dimensional.* Then have students listen to the first few pages of "A Meeting in Space" using the **Listening Library Audiocassette.** Have students listen for how the vocabulary words' meanings are implied in the text, whether through context clues, word structure, or apposition.

Assessment

✓ **Formal** To assess students' reading comprehension, have them complete **Skills Assessment,** page 22.

Listening Vocabulary

INTRODUCED: Unit 2, Lesson 3
REVIEWED: Unit 2, Lesson 6
Unit 2, Lesson 8

Vocabulary

Listening Vocabulary

Instruct Ask students what strategies they use to define the selection vocabulary and other unfamiliar words while they are reading *(word structure, context clues, apposition).* Prompt students to define each strategy. Then tell them that they can use these same strategies when they hear unfamiliar words in a speech, in a selection read aloud, or even during a conversation.

Practice Write the following three columns of words from "A Meeting in Space" on the chalkboard.

Column 1	Column 2	Column 3
multicolored (p. 176)	civilized (p. 179)	reverberations (p. 193)
corrugated (p. 176)	evolved (p. 179)	rotated (p. 195)
irregularities (p. 176)	magnified (p. 185)	supersaturated (p. 196)

Divide the class into three groups and assign each a column of words. Group members are responsible for finding their assigned words on the given page numbers in the selection. Have them take turns reading aloud the sentences or paragraph that puts each term in context. Then, have the other groups attempt to define the words using apposition, word structure, and context clues. Finally, have students consult a dictionary or glossary to see if the words were defined correctly.

Apply Have students write three original sentences using one word from each of the columns in the Practice exercise.

Grammar, Usage, and Mechanics

Subject and Verb Agreement

Instruct Tell students that the subject and the verb need to agree in order for a sentence to make sense. Point out the following rules for subject and verb agreement.

- The verb is the word that describes the action and the subject is the person or thing in a sentence that performs the action of the verb.
- The subject determines what form of the verb to use. If the subject is singular, the verb form is singular. If the subject is plural, the verb form must be plural.

Have students compare the subject and verb in this pair of example sentences: *A planet circles around the sun. Planets circle around the sun.* Point out that the verb form changes as the subject changes from singular to plural.

Practice Using the example above as a model, have students write more sentence pairs that illustrate how the verb changes to match a singular or plural subject. Have students use astronomy-related nouns from this selection as the subjects for their sentences. Invite volunteers to share their sentence pairs with the class.

Apply Have the students look through their Writing Journals, checking for subject and verb agreement. For additional practice, have students complete *Reading and Writing Workbook* pages 69–70.

Reading and Writing Workbook pp. 69–70

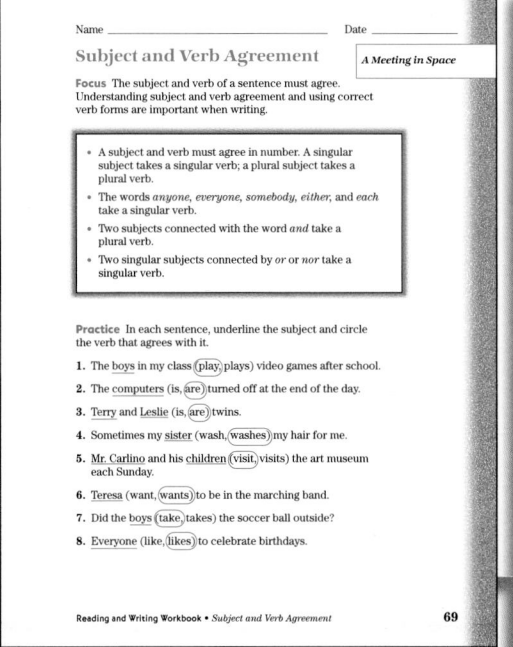

Meeting Individual Needs

Reteach

Subject and Verb Agreement Have students who need additional instruction and practice with this concept complete *Reteach,* pages 69–70.

Challenge

Subject and Verb Agreement Challenge students to find three examples of subject and verb agreement between a singular subject and verb, and three examples of subject and verb agreement between a plural subject and verb in the selection "A Meeting in Space." Have students who understand this concept complete *Challenge,* page 37.

Skills Strand

Subject and Verb Agreement
INTRODUCED: Unit 2, Lesson 6
REVIEWED: Unit 3, Lesson 4
Unit 6, Lesson 2

Remind students to check their expository papers for subject and verb agreement.

 **Integrating the Curriculum**

Meeting Individual Needs

ESL

Dramatizations Because the entire class will be creating these dramatizations, this exercise provides an excellent opportunity for English-language learners to practice their fluency and communications skills.

Listening/Speaking/Viewing

Dramatizations

Aliens have been the subject of a number of books and movies. Have students discuss some of the books they have read or shows they have seen that include aliens. Then ask students to think about the story from the aliens' perspective or point of view. What might they think of earthlings? How would our world be different from theirs?

Have student pairs write a dialogue that might take place between Barbary and the aliens later in the story. Tell students to keep in mind what they already know about the aliens in this story and use that as a basis for their dialogues. Then have students assume the roles of the characters they created and play them out with partners. After enough practice, students may want to perform their dialogue for the class or tape it and have the class listen to the tape.

Study and Research

Create Diagrams Using Technology

Instruct Ask students what they know about creating diagrams to enhance their writing. If necessary, remind them that diagrams are used to organize information in such a way as to make it easily understandable for the reader.

Practice Have students consider ways to incorporate diagrams into their papers and present them at the publishing stage of the writing process. Give the students several media options for their presentations, such as:

■ Transfer rough drafts of diagrams onto posterboard, using colored pencils or markers.

■ Create an overhead transparency by drawing diagrams on a blank transparency.

■ Use a draw or paint program to illustrate diagrams on the computer. Then print the diagram to be inserted into the text of the paper or mounted on posterboard.

■ Use a multimedia program to illustrate diagrams and insert audio readings of the captions.

Remind students that the options they choose for their diagrams must relate to their writing topics and enhance their papers by making the content easier to understand.

Apply Have students begin working on diagrams to insert into their expository papers. Be on hand to give suggestions or provide help with computer programs. For more practice, have students complete *Inquiry Journal,* page 34.

 Most word processing programs have a paint or draw feature.

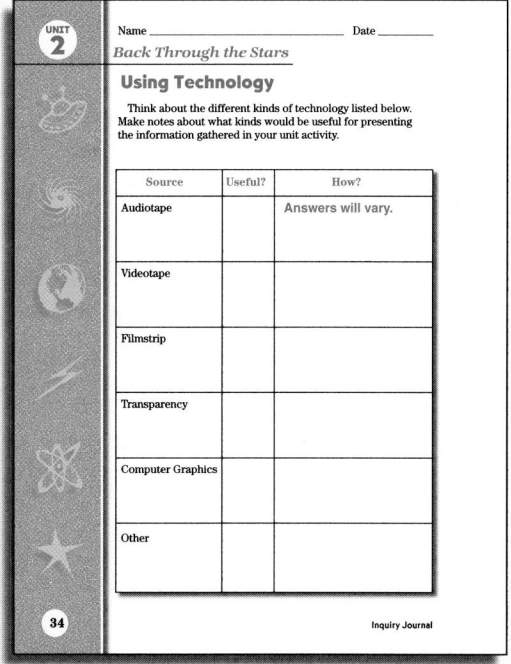

Inquiry Journal p. 34

Across the Curriculum

Math

Word Problem Invasion

Purpose

To have students practice using word problems and make a connection about how they could be used in real-life situations

Procedure

Tell students that in the story, Barbary wished that she had paid more attention to word problems in school. She had never seen the point of figuring out when a train would arrive somewhere *until* she was trying to calculate how to meet Mick's raft without passing it. Write this word problem on the board.

Leonard needs $120.00 to buy a CD player. He has $40.00. If he saves $10.00 each week, how long will it take him to save enough money? (Answer: Eight weeks)

Ask students in what real-life situation they could use this type of math to solve a problem.

Have student pairs work the following word problems and have them come up with a real-life application for each. After students have solved the problems, have them share their answers with the class.

Word Problems:

■ Tina bought 3 pens that cost 1.25 each. Then she bought a backpack that cost $16.00. If Tina gave the clerk $20.00, how much change should she get back? (Answer: $0.25)

■ Mr. Saunders drives 3 miles to and from work. On Sunday he visited his nephew 25 miles away. How far did he drive round-trip on Sunday? (Answer: 50 miles)

■ David sold 25 sports cards for $5.00 each. He paid $2.50 for each sports card. How much profit did he make on the sports cards? (Answer: $62.50)

You may want to have students create their own word problems and exchange them for others to solve.

Art

Alien Creatures

Purpose

To create models of alien creatures

Materials

clay, modeling dough, papier-mâché, paper, glue, or other modeling materials

Procedure

■ Have students recall what Barbary thought the aliens would look like and why she had these ideas. Brainstorm other books or movies where students have gotten different impressions of alien beings. If students have Internet access, have them use a search engine to find other ideas about extraterrestrials.

■ Have students work in pairs to visualize and create their own aliens. Have them write information about their aliens such as where they are from, why they came to Earth, and how they communicate.

■ As an optional activity, have an Alien Invasion Day and have students dress like aliens. Serve food that aliens may eat and communicate using the alien's language. Display students' work in the classroom or hallway for others to view.

Across the Curriculum

 ## Science

Drafting a Model Space Station

Purpose

To create a sketch of a space station that could support life in space

Procedure

- Explain to students that living in space creates unique problems for scientists who design spaceships. Tell students they will be working in groups of three to design a space station that could support human life.
- Discuss what things would be necessary to support life in space. Help students see that they will need to have room in their space stations for air, food, water, safety kits, and even a method to dispose of waste.
- Have students brainstorm a list of items to include on their space station.
- Have students create diagrams of their space stations.
- Encourage them to label the different areas and components of their space stations.
- Encourage students to share their drafts with the rest of the class, explaining the features of their space stations.

 ## Art

Picture Books

Purpose

To show that pictures can tell a story as effectively as words can

Materials

paper, pens, pencils, markers, and crayons

Procedure

- Have students think about books that they enjoyed before they learned to read. Ask them what they remember about the pictures in the books. Were they in color, or were they in black and white? Were the colors bright or soft? Were the pictures funny or serious? Did the pictures show many details of the people or things represented?
- Now have students look at the illustrations for "A Meeting in Space." How do these pictures help to tell the story? Can one tell what is going to happen in the story just by looking at the pictures? Are the illustrations colorful or detailed?
- Have the students work with partners. Invite each student to draw a series of pictures that tells a story, similar to a comic strip. Encourage students to use color and detail in a way that helps to communicate the story. Then have students trade pictures with their partners. Can their partners tell the story just by looking at the picture?

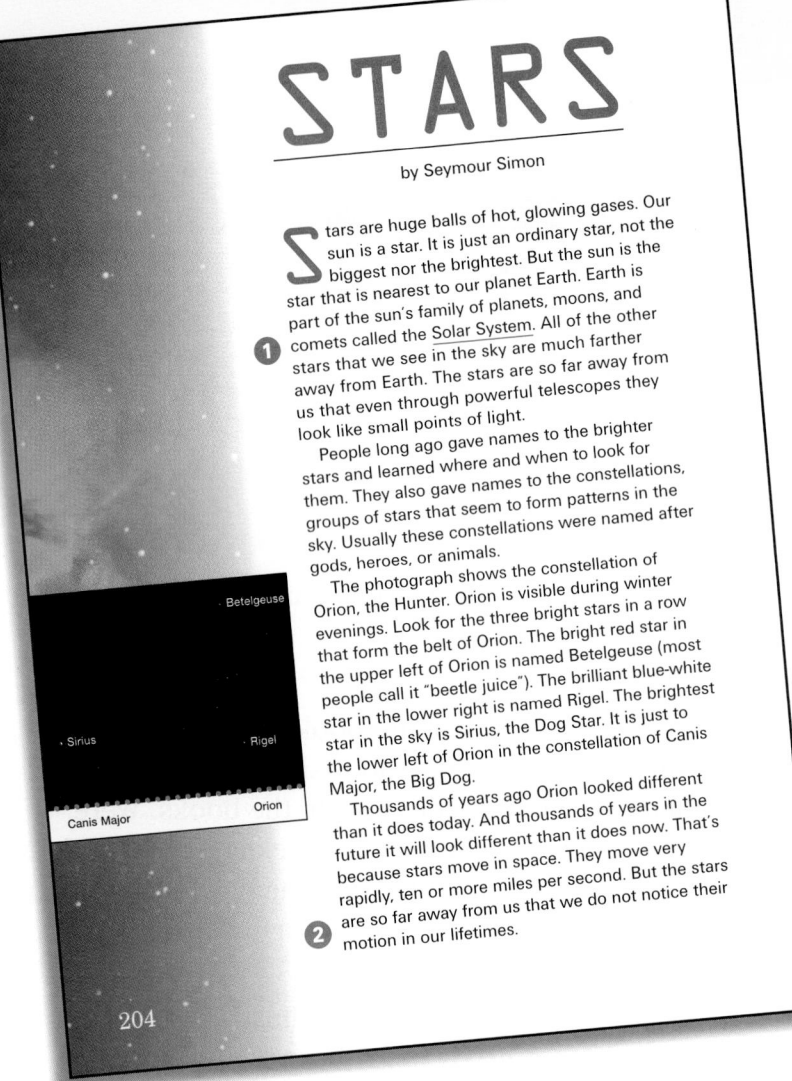

STARS
by Seymour Simon

Stars are huge balls of hot, glowing gases. Our sun is a star. It is just an ordinary star, not the biggest nor the brightest. But the sun is the star that is nearest to our planet Earth. Earth is part of the sun's family of planets, moons, and comets called the Solar System. All of the other stars that we see in the sky are much farther away from Earth. The stars are so far away from us that even through powerful telescopes they look like small points of light.

People long ago gave names to the brighter stars and learned where and when to look for them. They also gave names to the constellations, groups of stars that seem to form patterns in the sky. Usually these constellations were named after gods, heroes, or animals.

The photograph shows the constellation of Orion, the Hunter. Orion is visible during winter evenings. Look for the three bright stars in a row that form the belt of Orion. The bright red star in the upper left of Orion is named Betelgeuse (most people call it "beetle juice"). The brilliant blue-white star in the lower right is named Rigel. The brightest star in the sky is Sirius, the Dog Star. It is just to the lower left of Orion in the constellation of Canis Major, the Big Dog.

Thousands of years ago Orion looked different than it does today. And thousands of years in the future it will look different than it does now. That's because stars move in space. They move very rapidly, ten or more miles per second. But the stars are so far away from us that we do not notice their motion in our lifetimes.

Betelgeuse

Sirius · Rigel

Canis Major   Orion

204

Selection Summary

Genre: Nonfiction

Beautiful photographs of nebulas, quasars, supernovas, and other stellar phenomena illuminate this exceptionally lucid text. Award-winning children's nonfiction author Seymour Simon presents a great deal of sophisticated and fascinating information in clear, simple language. His rich detail illuminates the nearly incomprehensible vastness of space and the role of technology in unlocking the mysteries of the universe.

About the Author

Seymour Simon, who spent 20 years teaching science in New York City public schools, has written more than 100 science books for preschool to middle school students. He believes that it is important for students to begin reading about science at an early age. "If we want a literate citizenry, we have to start children on science books when they're young. They have no fear at a young age, and they will stay familiar with science all of their lives." He calls his works "guidebooks to unknown territories. Each territory has to be discovered again by a child venturing into it for the first time." His book *The Paper Airplane Book* was named a Children's Book Showcase title.

Students can read more about Seymour Simon on page 212 of the ***Student Anthology.***

Other Books by Seymour Simon
- *Chemistry in the Kitchen*
- *Science at Work: Projects in Space Science*
- *Science Projects in Pollution*
- *Let's Try It Out: Hot and Cold*

Exploring the Theme

Selection Concepts

"Stars" underscores the importance of sophisticated tools in learning about the universe. With the aid of high-powered telescopes, scientists have discovered not only what a mind-boggling number of stars there are, but also what stars are made of, how they were born, how they die, and much more. This selection also demonstrates how discovering and exploring one phenomenon can lead to further discoveries. Key concepts explored are:

- Sophisticated equipment makes it possible to study nebulas, quasars, supernovas, and other stellar phenomena.
- Information gathered from studying the stars has helped scientists learn more about how the universe itself began.

Check the Reading link of the **SRA** Web page for links to theme-related Websites.
http://www.sra4kids.com

Exploration Activity Tips

Before Reading, ask the students if they have heard of the terms *light-year, nova, supernova, galaxy,* and *quasar.* Explain that the article they are going to read includes these and other content-area words that are important for understanding the stars. Have students browse the text for clues to the the meanings of unfamiliar terms.

During Reading, after each paragraph, allow students to pose questions for others to answer. Because this article contains a great deal of factual material, students may have many questions.

After Reading, have students tell what conclusions they have drawn from this selection that will be useful in their research. Then have students update the Concept/Question Board. Some may want to revise their activity plans based on what they have learned from the selection.

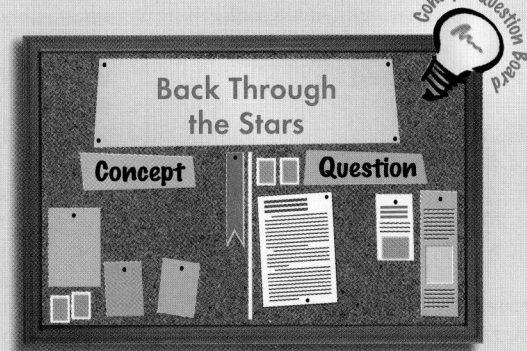

Unit 2 Exploration Management	
Lesson 1	Brainstorm research problems. Form interest-based groups. Develop and discuss initial research plans.
Lesson 2	Groups finalize plans, allocate tasks, and begin research. Discuss initial findings and resources.
Lesson 3	Research continues as groups consider revision of their activity focus.
Lesson 4	Students continue with research and present their initial findings.
Lesson 5	Research continues. Students present interesting findings or problems.
Lesson 6	Research continues. Students present interesting findings or problems.
Lesson 7 Stars	**Collaborative Exploration** Students organize research findings and prepare presentations. **Supplementary Activity** Organize information in a chart. Groups make informal presentations in the form of mini-debates, problem presentations, or poster sessions.
Lesson 8	Students present their activities.

Lesson Planner

Suggested Pacing: 3–5 days	DAY 1	DAY 2	
	DAY 1	**DAY 2**	
Part 1 **Preparing to Read** **Materials** ■ Student Anthology, pp. 204–213 ■ Transparencies 13, 44	**Word Knowledge** ■ Reading the Words and Sentences, p. 204G ■ Developing Oral Language, p. 204G **Build Background, p. 204H** **Preview and Prepare, p. 204I** **Selection Vocabulary, p. 204I** *variable, particle, visible, globular*	**Preview and Prepare, p. 204I** ■ Review Transparency 44	
Part 2 **Reading and Responding** **Materials** ■ Student Anthology, pp. 204–217 ■ Teacher Observation Log ■ Reading and Writing Workbook, pp. 71–72 ■ Inquiry Journal, p. 23 ■ Home Connection, p. 29	**Student Anthology, pp. 204–213** **Comprehension Strategies** ■ Asking Questions, pp. 204, 206, 210 ■ Clarifying, pp. 204, 208 ■ Summarizing, p. 206 **Discussing Strategy Use, p. 210**	**Student Anthology, pp. 204–213** **Comprehension Skills** ✓ ■ Compare and Contrast, p. 205 ✓ ■ Discussing the Selection, p. 211 **Exploring the Theme** ■ Selection Vocabulary, p. 217A *variable, particle, visible, globular*	
Part 3 **Integrating the Curriculum** **Materials** ■ Student Anthology, pp. 204–213 ■ Reading and Writing Workbook, pp. 73–76 ■ Inquiry Journal, pp. 35–36	**Writing** ■ Evaluating the Author's Writing, p. 217C **Literary Elements** ✓ ■ Organizing Information, p. 217D	**Writing Process** ■ Student's Choice, p. 217C **Vocabulary** ✓ ■ Content-Area Words, p. 217E	
Independent Work Time **Materials** ■ Reteach, pp. 71–76 ■ ESL Supplement ■ Challenge, pp. 38–40 ■ Intervention Guide ■ Listening Library Audiocassette	**Writing Process Continued** **ESL** ■ Word Meaning, p. 204G ■ Vocabulary, p. 204J **Intervention** ■ Antonyms, p. 204G ■ Summarizing, p. 206 **Unit Project** ■ Organize Research Findings ■ Prepare Presentations	**Writing Process Continued** **Reteach** ✓ ■ Organizing Information, *Reteach*, pp. 73–74 **ESL** ■ Picture Story, p. 217E **Challenge** ✓ ■ Organizing Information, *Challenge*, p. 39 **Intervention** ■ Comprehension, p. 204 ■ Evaluating Author's Writing, p. 217C **Unit Project Continued**	

✓ Informal **Assessment Available**   ✓ **Formal Assessment Available**

DAY 2 continued	DAY 3	
DAY 3	**DAY 4**	**DAY 5**
General Review	**General Review**	**Review Word Knowledge**
Student Anthology, pp. 204–213 **Comprehension Skills** ✓■ Classifying and Categorizing, pp. 207, 209 **Theme Connections** ■ Think About It, p. 213 ■ Research Ideas, p. 213	**Student Anthology, pp. 204–217** **Poetry, pp. 214–217** **Exploring the Theme** ■ Reading/Writing Connections, p. 217A ■ View Fine Art, p. 217A ■ Supporting Student Explorations, p. 217B	**Student Anthology, pp. 204–213** ■ Review Selection ■ Complete Discussion ■ Reread Selection in Pairs **Home Connection, p. 217A** ■ Discuss "Stars" ■ Write a description of each phase of a star's life
Writing Process Continued **Grammar, Usage, and Mechanics** ✓■ Commas in Direct Address, p. 217F **Listening/Speaking/Viewing** ■ Major Ideas and Supporting Evidence Speech, p. 217G	**Writing Process Continued** **Study and Research** ✓■ Note-Taking, p. 217H	**Across the Curriculum** **Science** ■ Planets of Our Solar System, p. 217I **Social Studies** ■ Astronaut Heroes, p. 217I **Art** ■ Making Star Models, p. 217J **Math** ■ Measurement, p. 217J
Writing Process Continued **Reteach** ✓■ Content-Area Words, *Reteach*, pp. 75–76 **Challenge** ■ Classifying and Categorizing, p. 207 ✓■ Content-Area Words, *Challenge*, p. 40 **Unit Project Continued**	**Writing Process Continued** **Reteach** ✓■ Classifying and Categorizing, *Reteach*, pp. 71–72 **Challenge** ✓■ Classifying and Categorizing, *Challenge*, p. 38 **Unit Project Continued**	**Writing Process Continued** **Challenge** ■ Commas in Direct Address, p. 217F **Unit Project Continued**

Meeting Individual Needs
Independent Work Time

Part 1
Preparing to Read

Meeting Individual Needs

ESL
- Word Meaning, p. 204G
- Vocabulary, p. 204J

Intervention
- Antonyms, p. 204G

Part 2
Reading and Responding

Meeting Individual Needs

Reteach
- Classifying and Categorizing, *Reteach*, pp. 71–72

ESL
- Public Speaking, p. 206

Challenge
- Classifying and Categorizing, p. 207
- Classifying and Categorizing, *Challenge*, p. 38

Intervention
- Comprehension, p. 204
- Compare and Contrast, p. 205
- Summarizing, p. 206
- Classifying and Categorizing, p. 207
- Clarifying, p. 208

Part 3
Integrating the Curriculum

Meeting Individual Needs

Reteach
- Organizing Information, *Reteach*, pp. 73–74
- Content-Area Words, *Reteach*, pp. 75–76

ESL
- Picture Story, p. 217E

Challenge
- Organizing Information, *Challenge*, p. 39
- Content-Area Words, *Challenge*, p. 40
- Commas in Direct Address, p. 217F

Intervention
- Evaluating Author's Writing, p. 217C

Formal Assessment Options

Use these assessment pages along with your informal observations to gauge student progress.

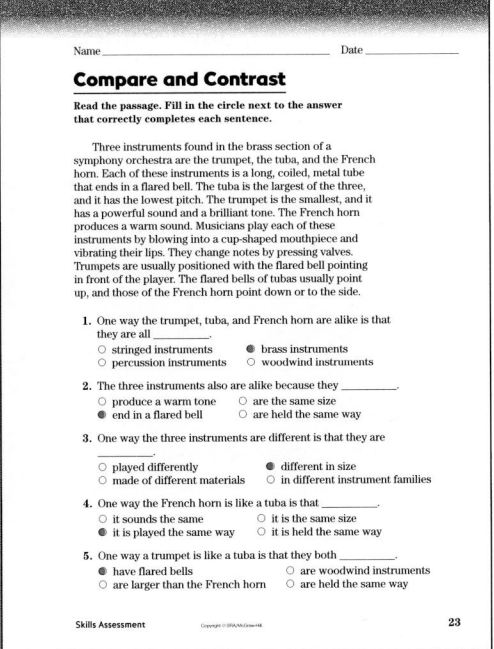

Skills Assessment, p. 23

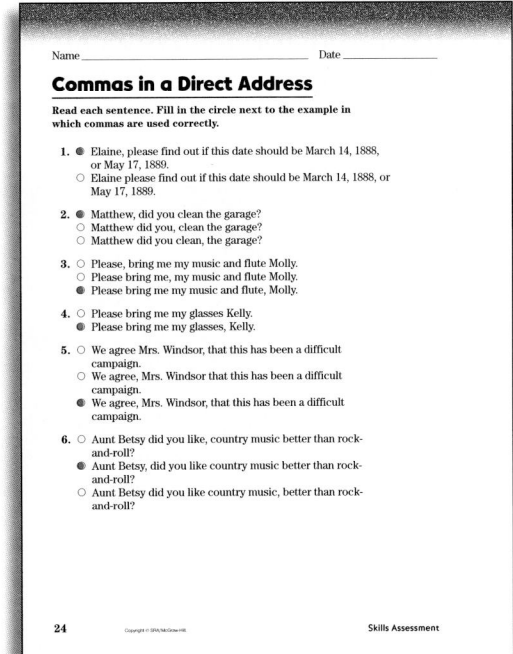

Skills Assessment, p. 24

Skills Assessment, p. 25

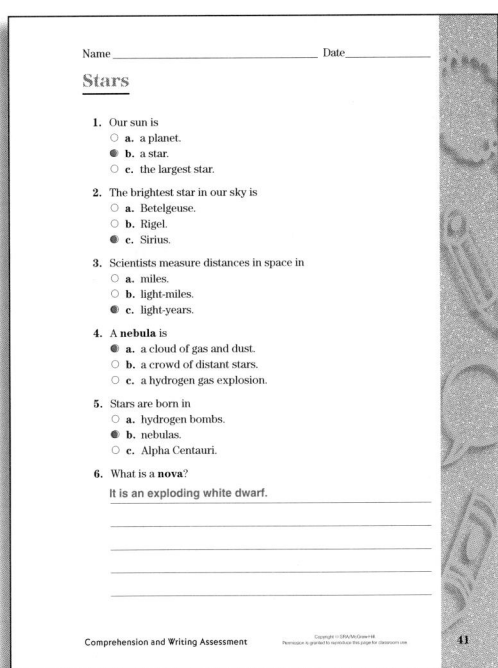

Comprehension and Writing Assessment, p. 41

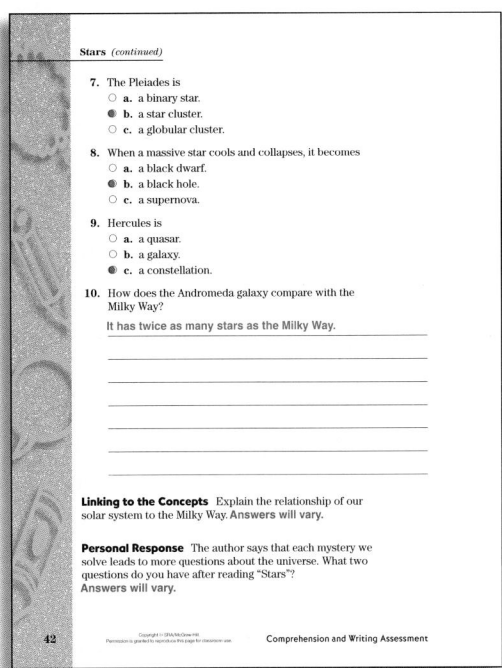

Comprehension and Writing Assessment, p. 42

① Preparing to Read

Word Knowledge

Reading the Words and Sentences

Write each word and sentences on the chalkboard. Have students read each word together. After all the words have been read, have students read each sentence in natural phrases or chunks. Use the suggestions in About the Words to discuss the different features of the listed words.

Line 1:
Line 2:
Line 3:
Sentence 1:
Sentence 2:

Sentence 3:

distant near ordinary unusual powerful weak
cloud thousands sound
hydrogen gigantic edge
The Andromeda Galaxy lies in distant space.
About two thousand stars are visible without a telescope.
Stars begin to run out of hydrogen fuel.

About the Words

- Line 1 contains words that are antonyms. Antonyms are words that mean the opposite of each other.
- In Line 2 the words contain the /ow/ sound spelled *ou*. Invite students to think of other words in which the /ow/ sound is spelled *ou*.
- The words in Line 3 contain the /j/ sound spelled *g*. The letter *g* takes on the /j/ sound whenever it comes before an *i* or an *e*.

Developing Oral Language

To review the words, have students do one or both of the following activities.

- Write the words *create* and *gigantic* on the chalkboard. Ask students to think of antonyms for these words, such as *destroy* and *tiny*.
- Have a student choose a word from Lines 1, 2, or 3 and use it in a sentence. Next, have another student extend the sentence by adding another word from the lines in a way that makes sense. Example: *I see clouds in the sky. I see thousands of clouds in the sky.* Have students see how many words they can fit into the sentence logically, encouraging them to extend both the beginning and the end of the sentence.

Build Background

Activate Prior Knowledge

Have students check the Concept/Question Board to refresh their memories about astronomy. Discuss the following with students to find out what they may already know about stars and have already learned about the unit theme. Tell students to use their prior knowledge to help them comprehend the selection they are about to read.

- Have students review what they learned about stars from Barbary's observations as she travels through space in "A Meeting in Space."
- Ask students whether they are familiar with the selection they are about to read, and if so, to tell a little about it.
- Have students share any other stories involving stars. List additional facts students may recall about stars on the Concept/Question Board.

Background Information

The following information may help the students better understand the selection they are about to read.

- This text contains many facts about stars. Have students identify unfamiliar terms and then look for definitions as they read.
- Many large numbers appear in the text. Write out the numbers one thousand, one hundred thousand, one million, one billion, one trillion, and so on to help students conceptualize the sizes and distances the author describes.

Writing Journal Tell students that after reading they will be jotting down in their Writing Journals their reactions to the selection. Have them be on the lookout for any ideas they may have for using information about stars in a story.

1 Preparing to Read

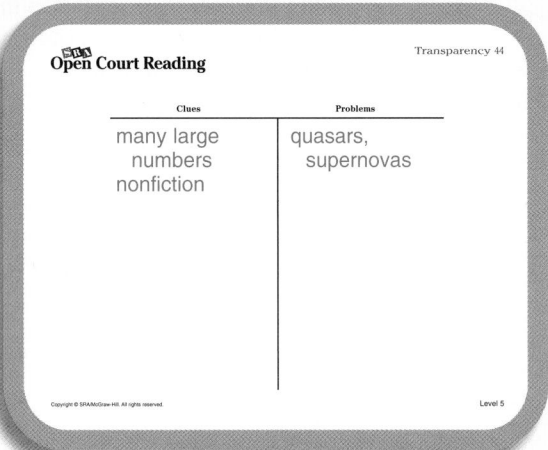

Transparency 44

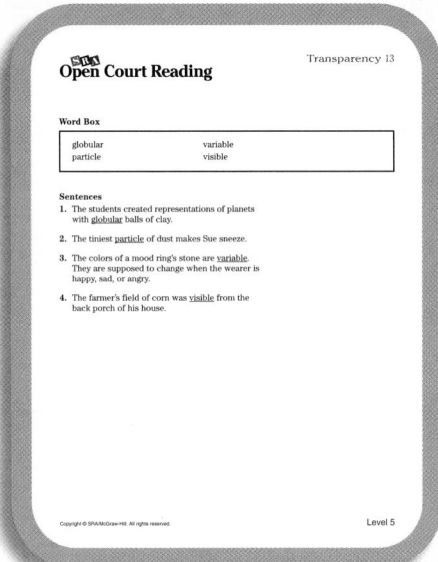

Transparency 13

To help students decode words, divide
them into the syllables shown below.
The information following each word
tells how students can figure out the
meaning of each word from the
sentences on the transparency.

var·i·a·ble	context clues, word structure
par·ti·cles	context clues, word structure
vis·i·ble	context clues, word structure
glob·u·lar	context clues, word structure

Preview and Prepare

Browse

- Have a volunteer read the title and author's name aloud. Have students share what they know about nonfiction.

- Because this is nonfiction, have students browse through the entire story, skimming the text and looking at photos and captions. Have students search for words and phrases that connect to what they already know. Record these in the Clues column on **Transparency 44.** Discuss with them what they think this story might have to do with astronomy.

- Encourage students to ask questions as they browse. Have them identify any problems they notice while reading in the Problems column.

Set Purposes

As students read, have them think about their own observations of the night sky. Do they recognize favorite constellations? Have they wondered why some stars appear brighter than others? In addition, have students think about information in the selection that may be useful to them as they work on their activities.

Selection Vocabulary

As students study vocabulary, they will use context clues, word structure, and apposition to clarify these and other unfamiliar words.

Display **Transparency 13** to introduce and discuss the following words and their meanings.

var·i·a·ble: likely to change (page 207)
par·ti·cles: very small pieces or portions of something (page 208)
vis·i·ble: able to be seen or noticed (page 208)
glob·u·lar: having the shape of a globe (page 209)

Have students read the words in the Word Box. Help students decode multisyllabic words by reading them syllable by syllable.

Have students read the sentences on **Transparency 13** to determine the meaning of the underlined words. Remind them to use clues in the sentences and structural clues to figure out the meaning. See the teacher tip on the left for information on how the words in each sentence can be defined.

Reading Recommendations

Your first reading of the selection should focus on developing the reading strategies found to the left of the reduced pages. We recommend that the students revisit the selection to focus on the comprehension skills found to the right of the reduced pages.

Oral Reading

Because of the high information load and technical vocabulary in this selection, students may want to work together in small groups so that they can ask each other questions and help each other with difficult passages. As this is a nonfiction selection and students are reading to be informed, allow students more time for reading. Have students adjust their reading rate by reading more slowly or by rereading certain sections of the selection in order to comprehend the information presented.

As students read aloud, have them read expressively at an appropriate pace, in natural phrases and chunks. By reading the selection with fluency, students will demonstrate an understanding of the text and an ability to engage the listeners in an effective manner. If students encounter difficulties, have them use the reading strategies below or refer to the Blending Procedure (Program Appendix 15–16).

Using Reading Strategies

Reading strategy instruction allows students to become aware of how good readers read. Skilled readers recognize when they are having problems and stop to use various reading strategies to help them make sense of what they are reading.

During the reading of "Stars," you will model the use of the following reading strategies:

- Asking Questions
- Clarifying
- Summarizing

Before reading, have students share how they have used these strategies in the past and any tips they can give each other on their use.

Building Comprehension Skills

Revisiting and rereading a selection allows students to apply skills that give them a more complete understanding of the text. Some follow-up comprehension skills, such as *Main Idea and Details* and *Compare and Contrast*, help students organize information. Others, such as *Author's Purpose*, *Making Inferences*, and *Drawing Conclusions*, lead to deeper understanding—to "reading between the lines," as mature readers do. In this selection, students will apply the follow-up comprehension skills of *Compare and Contrast* and *Classifying and Categorizing*.

Teacher Tip By this time in the fifth grade, good readers should be reading approximately 126 words per minute with fluency and expression. The only way to gain fluency is through practice. As explained in Reading Recommendations, have students reread all or part of the selection to you and to each other during class or Independent Work Time to focus on the comprehension skills and to build fluency.

Meeting Individual Needs

ESL

Vocabulary Pair English-language learners with English-speaking students. Have the students review the vocabulary words, their meanings and pronunciations, in pairs.

Teacher Tip Have students who may need extra help reading "Stars" reread the selection using the *Listening Library Audiocassette*.

② Reading and Responding

Read pages 204–217.

Comprehension Strategies

Modeling

① Asking Questions *Good readers ask questions to help them focus on what they would like to learn from the text. I wonder what a solar system is. Let's read this page so that we can know for sure. It says that the solar system is the sun's family of planets, moons, and comets. Do any of you have questions you want to ask before we read on?*

Modeling

② Clarifying *Photographs often contain information useful in clarifying text. If we look at the photographs as we read, we can use them to help identify some of the things mentioned in the text. On page 204 there's a photograph that helps me understand the belt of Orion. Can all of you see Orion's belt in the photograph?*

Word Knowledge

Rigel, huge, imagine

Students can use the skills they learned in the Word Knowledge section of this lesson to read these words. Remind students of this if they have difficulty reading these words.

Reading Recommendation

ORAL · CHORAL · SILENT

STARS
by Seymour Simon

S tars are huge balls of hot, glowing gases. Our sun is a star. It is just an ordinary star, not the biggest nor the brightest. But the sun is the star that is nearest to our planet Earth. Earth is part of the sun's family of planets, moons, and ① comets called the <u>Solar System</u>. All of the other stars that we see in the sky are much farther away from Earth. The stars are so far away from us that even through powerful telescopes they look like small points of light.

People long ago gave names to the brighter stars and learned where and when to look for them. They also gave names to the constellations, groups of stars that seem to form patterns in the sky. Usually these constellations were named after gods, heroes, or animals.

The photograph shows the constellation of Orion, the Hunter. Orion is visible during winter evenings. Look for the three bright stars in a row that form the belt of Orion. The bright red star in the upper left of Orion is named Betelgeuse (most people call it "beetle juice"). The brilliant blue-white star in the lower right is named Rigel. The brightest star in the sky is Sirius, the Dog Star. It is just to the lower left of Orion in the constellation of Canis Major, the Big Dog.

Thousands of years ago Orion looked different than it does today. And thousands of years in the future it will look different than it does now. That's because stars move in space. They move very rapidly, ten or more miles per second. But the stars are so far away from us that we do not notice their ② motion in our lifetimes.

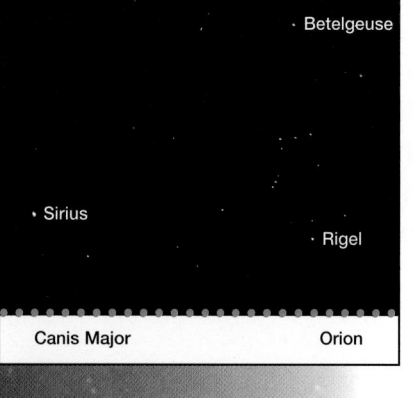

· Betelgeuse

· Sirius

· Rigel

Canis Major　　　　　Orion

204

Meeting Individual Needs

Imagine traveling in a spaceship going ten miles a second. Even at that speed, it would still take you about three and a half months to reach the sun. But it would take more than seventy thousand *years* to reach the next nearest star, Alpha Centauri.

Alpha Centauri is about twenty-five trillion miles away. There are other stars *millions* of trillions of miles away. These numbers are so big that they are hard to understand. Measuring the distance between the stars in miles is like measuring the distance around the world in inches.

Because of the great distances between stars, scientists measure with the light-year instead of the mile. Light travels at a speed of about 186,000 miles every second. A light-year is the distance that light travels in one year: a bit less than six trillion miles. Alpha Centauri is a little more than four light-years away. The stars shown in this giant cloud of gas in the constellation of Orion are fifteen hundred light-years away.

How many stars do you think you can see on a clear, dark night? Can you see thousands, millions, countless numbers? You may be surprised that in most places only about two thousand stars are visible without a telescope.

When the great scientist Galileo looked through his low-power telescope in the year 1610, he saw thousands and thousands of stars that no one on Earth had ever seen before. As more powerful telescopes were made, millions and millions of other stars were seen.

What look like clouds in the photograph of the Milky Way galaxy are really millions of stars too far away to be seen as separate points of light. With powerful telescopes we can see that the stars are as many as the grains of sand on an ocean beach.

Alpha Centauri

Some of the millions and millions of stars in the Milky Way.

205

Comprehension Skills

Compare and Contrast

Explain to the students that good readers gain a deeper understanding of ideas they read about by determining their similarities and differences. Point out to the students that this author is presenting two types of information about stars. He gives the reader scientific facts about stars, and he tells the reader how people have viewed stars through the ages.

Have the students identify the places in which the author is telling us scientific facts and when he is telling about how people view the stars. Then have them read just the scientific parts. Does this make the information easier to read or harder?

The author also makes comparisons to help the reader understand the size and distances of the stars. For example:

- It would take $3\frac{1}{2}$ months to reach the sun, but 70,000 years to reach the nearest star, Alpha Centauri.

Have the students find other comparisons that help them understand the distances of stars in our galaxy.

Skills Strand

Compare and Contrast

INTRODUCED: Unit 2, Lesson 5
REVIEWED: Unit 2, Lesson 7
Unit 3, Lesson 2
Unit 3, Lesson 5
Unit 4, Lesson 1

Teacher Tip

Help the students pronounce the names of stars they may find unfamiliar. Betelgeuse is pronounced bē´təl jüs. Alpha Centauri is pronouned äl´fa sen tô´rē.

Assessment

✓ **Formal** To assess students' ability to compare and contrast, use Skills Assessment page 23.

Meeting Individual Needs

Intervention

Compare and Contrast If students are having difficulty contrasting factual information from people's views about the stars, tell them that in this selection, factual information often contains numbers, measurements, and technical terminology.

Reading and Responding

Comprehension Strategies

Prompting

3 Asking Questions *Have you had any questions that naturally occurred to you as you were reading?*

Student Sample

Asking Questions *I wonder how big a star can be. As we read on, it says that a red giant star may be 40 or 50 million miles across. Wow! That seems really big to me.*

Modeling

4 Summarizing *This seems like a good point to stop and summarize the main ideas in this section. This will help us to remember and to check our understanding of what we have read so far. In short, we have been reading about the birth, life, and death of most stars within these last couple of pages. Who can summarize this part in your own words?*

Teacher Tip Showing other pictures of stars, or a videotape or film documentary on the subject, can help bring this subject to life for the students.

Word Knowledge

There are many multisyllabic words in this selection. Be sure students are using the skills they learned in the Word Knowledge section of this lesson.

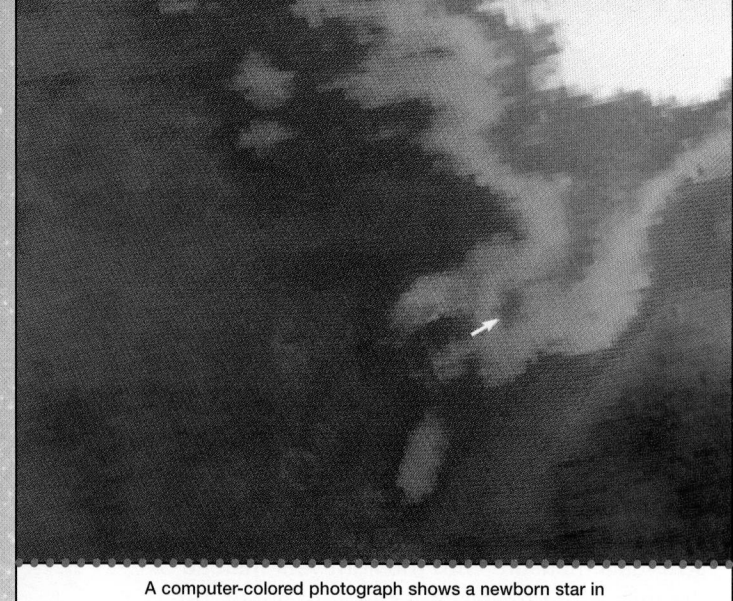
A computer-colored photograph shows a newborn star in the cloud of gas and dust known as Barnard 5.

Stars are born in giant clouds of gas and dust called nebulas. Most of the gas is hydrogen with a small amount of helium. Over millions of years, gravity pulls the gas and dust particles together and squeezes them so that they heat up. When the gas gets hot enough, it sets off a <u>nuclear reaction</u> like that of a super hydrogen bomb and a star is born. This computer-colored photograph shows a newborn star (*arrow*) in the cloud of gas and dust known as Barnard 5.

Stars change as they grow older. For example, young stars (10 to 200 million years old) are very hot——with surface temperatures of more than 12,000 degrees (F)——and are usually blue or blue-white in color. Middle-aged stars like our sun are yellow and not as hot——10,000 degrees (F).

After about ten billion years stars begin to run out of their hydrogen fuel. Most of these old stars collapse upon themselves and they get hotter and hotter. Then, like a piece of popcorn when it "pops," the stars balloon out and become hundreds of times larger. They become what are known as red giant stars.

206

Meeting Individual Needs

Intervention

Summarizing This section contains a good deal of technical information. For students who may have difficulty with this type of text, preread together in a small group, stopping frequently to let them sum up and clarify difficult points.

ESL

Public Speaking Encourage English-language learners to speak in front of the whole group. Knowing that they will be heard and receive some response helps build confidence in speaking.

A red giant star may be 40 or 50 million miles across. Some are even larger. Betelgeuse is a red supergiant star 250 million miles across. If Betelgeuse were put in place of our sun in the center of the Solar System, it would swallow up Mercury, Venus, Earth, and Mars.

Some older stars go through a stage where they keep growing and then shrinking. These stars are called variable stars because at times they appear bright and at other times they are dim.

Other older stars shoot out a large cloud of gas into space. These stars are called planetary nebulas because through low-power telescopes they look like round planets. This photograph taken with a high-power telescope shows the real nature of a planetary nebula. This is the Ring Nebula in the constellation Lyra.

Finally, older stars cool and start collapsing. They shrink down to about the size of a small planet and are called white dwarf stars. As the white dwarfs slowly cool off they become black dwarf stars. And then the stars are dead.

Sometimes a star, usually a white dwarf, suddenly explodes and becomes much brighter. To people long ago it looked like a new bright star had appeared in the sky. They called the star a nova (*nova* means "new"). Even though most novas are too far away for us to see, scientists think that two or three dozen novas appear in the Milky Way every year.

Much rarer are the gigantic explosions known as supernovas. A supernova star flares up and becomes millions of times brighter than normal.

A supernova may appear only once every few hundred years. In the year 1054, Chinese astronomers saw a supernova in the constellation of Taurus. Today we can see the gaseous remains of that exploding star. We call it the Crab Nebula.

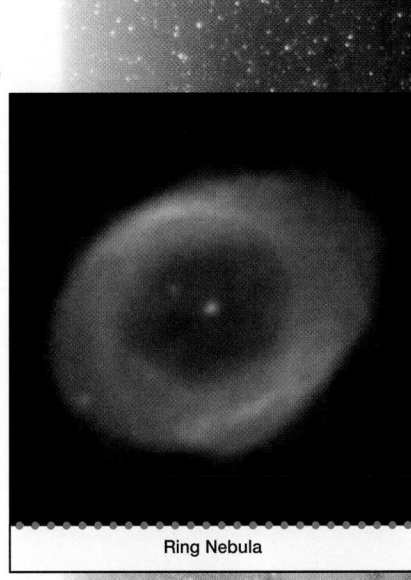

Ring Nebula

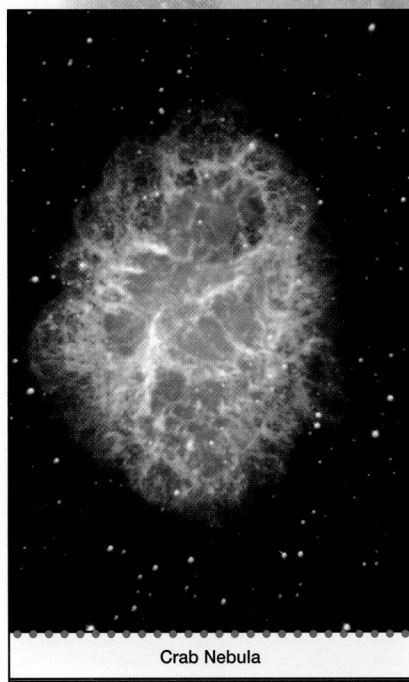

Crab Nebula

207

Comprehension Skills

Classifying and Categorizing

Remind the students that authors classify and categorize things according to how they are alike. In this selection, astronomers have classified and categorized stars according to their characteristics.

Help the students find the following classifications of stars on pages 206–207: *red giants*, *planetary nebulas*, *white dwarfs*, *novas*, and *supernovas*. List these on the chalkboard. Call on volunteers to provide characteristics of stars in each of these classifications.

Classifying and Categorizing

Meeting Individual Needs

Intervention

Classifying and Categorizing Remind students who are having difficulty with this comprehension skill that objects are classified and categorized in their everyday lives. For example, their clothes are classified as warm-weather clothes and cool-weather clothes.

Challenge

Classifying and Categorizing Have the students practice this skill by classifying and categorizing objects in the classroom.

② Reading and Responding

Comprehension Strategies

Modeling

⑤ Clarifying *I know what X rays are because I know about getting an X ray at the hospital, but I didn't know you could take an X ray of a star! It's a good thing the author included some photographs. Maybe looking at them will help us understand more about how scientists see X rays from stars. What do these photographs tell us?*

Teacher Tip Cygnus is pronounced sig´nəs. Pleiades is pronounced plā´ə dēz.

Teacher Tip Because this article contains a great deal of factual information, students may want to pose questions for others to answer after each paragraph is read.

Word Knowledge

lighthouse, average, surrounded

Students can use the skills they learned in the Word Knowledge section of this lesson to read these words. Remind students of this if they have difficulty reading these words.

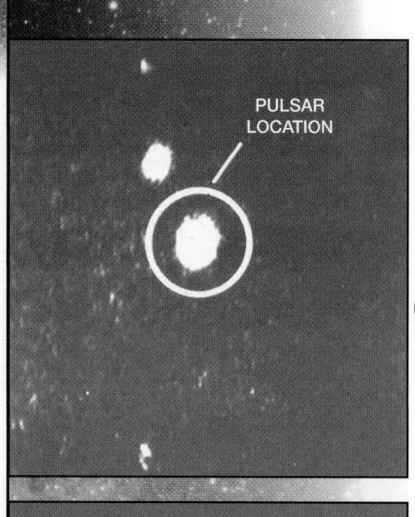

PULSAR LOCATION

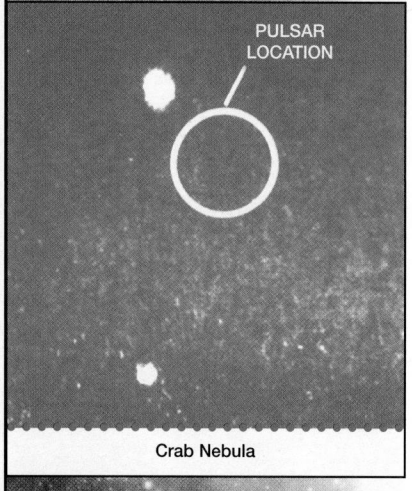

PULSAR LOCATION

Crab Nebula

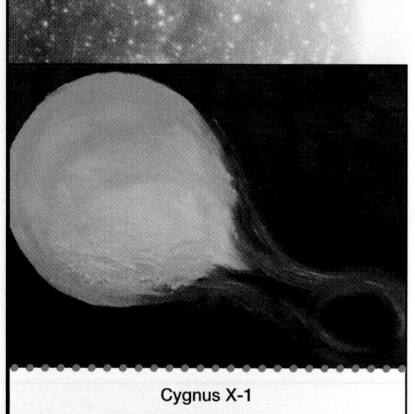

Cygnus X-1

208

Some supernovas shatter completely, leaving behind only the wispy gases of a nebula. But a few supernovas leave a small, tightly packed ball of particles called a neutron star. A tiny drop of a neutron star would weigh a billion tons on earth.

⑤ The sudden collapse of a supernova causes a neutron star to spin very rapidly and give off a beam of X-ray radiation. Like the beam from a lighthouse, we can detect the X rays as a pulse. So a <u>rotating</u> neutron star is called a pulsar.

This X-ray photograph shows a pulsar in the middle of the Crab Nebula. The X rays from the pulsar in the Crab blink on and off thirty times every second. The star is visible when the X rays are "on" and invisible when the X rays are "off."

Some stars are much larger than the average star. When such a massive star cools and collapses, it becomes something very special. The star is crushed together by the huge weight of the collapsing gases. Gravity keeps squeezing and squeezing until the star seems to disappear. The star has become a black hole.

Anything passing too close to a black hole will be pulled into it and never get out again. Even light is pulled in and cannot escape, so a black hole is invisible. Yet, scientists think they have located several black holes.

This drawing is of a double star called Cygnus X-1. Only one of the stars is visible: a hot, blue giant star. Near it is a black hole that pulls gases from its neighbor. As the gases are sucked in they become so hot that they give off huge amounts of X rays. Some scientists think that there are many such black holes scattered throughout space.

Meeting Individual Needs

Intervention

Clarifying Have students share different methods that can be used to clarify an unfamiliar passage or word. Model clarifying yourself, only if students are not able to suggest an effective method for clarifying a passage.

Our sun is an unusual star. It does not have any nearby stars circling it. Most stars have one or more companion stars and they revolve around each other. The star groups are so far from us that most look like single points of light to our eyes.

About half of all the stars we can see are double, or binary, stars. There are also many groups with three, four, a dozen, or even more stars in them. These groups of stars move through space together like flocks of birds in flight. Scientists think that the stars in such a group were all formed at the same time.

Very large groups of stars are called star clusters. This is a photograph of the Pleiades, an open cluster of stars. It contains several hundred stars that form a loose group with no special shape. These are young stars and they are surrounded by clouds of gas and dust.

Here is a different kind of star cluster called a globular cluster. A globular cluster contains many thousands, or even millions, of stars very close together.

This is the great globular cluster known as M.13 in the constellation of Hercules. It is visible just as a dot of light to the naked eye. But through a telescope we can see that it has at least a million stars. Most of these stars are very old and they have stayed together throughout their lifetime.

The biggest star clusters of all are called galaxies. Galaxies are the largest kind of star systems. Our sun and its planets are a member of a galaxy called the Milky Way. There are more than one hundred billion stars in the Milky Way galaxy.

Pleiades

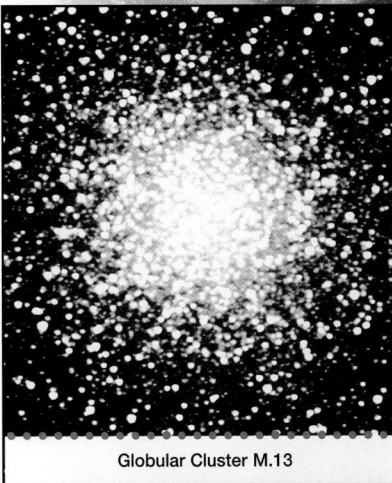

Globular Cluster M.13

209

Comprehension Skills

Classifying and Categorizing

For additional practice with *classifying and categorizing*, have students complete pages 71–72 of the *Reading and Writing Workbook*.

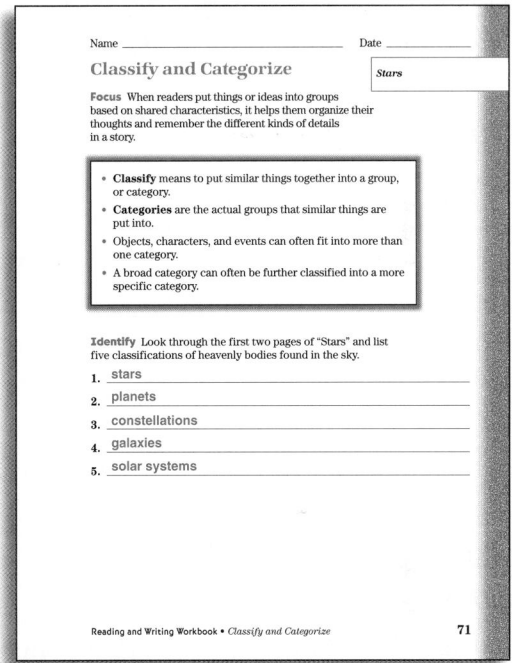

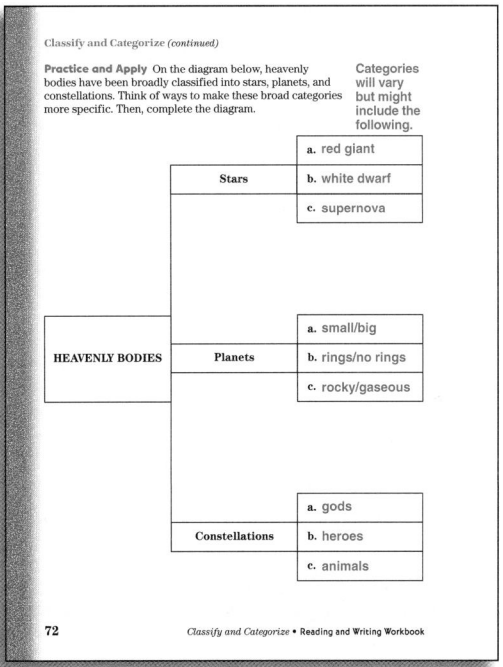

Reading and Writing Workbook pp. 71–72

Meeting Individual Needs

Reteach	Challenge
Classifying and Categorizing Have students who need additional help and instruction with this concept complete **Reteach,** pages 71–72.	**Classifying and Categorizing** Have students who understand this concept complete **Challenge,** page 38.

② Reading and Responding

Comprehension Strategies

Modeling

⑥ Asking Questions *Not only is there a photograph of another solar system, but scientists think there may be millions of other planets similar to Earth! What does this photograph make you wonder about?*

Discussing Strategy Use

After they have read the selection, have students share any problems they encountered and tell what strategies they used to solve them. Then, have them answer the following questions. If they answer "no" to any of the questions, have them reread part of the selection to find the answer.

- Did they ask themselves questions to focus their reading?
- Did they stop to summarize at the end of major sections in the text?
- What did they do to clarify parts of the text they found confusing?

Make sure that students explain how using the strategies helped them understand the selection better and how they read effectively to find answers to the questions they asked as they set purposes.

Word Knowledge

earliest, all-powerful, journeyed

Students can use the skills they learned in the Word Knowledge section of this lesson to read these words. Remind students of this if they have difficulty reading these words.

Beta Pictoris

The sun is located almost out on the edges of the Milky Way. All the stars in the Milky Way whirl around the center of the galaxy, each at its own speed. The sun along with the Solar System moves at about 150 miles a second around the center of the galaxy. But the galaxy is so big that the sun takes about 225 million years to go around once.

Are there planets circling other stars in our galaxy? The answer is almost definitely yes. This picture shows a ring of material surrounding the star Beta Pictoris. This material is thought to be a young solar system in the making.

⑥ Planets form at the same time and from the same gases as do stars. So scientists think it is likely that some or even many stars have planets circling them. If even a tiny percentage of these planets are similar to Earth, then there may be millions of Earth-like planets in the galaxy.

Do any of these planets have life on them? No one knows. But scientists are using radio telescopes to listen for signals of intelligent life in outer space. They think the signals will come in the form of radio waves much like those of our own radios and televisions. So far scientists have not found anything, but they are not discouraged. Until they have examined every star that may have planets they won't know for sure.

The Milky Way is only one galaxy among millions of others in the universe. Galaxies—large and small, single or in groups and clusters, and in many different shapes—are found in every direction.

210

Research in Action

Strategy Use

Good readers develop their own strategies for dealing with difficult text. Encourage the students to share and discuss the strategies they have developed on their own as well as those discussed in this lesson.

(Michael Pressley)

The Andromeda galaxy, shown here, is a spiral galaxy with almost twice as many stars as there are in the Milky Way. The Andromeda galaxy lies in far distant space, almost twelve quintillion miles away. That's 12,000,000,000,000,000,000! Light from this galaxy has been traveling for more than two million years by the time we see it in our telescopes.

How many galaxies are there in the universe? No one knows. But scientists think that there are about one hundred billion other galaxies. And each one of these galaxies contains hundreds of thousands of millions of stars.

Many mysteries confront us in the distant reaches of space. Beyond most of the galaxies that we can see with our largest telescopes are bright starlike objects called quasars. Each quasar gives off more than one hundred times the energy of all the stars in the Milky Way galaxy put together.

This is a computer-colored photo of a quasar-galaxy pair. Scientists think that quasars may be the centers of young galaxies that are just forming. Light from most quasars has been traveling for ten to fifteen billion years by the time it reaches Earth. That means that we are viewing quasars as they were ten to fifteen billion years ago, just after the universe began.

Powerful telescopes orbiting above Earth's atmosphere may soon show us the very edges of the universe and the beginning of time itself. Will all our questions about stars then be answered? It's not likely. Each mystery that we solve about space seems to lead to many more unsolved questions about the nature of the universe.

Andromeda Galaxy

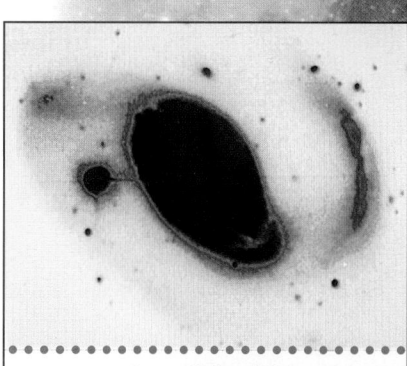

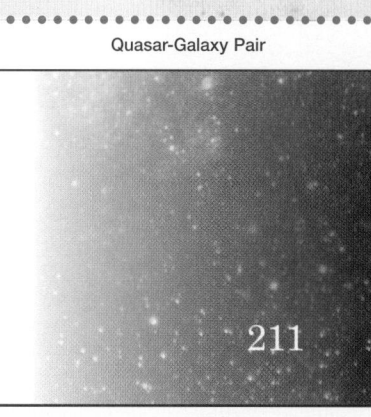

Quasar-Galaxy Pair

211

Comprehension Skills

Discussing the Selection

Following reading, engage the students in discussion of the selection. Using the *handing-off process* will help the students take responsibility for the discussion. In addition to the following questions, have them revisit any questions asked when they set purposes before reading.

- What are stars? *(huge balls of hot, glowing gases)*
- What is the name of a star in our solar system? *(the sun)*
- What is a light-year? *(the distance light travels in one year)*
- How has this selection connected with your knowledge of the unit theme? *(Answers will vary—students should compare/contrast examples of astronomy from this selection with their own experiences or past reading and use these connections to make a general statement about the unit theme.)*

During this time, have the students return to the clues and problems that they noted on the transparency before reading. Let the students decide which items deserve further discussion.

If students want to remember thoughts about, or reactions to, a selection, suggest that they record these in the Writing Journal.

Teacher Tip

Beta Pictoris is pronounced bā´ta pik tôr´is. Andromeda is pronounced än dro´mə də.

Assessment

✓ **Formal** To assess students' reading comprehension, have them complete *Comprehension and Writing Assessment,* pages 41–42.

Teacher Tip

Check for students' comprehension of the selection by asking the following true-false questions.

- Stars move in space. *(true)*
- Supernovas are fairly common. *(false)*
- Quasars may be the centers of young galaxies. *(true)*
- Scientists know all there is to know about space. *(false)*

② Reading and Responding

Meet the Author and Illustrator

After the students read the information about Seymour Simon, discuss the following questions with them.

Why does Seymour Simon like to use photographs as tools for teaching science? *(Possible answer: He likes to use photographs because they can "freeze" images for as long as one wants to look at them.)*

Why does Seymour Simon like to study and teach science? *(Possible answer: He likes to study science because it is about fascinating things such as dinosaurs, space, earthquakes, and the human body.)*

STARS

Meet the Author

Seymour Simon taught science in the New York City schools for 23 years but now devotes all of his time to writing. Simon is the author of nearly 150 science books written especially for students from preschool to junior high. Most of his books are about astronomy and animals. One of the reasons why his books are so wonderful is because they contain many spectacular photos. He likes picture books because, unlike television, they can "freeze" images for as long as the reader wants to look at them. He hopes children will be as amazed as he is by the photos' subjects. He says, "Children need to develop a lifelong enjoyment and appreciation for science. Science is fascinating stuff like dinosaurs, space, earthquakes, and the human body."

212

Theme Connections

Think About It

With a small group of classmates, discuss what scientists have learned from studying the stars.

- Compare ancient people's impressions of the stars with that of modern scientists.
- Why would it be important for scientists to learn about the life cycles of stars?

Check the Concept/Question Board to see if there are any questions there that you can answer now. If the selection or your discussions about the selection have raised any new questions about astronomy, put the questions on the Concept/Question Board. Maybe the next selection will help answer the questions.

Record Ideas

How does the appearance of stars in the night sky correspond to what you have learned about their composition? Use your Writing Journal to record notes and ideas about any disparities.

Research Ideas

- Find out more about the likelihood that other stars—like our sun—are orbited by planets, forming solar systems that may house intelligent life forms.

213

Theme Connections

Think About It

- As students discuss information gained from studying the stars, circulate and observe the discussions.

- Suggest that students review what people have learned from and about the stars from ancient times to the present.

- Have the students report what they discussed. Encourage them to record on the Concept/Question Board any questions they may have.

Research Ideas

If there is a planetarium in your area, suggest that students visit for more information about the stars.

Teacher Tip Have students tell what they've learned from this selection that will be useful in their research. Some may want to revise their activity plans based on what they've learned from this selection.

Reading and Responding

Sun
by **Myra Cohn Livingston**

Activating Prior Knowledge

- Remind the students about the information they have read in this unit about the sun and other stars.

- Direct the students' attention to the title and have them share their feelings about the sun.

Reading the Poem

- Read the poem aloud twice in a voice that expresses the magnitude of space. Use the repetition of sounds, such as the double *b* in *bubbling*, to emphasize the sounds of the words. Have the students close their eyes as you read and to listen very carefully. Then have the students read the poem.

- In the time you designate for independent work, have the students listen to the poem recording on the ***Listening Library Audiocassette.***

Literary Techniques

Onomatopoeia

- Explain to students that the poet uses many words to create sounds that convey the power and excitement of the exploding gases in the sun. Tell them that some of these words are examples of *onomatopoeia*, or a word that sounds like the thing it names (for example, *buzz*).

  Invite students to find examples of this technique in the poem and describe how the word sounds affect and convey meaning to the listener.

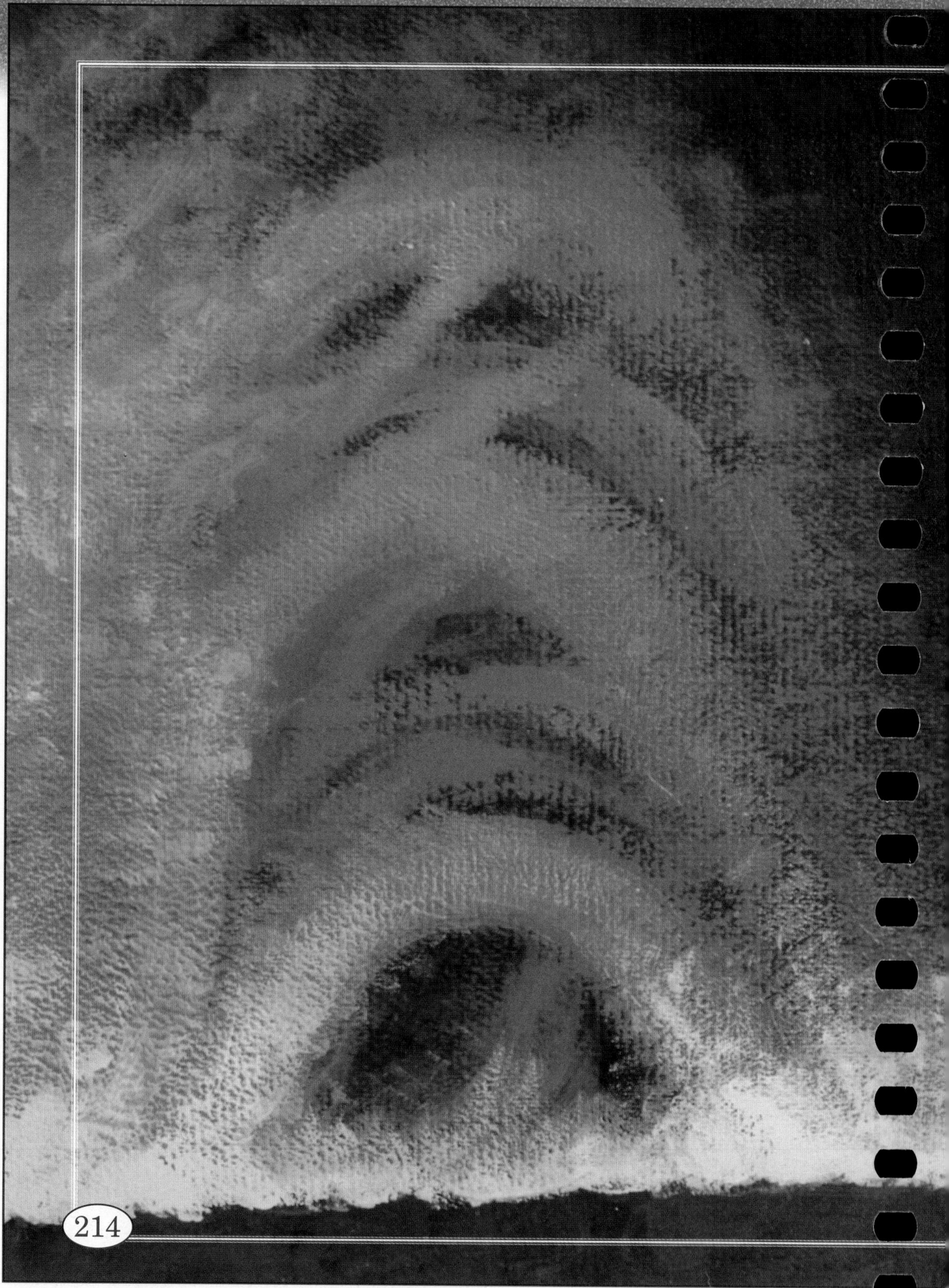

214

Teacher Tip Have students take notice of the poem's shape, and discuss how it affects the meaning of the poem.

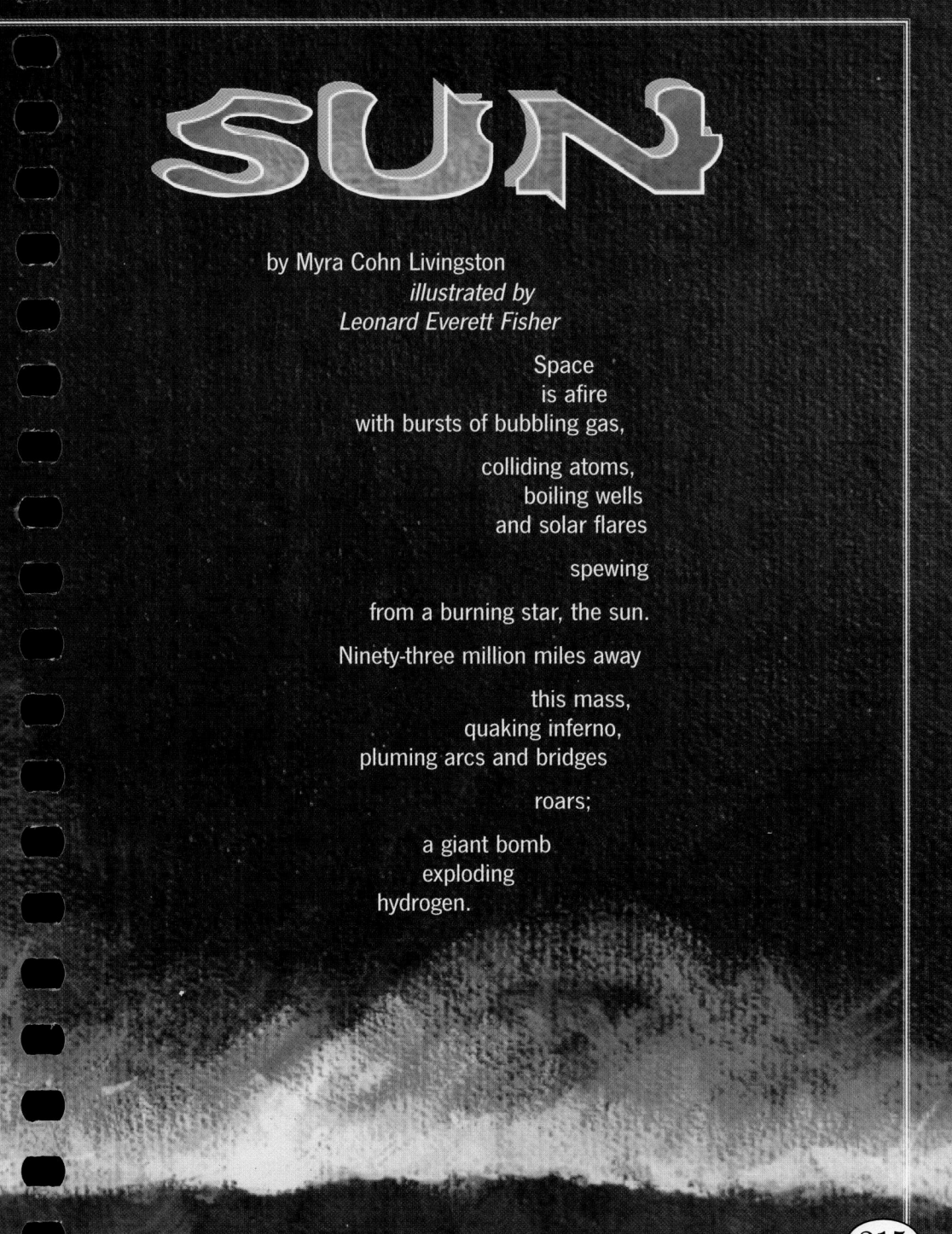

SUN

by Myra Cohn Livingston
illustrated by
Leonard Everett Fisher

Space
is afire
with bursts of bubbling gas,

colliding atoms,
boiling wells
and solar flares

spewing

from a burning star, the sun.

Ninety-three million miles away

this mass,
quaking inferno,
pluming arcs and bridges

roars;

a giant bomb
exploding
hydrogen.

215

Theme Connection

■ Have the students discuss how this poem reflects the information they have read about stars and space. *(Answers may vary; however, students might note that the poem is based on scientific facts about the sun.)*

Meet the Poet

Myra Cohn Livingston was born in Omaha, Nebraska, and now lives in southern California. She enjoys collecting and making books and doing word puzzles. She says this about poetry:

"It is difficult to define why poetry is important to the individual. Poetry is, after all, a personal thing; its meaning to each human being is private. It invades the innermost thoughts, it clings to and bolsters the inner life.... The degree to which the reader is provoked to find the part, the fraction that is missing or not understood, is [a] measure of the poem's worth."

Myra Cohn Livingston has numerous awards, including the Golden Kite Honor Award from the Society of Children's Book Writers for *The Way Things Are and Other Poems*; The Parent's Choice Award for *Why Am I Grown So Cold?*; and the National Jewish Book Award for *Poems for Jewish Holidays*.

The poems "Sun" and "Secrets" appear in her book *Space Songs*.

2 Reading and Responding

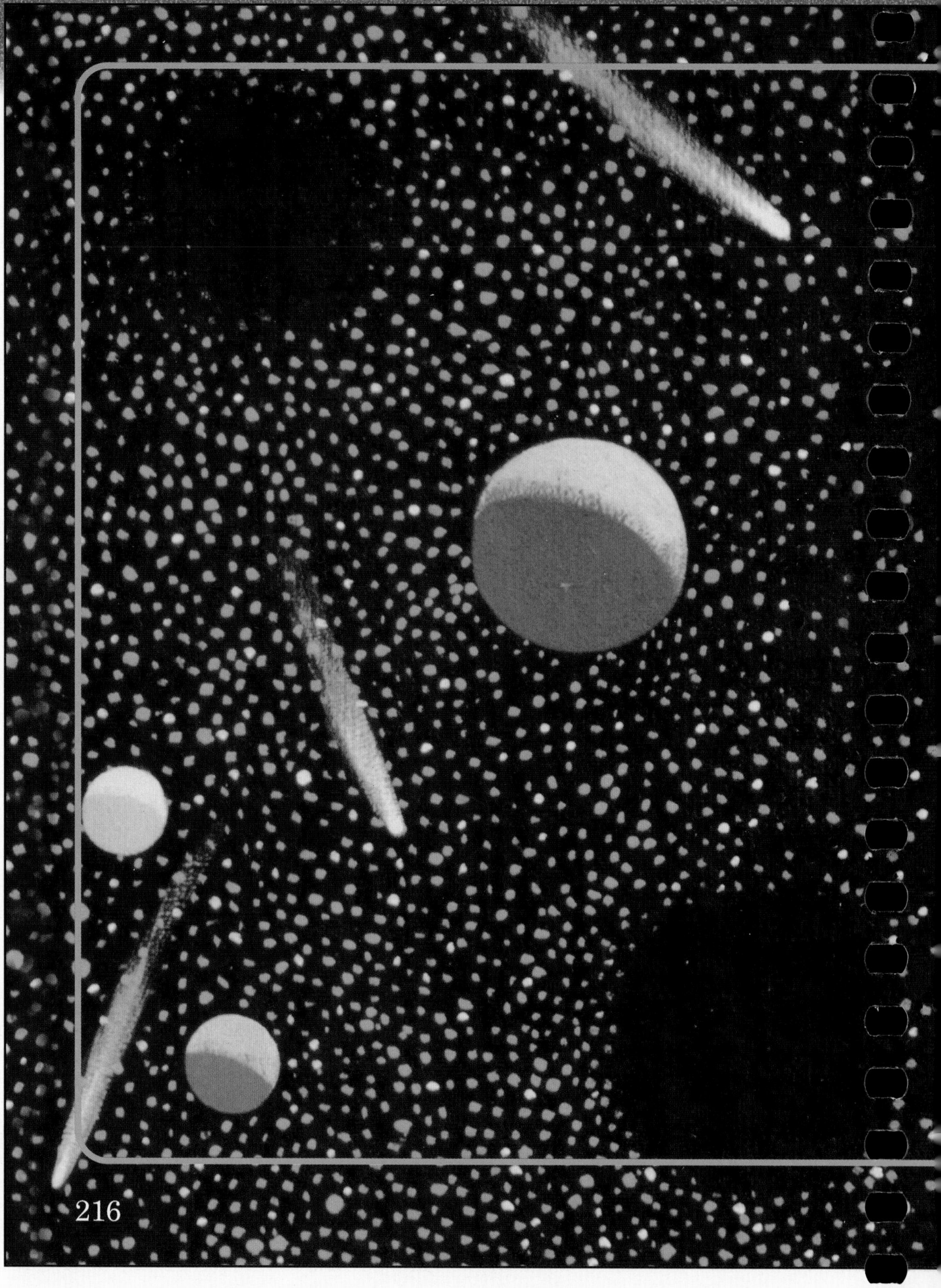

Secrets
by **Myra Cohn Livingston**

Activating Prior Knowledge

- Remind the students about the information they have learned in this unit about space.

- Have them discuss what the poet might mean by secrets. Discuss how dark and mysterious space seems, with many unanswered questions.

Reading the Poem

- Read the poem aloud twice with a voice that depicts the mystery and vastness of space. Emphasize the pauses between lines and the *s* sounds in the words. Have the students close their eyes and picture what you are reading. Then have the students read the poem.

- In the time you designate for independent work, have the students listen to the poem recording on the *Listening Library Audiocassette.*

Literary Techniques

Rhythm

Explain that the poet uses a set rhythm to help readers understand the mystery of space. The short, choppy sentences imply a lot of empty space, with much silence. They help convey the idea that we know only bits and pieces of the puzzle.

Have the students reread the poem quietly to themselves, being silent in the pauses between lines. Have them discuss how these pauses affected the tone and meaning of the poem differently as they listened to it.

216

Have students compare how they felt while reading the poem "Secrets" with how they felt while reading "Sun."

Secrets

by Myra Cohn Livingston
illustrated by Leonard Everett Fisher

Space keeps its secrets
                    hidden.
It does not tell.
            Are black holes time machines?
            Where do lost comets go?

            Is Pluto moon or planet?

How many, how vast
   unknown galaxies beyond us?

      Do other creatures
      dwell   on distant spheres?

            Will we ever know?

Space is silent.
It seldom answers.

      But we ask.

217

Theme Connection

■ Have the students discuss how this poem
reflects the information they have read
about space. Is the poet using the idea of
secrets literally, or is she using it as a
metaphor for something about space?

Meet the Illustrator

   Leonard Everett Fisher was born in
New York. He has written books on Colonial
crafts and trades, nineteenth-century trades,
the Great Wall of China, the Tower of London,
and the pyramids of Teotihuacán. He has
illustrated more than 150 books for children.
The acrylic paintings he created for the
several books on which he collaborated with
Myra Cohn Livingston have been especially
praised by critics.

Teacher Tip Give students opportunities to respond to
various types of poetry and to hear both
serious and humorous poetry. Have them
respond to poetry by writing in their
Writing Journals, creating music for the
poem, discussing their feelings about the poem in
class, or writing a poem of their own.

② Responding

✦ Exploring the Theme

Teacher Tip Have students write sentences using the selection vocabulary words. In order to provide additional help in remembering words, students can write synonyms or antonyms for the words if it is appropriate. Some students may even draw something to help them remember the meanings of the words.

Orion in December. 1959. *Charles Burchfield.* Watercolor and pencil on paper. 39 ⁷/₈ x 32 ⁷/₈ in. National Museum of American Art, Smithsonian Institution, Washington, DC. Photo: Art Resource, NY.

Student Anthology p. 155

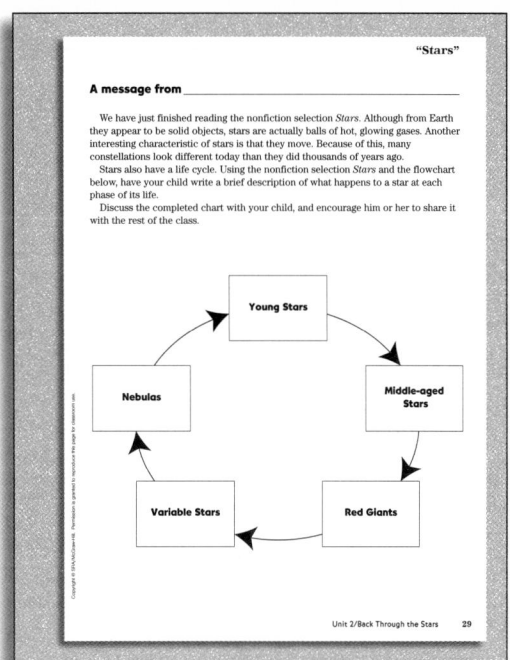

Home Connection p. 29

Selection Vocabulary

Have students write in their Writing Journals, the definitions for words discussed before the reading of the selection and any other interesting words they clarified while reading. Students should be encouraged to refer to these words throughout the unit as they work on student and writing projects. The words from this selection are:

globular   particles   variable   visible

Reading/Writing Connections

Point out that the author of "Stars" presents a great deal of sophisticated and fascinating information in clear, simple language. Point out to the students that the author provides definitions for many different kinds of stars, and explains extremely large numbers in a way that gives them meaning to his readers. The author also describes the size of the supergiant red star, Betelgeuse, in a way that can be pictured by the readers.

Have students share other things they think the author did especially well. They might think back to a section of the article that they particularly enjoyed.

View Fine Art

Tell students that this is *Orion in December,* by **Charles Burchfield,** found on page 155 of their *Student Anthologies.* Have students look at the picture and discuss other selections in this unit with which they can connect it. Then point out that the star outlined in red represents Betelgeuse, one of the largest known stars. If necessary, remind them that Betelgeuse marks the right shoulder of the constellation Orion.

Home Connection

The class has just finished reading "Stars," an award-winning nonfiction selection about the role of technology in unlocking the mysteries of our vast universe. An informational letter on "Stars," in both English and Spanish, can be found in the *Home Connection* guide.

Supporting Student Explorations

Have students continue with their research. You may want to do the following:

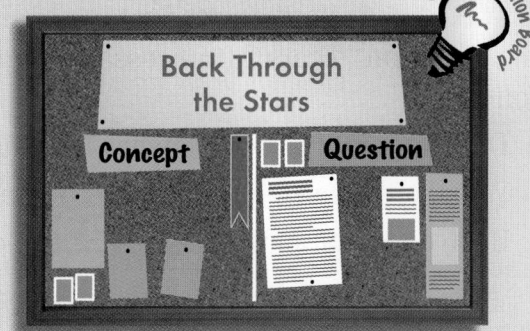 **Whole Group** Have researchers present interesting conclusions they have drawn or problems they have found to the class for discussion. Some groups may want to make preliminary, informal presentations.

If the students have not already done so, suggest that they select an organized way to store their research information.

Small Group Meet with research groups to arrange presentation schedules and update progress charts. Some groups might be ready to present their final projects. Set aside time for presentations and class discussions of presentations.

Suggest that students post on the Concept/Question Board brief descriptions of books, magazine articles, computer Websites, or other sources of information that they have found to be especially helpful in their explorations of astronomy. Encourage students who are having difficulty finding information to check sources on the board and to post their questions as well.

Concept/Question Board

Back Through the Stars

Concept   **Question**

Inquiry Journal Have students complete page 23 of the *Inquiry Journal.* Have them record their ideas about how "Stars" added to their knowledge about astronomy.

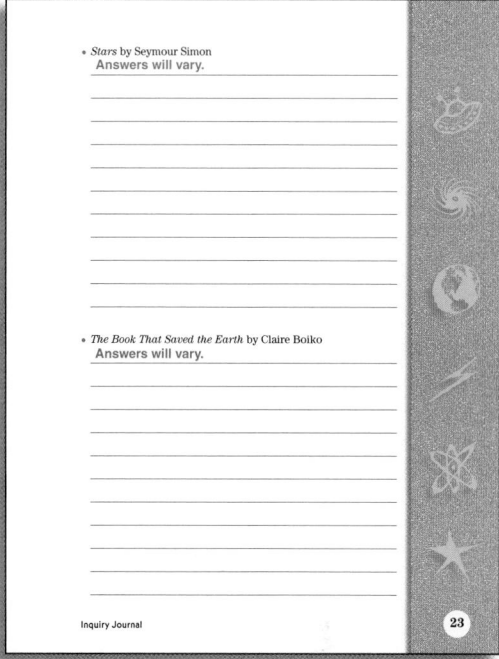

* *Stars* by Seymour Simon
Answers will vary.

* *The Book That Saved the Earth* by Claire Boiko
Answers will vary.

Inquiry Journal   23

Inquiry Journal p. 23

Teacher Tip   Informal presentations should take some of the emphasis off the final research product and give students a better sense of research as a continuous process.

Assessment

✔ **Informal** At this stage, students are making informal presentations of their research findings and organizing their final presentations. Check to see that students:
- are prepared to make their presentations.
- display appropriate audience behavior.

③ Integrating the Curriculum

Assessment

✓ **Informal** Take this opportunity to assess students' progress with the writing process by commenting on the entries in their Writing Journals.

Meeting Individual Needs

Inter**v**ention

Evaluating Author's Writing Locate a movie review from a newspaper or magazine movie critic's column. Sit with students who are having difficulty evaluating authors' writing and identify the ways that the movie critic made judgments about the movie in question. Explain the ways in which an analysis of an author's writing is similar to the movie critique. Have students write a short critique of a movie or television show that they have seen recently. Check to see if the students understood the concept of evaluating writers' work.

Language Arts

Writing

Evaluating the Author's Writing

Instruct Tell students that it is important to be able to evaluate an author's writing. This means that one decides what information in the work is valuable, while judging the quality of its presentation. Readers do this to check their understanding of the text and to get new ideas on how to effectively present information in their own writing.

Practice Call on students to evaluate Seymour Simon's writing in the selection, "Stars." If necessary, begin the discussion by asking the following.

- Does something about the writing stand out?
- Was there a particular part of the selection that you especially enjoyed?
- If so, does that part contain a clue about what makes the writing good?

Allow students time to skim the selection to refresh their memories. Call on volunteers to read passages from the selection that they found especially interesting and to talk about anything in the writing that made the passages enjoyable to them. If the students have difficulty expressing their feelings about the writing, model a response, pointing out things you found noteworthy, such as how the author provided definitions for many different stars.

Apply Encourage the students to use in their own writing any of the techniques that stood out in "Stars." Have them review their Writing Journals for a piece of writing to revise including a particular writing technique that was used well in the selection.

Writing Process

Students' Choice Although no new writing assignment is recommended here, the students may concentrate on an appropriate phase of the writing process for the expository paper on which they are currently working.

Literary Elements

Authors Organize Information in Specific Ways

Instruct Tell students that authors organize information in ways specific to their purpose for writing. They do this so that the message will be communicated clearly and effectively.

Have students brainstorm different ways that nonfiction can be organized, based on the selections they have read in Unit 2. Students may mention that most nonfiction is organized either chronologically or as a series of steps. It also frequently contains headings, captions, photos, and diagrams. Tell students that this type of organization is particularly helpful in text that instructs or explains because it leaves as little as possible for readers to infer for themselves.

Practice Lead students to notice how the author of this selection builds on his readers' knowledge of stars by starting with the one they are most familiar with, the Sun. From there, he talks about how each star is born, what the different types of stars are, and then about different galaxies of stars. Discuss with students how their understanding of stars might have been affected if the author had begun the selection with information on the Andromedia galaxy.

Apply Have students outline their expository papers as a check on the clarity of their papers' organization. For additional practice, have students complete **Reading and Writing Workbook,** pages 73–74.

Meeting Individual Needs

Reteach

Organizing Information Have students who need additional instruction and practice with this concept, complete **Reteach,** pages 73–74.

Challenge

Organizing Information Have students who understand this concept complete **Challenge,** page 39.

 **Teacher Tip** You may wish to explain to students that when they are writing an expository text that requires the inclusion of many facts or detailed information, it might be a good idea to write their first draft in outline form. An outline would help them develop a plan for a second rough draft and might ensure that they don't forget to include important information.

Reading and Writing Workbook pp. 73–74

Name _____ Date _____

Authors Organize Information in Specific Ways

Stars

Focus Good writers try to organize their information in a way that best communicates their ideas. They also want their writing to be interesting and easy to understand.

Here are some ways you might organize information.

* Make a statement that contains the main idea at the beginning of a paragraph. Then, use the body of the paragraph to explain or provide examples.
* Begin a paragraph with examples and explanations. Then, sum them up at the end of a paragraph with a statement that contains the main idea.

Practice Prepare to write an informational paragraph on what you find interesting about stars. Use one of the ways to organize information described above. Use the lines below to plan your paragraph.

Answers will vary. Possible answers are provided below.

Stars vary in temperature depending on their ages.

1. Young stars (10-200 million years old) are very hot.
2. Middle-aged stars are not as hot.
3. Older stars start to cool.

Reading and Writing Workbook • *Organizing Information*　73

Authors Organize Information in Specific Ways *(continued)*

Apply Write your paragraph, using your plan on the previous page to help you. Answers will vary.

74　*Organizing Information* • Reading and Writing Workbook

3 Integrating the Curriculum

Meeting Individual Needs

Reteach

Content-Area Words For students who need additional instruction and practice with this concept, have them complete **Reteach,** pages 75–76.

ESL

Picture Story If writing a story is beyond the skills of English-language learners, have them write a list of astronomy-related words, draw a sequence of pictures that tell a story, and illustrate some of the words in their lists. Help the students write labels for the pictures. If necessary, they can copy your suggested labels.

Challenge

Content-Area Words Challenge students to incorporate some of the new astronomy vocabulary words they have been learning into the theme-related papers they have been working on throughout Unit 2. For students who understand this concept, have them complete **Challenge,** page 40.

← Skills Strand →

Content-Area Words

INTRODUCED: Unit 2, Lesson 1
REVIEWED: Unit 2, Lesson 2
Unit 2, Lesson 7

Teacher Tip

In order to reinforce the idea that many professionals develop their own "language," brainstorm with students various computer terms, such as *Website, Internet, software, hardware, disk drive,* or *format.*

Vocabulary

Content-Area Words

Instruct Explain to students the importance of using technical or identifying words when writing an expository paper. Tell them that, over time, most professions develop a "language" that contains words that have special meaning for their particular work. Point out that Simon uses and defines many astronomy-related words in the selection. Ask the students which terms were familiar to them as they read. Which words were unfamiliar?

Practice Have students scan the text for astronomy-related words (for example, *particles, planetary nebula, nova, super nova, neutron star, globular cluster*). List these specialized terms on the chalkboard.

■ Ask the students to locate in the selection the definition for one or two of those words.

■ Have students share terms and definitions. Create a class list of astronomy-related words and post this in the classroom for reference.

■ Have students brainstorm other types of writing in which they may find the terms listed above (for example, science fiction).

Apply Have students write an article or story that uses their new astronomy vocabulary.

For additional practice, have students complete **Reading and Writing Workbook** pages 75–76.

Reading and Writing Workbook pp. 75–76

Name _____ Date _____

Content-Area Words | Stars |

Focus A word you use in everyday conversation may have a different meaning in a specific content area.

A **content area** can be
- a subject area, such as math, science, social studies, art, or language arts.
- a field or area of study, such as education, finance, law, family, or religion.
- an industry, such as technology, entertainment, banking, or sports.

Identify Below are some familiar science-related words from "Stars." Use context clues in the story to help you write science-related meanings for the words. Then, write a different meaning for each word.

Word	Science-Related Meaning	Alternate Meaning
1. banded	striped	to have formed a group of something
2. bright	shining with much light	smart or intelligent
3. nature	qualities of a person, thing, or animal	plants, animals, geography, climate
4. gas	a substance that is not solid or liquid	a liquid used as fuel for automobiles

Reading and Writing Workbook • Content-Area Words   75

Content-Area Words *(continued)*

Practice Select a word from the box to complete each sentence. Use clues in the sentence to help you figure out the correct word.

| magnified astronomical frequency concave |

1. Many signals were registering on the computer. The high **frequency** of the signals helped the scientists determine the location of the star.

2. An **astronomical** telescope is used to view far-off planets, stars, and galaxies.

3. A **concave** mirror is one that curves inward like the inside of a bowl.

4. When students looked through the telescope, the stars looked much closer because they were **magnified**

Apply Write a paragraph explaining what you learned about the different kinds of telescopes. Include in your paragraph some of the science-related words from the selection. Paragraphs will vary.

_____

_____

_____

_____

_____

76   *Content-Area Words • Reading and Writing Workbook*

Grammar, Usage, & Mechanics

Commas in Direct Address

Instruct Ask students what they know about commas. Remind them that a comma is used to set apart the name of the person being spoken to, or addressed. The following are rules for using commas in direct address.

- When the first word in a sentence is the name of the person being addressed, a comma follows the name.
- When the name of the person being addressed is last, a comma comes before it.
- When the name of the person being addressed is in the middle of a sentence, a comma comes before and after the name.

  Tell students to look at the following examples of each use. Have individual students read the sentences aloud, pausing at each comma.

- "Michael, I thought you knew we had a test today."
- "I didn't hear the teacher announce it, Cindy."
- "Well, Michael, you still have time to study."

Practice Remind students that in written dialogue, it is helpful to include the name of the person being spoken to, so that readers can tell who is speaking. Have students copy the following conversation between Ruby and her mother, adding the comma of address wherever it is needed.

> "You're late Ruby. Where have you been?" *("You're late, Ruby.")*
> "Mom I told you I was going to the library with Jeanie."
> *("Mom, I told you that I was going to the library with Jeanie.")*
> "Today? I thought that was tomorrow. I'm sorry Honey."
> *("I'm sorry, Honey.")*
> "It's okay Mom. I don't mind. I know you were worried."
> *("It's okay, Mom.")*

Apply Remind students to check any writing they are currently working on to make sure they have placed commas correctly.

Meeting Individual Needs

Challenge

Commas in Direct Address Challenge students to write an original skit based on a dialogue between two characters. Remind them to include the name of the person being addressed to help readers determine who is speaking. Have them proofread the skit to make sure they have punctuated the dialogue correctly.

Assessment

✓ **Formal** To assess students' ability to identify correctly used commas in direct address, use *Skills Assessment,* page 24.

Commas in Direct Address

INTRODUCED:	Unit 1, Lesson 5
REVIEWED:	Unit 2, Lesson 7
	Unit 4, Lesson 8

Integrating the Curriculum

Teacher Tip Encourage students to refer to the Concept/Question Board for ides for their astronomy-related speeches.

Listening/Speaking/Viewing

Major Ideas and Supporting Evidence Speech

Explain that when listening to someone speak formally or informally on a topic, it is important to be able to distinguish the main idea of what he or she is saying from the supporting evidence or details. Have students practice this skill by participating in the following exercise.

- Have each student think of and take a position on an astronomy-related issue he or she is interested in, such as whether or not it is possible that humans may someday be able to travel to another galaxy.

- Have students support their arguments by connecting information from the selections in this unit that relates to their positions.

- Have students break into small groups. Have each student present to the group his or her position and argument for a certain issue. As each student speaks, have the other students in the group listen for and jot down the speaker's main ideas and supporting evidence.

- After each student speech, have the group members review their notes. Have each group member respond to the speaker's argument by citing a piece of information from the selections in this unit that supports or disputes one of the details of the speaker's argument.

Study and Research

Note Taking

Instruct Ask students what they know about note-taking and when they should take notes. As an example, point out that, after defining a research question or problem and finding appropriate sources, a researcher must have a way to remember and organize the information that he or she finds. Photocopy the following guidelines for note taking and discuss them with students.

1. Organize your notes under subject headings.
2. Write notes in your own words.
3. Summarize the most important information about your research question or problem.
4. Keep your notes short. Use abbreviations, key phrases, and short sentences.
5. If you use an author's exact words, put them within quotation marks. Include the author's name, the book title (or magazine and article titles), and the page number.
6. Write neatly and clearly.

Practice Have a volunteer suggest a research topic based on one of the selections in the **Student Anthology** (for example, Alpha Centauri in "Stars"). Turn this topic into a heading and write it on the chalkboard. Have students skim the selection for facts and summarize information about the heading as they find it. Write the information on the chalkboard, modeling the guidelines for note taking.

Apply Have students complete **Inquiry Journal,** pages 35–36.

Inquiry Journal pp. 35–36

Teacher Tip Point out to students that when note taking, they will sometimes want to quote the author directly if the author's words are especially important, interesting, or original. Explain the following guidelines for using an author's exact words.

- Copy the author's words exactly as they appear on the page.
- Put quotations marks around the author's words.
- Record the author's name, the book title (or magazine and article title), and the page number of the quotation.

Teacher Tip Make sure students understand the difference between summarizing and paraphrasing. Summarizing is restating just the main points or ideas of a body of material. Paraphrasing is restating in different words a passage or a part of a text to clarify its meaning.

Assessment

✓ **Formal** To assess students' understanding of this concept, have them complete **Skills Assessment,** page 25.

Across the Curriculum

 ## Science

Planets of Our Solar System

Purpose

To help students understand the vast differences between the planets of Earth's solar system

Materials

posterboard, markers, paints

Procedure

Divide the class into nine groups and assign each group to research one of the nine planets in Earth's solar system. Have them concentrate on the physical aspects of their particular planet—its shape, color, size, and accompanying moons or rings.

Have each group create a poster illustrating their planet. Have them add any details that they learned about, for example, Jupiter's red spot.

Display the posters around the classroom and provide time for informal panel discussions where each group can inform the class about what they learned about their planet.

 ## Social Studies

Astronaut Heroes

Purpose

To acquaint students with America's astronauts, who risked their lives to explore the heavens

Procedure

Have students select one of America's many astronaut heroes and prepare a short (5-minute) oral report on one of that astronaut's space missions. They may choose any American astronaut, from the first human to ride a rocket up into the heavens, to any member of the crew on the latest spaceflight.

Have students search the Internet, encyclopedias, and available expository texts to find information about their chosen hero.

Encourage students to be creative in the way they choose to give their presentation. Some students may wish to role-play, taking the part of their hero and talking to the audience directly in his or her "voice." Other students may decide to use lots of pictures, diagrams, three-dimensional models, or statistical charts or graphs as visual aids. Other students might decide to add musical accompaniment to their report.

Schedule time for four or five students to give their oral presentations each day.

Across the Curriculum

Art

Making Star Models

Purpose

To help students appreciate the variety among stars

Materials

posterboard, paint, markers, clay, papier mâché, materials from nature

Procedure

- Ask students to select an interesting type of star or stage of a star's existence mentioned in the selection.

- Have students choose an art medium with which to represent this star.

- Help students list and gather materials for their model.

- Ask students to write a short caption to identify and describe their star.

- Invite students to share their models with the class.

- Display these models in the classroom as sources of information.

Math

Measurement

Purpose

To help students understand the importance of measurement in astronomy and in their lives

Procedure

- Review with students the many references to vast distances in the selection "Stars." Remind them that measurement is important to the study of astronomy.

- Invite students to brainstorm some ways we measure our world (rulers, yardsticks, measuring tapes, measuring spoons or cups, scales, speedometers, and so on). List the measuring devices the students suggest on the chalkboard.

- Ask students to recall times in their own lives when accurate measurement was important.

- Display pictures of people in different careers, such as doctors, builders, architects, and surveyors, using measurement in their work. Have students note how measurement helps each of these professionals do a better job.

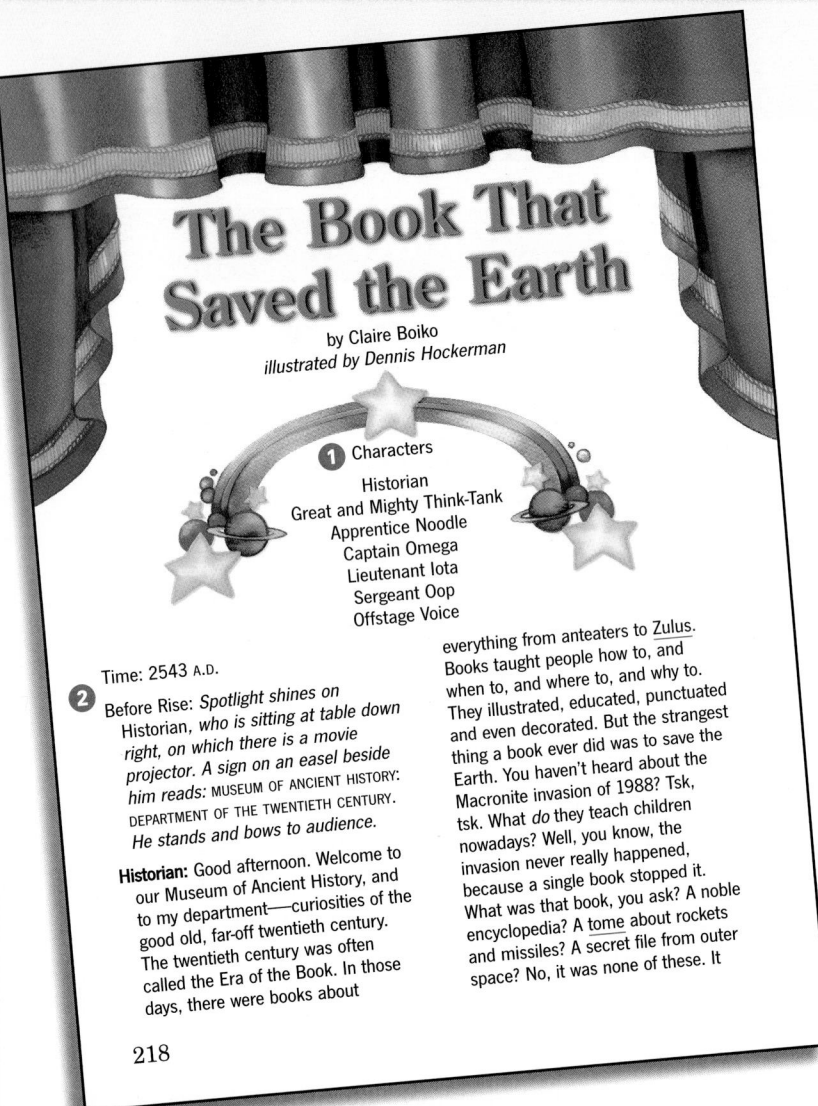

About the Author

Claire Taylor Boiko was born in Oakland, California. Before her writing career took off, Claire was an actress in Clare Tree Major Children's Theater. She then worked in the Army Special Services as a civilian entertainment and music technician. She has written and published many plays, including *Children's Plays for Creative Actors* and *Plays and Programs for Boys and Girls.*

Students can read more about Claire Taylor Boiko on page 226 of the **Student Anthology.**

Other Books by Claire Taylor Boiko:

- *The Cry-Baby Princess: A Play*
- *Dramatized Parodies of Familiar Stories*
- *My Hero!*
- *Who's Afraid of the Big, Bad, W-h-h-a-a-t?*

Selection Summary

Genre: Science Fiction Play

This science fiction play looks back at a pivotal moment in Earth history: the day a book saved Earth from invasion. The Mighty Think-Tank, ruler of the planet Macron, has sent a space probe to take over "the ridiculous, little planet" Earth, but the probe has landed in a library. When the Macronites decipher the code and read one of the books, they "discover" that Earthlings are more advanced than they thought, and they quickly leave the planet. What powerful book could have changed the invasion plans of the Macronites?

Exploring the Theme

Selection Concepts

"The Book That Saved the Earth" is another science fiction selection, this time in play form. Because much of students' exposure to science fiction is likely to have been through television, they should already be familiar with the drama form and should find it easy to turn the play into a production. Key concepts explored are:

- This play makes fun of the notion of superintelligent extraterrestrials.
- Treatment of this selection should emphasize production of the play rather than analysis and comprehension.

 Check the Reading link of the **SRA** Web page for links to theme-related Websites.
http://www.sra4kids.com

Exploration Activity Tips

Before Reading, have students recall the different kinds of characters they have seen in science fiction programs. Ask the students how extraterrestrials are usually portrayed and how they would portray extraterrestrials.

During Reading, have students think of ideas for producing this play. They should consider casting, setting, props, and so on.

After Reading, have students discuss the humorous intent of the play. Ask them to point out anything in the play that didn't make sense, such as the Macrons knowing how to read English, yet having no idea of fiction or fantasy. Then have students update the Concept/Question Board.

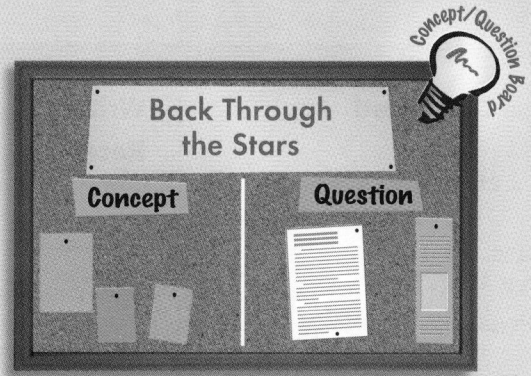

Unit 2 Exploration Management

Lesson 1	Brainstorm research problems. Form interest-based groups. Develop and discuss initial research plans.
Lesson 2	Groups finalize plans, allocate tasks, and begin research. Discuss initial findings and resources.
Lesson 3	Research continues as groups consider revision of their activity focus.
Lesson 4	Students continue with research and present their initial findings.
Lesson 5	Research continues. Students present interesting findings or problems.
Lesson 6	Research continues. Students present interesting findings or problems.
Lesson 7	Students organize research findings and prepare presentations.
Lesson 8 **The Book That Saved the Earth**	**Collaborative Exploration** **Students present their activities.** **Supplementary Activity** **Groups present their research activities and raise new questions for further investigation.**

Lesson Planner

Suggested Pacing: 3–5 days	DAY 1	DAY 2

Part 1 — Preparing to Read

Materials
- Student Anthology, pp. 218–227
- Transparencies 14, 44

DAY 1

Word Knowledge
- Reading the Words and Sentences, p. 218G
- ✓ Developing Oral Language, p. 218G

Build Background, p. 218H

Preview and Prepare, p. 218I

Selection Vocabulary, p. 218I
apprentice, insignificant, primitive, pantomimes, cease

DAY 2

Preview and Prepare, p. 218I
- Review Transparency 44

Part 2 — Reading and Responding

Materials
- Student Anthology, pp. 218–227
- Teacher Observation Log
- Reading and Writing Workbook, pp. 77–78
- Inquiry Journal, p. 23
- Home Connection, p. 31

DAY 1

Student Anthology, pp. 218–227
Comprehension Strategies
- Clarifying, pp. 218, 220, 222
- Visualizing, p. 222
- Predicting, pp. 222, 224

Discussing Strategy Use, p. 224

DAY 2

Student Anthology, pp. 218–227
Comprehension Skills
- ✓ Main Idea and Details, pp. 219, 221, 223
- ✓ Discussing the Selection, p. 225

Exploring the Theme
- Selection Vocabulary, p. 227A
apprentice, insignificant, primitive, pantomimes, cease

Part 3 — Integrating the Curriculum

Materials
- Student Anthology, pp. 218–227
- Reading and Writing Workbook, pp. 79–82
- Inquiry Journal, p. 37

DAY 1

Writing
- Publishing, p. 227C

Literary Elements
- Literary Terms Related to Plays, p. 227E

DAY 2

Writing Process
- Publishing, p. 227D

Vocabulary
- ✓ Develop Vocabulary by Listening, p. 227F

Independent Work Time

Materials
- Reteach, pp. 77–82
- ESL Supplement
- Challenge, pp. 41–43
- Intervention Guide
- Research CD-ROM
- Listening Library Audiocassette

DAY 1

Writing Process Continued
ESL
- Word Meaning, p. 218G

Intervention
- Synonyms, p. 218G
- Comprehension, p. 218

Unit Project: Present Activities

DAY 2

Writing Process Continued
Reteach
- ✓ Main Idea and Details, *Reteach*, pp. 77–78

Challenge
- ✓ Main Idea and Details, *Challenge*, p. 41

Intervention
- Main Idea and Details, p. 221
- Publishing, p. 227D

Unit Project Continued

✓ Informal **Assessment Available**   ✓ Formal **Assessment Available**

DAY 2 continued	DAY 3	
DAY 3	**DAY 4**	**DAY 5**
General Review	**General Review**	**Review Word Knowledge**
Student Anthology, pp. 218–227 **Theme Connections** ■ Think About It, p. 227 ■ Research Ideas, p. 227	**Student Anthology, pp. 218–227** **Exploring the Theme** ■ Reading/Writing Connections, p. 227A ■ Literature Appreciation, p. 227A ■ Supporting Student Explorations, p. 227B	**Student Anthology, pp. 218–227** ■ Review Selection ■ Complete Discussion ■ Reread Selection in Pairs **Home Connection, p. 227A** ■ Discuss "The Book That Saved the Earth" ■ Write about one of Earth's leaders
Writing Process Continued **Grammar, Usage, and Mechanics** ✓■ Commas in a Series, p. 227G **Listening/Speaking/Viewing** ■ Dramatic Interpretation of Poetry, p. 227H	**Writing Process Continued** **Study and Research** ■ Evaluating Research, p. 227I	**Across the Curriculum** **Art** ■ Design an Astronomical Set, p. 227J **Social Studies** ■ U.S. Space Missions, p. 227J **Unit 2 Test**
Writing Process Continued **Reteach** ✓■ Listening Vocabulary, *Reteach*, pp. 79–80 **ESL** ■ Commas in a Series, p. 227G **Challenge** ✓■ Listening Vocabulary, *Challenge*, p. 42 **Unit Project Continued**	**Writing Process Continued** **Reteach** ✓■ Commas in a Series, *Reteach*, pp. 81–82 **Challenge** ✓■ Commas in a Series, *Challenge*, p. 43 **Unit Project Continued**	**Complete Writing Process** **Complete Unit Project**

Meeting Individual Needs
Independent Work Time

Part 1
Preparing to Read

Meeting Individual Needs

ESL
- Word Meaning, p. 218G

Inter∧vention
- Synonyms, p. 218G

Part 2
Reading and Responding

Meeting Individual Needs

Reteach
- Main Idea and Details, *Reteach*, pp. 77–78

ESL
- Participation, p. 219
- Choral Reading, p. 221

Challenge
- Main Idea and Details, *Challenge*, p. 41

Inter∧vention
- Comprehension, p. 218
- Clarifying, p. 220
- Main Idea and Details, p. 221
- Predicting, p. 224

Part 3
Integrating the Curriculum

Meeting Individual Needs

Reteach
- Listening Vocabulary, *Reteach*, pp. 79–80
- Commas in a Series, *Reteach*, pp. 81–82

ESL
- Commas in a Series, p. 221G

Challenge
- Listening Vocabulary, *Challenge*, p. 42
- Commas in a Series, *Challenge*, p. 43

Inter∧vention
- Publishing, p. 227D

Formal Assessment Options

Use these assessment pages along with your informal observations to gauge student progress.

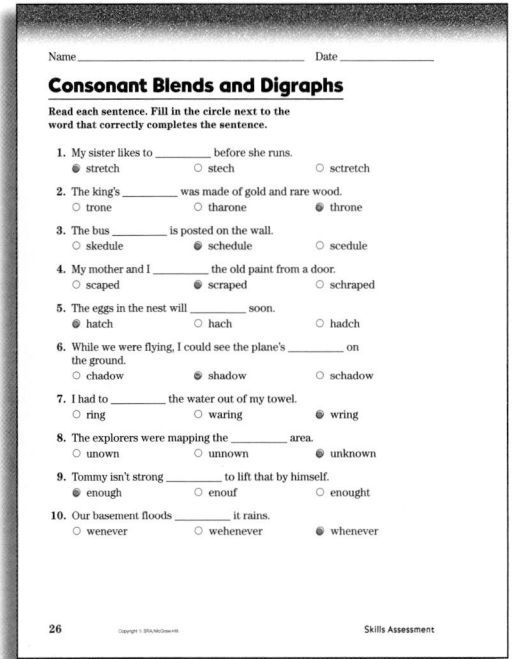

Skills Assessment, p. 26

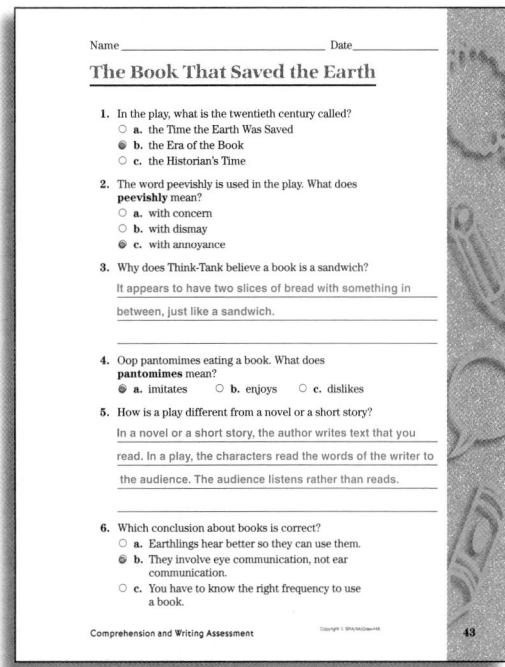

Comprehension and Writing Assessment, p. 43

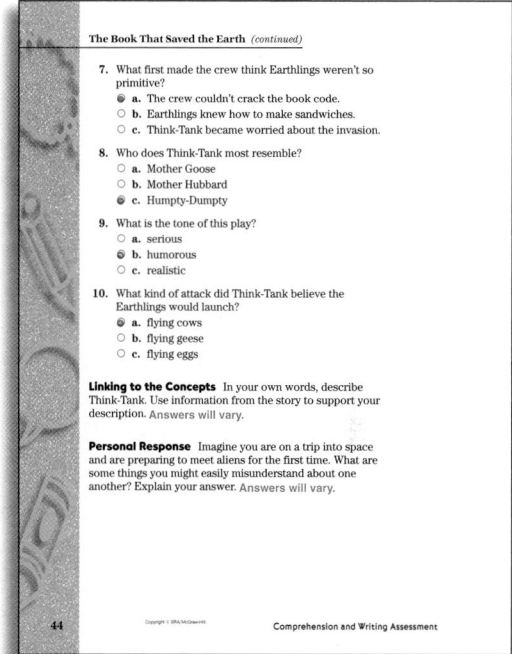

Comprehension and Writing Assessment, p. 44

① Preparing to Read

Meeting Individual Needs

ESL

Word Meaning Make sure English-language learners understand the meanings of the words before they do the exercises. Refer to Unit 2, Lesson 8, of the **ESL Supplement** for specific suggestions.

Intervention

Synonyms Explain to students who need more help with synonyms that synonyms are words that have the same or nearly the same meanings. For example, *laugh* means the same, or nearly the same, as *giggle*. Therefore, *laugh* and *giggle* are synonyms. Give students the following list of words and ask them to name a synonym for each. Tell them to use this sentence and fill in the blanks:

_____ means the same as _____; therefore, _____ and _____ are synonyms.

small	angry
big	smile
eat	nice
cold	child
warm	happy

For students who need more help, see Unit 2, Lesson 8, of the **Intervention Guide.**

Assessment

✓ **Formal** To assess students' knowledge of consonant blends and digraphs, use **Skills Assessment,** page 26.

Word Knowledge

Reading the Words and Sentences

Write each word and sentence on the chalkboard. Have students read each word together. After all the words have been read, have students read each sentence in natural phrases or chunks. Use the suggestions in About the Words to discuss the different features of the listed words.

Line 1: insignificant trifling decipher decode
Line 2: twentieth chart sandwich wish
Line 3: certainly closely breathlessly slowly
Sentence 1: Pay no attention to the insignificant details.
Sentence 2: The twentieth century ended when the new millennium began.
Sentence 3: "I've just run a long race," she said slowly and breathlessly.

About the Words

- The words in Line 1 are synonyms. Synonyms are words that have the same, or nearly the same, meanings. Discuss the meaning of each pair.
- Line 2 contains words that have consonant digraphs. Digraphs are two letters which, when placed together, create a single sound.
- In Line 3, the words each have an *-ly* ending. Adverbs are formed with the addition of this suffix to an adjective.

Developing Oral Language

To review the words, have them do the following activities.

- Have students choose two of the words in the lines above, and say one or two synonyms for each word (for example, *wish/hope*).
- Have students circle the consonant digraphs in the words in Line 2 (th, ch, and sh). Then have them say other words that use the same digraphs (for example, *th*ink, *ch*ange, *sh*ield).
- Have the children circle the root words in Line 3. Have them use the root words (adjectives) in a sentence.
- Then have them rewrite the word with the *-ly* suffix and use the adverbs in new sentences. You can do this activity as an entire class at the chalkboard, or have the students write the sentences down and then call on students to read their sentences to the class.

Build Background

Activate Prior Knowledge

Have students check the Concept/Question Board to refresh their memories about astronomy. Discuss the following with students to find out what they may already know about aliens or plays and have already learned about the unit theme. Tell students to use their prior knowledge to help them comprehend what they are about to read.

■ Have students recall "A Meeting in Space," in which aliens from outer space expressed a curiosity about humans from Earth.

■ Ask students whether they are familiar with the story they are about to read, and if so, to tell a little about it. Remind students not to give away the ending of the selection.

■ Have students share any other stories that have aliens from outer space as characters.

Background Information

The following information may help the students better understand the selection they are about to read.

■ Review nursery rhymes with students. Provide a few nursery rhyme books and have students take turns reading them aloud to each other. Or, if you have access to a kindergarten class, have students buddy up with younger students and have them read nursery rhymes together.

■ Some students may need supportive information about how a play is written and how it is read differently than other writing formats. Tell students that plays are writings to be performed by two or more readers reading the part of the characters. Point out the character list, time, and setting on the first page of this selection. Note that the speaker of each line is written in capital letters followed by a colon. The words after the colon are what the speaker says. Words in italics are stage directions.

 Tell students that after reading they will be jotting down in their Writing Journals their reactions to this selection. Have them be on the lookout for any ideas they may have for writing a play or a skit of their own.

 Encourage the students to discuss the qualities of science fiction characters.

1 Preparing to Read

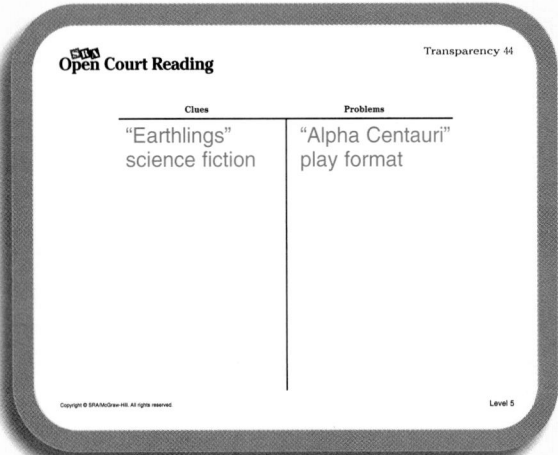

Transparency 44

Teacher Tip To help students decode words, divide them into the syllables shown below. The information following each word tells how students can figure out the meaning of each word from the sentences on the transparency.

ap·pren·tice	context clues
in·sig·nif·i·cant	context clues, word structure
prim·i·tive	context clues
pan·to·mimes	context clues
cease	context clues

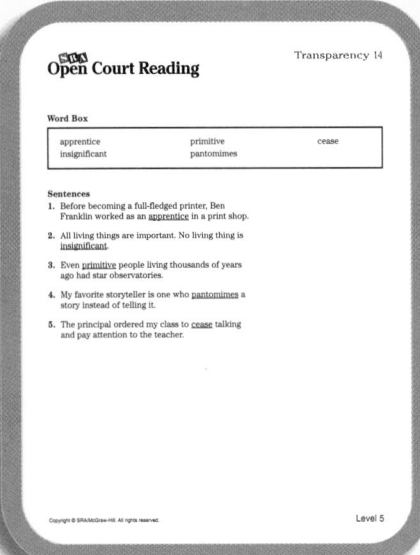

Transparency 14

Preview and Prepare

Browse

- Have a volunteer read the title and author's name aloud. Have students share what they know about plays and science fiction.

- Because this selection is fiction, have the students browse through the first half of the play. Have students search for words and phrases that connect to what they already know. Record these in the Clues column on *Transparency 44*. Discuss with them what they think this play might have to do with astronomy.

- Encourage the students to ask questions as they browse. Have them identify any problems they notice while reading and record them in the Problems column.

Set Purposes

As they read, have students think about inventions inspired by knowledge of astronomy.

Selection Vocabulary

As students study vocabulary, they will use context clues, word structure, and apposition to clarify these and other unfamiliar words.

Display *Transparency 14* before reading the selection to introduce and discuss the following words and their meanings.

ap·pren·tice:	a person learning a trade (page 218)
in·sig·nif·i·cant:	not important (page 219)
prim·i·tive:	living in the ways of long ago (page 220)
pan·to·mimes:	uses bodily movements or facial expressions, instead of speech, to tell a story (page 221)
cease:	to bring an activity or action to an end (page 225)

Have students read the words in the Word Box. Help students decode multisyllabic words by reading them syllable by syllable.

Have students read the sentences on the *Transparency 14* to determine the meaning of the underlined words. Remind them to use clues in the sentences to figure out the meaning. See the teacher tip on the left for information on how the words in each sentence can be defined.

Reading Recommendations

Your first reading of the selection should focus on developing the reading strategies found to the left of the reduced pages. We recommend that the students revisit the selection, rereading sections or the entire selection to focus on the comprehension skills, found to the right of the reduced pages.

Oral Reading

Since it is a play, this selection lends itself well to oral reading. Tell students to take roles and read it aloud together. Have students adjust their reading rate to suit the action of the text. For example, if a character were very excited, his or her part might be read quickly, while the part of a character that is pondering something might be read more slowly. As students read aloud, have them read expressively, at an appropriate pace, in natural phrases and chunks. By reading the selection with fluency, students will demonstrate an understanding of the text and an ability to engage the listeners in an effective manner. If students encounter difficulties, have them use the reading strategies below or refer to the Blending Procedure (Program Appendix 15–16).

Using Reading Strategies

Reading strategy instruction allows students to become aware of how good readers read. Good readers recognize when they are having problems and stop to use various reading strategies to help them make sense of what they are reading.

During the reading of "The Book That Saved the Earth," you will model the use of the following reading strategies:

■ Clarifying   ■ Visualizing   ■ Predicting

Before reading, have students share how they have used these strategies in the past and any tips they can give each other on their use.

Building Comprehension Skills

Revisiting or rereading a selection allows students to apply skills that give them a more complete understanding of the text. Some follow-up comprehension skills, such as *Main Idea and Details* and *Compare and Contrast*, help students organize information. Others, such as *Author's Purpose, Making Inferences*, and *Drawing Conclusions*, lead to deeper understanding—to "reading between the lines," as mature readers do. In this selection, students will apply the follow-up comprehension skill of *Main Idea and Details*.

Teacher Tip Have students who may need extra help reading "The Book that Saved the Earth" reread the selection using the *Listening Library Audiocassette*.

Teacher Tip By this time in the fifth grade, good readers should be reading approximately 126 words per minute with fluency and expression. The only way to gain fluency is through practice. As explained in Reading Recommendations, have students reread all or part of the selection to you and to each other during class or Independent Work Time to focus on the comprehension skills and to build fluency.

Teacher Tip So that the action of the play will not be interrupted, you may find it appropriate to save some strategy modeling and discussion until after a complete read-through of the play. Encourage students to ask questions as needed.

② Reading and Responding

Read pages 218–227.

Comprehension Strategies

Prompting

❶ Clarifying *I wonder what this list is. It says characters above it. Let's see if there are clues in the text that will help us clarify the list's purpose. I see that the people from the list are speaking in the play. This must be a list of who will be in the play. What else about the format of this play should we clarify?*

Student Sample

❷ Clarifying *There are some lines here before the first character speaks. They are different from the other paragraphs on these pages where characters speak. Let's read the paragraph again.*

It seems to me that this is telling how the stage is set up and which character is about to speak. These must be the stage directions that playwrights put in plays to help the actors know where to stand and where to move during the play.

Word Knowledge

illustrated, unpunctuated, insignificant

Students can use the skills they learned in the Word Knowledge section of this lesson to read these words. Remind students of this if they have difficulty reading these words.

Reading Recommendation

ORAL · CHORAL · SILENT

The Book That Saved the Earth

by Claire Boiko
illustrated by Dennis Hockerman

❶ Characters

Historian
Great and Mighty Think-Tank
Apprentice Noodle
Captain Omega
Lieutenant Iota
Sergeant Oop
Offstage Voice

Time: 2543 A.D.

❷ **Before Rise:** *Spotlight shines on Historian, who is sitting at table down right, on which there is a movie projector. A sign on an easel beside him reads:* MUSEUM OF ANCIENT HISTORY: DEPARTMENT OF THE TWENTIETH CENTURY. *He stands and bows to audience.*

Historian: Good afternoon. Welcome to our Museum of Ancient History, and to my department—curiosities of the good old, far-off twentieth century. The twentieth century was often called the Era of the Book. In those days, there were books about everything from anteaters to Zulus. Books taught people how to, and when to, and where to, and why to. They illustrated, educated, punctuated and even decorated. But the strangest thing a book ever did was to save the Earth. You haven't heard about the Macronite invasion of 1988? Tsk, tsk. What *do* they teach children nowadays? Well, you know, the invasion never really happened, because a single book stopped it. What was that book, you ask? A noble encyclopedia? A tome about rockets and missiles? A secret file from outer space? No, it was none of these. It

218

Meeting Individual Needs

Intervention

Comprehension Intervention strategies for those students having difficulty with reading "The Book That Saved the Earth" can be found in Unit 2, Lesson 8, of the *Intervention Guide.*

Assessment

✓ **Informal** Observe individual students as they read and use the Teacher Observation Log found in the *Assessment Guide* to record anecdotal information about each student's strengths and weakness.

was *(Pauses, then points to projector)*——here, let me turn on the historiscope and show you what happened many, many centuries ago, in 1988. *(He turns on projector, and points it left. Spotlight on Historian goes out, and comes up down left on Think-Tank, who is seated on raised box, arms folded. He has huge, egg-shaped head, and he wears long robe decorated with stars and circles. Apprentice Noodle stands beside him at an elaborate switchboard. A sign on an easel reads:* MACRON SPACE CONTROL. GREAT AND MIGHTY THINK-TANK, COMMANDER-IN-CHIEF. BOW LOW BEFORE ENTERING.*)*

Noodle *(Bowing)*: O Great and Mighty Think-Tank, most powerful and intelligent creature in the whole universe, what are your orders?

Think-Tank *(Peevishly)*: You left out part of my <u>salutation</u>, Apprentice Noodle. Go over the whole thing again.

Noodle: It shall be done, sir. *(In singsong)* O Great and Mighty Think-Tank, Ruler of Macron and her two moons, most powerful and intelligent creature in the whole universe——*(Out of breath)* what-are-your-orders?

Think-Tank: That's better, Noodle. I wish to be placed in communication with our manned space probe to the ridiculous little planet we are going to put under our generous rulership. What do they call it again?

Noodle: Earth, Your Intelligence.

Think-Tank: Earth——of course. You see how insignificant the place is? But first, something important. My mirror. I wish to consult my mirror.

Noodle: It shall be done, sir. *(He hands Think-Tank hand mirror.)*

Think-Tank: Mirror, mirror, in my hand, who is the most fantastically intelligently gifted being in the land?

Offstage Voice *(After a pause)*: You, sir.

Think-Tank *(Striking mirror)*: Quicker. Answer quicker next time. I hate a slow mirror. *(He admires himself.)* Ah, there I am. Are we Macronites not a handsome race? So much more attractive than those ugly earthlings with their tiny heads. Noodle, you keep on exercising your mind, and some day you'll have a balloon brain just like mine.

Noodle: I certainly hope so, Mighty Think-Tank.

219

Comprehension
Skills

Main Idea and Details

Explain to the students that plays contain *a main idea* and *details*, just like other forms of writing. The *main idea* is what the play is mainly about. The *details* provide more information about the main idea.

- Have students read the Historian's speech on pages 218–219. What is the main idea? *(The twentieth century was often called the Era of the Book.)*

- Have the students find details that support this main idea. *(There were books about everything from anteaters to Zulus. Books taught people how to, and when to, and where to, and why to. The strangest thing a book ever did was to save Earth.)*

This play contains many space alien characters. They do not have to sound or act like human beings. Encourage the students to have fun and exaggerate their parts as much as they like while they are reading.

<←Skills Strand→

Meeting Individual Needs

ESL

Participation Those students who are not reading parts can still participate in the "production" of this play. Have them think about costumes or set designs based on the descriptions and personalities of the characters in the play, and to create sketches of them.

2 Reading and Responding

Comprehension Strategies

Modeling

3 Clarifying *The playwright has the curtain rising at this point. I don't understand. Wasn't it opened before? Let's reread. In the first scene, there is a spotlight on the Historian down right. The next scene takes place down left.*

Oh. I see. They both take place in front of the main curtain with just a little bit of scenery. That way, there can be a big set behind the curtain for the library.

Teacher Tip Draw a diagram of the stage set on the chalkboard with "Down Right" and "Down Left" marked on them to help students visualize the action of the play. Explain that down right is the part of the stage closest to the audience's right hand and down left is closest to the audience's left hand.

Word Knowledge

undoubtedly, brightly, unhappily

Students can use the skills they learned in the Word Knowledge section of this lesson to read these words. Remind students of this if they have difficulty reading these words.

Think-Tank: Now, contact the space probe. I want to invade that primitive ball of mud called Earth before lunch.

Noodle: It shall be done, sir. *(He twists knobs and adjusts levers on switchboard. Electronic buzzes and beeps are heard. Noodle and Think-Tank remain at controls, as curtain rises.)*

* * *

Setting: *The Centerville Public Library.*

At Rise: Captain Omega *stands at center, opening and closing card catalogue drawers, looking puzzled.* Lieutenant Iota *is up left, counting books in bookcase.* Sergeant Oop *is at right, opening and closing book, turning it upside down, shaking it, and then riffling pages and shaking his head.*

Noodle *(Adjusting knobs)*: I have a close sighting of the space crew, sir. (Think-Tank *puts on pair of huge goggles and turns toward stage to watch.)* They seem to have entered some sort of Earth structure.

Think-Tank: Excellent. Make voice contact.

Noodle *(Speaking into a microphone)*: Macron Space Control calling the crew of Probe One. Macron Space Control calling the crew of Probe

One. Come in, Captain Omega. Give us your location.

Captain Omega *(Speaking into disc which is on chain around his neck)*: Captain Omega to Macron Space Control. Lieutenant Iota, Sergeant Oop and I have landed on Earth without incident. We have taken shelter in this *(Indicates room)*—this square place. Have you any idea where we are, Lieutenant Iota?

Iota: I can't figure it out, Captain. *(Holding up book)* I've counted two thousand of these peculiar things. This place must be some sort of storage barn. What do you think, Sergeant Oop?

Oop: I haven't a clue. I've been to seven galaxies, but I've never seen anything like this. Maybe they're hats. *(He opens book and puts it on his head.)* Say, maybe this is a haberdasher's store!

Omega *(Bowing low)*: Perhaps the Great and Mighty Think-Tank will give us the benefit of his thought on the matter.

Think-Tank: Elementary, my dear Omega. Hold one of the items up so that I may view it closely. (Omega *holds book on palm of his hand.)* Yes, yes, I understand now. Since Earth

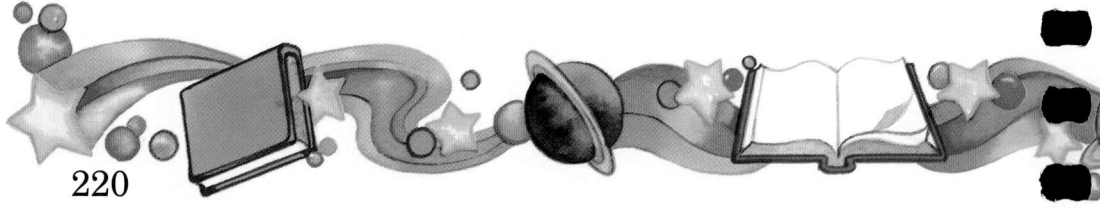

220

Meeting Individual Needs

Intervention

Clarifying Have students clarify anything they might find confusing on these pages. Remind them that clarifying is a process. Tell students to work together to clarify confusing ideas and words.

creatures are always eating, the place in which you find yourselves is undoubtedly a crude refreshment stand.

Omega *(To* Iota *and* Oop): He says we're in a refreshment stand.

Oop: The Earthlings certainly do have a strange diet.

Think-Tank: That item in your hand is called a "sandwich."

Omega *(Nodding)*: A sandwich.

Iota *(Nodding)*: A sandwich.

Oop *(Taking book from his head)*: A sandwich?

Think-Tank: Sandwiches are the main staple of Earth diet. Look at it closely. (Omega *squints at book.)* There are two slices of what is called "bread," and between them there is some sort of filling.

Omega: That is correct, sir.

Think-Tank: To confirm my opinion, I order you to eat it.

Omega *(Gulping)*: Eat it?

Think-Tank: Do you doubt the Mighty Think-Tank?

Omega: Oh, no, no. But poor Lieutenant Iota has not had his breakfast. Lieutenant Iota, I order you to eat this—this sandwich.

Iota *(Dubiously)*: Eat it? Oh, Captain! It's a very great honor to be the first Macronite to eat a sandwich, I'm sure, but—but how can I be so impolite as to eat before my Sergeant? *(Handing* Oop *book; brightly)* Sergeant Oop, I order you to eat the sandwich.

Oop *(Making a face)*: Who, sir? Me, sir?

Iota and **Omega** *(Slapping their chests in a salute)*: For the glory of Macron, Oop.

Oop: Yes, sirs. *(Unhappily)* Immediately, sirs. *(He opens his mouth wide. Omega and* Iota *watch him breathlessly. He bites down on corner of book, and pantomimes chewing and swallowing, while making terrible faces.)*

Omega: Well, Oop?

Iota: Well, Oop? (Oop *coughs.* Omega *and* Iota *pound him on back.)*

Think-Tank: Was it not delicious, Sergeant Oop?

221

Comprehension Skills

Main Idea and Details

Have students tell you what the main idea and details are. *(The main idea is what a paragraph or play is mainly about. Details provide more information about the main idea.)*

- Have the students identify the main idea of what Oop says first on page 220. *(He doesn't know what books are.)*

- Which details support this main idea? *(Students should choose any sentence from the paragraph.)*

Teacher Tip Have students think of ideas for producing this play. They should consider casting, setting, props, and so on.

Meeting Individual Needs

ESL

Choral Reading Have three or four students, including English-language learners, read the part of "Great and Mighty Think-Tank" simultaneously. This will maximize the participation of English-language learners, and give them a good reason to practice and become familiar with the words, and be in character since Think-Tank believes he is four times smarter than other mere aliens.

Intervention

Main Idea and Details Have those students who are having difficulty with main idea and details chart the main idea and details of each section. Have volunteers explain why they included each main idea and detail on their chart.

② Reading and Responding

Comprehension Strategies

Modeling

④ Visualizing *Forming a mental image of what is happening in a play would be especially important to someone who wanted to stage it. When you visualize what is happening, do you picture the characters as they would speak and move, or do you picture actors performing the character roles on stage? I tend to see the actual characters—they're kind of cartoonish looking. What do you see?*

Modeling

⑤ Predicting *Making predictions helps readers to focus on what they would like to learn from the text. These aliens don't seem very smart. Eating the vitamins will probably help them read the book, but I predict they're not going to understand it. We'll find out soon. (This prediction is confirmed on page 224.)*

 **Teacher Tip** Continue to encourage the students to model for one another when they use strategies, or work out problems as they read.

Word Knowledge

naturally, important, department

Students can use the skills they learned in the Word Knowledge section of this lesson to read these words. Remind students of this if they have difficulty reading these words.

Oop *(Slapping his chest in salute):* That is correct, sir. It was *not* delicious. I don't know how the Earthlings can get those sandwiches down without water. They're dry as Macron dust.

Noodle: Sir—O Great and Mighty Think-Tank. I beg your pardon, but an insignificant bit of data floated into my mind about those sandwiches.

Think-Tank: It can't be worth much, but go ahead. Give us your <u>trifling</u> bit of data.

Noodle: Well, sir, I have seen surveyor films of those sandwiches. I noticed that the Earthlings did not *eat* them. They used them as some sort of communication device.

Think-Tank *(Haughtily):* Naturally. That was my next point. These are actually communication sandwiches. Think-Tank is never wrong. Who is never wrong?

All *(Saluting):* Great and Mighty Think-Tank is never wrong.

Think-Tank: Therefore, I order you to listen to them.

Omega: Listen to them?

Iota and Oop *(To each other; puzzled):* Listen to them?

Think-Tank: Do you have marbles in your ears? I said, listen to them. *(Macronites bow very low.)*

Omega: It shall be done, sir. *(They each take two books from case, and hold them to their ears, listening intently.)*

Iota *(Whispering to Omega):* Do you hear anything?

Omega *(Whispering back):* Nothing. Do you hear anything, Oop?

Oop *(Loudly):* Not a thing! (Omega *and* Iota *jump in fright.)*

Omega *and* **Iota:** Sh-h-h! *(They listen intently again.)*

Think-Tank: Well?, Well? Report to me. What do you hear?

Omega: Nothing, sir. Perhaps we are not on the correct frequency.

Iota: Nothing, sir. Perhaps the Earthlings have sharper ears than we do.

Oop: I don't hear a thing. Maybe these sandwiches don't make sounds.

Think-Tank: What? What? Does someone suggest the Mighty Think-Tank has made a mistake?

Omega: Why, no, sir. No, sir. We'll keep listening.

222

Research in Action

Visualizing

As they read, good readers envision the action being described in a text. This process heightens their enjoyment of the text but also improves comprehension and long-term memory. The mental images created while visualizing are a form of interpretation. They reflect the interaction between what the reader receives from the text and what he or she brings to the reading of the text. These images are a type of nonverbal coding that is deeper and more meaningful than the verbal coding that follows from reading the words of the text. *(Michael Pressley)*

Noodle: Please excuse me, Your Brilliance, but a cloudy piece of information is rolling around in my head.

Think-Tank: Well, roll it out, Noodle, and I will clarify it for you.

Noodle: I seem to recall that the Earthlings did not *listen* to the sandwiches. They opened them, and watched them.

Think-Tank: Yes, that is quite correct. I will clarify that for you, Captain Omega. Those sandwiches are not for ear communication, they are for eye communication. Now, Captain Omega, take that large, bright-colored sandwich over there. It appears to be important. Tell me what you observe. (Omega *picks up very large copy of "Mother Goose," holding it so that the* *audience can see title.* Iota *looks over* Omega's *left shoulder, and* Oop *squints over his right shoulder.*)

Omega: It appears to contain pictures of Earthlings.

Iota: There seems to be some sort of code.

Think-Tank *(Sharply interested)*: Code? Code? I told you this was important. Describe the code.

Oop: It's little lines and squiggles and dots. Thousands of them, next to the pictures.

Think-Tank: Code. Perhaps the Earthlings are not so primitive as we have thought. We must break the code. We must.

Noodle: Forgive me, Your Cleverness, but did not the chemical department give our spacemen a supply of Vitamin X to increase their intelligence?

Think-Tank: Stop! A thought of magnificent brilliance has come to me. Spacemen, our chemical department has given you a supply of Vitamin X to increase your intelligence. Take it immediately and then watch the sandwich. The meaning of the code will slowly unfold before you.

Omega: It shall be done, sir. Remove pill. (Crew take vitamins from boxes *on their belts.)* Present Vitamin X. *(They hold vitamins out in front of them, stiffly.)* Swallow. *(They put vitamins into their mouths and gulp* simultaneously. *They open their eyes wide, shake their heads, and they put their hands to their foreheads.)* The cotangent of a given angle in a right

223

Meeting Individual Needs

Reteach	**Challenge**
Main Idea and Details Have students who need additional help and instruction with this concept complete **Reteach,** pages 77–78.	**Main Idea and Details** Have students who understand this concept complete **Challenge,** page 41.

Main Idea and Details

For additional help in *main idea and details*, have the students complete **Reading and Writing Workbook,** pages 77–78.

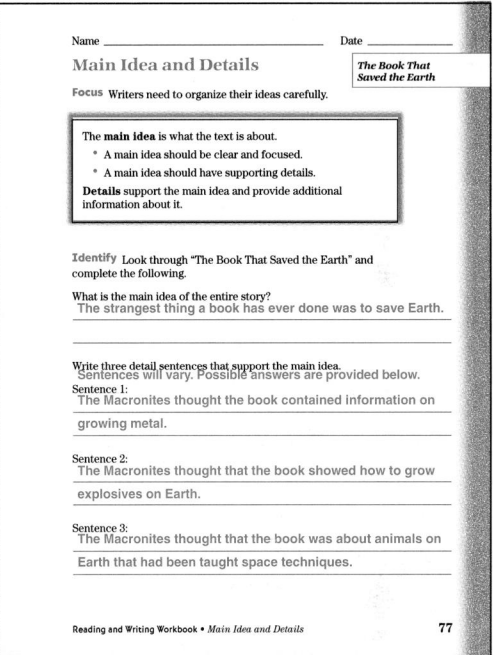

Reading and Writing Workbook pp. 77–78

② Reading and Responding

Comprehension Strategies

Modeling

⑥ Confirming Predictions *Earlier, I predicted that none of the aliens would understand the rhymes in* Mother Goose. *I was halfway right. Oop understands that they are funny, but Think-Tank is confused.*

Discussing Strategy Use

After they have read the selection, have students share any problems they encountered and tell what strategies they used to solve them. Then, have them answer the following questions. If they answer "no" to any of the questions, have them reread part of the selection to find the answer.

- Did they clarify words, phrases, and ideas that they didn't understand?

- Did they predict what might happen and then check to see if they were correct?

- Did they get images in their heads about what was happening in the play?

Make sure that students explain how using the strategies helped them understand the selection better and how they read effectively to find answers to the questions they asked as they set purposes.

Word Knowledge

transcribe, discovered, domesticated

Students can use the skills they learned in the Word Knowledge section of this lesson to read these words. Remind students of this if they have difficulty reading these words.

triangle is equal to the <u>adjacent</u> side divided by the <u>hypotenuse</u>.

Iota: *Habeas corpus ad faciendum et recipiendum!*

Oop: There is change of pressure along a radius in <u>curvilinear</u> motion.

Think-Tank: Excellent. Now, <u>decipher</u> that code.

All: It shall be done, sir. *(They frown over book, turning pages.)*

Omega: *(Brightly):* Aha!

Iota: *(Brightly):* Oho!

Oop: *(Bursting into laughter):* Ha, ha, ha!

Think-Tank: What does it say? Tell me this instant. <u>Transcribe</u>, Omega.

Omega: Yes, sir *(He reads with great seriousness.)*

"Mistress Mary, quite contrary,
How does your garden grow?
With cockle shells and silver bells
And pretty maids all in a row."

⑥ Oop: Ha, ha, ha. Imagine that. Pretty maids growing in a garden.

Think-Tank: *(Alarmed):* Stop! This is no time for <u>levity</u>. Don't you realize the seriousness of this discovery? The Earthlings have discovered how to

combine agriculture and mining. They can actually *grow* crops of rare metals such as silver. And cockle shells. They can grow high explosives, too. Noodle, contact our invasion fleet.

Noodle: They are ready to go down and take over Earth, sir.

Think-Tank: Tell them to hold. Tell them new information has come to us about Earth. Iota, continue transcribing.

Iota: Yes, sir. *(He reads very gravely.)*

"Hey diddle diddle! The cat and
the fiddle,
The cow jumped over the moon,
The little dog laughed to see
such sport,
And the dish ran away with
the spoon."

Oop *(Laughing):* The dish ran away with the spoon!

Think-Tank: Cease laughter. <u>Desist</u>. This is more and more alarming. The Earthlings have reached a high level of civilization. Didn't you hear? They have taught their <u>domesticated</u> animals musical culture and space techniques. Even their dogs have a sense of humor. Why, at this very moment, they may be launching an interplanetary

224

Meeting Individual Needs

Inter√ention

Predicting Tell students to base their predictions on prior knowledge. Ask if students based their predictions about the intelligence of the aliens on their knowledge of the aliens in "A Meeting in Space." If so, how did that affect their predictions?

attack of millions of *cows!* Notify the invasion fleet. No invasion today. Oop, transcribe the next code.

Oop: Yes, sir. *(Reading)*

"Humpty Dumpty sat on the wall,
Humpty Dumpty had a great fall;
All the King's horses and all the
    King's men,
Couldn't put Humpty Dumpty
    together again."

Oh, look, sir. Here's a picture of Humpty Dumpty. Why, sir, he looks like—he looks like—*(Turns large picture of Humpty Dumpty toward Think-Tank and audience)*

Think-Tank *(Screaming and holding his head)*: It's me! It's my Great and Mighty Balloon Brain. The Earthlings have seen me. They're after me. "Had a great fall!" That means they plan to capture Macron Central Control and me! It's an invasion of Macron! Noodle, prepare a space capsule for me. I must escape without delay. Spacemen, you must leave Earth at once, but be sure to remove all traces of your visit. The Earthlings must not know that I know—*(Omega, Iota and Oop rush about, putting books back on shelves.)*

Noodle: Where shall we go, sir?

Think-Tank: A hundred million miles away from here. Order the invasion fleet to evacuate the entire planet of Macron. We are heading for Alpha Centauri, a hundred million miles away. *(Omega, Iota, and Oop run off right, as Noodle helps Think-Tank off left and curtain closes. Spotlight shines on Historian down right.)*

Historian *(Chuckling)*: And that's how one dusty old book of nursery rhymes saved the world from an invasion from Macron. As you all know, in the twenty-fifth century, five hundred years after all this happened, we Earthlings resumed contact with Macron, and we even became very chummy with the Macronites. By that time, Great and Mighty Think-Tank had been replaced by a very clever Macronite—the Wise and Wonderful Noodle! Oh, yes, we taught the Macronites the difference between sandwiches and books. We taught them how to read, too, and we established a model library in their capital city of Macronopolis. But, as you might expect, there is still one book that the Macronites can never bring themselves to read. You've guessed it—*Mother Goose!* (He bows and exits right.)

The End

225

Teacher Tip

Tell students that production notes are often provided at the end of a play script. The production notes are for the director's use. They include information on the gender and number of characters in the play; the amount of time it takes to stage the production; a list of properties, or objects used in the play; and recommendation for setting, costumes, lighting and sound. If possible, check out from the library copies of "The Book That Saved the Earth" and some other plays so students can see what production notes look like. Then have students create their own production notes for this selection.

Comprehension Skills

Discussing the Selection

Following reading, engage the students in discussion of the selection. Using the *handing-off process* will help them take responsibility for the discussion. Also have them revisit any questions asked when they set purposes before reading. Have students support their responses with text evidence.

- Could there possibly be aliens like the Macronites in other solar systems? *(Answers may vary. Students might note that these aliens don't seem smart enough to have developed space travel.)*

- Which character was the "star" of this play? Why? *(Answers may vary, but most students will probably answer Think-Tank because he had the most lines and told the others what to do.)*

- If we were visited by aliens, what do you think they'd be impressed by? *(Answers will vary.)*

- How has this selection connected with your knowledge of the unit theme? *(Answers will vary—students should compare/contrast examples of astronomy from this selection with their own experiences or past reading and use these connections to make a general statement about the unit theme.)*

During this time, invite the students to return to the clues and problems that they noted on the transparency before reading. Let the students decide which items deserve further discussion.

When the student finishes his or her comments, that student should hand off the discussion to the next speaker. In this way, students maintain a discussion without relying on the teacher to decide who speaks.

Reading and Responding

Meet the Author

After students read the information about Claire Taylor Boiko, discuss the following questions with them.

What are three jobs that Claire Taylor Boiko has had in the theater?
(Possible answer: Three jobs that she has had in the theater are as an actress, a behind-the-scenes worker, and a playwright.)

Claire Taylor Boiko likes to write about the things that interest her. How is this reflected in her play "The Book That Saved the Earth"?
(Possible answer: Her interests are reflected in the play because it is for children, and it is based on things we have learned in astronomy, which is a science.)

The Book That Saved the Earth

Meet the Author

Claire Taylor Boiko has worked at many different jobs in theater ever since she was a young woman. While in her twenties, she worked as an actress in Children's Theater. Later, she worked behind-the-scenes on musical shows for soldiers in the Army. Now she writes plays for children. Her plays are found in books such as *Children's Plays for Creative Actors* and *Plays and Programs for Boys and Girls*. Ms. Boiko writes plays about things that interest her, including science, myths, and folk music.

Meet the Illustrator

Dennis Hockerman has been a freelance designer and illustrator for the last 23 years. Besides illustrating children's books, he has done work for the greeting card, gift wrap, and toy industries. In his spare time, Mr. Hockerman enjoys working at his printing press creating limited edition, hand-colored etchings.

226

Theme Connections

Think About It

With a small group of classmates, talk about the plots of some science fiction programs you have seen.

- Would the play you just read be more realistic if it weren't written as a comedy?
- If intelligent aliens came to Earth, where do you think they should go to learn the most important information about earthlings and our planet?

Check the Concept/Question Board to see if there are any questions there that you can answer now. If the selection or your discussions about the selection have raised any new questions about astronomy, put the questions on the Concept/Question Board.

Record Ideas

What do you like or dislike about the science fiction genre? Record your notes and ideas in your Writing Journal.

Research Ideas

Write a science fiction story or play based on research you have conducted about astronomy.

227

Theme Connections

Think About It

- As students discuss science fiction programs, circulate and observe the discussions.

- Have students compare this work of science fiction with the selection "A Meeting in Space."

- Have the students report what they discussed. Encourage them to record on the Concept/Question Board any questions they may have.

Research Ideas

Students should be ready to give their presentations.

Teacher Tip Have students discuss the humorous intent of this play. Tell them to point out anything that did not make sense, such as the Macrons knowing how to read English, yet having no idea of fiction or fantasy.

 **Responding**

Research

As students continue their explorations, have them use the **Research** CD-ROM Program to help organize and share their findings.

Home Connection p. 31

Selection Vocabulary

Have students write in their Writing Journals the definitions for words discussed before the reading of the selection and any other words they clarified while reading. Students should be encouraged to refer to these words throughout the unit as they work on student and writing projects. The words from this selection are:

apprentice	insignificant	primitive
pantomimes	cease	

Reading/Writing Connections

Point out that in "The Book That Saved the Earth," it took Think-Tank three tries to figure out how to use the book he found at the Centerville Library. First, he tried to eat it; then, he tried to listen to it; and finally, he tried to read it. Ask students if they can think of any other stories where it took the characters three tries to solve a problem (for example, *The Three Bears* and *The Three Little Pigs*). This pattern of organizing the action of a story around three events (or tries) is an example of plot structure. Have students choose a story idea from their Writing Journals, and expand their idea to include three events or attempts to solve a problem.

Literature Appreciation

Think-Tank is a character who enjoyed being considered powerful, yet benevolent. Have students find passages from "The Book That Saved the Earth" that support this statement. Then have students identify Apprentice Noodle's character traits using evidence from the play.

Home Connection

The class has just finished reading "The Book That Saved the Earth," a humorous science fiction play about how aliens from outer space might interpret our culture. An informational letter on "The Book That Saved the Earth," in both English and Spanish, can be found in the *Home Connection* guide.

Supporting Student Explorations

Whole Group Set aside time for students to present their research activities. This will likely take more than one class period. Tell students that, as researchers, once they have drawn conclusions about the information they have gathered, they must use this compiled information and knowlege to raise additional unanswered questions. Have students ask questions about the presentations and suggest ideas for further research.

Once all groups have presented their research, discuss the presentations. Although much of the discussion may center on particularly interesting facts or issues, direct the conversation so that students talk about what they learned about astronomy from their own research and from that of their classmates.

Suggest that students post on the Concept/Question Board brief descriptions of books, magazine articles, computer Websites, or other sources of information that they have found to be especially helpful in their explorations of astronomy.

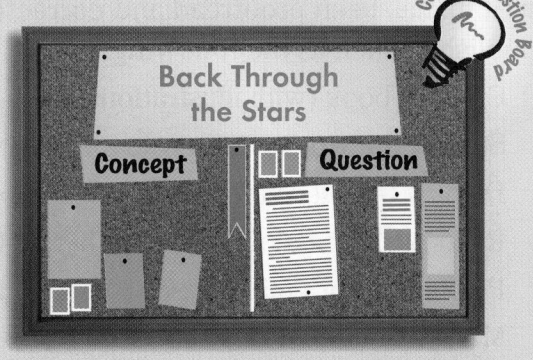

Inquiry Journal
Have students complete page 23 of the *Inquiry Journal.* Have them record their ideas about how "The Book That Saved the Earth" added to their knowledge of astronomy.

* *Stars* by Seymour Simon
Answers will vary.

* *The Book That Saved the Earth* by Claire Boiko
Answers will vary.

Inquiry Journal   23

Inquiry Journal p. 23

Assessment

✓ **Informal** At this point, students are making formal presentations of their research projects. Check to be sure that students:
- participate appropriately in whole group discussions.
- display good audience behavior.
- relate research findings to their knowledge of the unit theme.

③ Integrating the Curriculum

Language Arts

Writing

Publishing

Instruct Point out that the purpose of writing is to communicate. *Publishing* is the process of preparing a piece of writing so that its content is communicated clearly and effectively. Tell students that after a piece of writing has been proofread and corrected there are many ways they can publish it, such as the following.

- Create a book (with illustrations, photographs, or diagrams if appropriate).
- Submit the work to a newspaper or magazine.
- Display the piece (with artwork, if appropriate) on a bulletin board.
- Read the piece aloud to an audience (with or without music).
- Perform an original play or puppet show for the class.
- Make a comic book.
- Give a speech or dramatic reading of original work for the class.
- Present the piece as a pamphlet or letter to a specific audience.

Practice Have students select a paragraph from their *Writing Folders* to prepare for publication. First, have them proofread it for any spelling or grammatical errors. After making any necessary corrections, have them copy the paragraph onto a clean sheet of paper. Then, if appropriate, have students create visuals, such as diagrams or illustrations, to enhance or clarify their paragraphs.

Apply Have students use the following checklist to help them as they publish their works. They should note, however, that not every question applies to every form of publishing.

_____ Have I chosen my best piece?

_____ Have I revised it to make it better?

_____ Have I proofread it carefully?

_____ Have I decided upon my illustrations?

_____ Have I recopied my piece carefully and illustrated it?

_____ Have I numbered the pages?

_____ Have I made a cover that tells the title and my name?

Assessment

✓ **Informal** Take this opportunity to assess students' progress with the writing process by commenting on the entries in their Writing Journals.

Teacher Tip For students who want to create a book, three simple ways are listed below.

- Create a simple book by stapling together on the left side all of the pages, plus the front and back covers.
- Make an accordion book by pleating a long piece of paper.
- Make a plank book by binding together heavy pages of cardboard or thin wood with a string looped through holes in the pages.

Writing Process

Publish In general, if a student has brought a work to the proofreading stage, he or she should publish it. However, the decision to publish is the student's. Students may want to publish the expository writing pieces that they have been working on throughout this unit. If so, have them decide what form of publication they want to take for their work. An individual publishing conference may be useful in helping them give form to their ideas and make final corrections. Remind students that the diagrams they have been working on would be a nice way to enhance their publication.

3 Integrating the Curriculum

The Book That Saved the Earth

Teacher Tip Prompt students to tell you the meanings of the literary terms related to plays. Ask them how many of these are familiar after having created a dramatic play for the Unit 1 activity.

Literary Elements

Literary Terms Related to Plays

Instruct Explain that the theater profession developed a "language" to facilitate understanding among actors, writers, producers, directors, and others who work in theater productions. Tell students that in order for them to understand, appreciate, and perform plays, it is necessary for them to understand this specialized terminology.

Ask students what theater vocabulary they know. List terms on the chalkboard. Examples are *playwright, act, stage, director, lighting, rehearsal, script, lead, scene, monologue, dialogue, costumes, prompt,* and *actor.* As students propose terms, ask them to define each term and explain how it relates to theater. If any terms remain unclear, have students look them up in the dictionary, then discuss why they are important to the production of plays. You may want to point out that this terminology is also used in movie and television productions.

Practice Have students create a brief dictionary of theater terms in the Personal Dictionary section of their Writing Journals. Have them begin by listing the terms in alphabetical order. Then have them supply a definition and a sentence that illustrates the meaning of the term.

Apply Have students make a poster or a television ad for "The Book That Saved the Earth." Their poster or TV ad should advertise the play using literary terms, examples of dialogue, and descriptions of scenes that will entice an audience to their performance.

Vocabulary

Develop Vocabulary by Listening

Instruct Inform students that one way for them to increase their vocabulary is for them, as they listen to stories or informational text, to identify unfamiliar words and then use context clues, word structure, and apposition to figure out their meanings. It always is wise to check these inferred meanings in a dictionary, a thesaurus, or a glossary. Have students listen as you read the first paragraph of dialogue in "The Book That Saved the Earth" on page 218. Model for students how context clues help define the word *tome* as meaning "a book or volume."

Practice As you read aloud the play "The Book That Saved the Earth," have students listen for any unfamiliar words and use the appropriate clues to figure out the meaning of each word. As a group, discuss how listening to a word used in context helped them to discern its meaning.

Apply Choose an expository text having to do with the unit theme, Back Through the Stars. Read it aloud to the students and have them listen for and jot down unfamiliar words, then practice the skills they have learned in order to build their vocabulary.

Meeting Individual Needs

Reteach

Listening Vocabulary Have students who need additional instruction and practice with this concept complete **Reteach,** pages 79–80.

Challenge

Listening Vocabulary Choose five to ten sentences from any selection in Unit 2 of the **Student Anthology.** Make sure that each sentence contains at least one particularly challenging vocabulary word. Challenge students to determine the meanings of the words you identify using context clues instead of the glossary or dictionary. Have students who understand this concept complete **Challenge,** page 42.

Skills Strand

Listening Vocabulary

INTRODUCED:	Unit 2, Lesson 3
REVIEWED:	Unit 2, Lesson 6
	Unit 2, Lesson 8

Reading and Writing Workbook pp. 79–80

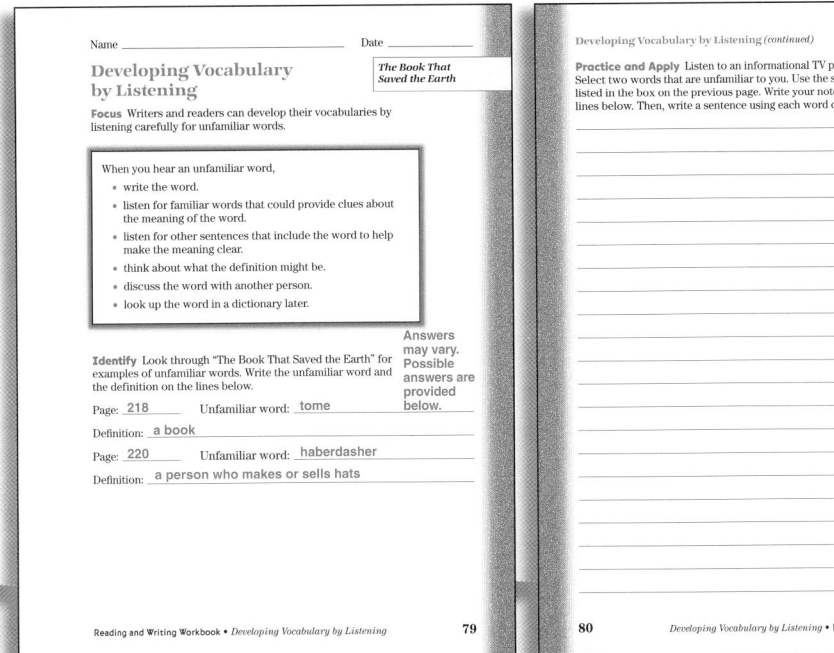

3 Integrating the Curriculum

Meeting Individual Needs

Reteach
Commas in a Series Have students who need additional instruction and practice with this concept complete **Reteach,** pages 81–82.

ESL
Commas in a Series You may wish to work with English-language learners to make sure that they understand the placement of commas in a series. Many languages have rules for the use of commas that do not follow those of the English language. Therefore, these students may be confused by the whole concept of commas and require additional instruction.

Challenge
Commas in a Series Challenge students to write a sentence using commas in a series correctly for each of the following prompts:
- at least three subjects in school
- at least three places you would like to visit during the summer
- at least three things in a room in your home
- at least three things you can do at a playground

Have students who understand this concept complete **Challenge,** page 43.

←Skills Strand→

Commas in a Series
INTRODUCED: Unit 2, Lesson 8
REVIEWED: Unit 3, Lesson 7
Unit 4, Lesson 8

Grammar, Usage, & Mechanics

Commas in a Series

Instruct Write this sentence on the chalkboard: *Marbles may be made of stone, glass, steel, clay, or plastic.* Ask a volunteer to read the five words in this list. Then have a student circle the four commas in the sentence. Remind students that a comma is used to set off and separate words and groups of words. Tell them that in the example sentence, the commas separate the words that are used in a series. When there are three or more words used as in a list, that is, in a series, then commas separate the words that precede the conjunction.

Practice Have students skim the selection, "The Book That Saved the Earth" for sentences in which commas in a series are used. As they find these sentences, allow students to read them aloud to the class, pausing whenever they come to a comma.

Apply Have students choose a classroom object and write three adjectives to describe it. Then have them write a sentence describing the object, using the three adjectives in a series. Did they remember to use commas correctly?

For additional practice, have students complete **Reading and Writing Workbook** pages 81–82.

Reading and Writing Workbook pp. 81–82

Listening/Speaking/Viewing

Dramatic Interpretation of Poetry

Explain that not all poetry rhymes, but that many poems are structured with the intention of bringing emphasis to certain words, ideas, or word sounds. For example, sometimes a poet ends a line of poetry in the middle of a sentence or at other intervals that at first may seem awkward. Reading the poem aloud can help the reader sense how the line breaks have been used to enhance the meaning, rhythm, or tone of the poem.

Have students turn to the poem "Sun" by Myra Cohn Livingston on pages 214–215. Do a dramatic reading of the first sentence in this poem; use vocal inflections that communicate the mood of the poem, and pause deliberately after each line break and between stanzas. Then ask students what kind of effect the pauses created. If necessary, offer that each line break occurs after a description of something that happens on the sun. This gives the reader a chance to form a mental image of each individual activity, creating an awed tone and accentuating the idea of the sun being very dynamic and powerful. Have a volunteer do a dramatic reading of the second sentence in the poem, pausing after each line break. Have students comment on how the delivery of the poem's second sentence affected the tone of its message.

Repeat the exercise above with a dramatic reading and discussion of the poem "Secrets" on pages 216–217. Have students implement the *handing-off process* during the discussion (see Program Appendix page 28 for information on *handing off*).

Teacher Tip You may wish to have students plan and perform a formal, dramatic reading of these two poems. You could invite a neighboring class to be the audience. Suggest that your students create several large, poster-sized illustrations, incorporating some of the visual images that they pictured as they read the poems. Individual students might wish to supplement the formal class reading of these two poems with personal recitations of their particular interpretations. Other students might like to find and read other poems about space, stars, planets, or the sun.

Teacher Tip Explain that before television introduced moving pictures into America's living rooms, people gathered together around the radio to listen to dramatic presentations in much the same way that students will listen in this lesson. Radio performers used vocal inflections to add dramatic qualities to their work. Proper diction was also necessary to ensure that the audience heard the correct dialogue. Have students practice these skills as they perform their auditory play.

3 Integrating the Curriculum

Study and Research

Evaluating Writing

Instruct Ask students what they usually do after they have finished a research project or paper. Though some students may mention that they continue their interest in and research of the subject, many just forget about all the work they put into it. Explain to students that they should always take time to assess their research as part of making a thorough evaluation of their writing. They should reflect on what they have learned and what they still want to know about their subject. Tell them they can conduct a good evaluation by asking themselves the following questions.

- Did my research sources contain the most current information available on my subject?
- Did did my research answer the questions posed in my research topic?
- Is my research reflected clearly and completely in my paper or project?
- What new questions came up during my research, and was I able to answer them?

Practice Have students look back at their expository papers and expository papers from this unit and ask themselves each of the questions above. Tell students that it is never too late to go back and research more fully any questions that may have been left unanswered in their projects.

Apply For more practice, have students complete *Inquiry Journal,* page 37.

Teacher Tip Students can evaluate their writing at any stage of the writing process. Drafting, revising, and publishing are particularly appropriate phases for students to reflect on the work they have done.

Name _____ Date _____

Back Through the Stars

UNIT **2**

Evaluating Writing

It is important for writers to think about what they have written and how they might improve it. Reread the persuasive paper you wrote for Unit 1 and the expository paper you wrote for this unit. Then, answer the following questions.

- In which paper do you think you more successfully achieved your purpose? Why?
  Answers will vary.
  _____
  _____
  _____

- Do you think details, facts, and supporting evidence are more important in a persuasive paper or an expository paper? Why?
  Answers will vary.
  _____
  _____
  _____

- How did you apply what you learned from writing the Unit 1 paper to writing the Unit 2 paper?
  Answers will vary.
  _____
  _____
  _____

Inquiry Journal

37

Inquiry Journal p. 37

Across the Curriculum

 **Art**

Design an Astronomical Set

Purpose

To help students express their ideas about astronomy in science fiction by designing a stage set for the play "The Book That Saved the Earth"

Materials

small boxes, markers, construction paper, glue, scissors

Procedure

Although stage and set directions are provided with the text of the play, there is much room for artistic expression. Have students elaborate on the astronomy theme with their own design for one of the three sets needed for this play.

- Suggest that students build their sets in small boxes or shoeboxes.
- Students will use art materials to build their model sets.
- Help students identify and choose one of the three sets used in the play—the Historian's set, Think-Tank's set, and the Centerville Library.
- Instruct students to follow the sketchy descriptions given in the play, but to be creative and elaborate on the information given.
- Students could take their designs one step further and place models of actors in their sets. They will need to design costumes for their models.

 **Social Studies**

U.S. Space Missions

Purpose

To help students become aware of the history of the U.S. space program and the role Americans have had in learning about outer space

Materials

astronomy-related books and articles, index cards, paper, markers, paints

Procedure

Have students discover the extensive space exploration history of the United States by researching the major events of the U.S. space program. Students will share their research by displaying the events and achievements on a classroom time line.

- Assign small groups to research different decades of space history beginning with the 1960s.
- Students may wish to post on the Concept/Question Board their resources from books, magazines, newspapers, and computer searches.
- Have students write each important event and achievement of their assigned decade on index cards.
- Assign one group to develop/draw the time line. Perhaps they will want to make the time line the size of a wall mural or do a vertical time line in the shape of a launching rocket. They might wish to add illustrations of some of the space events along the time line.
- Have students present their events to the class as they attach their index cards to the historical time line.

Bibliography

Extending the Unit Theme

Have students explore other dimensions of astronomy through reading and discussing the books listed on these pages.

Promoting Reading for Pleasure

There are several ways you can promote reading for pleasure.

- Develop a classroom library and reading area that includes unit theme-related selections brought in by the students, as well as a comfortable chair, a globe, posters, and so on.
- Take students to the school or local public library regularly. Help them locate books by subject, author, or genre.
- Invite a local authority or amateur astronomy enthusiast to speak to your class and suggest their favorite age-appropriate books on astronomy.

Using the Bibliography Pages

To get started, have students read each of the book descriptions on pages 228–229. Ask if anyone has read any of these books or is familiar with any of the authors represented. Encourage students to share what they know about the authors and the books, without giving away important parts of a story.

Tips for Reading

- Have students visualize processes or events step by step as they are described in their selections.
- As students encounter unfamiliar words in their selections, expect them to figure them out using sound/spelling skills to decode a word.
- Have students consult these books for information on astronomy.

Back Through the Stars

Bibliography

Astronomy for Every Kid: 101 Easy Experiments That Really Work

by Janice VanCleve. Try these experiments and learn about the universe. Average

Comets, Meteors, and Asteroids

by Seymour Simon. Explore the solar system, and spin around with the meteors, asteroids, and comets. Easy

Cosmic Science

by Jim Wiese. Marshmallow constellations, toilet paper planets, and straw rockets are just a few "space-cruising" activities you can enjoy. Average

Edwin Hubble: American Astronomer

by Mary Virginia Fox. Ever heard of the Hubble telescope? Read about the man for whom the telescope is named. Average

228

Flight, Space & Astronomy

by Bob Bonnet and Dan Keen. Try at least one of these fifty-seven projects and experiments and find out how much you can learn about space science. Average

Tales of the Shimmering Sky

retold by Susan Milord. People everywhere all look at the same sky. Meet people from all over the world through these sky tales. Advanced

Voyager: An Adventure to the Edge of the Solar System

by Sally Ride. Take a look at the Voyager spacecraft. Then travel on a mission to Saturn, Uranus, or Neptune. Easy

The Young Astronomer

by Harry Ford. Chart the phases of the moon, watch meteor showers, and read a map of the constellations. This book will teach you how to do those things and more. Average

229

Discussing the Books

Have each student select one or more of the books for reading and discussion. Use the following questions as discussion starters:

- After reading your selection, are you more inclined to want to read more about astronomy? Explain.
- What did you learn about astronomy through your selection? What are you curious about?
- What suggestions would you give to this book's author?
- What is the most interesting thing about astronomy? What is the least?

Tips for Discussion

- Have students discuss how their selections were the same and different from the others. Suggest that students with unanswered questions raise them during discussions so that if others came across that information in their text, they may share it.
- When a question is presented, silently allow "wait time" to give students the opportunity to come up with suggestions or answers of their own. If students have difficulty, you may want to give a hint rather than a complete answer to provide another opportunity for them to work it out.

Student Recommendations

Encourage students to make one of the projects from *Cosmic Science* or *Flight, Space & Astronomy*, if they chose one of these selections, or to make a model or poster of information in one of the other texts to get students' attention as they recommend the selection. These projects can then be displayed in the classroom library/reading area.

Note: Teachers should preview any trade books for appropriateness in their classrooms before recommending them to students.

Exploration Wrap-Up

Whole-Group Discussion

- Initiate a class discussion of the unit selections, focusing on astronomy.

- Have students refer to page 20 of their *Inquiry Journal* to remind themselves of what they knew about astronomy when they began the unit and what they expected to learn from the unit.

- Remind students to think about their previous discussions of ideas from the Concept/ Question Board.

Inquiry Journal p. 20

Small-Group Discussion

- As an alternative to whole-group discussion, have students work in small groups to discuss the unit. Have group participants refer to the Concept/ Question Board, browse unit selections, and review their *Inquiry Journal* pages for Unit 2 to refresh their memories for important ideas raised in the unit.

- Call on the groups to share with classmates important points and conclusions from their discussions.

Unit Celebration

Have students suggest ways to celebrate the completion of this unit. If necessary, offer your own suggestions, such as the following:

- Create a classroom gallery of pictures of important people in the field of astronomy. Include information about their contributions.

- Students could make up a game about astronomy in which they write questions and use them to quiz each other.

Extending the Discussion

- Have the students evaluate the unit selections, identifying those they found most interesting and those they found least interesting.

- Have the students evaluate the unit activities. Which activities did they find most enjoyable or informative?

- Have students evaluate the overall unit. They should consider how well the unit topic was covered and whether the topic was worth examining.

- Have students suggest aspects of astronomy that are worth further exploration, possibly beginning with any questions left on the Concept/Question Board.

 **Review the Concepts**

- After all of the collaborative groups have shared their ideas about astronomy with the class, ask the students if there are additional ideas that they wish to discuss or explore.
- Encourage students to discuss how their original perceptions of astronomy have changed.
- Remind students to review any questions they may have had throughout the unit.
- As always, students' ideas should determine the discussion.

- Remind students that they can continue to research astronomy even though they have finished the unit.

Review Fine Art

Have students look again at the Fine Art shown on pages 154–155 of their anthologies. Invite them to review the aspect of astronomy that is represented by each work.

Assessment

✓ Informal Assessment

- Give the children the opportunity to evaluate their personal learning experiences during this unit by completing *Inquiry Journal* pages 38–39.
- Meet individually with students to discuss their evaluations.

Inquiry Journal pp. 38–39

UNIT 2	Name _____ Date _____
Back Through the Stars	

Unit Wrap-Up

- How did you feel about this unit?
  ☐ I enjoyed it very much. ☐ I liked it.
  ☐ I liked some of it. ☐ I didn't like it.
- How would you rate the difficulty of this unit?
  ☐ easy ☐ medium ☐ hard
- How would you rate your performance during this unit?
  ☐ I learned a lot about astronomy.
  ☐ I learned some new things about astronomy.
  ☐ I didn't learn much about astronomy.
- Why did you choose this rating?
  Answers will vary.
- What was the most interesting thing you learned about astronomy?
  Answers will vary.
- Is there anything else about astronomy that you would like to learn? What?
  Answers will vary.

38   Inquiry Journal

Inquiry Journal

- What did you learn about astronomy that you didn't know before?
  Answers will vary.
- What did you learn about yourself as a learner?
  Answers will vary.
- What do you need to work on as a learner?
  Answers will vary.
- What resources (books, films, magazines, interviews, other) did you use on your own during this unit? Which of these were the most helpful? Why?
  Answers will vary.

39

✓ Formal Assessment

You can find the unit assessment for Unit 2 on pages 45–53 of the *Comprehension and Writing Assessment*. See the *Assessment Guide* for specific suggestions on how to use these skills.

Comprehension Assessment

- Understanding the Selection
- Making Connections Across Selections
- Vocabulary
- Skills

Writing Assessment

- Personal Response—Students write an essay about what it would be like to travel to another star system.
- Exploring Unit Concepts—Students write an essay comparing ancient and present astronomy.

Exploring the Theme

UNIT 3

Heritage

Every family has a story. And each of those stories tells of many people and different times and places. Each story tells of the rich heritage that makes up the fabric and texture of the family and out of this fabric and texture, the family members learn their identity.

230

231

Introduction

The family is a basic unit of social organization all over the world. Sociologists, anthropologists, and historians have studied many aspects of the family— why it takes the form it does in different societies and how traditions and customs are played out across generations. Writers of literature have explored these same topics, illustrating the effects of heritage on fictional characters with whom we can identify.

The selections in this unit introduce students to a variety of families, customs, and traditions. Because fifth graders often take the concept of family for granted, it can be difficult for them to think about their heritage. These selections will facilitate the reflection process for students by presenting diverse family forms and values, some of which will be very different from their own. As they enter the worlds of the story characters, students will extend their understanding of heritage as well as explore authors' methods of depicting life within the family, whatever its form.

Exploration and Reflection Goals

Wherever the students' ideas about heritage begin, it is important that they broaden and deepen their understanding of both the variety of family forms and the approaches various writers have taken to convey the idea of heritage. The goals for this unit are:

■ to extend knowledge of heritage, including how it varies across cultures.

■ to analyze the characteristics of various genres and build thematic links among the selections.

■ to develop understanding of creative story-writing, including how to generate ideas, how to transform ideas into a literary form, and how to utilize literary elements and techniques.

Learning Goals

Throughout this unit, the students will have the opportunity to share information about their own heritage or another heritage with which they are familiar. Within each of the general reflection and exploration goals, a number of more specific learning goals are pursued.

The learning goals of this unit are:

■ to connect personal ideas, experiences, information, and insights about heritage with those of others.

■ to determine distinctive and common characteristics of cultures through reading about heritage.

■ to understand how an author's point of view affects the text.

■ to recognize the distinguishing features and purposes of genres, including biography, nonfiction, and realistic fiction.

■ to understand and identify literary terms such as *title*, *author*, *illustrator*, and *dialogue*.

■ to analyze characters, including their traits, motivations, conflicts, points of view, and relationships, and the changes they undergo.

■ to use literary conventions to express thoughts about heritage.

■ to develop and revise drafts about heritage in order to publish for general and specific audiences.

■ to proofread one's own work as well as that of peers and respond constructively to the work of others.

Teacher Tip

The topic of heritage raises a broad range of questions. In order to prepare for this unit, you might ask yourself the following questions.

• What do I know about my heritage? How did I learn about it?

• What role does culture play in one's heritage? What effect does our modern culture have on one's heritage?

• What are some ways in which one's heritage can be preserved?

• Do I have a story related to my heritage that I want to share with my students?

Exploring the Theme

Unit Activities

Unit activities are student-driven and should emerge from students' interests, encouraged or ignited by their reading and class discussions. Unit activities should involve reading beyond the program material and address the conceptual aims of the unit.

Exploration Activities

- Students might enjoy creating a heritage album. They could interview family members or friends for biographical data and stories about family events and traditions, then present the information in a variety of written forms. The students might write stories, poetry, songs, and newspaper articles for inclusion in their albums.

- Some students might prefer to learn about and report on a heritage other than their own. Offer these students the choice of interviewing and writing about a neighbor, family friend, or community member to create their albums.

	The Land I Lost	In Two Worlds	The Night We Started Dancing
Overview of Selection	■ In this autobiography, a Vietnamese boy relates memories of his life before it was disrupted by war.	■ This selection is a nonfiction account of life in Alaska and how contact with outsiders has affected family customs through generations.	■ In this piece of realistic fiction, an eight-year-old boy whose parents have died helps his grandfather get past his grief.
Link to the Theme	■ Immigrants often feel lonesome for the land they left behind.	■ People can retain traditional values, even while adopting modern practices.	■ Customs and traditions help bring and hold families together.
Unit Activities	■ Students listen to and interview a class guest about heritage. ■ Students select and read library books about heritage.	■ Students plan genres and selections for their albums. ■ Students reflect on their heritage, interview family members and friends about customs and traditions, and begin writing.	■ Students identify and utilize various literary techniques used by published authors to communicate their heritage. ■ Students begin writing the second piece for their albums.
Supporting Student Explorations	■ Introduce the unit activity. ■ Discuss interviewing techniques, prepare questions about heritage, and invite a guest to class. ■ Schedule a library visit.	■ Discuss with students some appropriate genres for their heritage albums. ■ Students meet in small groups to share heritage stories.	■ Highlight various literary techniques and suggest that students consider creating a photographic essay. ■ Encourage students to discuss customs and traditions with relatives and friends.

Supporting Student Explorations

Throughout the unit, the students will engage in activities of their own choosing—such as those shown in the chart below—that allow them to explore heritage more deeply and to use the questions they have raised to do so. These activities may relate to the selection the students are reading or to a number of selections, but they must revolve around the theme concept.

For their activities, the students might choose to do one of the following:

- conduct audio- or videotaped interviews of family members and friends about their thoughts on heritage
- take notes from tape-recorded interviews and identify direct quotations for use in original stories
- ask family members and friends to share a folktale from their cultural heritage, then write an original retelling
- conduct a panel discussion about how parents' and guardians' attitudes toward education affect their children and why this is an important part of heritage
- write letters to request information from relatives and friends who live in other cities
- create a family tree

Explain to the students that they may work on their unit activities alone, with partners, or in small groups. Throughout each lesson, monitor student progress and encourage students to report problems they encounter in preparing their activities.

West Side	Chinatown	The Night Journey	Parmele
■ In this piece of realistic fiction, a young boy feels isolated after immigrating to New York City until he discovers a Puerto Rican enclave.	■ In this piece of realistic fiction, a Chinese girl comes to appreciate the richness of her Chinese heritage.	■ In this piece of realistic fiction, a 13-year-old Jewish girl learns about her great-grandmother's narrow escape from Russia and about the importance of the family's samovar.	■ In this autobiography, the author recalls happy times spent visiting her grandparents in the rural South.
■ Heritage need not be left behind when leaving one's homeland.	■ Children can learn the importance of their heritage from their grandparents.	■ Artifacts and storytelling can link the generations of a family.	■ Visits with grandparents can provide valuable information and insight about heritage.
■ Students continue working on the second pieces for their albums. ■ Students discuss with relatives and friends what they want to communicate about their heritage.	■ Students write an autobiographical sketch for their author pages. ■ Students consider using a family member as a model for a character in a piece of realistic fiction.	■ Students prepare final drafts, complete illustrations, prepare title and copyright pages, and bind their books. ■ Students write thank-you notes to those who assisted them with their work.	■ Students select a piece from their heritage albums, practice reading it, and share it with the class.
■ Conduct class discussion of students' progress with their heritage albums. ■ Discuss use of literary conventions to express thoughts.	■ Arrange peer-editing sessions for students' autobiographical sketches. ■ Discuss effective use of point of view in students' stories about heritage.	■ Discuss the process of preparing text for publication for general and specific audiences. ■ Conduct a class review of writing letters of thanks.	■ Schedule readings of student selections. ■ Plan the unit celebration.

Program Resources

Student Materials

Student Anthology
Pages 230–253

Reading and Writing Workbook
Pages 83–110

Inquiry Journal
Pages 40–55

Writing Folder

Listening Library Audiocassettes

Teacher Materials

Teacher's Guide, Book 1

Reteach
Pages 83–110

Challenge
Pages 44–57

Home Connection
Pages 33–48

Skills Assessment
Pages 27–34

Comprehension and Writing Assessment
Pages 55–78

Assessment Guide

ESL Supplement
Unit 3, Lessons 1–7

Overhead Transparencies
Numbers 15–21, 44–47, 51

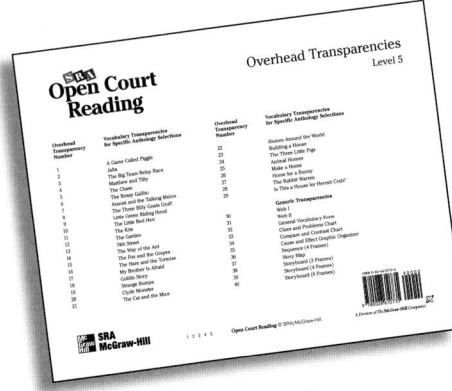

Intervention Guide
Unit 3, Lessons 1–7

Additional Materials
- **Visual Glossary**
- **Intervention Package**
- **Teacher's Professional Guides**

Program Resources

Classroom Library*

Appalachia: The Voices of Sleeping Birds

BY CYNTHIA RYLANT. VOYAGER, 1998.

Rylant's poetic recollections of Appalachia—the life, the people, and their heritage—are enhanced by full-color portraits. (Boston Globe Horn Book Nonfiction Award, Notable Children's Trade Book in the Field of Social Studies, SLJ Best, ALA Notable, Parents Choice Award Illustrations in Children's Books) **(Average)**

Childtimes: A Three-Generation Memoir

BY ELOISE GREENFIELD. HARPERTROPHY, 1993.

Greenfield tells the story about three generations of her family. **(Average)**

Immigrant Kids

BY RUSSELL FREEDMAN. PUFFIN, 1995.

Photographs from the late 1800s to the early 1900s illustrate the experience of young European immigrants. (ALA Notable) **(Average)**

My Daniel

BY PAM CONRAD. HARPERCOLLINS JUVENILE, 1991.

Ellie and Steve learn about a family legacy when their grandmother tells them stories of her brother's historic quest for dinosaur bones on their late nineteenth-century Nebraska farm. **(Average)**

Note: Teachers should preview any trade books and videos for appropriateness in their classrooms before recommending them to students.

* These books, which all support the unit theme of Heritage, are part of a 24-book *Classroom Library* available for purchase from SRA/McGraw-Hill.

*Amos Fortune, Free Man

Born the son of an African king, Amos Fortune is kidnapped and sold into slavery at age 15. In spite of his royal heritage, Amos remains a slave for 45 years, until he can buy his freedom. Videocassette; 45 min.

Different Dance
CORONET/MTI

Lily is taunted because of her Sioux ancestry, but when her peers visit the local Native American museum, they gain an understanding of her people and her noble heritage. Videocassette or videodisc; 22 min.

*M. C. Higgins, the Great

When two strangers come to town, M. C. Higgins must come to terms with his family heritage in order to realize his dream of saving their home from strip mining. Videocassette; 42 min.

*Roll of Thunder, Hear My Cry

Cassie and her family fight to keep their land as they struggle against racism. Videocassette; 46 min.

Family Tree Maker
DELUXE EDITION II

Have students use this interactive program, which includes an index of 115 million names and 12,000 actual family trees, to help students research their ancestry and create family trees. CD-ROM.

*Listening Library: Heritage
SRA/MCGRAW-HILL, 2000

Students will enjoy listening to the selections they have read. Have them use the audiocassette during Independent Work Time. Audiocassette.

*Lesson Planner
SRA/MCGRAW-HILL, 2000

Use the Lesson Planner to adjust and refine lessons to meet the specific needs of your students. CD-ROM.

*Research
SRA/MCGRAW-HILL, 2000

As students continue their exploration of Heritage, have them use the Research program to help them organize and share their findings. CD-ROM.

Heritage Websites

Have students find information about Heritage and links to sites concerning heritage at: **http://www.sra4kids.com**

*Basic Computer Skills Connection

Have students use the Graphics/Multimedia unit of the **SRA Basic Computer Skills** program to help them develop computer skills within the context of the unit theme. The Applying Computer Skills in Reading activity contains a computer skills application specific to this unit.

Titles preceded by an asterisk (✱) are available through SRA/McGraw-Hill. Other titles can be obtained by contacting the publisher listed with the title. See page 38 of the Program Appendix for ordering information.

Unit Skills Overview

	WORD KNOWLEDGE	COMPREHENSION SKILLS & STRATEGIES	LITERARY ELEMENTS	VOCABULARY & SPELLING
The Land I Lost: Adventures of a Boy in Vietnam **Genre: Autobiography**	■ Antonyms ■ Long e spelled *ea* ■ Consonant Digraph *wh*	■ Author's Purpose ■ Author's Point of View ■ Visualizing ■ Making Connections ■ Summarizing	■ Autobiography	■ Syllable Boundary Patterns
In Two Worlds: A Yup'ik Eskimo Family **Genre: Nonfiction**	■ Synonyms ■ *s*-family Consonant Blends ■ /oo/ spelled *oo*	■ Compare and Contrast ■ Main Idea and Details ■ Asking Questions ■ Clarifying ■ Summarizing	■ Purposes of Types of Texts	■ Use a Dictionary
The Night We Started Dancing **Genre: Realistic Fiction**	■ Compound Words ■ /j/ spelled *dge* ■ The Suffix *-dom*	■ Making Inferences ■ Sequence ■ Asking Questions ■ Summarizing ■ Predicting	■ Analyzing Character Traits	■ Regular and Irregular Plurals
The West Side **Genre: Realistic Fiction**	■ Homophones ■ Three-letter Consonant Blends ■ /ch/ spelled *tch*	■ Drawing Conclusions ■ Summarizing ■ Clarifying ■ Predicting	■ Analyzing Character Traits	■ Syllable Boundary Patterns
Chinatown **Genre: Realistic Fiction**	■ Hyphenated Compound Words ■ Long a spelled *ai* ■ /n/ spelled *kn*	■ Compare and Contrast ■ Fact and Opinion ■ Making Connections ■ Clarifying ■ Summarizing	■ Setting, Plot, and Problem Resolution	■ Consonant Before *-le* Endings
The Night Journey **Genre: Adventure**	■ Synonyms ■ Consonant Digraph *sh* ■ /k/ spelled *ck*	■ Author's Point of View ■ Drawing Conclusions ■ Summarizing ■ Asking Questions ■ Making Connections	■ Literary Elements of a Story	■ Words in Context
Parmele **Genre: Autobiography**	■ Open Compound Words ■ /f/ spelled *gh* ■ Long o spelled *ow*	■ Main Idea and Details ■ Visualizing ■ Making Connections ■ Clarifying	■ Autobiography	■ Use a Dictionary to Clarify Meanings

WRITING	LISTENING/ SPEAKING/VIEWING	GRAMMAR, USAGE, & MECHANICS	STUDY & RESEARCH	ACROSS THE CURRICULUM

■ Writing a Narrative
■ Prewrite
	■ Interview Questions	■ Pronoun Referents	■ Using a Dictionary or Glossary	Social Studies
				  ■ Heritage Map
				  ■ A Letter to Future
				    Grandchildren
				Art
				  ■ A Coat of Arms
				Math
				  ■ Graphing Family History

■ Indicators of Time and Order
■ Prewrite
	■ Interpret Speaker's Messages	■ Regular and Irregular Verbs	■ Interviewing	Social Studies
				  ■ Come to Alaska
				  ■ Trade with Scammon Bay
				Science
				  ■ Wildlife in Alaska
				Art
				  ■ Animal Carving

■ Plot
■ Draft
	■ Listening to and Appreciating Spoken Language	■ Adverbs	■ Using a Thesaurus	Social Studies
				  ■ Occupations
				Music
				  ■ Songs of Other Countries

■ Evaluating the Author's Writing
■ Revise
	■ Connect Experiences	■ Subject and Verb Agreement	■ Using Graphs	Social Studies
				  ■ Learning Español
				Math
				  ■ Money Word Problems

■ Dialogue
■ Revise
		■ Compound Sentences and Conjunctions	■ Draw Conclusions from Multiple Sources	Social Studies
				  ■ Writing an Article
				Art
				  ■ Creating a Picture Album

■ Using and Punctuating Dialogue
■ Proofread
	■ Language Reflecting a Region and Culture	■ Capitalizing Titles	■ Using Technology in Presentations	Music
				  ■ A Heritage of Folk Dancing
				Social Studies
				  ■ Ellis Island

■ Publishing a Personal Narrative	■ Verbal and Nonverbal Messages	■ Commas in a Series	■ Multimedia Presentations	Art
				  ■ Making a Tradition Quilt
				Social Studies
				  ■ Planning a Traditional
				    Evening

Meeting the Needs of All Children

Meeting Individual Needs

	Reteach	ESL	Challenge
The Land I Lost: Adventures of a Boy in Vietnam **Genre: Autobiography**	**Reading and Responding** ■ Author's Purpose **Integrating the Curriculum** ■ Autobiography ■ Syllable Boundary Patterns ■ Pronouns and Pronoun Referents	**Preparing to Read** ■ Word Meaning ■ Vocabulary **Reading and Responding** ■ Discussing the Selection	**Reading and Responding** ■ Author's Point of View ■ Author's Purpose **Integrating the Curriculum** ■ Autobiography ■ Syllable Boundary Patterns ■ Pronouns and Pronoun Referents
In Two Worlds: A Yup'ik Eskimo Family **Genre: Nonfiction**	**Reading and Responding** ■ Compare and Contrast **Integrating the Curriculum** ■ Using a Dictionary ■ Regular and Irregular Verbs	**Preparing to Read** ■ Word Meaning ■ Vocabulary **Reading and Responding** ■ Main Idea and Details **Integrating the Curriculum** ■ Sharing Ideas	**Reading and Responding** ■ Main Idea and Details ■ Compare and Contrast **Integrating the Curriculum** ■ Using a Dictionary ■ Regular and Irregular Verbs
The Night We Started Dancing **Genre: Realistic Fiction**	**Integrating the Curriculum** ■ Regular and Irregular Plurals ■ Adverbs	**Preparing to Read** ■ Word Meaning ■ Accepting Change ■ Vocabulary **Reading and Responding** ■ Sequence **Integrating the Curriculum** ■ Analyzing Character Traits	**Reading and Responding** ■ Sequence ■ Making Inferences **Integrating the Curriculum** ■ Regular and Irregular Plurals ■ Adverbs
The West Side **Genre: Realistic Fiction**		**Preparing to Read** ■ Word Meaning ■ Cultural Context ■ Vocabulary **Reading and Responding** ■ Clarifying **Integrating the Curriculum** ■ Writing and Revising	**Reading and Responding** ■ Drawing Conclusions **Integrating the Curriculum** ■ Syllable Boundary Patterns ■ Subject and Verb Agreement
Chinatown **Genre: Realistic Fiction**	**Reading and Responding** ■ Fact and Opinion **Integrating the Curriculum** ■ Spelling *-le* Endings ■ Compound Sentences	**Preparing to Read** ■ Word Meaning ■ Cultural Context ■ Vocabulary **Reading and Responding** ■ Movies ■ Discussing Strategy Use **Integrating the Curriculum** ■ Revise	**Reading and Responding** ■ Fact and Opinion **Integrating the Curriculum** ■ Spelling *-le* Endings ■ Compound Sentences
The Night Journey **Genre: Adventure**	**Integrating the Curriculum** ■ Literary Elements of a Story ■ Words in Context	**Preparing to Read** ■ Word Meaning ■ Vocabulary **Reading and Responding** ■ Making Connections **Integrating the Curriculum** ■ Proofreading ■ Foreign Language as a Literary Device	**Reading and Responding** ■ Drawing Conclusions ■ Author's Point of View **Integrating the Curriculum** ■ Literary Elements of a Story ■ Words in Context ■ Capitalizing Titles
Parmele **Genre: Autobiography**		**Preparing to Read** ■ Word Meaning ■ Vocabulary **Reading and Responding** ■ Reread **Integrating the Curriculum** ■ Cooperative Activities	**Reading and Responding** ■ Main Idea and Details **Integrating the Curriculum** ■ Using a Dictionary ■ Commas in a Series

Assessment

Intervention	✓ Informal	✓ Formal
Preparing to Read ■ Antonyms **Reading and Responding** ■ Comprehension ■ Author's Purpose ■ Visualizing ■ Summarizing ■ Author's Point of View ■ Making Connections	Reading and Writing Workbook pp. 83–90 Reteach pp. 83–90 Challenge pp. 44–47 Teacher Observation Log Project Assessment	Comprehension and Writing Assessment pp. 55–56 ■ "The Land I Lost: Adventures of a Boy in Vietnam" Skills Assessment p. 27 ■ Author's Purpose
Preparing to Read ■ Word Knowledge **Reading and Responding** ■ Comprehension ■ Summarizing ■ Main Idea and Details ■ Compare and Contrast ■ Clarifying	Reading and Writing Workbook pp. 91–96 Reteach pp. 91–96 Challenge pp. 48–50 Teacher Observation Log Project Assessment	Comprehension and Writing Assessment pp. 57–58 ■ "In Two Worlds: A Yup'ik Eskimo Family" Skills Assessment p. 28 ■ Using a Dictionary or Glossary
Preparing to Read ■ Compound Words **Reading and Responding** ■ Comprehension ■ Summarizing ■ Sequence ■ Making Inferences ■ Predicting	Reading and Writing Workbook pp. 97–100 Reteach pp. 97–100 Challenge pp. 51–52 Teacher Observation Log Project Assessment	Comprehension and Writing Assessment pp. 59–60 ■ "The Night We Started Dancing" Skills Assessment pp. 29, 37 ■ Using a Thesaurus ■ Sequence
Preparing to Read ■ Homophones **Reading and Responding** ■ Comprehension ■ Clarifying ■ Predicting ■ Summarizing ■ Drawing Conclusions **Integrating the Curriculum** ■ Revise	Teacher Observation Log Project Assessment	Comprehension and Writing Assessment pp. 61–62 ■ "The West Side" Skills Assessment p. 30 ■ Subject and Verb Agreement
Preparing to Read ■ Word Knowledge **Reading and Responding** ■ Comprehension ■ Clarifying ■ Fact and Opinion ■ Making Connections **Integrating the Curriculum** ■ Revise	Reading and Writing Workbook pp. 101–106 Reteach pp. 101–106 Challenge pp. 53–55 Teacher Observation Log Project Assessment	Comprehension and Writing Assessment pp. 63–64 ■ "Chinatown" Skills Assessment p. 31 ■ Setting
Preparing to Read ■ Synonyms **Reading and Responding** ■ Comprehension ■ Asking Questions ■ Drawing Conclusions ■ Author's Point of View ■ Making Connections **Integrating the Curriculum** ■ Punctuating Dialogue	Reading and Writing Workbook pp. 107–110 Reteach pp. 107–110 Challenge pp. 56–57 Teacher Observation Log Project Assessment	Comprehension and Writing Assessment pp. 65–66 ■ "The Night Journey" Skills Assessment p. 32 ■ Capitalizing Titles
Preparing to Read ■ Word Knowledge **Reading and Responding** ■ Comprehension ■ Main Idea and Details ■ Clarifying	Teacher Observation Log Project Assessment	Comprehension and Writing Assessment pp. 67–78 ■ "Parmele" ■ Unit 3 Review Skills Assessment p. 33 ■ Commas in a Series

Previewing the Unit

Activating Prior Knowledge

Have the students take some time to consider what they already know and believe about heritage. Tell them that throughout the unit they will share stories and that you are looking forward to learning more about each student's heritage. Suggest that students consider the following:

- What do you know about your heritage? How did you learn about it?
- Does your heritage make you different from others? Why or why not?
- Is there a special artifact, memento, or photograph that is cherished by a friend or family member? What makes it so valuable?

When students have had some time to compose their thoughts and ideas, call on volunteers to speak. Over the next several days, allow students to express themselves, after which they can be asked questions. Add students' ideas to the Concept/Question Board.

Concept/Question Board

- Start the Concept/Question Board for this unit.
- Remind the students that the Concept/Question Board is where they are to post new information and ideas about heritage that they gather as they explore the theme.
- Record the students' contributions on the Concept/Question Board.
- Have those students who have chosen not to contribute orally add their ideas to the written record.
- Draw students' attention to the array of content and the various presentation modes.

Over the course of the first week of the unit, have the students reread and reflect on the contributions listed on the Concept/Question Board. Have them note, in their Writing Journals, the contributions that mean the most to them. Suggest that they expand on the original contributions by adding their own thoughts and associated material—stories, articles, pictures, and so on.

Home Connection

In our unit on Heritage, the students will read stories that range from realistic fiction about moving to a strange country to autobiographies about family history. An informational letter on Heritage, in both English and Spanish, can be found in the **Home Connection** guide.

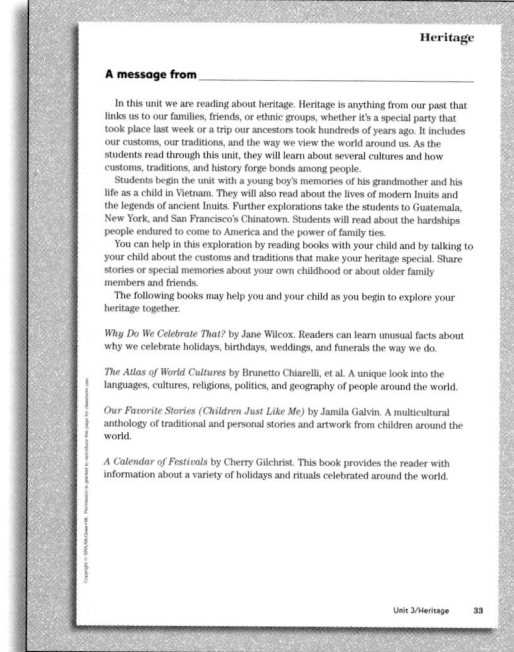

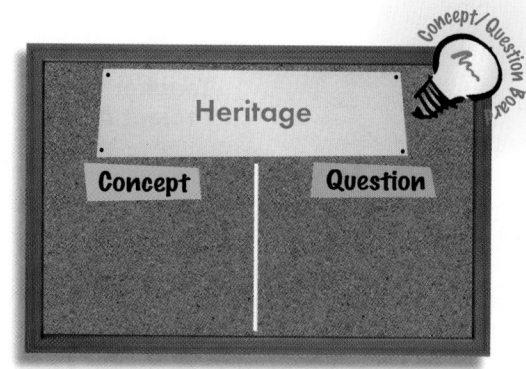

Home Connection p. 33

Setting Reading Goals

Have the students open their anthologies to the first page of the Heritage unit. Discuss the unit opener illustration on pages 230–231. It may prompt questions about the unit.

- Have the students spend a few minutes browsing the selections in the unit. Ask the students to share what interests them most about the subject of heritage. Record their ideas on the Concept/Question Board.

- Have the students report and discuss what they have noticed in their browsing, raise any questions they have, and post their questions on the Concept/Question Board.

- If there are different opinions as to what this unit will be about, record these on the chalkboard and discuss them after students have read some of the selections.

- Tell the students to think about how their heritage is similar to and different from that of the families in the selections.

Inquiry Journal

- After the students have discussed what they think this unit might be about, have them complete page 40 in their *Inquiry Journals.*

- Share ideas about heritage that they would like to learn more about.

Inquiry Journal p. 40

Research in Reading

Dr. Marsha Roit on Writing

The writing classroom is changing, and adjusting to this change is one of the many challenges facing today's teacher. Currently, instruction encourages the expression of ideas and feelings, the development of fluency, the building of knowledge, the sharing of learning, and the development of self-esteem.

What has caused this change in writing instruction? Much of our insight comes from our growing understanding of what good writers do. They have ownership of their work and are actively involved in the process from start to finish. The same should be true for the young authors in classrooms.

Successful writers spend time planning, drafting, revising, editing, and presenting their work. Writing is a recursive process as authors move back and forth through writing activities, from drafting to revising and back to drafting, to create their final pieces.

Check the Reading link of the **SRA** Web page for information about Research in Reading.
http://www.sra4kids.com

The Land I Lost:

Adventures of a Boy in Vietnam

from the book by Huynh Quang Nhuong
illustrated by Neil Waldman

I was born on the central highlands of Vietnam in a small hamlet on a riverbank that had a deep jungle on one side and a chain of high mountains on the other. Across the river, rice fields stretched to the slopes of another chain of mountains.

There were fifty houses in our hamlet, scattered along the river or propped against the mountainsides. The houses were made of bamboo and covered with coconut leaves, and each was surrounded by a deep trench to protect it from wild animals or thieves. The only way to enter a house was to walk across a "monkey bridge"—a single bamboo stick that spanned the trench. At night we pulled the bridges into our houses and were safe.

There were no shops or marketplaces in our hamlet. If we needed supplies—medicine, cloth, soaps, or candles—we had to cross over the mountains and travel to a town nearby. We used the river mainly for traveling to distant hamlets, but it also provided us with plenty of fish.

232

Selection Summary

Genre: Autobiography

Huynh Quang Nhuong (Hwoon Kwan Nyoon) planned to live his life in Vietnam. He wanted to be a teacher like his father, and a farmer and a hunter like the other men in his village. But war and paralysis from a gunshot wound forced him to leave his homeland. In his book "The Land I Lost: Adventures of a Boy in Vietnam," the author tells warm and humorous stories of his childhood. The selection consists of two chapters from his book. The first describes the Nhuong family's way of life before the war. The second is about his grandmother, who was a colorful character.

About the Author

Huynh Quang Nhuong graduated from the University of Saigon with a degree in chemistry. He was drafted into the South Vietnamese army and was left permanently paralyzed by a gunshot wound. Huynh came to the United States for medical treatment and decided to stay. Here he earned bachelor's and master's degrees in French and comparative literature. He now lives in Columbia, Missouri.

The Land I Lost: Adventures of a Boy in Vietnam was the first children's book written by Mr. Nhuong and was published in five different languages. This book received the William Allen White Children's Book Award, the Blue Cobra Award, the Friends of American Writers Award, and the German Youth Literature Prize.

Students can read more about Huynh Quang Nhuong on page 242 of the ***Student Anthology.***

About the Illustrator

Neil Waldman says, "It is no coincidence that I chose to become a children's book illustrator. As a child, I would retreat to my bedroom, close the door, and sit down with crayon and a sketchpad. For me each new picture book is an adventure."

Students can read more about Neil Waldman on page 242 of the ***Student Anthology.***

Other Books Illustrated by Neil Waldman

- *The Never-Ending Greenness*
- *Bayou Lullaby*
- *Quetzal*

Exploring the Theme

Selection Concepts

"The Land I Lost" is excerpted from an autobiography of the same title. These two chapters describe the traditions and customs of country life in Vietnam before the war and the author's memories of his family members. Key concepts to be explored are:

- Immigrants often feel lonesome for the land they left behind.
- Family stories about parents and grandparents are important for preserving one's heritage.

Check the Reading link of the **SRA** Web page for links to theme-related Websites.
http:// www.sra4kids.com

Exploration Activity Tips

Before Reading, have the students browse the selection to determine what it is about. As they browse, students should consider how this selection might help them with their unit activities.

During Reading, have students ask themselves what the selection tells them about heritage and what type of narrative genre the author has used.

After Reading, have the students discuss the story and their thoughts on whether autobiography is an effective genre for writing about heritage. Then have students update the Concept/Question Board. Some may want to revise their activity plans based on what they have learned from the selection.

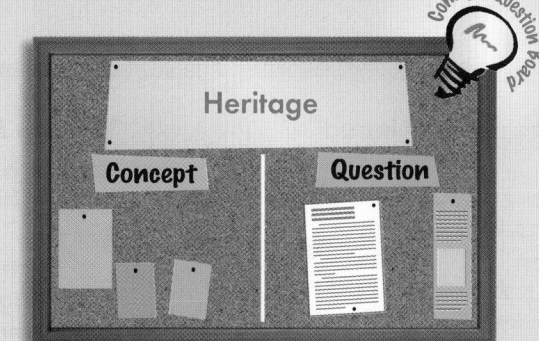

Unit 3 Exploration Management

Lesson 1 The Land I Lost: Adventures of a Boy in Vietnam	**Collaborative Exploration** Listen to and interview a class guest about heritage. Select and read library books about heritage. **Supplementary Activity** Introduce the unit activity. Discuss interviewing techniques, prepare questions about heritage, and invite a guest to class. Schedule a library visit.
Lesson 2	Identify genres for inclusion in heritage albums. Reflect on one's own heritage, interview family members and friends about customs and traditions, and begin writing.
Lesson 3	Identify and utilize various literary techniques. Writing begins on second selection for student albums.
Lesson 4	Work on unit activity continues. Discuss with relatives and friends what they want to communicate about their heritage.
Lesson 5	Write autobiographical sketches for author pages and consider modeling a character after a family member or friend.
Lesson 6	Prepare final drafts, complete illustrations, prepare title and copyright pages, and bind books. Write thank-you notes to those who helped with activity.
Lesson 7	Students present a selected piece from their heritage albums.

Lesson Planner

Suggested Pacing: 3–5 days	DAY 1	DAY 2	
	DAY 1	**DAY 2**	
Part 1 **Preparing to Read** **Materials** ■ Student Anthology, pp. 232–243 ■ Transparencies 15, 44	**Word Knowledge** ■ Reading the Words and Sentences, p. 232G ■ Developing Oral Language, p. 232G **Build Background, p. 232H** **Preview and Prepare, p. 232I** **Selection Vocabulary, p. 232I** *hamlet, cultivate, passion, mythology*	**Preview and Prepare, p. 232I** ■ Review Transparency 44	
Part 2 **Reading and Responding** **Materials** ■ Student Anthology, pp. 232–243 ■ Teacher Observation Log ■ Reading and Writing Workbook, pp. 83–84 ■ Inquiry Journal, p. 41 ■ Home Connection, p. 35	**Student Anthology, pp. 232–243** **Comprehension Strategies** ■ Visualizing, pp. 232, 234 ■ Making Connections, pp. 232, 236, 238 ■ Summarizing, pp. 234, 240 **Discussing Strategy Use, p. 240**	**Student Anthology, pp. 232–243** **Comprehension Skills** ■ Author's Point of View, pp. 233, 235 ✓■ Discussing the Selection, p. 241 **Exploring the Theme** ■ Selection Vocabulary, p. 243A *hamlet, cultivate, passion, mythology*	
Part 3 **Integrating the Curriculum** **Materials** ■ Student Anthology, pp. 232–243 ■ Reading and Writing Workbook, pp. 85–90 ■ Inquiry Journal, p. 44	**Writing** ■ Writing a Narrative, p. 243C **Literary Elements** ✓■ Autobiography, p. 243D	**Writing Process** ■ Brainstorm, p. 243C **Spelling** ✓■ Syllable Boundary Patterns, p. 243E	
Independent Work Time **Materials** ■ Reteach, pp. 83–90 ■ ESL Supplement ■ Challenge, pp. 44–47 ■ Intervention Guide ■ Listening Library Audiocassette	**Writing Process Continued** **ESL** ■ Word Meaning, p. 232G ■ Vocabulary, p. 232G **Intervention** ■ Antonyms, p. 232G ■ Comprehension, p. 232	**Writing Process Continued** **Reteach** ✓■ Autobiography, *Reteach*, pp. 85–86 **ESL** ■ Discussing the Selection, p. 241 **Challenge** ■ Author's Point of View, p. 235 ✓■ Autobiography, *Challenge*, p. 45 **Intervention** ■ Author's Point of View, p. 235	

✓ Informal **Assessment Available**   ✓ Formal **Assessment Available**

DAY 2 continued	DAY 3	
DAY 3	DAY 4	DAY 5

General Review	**General Review**	**Review Word Knowledge**

Student Anthology, pp. 232–243

Comprehension Skills

✓✓ ■ Author's Purpose, pp. 237, 239

Theme Connections

■ Think About It, p. 243
■ Improvise a Scene, p. 243

Student Anthology, pp. 232–243

Exploring the Theme

■ Reading/Writing Connections, p. 243A
■ View Fine Art, p. 243A
■ Supporting Student Explorations, p. 243B

Student Anthology, pp. 232–243

■ Review Selection
■ Complete Discussion
■ Reread Selection in Pairs

Home Connection, p. 243A

■ Discuss "The Land I Lost: Adventures of a Boy in Vietnam"
■ Write a paragraph about personal heritage

Writing Process Continued

Grammar, Usage, and Mechanics

✓ ■ Pronouns and Pronoun Referents, p. 243F

Listening/Speaking/Viewing

■ Interview Questions, p. 243G

Writing Process Continued

Study and Research

■ Multiple Sources, p. 243H

Across the Curriculum

Social Studies

■ Heritage Map, p. 243I
■ A Letter to Future Grandchildren, p. 243J

Art

■ A Coat of Arms, p. 243I

Math

■ Graphing Family Holidays, p. 243J

Writing Process Continued

Reteach

✓ ■ Syllable Boundary Patterns, *Reteach*, pp. 87–88

Challenge

■ Author's Purpose, p. 237
✓ ■ Syllable Boundary Patterns, *Challenge*, p. 46

Intervention

■ Author's Purpose, p. 237

Writing Process Continued

Reteach

✓ ■ Author's Purpose, *Reteach*, pp. 83–84

Challenge

✓ ■ Author's Purpose, *Challenge*, p. 44

Unit Project

■ Interview a Class Guest
■ Read Books About Heritage

Writing Process Continued

Reteach

✓ ■ Pronouns and Pronoun Referents, *Reteach*, pp. 89–90

Challenge

✓ ■ Pronouns and Pronoun Referents, *Challenge*, p. 47

Unit Project Continued

Meeting Individual Needs
Independent Work Time

Part 1
Preparing to Read

Meeting Individual Needs

ESL
- Word Meaning, p. 232G
- Vocabulary, p. 232J

Intervention
- Antonyms, p. 232G

Part 2
Reading and Responding

Meeting Individual Needs

Reteach
- Author's Purpose, *Reteach*, pp. 83–84

ESL
- Discussing the Selection, p. 241

Challenge
- Author's Point of View, p. 235
- Author's Purpose, *Challenge*, p. 44

Intervention
- Comprehension, p. 232
- Visualizing, p. 234
- Summarizing, p. 234
- Author's Point of View, p. 235
- Making Connections, p. 236
- Author's Purpose, p. 237

Part 3
Integrating the Curriculum

Meeting Individual Needs

Reteach
- Autobiography, *Reteach*, pp. 85–86
- Syllable Boundary Patterns, *Reteach*, pp. 87–88
- Pronouns and Pronoun Referents, *Reteach*, pp. 89–90

ESL
- Interview Questions, p. 243G

Challenge
- Autobiography, *Challenge*, p. 45
- Syllable Boundary Patterns, *Challenge*, p. 46
- Pronouns and Pronoun Referents, *Challenge*, p. 47

Formal Assessment Options

Use these assessment pages along with your informal observations to gauge student progress.

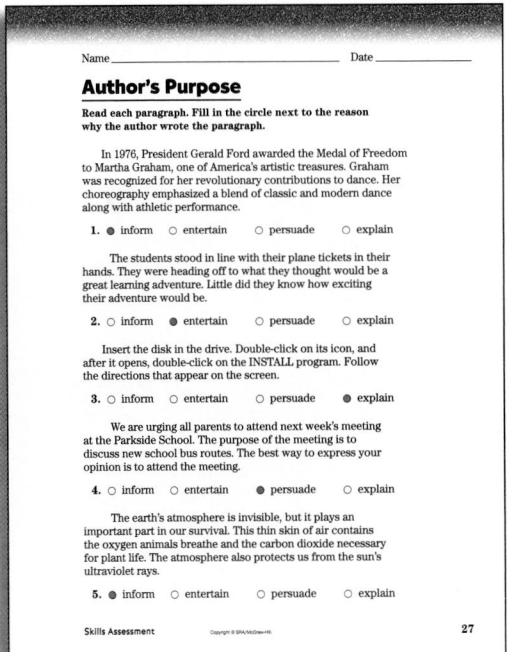

Skills Assessment, p. 27

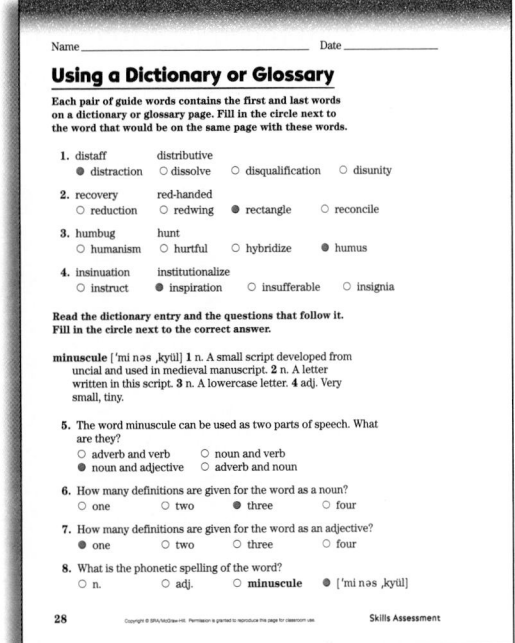

Skills Assessment, p. 28

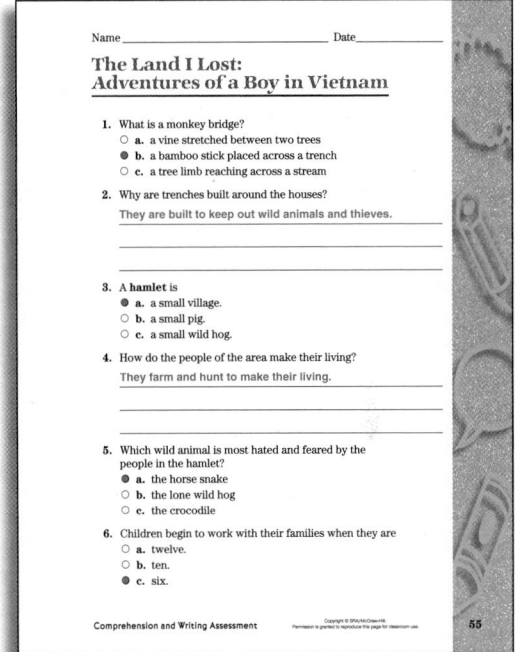

Comprehension and Writing Assessment, p. 55

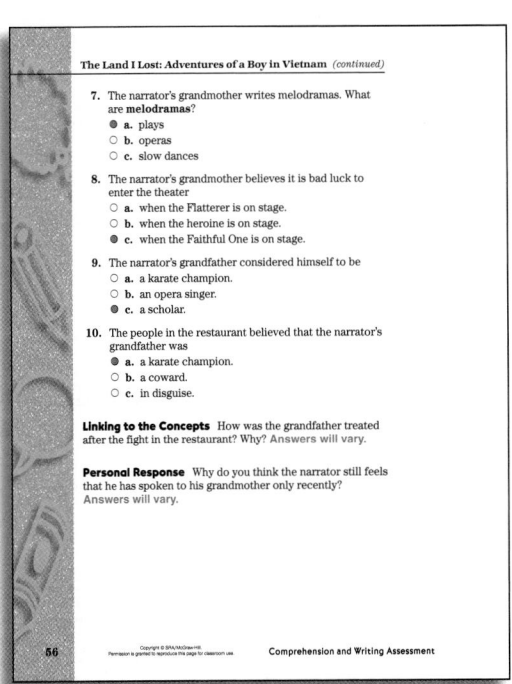

Comprehension and Writing Assessment, p. 56

① Preparing to Read

ESL

Word Meaning Make sure English-language learners understand the meanings of the blending words before they do the blending exercise. Refer to Unit 3, Lesson 1, of the **ESL Supplement** for specific suggestions.

Intervention

Antonyms Explain that antonyms are words that have opposite meanings. For example, *high* is the opposite of *low*. Therefore, *high* and *low* are antonyms.

Write ten words that have opposites on the chalkboard and have students work in pairs to find the antonym for each word. Encourage them to use a dictionary if necessary. For students who need more help see Unit 3, Lesson 1, of the **Intervention Guide.**

Word Knowledge

Reading the Words and Sentences

Write each word and sentence on the chalkboard. Have students read each word together. After all the words have been read, have students read each sentence in natural phrases or chunks. Use the suggestions in About the Words to discuss the different features of the listed words.

Line 1:	deep shallow enter exit lead follow
Line 2:	feared season weak sneaky
Line 3:	whined wherever when whole
Sentence 1:	My little brother whined and followed me wherever I went.
Sentence 2:	I feared this season's whole crop would be ruined by the heat.
Sentence 3:	Weak swimmers should stay in the shallow end of the pool.

About the Words

Discuss with the students the following elements as illustrated in each line of words:

■ Line 1 contains words that are antonyms. Antonyms are two words that mean the opposite of each other.

■ The words in Line 2 all contain the vowel digraph *ea*. These letters, when placed together, make one sound.

■ All of the words in Line 3 contain the consonant digraph *wh*. These letters, when placed together, make one sound.

Developing Oral Language

To review the words, have students do one or both of the following activities.

■ Give students a word from Line 1 and ask them to supply its antonym. Then have a volunteer use both words in a sentence.

■ Have a student choose a word from Lines 1, 2, or 3 and use it in a sentence. Next, have another student extend the sentence by adding another word from the lines in a way that still makes sense. Have students see how many words they can fit in the sentence logically, encouraging them to extend both the beginning and end of the sentence.

Teacher Tip Gaining a better understanding of the spellings of sounds and the structure of words will help students as they encounter unfamiliar words in their reading. By this time in fifth grade, students should be reading approximately 143 words per minute with fluency and expression.

Build Background

Activate Prior Knowledge

Discuss the following with students to find out what they may already know about the selection or about heritage. Tell students to use their prior knowledge to help them comprehend the selection they are about to read.

- Tell students that *culture* is the arts, beliefs, and customs that make up a way of life for a group of people at a certain time; *heritage* is something handed down from earlier generations or from the past. Have students discuss the role that *culture* plays in a person's *heritage*.
- Have students share anything they know about the country Vietnam.
- Ask students if they are familiar with the story they are about to read, and if so, to tell a little about it. Remind students, however, not to give away the ending of the selection.
- Have students share any other stories that involve grandparents or heritage.

Background Information

The following information may help the students better understand the selection they are about to read.

- In 1954, Vietnam was divided into North Vietnam and South Vietnam as part of a peace settlement between the French, who formerly controlled the country as a colony, and communist forces.
- In 1957, the Vietnam War began when South Vietnamese communists, supported by North Vietnam, began to rebel against the government. The United States sent military forces to aid South Vietnam.
- In l973, a cease-fire agreement was signed, and American troops left the country. In l975, the capital of South Vietnam fell to the communists, and the country was unified under one government. Since that time many people have left the country as refugees.

Teacher Tip Remind students that reading should always bring to mind their own experiences and things they have already learned. Students can make connections to the text, to themselves, and to the world.

Teacher Tip You may want to further discuss the terms *communist* and *refugees*.

Writing Journal Tell students that after reading they will be jotting down in their Writing Journals their reactions to the story. Have them be on the lookout for any ideas they may have about heritage and questions about heritage as it relates to their unit activity.

Research in Action

Background Information

To "read as a writer" means we notice *how* the authors express ideas and why—not just what ideas they express. For example, authors use vivid imagery so that readers can imagine, and almost experience, what story characters experience. They use flashbacks and memories to help readers understand characters' unique response to events. *(Anne McKeough)*

Preparing to Read

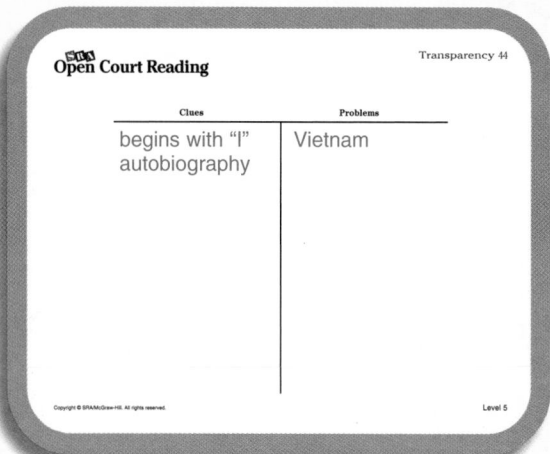

Transparency 44

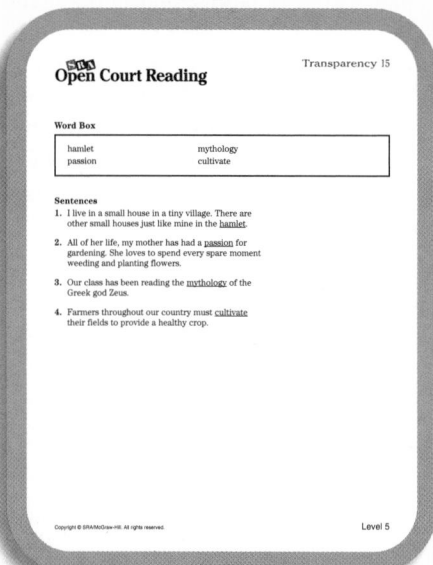

Transparency 15

Teacher Tip To help students decode words, divide them into the syllables shown below. The information following each word tells how students can figure out the meaning of each word from the sentences on the transparency.

ham•let	context clues
cul•ti•vate	context clues
pas•sion	context clues
my•thol•o•gy	context clues, word structure

Preview and Prepare

Browse

- Have a volunteer read the title and author's and illustrator's names aloud. Have students share what they know about autobiography.

- Because this selection is nonfiction, have the students browse through the entire selection, looking for words and phrases that connect to what they already know. Record these in the Clues column on the **Transparency 44.** Discuss with the students what they think this story might have to do with heritage.

- Encourage students to ask questions as they browse. Have them identify any problems they notice while reading in the Problems column.

Set Purposes

As they read, have students think about their family and what events they would choose if they were to write an autobiography.

Selection Vocabulary

As students study vocabulary, they will use context clues, word structure, and apposition to determine the meaning of these and additional unfamiliar words.

Display **Transparency 15** before reading the selection to introduce and discuss the following words and their meanings.

> **ham•let:** a group of houses that make up a small village (page 232)
>
> **cul•ti•vate:** to take care of something so it will grow (page 233)
>
> **pas•sion:** a strong feeling for something (page 236)
>
> **my•thol•o•gy:** stories about gods and heroes (page 236)

Have students read the words in the Word Box. Help students decode multisyllabic words by reading them syllable by syllable. *Mythology* may be difficult for students to decode.

Have students read the sentences on **Transparency 15** to determine the meaning of the underlined words. Remind them to use clues in the sentences and structural clues to figure out the meaning. See the teacher tip on the left for information on how the words in each sentence can be defined.

Other words that may be unfamiliar to the students should be clarified during reading.

Reading Recommendations

Your first reading of the selection should focus on developing the reading strategies found to the left of the reduced pages. We recommend that the students revisit the selection, rereading sections or the entire selection as a way to enhance their understanding and appreciation of the text. During rereading they should focus on the comprehension skills found to the right of the reduced pages.

Oral Reading

Because this selection is a first-person account, students will enjoy reading it aloud. Have students help each other with unfamiliar words and difficult ideas. As students read aloud, have them read expressively at an appropriate pace, in natural phrases and chunks. By reading the selection with fluency, students will demonstrate an understanding of the text and an ability to engage the listeners in an effective manner. If students encounter difficulties, have them use the reading strategies below or refer to the Blending Procedure (Program Appendix 15–16).

Using Reading Strategies

Reading strategy instruction allows students to become aware of how good readers read. Good readers constantly check their understanding as they are reading and ask themselves questions. In addition, skilled readers recognize when they are having problems and stop to use various reading strategies to help them make sense of what they are reading.

During the reading of "The Land I Lost," you will model the use of the following reading strategies:

- Making Connections
- Visualizing
- Summarizing

Before reading, have students share how they have used these strategies in the past and any tips they can give each other on their use.

Building Comprehension Skills

Revisiting or rereading a selection allows students to apply skills that give them a more complete understanding of the text. Some follow-up comprehension skills, such as *Main Idea and Details* and *Compare and Contrast*, help students organize information. Others, such as *Author's Purpose*, *Making Inferences*, and *Drawing Conclusions*, lead to deeper understanding—to "reading between the lines," as mature readers do. In this selection, students will apply the follow-up comprehension skills of *Author's Point of View* and *Author's Purpose*. Because two skills are reviewed, you may want to do all the sections related to one skill before doing the other skill.

Teacher Tip Have students who may need extra help reading "The Land I Lost" reread the selection using the *Listening Library Audiocassette*.

Meeting Individual Needs

ESL

Vocabulary Check that English-language learners know the meanings of idioms and more difficult vocabulary in the story, including: *central highlands; hamlet; cultivate; water buffaloes; recognize; poisonous; damage; youthful spirit; never diminished with age; melodramas; young at heart; scold; vindicate; something was amiss;* and *passed away.* Explain and show pictures as needed. Model example sentences and help English-speaking students make their own sentences. Refer to Unit 3, Lesson 1, in the *ESL Supplement* for teaching suggestions.

Teacher Tip Remind students to keep their unit activities in mind while reading the selection.

Teacher Tip By this time in the fifth grade, good readers should be reading approximately 143 words per minute with fluency and expression. The only way to gain fluency is through practice. As explained in Reading Recommendations, have students reread all or part of the selection to you and to each other during class or Independent Work Time to focus on the comprehension skills and to build fluency.

② Reading and Responding

Read pages 232–243.

Comprehension Strategies

Modeling

① Visualizing *When a new term is introduced, sometimes visualizing its meaning can help a reader understand it. I am not familiar with what a hamlet is. The text says that a hamlet has many houses in it, but this one has no shops or marketplaces. A hamlet must be like a village. It might help me to draw a quick sketch. How do you visualize the author's homeland?*

Modeling

② Making Connections *Readers can enhance their current stores of knowledge by making connections. I can connect river travel in the author's homeland to river travel in American culture. I know that in the past, Americans used rivers as a means of travel and for the transport of goods. Now we usually use cars or airplanes instead of rivers. This connection has helped me understand how my culture is similar to and different from the author's. What connections have you made, and how do they enhance your store of knowledge?*

Reading Recommendation

ORAL • CHORAL • SILENT

The Land I Lost:

Adventures of a Boy in Vietnam

from the book by Huynh Quang Nhuong
illustrated by Neil Waldman

I was born on the central highlands of Vietnam in a small <u>hamlet</u> on a riverbank that had a deep jungle on one side and a chain of high mountains on the other. Across the river, rice fields stretched to the slopes of another chain of mountains.

There were fifty houses in our hamlet, scattered along the river or propped against the mountainsides. The houses were made of bamboo and covered with coconut leaves, and each was surrounded by a deep <u>trench</u> to protect it from wild animals or thieves. The only way to enter a house was to walk across a "monkey bridge"—a single bamboo stick that spanned the trench. At night we **①** pulled the bridges into our houses and were safe.

There were no shops or marketplaces in our hamlet. If we needed supplies—medicine, cloth, soaps, or candles— we had to cross over the mountains and travel to a town **②** nearby. We used the river mainly for traveling to distant hamlets, but it also provided us with plenty of fish.

232

Meeting Individual Needs

Intervention

Comprehension Intervention strategies for those students having difficulty reading "The Land I Lost: Adventures of a Boy in Vietnam" can be found in Unit 3, Lesson 1, of the *Intervention Guide.*

Assessment

✓ **Informal** Observe individual students as they read, and use the Teacher Observation Log found in the *Assessment Guide* to record anecdotal information about each student's strengths and weaknesses.

During the six-month rainy season, nearly all of us helped plant and <u>cultivate</u> fields of rice, sweet potatoes, Indian mustard, eggplant, tomatoes, hot peppers, and corn. But during the dry season, we became hunters and turned to the jungle.

Wild animals played a very large part in our lives. There were four animals we feared the most: the tiger, the lone wild hog, the crocodile, and the horse snake. Tigers were always trying to steal cattle. Sometimes, however, when a tiger became old and slow it became a maneater. But a lone wild hog was even more dangerous than a tiger. It attacked every creature in sight, even when it had no need for food. Or it did crazy things, such as charging into the hamlet in broad daylight, ready to kill or to be killed.

The river had different dangers: crocodiles. But of all the animals, the most hated and feared was the huge horse snake. It was sneaky and attacked people and cattle just for the joy of killing. It would either crush its victim to death or poison it with a bite.

233

Comprehension Skills

Author's Point of View

Remind the students that writers choose a *point of view* when they write. A first-person point of view tells the story through the eyes of a character. A third-person point of view tells the story through the eyes of an outside narrator.

Point out the following examples from pages 232 and 233 of this selection:

- "*I* was born . . ."
- "There were fifty houses in *our* hamlet . . ."
- "At night, *we* pulled the bridges into *our* houses and were safe."

Have students tell you what point of view the author uses to tell this story. (*first person*)

Explain to the students that *I*, *our*, and *we* are clue words, letting the reader know that the story is written in the first person. Discuss what they are likely to find out about the narrator compared with what they will find out about other characters.

←Skills Strand→

Author's Point of View
INTRODUCED: Unit 1, Lesson 3
REVIEWED: Unit 1, Lesson 5
Unit 1, Lesson 6
Unit 3, Lesson 1
Unit 3, Lesson 6

Teacher Tip Invite the students to compare the chores they do around their homes with the ones in this selection.

② Reading and Responding

Comprehension Strategies

Modeling

③ Visualizing *Can you picture the jungle? I imagine it being very hot and humid, with very tall trees and lots of green leafy plants covering the ground. What do you imagine?*

Prompting

④ Summarizing *Before we read about the author's memories, let's sum up the story so far to see if we understand everything. Huynh's family lived in a small hamlet or town on the river. For half of the year, they planted. The other half of the year, they hunted in the jungle. Who wants to continue the summary?*

Student Sample

Summarizing *His father had a college education, but also taught him how to hunt and look for food in the jungle. The war changed everything and his world was lost. Now, all he has are memories.*

Word Knowledge

Students learned about antonyms in the Word Knowledge section of this lesson. Have them identify antonyms they find on these pages *(edible, poisonous)*.

Like all farmers' children in the hamlet, I started working at the age of six. My seven sisters helped by working in the kitchen, weeding the garden, gathering eggs, or taking water to the cattle. I looked after the family herd of <u>water buffaloes</u>. Someone always had to be with the herd because no matter how carefully a water buffalo was trained, it always was ready to nibble young rice plants when no one was looking. Sometimes, too, I fished for the family while I guarded the herd, for there were plenty of fish in the flooded rice fields during the rainy season.

234

Meeting Individual Needs

Inter**v**ention

Summarizing If students have difficulty summarizing, you might ask, "What should you do when you have trouble summarizing?" *(reread)*

Inter**v**ention

Visualizing Review with students that good readers try to visualize what is happening in the text as they read it. This helps them to comprehend and remember the text. Point out that if students are having difficulty picturing something, it may be because they need to clarify terms or ideas in the description.

I was twelve years old when I made my first trip to the jungle with my father. I learned how to track game, how to recognize useful roots, how to distinguish edible mushrooms from poisonous ones. I learned that if birds, raccoons, squirrels, or monkeys had eaten the fruits of certain trees, then those fruits were not poisonous. Often they were not delicious, but they could calm a man's hunger and thirst.

My father, like most of the villagers, was a farmer and a hunter, depending upon the season. But he also had a college education, so in the evenings he helped to teach other children in our hamlet, for it was too small to afford a professional schoolteacher.

My mother managed the house, but during the harvest season she could be found in the fields, helping my father get the crops home; and as the wife of a hunter she knew how to dress and nurse a wound and took good care of her husband and his hunting dogs.

I went to the lowlands to study for a while because I wanted to follow my father as a teacher when I grew up. I always planned to return to my hamlet to live the rest of my life there. But war disrupted my dreams. The land I love was lost to me forever.

3

4 These stories are my memories. . . .

235

Comprehension Skills

Author's Point of View

A first-person point of view gives us a lot of information about how one character thinks and feels. A third-person point of view tells us about all of the characters.

■ Discuss with the students possible reasons the author had for choosing to write this selection in the first person.

■ How might the experience of reading this selection have changed if it were written in the third-person point of view? *(Answers may vary, but students may note that writing in the third person might make stories more distant or less realistic.)*

Teacher Tip Huynh Quang Nhuong mentions many animals. Students might enjoy making a picture book of the animals in Vietnam. Have them research animals that live in Vietnam. If possible, have them include photocopies of photographs or their own sketches of the animals.

Meeting Individual Needs

Challenge

Author's Point of View Have students practice using author's point of view by selecting a paragraph from this part of the selection and rewriting it in the third person. Have a volunteer reread his or her paragraph to the class. Then, have students comment on how writing the paragraph from a different point of view changes the meaning of the paragraph.

Intervention

Author's Point of View Have students look through other selections they have read and identify the point of view in these selections.

 **Reading and Responding**

Comprehension
Strategies

Modeling

5 **Making Connections** *His grandmother sounds very strong. My grandmother still plays tennis and walks a mile every day. But I'm not sure she would want to walk an hour to the market with a heavy load on her back! She'd take the car. I never thought about what she looked like when she was young, even though I've seen pictures of her. I think I'm going to see her in a new way, after reading this story.*

Modeling

6 **Making Connections** *I've never been to a Chinese Opera before, but I can better understand what it might be like by connecting it to theater productions I have seen here in the United States. Chinese Opera sounds a lot different from the kind of theater I've been to in this country. No one here would walk into the theater after the play has already started. And our theater doesn't usually last for five hours! Do any of you have connections with this part of the selection that you would like to share?*

> ### Word Knowledge
> *when, what*
>
> Students can use the skills they learned in the Word Knowledge section of this lesson to read these words. Remind students of this if they have difficulty decoding these words.

Opera and Karate

When she was eighty years old grandmother was still quite strong. She could use her own teeth to eat corn on the cob or to chew on sugar plants to extract juice from them. Every two days she walked for more than an hour to reach the marketplace, carrying a heavy load of food with her, and then spent another hour walking back home. And even though she was quite old, traces of her beauty still lingered on: Her hands, her feet, her face revealed that she had been an attractive young woman. Nor did time do **5** much damage to the youthful spirit of my grandmother.

One of her great <u>passions</u> was theater, and this passion never <u>diminished</u> with age. No matter how busy she was, she never missed a show when there was a group of actors in town. If no actors visited our hamlet for several months, she would organize her own show in which she was the manager, the producer, and the young leading lady, all at the same time.

My grandmother's own plays were always <u>melodramas</u> inspired by books she had read and by what she had seen on the stage. She always chose her favorite grandson to play the role of the hero. who would, without fail, marry the heroine at the end and live happily ever after. And when my sisters would tell her that she was getting too old to play the role of the young heroine anymore, my grandmother merely replied: "Anybody can play this role if she's young at heart."

When I was a little boy my grandmother often took me to see the opera. She knew Chinese <u>mythology</u> by heart, and the opera was often a <u>dramatization</u> of this mythology. On one special occasion, during the Lunar New Year celebrations—my favorite holiday, because children could do anything they wanted and by tradition no one could scold them—I accompanied my grandmother to the opera.

236

Meeting Individual Needs

> ### Intervention
>
> **Making Connections** Have students make connections to the story as they read. Parts of the selection may remind them of things they have experienced, seen, read about, or learned. Have students share these connections, comparing and contrasting them with those of others.

When we reached the theater I wanted to go in immediately. But my grandmother wanted to linger at the entrance and talk to her friends. She chatted for more than an hour. Finally we entered the theater, and at that moment the "Faithful One" was onstage, singing sadly. The "Faithful One" is a common character in Chinese opera. He could be a good minister, or a <u>valiant</u> general, or someone who loved and served his king faithfully. But in the end he is unjustly <u>persecuted</u> by the king, whose opinion of him has been changed by the lies of the "Flatterer," another standard character.

⑥   When my grandmother saw the "Faithful One" onstage she looked upset and gave a great sigh. I was too interested in what was happening to ask her the reason, and we spent the next five hours watching the rest of the opera. Sometimes I cried because my grandmother cried at the pitiful situation of the "Faithful One." Sometimes I became as angry as my grandmother did at the wickedness of the "Flatterer."

237

Meeting Individual Needs

Intervention

Author's Purpose Have the students review other selections in the anthology and discuss the author's purpose or purposes for writing them.

Comprehension
Skills

Author's Purpose

Explain to students that authors always have a purpose when they write. That purpose might be to *inform* the reader, to *explain* something to the reader, to *entertain* the reader by telling a good story, or to *persuade* the reader to think in a certain way.

Remind the students of the author's statement about having only his memories left. Have students discuss the possible purposes for the author writing this selection and how that statement might relate to his purpose.

←Skills Strand→

Author's Purpose

INTRODUCED: Unit 1, Lesson 1
REVIEWED: Unit 3, Lesson 1
                   Unit 4, Lesson 6
                   Unit 4, Lesson 7
                   Unit 5, Lesson 6

Teacher Tip   Remind students to think about what the selection tells them about heritage and how an autobiography is effective in communicating the unit theme.

② Reading and Responding

Comprehension Strategies

Modeling

❼ Making Connections *It's interesting to see how different other cultures can be. There are ways that I can connect with what I know of Chinese culture. I do know about chopsticks. I even use them sometimes. I know about karate, too, but imagine being taught karate from your great-great uncle. One thing never changes, though. There are bullies in every culture.*

Can anyone tell me why it was important for me to stop here and make a connection? Have any of you seen someone performing karate or using chopsticks? What do these things look like?

Teacher Tip To model making connections, share with the students thoughts or memories that come to mind as you read the selection aloud. Use as examples people you know who remind you of the characters in the selection, or articles you have read that correlate in some way with the subject of the reading.

Word Knowledge

There are many multisyllabic words in this selection. Be sure students are using the skills they learned in the Word Knowledge section of this lesson.

When we went home that night my grandmother was quite sad. She told my mother that she would have bad luck in the following year because when we entered the theater, the "Faithful One" was onstage. I was puzzled. I told my grandmother that she was confused. It would be a good year for us because we saw the good guy first. But my mother said, "No, son. The 'Faithful One' always is in trouble and it takes him many years to vindicate himself. Our next year is going to be like one of his bad years."

So, according to my mother's and grandmother's logic, we would have been much better off in the new year if we had been lucky enough to see the villain first!

My grandmother had married a man whom she loved with all her heart, but who was totally different from her. My grandfather was very shy, never laughed loudly, and always spoke very softly. And physically he was not as strong as my grandmother. But he excused his lack of physical strength by saying that he was a "scholar."

About three months after their marriage, my grandparents were in a restaurant and a rascal began to insult my grandfather because he looked weak and had a pretty wife. At first he just made insulting remarks, such as, "Hey! Wet chicken! This is no place for a weakling!"

My grandfather wanted to leave the restaurant even though he and my grandmother had not yet finished their meal. But my grandmother pulled his shirt sleeve and signaled him to remain seated. She continued to eat and looked as if nothing had happened.

Tired of yelling insults without any result, the rascal got up from his table, moved over to my grandparents' table, and grabbed my grandfather's chopsticks. My grandmother immediately wrested the chopsticks from him and struck the rascal on his cheekbone with her elbow. The blow was so quick and powerful that he lost his balance and fell on the floor.

238

Instead of finishing him off, as any street fighter would do, my grandmother let the rascal recover from the blow. But as soon as he got up again, he kicked over the table between him and my grandmother, making food and drink fly all over the place. Before he could do anything else, my grandmother kicked him on the chin. The kick was so swift that my grandfather didn't even see it. He only heard a heavy thud, and then saw the rascal tumble backward and collapse on the ground.

All the onlookers were surprised and delighted, especially the owner of the restaurant. Apparently the rascal, one of the best karate fighters of our area, came to this restaurant every day and left without paying for his food or drink, but the owner was too afraid to <u>confront</u> him.

7 While the rascal's friends tried to revive him, everyone else surrounded my grandmother and asked her who had taught her karate. She said, "Who else? My husband!"

239

Comprehension Skills

Author's Purpose

For more practice with author's purpose, have students complete pages 83–84 of the *Reading and Writing Workbook.*

Name _____ Date _____

Author's Purpose   *The Land I Lost*

Focus Writers have a purpose in mind when they write a selection.

> **An author's purpose**, or reason for writing a selection, can be
> • to inform.
> • to explain.
> • to persuade.
> • to entertain.

Identify Look through "The Land I Lost" and complete the following. What was the author's purpose for writing this story? Give examples from the story that support your opinion.

Answers will vary but may include the following.

Author's purpose: to explain what life was like for a young boy who was born and raised in Vietnam

Page: first page of the story

Example: "I was born on the central highlands of Vietnam in a small hamlet on a riverbank that had a deep jungle on one side and a chain of high mountains on the other."

Page: fourth page of the story

Example: "I went to the lowlands to study for a while because I wanted to follow my father as a teacher when I grew up. . . . But war disrupted my dreams. The land I loved was lost to me forever. These stories are my memories. . . ."

Reading and Writing Workbook • *Author's Purpose*   83

Author's Purpose *(continued)*

Practice Read the paragraphs below and write the author's purpose for each one.

To grow tomatoes, first plant seeds in soil in small starter pots. Water the pots and set them in a sunny place. Within a few days, you should see the seedlings coming up. Be sure to keep the soil moist. When the seedlings are about a foot high, plant them outside. Water them immediately.

Author's purpose: to explain

Tomatoes are one of the most popular items in the fresh produce section of the grocery store. Although most people think tomatoes are vegetables, they are actually fruits. In the early 1500s, tomatoes were called "love apples" and thought to be poisonous.

Author's purpose: to inform

Apply Write a paragraph about a person in history. Decide whether this paragraph will inform, explain, persuade, or entertain. Write its purpose. Then, write the paragraph.

Paragraphs will vary.

84   *Author's Purpose* • Reading and Writing Workbook

Reading and Writing Workbook pp. 83–84

Assessment

✔ **Formal** To assess students' progress with Author's Purpose, have them complete *Skills Assessment,* page 27.

Meeting Individual Needs

Reteach

Author's Purpose Have students who need additional instruction and practice with this concept complete *Reteach,* pages 83–84.

Challenge

Author's Purpose Have students who understand this concept complete *Challenge,* page 44.

2 Reading and Responding

Comprehension Strategies

Prompting

8 **Summarizing** *Now that we've come to the end of the selection, we should summarize again, to help us remember what happened. Huynh Quang Nhuong remembered his grandmother. She loved the theater and put on her own plays when she couldn't go. Who can continue the summary?*

Student Sample

Summarizing *She was great at karate. She once fought a bully who was bothering her and her husband. One day, she seemed to know that she was dying and that night she died.*

Discussing Strategy Use

After they have read the selection, have students share any problems they encountered and tell what strategies they used to solve them. Then, have them answer the following questions. If they answer "no" to any of the questions, have them reread part of the selection to find the answer.

■ Did they visualize events in the story?

■ Were they able to find connections between this story and experiences they have had in their own lives?

■ Did they summarize in order to help them understand what they've read?

Make sure that students explain how using the strategies helped them understand the selection better and how they read effectively to find answers to the questions they asked as they set purposes.

After the fight at the restaurant people assumed that my grandfather knew karate very well but refused to use it for fear of killing someone. In reality, my grandmother had received special training in karate from my great-great uncle from the time she was eight years old.

Anyway, after that incident, my grandfather never had to worry again. Anytime he had some business downtown, people treated him very well. And whenever anyone happened to bump into him on the street, they bowed to my grandfather in a very respectful way.

One morning my grandmother wanted me to go outside with her. We climbed a little hill that looked over the whole area, and when we got to the top she looked at the rice field below, the mountain on the horizon, and especially at the river. As a young girl she had often brought her herd of water buffaloes to the river to drink while she swam with the other children of the village. Then we visited the graveyard where her husband and some of her children were buried. She touched her husband's tombstone and said, "Dear, I will join you soon." And then we walked back

240

Teacher Tip Have students identify the techniques the author uses to communicate his ideas about heritage—vivid *imagery* to help the reader visualize his home, and *characterization* to help the reader make connections with the author's relationship with his grandmother. Remind students to apply those techniques when creating their heritage albums.

to the garden and she gazed at the fruit trees her husband had planted, a new one for each time she had given birth to a child. Finally, before we left the garden my sister joined us, and the two of them fed a few ducks swimming in the pond.

That evening my grandmother did not eat much of her dinner. After dinner she combed her hair and put on her best dress. We thought that she was going to go out again, but instead she went to her bedroom and told us that she didn't want to be disturbed.

The family dog seemed to sense something was <u>amiss</u>, for he kept looking anxiously at everybody and whined from time to time. At midnight my mother went to my grandmother's room and found that she had died, with her eyes shut, as if she were sleeping normally.

8 It took me a long time to get used to the reality that my grandmother had passed away. Wherever I was, in the house, in the garden, out on the fields, her face always appeared so clearly to me. And even now, many years later, I still have the feeling that my last conversation with her has happened only a few days before.

241

Comprehension Skills

Discussing the Selection

Following reading, engage the students in a discussion of the selection. Using the *handing-off process* will help the students to take responsibility for the discussion. In addition to the following questions, have them revisit any questions asked when they set purposes before the reading.

■ What did the author mean when he said that all he had now were memories? (*Answers may vary, but students should mention the disruption war causes.*)

■ What was the most interesting thing you remember about the author's family? (*Answers may vary. Students might mention the grandmother or learning to hunt in the jungle as the most interesting thing they remember.*)

■ How has this selection connected with your knowledge of the unit theme? (*Answers will vary—students should compare/contrast examples of heritage from this selection with their own experiences of past reading and use these connections to make a general statement about the unit theme.*)

During this time, have the students return to the clues and problems that they noted on the transparency before reading to determine whether the clues were borne out by the selection. Let the students decide which items deserve further discussion.

Teacher Tip In order for handing off to work effectively, a seating arrangement that allows students to see one another is essential. A circle or a semicircle is effective. In addition, all of the students need to have copies of the materials being discussed.

Meeting Individual Needs

ESL

Discussing the Selection Have English-language learners express themselves in either oral or written form. Emphasize their good ideas rather than error-free English.

Assessment

✓ **Formal** To assess students' reading comprehension, have them complete *Comprehension and Writing Assessment,* pages 55–56.

2 Reading and Responding

Meet the Author

After the students read the information about Huynh Quang Nhuong, discuss the following questions with them.

> **Huynh Quang Nhuong writes both fiction and nonfiction. Why would it be helpful to know how to do both styles of writing?** *(Possible answer: Knowing how to do both types of writing allows one's nonfiction to be more creative.)*

> **Huynh Quang Nhuong believes that "good literature reaches into the hearts of those who read it, no matter what country they are from." Why might he believe this?** *(Possible answer: He knows firsthand that good literature can affect a person, no matter what his or her nationality is, because he has lived in both Vietnam and the United States.)*

Meet the Illustrator

After the students read the information about Neil Waldman, discuss the following questions with them.

> **Why did Neil Waldman start drawing when he was a child?** *(Possible answer: He had a painful childhood, and drawing helped ease his pain and fear.)*

> **Why did Neil Waldman decide to become an illustrator?** *(Possible answer: He could earn a living doing what he loved the most.)*

The Land I Lost:

Adventures of a Boy in Vietnam

Meet the Author

Huynh Quang Nhuong was born in My Tho, Vietnam. He was a first lieutenant in the South Vietnamese Army, and was wounded during the Vietnam War. He came to the United States for medical treatment. Once in the U.S., he became a naturalized citizen. He now makes his home in Columbia, Missouri.

Mr. Nhuong is the first Vietnamese writer to write both fiction and nonfiction in English. He says, "I hope my books will make people from different countries happy. . . " He believes that good literature reaches into the hearts of all those who read it, no matter what country they are from, what age they are, or what they believe.

The Land I Lost was Mr. Nhuong's first book for children. It was published in five different languages and has received awards worldwide.

Meet the Illustrator

Neil Waldman had a painful childhood and art became his outlet. When he was young, he says, "I would retreat to my bedroom, close the door, and sit down with crayons and a sketch pad. As I watched amazing shapes and colors pour from my crayons onto the blank sheets of paper, I could feel the fear and tension dissolve." As an adult, he chose to be a children's book illustrator because it allowed him to earn a living while doing what he loved most. Some of Mr. Waldman's favorite books that he has illustrated are *The Never Ending Greenness*, *Bayou Lullaby*, and *Quetzal*.

242

Teacher Tip Ask students if they think an autobiography is an effective way to communicate ideas about heritage. Encourage them to incorporate what they have learned from the selection into the activities they will be working on for this unit.

Theme Connections

Think About It

With a small group of classmates, discuss the following questions.

- What were some of the important memories the author had of his childhood?
- Why were these memories so important to him?
- Do you have any memories of friends or family members that are important to you? Why are they important?

Record Ideas

Record in your Writing Journal what you have learned about heritage from this selection. Also note any new questions you have about the unit theme.

Improvise a Scene

The author's grandmother loved the theater so much that, when there were no actors in town, she created plays of her own and recruited people from town to act in them. With a partner, think of a part of the story, "The Land I Lost," that you particularly liked. Together, briefly outline the scene's sequence of events. Then, with your partner, act out the scene for two other people in your class, improvising character roles and dialogue.

243

Theme Connections

Think About It

- Ensure that students understand that our memories of friends and family help us develop a sense of who we are.
- Circulate among the groups, encouraging all students to contribute to the discussion.
- Remind students that *culture* is the arts, beliefs, and customs that make up a way of life for a group of people at a certain time; *heritage* is something handed down from earlier generations or from the past. Have students discuss the arts, beliefs, and customs that were part of the author's heritage. Then, have students discuss how the author's culture is similar to and different from their own.

Improvise a Scene

If necessary, point out that when improvising a scene, actors do not memorize lines from a script. Instead, they take a story that they already know, and then make up lines for the characters on the spot. Have students act out any part of the selection they choose and tell them to be creative in their interpretation of different character roles. However, emphasize that all action and dialogue must be based on the text.

2 **Responding**

Exploring the Theme

Selection Vocabulary

Have students write in their Writing Journals the definitions for words discussed before the reading of the selection and any other interesting words they clarified while reading. Students should be encouraged to refer to these words throughout the unit as they work on writing and unit activities. The words from this selection are:

hamlet   cultivate   passion   mythology

You may want to create a semantic map on the Concept/Question Board of key words from other resources, student activities, and family discussions, and add them to this semantic map.

Naranjas (Oranges).
1988. Carmen
Lomas Garza.
Gouache.20 × 14 in.
Collection of
Mr. and Mrs. Ira
Schneider,
Scottsdale, Arizona.
Photo by Wolfgang
Dietze.

Student Anthology p. 299

Reading/Writing Connections

Reread the paragraph where Huynh described his grandmother and discuss the details he used to create a vivid picture. Have students reflect on an incident in their lives involving an older member of their family. Have students write about that incident using specific details to describe the family member. Have students include descriptions of how the person talks, feels, and thinks about things.

View Fine Art

Naranjas, found on page 299 of the ***Student Anthology,*** was painted by an Hispanic artist, **Carmen Lomas Garza.** *Naranjas* is Spanish for *oranges.* Have students tell you what is happening in the painting. Lead them to see that woman's act of picking oranges is probably an everyday activity that is done out of necessity. Have students compare the type of food this woman is gathering with the types of food gathered by Huynh Quang Nhuong in "The Land I Lost: Adventures of a Boy in Vietnam."

Home Connection p. 35

Home Connection

The class has just finished reading "The Land I Lost," a selection that speaks of the author's memories of his childhood. An informational letter on "The Land I Lost," in both English and Spanish, can be found in the ***Home Connection*** guide.

Supporting Student Explorations

To help students with their unit activity topics, do the following:

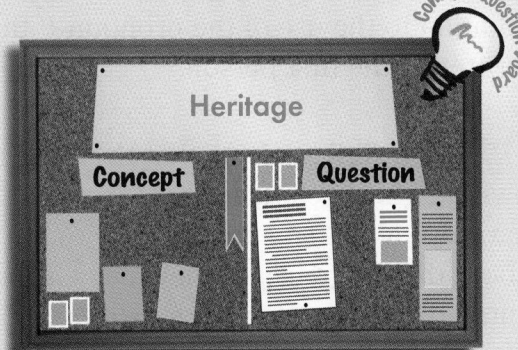 **Whole Group** Tell the students that they will interview family members and friends to learn more about their own heritage, then write several pieces to include in a heritage album. Explain that they will work at their own pace, but that they should try to complete at least two selections.

Schedule a library visit for your class. Ask the librarian to select books about heritage, and have each student check out several books. Have the students discuss their library books as they read them throughout the unit. Have them compare and contrast their own experiences with those of the story characters and post short summaries of the books on the Concept/Question Board. Also have them include an interesting technique that the authors of their library books may have used to communicate ideas about heritage, such as characterization or imagery, along with a brief review of the books and any questions they may have.

Have the students work in pairs to think of two or three questions they would like to ask the guest who will be visiting the class. Record the questions on chart paper. Then, as a class, decide on a final set of questions to ask the guest speaker.

Individual Have the students compare and contrast their own heritages with that of the guest and record their ideas in their Writing Journals.

Have students select books, magazine articles, Websites, and other sources to aid their research. Suggest that students post on the Concept/Question Board brief descriptions of sources of information that they have found to be especially helpful in their explorations of heritage. Encourage students who are having difficulty finding information to check sources on the Board and to post their questions as well.

Inquiry Journal Have students complete page 41 of the *Inquiry Journal.* Have them record their ideas about how "The Land I Lost: Adventures of a Boy in Vietnam" added to their knowledge of heritage.

Teacher Tip Many of the selections in this unit are by well-known children's authors. Give the librarian a list of their names so that he or she may find other books by these authors for the students to choose from.

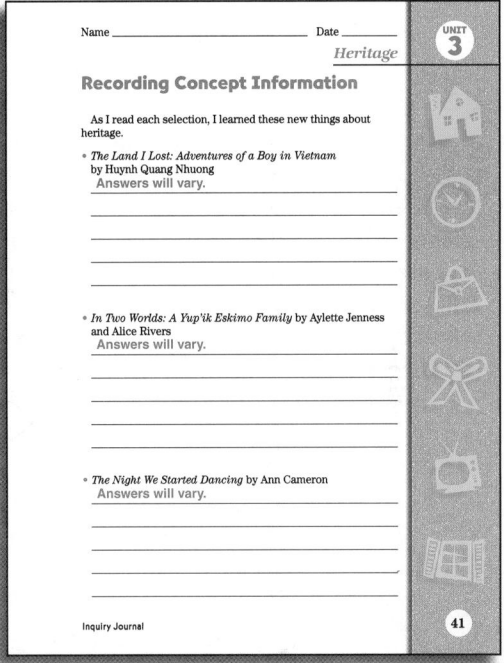

Inquiry Journal p. 41

Assessment

✔ **Informal** Keeping an anecdotal record of students' progress is an effective method of informal assessment. Note whether students:

- compare and contrast their heritage with that of story characters and the guest speaker.
- identify techniques authors use to inform readers about heritage.

③ Integrating the Curriculum

Teacher Tip Discuss why an author might choose to use a first-person narrator or a third-person narrator. Students might suggest that authors write in the first-person in order to bring readers closer to one particular character and experience the story from inside that character's mind. If an author wants to "get inside the heads" of other characters as well, he or she may write in the third person.

Teacher Tip Remind students to use what they have learned about brainstorming and writing narratives in their unit activities.

Assessment

✓ **Informal** Take this opportunity to assess students' progress with the writing process by commenting on the entries in their Writing Journals.

Language Arts

Writing

Writing a Narrative

Instruct Explain to students that one of the first things an author must do when writing a story or *narrative* is decide who will tell the story.

- Prompt students to tell you that stories written in the *first person* are narrated by one of the characters in a story. In these narratives, first-person pronouns such as *I, me, we,* and *us* are used and the narrator can describe his or her own experiences, thoughts, and feelings but not those of other characters.

- When a story is told by a narrator who is not a character in the story, then the story is written in the *third person*. These stories use third-person pronouns such as *he, she,* and *they,* and the narrator can reveal how all of the characters in a story think and feel about story events. However, many of these stories focus on only one main character.

Practice Ask the students whether Huynh Nhoung used a first-person or a third-person narrator in this selection, and how they know.

Have students look through the text to see if they notice anything, in addition to the use of the pronoun *I,* that tells them that this story is written in the first person.

Apply Tell students that they will be writing a narrative about their own heritage. Tell them that they may want to write a third-person narrative about an experience with a friend or relative that taught them about their heritage, or they may choose to write their own autobiographies, in the first person.

Writing Process

Prewrite Students will begin the process of writing a narrative by brainstorming ideas. Encourage them to think, talk to other students, and jot down story ideas as they come to mind. Encourage them to list key words and phrases they want to develop in their stories. Remind them to consider whether they want to write from the first-person or third-person point of view.

Literary Elements

Recognizing Autobiography

Instruct Ask students to tell what characteristics of an autobiography they already know and create a list on the chalkboard. Discuss the differences between biographies and autobiographies. A *biography* is nonfiction that tells about the life of a real person. An *autobiography* is a story about a person's life written by herself or himself.

Have students look at the first page of "The Land I Lost." Point out that the story was written in the first person. The author uses the word *I* to let readers know whom the story is about. Have students discuss any other autobiographies they may have read. Have books for students to browse through as examples, such as *When I Was Young in the Mountains* by Cynthia Rylant; *Boy: Tales of Childhood* by Roald Dahl; *A Grain of Wheat: A Writer Begins* by Clyde Bulla; or *My Life with Martin Luther King, Jr.* by Coretta Scott King.

Practice Using the books you have made available, have students select one and skim through it. Have them write down five sentences that the author uses to notify the readers that the book is an autobiography.

Apply Remind students that if they write their own autobiographies or personal narratives, the writing should be from their point of view.

For more practice with autobiography, have students complete *Reading and Writing Workbook* pages 85–86.

Meeting Individual Needs

Reteach

Recognizing Autobiography Have students who need additional instruction and practice with this concept complete *Reteach,* pages 85–86.

Challenge

Recognizing Autobiography Have students who understand this concept and could benefit from extended practice complete *Challenge,* page 45.

Teacher Tip It is important to review books before recommending them to students, to evaluate whether or not they are appropriate for use in your classroom.

Teacher Tip Discuss with students that an autobiography:
- is written by a person about his or her own life.
- contains important information about a person's life, such as how he or she talks, feels, and thinks about things.
- spans the person's life, or part of the person's life.
- is usually told in chronological order.
- focuses on the most important events in a person's life, such as that person's achievements or talents.

Reading and Writing Workbook pp. 85–86

Name _____ Date _____

Recognizing Autobiography
The Land I Lost

Focus An **autobiography** is the true story of a person's life. It is written by a person about his or her own life.

> An **autobiography**
> - allows the reader to learn a lot about the person.
> - allows the writer to share his or her feelings and life experiences with others.
> - allows the writer to share what it was like to live in a certain place and during a certain time.

Identify Look through "The Land I Lost: Adventures of a Boy in Vietnam" for the following information.

1. What parts of the title are clues that this story is an autobiography?
   the pronoun "I"; the subtitle which explains who "I" refers to

2. What does Huynh give the most details about on the first two pages of the story? What are his feelings toward what he describes?
   He describes where he lives—the country, the land, his village, the weather, and the animals. He loved the land where he lived.

3. What person, other than Huynh, is the rest of the story mainly about, and how did Huynh feel about the person?
   He mainly talks about his grandmother. Huynh loved and admired his grandmother.

Reading and Writing Workbook • Recognizing Autobiography **85**

Recognizing Autobiography *(continued)*

Practice Read each pair of book titles. Underline the titles that are likely to be autobiographies.

1. *How the West Was Won*   *How I Helped Tame the West*
2. *My Life As a Clown*   *Clowns in the Circus of Life*
3. *The Way I See It: My Ideas on Education*   *The Opinions of Two Scholars*
4. *Memories of a Globetrotter*   *The Day the Globetrotters Came to Town*
5. *The Land Beyond the Mountains*   *My Life Beyond the Mountains*

Apply Write an autobiographical paragraph about an important event, experience, or time in your life. Paragraphs will vary.

_____
_____
_____
_____
_____
_____
_____
_____
_____
_____

86 *Recognizing Autobiography • Reading and Writing Workbook*

3 Integrating the Curriculum

Meeting Individual Needs

Reteach

Syllable Boundary Patterns Have students who need additional instruction and practice with this concept complete **Reteach,** pages 87–88.

Challenge

Syllable Boundary Patterns Challenge students to divide the following words into syllables: *marketplace, eggplant, grandmother, unfaithfulness,* and *delight.* Have students who might benefit from extended practice of this concept complete **Challenge,** page 46.

Syllable Boundary Patterns

INTRODUCED: Unit 3, Lesson 1

REVIEWED: Unit 3, Lesson 4

Unit 5, Lesson 6

Have students check for correct spelling of syllable boundary patterns when proofreading their narrative writing and unit activities.

Spelling

Syllable Boundary Patterns

Instruct Tell students that breaking a word into syllables sometimes can help them figure out how to pronounce or spell an unfamiliar word. Write the word *hamlet* on the chalkboard. Ask students if they know how to divide this word into syllables; you may want to remind them that each syllable must contain a single vowel sound. Point out that *hamlet* has two consonants between the vowels. This word can be divided into syllables between the two consonants. *(ham/let)* Have students take turns dividing the words *active, shallow, elbow,* and *husband. (ac/tive, shal/low, el/bow, hus/band)*

Let students know that in this type of word, the vowel in the first syllable is often a short vowel. Also, some words of this type have double consonants, and the words can often be broken into syllables between the double consonants.

Tell students that when a word has three consonants between vowels, they should divide the word between the consonant and the consonant blend, or digraph, as in *cen/tral and pan/ther.* Have them divide the words *explore, control, approve,* and *instant. (ex/plore, con/trol, ap/prove, in/stant)*

Practice Have students skim the selection and write down at least five words that follow either of these syllable patterns. Have them exchange papers with a classmate and divide the partner's words into syllables. Have them check their work with a dictionary.

Apply For additional practice, have students complete **Reading and Writing Workbook** pages 87–88. *Reading and Writing Workbook pp. 87–88*

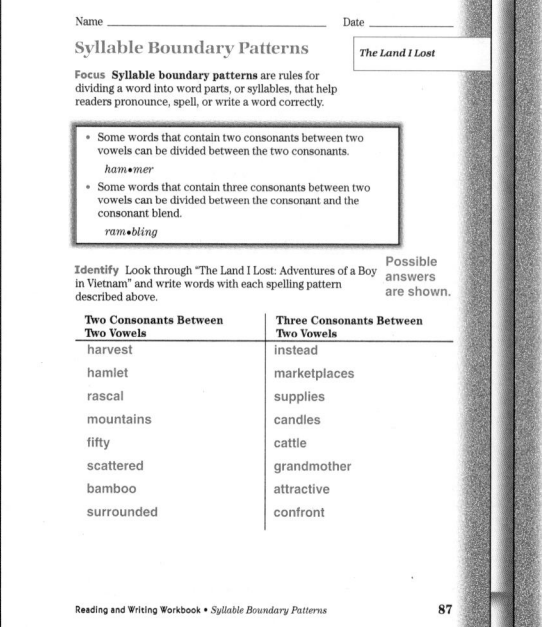

Grammar, Usage, and Mechanics

Pronoun Referents

Instruct Remind students that pronouns are words that take the place of nouns. The nouns they replace are called pronoun referents, or antecedents. Pronouns must agree in number, gender, and person with the nouns that they replace. Refer to the Teacher Tip for rules.

Practice Write the following paragraph on a transparency or the chalkboard, and have students identify the pronouns and the nouns to which they refer.

> Jacob has always liked to write stories. He writes everyday in his journal. Yesterday, Jacob wrote about his trip to the beach. It was fun. Jacob's parents let him swim in the ocean. They are planning another trip for next year.

Apply Remind students that when they are writing, they need to be sure to use the correct pronoun to replace a noun. Have students look through their *Writing Folders* for a piece that contains several pronouns. Have them circle each pronoun, underline the noun or nouns to which each refers, and then trade papers with a classmate to check each other's work.

For additional practice, have students complete ***Reading and Writing Workbook*** pages 89–90.

Teacher Tip

Rules for Using Pronouns
- Use singular pronouns such as *I*, *you*, *he*, *she*, or *it* to take the place of singular nouns.
- Use plural pronouns such as *we*, *you*, or *they* to take the place of plural nouns.
- Use possessive pronouns to take the place of possessive nouns. Possessive pronouns, such as *my*, *your*, *his*, *her*, *its*, *our*, and *their*, show ownership. They appear before the noun. Possessive pronouns, such as *yours*, *his*, *hers*, *its*, *ours*, and *theirs*, stand alone.
- The antecedent, or referent, of a pronoun should always be clear. If it is not clear, use the noun again.

Meeting Individual Needs

Reteach

Pronoun Referents Have students who need additional instruction and practice with this concept complete *Reteach,* pages 89–90.

Challenge

Pronoun Referents Have students discuss the ambiguity of the following sentence: *Yusuf saw Ted eating his sandwich.* Have the students invent a context that will let the reader know that the sandwich belonged to Yusuf, such as . . . *so he yelled "Stop, thief!"* Have students who might benefit from extended practice with this concept complete *Challenge* page 47.

Reading and Writing Workbook pp. 89–90

Name _____ Date _____

Pronoun Referents   [*The Land I Lost*]

Focus Knowing how to make pronouns agree with the nouns they refer to can make your writing clearer and more accurate.

> A **pronoun** is a word that takes the place of and refers to a noun. The noun is the **antecedent** or **referent** that the pronoun replaces. A pronoun must agree in number, gender, and person with its antecedent.
> - Use singular pronouns to replace singular nouns.
> - Use plural pronouns to replace plural nouns.
> - Use subject pronouns to replace nouns used as subjects.
>   Byron ran the marathon. He won the race.
> - Use object pronouns to replace nouns used as objects.
>   Byron told his friends that he won. He told them on Saturday.
> - Use possessive pronouns to replace possessive nouns.
>   Byron's friends were happy. His friends were also surprised.

Practice Read each sentence. Write a pronoun that can replace the underlined word or words.

1. Martin no longer goes to this school. __He__
2. Last week I fixed the computer's disk drive. __its__
3. This bike belongs to Harry and Michelle Jones. __them__
4. Did Betsy say she was going to attend the meeting? __she__
5. The presents are for Allen and me. __us__
6. Maybe the flowers will last until Sunday. __they__

Reading and Writing Workbook • *Pronoun Referents*   89

Pronoun Referents *(continued)*

Write the correct pronoun in each blank to complete each sentence or pair of sentences.

7. Mario's bike is new. __His__ bike is quite expensive.
8. The car has a dent on __its__ rear fender.
9. Maggie is a police officer. __She__ graduated from the police academy last week.
10. Ali called her cousins on the phone. She told __them__ to meet her at the mall at noon.

Apply Rewrite the following paragraphs, replacing the underlined word or words with the correct pronouns.

> Margaret works in a day care center. Margaret takes care of four-year-olds. Margaret thinks four-year-olds are lots of fun. Last week one of the four-year-olds made a car out of clay. Margaret didn't think the clay looked much like a car, but four-year-old Michael did.
> "Look," said Michael. "Here's the car's steering wheel, and these are the tires." Then Michael picked up Michael's clay car and changed the clay car into a pancake!

Margaret works in a day care center. She takes care of four-year-olds. She thinks they are lots of fun. Last week one of them made a car out of clay. Margaret didn't think it looked much like a car, but four-year-old Michael did.

"Look," said Michael. "Here's its steering wheel, and these are the tires." Then he picked up his clay car and changed it into a pancake!

90   *Pronoun Referents* • Reading and Writing Workbook

 Skills Strand

Pronoun Referents

INTRODUCED: Unit 3, Lesson 1
REVIEWED: Unit 5, Lesson 2
Unit 6, Lesson 5

3 Integrating the Curriculum

Teacher Tip Tell students that they will be interviewing people for information to use in their unit activities.

Meeting Individual Needs

ESL

Interview Questions Set up opportunities for conversational practice. Have English-language learners pair up with native English-speaking students to brainstorm interview questions.

Listening/Speaking/Viewing

Interview Questions

Have students brainstorm a list of questions about their own heritage that they would like to have answered, and then work in small groups to revise and refine their questions. Ask them to be on the lookout for questions that are either too narrow (such as questions that have *yes* or *no* answers) or too broad (such as, "What was life like when you were young?"). Have students use these questions to interview older family members or friends and then record the answers in their ***Writing Folders***. Have students use the information they gathered while working on their personal narratives during the course of this unit.

In a group discussion, have students take turns telling the class one interesting and appropriate thing they learned about their heritage that they did not already know. (Hold one-on-one conferences with the students so that you can assess whether or not their stories are appropriate in nature before having students share them with the class.) Then, have students discuss connections, differences, and similarities between the types of information they all shared to deepen their understanding of their own heritage and that of their peers.

Study and Research

Using a Dictionary or Glossary

Instruct   Have students tell you where they can find the meanings, pronunciations, derivations, and parts of speech for unfamiliar words. Students should mention that all of these things are found in a dictionary. If necessary, tell them that they are also found in a *glossary*. A *glossary* is the section in the back of a book that gives the meanings of words that appear in that book.

Have students turn to their ***Student Anthology*** glossary and compare it to a dictionary. Point out that, like a dictionary, their glossary contains *entry words* (each word defined in a dictionary or glossary) listed in alphabetical order. There are also *guide words* at the top of each page— one on the left indicating the first word defined on the page and one on the right indicating the last word defined on the page. Have students also note that in their glossary they can find a word's part of speech, definition, and, in some cases, a word's derivations and history.

Practice   Have students compare the dictionary and glossary entries for the words *arc* and *bow*. Students should note that their glossary contains only the meanings and parts of speech for those words as they are used in their ***Student Anthology*** selections. The dictionary, however, contains more than one part of speech and many other definitions for the same words. They may find that the word history for *bow* is written very differently in each resource; oftentimes, in a dictionary, the word's history is abbreviated in brackets (the meanings of the abbreviations can be found in the front of the dictionary). The list of word derivations for *arc* is probably more detailed in their glossary than students will find under a single dictionary entry for the same word.

Apply   Tell students to compare dictionary and glossary entries for *forlorn, sphere, perspective,* and *recede* and discuss their findings. Then, have students complete ***Inquiry Journal*** page 44 as a group.

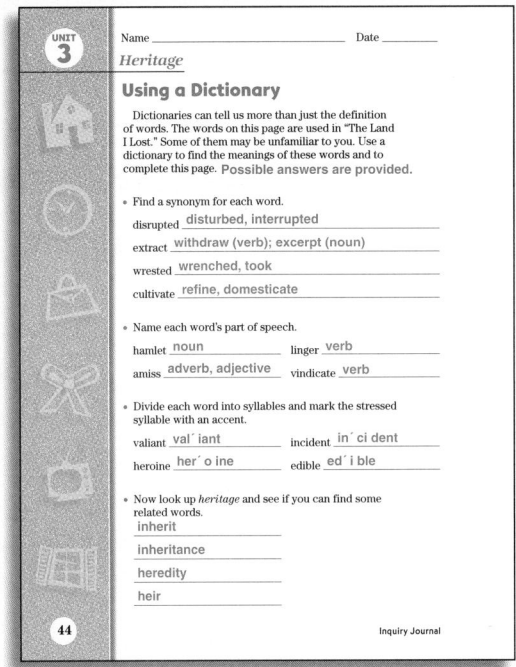

Inquiry Journal p. 44

Teacher Tip   Tell students that most dictionaries include the spelling, pronunciation, part of speech, and meaning of the word. Other types of information they may find include the following:

- synonyms, antonyms, or cross-references
- sentences using the word in context
- spelling of the word's plural form
- spelling of the word with different affixes
- history of the word

Assessment

✓ **Formal** To assess students' understanding of this concept, have them complete ***Skills Assessment,*** page 28.

Across the Curriculum

 ## Social Studies

Heritage Map

Purpose

To help students learn more about their heritage and geography

Materials

world map, photo or drawing of family member or friend, straight pins

Procedure

Students will create a heritage map to help them find a friend's or their own roots.

- Have students ask a family member or friend from what region of the United States or another country their family comes.

- Provide a large map of the world to hang on the wall. Model the procedure by pinning a photo or drawing of a family member or friend on the map on the place he or she came from.

- Have students pin their photos or drawings on the map.

- Display the heritage map in the classroom and discuss the diversity of origins of people who have come to live in the United States.

 ## Art

A Coat of Arms

Purpose

To help students focus on family characteristics and heritage

Materials

drawing paper, colored pencils or crayons

Procedure

- Begin by explaining that a flag tells something about the country it represents. On the United States flag, for example, the red stripes stand for courage; the white for purity; the thirteen stripes for the thirteen original colonies; and the fifty stars for the fifty states of today. A family, too, may have an emblem, or coat of arms, with elements that represent something about their heritage.

- Ask students what Huynh's family's coat of arms might have on it. They may think of such things as a water buffalo to represent the hard work they did on the family farm; a jungle, where Huynh learned to hunt with his father; or a theater stage because it played a large role in their lives.

- Tell students to think about their heritage. Have them talk with other family members and friends to decide what is important about their heritage.

- When students have decided what symbols to use to represent their heritage, distribute the drawing materials. Have students draw their coats of arms.

- Display the coats of arms in the classroom, and allow the students to take turns explaining to the rest of the class the meaning of the symbols and colors they chose.

Across the Curriculum

 **Math**

Graphing Family Holidays

Purpose

To practice graph and chart skills by creating graphs and charts

Procedure

Tell students that they will make a graph showing how many people in the classroom celebrate various common holidays.

- Generate holidays to be graphed by asking students to call out various holidays they celebrate with their families and friends, and write them on the chalkboard.

- Poll students to find out how many celebrate each holiday, and write the number next to the holiday.

- Have students record this information in a bar graph.

- For further practice, the information could also be put into a pie chart.

 **Social Studies**

A Letter to Future Grandchildren

Purpose

To encourage students to think about what they may pass on to future generations

Procedure

Encourage discussion by asking questions such as the following:

Has an older relative or friend ever given you something special that belonged to them? If you could pass something along to your future grandchildren or great grandchildren, what would it be?

- Ask students to think of one special item they own that they could pass on to a grandchild. It could be a favorite toy, a picture, a book, a piece of clothing, or anything that is special to the student.

- Ask students to write a letter to the imaginary grandchild, explaining why they have chosen this item and passing along any personal information they would like to include.

- Students may share their items and letters with partners if they wish to do so.

About the Authors

Aylette Jenness worked on her two previous books about life in Alaska while living in Scammon Bay.

Alice Rivers was a teenager at the time and worked for Jenness as a baby-sitter. Twenty-five years later, the two women decided to collaborate on a book. Jenness wrote the accounts of changes in Scammon Bay. Rivers provided a first-person account of growing up in Scammon Bay and of her life today. She also encouraged her mother, sister, husband, and children to contribute to the book.

Students can read more about Aylette Jenness and Alice Rivers on page 260 of the *Student Anthology.*

Other Books by Aylette Jenness
- *Gussuk Boy*
- *A Life of Their Own: An Indian Family in Latin America*
- *Dwellers of the Tundra*
- *Along the Niger River*
- *Families*

Selection Summary

Genre: Nonfiction

This vivid photographic portrait features a family living in Alaska on the coast of the Bering Sea. Three generations tell about their lives and customs, and about how they strive to adopt the best of modern ways without abandoning their traditional values.

Exploring the Theme

Selection Concepts

"In Two Worlds," excerpted from a book by the same name, is a vivid portrait of a family living in Alaska. Three generations tell about their lives and customs and about how they adopted the best of the modern world without abandoning their traditional values. Key concepts to be explored are:

- Families can maintain traditional values while adopting modern ways.
- Physical environment has a significant impact on a society's customs.

 Check the Reading link of the **SRA** web page for links to theme-related Websites.
http://www.sra4kids.com

Exploration Activity Tips

Before Reading, have the students browse the selection illustrations and predict what the story might be about. Have them formulate some questions they think the selection can answer.

During Reading, have students pay particular attention to *point of view* and share how they might make interesting use of this skill in their heritage albums.

After Reading, have students discuss ways that tradition and customs can be passed from one generation to the next. Then have students update the Concept/Question Board. Some may want to revise their activity plans based on what they have learned from the selection.

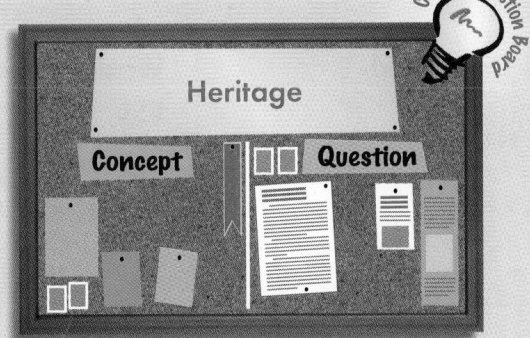

Unit 3 Exploration Management

Lesson 1	Listen to and interview a class guest about heritage. Select and read library books about heritage.
Lesson 2 In Two Worlds: A Yup'ik Eskimo Family	**Collaborative Exploration** **Identify genres for inclusion in heritage albums. Reflect on one's own heritage, interview family members and friends about customs and traditions, and begin writing.** **Supplementary Activity** **Discuss appropriate genres for pieces in heritage albums. Students meet in small groups to share stories about their heritage.**
Lesson 3	Identify and utilize various literary techniques. Writing begins on second selection for student albums.
Lesson 4	Work on unit activity continues. Discuss with relatives what they want to communicate about their heritage.
Lesson 5	Write autobiographical sketches for author pages and consider modeling a character after a family member or friend.
Lesson 6	Prepare final drafts, complete illustrations, prepare title and copyright pages, and bind books. Write thank-you notes to those who helped with activity.
Lesson 7	Students present a selected piece from their heritage albums.

Lesson Planner

Suggested Pacing: 3–5 days	DAY 1	DAY 2	
	DAY 1	**DAY 2**	
Part 1 **Preparing to Read** **Materials** ■ Student Anthology, pp. 244–261 ■ Transparencies 16, 44	**Word Knowledge** ■ Reading the Words and Sentences, p. 244G ■ Developing Oral Language, p. 244G **Build Background, p. 244H** **Preview and Prepare, p. 244I** **Selection Vocabulary, p. 244I** *intricate, precarious, resource, secluded, traditional*	**Preview and Prepare, p. 244I** ■ Review Transparency 44	
Part 2 **Reading and Responding** **Materials** ■ Student Anthology, pp. 244–263 ■ Teacher Observation Log ■ Reading and Writing Workbook, pp. 91–92 ■ Inquiry Journal, p. 41 ■ Transparency 46 ■ Home Connection, p. 37	**Student Anthology, pp. 244–253** **Comprehension Strategies** ■ Asking Questions, pp. 244, 248, 252 ■ Clarifying, p. 246 ■ Summarizing, pp. 246, 250, 252	**Student Anthology, pp. 253–261** **Comprehension Strategies** ■ Clarifying, p. 254 ■ Summarizing, pp. 256, 258 **Discussing Strategy Use, p. 258** **Comprehension Skills** ■ Discussing the Selection, p. 259 **Exploring the Theme** ■ Selection Vocabulary, p. 263A *intricate, precarious, resource, secluded, traditional*	
Part 3 **Integrating the Curriculum** **Materials** ■ Student Anthology, pp. 244–261 ■ Reading and Writing Workbook, pp. 93–96 ■ Transparencies 45, 47 ■ Inquiry Journal, pp. 45–46	**Writing** ■ Indicators of Time and Order, p. 263C **Literary Elements** ■ Purposes of Types of Texts, p. 263D	**Writing Process** ■ Prewrite, p. 263C **Vocabulary** ✓■ Use a Dictionary, p. 263E	
Independent Work Time **Materials** ■ Reteach, pp. 91–96 ■ ESL Supplement ■ Challenge, pp. 48–50 ■ Intervention Guide ■ Listening Library Audiocassette	**Writing Process Continued** **ESL** ■ Word Meaning, p. 244G **Intervention** ■ Word Knowledge, p. 244G **Unit Project** ■ Reflect on Heritage ■ Interview Family and Friends ■ Begin Writing	**Writing Process Continued** **ESL** ■ Vocabulary, p. 244G **Intervention** ■ Comprehension, p. 244 **Unit Project Continued**	

✓ Informal **Assessment Available**   ✓ Formal **Assessment Available**

DAY 2 continued	**DAY 3**	
DAY 3	**DAY 4**	**DAY 5**

General Review	General Review	Review Word Knowledge

Student Anthology, pp. 244–261 **Comprehension Skills** ■ Main Idea and Details, pp. 245, 247, 249 **Theme Connections** ■ Think About It, p. 261 ■ Make a Time Line, p. 261	**Student Anthology, pp. 244–263** **Comprehension Skills** ✓■ Compare and Contrast, pp. 251, 253, 255, 257 **Poetry, pp. 262–263** **Exploring the Theme** ■ Reading/Writing Connections, p. 263A ■ View Fine Art, p. 263A ■ Supporting Student Explorations, p. 263B	**Student Anthology, pp. 244–261** ■ Review Selection ■ Complete Discussion ■ Reread Selection in Pairs **Home Connection, p. 263A** ■ Discuss "In Two Worlds: A Yup'ik Eskimo Family" ■ Compare and contrast lifestyles

Writing Process Continued **Grammar, Usage, and Mechanics** ✓■ Regular and Irregular Verbs, p. 263F **Listening/Speaking/Viewing** ■ Interpret Speakers' Messages, p. 263G	**Writing Process Continued** **Study and Research** ■ Interviewing, p. 263H	**Across the Curriculum** **Social Studies** ■ Come to Alaska, p. 263H ■ Trade with Scammon Bay, p. 263J **Science** ■ Wildlife in Alaska, p. 263H **Art** ■ Animal Carving, p. 263J

Writing Process Continued **Reteach** ✓■ Using a Dictionary, *Reteach*, pp. 93–94 **Challenge** ✓■ Using a Dictionary, *Challenge*, p. 49 ■ Main Idea and Details, p. 247 **Unit Project Continued**	**Writing Process Continued** **Reteach** ✓■ Regular and Irregular Verbs, *Reteach*, pp. 95–96 **Challenge** ✓■ Regular and Irregular Verbs, *Challenge*, p. 50 **Intervention** ■ Compare and Contrast, p. 253 **Unit Project Continued**	**Writing Process Continued** **Reteach** ✓■ Compare and Contrast, *Reteach*, pp. 91–92 **Challenge** ✓■ Compare and Contrast, *Challenge*, p. 48 **Unit Project Continued**

Meeting Individual Needs
Independent Work Time

Preparing to Read

Meeting Individual Needs

ESL
- Word Meaning, p. 244G
- Cultural Context, p. 244H
- Vocabulary, p. 244J

Intervention
- Word Knowledge, p. 244G

Reading and Responding

Meeting Individual Needs

Reteach
- Compare and Contrast, *Reteach*, pp. 91–92

ESL
- Main Idea and Details, p. 249

Challenge
- Main Idea and Details, p. 247
- Compare and Contrast, *Challenge*, p. 48

Intervention
- Comprehension, p. 244
- Summarizing, pp. 246, 252
- Main Idea and Details, p. 247
- Compare and Contrast, p. 253
- Clarifying, p. 254

Integrating the Curriculum

Meeting Individual Needs

Reteach
- Using a Dictionary, *Reteach*, pp. 93–94
- Regular and Irregular Verbs, *Reteach*, pp. 95–96

ESL
- Sharing Ideas, p. 263G

Challenge
- Using a Dictionary, *Challenge*, p. 49
- Regular and Irregular Verbs, *Challenge*, p. 50

Formal Assessment Options

Use these assessment pages along with your informal observations to gauge student progress.

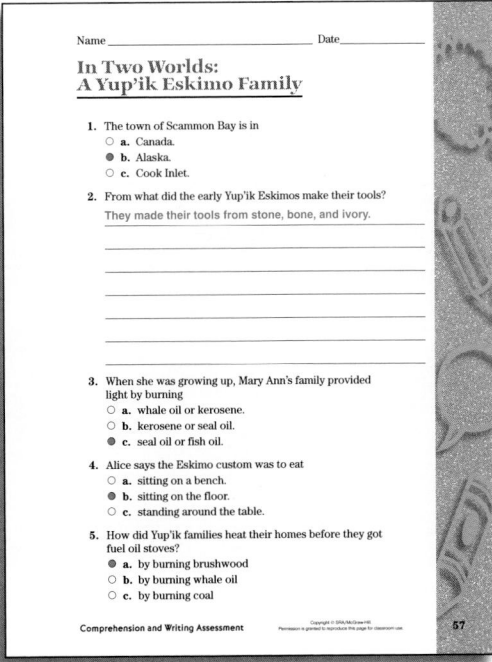

Comprehension and Writing Assessment, p. 57

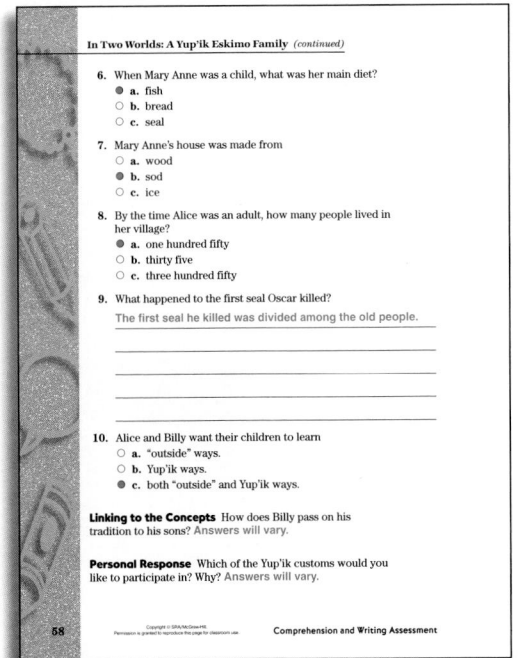

Comprehension and Writing Assessment, p. 58

① Preparing to Read

Meeting Individual Needs

ESL

Word Meaning Make sure English-language learners understand the meanings of the words before they do the exercises. Refer to Unit 3, Lesson 2, of the **ESL Supplement** for specific suggestions.

Intervention

Word Knowledge Have students scan the story for other words that have an s consonant blend or the /oo/ sound. Make a list of the new words and review them with the students. For students who need more help, see Unit 3, Lesson 2, of the **Intervention Guide.**

Teacher Tip Knowledge of the genre the author has chosen helps students anticipate the type of content they will encounter. For example, knowledge that this selection is a nonfiction biography primes them to expect to read about specific individuals.

Word Knowledge

Reading the Words and Sentences

Write each word and sentence on the chalkboard. Have students read each word together. After all the words have been read, have students read each sentence in natural phrases or chunks. Use the suggestions in About the Words to discuss the different features of the listed words.

Line 1:	small little withered shrank netted caught
Line 2:	Scammon vast spawned snow skimmed
Line 3:	tool school food
Sentence 1:	In the small lagoon, we netted the most fish we had ever caught.
Sentence 2:	In Scammon Bay, the vast, snow-covered tundra stretches as far as you can see.
Sentence 3:	At school, we use special tools in the kitchen to prepare food.

About the Words

- Line 1 contains words that are synonyms. Synonyms are words with similar meanings.

- The words in Line 2 all have an *s*-consonant blend. Invite students to think of other words with *s*-consonant blends.

- All of the words in Line 3 have the digraph *oo* pronounced /ōō/. Practice making this sound and then have the children find examples of other words with *oo* pronounced /ōō/ in their selections.

Developing Oral Language

To review the words, have students do one or both of the following activities.

- Give the opposites for the words in Line 1 and have students find the antonym, for example, *large*.

- Have a student choose two words from the chalkboard and use them in a sentence. Then have another student use the same two words, plus another word from the chalkboard in a sentence. Continue until no more words can be added. Have the students use the words in different sentence combinations.

Build Background

Activate Prior Knowledge

Have students check the Concept/Question Board to refresh their memories about heritage. Discuss the following with students to find out what they may already know about the selection and have already learned about the unit theme. Tell students to use their prior knowledge to help them comprehend what they are about to read.

- Ask students whether they are familiar with the selection they are about to read, and if so, to tell a little bit about it.

- Have students share what they know about Alaska or the Eskimo peoples. Have them discuss ideas about how the culture of these people is similar to or different from that of those living in the other 49 states.

- Ask students if they remember any other stories that are about family life in the past, present, or future.

Background Information

The following information may help the students to better understand the selection they are about to read.

- Tell students that in the selection "In Two Worlds: A Yup'ik Eskimo Family," the authors compare life as it was for parents and grandparents of the past, to life as it is for people today in the community of Scammon Bay, Alaska.

- A small map showing Alaska, the Bering Sea, and Scammon Bay can be found on page 246 of the selection. You might also help students to identify Alaska and the Bering Sea on a large map or globe.

- Tell students that the Yup'ik is one major group of Native Alaskan people. When questioned about the use of the term *Eskimo*, members of the group said that it is commonly used among the native peoples and that it is not considered offensive. However, they appreciate being called by the name of their specific Alaskan cultures, such as Inuit or Yup'ik.

Writing Journal Tell the students that after reading they will be jottting down in their Writing Journals their reactions to the story. Have them be on the lookout for any ideas they may have for using the past, present, and future in their heritage albums.

Teacher Tip Explain to students that in this selection the author uses comparisons and contrasts to highlight the similarities and differences between past and present.

Preparing to Read

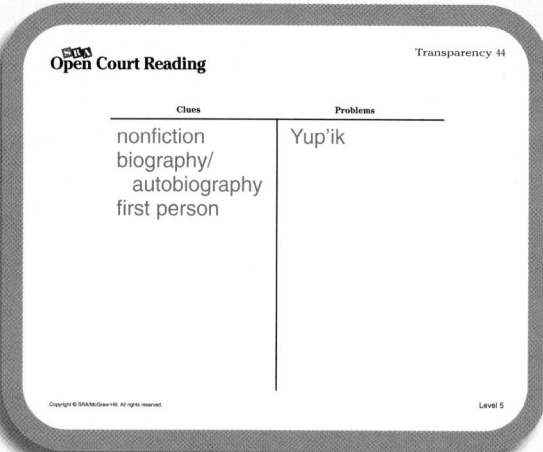

Transparency 44

Teacher Tip To help students decode words, divide them into the syllables shown below. The information following each word tells how students can figure out the meaning of each word.

in·tri·cate	context clues
pre·car·i·ous	context clues
re·source	context clues, word structure
se·clud·ed	context clues, word structure
tra·di·tion·al	context clues, word structure

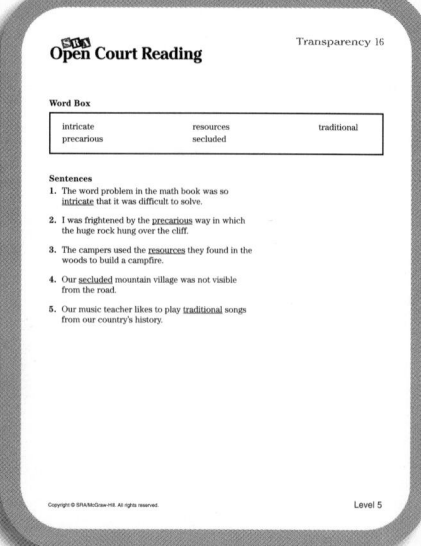

Transparency 16

Preview and Prepare

Browse

■ Have a volunteer read the title and authors' names aloud. Have students share what they know about nonfiction.

■ Because this selection is nonfiction, have the students browse through the entire selection, looking at photographs and maps and reading subtitles. Discuss with them what they think this selection might have to do with heritage.

■ Have students search for clues that tell them something about the selection. Record their observations in the Clues column on **Transparency 44.**

■ Encourage students to ask questions as they browse. Have them identify any problems they notice while reading in the Problems column.

Set Purposes

As they read, have students think about heritage and how ancient traditions can be incorporated into a modern lifestyle.

Selection Vocabulary

As students study vocabulary, they will use context clues, word structure, and apposition to determine the meaning of these and additional unfamiliar words.

Display **Transparency 16** before reading the selection to introduce and discuss the following words and their meanings.

in·tri·cate: very involved, having a lot of detail (page 246)
pre·car·i·ous: unsafe, dangerous (page 246)
re·source: something that can be used (page 247)
se·clud·ed: away from others (page 247)
tra·di·tion·al: passed from one generation to another (page 256)

Have students read the words in the Word Box. Help students decode multisyllabic words by reading them syllable by syllable.

Have students read the sentences on **Transparency 16** to determine the meaning of the underlined words. Remind them to use clues in the sentences and structural clues to figure out the meaning. See the teacher tip on the left for information on how the words in each sentence can be defined.

Reading Recommendations

Your first reading of the selection should focus on developing the reading strategies found to the left of the reduced pages. During rereading, they should focus on the comprehension skills found to the right of the reduced pages.

Oral Reading

Because this selection is a first-person account, students will enjoy reading it aloud. Have students help each other with unfamiliar words and difficult ideas. As students read aloud, have them read expressively, at an appropriate pace, in natural phrases and chunks. By reading the selection with fluency, students will demonstrate an understanding of the text and an ability to engage the listeners in an effective manner. If students encounter difficulties, have them use the reading strategies below or refer to the Blending Procedure (Program Appendix 15–16).

Using Reading Strategies

Reading strategy instruction allows students to become aware of how good readers read. Good readers constantly check their understanding as they are reading and ask themselves questions. In addition, skilled readers recognize when they are having problems and stop to use various reading strategies to help them make sense of what they are reading.

During the reading of "In Two Worlds: A Yup'ik Eskimo Family," you will model the use of the following reading strategies:

- Asking Questions
- Clarifying
- Summarizing

Before reading, have students share how they have used these strategies in the past and any tips they can give each other on their use.

Building Comprehension Skills

Revisiting or rereading a selection allows students to apply skills that give them a more complete understanding of the text. Some follow-up comprehension skills, such as *Main Idea and Details* and *Compare and Contrast*, help students organize information. Others, such as *Author's Purpose*, *Making Inferences*, and *Drawing Conclusions*, lead to deeper understanding—to "reading between the lines," as mature readers do. In this selection, students will apply the follow-up comprehension skills of *Main Idea and Details* and *Compare and Contrast*. Since two skills are reviewed, you may want to do all the sections related to one skill before doing the other skill.

Meeting Individual Needs

ESL

Vocabulary Check that English-language learners know the meanings of idioms and more difficult vocabulary in the story, including: *long ago; ancestors; tidal flats bordering the sea; melted; moved with the seasons; migrated north; precarious; had rights to certain places for hunting or fishing; no one owned the land; secluded; raise their family; missionaries; standard public elementary school curriculum; freighter; factory-made goods; dish antenna; satellite transmission; electric generator; sewage disposal system; modern conveniences; expensive;* and *invisibly connected to the whole world.* Explain and show pictures as needed. Model example sentences and help English-speaking students make their own sentences. Refer to Unit 3, Lesson 2 of the **ESL Supplement** for teaching suggestions.

Have students who may need extra help reading "In Two Worlds: A Yup'ik Eskimo Family" reread the selection using the **Listening Library Audiocassette**.

By this time in the fifth grade, good readers should be reading approximately 143 words per minute with fluency and expression. The only way to gain fluency is through practice. As explained in Reading Recommendations, have students reread all or part of the selection to you and to each other during class or Independent Work Time to focus on the comprehension skills and to build fluency.

② Reading and Responding

Read pages 244–263.

Comprehension Strategies

Modeling

① Asking Questions *Good readers ask questions to help them focus on what they want to learn from the text. I wonder what this title means? "In Two Worlds: A Yup'ik Eskimo Family"—what two worlds are the authors talking about? The first section has a heading that says "The Past." Maybe there's a part called "The Present." That could be two worlds, couldn't it? Let's check later as we read and see if we're right. (This question is answered on page 248.)*

What questions do you have about this selection?

Teacher Tip Some of the words in this selection will be unfamiliar to students. Help them pronounce these words. Yup'ik is pronounced Yōō´pik.

Scammon Bay

Anchorage

244

Word Knowledge

Scammon, Eskimos, spawned

Students can use the skills they learned in the Word Knowledge section of this lesson to read these words. Remind students of this if they have difficulty reading these words.

Meeting Individual Needs

Inter**v**ention

Comprehension Intervention strategies for those students having difficulty with reading "In Two Worlds" can be found in Unit 3, Lesson 2, of the ***Intervention Guide.***

Assessment

✓ **Informal** Observe individual students as they read, and use the Teacher Observation Log found in the ***Assessment Guide*** to record anecdotal information about each student's strengths and weaknesses.

Reading Recommendation

ORAL • CHORAL • SILENT

IN TWO WORLDS:

• A Yup'ik Eskimo Family •

from the book by Aylette Jenness and Alice Rivers
photographs by Aylette Jenness

1

THE PAST

• *Long Ago* •

Alice and Billy Rivers live with their children in the small town of Scammon Bay, Alaska, on the coast of the Bering Sea. They are Yup'ik Eskimos. Their story really begins long, long ago.

Alice and Billy's parents, grandparents, great-grandparents, great-great-grandparents—all their ancestors for several thousand years—have always lived here. They were part of a small group of Yup'ik Eskimos whose home was this vast area of <u>tidal flats</u> bordering the sea, with inland marshes, ponds, creeks, and rivers lacing the flat treeless <u>tundra</u>, broken only by occasional masses of low hills.

Each year, as the northern part of the earth tilted toward the sun, the long hours of sunlight here melted the snow, melted the sea ice, melted the rivers, melted, even, the frozen land down to the depth of a foot or so. Briefly, for a few months, birds came from the south to lay their eggs and raise their young. The fish <u>spawned</u>, plants grew, berries ripened. And then the earth tilted away from the sun. Days grew shorter, the sun weaker, temperatures fell. The rain turned to snow, plants withered, birds flew south. Ponds, creeks, rivers, and finally even the Bering Sea froze, and layers of snow covered the whole landscape. Fish, sea mammals, and land animals all moved beneath thick blankets of ice and snow.

(245)

Comprehension Skills

Main Idea and Details

Have students tell what they know about *main idea and details*. If necessary, remind them that a *main idea* is what a paragraph or section of text is mostly about. Supporting *details* give more information about this main idea.

Have the students read the three paragraphs on page 245 and point out these main ideas.

- Alice and Billy Rivers are Yup'ik Eskimos. (first paragraph)
- Their ancestors have always lived in this area (second paragraph)
- The third paragraph continues the main idea of the second paragraph with a more elaborate description of the tidal flats.

Have the students identify the main idea and supporting details in the paragraphs or sections as they read. Explain that identifying main ideas can help readers remember what a selection is about, especially one like this with many facts.

Skills Strand

Main Idea and Details
INTRODUCED: Unit 2, Lesson 2
REVIEWED: Unit 2, Lesson 4
Unit 2, Lesson 8
Unit 3, Lesson 2
Unit 3, Lesson 7

Teacher Tip Some students might enjoy finding out what their own area was like thousands of years ago. Encourage the students to research and write a short report describing the differences between their geographic region in the past and today.

2 Reading and Responding

Comprehension Strategies

Prompting

2 Clarifying *Are there any terms or ideas in this selection that we should clarify before reading further?*

Student Sample

Clarifying *"Their mark on the land was light." That's a weird phrase. I know that a "mark" is something that you leave behind, like a scratch on a table. It's always there but it can be hard to see. If their mark is light, then I guess it means that they didn't change the land much.*

Modeling

3 Summarizing *The main idea changes sharply here. That's a clue that we ought to stop and summarize to make sure we understand what we have read. The Rivers family has lived in Scammon Bay for thousands of years. There were lots of fish and other animals to provide food for them. They knew how to survive, but didn't change the land much. They shared with all the other families. Life changed very little until about fifty years ago. Is there anything we have left out of the summary?*

Word Knowledge
harpooned, footsteps

Students can use the skills they learned in the Word Knowledge section of this lesson to read these words. Remind students of this if they have difficulty reading these words.

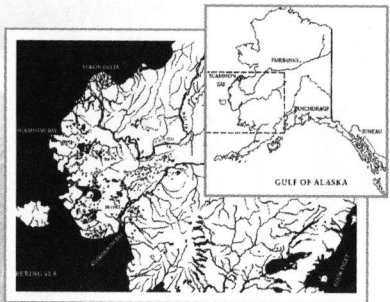

The small, scattered groups of Yup'ik Eskimos knew exactly how to survive here. Living as single families, or in small groups of relatives, they moved with the seasons to catch each kind of fish, bird, or mammal when and where each was most easily available. They harpooned the whales that migrated north along the coast in spring and south in the fall. They shot and snared birds nesting on the tundra, and they gathered the birds' eggs. They netted saltwater fish coming to lay their eggs in the rivers and creeks, and they caught freshwater fish moving beneath the ice of inland creeks. They trapped small mammals on the land for meat and for fur clothing. They knew where to find and how to catch dozens of different fish and animals for food, for clothing, even for light and heat for their small homes.

They had fire, but they didn't know how to use it to make metal. Everything they had they made themselves, with their hands, with stone, bone, or ivory tools—their many intricate snares and nets and traps, their boats and sleds, their homes and their clothing. Life was hard and precarious. Nothing was wasted.

2 Their mark on the land was light. Today their old sites are nearly part of the earth, not easy to see. These Yup'ik Eskimos didn't build monuments to gods or leaders. They believed that animals had spirits, and that the spirits survived the animals' death to inhabit other animals. After killing a seal, they put water in its mouth to show their caring and respect for it and to ensure that its spirit would return in the form of another seal another time. They made up stories and dances of awe, fear, and pleasure in the animals they knew so well.

246

Meeting Individual Needs

Intervention

Summarizing Tell the students that summarizing will help them see if they understand what they are reading. Have them summarize in their own words, so they can be sure they understand what they have read.

They shared with each other, and no one was much better or worse off than anyone else. Families, or groups of families, had rights to certain places for hunting or fishing, but no one owned the land or its resources.

They knew no outsiders, no one different from themselves. During those hundreds and hundreds of years, their way of life changed very little. People followed in the footsteps of their ancestors, children learning from their parents the vast body of knowledge necessary for survival in this environment.

③ But during the last fifty years, their lives have changed enormously. And these changes are within the memory of the older people living here now.

Listen to Alice Rivers's mother, Mary Ann, describe her childhood. She speaks in Yup'ik, and one of her daughters, Leota, translates into English.

● **Mary Anne Remembers** ●

"I was born, as I was told, in the late fall. My mother delivered me outside in the tundra, out in the open. My mother told me that after I was born I clutched some tundra moss and grass in my hand. I do not know why I was born outside, but it must have been because my mother was out in the tundra.

"When I was first aware of my surroundings, we lived on the other side of the mountains of Scammon Bay. The name of the place where I was born is called Ingeluk, and I think it's called this name because we are surrounded by small hills. We were the only people living in that area. We were <u>secluded</u> away from other people. There was my father, my mother, my two older sisters, and one older brother, and I am the youngest in the family.

(247)

Comprehension Skills

Main Idea and Details

Writers often present the *main idea* of a paragraph in the first or last sentence of a paragraph. This is called the topic sentence. The other sentences in the paragraph give supporting details. Point out the following examples of main ideas that come in the first sentence of a paragraph:

- "The small scattered groups of Yup'ik Eskimos knew exactly how to survive here." (paragraph 1, page 246)
- "Their mark on the land was light." (paragraph 3, page 246)
- "But during the last fifty years, their lives have changed enormously." (paragraph 3, page 247)

Have students identify details that support these main ideas. Have the students continue to look for main ideas and details as they reread.

Meeting Individual Needs

Challenge

Main Idea and Details Have students make a chart of the main ideas in "In Two Worlds." Under each main idea, have students list the details that support it. When they are finished, have students write a sentence or two that tells how they determined which were the main ideas and which were the details.

Intervention

Main Idea and Details Some students may have trouble retaining the information in this selection. Have them jot down main ideas as they read.

2 Reading and Responding

Comprehension Strategies

Modeling

4 Asking Questions *Where did they get kerosene? From what we've read so far, they made everything they had. You can't just make kerosene, can you? Come to think of it, where did they get the kettle? Let's keep reading and see if the mystery clears up.*

Modeling

5 Answering Questions *Here's an answer to our question. There was a man who traded goods for skins. I'll bet that's how they got the kettle and kerosene. It sounds as if their life was beginning to change even when Mary Ann was just a child!*

Modeling

6 Answering Questions *Here is the answer to my question from the beginning of the selection. Mary Ann is talking about two lives here, her life before the changes and her life after the changes. I think I was right about the two worlds. They are the past and the present. Have any of you been able to answer some of your questions from earlier?*

Word Knowledge

youngest, skimmed, Protestants

Students can use the skills they learned in the Word Knowledge section of this lesson to read these words. Remind students of this if they have difficulty reading these words.

"We lived in a sod house. The insides of our house had braided grass hanging on the walls as paneling. We had only one window, which was made out of dried seal guts, and it made a lot of noise when it was windy. Our floor was plain, hard, dried mud. Our beds were dried grass, piled high to keep us warm. We had no blankets. We mostly did with what we had at hand, and we used our parkas to keep us warm. I remember we had one kettle, a small half kerosene tank for our cooking pot, and the plates we had were carved from wood by my father. **4**

"For light, we used seal oil when we had the oil, and it smoked a lot. Other times we had no light because we had no oil. I remember my mother cooked whitefish, and she carefully skimmed off the oil from the pot we had, and what she took out of the cooking pot we used in our oil lamp. The oil from the fish made pretty good light; it never smoked like the seal oil did. There were lots of stories being told, that's what we did during the evenings.

"Our main diet was fish, caught in my father's traps. There were times that we were really hungry. We were very poor. Sometimes when we woke up in the morning, we had nothing at all to eat.

"We didn't have any kind of bread. We did not know what coffee and tea were.

"I saw my first white man when we were traveling by our skin boat. I did not know who he was, but later on I was told that the white man was trading goods for fur or skins. Maybe I was fifteen years old when I saw an airplane. **5**

> "*We lived in a sod house. The insides of our house had braided grass hanging on the walls as paneling. We had only one window, which was made out of dried seal guts, and it made a lot of noise when it was windy.*"

(248)

6 "I liked the life we used to live a long time ago, but we were always in need of something. I would say we live in comfort now. I don't go in hunger now. I say both lives I led were good, and I like both."

Mary Ann grew up and married a man who lived nearby, Teddy Sundown. They began to raise their family in Keggatmiut, as Scammon Bay is known in Yup'ik. It was a good site, and a number of families settled there. They built their small log houses on the lower slope of a range of hills that rose out of the flat tundra. A clear stream, racing down the hillside, flowed into the river that wound along the base of the hills, and finally emptied into a wide, shallow bay of the Bering Sea. Mary Ann and Teddy still moved to seasonal camps to fish, trap, and hunt, but as the village grew, they began to spend more and more of the year there.

The United States government set up a school in Scammon Bay and hired a Yup'ik teacher. All of the children were expected to attend school.

Missionaries had come to convert the people from their traditional religion, and the village was divided between Catholics and Protestants. Two churches were built.

Alice was the fourth child born to Mary Ann and Teddy. She is shown at the age of ten, standing on the far right of her family. She speaks of growing up in Scammon Bay.

249

Comprehension Skills

Main Idea and Details

Direct students to look at pages 248–249 and decide whether the following sentences contain the main idea of a paragraph, or give a supporting detail.

- "We lived in a sod house." *(main idea)*
- "Our floor was plain, hard, dried mud." *(supporting detail)*
- "For light, we used seal oil when we had the oil, and it smoked a lot." *(main idea)*
- "They built their small log houses on the lower slope of a range of hills that rose out of the flat tundra." *(supporting detail)*

Teacher Tip Have the students discuss how they might learn if there were no schools. Would they learn how to do their parents' work like Mary Ann did?

Meeting Individual Needs

ESL

Main Idea and Details Have English-language learners read paragraphs or passages and restate the main ideas in their own words. This may help them understand the main points being presented.

2 Reading and Responding

Comprehension Strategies

Prompting

7 Summarizing *Who would like to sum up what we have read in this part of the selection?*

Student Sample

Summarizing *Mary Ann is finished and now Alice is going to remember. I should go back and summarize what Mary Ann said. During her life, the Yup'iks went from moving all year to settling down in Scammon Bay. A school was started and missionaries came. Instead of learning the traditional ways of surviving and their ancestors' religion, the children attended school and church.*

Teacher Tip Accept students' comments as they are given, without turning them into what you have in mind.

Word Knowledge

straight, transportation, standard

Students can use the skills they learned in the Word Knowledge section of this lesson to read these words. Remind students of this if they have difficulty reading these words.

7 • Alice Remembers •

"Our home was a one-room building. Our beds were together—Mom and Dad's bed and our bed. All of us kids slept together in one bed. No table—the tables came later on. We used to eat sitting on the floor, Eskimo way. Mom used to cook bread on top of the stove, 'cause there was no oven. To me it used to be the best bread I've eaten. Then as I grew older, we got a stove and oven, and she started baking bread.

"We ate bread, birds, dried herrings, clams, mussels, fish—boiled and frozen—seals, mink, muskrats. There were two stores. We bought shortening, flour, tea, coffee—just what we needed.

"We were always together. We'd go to church every morning. Mom would wake us up early, we'd go to Mass. We never used to be lazy, we used to just go, get up and go, get up to a real cold morning, and by the time we were home, the house would be nice and warm.

"Right after church we used to go straight to school, all of us. I remember that learning to write my name was the hardest thing. I was maybe about six. We had Eskimo teachers. It was one room, and everything was there.

"After school, we'd have lots of things to do— bringing some wood in, dishes to wash, house to clean, babies to watch, water to pack. We had aluminum pails with handles. We used to run over to the stream and pack water until we had what we needed. In the winter we had to keep one hole in the ice open the whole winter. This was one of the things I used to do with my sisters, not only me.

(250)

"Planes came in maybe once a week with mail. We didn't know about telephones. We had a radio, just for listening. I think we listened to one station all the time. No TV.

"The teachers had a short-wave radio. If someone got sick, they would report us to the hospital. They would give us medication or send us to the hospital in Bethel."

● **Alice Grown Up** ●

By the time Alice was an adult, Scammon Bay was a village of a hundred and fifty people, with twenty-five log and frame homes. For transportation, each family had a dog sled and team, and a boat for use in summer.

The government began to take a larger role in the Yup'ik villages. A new school was built, with living quarters for non-Eskimo teachers from outside of Alaska. Children were taught a standard public elementary school curriculum, which had little reference either to their own lives or to what they knew and didn't know about life outside Scammon Bay. They were forbidden to speak Yup'ik in school, in the belief that this would help them to learn English, and that learning English was very important.

A postmaster was hired from among the village men, and a custodian for the school. A health aide was trained, and a small clinic built and stocked. More planes came to Scammon Bay, and it became easier to fly someone needing hospital care out—as long as the weather was good.

251

Comprehension
Skills

Compare and Contrast

Have students tell what they know about comparing and contrasting. If necessary, remind the students that *comparing and contrasting*, or identifying similarities and differences between two or more parts of a selection, can help them to understand each element more completely.

Have the students read the section with the heading "Alice Remembers" and point out some of the contrasts between what Alice remembers and what her mother, Mary Ann, remembers. For example:

■ Alice remembers Mary Ann cooking bread on the top of the stove. Mary Ann remembers no bread at all in her childhood.

■ Alice went to school and church. There were no schools or church when Mary Ann was growing up.

Skills Strand

Compare and Contrast
INTRODUCED: Unit 2, Lesson 5
REVIEWED: Unit 2, Lesson 7
Unit 3, Lesson 2
Unit 3, Lesson 5
Unit 4, Lesson 1

2 Reading and Responding

Comprehension Strategies

Modeling

8 Summarizing *Here's another major change in the text. Let's stop and summarize Alice's memories. As a child, she ate the same things as Mary Ann, except she had bread, tea, and coffee, too. She went to school and church. There was one plane that brought in mail, and one radio station. As she grew, a clinic was built in the town, and people bought more modern appliances. Some people moved away to other states.*

Prompting

Asking Questions *Are there any questions about Scammon Bay that you hope will be answered later in the text?*

Student Sample

9 Asking Questions *The author says that Scammon Bay has grown and changed in many ways. I wonder how it has changed.*

I see. The next paragraph answers my question by giving the details.

Government money became available for low-income families and for the elderly and disabled. There were few opportunities to earn cash, but almost all of the men in Scammon Bay were able to earn some money by hunting or trapping seals, mink, muskrats, and beaver and selling the skins to be made into luxury fur coats outside of Alaska. In summer they netted salmon in the river mouths north of Scammon Bay and sold this valuable fish to processors, who marketed it throughout the United States as smoked fish, or lox.

Each summer a freighter came up the coast from Seattle, Washington, with supplies for the villages. Everyone began to buy more factory-made goods. Some families bought stoves that burned fuel oil instead of relying on brush wood they cut nearby. Some bought windmills, which produced enough electricity for one or two light bulbs in their homes. Some bought snowmobiles, which enabled them to travel farther than they could by dog team to hunt and trap, but which, unlike dogs, required money for fuel and new parts.

And for the first time in the long history of the Yup'ik Eskimos, some people began to travel away from their homeland. Some teenagers went to boarding school in the state of Washington. Some men went to National Guard training, and some families moved away permanently, settling in Alaskan towns and cities, or even as far away as Oregon and California.

But most remained in Scammon Bay, and some new Yup'ik people came to live there from other towns. **8**

252

Word Knowledge

disposal, storage, lagoon

Students can use the skills they learned in the Word Knowledge section of this lesson to read these words. Remind students of this if they have difficulty reading these words.

Meeting Individual Needs

Intervention

Summarizing Remind the students to summarize in their own words, and to make sure that they summarize the events in the order they occurred. Remind the students to include only main points in their summaries.

NOW

Alice's life today is both very similar to that of her mother at the same age—and very different. Scammon Bay has grown and changed in many ways.

(9)

There are three hundred and fifty people in Scammon Bay now, living in fifty-six houses. Most of the old log homes are now used for storage, and many people, like the Riverses, have new houses provided by the government at low cost. A dish antenna relays television to all the homes. Satellite transmission enables families to make telephone calls anywhere in the world. Huge storage tanks hold fuel to run an electric generator that provides enough power for each home to have all the lights that people want. A water and sewage disposal system required building a water treatment plant and a lagoon on the tundra for waste water. The dump, full of cans, plastic, fuel drums, and broken machinery, is a reminder of the difficulty of disposing of modern trash.

For some years the state government made a great deal of money from taxes on oil found in Alaska, and this money paid for many of the modern conveniences in Scammon Bay and other rural towns. An airstrip was built so that planes could land more easily at all times of the year; it is regularly plowed in winter. Three small planes a day fly into Scammon Bay, bringing everything from cases of soft drinks to boxes of disposable diapers and, of course, the mail. A huge new gym has been built, and

> *Satellite transmission enables families to make telephone calls anywhere in the world.*

(253)

Comprehension Skills

Compare and Contrast

Have the students compare the following descriptions with those in Mary Ann's childhood. How do her memories differ from the present?

■ "There are three hundred and fifty people in Scammon Bay now, living in fifty-six houses." *(Mary Ann's family were the only people living there.)*

■ "Three small planes a day fly into Scammon Bay, bringing everything . . . " *(Mary Ann never saw an airplane until she was fifteen.)*

Discuss how comparing and contrasting is another useful way to summarize information. Make copies of ***Transparency 46*** and give each student several copies. Have students keep track of the similarities and differences in the way people live in Scammon Bay today, and the way they lived in the past.

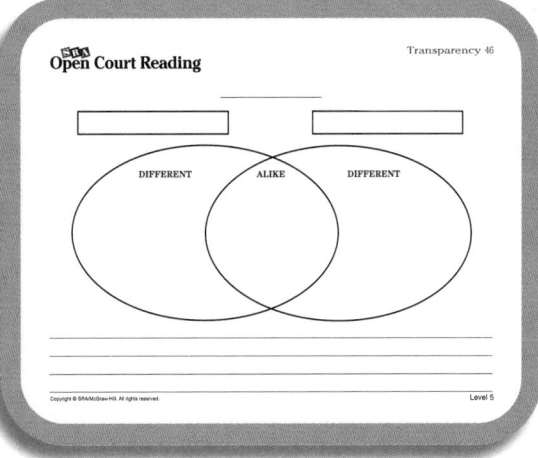

Transparency 46

Teacher Tip
Have students make use of the comprehension skill *compare and contrast* as they are working on their heritage album.

Meeting Individual Needs

Intervention

Compare and Contrast Have students make "now and then" charts to compare and contrast information from the story.

2 Reading and Responding

Comprehension Strategies

Modeling

🔟 **Clarifying** *I'm a bit confused here. This is something I should clarify. Why is the teacher writing words in Yup'ik on the chalkboard? Let's reread this section. I see. It says here that the class wants to be fluent in both English and Yup'ik. Is there anything else we should clarify before we go on?*

Teacher Tip Try to find out what students know about something before telling them what you know. If they have no ideas, help them rather than allowing them to make random guesses.

Word Knowledge

snowmobile, responsibility

Students can use the skills they learned in the Word Knowledge section of this lesson to read these words. Remind students of this if they have difficulty reading these words.

a new clinic, a preschool center, town offices, and a post office. The school is now run by the state, not the federal government, and goes all the way through the twelfth grade.

In spite of the changes, the traditional pattern of living from the land is still powerful. This can be seen most clearly as people move to seasonal camps during the summer months.

● School ●

During the school year the family's life falls into very different patterns from those of summer. Billy begins his winter rounds of hunting and fishing, going out by snowmobile nearly every day to get food or firewood for the family. Alice goes to work as the school cook, and the Rivers children go to their classrooms each morning.

Billy Junior, in the second grade, is learning to type. He says proudly, "I've already finished typing one book, and now I'm on another. We can read any kind of books. Now I'm on a hard one."

254

Meeting Individual Needs

Inter⌃vention

Clarifying Remind the students that clarifying is a process. Often this process involves identifying the idea or term that needs to be cleared up, then making connections, answering questions, or checking other resources until clarification is achieved. Have volunteers model this process for other students.

In Sarah and Isaac's combined third and fourth grade class, Clifford Kaganak teaches Yup'ik. Here he writes words in Yup'ik on the chalkboard, and the class practices reading and translating. They want to be fluent in both of their languages—English and Yup'ik. **10**

Down the hall, Jennifer Allison Keim works with the older Rivers boys—Oscar, Jacob and Abraham. Jacob enjoys using the computers, but generally the boys would rather be out hunting and fishing—or using the school skis. Jennifer says, "My goals are for the kids to be educated to the point where they can protect themselves from outsiders, so if something comes their way that they have to deal with, they'll know how to weigh and measure and make decisions."

The teachers all know that the school has a great responsibility to prepare the kids for the outside world, and they also want to encourage a sense of pride in Yup'ik Eskimo culture. Some students want to go on to college after graduating from high school in Scammon Bay, and the teachers work hard to make this happen.

255

Comprehension Skills

Compare and Contrast

Remind the students that comparing and contrasting allows the reader to see clearly the differences and similarities in the text.

Have the students compare and contrast the family's school year activities with the activities of the summer. Point out to them that adults and children have very different patterns during the school year than the ones they have during the summer. Have them continue to add to their *compare and contrast c*hart.

② Reading and Responding

Comprehension Strategies

Modeling

⑪ Summarizing *One final time, let's sum up the major ideas we've read. Mary Ann's family lived in isolation, making most of their things and hunting for almost all their food. They lived as their ancestors lived. Alice went to school and church. She ate bread and other foods brought in by plane, as well as the traditional food. Her children drink soda pop, but they also learn the traditional ways. Why was it important for us to sum up at this point?*

Teacher Tip Remind students that summarizing small sections at a time helps them remember the text.

Word Knowledge
mistake, understand

Students can use the skills they learned in the Word Knowledge section of this lesson to read these words. Remind students of this if they have difficulty reading these words.

● On the Weekends ●

During the school year, traditional ways of life are practiced mostly on the weekends. The end of each school week marks the beginning of two days of hunting and fishing for the whole Rivers family.

Alice says, "On the weekends, we get to go traveling with Billy. Usually we decide what we're going to do ahead of time, what's going to happen. Like if we want to go fishing, we go fishing, or hunting <u>ptarmigans</u>. We're out most of the day Saturday doing this and that."

This is where Billy becomes the teacher, training the kids in both the oldest methods of hunting and fishing, and the newest. Since the children spend so much time in school, this is an important time for them to learn how to survive as Eskimos.

"I teach my boys the way I've been taught, the way my dad taught me. What I think that's wrong, I try to do it better than my dad. And when I make a mistake, I try to correct it to my boys, so they'll do it better than I did.

256

(11) "I start taking them out as soon as they're old enough—like in the boat, when they're old enough to sit down and take care of themselves. I tell them little things like taking the anchor out, putting the anchor back up. As soon as they understand our words, we teach them from there. If they show you something that they know, you'll know they learned it—and then they can start doing it by themselves.

"Each one of them that goes with me, I talk to them, I tell them about little things—what's dangerous, what's not dangerous. I tell them about melting ice—even though it looks good on the surface, some places you can't see when it's covered with snow, it's thin. That's where they fall through. I teach them what thin ice looks like, and how it looks when it's safe.

"Oscar's been going with me first, 'cause he's the oldest one, then Jacob. One of them will know more, the one that pays attention more, just like in school. The one that doesn't listen, or doesn't pay attention, he'll make more mistakes or get more scolding.

"Oscar was about seven or eight when I first let him shoot a gun. He got his first seal when he was maybe eight or nine. In the boat I did the driving, and I had him do the shooting. He got a young mukluk that was a baby in springtime. He shot it, and after he shot it, he looked at me, looked back, and he smiled. 'I catch it.' "

257

Meeting Individual Needs

Reteach

Compare and Contrast For students who need additional instruction and practice with this concept, have them complete **Reteach,** pages 91–92.

Challenge

Compare and Contrast Have students compare and contrast their parents' and their grandparents' lives. Have students who may benefit from extended practice with this concept complete **Challenge,** page 48.

Comprehension Skills

Compare and Contrast

For more practice with compare and contrast, have students complete *Reading and Writing Workbook* pages 91–92.

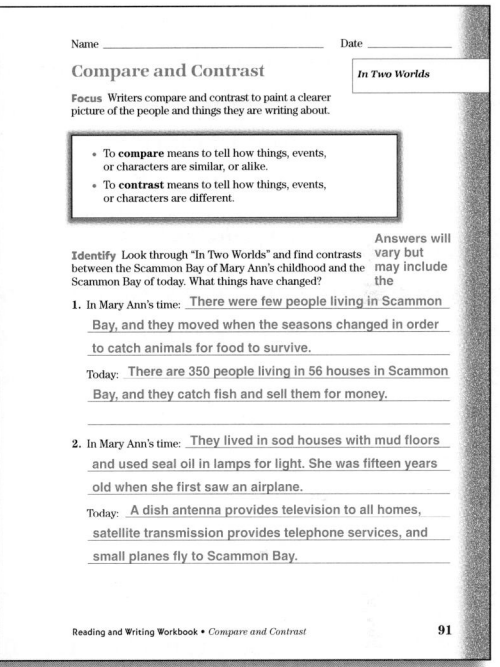

Reading and Writing Workbook pp. 91–92

② Reading and Responding

Comprehension Strategies

Prompting

⑫ Summarizing *Let's sum up what we've learned. The Yup'ik people have lived in Scammon Bay, Alaska, for several thousand years. They lived off the land until white people came to Scammon Bay. Who would like to continue the summary?*

Student Sample

Summarizing *The Yup'ik began to trade with the white people and adopt some of their ways. The children began to attend school and learn nontraditional ways to live. But the Yup'ik still teach their children traditional Yup'ik customs.*

Discussing Strategy Use

After they have read the selection, have students share any problems they encountered and tell what strategies they used to solve them. Then, have them answer the following questions. If they answer "no" to any of the questions, have them reread part of the selection to find the answer.

- Did they ask questions and check later to see if their questions were answered?

- Did they stop to clarify words, phrases, and ideas that they didn't understand?

- Did they summarize to help them understand what they've read?

Make sure that students explain how using the strategies helped them understand the selection better and how they read effectively to find answers to the questions they asked as they set purposes.

Oscar remembers this very clearly. He says, "My grandpa divided the seal up in circles and gave it to the old people." This is the traditional Yup'ik way of sharing a boy's first catch with the elders, still carried on, though motorboats have replaced kayaks, and rifles are used in place of thrown harpoons.

THE FUTURE

Alice and Billy know very well that life is changing fast here in Scammon Bay, and they want their children to be prepared for this.

Alice says, "When I was a kid, I used to do things with my mom. I used to watch her sew. Now I try to have Mattie knit, crochet, make things, but she thinks it's too boring. She knows how to do it, but she can't sit and look at one thing for a long time. I can't even teach her how to sew a skin. She doesn't have any patience.

"Now there's so many other things going on. In our time there was no basketball, no Igloo [community center], hardly any dances."

Billy says, "When I was Billy Junior's age, I used to run maybe twenty or thirty times around a pond with my little wooden boat. Just run around, play with it, put mud inside of it, and run around. I'd never think of TV, it wasn't in my mind."

(258)

Teacher Tip Reread this selection with students who had difficulty understanding it. Continue modeling and prompting the use of strategies and skills as you reread.

"Everything is not the same here in Alaska, not like before. Things are changing. Things are getting more expensive. Most of the people are depending on more jobs. I mean working, you have to have a job.

"I talk to the kids, I just say what we'd like them to do. I tell them, 'If you go to school, and be smart over there, and try to learn what you're taught, you guys will have good jobs, and good-paying jobs. I want you to have good-paying jobs, so we'll have the things that we need, anything we need'; like this I talk to them."

"I'd be happy to have them travel to see other countries, to have them learning something that's Outside——*if* they have a job. 'Cause Outside there's many people without jobs, no home. Here it's okay, as we help each other here in the villages."

"We get after the kids for not doing their homework. We want them to be more educated, more than us. I mean, learn more. I only went up to the fifth grade."

Alice agrees. She adds "I want them to learn other ways—Outside ways. And I want them to learn our ways, too—hunting for our kind of foods. We can't have store-bought food all the time. I want them to learn both ways."

12 Looking down on Scammon Bay from the hill, it seems like a very small settlement, nearly lost in the huge expanse of tundra around it. From this distance it doesn't look so different from the Scammon Bay of Alice's childhood. Yet it is invisibly connected to the whole world now. And so is the Rivers family.

> "*Now there's so many other things going on. In our time there was no basketball, no Igloo [community center], hardly any dances.*"

(259)

Teacher Tip

Have students discuss how traditions and customs are passed down through generations. Remind them to keep this idea in mind when working on their unit activities.

Assessment

✓ **Formal** To assess students' reading comprehension, have them complete *Comprehension and Writing Assessment*, pages 57–58.

Comprehension Skills

Discussing the Selection

Following reading, engage the students in a discussion of the selection. Using the *handing-off process* will help the students take responsibility for the discussion. In addition to the following questions, have them revisit any questions asked when they set purposes before the reading.

■ What two worlds did the Rivers family live in? *(The past of their heritage and the present, modern world.)*

■ What parts of their heritage did the Rivers lose during Alice's lifetime? *(They brought in food and other supplies from the outside and used some modern things like appliances.)*

■ Was it a bad thing that the Rivers family changed? Why or why not? *(Answers will vary. Students might mention that it is good that they still keep some of their ways alive.)*

■ How has this selection selection connected with your knowledge of the unit theme? *(Answers will vary—students should compare/contrast examples of heritage from this selection with their own experiences or past reading and use these connections to make a general statement about the theme.)*

During this time, have the students return to the clues and problems that they noted on the transparency before reading. Let the students decide which items deserve further discussion.

Have students take responsibility for the discussion. The teacher should not be the one who is expected to call on the next speaker and should not be a pivotal figure in the discussion.

2 **Reading and Responding**

Meet the Authors

After the students read the information about Aylette Jenness and Alice Rivers, discuss the following question with them.

Aylette Jenness and Alice Rivers have been friends for a long time. When Aylette Jenness returned to Scammon Bay after twenty years, why do you think she decided to write this story with and about her friend? *(Possible answer: Having lived in Scammon Bay herself, Aylette Jenness could see and understand the important changes that had taken place in Alice Rivers's life, and wanted to tell her friend's story.)*

Why do you think the changes in the Scammon Bay community might be both exciting and upsetting for Alice Rivers? *(Possible answer: The modern conveniences, such as store-bought food, radios, and electricity, are nice. However, it is also important to Alice Rivers that her children learn the old ways so that their culture, an important part of who they are, won't be lost.)*

IN TWO WORLDS:

• A Yup'ik Eskimo Family •

Meet the Authors

Aylette Jenness, a writer and photographer, met **Alice Rivers** when they were both young women. At the time, Aylette had moved to Alaska to write books about the people of Scammon Bay. While writing *Gussuk Boy* and *Dwellers of the Tundra*, she met Alice Rivers. After finishing the books, Aylette left Alaska. When she returned to Alaska for a visit more than twenty years later, she met up with her old friend, Alice Rivers. Alice told her about how different things were in Scammon Bay since she had lived there twenty years ago. The two decided to work together on the story of how Alice's family had grown and changed, and how the little community on the Bering Sea had changed as well. Rivers's mother, Mary Ann Sundown, also contributed to the book by telling about the way people lived during the years she herself was growing up near Scammon Bay.

260

Theme Connections

Think About It

With a small group of classmates, discuss the following questions.

- What are the differences between Scammon Bay and where you live?
- How does the place in which people live affect their culture?
- Why is it important for families to tell their stories? What purpose does it serve?
- Is heritage important to the Yup'iks? Have their feelings about their heritage changed over time?

Record Ideas

 Think about the ways the Yup'ik tribe's community has changed over the generations, and then try to predict what other changes may come in the future. Write a paragraph in your Writing Journal about what you think their community will be like in another twenty years.

Make a Chart

Draw a straight line across a piece of paper, then divide the line into three sections. Label the first section "The 1940s," the second section "The 1970s," and the third section "Present Day." The object is to find out what kinds of work and play activities children took part in during each of the years on your chart. You may get this information by interviewing friends or family members that were children during those years, or you may get your information from books, movies, television, or personal experience. List the activities below the chart date during which they occurred.

Compare and contrast the information for each date. Have the activities changed over three generations? Did they change as much over the years as the Yup'ik's culture did? Why or why not?

261

Theme Connections

Think About It

Ensure that students are aware that the Yup'iks pass on their traditional values, customs, and skills through stories, and that parents and grandparents were the children's primary teachers.

Have students discuss differences and similarities between the Rivers's culture and that of the author of "The Land I Lost: Adventures of a Boy in Vietnam." What aspects of these two cultures can students connect to their own?

Record Ideas

Consider responding to student's journal entries, expanding their thinking through questions and comments.

Make a Chart

Have students share their work with classmates. Have them compare and contrast the kinds of activities engaged in by different cultural groups. If any of your students' families or friends have immigrated fairly recently, discuss how the children's activities have changed as a result of the move.

 **Teacher Tip** Have students incorporate old customs and traditions into their heritage albums.

**2** **Reading and Responding**

History of the Tunrit: A Traditional Netsilik Eskimo Legend

translated by **Edward Field**
illustrated by **Pudlo**

Activating Prior Knowledge

- Remind the students about the information they have learned in this unit about the Yup'ik ways of life in "In Two Worlds."

- Direct the students' attention to the title and art and encourage them to discuss what the poem might be about.

Reading the Poem

- Read the poem out loud at least twice. Then allow the students to take turns reading aloud to each other.

- During Independent Work Time, have students listen to its recording on the ***Listening Library Audiocassette.***

Literary Techniques

Author's Purpose

Tell students that people tell stories to help them remember and communicate their heritage. Some stories such as "History of the Tunrit" are part of an *oral tradition,* or a collection of stories passed down through generations of people by word of mouth. Have students compare the Netsilik, Indian, and Greek oral traditions as exemplified by "History of the Tunrit" and the myths in "The Heavenly Zoo" in Unit 2.

History *of the* Tunrit

collected by Knud Rasmussen
a traditional Netsilik Eskimo Legend
translated by Edward Field
illustrated by Pudlo

When our Netsilik forefathers came to these hunting grounds
the Tunrit people already lived here.
It was the Tunrit who first learned
how to survive in this difficult country.
They showed us the caribou crossing places
and taught us the special way to fish in the rivers.

Our people came from inland
so we love <u>caribou</u> hunting more than anything else,
but the Tunrit were sea people
and preferred to hunt seal.
They actually went out on the salt sea in their <u>kayaks</u>,
hunting seal in open water. That takes nerve.
We only hunt them through the ice at breathing holes.
They also caught whales and walruses as they swam by:

    The bones of these creatures are still lying around
    in the wrecks of the Tunrit houses.
    And they hunted bear and wore their skins for clothes.
    We wear caribou.

262

The Tunrit were strong, but easily frightened.
In a fight they would rather run than kill. Anyway,
you never heard of them killing anyone.
And we lived among the Tunrit in those days peacefully,
for they let us come and share their land:
Until once by accident some of them killed one of our dogs
and ran away scared, leaving their homeland.

All of the Tunrit fled finally from their villages here,
although we cannot remember why anymore:
They just ran away or the land was taken from them.
And on parting from us they cried:
"We followed the caribou and hunted them down;
now it is your turn to follow them and do the hunting."

And so we do to this day.

263

Theme Connection

Review what the Netsilik learned from the Tunrit. Discuss how we are affected by living alongside people from other cultures (*food, holidays*). Then, discuss how our heritage is enriched by contact with other cultures.

The influence of outside cultures is a theme that connects "History of the Tunrit" with "The Land I Lost" and "In Two Worlds." Have students brainstorm other themes that connect these three selections (for example, ways of finding food and connections to one's homeland). Then, have students compare and contrast each selection's treatment of these themes.

Meet the Poet

Knud Rasmussen was an explorer who gathered information on Inuit culture while participating in an Arctic expedition. This song comes from *Stories and Songs of the Netsilik Eskimos*, a book based on material he gathered. He was part Eskimo and had grown up in Greenland speaking an Eskimo language.

Rasmussen found that the stories, songs, and languages of the various Arctic people were very similar, even though the groups lived thousands of miles apart. Eventually, he found the Netsilik, a group without any written language. This song was passed from generation to generation by word of mouth.

The translator of this poem, Edward Field, was born in Brooklyn just about the time Rasmussen was exploring the Arctic. He started writing poetry while he was in the army. When he left the army, he worked at various jobs and studied acting. Most of his poems "tell beautiful and believable stories of the indestructibility of the human spirit."

 **Responding**

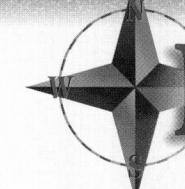Exploring the Theme

Teacher Tip If you created a semantic map on the Concept/Question Board of key words related to the unit theme, Heritage, have students find words from other resources, their projects and family discussions and add them to the appropriate category on the map.

Family Greeting, 1962. Eli Tikeayak. Canadian Inuit, Rankin Inlet. Light green-grey stone. Art Gallery of Ontario, Toronto. Gift of Robert C. Williamson, C. M., 1989.

Heritage

FINE Art

Family Greeting. 1962. Eli Tikeayak. Canadian Inuit, Rankin Inlet. Light green-grey stone. Art Gallery of Ontario, Toronto. Gift of Robert C. Williamson, C.M., 1989.

298

Student Anthology p. 298

"In Two Worlds: A Yup'ik Eskimo Family"

A message from _____

Our class has just read the story *In Two Worlds: A Yup'ik Eskimo Family,* which describes how, as time moves on, some aspects of the Yup'ik family life have changed, while others have remained the same.

Ask your child to explain some of the similarities and differences in this family's life as described in the selection we read in class. Have your child compare and contrast the lifestyles of the two women in the selection, Mary Ann and Alice, and complete the chart below. Remind your child that *compare* means to list things that are the same; *contrast* means to list things that are different.

Encourage your child to share this chart with the class.

		Compare	Contrast
Mary Ann	Food		
	Housing		
	Clothing		
	Religion		
Alice	Food		
	Housing		
	Clothing		
	Religion		

Unit 3/Heritage 37

Home Connection p. 37

Selection Vocabulary

Have students write in their Writing Journals the definitions for words discussed before the reading of the selection and any other interesting words they clarified while reading. Students should be encouraged to refer to these words throughout the unit as they work on student and writing projects. The words from the selection are:

intricate	traditional	secluded
precarious	resource	

Reading/Writing Connections

Discuss how the members of the older generation passed on their heritage to the younger generation. Have students make a list of the ways family and cultural customs and activities were communicated. Have volunteers share examples of similar forms of communication they might use in their unit activities—for example, having a grandparent or another adult tell them about what he or she did as a child.

View Fine Art

This is *Family Greeting,* a contemporary sculpture of an Inuit family that can be found on page 298. Scenes such as this one have become popular within the last 50 years, since advances in technology have made fishing and hunting less central to the lives of Inuits. Have students comment on how this trend in Inuit sculpture relates to what they read about in "In Two Worlds: A Yup'ik Eskimo Family." Lead them to see that, though *Family Greeting* depicts a contemporary scene, its artist is keeping alive a traditional art form that has been used by Inuits for thousands of years.

Home Connection

The class has just finished reading "In Two Worlds: A Yup'ik Eskimo Family," a selection about a family living in Alaska on the coast of the Bering Sea. An informational letter on "In Two Worlds: A Yup'ik Eskimo Family," in both English and Spanish, can be found in the *Home Connection* guide.

Supporting Student Explorations

To help the students decide what to include in their heritage albums, consider the following activities:

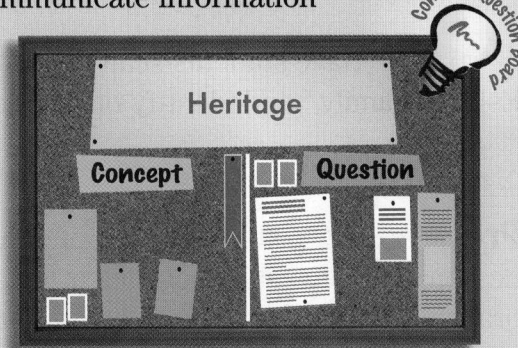 **Whole Group**   Help students create a list of the types of stories students might include in their albums, such as stories told by family members and friends; descriptions of important events, traditions, and customs; songs, poems, or stories shared by family members and friends; biographies of family members and friends; and descriptions of their homes or hometowns.

Small Group   Have small groups of students discuss the pros and cons of including the stories they're considering in their heritage albums.

Have the students list in their *Inquiry Journals* the family members, friends, or neighbors whom they might interview. Once students have contacted several people, have them use their interview notes to write summaries of the stories they were told in their journals.

Individual   Meet with students to review their summaries and ensure that they are appropriate for sharing with the class. If you feel that any of the stories are inappropriate, explain to the student why you consider the story to be private. Have students decide on the type of piece they wish to create for their first heritage album selection and begin writing.

Have students continue reading and sharing published stories. Have them look for ways authors communicate information about heritage and consider using similar techinques in their heritage album pieces. Suggest that students post on the Concept/Question Board brief descriptions of books, magazine articles, computer Websites, or other sources of information that they have found to be especially helpful in their explorations of heritage. Encourage students who are having difficulty finding information to check sources on the Board and to post their questions as well.

Inquiry Journal   Have students complete page 41 of the *Inquiry Journal.* Have them record how reading "In Two Worlds: A Yup'ik Eskimo Family" has added to their knowledge of the unit theme, Heritage.

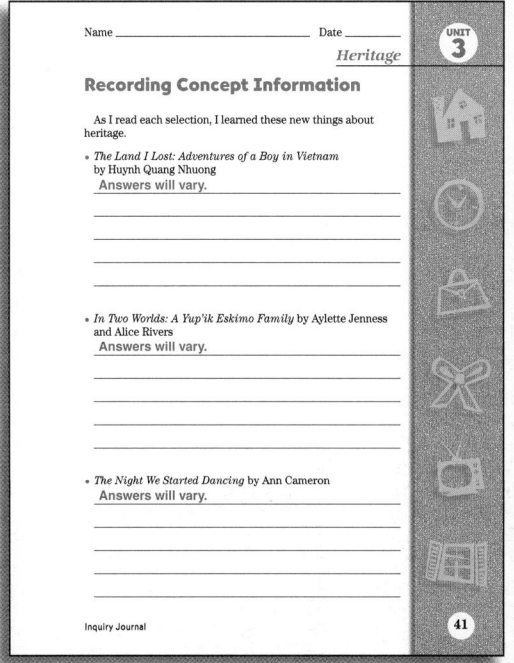

Inquiry Journal p. 41

Assessment

✓ **Informal** In the anecdotal record of students' progress, note whether they:
- gather useful information about their heritage by interviewing individuals.
- select a genre and begin to write their first heritage album piece.

Teacher Tip Send home a letter to inform students' families or guardians about the unit activity and to let them know that their contributions will be very valuable.

③ Integrating the Curriculum

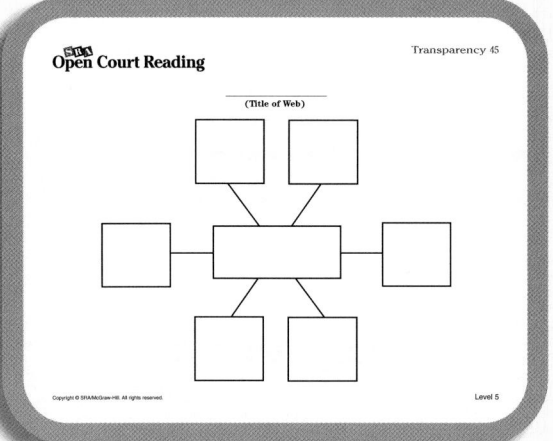

Transparency 45

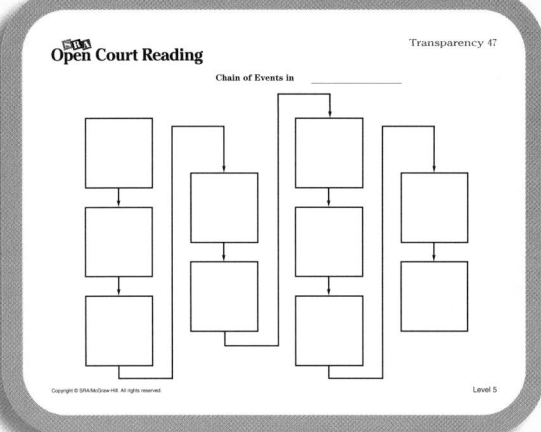

Transparency 47

Language Arts

Writing

Indicators of Time and Order

Instruct Explain to students that indicators of time and order are words that tell when events happen, and in what sequence they take place. Discuss the following guidelines and examples with students.

- Indicators of time tell when something happens. Examples are *last night*, *this morning*, and *in two weeks*.

- Indicators of order show the sequence of events. Examples are *first*, *next*, and *then*.

Practice Refer students to paragraph 3 on page 245 from "In Two Worlds: A Yup'ik Eskimo Family." Have students tell when the events in the paragraph occurred, and ask them how they know.

Students should point out the words that indicate time and order *(each year, for a few months, then)*. Tell students that these indicators are also called signal words.

Apply Have students scan the selection "In Two Worlds: A Yup'ik Eskimo Family," and identify other paragraphs that contain signal words.

Writing Process

Prewrite Have students continue the narrative writing they started in Lesson 1. Have each choose a story idea from the lists that they brainstormed. Using *Transparency 45,* demonstrate how to generate supporting details for their story ideas by using a web. Then, using *Transparency 47,* show students how to put the details they generated into sequential order. Distribute copies of the transparencies to students. Have them generate details for their narratives and then put the details in sequential order. Tell students that this will prepare them for the draft they will start in Lesson 3.

Literary Elements

Purposes of Types of Text

Instruct Ask the students what different purposes authors can have for writing various kinds of books, stories, and articles *(to entertain, to express opinions or feelings, to influence).* Remind them that an author can have several purposes at once.

Practice Ask students what purpose they think Aylette Jenness and Alice Rivers had for writing "In Two Worlds." Have students explain their answers. Then, have them compare and contrast this purpose(s) with that of "The Land I Lost: Adventures of a Boy in Vietnam."

Ask students whether any of them would choose to read another book like "In Two Worlds: A Yup'ik Eskimo Family." Discuss that many people enjoy reading factual material such as biographies, autobiographies, diaries or journals, and travelogues. Although these materials are factual, they are also meant to be entertaining.

Apply Have students use the table of contents in their anthologies to locate the titles of the selections in Unit 1 or Unit 2. Have them discuss what they think the author's purpose is for each selection and how students came to their conclusions.

Teacher Tip Tell students to keep in mind what their purpose is for writing their narratives and their heritage album entries.

Research in Action

Writing

Just as you and the student model reading strategies to help each other understand how good readers read, good writers can model effective writing strategies. Encourage students to use techniques from the selections they read in their efforts to become better writers. *(Marlene Scardamalia)*

3 Integrating the Curriculum

Meeting Individual Needs

Reteach

Using a Dictionary If students need extra help with using a dictionary, see *Reteach,* pages 93–94.

Challenge

Using a Dictionary Remind students that many words have more than one meaning. Write the following sentences on the board and have students use dictionaries to discover the meanings of the italicized words:

The teacher was shocked to learn what *transpired* while he was out of the room.

The plant *transpired* and took up more moisture from the ground.

Choose five other words that have more than one meaning. Ask students to write original sentences for at least two of the different meanings for each word.

If students would like to continue working with using a dictionary, see *Challenge,* page 49.

←Skills Strand→

Using a Dictionary
INTRODUCED: Unit 3, Lesson 2
REVIEWED: Unit 3, Lesson 7
Unit 4, Lesson 1

Vocabulary

Using a Dictionary

Instruct Review with students why they use a dictionary *(to check the spelling, meaning, derivation, or usage of a word).*

Remind students that every page in a dictionary has guide words. Discuss how guide words can help students find the word they are looking for.

Many words have more than one meaning. Students will need to know how an unfamiliar word is used in order to determine its meaning.

Entries also often include the word's part of speech, other forms of the word, examples of how the word can be used, and information about the history of the word.

Practice Have the students use their dictionaries to look up words from the selection: *ptarmigan, intricate, spawn, ancestor,* and *traditional.* Have students write each word, followed by the part of speech, the word's meaning as used in the selection, and the word's history and derivations, if included. Allow time for the students to share their findings.

Apply For additional practice, have students complete *Reading and Writing Workbook* pages 93–94.

Reading and Writing Workbook pp. 93–94

Name _____ Date _____

Use a Dictionary to Clarify Meaning and Usage

In Two Worlds

Focus Dictionaries are useful to both writers and readers.

The main parts of a dictionary are
- the **entry word**, which appears in alphabetical order and is usually in dark type. It shows how the word is spelled and how it can be divided in writing.
- the **guide words**, which appear at the top of each page and are usually in dark type. The word on the left indicates the first entry word listed on the page, while the word on the right indicates the last entry word listed on the page.
- the **pronunciation**, which follows the entry word and usually appears in parentheses.
- the **part-of-speech label**, which usually follows the pronunciation. It is usually an abbreviation (such as *n.* for *noun, v.* for *verb*) and appears in italic type.
- the **definition**, which usually follows the part of speech and tells what the word means. If a word has more than one meaning, the definitions will be numbered.

Identify Use a dictionary to look up the following words from "In Two Worlds" and complete the chart below. Answers will vary.

Entry Word	Pronunciation	Part of Speech	Definition
tundra	tən´drə	n.	vast, nearly treeless plain of the Arctic region
harpoon	här pōōn´	n.	1. spearlike weapon thrown or shot to kill during hunting
		v.	2. to strike or kill with a harpoon
precarious	pri kâr´ē əs	adj.	uncertain, unstable

Reading and Writing Workbook • Use a Dictionary to Clarify Meaning and Usage   93

Use a Dictionary to Clarify Meaning and Usage *(continued)*

Practice Find and write the definition for each of the following words. Then, use each word in a sentence. Answers will vary.

1. inhabit: _____

2. monument: _____

3. enormous: _____

Apply Choose one of the following words that have several different meanings. Find and write at least two different definitions for the word you chose. Then, write a sentence for each meaning of the word. Answers will vary.

present	counter	lead

94   *Use a Dictionary to Clarify Meaning and Usage* • Reading and Writing Workbook

Grammar, Usage, and Mechanics

Forming the Present Tense of Verbs

Instruct Prompt students to tell you that verbs in the present tense show action that is happening now and are formed by adding *s* or *es* to a verb. Verbs that do not follow this rule are called irregular verbs. Irregular verbs have special forms. Review the Grammar lesson from Unit 2, Lesson 3, if necessary.

Practice Prepare two sets of index cards as follows:

Set One Write the following nouns and pronouns, one per card: *I, the captain of the team, you, dogs and cats, my friends and I, the baby.*

Set Two Write the following verbs, one per card: *do, have, be, scream, eat, scratch, sleep.*

Place each set of index cards in a separate box, and have a volunteer draw one card out of each box. The volunteer will then show the cards to the rest of the class and say the correct verb form for the subject noun or pronoun. (For example, if the student selects pronoun card "I" and verb card "be," he or she will show both cards to the class and say "I am.") The rest of the class will then say "correct" or "incorrect" and supply the correct answer if the student was wrong. Have the volunteer put the cards back in the boxes. Call on another volunteer and repeat the procedure.

Apply For additional practice, have students complete *Reading and Writing Workbook,* pages 95–96.

Teacher Tip Remind students to check for correct use and spelling of regular and irregular verbs in their narratives and unit activities.

Meeting Individual Needs

Reteach

Regular and Irregular Verbs Have students who need additional instruction and practice with this concept complete *Reteach,* pages 95–96.

Challenge

Regular and Irregular Verbs Have each student create a puzzle for a partner by writing a paragraph in the present tense about life in Alaska, putting only a blank line where the verbs should be. Have students trade papers with their partners and try to fill in the blanks with the correct verbs in the correct forms.

Have students who may benefit from extended practice with this concept complete *Challenge,* page 50.

Regular and Irregular Verbs
INTRODUCED: Unit 2, Lesson 3
REVIEWED: Unit 2, Lesson 4
Unit 3, Lesson 2
Unit 6, Lesson 1

Reading and Writing Workbook pp. 95–96

Name _____ Date _____

Forming the Present Tense of Verbs

In Two Worlds

Focus Writers use present tense verbs to describe an action that is happening now or is ongoing.

The present tense is formed by adding *-s* or *-es* to a verb, except in the case of irregular verbs, such as *be, have,* and *do,* which have special present tense forms.

* If the subject of the sentence is singular (except *I* or *you*), add *-s* or *-es* to regular verbs to form the present tense.
* If the subject is plural, or if the subject is *I* or *you,* do not add an ending to regular verbs to form the present tense.
* In addition, remember that the verb of a sentence must agree with the subject. If the subject is singular, the verb must be singular. If the subject is plural, the verb must be plural.

Singular Subjects and Verbs
I call, watch, am
you call, watch, are
he, she, or *it* calls, watches, is

Plural Subjects and Verbs
we call, watch, are
you call, watch, are
they call, watch, are

Practice Write the present tense form of the underlined verb in each sentence.

1. Mrs. Jones <u>decided</u> to end class early. decides
2. We <u>traveled</u> to school by bus. travel
3. Father <u>wished</u> he could take a train to work. wishes
4. They <u>did</u> the laundry every Saturday. do
5. I <u>had</u> math homework. have
6. We <u>raked</u> the yard in one hour. rake
7. They <u>stopped</u> to eat at a restaurant. stop

Reading and Writing Workbook • *Forming the Present Tense of Verbs* 95

Forming the Present Tense of Regular and Irregular Verbs *(continued)*

Write sentences using the present tense forms of the following verbs. Make sure you use some singular and some plural subjects. Sentences will vary.

8. search: _____

9. am: _____

10. bounce: _____

11. identify: _____

12. change: _____

Apply Imagine that you are doing some exciting activity, such as running a race, riding a roller coaster, or some other activity. Write a paragraph describing your actions. Use some regular and some irregular verbs in the present tense. Paragraphs will vary.

96 *Forming the Present Tense of Verbs* • Reading and Writing Workbook

 **Integrating the Curriculum**

Listening/Speaking/Viewing

Interpret Speakers' Messages

Ask students what they know about persuasive techniques and interpreting a speaker's messages. If necessary, review the Listening/Speaking/Viewing lesson from Unit 1, Lesson 1.

Have students think about the two ways of life they read about in the selection—the modern way of life and the traditional Yup'ik way of life. Ask students whether they think the authors consider one of the lifestyles to be better than the other and have them explain why.

Make two columns on the chalkboard, one titled "Modern" and the other titled "Traditional." Tell the students that they will generate ideas that a person could use to persuade others that one of the lifestyles is better than the other. Help them brainstorm ideas, and write them on the chalkboard under the appropriate columns. Then divide the class into two groups. One group will represent the traditional way, and the other will represent the modern way. Have each group collaborate on planning a persuasive speech supporting their assigned way of life. Allow time for students to give their speeches to the class.

Meeting Individual Needs

ESL

Sharing Ideas Students who are English-language learners may need extra encouragement to share their ideas. They might prefer to share with other English-language learners.

Study and Research

Interviewing

Instruct Have students turn to *Inquiry Journal* page 45. Have students review the first page. As a class, generate a list of questions they would like to ask an older friend or family member to learn more about their heritages.

Practice Have students select a family member or close friend to interview. Point out to students that it is difficult to write down every word that the interviewee says, so they should practice writing down key words that will help them remember what the person said. Here are some tips students may want to follow when interviewing:

1. Contact the person and ask permission to conduct an interview. You might talk to the person face-to-face or on the phone.
2. Have your questions written in the order you want to ask them.
3. Be polite and allow plenty of time for the person to answer each question.
4. Listen carefully. Careful listening will help you take notes and remember what you heard.
5. Take notes as the person answers your questions, even if you use a tape recorder. You don't need to write every word but do write enough to remember later what the person said.
6. Read your notes as soon after the interview as possible. The interview will be fresh in your mind, and if your notes are unclear or incomplete, you can add information that you remember.

Apply After students have conducted their interviews, have them use their notes to organize their information on *Inquiry Journal* page 46. Remind students that they should observe the rules above for interviewing when working on their unit activities. Also, have students record some ideas for how they can use the information they obtained from the *Inquiry Journal* excercise in their unit activities.

Teacher Tip You may want to have students practice asking their questions to each other before they conduct their interviews.

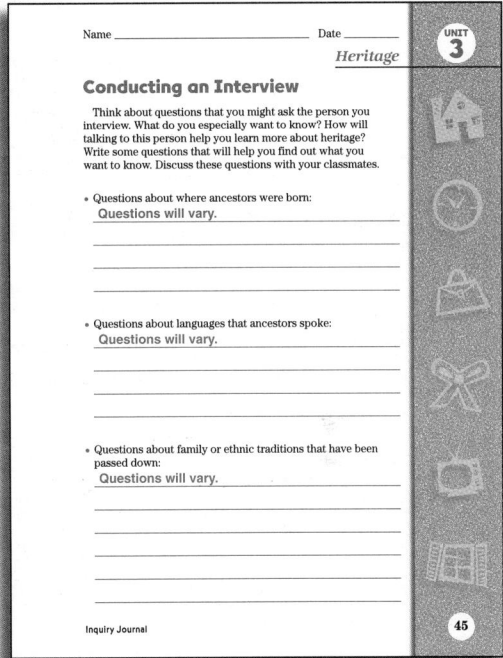

Inquiry Journal pp. 45–46

Across the Curriculum

 **Social Studies**

Come to Alaska

Purpose

To help students become aware of Alaska's geography, climate, and history

Materials

globe or map of Alaska, reference books about Alaska

Procedure

Use a map or globe to show students where Alaska is located. Provide encyclopedias, books about Alaska from the library, and travel brochures.

- Have students work in small groups. Have them use the encyclopedia, the Internet, books, and brochures to find information about the climate, topography, natural resources, cities, history, tourist sites, and anything else that interests them about Alaska.

- Have each group pretend that they are an advertising agency hired to promote tourism in Alaska. Discuss with the groups the types of promotional material they could produce, including travel brochures, posters, radio or television commercials, or billboards.

- Have each group select an idea from above to display their information about Alaska in a way that will attract visitors.

 **Science**

Wildlife in Alaska

Purpose

To help students become aware of Alaska's wildlife

Materials

encyclopedias, reference books about Alaskan animals, posterboard, markers, paints

Procedure

Provide encyclopedias and other reference books about Alaskan animals.

- Have students review "In Two Worlds: A Yup'ik Eskimo Family" and choose one of the animals mentioned to research.

- Have students research their chosen animals to determine their size, eating habits, enemies, habitat, and methods of raising their young.

- Have students present their findings in the form of an annotated poster. Display the completed posters in the classroom for everyone to enjoy.

Across the Curriculum

 **Social Studies**

Trade with Scammon Bay

Purpose

To help students recognize the economic interdependency of communities

Materials

posterboard, markers, paints

Procedure

Have the students review "In Two Worlds: A Yup'ik Eskimo Family" to find mention of items imported to and exported from Scammon Bay.

- Work with the students to create a list, if possible, of items being imported and where they are from and a list of items being exported and where they are going.

- Discuss with students the various ways they could depict this commerce. Students may suggest a flow chart, a map, or a line chart, among others.

- Have groups of students work together to create a graphic representation of the trade between Scammon Bay and the outside world.

- Students may also be interested in looking for products from Alaska in the grocery store and other stores. You may want to keep a separate list of these findings.

 **Art**

Animal Carving

Purpose

To help students appreciate sculpture

Materials

clay or soap, carving utensils such as wooden popsicle sticks, toothpicks, and emery boards

Procedure

Remind students that in the selection "In Two Worlds: A Yup'ik Eskimo Family," Alice Rivers talks about teaching her daughter Mattie to knit and sew and about wanting to teach Mattie the traditional skill of sewing a skin. Share the following information with the students:

In the past, native Alaskans had to make everything they used. Some of the materials they used were stone, bone, and ivory. Sometimes they carved figures using these materials. Some Alaskans today still carve things from bone and stone, especially from a stone called soapstone.

- Give each student a bar of soap or a small lump of clay and carving utensils.

- Suggest that students carve an animal, either one mentioned in the selection or one that they know well. Encourage them to include as many details as they can. (You may want to supply some wildlife books or magazines containing pictures of animals that live in Alaska, after which students can model their carvings.)

- Have each student use a small folded piece of cardboard to make a label for his or her animal carving. Suggest that they title their artwork and list themselves as the artist.

- Display the finished carvings in a classroom "gallery."

The Night We Started Dancing

by Ann Cameron
illustrated by Carlos Caban

I am named after my dad, Luis, but everybody calls me Luisito. I live with my grandfather and grandmother; my four uncles; my two aunts; my cousin, Diego; a girl named Maria who helps my grandmother; our two dogs, Chubby and Pilot; our two cats, Stripes and Hunter; and our big green parrot, Bright Star, that my grandmother always says she is going to bake and serve for dinner someday.

1 We live in a town called Santa Cruz, in Guatemala, Central America. Santa Cruz has a park where there are great band concerts, free, every week. It has a public school, and a big college for army cadets, and it has an electronics store where you could special-order a computer, but it doesn't have paved streets, it has only dirt streets that turn to dust in the winter when it's dry, and to mud in the summer when it rains.

I like dirt streets. It goes with the special thing about Santa Cruz, which is that it's a very old town. It was a town before Columbus discovered America, and before the Spaniards came from Spain to steal our land and our gold and make slaves of people, because they said their religion was the true one, and God liked them better than us.

On the edge of Santa Cruz there is a high hill covered with old pine trees and the ruins of pyramids and an ancient fortress. That's where the headquarters of our people was, the headquarters of the kingdom of the Quichés, where our ancestors fought the Spaniards harder than **2** anybody in Guatemala, before they lost for good.

264

About the Author

Ann Cameron is a master of writing stories set in different cultures. She believes you should write about things you care about, not just the things you know. She received the Children's Book Award of the Child Study Children's Book Committee, and *The Stories Julian Tells* was an American Library Association Notable Book, as well as the winner of a Parent's Choice Award. Students can read more about Ann Cameron on page 282 of the *Student Anthology*.

Other Books by Ann Cameron
- *The Most Beautiful Place in the World*
- *More Stories Julian Tells*
- *Julian's Glorious Summer*

Selection Summary

Genre: Realistic Fiction

In this excerpt from the book *Free to Be a Family*, eight-year-old Luisito lives in Guatemala with his grandparents and other family members. In a very authentic voice, he tells the story of what has happened to him and his family in the last few years and, especially, of what happened on Christmas Eve, the night they started dancing. He speaks of his town and of the achievements of his Mayan ancestors, of the accident that killed his parents and of the bad dreams he still has about it, and especially of his grandfather, who continues to grieve for his dead son.

About the Illustrator

Carlos Caban graduated from the Pratt Institute in New York and joined the Peace Corps where he worked with a nomadic tribe in Colombia. He particulary enjoyed illustrating this selection because of his love for the Mayan culture and people. His advice to young artists is, "All children draw when they are young, I just kept at it. So if you want to be an artist, just keep at it."

Students can read more about Carlos Caban on page 282 of the *Student Anthology*.

Exploring the Theme

Selection Concepts

"The Night We Started Dancing" is the story of a young boy who lives with his grandparents and other relatives after his parents are killed in an accident. In an authentic voice, the boy speaks of his family, his town, the achievements of his Mayan ancestors, and of his grieving grandfather. Key concepts to be explored are:

- Family members help each other survive and carry on despite the losses they suffer.
- Customs and traditions help bring and hold families together.

Check the Reading link of the **SRA** Web page for links to theme-related Websites.
http://www.sra4kids.com

Exploration Activity Tips

Before Reading, read aloud the title of the selection and have the students predict what the story will be about. Then have them browse the selection and add any additional comments.

During Reading, have students think about the impact the death of Luisito's parents had on the family members. Discuss why celebrating Christmas was so important to members of his family.

After Reading, have students discuss what Luisito's Mayan heritage meant to him and how the author conveyed its importance. Then have students update the Concept/Question Board. Some may want to revise their activity plans based on what they have learned from the selection.

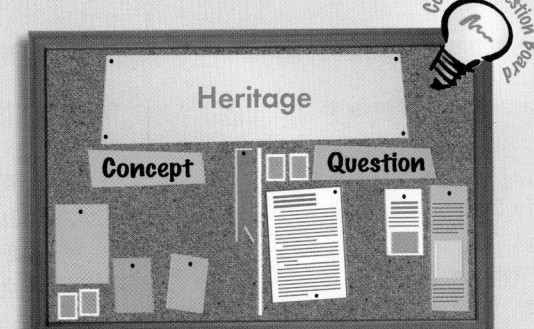

Unit 3
Exploration Management

Lesson 1	Listen to and interview a class guest about heritage. Select and read library books about heritage.
Lesson 2	Identify genres for inclusion in heritage albums. Reflect on one's own heritage, interview family members and friends about customs and traditions, and begin writing.
Lesson 3 **The Night** **We Started** **Dancing**	**Collaborative Exploration** **Identify and utilize various literary techniques. Writing begins on second selection for student albums.** **Supplementary Activity** **Discuss and demonstrate various literary techniques and suggest that students consider creating a photographic essay. Encourage students to discuss customs and traditions with relatives and friends.**
Lesson 4	Work on unit activity continues. Discuss with relatives what they want to communicate about their heritage.
Lesson 5	Write autobiographical sketches for author pages and consider modeling a character after a family member or friend.
Lesson 6	Prepare final drafts, complete illustrations, prepare title and copyright pages, and bind books. Write thank-you notes to those who helped with the activity.
Lesson 7	Students present a selected piece from their heritage albums.

Lesson Planner

Suggested Pacing: 3–5 days	DAY 1	DAY 2	
	DAY 1	**DAY 2**	
Part 1 — Preparing to Read **Materials** ■ Student Anthology, pp. 264–283 ■ Transparencies 17, 44	**Word Knowledge** ■ Reading the Words and Sentences, p. 264G ■ Developing Oral Language, p. 264G **Build Background, p. 264H** **Preview and Prepare, p. 264I** **Selection Vocabulary, p. 264I** *agriculture, foresee, develop, influence*	**Preview and Prepare, p. 264I** ■ Review Transparency 44	
Part 2 — Reading and Responding **Materials** ■ Student Anthology, pp. 264–283 ■ Teacher Observation Log ■ Inquiry Journal, p. 41 ■ Home Connection, p. 39	**Student Anthology, pp. 264–272** **Comprehension Strategies** ■ Asking Questions, pp. 264, 266, 268, 272 ■ Summarizing, p. 268 ■ Predicting, p. 270	**Student Anthology, pp. 273–283** **Comprehension Strategies** ■ Predicting, p. 274 ■ Asking Questions, pp. 276, 278 ■ Summarizing, p. 280 **Discussing Strategy Use, p. 280** **Comprehension Skills** ✓■ Discussing the Selection, p. 281 **Exploring the Theme** ■ Selection Vocabulary, p. 283A *agriculture, foresee, develop, influence*	
Part 3 — Integrating the Curriculum **Materials** ■ Student Anthology, pp. 264–283 ■ Reading and Writing Workbook, pp. 97–100 ■ Transparency 51 ■ Inquiry Journal, p. 47	**Writing** ■ Plot, p. 283C **Literary Elements** ■ Analyzing Character Traits, p. 283E	**Writing Process** ■ Draft, p. 283D **Vocabulary** ✓■ Regular and Irregular Plurals, p. 283F	
Independent Work Time **Materials** ■ Reteach, pp. 97–100 ■ ESL Supplement ■ Challenge, pp. 51–52 ■ Intervention Guide ■ Listening Library Audiocassette	**Writing Process Continued** **ESL** ■ Word Meaning, p. 264G ■ Vocabulary, p. 264J **Intervention** ■ Compound Words, p. 264G **Unit Project** ■ Identify Literary Techniques ■ Begin Writing Second Selection	**Writing Process Continued** **ESL** ■ Analyzing Character Traits, p. 283E **Intervention** ■ Comprehension, p. 264 **Unit Project Continued**	

✓ Informal **Assessment Available**   ✓ **Formal** Assessment Available

DAY 2 continued	DAY 3	
DAY 3	**DAY 4**	**DAY 5**
General Review	General Review	Review Word Knowledge
Student Anthology, pp. 264–283 **Comprehension Skills** ✓ ■ Sequence, pp. 265, 267, 269 **Theme Connections** ■ Think About It, p. 283 ■ Do a Character Sketch, p. 283	**Student Anthology, pp. 264–283** **Comprehension Skills** ■ Making Inferences, pp. 271, 273, 275, 277 **Exploring the Theme** ■ Reading/Writing Connections, p. 283A ■ Literature Appreciation, p. 283A ■ Supporting Student Explorations, p. 283B	**Student Anthology, pp. 264–283** ■ Review Selection ■ Complete Discussion ■ Reread Selection in Pairs **Home Connection, p. 283A** ■ Discuss "The Night We Started Dancing" ■ Write a paragraph about a favorite holiday
Writing Process Continued **Grammar, Usage, and Mechanics** ✓ ■ Adverbs, p. 283G **Listening/Speaking/Viewing** ■ Listening to and Appreciating Spoken Language, p. 283H	**Writing Process Continued** **Study and Research** ✓ ■ Using a Thesaurus, p. 283I	**Across the Curriculum** **Social Studies** ■ Occupations, p. 283J **Music** ■ Songs of Other Countries, p. 283J
Writing Process Continued **Reteach** ✓ ■ Regular and Irregular Verbs, *Reteach*, pp. 97–98 **Challenge** ✓ ■ Regular and Irregular Verbs, *Challenge*, p. 51 ■ Sequence, p. 267 **Unit Project Continued**	**Writing Process Continued** **Reteach** ✓ ■ Adverbs, *Reteach*, pp. 99–100 **Challenge** ✓ ■ Adverbs, *Challenge*, p. 52 **Unit Project Continued**	**Writing Process Continued** **Challenge** ■ Making Inferences, p. 275 **Unit Project Continued**

Meeting Individual Needs
Independent Work Time

Preparing to Read

Meeting Individual Needs

ESL
- Word Meaning, p. 264G
- Accepting Change, p. 264H
- Vocabulary, p. 264J

Intervention
- Compound Words, p. 264G

Reading and Responding

Meeting Individual Needs

ESL
- Sequence, p. 267

Challenge
- Sequence, p. 267
- Making Inferences, p. 275

Intervention
- Comprehension, p. 264
- Summarizing, p. 268
- Sequence, p. 269
- Making Inferences, p. 273
- Predicting, p. 274

Integrating the Curriculum

Meeting Individual Needs

Reteach
- Regular and Irregular Plurals, *Reteach*, pp. 97–98
- Adverbs, *Reteach*, pp. 99–100

ESL
- Analyzing Character Traits, p. 283E

Challenge
- Regular and Irregular Plurals, *Challenge*, p. 51
- Adverbs, *Challenge*, p. 52

Formal Assessment Options

Use these assessment pages along with your informal observations to gauge student progress.

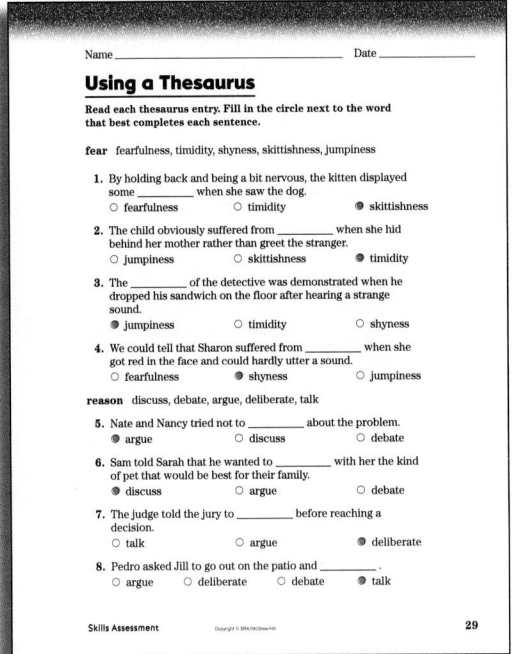

Skills Assessment, p. 29

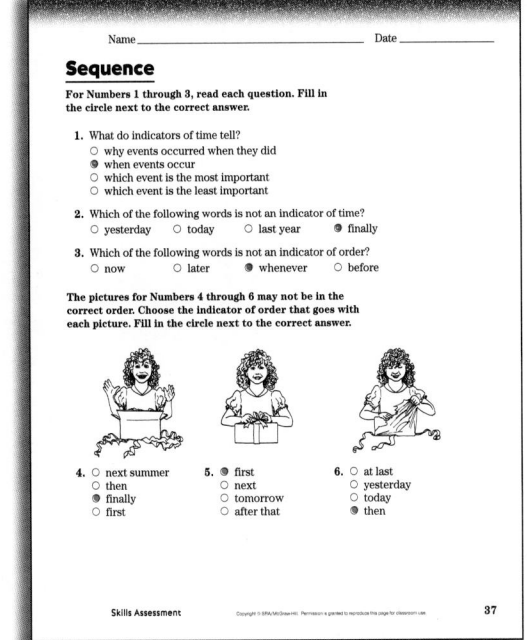

Skills Assessment, p. 37

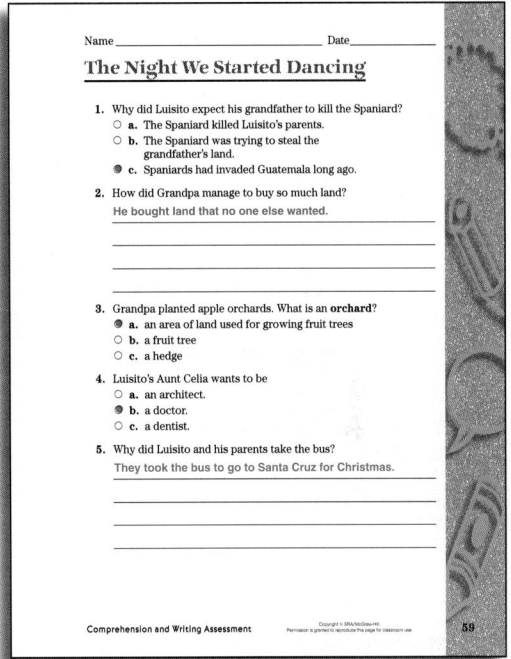

Comprehension and Writing Assessment, p. 59

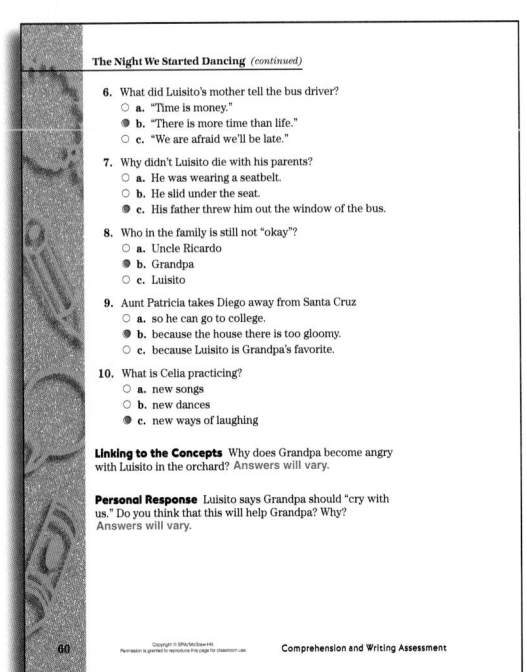

Comprehension and Writing Assessment, p. 60

① Preparing to Read

Meeting Individual Needs

ESL

Word Meaning Make sure English-language learners understand the meanings of the blending words before they do the blending exercises. Refer to Unit 3, Lesson 3, of the **ESL Supplement** for specific suggestions.

Intervention

Compound Words Have students read through the story and list some compound words. Then have them draw a picture equation for each word. Have students exchange papers and solve the equations. For students who need more help, see Unit 3, Lesson 3, of the **Intervention Guide.**

Word Knowledge

Reading the Words and Sentences

Write each word and sentence on the chalkboard. Have students read each word together. After all the words have been read, have students read each sentence in natural phrases or chunks. Use the suggestions in About the Words to discuss the different features of the listed words.

Line 1:   someday   daytime   hillside   houseboat
Line 2:   edge   judge   bridge   porridge   pledge
Line 3:   kingdom   wisdom   freedom
Sentence 1:   The animals graze on the hillside in the daytime.
Sentence 2:   The houseboat moved slowly under the bridge.
Sentence 3:   The judge was widely known for her wisdom.

About the Words

- Line 1 contains closed compound words. These are formed by joining together two words without the use of a hyphen.

- The words in Line 2 all have the /j/ sound spelled *-dge.* Invite students to think of other words that contain this spelling of the /j/ sound.

- All of the words in Line 3 have the suffix *-dom.* The suffix *-dom* is added to the base word to signify ownership.

Developing Oral Language

To review the words, have students do one or both of the following activities.

- Write several words from each line on the chalkboard. Sort them into categories according to their structural element. Have the students brainstorm more words for each list.

- Have students use some of the words on the chalkboard in sentences. Then have other students extend the sentences.

Build Background

Activate Prior Knowledge

Have students check the Concept/Question Board to refresh their memories about heritage. Discuss the following with students to find out what they already know about the selection and have already learned about the unit theme. Tell students to use their prior knowledge to help them comprehend what they are about to read.

- Ask students if they are familiar with the story they are about to read, and if so, to tell a little bit about it. Remind students, however, not to give away the ending of the selection.
- Have students share anything they know about Guatemala or the Mayans.
- Remind students that the story "In Two Worlds: A Yup'ik Eskimo Family" describes the changes in a family that occur when a small town in Alaska becomes more connected with the world. Have students discuss other types of events that would change the dynamics of family life.
- Have students share any other stories that involve traditions or holidays.

Background Information

The following information may help the students to better understand the selection they are about to read.

- "The Night We Started Dancing" is a story about a family living in Santa Cruz, Guatemala, in Central America. Show students where Guatemala is on a map or globe.
- Ann Cameron lives in Guatemala and got the idea for "The Night We Started Dancing" from a Christmas Eve celebration at the home of Guatemalan friends.
- Be aware that the death of the main character's parents may be a sensitive issue in your classroom. Focus on the positive ways family members in this selection help each other to cope with this tremendous loss.
- Tell students that the holidays that individuals and families celebrate can tell a lot about the traditions that are their heritage.

Meeting Individual Needs

ESL

Accepting Change Begin a discussion about how difficult change can be to accept. Ask English-language learners to talk about something that their own grandparents have difficulty accepting. Perhaps students can make suggestions about strategies for coping with and accepting those specific changes.

Writing Journal Tell the students that after reading they will be jotting down in their Writing Journals their reactions to the story, as well as any ideas they may have about the customs and traditions of their heritage.

 *Teacher Tip* Ask the students how knowing that this selection is realistic fiction prepares them for reading this story. Would they anticipate different types of information if the selection was an informational essay?

Preparing to Read

Transparency 44

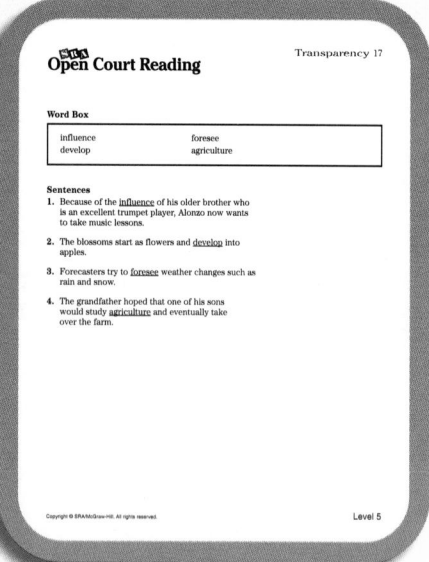

Transparency 17

Teacher Tip

To help students decode words, divide them into the syllables shown below. The information following each word tells how students can figure out the meaning of each word from the sentences on the transparency.

ag·ri·cul·ture   context clues
fore·see   context clues, word structure
de·vel·op   context clues
in·flu·ence   context clues

Preview and Prepare

Browse

■ Have a volunteer read the title and author's and illustrator's names aloud. Have students share what they know about realistic fiction.

■ Because this selection is fiction, have the students browse through the first half of the story searching for words and phrases that connect to what they already know. Record these in the Clues column on **Transparency 44.** Discuss with the students what they think this selection might have to do with family traditions or heritage.

■ Encourage students to ask questions as they browse. Have them identify any problems they notice while reading in the Problems column.

Set Purposes

As they read, have students think about heritage. You may also have students think about what ideas they may have for their heritage albums.

Selection Vocabulary

As students study vocabulary, they will use context clues, word structure, and apposition to determine the meaning of these and additional unfamiliar words.

Display **Transparency 17** before reading the selection to introduce and discuss the following words and their meanings.

ag·ri·cul·ture: farming; growing crops and raising animals (page 268)
fore·see: to know ahead of time; to see into the future (page 270)
de·vel·op: to create, progress, or improve (page 273)
in·flu·ence: the power of a person to affect another (page 276)

Have students read the words in the Word Box. Help students decode multisyllabic words by reading them syllable by syllable.

Have the students read the sentences on **Transparency 17** to determine the meaning of the underlined words. Remind them to use clues in the sentences and structural clues to figure out the meaning. See the teacher tip on the left for information on how the words in each sentence can be defined.

Reading Recommendations

Your first reading of the selection should focus on developing the reading strategies found to the left of the reduced pages. We recommend that the students revisit the selection, rereading sections or the entire selection as a way to enhance their understanding and appreciation of the text. During rereading, they should focus on the comprehension skills found to the right of the reduced pages.

Oral Reading

Because the pronunciation of Spanish names and words in this selection may be unfamiliar to students, oral reading is recommended. Have students practice pronouncing these words and names before reading (for your convenience, Teacher Tips on their pronunciations are featured beside and below the reduced **Student Anthology** pages in the **Teacher's Edition**). As students read aloud, have them read expressively at an appropriate pace, in natural phrases and chunks. By reading the selection with fluency, students will demonstrate an understanding of the text and an ability to engage the listeners in an effective manner. If students encounter difficulties, have them use the reading strategies below or refer to the Blending Procedure (Program Appendix 15–16).

Using Reading Strategies

Reading strategy instruction allows students to become aware of how good readers read. During the reading of "The Night We Started Dancing," you will model the use of the following reading strategies:

- Asking Questions
- Predicting
- Summarizing

Before reading, have students share how they have used these strategies in the past and any tips they can give each other on their use.

Building Comprehension Skills

Revisiting or rereading a selection allows students to apply skills that give them a more complete understanding of the text. Some follow-up comprehension skills, such as *Main Idea and Details* and *Compare and Contrast*, help students organize information. Others, such as *Author's Purpose*, *Making Inferences*, and *Drawing Conclusions*, lead to deeper understanding—to "reading between the lines," as mature readers do. In this selection, students will apply the follow-up comprehension skills of *Sequence* and *Making Inferences*. Because two skills are reviewed, you may want to do all the sections related to one skill before doing the other skill.

Meeting Individual Needs

ESL

Vocabulary Check that English-language learners know the meanings of idioms and more difficult vocabulary in the story, including: *pyramids; ancient fortress; they lost for good; I couldn't stand it; tortilla; a crazy parrot; judge people by what they do; hoeing; ashamed-looking; architecture; economics; dentistry; law; accounting; psychology; put the bus in gear; gloomy; treats me like a grown-up; waste of time; borrow a laugh; the influence of a man; be patient;* and *jokes*. Explain and show pictures as needed. Model example sentences and help English-speaking students make their own sentences. Refer to Unit 3, Lesson 3, of the **ESL Supplement** for teaching suggestions.

 By this time in the fifth grade, good readers should be reading approximately 143 words per minute with fluency and expression. The only way to gain fluency is through practice. As explained in Reading Recommendations, have students reread all or part of the selection to you and to each other during class or Independent Work Time to focus on the comprehension skills and to build fluency.

 Have students who may need extra help reading "The Night We Started Dancing" reread the selection using the **Listening Library Audiocassette.**

 You may want to encourage the students to reread the selection silently. Have them write down any questions they encounter and then conduct a whole-group discussion.

2 Reading and Responding

Read pages 264–283.

Comprehension Strategies

Modeling

1 Asking Questions *Good readers ask questions to help them focus on what they want to learn from the reading. I wonder what Santa Cruz is like. It's in a different country, so it will probably be very different from the places I'm familiar with. I'm sure we'll learn more as we keep reading.*

What question are you asking yourself about this new selection?

Modeling

2 Answering Questions *This part answers my question by telling me something of what Santa Cruz is like. Santa Cruz sounds very interesting. At first it didn't seem so different from a small town in this country. But the pyramids and fortress are things I couldn't find around here.*

Word Knowledge

grandfather, grandmother, someday, headquarters

Students can use the skills they learned in the Word Knowledge section of this lesson to read these words. Remind students of this if they have difficulty decoding these words.

Reading Recommendation

ORAL · CHORAL · SILENT

The Night We Started Dancing

by Ann Cameron
illustrated by Carlos Caban

I am named after my dad, Luis, but everybody calls me Luisito. I live with my grandfather and grandmother; my four uncles; my two aunts; my cousin, Diego; a girl named Maria who helps my grandmother; our two dogs, Chubby and Pilot; our two cats, Stripes and Hunter; and our big green parrot, Bright Star, that my grandmother always says she is going to bake and serve for dinner someday.

1 We live in a town called Santa Cruz, in Guatemala, Central America. Santa Cruz has a park where there are great band concerts, free, every week. It has a public school, and a big college for army cadets, and it has an electronics store where you could special-order a computer, but it doesn't have paved streets, it has only dirt streets that turn to dust in the winter when it's dry, and to mud in the summer when it rains.

I like dirt streets. It goes with the special thing about Santa Cruz, which is that it's a very old town. It was a town before Columbus discovered America, and before the Spaniards came from Spain to steal our land and our gold and make slaves of people, because they said their religion was the true one, and God liked them better than us.

On the edge of Santa Cruz there is a high hill covered with old pine trees and the ruins of pyramids and an ancient fortress. That's where the headquarters of our people was, the headquarters of the kingdom of the Quichés, where our ancestors fought the Spaniards harder than **2** anybody in Guatemala, before they lost for good.

264

Assessment

✓ **Informal** Observe individual students as they read, and use the Teacher Observation Log found in the *Assessment Guide* to record anecdotal information about each student's strengths and weaknesses.

Meeting Individual Needs

Intervention

Comprehension Intervention strategies for students having difficulty reading "The Night We Started Dancing" can be found in Unit 3, Lesson 3, of the *Intervention Guide.*

Once, when I was six, a real Spaniard from Spain came to our house for dinner. He was going to do some business with my grandfather, so my grandmother invited him.

The whole dinner I kept watching my grandfather and the Spaniard all the time, and looking at my grandfather's big machete knife that he keeps by the front door.

265

 There are several words in this selection that the students might find difficult. Help them to pronounce the following words:

Luis is pronounced lo͞o´ ēs
Luisito is pronounced lo͞o ē sē´ tō
Diego is pronounced dē ā´ gō
Santa Cruz is pronounced sän´ tä kro͞oz
Guatemala is pronounced gwä tä mä´ lä
Quiches is pronounced kē´ chäs

Comprehension Skills

Sequence

Have the students tell what they know about sequence. If necessary, remind them that *sequence* is the chronological order in which events happen in a story. Authors use time-order words to help their readers understand that time is passing in a story. Point out the following clue words in this story:

- "It was a town before Columbus discovered America, . . ." (page 264)
- "Once, when I was six, . . ." (page 265)

Have the students look for other time-order words in the story. Remind them to pay extra attention to the way this author handles time and sequence because she often skips back and forth in time.

Sequence
INTRODUCED: Unit 1, Lesson 4
REVIEWED: Unit 3, Lesson 3
Unit 4, Lesson 2
Unit 5, Lesson 7
Unit 6, Lesson 1

 Some students might like to learn more about Santa Cruz or Guatemala. Have them look in travel books, an encyclopedia, or on the Internet for more information.

② Reading and Responding

Comprehension Strategies

Modeling

❸ Asking Questions *Why does Luisito think his grandfather is going to kill the Spaniard? This is a strange story. I better keep reading and find out what happens.*

Oh, I see. Luisito was confused because he wasn't really aware that the battle with Spain was over a long time ago. Well, he was only six when this happened. It can be hard to understand time when you are young.

Prompting

❹ Asking Questions *Because Luisito is the main character in this story, do you have any questions about him that you would like answered?*

Student Sample

Asking Questions *Hmm. I know that Luisito lives with his grandparents, aunts, and cousin. He is named after his father. Now we are learning more about his grandfather. Where are his parents and why doesn't he live with them? I'll keep reading and hopefully find out about his parents. (This question is answered on page 268.)*

Word Knowledge

judge

Students can use the skills they learned in the Word Knowledge section of this lesson to read this word. Remind students of this if they have difficulty reading this word.

Finally, I couldn't stand it, I said, "*Con permiso,* excuse me," and got up from the table and followed my grandmother into the kitchen when she went to get more food, and I even ducked under Bright Star's perch to get there faster.

"When?" I asked my grandmother. "When is he going to do it?"

❸ "Who?" my grandmother said. "Do what?"

"When is Grandpa going to kill the Spaniard?" I whispered, and Bright Star hissed in his loudest voice, "Kill the Spaniard!" and the Spaniard looked around fast and dropped his fork.

My grandfather stopped munching his tortilla. "Don't be concerned," he said to the Spaniard, "we just have a crazy parrot," and my grandmother said, "One day I am going to bake you, Bright Star!"

Then she took me into one of the bedrooms and closed the door.

266

Continue to encourage the students to model for one another when they use strategies or work out problems as they read.

"What is this all about?" she said. "Why would Grandpa kill the Spaniard?"

"For being a Spaniard," I said.

"Are you crazy?" my grandmother said. "How can the Spaniard help being a Spaniard? He was born one, just like you were born a Guatemalan and a Quiché. Don't you know the battles with the Spaniards were over hundreds of years ago? We have to judge people by what they do, not by where they come from. And we have to fight our own battles, too, not the ones our ancestors fought."

So that was when I first found out that we'd never get our kingdom back—at least not the way it used to be.

My grandfather was born poor, and he never went to school. He worked from the time he was six years old, out in the wheat fields and the cornfields, hoeing. Every day when he finished work and went home, he would pass by his own dad in the street, drinking and spending all the family money. My great-granddad never helped my granddad at all. But my granddad just kept working, and when he was twenty, he started buying land—pieces nobody thought were good for anything—and on the land he planted apple orchards, and when the apples grew all over, big and beautiful, he got rich. He built a big house for my grandmother and our family, with five big bedrooms, and a patio in the middle full of flowers, and a living room where he and my grandmother put up all the pictures of both their families, except my grandfather never put up a picture of his dad. Then, last year, he must have finally started feeling sorry for his father, because he got his picture out of a drawer, and dusted it off, and put it up in the living room, only not with the rest of the pictures.

267

Comprehension Skills

Sequence

Point out the following examples of time-order words used to sequence Luisito's grandfather's story of growing up (page 267).

- "Every day . . ."
- "Then, last year . . ."

Explain that the author is using both long and short periods of time to tell a story that covers decades in the space of one paragraph. Discuss how time-order words and phrases help to clarify the author's message.

Teacher Tip There are several words in this selection that the students might find difficult. Help them pronounce the following word: con permiso is pronounced kon´pär mē´sō

Teacher Tip One of the hallmarks of narrative is that events follow a temporal sequence. There are, however, several ways authors sequence events. They can use a *standard* time line, in which events follow a chronological order, a *dual* time line in which two separate events occur simultaneously, or an *interrupted* time line, which is a standard time line, broken by flashbacks. Knowing these temporal organizational patterns helps students' story comprehension and composition skills.

Meeting Individual Needs

ESL	Challenge
Sequence Help English-language learners become more comfortable with sequencing by asking them about time-order words in their first language. Have them explain how these words are used and ask them if they can give the English equivalent for some of their time-order words.	**Sequence** Have students tape record grandparents' memories. Then, have the students write a summary of what they taped, in the sequence in which it was told. Have students identify any time-order words used to indicate the sequence of events.

2 Reading and Responding

Comprehension Strategies

Modeling

5 Answering Questions *Now I know what happened to Luisito's parents. How sad that they died.*

Prompting

6 Summarizing *Because the main story seems to be starting now, and there has been a lot of information before this point, I think we ought to sum up quickly to make sure we remember everything that has happened. Who wants to begin the summary?*

Student Sample

Summarizing *Luisito lives with his grandparents because his parents died. His grandfather worked all his life, and got rich planting orchards. His favorite son was Luisito's father. The only one of their children living with them is Celia, who is sixteen.*

Word Knowledge

grandparents, hometowns, suitcase

Students can use the skills they learned in the Word Knowledge section of this lesson to read these words. Remind students of this if they have difficulty reading these words.

So now my great-grandfather is staring out at the rest of the family, kind of ashamed-looking, from behind a fern.

My grandmother only learned to read four years ago, but she made my aunts and uncles study hard in school, and now she's making me do it, too. When I asked her why I had to study so hard, she said, "So that you aren't working with a hoe in the fields all your life, with the sun beating down on your head like a hammer."

When my grandparents' kids got to be old enough to study in the capital, my grandparents bought a house there for them to live in. So most of the year my aunts and uncles are there, studying architecture, and economics, and dentistry, and law, and accounting, and psychology. Only my youngest aunt, Celia, who is sixteen, is still living in Santa Cruz all the time. But next year she's going to the capital, too. She says she's going to study to be a doctor. My grandparents are very proud of all their children. The sad thing is, their oldest son, the only one who was studying agriculture and who loved the land the way my grandfather does, was my **5** father, and he died. My mother died with him. **6**

My mother was teaching grade school and my dad was in the last year of his agriculture studies when they died. I was four years old.

268

Meeting Individual Needs

Intervention

Summarizing If students have difficulty summarizing, you might ask "What should you do when you have trouble summarizing?" *(reread)*

It happened four years ago, when my mom and dad and I and Uncle Ricardo were taking a bus from the capital to go back to my grandparents' house for Christmas. The bus terminal was full of dust and people trying to sell ice cream and coconuts and last-minute Christmas presents. Lots of people were going back to their hometowns for the holidays, and there weren't enough buses. Everybody was pushing and shoving to get on the ones there were.

My mom had a suitcase, and my dad had me on his back because he figured I couldn't run fast enough, and Uncle Ricardo was staring toward the sun with his hand shading his eyes, trying to see the bus that goes to Santa Cruz.

"Santa Cruz! That's it! Run!" he shouted, and my mom and dad raced for the front door of the bus, and Uncle Ricardo raced for the back, and they did flying dives over the top of a bunch of other people. My mom and dad got seats right behind the driver, and I sat on my mom's lap. Uncle Ricardo got stuck at the back, standing up.

Everybody pushed the windows down to get more air, and the driver put the bus in gear, but it didn't move, and his helper, the ticket taker, got out a hammer and a wrench and raised the hood on the bus and hammered on something for a while, and then the driver tried to move the bus again, and it went, and Uncle Ricardo heard my mother say, "A miracle! What a miraculous miracle!" and the ticket taker ran after the moving bus and jumped in the open door with the hammer and the wrench in his hand, and we were off.

269

Comprehension
Skills

Sequence

Review with the students that good readers look for clues in the text that show what time it is, how time is passing, or the order of events.

Point out to the students that on page 268, the author slips from present-tense verbs to past-tense verbs.

Have the students discuss why the author shifted from the present to the past. Point out that telling about the past helps readers understand events and characters in the present.

Teacher Tip

There are many words in this selection that the students might find difficult. Help them pronounce the following words:

Celia is pronounced   sā´ lē ä
Ricardo is pronounced   rē kär´ dō

Meeting Individual Needs

Intervention

Sequence Help students better understand sequence by laying out the main ideas in the story and having them place them in the correct order. Explain that even though events that happened in the past are told after events that happened in the present, each section tells events in a set sequence.

Assessment

✓ **Formal** To assess students' understanding of this concept, have them complete **Skills Assessment**, page 37.

Reading and Responding

Comprehension Strategies

Modeling

7 Predicting *Predictions should be based on both the text and one's own knowledge. I'm getting a funny feeling from the way Luisito's parents keep warning the driver—something bad is going to happen. I'm not even sure I want to keep reading, but I'll never find out what happens if I don't.*

My prediction was right. Something bad did happen. Even though I knew earlier that Luisito's parents had died, this was still hard to read.

Teacher Tip The death of Luisito's parents could be a sensitive issue for some students in your classroom. Please keep this in mind and plan appropriate ways to address this issue with your students.

Word Knowledge

There are many multisyllabic words in this selection. Be sure students are using the skills they learned in the Word Knowledge section of this lesson.

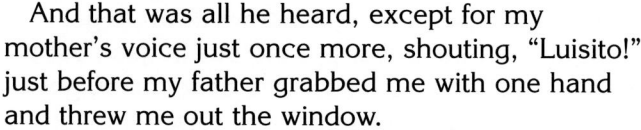

Uncle Ricardo settled in and tried to take his elbow out of the stomach of the person on his right, and get his feet out from under the feet of the person on his left. My mom and dad were probably about the only ones who could see out the window, and who knew how the driver was driving.

The bus didn't go very fast, because it couldn't with so many people on it, but after a while Uncle Ricardo felt the bus lurch, and he heard my dad say to the driver, "Be careful, brother!" so he figured that the bus driver must have been taking a chance passing on a mountain curve.

A little while later he felt the bus twist again, and he heard my father say to the driver, "A man who foresees trouble and prevents it, is worth two men." But it seemed like the driver didn't feel like listening, because a little while later Uncle Ricardo heard my father say, "No matter where you are going, you don't have to get there first. The thing is, to get there."

And after that he heard my mother say, "Driver, there is more time than life."

7 And that was all he heard, except for my mother's voice just once more, shouting, "Luisito!" just before my father grabbed me with one hand and threw me out the window.

270

The bus driver went head-on into another bus. And my mother was right, because time just keeps going on and on and on, but she and my dad and the bus driver and the ticket taker and a lot of other people ran out of life completely.

Uncle Ricardo was okay because he was at the back, and I was okay.

The only part I remember begins with the grip of my father's hand, and how it hurt when he shoved me through the window frame. But I don't like to remember. I like to think about daytime things, my aunts and uncles, and things that are happening now.

But sometimes I still dream about it, being thrown out the window. In the dream I am little again, the same age I was then, and I land down a hillside in a freshly hoed field, just the way I really landed, but it is not daytime, it is almost completely dark, and I get up and go back to the wrecked bus, to find my mom and dad, but it gets darker and darker, and I never can find them.

271

Comprehension Skills

Making Inferences

Have the students tell what they know about making inferences. Remind them that authors do not directly tell everything they want readers to know. Explain to the students that good readers use clues from the text and their own knowledge to better understand a character, thing, or event in a story. This is called making inferences.

Point out to the students that Luisito tells the story about the bus ride from his Uncle Ricardo's point of view.

■ Ask the students what they infer from this about Luis' memory of the event. *(He was too young or too scared to remember much of what happened.)*

■ Have students identify the clues in the story that led them to this inference.

■ What does Uncle Ricardo infer from the remarks he hears Luisito's parents make? *(The driver is driving the bus recklessly.)*

←Skills Strand→

Making Inferences
INTRODUCED: Unit 1, Lesson 2
REVIEWED: Unit 1, Lesson 6
Unit 2, Lesson 3
Unit 3, Lesson 3
Unit 4, Lesson 5

 **Reading and Responding**

Comprehension Strategies

Modeling

8 Asking Questions *Why is it that everyone in the family is "okay" about the death of Luisito's parents except his grandfather?*

Oh, I see. Luisito's father was more than a son to Luisito's grandfather—he was his best friend.

Modeling

9 Asking Questions *Why aren't they celebrating Christmas?*

Oh, I remember now. Luisito's parents were traveling back home for the holidays. They must have died around Christmas time. No wonder the grandfather is so sad! Even one year after their death, he wasn't able to celebrate Christmas.

Word Knowledge

anymore, anybody, everything

Students can use the skills they learned in the Word Knowledge section of this lesson to read these words. Remind students of this if they have difficulty reading these words.

Uncle Ricardo says one day I won't have the dream anymore. He says that my parents loved me a lot, and that I will always have them in my heart. He says one day my dream self will understand that, too. It will know that my parents are always with me when I remember them. It won't have to go back to the wrecked bus to look for them anymore.

And really I am okay, and Uncle Ricardo is okay, and my grandmother also is okay, because she loves all her children very much, but equally. The **8** only one who has not been okay is my grandfather, because he loved my dad more than anybody. My dad wasn't only his son, he was his best friend.

9 The first Christmas after the accident we didn't celebrate, because nobody wanted to. But the next Christmas we didn't celebrate either, because Grandpa didn't want to. On the anniversary of the accident, he cut a lot of white roses and put them in front of my parents' wedding picture that hangs in the living room, and we visited their graves at the cemetery, so that was all there was of Christmas that year, too.

And from the beginning my grandmother said we shouldn't mention my mom and dad in front of my grandfather because it might upset him too much. She said we should just wait, and in time he would get better.

But it got to be September of the third year after my father died, and my grandfather still wasn't any better. My aunt Patricia, who had been leaving my cousin Diego with us a lot in Santa Cruz, decided to take Diego to the city. She said it was because she didn't have so many courses and she would have more time to spend with him, but Uncle Ricardo told me it was really because she thought it was too gloomy for Diego around our house.

272

The only reason I liked being in the house is that I like my grandmother and Celia a lot, my grandmother because she never yells at anybody, and Celia because she treats me like a grown-up. She got me to help her with a lot of projects, especially her Laugh Development Project, in which she said she needed the opinion of a man.

She wanted to develop four new laughs, even though my grandmother said it was a waste of time, and she couldn't see what was wrong with the laugh Celia was born with.

Celia said these are modern times, and a person should have five of everything. She said her original laugh was for when she really felt like laughing, and the other four would be for when she couldn't afford to be serious. She wanted my

273

Comprehension Skills

Making Inferences

Authors don't include all the information in a story. Good readers use clues from the story plus what they already know to *make inferences* about why events happen in a certain way and why characters act as they do.

■ Have students think about a time when an adult tried to comfort them because they were sad or scared. What inference can the students make about why Uncle Ricardo is telling Luisito that he won't have the bad dream anymore? *(He wants Luisito to feel better and to know that one day he will work through his parents' death.)*

Have the students make other inferences as they read.

Teacher Tip Have students distinguish between ideas that are stated explicitly in the text and those that are triggered in their minds by clues in the text. Explain that when they write, they should make sure to include enough information to allow readers to gain meaning. This is what is meant by "writing as a reader."

Meeting Individual Needs

Intervention

Making Inferences Review with students that good readers use clues from the text and their own knowledge to make inferences about a character, thing, or event in a story. Present clues and ask the students to make inferences. Then, have students tell you what they can infer about the outcome of the story by reading its title.

2 Reading and Responding

Comprehension Strategies

Modeling

⑩ Predicting *Will Luisito's grandfather find out about the "Laugh Development Project?" I think he will. I also predict that he won't be happy about it. He doesn't seem to want to laugh at all anymore.*

When I read on, I see that he doesn't get angry when he finds out, but he does tell Luisito he wants to take him to the orchards.

Prompting

⑪ Predicting *What do you predict Luisito's grandfather will want to talk about while they are in the orchard?*

Student Sample

Predicting *I predict he is going to tell Luisito to stay away from Celia because of the "Laugh Development Project."*

I was right. He does feel that Luisito is around Celia too much. He feels Luisito should be around men more.

Word Knowledge

eyebrows, boyfriend, afternoon

Students can use the skills they learned in the Word Knowledge section of this lesson to read these words. Remind students of this if they have difficulty reading these words.

---

opinion because she wanted to make sure the four new laughs would be good enough to impress boyfriends.

So when Grandpa wasn't around, she practiced in front of the big cracked mirror on the patio.

"Ha, ha, HAH, HAH, hah," went the first laugh, which is a rapid one where she tosses her long black hair back behind her shoulders. That is her Rio de Janeiro laugh.

"Ho ho ho," she laughs slowly, and rubs her chin thoughtfully with the finger of one hand. That's her Paris laugh.

"Hee hee hee," she giggles, and covers her eyes with her hands. That's her Tahiti laugh.

"Hoo, hoo, hoo, hoo," she laughs, and raises her eyebrows very high. That's her Mexico City laugh.

274

Meeting Individual Needs

Intervention

Predicting Remind students that predictions are not wild guesses. Tell students having difficulty making predictions to summarize this section of the selection, and use their summaries as a basis for their predictions. Have them check their predictions as they read.

She got all the ideas for the laughs from TV and from fashion magazines. After she got them all worked out, I told her they were all good, except the Tahiti laugh, which looked like she was just waking up in the morning, so she decided to rename it a waking-up laugh, to throw a stretch into it.

So she did. But just when she had them all perfect, Bright Star got them perfect, too. He sang them all off in a row, and then he said, in my voice, "Laugh Development Project."

"Now I can't bring any boyfriend home!" Celia said. "Either I can't bring one home, or I can't use my laughs."

10 "Not only that," I said, "Grandpa is going to know about this for sure."

Celia shrugged. "Maybe he'll borrow a laugh," she said. "He doesn't seem to have one of his own. Anyway, what more can he do? We already don't have Christmas anymore."

Sure enough, when Grandpa came home, Bright Star talked. He laughed all four laughs, and then imitated me, saying "Laugh Development Project."

It happened at dinner. My grandfather looked at Bright Star, and he looked at Celia, and he looked at me, but all he said was, "After school tomorrow, **11** I want to take you out to the orchards, Luisito."

So I said okay, and the next afternoon we hiked out to the orchards.

275

Comprehension Skills

Making Inferences

Have the students continue to make inferences from the selection.

- Why did Celia practice her laugh when her father wasn't around? *(because he was sad and she was afraid he would get angry at her for laughing and being happy)*

- Why do you think Luisito's grandfather placed the white roses beside Luisito's parent's wedding picture on the anniversary of the accident? *(He wanted to honor them and remember them in a special way. That is also why they visited the cemetery. Luisito's grandfather probably wanted to make these special gestures instead of celebrating Christmas.)*

- Why does Celia say that she cannot bring home her boyfriends or cannot use her laughs? *(Because Bright Star is imitating Celia's laughs and repeating the name of the project, her boyfriends would know that they were not real laughs, that they were all rehearsed.)*

- Why does Luisito's grandfather say he wants to take Luisito out to the orchards? *(After Luisito's grandfather listens to Celia's story about the Laugh Development Project, he decides it is time for Luisito to start doing the things that his father used to do.)*

Teacher Tip Remind the students that inferences are solidly based on clues in the text.

Meeting Individual Needs

Challenge

Making Inferences Encourage students to break into small groups and discuss Celia's remark about her father, "Maybe he'll borrow a laugh . . . He doesn't seem to have one of his own." From that remark what can one infer about Celia. What can one infer about her father?

2 Reading and Responding

Comprehension Strategies

Modeling

12 Asking Questions *I wonder why grandma tells Luisito about the time his father set the cornfield on fire? When I think about it, I'm sure she wants Luisito to feel better about not listening or remembering things as well as his father used to. She probably wants him to see that his father was just a kid once, too.*

What do you wonder about this part of the selection?

Word Knowledge

kingdom

Students can use the skills they learned in the Word Knowledge section of this lesson to read this word. Remind students of this if they have difficulty reading this word.

"You are around your Aunt Celia too much," my grandfather said, but not unkindly. "You need the influence of a man."

"I am a man," I said.

"You are?" my grandfather said. "How do you know?"

"Celia said so."

He looked at me and said it took more than Celia's saying so to make somebody a man, and then he started telling me about the trees, and what you had to do to take care of them, and how many different kinds of apples there were, and how you could tell them apart.

276

Teacher Tip This selection is written in non-chronological order. That is, the narrator often goes back in time to tell about a past event and then returns to the present. Have students ask questions and sum up in order to clarify these shifts in time.

But a bad thing happened, because the orchards are right next to the pyramids and the forts of the old kingdom, and I kept thinking about them and wanting to go over there, instead of listening to my grandfather.

"Luisito," he said suddenly, "how many kinds of apples do I have?"

And I couldn't tell him.

"You're not listening! Your father understood and remembered everything when he was your age!" he shouted. "Go on home to your grandmother!"

So I left, and instead of going straight home, I went over to the pyramids and ran up to the top of the biggest and stood there listening to the branches of the pine trees in the wind. It didn't help anything. And then I walked home alone.

 When I told my grandma what happened, she said, "Your dad did understand and remember very well when he was your age. But when he was your age, he also played with matches once and set a whole cornfield on fire. It took us, the neighbors and the whole fire department to put it out."

"Tell Grandpa that!" I said. "Remind him about it!"

"I will sometime," my grandmother said, "but not now."

"When?" I asked. "You said Grandpa would get better and we just had to be patient. He used to make jokes, Celia says. He used to take everybody on trips. Now he never does, and he never gets any better."

277

Comprehension
Skills

Making Inferences

Have the students reread the first five paragraphs on page 277. Have them make inferences as to why the grandfather gets so angry at Luisito and why he mentions Luisito's father. Guide them to infer that he wants Luisito to be like his father was at his age. He misses Luisito's father very much and wants Luisito to be more like him.

Have the students continue to make inferences about events and characters as they read.

Teacher Tip

Remind students that this selection is realistic fiction. Discuss how knowing this information helps them make inferences. *(They can use what they know about why real people act as they do to figure out the characters' motives.)*

 **Reading and Responding**

Comprehension Strategies

Modeling

⓭ **Asking Questions** *I wonder why the grandfather doesn't want to dance. Maybe it's because he's so sad about Luisito's parents. After all, dancing is a happy thing to do and it's hard when other people are happy and you're sad. But it's very sad not to dance. I hope the grandfather feels better soon.*

Modeling

⓮ **Asking Questions** *I wonder if Luisito will be able to help his grandfather.*

Reading on, I see that he has, just by being there with him. I know that sometimes you can comfort someone without saying very much.

Word Knowledge

everybody, firecrackers, outside

Students can use the skills they learned in the Word Knowledge section of this lesson to read these words. Remind students of this if they have difficulty reading these words.

"You are right," my grandmother said.

"Besides," I said, "Christmas is coming, and I am tired of not having Christmas, and so is Celia."

"You're probably right," my grandmother said. "We should celebrate Christmas."

And she actually used the telephone, which she never uses, to call up Ricardo and talk to him about it.

And that night at dinner, she told my grandfather, "It's time we started to celebrate Christmas again."

"I would rather not," my grandfather said.

"The children say they won't come home for Christmas, unless we celebrate, like the old days. Luisito and Celia say they would rather go into the city to be with Ricardo and everybody if we don't celebrate Christmas."

"Um," my grandfather said.

"I might go, too," my grandmother said.

"*You* might go?" my grandfather said.

"Yes, I probably will go," my grandmother said.

"You would *leave* me?" my grandfather said.

"Just for Christmas," my grandmother said.

"It wouldn't be good," my grandfather said. "We've been together thirty-one years. You've never been away. Not one day!"

"Times change," my grandmother said.

⓭ "Well," my grandfather said, "we had better celebrate Christmas. But I won't dance."

"You don't have to dance," my grandmother said. "Nobody has to dance. But at least we will have dance music, anyway."

Celia and I made a beautiful golden Christmas tree out of corn husks that we cut to fasten on

278

wires and make the shape of branches. When we were done, the tree went all the way to the ceiling, and we draped it with red chains of tinsel. And my grandmother stood in front of the stove all Christmas Eve day making the tamales for the midnight dinner—corn stuffed with chicken and meat and olives and raisins and hot chili sauce, and wrapped in banana leaves to cook. And everybody arrived from the city about six-thirty at night, just in time for the supper we were going to have to tide us over to the real dinner at midnight.

Uncle Ricardo brought Diego and me about sixty firecrackers to set off at midnight, when all the kids in town go outside to set off firecrackers, so we were feeling good. And my grandfather had dressed up in his best and happiest clothes, new pants, and a cap that makes him look as young as my uncles.

Everybody hugged, and we all sat down to eat, but nobody talked much until we were almost finished, when Aunt Patricia said, "All the same, it's sad anyway."

And my Uncle Pedro, who had been an exchange student in the U.S. for one year of high school, said, "If the roads had shoulders, the way the highways do in the U.S., they never would have died."

And Celia said, "So in the great U.S.A. there are no traffic accidents?"

And before Pedro could answer her, my grandfather got up out of his chair and went out on the patio, and we all stopped talking.

14 "Luisito," my grandmother said, "go be with your grandfather."

279

Comprehension Skills

Making Inferences

Have volunteers explain how they make inferences. Write their answers on the chalkboard.

■ Ask the students to read page 278 carefully for clues to the relationship between Luisito's grandmother and grandfather. Have them infer why the grandfather finally agrees to have Christmas after all this time. *(He doesn't want to be left alone and away from his wife and family.)*

What other inferences can the students make? Discuss how making inferences keeps the reader actively involved with the story.

 **Teacher Tip**
Some students may be interested in knowing that Ann Cameron is also the author of the *Julian* books.

 **Teacher Tip**
There are many words in this selection that the students might find difficult. Help them to pronounce the following word: Pedro is pronounced pā′ drō.

2 Reading and Responding

Comprehension Strategies

Prompting

15 **Summarizing** *Let's summarize to make sure we got everything straight. The family isn't happy that grandfather is still sad. They want to have Christmas. Luisito is upset that he can't do as well as his father did in the orchards. Who can continue the summary?*

Student Sample

Summarizing *He learns that his father wasn't perfect either. Grandmother convinces Grandfather to celebrate Christmas. He realizes that he can't do anything about the death of his son and must continue with life.*

Discussing Strategy Use

After they have read the selection, have students share any problems they encountered and tell what strategies they used to solve them. Then, have them answer the following questions. If they answer "no" to any of the questions, have them reread part of the selection to find the answer.

- Did they ask questions and check to see if they were answered in the text?

- Did they predict what might happen and then check to see if they were correct?

- Did they summarize in order to help them understand what they've read?

Make sure that students explain how using the strategies helped them understand the selection better and how they read effectively to find answers to the questions they asked as they set purposes.

So I went out on the patio and stood by my grandfather, who was looking up at the sky and wouldn't look down.

I just stood there by him, looking up, too.

There was a full moon, shining down on the patio and on the papery violet leaves of the bougainvillea, and my grandfather spoke, in a choked voice.

"See the leaves? There are so many you can't see the branch, and all different.

"And we are like them, all different, but holding on to an invisible branch——but two of us are missing!"

"Why do they have to talk about it? Don't they know I've cried enough? What do they think I do out in the orchard, but cry?"

"You should cry with us," I said, and I saw my grandfather's eyes drop tears, and we stood there a long time.

Everybody else had gone into the living room, and while we were standing there, the dance music started, very slowly, low music, soft like smoke, winding into the moonlight.

"Oh, Luisito," my grandfather said. "What can we do? What can anybody do? Luisito, we should dance."

And so my granddad and I danced, around the cage of Bright Star, who was sleeping under a new Christmas blanket, and past the cracked mirror and the bougainvillea vine, and then, very slowly, into the living room. And then I danced with Celia, and my grandfather put his arms around my grandmother and danced with her, and everybody danced with everybody, straight through until midnight when the fireworks started going off in huge booms all over town, and we all held hands, and everyone of us kissed every other one, and I noticed for the first time in a long time that in the photo of my mom and dad, above Grandpa's white roses, they were smiling.

280

Teacher Tip Reread the selection with students who had difficulty understanding it. Continue modeling and prompting the use of strategies and skills as you reread.

Comprehension Skills

Discussing the Selection

Following reading, engage the students in a discussion of the selection. Using the *handing-off process* will help the students to take responsibility for the discussion. In addition to the following question, have them revisit any questions asked when they set purposes before the reading.

- How is Luisito's family different from the families we've read about so far in this unit? *(Answers may vary. Students may mention that Luisito doesn't have parents.)*

- What was Luisito's heritage and how did it affect him? *(Answers may vary. But students will probably mention the pyramids and the history of Spanish rule in the country. They can also talk about the orchards.)*

- How was Luisito's family different from your family? *(Answers may vary. Students might mention living with his grandparents, all the pets in the house, traditional foods eaten, and other differences.)*

- How has this selection connected with your knowledge of the unit theme? *(Answers will vary—students should compare/contrast examples of heritage from this selection with their own experiences or past reading and use these connections to make a general statement about the unit theme.)*

During this time, have the students return to the clues and problems that they noted on the transparency before reading. Let the students decide which items deserve further discussion.

Having the children "hand off" the discussion to other students instead of the teacher encourages them to retain complete control of the discussion.

Assessment

✓ **Formal** To assess students' reading comprehension, have them complete **Comprehension and Writing Assessment,** pages 59–60.

② Reading and Responding

Meet the Author

After the students read the information about Ann Cameron, discuss the following questions with them.

Ann Cameron grew up wondering about other people and often read to help satisfy her curiosity. Why might it be useful for a writer to be curious? *(Possible answer: The more curious you are, the more you learn about the world. Curiosity helps fuel the imagination, which is an important tool for writing.)*

Ann Cameron says, "When I do what really matters to me, I'm happy." Why do you think it is important to have a job that matters to you? *(Possible answer: When you like what you are doing, you are willing to try harder and you are more likely to be proud of your work.)*

Meet the Illustrator

After the students read the information about Carlos Caban, discuss the following question with them.

Why do you suppose living and working with a Native American tribe influenced Carlos Caban's illustrations? *(Possible answer: Carlos Caban must have had an interest in working with Native American cultures when he joined the Peace Corps. By this time, he already had developed his talent for art. He probably finds blending his two interests very gratifying.)*

The Night We Started Dancing

Meet the Author

Ann Cameron grew up filled with curiosity about other people and read to satisfy that curiosity. After graduating from Harvard, she became an editor so she could read books for a living. After two years of that, however, she knew she would rather be writing them. Today, Ann Cameron is an author who writes about the people who interest her.

Her friends and neighbors are always sources of inspiration. A South African friend, who told stories about his childhood, inspired her first children's book, *The Stories Julian Tells*. She also writes about the people that live around her. Her life is guided by her belief that, "when I do what really matters to me, I'm happy, and my friends are real friends who like me for what I really am."

Meet the Illustrator

Carlos Caban teaches painting and drawing at the Art Institute in San Miguel de Allende, Mexico. This is a small colonial city famous for its art. He grew up in New York but he became interested in Indian cultures while working for the Peace Corps in Colombia, South America. He says, "The story was especially exciting for me because I love the Mayan culture and people and my paintings have been influenced by them."

282

Theme Connections

Think About It

With a small group of classmates, discuss the following questions.

- What does this story tell you about the importance of family and traditions?
- When Luisito's grandfather began to dance with him, what do you think it meant?
- What might have happened to Luisito's grandfather if the family had not insisted on celebrating the Christmas holiday?
- Are there any traditions in your family? If so, do you know how they were developed?

Record Ideas

Think of something you might say to a person who is sad to make them feel better, and write it in your Writing Journal. Then make a list of activities you and your classmates can take part in together, to make people in your community happier.

Do a Character Sketch

Work with a partner and write a description of the characters in this story. Remember to include enough information to let someone who didn't read the story understand what each character is like. As you work, follow these guidelines.

- Plan with your partner what information to include.
- Share your plans with another pair of students.
- Revise your plan, as you see fit.
- Write your character description.

283

Theme Connections

Think About It

- Form small groups and encourage all students to contribute to the discussion.
- Tell students that over the course of this discussion they should try to find and share connections between their own traditions, those of their classmates, and those depicted in the selections. Have students discuss what insights they can gain into the values and beliefs of others by making a study of cultural traditions and holidays.

Do a Character Sketch

Have students post their character descriptions on the Concept/Question Board. Encourage them to read and comment on each other's work.

Teacher Tip Have students discuss what Luisito's Mayan heritage meant to him, and how the author conveyed its importance.

② Responding

✦Exploring the Theme

Some students may choose to conduct a computer search for additional books or information about heritage. Have them make a list of these books and sources of information to share with classmates and the school librarian. Check the Reading link of the **SRA** Web page for links to theme-related Websites.
http://www.sra4kids.com

Have students write sentences using the selection vocabulary words. In order to provide additional help in remembering words, students can write synonyms or antonyms for the words if it is appropriate. Some students may even draw something to help them remember the meanings of the words.

Selection Vocabulary

Have students write in their Writing Journals the definitions for words discussed before the reading of the selection and any other interesting words they clarified while reading. Students should be encouraged to refer to these words throughout the unit as they work on student and writing projects. The words from the selection are:

influence   develop   foresee   agriculture

Reading/Writing Connections

Ann Cameron does not write of the present and the past in chronological order. Have the students think about other books and selections they have read or heard which are written in a similar structure. Discuss with them how they could use a similar structure in their own writing.

Literature Appreciation

Luisito's relatives all attend or plan on attending a university. Several content-area words are used to describe different areas of study, including *architecture*, *economics*, and *dentistry*. Ask the students to think of other areas they might study in college, and write these down on chart paper, along with a definition of each word.

Home Connection

The class has just finished reading "The Night We Started Dancing," a selection that tells the story of eight-year-old Luisito and his family, and why they do not celebrate Christmas. An informational letter on "The Night We Started Dancing," in both English and Spanish, can be found in the **Home Connection** guide.

"The Night We Started Dancing"

A message from _____

We have just finished reading the story *The Night We Started Dancing*, in which a Guatemalan boy named Luisito explains why his family no longer celebrates Christmas. When Luisito was very small, his parents were killed in a bus crash that happened just before Christmas. Luisito now lives with his grandparents, who are still mourning and don't feel like celebrating the holiday anymore. Eventually, Luisito convinces his grandmother, and finally his grandfather, to revive the holiday traditions that make their family special.

Talk to your child about a favorite holiday or gathering. Discuss the things that make this holiday or gathering special.

Have your child use the space below to write a paragraph about this event, and encourage him or her to share it with the class.

Unit 3/Heritage   39

Home Connection p. 39

Supporting Student Explorations

At this point students should be finishing their first written pieces for their albums.

Whole Group Have the students use illustrations, photographs, and diagrams to complement their written work. Suggest that they include an illustration created by a family member or friend.

Remind the students that in each selection they have read so far, the author has used some technique to tell about heritage in an interesting and effective way (such as including memories of family members and past events, using the character's own "voice" to tell the story, comparisons of traditions and customs across generations, non-chronological event sequence, and songs that tell about heritage). Have the students discuss these techniques and consider those that they would like to use in their own stories.

Small Group Have the students read a rough draft of their second pieces to a small group of classmates. Have them make revisions based on the feedback they receive.

Individual Have students begin a second piece for their heritage album. Suggest that they discuss what the next piece might be about with family members or older friends.

Suggest that students post on the Concept/Question Board brief descriptions of books, magazines articles, computer Websites, or other sources of information that they have found to be especially helpful in their explorations of heritage. Encourage students who are having difficulty finding information to check sources on the Board and to post their questions as well.

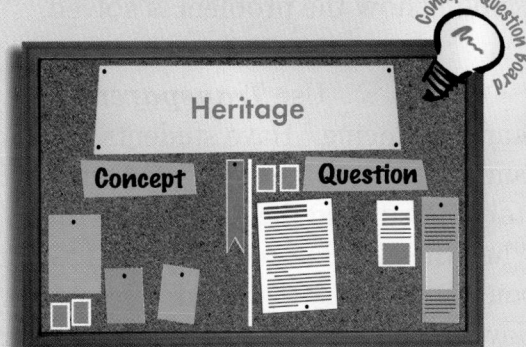

Inquiry Journal Have students complete page 41 of the *Inquiry Journal* to record some of the information learned in "The Night We Started Dancing."

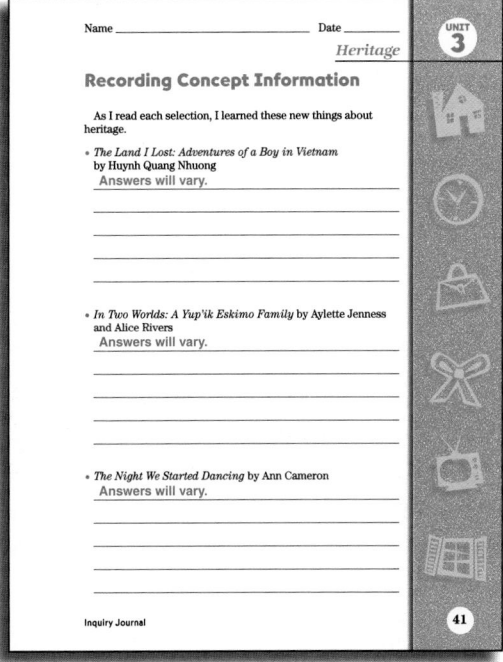

Inquiry Journal p. 41

Assessment

✓ **Informal** Continue your anecdotal record of students' progress. Note whether the students:

- use an author's techniques for communicating about heritage.
- complete one heritage album piece and begin another.
- identify and share informational sources.

 **Integrating the Curriculum**

Language Arts

Writing

Plot

Instruct Explain to students that the chain of events in a story is called the *plot*. The plot introduces a problem and follows the characters as they solve it. Write the elements of plot on a transparency or the chalkboard, and then discuss the elements with students.

■ Every good plot has a beginning, a middle, and an end.

■ A problem that one or more main characters have is introduced at the beginning of the story.

■ In the middle of the story, the characters go through one or more conflicts as they try to solve the problem. Excitement occurs when the conflicts take place.

■ The highest point of interest in the story is called the climax. At the climax the problem begins to be resolved.

■ The conclusion occurs after the climax. The conclusion finishes telling how the problem is solved.

Practice Use **Transparency 51** to summarize "The Night We Started Dancing." Have students tell about the problem Luisito and his family had, how they struggled with it, how they solved it, and how the story ended. Add their responses to the appropriate spots on the plot line. When the plot line is completed, have students tell where the most intense point in the story occurred. If necessary, point out that this is the *climax*. Have them identify where each event on their plot line takes place in the story—beginning, middle, or end.

Apply Have students use the table of contents to locate another story from the **Student Anthology** that they particularly enjoyed reading. Ask them to create a plot line for the story they choose. Point out to students that when creating a plot line for a story, it is important to list the events in sequential order so that one can easily identify how the plot builds toward its climax.

Assessment

✓ **Informal** Take this opportunity to assess students' progress with the writing process by commenting on the entries in their Writing Journals.

 **Teacher Tip** While students are encouraged to write quickly, remind them that it is important to make their ideas clear to readers. Encourage them to keep in mind the rules for writing paragraphs, which include having topic sentences. You may want to copy the rules for writing paragraphs onto the chalkboard or an overhead transparency for students to refer to as they write their drafts.

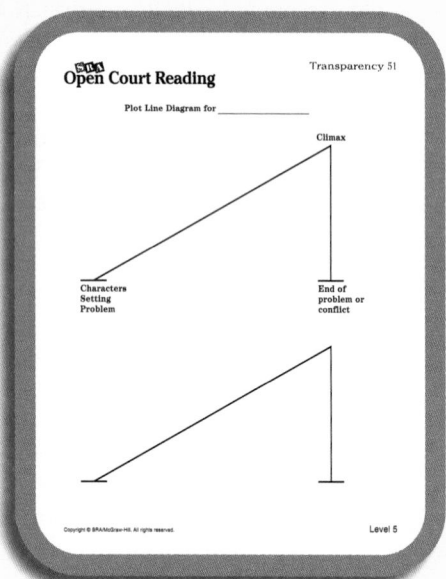

Transparency 51

Writing Process

Draft Have students begin drafting their narratives using the Sequence of Events organizer they created in Lesson 2. Tell them to be sure they have all the details they need to support their story ideas, in the right order, before they begin writing.

Remind students that when drafting, the idea is to get their ideas down on paper as quickly as possible, so they can use abbreviations, cross out words, leave blanks, and so on.

Teacher Tip Remind students to use what they have learned about plot and drafting when working on entries for their heritage albums.

Research in Action

Writing

An environment in which writing is central provides a multifaceted context for the development of higher-order thinking. Students learn to plan, which allows them to work out ideas in their heads; to set goals, which promotes interest and the ability to monitor progress; to edit, which enables the creation of the text that conforms to conventional standards and heightens its acceptability; and to revise content, which engages students in the reworking and rethinking activities that elevate writing from a craft to a tool for discovery. *(Marsha Roit)*

3 Integrating the Curriculum

Teacher Tip Encourage students to generate and direct discussion of character traits and to take over the process of instruction, when appropriate.

Meeting Individual Needs

ESL

Analyzing Character Traits English-language learners may need additional guidance from you as they participate in reflective activities such as this one. Have them summarize ideas in their own language before dictating them to you and the class.

Literary Elements

Analyzing Character Traits

Instruct Have students talk about ways that authors tell about their characters. The most obvious way, of course, is simply to describe the character. Ann Cameron, the author of "The Night We Started Dancing," shows many things about her characters by revealing what they say, think, or do. For example, Ms. Cameron tells more about Celia by describing her laugh project than by using a list of adjectives.

Practice Have the students go back to "The Night We Started Dancing" and find other examples of ways that the author tells her readers about the character in her story. Remind them to consider how Ms. Cameron lets readers know about the character of Luisito himself.

Examples of characterization in the selection include the following:

■ page 267, last paragraph: Luisito describes his grandfather as being born poor and having never gone to school, working from the time he was six years old. *(He has been ambitious and hard-working his whole life.)*

■ page 268, second paragraph: Luisito describes how his grandmother only learned to read four years earlier and was making his aunts and uncles as well as himself study hard in school. *(She is ambitious for her children and grandchildren; she is courageous to learn to read so late in life.)*

Apply Tell students to break into groups and choose a character with whom they identified. Have them discuss this character's actions and motivations with their group.

Remind students to develop the characters in their narratives and their heritage album entries.

Spelling

Regular and Irregular Plurals

Instruct A plural noun names two or more persons, places, or things. Discuss the rules for regular and irregular plurals.

Regular Plurals are made by:

- adding *-s* inflectional ending to a word. *(program/programs)*
- adding *-es* inflectional ending to words ending in *ch, s, ss, sh, x,* and *z.* *(porch/porches, guess/guesses, flash/flashes, reflex/reflexes, quiz/quizzes)*
- changing a *y* ending to *i* and adding *-es.* *(hobby/hobbies)*
- changing some *f* and *fe* endings to *v* and adding *-es.* *(loaf/loaves; wife/wives)* Other nouns that end in *f* or *fe* do not change their spellings.

Irregular plurals are made by:

- Changing their spellings. *(tooth/teeth)*
- Changing nothing at all. *(sheep/sheep)*

Practice Write the singular forms of these nouns on the chalkboard. Have volunteers give the plural form of each noun.

stamp (stamps)	mix (mixes)	virus (viruses)
goose (geese)	leaf (leaves)	deer (deer)
berry (berries)	belief (beliefs)	leash (leashes)

Apply For more practice with regular and irregular plurals, have students complete **Reading and Writing Workbook** pages 97–98.

Reading and Writing Workbook pp. 97–98

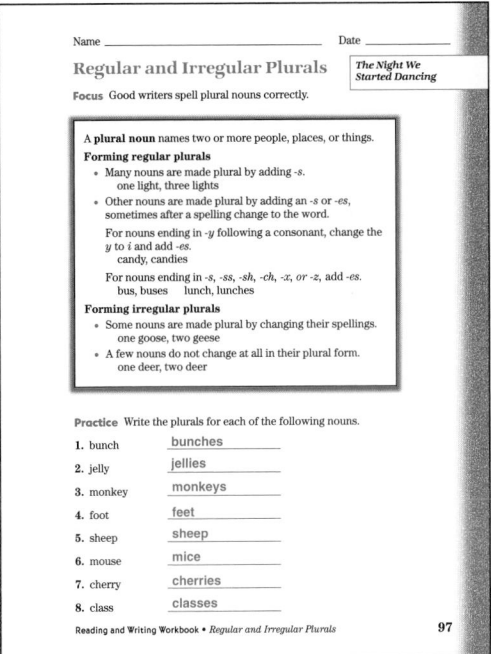
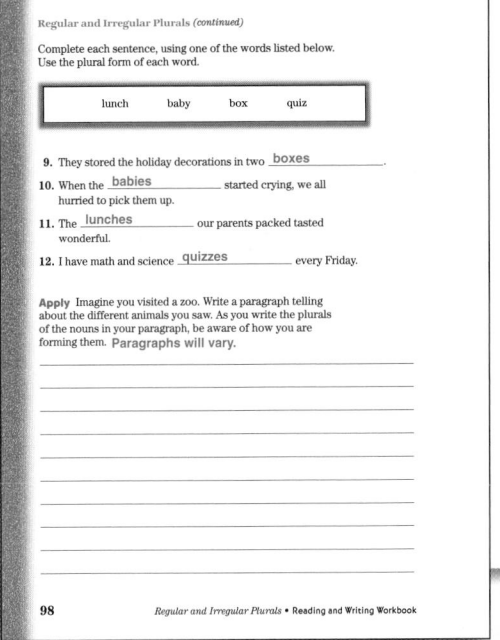

Meeting Individual Needs

Reteach

Regular and Irregular Plurals Have students who need additional instruction and practice with this concept complete **Reteach,** pages 97–98.

Challenge

Regular and Irregular Plurals Give students a list of ten singular nouns, five of which have regular plural forms and five of which have irregular plural forms. Have students write the plural form of the noun and use each plural in a sentence. Have students who can benefit from extended practice of this concept complete **Challenge,** page 51.

 Have students check for correct spelling of plural nouns as they proofread their narratives and heritage album entries.

Regular and Irregular Plurals
INTRODUCED: Unit 3, Lesson 3
REVIEWED: Unit 4, Lesson 7
Unit 5, Lesson 1

3 Integrating the Curriculum

Teacher Tip Whenever you are introducing a new skill, let students tell you what they already know about it before beginning instruction.

Meeting Individual Needs

Reteach

Adverbs Have students who need additional instruction and practice with this concept complete **Reteach,** pages 99–100.

Challenge

Adverbs Provide students with the following pair of sentences:

"We took the <u>final</u> test. The test was <u>finally</u> over."

Have students tell whether *final* is an adjective or an adverb. Discuss ways they can tell that *final* is an adjective: it describes the noun *test,* and it tells *what kind.* Do the same for *finally,* pointing out that it tells *when* about the word *over.* Follow the same procedure for several pairs of sentences.

Have students who can benefit from extended practice of this concept complete **Challenge,** page 52.

Adverbs

INTRODUCED: Unit 3, Lesson 3
REVIEWED: Unit 5, Lesson 4
Unit 6, Lesson 3

Grammar, Usage, and Mechanics

Adverbs

Instruct Copy the following list of rules for using adverbs onto the chalkboard or a transparency and review them with students:

1. An *adverb* describes a verb, an adjective, or another adverb. For example, in the sentence "The dancers move gracefully," the adverb *gracefully* describes the verb *move.*
2. An *adverb* may answer the question *When? Where? How? How much?* or *How often?* For example, in the sentence above, the adverb *gracefully* answers the question, "How did the dancers move?"
3. Many *adverbs* are formed by adding *-ly* to an adjective. The spelling of the word may change when the *-ly* ending is added. For example, in the sentence above, the adverb *gracefully* was formed by adding *-ly* to the adjective *graceful.*

Practice Write two or three sentences on the chalkboard that could be made more descriptive with the addition of adverbs. Have students work in small groups and copy the sentences on paper. Have them brainstorm a list of adverbs that could be added to the sentences. Then have them rewrite the sentences adding adverbs.

Apply Encourage students to make their writing more descriptive using adverbs. For additional practice, have students complete *Reading and Writing Workbook* pages 99–100.

Reading and Writing Workbook pp. 99–100

Listening/Speaking/Viewing

Listening to and Appreciating Spoken Language

Share with students the joys of listening to a story being read by an effective reader. Play excerpts from audiocassettes of classical and contemporary stories read by professional readers. First, ask students to recall times when they were read to when they were younger, and discuss the reasons they enjoyed it. Discuss the qualities that a good storyteller might possess. Play excerpts suggested in the Teacher Tip and then have students discuss the following:

- Which reader did they enjoy the most?
- What kind of vocal qualities did they notice (loudness, softness, animated tone, relaxed tone)?
- How did the readers distinguish the voices of the different characters?
- Did their reading style change at all during the reading?
- How did the author's language choices and the reader's delivery of each story work together to affect the tone of each author's message?
- How did the delivery of each story make the students feel?

You may want to play the tapes again after the discussion so students can reevaluate their responses and confirm what they discussed. Encourage them to read stories and books to younger relatives at home.

Teacher Tip Consider using a *Listening Library Audiocassette* of a selection students have already read in Units 1, 2, or 3 that they particularly enjoyed.

③ Integrating the Curriculum

Teacher Tip Have students use words from a thesaurus to enhance their narratives and unit activities.

Inquiry Journal p. 47

Assessment
✓ **Formal** To assess students' knowledge of using a thesaurus, use *Skills Assessment,* page 29.

Study and Research

Using a Thesaurus

Instruct Ask students where they would look if they needed to find a word that has the same meaning as *happy.* Tell students that they could use a thesaurus, or synonym finder. A *thesaurus* is a listing of synonyms and antonyms. It may be a book or part of a word-processing program. In books, the words are usually arranged alphabetically. A thesaurus is a valuable tool for clarifying a word's meaning and usage or for avoiding using the same word too often. Explain that a thesaurus is a tool writers can use to make their writing more specific and more interesting. Write the following sentence on the chalkboard:

Do you think the president understands our problem?

Ask a volunteer to find the word *understand* in a thesaurus. Discuss what words are listed in the entry and how they are similar or different. Read the sentence substituting a synonym from the thesaurus for the word *understand.*

Have students brainstorm a list of words that they frequently overuse when they write. Some examples might be *nice, said, went,* or *great.*

Practice Have students copy the list of overused words from the chalkboard. Tell them to write a sentence for each word and underline the word from the chalkboard. Then have students look up the underlined word in a thesaurus and write a more interesting word to the left of the sentence.

Apply Have students look through their **Writing Folders** for places where they could use a thesaurus to enhance their writing. Suggest that they try several synonyms and choose the one that comes closest to their intended meaning.

For additional practice, have students complete **Inquiry Journal** page 47.

Across the Curriculum

 **Social Studies**

Occupations

Purpose

To help students understand the ways people prepare for their future jobs

Procedure

Ask students what kind of jobs they would like to have when they are adults. Have they seen someone in their community doing a job they think would be a good one to have? Ask them to think about how they might prepare themselves for these jobs. You might offer information on how you prepared to be a teacher—education, on-the-job training, talking to your family and friends, and so on.

■ Ask students to recall the fields of study pursued by Luisito's aunts and uncles. Have them create a list of possible occupations that they would like to have. Discuss ways they may have learned job skills, such as helping on the farm or learning from their grandparents.

■ Have students select one occupation they would like to pursue and write a paragraph about it. Have them tell why it interests them and how they will prepare themselves for these jobs.

 **Music**

Songs of Other Countries

Purpose

To learn the music of other countries

Procedure

Discuss with the students any music that is traditionally sung at home or at social gatherings. From which regions or cultures do the songs come? Do these songs tell stories that are important to the students' heritage?

■ Have students select a traditional song from another country and research the country. They may want to choose the country of their origin.

■ Use books or the Internet to find information about the particular music from a chosen country or a specific song. Have students write a short report using the information they find.

■ If possible, have students sing or record some music from their chosen country and share it with the class.

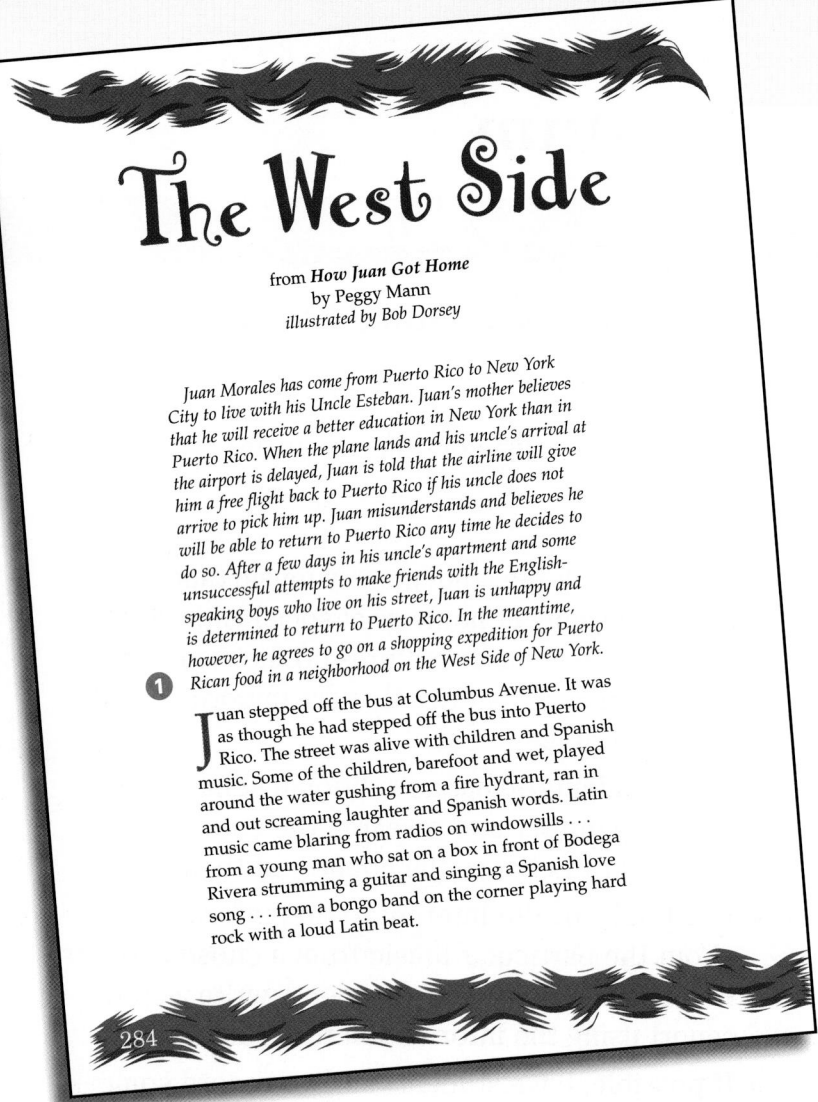

The West Side

from *How Juan Got Home*
by Peggy Mann
illustrated by Bob Dorsey

Juan Morales has come from Puerto Rico to New York City to live with his Uncle Esteban. Juan's mother believes that he will receive a better education in New York than in Puerto Rico. When the plane lands and his uncle's arrival at the airport is delayed, Juan is told that the airline will give him a free flight back to Puerto Rico if his uncle does not arrive to pick him up. Juan misunderstands and believes he will be able to return to Puerto Rico any time he decides to do so. After a few days in his uncle's apartment and some unsuccessful attempts to make friends with the English-speaking boys who live on his street, Juan is unhappy and is determined to return to Puerto Rico. In the meantime, however, he agrees to go on a shopping expedition for Puerto Rican food in a neighborhood on the West Side of New York.

1

Juan stepped off the bus at Columbus Avenue. It was as though he had stepped off the bus into Puerto Rico. The street was alive with children and Spanish music. Some of the children, barefoot and wet, played around the water gushing from a fire hydrant, ran in and out screaming laughter and Spanish words. Latin music came blaring from radios on windowsills . . . from a young man who sat on a box in front of Bodega Rivera strumming a guitar and singing a Spanish love song . . . from a bongo band on the corner playing hard rock with a loud Latin beat.

284

Selection Summary

Genre: Realistic Fiction

"The West Side" is from the final chapters of *How Juan Got Home*. Juan Morales wants to go home to Puerto Rico. Although he likes his uncle's comfortable New York City apartment, he fears he'll never find friends. None of the boys in the East Side neighborhood where his uncle lives speaks Spanish. Then, on a search for Puerto Rican food, he goes to the West Side. Here he finds some reminders of Puerto Rico, and here, for the first time since being in New York, he finds a friend.

About the Author

Peggy Mann's book *How Juan Got Home* is one of a series of books based on the experiences of Mann's family after they had bought, renovated, and moved into a home in a poor neighborhood in New York City's Upper West Side. The first of these books, *The Street of Flower Boxes*, was made into a TV film and won a Peabody Award. Carlos, a character in "The West Side," also appears in these books. The other books in the series are *The Clubhouse*, *When Carlos Closed the Street*, and *The Secret Dog of Little Luis*.

Students can read more about Peggy Mann on page 296 of the *Student Anthology.*

Other Books by Peggy Mann
- *My Dad Lives in a Downtown Hotel*
- *The Boy with a Billion Pets*
- *Amelia Earhart: Pioneer of the Skies*

About the Illustrator

Bob Dorsey's work has appeared in books, advertising campaigns, and magazines. He is well known for the many portraits that he has completed for the National Baseball Hall of Fame. He has received an Award of Excellence from the Beckett National Sports Art Gallery. Bob Dorsey's illustrations capture characters with their use of light and color. He currently lives in Penfield, New York, with his wife and three children. Students can read more about Bob Dorsey on page 296 of the *Student Anthology.*

Exploring the Theme

Selection Concepts

"The West Side" is a work of realistic fiction in which a young boy longs for his home in Puerto Rico. While shopping in the Puerto Rican district on the west side of New York City, Juan Morales finds reminders of his homeland and, finally, a friend. Key concepts to be explored are:

- Familiar traditions and customs can make one feel both more comfortable and homesick in a foreign land.
- People can find ways to communicate even if they speak different languages.

Check the Reading link of the **SRA** Web page for links to theme-related Websites.
http:// www.sra4kids.com

Exploration Activity Tips

Before Reading, have the students browse the selection looking for clues about the story.

During Reading, suggest that students also read "The West Side" silently on their own. Tell them to note how Juan feels at various points throughout the selection and think about the reasons for his feelings.

After Reading, have students talk about why Juan wanted to go home and whether they think he liked everything about Puerto Rico as much when he lived there as he seems to now. Then have students update the Concept/Question Board. Some may want to revise their activity plans based on what they have learned from the selection.

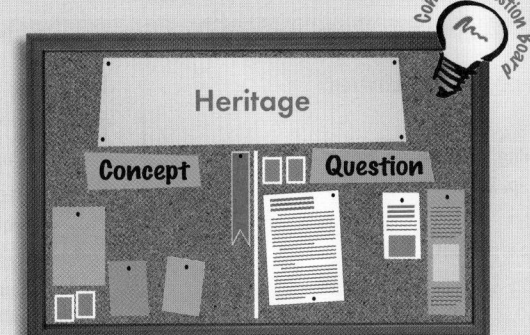

Unit 3 Exploration Management

Lesson 1	Listen to and interview a class guest about heritage. Select and read library books about heritage.
Lesson 2	Identify genres for inclusion in heritage albums. Reflect on one's own heritage, interview family members and friends about customs and traditions, and begin writing.
Lesson 3	Identify and utilize various literary techniques. Writing begins on second selection for student albums.
Lesson 4 **The West Side**	**Collaborative Exploration** **Work on unit activity continues. Discuss with relatives and friends what they want to communicate about their heritage.** **Supplementary Activity** **Conduct class discussion of students' progress with their heritage albums. Discuss use of literary conventions to express thoughts.**
Lesson 5	Write autobiographical sketches for author pages and consider modeling a character after a family member or friend.
Lesson 6	Prepare final drafts, complete illustrations, prepare title and copyright pages, and bind books. Write thank-you notes to those who helped with the activity.
Lesson 7	Students present a selected piece from their heritage albums.

Lesson Planner

Suggested Pacing: 3–5 days	DAY 1	DAY 2
	DAY 1	**DAY 2**
Part 1 **Preparing to Read** **Materials** ▪ Student Anthology, pp. 284–297 ▪ Transparencies 18, 44	**Word Knowledge** ▪ Reading the Words and Sentences, p. 284G ▪ Developing Oral Language, p. 284G **Build Background, p. 284H** **Preview and Prepare, p. 284I** **Selection Vocabulary, p. 284I** scowled, jabbering, manager, embarrassed, impressed	**Preview and Prepare, p. 284I** ▪ Review Transparency 44
Part 2 **Reading and Responding** **Materials** ▪ Student Anthology, pp. 284–299 ▪ Teacher Observation Log ▪ Inquiry Journal, p. 42 ▪ Home Connection, p. 41	**Student Anthology, pp. 284–297** **Comprehension Strategies** ▪ Summarizing, pp. 284, 294 ▪ Clarifying, pp. 286, 288, 290, 292 ▪ Predicting, pp. 288, 290 **Discussing Strategy Use, p. 294**	**Student Anthology, pp. 284–297** **Comprehension Skills** ✓▪ Discussing the Selection, p. 295 **Exploring the Theme** ▪ Selection Vocabulary, p. 299A scowled, jabbering, manager, embarrassed, impressed
Part 3 **Integrating the Curriculum** **Materials** ▪ Student Anthology, pp. 284–297 ▪ Inquiry Journal, pp. 48–49	**Writing** ▪ Evaluating the Author's Writing, p. 299C **Literary Elements** ▪ Analyzing Character Traits, p. 299D	**Writing Process** ▪ Revise, p. 299C **Spelling** ▪ Syllable Boundary Patterns, p. 299E
Independent Work Time **Materials** ▪ ESL Supplement ▪ Intervention Guide ▪ Research CD-ROM ▪ Listening Library Audiocassette	**Writing Process Continued** **ESL** ▪ Word Meaning, p. 284G ▪ Vocabulary, p. 284J **Intervention** ▪ Homophones, p. 284G **Unit Project: Discuss Heritage with Relatives and Friends**	**Writing Process Continued** **ESL** ▪ Writing and Revising, p. 299C **Challenge** ▪ Syllable Boundary Patterns, p. 299E **Intervention** ▪ Comprehension, p. 284 ▪ Revising, p. 299C **Unit Project Continued**

✓ Informal **Assessment Available**   ✓ Formal **Assessment Available**

DAY 2 continued	**DAY 3**	
DAY 3	**DAY 4**	**DAY 5**
General Review	General Review	Review Word Knowledge
Student Anthology, pp. 284–297 **Comprehension Skills** ■ Drawing Conclusions, pp. 285, 287, 289, 291, 293 **Theme Connections** ■ Think About It, p. 297 ■ Share a Story, p. 297	**Student Anthology, pp. 284–297** **Fine Art, pp. 298–299** **Exploring the Theme** ■ Reading/Writing Connections, p. 299A ■ Supporting Student Explorations, p. 299B	**Student Anthology, pp. 284–297** ■ Review Selection ■ Complete Discussion ■ Reread Selection in Pairs **Home Connection, p. 299A** ■ Discuss "The West Side" ■ List skills needed for favorite sport or game
Writing Process Continued **Grammar, Usage, and Mechanics** ✓ ■ Subject and Verb Agreement, p. 299E	**Writing Process Continued** **Study and Research** ■ Using Graphs, p. 299G	**Across the Curriculum** **Social Studies** ■ Learning Español, p. 299H **Math** ■ Money Word Problems, p. 299H
Writing Process Continued **Challenge** ■ Subject and Verb Agreement, p. 299F **Unit Project Continued**	**Writing Process Continued** **Unit Project Continued**	**Writing Process Continued** **Unit Project Continued**

Meeting Individual Needs
Independent Work Time

Preparing to Read

Meeting Individual Needs

ESL
- Word Meaning, p. 284G
- Cultural Context, p. 284H
- Vocabulary, p. 284J

Intervention
- Homophones, p. 284G

Reading and Responding

Meeting Individual Needs

ESL
- Clarifying, p. 286

Challenge
- Drawing Conclusions, p. 289

Intervention
- Comprehension, p. 284
- Predicting, p. 290
- Drawing Conclusions, p. 291
- Clarifying, p. 292
- Summarizing, p. 294

Integrating the Curriculum

Meeting Individual Needs

ESL
- Writing and Revising, p. 299C

Challenge
- Syllable Boundary Patterns, p. 299E
- Subject and Verb Agreement, p. 299F

Intervention
- Revise, p. 299C

Formal Assessment Options

Use these assessment pages along with your informal
observations to gauge student progress.

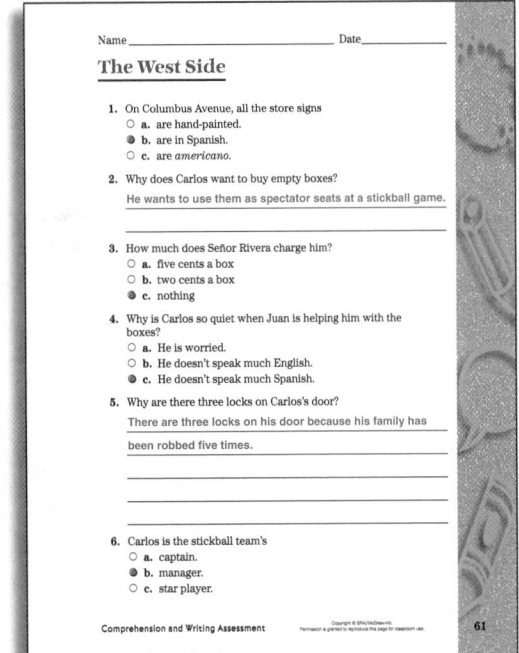

Name _____ Date _____

Subject and Verb Agreement

**Read each sentence. Fill in the circle next to the
verb that correctly completes each sentence.**

1. Janine _____ her sister to the park every afternoon.
   ○ take ● takes ○ taking ○ taken

2. She and her sister _____ happy to spend time together.
   ○ be ○ is ● are ○ being

3. The ducks at the pond _____ forward to seeing Janine
   and her sister.
   ○ looks ○ looking ○ has looked ● look

4. Either Janine or her sister usually _____ some food
   for them.
   ● brings ○ bring ○ bringing ○ are bringing

5. Both Janine and her sister _____ on the swings for a
   while.
   ○ plays ○ playing ○ is playing ● play

6. One of the other children at the park _____ on the slide.
   ○ are ○ be ● is ○ being

7. Everyone _____ that Janine's sister likes to feed the
   ducks.
   ● knows ○ know ○ are knowing ○ knowing

8. The slide or the swing set _____ to be repaired soon.
   ● needs ○ need ○ needing ○ is needing

9. Somebody _____ to add some new equipment to the
   playground.
   ● wants ○ want ○ wanting ○ are wanting

10. Everyone _____ that is a terrific idea.
    ○ thinking ○ think ○ are thinking ● thinks

30 Copyright © SRA/McGraw-Hill. Permission is granted to reproduce this page for classroom use. Skills Assessment

Skills Assessment, p. 30

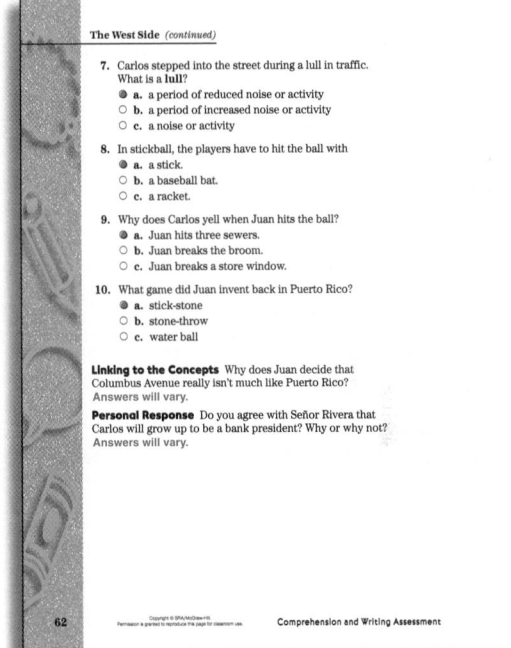

Name _____ Date _____

The West Side

1. On Columbus Avenue, all the store signs
   ○ a. are hand-painted.
   ● b. are in Spanish.
   ○ c. are *americano*.

2. Why does Carlos want to buy empty boxes?
   He wants to use them as spectator seats at a stickball game.
   _____

3. How much does Señor Rivera charge him?
   ○ a. five cents a box
   ○ b. two cents a box
   ● c. nothing

4. Why is Carlos so quiet when Juan is helping him with the
   boxes?
   ○ a. He is worried.
   ○ b. He doesn't speak much English.
   ● c. He doesn't speak much Spanish.

5. Why are there three locks on Carlos's door?
   There are three locks on his door because his family has
   been robbed five times.
   _____
   _____
   _____

6. Carlos is the stickball team's
   ○ a. captain.
   ● b. manager.
   ○ c. star player.

Comprehension and Writing Assessment Copyright © SRA/McGraw-Hill. Permission is granted to reproduce this page for classroom use. 61

**Comprehension and Writing
Assessment, p. 61**

The West Side *(continued)*

7. Carlos stepped into the street during a lull in traffic.
   What is a **lull**?
   ● a. a period of reduced noise or activity
   ○ b. a period of increased noise or activity
   ○ c. a noise or activity

8. In stickball, the players have to hit the ball with
   ● a. a stick.
   ○ b. a baseball bat.
   ○ c. a racket.

9. Why does Carlos yell when Juan hits the ball?
   ● a. Juan hits three sewers.
   ○ b. Juan breaks the broom.
   ○ c. Juan breaks a store window.

10. What game did Juan invent back in Puerto Rico?
    ● a. stick-stone
    ○ b. stone-throw
    ○ c. water ball

Linking to the Concepts Why does Juan decide that
Columbus Avenue really isn't much like Puerto Rico?
Answers will vary.

Personal Response Do you agree with Señor Rivera that
Carlos will grow up to be a bank president? Why or why not?
Answers will vary.

62 Copyright © SRA/McGraw-Hill. Permission is granted to reproduce this page for classroom use. Comprehension and Writing Assessment

**Comprehension and Writing
Assessment, p. 62**

1 Preparing to Read

Meeting Individual Needs

ESL

Word Meaning Make sure English-language learners understand the meanings of the words before they do the exercises. Refer to Unit 3, Lesson 4, of the **ESL Supplement** for specific suggestions.

Intervention

Homophones Have students skim the story for homophones. List the words they find on the chalkboard. Have volunteers take turns telling you the spelling of the homophone until the list is completed. Some examples of words from the story are: *here, you, made, not, knew, where.* For students who need more help, see Unit 3, Lesson 4, of the **Intervention Guide.**

Word Knowledge

Reading the Words and Sentences

Write each word and sentence on the chalkboard. Have students read each word together. After all the words have been read, have students read each sentence in natural phrases or chunks. Use the suggestions in About the Words to discuss the different features of the listed words.

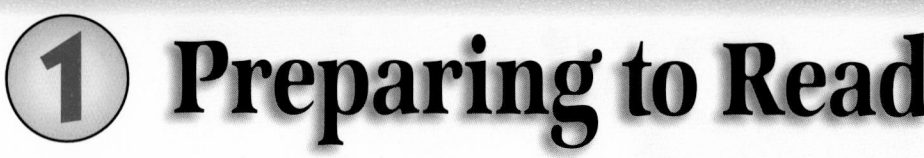

Line 1: blue blew to two red read break brake
Line 2: sprint splendid stranger scream
Line 3: watch catch scratch
Sentence 1: The two girls will sprint across the playground.
Sentence 2: I have a red scratch on my arm from my fall.
Sentence 3: I screamed when the stranger tried to catch my blue balloon.

About the Words

- Line 1 contains homophones. A homophone is a word that sounds the same as another word but has a different meaning and spelling.

- The words in Line 2 all begin with three-letter consonant blends. Have the students think of other words that start with the blends used in these words.

- All of the words in Line 3 have the /ch/ sound spelled *tch*. The *tch* spelling occurs only at the end of words or syllables.

Developing Oral Language

To review the words, have students do the following activities.

- Write one word from each pair in Line 1 on the chalkboard. Say the word *blue* and ask a student to give the homophone *(blew)*. Then have the student say a word and choose another student to give the homophone. Have students brainstorm more words and their homophones.

- Write several words on the chalkboard. Have a student use one word in a sentence. Next, have another student add a word from the list to the sentence. See how many words they can fit in the sentence logically.

Build Background

Activate Prior Knowledge

Have students check the Concept/Question Board to refresh their memories about heritage. Discuss the following with students to find out what they already know about the selection and have already learned about the unit theme. Tell students to use their prior knowledge to help them comprehend the selection they are about to read.

■ Ask students if they are familiar with the story they are about to read, and if so, to tell a little bit about it. Remind students, however, not to give away the ending of the selection.

■ Have students share what they know about Puerto Rico.

■ Have students discuss how they would feel about moving to a strange place or being away from home for a long period of time.

■ Have students share any other stories that involve moving to a new place or feeling homesick.

Background Information

The following information may help the students to better understand the selection they are about to read.

■ Although there are many Spanish words in the story, most of them are made clear by their context. Pronunciations of these words are printed with the miniature pages. The pronunciations are only approximations written in English respellings. If you have Spanish-speaking students in your class, you might ask them to pronounce the words for their classmates after the story has been read.

■ Stickball is a form of baseball that children play in the streets of large cities using a stick and some type of ball.

■ Eating ethnic foods is part of a family's heritage.

■ Children with parents from other countries may not always speak their native language.

■ Point out both Puerto Rico and New York City on a map in order to demonstrate how far Juan is from home.

■ Be aware that the description of Carlos's home on page 293 may be a sensitive issue in your classroom.

Meeting Individual Needs

ESL

Cultural Context English-language learners may be able to identify with Juan. Ask those students to say what sounds, sights, and tastes make them homesick for their first culture or homeland. Also, have them explain how they think Juan feels after he makes friends with Carlos.

 *Writing Journal* Tell the students that after reading they will be jotting down in their Writing Journals their reactions to the story. Have them be on the lookout for any ideas they may have for adding Juan's experience to their activity.

Teacher Tip Review some of the techniques the authors of the unit's other selections used. Remind students that they should be "reading as writers"— noticing the authors' writing techniques so that they can use them in their own writing.

Preparing to Read

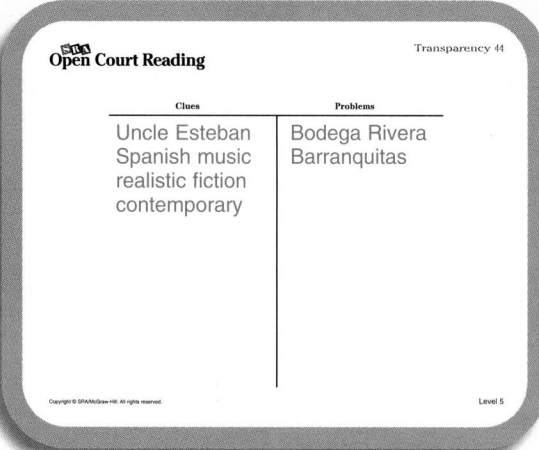

Transparency 44

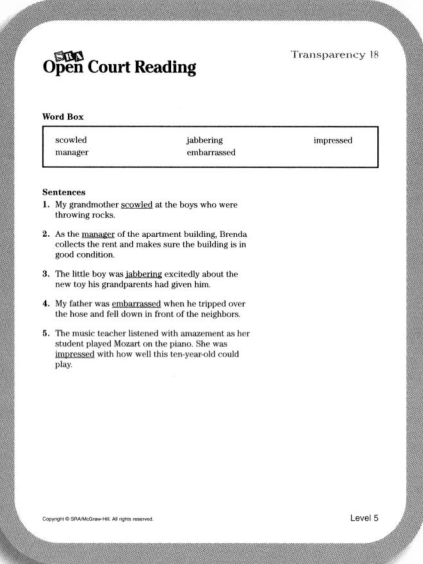

Transparency 18

Teacher Tip To help students decode words, divide them into the syllables shown below. The information following each word tells how students can figure out the meaning of each word from the sentences on the transparency.

scowled	context clues, word structure
jab•ber•ing	context clues, word structure
man•a•ger	context clues, word structure
em•bar•rassed	context clues, word structure
im•pressed	context clues, word structure

Preview and Prepare

Browse

- Have a volunteer read the title and author's and illustrator's names aloud. Have students share what they know about realistic fiction.
- Because this selection is fiction, have the students browse through the first half of the selection, looking for words and phrases that connect to what they already know. Record these in the Clues column on **Transparency 44.** Discuss with them what they think this selection might have to do with family heritage.
- Encourage students to ask questions as they browse. Have them identify any problems they notice while reading in the Problems column.

Set Purposes

As they read, have students think how they would feel, or have felt, if they had to move to a strange place to live and go to school.

Selection Vocabulary

As students study vocabulary, they will use context clues, word structure, and apposition to clarify these and additional unfamiliar words.

Display **Transparency 18** before reading the selection to introduce and discuss the following words and their meanings.

scowled: frowned (page 287)

jab•ber•ing: talking a lot and very fast (page 290)

man•a•ger: a person who takes care of or organizes something like an office or a sports team (page 293)

em•bar•rassed: feeling bad or silly about something you've done (page 294)

im•pressed: describes someone who thinks another person is good at something (page 295)

Have students read the words in the Word Box. Help students decode multisyllabic words by reading the words syllable by syllable. If the word is not decodable, give the students the pronunciation.

Have the students read the sentences on **Transparency 18** to determine the meaning of the underlined words. Remind them to use clues in the sentences and structural clues to figure out the meaning. See the teacher tip on the left for information on how the words in each sentence can be defined.

Reading Recommendations

Your first reading of the selection should focus on developing the reading strategies found to the left of the reduced pages. We recommend that the students revisit the selection, rereading sections or the entire selection as a way to enhance their understanding and appreciation of the text. During rereading, they should focus on the comprehension skills, found to the right of the reduced pages.

Oral Reading

Because the pronunciation of Spanish names and words in this selection may be unfamiliar to students, oral reading is recommended. Have students practice pronouncing these words and names before reading (for your convenience, Teacher Tips on their pronunciations are featured beside and below the reduced **Student Anthology** pages in the **Teacher's Edition**). As students read aloud, have them read expressively at an appropriate pace, in natural phrases and chunks. By reading the selection with fluency, students will demonstrate an understanding of the text and an ability to engage the listeners in an effective manner. If students encounter difficulties, have them use the reading strategies below or refer to the Blending Procedure (Program Appendix 15–16).

Using Reading Strategies

Reading strategy instruction allows students to become aware of how good readers read. Skilled readers recognize when they are having problems and stop to use various reading strategies to help them make sense of what they are reading.

During the reading of "The West Side," you will model the use of the following reading strategies:

- Clarifying
- Summarizing
- Predicting

Before reading, have students share what they know about these strategies and how they have used them in the past.

Building Comprehension Skills

Revisiting or rereading a selection allows students to apply skills that give them a more complete understanding of the text. Some follow-up comprehension skills, such as *Main Idea and Details* and *Compare and Contrast*, help students organize information. Others, such as *Author's Purpose* and *Making Inferences*, lead to deeper understanding—to "reading between the lines," as mature readers do. In this selection, students will apply the follow-up comprehension skill of *Drawing Conclusions*.

Meeting Individual Needs

ESL

Vocabulary Check that English-language learners know the meanings of idioms and more difficult vocabulary in the story, including: *a better education; fire hydrant; bongo band; umpire the game; give me a hand; the mainland; their Spanish is nothing to speak of; pun; I myself am not so hot at this game;* and *sewer.* Explain and show pictures as needed. Model example sentences and help English-speaking students make their own sentences. Refer to Unit 3, Lesson 4, of the **ESL Supplement** for teaching suggestions.

 Have students who may need extra help reading "The West Side" reread the selection using the **Listening Library Audiocassette.**

 By this time in the fifth grade, good readers should be reading approximately 143 words per minute with fluency and expression. The only way to gain fluency is through practice. As explained in Reading Recommendations, have students reread all or part of the selection to you and to each other during class or Independent Work Time to focus on the comprehension skills and to build fluency.

② Reading and Responding

Read pages 284–299.

Comprehension Strategies

Modeling

❶ **Summarizing** *I see that this is an excerpt from a larger story. I think I'll summarize the information in the introduction to make sure I understand all of the details. Juan came from Puerto Rico and is living with his uncle. He hasn't made any friends in his uncle's neighborhood and wants to go home. Today he is going to another neighborhood to buy some Puerto Rican food.*

Teacher Tip Some children may not be familiar with the concentration of cultures in New York City. Explain that many immigrant groups settle in specific neighborhoods in the city and retain much of the feeling, flavor, and culture of their homelands.

Word Knowledge

street, strumming

Students can use the skills they learned in the Word Knowledge to read these words. Remind students of this if they have difficulty decoding these words.

Reading Recommendation

ORAL · CHORAL · SILENT

The West Side

from *How Juan Got Home*
by Peggy Mann
illustrated by Bob Dorsey

Juan Morales has come from Puerto Rico to New York City to live with his Uncle Esteban. Juan's mother believes that he will receive a better education in New York than in Puerto Rico. When the plane lands and his uncle's arrival at the airport is delayed, Juan is told that the airline will give him a free flight back to Puerto Rico if his uncle does not arrive to pick him up. Juan misunderstands and believes he will be able to return to Puerto Rico any time he decides to do so. After a few days in his uncle's apartment and some unsuccessful attempts to make friends with the English-speaking boys who live on his street, Juan is unhappy and is determined to return to Puerto Rico. In the meantime, however, he agrees to go on a shopping expedition for Puerto
❶ *Rican food in a neighborhood on the West Side of New York.*

Juan stepped off the bus at Columbus Avenue. It was as though he had stepped off the bus into Puerto Rico. The street was alive with children and Spanish music. Some of the children, barefoot and wet, played around the water gushing from a fire hydrant, ran in and out screaming laughter and Spanish words. Latin music came blaring from radios on windowsills . . . from a young man who sat on a box in front of Bodega Rivera strumming a guitar and singing a Spanish love song . . . from a bongo band on the corner playing hard rock with a loud Latin beat.

284

Meeting Individual Needs

Intervention

Comprehension Intervention strategies for those students having difficulty reading "The West Side" can be found in Unit 3, Lesson 4, of the **Intervention Guide.**

Assessment

✓ **Informal** Observe individual students as they read, and use the Teacher Observation Log found in the **Assessment Guide** to record anecdotal information about each student's strengths and weaknesses.

285

Comprehension
Skills

Drawing Conclusions

Tell the students that good readers often draw conclusions about a story based on information in the text. The conclusion is not directly stated in the text.

Point out to the students that Juan draws some conclusions in this story, based on clues he has seen or heard. Direct the students' attention to the following examples.

- Juan concludes that when the airline offers him a ticket home, he can use the ticket at any time.

- Juan concludes that the West Side of New York is just like Puerto Rico.

Have students discuss whether or not Juan is correct in his conclusions. Explain that Juan's conclusions might change during the story as he receives more information.

⇐ **Skills Strand** ⇒

Drawing Conclusions
INTRODUCED: Unit 1, Lesson 1
REVIEWED: Unit 1, Lesson 5
Unit 2, Lesson 1
Unit 3, Lesson 4
Unit 3, Lesson 6

Teacher Tip There are many words in this selection that may not be familiar to students. Help students pronounce these words. Juan Morales is pronounced hwän mō rä´ läs. Esteban is pronounced ä stä´ bän. Bodega is pronounced bō dä´ gä.

Teacher Tip If the class contains Spanish-speaking students, invite them to model pronunciation and to help translate the words and phrases. However, keep in mind that many of the food items mentioned are specific to the Caribbean and may be unfamiliar to Hispanic students from other areas of the world.

2 Reading and Responding

Comprehension Strategies

Modeling

2 Clarifying *There are a lot of Spanish words and names here. I know that a Bodega is a small grocery, but I don't know the others. I could look up these words in a Spanish/English dictionary. Who will volunteer to look up meanings and pronunciations for some of these words?*

Prompting

3 Clarifying *What are some other terms or ideas that should be clarified before we continue reading?*

Student Sample

Clarifying *I wonder what "stickball" is? According to what the boy is saying, it's something that's played on the street. It must be popular if he's sold twenty box seats for it! Maybe I'll learn more about it as I read on. (There is further clarification on what "stickball" is on page 292.)*

Word Knowledge

shrilling, strode, stranger

Students can use the skills they learned in the Word Knowledge to read these words. Remind students of this if they have difficulty decoding these words.

Women leaned out of windows shrilling in Spanish to children on the street. A group of men sat around a bridge table on the sidewalk, playing dominoes. Women in bright cotton dresses sat on the front steps gossiping in Spanish. And the stores! At home the stores often had *americano* names: the Blue Moon Bar Restaurant . . . Joe's Shop . . . the Cooperative . . . Mercado's Barbershop . . . . But here: everything Spanish! Farmacia Flores . . . Tienda La Favorita . . . Zapatería El Quijote . . . Repostería Borinquén. . . .

All crowded together like this, the store signs, the music, the look and the sound of the Spanish people, it seemed somehow *more* Puerto Rican than anything he had seen in Puerto Rico. He was no longer a stranger. He didn't even need to ask directions. With a smile on his face he strode into Bodega Rivera.

He *was* home. The small crowded grocery store was just like the one on his street in Barranquitas. The same small, sweet *niños* bananas hung in clumps in the dusty window; and the long, green *plátanos* hung next to *cooking bananas* them on iron hooks. The same bins of tropical fruits and vegetables. The same cans and bottles on the shelves: guava juice, papaya juice, *asopao de jueyes*, red beans, pink beans, white beans, pinto beans, chick peas, *Doraditos, Florecitas, coco rico* and *chinita*. Even the same penny candy machine. And the same packets of ladies' panty hose on the rack behind the counter.

The shopkeeper, who wore a large black mustache and a dirty white apron, was arguing with a customer about the price of his *batatas*. Loudly Señor Rivera informed her that he had to import the *batatas* from the island. If she could not pay for special Spanish food she **2** should eat American.

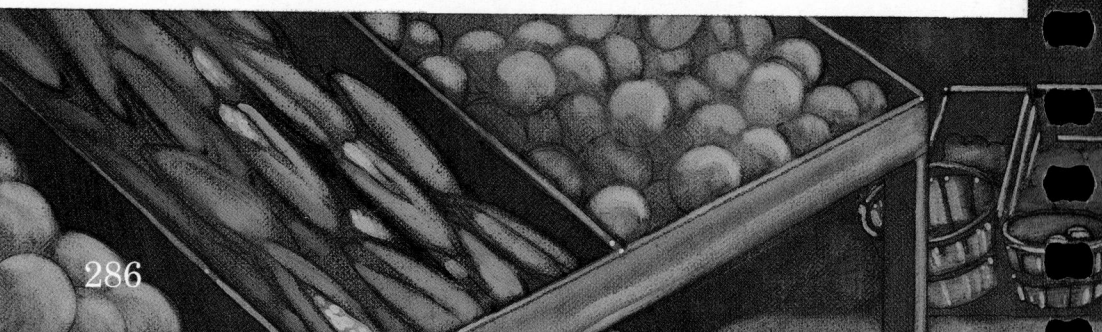

286

Meeting Individual Needs

ESL

Clarifying Encourage the students to react freely to the text identifying words that need clarification, asking their own questions, and sharing ideas they wish to talk about. Students will then be able to contribute more in a whole-group discussion because the focus on meaning will be easier, and problems with vocabulary and unfamiliar concepts will have been addressed.

When, grumbling, she counted out her money and left, a boy about Juan's age stood on tiptoe in front of the counter and asked in a loud voice whether Señor Rivera would sell him some boxes.

"Boxes of *what?*" Señor Rivera said.

"Empty boxes," the boy said. "We're having a stickball game on the street tomorrow afternoon and we already sold twenty box seats to people who want to watch from the sidewalk. Now we gotta get the boxes."

"Get out of here, Carlos," Señor Rivera said. "I'm busy."

"But Señor Rivera!" Carlos persisted. "I'm willing to pay for the boxes. Usually you give them out free to customers. I'm going to *pay!*"

"Yes?" Señor Rivera said. "And how are my customers going to carry home their groceries if I got no more boxes?"

"Listen," Carlos said, "I'll make you a deal. If you let us have the boxes, I'll let your son Willie umpire the game."

Señor Rivera said nothing. He scowled.

"As you know," Carlos said, "your boy Willie is kind of a pain-in-the-neck kid. That's why he gets beat up so much. But nobody beats up an umpire. You got to respect an umpire."

"How much did you sell the box seats for?" said Señor Rivera.

287

Comprehension Skills

Drawing Conclusions

Have the students read the description of the neighborhood on page 286. Then have them discuss the following questions:

- What conclusions can you draw from the statement that Juan was "no longer a stranger"? (*Because everything was so familiar to him, he felt as if he belonged.*)

- What conclusion can you reach about the woman who bought the food even though she thought it was too expensive? (*She wanted Spanish food even though it is expensive.*)

Teacher Tip Americano is pronounced ä mä rē kä´ nō. Farmacia Flores is pronounced fär mä sē´ ä flō´räs. Tienda La Favorita is pronounced tē yen´ dä lä fä vō rē´ tä. Zapateria El Quijote is pronounced zä pä tä rē´ ä äl kē hō´ tä. Reposteria Borinquén is pronounced rā pōs tä rē´ ä bō rēn kän´. Barranquitas is pronounced bä rän kē´ täs. Niños is pronounced nēn´ yōs. Plátanos is pronounced plä´ tä nōs. Asopao de jueges is pronounced ä sō pä´ ō dā hwā´ yās. Doraditos is pronounced dō rä dē´ tōs. Florecitas is pronounced flō rä sē´ täs. Coco rico is pronounced kō´ kō rē´ kō. Chinita is pronounced chē nē´ tä. Batatas is pronounced bä tä´ täs.

2 Reading and Responding

Comprehension Strategies

Modeling

4 Predicting *Carlos looks like an interesting person, and we just spent a lot of time listening to him and the shopkeeper. Based on how characters have been introduced in other stories I've read, I think that he's going to have more to do in this story. I'll bet he and Juan become friends. Let's read on to see.*

Modeling

5 Clarifying *Here are some more Spanish words. I don't know what* gardules *and* ajíes *are, and I can't guess from looking at this paragraph. I'll have to look them up in a Spanish/English dictionary.*

Modeling

6 Confirming Predictions *I think I was right about Carlos. He and Juan are hitting it off great. Maybe now Juan will feel better about living with his Uncle.*

Encourage students to make connections with Juan. Ask them to share experiences they have had with trying to make new friends and compare and contrast these experiences with Juan's.

Word Knowledge

wood/would, to/two

Remind students if they have difficulty decoding these words that they learned about homophones in the Word Knowledge section of this lesson.

"Five cents a box for cardboard, ten cents for wood. I told them they could take the seats home with them."

"And how much are you planning to pay me, Carlos, for every box I give you?"

"Well," Carlos said, "a penny for cardboard. Two cents for wood."

Señor Rivera laughed. "Carlos," he said, "you're going to grow up to be the president of the First National Bank. Listen," he added, "go down in my cellar and haul yourself up twenty boxes. You can have them for free."

Carlos grinned and started for the flight of steps leading down to the cellar.

4 "Save a box seat for me," Señor Rivera called after him. "I want to come watch my son Willie be umpire."

288

Plátanos verdes is pronounced plä´ tä nōs vär´ dās. Gardules is pronounced gär dōō´ lās. Ajíes is pronounced ä hē´ yās.

Juan then stood on tiptoe in front of the greasy glass counter. He ordered twelve *plátanos verdes*, two pounds of *gandules* and one ounce of *ajíes*. But when he paid his money, and held the three paper bags in his hands, he

⑤ still did not want to leave.

If only his uncle had the job of maintenance engineer on Columbus Avenue! Then he, Juan, might not even want to go home. If he lived over here, then he could go to school over here. Maybe here they even had Spanish schools and he'd never need to learn English at all!

But Uncle Esteban had explained that a boy must go to school in the district where he lived. He would have to go to school on the rich East Side of Manhattan; a school which would, no doubt, be filled up tight with *americanos*.

He noticed the boy called Carlos who came staggering up from the cellar with an armload of cardboard boxes. "Hey!" He walked over to Carlos. "You want me to help you carry those boxes to wherever you're going?"

"Sure," Carlos said in English. "Matter of fact, I was going to ask you to give me a hand." He smiled.

Juan didn't understand the English, but a smile was the same in any language.

⑥ He smiled back.

They made two trips from the Bodega Rivera to the basement of the brownstone rooming house where Carlos lived. Juan kept talking almost nonstop all the way. He had so much talk inside him it seemed he just couldn't get it all said.

289

Comprehension Skills

Drawing Conclusions

Explain that readers can draw conclusions about characters in a story. Have the students reread the exchanges between Señor Rivera and Carlos on pages 288–289.

Have the students draw conclusions about the characters of Señor Rivera and Carlos. *(Señor Rivera is a good father and supportive of kids in the neighborhood. Carlos is determined and good at making deals for himself. He has no problem asking for help.)*

Encourage the students to tell how they reached their conclusions. What clues did they use?

Meeting Individual Needs

Challenge

Drawing Conclusions Discuss why authors do not include everything in the text. Have students reread a selection and explain all the conclusions they reach.

2 Reading and Responding

Comprehension Strategies

Prompting

7 **Clarifying** *Here's another Spanish word:* puertorriqueño. *Who wants to clarify this term for me and tell me what you did to clarify it?*

Student Sample

Clarifying *I think I can figure this one out by myself.* Puertorriqueño *looks a lot like* Puerto Rican *to me, and it makes sense with what is being said in the sentence.*

Modeling

8 **Confirming Predictions** *Uh-oh. I might have been wrong about Carlos. It doesn't look as if Juan wants to be friends with Carlos after all. That's too bad, because I'm beginning to like Carlos a lot, and at least Carlos can speak a little Spanish. I still think he and Juan have a lot they could teach each other and a lot in common.*

Teacher Tip Many students may, like Carlos, have grandparents who speak mostly in a foreign language, while they grew up speaking English. Invite them to share their experiences with the class.

Word Knowledge

The word *watched* appears on page 290. Remind students that they learned words with the /ch/ sound spelled *tch* in the Word Knowledge section of the lesson.

Carlos spoke very little. When they had finished piling the boxes in a corner of the basement, Carlos explained why he always answered Juan in such short sentences. He knew very little Spanish.

7 Juan stared at him through the basement gloom, astounded. A *puertorriqueño* who didn't know Spanish?

Carlos shrugged and explained that they'd come from the mainland when he was three years old to live with his grandmother. He'd been brought up on English, in the streets and in school. In fact, the only Spanish he knew came from talking to his grandmother.

Juan nodded. He felt he had found a friend—only to lose him. What was worse, he felt like a fool. Here he'd been jabbering away to this boy all about Barranquitas and his house and his mother and sisters and friends and his miniature car collection and the Piñonas River and his school and the TV programs he watched at home. And all the time Carlos had hardly understood a single word!

"As a matter of fact," Carlos said in English as he started up the basement stairs, "you'll find that most of the Spanish kids on this street don't speak Spanish. At least, their Spanish is nothing to speak of!" Then, having made a kind of <u>pun</u>, Carlos laughed.

But Juan trudging up the stairs behind him did not laugh. He had not understood a word Carlos said.

Carlos turned then and repeated the sentences in a stiff and inaccurate Spanish.

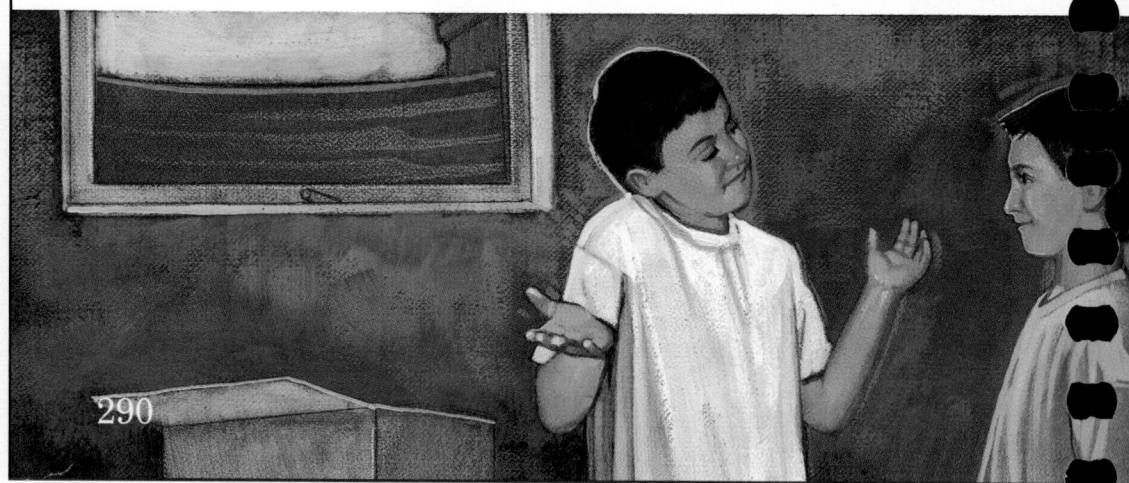

290

Meeting Individual Needs

Intervention

Predicting Students should notice that predicting, once learned, comes naturally and enhances the meaning and enjoyment of a selection. Encourage them to discuss with classmates the predictions they have made during the selection. Remind students that regardless of whether or not their predictions come true, the best predictions are based on the text and one's own experiences.

Juan nodded glumly. He felt betrayed. Even if he took the bus over here every day to play with the *puertorriqueño* kids on Columbus Avenue, it would be no good. He would still be a stranger—among his own people. Only they weren't his own people anymore. ⑧ They were *americanos*.

When they reached the street Carlos said, in Spanish, "Well, thanks for helping me out."

And, in Spanish, Juan replied. "That's okay." Then he added, "I better say good-bye now. I'll be going back home at the end of the week."

"To the island?" Carlos said, in some surprise.

Juan nodded.

"You must be pretty rich," Carlos said, "to come hopping all the way over here just for one week. How much is the plane fare?"

Juan explained that the trip home wouldn't cost him anything. The airline would fly him home free.

Carlos frowned. He did not understand. "Free? How could that be?"

Juan, speaking in slow careful Spanish as though he were addressing a very small child, explained how the airline had promised to send him home free the night he arrived. So since he hadn't taken them up on their offer then, he would do so at the end of the week.

"Listen, you stupid kid," Carlos said. "Sure they were going to send you home free when your uncle didn't show up. I mean they can't let a little kid like you just be hanging around the airport at night all alone. But your uncle *did* show up. So the offer's over. Now you're *his* worry. Not theirs. How could they ever make any money if they kept dealing out free tickets to anyone wanting to make a trip back home?"

291

Teacher Tip Puertorriqueño is pronounced pwer tō rē kān´ yo. Piñonas is pronounced pēn yo´ näs.

Meeting Individual Needs

Inter**V**ention

Drawing Conclusions To help students draw conclusions, carefully spell out some clues. Lead the students to use these clues to reach a conclusion.

Drawing Conclusions

Remind the students that characters in a story often draw conclusions themselves. These conclusions may or may not be correct. Point out the following examples:

- Juan concludes that he's lost a friend when he realizes Carlos doesn't understand much Spanish.

- Carlos concludes that Juan must be rich because he's going back to Puerto Rico so soon.

- After getting more information, Carlos concludes that Juan misunderstood the airline.

What conclusions can the students make about characters in the selection?

2 Reading and Responding

Comprehension Strategies

Prompting

9 **Clarifying** *As you read, remember that it is important to continue gathering information that helps you clarify unfamiliar words and ideas. Have any of you been able to clarify further anything you found confusing or unfamiliar earlier in the selection?*

Student Sample

Clarifying *Here's some more information about "stickball." From the way Carlos explains this game, it sounds like baseball to me.*

Word Knowledge

no, know

Remind students if they have difficulty decoding these words that they learned about homophones in the Word Knowledge section of this lesson.

He spoke now in English. Juan kept nodding. Then he said, "*No entiendo.* I not onnerstan'."

So, with some effort, Carlos repeated it all in Spanish. Juan nodded again. This time he understood all too well, and knew with certainty that Carlos was correct. In fact, this very thought had been lurking in the back of his mind. But he hadn't allowed it to come forward before. Because he didn't want to know the truth. The truth that he *could* not go home.

"Listen, kid," Carlos said suddenly, in Spanish, "since you helped me with the boxes, how'd you like a free box seat for the game tomorrow afternoon?"

"What kind of game?" Juan asked.

"Stickball."

"What's stickball?"

"Stickball's what it says it is," Carlos said. "You hit a ball with a stick. Want me to show you?"

Juan nodded.

"C'mon," Carlos said. "I got my equipment upstairs." He shoved open the front door and Juan followed him into the hallway. The place smelled strongly of cats and rancid cooking oil and the garbage which sat outside each doorway in overflowing pails or paper bags.

Juan felt like holding his breath and holding his nose. Who would want to live in such a place when they could be back in the fresh mountain air of Barranquitas where the only smell one noticed was that of flowers?

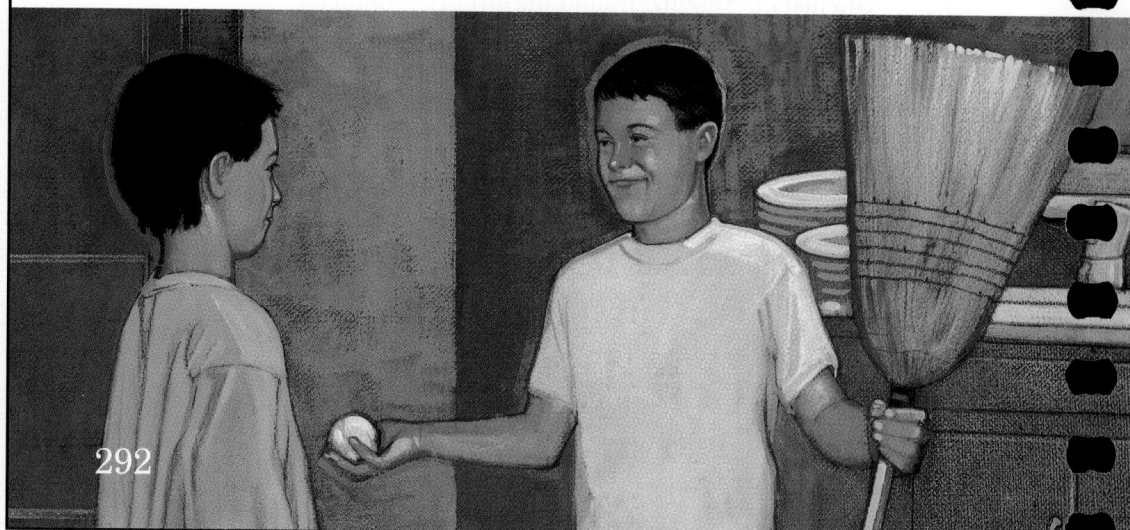

292

Meeting Individual Needs

Intervention

Clarifying Remind the students that clarifying is a process. If the students have trouble clarifying, you may wish to have them work with partners as they read through the story, and work together to clarify confusing words or ideas.

Teacher Tip No entiendo is pronounced nō ān tē ān´dō.

When they reached the third floor Carlos took a ring of keys from his pocket and started unlocking one of the doors. "We got three different locks," he explained to Juan, "because we have been robbed five times."

Juan was impressed. Carlos must live in a pretty big place with some valuable things in it for anyone to bother robbing his apartment five times. After all, even though the hallways smelled, that didn't mean the apartments weren't beautiful inside.

But inside there was nothing much either. Just one room with a flowered curtain drawn across the middle. The whole place was not much bigger than the bedroom he shared at home with his two sisters. There was a wooden table and four wooden chairs all painted bright green. There was a picture of the Virgin Mary tacked to the wall. And in the corner a small stove and large sink, stacked with dishes. Sunlight fell in through the open window and lay in a long <u>oblong</u> pattern across the worn green linoleum on the floor. There was a flower box on the windowsill with some geraniums in it.

Not a bad place, Juan thought. At least it looked friendly. He'd a lot rather live here than in Uncle Esteban's fine basement apartment where all the windows had bars like a jail.

Carlos meanwhile had gone behind the curtain. He came back with a small rubber ball and a broom. "Of course," he said, "the bat we play with is a mop handle without the mop. But our captain keeps that in his house. I'm the manager of the team," he added, with an edge of pride in his voice. "That means I set up the games and arrange everything. The big game we got on tomorrow is against the Young Princes. Come on. I'll show you how we play." **9**

293

Comprehension Skills

Drawing Conclusions

Have volunteers explain how to draw conclusions based on information in a story.

Have the students look at the following two conclusions that Juan draws.

■ After Carlos explains about the airline tickets, Juan concludes that he can't go home after all.

■ When Carlos tells Juan that he's been robbed five times, Juan concludes that Carlos must be rich.

Have the students discuss Juan's conclusions. Is he right or wrong? Have the students support their answers with examples from the text or their own knowledge about the world.

Teacher Tip Have students share what they know of being far away from home in a strange place. Then, have them discuss how their experiences compare with Juan's.

② Reading and Responding

Comprehension Strategies

Prompting

🔟 **Summarizing** *This was a good story. While it's still fresh in our minds, let's sum up what happened. Who would like to begin?*

Student Sample

Summarizing *Juan was unhappy living in New York City because it was so different from Puerto Rico. But on a trip to buy food, he found a whole neighborhood that reminded him of home. He met a boy named Carlos, and, even though they couldn't always understand each other, they became friends.*

Discussing Strategy Use

After they have read the selection, have students share any problems they encountered and tell what strategies they used to solve them. Then, have them answer the following questions. If they answer "no" to any of the questions, have them reread part of the selection to find the answer.

- Did they stop to clarify words, phrases, and ideas that they didn't understand?

- Did they predict what might happen and then check to see if they were correct?

- Did they summarize in order to help understand what they've read?

Make sure that students explain how using the strategies helped them understand the selection better and how they read effectively to find answers to the questions they asked as they set purposes.

Juan followed Carlos into the hallway again, waited while his new friend locked the door with three different keys, and went down the stairs after him, taking two at a time as Carlos did.

In the street Carlos waited until a few cars had gone by. Then, when there was a <u>lull</u> in the traffic, he stepped out, threw the ball into the air, swung the broom handle hard. And missed.

<u>Shamefaced</u>, he picked up the ball. "Well, I myself am not so hot at this game," he said in English. "I'm better at organizing than playing. But the idea is, if you hit the ball past the first sewer that's pretty good. If you hit it past the second sewer, that's sensational. And if you hit it past the third sewer, that's impossible. The third sewer's right down at the end of the street. You can hardly even see it from here."

Juan nodded. He had barely understood a word that Carlos said. But he was embarrassed to ask his friend to repeat it all over again in Spanish. So he asked instead, "I try?"

"Sure," Carlos said and threw him the broom which Juan caught in one hand. Then Carlos threw the ball which Juan caught in the other hand. And stepped out into the street.

"Hey! *Watch it!*" Carlos screamed in English.

Juan stepped back just as a yellow taxi sped by his toes. He'd been so intent about showing Carlos that he could hit this ball with the broom that he forgot about everything else—including getting run over. His heart now started thudding with fear at his narrow escape.

"Listen!" Carlos said sternly. "They got such things as cars in this city and don't you ever forget that!"

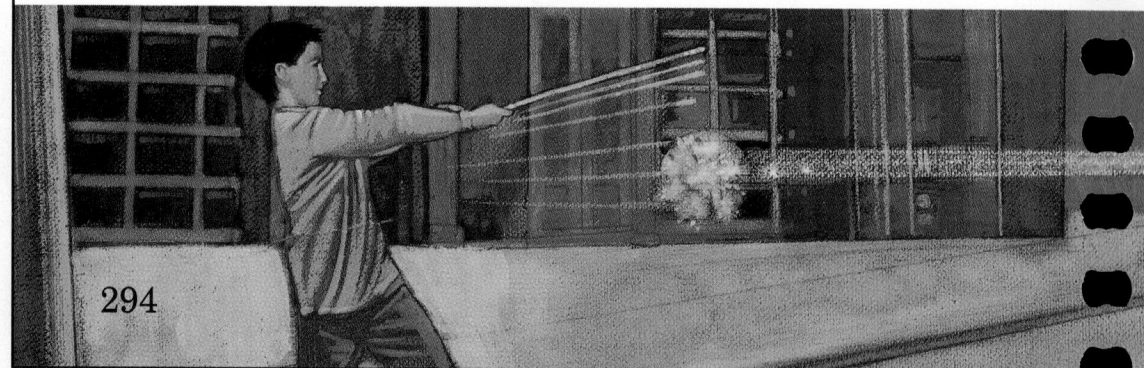

294

Meeting Individual Needs

Intervention

Summarizing Tell the students that summarizing will help them see if they understand what they are reading. Encourage them to summarize the events in the order in which they occurred.

Reread the selection with students who had difficulty understanding it. Continue modeling and prompting the use of strategies and skills as you reread.

Juan nodded. He looked carefully up and down the street.

"It's okay now," Carlos said. "Nothing coming."

But still Juan felt afraid.

"Hurry up! *Avanza!*" Carlos said. "Take your chance while you got it."

So Juan, his heart still pounding, stepped out into the street, threw the rubber ball into the air, and hit it with the broom handle. Hard.

He watched the ball proudly as it sped through the air.

Carlos screamed again. And again Juan rushed back to the safety of the sidewalk. But this time there were no cars coming. This time Carlos screamed for another reason. "You hit three sewers!" he kept screaming. "Man, don't you understand, you hit *three sewers!*"

"Yes," said Juan. "I onnerstan'." He did not know what "three sewers" meant. But he did understand that Carlos was impressed at how he had hit the ball.

"Listen," Carlos said. "You must be puttin' me on, man. Telling me you never played stickball before." He repeated the question in Spanish. The words were charged with suspicion. "You sure you never played stickball before?"

Juan shook his head. "No," he said. "I have never played stickball before." He saw no reason to explain that he had been playing stick-stone ever since he was seven years old. Hitting a stone with a stick across the Piñonas River in the Contest game he had invented.

"Listen, kid," Carlos said suddenly. "How'd you like to play on our team tomorrow afternoon?" Then, slowly, carefully he tried the words in Spanish. "*¿Vas a jugar con nosotros mañana?*"

Juan grinned. "Sure, man," he said in English. "Hokay!"

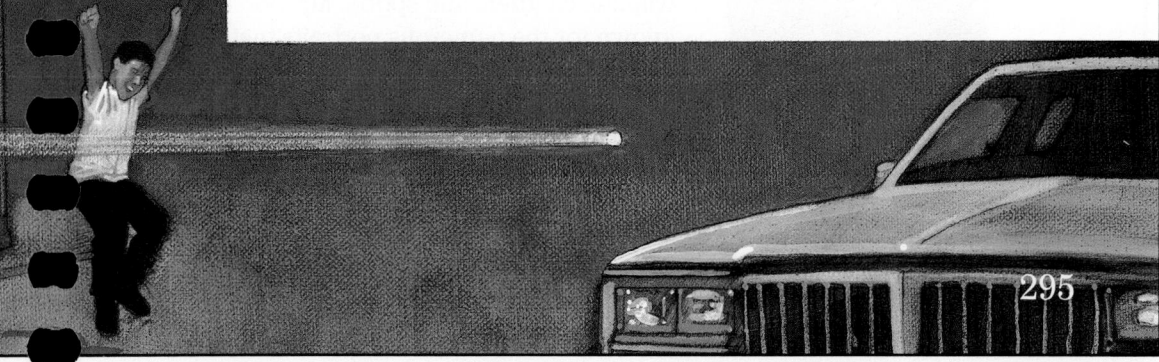

295

Teacher Tip

Avanza is pronounced ä vän′ zä. Vas a jugar con nosotros mañana is pronounced väs′ ä hōō gär′ kōn′ nō sō′tros män yä′ nä.

Assessment

✔ **Formal** To assess students' reading comprehension, have them complete *Comprehension and Writing Assessment,* pages 61–62.

Discussing the Selection

Following reading, engage the students in a discussion of the selection. Using the *handing-off process* will help the students to take responsibility for the discussion. In addition to the following questions, have them revisit any questions asked when they set purposes before reading.

- How do you think the West Side neighborhood was similar to Juan's hometown? What was different? *(Many of the stores had Spanish names and sold Spanish food. Many of the people, however, did not speak Spanish.)*

- Why do you think Juan wants to become friends with Carlos? *(He wants to fit in.)*

- How has this selection connected with your knowledge of the unit theme? *(Answers will vary—students should compare/contrast examples of heritage from this selection with their own experiences or past reading and use these connections to make a general statement about the unit theme.)*

During this time, have the students return to the clues and problems that they noted on the transparency before reading. Let the students decide which items deserve further discussion.

As the year progresses, the students take more and more responsibility for discussions of the selections and how they progress. This *handing-off process* encourages them to retain complete control of the discussion and to become more actively involved in the learning process.

2 Reading and Responding

Meet the Author

After the students read the information about Peggy Mann, discuss the following questions with them.

Peggy Mann wrote a whole series about her years living in a brownstone. Why do you think she wanted to write a series? *(Possible answer: Writing a series allowed her to tell many different stories about a subject that was very dear to her.)*

Why do you think it is so important to Peggy Mann to support urban renewal projects? *(Possible answer: Her love for her own home makes her want to reach out and make good homes for people in her community.)*

How does Peggy Mann's writing help to support these urban renewal projects? *(Possible answer: It helps by showing other people why these brownstone buildings are important to urban communities.)*

Meet the Illustrator

After the students read the information about Bob Dorsey, discuss the following question with them.

Bob Dorsey likes to illustrate portraits, children, wildlife, and sports. How do you think this helped him when illustrating this story? *(Possible answer: Because this is a children's story, he probably enjoyed illustrating the children. He also illustrated children playing stickball.)*

The West Side

Meet the Author

Peggy Mann is a native New Yorker. She has based a lot of her writing on childhood experiences that she had when her family restored a brownstone building on a slum street in Manhattan. Her first book, called *The Street of the Flower Boxes*, was about her years in the brownstone. It was made into a children's television special. Other books in the series include *The Clubhouse, When Carlos Closed the Street, How Juan Got Home,* and *The Secret Dog of Little Luis.*

Today, the slum block she lived on as a little girl is a showplace. Families from the area got together and fixed up all the old brownstones as part of an urban renewal project. Now, that block stands as an example to other urban renewal projects around the country. Peggy Mann started, and became the president of, one of the committees that makes these projects possible.

Meet the Illustrator

Bob Dorsey has been a professional illustrator for 17 years, working with a wide range of media and a variety of subject matter. Some of his favorite subjects include portraits, wildlife, children, and sports. Mr. Dorsey is well known for the numerous portraits that he has done for the National Baseball Hall of Fame in Cooperstown, New York. His paintings have been exhibited throughout the country.

Theme Connections

Think About It

In small groups, share the experience of someone you know who has had to move from another place. Have you had the experience of moving to a new place? If so, consider sharing that experience with your group members.

Record Ideas

In your Writing Journal, write about a time when you had to move and how the move affected you. If you have never moved, try to imagine what it would be like if you did, and record this in your Writing Journal.

Share a Story

Think of a book you have read, a movie you have seen, or a story you have heard about someone who has left his or her home to live in a new place. Share the story with a small group of classmates. Be sure to explain how the person felt when he or she had to move. What are some things that that person worried about? What kinds of things did they need to figure out about the place where they moved? Did the person move to a place with new traditions and customs? If so, did the person continue to practice his or her customs, or leave them behind?

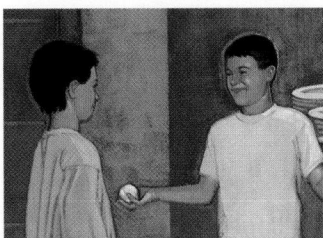

297

Theme Connections

Think About It

If students have not had any experiences with moving to a new place, suggest that they think about how Juan felt about his move, and compare that to how they think they would feel.

Have students who have experienced a move share with other group members how their experiences were the same as or different from Juan's. Tell students to make connections with each other's experiences and comment on any new insights these connections give them into Juan's character.

Share a Story

Ensure that students understand that immigrants usually try to maintain some of their customs and traditions in their adopted home. Have them discuss how, even though Carlos did not speak a lot of Spanish, the customs and traditions of his native land surrounded him.

Teacher Tip
Have students talk about why Juan wanted to go home and whether he liked everything in Puerto Rico as much when he was there.

Fine Art

Heritage

Viewing the Theme Through Fine Art

Students can use the artworks on these pages to explore the unit theme, Heritage, in images rather than words. Encourage them to talk about their impressions of the artworks and how each one might relate to heritage.

Following is some background information about each of the artworks. Share with students whatever you feel is appropriate. You may also wish to encourage students to find out more about artists and artistic styles that interest them.

Family Greeting

The word *Inuit* means "people." Inuits are the group of Eskimos from the Canadian Arctic. Originally, Eskimo art was used for rituals or ornamentation; amulets were made to be worn on clothing and animals were carved to be used as toys for children. During the twentieth century, tourism introduced a demand for souvenirs and carving became a major occupation. Men usually hold the prestigious position of carver.

Family Greeting portrays a family of Eskimos; the father figure waves his hand in greeting to the viewer. Contemporary sculptures like this piece first emerged during the late 1940s and became increasingly popular by the 1960s. Sculptors carve domestic and social scenes rather than hunting and fishing which are no longer central to their lives.

Heritage

FINE Art

Family Greeting. 1962. **Eli Tikeayak.** Canadian Inuit, Rankin Inlet. Light green-grey stone. Art Gallery of Ontario, Toronto. Gift of Robert C. Williamson, C.M., 1989.

298

Mother and Child. 1922. **Pablo Picasso.** Oil on canvas. 100 × 81 cm. The Baltimore Museum of Art: The Cone Collection formed by Dr. Claribel Cone and Miss Etta Cone of Baltimore, Maryland. ©1998 Estate of Pablo Picasso/Artist Rights Society (ARS), New York.

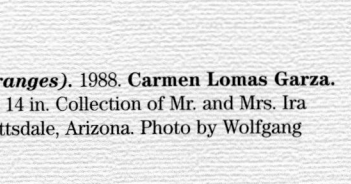

Naranjas (Oranges). 1988. **Carmen Lomas Garza.** Gouache. 20 × 14 in. Collection of Mr. and Mrs. Ira Schneider, Scottsdale, Arizona. Photo by Wolfgang Dietze.

299

Mother and Child

Pablo Picasso (1881–1973) was born in Spain and is considered one of the most influential artists of the twentieth century. His work changed throughout his life: from realistic, to the monochrome (using mainly one color) palettes of his Rose and Blue periods, to cubism, which he invented. Picasso was a painter, sculptor, graphic artist, designer, and ceramist. He completed approximately 50,000 works of art by the age of ninety.

Mother and Child was painted during Picasso's Classical period. The image of the mother and child was inspired by the classical Greek and Roman art Picasso viewed after visiting Rome. See how he uses simple lines to portray the complex image of the mother affectionately holding her child.

Naranjas

Carmen Lomas Garza (1948 –) is a Hispanic American who was born in Kingsville, Texas. She received a master's degree in art from San Francisco State University. Her use of bright colors, repeated patterns, and simple shapes is reminiscent of Chicano culture. Lomas Garza explores her heritage through her paintings, often portraying families and people participating in daily activities.

Naranjas is a *monito*, or "little people" painting. These small paintings tell stories of families participating in common daily activities. Notice how the woman places the oranges, or *naranjas*, which the children are gathering, in her apron.

Teacher Tip Encourage students to use art to enhance their heritage albums. They may want to illustrate one of their written pieces or use photographs from home. Students may also wish to use a culturally traditional style of art to decorate their albums.

 **Responding**

 Research

As students continue their explorations, have them use the **Research** CD-ROM program to help organize and share their findings.

 **Teacher Tip** If you created a semantic map on the Concept/Question Board of key words related to the unit theme, Heritage, have students find words from other resources, their projects, and family discussions and add them to the appropriate category on the map.

Exploring the Theme

Selection Vocabulary

Have students write in their Writing Journals the definitions for words discussed before the reading of the selection and any other interesting words they clarified while reading. Students should be encouraged to refer to these words throughout the unit as they work on unit and writing activities. The words from the selection are:

jabbering   scowled   manager
embarrassed impressed

Reading/Writing Connections

Have students identify techniques that the author used to tell about Juan's heritage—for example, memory sequences and vivid descriptions of scenes that caused Juan to remember his homeland. Have students discuss how they have used or will use these techniques in their heritage albums.

Home Connection

The class has just finished reading "The West Side," a fictional selection about a boy who must adjust to a move he has made from Puerto Rico to the United States. An informational letter on "The West Side," in both English and Spanish, can be found in the **Home Connection** guide.

Research in Action
Writing and Reading Strategies

Writing and reading strategies are complementary. Reading is the ultimate source of good models for writing. Learning to read with an eye to possibilities for personal style and subject matter can dramatically expand a writer's repertoire and skills. *(Marlene Scardamalia)*

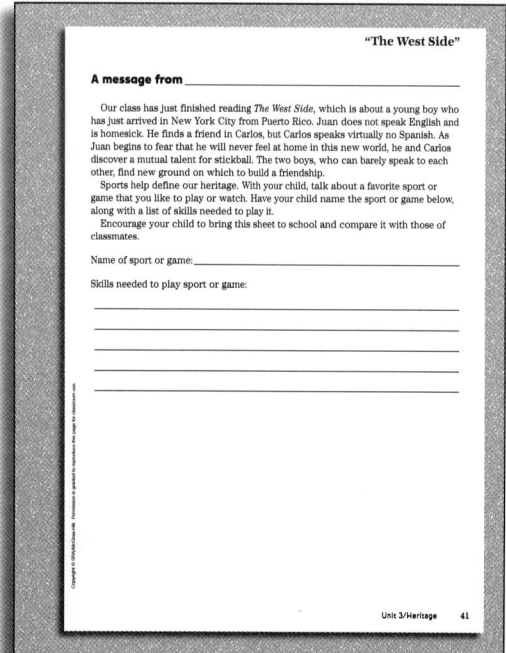

Home Connection p. 41

Supporting Student Explorations

Students should continue to work on the second pieces for their albums. You may want to do the following:

Whole Group Tell the students to use vivid descriptions in order to give readers a clear sense of people, places, and events. Suggest that they revise their work as needed to include such descriptions, then prepare a final draft. Tell the students to add illustrations to complement the text.

Individual Meet with students individually to review the work they have completed thus far. Talk with them about what they want to share about their heritage, and review possible ways of presenting the information. Explore the possibility of creating a photographic essay on a particular theme, such as birthdays.

Have the students continue to read their library books and to share any questions or interesting information they encounter. Explain that if they "read as writers," it will help them learn the techniques that authors use to tell about heritage.

Suggest that students post on the Concept/Question Board brief descriptions of books, magazines articles, computer Websites, or other sources of information that they have found to be especially helpful in their explorations of heritage. Encourage students who are having difficulty finding information to check sources on the board and to post their questions as well.

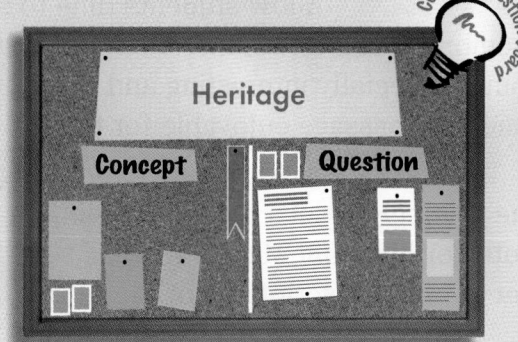

Inquiry Journal Have students complete page 42 of the *Inquiry Journal*. Have them record their ideas about how "The West Side" added to their knowledge of heritage.

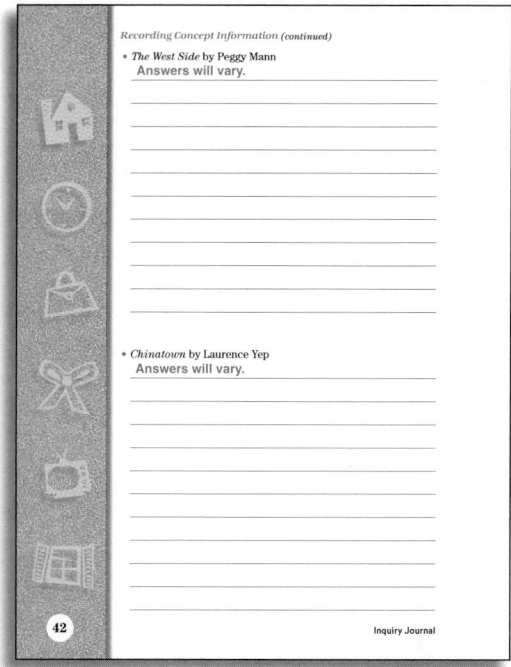

Inquiry Journal p. 42

Teacher Tip After reading their library books, have students tell what writing techniques they have learned from the authors.

Assessment

✓ **Informal** Continue making anecdotal records of students' progress. Note whether they:
- complete a second piece for their heritage albums.
- access a range of sources for information about their exploration of their heritage.
- identify and use techniques, such as description, to communicate their own heritage.

③ Integrating the Curriculum

Teacher Tip
Sentence Lifting The students' own writing provides the best vehicle for teaching language and writing skills. Lift sentences from student writing that show good elements as well as those that need correction.

Teacher Tip
Writing Seminar Students have been working on a draft of a narrative paper. Either have volunteers read their drafts to the rest of the class, or select students to do so. Since the purpose of this seminar is to provide students with usable and thoughtful feedback, no more than two students should present their work on any given day. If students seem rushed when two students present their work, have only one present.

Meeting Individual Needs

ESL
Writing and Revising Peer tutoring increases the amount of understandable input English-language learners receive in English and therefore, helps to increase their language mastery. Pair English-language-learners with native English-speaking students for tutoring in writing and revising whenever possible.

Intervention
Revise For students who need more help with this stage of the writing process, see Unit 3, Lesson 4, of the *Intervention Guide.*

Teacher Tip
When revising, remind students to incorporate what they have learned in the grammar and spelling lessons in this unit, about syllable boundary patterns, pronoun referents, regular and irregular verbs, regular and irregular plural nouns, and adverbs.

Language Arts

Writing

Evaluating the Author's Writing

Instruct Ask students to think back to any part of "The West Side" that they reacted to strongly or particularly enjoyed as they read. Call on students to discuss something that Peggy Mann, the author of "The West Side," did particularly well. If necessary, begin the discussion by asking a question, such as the following:

- Does something about the writing in this story stand out?
- What made this story seem real?
- Was there a particular part of the story that you especially enjoyed? If so, does that part contain a clue about what makes writing good?

Practice Allow students time to skim the story to refresh their memories. Call on volunteers to read passages from the story that they found especially interesting and to talk about anything in the writing that made the passage enjoyable for them.

If students have difficulty expressing their thoughts and feelings about the writing, model a response, pointing out the things that you found noteworthy about Mann's writing, such as how she used Spanish words or her detailed descriptions of the setting.

Apply Have students use in their own writing any of the techniques that stood out in "The West Side." Have students review their narratives and revise them to include a particular writing technique that was used well in the selection.

Writing Process

Revise Have students revise the rough draft of their personal narratives. Remind students that the purpose of revising is to make sure that their writing expresses their ideas clearly. As they work to make their writing better, they may need to move or change sentences, add new ideas or details, take out ideas or details that do not fit, or change words. Have them use what they learned when they evaluated the author's writing as they revise their personal narratives.

Literary Elements

Analyze Character Traits

Instruct Remind students that writers reveal traits about a character in different ways—by describing the character's actions, by telling what the character is thinking, by including dialogue between the characters in the story, or by revealing what others think about the character.

Practice If the following activity, students will make inferences about Juan by analyzing what he does, says, and thinks in the story. Have pairs of students work together. Have each pair make a two-column chart on a sheet of paper. The heading for the first column should read *Juan's Character Traits*. The heading for the second column should read *What We Learn About Juan*. As a class, fill in the first column with things that Juan says, does, and thinks, and others' reactions to him. Then have the pairs of students write in the other column what the reader learns about Juan from these clues.

Apply Have students do character analyses to enhance their narratives and their unit activities.

Spelling

Syllable Boundary Patterns

Instruct Point out that words can often be divided into syllables between the two consonants, as in the word *suc/cess*. Write this word on the chalkboard.

Point out that a word cannot be broken into syllables between two consonants if the consonants are a blend or digraph. Write the word *respect* on the chalkboard, and ask a student to divide this word into syllables. *(re/spect)* Remind students that *sp* is a blend. Then tell students that when a word has a vowel and three consonants, they should divide the word between the consonant blend and the other consonant, as in the word *em/ploy*.

Practice Have students practice dividing words into syllables with these words from "The West Side": *strum/ming, mus/tache, cur/tain, bar/ber/shop, stick/ball, af/ter/noon, brown/stone, un/der/stand.*

Apply Have students skim the selection and write down eight to ten words that follow either of these syllable patterns. Have them exchange papers and divide the words into syllables.

Meeting Individual Needs

Challenge
Syllable Boundary Patterns Have students select five words from the story that do not follow these patterns. Have them try to figure out the syllable pattern of the words they have chosen.

Skills Strand

Syllable Boundary Patterns
INTRODUCED: Unit 3, Lesson 1
REVIEWED: Unit 3, Lesson 4
Unit 5, Lesson 6

Teacher Tip Remind students that sometimes breaking a word into syllables can help them spell or pronounce the word.

3 Integrating the Curriculum

Grammar, Usage, & Mechanics

Subject and Verb Agreement

Instruct Review subject and verb agreement with students by writing this sentence on the chalkboard: *Pepe plays soccer.* Ask students to give the subject and verb of the sentence. Point out that the *subject* is the word(s) that refers to the person(s) or thing(s) that performs or receives the action of the verb. The *verb* is the word that refers to the action. The verb must agree with the subject. A singular subject takes a singular verb. A plural subject takes a plural verb.

Practice Write these sentences on the chalkboard and have students fill in the blank with the correct verb choice.

The goalie _____ the ball with his hands. (touch/<u>touches</u>)

The sun _____ the playing field. (dry/<u>dries</u>)

Maria and Franco _____ in the woods. (<u>play</u>/plays)

One of the English teachers _____ in charge of the play. (are/<u>is</u>)

Sid _____ home. (<u>goes</u>/go)

My mother _____ pepperoni pizza. (<u>likes</u>/like)

Apply Tell students to look in their **Writing Folders** for their narratives and their heritage albums. Have them make sure the subject and verb agree in both activities.

Meeting Individual Needs

Challenge

Subject and Verb Agreement Have students write sentences similar to the ones in the Practice exercise and exchange papers to fill in the blanks.

Assessment

✓ **Formal** To assess students' knowledge of Subject and Verb Agreement, use **Skills Assessment,** page 30.

Subject and Verb Agreement
INTRODUCED: Unit 2, Lesson 6
REVIEWED: Unit 3, Lesson 4
Unit 6, Lesson 2

Listening/Speaking/Viewing

Connect Experiences

Ask students if they have ever been in a situation similar to Juan's. How did they feel? What did they do to feel better if they were homesick? Do they think they will ever be in a situation like that again? Allow time for discussion within the classroom.

Then divide the class into small groups and have them discuss the following questions based on their own experiences and what they know of Juan's character.

1. What could Juan's family in Puerto Rico have done to prepare him better for this trip?
2. What could Juan's uncle have done to make Juan feel more comfortable in New York City?
3. How do you think Juan will react the next time he meets a Puerto Rican boy or girl?
4. What might happen between Juan and Carlos after their first meeting?

Teacher Tip If students are having difficulties answering questions 1–4 in this activity, emphasize that they should try to imagine themselves as if they were Juan and then try to answer the question.

3 **Integrating the Curriculum**

Encourage students to use graphs to enhance their heritage albums if graphs are appropriate.

Study and Research

Using Graphs

Instruct   Remind students of the uses of graphs. Tell them that a *bar graph* is a graph in which quantities are shown by bars. Draw the example below to show students the number of days it rained in Anytown for the months of April, May, and June.

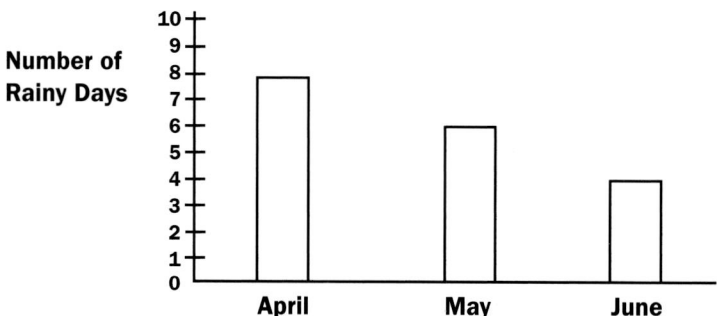

Practice   Have the class help you create a bar graph showing the number of boys and the number of girls in the classroom. Draw the outline of a graph on the chalkboard that shows the numbers 1 through 15 on the left-hand side. Write the label *Number of Students* to the left of the numbers. At the bottom of the graph, write the labels *Boys* and *Girls*. Have students count the number of boys and the number of girls in the classroom. Write those numbers on the chalkboard. Then have a volunteer come to the chalkboard and draw bars representing the numbers of boys and girls in the classroom.

Apply   For additional practice with using graphs, have students complete *Inquiry Journal* pages 48–49.

Inquiry Journal pp. 48–49

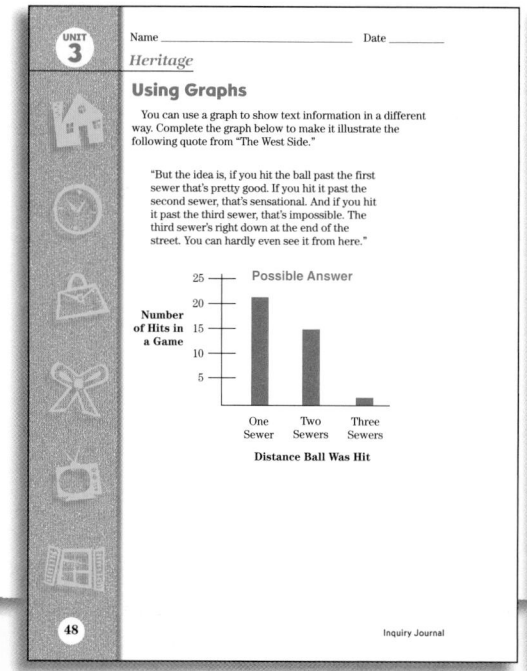

Across the Curriculum

 ## Social Studies

Learning Español

Materials

Spanish/English picture dictionaries or word dictionaries

Purpose

To help students learn some Spanish words

Procedure

Many Spanish words are used in the story "The West Side," and there are also many people in the United States who speak Spanish. Students will work together to learn Spanish words.

- Gather some Spanish/English picture dictionaries for students to browse.

- Have students skim the story "The West Side" for Spanish words and list them on the board as they find them. Using the pronunciation key in the book, have students pronounce the words together orally. Ask students if they can figure out what the words mean in English.

- If you have students who speak Spanish, have them teach the class how to count from one to ten. You may want to record the Spanish counting for students to use later.

- Have small groups select some conversational words and phrases such as *hello*, *good-bye*, and *How are you?* Using the dictionaries or other sources, have students make a list of English words. Then have them find the Spanish words that correlate with their English list.

- Have student practice greeting each other in Spanish.

 ## Math

Money Word Problems

Purpose

To help students apply some of their math skills

Procedure

Brainstorm with students a list of ways that children can make money such as lemonade stands, paper routes, car washes, and pet-sitting.

- Write this problem based on the story on the chalkboard:

  If Carlos buys 20 cardboard boxes from Señor Rivera for a penny each and sells the boxes for five cents each, how much money will Carlos make altogether?

- Have students work in pairs to write math word problems using the list of money making projects. Then have them exchange their word problems with a partner and solve the problems.

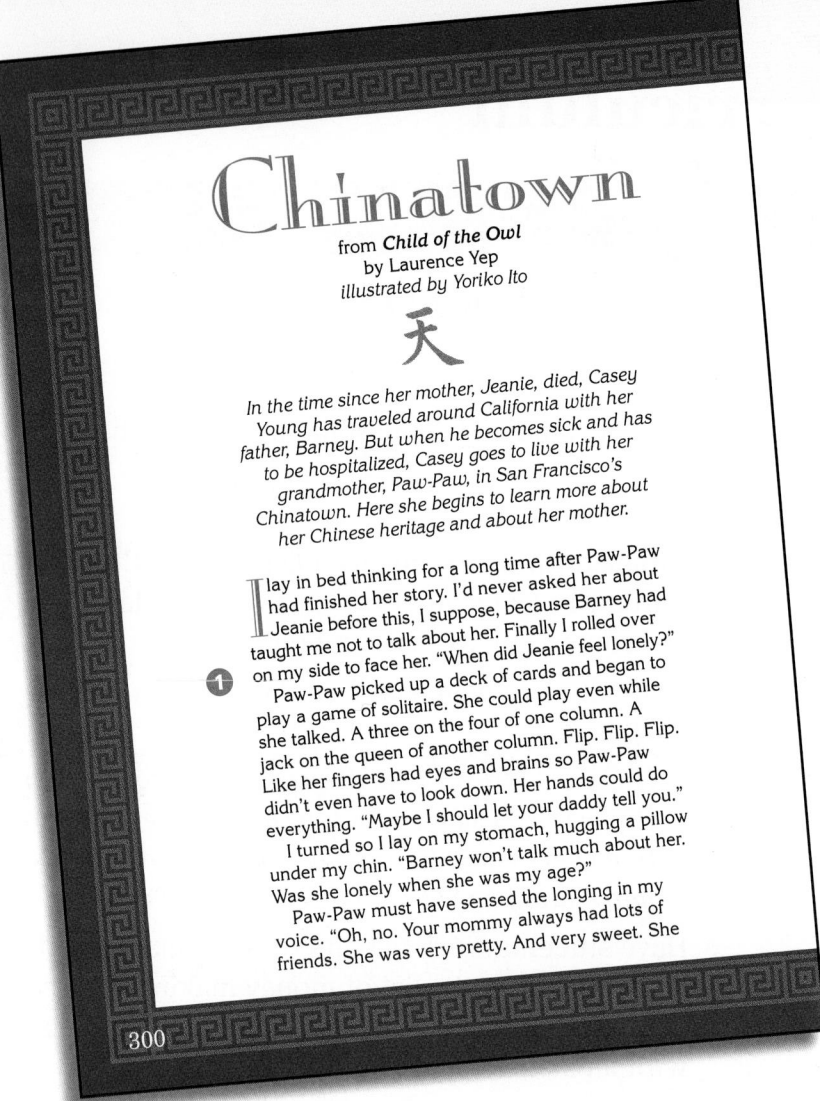

About the Author

Laurence Yep has written many historical fiction, science fiction, fantasy, and realistic fiction books. Many of the books reveal his own experiences of "otherness" as a Chinese adolescent in American culture. All of his books have similar themes of family, the past, and imagination. Yep has done doctoral work in literature and psychology at State University in New York.

"Chinatown" is taken from Yep's book *Child of the Owl*, which won an American Library Association Notable Children's Book Award and the Boston Globe-Horn Book Award for Fiction. Yep's *Dragonwings* won the Newbery Honor Book and the Phoenix Award for being a book of lasting importance.

Students can read more about Laurence Yep on page 314 of the **Student Anthology.**

Other Books by
Laurence Yep:
- *Dragon of the Lost Sea*
- *Liar, Liar*
- *The Star Fisher*
- *Later, Gator*

Selection Summary

Genre: Realistic Fiction

Casey Young is Chinese, but she has never lived among Chinese people nor even met her Chinese grandmother. So, when she comes to San Francisco's Chinatown to live with her grandmother, she has a lot to learn—about being Chinese, about her late mother's early life, and especially about herself.

Walking one rainy evening with her grandmother, Casey sees Chinatown transformed into a fantasy place. She begins to feel that finally she has found the place where she belongs.

About the Illustrator

Yoriko Ito was raised in Japan. She now lives in California, where, in addition to illustrating books, she works as an artist and designer.

Students can read more about Yoriko Ito on page 314 of the **Student Anthology.**

Other Books illustrated by
Yoriko Ito:
- *Child of the Owl*
- *Lily and the Wooden Bowl*
- *Jojofu*

Exploring the Theme

Selection Concepts

"Chinatown" is a work of realistic fiction about a young girl who comes to appreciate the richness of her Chinese heritage. After she moves to San Francisco's Chinatown to live with her grandmother, Casey feels that she has found the place where she belongs. Key concepts to be explored are:

- Grandparents can play an important role in helping children learn about and appreciate their heritage.
- Mementos can carry deep symbolic meaning that links generations of a family.

Check the Reading link of the **SRA** Web page for links to theme-related Websites. **http://www.sra4kids.com**

Exploration Activity Tips

Before Reading, have the students browse the selection to determine the genre used by the author *(realistic fiction).* Then have them read the "Meet the Author" feature at the end of the story and discuss the advantages and challenges of modeling a fictional character after a real person.

During Reading, have the students reflect on how Casey might have felt about not having much knowledge of her Chinese heritage. Tell them to consider the reasons Casey felt as she did while watching the Chinese movie.

After Reading, as a class, discuss what Casey learned from her grandmother and what this selection taught the students about heritage. Then have students update the Concept/Question Board. Some may want to revise their activity plans based on what they have learned from the selection.

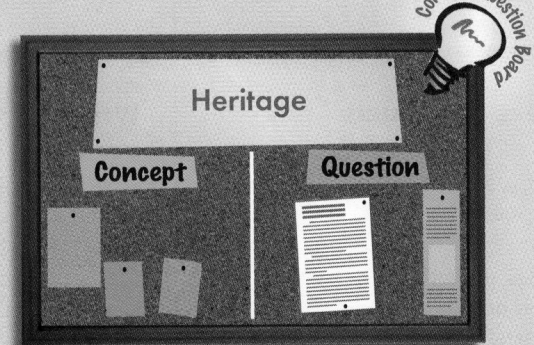

Unit 3 Exploration Management

Lesson 1	Listen to and interview a class guest about heritage. Select and read library books about heritage.
Lesson 2	Identify genres for inclusion in heritage albums. Reflect on one's own heritage, interview family members and friends about customs and traditions, and begin writing.
Lesson 3	Identify and utilize various literary techniques. Writing begins on second selection for student albums.
Lesson 4	Work on unit activity continues. Discuss with relatives and friends what they want to communicate about their heritage.
Lesson 5 Chinatown	**Collaborative Exploration** **Write autobiographical sketches for author pages and consider modeling a character after a family member or friend.** **Supplementary Activity** **Arrange peer-editing sessions for students' autobiographical sketches. Discuss effective use of point of view in students' stories about heritage.**
Lesson 6	Prepare final drafts, complete illustrations, prepare title and copyright pages, and bind books. Write thank-you notes to those who helped with the activity.
Lesson 7	Students present a selected piece from their heritage albums.

Lesson Planner

Suggested Pacing: 3–5 days	DAY 1	DAY 2
	DAY 1	**DAY 2**

Part 1 — Preparing to Read

Materials
- Student Anthology, pp. 300–315
- Transparencies 19, 44

DAY 1

Word Knowledge
- Reading the Words and Sentences, p. 300G
- Developing Oral Language, p. 300G

Build Background, p. 300H

Preview and Prepare, p. 300I

Selection Vocabulary, p. 300I
longing, souvenirs, gaudy, immortality, meditate

DAY 2

Preview and Prepare, p. 300I
- Review Transparency 44

Part 2 — Reading and Responding

Materials
- Student Anthology, pp. 300–317
- Teacher Observation Log
- Reading and Writing Workbook, pp. 101–102
- Inquiry Journal, p. 42
- Transparency 46
- Home Connection, p. 43

DAY 1

Student Anthology, pp. 300–307

Comprehension Strategies
- Making Connections, pp. 300, 302, 306
- Clarifying, p. 304
- Summarizing, p. 306

DAY 2

Student Anthology, pp. 308–315

Comprehension Strategies
- Clarifying, p. 308
- Making Connections, p. 310
- Summarizing, p. 312

Discussing Strategy Use, p. 312

Comprehension Skills
✓ Discussing the Selection, p. 313

Exploring the Theme
- Selection Vocabulary, p. 317A
longing, souvenirs, gaudy, immortality, meditate

Part 3 — Integrating the Curriculum

Materials
- Student Anthology, pp. 300–315
- Teacher Observation Log
- Reading and Writing Workbook, pp. 103–106
- Inquiry Journal, p. 50

DAY 1

Writing
- Dialogue, p. 317C

Literary Elements
✓ Setting, Plot, and Problem Resolution, p. 317D

DAY 2

Writing Process
- Revise, p. 317C

Spelling
✓ Spelling -le Endings, p. 317E

Independent Work Time

Materials
- Reteach, pp. 101–106
- ESL Supplement
- Challenge, pp. 53–55
- Intervention Guide
- Listening Library Audiocassette

DAY 1

Writing Process Continued

ESL
- Word Meaning, p. 300G
- Vocabulary, p. 300J

Intervention
- Word Knowledge, p. 300G
- Comprehension, p. 300

Unit Project: Write Autobiographical Sketches

DAY 2

Writing Process Continued

ESL
- Discussing Strategy Use, p. 312
- Revise, p. 317C

Intervention
- Making Connections, p. 302
- Revise, p. 317C

Unit Project Continued

✓ **Informal** Assessment Available   ✓ **Formal** Assessment Available

DAY 2 continued	DAY 3	
DAY 3	**DAY 4**	**DAY 5**
General Review	**General Review**	**Review Word Knowledge**
Student Anthology, pp. 300–315 **Comprehension Skills** ✓ ■ Fact and Opinion, pp. 301, 303, 305 **Theme Connections** ■ Think About It, p. 315 ■ Draw a Special Family Object, p. 315	**Student Anthology, pp. 300–317** **Comprehension Skills** ■ Compare and Contrast, pp. 307, 309, 311 **Poetry, pp. 316–317** **Exploring the Theme** ■ Reading/Writing Connections, p. 317A ■ Literature Appreciation, p. 317A ■ Supporting Student Explorations, p. 317B	**Student Anthology, pp. 300–315** ■ Review Selection ■ Complete Discussion ■ Reread Selection in Pairs **Home Connection, p. 317A** ■ Discuss "Chinatown" ■ Complete similarities/differences chart
Writing Process Continued **Grammar, Usage, and Mechanics** ✓ ■ Compound Sentences and Conjunctions, p. 317F	**Writing Process Continued** **Study and Research** ■ Draw Conclusions from Multiple Sources, p. 317G	**Across the Curriculum** **Social Studies** ■ Writing an Article, p. 317H **Art** ■ Creating a Picture Album, p. 317H
Writing Process Continued **Reteach** ✓ ■ Spelling -le Endings, *Reteach*, pp. 103–104 **Challenge** ■ Fact and Opinion, p. 303 ✓ ■ Spelling -le Endings, *Challenge*, p. 54 **Unit Project Continued**	**Writing Process Continued** **Reteach** ✓ ■ Fact and Opinion, *Reteach*, pp. 101–102 **Challenge** ✓ ■ Fact and Opinion, *Challenge*, p. 53 **Unit Project Continued**	**Writing Process Continued** **Reteach** ✓ ■ Compound Sentences, *Reteach*, pp. 105–106 **Challenge** ✓ ■ Compound Sentences, *Challenge*, p. 55 **Unit Project Continued**

Meeting Individual Needs
Independent Work Time

Preparing to Read

Meeting Individual Needs

ESL
- Word Meaning, p. 300G
- Cultural Context, p. 300H
- Vocabulary, p. 300J

Intervention
- Word Knowledge, p. 300G

Reading and Responding

Meeting Individual Needs

Reteach
- Fact and Opinion, *Reteach*, pp. 101–102

ESL
- Movies, p. 308
- Discussing Strategy Use, p. 312

Challenge
- Fact and Opinion, p. 303
- Fact and Opinion, *Challenge*, p. 53

Intervention
- Comprehension, p. 300
- Fact and Opinion, p. 301
- Making Connections, p. 302
- Clarifying, p. 304

Integrating the Curriculum

Meeting Individual Needs

Reteach
- Spelling -*le* Endings, *Reteach*, pp. 103–104
- Compound Sentences, *Reteach*, pp. 105–106

ESL
- Revise, p. 317C

Challenge
- Spelling -*le* Endings, *Challenge*, p. 54
- Compound Sentences, *Challenge*, p. 55

Intervention
- Revise, p. 317C

Formal Assessment Options

Use these assessment pages along with your informal observations to gauge student progress.

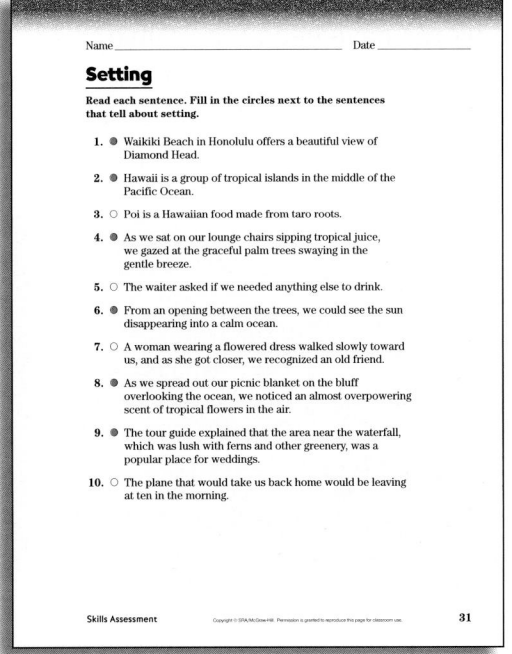

Skills Assessment, p. 31

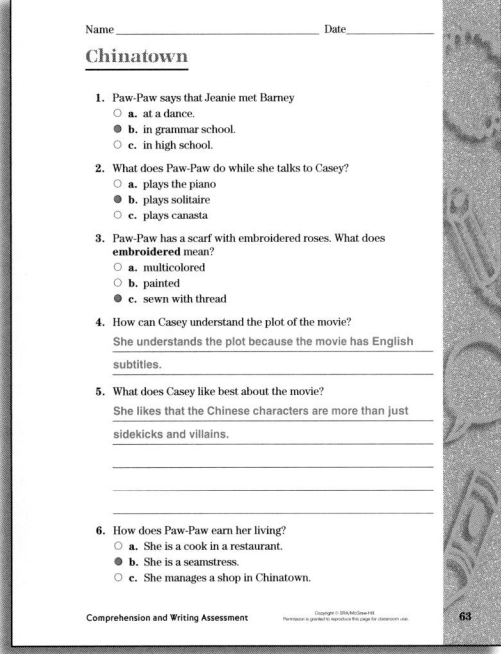

Comprehension and Writing Assessment, p. 63

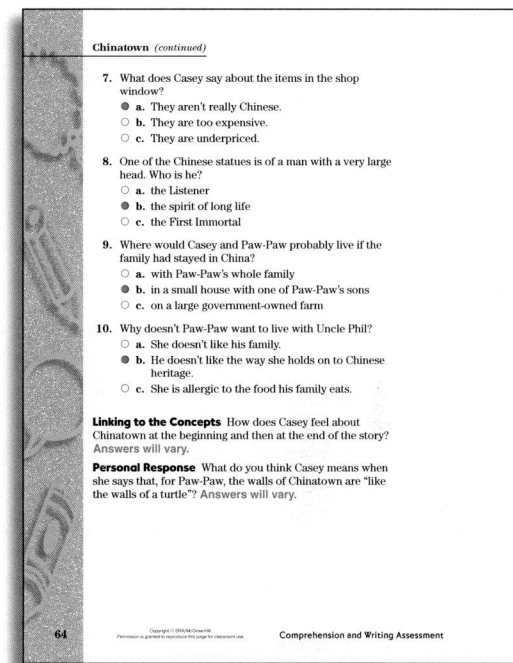

Comprehension and Writing Assessment, p. 64

① Preparing to Read

Meeting Individual Needs

ESL

Word Meaning Make sure English-language learners understand the meanings of the words before they do the blending exercises. Refer to Unit 3, Lesson 5, of the **ESL Supplement** for specific suggestions.

Intervention

Word Knowledge Have students skim the story for words that contain the *ai* spelling. List the words they find on the chalkboard. Have volunteers take turns using the words in a sentence. Some examples of words from the story are *plain, mainly, entertain,* and *brains*. For students who need more help, see Unit 3, Lesson 5, of the **Intervention Guide.**

 **Teacher Tip** Gaining a better understanding of the spellings of sounds and the structure of words will help students as they encounter unfamiliar words in their reading.

Word Knowledge

Reading the Words and Sentences

Write each word and sentence on the chalkboard. Have the students read each word together. After all the words have been read, have students read each sentence in natural phrases or chunks. Use the suggestions in About the Words to discuss the different features of the listed words.

> Line 1: well-being sister-in-law high-rise
> Line 2: remains wait rain
> Line 3: knew knit knight
> Sentence 1: She cared about the well-being of her sister-in-law.
> Sentence 2: I'll wait and see who remains in the high-rise.
> Sentence 3: The knight knew the rain would rust his armor.

About the Words

- Line 1 contains hyphenated compound words. A compound word is formed by joining two or more words.
- The words in Line 2 all contain Long a spelled *ai*. In this digraph, the *a* and the *i*, when placed together, take on the Long a sound.
- All of the words in Line 3 have the /n/ sound spelled *kn*. Invite students to think of other words containing this spelling of the /n/ sound.

Developing Oral Language

To review the words, have students do one or both of the following activities.

- Have a student point to one word in the lines above and select a classmate to read it and use it in a sentence.
- Ask a question using one of the words in the lines above. Challenge students to answer your question using another word in the lines. For example, "Can you *knit?*" "I once *knew* how but forgot."

Build Background

Activate Prior Knowledge

Have students check the Concept/Question Board to refresh their memories about heritage. Discuss the following with students to find out what they already know about the selection and have already learned about the unit theme. Tell students to use their prior knowledge to help them comprehend the selection they are about to read.

■ Ask students if they are familiar with the story they are about to read, and if so, to tell a little bit about it. Remind students, however, not to give away the ending of the selection.

■ Have students share what they know about China, Chinese culture, or Chinatown in San Francisco.

■ Have students exchange other stories that tell of a close relationship between a grandparent and a grandchild.

Background Information

The following information may help the students to better understand the selection they are about to read.

■ "Chinatown" is an excerpt from the book *Child of the Owl*. The owl of the title refers to a traditional Chinese tale told in the chapter that precedes this selection. One afternoon, Casey's grandmother sees that Casey is lonely and unhappy. She shows Casey a beautiful jade carving of an owl that she wears around her neck and tells her that it was given to the women of their family by an ancestor who was an owl spirit. This owl spirit was forced to take on human form for a time and lived as the wife of a human man. Although she bore several children, she missed the freedom she had known as an owl. After many years, she left her human family and resumed her owl form. Casey's grandmother says that because the women of their family are descended from this owl spirit, they often feel lonely in the ordinary human world.

■ Casey feels better after hearing this story. She says, "It was like there had always been this person inside of me that I had never been able to name or describe—a small feathery me lost inside this body—and now I not only knew her name but I could tell part of her story."

■ The selection is set in San Francisco in 1964, in an area referred to as Chinatown. In many large cities, there are neighborhoods in which people who speak a language other than English or have similar ethnic backgrounds live together.

Teacher Tip Remind students that this selection is fiction, yet the character of the grandmother is modeled after the author's own grandmother. Ask the students how knowing this might help them use their background knowledge.

Writing Journal Tell students that after reading they will be jotting down in their Writing Journals their reactions to the story. Have them be on the lookout for any ideas they may have about family members or friends who may serve as good character models in their heritage albums.

Meeting Individual Needs

ESL

Cultural Context English-language learners may be able to talk about which neighborhoods in town, or in the nearest city, are inhabited by which ethnic groups and which languages are commonly spoken in these areas. Perhaps English-language learners can take the lead in describing the restaurants and stores run by bilingual people.

Preparing to Read

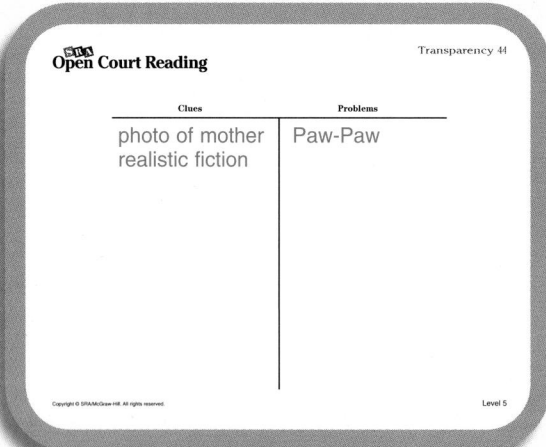

Transparency 44

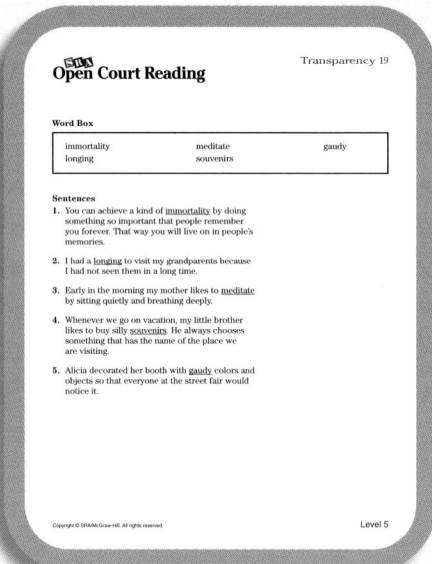

Transparency 19

To help students decode words, divide them into the syllables shown below. The information following each word tells how students can figure out the meaning of each word from the sentences on the transparency.

long·ing	context clues
sou·ve·nirs	context clues
gaud·y	context clues
im·mor·tal·i·ty	context clues, word structure
med·i·tate	context clues

Preview and Prepare

Browse

- Have a volunteer read the title and author's and illustrator's names aloud. Have students share what they know about realistic fiction.

- Because this selection is fiction, have the students browse through the first half of the story, looking for words and phrases that connect to what they already know. Record these in the Clues column on *Transparency 44.* Discuss with the students what they think this selection might have to do with family traditions or heritage.

- Encourage students to ask questions as they browse. Have them identify any problems they notice while reading in the Problems column.

Set Purposes

As they read, have students think about their own families and how they would feel if they had to move and live with someone else.

Selection Vocabulary

As students study vocabulary, they will use context clues, word structure, and apposition to clarify these and additional unfamiliar words.

Display *Transparency 19* before reading the selection to introduce and discuss the following words and their meanings.

long·ing:	the feeling of really wanting something (page 300)
sou·ve·nirs:	things to buy to remember a place you have visited (page 303)
gaud·y:	bold, flashy, overdone (page 306)
im·mor·tal·i·ty:	the ability to live forever (page 310)
med·i·tate:	thinking deeply and quietly (page 297)

Have students read the words in the Word Box. Help students decode multisyllabic words by reading the words syllable by syllable. If the word is not decodable, give the students the pronunciation.

Have the students read the sentences on *Transparency 19* to determine the meaning of the underlined words. Remind them to use clues in the sentences and structural clues to figure out the meaning. See the teacher tip on the left for information on how the words in each sentence can be defined.

Reading Recommendations

Your first reading of the selection should focus on developing the reading strategies found to the left of the reduced pages. We recommend that the students revisit the selection, rereading sections or the entire selection as a way to enhance their understanding and appreciation of the text. During rereading, they should focus on the comprehension skills found to the right of the reduced pages.

Oral Reading

Because this story is full of colorful descriptions of Chinatown, students will enjoy reading it aloud. Have students help each other with unfamiliar words and difficult ideas. As students read aloud, have them read expressively in natural phrases and chunks to show that they understand the text and can engage the listeners. If students encounter difficulties, have them use the reading strategies below or the Blending Procedure (Program Appendix 15–16).

Using Reading Strategies

Reading strategy instruction allows students to become aware of how good readers read. Good readers constantly check their understanding as they are reading and ask themselves questions. In addition, skilled readers recognize when they are having problems and stop to use various reading strategies to help them make sense of what they are reading.

During the reading of "Chinatown," you will model the use of the following reading strategies:

- Making Connections
- Clarifying
- Summarizing

Before reading, have students share how they have used these strategies in the past and any tips they can give each other on their use.

Building Comprehension Skills

Revisiting or rereading a selection allows students to apply skills that give them a more complete understanding of the text. Some follow-up comprehension skills, such as *Main Idea and Details* and *Compare and Contrast*, help students organize information. Others, such as *Author's Purpose, Making Inferences,* and *Drawing Conclusions,* lead to deeper understanding—to "reading between the lines," as mature readers do. In this selection, students will apply the follow-up comprehension skills of *Fact and Opinion* and *Compare and Contrast.* Because two skills are reviewed, you may want to do all the sections related to one skill before doing the other skill.

Meeting Individual Needs

ESL

Vocabulary Check that English-language learners know the meanings of idioms and more difficult vocabulary in the story including *heritage; game of solitaire; shuffle her cards; the bureau; made me feel less lonely; there would be no arguing with her; the small world of Chinatown; tightly-knit world; subtitles in English; the second feature; synchronized; immortality; invisible walls;* and *two small owls clawing their way along a branch.* Explain and show pictures as needed. Model example sentences and help English-speaking students make their own sentences. Refer to Unit 3, Lesson 5, of the *ESL Supplement* for teaching suggestions

Have students who may need extra help reading "Chinatown" reread the selection using the *Listening Library Audiocassette.*

By this time in fifth grade, good readers should be reading approximately 143 words per minute with fluency and expression. The only way to gain fluency is through practice. As explained in Reading Recommendations, have students reread all or part of the selection to you and to each other during class or Independent Work Time to focus on the comprehension skills and to build fluency.

② Reading and Responding

Read pages 300–317.

Comprehension Strategies

Prompting

❶ Making Connections *Let's try to think of connections to Casey and her grandmother as we read so that it is easier for us to relate to them. Casey is asking her grandmother when her mother felt lonely. I think she's asking that because she's feeling lonely. I know that I feel lonely when I have to be in a strange place without my parents or friends. How do you connect with Casey and her grandmother?*

Student Sample

❷ Making Connections *I can connect with Casey looking at the pictures of her mom. I remember pictures of my mother going to parties when she was about sixteen. Her clothes looked so different from what I wore at her age. It's always a little strange to see pictures of your parents before you were born, with different hairstyles and clothes.*

Word Knowledge

brains, good-looking, late-night

Students can use the skills they learned in the Word Knowledge section of this lesson to read these words. Remind students of this if they have difficulty reading these words.

Reading Recommendation

ORAL • CHORAL • SILENT

Chinatown

from *Child of the Owl*
by Laurence Yep
illustrated by Yoriko Ito

In the time since her mother, Jeanie, died, Casey Young has traveled around California with her father, Barney. But when he becomes sick and has to be hospitalized, Casey goes to live with her grandmother, Paw-Paw, in San Francisco's Chinatown. Here she begins to learn more about her Chinese heritage and about her mother.

I lay in bed thinking for a long time after Paw-Paw had finished her story. I'd never asked her about Jeanie before this, I suppose, because Barney had taught me not to talk about her. Finally I rolled over on my side to face her. "When did Jeanie feel lonely?"

Paw-Paw picked up a deck of cards and began to play a game of solitaire. She could play even while she talked. A three on the four of one column. A jack on the queen of another column. Flip. Flip. Flip. Like her fingers had eyes and brains so Paw-Paw didn't even have to look down. Her hands could do everything. "Maybe I should let your daddy tell you."

I turned so I lay on my stomach, hugging a pillow under my chin. "Barney won't talk much about her. Was she lonely when she was my age?"

Paw-Paw must have sensed the longing in my voice. "Oh, no. Your mommy always had lots of friends. She was very pretty. And very sweet. She

300

Assessment

✓ **Informal** Observe individual children as they read, and use the Teacher Observation Log found in the **Assessment Guide** to record anecdotal information about each child's strengths and weaknesses.

Meeting Individual Needs

Intervention

Comprehension Intervention strategies for those students having difficulty with reading "Chinatown" can be found in Unit 3, Lesson 5, of the **Intervention Guide.**

was always a big help to me." Paw-Paw finished her game and began to sweep the cards into the middle of the table so she could gather them into a deck. "And your daddy was thought to be a very good-looking boy so they were always a natural couple. From grammar school on."

"Grammar school?"

"They both went to Commodore Stockton just a little way from here. And then they went through junior high and high school together." Paw-Paw began to shuffle her cards to get them ready for the next time she wanted to play.

"Were they very popular?"

"Oh, yes. Very popular. You'd always see them together at all the dances in Chinatown. Your momma liked dancing."

Paw-Paw went to the bureau and opened a middle drawer, rummaging around till she took out an old, worn brown bag and drew a small pile of photos out of it. She set them down on the table and sorted through them. "That's your momma. She was going to a dance that night." Paw-Paw tapped one photo of a pretty girl of about sixteen in bobby sox and a long skirt like all the American girls used to wear—or at least that's what Barney and some of the older people used to tell me when we had watched late-night

2

301

Comprehension Skills

Fact and Opinion

Explain to the students that good readers try to distinguish facts from opinions when they read a piece of writing. *Facts* can be proven. *Opinions* are what someone thinks or believes, and can be supported but not proven.

Point out the following examples from the text.

- *Fact:* "She [Paw-Paw] could play even while she talked." *Opinion:* "Her hands could do everything." (page 300)

- *Fact:* "Your mommy always had lots of friends." *Opinion:* "She was very pretty. And very sweet." (page 300)

- *Fact:* "They both went to Commodore Stockton [School]." *Opinion:* "[They were] very popular." (page 301)

Have students look for other examples of fact and opinion.

Fact and Opinion
INTRODUCED: Unit 3, Lesson 5
REVIEWED: Unit 4, Lesson 1
Unit 5, Lesson 5

Meeting Individual Needs

Intervention

Fact and Opinion Help students to identify other facts and opinions from the text. Then have students tell how they know which is a fact and which is an opinion.

Students may be confused about "facts" in a piece of fiction. Explain that a fact is something that could be proven if the events in the story were real.

② Reading and Responding

Comprehension Strategies

Prompting

❸ Making Connections *Casey's grandmother is talking about sewing shirts for extra money. I know that many women have worked as seamstresses in small factories. Sometimes they get paid by the piece, so they can make extra money that way. But the work is very hard, and they don't earn very much.*

Does anyone else have connections to share with the group?

Student Sample

❹ Making Connections *The description of Chinatown reminds me of Columbus Avenue in "The West Side." All of the stores and the people are from one culture. I can see why Juan was comfortable on Columbus Avenue and Paw-Paw feels at home in Chinatown.*

Word Knowledge

cinnamon-flavored, knit, know

Students can use the skills they learned in the Word Knowledge section of this lesson to read these words. Remind students of this if they have difficulty reading these words.

---

movies in different hotel lobbies. "I used to sew all your momma's clothes but only with the best material." She glanced at me briefly and then went through some of the other old photos of Jeanie, who had a different outfit in each one. And while I didn't much care about the clothes, somehow talking with Paw-Paw about Jeanie made me feel less lonely.

"But she couldn't have always gone out with Barney. What did she do with you for fun? I mean, besides playing cards."

"We went to see Chinese movies." Paw-Paw put her cards down in a neat stack by the little cup that held her toothpicks. They were cinnamon-flavored and each was wrapped in a little paper envelope. "Would you like to see a movie like your mommy and I used to see?"

I wasn't doing much of anything so I figured why not. "I've got money for myself."

❸ "Why spend your money? I can sew some extra shirts this week."

"Are you sure it's okay?" I asked.

"Of course, it's okay," she snapped and I could see there would be no arguing with her.

Paw-Paw bundled up as usual, putting on a blouse over her pajama top and then a sweater and a heavy silk jacket over the sweater so that by the time she had on her heavy cloth coat, she looked twice as round. Over her head she put her favorite <u>vermilion</u> <u>chiffon</u> scarf with the roses embroidered on it with gold thread.

302

Meeting Individual Needs

Intervention

Making Connections Casey talks about the neighborhood her grandmother lives in. Have students draw maps of their neighborhoods. Encourage them to include landmarks, such as stores, parks, and schools. Have them compare and contrast their own neighborhoods with Paw-Paw's. Tell students that by comparing and contrasting their neighborhoods with Paw-Paw's, they are making connections with her.

Paw-Paw seemed very comfortable within the small world of Chinatown; I wondered if Jeanie had been too. It didn't cover more than half a square mile or so then, and within those boundaries, as I was to find out, it is a very small, tightly knit world where everyone knows your business and you know theirs. To the west lay the souvenir shops and on the east, <u>delicatessens</u> and grocery stores and meat markets, some of which had fish tanks in the bottom half of their windows in which a hundred fish would be squeezed, all staring out at you with cold, black eyes, or even turtles, or sometimes cages of snakes, all to be sold and eaten.

4

303

Meeting Individual Needs

Challenge

Fact and Opinion Have students make a chart comparing the facts and opinions in this story. Students may want to chart other stories in this way as well.

Comprehension
Skills

Fact and Opinion

Have students read page 303. Ask the following questions:

■ Which sentences or parts of sentences show facts? *("It didn't cover more than a half a square mile or so then, . . . "* and *"To the west lay the souvenir shops and on the east, delicatessens and grocery stores and meat markets . . . ")*

■ What parts of the paragraph show Casey's opinion of Chinatown? *("Paw-Paw seemed very comfortable within the small world of Chinatown"* and *". . . and within those boundaries, as I was to find out, it is a very small, tightly knit world where everyone knows your business and you know theirs.")*

Have students justify their answers.

Teacher Tip Have students give definitions for the following words: *believe, conclude, know, guess,* and *think.* Write *Fact* on one side of the chalkboard, and *Opinion* on the other side. Have students categorize the words under these headings. Have them explain their decisions. Tell students to keep their own lists of Fact and Opinion words as they read.

2 Reading and Responding

Comprehension Strategies

Modeling

5 Clarifying *In order to clarify a passage you are reading, you must first be able to identify what about the passage does not make sense to you, whether that might be an unfamiliar word or idea. For example, I wonder why the ladies with no English could only work doing sewing. Maybe it is because they could use their skills at sewing even without being able to speak English. Maybe I can think of some other jobs that people who cannot speak English could do.*

Word Knowledge

plain, sun-bleached, knew

Students can use the skills they learned in the Word Knowledge section of this lesson to read these words. Remind students of this if they have difficulty reading these words.

Teacher Tip Ask the students if they have ever seen a movie with subtitles. Discuss how Casey may have felt watching a Chinese movie with English subtitles.

To the north was Stockton Street, where my school was. Mostly it was sewing-machine shops up that way: plain storefronts sometimes with wallpaper covering the windows or old, sun-bleached curtains. From within would come the steady whir and whine of the machines of the ladies sewing dresses, shirts, even jeans and expensive wedding outfits for American stores. A lot of ladies with no English could only do that. Just above Stockton Street was the public grammar school, Commodore Stockton, or "Commodore" to the kids. Across from it lay the <u>YWCA</u> and Cameron House, a kind of club for Chinese kids. Above that, where Paw-Paw never went, were the cable-car lines and the apartment houses for Americans, including the

5 fancy hotels and limousines of Nob Hill.

But at that moment I was thinking mainly about the movies we were going to see. I had my doubts because all I had seen up to then were Charlie Chan movies or silly houseboys on TV shows or funny laundrymen in westerns. But even so, one of those kinds of movies was better than nothing because I knew Paw-Paw never left Chinatown to see any of the Hollywood movies just a few blocks away.

We went to the Chinese Globe that had a bright neon sign outside in front and looked like a regular theater except for the fact that there was a guy selling newspapers by the ticket booth. He had about a dozen different Chinese newspapers laid in neat piles on a board that he laid over some boxes. But I saw a dozen portable newsstands like that set

304

Meeting Individual Needs

Intervention

Clarifying Tell the students to clarify parts of the text that they find unclear as they read. Clues in the text, sharing knowledge with other students, and outside references can all help them understand the story better.

up all over Chinatown——in doorways or in corners or in front of busy stores. He nodded familiarly to Paw-Paw as she bought our tickets at the booth.

When I finally got to see the movies, they were completely different than I thought. I could see why Jeanie had liked them. For one thing, the Chinese were actually people who could be brave or sad. They had subtitles in English, too, which was good. It was something to see Chinese do more than be the sidekick to some white guy in a fight, or see the Chinese actually win. I mean, I almost felt like crying when I saw it: a kind of bubbling feeling deep down inside that had me almost cheering and crying while this Chinese mother led her three sons in beating up the bad guys. And it was even better when I saw the Chinese girls fighting.

305

Meeting Individual Needs

Reteach	Challenge
Fact and Opinion Have students who need additional instruction and practice with this concept complete **Reteach,** pages 101–102.	**Fact and Opinion** Have students who understand this concept complete **Challenge,** page 53.

Comprehension Skills

Fact and Opinion

For more practice with Fact and Opinion, have students complete **Reading and Writing Workbook** pages 101–102.

Name _____ Date _____

Fact and Opinion

Chinatown

Focus Writers may use both facts and opinions in their writing. A good reader can tell one from the other.

- **Facts** are details that can be proven true or false. They provide additional information about main ideas.
- **Opinions** are people's thoughts or feelings about a subject. They can be supported, but cannot be proven true or false.

Identify Look through "Chinatown" for examples of facts and opinions. Write the page numbers and examples below and tell whether each is a fact or an opinion. *Answers will vary but may include the*

Page: 304

Example: To the north was Stockton Street, where my school was.

Fact or opinion: Fact

Page: 300

Example: "Oh, no. Your mommy always had lots of friends. She was very pretty. And very sweet. She was always a big help to me."

Fact or opinion: Opinion

Reading and Writing Workbook • *Fact and Opinion* 101

Fact and Opinion *(continued)*

Practice Each of the sentences below states either a fact or an opinion. After each sentence, identify it as *fact* or *opinion*. Then, write a second sentence. If you identified a sentence as a fact, make your sentence an opinion. If you identified a sentence as an opinion, make your sentence a fact. *Sentences will vary.*

1. Pizza is the best food. opinion

2. Almost all of the major rivers in this country flow south. fact

3. Country and western music sounds better than most other kinds of music. opinion

Apply Write a paragraph that states your opinion about something. It could be about an issue in your community or school, or some other issue of your choice. Remember that you can use facts to support your opinion. *Paragraphs will vary.*

102 *Fact and Opinion • Reading and Writing Workbook*

Reading and Writing Workbook pp. 101–102

2 Reading and Responding

Comprehension Strategies

Modeling

6 Summarizing *This seems like a good point in the story to summarize what has been happening so far. Summarizing a story's events helps us remember the plot, the characters, and the setting. It also helps us clarify information. Casey and Paw-Paw went to the movies. Casey really liked the second feature, "Princess of the Streets." She liked how the girls were portrayed as strong characters.*

Modeling

7 Making Connections *What does Casey mean when she says she felt as if she had "just come home?" She mentioned that the Chinatown she was seeing as she stepped outside the movie theater must have been just like the Chinatown her mother had seen. Sometimes sights and sounds and even scents can remind us of other people and events from our lives. Sometimes these memories can make us feel as if we are right back in that same place and at the same time. I see. Casey must have felt a connection to her mother right at that moment. Does anybody have a similar experience you would like to share?*

Word Knowledge

rain, entertain

Students can use the skills they learned in the Word Knowledge section of this lesson to read these words. Remind students of this if they have difficulty reading these words.

The second feature, you see, was *Princess of the Streets,* which is about this girl who grows up in the back streets of Hong Kong. She gets friendly with this other girl who does juggling and fighting displays in a medicine show. And together she and her friend wipe out the big crime boss. I don't think I ever saw anyone jump as high in the air to kick someone.

It must have rained while we were inside the theater because when we came out later, the streets were slick and black, like they were made of shining crystal. I saw a Chinatown I'd never seen before. It was the Chinatown Jeanie must have seen. Suddenly all the gaudy neon signs were no longer a bunch of words but were like snakes of colored lights crawling up the faces of the buildings and their reflections smashed themselves on the streets, looking like broken stars sliding back and forth and trying to put themselves back together. Funny, but it seemed, right then, like I'd just come home.

A radio store had begun playing music over an outside loudspeaker. Some of the stuff, especially the opera, sounded terrible to me—a high whiny kind of noise—but this sounded different. Some people might have thought there was too much of a clutter of sound with the cymbals crashing and the drums beating and everybody playing like mad, but there was something inside of me that liked it—like it <u>synchronized</u> right with the pulsing of my blood through my body. And the sound wound its way through the chatter of the nighttime crowds.

Humming with the tune, Paw-Paw took my arm for support as we made our way along the slippery

306

Teacher Tip Casey writes a very interesting description of the lights in her neighborhood. Some students might enjoy writing their own descriptions of their communities. Have them write a short description or poem, using vivid images like Casey has done.

pavements of Grant Avenue. We passed by the delicatessens, where Paw-Paw pointed to the dark-brown, roasted ducks dangling from hooks in the windows. "That's what I like," she said. "Jeanie too."

"I've never had duck in my life," I said.

She patted my arm, the one she was holding on to. "Maybe I'll sew some extra shirts and dresses someday and we'll buy half of one so you can try it."

We went about two blocks before the rain started to fall again. It was falling pretty hard so we stopped under the awning of this one souvenir shop. Paw-Paw acted like the window display had been put there just to entertain us. "Look at that whirly thing." She pointed at one of those little solar windmills that rotate whenever they're near a source of light like the light bulb <u>illuminating</u> the window.

307

Comprehension Skills

Compare and Contrast

Explain to the students that authors often use *comparing* or *contrasting* to make their writing more interesting to the reader. Have students find these examples in the story:

- "It must have rained while we were inside the theater because when we came out later, the streets were slick and black, like they were made of shining crystal." (page 306, paragraph 2)

- "I saw a Chinatown I'd never seen before. It was the Chinatown Jeanie must have seen. Suddenly all the gaudy neon signs were no longer a bunch of words but were like snakes of colored lights crawling up the faces of the buildings and their reflections smashed themselves on the streets, looking like broken stars sliding back and forth and trying to put themselves back together." (page 306, paragraph 2)

- "A radio store had begun playing music over an outside loudspeaker . . . there was something inside of me that liked it—like it synchronized right with the pulsing of my blood through my body." (page 306, paragraph 3)

Compare and Contrast

 Review with the students how similes and metaphors are used to show comparisons.

 Give students copies of *Transparency 46.* Encourage them to use the diagram to compare and contrast as they read.

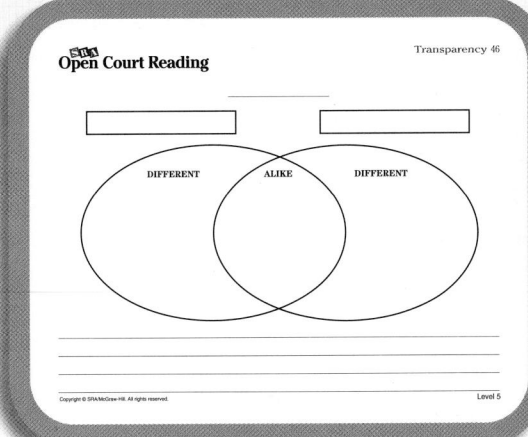

Transparency 46

(2) Reading and Responding

Modeling

8 Clarifying *Paw-Paw says that the Americans won't let the Chinese bring things in from China. I'm not sure I understand why that is. It's not as though we were ever at war with China. Perhaps if I look in an encyclopedia under China, I can clarify why this would be. Or I could ask someone who knows about politics and history.*

Word Knowledge

two-headed, back-scratchers

Students can use the skills they learned in the Word Knowledge section of this lesson to read these words. Remind students of this if they have difficulty.

There was something wrong about the window. At first I couldn't figure it out but as Paw-Paw went on mentioning things in the window, I realized she hadn't talked about one Chinese thing yet. I started to study the window then. There didn't seem to be anything as beautiful or as old as the owl charm Paw-Paw wore about her neck. There was just a lot of silly stuff like two-headed back-scratchers. Paw-Paw didn't point at any of those or at some of the things that were downright nasty—like pellet guns and various types of knives, from simple pocket- and hunting knives to switchblades and gravity blades that snap out with a flick of a wrist. The only thing vaguely Oriental that I saw at first in the window were the Japanese kimonos and geisha dolls they sold.

"It doesn't seem right somehow," I said. "I mean, if it's a Chinatown souvenir shop, shouldn't it be selling Chinese stuff?"

8 "The Americans won't let us bring in things from China." She shrugged. "And the Taiwan government's too busy to bother with souvenirs. You have to sell the Americans something."

"But we're selling things as if they're Chinese when it's really . . . well, I don't know . . . this stuff just seems like junk compared to your owl charm. There's no story behind most of this stuff. There's no meaning to this stuff. This junk is probably not even much fun."

"They do have a few real Chinese things. See?" She moved a little to the side and bent down, pointing to one dark corner of the window. "See down there in the back?"

308

Meeting Individual Needs

ESL

Movies Have the English-language learners discuss movies from their own cultures: the characters, plots, and settings. Ask them if they have seen movies in their first language with English subtitles. Tell them to compare and contrast their experiences with Casey's.

I leaned forward slightly and looked where her finger was pointing and saw a bunch of dusty statues crowded together like they were making a last stand. "They've got some of the stuff you've got on your bureau. Look, there's that pretty lady with the flower."

Paw-Paw studied me. I hadn't laughed about the owl story and I had even liked the Chinese movies so I guess she decided to go ahead. "That lady is the Listener. She could have gone to heaven, but when she was just about to enter the gate, she could hear all the poor souls back on earth groaning and she turned her back on heaven, saying she could not enter until everyone else had gone before her, so she spends all her time trying to help the rest of us to heaven."

309

Comprehension Skills

Compare and Contrast

Have the students continue looking through selections to locate examples of phrases that show comparisons or contrasts. Point out the following examples from this story.

- "…this stuff just seems like junk compared to your owl charm." (page 308, paragraph 4)

- "…a bunch of dusty statues crowded together like they were making a last stand." (page 309, paragraph 1)

Teacher Tip — Students who enjoy this selection may want to read the book from which it was excerpted, called *Child of the Owl.*

② Reading and Responding

Comprehension Strategies

Modeling

❾ **Making Connections** *I've never heard much about Chinese mythology. This story, though, reminds me of a Greek myth. The goddess of the dawn fell in love with a man and asked the gods to make him immortal. They did, but she forgot to ask for eternal youth for him. So he got older, and older, and older, until he shriveled up into a cricket. And you can still hear him chirping at dawn and dusk.*

Teacher Tip Ask students how they can connect Chinese mythology with what they read in "The Heavenly Zoo," from the Back Through the Stars unit.

Word Knowledge

explaining, ninety-one, dream-soul

Students can use the skills they learned in the Word Knowledge section of this lesson to read these words. Remind students of this if they have difficulty reading these words.

Though it was a cold, rainy night outside, I felt warm inside now that Paw-Paw was finally explaining things to me. "Hey, there's the guy with the big head."

"He's the spirit of long life," Paw-Paw corrected me. "His head swelled up because he's so full of life. He helps keep the record of your life and sometimes with special people he juggles his books and they live longer, so maybe someone dies when they're ninety-one instead of nineteen. He's got a magic peach in his hand, grown in heaven for the gods. A person eats that peach and that person lives forever."

And she told me the eight statues—not as small as hers—were the Eight Immortals who had once been simple men and women but had gained the secret of <u>immortality</u>. One of them had <u>meditated</u> so long and let his dream-soul wander so far away that his body died in the meantime and his dream-soul had to take the bony body of a crippled beggar ❾ when it got back.

She told me about a few more of the statues and when she stopped, I asked her a new question I'd been thinking about. "What would it be like if we were in China, Paw-Paw?"

Paw-Paw shut her eyes but kept her face turned toward the window as if she were trying to picture it herself. "It'd be very noisy and you'd have much less time to yourself than here. You have to go through the rain to the village lavatory. Or maybe you have to empty out a . . . a . . . what is the word? . . . a chamber pot."

"Ugh."

"No heat except the stuff in the stove so you

310

have to go and look for every leaf and every bit of grass and all your neighbors would be doing the same thing."

"Would you have a whole bunch of families together in the same big house? Like Uncle Phil and Uncle Chester would live with you?" Uncle Chester was a year younger than Jeanie and lived down in L.A.

Paw-Paw shook her head. "Only if we were rich, but we'd probably be poor farmers if we had stayed back in China. Each of them would have their own little house and you and I would be crowded in somehow into one of those two."

311

Comprehension Skills

Compare and Contrast

Discuss the following phrases from this selection. Have the students tell whether each phrase shows a comparison or a contrast. Tell the students to also explain why they think the author chose to express his thoughts using the comparison or the contrast.

■ "Though it was a cold, rainy night outside, I felt warm inside now that Paw-Paw was finally explaining things to me." (page 310, paragraph 1)

■ "What would it be like if we were in China, Paw-Paw?" . . . "It'd be very noisy and you'd have much less time to yourself than here." (page 310, paragraphs 4 and 5)

② Reading and Responding

Comprehension Strategies

Modeling

⑩ Summarizing *Now that we finished, let's quickly sum up what we've read. Casey was happy that Paw-Paw was talking about Casey's mother who had died. Then they decided to go see a movie. The movie surprised Casey because it showed Asians in leading roles, and as heroes. She and Paw-Paw walked around Chinatown. Casey started seeing Chinatown through her mother's eyes. She and Paw-Paw became closer.*

Discussing Strategy Use

After they have read the selection, have students share any problems they encountered and tell what strategies they used to solve them. Then, have them answer the following questions. If they answer "no" to any of the questions, have them reread part of the selection to find the answer.

- Did they stop to clarify words, phrases, and ideas that they didn't understand?

- Were they able to find connections between this story and experiences they have had in their own lives?

- Did they summarize in order to help them understand what they've read?

Make sure that students explain how using the strategies helped them understand the selection better and how they read effectively to find answers to the questions they asked as they set purposes.

I drew my finger down the glass slowly. Rain dribbled down from the awning overhead. "But still, would you like that better than the way you live now? I mean if we were in China, you'd really be in charge, like the mother was in the first movie, bossing all her grown-up sons around."

Paw-Paw sighed. "I don't know. It's too easy to worry about the way things might have been. I'd rather live with the way things are now. That's what the Owl Spirit did after all."

"Well, why don't you live with one of your children now?"

"I could live with your Uncle Phil anytime I want, but they always get this rotten chicken meat from the freezer, when chickens should be fresh. But no, the feathers make too much mess and they don't like it when I take out the blood and guts. And I say, 'What do you think's inside of you?' Or they give me steak in a huge chunk and they hand me a knife and that thing with the four sharp points."

"A fork?"

"Yes, and I say, 'When I come to the dinner table, I come to eat, not to cook. Meat should be cut up and cooked properly in the kitchen before dinner.'"

"They'd probably let you make your own meals," I said.

"Well, I guess I could make my peace with them on that, but there are other things." Her eyes glanced at the statues in the window. "They tell me those things are only for stupid, old people."

I realized that it all depended on how I looked around myself—if there were invisible walls around Chinatown for Paw-Paw, they were like the walls of

312

Meeting Individual Needs

ESL

Discussing Strategy Use Have English-language learners work with you to identify aspects of a text that make it difficult, then share and evaluate their strategies for resolving those difficulties.

Word Knowledge

grown-up, remain

Students can use the skills they learned in the Word Knowledge section of this lesson to read these words. Remind students of this if they have difficulty reading these words.

a turtle, walls behind which you could remain warm and alive, and for someone like me, those walls didn't have to be any more of a trap than I let them. They could be like something to give me shape and form and when I couldn't grow anymore inside them, I could break out of those invisible walls.

Paw-Paw began to retie her scarf but her fingers had begun to stiffen in the cold and the wet. I reached my hands out. "Here, Paw-Paw, let me help you." So Paw-Paw leaned forward, waiting patiently until I had retied her scarf. She checked the knot under the chin of her reflection in the window, smoothing her hand over it.

She smiled, pleased. "You did that very well. Such strong young fingers."

She gripped my fingers tightly in her hand for a moment with what seemed like an immense strength. "Now help an old lady up the hills. It's wet and I'm afraid I'm going to fall."

I let her take my arm then and once again she was just a little old lady and we climbed slowly up the steeply slanting hillside, like two small owls clawing their way along a branch that twisted upward into the **10** night sky.

313

Teacher Tip Reread the selection with students who had difficulty understanding it. Continue modeling and prompting the use of strategies and skills as you reread.

Assessment
✓ **Formal** To assess students' reading comprehension, have them complete *Comprehension and Writing Assessment,* pages 63–64.

Comprehension Skills

Discussing the Selection

Following reading, engage the students in a discussion of the selection. Using the *handing-off process* will help the students to take responsibility for the discussion. In addition to the following question, have them revisit any questions asked when they set purposes before the reading. Have students support their responses with text evidence.

- Why was Casey staying with her grandmother and not her parents? *(Her mother had died, and her father was in the hospital.)*

- How do you think Casey felt about living with her grandmother? *(Answers may vary. Students may mention how lonely Casey was without her friends.)*

- What did Casey find out about her heritage in this story? *(Answers may vary, but students should mention the movie Casey saw, the meanings behind the statues, and how life would be different if they were in China.)*

- How has this selection connected with your knowledge of the unit theme? *(Answers will vary—students should compare/contrast examples of heritage from this selection with their own experiences or past reading and use these connections to make a general statement about the unit theme.)*

During this time, have the students return to the clues and problems that they noted on the transparency before reading. Let the students decide which items deserve further discussion.

Actively encourage this handing-off process by letting students know that they, not you, are in control of the discussion.

② Reading and Responding

Meet the Author

After the students read the information about Laurence Yep, discuss the following questions with them.

Laurence Yep likes writing about being an outsider. Why do you think this makes his writing popular with young readers? *(Possible answer: Everyone feels like an outsider from time to time, especially young people.)*

Why do you think it is important to Laurence Yep to break down racial stereotypes? *(Possible answer: He knows firsthand that people can get wrong ideas about unfamiliar cultures because they don't have all the facts. Therefore, he wants to make sure that correct information is available to readers.)*

Meet the Illustrator

After students read the information about Yoriko Ito, discuss the following question with them.

Why do you think Yoriko Ito may have wanted to illustrate a story about a young girl who learns more about her heritage from her grandmother? *(Possible answer: She knows firsthand the beauty of Asian cultures and wants to depict it for young readers. She may also identify with the grandmother, who wants to keep her heritage alive in herself and her family, even though she is living far from her homeland.)*

Chinatown

Meet the Author

Laurence Yep was born in San Francisco, California. His Chinese-American family lived in an African-American section of the city, so he had to commute to a bilingual school in Chinatown. Yep says he never encountered white culture in America until high school, and always felt like an outsider. Growing up, he found few books that dealt with being a Chinese-American. Because of this, he used his own writing to fight racial stereotypes. He likes to write about this feeling of being an outsider and believes this is the reason he is so popular with young adult readers.

Meet the Illustrator

Yoriko Ito was raised in Japan, but moved to the United States when she was about 21 years old. Says Yoriko Ito, "Even when I was little, I knew I wanted to paint, but my parents would say, 'What are you talking about?' I dreamed about pursuing art in high school, but it was when I came to the United States that I actually decided to pursue art."

She now works painting backgrounds for animated films. Some of the movies she has worked on are "The Prince of Egypt" and "El Dorado." She advises other aspiring artists, "You have to do your best always—don't doubt your ability. Trust yourself, especially if you enjoy art." She especially encourages trying new, fun ways to test one's artistic abilities.

314

Theme Connections

Think About It

A visit to Chinatown helped Casey to become more aware of her Chinese heritage. With a small group of students, discuss the following questions.

- What traditional figures did Paw-Paw describe?
- What did the figures mean to Paw-Paw?
- Did they mean the same to other people?
- What family traditions did Paw-Paw describe?
- What did Casey's experiences with her grandmother teach her?

Record Ideas

Do you own an object that means something special to you? If not, can you think of a friend or a family member that owns or carries an object that is of some significance to him or her? Describe that object in your Writing Journal, and tell why it is meaningful or important.

Draw a Special Family Object

Draw a picture of the object described in your Writing Journal, and then give your drawing a title or caption. Prepare a final draft of the object's description and attach it with your drawing. Share your drawing and description with other students, and post it on the Concept/Question Board for possible use in your unit activity.

315

 **Have students include cultural myths and legends in their heritage albums.**

Theme Connections

Think About It

Ensure that students understand the symbolism that was inherent in what Paw-Paw was teaching Casey.

Record Ideas

Have students discuss this question with their families or with a trusted friend.

Draw a Special Family Object

If students cannot identify a special object, have them find a photograph of people who are special to them and tell why the photo is important to them.

② Reading and Responding

Women
by Alice Walker

Activating Prior Knowledge

■ Remind the students about some of the women and grandmothers they have read about in this unit. Discuss if they were strong women who governed their family.

■ Direct their attention to the title and discuss their feelings about women from a mother's or grandmother's generation. How do they differ from some younger women they know?

Reading the Poem

■ Read the poem aloud for the students, slowly. Pause at the end of each line, and a bit longer at the end of each thought. Read it a second time and tell the students to try to visualize each image.

■ In the time you designate for independent work, have the students listen to the poem recording on the *Listening Library Audiocassette.*

Literary Techniques

Metaphor

Writers often use metaphor to make their descriptions more vivid or produce more striking effects. A metaphor is a comparison of two things that are not alike in most ways, but are alike in a certain way, a way that the poet wants to emphasize. In "Women," Alice Walker compares women like her mother to generals. Have students identify all the references to women being like generals. Then have students comment on how metaphors affect the mood of the poem.

WOMEN

by Alice Walker
illustrated by Tyrone Geter

They were women then
My mama's generation
Husky of voice—Stout of
Step
With fists as well as
Hands
How they battered down
Doors
And ironed
Starched white
Shirts

316

Teacher Tip You may want to tell students that *simile*, like *metaphor*, compares two things that are unlike in most ways. However, similes, unlike metaphors, use the word *like* or *as* (for example, *the tornado sounded* like *a train*).

How they led
Armies
Headragged Generals
Across mined
Fields
Booby-trapped
Ditches
To discover books
Desks
A place for us
How they knew what we
Must know
Without knowing a page
Of it
Themselves.

317

Theme Connection

■ Have the students discuss the hardships of women during the 1940s and 1950s (the time period that Alice Walker is writing about). Have them discuss how Alice Walker's vision of her mother relates to their own heritage.

Meet the Poet

Alice Walker was born in Eatonian, Georgia, to a family of sharecroppers. She was the eighth child. When she was young, her brother accidentally shot her with a BB gun and blinded her in one eye. Because she felt self-conscious about the scar, she spent much of her time alone, reading.

When she was fourteen, the scar tissue from the wound was removed, and she became more outgoing. Her first poems were published while she was still in college. Her first novel was published in 1970, and her first short story collection, *In Love & Trouble,* won the Rosenthal Award of the National Institute of Arts and Letters.

Her other books include *Revolutionary Petunias and Other Poems* (in which her poem "Women" appears); *Meridian; The Color Purple;* and *In the Temple of My Familiar.*

 **Teacher Tip** Help the students remember that each person's response to a text is a very individual matter and that no two people will have the exact same response.

② Responding

✦Exploring the Theme

Some students may choose to conduct a computer search for additional books or information about heritage. Have them make a list of these books and sources of information to share with classmates and the school librarian. Check the reading link of the **SRA** Web page for links to theme-related Websites. **http://www.sra4kids.com**

Have students write sentences using the selection vocabulary words. In order to provide additional help in remembering words, students can write synonyms or antonyms for the words if it is appropriate. Some students may even draw something to help them remember the meanings of the words.

Selection Vocabulary

Have students write in their Writing Journals the definitions for words discussed before the reading of the selection and any other interesting words they clarified while reading. Students should be encouraged to refer to these words throughout the unit as they work on student and writing projects. The words from the selection are:

immortality	**longing**	**meditate**
souvenirs	**gaudy**	

Reading/Writing Connections

On the chalkboard, create a diagram to record the development of Casey's awakening in "Chinatown." Draw a series of wide steps that climb from left to right. Put a stick drawing of Casey at the bottom and a sun at the top. Tell students to identify the different steps that lead to Casey's recognition that she is part of her mother and grandmother's world of Chinatown. Write each answer on one of the steps. Then, tell students to think of other stories they know that have similar structure to that of "Chinatown." Discuss with them how they could use the structure for one of their story ideas.

Literature Appreciation

Remind students that in "Chinatown" Paw-Paw tells Casey legends from her Chinese traditions. Have students think of stories from their families' traditions. Tell each student to select one, rehearse the story, and then retell it to the class. Some students may be able to place the legend or story in a modern setting. Meet with each student briefly beforehand to determine if his or her story is appropriate to share with the class.

Home Connection

The class has just finished reading "Chinatown," a fictional selection about a Chinese-American girl who gains insight into her heritage when she goes to live with her grandmother. An informational letter on "Chinatown," in both English and Spanish, can be found in the ***Home Connection*** guide.

Home Connection p. 43

Supporting Student Explorations

Students should be continuing to work on the unit activity. You may want to do the following:

Whole Group Explain to the students that they can include works of realistic fiction in their heritage albums and that modeling a character after a family member or friend is a helpful way to get started. Have them write about a problem or goal of the main character. Remind them that they need to let their readers know about what their characters think and feel and why. Have them show in their story how traditions and customs might have shaped the characters. Explain that they can show more about characters by "flashing back" to an important event in their past that explains why they act, think, and feel as they do. Also remind students that dialogue is an effective way to communicate what characters think and feel.

Small Group Have the students work as partners to review the two other works of realistic fiction they have read in this unit ("The Night We Started Dancing" and "The West Side"). Tell them to identify the main characters' problems or goals and to discuss how each character's past affected his thoughts and actions. Have students use the treatment of these characters as a model for the characters in their heritage albums.

Individual Have the students begin an "About the Author" page for their heritage albums. Tell them to use the Meet the Author features in their anthologies as models. Suggest that students exchange their work with a classmate for peer editing.

Suggest that students post on the Concept/Question Board brief descriptions of books, magazine articles, computer Websites, or other sources of information that they have found to be especially helpful in their explorations of heritage. Encourage students who are having difficulty finding information to check sources on the Board and to post their questions as well.

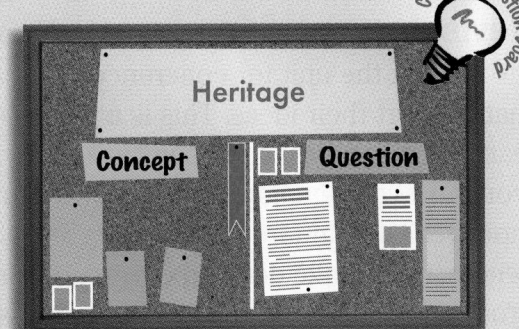

Inquiry Journal Have
students complete page 42 of the *Inquiry Journal.*

Recording Concept Information (continued)
- *The West Side* by Peggy Mann
  Answers will vary.

- *Chinatown* by Laurence Yep
  Answers will vary.

42   Inquiry Journal

Inquiry Journal p. 42

Assessment

✓ **Informal** Continue making anecdotal records of students' progress. Note whether they:
- communicate what characters in their stories think and feel about their heritage and why.
- explore how past events impact how characters feel about their heritage.

3 Integrating the Curriculum

Meeting Individual Needs

ESL

Revise You might want to work with English-language learners during Independent Work Time to help them revise their drafts.

Intervention

Revise If a student doesn't see anything that needs to be changed, get him or her to do something to the paper—number the details in a description or the steps in a process, circle exact words, or underline the best parts of the paper. Once a paper is marked, the student may not be so reluctant to change it.

Assessment

✓ **Informal** Take this opportunity to assess students' progress with the writing process by commenting on the entries in their Writing Journals.

Writing Seminar Continue to hold seminars in which students share their work with the class in order to gain feedback. Reading their pieces-in-progress will help them to identify any pertinent information that needs to be added.

Language Arts

Writing

Dialogue

Instruct Ask students what they know about dialogue. If necessary, explain that *dialogue* is written conversation between two or more characters in a story. Discuss with students ways that dialogue makes a story believable by showing how characters think and feel, and keeps readers interested in the story by moving the action along. Also, point out that when writing dialogue, one begins a new paragraph every time a different person talks.

Practice Have students reread the dialogue between Casey and Paw-Paw on pages 300–302 of "Chinatown." Then call on volunteers to discuss how Laurence Yep's use of dialogue improves the story. List their ideas on the chalkboard. Add to the list any purposes of dialogue from the list above that students do not mention.

Apply Ask students to skim through the rest of "Chinatown" to find other examples of dialogue that make the story more realistic and interesting.

Writing Process

Revise Have students revise the narratives they have been working on throughout the unit for coherence, natural progression of events, and details that support their ideas. This is a good time to implement what they have learned in many of the lessons in Unit 3, such as time words and order words. Have them add dialogue between the characters to make the story more realistic and interesting. However, remind them that it is not necessary to make detailed corrections, as those will be taken care of in the proofreading stage of the writing process.

Literary Elements

Setting, Plot, and Problem Resolution

Instruct Have students define and discuss *plot*, *setting*, and *problem resolution*. If necessary, explain to students that *plot* consists of a problem or goal, introduced by the main character of the story, and the chain of events that leads to its resolution. *Setting* is where the events of the story take place. *Problem resolution* occurs when the problem is solved or the goal is realized.

Practice Have students analyze the setting of "Chinatown" by drawing two vertical lines on the chalkboard to represent Grant Avenue. Add a standard compass rose, with north at the top. At the bottom end of the street, write "Paw-Paw's apartment." Then ask students to begin reading on page 304 to name other sites along the avenue. As students respond, add stores and other places to the map. Make a large X on any location at which Casey and her grandmother stop. Then discuss what happens at each site; for example, at the movie theater Casey sees for the first time movies in which Chinese people are noble characters.

Apply Ask students how the changes in the setting affect the story's plot and correspond with Casey's resolution of her problem. *(Casey makes two kinds of trips. One is a journey along Grant Avenue; the other takes her from a feeling of loneliness and not belonging to a sense that she has found her way home.)*

Assessment

✓ **Formal** To assess students' knowledge of setting, use *Skills Assessment,* page 31.

3 Integrating the Curriculum

Meeting Individual Needs

Reteach
Spelling -le endings Have students who need additional instruction and practice with this concept complete **Reteach,** pages 103–104.

Challenge
Spelling -le endings Have students read through the story for words that end in -le. Ask them to list the words, scrambling the letters in each. Have students exchange papers with other students and write the correct spelling for each word.

Have students who understand this concept and could benefit from extended practice complete **Challenge,** page 54.

← Skills Strand →

Spelling -le Endings
INTRODUCED: Unit 1, Lesson 2
REVIEWED: Unit 1, Lesson 3
Unit 3, Lesson 5

Spelling

Spelling -le Endings

Instruct The consonant before -le, -el, -al, -il, or -ol is a different spelling of the same vowel sound in the unstressed ending syllable of some words (for example, *possible, barrel, literal, pupil,* and *symbol*). The consonant before -le syllable pattern is the most common spelling of that sound.

Practice Have students think of at least five words with the consonant before -le spelling pattern. Have students write sentences with these words and trade papers with a partner. Partners should check the words to make sure they are spelled correctly.

Apply Remind students to always check their writing for the correct spellings of words ending in the consonant before -le, -el, -al, -il, or -ol pattern. For additional practice, have students complete **Reading and Writing Workbook** pages 103–104.

Reading and Writing Workbook pp. 103–104

Grammar, Usage, and Mechanics

Compound Sentences

Instruct Ask students what they know about compound sentences. If necessary, tell students that a *compound sentence* is two complete sentences that are combined into one by using a comma and a conjunction such as *so, and, or, nor, yet,* or *but.*(Example: "She loves the ferris wheel, *but* she hates roller coasters.")

Then tell students a compound sentence can also be formed by combining two complete sentences using a semicolon. (Example: "She loves the ferris wheel; she hates roller coasters.")

Writers use compound sentences to add style and variety to their writing. Students should avoid using too many short, choppy sentences.

Practice Copy the following paragraph on the chalkboard or transparency. Have students improve it by explaining how some sentences could be combined.

> We came out of the theater. We decided to get something to eat. It wasn't raining anymore. We walked to a restaurant. The restaurant was crowded and noisy. It was too expensive. We left. We found a cheaper place to eat.

Apply For additional practice, have students complete ***Reading and Writing Workbook*** pages 105–106.

Reading and Writing Workbook pp. 105–106

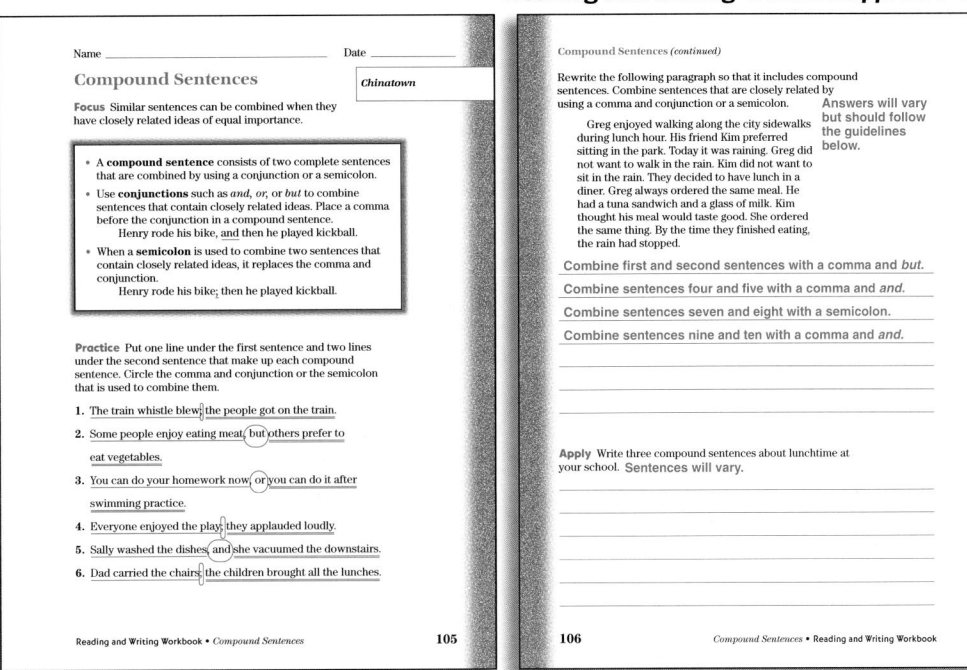

Teacher Tip Remind students to keep in mind what they have learned about compound sentences and conjunctions when revising their narratives and unit projects.

Meeting Individual Needs

Reteach

Compound Sentences Have students who need additional instruction and practice with this concept complete *Reteach,* pages 105–106.

Challenge

Compound Sentences Have students use the newspaper and copy five simple sentences. Have them add to each sentence to make compound sentences. Challenge students to combine sentences using both semicolons and commas and conjunctions.

Have students who understand this concept and could benefit from extended practice complete *Challenge,* page 55.

Compound Sentences

INTRODUCED: Unit 3, Lesson 5
REVIEWED: Unit 5, Lesson 5
Unit 6, Lesson 6

3 Integrating the Curriculum

Teacher Tip Encourage students to use these skills in their unit activity or in writing their narratives, if appropriate.

Study and Research

Draw Conclusions from Multiple Sources

Instruct Remind students that good writers use reliable sources and, when necessary, cross-check information in different sources. They can then be assured that what they write is accurate. Because "Chinatown" takes place in San Francisco, it may be interesting to do some research about the city. Have students brainstorm a list of questions they would like to answer about San Francisco. Some examples may be: Where is it located? What tourist attractions are there? What is its main source of economy? What is the climate? Who lives there? Are there any colleges or universities there?

Then tell students that they can draw logical conclusions based on the information they have learned, such as: *Would they want to live there? Why or why not? What kind of occupation would be best to find a job there? Would it be a good place to take a vacation?*

Practice Have students use their lists of questions and find the answers using reference materials. Remind students that they should use multiple sources of information.

Apply Have students complete *Inquiry Journal* page 50 to draw conclusions based on their research.

Inquiry Journal p. 50

Across the Curriculum

 **Social Studies**

Writing an Article

Purpose

To help students appreciate the richness of their heritage

Materials

paper, pencils, markers, crayons

Procedure

Have students discuss the selection and any personal thoughts or questions that it raises. Ask students whether it reminds them of anything in their own lives—people, places, events, relationships, or emotions.

- Have students explore their heritage. Provide time for them to discuss what they wish to explore and how they wish to go about it.

- Have students ask adults, friends, or family members about folktales or other stories from a particular heritage. Students may also choose to visit the library and do some research about the history and culture of a particular heritage.

- Have students write and illustrate a news article. Tell them to think about how pictures contribute to a newspaper article. What can pictures tell that words cannot? Have them write an article about something that is important to them about their heritage. Have students use some examples of descriptive language in their writing, then draw some pictures that relate to the points made in their article.

- Have students share their articles and illustrations with their classmates.

 **Art**

Creating a Picture Album

Purpose

To awaken students to the similarities between different cultures

Materials

paper, pencils, markers, crayons

Procedure

Explain to students that although people may come from different backgrounds and have different cultures, there are certain things we all have in common.

- Have students brainstorm what those things might be as you write their ideas on the chalkboard. Invite ideas about major celebrations or observances, but also ask for suggestions about such everyday events as eating together, working in and around the home, and leisure-time activities.

- Tell students to narrow the list to two or three activities that are common to all or most cultures. Circle those activities on the chalkboard, and discuss them briefly. Stress that though there may be differences in the ways these activities are carried out, there are also similarities.

- Have students draw a picture of themselves taking part in one of the three activities you discussed. Suggest that they make several rough sketches of what they want the scene to look like, and then choose one sketch as a model for their final version.

- Bind the student drawings into a single class album. Have students think of a title for the album that reflects what they have discussed about the similarities between people of different cultures.

318

About the Author

Kathryn Lasky has written picture books and novels, and she has collaborated on several books with her photographer husband, Christopher G. Knight. "The Night Journey" won the Association of Jewish Libraries Award, the National Jewish Book Award, and the Sydney Taylor Book Award. In addition, *The Weaver's Gift* won The Boston Globe-Horn Book Award for nonfiction, and *Sugaring Time* won a Newbery Honor Book Award.

Students can read more about Kathryn Lasky on page 340 of the **Student Anthology.**

Other Books by Kathryn Lasky
- *Dreams in the Golden Country: The Diary of Zipporah Feldman, a Jewish Immigrant Girl*
- *Alice Rose & Sam*
- *Days of the Dead*

Selection Summary

Genre: Adventure

Thirteen-year-old Rache's great-grandmother Sashie has stories to tell of her childhood in old Russia, and the telling begins when the gift of a restored samovar elicits Sashie's memories. In this excerpt from the book, "The Night Journey," Sashie recalls the time when she and her family fled the persecution of Jews under Tsar Alexander. Hiding in a poultry wagon, keeping babies quiet, and fighting off fear make for a suspenseful, yet precious, family history.

About the Illustrator

Trina Schart Hyman's career began in Sweden where she worked for two weeks on the illustrations for *Pippi Longstocking*. She has received many awards, including the Caldecott Medal for *St. George and the Dragon*, and the Caldecott Honor Book for *The Adventures of Herschel of Ostropol.*

Students can read more about Trina Schart Hyman on page 340 of the **Student Anthology.**

Other Books Illustrated by Trina Schart Hyman
- *The Boggart and the Monster*
- *The Fortune-Tellers*

Exploring the Theme

Selection Concepts

"The Night Journey" tells the story of 13-year-old Rache's daily visits with her grandmother. During this time together, Rache learns about her grandmother's childhood and about her family's dangerous escape from persecution in tsarist Russia. Key concepts to be explored are:

- Artifacts and storytelling can link the generations of a family.
- The pain and hardships a family endures are as binding as its joyful celebrations.

Check the Reading link of the **SRA** Web page for links to theme-related Websites.
http://www.sra4kids.com

Exploration Activity Tips

Before Reading, have the students browse the selection for clues about what will happen and how this selection relates to the theme of heritage.

During Reading, have the students note the use of symbolism in "The Night Journey." Tell them to think about symbols that are important in their own lives and those of family and friends.

After Reading, have students discuss artifacts or treasured possessions that are important to their friends or family members. Then have students update the Concept/Question Board. Some may want to revise their activity plans based on what they have learned from the selection.

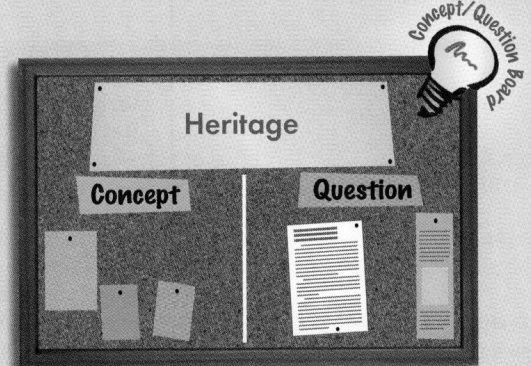

Unit 3 Exploration Management

Lesson 1	Listen to and interview a class guest about heritage. Select and read library books about heritage.
Lesson 2	Identify genres for inclusion in heritage albums. Reflect on one's own heritage, interview family members or friends about customs and traditions, and begin writing.
Lesson 3	Identify and utilize various literary techniques. Writing begins on second selection for student albums.
Lesson 4	Work on unit activity continues. Discuss with relatives or friends what they want to communicate about their heritage.
Lesson 5	Write autobiographical sketches for author pages and consider modeling a character after a family member or friend.
Lesson 6 The Night Journey	**Collaborative Exploration** Prepare final drafts, complete illustrations, prepare title and copyright pages, and bind books. Write thank-you notes to those who helped with the activity. **Supplementary Activity** Discuss the process of preparing text for publication for general and specific audiences. Conduct a class review of writing letters of thanks.
Lesson 7	Students present a selected piece from their heritage albums.

Lesson Planner

Suggested Pacing: 3–5 days	DAY 1	DAY 2
	DAY 1	**DAY 2**
Part 1 Preparing to Read **Materials** ■ Student Anthology, pp. 318–341 ■ Transparencies 20, 44	**Word Knowledge** ■ Reading the Words and Sentences, p. 318G ■ Developing Oral Language, p. 318G **Build Background, p. 318H** **Preview and Prepare, p. 318I** **Selection Vocabulary, p. 318I** *tantrum, imperial, regiment, kosher, ingratiate*	**Preview and Prepare, p. 318I** ■ Review Transparency 44
Part 2 Reading and Responding **Materials** ■ Student Anthology, pp. 318–341 ■ Teacher Observation Log ■ Inquiry Journal, p. 42 ■ Home Connection, p. 45	**Student Anthology, pp. 318–327** **Comprehension Strategies** ■ Summarizing, pp. 318, 322 ■ Asking Questions, pp. 320, 322, 324, 326	**Student Anthology, pp. 328–341** **Comprehension Strategies** ■ Asking Questions, pp. 328, 332, 334, 336 ■ Making Connections, p. 330 ■ Summarizing, p. 338 **Discussing Strategy Use, p. 338** **Comprehension Skills** ✓■ Discussing the Selection, p. 339 **Exploring the Theme** ■ Selection Vocabulary, p. 341A *tantrum, imperial, regiment, kosher, ingratiate*
Part 3 Integrating the Curriculum **Materials** ■ Student Anthology, pp. 318–341 ■ Reading and Writing Workbook, pp. 107–110 ■ Inquiry Journal, pp. 51–52	**Writing** ■ Using and Punctuating Dialogue, pp. 341C, D **Literary Elements** ✓■ Literary Elements of a Story, p. 341E	**Writing Process** ■ Proofreading, p. 341D **Vocabulary** ✓■ Words in Context, p. 341F
Independent Work Time **Materials** ■ Reteach, pp. 107–110 ■ ESL Supplement ■ Challenge, pp. 56–57 ■ Intervention Guide ■ Research CD-ROM ■ Listening Library Audiocassette	**Writing Process Continued** **ESL** ■ Word Meaning, p. 318G ■ Vocabulary, p. 318J **Intervention** ■ Synonyms, p. 318G ■ Comprehension, p. 318 **Unit Project** ■ Prepare Final Drafts ■ Write Thank-You Notes	**Writing Process Continued** **Reteach** ✓■ Literary Elements of a Story, *Reteach*, pp. 107–108 **ESL** ■ Proofreading, p. 341D **Challenge** ✓■ Literary Elements of a Story, *Challenge*, p. 56 **Intervention** ■ Asking Questions, p. 332 ■ Punctuating Dialogue, p. 341D **Unit Project Continued**

✓ Informal Assessment Available ✓ Formal Assessment Available

| DAY 2 continued | DAY 3 | |
DAY 3	DAY 4	DAY 5
General Review	**General Review**	**Review Word Knowledge**
Student Anthology, pp. 318–341 **Comprehension Skills** ■ Drawing Conclusions, pp. 319, 321, 323, 329, 335 **Theme Connections** ■ Think About It, p. 341 ■ Draw a Family Tree, p. 341	**Student Anthology, pp. 318–341** **Comprehension Skills** ■ Author's Point of View, pp. 325, 327, 331, 333, 337 **Exploring the Theme** ■ Reading/Writing Connections, p. 341A ■ Supporting Student Explorations, p. 341B	**Student Anthology, pp. 318–341** ■ Review Selection ■ Complete Discussion ■ Reread Selection in Pairs **Home Connection, p. 341A** ■ Discuss "The Night Journey" ■ Write a summary
Writing Process Continued **Grammar, Usage, and Mechanics** ✓ ■ Capitalizing Titles, p. 341G **Listening/Speaking/Viewing** ■ Language Reflecting a Region and Culture, p. 341H	**Writing Process Continued** **Study and Research** ■ Using Technology in Presentations, p. 341I	**Across the Curriculum** **Music** ■ A Heritage of Folk Dancing, p. 341J **Social Studies** ■ Ellis Island, p. 341J
Writing Process Continued **Reteach** ✓ ■ Words in Context, *Reteach*, pp. 109–110 **ESL** ■ Foreign Language as a Literary Device, p. 341H **Challenge** ■ Drawing Conclusions, p. 321 ✓ ■ Words in Context, *Challenge*, p. 57 **Unit Project Continued**	**Writing Process Continued** **Challenge** ■ Author's Point of View, p. 331 ■ Capitalizing Titles, p. 341G **Intervention** ■ Author's Point of View, p. 327 **Unit Project Continued**	**Writing Process Continued** **Unit Project Continued**

Meeting Individual Needs
Independent Work Time

Part  1
Preparing to Read

Meeting Individual Needs

ESL
- Word Meaning, p. 318G
- Cultural Keepsakes, p. 318H
- Vocabulary, p. 318J

Intervention
- Synonyms, p. 318G

Part  2
Reading and Responding

Meeting Individual Needs

ESL
- Making Connections, p. 330

Challenge
- Drawing Conclusions, p. 321
- Author's Point of View, p. 331

Intervention
- Comprehension, p. 318
- Drawing Conclusions, p. 323
- Author's Point of View, p. 327
- Making Connections, p. 330
- Asking Questions, p. 332

Part 3
Integrating the Curriculum

Meeting Individual Needs

Reteach
- Literary Elements of a Story, *Reteach*, pp. 107–108
- Words in Context, *Reteach*, pp. 109–110

ESL
- Proofreading, p. 341D
- Foreign Language as a Literary Device, p. 341H

Challenge
- Literary Elements of a Story, *Challenge*, p. 56
- Words in Context, *Challenge*, p. 57
- Capitalizing Titles, p. 341G

Intervention
- Punctuating Dialogue, p. 341D

Formal Assessment Options

Use these assessment pages along with your informal
observations to gauge student progress.

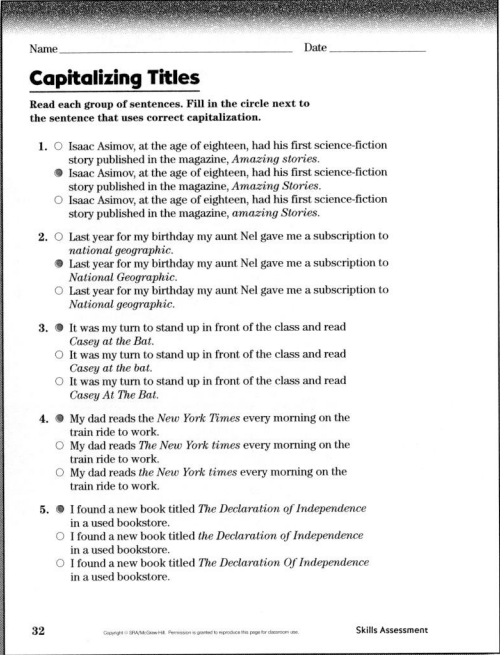

Name _____ Date _____

Capitalizing Titles

**Read each group of sentences. Fill in the circle next to
the sentence that uses correct capitalization.**

1. ○ a. Isaac Asimov, at the age of eighteen, had his first science-fiction story published in the magazine, *Amazing stories.*
   ● b. Isaac Asimov, at the age of eighteen, had his first science-fiction story published in the magazine, *Amazing Stories.*
   ○ c. Isaac Asimov, at the age of eighteen, had his first science-fiction story published in the magazine, *amazing Stories.*

2. ○ a. Last year for my birthday my aunt Nel gave me a subscription to *national geographic.*
   ● b. Last year for my birthday my aunt Nel gave me a subscription to *National Geographic.*
   ○ c. Last year for my birthday my aunt Nel gave me a subscription to *National geographic.*

3. ● a. It was my turn to stand up in front of the class and read *Casey at the Bat.*
   ○ b. It was my turn to stand up in front of the class and read *Casey at the bat.*
   ○ c. It was my turn to stand up in front of the class and read *Casey At The Bat.*

4. ● a. My dad reads the *New York Times* every morning on the train ride to work.
   ○ b. My dad reads *The New York times* every morning on the train ride to work.
   ○ c. My dad reads *the New York times* every morning on the train ride to work.

5. ● a. I found a new book titled *The Declaration of Independence* in a used bookstore.
   ○ b. I found a new book titled *the Declaration of Independence* in a used bookstore.
   ○ c. I found a new book titled *The Declaration Of Independence* in a used bookstore.

32   Copyright © SRA/McGraw-Hill. Permission is granted to reproduce this page for classroom use.   Skills Assessment

Skills Assessment, p. 32

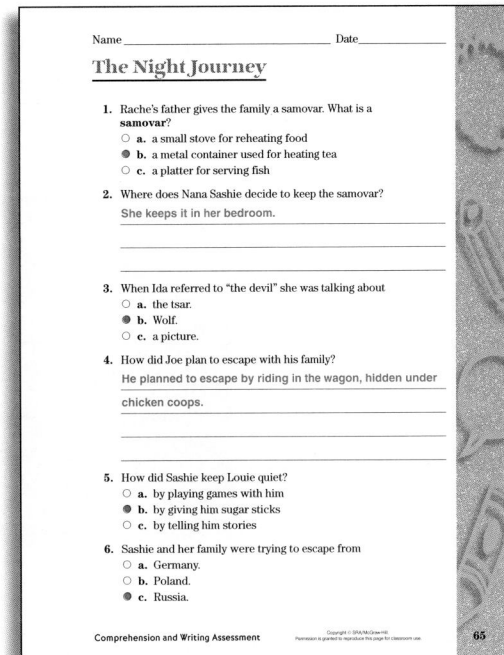

Name _____ Date _____

The Night Journey

1. Rache's father gives the family a samovar. What is a **samovar**?
   ○ a. a small stove for reheating food
   ● b. a metal container used for heating tea
   ○ c. a platter for serving fish

2. Where does Nana Sashie decide to keep the samovar?
   She keeps it in her bedroom.
   _____
   _____

3. When Ida referred to "the devil" she was talking about
   ○ a. the tsar.
   ● b. Wolf.
   ○ c. a picture.

4. How did Joe plan to escape with his family?
   He planned to escape by riding in the wagon, hidden under
   chicken coops.
   _____

5. How did Sashie keep Louie quiet?
   ○ a. by playing games with him
   ● b. by giving him sugar sticks
   ○ c. by telling him stories

6. Sashie and her family were trying to escape from
   ○ a. Germany.
   ○ b. Poland.
   ● c. Russia.

Comprehension and Writing Assessment   Copyright © SRA/McGraw-Hill. Permission is granted to reproduce this page for classroom use.   65

**Comprehension and Writing
Assessment, p. 65**

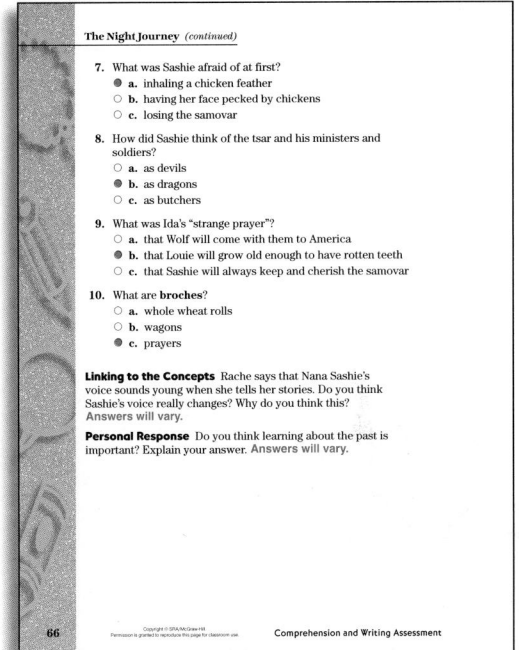

The Night Journey *(continued)*

7. What was Sashie afraid of at first?
   ● a. inhaling a chicken feather
   ○ b. having her face pecked by chickens
   ○ c. losing the samovar

8. How did Sashie think of the tsar and his ministers and soldiers?
   ○ a. as devils
   ● b. as dragons
   ○ c. as butchers

9. What was Ida's "strange prayer"?
   ○ a. that Wolf will come with them to America
   ● b. that Louie will grow old enough to have rotten teeth
   ○ c. that Sashie will always keep and cherish the samovar

10. What are **broches**?
    ○ a. whole wheat rolls
    ○ b. wagons
    ● c. prayers

Linking to the Concepts Rache says that Nana Sashie's
voice sounds young when she tells her stories. Do you think
Sashie's voice really changes? Why do you think this?
Answers will vary.

Personal Response Do you think learning about the past is
important? Explain your answer. Answers will vary.

66   Copyright © SRA/McGraw-Hill. Permission is granted to reproduce this page for classroom use.   Comprehension and Writing Assessment

**Comprehension and Writing
Assessment, p. 66**

① Preparing to Read

Reading the Words and Sentences

Write each word and sentence on the chalkboard. Have students read each word together. After all the words have been read, have students read each sentence in natural phrases or chunks. Use the suggestions in About the Words to discuss the different features of the listed words.

Line 1: lambent luminous stony inexorable
Line 2: short sharp shutters sheer
Line 3: cackle chicken clucking thickness
Sentence 1: We could see the lambent flickers of light through the sheer curtains.
Sentence 2: Sharp, short beeps emanated from a car alarm.
Sentence 3: The farmer was greeted with the cackle and clucking of the chickens.

About the Words

- Line 1 contains synonyms. Synonyms are words that have the same meaning.
- The words in Line 2 all contain consonant digraph *sh*. In this spelling pattern, the *s* and the *h*, when placed together, make the single /sh/ sound.
- All of the words in Line 3 have the /k/ sound spelled *ck*. The spelling *ck* is preceded by a short vowel. Invite students to think of other words containing this spelling of the /k/ sound.

Developing Oral Language

To review the words, have students do one or more of the following activities.

- Have students give a synonym for one of the words from Lines 1–3 and then challenge a classmate to identify the word to which the synonym refers.
- Encourage students to say a sentence that uses alliteration. A sentence could use words that begin or end with *sh*, or words that end with the /k/ sound spelled *ck*. For example, *The shabby sheep shivered in the wind.*
- Have volunteers make up a sentence that uses one word from Line 2 and one word from Line 3.

Meeting Individual Needs

ESL

Word Meaning Make sure the English-language learners understand the meaning of the words before you do the exercises with them. Refer to Unit 3, Lesson 6, of the *ESL Supplement* for specific suggestions.

Intervention

Synonyms Explain to students that synonyms are words that have the same or nearly the same meaning. For example, *thin* and *lean* have the same meaning. Therefore, they are synonyms. Have students scan the story for synonyms and make a list of ten words. Then have them write the synonyms for the words they have listed. They may use a thesaurus or synonym finder if needed. Examples are: worried, young, strict, and easy. For students who need more help, see Unit 3, Lesson 6, of the *Intervention*

Teacher Tip Have the students write original sentences using words with the digraph *sh*, the /k/ sound spelled *ck*, and synonyms from the selection.

Build Background

Activate Prior Knowledge

Have students check the Concept/Question Board to refresh their memories about heritage. Discuss the following with students to find out what they may already know about the selection and have already learned about the unit theme. Tell students to use their prior knowledge to help them comprehend the selection they are about to read.

- Ask students if they are familiar with the story they are about to read, and if so, to tell about it. Remind students, however, not to give away the ending of the selection.

- Have students exchange what they know about Russia.

- Have students share any other stories that involve a daring escape.

Background Information

The following information may help the students better understand the selection they are about to read.

- During the reign of the Russian emperor Alexander III there were discriminatory laws against Jews. The laws determined where Jews could live and what education they could receive. At the same time, the Russian government did little to control the anti-Jewish riots. At the end of the 19th century, hundreds of thousands of Jews emigrated to Western Europe and the United States. Things did not improve under Tsar Alexander's son, Nicholas II. Nicholas II was the emperor, or tsar, from 1894–1917, the time of this story. Nicholas was the last emperor of Russia.

- A samovar is a metal urn that is used for heating water for tea and is used mainly in Russia. The word actually means "self-boiler."

- The genre of this piece is adventure. Adventure stories are exciting and suspenseful stories about realistic characters, places, and events.

- The Russian treatment of Jewish people depicted in this story may be a sensitive issue in your classroom.

Writing Journal Tell the students that after reading they will be jotting down in their Writing Journals their reactions to the story. Have them be on the lookout for any ideas they may have for including stories of daring escapes in their heritage albums.

1 Preparing to Read

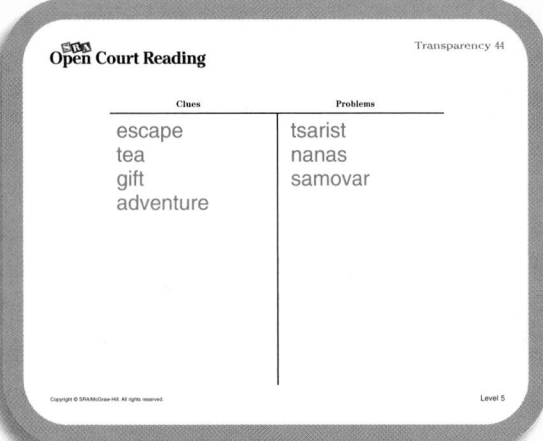

Transparency 44

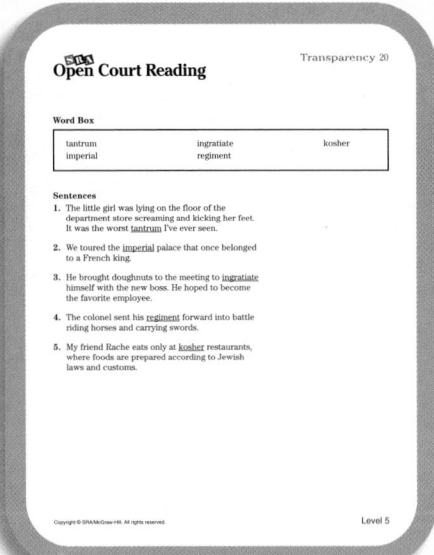

Transparency 20

To help students decode words, divide them into syllables shown below. The information following each word tells how students can figure out the meaning of each word in the sentences on _Transparency 20._

tan·trum	context clues
im·pe·ri·al	context clues
re·gi·ment	context clues
ko·sher	context clues
in·gra·ti·ate	context clues, word structure.

Preview and Prepare

Browse

■ Have a volunteer read the title and the author's and illustrator's names aloud. Have students share what they know about adventure.

■ Because this selection is fiction, have the students browse through the first half of the story, looking for words and phrases that connect to what they already know. Record these in the Clues column on _Transparency 44._ Discuss with the students what they think this selection might have to do with heritage.

■ Encourage students to ask questions as they browse. Have them identify any problems they notice and record them in the Problems column.

Set Purposes

As they read, have students think about how both hardships and celebrations can bring a family together.

Selection Vocabulary

As students study vocabulary, they will use context clues, word structure, and apposition to determine the meaning of these and additional unfamiliar words.

Display _Transparency 20_ before reading the selection to introduce and discuss the following words and their meanings.

tan·trum:	a screaming, crying fit of childish anger (page 333)
im·pe·ri·al:	describes something that is part of or belongs to a king's empire (page 333)
re·gi·ment:	a military word that means a group of soldiers (page 333)
ko·sher:	proper or acceptable according to Jewish law (page 335)
in·gra·ti·ate:	to do something to try to get someone to like you (page 336)

Have students read the words in the Word Box. Help students decode multisyllabic words by reading the words syllable by syllable. If the word is not decodable, give the students the pronunciation.

Have the students read the sentences on _Transparency 20_ to determine the meaning of the underlined words. Remind them to use clues in the sentences and structural clues to figure out their meanings.

Reading Recommendations

Your first reading of the selection should focus on developing the reading strategies found to the left of the reduced pages. We recommend that the students revisit the selection, rereading sections or the entire selection as a way to enhance their understanding and appreciation of the text. During rereading, they should focus on the comprehension skills found to the right of the reduced pages.

Silent Reading

Because this story is quite long, have students read it silently, stopping after the first part to sum up before continuing. The second part of the selection begins on page 328. Have students practice reading on their own for at least 10 minutes at a time. As they become better readers, students will read silently with increasing ease, over longer periods of time.

Have students make use of the reading strategies listed below to help them understand the selection. Have them stop reading periodically or wait until they have completed the selection to discuss the reading strategies. After the students have finished reading the selection, use the "Discussing the Selection" questions to see if they have understood what they have read. If they have not, refer to the **_Intervention Guide_** for further strategies.

Using Reading Strategies

Reading strategy instruction allows students to become aware of how good readers read. During the reading of "The Night Journey," you will model the use of the following reading strategies:

- Summarizing
- Asking Questions
- Making Connections

Before reading, have students share how they have used these strategies in the past and any tips they can give each other on their use.

Building Comprehension Skills

Revisiting or rereading a selection allows students to apply skills that give them a more complete understanding of the text. Some follow-up comprehension skills help students organize information. Others lead to deeper understanding—to "reading between the lines," as mature readers do. In this selection, students will apply the follow-up comprehension skills of _Drawing Conclusions_ and _Author's Point of View_. Since two skills are reviewed, you may want to do all the sections related to one skill before doing the other skill.

Have students who may need extra help reading "The Night Journey" reread the selection using the **_Listening Library Audiocassette_**.

By this time in the fifth grade, good readers should be reading approximately 143 words per minute with fluency and expression. The only way to gain fluency is through practice. As explained in Reading Recommendations, have students reread all or part of the selection to you and to each other during class or Independent Work Time to focus on the comprehension skills and to build fluency.

Meeting Individual Needs

ESL

Vocabulary Check that English-language learners know the meanings of idioms and more difficult vocabulary in the story, including: _tsarist Russia; persecution; samovar; pantry; apprehension; din; brass; tightening several bolts; trial run; consequently; recoiled in horror; unseeing sockets; Jewish statement of faith; coops; four-wheel vehicle; the tsarless region; sabotaged; suffocating; tantrum; and conserving energy._ Explain and show pictures as needed. Model example sentences and help English-speaking students make their own sentences. Refer to Unit 3, Lesson 6, of the **_ESL Supplement_** for teaching suggestions.

② Reading and Responding

Read pages 318–341.

Comprehension Strategies

Modeling

① Summarizing *The story starts in the middle, and this is a long introduction. Let's sum up, so that we can start reading without getting too confused. Rache's parents told her not to talk to her great-grandmother about tsarist Russia, but Rache and Sashie have been talking anyway. Rache found part of a samovar, or tea urn, that Sashie's mother carried out from Russia. Rache's father took the part and built a new samovar.*

318

Word Knowledge

There are many multisyllabic words in this selection. Be sure students are using the skills they learned in the Word Knowledge section of this lesson.

Assessment

✓ **Informal** Observe individual students as they read, and use the Teacher Observation Log found in the **Assessment Guide** to record anecdotal information about each student's strengths and weaknesses.

Meeting Individual Needs

Intervention

Comprehension Intervention strategies for those students having difficulty with reading "The Night Journey" can be found in Unit 3 Lesson 6, of the **Intervention Guide.**

Reading Recommendation

ORAL · CHORAL · **SILENT**

The Night Journey

from the book by Kathryn Lasky
illustrated by Trina Schart Hyman

Rache lives with her parents, Ed and Leah; her grandmother, Rose; and her great-grandmother, Sashie. Rache's parents and grandmother warn her not to upset Nana Sashie by asking about tsarist Russia and the persecution Jewish people were subjected to there. However, Rache is fascinated by the story Nana Sashie has begun to tell about her family's dangerous escape from that country.

✽

In an old trunk Rache finds a piece of the brass samovar, or tea urn, that figures largely in Nana Sashie's story. The samovar was the one thing that Sashie's mother, Ida, chose to take with her from Russia. The selection begins on the evening when Rache's father surprises the family with a rebuilt samovar. That night, Nana Sashie continues her story for Rache after the others have gone to bed.

"I have one last gift," said Ed.
"Oh, Ed, enough already!"
"This is actually a gift for the whole family."
"Oooooh!" Rache, Leah, and the nanas exclaimed in <u>unison</u>.

319

Comprehension Skills

Drawing Conclusions

Explain to the students that writers don't always directly supply all the information in a story. Good readers *draw conclusions* from clues in the text to make statements about the characters, things, and events in a story.

Have the students read page 319 and then ask them to draw conclusions:

- Is the family excited to receive a gift for the whole family? *(yes)*

Have students identify the clues in the text that led them to their conclusions.

Teacher Tip

There are many unfamiliar words in this selection. Help the students pronounce these words. Rache is pronounced rā´ kə.

Skills Strand

Drawing Conclusions
INTRODUCED: Unit 1, Lesson 1
REVIEWED: Unit 1, Lesson 5
Unit 2, Lesson 1
Unit 3, Lesson 4
Unit 3, Lesson 6

2 Reading and Responding

Comprehension Strategies

Modeling

2 Asking Questions *Good readers many times will find that questions occur to them naturally as they are clearing up confusion or wondering why something in the text is as it is. For example, this is strange. I wonder why the type in this part of the text had suddenly changed. In the introduction, it says that Sashie has been telling Rache about her childhood. Maybe Rache is remembering something Sashie said to her.*

Continue to encourage the students to model for one another when they use strategies or work out problems as they read.

Students may need to use context clues to clarify that the sentences in italic type are Rache's thoughts as her family's conversation is going on around her. She is remembering pieces of Sashie's story.

Word Knowledge

Yiddish, Sashie, polished

Students can use the skills they learned in the Word Knowledge section of this lesson to read these words. Remind students of this if they have difficulty reading these words.

"Just one minute while I get it." Ed went to the pantry and returned with something large and fairly tall wrapped in cloth. "It was too big to wrap in paper so I just put this cloth around it." As he set it on the table he asked, "Who wants to unwrap it?"

Rache was puzzled. There were not the usual hesitations, the if-you-don't-like-it statements.

"Rache, why don't you unwrap it?"

"Well, okay," said Rache with slight apprehension. She leaned forwards and gave a light tug. The cloth fell off. There was a sharp gusty sound as each of the women sucked in her breath in shock. Then silence. A samovar—polished and bright—stood before them. Rache heard Nana Sashie whisper something in Yiddish. The top piece—the crown, Ida's crown—flickered unquenchably in the candlelight. The good soldier was back! Rache sat stunned as conversation bubbled up around her.

"It's a samovar!"

2 *Even the babies liked a glass of tea from the samovar.*

"Ed, however did you do it?"

From my bed I could see the samovar.

"Well, the part that Rache found started me off."

"Were you here that day?"

Like a polished good soldier.

The words floated back to Rache through the din.

"So I started hunting in antique shops and got some leads from the museum—you know, just to find the other brass parts."

Its brass catching the glow of the gas lamp in the street outside.

"I'll tell you who was really incredibly helpful and who did most of the rebuilding when we got the parts was . . ."

I used to pretend it was a good soldier . . .

"Bo Andersen of Andersen's Jewelry. You know, the son, the kid . . ."

"You mean the one who's about forty?"

"Yes. Well, he just loved working on this."

"Nana Sashie?" Leah suddenly looked worried. "Ed, I hope this doesn't . . . Nana Sashie, are you all right?"

A sentry in the darkness standing watch over us.

320

There were two small pockets of loud silence in the happy din—one was Nana Sashie, whose face seemed lost in a gentle reverie, and the other was Rache, who, now over her initial astonishment, felt a confusing mixture of emotions. When she had first discovered the samovar part, Rache had been disgusted by Leah's and Nana Rose's ignorance of Sashie's Russia. But now she felt a real apprehension, as if the gulf between the two worlds had closed too quickly and the one world that she had explored with Sashie would no longer be just theirs alone. Sashie! Funny, she had never thought of her as just Sashie before. She had always been Nana Sashie. It was odd. Odder still was her father. Did he know about the meetings with Nana Sashie? Had he seen her go into Nana's room that night?

"Rache! Come back to the world of the living. Thank you."

"Oh, sorry!"

"Nana Sashie asked you a question."

"Oh! What? What, Nana?"

"Would you kindly fetch the toolbox. There are a few bolts that need tightening if we are going to use this for making tea—which we are!"

After tightening several bolts, Nana Sashie declared the samovar fit for a trial run and insisted that they bring it to her bedroom.

321

Meeting Individual Needs

Challenge

Drawing Conclusions It's likely that Nana Sashie told Rache that she used to think of the samovar as looking like a soldier. Have students draw their idea of what the samovar looks like based on the description in the text.

Comprehension Skills

Drawing Conclusions

Authors often provide hints in a text, without stating something outright. Good readers use these hints to *draw conclusions.*

■ Have the students read up to the words "Like a polished good soldier" on page 320. Ask students what the "good soldier" is. *(the samovar)*

■ What clues did the students use to draw their conclusion? *(They just received the gift of the samovar and are talking about it.)*

2 Reading and Responding

Comprehension Strategies

Prompting

3 **Summarizing** *Since Sashie is about to begin talking about the past, this is a good place for us to stop and summarize. Who would like to sum up this section?*

Student Sample

Summarizing *Ed brought in the rebuilt samovar. Nana Rose seemed a bit afraid that the samovar was dangerous, but Nana Sashie was delighted. She insisted that the samovar be placed in her room. Rache worries that she'll have to share Sashie.*

Modeling

4 **Asking Questions** *I think this part of the text is Sashie talking about her life in tsarist Russia, but what is going on? I feel as if we're coming in on the middle of this story. I think this is just where Sashie left off the last time she and Rache talked.*

Word Knowledge
flickered

Students can use the skills they learned in the Word Knowledge section of this lesson to read this word. Remind students of this if they have difficulty reading this word.

"I don't like the idea of her sleeping with that thing burning in her room," said Nana Rose to Ed and Leah.

"What do you mean? I slept with 'that thing' burning every night in my room for my first nine years!"

"Sparks could fly."

"No, it's very well designed," said Ed. "It's probably safer than our electric toaster."

"Well, I don't like the idea."

"Well, I do," Nana Sashie said bluntly.

"I thought it was supposed to be for the whole family?" Nana Rose persisted.

"It is. You can come up to my room for tea any time. It's easier for you to come upstairs than for me to come down."

That seemed to settle it; the samovar went to Nana Sashie's room. If people wanted a cup of tea, they had to go to her **3** bedroom, which consequently became quite socially active.

But that first night the samovar would belong to Nana Sashie and Rache alone. At least, that was the thought in Rache's mind as she moved across the hall carpeting to Sashie's room. It was 2:30 in the morning and Rache had not even needed the alarm to wake her for this short hike toward the long journey through time, through Nana Sashie's time, to the world that might not be strictly their preserve for much longer. She stepped into the bedroom. The polished good soldier loomed before her in the night. The street lights were lawns away in the suburbs, and yet the samovar seemed <u>lambent</u> and luminous, as if catching the reflections from a distant mirror.

"I knew you'd come tonight."

Rache jumped in surprise. The voice sounded so young.

"Nana Sashie!"

"Who else?"

322

"You're awake?"

"Yes."

"How's your stomach?"

"What about my stomach?"

"The garlic didn't upset it?"

"Of course not! Stop with the stomach already! Come sit down here beside me." She patted the covers. "Quite remarkable, isn't it? With just one piece to start with, your father did an amazing job! And now he's back, the good soldier." Nana Sashie gave Rache's hand a squeeze.

Like iron filings pulled to a magnet, Rache's and Sashie's eyes were drawn to the glow of the samovar. The old eyes flickered with new color. Time melted. A century bent. There was a young voice.

4 "We're going with him?"

A strange waxy face with dreadful eyes had melted out of the mist of the <u>cobbler's</u> alley. Sashie felt a stinging cuff on her ear as soon as she asked the question.

323

Comprehension Skills

Drawing Conclusions

Point out the following clues from the text and have students tell you the possible *conclusions* that can be *drawn* from them:

- "I knew you'd come tonight." *(Rache and Sashie don't meet every night, but this night is special.)*

- "You're awake!" *(Rache often finds Sashie asleep.)*

- "Time melted. A century bent. There was a young voice." *(Sashie began to tell more of her story.)*

Explain to the students that writers depend on readers to fill in the blanks as they read. Discuss how different a story would be if the author explained everything.

Teacher Tip Some students might want to learn more about Russia and the pogroms that took place. Suggest that they search their local library for information. Students might also try asking older members in their family or community for stories they might have heard from their parents or grandparents.

Meeting Individual Needs

Inter\/ention

Drawing Conclusions Provide the clues to lead the students to draw conclusions. Then reverse the process. Write the conclusion and ask the students to tell the clues that led to the conclusion.

Reading and Responding

Comprehension Strategies

Modeling

5 **Asking Questions** *I wonder why Sashie's mother is so horrified by Wolf. All we know about him is that he has a waxy face. That might look frightening and this seems to be late at night. But he's obviously here to help them escape.*

When we keep reading we see that he is described as unsociable and Sashie's mother thinks he's the devil. I guess people just didn't like him, but the family really needed him.

Do you have any questions about Wolf, or Sashie and her family?

Modeling

6 **Asking Questions** *I wonder what language this is that Joe has started speaking. Since it mentions Israel, I think it's Hebrew. I'm glad the author translated it for us. But it's also nice to have it written in the original language, because when we read it out loud, it sounds very much like a prayer.*

Modeling

7 **Asking Questions** *I remember the father introducing his family to Wolf, but he didn't mention any babies. Who are they? Maybe we'll find out if we keep reading. (This question is answered on page 326.)*

Teacher Tip Point out to the students that on page 324 of the *Student Anthology* they can tell by drawing conclusions that Sashie is remembering being a young girl. This answers the question posed on page 322 of the *Teacher's Edition*.

"Be quiet!" Her father's voice was sharp. He leaned forward and greeted Wolf warmly.

As Sashie saw her father's hand actually touch the other man's flesh, she felt her stomach turn, and she <u>recoiled</u> in horror. She sought her mother's hand, but Ida was like a statue, rigid, her eyes unseeing sockets. Through the fog came the <u>disembodied</u> cluckings of chickens. Sounds, even the strangest ones, took on a peculiar <u>intimacy</u> in the thickness of a fog, and Sashie shivered as she heard these.

"Wolf Levinson," said Joe. "My family—Sashie; my wife, Ida; my sister, Ghisa; and my father, Sol."

Wolf nodded and touched his hand to his hat in his first social gesture in twenty-five years.

"We have no time to waste, Joe." Sashie felt her mother <u>wince</u> at hearing her husband's name spoken by this man. "So if you will follow me, the wagon's right here. I have arranged the coops so you can get in and lie flat. Then I'm afraid after you're settled I must put them back to cover you."

"Yes. Yes, Wolf, we understand," said Joe.

"Well then, this way and we can lay out the bedclothes to make it more comfortable." There was a bustling as bundles were taken off backs and rearranged in the wagon. Sashie was busy untying her own, but she suddenly was aware of a stony, <u>inexorable</u> stillness directly behind her. It was as if Ida were not even breathing. Joe put down his toolbox and moved quickly to

324

Teacher Tip Ghisa is pronounced gē′ sə. She′ma y′Isoreal is pronounced shə mä′ yis ro′ āl. Adonai is pronounced ä dō nī. Aloujanou is pronounced elō hä′nōō. Echod is pronounced e hod′.

her side. He spoke gently. "Come on now, Ida." He began to untie her bundle quickly. "It's going to be all right."

(5) "The chickens are one thing, but the devil is something else!"

"Don't be silly, Ida." But Ida did not answer.

Crawling down a temporary center aisle Wolf had made, Sashie was helping Ghisa spread the bedclothes on the floor of the wagon. As long as she kept helping Ghisa she did not have to look at or really think about the strange face with the awful eyes. But now there was trouble. She could sense it. Ida was not moving and Joe was desperate. Sashie peeked around a coop. Her mother's <u>bedrock</u> <u>stance</u> shocked her. She felt the real possibility that the escape might never begin, that they were doomed to stand here until morning, when they would be discovered. And then what? She had absolutely no idea how her father could ever move her mother onto the wagon. It would take a miracle. Sashie suddenly thought of Moses standing by the Red Sea before it parted. Next to Ida, the Red Sea was a puddle to jump. Sashie had never seen anything as unmovable as Ida. Partially hidden by the coop, Sashie listened to the drama taking place between her parents.

"Ida, you must!" pleaded Joe.

"Who is this man?"

"Ida, he is our only chance."

"What hell has he been to?"

"Ida!" Joe swallowed hard and brought his face close to hers. "For the love of our children, get in that wagon!" What in the world was he going to do, Sashie wondered. Carry her?

(6) "Ida, say this with me." And Joe began a soft chant: *"She'ma Y'Isoreal! Adonai Aloujanou! Adonai Echod!* Hear, O Israel! The Lord our God! The Lord is One!"

Sashie's eyes widened as she saw her mother lean on her father's arm and begin to move. As she took these first steps on the longest journey, Sashie could hear her mother whispering softly the words of the *Shema*, the Jewish statement of faith.

The blankets had been spread. Ida and Sashie stretched out in **(7)** the most forward part of the wagon, each with a baby tucked in at her side. The space left between them was for Joe. At their toes

325

Comprehension Skills

Author's Point of View

Ask the students what they already know about *author's point of view*. If necessary, explain to the students that the *author's point of view* is how an author chooses to tell a story. In a *first-person narrative*, the story is told through the eyes of a character in the story. In a *third-person narrative*, the story is told by a character outside of the story. Third-person narratives use the pronouns *he*, *she*, and *they*. For example:

■ "*She* had absolutely no idea how *her* father could ever move *her* mother onto the wagon."

■ "*Sashie's* eyes widened as *she* saw *her* mother lean on *her* father's arm and begin to move."

Remind the students that these pronouns show that the author is writing in the third person. However, even in third-person narratives, one character's point of view can be dominant. Discuss from whose point of view the author is mostly writing.

Skills Strand

Author's Point of View

INTRODUCED: Unit 1, Lesson 3

REVIEWED: Unit 1, Lesson 5

Unit 1, Lesson 6

Unit 3, Lesson 1

Unit 3, Lesson 6

2 Reading and Responding

Comprehension Strategies

Modeling

8 Answering Questions *Well, this answers our question about the babies. One is named Louie, and the other one is Cecile. They must be Sashie's little brother and sister.*

Modeling

9 Asking Questions *I'm still a little confused about what is happening. Where is Sashie's family going, and why are they going in a chicken wagon? Let's go back to the introduction and reread it. It says that Jewish people were subjected to abuse and persecution in tsarist Russia, and that Sashie and her family escaped. This must be the start of their escape.*

> ### Word Knowledge
> *clacking, chickens*
>
> Students can use the skills they learned in the Word Knowledge section of this lesson to read these words. Remind students of this if they have difficulty reading these words.

were the tops of Ghisa's and Zayde Sol's heads, who were stretched out from the midsection of the wagon to the back end. Ida and Sashie settled in as best they could. With a small pillow under their heads, they had about twelve or fifteen inches clearance between their faces and the chicken coops. This seemed much more <u>ample</u> than Sashie had imagined. There was plenty of room to place a tier of the samovar over her face as a shield.

"This isn't bad, Mama," said Sashie, trying on the samovar face mask. "Here, try it." Sashie turned toward her mother to hand her the brass piece.

"No, I want to see," Ida said <u>emphatically</u>.

"So much for the samovar!" muttered Ghisa, whose voice floated up from Sashie's feet. There was no way that Sashie could see Ghisa's or Zayde Sol's face, and she found that she missed the smirk that must have punctuated her aunt's remark.
8 She could just see her mother's face by turning her head to the side, and she could see Louie's chubby face, tucked in under her own arm and sleeping for now. Cecile's face was mostly buried under her mother's blouse, but Sashie listened hard and through the clucking gale of the chickens above could hear the deep, throaty sucking noises of the infant as she nursed, a sound she had heard a thousand times but which thrilled her in a new way. Her father had arranged himself between Ida and Sashie. His head was a little forward of theirs, so he did not block their view of each other, and in order to see Joe, Ida and

326

Teacher Tip Zayde is pronounced zāˊ də.
Sashela is pronounced
sä shāˊ lä.

Sashie needed only to crane their necks and look up a bit. He quickly put a hand on each of their shoulders.

"Well, is everything as comfortable as possible here? You know, you don't need to be on your backs; you can turn over on your stomachs. Everyone all right?" Joe asked. "Ida?"

"All right." She replied flatly.

"Sashie?"

"Fine, Papa."

"Ghisa?"

"Lovely!" Darn, Sashie thought. She wished she could see Ghisa's face.

"Papa?" Joe asked.

There was a slight pause, then, "I'm alive?"

"All ready?" Wolf's face loomed at the end of the aisle.

"All set," Joe answered. His voice seemed tinged with excitement that bordered more on joy than fear.

"All right, I'll put on the last coops."

9 There was a great clatter and clacking as Joe dropped the first coop into the center aisle where it rested on the edges of the flanking coops. A little chunk of white night disappeared, and Sashie felt her heart beat faster. More clatter and clucks, and another piece of the night vanished. One by one the coops were dropped, and piece by piece the world above Sashie and her family was eaten up. The clucking of chickens choked the air around her, and Sashie found herself gulping for breath. Terrified of inhaling one of the white feathers that tumbled crazily through the air, she tried to screen her mouth with her scarf, but then it was harder to breathe.

"Sashie!" Her father's voice came through strong and gentle. "Look at me, Sashela." She craned her neck towards her father. "You breathe like me now. Do just what I do. First in through the nose, not too deep, then out through the mouth blowing softly. Slowly. Take your time, Sashela. There's plenty of air. And you think of nice things, like the smell of bread baking and kites flying and the first leaves of May and lighting Hanukkah candles."

327

Comprehension Skills

Author's Point of View

Remind the students that writers use the point of view of their characters to make stories interesting and exciting for the reader.

Have students reread pages 326–327. Point out that the author is confining the story to Sashie's point of view. While she isn't telling the story, the things she sees, hears, and feels are what is described. This puts the reader into the wagon with Sashie as she escapes.

Have the students discuss how the story might be told differently, if the author told it through another character's eyes.

Discuss why the author chose to write a third-person narrative rather than a first-person narrative. How would the story be different if it had been told in the first person?

Teacher Tip Remind students to choose a point of view for their heritage albums.

Meeting Individual Needs

Intervention

Author's Point of View Give the students more practice with author's point of view. Have them look through other selections in the anthology and determine the author's point of view.

2 Reading and Responding

Comprehension Strategies

Modeling

10 Asking Questions *Why is the wagon stopping? Since Sashie and her family are hiding in the bottom of the wagon, they must not be able to leave the city freely. What if the guards search the cart? What will happen? Will Wolf be able to get them past without getting searched? We'll have to keep reading.*

Modeling

11 Answering Questions *Whew! I thought that Sashie and her family were really in trouble there for a minute! I'm glad they weren't discovered.*

Word Knowledge

There are many multisyllabic words in this selection. Be sure students are using the skills they learned in the Word Knowledge section of this lesson.

Teacher Tip Vaskeyevka is pronounced väs ke yev´ kä.
Zolodievka is pronounced zō lō dyev´ kä .

"Harruh!" They heard Wolf grunt and slap the reins on the horse's back. The wagon groaned and lurched forwards, the wheels creaking, and they were on their way. Sashie thought she could count every cobblestone as the wagon rolled down the cobbler's alley. But she kept breathing just as her father had told her to and tried to think of nice things——things that now seemed rare and wondrous, like an open window on a starry summer night, a raindrop's path on glass, April branches with leaves curled tight as babies' fists.

They must be on Vaskeyevka Street. She would try and guess their route as they went. But she certainly could not see, and at this hour there were no sounds except the blizzard of cluckings that raged inches above them. She wondered if they would go by the park. And then after the park, what? She had never gone beyond the park. The Alexandra Gate of the park was the farthest perimeter of her life. Some chicken droppings splattered on her cheek, but just as disgust welled up inside Sashie a new noise split the cluckings——iron spikes hitting stone. The world above was laced with the rhythmic strikes.

10 "Whoa! Whoa!" She felt the wagon stop. Ghisa slid forwards a bit, her head pressing on Sashie's feet, and Sashie's head pressed against her father's arm. Louie's eyes flew open. Sashie opened her eyes as wide as she could and, staring directly into the little boy's, commanded his silence with an unblinking and fierce gaze that was intended to freeze his tongue. Quickly she reached up her sleeve for a sugar stick and popped it into his mouth. It worked, this time. Outside she could hear Wolf conversing in Russian with some men. The street was being repaired and impassable for a four-wheel vehicle. They must turn around and take Zolodievka Street. There followed

328

a great deal of jangling and jolting shot through with Wolf's grunts and barks at the horse. Sashie felt the wagon roll backwards a few feet, then forwards. There were more barks. From the noise Sashie thought that Wolf must be off the wagon and guiding the horse around by pushing and pulling on the harness. Louie cried out once, but the sound was drowned by the tumult of the horse whinnying in protest, chickens clucking, harness jangling, wheels creaking, not to mention the string of curses and barks emanating from Wolf.

"Old man!" said one of the street workers jovially. "Watch your tongue. You know there are not just roosters aboard your wagon. I see some hens!"

The swirl of feathers seemed to freeze in the air above Sashie. She felt Ghisa grab her foot and her father's hand bite into her shoulder.

"Just joking!" She heard the man protest innocently. "Can't you take a joke, old man?"

Sashie had not heard Wolf say anything to the street worker, but she had a sense that Wolf need not say much to fill another with dread. The wagon was finally turned around. The street worker stood just by Sashie's side of the wagon now. With only the boards between them, she could hear him mutter nervously to the other, "Queer eyes!" Sashie could feel Wolf climbing into the driver's seat.

11 "Harruh!" he yelled. The wagon lurched forwards and clattered out of the street.

If they had to take Zolodievka Street instead of this one, it must be fairly near, and if it were fairly near, reasoned Sashie, the Alexandra Gate of the park was not that far away. Approaching the edge of her known world, Sashie felt a ripple of excitement run through her body. She remembered suddenly a book her father had shown her that had a picture of a map from long long ago, from before Columbus had discovered the new world. The map showed a world with the continents and oceans known in the early fifteenth century. At a certain

329

Drawing Conclusions

Tell students that Sashie must draw conclusions herself, as she listens to what is happening outside of her hiding space. Direct the students to the following examples. Then have them find other examples.

- "From the noise, Sashie thought that Wolf must be off the wagon and guiding the horse around by pushing and pulling on the harness."

- "Sashie had not heard Wolf say anything to the street worker, but she had a sense that Wolf need not say much to fill another with dread."

Teacher Tip Students may remember that in "The West Side," Juan was sent to New York from Puerto Rico so that he might have a better life. Paw-Paw, the grandmother in "Chinatown," probably left her homeland for similar reasons. In the same way, Sashie's family hopes to find a better life somewhere outside of Russia.

Reading and Responding

Comprehension Strategies

Modeling

12 Making Connections *Good readers make connections between what they are reading and what they already know from experience or previous reading. Sometimes they use these connections to help them relate to a character in the text. For example, we've been reading so much about Sashie and what her family had to go through. It's hard to imagine having to suffer so much. How would you react to hiding under chicken coops? I don't know if I could be as brave as Sashie. I can't wait to see if they make it out safely.*

Can you imagine what it would be like to have to hide under chicken coops?

Tsar is pronounced zär. Tsarina is pronounced zä rē´nä. Nikolayev is pronounced nē kō lä´ yev.

Word Knowledge

shoulder, bucket, shutters

Students can use the skills they learned in the Word Knowledge section of this lesson to read these words. Remind students of this if they have difficulty reading these words.

---

distance from the land, sea serpents were drawn riding through the crests of waves, with the legend HERE BEGINNETH THE REGION OF THE DRAGONS. Except, thought Sashie, in Russia the dragons live everywhere, and she and her family were supposed to be escaping from them to the tsarless region of what angels? She was not sure. Although she herself had not dealt directly with the dragons, Sashie never once doubted their existence. One did not have to have tea with the tsar and tsarina to have his life sabotaged by them, or their ministers, or the notorious Black Hundreds, who were nothing but street thugs glorified by the tsar and given a license to kill Jews. She remembered her father's stories of the army and she had the feeling that that was not the half of it. And she would never forget the night the news came of her grandparents. She had been only three years old at the time, but she would never forget it—the hollow, stunned voice of her mother repeating over and over, "Both of them?" No, Sashie believed in these dragons, and something deep, deep inside told her that the dragon's fire had scorched Wolf. His eyes were queer because he had looked straight down the fiery throat. She wondered what it was he had seen. She would probably never know, Sashie thought, and she could certainly never ask.

Louie had finished his sugar stick and was demanding more. Sashie felt the wagon turn another corner. They must be near the Alexandra Gate. Had Columbus been forced to begin the region of the dragons with a baby wailing for more and twisting his nose, as Louie was now twisting Sashie's? "Hush, hush!" commanded everyone, but Louie would not be quiet.

"Give him another one!" hissed Ghisa from Sashie's feet. Sashie groped up her sleeve for another sugar stick. "Here," she huffed, "what do I care if you grow up to have rotten teeth!"

Ida prayed a strange prayer—that her baby boy would grow old enough to have rotten teeth. And Joe, buoyed by Sashie's relentless optimism, smiled quietly to himself and patted his daughter on the shoulder.

330

Meeting Individual Needs

ESL

Making Connections Give English-language learners an opportunity to relate what they know. Call on volunteers to tell what they know about their country of origin.

Intervention

Making Connections Have the students make connections between what they are reading and what they know. Have them share their impressions and feelings as they read.

Sashie had fifteen sugar sticks. At this rate, she calculated, they would not last the day. "We might need the b-o-t-t-l-e." Ida and Joe weren't overjoyed at the prospect of drugging babies, but such a possibility had had to be planned for on this trip and a bottle of milk with a light sleeping <u>draught</u> had been prepared. Just then Sashie heard a torrent of water from a slop bucket being thrown out a high window. The chickens on the left side of the wagon forward of her sent up a loud cackle. They must have caught some of it, and then under the layer of cackles was another noise—a steamy hiss of curses from Ghisa. There seemed to be more street noises now—shutters being opened, dogs barking, more wheels creaking, fragments of early morning talk drifting out of doorways as shopkeepers readied for trade. But where were they? It sounded nothing like the noises one would hear around the Alexandra Gate. There were not any buildings near the gate from whose windows slop buckets would be emptied. They must be beyond the gate and near the outskirts of Nikolayev, Sashie thought. As if to answer her question, there was suddenly a new sound and a new motion as the wheels of the wagon rolled from cobblestones to wood. The bass tones of the wooden planks rumbled beneath the wheels and the rush of coursing spring waters muted the <u>manic</u> cluckings. Even Louie, who had managed to sit up, stopped sucking on his sugar stick.

"What dat?" the baby demanded softly.

331

Comprehension Skills

Author's Point of View

Ask students for the meaning of author's point of view and how to determine which point of view an author is using—first or third person.

Have the students read the last paragraph on page 329, which continues on page 330. Explain that the author is describing the conditions for Jewish people in Russia during this time period. She is describing it from the point of view of a young girl, however, who doesn't completely understand all that is going on, or why.

Have the students discuss how this description might be different if the author had used another character's point of view, such as Sashie's father's. What kind of information does Sashie's father have that Sashie does not?

Meeting Individual Needs

Challenge

Author's Point of View Challenge the students to rewrite passages of their choice either from the first-person point of view or through the eyes of another narrator. Have them share their passages.

2 Reading and Responding

Comprehension Strategies

Prompting

13 Asking Questions *Uh-oh. This sounds even worse than the first time the wagon stopped. These aren't street workers. These are real soldiers, probably the very people Sashie and her family are trying to avoid. The story is getting pretty exciting. Do any of you have questions going through your mind right now? What are they?*

Student Sample

Asking Questions *What is going to happen? This seems like a really dangerous situation. I hope they will get out of it soon.*

Have students visualize the scene where the wagon is stopped for the second time. Ask them to imagine what things they would see, hear, smell, and feel if they were in the wagon with Sashie.

Word Knowledge

sucking, kicking

Students can use the skills they learned in the Word Knowledge section of this lesson to read these words. Remind students of this if they have difficulty reading these words.

"It's the river." Sashie whispered. "We're leaving Nikolayev now."

"Oh."

"Be a good boy, Louie!" Sashie patted his knee. Louie was now starting to crawl around, exploring under the chicken coops. It seemed to keep him quiet and drain off some of his energy, so nobody tried to stop him. There wasn't far he could go.

As the wagon moved from the bridge to the dirt road, the clucks and cackles rolled up once more in a <u>suffocating</u> swarm. Oh, to hear water again! thought Sashie. But the liquid <u>resonance</u> of the flowing river was soon a memory <u>obliterated</u> by the cackles that seemed to bristle right inside Sashie's brain. She would go mad if she listened to the chickens another minute! She would think of a song. But she could not think of one. She would try to hear the road under the wheels. But she could not hear it. The road did, however, feel different from the cobblestone streets. It was softer. The speed seemed slower—not just slower, but thicker, Sashie thought. How can motion feel thick? It was not a bad feeling. And the noise, it wasn't noise. She caught herself. How can I hear noise, Sashie thought, above the cackles? But she did. And it was different. It wasn't noise that was reflected from hard surfaces like cobblestones, wood, and granite. It came from a deep quiet center. They were soft and sucking sounds; the sound of things being absorbed, soaked up. It's mud sounds, thought Sashie, ecstatically. "I am listening to spring mud." It was like beautiful music to Sashie.

Just above the mud but not as high as the wagon top she heard another sound. It was the whispering of a south wind blowing through winter grass. Sashie had never in her life been outside the city. She had never known the sound of the vast quietness of the country, which absorbed noise to make new sound. She lay perfectly still, listening as the country sounds bloomed around her like huge flowers.

Through the minutes and in and out of hours they slept, whispered, ate a hunk of bread or piece of potato. The babies were doing tolerably well and the sleeping draught had not yet

332

Meeting Individual Needs

Intervention

Asking Questions Students should keep a chart of all their questions and the corresponding answers to make sure that they don't have any unanswered questions when the story is finished.

been needed. A huge baked potato kept Louie busy for twenty minutes. A medley of whispered nursery rhymes delivered by Sashie and her father averted a near tantrum.

Sashie had just finished drawing tiny faces on both her thumb and index finger for a puppet finger show to entertain Louie when she felt Wolf slow the horse.

"Whoa!" he said.

The horse and the wagon stopped. Just as Wolf had begun to speak to the horse, Sashie had heard distant rapid beats, like small explosions in the earth.

"Trouble!" Wolf's voice was tight with fear. "Everybody must be quiet! It's soldiers." He paused, and Sashie thought she could hear the breath catch in his throat. "My God, it's an imperial regiment!"

Then there was a timpani of cold metal as sabers and spurs jangled in the air. Sashie had managed to grab Louie and press him flat on the floor. Her father lay his leg over the little boy's kicking ones and Sashie clapped her hand over his mouth.

"Hail! In the name of their imperial majesties, the Tsar Nicholas and the Tsarina Alexandra!"

Wolf mumbled something conciliatory, but Sashie could not hear the exact words, for the only noise was that of metal clanging, leather squeaking, hooves striking the ground, animals panting, and occasional coughs. The chickens' clucking was eclipsed by the noises that accompanied the tsar's regiment of twenty on an exercise in the countryside. And beneath the chicken coops the human cargo lay in frozen terror.

"You carry chickens, I see . . ." The commander spoke. "And where are you bound for?"

333

Comprehension Skills

Author's Point of View

Sometimes a story is told in a third-person point of view, but through the eyes of one character.

Have students read pages 332–333. Point out to students that the author is describing the journey in terms of Sashie's thoughts and feelings. Ask them to discuss whether or not a description of the journey would be as interesting if it were being described from "outside" the wagon.

Have them describe the scene from outside the wagon. Be sure the students understand that an "outside" narrator doesn't know much about thoughts and feelings.

Reading and Responding

Comprehension Strategies

Prompting

⑭ **Asking Questions** *Now what is happening? Are they hurting Wolf? Can he stop the soldiers from finding Sashie and her family? I hope so. What questions do you have? (This question is answered on page 336.)*

Modeling

⑮ **Asking Questions** *What are "pogroms?" Maybe I'll look in a book of Russian history, or in the encyclopedia to get a better understanding.*

Teacher Tip Borisov is pronounced bō rē´ sôv. Zhidi is pronounced zhē´ dē. Kosher is pronounced kō´ shər. Kliminsky is pronounced klē min´ skē. Kasha is pronounced kä´ shä.

Teacher Tip To help students visualize and relate to the selection, have them look up "pogrom" in an encyclopedia. Give students an opportunity to discuss the context of this selection.

"Oh, just to Borisov to deliver them for my boss to a client."

"How generous of your boss. I am sure he would not begrudge a few chickens for the tsar's regiment, and the client will never miss them."

"Lieutenant, if you please, two or three coops." Sashie heard a man jump from a horse.

⑭ "Aaaaagggg!" screamed Wolf. "Hold it!"

⑮ " 'Hold it!' You old Zhidi!" The last word hung in the air like a dagger dripping blood. "Zhidi," the abusive word for "Jew," had become quite popular with the latest wave of <u>pogroms</u>. Sashie trembled all over. She pressed her hand harder on Louie's mouth.

The commander spoke slowly. "You deny one of the tsar's most loyal and favored regiments a few chickens? To deny the tsar's officers is to deny the tsar, and to deny the tsar is to deny God!" the voice thundered.

"No! No! I do not deny anything to you, your . . . your excellency. It's just that the coops are in bad repair and if you carry them with you they are bound to come apart and the chickens escape. Better you take the chickens slaughtered."

"Fine. Lieutenant, skewer a few chickens then, if you will."

There was a bright flash and Sashie's breath suddenly locked in her throat. Her eyes widened in terror as she saw the tip of a thin silver blade slice through the mesh and come within three inches of her face. Time stopped as her eyes focused on the glinting sliver of death that played above her. She could even see the scarlet sleeve of the officer's jacket. The three gold buttons blazed through a small flurry of white feathers, and the black decorative braid at the cuff was like four coiled snakes ready to strike. The silvery death dance went on raging above her face and throat. The moist still air from her half-open mouth fogged the blade tip.

"Here! I find you a fat one. Those are all skinny." The blade stilled. The silver death retreated through the slashed mesh to the world above, and Sashie fainted.

A few seconds later she came to and heard Wolf talking rapidly.

334

"Those are the scrawny ones. Good breeders, but no good eating. Now over here we have your scratchers."

"Scratchers?" asked the commander.

"Yeah, scratchers. They have to scratch for their food. Makes 'em tough. Stringy. They're big chickens, mind you. Weighty, but quite tough. No flavor. But here. Here in the middle we have our plumpsters—we call them plumpsters." Wolf prattled on faster than a runaway cart down Kliminsky Street on the science and technology of poultry. "With the plumpsters you get more meat per cubic centimeter than any other kind of chicken. Succulent! Juicy! You see, the plumpsters are not required to scratch for their food. And what food it is! Whole-grain bread soaked in gravy, pumpkin seeds, kasha. We Zhidi should only eat like that! The plumpsters' main job in life is eating, with an occasional stroll in a very small area. A chicken, one might say, truly fit for a tsar. Please sire, your sword. I will fetch you the plumpest of the plumpsters. Yes, a rare bird indeed!"

Sashie felt the wagon shake as Wolf pulled himself up on the side. "Kosher is quick!" She heard Wolf mutter to himself in Yiddish. In less than three minutes he had slaughtered

335

Drawing Conclusions

Have the students read pages 334–335, paying particular attention to what Wolf is doing and saying. Prompt them to draw conclusions about his actions by asking:

- What conclusion can you draw about Wolf's screaming? *(He wants to keep the lieutenant from lifting off the coops and finding the people in the wagon.)*

- Why does he talk so much about the chickens? *(to distract the soldiers)*

- Why does he call himself a "Zhidi"? *(Answers may vary. Some students may answer to seem weak and harmless to the soldiers.)*

Teacher Tip

Be sure the students back up their conclusions with information from the text.

Reading and Responding

Comprehension Strategies

Modeling

16 **Answering Questions** *Whew! I was scared there for a long time. The soldiers seemed very close to finding Sashie and her family. Wolf did some pretty quick thinking to keep them all safe.*

Whenever possible, encourage students to generate and direct discussion, and to take over the process of instruction.

Word Knowledge

There are many multisyllabic words in this selection. Be sure students are using the skills they learned in the Word Knowledge section of this lesson.

---

ten chickens. Blood dripped down the center aisle onto the bedclothes.

"Your chickens, your excellency. May you and your officers eat them in good health!"

"Your client will never miss them," came the reply.

As the spurs dug into flanks, whinnies mixed with leathery squeaks and metallic janglings filled the air. The command finally came—"Forward!"—and then the rapid explosive noises of eighty hooves striking the earth as they moved off with their imperial load.

16 Zhidi, Sashie thought, when at last she could think again. Wolf called himself a Zhidi. How very strange that he could do this—abuse himself with this foul word even though it was done to <u>ingratiate</u> himself with the commander. For the first hours after the encounter with the regiment, Sashie lay in a state of total exhaustion. It was as if her nerves, her brain, and each muscle in her body had used every bit of energy available. Gradually, however, she began to realize that she was alive. It was a miracle. It was as if she were a newborn baby with an older mind that could appreciate the wonder of its own birth— of being born a whole, complete human being. She tingled all over with the sheer excitement of her own living body. She touched her throat and face. She traced the gullies and curves of her ears. She pressed hard through all the layers of clothing and felt a rib. She took a joyous inventory of her body. Then after the miracle of survival was confirmed, she thought of Wolf and the word he had used in reference to himself. How absolutely confounding and unfathomable it was. She could not imagine ever calling herself by this horrible name, no matter what the danger was.

336

Sashie had stared unblinkingly as Death sliced the air just inches from her face and throat. She was sure Wolf had seen something worse, but what was it? The haunted man contained a death riddle. Sashie had been brought to the edge, but Wolf in some way had crossed over.

The fog had long ago burned off and slants of sunlight had pierced through the mesh and feather storm into the netherworld of the coops. But now the sun was at too low an angle to light the wagon, and Sashie felt a twilight chill. If she could only move more, she would feel warmer. Louie was warm as a puppy from crawling around under the coops, and though he was now sleeping, his short little body could curl up into a nice ball perfect for conserving energy. Sashie tucked him in closer to her own body to steal a little heat. Soon she drifted in and out of a troubled sleep that jolted and lurched and flashed with silver blades dripping blood. Then everything stopped and she woke up into a night-still world with her own hand fast at her throat.

"All right!" Wolf shouted. She felt him jump down from the driver's seat. "We're here."

"My God!"

"Thank God!"

"Am I dead or alive?"

"Or a chicken!"

"It's all right, Ida, we're here!"

"Oh, Joe!"

"Hang on, folks. I'll get the coops off in half a second." Sashie felt Wolf climb on the back end of the wagon. She heard the clatter of the first coop being removed.

"Ah!" exclaimed Ghisa with wonder as she saw the first piece of the world above. Another two coops were removed and

337

Comprehension Skills

Author's Point of View

Explain that because the story of the journey is being told through Sashie's point of view, the reader must filter everything through Sashie's thoughts and feelings.

Have the students read page 336. Point out that they get to share with Sashie the joy of being alive after going through such a dangerous experience.

Point out, too, the thoughts and feelings Sashie has about Wolf. Have the students discuss Sashie's attitude towards Wolf and whether or not they share her feelings.

2 Reading and Responding

Comprehension Strategies

Prompting

17 Summarizing *Now that we have finished reading this selection, how would we summarize what happened in Sashie's story?*

Student Sample

Summarizing *Sashie and her family hid in the bottom of a chicken wagon to escape from Russia. They had to stop once before they left the city, but it was outside that they really got into danger. The imperial regiment stopped the wagon and demanded chickens. Luckily, the family wasn't found, and Sashie realized how wonderful it was to be alive.*

Discussing Strategy Use

After they have read the selection, have students share any problems they encountered and tell what strategies they used to solve them. Then, have them answer the following questions. If they answer "no" to any of the questions, have them reread part of the selection to find the answer.

- Did they ask questions and check later to see if their questions were answered?

- Did they stop to clarify words, phrases, and ideas that they didn't understand?

- Did they summarize in order to help them understand what they've read?

Make sure that students explain how using the strategies helped them understand the selection better and how they read effectively to find answers to the questions they asked as they set purposes.

Sashie heard Zayde Sol recite a *broche*, a prayer, upon seeing the evening again. Then another coop was removed and a square of night sky reappeared, black velvet chinked with stars. Piece by piece the sky came back and the wind, with the smell of winter grass and earth, blew across Sashie's face.

Each person had to be helped off the wagon by Wolf and, except for Louie, walked around a few feet by him until their legs and back regained their strength. Sashie needed Wolf's arm only for a couple of steps. Almost immediately she was off on her own trying out her new legs. First she tried walking a few meters, but the night was so warm, the air so gentle, and the field so vast that Sashie felt she must dance, leap, fly through this startling country. Under the starry dome of the Russian night Sashie whirled and jumped. Her head thrown back, she watched the stars spin and smelled the thawing earth and listened to the wind songs in the grass.

Ghisa too was soon running and skipping in jerky little circles around a moonlit tree stump. The babies squealed and Ida and Joe said soft prayers of thanksgiving and laughed gently with each other in the night. And Zayde Sol said more *broches*—*broches* for seeing stars again, *broches* for seeing the moon, *broches* for seeing a baby walk, and *broches* for seeing a **17** granddaughter dance.

338

Teacher Tip Broche is pronounced brō´ kə.

Teacher Tip Reread the selection with students who had difficulty understanding it. Continue modeling and prompting the use of strategies and skills as you reread.

339

Comprehension Skills

Discussing the Selection

Following reading, engage the students in a discussion of the selection. Using the *handing-off process* will help the students to take responsibility for the discussion. In addition to the following question, have them revisit any questions asked when they set purposes before the reading.

- What is Rache learning about her heritage from Nana Sashie in these stories? *(that her family had to flee Russia during the pogroms)*

- What might have happened to the family if they hadn't been able to escape? *(They might have been imprisoned or killed.)*

- Why did Wolf risk his life to help the family? *(Answers may vary. Students might suggest that he was paid to help them, or that he was a friend of the father's.)*

- How has this selection connected with your knowledge of the unit theme? *(Answers will vary—students should compare/contrast examples of heritage from this selection with their own experiences or past reading and use these connections to make a general statement about the unit theme.)*

During this time, have the students return to the clues and problems that they noted on the transparency before reading. Let the students decide which items deserve further discussion.

When handing off is in place, the teacher's main roles are to occasionally remind students to hand off and to monitor the discussion to ensure that everyone gets a chance to contribute.

Teacher Tip Invite students to discuss artifacts or treasured possessions that are important to their friends or family members. Encourage them to use what they've learned in their unit activities.

Assessment

✓ **Formal** To assess students' reading comprehension, have them complete *Comprehension and Writing Assessment,* pages 65-66.

② Reading and Responding

Meet the Author

After the students read the information about Kathryn Lasky, discuss the following questions with them.

Kathryn Lasky has received a number of awards and honors for "The Night Journey." Why do you think this is? *(Possible answer: Not only was her book good to read, but it also teaches important information about the heritage of Jewish people.)*

Why do you think it might be especially important to Kathryn Lasky to have received awards from libraries? *(Possible answer: Libraries are important centers for learning. For this reason, it shows that the book is not only well-written, it also has important educational value.)*

Meet the Illustrator

After the students read the information about Trina Schart Hyman, discuss the following question with them.

What are some ways Trina Schart Hyman's illustrations might tell you about who she is and what she cares about? *(Possible answer: The people in her illustrations are very active and expressive, which may show that she is interested in the things people do and the way they feel.)*

The Night Journey

Meet the Author

Kathryn Lasky says she has always been a "compulsive story maker" and today writes books for children, teenagers, and adults. She enjoys being her own boss, setting her own hours, and being able to wear anything she wants to work.

Her book *The Night Journey* won the Association of Jewish Libraries Sydney Taylor Book Award and was named a Notable Book by the American Library Association.

Other works by Lasky include *Sugaring Time, The Weaver's Gift, Puppeteer, Beyond the Divide, Prank,* and *Pageant.*

Meet the Illustrator

Trina Schart Hyman started drawing at a very young age but attended five art schools and rode her bike 3,000 miles through the Netherlands and England before she started taking her art portfolio to publishers. They rejected her work for three years, but today she is a Caldecott Award-winning artist for children's books.

Hyman says her illustrations are full of her friends, family, and neighbors. In *Snow White,* some of the dwarfs are people she knows!

340

Teacher Tip Reinforce student commentary only when absolutely necessary (for example, when a student who has been especially reticent offers a comment and no reinforcement is coming from other students.)

Theme Connections

Think About It

With a small group of students, discuss the following questions.

- How did Nana Sashie feel about the samovar? Why?
- Why did Nana Sashie get to keep the samovar in her room?
- Why did Rache visit Nana Sashie's room in the middle of the night, just after they got the samovar?
- Why did Rache visit Nana Sashie's room on other nights as well?
- Why did Rache want to hear Nana Sashie's stories?

Record Ideas

What have you learned about heritage from this story? What do you want to learn about your own heritage? Write your thoughts in your Writing Journal.

Draw a Family Tree

To help you remember the characters in "The Night Journey," and the generations to which they belong, make a family tree. Whose names should go on the roots? Whose names should be written on the biggest branches? Whose names should be written on the smaller branches?

341

Theme Connections

Think About It

- Have students connect this selection to "Chinatown" by discussing how they can compare and contrast the importance of the samovar to the value Paw-Paw placed on her owl charm and statues. Then, have students recall objects that are important to them, their friends, and their family members. What makes these objects important?

- Have students discuss reasons why they agree or disagree that it is common for people of different cultures to have objects that symbolize their heritage.

Record Ideas

Challenge students to think of ways they might pursue finding out more about their own heritage and include them in their journals.

Draw a Family Tree

Encourage students to consult with each other, sharing their work. Post the family trees on the Concept/Question Board.

 **Teacher Tip** Encourage students to discuss the symbolism used in this selection. Ask them to think about symbols that are important in their own lives, and in those of family and friends.

2 Responding

⟡Exploring the Theme

Research

As students continue their explorations, have them use the **Research** CD-ROM Program to help organize and share their findings.

> **Teacher Tip**
> If you created a semantic map on the Concept/Question Board of key words related to the unit theme, Heritage, have students find words from other resources, their projects, and family discussions and add them to the appropriate category on the map.

Selection Vocabulary

Have students write in their Writing Journals the definitions for words discussed before the reading of the selection and any other interesting words they clarified while reading. Students should be encouraged to refer to these words throughout the unit as they work on student and writing projects. The words from this selection are:

tantrum	**ingratiate**	**imperial**
regiment	**kosher**	

Reading/Writing Connections

Draw students' attention to how the author created suspense. Explain that she offered vivid descriptions of sights and sounds, and that tension was not resolved quickly, but moments seemed to last forever. Have students review their Exploration Activities and consider how they might make the stories more suspenseful.

Home Connection

The class has just finished reading "The Night Journey," an adventure story about a Jewish family's heroic escape from their Russian persecutors. An informal letter on "The Night Journey," in both English and Spanish, can be found in the **Home Connection** guide.

"The Night Journey"

A message from _____

Our class has just finished reading *The Night Journey*. In this story Rache's grandmother tells her about the terrible risks her family took to leave Russia and come to America. Many people who came to America suffered hardships on their journeys. Their stories are an important part of their heritage.

Share with your child stories of a friend's or your family's journey to America. How long have they been in America? What generation came here? From where did they come? Was their journey easy or difficult? What was life in a new country like for them? If your family is Native American, tell your child about your family's journey to the place where you now live.

Have your child write a paragraph summarizing the story of your family's or friend's journey, and encourage her or him to bring it to school to share with the class.

Unit 3/Heritage   45

Home Connection p. 45

Supporting Student Explorations

Students should be finishing their work on the unit activity. You may want to do the following:

Individual Have the students prepare final drafts of their stories. Offer assistance with editing and suggestions about where illustrations would enhance the text.

Tell the students to decide how to organize their heritage albums, then prepare tables of contents. Remind them to create title pages as well and to include their autobiographical sketches. Suggest that the students consider making copies of their work to give as gifts to family members or friends. They should make copies before binding their books.

Individual Have the students write thank-you letters to family members, friends, and others who helped them with their unit activity.

Suggest that students post on the Concept/Question Board brief descriptions of books, magazine articles, computer Websites, or other sources of information that they have found to be especially helpful in their explorations of heritage. Encourage students who are having difficulty finding information to check sources on the Board and to post their questions as well.

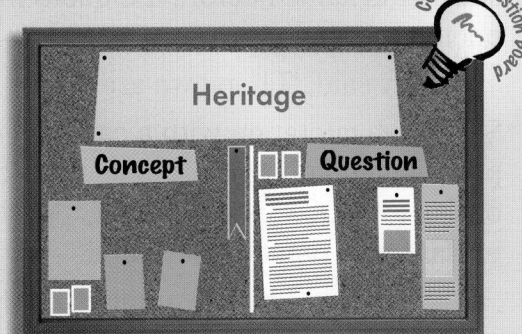

Inquiry Journal Have students complete page 43 of the *Inquiry Journal.* Have them record some ideas of how reading "The Night Journey" has added to their knowledge of heritage.

Inquiry Journal p. 43

Assessment

✓ **Informal** Continue making anecdotal record of students' progress. Note whether they:
■ complete at least two pieces for their heritage albums.
■ prepare thank-you letter for individuals who helped them.

③ Integrating the Curriculum

Language Arts

Writing

Using and Punctuating Dialogue

Instruct Ask students what they remember about dialogue. If necessary, remind them that a *dialogue* is a conversation. In a story, dialogue shows the words the characters are saying. Tell students that a speaker's exact words are called a quotation. A direct quotation shows the speaker's exact words enclosed in quotation marks (" "). Share with students the following rules for using and punctuating dialogue, and review them aloud:

■ Use quotation marks (" ") to set off a speaker's exact words. If the speaker is named before the quotation, put a comma before the opening quotation marks. For example:

> Cindy said, "I hope we are having pizza for lunch."

■ Start each quotation with a capital letter. When the spoken part ends, put a punctuation mark inside the closing quotation marks. Depending on the sentence, use a comma, a period, a question mark, or an exclamation point. For example:

> "Michael is a hard worker," Mr. Philips said. "He studies every evening after basketball practice."

■ Begin a new paragraph with each new speaker. For example:

> Marty yelled, "Coach, he wasn't safe! I tagged him! I know he was out!"
>
> "Stop yelling, Marty!" the coach replied.

■ Use two sets of quotation marks when a speaker tag interrupts a quotation. If the second part of the quotation is not a new sentence, put a comma after the speaker tag and do not capitalize the first word. If the interrupted quote contains two complete sentences, use a period and a capital letter. For example:

> "Let me in," cried my little brother. "I want to come in right now!"
>
> "You can't come in," said my older brother, "until you quit crying!"

Practice Copy paragraphs 1–4 from page 322 of "The Night Journey" onto the chalkboard or an overhead transparency. Omit the quotation marks and accompanying punctuation. Have students tell where the punctuation belongs in each sentence.

Choose other passages from the story, and repeat this exercise. Through discussion, verify students' understanding of each of the rules above.

Apply In Lesson 5, students incorporated dialogue into their narrative drafts. Have them now return to those drafts and check to see that any dialogue has been properly punctuated. Have students exchange drafts and check each other's papers for proper use and punctuation of dialogue.

Writing Process

Proofread Have students proofread their revised narratives. They might also exchange papers and use their proofreading skills to review a classmate's draft. During the proofreading stage of the writing process, students will check for and correct any errors in capitalization, punctuation, grammar, and spelling. Students should use dictionaries and other reference materials to make any necessary corrections. They can also confer with peers or the teacher about any questions they have.

Remind students to check especially for correct subject and verb agreement, pronoun referents, comma usage, and punctuation of compound sentences and dialogue. They should also check for correct use of adverbs, regular and irregular plurals, and verbs.

Research in Action
Writing

Proofreading sessions allow the students to apply grammar, usage, and mechanics skills to their writing. Encourage the students to proofread their writing at every phase of the writing process. Because you have samples of the students' writing at your disposal, evaluate each student's strengths and weaknesses in the mechanics of writing and provide them with constructive criticism when necessary. *(Marsha Roit)*

Teacher Tip

Sentence Lifting When reading student writing, keep an eye out for common errors. Lift sentences from student writing that contains these errors to help students see the relevance of the different writing, spelling, and grammar skills they are learning.

Meeting Individual Needs

ESL

Proofreading Using the proofreading checklist detailed in the Writing Process section may be tedious for English-language learners. Suggest that they concentrate on a couple of items on the list and a few misspelled words.

③ Integrating the Curriculum

Teacher Tip

Remind students that their narratives should contain plot, characters, setting, and point of view. Tell them these story elements should be kept in mind for their unit activities as well.

Literary Elements

Literary Elements of a Story

Instruct Ask students what elements distinguish a story from other forms of writing such as poems, autobiographies, or plays. Guide students to list these story elements on the chalkboard:

- Plot: beginning, middle, and end of a story
- Characters: the people, animals, or things the story is about
- Setting: the time and place in which the story happens
- Point of view: who is telling the story

Elicit from students that while a story can be based on true events, the specific details of character, setting, and plot are usually invented by the writer.

Practice Use "The Night Journey" as an example, and have volunteers tell about the plot, including the beginning, middle, and end. Ask other students to identify the characters, the setting, and the point of view of the story.

Apply Have students look in their Writing Journals for a story they have written and find and list the four elements for that story. If they discover an element poorly defined or missing, have them revise that portion of the story. For additional practice, have students complete *Reading and Writing Workbook* pages 107–108.

Meeting Individual Needs

Reteach

Literary Elements of a Story Have students who need additional instruction and practice with this concept complete *Reteach,* pages 107–108.

Challenge

Literary Elements of a Story Have students who understand this concept and could benefit from extended practice complete *Challenge,* page 56.

Reading and Writing Workbook pp. 107–108

Name _____ Date _____

Literary Elements of a Story | *The Night Journey* |

Focus Good readers recognize the elements that distinguish a story from other literary forms, such as a play or a poem.

The elements of a story include
- a **plot**, with a beginning, middle, and end.
- **characters**, including a main character who changes in some way or learns something about himself or herself.
- a **setting**, the time and place of the story.
- a **viewpoint**, a perspective from which the story is told.

Identify Answer the following questions about "The Night Journey." Answers will vary but may include the following.

1. Who is the main character in this story? _Sashie_
How did the character change?
Sashie is a young girl in the story she tells Rache.
She is a grandmother as she tells the story.

2. Why is "The Night Journey" a good title for this story?
The title is a good summary of the plot of the story.

Reading and Writing Workbook • *Literary Elements of Story*   **107**

Literary Elements of a Story *(continued)*

3. "The Night Journey" is actually a story within a story. Explain what that means.
The story of the escape from Russia long ago when
Sashie was a child is part of the larger story of life in the
present when Sashie is a grandmother.

Apply Write the title of another story that you have read in this unit. Then, briefly describe each of the story elements it included and tell a little about each.   Titles and descriptions will vary.

108   *Literary Elements of Story* • Reading and Writing Workbook

Vocabulary

Words in Context

Instruct Ask students how they determine the meaning of figures of speech and multiple-meaning words. If necessary, tell them that they must do so by looking at the context clues in the sentence in which the word appears.

Practice Write these sentences from "The Night Journey" on the chalkboard.

"At this hour, there were no sounds except the blizzard of clucking."

"The polished good soldier loomed before her in the night."

Have students read the first sentence. Prompt them to tell you that the meaning of *blizzard* in the first sentence is figurative, and have them point out the context clues they used to determine this. Ask students what this figure of speech means, and why they think the author used it. Students may answer that the author was vividly describing the sound of the clucking by comparing it to the sound of a blizzard.

Now, have students read the second sentence. Tell students that the word *loom* can mean "a frame for weaving yarn into cloth" or "to appear dimly or vaguely." Ask students how they know which is the correct meaning in the sentence. Students should mention that the context tells them that the correct meaning is "to appear dimly or vaguely."

Apply For additional practice, have students complete *Reading and Writing Workbook* pages 109–110.

Teacher Tip If necessary, remind students that words used figuratively, or figures of speech, are expressions in which words do not have their real meanings, but are used to create pictures in the reader's mind.

Meeting Individual Needs

Reteach

Words in Context Have students who need additional instruction and practice with this concept complete *Reteach,* pages 109–110.

Challenge

Words in Context Have students brainstorm a list of figures of speech and draw pictures of their literal meanings. *Amelia Bedelia* books are a good reference for literal interpretation of figurative language.

Have students who understand this concept and could benefit from extended practice complete *Challenge,* page 57.

←Skills Strand→

Words in Context

INTRODUCED: Unit 3, Lesson 6
REVIEWED: Unit 4, Lesson 3
Unit 6, Lesson 4

Reading and Writing Workbook pp. 109–110

Name _____ Date _____

Words in Context: Figurative and Multiple Meaning

The Night Journey

Focus Good readers use context clues and their own experiences to help them understand phrases with figurative language or words with multiple meanings.

- **Figurative language phrases** have vivid, descriptive words that have no literal meaning.
- **Multiple-meaning words** have more than one meaning.

Identify Look through "The Night Journey" for examples of a multiple-meaning word and a figurative language phrase. Use the context to help you explain what you think each means.

Answers will vary but may include the following.

Page: 320

Multiple-meaning word: leads

What it means: Clues or pieces of information that may result in an answer or the completion of a task

Page: 321

Figurative language phrase: two small pockets of silence in the happy din

What it means: Two people in the group of happy, talkative people were not talking at all.

Reading and Writing Workbook • Words in Context   109

Words in Context: Figurative and Multiple Meaning *(continued)*

Practice Read each passage below and decide what the underlined words or phrases mean. Write definitions for each underlined word or phrase. Use the context of the passages as clues, as well as your own knowledge, to help you understand what the words and phrases mean.

Answers will vary, but should be similar to the following.

1. The clown rode a <u>unicycle</u>. He perched above the big wheel, moving the pedals back and forth to keep his balance.

   unicycle—a one-wheeled vehicle that is moved by
   pedaling

2. The play opening on Saturday night was cause for <u>many tongues wagging</u> around town. Everybody was planning to attend. The star performer was not your <u>run-of-the-mill</u> community performer, but a legendary star who had grown up there and was finally coming home.

   many tongues wagging—lots of people talking;
   run-of-the-mill—ordinary

Apply Think about a journey you have taken. A journey can be a physical trip or a journey in your imagination. Write a paragraph about your journey being sure to use multiple-meaning words and figurative language phrases. Paragraphs will vary.

110   *Words in Context • Reading and Writing Workbook*

3 Integrating the Curriculum

Capitalizing Titles

Teacher Tip Remind students that their narratives and their heritage album entries will need titles. Have them pay close attention to capitalizing these titles correctly.

Meeting Individual Needs

Challenge

Capitalizing Titles Have students look through a newspaper and find examples of titles in print. Have them highlight the titles they find.

Assessment

✓ **Formal** To assess students' progress with capitalizing titles, have students complete **Skills Assessment** page 32.

Capitalizing Titles

INTRODUCED: Unit 1, Lesson 6
REVIEWED: Unit 3, Lesson 6
Unit 5, Lesson 6

Instruct Remind students that the first word and all important words in a title are capitalized. Words such as *a*, *the*, *in*, and *of* are not. This rule applies to books, short stories, and magazine titles. Also point out titles used with people's names, such as *Dr. Sutton*, *Mrs. Littman*, *Mr. McNeely*, and *Ms. Downard*.

Practice Write the following sentence on the chalkboard.

"Last week my friend and I went to see the movie, star wars."

Have students read the sentence and decide what mistake has been made. If no one mentions that the title should be capitalized and underlined, ask students to recall what is done to titles in a sentence. Capitalize and underline *Star Wars* when the correct response is given.

Write the following uncapitalized titles of these imaginary stories on the board and have the students capitalize them.

the day the elephants danced
a story from my heart
a friend to lean on

Apply Tell students to look over the titles in their own writing. Do they notice any errors in capitalization? Is there a pattern in the errors to which they need to pay attention?

Listening/Speaking/Viewing

Language Reflecting a Region and Culture

Have students look through "The Night Journey" for examples of how the author indicates the culture and region from which the characters in the story come. List students' ideas on the chalkboard. If students do not mention it, tell them that one indicator is the author's use of names, words, phrases, and titles from the Russian, Hebrew, and Yiddish languages.

Have students look through the story for references to place names, titles, and words that are distinctly Russian (for example, *Vashayevka Street*, *The Alexandra Gate*, *Zolodievka Street*, *Nikolayev*, the titles *tsar* and *tsarina*, and the food *kasha*). Have them also look for words and phrases from the Hebrew and Yiddish languages (for example, *kosher*, *Shema*, *Hanukkah*, *broches*, and "*She'ma Y'Isoreal! Adonai Aloujanou! Adonai Echod!*"). Tell students that some of these words can be found in a standard dictionary. If possible, make available Russian-, Hebrew-, and Yiddish-to-English dictionaries, also. Have students look up these words and share their definitions and word histories with the rest of the class. Have students discuss how these words are linked to region and culture. Then, have students discuss how this use of language enhances the readers' understanding of the story's setting and characters.

Meeting Individual Needs

ESL

Foreign Language as Literary Device Ask English-language learners to talk about the effect of seeing words in more than one language in a story, in this case English and Hebrew. Discuss the author's reason for including Hebrew. Do the unfamiliar words add to the suspense and mystery? Do they add to the feeling of traveling to a new world and going outside one's familiar comfort zone? Do they demonstrate the effort being made by people crossing from one culture to another? Have English-language learners write phrases on the chalkboard from their own first language and suggest ways those phrases might be used in a story. Encourage students to copy a few non-English words from the chalkboard into their Writing Journals.

3 Integrating the Curriculum

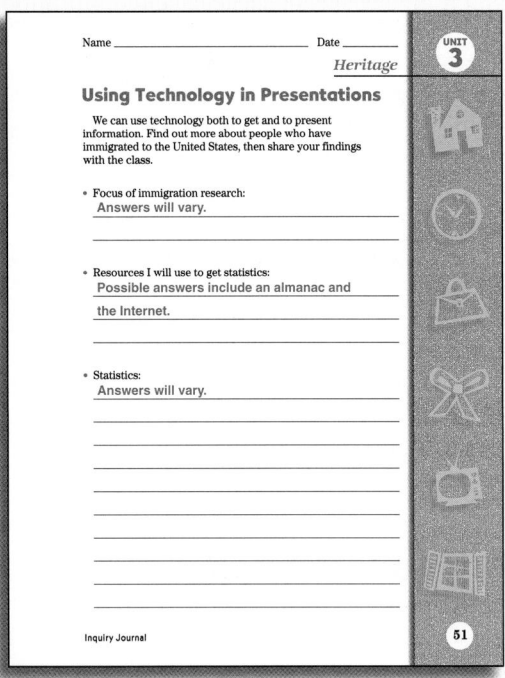

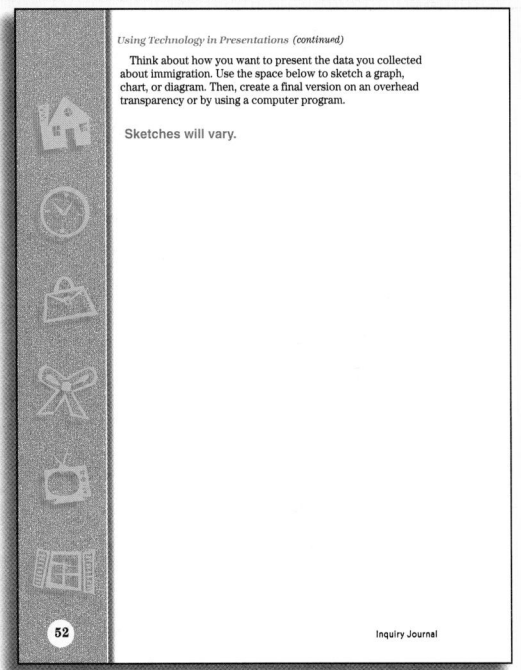

Inquiry Journal pp. 51–52

Teacher Tip Encourage students to research immigration statistics relevant to their own heritages, to incorporate into their narratives or heritage albums, if appropriate.

Study and Research

Using Technology in Presentations

Instruct In "The Night Journey," Sashie's family immigrates to a new land. Explain to students that the United States has long been a nation of immigrants and that immigration continues across our borders and in our port cities, as it does in many parts of the world. Tell students that facts and figures for current immigration can be found in world almanacs or on the Internet. Guide students as they research immigration statistics using available technology. If possible, demonstrate how students can find a Website containing immigration statistics. If this technology is unavailable, have an almanac available and talk with students about information it contains. Tell them that you will be helping them to order their findings and prepare graphs to be used in individual oral presentations.

Practice As students research immigration statistics, have them limit their focus to one aspect of immigration, such as immigration to a single state, or to a metropolitan area. Students should also focus on a specific time period. Have them use page 51 of the ***Inquiry Journal*** to gather and organize the information.

Apply After students have collected the data, have them prepare visual aids to be used with their oral presentations. Let students choose the form in which they wish to present their findings. They could use posterboard, an overhead transparency, or a computer spreadsheet or a draw-and-paint program to create a chart, graph, or diagram. Have students give their oral presentations to the class. Have the class discuss any conclusions or possible trends determined from the presentations.

Then have students complete ***Inquiry Journal*** page 52.

Across the Curriculum

 **Music**

A Heritage of Folk Dancing

Purpose

To help students become familiar with dances that are passed down from generation to generation

Procedure

In "The Night Journey," Sashie and Ghisa dance for joy at the end of their journey. Their dance was probably based on a traditional Russian dance. Even today, folk dances like this are often performed on special occasions, such as weddings and celebrations.

- Have students research the Hora, a simple folk dance that is easy to learn. They could learn about its history, where it comes from, and when it is danced.

- Instructions can be found on CDs, tapes, records, or videotapes, or can be learned from books that illustrate the steps.

- Have students work together to learn the steps, and then put on the music and let the dancing begin.

- If desired, they could then teach the dance to another class.

 **Social Studies**

Ellis Island

Purpose

To help students learn about the history of immigration in the United States

Materials

posterboard, markers, paints

Procedure

Ask students what they know about Ellis Island. If necessary, explain that from 1892 to 1943, this was the governmental checkpoint through which nearly all immigrants to the United States, such as Sashie and her family, had to pass upon arrival. Tell students that they will create an informational poster about Ellis Island.

- Have students work in small groups or pairs to research Ellis Island. They can find information in social studies and history books, or perhaps on the Internet. Tell them to find out what happened on Ellis Island: what purpose it served, what procedures the immigrants had to go through there, how many immigrants passed through, why it was opened, why it was closed, and any other information that piques their interest.

- Have them present their findings on an informational poster.

- Display the posters in the classroom for all to share.

Parmele

from *Childtimes: A Three-Generation Memoir*
by Eloise Greenfield and Lessie Jones Little

1 Every summer we took a trip down home. Down home was Parmele.

To get ready for our trip, Daddy would spend days working on our old car, putting it in shape to go on the road, and Mama would wash and iron all of our clothes. Then everything would be packed in the tan leather suitcase and the black cardboard suitcase, and we'd be ready to go.

Mama and Daddy would sit in the front with Vedie in Mama's lap, and Wilbur, Gerald, and I sat in the back with our legs on top of the suitcases. This was before cars had trunks. Or radios. Or air conditioners or heaters. And there were no superhighways. The speed limit was forty-five miles an hour, and we went thirty-five to keep from straining the car.

It was an eight-hour trip to Norfolk, Virginia, where we always went first. Grandma Pattie Ridley Jones and Grandpa had moved there by that time, and we'd spend about a week with them, then go on to Parmele for another week.

On the road, I played peek-a-boo with Vedie between her naps. Or my brothers and I would count all the cars on the road. We'd say, "There go one! That's twenty-two. There go another one!" And we'd read out loud the rhymes on the red signs advertising Burma shaving cream, and wave at people sitting on their porches, and argue with each other until one of us got real mad and real loud and Mama told us we were giving her the jimjams and to be quiet.

2 One thing that we saw on the road frightened me. Chain gangs. We saw them often, the lines of black men in their black-and-white-striped jail suits, chained by their ankles and watched over, as they repaired the roads, by white men with guns.

342

Selection Summary

Genre: Autobiography

In this excerpt, Eloise Greenfield recalls her family's annual visits with her grandparents in Parmele, North Carolina. The author shares her experiences: leaving the city to make the long automobile trip along country roads, her grandfather's scary stories, and the reluctant parting when the visit is over.

About the Authors

Eloise Greenfield has put together her love of words and music to create many works of poetry, picture books, biographies, essays, and novels. Her desire to provide more books for and about African-American children has been celebrated by many, including: the Recognition of Merit Award presented by the George C. Stone Center for Children's Books; the Coretta Scott King Award; and an ALA Notable Book for *Honey, I Love*. Greenfield and her mother, Lessie Jones Little, worked together to share this book of family stories told by Little's mother and other family members.

Students can read more about Eloise Greenfield on page 348 of the ***Student Anthology.***

Other Books by Eloise Greenfield:
- *Nathaniel Talking*
- *Rosa Parks*

Lessie Jones Little collaborated on two books with her daughter, Eloise Greenfield. *Childtimes* was selected as one of Child Study Association of America's Children's Books of the Year, and also received a *Boston Globe-Horn* Book Award. She received a Parents' Choice Award for *Children of Long Ago.*

Students can read more about Lessie Jones Little on page 348 of the ***Student Anthology.***

Other Books by Lessie Jones Little
- *I Can Do It by Myself* (with Eloise Greenfield)

Exploring the Theme

Selection Concepts

In "Parmele," an excerpt from the memoir *Childtimes*, the author recalls her family's annual visits with her grandparents in Parmele, North Carolina. Key concepts to be explored are:

■ Storytelling can provide an important link for generations of a family.

■ Happy times shared by family members build bonds and special memories.

 Check the Reading link of the **SRA** Web page for links to theme-related Websites.
http:// www.sra4kids.com

Exploration Activity Tips

Before Reading, have the students browse the selection to identify the genre. Draw their attention to the family photograph and ask if that provides a clue about the selection's genre.

During Reading, have students think about why the family made this annual trip. Have them note the comparisons between the city and country cultures and think about whether they use or could have used comparison in their heritage selections.

After Reading, have the students meet in small groups to discuss how this selection relates to the theme of Heritage. Have the students share with the class something they have learned about heritage over the course of the unit. Then have students update the Concept/Question Board.

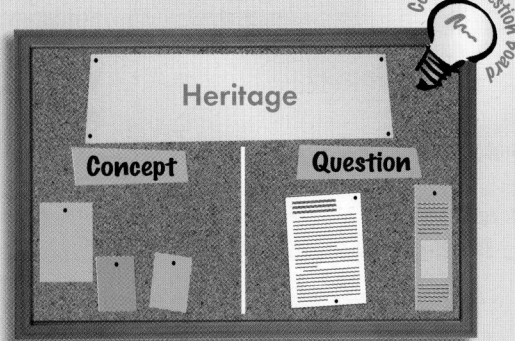

Unit 3 Exploration Management

Lesson 1	Listen to and interview a class guest about heritage. Select and read library books about heritage.
Lesson 2	Identify genres for inclusion in heritage albums. Reflect on one's own heritage, interview family members or friends about customs and traditions, and begin writing.
Lesson 3	Identify and utilize various literary techniques. Writing begins on second selection for student albums.
Lesson 4	Work on unit activity continues. Discuss with relatives or friends what they want to communicate about their heritage.
Lesson 5	Write autobiographical sketches for author pages and consider modeling a character after a family member or friend.
Lesson 6	Prepare final drafts, complete illustrations, prepare title and copyright pages, and bind books. Write thank-you notes to those who helped with the activity.
Lesson 7 Parmele	**Collaborative Exploration** **Students present a selected piece from their heritage albums.** **Supplementary Activity** **Schedule readings of student selections and plan the unit celebration.**

Lesson Planner

Suggested Pacing: 3–5 days	DAY 1 DAY 1	DAY 2 DAY 2	
Part 1 Preparing to Read **Materials** ■ Student Anthology, pp. 342–349 ■ Transparencies 21, 44	**Word Knowledge** ■ Reading the Words and Sentences, p. 342G ■ Developing Oral Language, p. 342G **Build Background, p. 342H** **Preview and Prepare, p. 342I** **Selection Vocabulary, p. 342I** *patchwork quilts, collards, commence, mantel, haint, hovering*	**Preview and Prepare, p. 342I** ■ Review Transparency 44	
Part 2 Reading and Responding **Materials** ■ Student Anthology, pp. 342–349 ■ Teacher Observation Log ■ Inquiry Journal, p. 43 ■ Home Connection, p. 47	**Student Anthology, pp. 342–349** **Comprehension Strategies** ■ Visualizing, p. 342 ■ Making Connections, pp. 342, 346 ■ Clarifying, p. 344 **Discussing Strategy Use, p. 346**	**Student Anthology, pp. 342–349** **Comprehension Skills** ■ Main Idea and Details, pp. 343, 345 ✓■ Discussing the Selection, p. 347 **Exploring the Theme** ■ Selection Vocabulary, p. 349A *patchwork quilts, collards, commence, mantel, haint, hovering*	
Part 3 Integrating the Curriculum **Materials** ■ Student Anthology, pp. 342–349 ■ Inquiry Journal, p. 53	**Writing** ■ Publishing a Personal Narrative, p. 349C **Literary Elements** ■ Autobiography, p. 349D	**Writing Process** ■ Publish, p. 349C **Vocabulary** ■ Use a Dictionary to Clarify Meanings, p. 349E	
Independent Work Time **Materials** ■ ESL Supplement ■ Intervention Guide ■ Listening Library Audiocassette	**Writing Process Continued** **ESL** ■ Word Meaning, p. 342G **Intervention** ■ Word Knowledge, p. 342G **Unit Project: Present Projects**	**Writing Process Continued** **ESL** ■ Vocabulary, p. 342J **Challenge** ■ Main Idea and Details, p. 343 **Intervention** ■ Comprehension, p. 342 ■ Main Idea and Details, p. 343 **Unit Project Continued**	

✓ Informal **Assessment Available**   ✓ Formal **Assessment Available**

DAY 2 continued		
DAY 3	**DAY 4**	**DAY 5**
General Review	General Review	Review Word Knowledge
Student Anthology, pp. 342–349 **Theme Connections** ■ Think About It, p. 349 ■ Write a Critique, p. 349	**Student Anthology,** pp. 342–349 **Exploring the Theme** ■ Reading/Writing Connections, p. 349A ■ Literature Appreciation, p. 349A ■ Supporting Student Explorations, p. 349B	**Student Anthology,** pp. 342–349 ■ Review Selection ■ Complete Discussion ■ Reread Selection in Pairs **Home Connection,** p. 349A ■ Discuss "Parmele" ■ Write about a trip
Writing Process Continued **Grammar, Usage, and Mechanics** ✓ ■ Commas in a Series, p. 349F **Listening/Speaking/Viewing** ■ Verbal and Nonverbal Messages, p. 349G	**Writing Process Continued** **Study and Research** ■ Multimedia Presentations, p. 349G	**Across the Curriculum** **Art** ■ Making a Tradition Quilt, p. 349H **Social Studies** ■ Planning a Traditional Evening, p. 349H **Unit 3 Test**
Writing Process Continued **ESL** ■ Reread, p. 344 **Challenge** ■ Using a Dictionary, p. 349E **Unit Project Continued**	**Writing Process Continued** **Challenge** ■ Commas in a Series, p. 349F **Unit Project Continued**	**Complete Writing Process** **ESL** ■ Cooperative Activities, p. 349G **Complete Unit Project**

Meeting Individual Needs
Independent Work Time

Part 1
Preparing to Read

Meeting Individual Needs

ESL
- Word Meaning, p. 342G
- Story Writing, p. 342H
- Vocabulary, p. 342J

Intervention
- Word Knowledge, p. 342G

Part 2
Reading and Responding

Meeting Individual Needs

ESL
- Reread, p. 344

Challenge
- Main Idea and Details, p. 343

Intervention
- Comprehension, p. 342
- Main Idea and Details, p. 343
- Clarifying, p. 344

Part 3
Integrating the Curriculum

Meeting Individual Needs

ESL
- Cooperative Activities, p. 349G

Challenge
- Using a Dictionary, p. 349E
- Commas in a Series, p. 349F

Formal Assessment Options

Use these assessment pages along with your informal observations to gauge student progress.

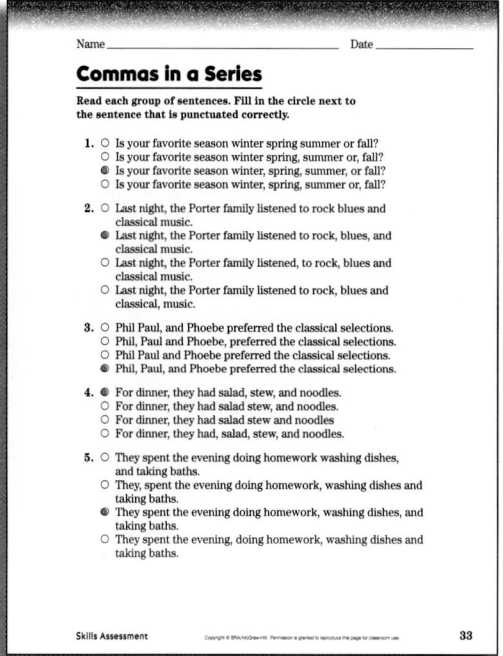

Skills Assessment, p. 33

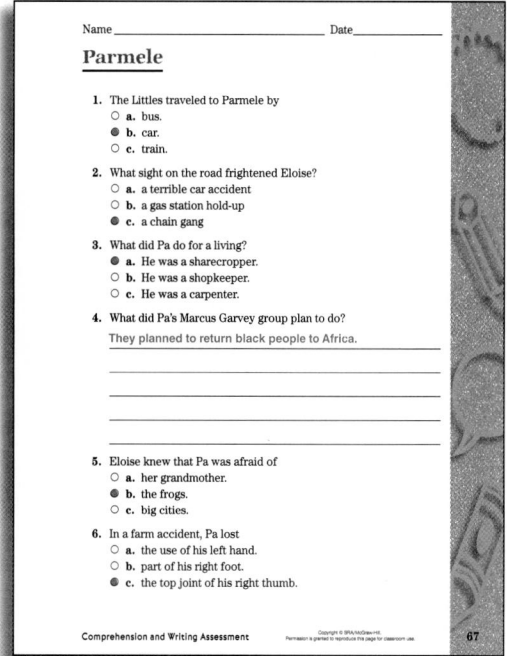

Comprehension and Writing Assessment, p. 67

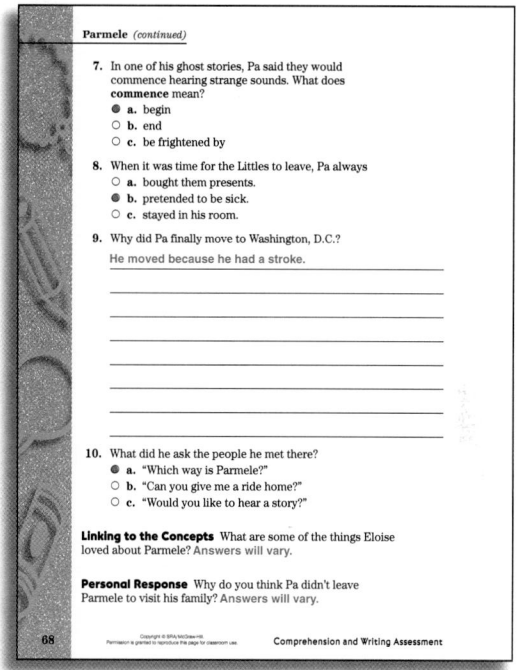

Comprehension and Writing Assessment, p. 68

① Preparing to Read

Meeting Individual Needs

ESL

Word Meaning Make sure English-language learners understand the meanings of the blending words before they do the blending exercises. Refer to Unit 3, Lesson 7, of the **ESL Supplement** for specific suggestions.

Intervention

Word Knowledge Help students think of more words that have the /f/ sound spelled *gh*. If they have trouble, give them simple definitions of some words and have them guess. Some sample words might include *cough, trough,* and *rough.* Have them copy the words into their notebooks. For students who need more help, see Unit 3, Lesson 7, of the **Intervention Guide.**

Teacher Tip Encourage students to come up with other compound words by putting together familiar words such as *mail* and *box,* and to look for more compound words in the selection.

Word Knowledge

Reading the Words and Sentences

Write each word and sentence on the chalkboard. Have students read each word together. After all the words have been read, have students read each sentence in natural phrases or chunks. Use the suggestions in About the Words to discuss the different features of the listed words.

Line 1:	gas station firefighter punching bag
Line 2:	laugh enough tough
Line 3:	narrow fellow grow
Sentence 1:	The fire engine raced to the gas station.
Sentence 2:	That tough fellow seems to think I'm his punching bag.
Sentence 3:	I've grown too tall to fit in those pants.

About the Words

- Line 1 contains open and closed compound words. Remind the students that open compound words have a space between the words, and closed compound words have no space between the words.

- The words in Line 2 all contain the digraph *gh.* In this spelling pattern, the *g* and *h*, when placed together, make the /f/ sound.

- All of the words in Line 3 have the /ō/ sound spelled *ow.* Invite students to think of other words that contain this spelling of the /ō/ sound.

Developing Oral Language

To review the words, have students do one or both of the following activities.

- Line 1 provides practice reading compound words. Have students identify the two words that make up each compound word. Ask them to discuss the meanings of the words individually, as well as the compound they make.

- Have a student choose one word and use it in a sentence. For example, "This example is tough." Have the next student create a sentence that uses the original word plus another from the list, as in "A firefighter has a tough job." Continue the game to see how many words from the list students can use to create sentences.

Build Background

Activate Prior Knowledge

Have students check the Concept/Question Board to refresh their memories about heritage. Discuss the following with students to find out what they may already know about the selection and have already learned about the unit theme. Tell students to use their prior knowledge to help them comprehend the selection they are about to read.

- Ask students if they are familiar with the story they are about to read, and if so, to tell a little about it. Remind students, however, not to give away the ending of the selection.
- Have students share any other stories that involve visiting grandparents or going on family road trips.

Background Information

The following information may help the students better understand the selection they are about to read.

- Eloise Greenfield collaborated with her mother, Lessie Jones Little, to write *Childtimes*, the memoir from which "Parmele" is an excerpt. Mrs. Little was, in turn, inspired to write by the stories of her mother, who began writing about her life when she was in her eighties.
- Have volunteers find North Carolina and Parmele on a map. Parmele is in the eastern part of the state. Students should also find Norfolk, Virginia, and Washington, DC.
- Marcus Garvey, referred to on page 345, was a Jamaican black nationalist. He brought the idea of a Universal Negro Improvement Association (UNIA) to the United States in 1916. Worldwide membership in UNIA after World War I reached six million people, with about two million in the United States. A central tenet of the organization's philosophy was closer ties between African blacks and those outside the continent.

Tell the students that after reading they will be jotting down in their Writing Journals their reactions to the story, as well as any ideas they may have for including visits to family members or friends in their future writing.

1 Preparing to Read

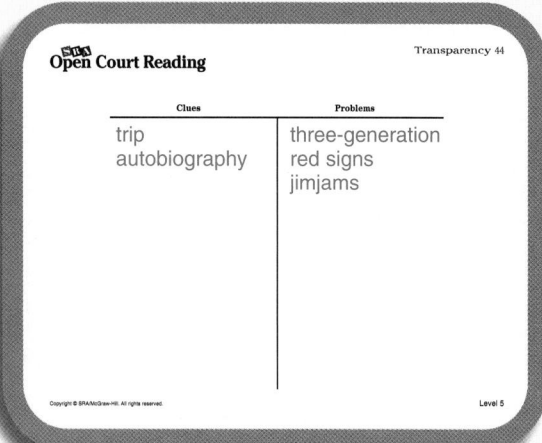

Transparency 44

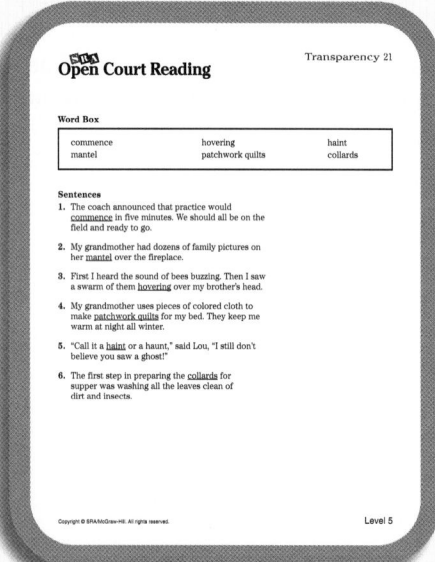

Transparency 21

Teacher Tip

To help students decode words, divide them into the syllables shown below. The information following each word tells how students can figure out the meaning of each word from the sentences on the transparency.

col·lards context clues
patch·work quilts context clues, word structure
man·tel context clues
com·mence context clues
haint context clues
hov·er·ing context clues, word structure

Preview and Prepare

Browse

- Have a volunteer read the title and authors' names aloud. Have the students share what they know about autobiography.
- Because this is an autobiography, have the students browse through the entire selection, looking for words and phrases that connect to what they already know. Record these in the Clues column on **Transparency 44.** Discuss with students what they think this selection might have to do with heritage.
- Encourage students to ask questions as they browse. Have them identify any problems that they notice while reading in the Problems column.

Set Purposes

As they read, have students think about information in the selection that may be useful to them as they work on their activities.

Selection Vocabulary

As students study vocabulary, they will use context clues, word structure, and apposition to clarify these and additional unfamiliar words.

Display **Transparency 21** before reading the selection to introduce and discuss the following words and their meanings.

col·lards: green leafy vegetable (page 345)
patch·work quilts: blankets made from scraps of material sewn together (page 345)
man·tel: shelf over a fireplace (page 346)
com·mence: begin (page 346)
haint: a ghost (page 346)
hov·er·ing: hanging low above something as if floating in air (page 346)

Have students read the words in the Word Box. Help students decode multisyllabic words by reading the words syllable by syllable. If the word is not decodable, give the students the pronunciation.

Have students read the sentences on **Transparency 21** to determine the meaning of the underlined words. Remind them to use clues in the sentences and structural clues to figure out their meanings. See the teacher tip on the left for information on how the words in each sentence can be defined.

Reading Recommendations

Your first reading of the selection should focus on developing the reading strategies found to the left of the reduced pages. We recommend that the students revisit the selection, rereading sections or the entire selection as a way to enhance their understanding and appreciation of the text. During rereading, they should focus on the comprehension skills found to the right of the reduced pages.

Oral Reading

This story's easygoing style lends itself to oral reading as listeners visualize the people and events described. Have students adjust their reading rate to suit the action of the text. For example, dialogue might be read more quickly or slowly depending on the personality and agenda of its speaker. As students read aloud, have them read expressively, at an appropriate pace, in natural phrases and chunks. By reading the selection with fluency, students will demonstrate an understanding of the text and an ability to engage the listeners in an effective manner. If students encounter difficulties, have them use the reading strategies below or refer to the Blending Procedure (Program Appendix 15–16).

Using Reading Strategies

Reading strategy instruction allows students to become aware of how good readers read. Good readers constantly check their understanding as they are reading and ask themselves questions. In addition, skilled readers recognize when they are having problems and stop to use various reading strategies to help them make sense of what they are reading.

During the reading of "Parmele," you will model the use of the following reading strategies:

- Making Connections   - Clarifying   - Visualizing

Before reading, have students share how they have used these strategies in the past and any tips they can give each other on their use.

Building Comprehension Skills

Revisiting or rereading a selection allows students to apply skills that give them a more complete understanding of the text. Some follow-up comprehension skills, such as *Main Idea and Details* and *Compare and Contrast*, help students organize information. Others, such as *Author's Purpose*, *Making Inferences*, and *Drawing Conclusions*, lead to deeper understanding—to "reading between the lines," as mature readers do. In this selection, students will apply the follow-up comprehension skill of *Main Idea and Details*.

Teacher Tip Have students who may need extra help reading "Parmele" reread the selection using the *Listening Library Audiocassette*.

Meeting Individual Needs

ESL

Vocabulary Check that English-language learners know the meanings of idioms and more difficult vocabulary in the story, including: *a trip; speed limit; played peek-a-boo; collards; leftover material; branches; a jar of preserving liquid; front-room mantel; nervous laughs;* and *an excuse.* Explain and show pictures as needed. Model example sentences and help English-language learners make their own sentences. Refer to Unit 3, Lesson 7 of the *ESL Supplement* for teaching suggestions.

Teacher Tip By this time in the fifth grade, good readers should be reading approximately 143 words per minute with fluency and expression. The only way to gain fluency is through practice. As explained in Reading Recommendations, have students reread all or part of the selection to you and to each other during class or Independent Work Time to focus on the comprehension skills and to build fluency.

② Reading and Responding

Read pages 342–349.

Comprehension Strategies

Prompting

❶ Visualizing *Though you aren't really into the story yet, have you begun to form a mental image that helps you relate to this family trip?*

Student Sample

Visualizing *I visualize a bright, hot summer day and a small, red car that is crowded with family members. They are excited about where they are going, but probably uncomfortable from being in the car so long.*

Modeling

❷ Making Connections *Relating our own experiences or knowledge to what we read can help us understand it better. For example, I have never seen a chain gang before, but their suits remind me of something I saw in a movie from the 1920s or 1930s. Maybe this story is from the same time period.*

Word Knowledge

There are many multisyllabic words in this selection. Be sure students are using skills they learned in the Word Knowledge section of this lesson.

Reading Recommendation

ORAL · CHORAL · SILENT

Parmele

from *Childtimes: A Three-Generation Memoir*
by Eloise Greenfield and Lessie Jones Little

❶ Every summer we took a trip down home. Down home was Parmele.

To get ready for our trip, Daddy would spend days working on our old car, putting it in shape to go on the road, and Mama would wash and iron all of our clothes. Then everything would be packed in the tan leather suitcase and the black cardboard suitcase, and we'd be ready to go.

Mama and Daddy would sit in the front with Vedie in Mama's lap, and Wilbur, Gerald, and I sat in the back with our legs on top of the suitcases. This was before cars had trunks. Or radios. Or air conditioners or heaters. And there were no superhighways. The speed limit was forty-five miles an hour, and we went thirty-five to keep from straining the car.

It was an eight-hour trip to Norfolk, Virginia, where we always went first. Grandma Pattie Ridley Jones and Grandpa had moved there by that time, and we'd spend about a week with them, then go on to Parmele for another week.

On the road, I played peek-a-boo with Vedie between her naps. Or my brothers and I would count all the cars on the road. We'd say, "There go one! That's twenty-two. There go another one!" And we'd read out loud the rhymes on the red signs advertising Burma shaving cream, and wave at people sitting on their porches, and argue with each other until one of us got real mad and real loud and Mama told us we were giving her the jimjams and to be quiet.

❷ One thing that we saw on the road frightened me. Chain gangs. We saw them often, the lines of black men in their black-and-white-striped jail suits, chained by their ankles and watched over, as they repaired the roads, by white men with guns.

342

Meeting Individual Needs

Intervention

Comprehension Intervention strategies for those students having difficulty with reading "Parmele" can be found in Unit 3, Lesson 7, of the *Intervention Guide.*

Assessment

✓ **Informal** Observe individual students as they read, and use the Teacher Observation Log found in the *Assessment Guide* to record anecdotal information about each student's strengths and weaknesses.

Eloise Greenfield stands at the far right of this photograph taken at Parmele in 1941. With her are her grandfather, her mother, her grandmother, Wilbur, Vedie, and Gerald.

〈343〉

Comprehension
Skills

Main Idea and Details

Ask students what they know about *main idea and details.* If necessary remind the students that the *main idea* is what a paragraph or passage is mostly about. *Details* give more information about the main idea. Sometimes the main idea is found in the first sentence in a paragraph. Sometimes it is found in the last sentence.

■ "One thing that we saw on the road frightened me. Chain gangs." What are some details that support this main idea? *(Students can choose any sentence in the paragraph.)*

Have the students look at the first five paragraphs on page 342 and discuss what the main idea is for that section.

Skills Strand

Main Idea and Details
INTRODUCED: Unit 2, Lesson 2
REVIEWED: Unit 2, Lesson 4
Unit 2, Lesson 8
Unit 3, Lesson 2
Unit 3, Lesson 7

Teacher Tip As students read "Parmele," they should think about why the family made this annual trip. Encourage them to note the differences between the city and the country.

Meeting Individual Needs

Challenge	Intervention
Main Idea and Details Prepare a paragraph without a stated main idea. Have the students write a main idea for the paragraph.	**Main Idea and Details** Have students state a main idea for this selection and list details that support the main idea.

2 Reading and Responding

Comprehension Strategies

Prompting

3 Clarifying *It is important to clarify anything that might hinder a complete understanding of what you are reading. For example, who is Marcus Garvey?*

Student Sample

Clarifying *According to the text, Marcus Garvey was head of the United Negro Improvement Association. We could probably find out more about him and this organization by looking them up in the encyclopedia or doing a search on the Internet. Perhaps we'll even find a picture of him.*

I wasn't afraid of the men, and I didn't think about maybe getting shot. But for a reason I didn't understand, I was afraid of the whole thing. Those bent-over striped backs, the sharp points of the picks the men swung, the sound of the picks hitting the concrete, the sight of men with long guns, pacing. It scared me.

After a few miles, that scared feeling would fade away, and I'd start to have fun again, or I might take a nap, and it always seemed as if days had passed before we finally crossed the line into Parmele.

By the time of my visits there, only a few trains were still passing through. My Parmele wasn't a train town or a <u>mill</u> town. It was a quiet town. Chinaberry trees and pump water and tree swings and figs and fat, pulpy grapes on the vine. People saying, "hey" instead of "hi," the way they did in Washington, *hey-ey*, sending their voices up, then down, softly, singing it through their noses. Parmele was me running from the chickens when I was little, riding around the yard in a goat-pulled cart, sitting on the porch and letting people going by in their cars wave at me, reading in the rocking chair, taking long walks to the gas station for soda pop with the children of Mama's and Daddy's childtime friends. Parmele was uncles and aunts and cousins. And Granny. And Pa.

Mack and Williamann Little, 1890s.

344

Word Knowledge

gas station, soda pop, rocking chair

Remind students if they have difficulty decoding these words that they learned about open compounds in the Word Knowledge section of this lesson.

Meeting Individual Needs

ESL

Reread Pair English-language learners with native speakers. Have the partner pairs reread parts or all of the selection to each other.

Intervention

Clarifying Remind students that one can clarify unfamiliar terms, names, and ideas by asking questions, checking outside resources for information, and rereading the text. Help students to come up with other resources they could use to look up information on Marcus Garvey.

They were Daddy's parents, Mack and Williamann Little. Black people in Parmele called them Mr. Mack and Miss Williamann. White people called them Uncle Mack and Ain' Williamann.

Granny was thin and whitehaired. She kept snuff tucked inside her bottom lip and wore aprons over her long dresses. I remember her most bending over the collards in her garden or feeding the chickens. She used to sew leftover material from my dresses into her patchwork quilts. She used to make apple jelly and green tomato pickles. Anything her grandchildren wanted, she wanted them to have.

And so did Pa.

"Leave the children alone," he used to tell mamas and daddies. "They ain't doing nothing."

Pa was a <u>sharecropper</u>. He worked in the fields, farming the land for the white man who owned it, and got paid in a share of the crops he raised. Along with that, he had almost always had some kind of little business going, even when Daddy was a boy—a meat market, an icehouse, a cleaner's, a grocery store.

Long before I was born, Pa had been a member of the Marcus Garvey group that used  to meet in Parmele on Sunday afternoons. It was one of thousands of branches of the United Negro Improvement Association headed by Marcus Garvey. They met to talk about the beauty and strength of blackness, and to plan the return of black people to Africa.

I didn't think my grandfather was afraid of anything except the frogs that came out of the

Eloise Little, 1932

345

Comprehension Skills

Main Idea and Details

Ask the students to restate what main idea and details are. If necessary, remind them that the main idea is what the author wants the reader to know in the story or paragraph. Details help to explain or give more information about the main idea.

Have the students read paragraph 5 on page 345.

- Ask them to state the main idea. *(Pa was a sharecropper and a businessman.)*
- Have them find the details that support the main idea. *(He worked in the fields, farming the land for the man who owned it, and got a share of the crops he raised. He also always had a business of his own, such as a meat market, an icehouse, a cleaner's, and a grocery store.)*

Teacher Tip Have students meet in small groups to discuss how this selection relates to the unit theme. Then have students update the Concept/Question Board.

Reading and Responding

Comprehension Strategies

Prompting

4 Making Connections *I know just how they must have felt. I've heard stories before that scared me. It can be fun to listen to spooky stories, but they make me nervous too. Can you make a connection to how they felt?*

Student Sample

5 Making Connections *I remember visiting friends and family when I was younger. People hate to see visitors leave, especially if the visits only happen once in a while. I can see why Pa tried everything he could to get them to stay longer.*

Discussing Strategy Use

After they have read the selection, have students share any problems they encountered and tell what strategies they used to solve them. Then, have them answer the following questions. If they answer "no" to any of the questions, have them reread part of the selection to find the answer.

- Did they stop to clarify words, phrases, and ideas that they didn't understand?
- Did they make connections between what they are reading and what they know?
- Did they visualize story events?

Make sure that students explain how using the strategies helped them understand the selection better and how they read effectively to find answers to the questions they asked as they set purposes.

---

mud-filled ditches at night and flopped across the yard, and he knew plenty of names to call them. The thumb on his right hand looked like a little baldheaded man. The top joint had been cut off in a farm accident, and he had put it in a jar of preserving liquid that stayed on the front-room mantel. I never got tired of looking at it.

Children hung around Pa, nieces and nephews and neighbors, listening to his stories, giggling at his jokes. Some nights there would be just us—Wilbur, Gerald, and me, with our grandfather—sitting on the porch where the only light was that of the stars and the nearest house was a long way down the road. He'd tell scary stories, and get really tickled when we got scared. He swore his ghost stories were true.

"One night," he'd say, "me and my brother John was coming 'cross that field over yonder." He'd make his arm tremble and point toward the woods across the highway. "And we commence to hearing this strange sound. Ummmmm-*umph!* Ummmmm-*umph!* And we looked up and saw this . . . this *haint!*"

He'd twist his face and narrow his eyes in horror as he stared out into the darkness, and I could just feel all those haints hovering behind us, daring us to turn around and run for the door.

Sometimes Pa would stop right in the middle of a story.

"Then what happened, Pa?" one of us would ask.

"Oh, I left after that," he'd say, and he'd laugh. Then we'd laugh, small nervous laughs, wanting to believe that it had all been just a joke.

4 Every year when it was time for us to leave, a sudden change would come over Pa. One minute he'd be challenging

Eloise Little and Bobby Greenfield, 1948

346

Teacher Tip Reread the selection with students who had difficulty understanding it. Continue modeling and prompting the use of strategies and skills as you reread.

Vera and Vedie Little, Langston Terrace, 1949

Daddy to a foot race that never took place, and the next minute he was weak and sick, trying to get us to stay. He didn't think he would live to see us the following summer, he'd say. At breakfast he'd begin the blessing with, "Lord, I sure do thank You for allowing me to see my family one last time before You call me home," and he'd pray a long, sad prayer that brought tears to our eyes.

But finally, when nothing worked, Pa would give up and help Daddy load the car with suitcases and with sacks of fresh corn and peanuts. There'd be hugs and kisses and more tears, and then we'd drive away, leaving him and Granny standing on the side of the road, waving, waving, waving, getting smaller and smaller, until they blended into one and disappeared.

Pa never liked to leave home. Granny came to visit us a few times over the years, but Pa always made an excuse. He couldn't get away right then, he had too much work to do, or something. One year, though, he had to come. He'd had a stroke, and Mama and Daddy brought him to Washington to take care of him. The stroke had damaged his body and his mind, so that he didn't understand much of what was going on around him, but he knew he wasn't where he wanted to be. Mama would take him for a walk and he'd ask people on the street, "Which way is Parmele?"

My grandfather never got back to Parmele. He lived in Washington for eighteen months, and then, in 1951, at the age of seventy-eight, he died.

347 ▷

Teacher Tip

Have students meet in small groups to discuss how this selection relates to the unit theme. Then have students update the Concept/Question Board.

Assessment

✓ **Formal** To assess students' reading comprehension, have them complete **Comprehension and Writing Assessment,** pages 67–68.

Comprehension Skills

Discussing the Selection

Following reading, engage the students in a discussion of the selection. Using the *handing-off process* will help the students to take responsibility for the discussion. In addition to the following question, have them revisit any questions asked when they set purposes before the reading.

■ What does this selection tell us about the author's heritage? *(Answers may vary. Students might mention that her family was poor but respected in their community, that there was always an undercurrent of unease because of the oppression African-Americans suffered, and that her family had rural roots.)*

■ How important is family to the author? *(Answers may vary. Students will probably say very important, since the whole family traveled back to their hometown every year.)*

■ What are some differences and similarities between your family and Eloise Greenfield's family? *(Answers will vary.)*

■ How has this selection connected with your knowledge of the unit theme? *(Answers will vary—students should compare/contrast examples of heritage from this selection with their own experiences or past reading and use these connections to make a general statement about the unit theme.)*

During this time, have the students return to the clues and problems that they noted on the transparency before reading. Let the students decide which items deserve further discussion.

Encourage students to record the thoughts, feelings, or reactions that are elicited by any reading they do.

② Reading and Responding

Meet the Author

After the students read the information about Eloise Greenfield, discuss the following questions with them.

Eloise Greenfield felt that too few books told the truth about her heritage. Why do you think this was a concern for her? *(Possible answer: She believes that books are powerful. People receive a great deal of their education through books of all kinds, so it is important for books to reflect a variety of beliefs and values.)*

Elosie Greenfield's father used to take the family to the library once a week for books. How do you think this affected her as a writer? *(Possible answer: She knew from an early age that reading and writing could be important tools for teaching and learning, which fueled her determination to write stories.)*

Why do you think Eloise Greenfield teaches creative writing to elementary and junior high students? *(Possible answer: She wants to develop in them a love for writing, and show them how they can use it both for enjoyment and as a way of expressing themselves.)*

Parmele

Meet the Authors

Eloise Greenfield was born during the Great Depression in Parmele, North Carolina. However, she did most of her growing up in Washington, DC. Her father used to pile the family into the car once a week to visit the library for a supply of books. She says she found far too few books that told the truth about African-Americans, and she wanted to change that.

Today she is a member of the African-American Writers Guild. She uses grant money to teach creative writing to elementary and junior high students, and has written many award-winning books.

Lessie Jones Little was born in Parmele, North Carolina, and spent most of her childhood there. Like many of the people in her town, she and her family made their money working on farms. The work was very hard and tiring, and didn't pay well. The money she earned went toward buying schoolbooks and cloth for her dresses.

When she graduated from high school, she was awarded a pin that signified she had earned the best grades. She went on to work as a teacher and then a clerk at the Office of the Surgeon General. It wasn't until she was sixty-seven years old that she began writing children's books. She collaborated on two books with her daughter, Eloise Greenfield, and also wrote an award-winning book of poems.

⟨348⟩

Theme Connections

Think About It

With a small group of students, discuss the following questions.

- What did the author enjoy about visiting her grandparents?
- What heritage was passed on during the author's visits?
- What do you enjoy about visiting your grandparents and older family friends?
- During these visits, how do they pass on pieces of their own heritage to you?

Record Ideas

What have you learned about heritage from your group discussion? Record your thoughts and ideas in your Writing Journal.

Write a Critique

Write a critique of the selection "Parmele." Give examples of what you liked and didn't like about the story, what you learned from it, and what characters you particularly liked or disliked. Share your critique with other students, comparing and contrasting your ideas.

349

Theme Connections

Think About It

Explain to students that *oral tradition* is the passing down of stories through generations by word of mouth. Tell students that an example of oral tradition is the stories that Pa told his grandchildren when they came to visit him in Parmele.

- Have students think about favorite stories that they tell with their friends and family, or if they know of any stories that are commonly told within their own culture. What do these stories mean to them?

- Explain to students that heritage allows people to feel connected to each other and to the past. Have students discuss how being connected makes oral tradition an important part of heritage.

Record Ideas

Respond to students' entries, extending their thinking through comments and questions.

Write a Critique

Encourage students to write critiques that are one to two paragraphs long. After they share their critiques with fellow students, encourage them to note any interesting ideas that may have been exchanged. Post critiques on the Concept/Question Board.

Teacher Tip Remind students to think about how the text makes them feel. Well-written stories touch the reader's emotions and spark ideas. This emotional and intellectual involvement makes each story the reader's own.

② Responding

✦Exploring the Theme

Some students may choose to conduct a computer search for additional books of information about heritage. Have them make a list of these books and sources of information to share with classmates and the school librarian. Check the Reading link of the **SRA** Web page for links to theme-related Websites.
http://www.sra4kids.com

Have students write sentences using the selection vocabulary words. In order to provide additional help in remembering words, students can write synonyms or antonyms for the words if it is appropriate. Some students may even draw something to help them remember the meanings of the words.

Selection Vocabulary

Have students write in their Writing Journals the definitions for words discussed before reading the selection and any other interesting words they clarified while reading. Students should be encouraged to refer to these words throughout the unit as they work on student and writing projects. The words from the selection are:

patchwork quilts	collards	commence
mantel	haint	hovering

Reading/Writing Connections

Ask students to think of other memoirs they have read, heard, and told that use a structure similar to "Parmele." Point out that "Parmele" does not have a plot line, as a work of fiction does. The author does, however, use a central idea—family relationships—to tie together a series of episodes. Have students use this structure to lay out the plan for a personal memoir.

Literature Appreciation

Tell volunteers to locate Washington, DC, and Parmele, North Carolina, on a map. (Parmele is in the eastern part of the state, slightly southwest of Norfolk, Virginia, where the family made its first stop.) Have students trace the route the family might have taken. Remind them that, as the author states, there were no superhighways then. Have students suggest other ways the route and sights along the way might have changed. If any students have visited places along this route, have them tell what they know about them.

Home Connection

The class has just finished reading "Parmele." This selection is about author Eloise Greenfield's recollection of her family's annual visits with her grandparents in Parmele, North Carolina. An informational letter on "Parmele," in both English and Spanish, can be found in the ***Home Connection*** guide.

Home Connection p. 47

Supporting Student Explorations

Students should be ready to share the results of their work with the class.

Whole Group Talk with the class about effective oral reading. Discuss strategies the students can use to get and keep an audience's attention. Record their ideas on chart paper for students' reference as they prepare to make their presentations.

Small Group Have the students work in pairs to practice reading their selections aloud in a way that reflects understanding of the text and engages the listeners. Have the partners give each other constructive feedback during practice sessions.

Schedule time for students to make their presentations. Remind them that they should explain why they chose the particular piece before presenting it.

After all of the students have had a chance to give their presentations, have them share and discuss what they have learned about heritage and culture over the course of this unit. Tell them to use the presentations, this unit's selections, and the research they did for their heritage albums as a basis for determining the common and distinctive characteristics of the cultures they have studied.

Suggest that students post on the Concept/Question Board brief descriptions of books, magazine articles, computer Websites, or other sources of information that they have found to be especially helpful in their explorations of heritage.

Inquiry Journal Have students complete page 43 of the *Inquiry Journal*. Have them record how reading "Parmele" has added to their knowledge of heritage.

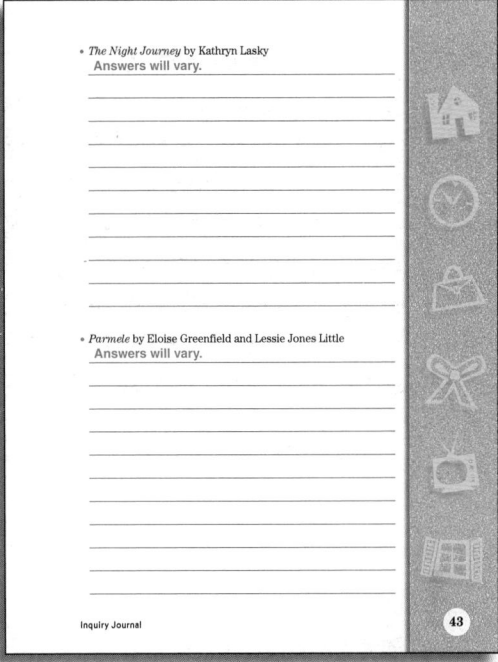

Inquiry Journal p. 43

Assessment

✓ **Informal** In your final anecdotal entry, note whether students:
- presented their work effectively, keeping the attention of the audience.
- used appropriate audience behavior.

3 Integrating the Curriculum

Teacher Tip Point out to students that they can use a spell checker to proofread their stories. However, remind students who use a spell checker that they will still have to "eyeball" their work. They need to check for homophones, such as *their, they're,* and *there.* Also, omitting or adding a letter may still create a real word. For example, they might want to write *niece,* leave out the first *e,* and still have a word (*nice*) that the spell checker software program would consider correct.

Language Arts

Writing

Publishing a Personal Narrative

Instruct Once students have written, revised, proofread, and made final corrections to a piece of writing, they may want to share the completed work with others by publishing it.

Before students have made their final corrections, have a brief publishing conference with each student. At this time, help the students make any last-minute changes that are necessary before the piece can be published.

Practice Provide materials for a publishing center and explain their use to the students. A word processor or typewriter might be located in this center along with other tools for writing and illustrating books and for making covers.

Apply Have students write a final draft of their writing activity and put it into a booklet. Have them make covers for their stories. Students may want to illustrate their stories with photographs of themselves or other family members included in the stories.

Writing Process

Publish Writing can be published in a variety of ways:

- It can be displayed on a bulletin board.
- It can be made into a book by putting the pages between covers.
- It can be collected with other pieces of writing and published in an anthology.
- It can be submitted for publication to a local newspaper or a national magazine.
- It can be published in a school newspaper.
- It can be read aloud to the class, to other classes, to younger students in the school, or to another group.

Encourage students to consider publishing their narratives in one of the above ways.

Literary Elements

Autobiography

Instruct Remind students that an autobiography tells the story of a person's life. Ask them how it differs from a biography. *(A biography is about someone else's life, not the writer's life.)* Review the autobiography in Lesson 1 of this unit, "The Land I Lost."

Practice Discuss with students who might write an autobiography and why people might be interested in reading it. Then have students answer such questions as these:

- What kinds of people write autobiographies?
- Who might be interested in reading such books?
- What autobiographies have you read? Why did you read it? What did you learn from reading about that person's life?
- Might someone your age write an autobiography? Give examples of someone around your age whose autobiography you would read and tell why.

  Point out that "Parmele" comes from a book called *Childtimes: A Three-Generation Memoir* by Eloise Greenfield and her mother Lessie Jones Little. Explain that a memoir is a kind of autobiography. If students are keeping a journal, point out that autobiographers often use their own journals as the basis for their memoirs.

Apply Have students think about how their heritage albums could be considered autobiographies. Discuss this with the class.

3 Integrating the Curriculum

Teacher Tip Have students clarify the meanings and spellings of words in their unit activities with the use of a dictionary.

Meeting Individual Needs

Challenge

Using a Dictionary Have students look up these words in the dictionary and select a meaning: *bow, present, wind, fly, top.* Then have them write and draw a picture of each word they have chosen.

Using a Dictionary
INTRODUCED: Unit 3, Lesson 2
REVIEWED: Unit 3, Lesson 7
Unit 4, Lesson 1

Vocabulary

Using a Dictionary Or Glossary

Instruct Have students tell you all the things they know about using a dictionary or glossary. They should recall that a dictionary is used to clarify the spelling, pronunciation, usage, and definition of words; it is arranged in alphabetical order; and it has guide words. Word histories and derivatives are also shown for some entries. Tell students that their *Student Anthology* glossary shares all of these characteristics, although it will only give the meaning and part of speech of a word as it is used in their *Student Anthology* selection(s). They should also recall the differences between how glossary and dictionary information is presented. For example, students can compare word histories and derivations as shown in both a dictionary and their glossary.

Practice Have students skim the selection "Parmele" for sentences containing these words: *commence* and *hover*. Have volunteers read these sentences aloud. Then have students use the context to figure out the meaning of the words. Have students use both a dictionary and their *Student Anthology* glossary to check the words' meanings.

Apply Have students list five more words from "Parmele" that are unfamiliar to them. Have students look up these words in the dictionary. Using the dictionary, have students create glossary entries for these words, modeling them after entries found in their *Student Anthology.* Tell them to remember that glossary entries contain only the meaning and usage of a word as it appears in the selection—students will have to use context clues to figure out how to do this appropriately.

Grammar, Usage, and Mechanics

Commas in a Series

Instruct Write the following sentence on the chalkboard:

Some nights there would be just us—Joe Tyler and me.

Ask a volunteer to read aloud the sentence. Then place commas after *Joe* and after *Tyler*, and have the sentence read aloud again. Ask students how adding the commas changed the way the sentence was read and its meaning.

Remind students that a comma is used to set off and separate words and groups of words. In sentences like the one above, they can help avoid confusion. In this sentence, the commas separate the names that are used in a series.

Practice Ask students how they would use commas in the following:

- cats dogs *(no commas: cats and dogs)*
- carrots tomatoes turnips *(carrots, tomatoes, and turnips)*
- tennis basketball football volleyball *(tennis, basketball, football, and volleyball)*

Apply Have students check their unit activities for any occurrences of commas in a series to make sure they are punctuated correctly.

 **Integrating the Curriculum**

Meeting Individual Needs

ESL

Cooperative Activities Cooperating in the production of classroom projects increases the students' opportunities to hear and produce language and to negotiate with others. Cooperative activities also develop students' self-esteem and friendship with students from other backgrounds.

 **Teacher Tip** When creating their video commercials, encourage students to be creative and persuasive. Have students think of their own advertising strategies and then choose the technology best suited to each idea.

Inquiry Journal p. 53

Listening/Speaking/Viewing

Verbal and Nonverbal Messages

In the story "Parmele," Pa tells the children some scary stories. He uses verbal and nonverbal messages to make his stories more realistic. Remind students that speakers use nonverbal messages, such as facial expressions, hand movements, and body language, to make a point without talking.

Have students read aloud the part of the selection that tells about Pa telling stories. Have one student be Pa and another be the narrator. Remind the students to be sure to include the nonverbal language too. Try to choose a student who is not afraid to "ham it up" for the role of Pa.

After the reading, ask students the following questions:

■ How did the verbal and nonverbal messages work together to frighten the children?

■ Would the story have frightened them if Pa had told it in a normal, matter-of-fact manner?

Study and Research

Multimedia Presentations

Instruct Previously, students were introduced to the idea of using technology as a part of an oral presentation of information. Tell students that there are a variety of tools that could be used to enhance any presentation of data. Ask students to name devices used for this purpose. If not mentioned, add posters, slides, overheads, video, audiotapes, or various computer programs. Gather examples of these items and explain or demonstrate how they could be used to enhance an oral presentation.

Practice Have students create a short video commercial. Help them use video equipment if it is available. Otherwise, tell them to create storyboard "stills" of the frames of the video. Tell them that the purpose of the video is to persuade people to buy a brand new invention—wind-up in-line skates. Have students brainstorm advertising slogans and ways to perform the action for their video. Encourage students use available technology to implement as many of their ideas as possible.

Apply For additional practice, have students complete page 53 in the *Inquiry Journal.*

Across the Curriculum

 **Art**

Making a Tradition Quilt

Purpose

To have students simulate a traditional method of preserving traditions of their own

Materials

colored paper, pencils, markers

Procedure

Encourage students to share what they know about patchwork quilts and how they are made. Start by asking questions such as these:

- In "Parmele," you read that Granny "used to sew leftover material from" young Eloise's dresses into her patchwork quilts. Can you think of reasons for making a quilt out of parts of clothing that have been worn?

- Explain that such quilts have been made in the United States since colonial times. It was not only a way of economizing but also of creating works of art. Quilting bees were social events to which whole families came to help put the quilts together. These were often big celebrations with good food and talk, as well as games for the children.

- Tell students that they are going to make a paper patchwork quilt that celebrates heritage. Explain that some quilt squares have pictures or designs. Suggest that students think of what design they would contribute to the quilt. It might be a house, the outline of a state or tree, or an animal. Have students design their piece of the quilt.

- Line a bulletin board with construction paper. Have each student staple his or her design on the background. Add strips of a contrasting color to separate the designs.

 **Social Studies**

Planning a Traditional Evening

Purpose

To help students become aware of how their ancestors spent their evenings

Procedure

Tell students to think about how they spend their evenings compared to the way their ancestors did. Stimulate discussion with such questions as the following:

Do you think your great-grandparents and their families spent more time talking to each other after dinner than you do now? What did you learn in "Parmele" that might make you think so?

What other activities might they have engaged in? Do any of these activities resemble what you do now?

Display reference book or encyclopedia pictures of families of the 1920s and 1930s engaged in activities. Have students identify the activities.

- On the chalkboard, write a list of traditional activities that students think they would enjoy. These might include watching the stars, telling ghost stories, playing board games, putting together a puzzle, preparing fudge, or making shadow pictures on the wall.

- Tell students they are to plan an evening of such activities, using the list as a starting point. Since they are to be traditional, they would *not* include such things as watching television, listening to the stereo, or playing electronic games.

- Have students imagine that they live in the past and have just spent the evening as they planned it in the previous step. Have them write a journal entry describing their evening.

Bibliography

Extending the Unit Theme

Have students explore other dimensions of heritage through reading and discussing one or more of the books on these pages. Students may also read for pleasure a book that appeals to them.

Promoting Reading for Pleasure

- Invite grandparents and older friends to come in and share stories of their heritage. Encourage them to read an appropriate book related to their story, if possible, or be prepared to suggest appropriate books to your students.

- Take your students to the school or local library regularly. Encourage them to explore different genres.

Using the Bibliography Pages

To get started, have students read each of the brief descriptions of books on pages 350–351. Ask if anyone has read any of these books or is familiar with any of the authors' books, without giving away important parts of the story.

Tips for Reading

Remind students to make connections as they read. Encourage them to relate characters and events in their selections to people they know or situations they have experienced.

Tell students to interpret as they read. Remind them that writers do not always state explicitly what they mean, so students may need to make inferences that help them understand and appreciate what they are reading.

Heritage

Bibliography

The Cook's Family

by Laurence Yep. What happens when you pretend to be someone's long-lost granddaughter? You might become part of the cook's family! Average

Do People Grow on Family Trees? Genealogy for Kids and Other Beginners

by Ira Wolfman. Learning something about your ancestors' lives means learning something about yourself. This fascinating guidebook shows you the steps to discovering your genealogy. Advanced

Going Back Home: An Artist Returns to the South

by Michele Wood and Toyomi Igus. Michele Wood goes home to learn about the place and people of her origin. She shares her story through her paintings. Average

The Great Ancestor Hunt: The Fun of Finding Out Who You Are

by Lila Perl. If you want to search for your roots, this is the book that will help you get started. Advanced

350

In My Family: En Mi Familia

by Carmen Lomas Garza. Share this Mexican American's family activities and fun. Learn how family history has shaped their lives. Easy

Journey to Ellis Island

by Carol Bierman. Imagine leaving your home in Russia and traveling to America with your mother and sister with only what you can carry in a suitcase. That's what Julius Weinstein did when he was 12 years old in 1922. Julius grew up to become a great storyteller, and this book captures these fascinating and often funny tales about Europe, Ellis Island, and America. Average

Secret of the Andes

by Ann Nolan Clard. Without a past or a family, an Incan boy lives in a hidden valley high in the mountains of Peru. What are the secrets of his Inca ancestors that he must discover to understand his destiny? Average

This Land is My Land

by George Littlechild. Through his art and words George Littlechild shares his feelings about being Native American in this time and place. Easy

351

Discussing the Books

Have each student select one or more of the books for reading and discussion. Use the following questions as discussion starters:

- How did you choose your selection? Did it prove to be a good strategy?
- What characters or events did you personally connect to? Explain.
- Has your selection inspired you to find our more about your heritage? Why or why not?
- What new information was presented in your selection? How is this information significant?

Tips for Discussion

Discussions offer a prime opportunity for you to introduce new ideas about concepts. If students do not mention an important idea that is necessary to the understanding of some larger issue, "drop" that idea into the conversion and repeat it several times to make sure it gets picked up.

The more you turn discussions over to the students, the more involved they will become, and the more responsibility they will take for their own learning.

Student Recommendations

Find out which students have read *Do People Grow on Family Trees? Genealogy for Kids and Other Beginners* or *The Great Ancestor Hunt: The Fun of Finding Out Who You Are.* Suggest that they share a helpful hint or two about searching for one's ancestors to get others interested in these selections. Also, encourage students to recommend and share other books they have read that contain characters or events that portray the rich tradition of their heritage.

Note: Teachers should preview any trade books for appropriateness in their classrooms before recommending them to students.

Exploration Wrap-Up

Whole-Group Discussion

- Initiate a class discussion of the unit selections, focusing on the theme of heritage.
- Have the students refer to page 40 of their **Inquiry Journals** to remind themselves of what they knew about heritage when they began the unit and what they expected to learn from the unit.
- Remind students to think about their previous discussions of ideas from the Concept/Question Board.

> **UNIT 3**
> Name _____ Date _____
> *Heritage*
> **Knowledge About Heritage**
> • This is what I know about heritage before reading the unit.
>   Answers will vary.
> _____
> _____
> _____
> _____
> • These are some things I would like to know about heritage.
>   Answers will vary.
> _____
> _____
> _____
> _____
> _____
> Reminder: I should read this page again when I get to the end of the unit to see how much I've learned about heritage.
> **40**   Inquiry Journal

Inquiry Journal p. 40

Extending the Discussion

- Have the students evaluate the unit selections, identifying those they found the most interesting and those they found the least interesting.
- Have the students evaluate the unit activities. Which activities did they find the most enjoyable or informative?
- Tell students to evaluate the overall unit. They should consider how well the unit topic was covered and whether the topic was worth examining.
- Tell students to suggest aspects of heritage that are worth further exploration, possibly beginning with any questions left on the Concept/Question Board.

Small-Group Discussion

- As an alternative to whole-group discussion, have students work in small groups to discuss the unit. Encourage group participants to refer to the Concept/Question Board, browse unit selections, and review their **Inquiry Journals** for Unit 3 to refresh their memories of important ideas raised in the unit.
- Call on the groups to share with their classmates any important points and conclusions from their discussions.

Unit Celebration

Have students suggest ways to celebrate the completion of this unit. If necessary, offer your own suggestions, such as the following:

- Make arrangements to display the students' heritage albums in the school library. Be sure to get permission from students' families.
- Invite students' family members to attend an afternoon or evening presentation of the students' selected pieces.

Review the Concepts

After all of the collaborative groups have shared their ideas about heritage with the class, ask the students if there are additional ideas that they wish to discuss or explore.

- Have students discuss how their original perceptions of heritage have changed.
- Have students review any questions they may have had throughout the unit.
- As always, students' ideas should direct the discussion.
- Remind students that they can continue to research heritage, even though they have finished the unit.

Review Fine Art

Have students look again at the fine art shown on pages 298–299 of their anthologies. Invite them to discuss the aspects of heritage that are represented by each piece.

Assessment

✓ Informal Assessment

- Give the children the opportunity to evaluate their learning experiences during this unit by completing **Inquiry Journal** pages 54–55.
- Meet individually with students to discuss their evaluations.

Inquiry Journal pp. 54–55

✓ Formal Assessment

You can find the unit assessment for Unit 3 on pages 69–78 of the **Comprehension and Writing Assessment**. See the **Assessment Guide** for specific suggestions on how to use these skills.

Comprehension Assessment

- Understanding the Selection
- Making Connections Across Selections
- Vocabulary
- Skills

Writing Assessment

- Personal Response—Students write an essay about a gift they received from a friend or family member that has special meaning to them.
- Exploring Unit Concepts—Students write an essay comparing one of their family traditions with a tradition from one of the stories.

Table *of* Contents

Grammar, Mechanics, and Usage

Study Skills

Writing and Technology

Complete and Incomplete Sentences

Rule: A **sentence** is a group of words that expresses a complete thought.

A sentence must have a subject and a predicate to be complete. The **subject** of a sentence tells *who* or *what*.

Subjects:
The experiment with sand was interesting.
(What? The experiment with sand)

Ted and Janet reported their observations.
(Who? Ted and Janet)

The **predicate** of a sentence tells *what happens* or *happened*.

Predicates:
The sand worked as an insulator.
(What happened? Worked as an insulator.)

The other insulators did not work as well.
(What happened? Did not work as well.)

A sentence is incomplete if it is missing a subject.

Incomplete:
Left the containers in the sun.
(Who left the containers in the sun?)

Checked them every hour.
(Who checked them every hour?)

A sentence is incomplete if it is missing a predicate.

Incomplete:
Each team of students.
(What happened to each team of students?)

Our science teacher, Ms. Kemp.
(What happened to our science teacher, Ms. Kemp?)

Compound Subject and Predicate

Rule: A subject of a sentence that has two or more parts is called a **compound subject**. A predicate of a sentence that has two or more parts is called a **compound predicate**. **Conjunctions** are words used to join sentence parts.

A compound subject has two or more parts. The parts are usually connected with the conjunctions *and*, *but*, or *or*.

Subjects with one part:
King Midas lived in a fine castle.
His daughter lived in a fine castle.

Compound subject:
King Midas and his daughter lived in a fine castle.

A compound predicate has two or more parts. The parts are usually connected with the conjunctions *and*, *but*, or *or*.

Predicates with one part:
The king counted his money every day.
The king arranged it in piles every day.

Compound predicate:
The king counted his money and arranged it in piles every day.

If a compound subject or compound predicate has three or more parts, use commas to separate the parts. Put the conjunction just before the last part.

Compound subject: Gold, jewels, and money were the king's most prized possessions.

Compound predicate: The King counted, hoarded, and hid his prized possessions.

Writer's Handbook

Grammar, Mechanics, and Usage

Compound Sentences

Rule: You can combine two sentences expressing related ideas. The combined form is called a **compound sentence**.

Follow these rules to form compound sentences:

Use conjunctions such as *and, or,* and *but* to combine sentences expressing closely related ideas. Place a comma before the conjunction.

Two sentences:
The library opens at eight o'clock.
It closes at six o'clock.

Compound sentence:
The library opens at eight o'clock, <u>and</u> it closes at six o'clock.

Two sentences:
The books could be due today.
The books could be due next week.

Compound sentence:
The books could be due today, <u>or</u> they could be due next week.

Two sentences:
The books were due today.
I renewed them.

Compound sentence:
The books were due today, <u>but</u> I renewed them.

672

Grammar, Mechanics, and Usage

Compound Sentences (continued)

Use a semicolon to combine two closely related sentences. The semicolon takes the place of the comma and conjunction.

Two sentences:
The library opens at eight o'clock. It closes at six o'clock.

Compound sentence:
The library opens at eight o'clock; it closes at six o'clock.

If two sentences do not express closely related ideas, keep them separate. For example, do not combine these sentences:

Jim lives near the library.
His favorite books are adventure stories.

673

Writer's Handbook

Grammar, Mechanics, and Usage

Phrases and Clauses

Rule: A **phrase** is a group of words that does not contain a subject and a predicate. A **clause** is a group of words containing a subject and a predicate.

Use phrases to add precise or interesting details to your writing. One type of phrase is the prepositional phrase. A **preposition** shows how one word is related to another word in the sentence. A **prepositional phrase** always begins with a preposition and is followed by a noun or a pronoun and any of its modifiers.

The prepositional phrases are underlined in the following sentences:

We stayed <u>at the park</u> and played <u>on the swings</u>.

<u>Up the tree</u> scurried the cat.

<u>Near the ocean</u> you can hear the waves as they crash <u>against the shore</u>.

In your writing, place a phrase as close as possible to the word the phrase modifies. Study these two examples:

Misleading: I saw a little monkey <u>in a magazine photo</u> <u>with a very long tail</u>.
(What has a very long tail?)

Clearer: I saw a little monkey <u>with a very long tail</u> <u>in a magazine photo</u>.

Use different kinds of clauses to show connections between ideas. There are two types of clauses, independent and dependent.

An **independent clause** can stand by itself as a sentence. A **dependent clause** has a subject and a predicate, but it cannot stand by itself because it begins with a connecting word. It depends on the

674

Grammar, Mechanics, and Usage

Phrases and Clauses (continued)

independent, or main, clause. Often, a dependent clause tells how, when, where, or why the action in the independent, or main, clause takes place.

dependent clause	independent clause
although I like soccer	I am not good at it

independent clause	dependent clause
Jill and I play tennis	after we leave school

Here are some connecting words that are used to introduce a dependent clause:

after	because	since	until	which
although	before	that	when	while
as	if	though	where	who

If a dependent clause is not necessary to the meaning of the sentence, put a comma between the clauses.

Examples:
I like fishing, which is Dad's favorite sport.
I fish with Dad, who likes to go out in a boat.

If a dependent clause is necessary to the meaning of the sentence, do not put a comma between the clauses.

Examples:
Dad knows the man who sold us our boat.
We looked for a boat that we could rent.

Use a comma after a dependent clause that begins a sentence.

Examples:
After we caught our limit, we went home.
Because we like fish, we had some for supper.

675

Writer's Handbook

Grammar, Mechanics, and Usage

Using Commas

Rule: Use a **comma** when you write a series of three or more nouns, adjectives, verbs, or phrases. Use a comma when you write dates and addresses, in direct address, and in certain letter parts.

In a **series** of three or more **nouns**, use a comma after each noun that comes before *and* or *or*.

> **Nouns:** Foxes eat lizards, birds, mice, and other small animals.

In a **series** of three or more **adjectives**, use a comma after each adjective that comes before *and* or *or*.

> **Adjectives:** The fur of the Arctic fox is long, white, and silky.

In a **series** of three or more **verbs**, use a comma after each verb that comes before *and* or *or*.

> **Verbs:** Fox cubs wrestle, jump, and play with each other.

In a **series** of three or more **phrases**, use a comma after each phrase that comes before *and* or *or*.

> **Phrases:** Foxes may live among rocks, in underground dens, in caves, or in the hollows of trees.

Follow these guidelines when you use commas in other places:

- In writing **dates**, use a comma to separate the day from the year. When you write a date in a sentence, also place a comma after the year (except at the end of a sentence) to separate it from the rest of the sentence.

676

Grammar, Mechanics, and Usage

Using Commas (continued)

> **Date:** January 3, 1959, is the date Alaska was admitted to the Union as the forty-ninth state.

- Use a comma to separate the parts of a **place name**. When you write a place name in a sentence, also use a comma after the last word in the place name (except at the end of a sentence) to separate it from the rest of the sentence.

> **Place name:** Nome, Alaska, is south of the Arctic Circle.

- When you address the person you're speaking to by name, use one or two commas, as necessary, to separate the person's name from the rest of the sentence.

> **Address a person:**
> Dad, may we visit Aunt Ada next summer?
> Yes, Kayla, we will visit your aunt.

- Use a comma after the greeting and after the closing of a friendly letter.

> **Friendly letter:** Dear Aunt Ada,
> Love,

- Use a comma after the closing of a business letter. Note that the greeting of a business letter ends with a colon, not a comma. For examples, see page 681, **Using Semicolons and Colons**.

> **Business letter:** Very truly yours,
> Sincerely,

677

Writer's Handbook

Grammar, Mechanics, and Usage

Using Parentheses, Dashes, and Ellipses

Rule: Parentheses, dashes, and ellipses are special kinds of punctuation marks. Use **parentheses** to show extra information within a sentence. Use **dashes** to show an interruption. Use **ellipses** to show a pause in speech, an unfinished sentence, or a place where words are left out of a quotation.

Put parentheses around extra information in a sentence. The information may tell what one of the words in the sentence means.

> ***Tyrannosaurus rex* was a carnivore (meat eater).**

The words in parentheses may give the reader more information.

> **A *Tyrannosaurus rex* was about 40 feet (12 meters) in length.**

You may also use dashes to set off a phrase that breaks the even flow of a sentence.

> **The Mesozoic Era—the period when the dinosaurs lived—lasted more than 175 million years.**

In dialogue, you can use a dash to show that a sentence was interrupted before it could be finished.

> **Terry pointed at the dinosaur skeleton and exclaimed, "What an enormous —"**

678

Grammar, Mechanics, and Usage

Using Parentheses, Dashes, and Ellipses (continued)

Use ellipses to show a pause in speech.

> **The teacher said, "I think that was the largest of the plant-eating dinosaurs . . . or was there a bigger one?"**

Use ellipses to show that a sentence was not finished. A period is placed after the sentence, followed by three dots.

> **I have read about so many dinosaurs: tyrannosaurs, stegosaurs, brachiosaurs. . . .**

Use ellipses to show that one or more words from a quotation have been left out.

> **She wrote, "Nobody knows . . . why the dinosaurs died out."**

679

Writer's Handbook

Grammar, Mechanics, and Usage

Using Semicolons and Colons

Rule: Semicolons and colons are punctuation marks. A **semicolon** (;) is used to separate two connected and complete thoughts in one sentence. A **colon** (:) shows that something more is to follow.

Colons and semicolons look similar, but serve different purposes.

Follow these rules when you use them:

Use a **semicolon** (;) to separate two connected and complete thoughts in one sentence. You may use a semicolon instead of a comma and a conjunction such as *and, but, or,* or *so.*

Sentence using comma and conjunction:
The fifth graders voted for dogs as their favorite animals, and cats came in second.

Sentence using semicolon:
The fifth graders voted for dogs as their favorite animals; cats came in second.

Notice that the semicolon separates a sentence into two parts. Each part is a complete thought with a subject and a predicate.

Use a **colon** (:) in a sentence to show that something is to follow. What follows might be a list of items or names, or it might be a complete thought that explains the first part of a sentence. If what follows is a complete thought, begin the sentence with a capital letter.

Grammar, Mechanics, and Usage

Using Colons and Semicolons (continued)

Colon introduces a list:
These animals also received two or more votes: parakeets, hamsters, and goldfish.

Second part of the sentence explains the first part:
There was only one surprise: Three people voted for snakes!

Use a colon between hours and minutes when you write a time.

Use a colon after the greeting in a business letter.

Examples: 6:45 A.M.   6:50 P.M.

Examples: Dear Mr. Cobra: Dear Ms. Windsor:

Writer's Handbook

Grammar, Mechanics, and Usage

Parts of Speech

Rule: All words can be classified into groups called parts of speech. They include **nouns**, **pronouns**, **verbs**, **adjectives**, **adverbs**, **prepositions**, **conjunctions**, and **interjections**.

A **noun** names a person, place, thing, or idea.

The football <u>players</u> practice on the <u>field</u>.

A **pronoun** takes the place of a noun.

The football players practice on the field. <u>They</u> practice for two hours.

A **verb** names an action or tells what someone or something is, was, or will be.

The players <u>practice</u> hard. They <u>are</u> determined to do well. They <u>will listen</u> to their coach.

An **adjective** describes a noun or a pronoun.

The <u>football</u> players enjoy playing the game. They are <u>strong</u> athletes.

An **adverb** describes a verb, an adjective, or another adverb. An adverb may answer the questions *How? How often? When?* or *Where?*

The football team plays <u>skillfully</u>. The players are <u>now</u> the best in the league. The fans cheer <u>frequently</u>. TV camera crews and reporters are <u>everywhere</u>.

Grammar, Mechanics, and Usage

Parts of Speech (continued)

A **preposition** shows the relationship between a noun or pronoun and a verb, an adjective, or another noun in a sentence.

The bleachers are <u>behind</u> the school.
Meet me <u>after</u> the game.

A **conjunction** is used to connect words, phrases, or sentences.

Cal <u>and</u> Jake are the best players.
They are tired <u>but</u> determined.

An **interjection** is a word or phrase that expresses strong emotion.

<u>Wow</u>! Jake can really run fast.
<u>Great</u>! He just made a touchdown.

Writer's Handbook

Grammar, Mechanics, and Usage

Using Possessive Nouns

Rule: A **possessive noun** is used to show ownership. Possessive nouns can be singular or plural.

Follow these rules to form possessive nouns:

A **singular noun** names only one person, place, or thing. Form the possessive of a singular noun by adding an apostrophe and *s* (*'s*).

Singular noun:
Juan had a special party for his birthday.

Possessive noun:
Juan's cousin plays in a rock band.

A **plural noun** names more than one person, place, or thing. Form the possessive of a plural noun that ends in *s* by adding an apostrophe after the *s* (*s'*).

Plural noun ending with *s*:
The band members all owned instruments.

Possessive noun:
The band members' instruments were beautiful.

To form the possessive of a **plural noun** that does not end in *s*, add an apostrophe and *s* (*'s*).

Plural noun not ending with *s*:
All the children clapped and cheered.

Possessive noun:
The children's applause made the band feel happy.

684

Writer's Handbook

Grammar, Mechanics, and Usage

Using the Right Pronoun for the Right Noun

Rule: **Pronouns** are words that take the place of nouns. Pronouns must agree in number, gender, and person with the nouns that they replace.

Use **singular pronouns** to take the place of singular nouns. Singular pronouns, such as *I, you, he, she,* or *it,* stand for one person or thing.

Singular nouns and pronouns:
Sonia went to the park. She took out her lunch and ate it happily.

Use **plural pronouns** to take the place of plural nouns. Plural pronouns, such as *we, you,* or *they,* stand for more than one person or thing.

Plural nouns and pronouns:
Sonia and her classmates went to the museum. They returned at three o'clock.

Use **subject pronouns** to take the place of subject nouns. The subject noun of a sentence tells who or what the sentence is about. Subject pronouns include *I, you, she, he, it, we,* and *they.*

Subject pronouns:
Sonia went to the park. She sat under a tree.

685

Grammar, Mechanics, and Usage

Using the Right Pronoun for the Right Noun (continued)

Use **object pronouns** to take the place of object nouns. The object noun of the sentence follows the verb. Sometimes an object pronoun follows words such as *to, for, with, at,* or *from.* Object pronouns include *me, you, him, her, it, us,* and *them.*

Object pronoun:
Sonia ate some grapes.
She ate them in the shade of a maple tree.

Use **possessive pronouns** to take the place of possessive nouns. Possessive pronouns show who owns or has something. Such possessive pronouns as *my, your, his, her, its, our,* or *their* appear before a noun. Other possessive pronouns, including *mine, yours, his, hers, its, ours,* or *theirs,* stand alone.

Possessive pronouns:
Sonia's father is a dentist. His office is on the fifth floor. The entire floor is his.

Always be sure your readers know exactly to *whom* or *what* each pronoun refers. If it is not clear to which noun your pronoun refers, use the noun again.

Not clear: Alex and Ben went to a café for lunch. He ordered cake.

Clear: Alex and Ben went to a café for lunch. Ben ordered cake.

686

Writer's Handbook

Grammar, Mechanics, and Usage

Using Present-Tense Verbs

Rule: A **verb tense** is a form of a verb that tells the time an action takes place—in the present, in the past, or in the future. A verb in the **present tense** shows action that happens now or action that happens again and again.

Follow these rules when you use present-tense verbs:

If the subject of a sentence is singular (except for the words *I* or *you*), add *-s* or *-es* to the verb to form the present tense. For most verbs, add *-s* to the end of the verb. With some verbs, you add *-es.* For example, if the verb ends with *-ch, -sh, -s, -ss, -x,* or *-z,* add *-es.*

Also, if the verb ends with a consonant followed by *y,* change the *y* to *i* and add *-es.*

Add *-s*: Margaret sees plays often.

Add *-es*: She coaches the school drama club.

Change *y* to *i* and add *-es*:
She tries to remember all of the lines.

If the subject of a sentence is plural, do not add an ending to the verb. Also, do not add an ending to the verb if the subject of the sentence is *I* or *you.*

No ending:
The girls love musicals. They buy recordings of their favorite plays. They listen to the songs over and over again. Sometimes I lend them my CDs.

687

Grammar, Mechanics, and Usage

Using Present-Tense Verbs (continued)

Irregular verbs have special present-tense forms that you must remember. Here are some examples:

Irregular Verbs	Present-Tense Forms
be	I <u>am</u>. You <u>are</u>. We <u>are</u>. They <u>are</u>. He <u>is</u>. She <u>is</u>. It <u>is</u>.
do	I <u>do</u>. You <u>do</u>. We <u>do</u>. They <u>do</u>. He <u>does</u>. She <u>does</u>. It <u>does</u>.
have	I <u>have</u>. You <u>have</u>. We <u>have</u>. They <u>have</u>. He <u>has</u>. She <u>has</u>. It <u>has</u>.

Writer's Handbook

Grammar, Mechanics, and Usage

Using Past-Tense Verbs

Rule: A **verb tense** is a form of a verb that tells the time an action takes place—in the present, in the past, or in the future. A verb in the **past-tense** form tells about an action that happened in the past.

Follow these rules when you use verbs in the past tense:

- Add *-ed* to form the past tense of most verbs.

  Add *-ed*: Ashley <u>played</u> the drums in a band. She <u>taped</u> her group's performance. Her dad <u>asked</u> her opinion. "It <u>sounded</u> good," she <u>replied</u>. "We really <u>jammed</u>."

For some verbs you need to change the spelling before you add *-ed*.

- If the verb ends with *e*, drop *e* when you add *-ed*.

  Drop *e*: tape <u>taped</u>

- If the verb ends with a consonant plus *y*, change the *y* to *i* and add *-ed*.

  Change *y* to *i* and add *-ed*: reply <u>replied</u>

- For most verbs that have one syllable, one short vowel, and one final consonant, double that final consonant before adding *-ed*.

  Double final consonant: jam <u>jammed</u>

Grammar, Mechanics, and Usage

Using Past-Tense Verbs (continued)

Irregular verbs have special forms in the past tense. Here are some common examples:

Irregular Verbs	Past-Tense Forms
be	I <u>was</u>. He <u>was</u>. She <u>was</u>. It <u>was</u>. You <u>were</u>. We <u>were</u>. They <u>were</u>.
do	did
have	had
go	went
come	came
say	said
give	gave

Writer's Handbook

Grammar, Mechanics, and Usage

Making Subject and Verb Agree

Rule: In a sentence, the verb must **agree** with the subject. A singular subject takes a singular verb. A plural subject takes a plural verb.

The **subject** of a sentence is the word or words that refer to the person(s) or thing(s) that performs or receives the action of the verb. The **verb** is the word that refers to the action.

Most verbs follow this pattern in the present tense:

Present Tense	
Singular	*Plural*
I work.	We work.
You work.	You work.
He, she, it works.	They work.

If the subject is a singular noun, or *he*, *she*, or *it*, add *-s* to the verb.

  Takes *-s* ending: Juan <u>plays</u> tennis. He <u>plays</u> tennis.

However, verbs that end in *-s, -z, -x, -ss, -ch,* or *-sh* take the ending *-es*. In verbs that end in a consonant plus *y*, the *y* changes to *i* before the *-es* ending.

  Takes *-es* ending:
  The player <u>smashes</u> the ball across the net.
  Final *y* changes to *i* before *-es*:
  The player <u>tries</u> a new grip.

Some common verbs, such as *be* and *have*, are irregular. They have special patterns that you must memorize.

Grammar, Mechanics, and Usage

Making Subject and Verb Agree (continued)

Be: Present Tense	
I am.	We are.
You are.	You are.
He, she, it is.	They are.

Have: Present Tense	
I have.	We have.
You have.	You have.
He, she, it has.	They have.

The words *anyone, everyone, somebody, either,* and *each* are singular and take a singular verb.

Everyone plans to attend the assembly.

A subject consisting of two singular words connected by *and* is usually plural and takes a plural verb.

Maria and Franco play outside.

A subject consisting of two singular words connected by *or* or *nor* takes a singular verb.

Neither Betty nor Tim takes the class.

A subject consisting of a singular word and a plural word connected by *or* or *nor* takes a verb that agrees with the word nearer the verb.

Will the football player or the cheerleaders talk at the assembly?

Sometimes other words come between the subject and the verb. Make sure that the verb agrees with the subject.

One of the English teachers is in charge of the debate.

Writer's Handbook

Grammar, Mechanics, and Usage

Using Adjectives and Adverbs

Rule: An **adjective** describes a noun or a pronoun. An **adverb** describes a verb, an adjective, or another adverb. Adverbs answer the question *Where? When? How much?* or *How often?*

Remember these guidelines when you use adjectives and adverbs:

An **adjective** describes a noun. An adjective can also describe a pronoun such as *he, she, it,* or *they.*

Adjectives: The box had a plastic cover on it. The two boys opened the box. They were curious.

An **adverb** describes a verb, an adjective, or another adverb. Adverbs tell *where, when, how much,* or *how often.*

Adverbs: The boys were slightly nervous. Soon they discovered what was in the box. They closed the box quickly.

You can form many adverbs by adding *-ly* to an adjective. Notice that the spelling of a word may change when *-ly* is added to it.

Adverbs:
Several snakes lay quietly in the box.   (quiet + -ly)
The boys put the box down gently.   (gentle + -ly)

Writer's Handbook

Grammar, Mechanics, and Usage

Using and Punctuating Dialogue

Rule: In a story, what characters say to each other is called **dialogue.** A speaker's exact words are called a **quotation.** These words are put inside **quotation marks** (" ").

Place quotation marks (" ") around a speaker's exact words.

Quotation marks: Janell said, "My telescope is assembled."

Begin the first word of a quotation with a capital letter, even if it is not at the beginning of a sentence.

Capital letter: Ben called, "My turn, my turn."

In most cases, use a comma to separate a quotation from the speaker tag.

Comma: "Sure, be my guest," replied Janell.

Put the end punctuation mark for the quotation inside the closing quotation marks.

End marks:
Ben exclaimed, "The moon looks so close!"
"Can you see any craters?" asked Sue.

Use two sets of quotation marks when a speaker tag interrupts a quotation. Separate the speaker tag from

---

Grammar, Mechanics, and Usage

Using and Punctuating Dialogue (continued)

the quotation with commas. Do not capitalize the first word after the speaker tag because it is part of the first sentence of the quotation, not a new sentence. If the interrupted quote contains two complete sentences, use a period and a capital letter.

One sentence:
"Yes," said Ben, "they look huge."

Two sentences:
"They are really big," said Sue. "One crater is about 700 miles across."

Always start a new paragraph when the speaker changes.

Example:
"Sue, did you bring the soccer ball?" Ben asked.
"I put it in the green bag, Ben," replied Sue.

Writer's Handbook

Study Skills

Parts of a Book

A book has other parts besides the main part, the part containing a story or information. All books do not have the same number of parts, but each part is usually found in the same place in every book. Many fiction books have only a **title page** and a **copyright page**, but some will also have a **table of contents** and a **glossary**. Nonfiction books have a title page and a copyright page and often a table of contents, glossary, **bibliography**, and **index**.

When you look for information about a story, question, or problem, you usually use several books. However, you will not have time to read every page of every book. Instead, use the parts of a book to help you find the information you need.

The title page, copyright page, and table of contents are at the front of the book.

- The **title page** gives the title of the book, the name of the author or editor, and the name of the publisher.
- The **copyright page** comes after the title page. It gives the publisher's name and location and the year in which the book was published.
- The **table of contents** is a list, in order of appearance, of the units, chapters, or stories in the book, with the page number on which each item begins.

Study Skills

Parts of a Book (continued)

The glossary, bibliography, and index are at the back of the book. Sometimes a bibliography is found, instead, at the end of each chapter or unit.

- The **glossary** is an alphabetical listing of new or special words that are used in the book along with their definitions.
- The **bibliography** is an alphabetical listing of books in which the author of the book found information about the subject. It may also include other writings that the author thinks would interest the reader.
- The **index** is an alphabetical listing of names, places, and topics covered in the book, with the numbers of the pages on which they are mentioned or discussed.

Writer's Handbook

Study Skills

Using the Card Catalog

Each library has a **card catalog**—a list of all the books in a library. Some libraries list the books on cards found in small cabinet drawers. Other libraries have the card catalog on computers. In both systems, you can find a book listed in three ways: by the author's last name, by the title of the book, or by the subject of the book.

The card catalog is a good place to start your research about a subject. The following information can help you get the most out of it:

- The **author** card lists the author's name at the top of the card. A **title** card lists the book's title at the top. A **subject** card lists the subject of the book at the top. On a computer, you can look up an author's name, a book title, or a subject.
- A book entry may contain a **call number**. On each card, the call number is in the upper left-hand corner. This number matches the numbers and letters on the spine of the book. The call number also matches numbers and letters on the shelf on which you can find the book. An *R* means that a book is in the reference section. A *J* or *JUV* before the number means that the book is in the juvenile section.
- Every card shows the year in which the book was published. Make sure you check the **publication date** if you need to obtain recent information.
- The card lists the **number of pages** in the book. This number can give you some idea of how much information is in a book. It might also suggest whether the book is too hard or too easy.

Study Skills

Using the Card Catalog (continued)

- If the book has **illustrations**, the abbreviation *ill.* is shown. Sometimes the abbreviation *col ill.* is shown to let you know that the illustrations are in color. Depending on your research problem, pictures might help you in your research.
- The entry includes a **summary** of the book. The summary briefly tells what the book is about. It will help you decide whether the book has the information you need.
- If the book includes an **index** or **bibliography**, the card also provides that information. An index will help you locate pages where your subject appears. A bibliography might lead you to other books related to your subject.
- At the bottom of each card is a list of **headings**. This list gives all the headings under which the book is listed in the card catalog. If you look under the other headings in the subjects cards, you may find more books on your research problem.

Writer's Handbook

Study Skills

Using a Dictionary, Glossary, or Thesaurus

A **dictionary** is a book that tells the meanings of most of the words that people use when they speak, read, and write. A **glossary** is the section in the back of a book that gives the meaning of words that appear in that book. A **thesaurus** is a dictionary of synonyms and antonyms. Words in it may be organized in alphabetical order or by subject. In that case, check the index to see how to find a certain word.

- Each word listed in a dictionary, glossary, or thesaurus is called an **entry word**. All entry words are listed in alphabetical order and are printed in dark type.

- At the top of each dictionary, thesaurus, or glossary page are two words called **guide words**. These words are usually printed in dark type. The word on the left is the first entry word listed on the page. The word on the right is the last entry word listed on the page. All other words on the page fall in alphabetical order between the two guide words. (A thesaurus may use guide numbers instead of words.) Guide words can help you find the page on which the word you are looking for is listed.

- A **dictionary** or **glossary entry** gives the word's spelling, pronunciation, part of speech, and meaning or meanings. The part of speech is abbreviated; for example, *n.* stands for *noun*. Entries may also give synonyms for the word, spellings of the word with endings added, and the word's history or etymology.

Study Skills

Using a Dictionary, Glossary, or Thesaurus (continued)

> **flan·nel** (flan´ əl) *n.* A soft, woven material made of wool and/or cotton. [Middle English *flanen*, from Welsh *gwlanen*, "woolen cloth," from *gwlân*, "wool."]

- A **pronunciation key** is found at the beginning of a dictionary or glossary. The key has symbols that stand for vowel and consonant sounds. The symbols are shown with example words. Pronounce these to hear the sounds. Then use the symbols to pronounce unfamiliar words.

- A **thesaurus entry** shows a list of synonyms for that word and perhaps an antonym or two.

> **neat** *adj.* orderly, organized, tidy, uncluttered, well-organized, trim. Antonym—see MESSY

- Select the word that best conveys your meaning. Remember that synonyms have meanings that are similar but not exactly the same. If you are unsure which word to use in your context, you may wish to check the meanings of the word in a dictionary.

Writer's Handbook

Study Skills

Using an Encyclopedia

Encyclopedias are reference books that contain articles on a wide range of subjects. The articles in encyclopedias usually are arranged in alphabetical order (a few are thematic).

An encyclopedia is a good place to start when you begin doing research. It gives you information about your topic in its articles. It can also lead you to other materials about your topic.

Follow these guidelines when you use an encyclopedia:

- Locate the encyclopedia's index. It is usually at the back of a one-volume encyclopedia or a separate volume of a multivolume set. The index is an alphabetical list of all the articles in the encyclopedia.

- Decide what the key word or words in your research question or problem are. Look up those words in the index of an encyclopedia. For a question about *how the Underground Railroad helped slaves*, you might look in the index under "Underground Railroad." If you need information about a person, look under the person's last name.

> **Lincoln, Abraham**
> **Tubman, Harriet**

- In the index of a multivolume encyclopedia, after each main article title, you will see a volume number or letter first, then a page number. Other articles that have additional information might be

Study Skills

Using an Encyclopedia (continued)

listed as well. Make a list of the titles, volume numbers or letters, and page numbers of articles that might have information about your topic.

> **Underground Railroad 18:329; 2:9**
> **Brown, John 3:328**
> **Tubman, Harriet 18:254**
> **Vermont 19:69**

- Look at your list and select the encyclopedia volumes that you think will be most helpful. Turn to the given pages to locate the articles.

- Read any headings or subheadings within each article. Headings tell you what information you will find in the article's sections. They might give you some idea of how to narrow your topic or arrange the information in your own report.

- Throughout the article and at its end, look for suggestions of other places in the encyclopedia where you might find more information about your topic. These suggestions are called cross-references.

> *(See* **Quakers***) See also* **Fugitive Slave Law**.

Also, a list of books with more information about your topic may be given at the end of an article.

> **Blockson, Charles L. *Underground Railroad***
> **Brandt, Nat. *The Town That Started the Civil War***

Writer's Handbook

Study Skills

Using Maps

Maps are drawings that show where places are located or where important events happened. Maps are made and used for many purposes. Each kind of map gives different information. For example, **historical maps** show information about the past such as where battles were fought, what trails the pioneers followed, or how land was once divided.

Maps can present a great deal of information more quickly than it can be explained in words. Most maps have these features:

- The **title** tells what information the map shows or what its purpose is. The map shown on this page shows which states remained in the Union during the Civil War and which became Confederate states.

Study Skills

Using Maps (continued)

- The **key** explains what each symbol or color on the map stands for. Notice the key with the map on page 704. It shows that a dot stands for a capital city.

- The **scale** shows how many miles or kilometers are represented by a given measure, usually some fraction of an inch or centimeter, on the map. This map, for instance, shows that one half-inch equals 600 kilometers.

- The **direction arrows** or **compass rose** shows north, south, east, and west on the map.

Use the map features to find more information about states you are researching. For example, this map shows that 34 states were in existence in the year 1861.

Writer's Handbook

Study Skills

Making and Using a Time Line

A **time line** is a graphic device used to show the sequence of important events over a particular period of time and the relative amount of time between them. A time line may cover any chosen length of time, from the lifetime of a person to a historical period of hundreds or thousands of years.

Reading a time line can help you understand and remember the order of important past events. Making a time line can help you present the most important facts gathered in your research.

Here are guidelines for making a time line:

- Decide what you want to show in your time line. Choose a title for it.

  Example: Amelia Earhart

- Make a list of the main events and the time of each one. Use concise, descriptive phrases.

  Examples:

  Born Atchison, Kansas—1897
  First woman to fly across Atlantic as
  passenger—1928
  Solo flight across Atlantic—1932
  Lost on flight around world—1937

Study Skills

Making and Using a Time Line (continued)

- Draw a line across a sheet of paper. Leave space above and below the line for writing the events and the times—in order, from left to right.

- On the line, make a dot for the time of each event. Vary the space between the dots, according to the length of time between events.

- Below each dot, write a time.

- Above each dot, write an event.

Born Atchison, Kansas	First woman to fly across Atlantic as passenger	Solo flight across Atlantic	Lost on flight around the world
1897	1928	1932	1937

Writer's Handbook

Study Skills

Using Diagrams

A **diagram** is an illustration that shows the parts of an object or shows how something works. Labels on a diagram help explain the parts or steps in the illustration. Diagrams often help readers visualize information that is mechanical or scientific.

Diagrams can show the following kinds of information:

- how something is put together, such as a bicycle
- how something is arranged, such as clothing in a suitcase
- how something works, such as a telescope
- how to make something, such as a quilt
- how two or more things are connected, such as the strings on a violin
- what steps make up a process, such as making lemonade
- what stages make up a cycle, such as the seasons of the year

When you read, diagrams can help you understand technical or scientific material. When you write, you can help your readers understand technical material by using diagrams.

Study Skills

Using Diagrams (continued)

These are the features of a diagram:

Parts of a Telescope

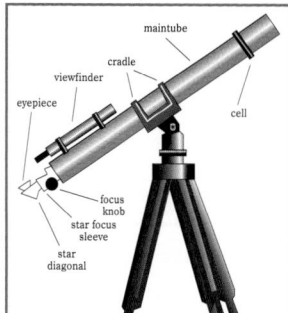

- The **title** of the diagram tells what the diagram is about.
- **Labels** of a diagram tell what each part of an object or step in a process is. On this diagram, for instance, a label tells you that a telescope has both a viewfinder and an eyepiece.
- **Lines** lead from each label to the part or step being identified.
- **Arrows** show in what order the steps of the process or the stages in a cycle take place. Arrows can also show movement or direction. This diagram contains no arrows. However, someone might add an arrow that shows which direction the focus knob turns or what path the light takes.

Writer's Handbook

Study Skills

Organizing Information in a Chart

A **chart** can present much information in a small amount of space. A chart helps organize information so that readers can understand it more easily and quickly.

Sometimes when you are doing research, you might find that you can better understand and compare information if you organize it in a chart. Charts are used for time schedules, work schedules, and other information.

The following guidelines will help you make charts and also understand them:

- Choose information that would be easier and faster to read and understand in a chart. For example, if you want to share information about money from around the world, your chart might include names and symbols for forms of money and different countries.

Money Around the World			
Name	*Symbol*	*Subdivision*	*Country*
Dollar	$	100 cents	United States
Drachma	Dr	100 lepta	Greece
Ruble	R *or* Rub	100 kopeks	Russia

Study Skills

Organizing Information in a Chart (continued)

- Give the chart a **title** that tells what it is about.
- Create **row headings** and write them down the left side of the page. Row headings are the names of the items you will give information about.
- Write short **column headings** across the top of the chart. These headings tell the kinds of information you will give about the items in the row headings.
- To help make the chart easy to read, draw lines between the column headings and between the row headings.
- In the blank spaces, write brief information about the items in the row headings. Complete sentences are not needed.
- To read a chart, find the row or column heading that shows the kind of information you are seeking. Read down or across until you find the information.

Writer's Handbook

Study Skills

Note Taking

Researchers take **notes** to help them remember important information about their research. Notes contain key phrases and short sentences that sum up important facts and ideas.

Follow these guidelines when you take notes:

- Use a different note card for each kind of information that you collect.

- Create a heading for each kind of information. Use the headings to organize your notes.

  Differences Between the North and South
  　Before the Civil War
  Different views on states' rights
  South was agricultural; North was industrial.
  South wanted to take slavery to the West.

- Sum up the source's ideas in our own words. Often you need to use only a few meaningful words, phrases, or abbreviations that will remind you of important information.

  Many diffs between N and S eventually led to CW.

- If the author uses especially interesting language to express an idea, you may want to quote her or his words exactly. If so, put quotation marks around the words. Also, record the author's name, the book title (or magazine and article title), and the page number of the quotation.

Study Skills

Note Taking (continued)

"Slowly, darkness lifted and Sumter's shape became more and more distinct. Confederate gunners adjusted the firing angle of their weapons, torches poised near the fuses. At exactly 4:30 a.m., General P. G. T. Beauregard gave the command, and the bombardment—and with it the Civil War—began."

Jim Murphy, "So I Became a Soldier," *The Boys' War: Confederate and Union Soldiers Talk About the Civil War*, page 1.

- Take notes on only the most important information about your research or problem.

- Write neatly and clearly so that you can easily read your notes as you write your report.

Writer's Handbook

Study Skills

Outlining

An **outline** is a written plan that writers use to organize their notes and ideas before they begin to write a first draft. An outline arranges information into main topics and subtopics.

When you are doing research, put your ideas into outline form before you start writing. Then you can be sure that your report or project is organized logically.

Follow these guidelines:

- On a sheet of paper, write the **title** for your outline. This title will be the title of your paper or project.

- Check the **headings** on your note cards. Then separate the cards into piles by their headings. The large, obvious divisions will be **main topics**.

- Next, check your note cards to see how each main topic can be divided. These divisions will be **subtopics** and must relate to the main topic. In the outline here, the two main topics are "Locations of most active volcanoes" and "Famous volcanic eruptions."

- Number each main topic with a Roman numeral (I, II, III, and so on) followed by a period. Your completed outline should include at least two main topics.

- Under each main topic, indent and number each subtopic with a capital letter followed by a period, as shown in the sample outline. Include at least two subtopics under each main topic—or none at all.

Study Skills

Outlining (continued)

- If subtopics need to be divided further, under each subtopic indent again as shown and number each subtopic with an Arabic numeral (1, 2, 3, and so on) followed by a period. If you use **sub-subtopics**, you should have at least two—or none at all.

  VOLCANIC ACTIVITY

  I. Locations of most active volcanoes

  　A. Ring of Fire

  　　1. Western coast of North and South America

  　　2. Eastern coast of Asian and Pacific Islands

  　B. Mediterranean Sea

  II. Famous volcanic eruptions

  　A. Mount Mazama

  　　1. Date

  　　2. Location

  　　3. Results

  　B. Mount Vesuvius

  　　1. Date

  　　2. Location

  　　3. Results

Writer's Handbook

Study Skills

Making a Bibliography

A **bibliography** is a list of writings about a particular subject. It may include books and other written material, recordings, and photographic collections in which the author found information to use in a book, an article, or a report. A bibliography may also be a list of books in which the reader can find more information about the subject.

A bibliography tells readers where the writer got her or his information. It also tells readers where they can read more about the subject. Provide a bibliography when you write about your research.

Follow these guidelines:

- Make a separate note or card for each book you use in your research. On the card, put the author's full name, with the last name first; the title of the book; the publisher's name; and the date of publication. The publisher's name is found at the bottom of the title page. The date of publication is found on the back of the title page.

  When you create your bibliography, put the information in this form:

  Meltzer, Milton. Voices from the Civil War: A Documentary History of the Great American Conflict. New York: HarperCollins Children's Books, 1989.

716

Study Skills

Making a Bibliography (continued)

- Note the form and punctuation: the first and last names are inverted; a comma is placed after the last name and a period after the middle name. The title is underlined or italicized and followed by a period. A colon is placed after the city of the publisher. A comma is placed after the name of the publisher. A period is placed after the date of publication.

- Write the title *Bibliography* in the center of the line at the top of the page. Leave a line space between the title and the first entry. Arrange your entries in alphabetical order by the last name of the author. If a source does not provide an author's name, list the work alphabetically by its title, ignoring the initial word *a*, *an*, or *the*. Leave a space between entries.

Bibliography

Arnold, Caroline. The Ancient Cliff Dwellers of Mesa Verde. New York: Clarion Books, 1992.

Lauber, Patricia. Painters of the Caves. Washington, D.C.: National Geographic Society, 1998.

717

Writer's Handbook

Writing and Technology

Doing On-Line Research

On-line research can be interesting, fun, and rewarding. On-line you can find newspaper articles, encyclopedia articles, interviews, dictionaries, and many other kinds of information.

When you do research, you will probably use a **search engine** or a **directory**. A search engine looks for certain keywords. A directory is a list of categories that you can look at and browse through. Many Websites contain both, so they are listed together here. Some of the best-known directories and search engines can be found at the following addresses:

    http://www.altavista.digital.com
    http://www.hotbot.com
    http://www.yahoo.com

These tools will provide you with lists of **URL's** (uniform resource locator), or Internet addresses. To access that site, just click or type the URL. If you type it, be sure you copy every letter, colon, and slash correctly. Type capital letters correctly and include all punctuation except for any at the end. Leave off an end punctuation mark, unless it is a slash (/).

Most sites offer either **search tips** or a **help file**. Read these carefully. They will help you search successfully. For example, at some sites, you can use words such as *AND* to join terms or names. Other sites use symbols or punctuation marks instead. At these sites, you may have to place a name inside quotation marks to search for it.

718

Writing and Technology

Doing On-Line Research (continued)

When you do research on-line, you should remember and follow a few simple guidelines:

- Use more than one search engine or directory, since each finds Websites in a special way. You may be unsuccessful at one site and successful at another.

- Check the most likely sources first. The Library of Congress or a major university is apt to be a better source of accurate historical information than a personal Website.

- Save information about your sources. If you used an on-line reference book, print out the page that gives its name, publisher, and date. If you used a Website, write down its URL, or Internet address.

719

Writer's Handbook

Writing and Technology

Comparing Information from Different On-Line Sources

When you select a book or magazine from a library, that document has gone through many people's hands: the writer's, one or more editors', fact checkers', and proofreaders', to name a few. Such material also contains the name of the publisher, whose reputation rests on printing reliable material. Printed material is usually evaluated before it is published.

Web material is different. Material that you find online may be just as reliable as material that you find in print. However, since anyone can publish on the Web, there is a greater chance that material may be inaccurate, wrong, or misleading. Therefore, you must learn to evaluate on-line information carefully.

The following guidelines can help you:

- Look at the person or organization that is sponsoring the site. To do this, look at the home page. Whose name appears on it? Is this a major university or a government organization? Is it a reputable professional person or group? Is it a commercial business, a political organization, or a private person?

- Sometimes the URL address can help you identify the source. Addresses of educational sites end in *edu*; those of government sites end in *gov*; those of businesses end in *com*. However, a personal Web page of a university student might also end in *edu*, so look further.

Writing and Technology

Comparing Information from Different On-Line Sources (continued)

- What is the purpose of the page? Is it designed to inform, persuade, or entertain you? Does it contain advertisements?

- Often, a home page will have a link to more information about the sponsoring organization or person. Click on it to learn more. Is this source likely to be an authority on the subject?

- Where does the information on the site come from? Most reliable sites provide this information somewhere. Sources that are quoted are named.

- Is the information up-to-date? Many pages tell when they were last updated.

- Does it contain links to other valuable sites?

Writer's Handbook

Writing and Technology

On-Line Safety Tips

Computers can connect you to people all over the world. You can look at Websites that were created in another country, and you can post and read messages on bulletin boards that are read throughout the world. You can communicate by e-mail and make new friends all over the world. Computers give you an opportunity to make new friends that you might otherwise never meet.

Meeting people on-line can be fun and exciting. However, you need to follow certain safety rules, just as you do when you meet any stranger.

- Do not believe everything that you read online. Many people make up special online personalities, either for fun or for deception. They may pretend to be older or younger than they really are. They may pretend to have another name or come from a different country.

- Never give out personal information online, unless you are sure that you are dealing with someone that you and your family knows well. Be careful what you post on bulletin boards. Do not give out any of the following information:

      your full name or address
      your school's name or location
      your phone number
      your Social Security number
      your parent's or guardian's name
      where your parent or guardian works

Writing and Technology

On-Line Safety Tips (continued)

- Never reply if someone asks for personal information. If someone writes anything that makes you feel uncomfortable or scared, do not write back. Instead, print out the other person's letter or message and give it to an adult.

- Never send a picture of yourself to someone you don't know. If someone asks for a picture, check with an adult.

- Never give out your password. Do not even tell it to your friends.

- Never agree to meet anyone in person unless you first tell a responsible adult and get that person's permission. Any meetings should be in a public place, not in a car or private home. Do not go alone.

- Never download a file from an unknown source. The file might contain a virus that will harm your computer. It might also contain a program that can damage your computer or gather information about you.

Glossary

Pronunciation Key

a as in at	ī as in kite	o͞o as in too	ə as in about, chicken, pencil, cannon, circus	sh as in shop
ā as in late	o as in ox	or as in form		th as in thin
â as in care	ō as in rose	ou as in out		th̸ as in there
ä as in father	ô as in bought and raw	u as in up		zh as in treasure
e as in set		y͞oo as in use	ch as in chair	
ē as in me	oi as in coin	ûr as in turn, germ, learn, firm, work	hw as in which	
i as in it	o͞o as in book		ng as in ring	

The mark (ˊ) is placed after a syllable with a heavy accent, as in **chicken** (chikˊ ən).

The mark (ˊ) after a syllable shows a lighter accent, as in **disappear** (disˊ ə pērˊ).

A

abacus (aˊ bə kəs) *n.* A tool used to figure math problems by sliding counters.

abolish (ə bolˊ ish) *v.* To put an end to.

Word Derivations

Below are some words related to *abolish*.

abolishable	abolishment	abolitionism
abolisher	abolition	abolitionist
abolishes	abolitionary	

abolitionist (abˊ ə lishˊ ən ist) *n.* A person who wants to end slavery.

acceleration (ak selˊ ə rāˊ shən) *n.* An increase in speed.

accumulation (ə ky͞ooˊ myə lāˊ shən) *n.* A piled-up mass.

ace (ās) *v.* To easily get all or most answers correct.

adjacent (ə jāˊ sənt) *adj.* Next to; touching.

adobe (ə dōˊ bē) *n.* Sun-dried brick.

agate (aˊ gət) *n.* A striped marble.

agitation (ajˊ i tāˊ shən) *n.* Disturbance; excitement.

ailment (ālˊ mənt) *n.* An illness; a sickness.

alder (ôlˊ dər) *n.* A tree in the birch family.

alien (āˊ lē an) *adj.* From another world.

align (ə līnˊ) *v.* To place in a straight line.

alignment (ə līnˊ mənt) *n.* The arrangement of things in a straight line.

---

allegiance · avocation

Pronunciation Key: at; lāte; câre; fäther; set; mē; it; kīte; ox; rōse; ô in bought; coin; bo͞ok; to͞o; form; out; up; ūse; tûrn; ə sound in about, chicken, pencil, cannon, circus; hw in which; ring; shop; thin; th̸ere; zh in treasure.

allegiance (ə lēˊ jəns) *n.* Loyalty.

amid (ə midˊ) *adv.* In the middle of; among.

amiss (ə misˊ) *adv.* Wrong; not as expected.

ample (amˊ pəl) *adj.* More than enough.

anomaly (ə nomˊ ə lē) *n.* Something that is different from the usual arrangement.

anticipate (an tisˊ ə pātˊ) *v.* To know or feel in advance.

anticipation (an tisˊ ə pāˊ shən) *n.* The act of expecting; hope.

applicant (apˊ li kənt) *n.* A person who asks for a position or job.

apprehension (apˊ ri henˊ shən) *n.* Fear.

apprentice (ə prenˊ tis) *v.* To bind oneself to a craft worker in order to learn a trade.

arc (ärk) *v.* To move in a curved line. —*n.* A curve.

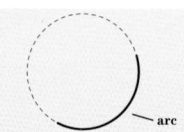

arc

Word Derivations

Below are some words related to *arc*.

arcade	arcading	arcing
arcaded	arced	arcs

archaeology or **archeology** (ärˊ kē olˊ ə jē) *n.* The scientific study of people of the past by digging up things they left behind.

Word History

Archaeology, or **archeology,** came into English in the year 1837. It is from the Latin word *archaeologia,* meaning "knowledge gained through the study of ancient objects." This Latin word's origins are with the Greek words *archē,* meaning "beginning," and *logos,* meaning "word."

aroma (ə rōˊ mə) *n.* A smell or odor, usually pleasant.

array (ə rāˊ) *n.* The order or arrangement of something.

arthritis (är thrīˊ tis) *n.* A disease of inflamed joints, often associated with advanced age.

artifice (ärˊ tə fis) *n.* A clever trick in the way a story's plot is constructed.

artillery (är tilˊ ə rē) *n.* Mounted guns.

ascend (ə sendˊ) *v.* To climb up; to rise.

assault (ə sôltˊ) *n.* A sudden attack.

astronomical (asˊ trə nomˊ i kəl) *adj.* Having to do with the study of the stars and planets.

astronomy (ə stronˊ ə mē) *n.* The scientific study of stars and planets.

atavistic (atˊ ə visˊ tik) *adj.* Characteristic of people from a much earlier time.

automated (ôtˊ ə māˊ təd) *adj.* Automatic; run by machines.

avert (ə vûrtˊ) *v.* To avoid.

avocation (avˊ ə kāˊ shən) *n.* Something a person does in addition to or aside from his or her regular job.

---

banish · brushpopper

B

banish (banˊ ish) *v.* To drive away; to force away.

bastion (basˊ chən) *n.* A part of a fortified structure that juts out so that defenders can fire at attackers from several angles.

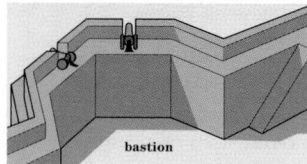

bastion

battery (batˊ ə rē) *n.* A group of mounted guns or cannons.

bayonet (bāˊ ə net) *n.* A swordlike weapon attached to the end of a rifle.

beanie (bēˊ nē) *n.* A small bill-less cap worn on the crown of the head.

bedclothes (bedˊ klōz) *n.* Items used to cover a bed, such as sheets, blankets, and quilts.

bedrock (bedˊ rok) *n.* Solid rock.

benevolent (bə nevˊ ə lənt) *adj.* Kind; generous.

berate (bi rātˊ) *v.* To scold harshly.

bewilderment (bi wilˊ dər mənt) *n.* Confusion.

bice (bīs) *adj.* Blue or blue-green.

billowing (biˊ lōˊ ing) *adj.* Swelled up by the wind.

blemish (blemˊ ish) *n.* A stain; a defect.

blintze (blints) *n.* Cheese or fruit wrapped in a thin pancake.

blocade (blo kādˊ) *v. An old-fashioned spelling of* **blockade.** To

cut off an enemy's supplies.

bloody (bluˊ dē) *adj.* A word used to indicate an extremely negative feeling.

bolt (bōlt) *n.* A roll of material or cloth.

bombard (bomˊ bärd) *n.* A leather jug or bottle.

bombardment (bom bärdˊ mənt) *n.* A battering with shots and shells.

boost (bo͞ost) *v.* To push up.

bore (bor) *v.* To drill into; to pierce.

bow (bou) *n.* The front part of a ship.

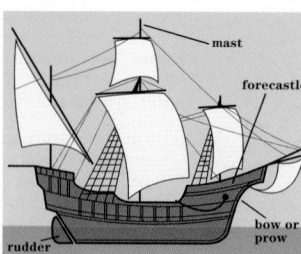

mast
forecastle
bow or prow
rudder

Word History

Bow came into English about 500 years ago. It probably came from the Dutch word *boech,* meaning "bow" or "shoulder." It is also related to *bōg,* a word meaning "bough" (a large tree branch) that dates back more than 800 years.

brazen (brāˊ zən) *adj.* Bold; cocky.

break (brāk) *v.* To tame a horse.

brocade (brō kādˊ) *n.* Woven cloth that has a raised pattern.

bronc (bränk) *n.* A wild or poorly broken horse.

brushpopper (brushˊ pŏ pər) *n.* A person who works in an area covered with low-growing bushes and weeds.

Pronunciation Key: at; lāte; câre; fäther; set; mē; it; kīte; ox; rōse; ô in bought; coin; boŏk; toō; form; out; up; ūse; tûrn; ə sound in about, chicken, pencil, cannon, circus; chair; hw in which; ring; shop; thin; thĕre; zh in treasure.

bulldog (boŏl´ dôg´) v. To wrestle a steer, usually by grabbing its horns and twisting its neck.

buttress (bu´ tris) n. A structure built outside a wall to give the wall support.

C

cairn (kârn) n. A pile of stones left as a landmark or a monument.

cairn

calculation (kal´ kyə lā´ shən) n. 1. Counting, computing, or figuring. 2. The result of counting, computing, or figuring.

calibrate (kal´ ə brāt´) v. To measure by marking off equal amounts.

candor (kan´ dər) n. Honesty.

capital (kap´ i tl) adj. Excellent.

carcass (kär´ kəs) n. The body of a dead animal.

caribou (kar´ ə boō´) n. A reindeer.

catapult (kat´ ə pult´) v. To move very quickly or with great force.

celandine (sel´ ən dīn´) n. A plant in the buttercup family with single yellow flowers.

ceremonial (ser´ ə mō´ nē əl) adj. Having to do with a formal celebration.

chance (chans) v. To take a risk and try something difficult.

chaparral (shap´ ə ral´) n. An area thick with shrubs and small trees.

cheder (hā´ dər) n. Religious school for teaching Judaism.

chiffon (shi fon´) n. A soft, see-through material made of silk, nylon, or rayon.

cinder (sin´ dər) n. Ash or a piece of partially burnt coal or wood.

circuit (sûr´ kit) n. 1. A journey around an established territory. 2. The path of an electrical current. **short circuit:** A condition in which something gets in the way of the path of an electrical current and causes either too much electricity or not enough.

clamber (klam´ bər) v. To climb with difficulty.

clarify (klâr´ ə fī´) v. To make something clear; to explain.

cloister (kloi´ stər) n. A place where religious people live away from the world; a convent or a monastery.

cobbler (kob´ lər) n. A person who repairs shoes and boots.

commence (kə mens´) v. To begin.

Word History

Commence came into English about 600 years ago. It came from the French word *comencer*, and its assumed origin is the Latin word *cominitiare*. This Latin word is a derivative of *initiare*, meaning "to initiate." (Also note that the word *commence* contains the *-ence* suffix, which in this word means "the action of" or "the process of.")

728

communal (kə myoōn´ l) adj. Public; shared by all.

compassion (kəm pash´ ən) n. Sympathy; pity.

compel (kəm pel´) v. To force.

compensate (kom´ pən sāt´) v. To make up for; to offset.

Word Derivations

Below are some words related to *compensate.*

compensated   compensative
compensating   compensator
compensation   compensatory
compensational

compensation (kom´ pən sā´ shən) n. Payment.

composition (kom´ pə zish´ ən) n. What something is made of.

compromise (kom´ prə mīz´) n. A settlement made by both sides each giving up a little.

concave (kon kāv´) adj. Curved inward; hollow; like the inner curve of a contact lens.

conceive (kən sēv´) v. 1. To start something with a certain point of view. 2. To understand.

conciliatory (kən sil´ ē ə tor´ ē) adj. Causing peace to be made.

concrete (kon´ krēt) adj. Real.

confine (kən fīn´) v. 1. To limit. 2. To keep in a place.

confounded (kon foun´ did) adj. Darned.

confront (kən frunt´) v. To face.

confrontation (kon´ frən tā´ shən) n. A face-to-face meeting.

consecrate (kon´ si krāt´) v. To make sacred.

consent (kən sent´) n. Permission.

consume (kən soōm´) v. To destroy.

Word Derivations

Below are some words related to *consume.*

consumed   consumerism   consuming
consumer   consumes   consumption

convex (kon veks´) adj. Curved outward; like the outer curve of a contact lens.

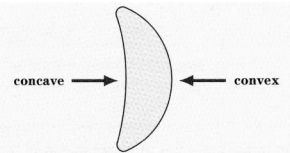
concave   convex

corn pone (korn´ pōn´) n. Baked or fried corn bread.

cotangent (kō tan´ jənt) n. A term used in trigonometry.

course (kors) v. To flow.

cradleboard (krād´ l bord´) n. A wooden frame that Native American women wore on their backs to carry their babies.

cringe (krinj) v. To back away from something unpleasant; to physically shrink because of fear or excessive humility.

croaker-sack (krō´ kər sak) n. A sack usually made of burlap.

crocheted (krō´ shād) adj. Made by looping one piece of yarn or thread through itself in an intricate pattern using a hooked needle.

crucial (kroō´ shəl) adj. Very important.

crusader (kroō sād´ ər) n. A person who fights for a cause.

729

Pronunciation Key: at; lāte; câre; fäther; set; mē; it; kīte; ox; rōse; ô in bought; coin; boŏk; toō; form; out; up; ūse; tûrn; ə sound in about, chicken, pencil, cannon, circus; chair; hw in which; ring; shop; thin; thĕre; zh in treasure.

cultivate (kul´ tə vāt´) v. To till the ground; to grow crops.

curvilinear (kur´ və li´ nē ər) adj. Having rounded or curving lines.

D

decipher (dē sī´ fər) v. To read or translate something written in code; decode.

deduction (di duk´ shən) n. A fact or conclusion figured out by reasoning.

defeatist (di fē´ təst) adj. Expecting and accepting that one will lose or be defeated.

defect (dē´ fekt) n. A fault; a flaw.

defect (di fekt´) v. To leave one's home country for another.

defiant (di fī´ ənt) adj. Openly disobedient; challenging.

Word History

Deliberately came into English about 500 years ago. It is the adverb form of the word *deliberate*, which came from the Latin word *deliberare*, meaning "to consider carefully." It is assumed that the Latin word *libra*, meaning "pound" or "scale," is also in its word history. This brings to mind the modern figure of speech "to weigh one's options." (Also note that *deliberately* contains the *-ly* suffix, which in this word means "in the manner of being.")

degradation (deg´ ri dā´ shən) n. Disgrace; shame.

deign (dān) v. To lower oneself; to stoop to do something that is beneath one.

deliberately (di li´ bə rət lē) adv. On purpose; meaning to.

delicatessen (del´ i kə tes´ ən) n. A shop selling prepared foods such as cooked meats and salads.

democracy (di mok´ rə sē) n. A government run by the people who live under it.

demolish (di mol´ ish) v. To do away with.

depredation (dep´ ri dā´ shən) n. The act of attacking and robbing.

desist (di sist´) v. To stop.

devise (di vīz´) v. To plan; to invent.

diffusion (di fyoō´ zhən) n. A spreading out or scattering.

dike (dīk) n. A bank or wall of earth built to hold back the water of a river or the sea.

diligence (dil´ i jens) n. Steady effort put forth to accomplish a task.

Word History

Diligence came into English about 600 years ago. It is a derivative of the word *diligent*, which has origins in the French word *diligere*, meaning "to love" or "to esteem." *Diligere* can also be divided into the word parts *di-*, meaning "apart," and *legere*, meaning "to select." (Also note that *diligence* contains the *-ence* suffix, which in this word means "the quality of" or "the state of.")

diminish (di min´ ish) v. To decrease; to lessen; to get smaller.

din (din) n. Clamor; uproar; racket.

730

discernible (di sûrn´ ə bəl) adj. Easy to recognize as different.

disconsolately (dis kon´ sə lit lē) adv. In a very unhappy way; hopelessly.

disembodied (dis´ em bod´ ēd) adj. Without a body.

disown (di´ sōn) v. To deny a connection to; to refuse to admit a relationship to.

dissipate (dis´ ə pāt´) v. To scatter.

Word Derivations

Below are some words related to *dissipate.*

dissipated   dissipates   dissipation
dissipater   dissipating   dissipative

distinct (di stingkt´) adj. 1. Clear; plain. 2. Separate.

distort (di stort´) v. To change the meaning of something; to misrepresent.

doctrine (dok´ trin) n. A principle or position that one believes in.

dogie (dō´ gē) n. A calf with no mother.

domesticated (də mes´ ti kāt´ əd) adj. Able to exist closely with humans.

domino (do´ mə nō´) n. A flat, rectangular game piece made of wood or plastic and divided into two equal parts with a varying number of dots on each part.

downpour (doun´ por´) n. A heavy rain.

dramatization (dram´ ə tə zā´ shən) n. An acting out of a story.

draught (draft) n. *chiefly British.* A liquid that is drunk; a dose.

dribble (dri´ bəl) v. In soccer, to move a ball down the field with a series of short, controlled kicks.

drought (drout) n. Dry weather that lasts a very long time.

dubiously (doo´ bē əs lē) adv. In a doubtful way.

dwindle (dwin´ dl) v. To get smaller gradually.

E

eclipse (i klips´) v. To darken; to cover over.

ecstatically (ek stat´ ik lē) adv. With great joy.

eddy (ed´ ē) v. To whirl into circle shapes.

edible (ed´ ə bəl) adj. Eatable.

emancipation (i man´ sə pā´ shən) n. The act of setting free.

embattled (em bat´ ld) adj. Struggling.

embellish (em bel´ ish) v. To make something better or more beautiful by adding to it.

encampment (en kamp´ mənt) n. A camp; a temporary stopping place.

encompass (en kum´ pəs) v. To include.

encounter (en koun´ tər) v. To meet by chance.

emphatically (em fat´ ik lē) adv. With spoken firmness or force.

engage (en gāj´) v. To take part; to be involved.

enumerate (i noō´ mə rāt´) v. To list; to count.

equinox (ē´ kwə noks´) n. The two times of the year when day and night are equal in length.

ermine (ûr´ min) n. A valuable white fur; the winter white fur coat of some weasels.

erroneous (ə rō´ nē əs) adj. Wrong; mistaken.

731

Student Reference

escort (e skort´) *v.* To go with and help or protect.
establish (i stab´ lish) *v.* To settle in a place.

Word Derivations

Below are some words related to *establish*.
establishable establisher establishment
established establishes

estate (i stāt´) *n.* A large piece of land owned by one individual or family.
eternal (i tûr´ nl) *adj.* Everlasting; always; endless.
ewe (yōō) *n.* A female sheep.
excursion (ik skûr´ zhən) *n.* A pleasure trip; an outing.
exhilarated (ig zil´ ə rāt´ əd) *adj.* Excited.

F
---

faction (fak´ shən) *n.* A group of people within a larger group or party.
fanatic (fə nat´ ik) *n.* A person whose devotion to a cause goes beyond reason; a person with extreme devotion.
feisty (fī´ stē) *adj.* Having a lively and aggressive personality.
fervently (fûr´ vənt lē) *adv.* With great feeling; with emotion.
festive (fes´ tiv) *adj.* Merry.

festoon (fe stōōn´) *v.* To hang ribbons or banners in curved shapes.
floe (flō) *n.* A large sheet of floating ice.
flounder (floun´ dər) *v.* To struggle.
forage cap (for´ ij kap´) *n.* A small, low military cap.
forlornly (for lorn´ lē) *adv.* Sadly; hopelessly.

Word History

Forlornly is the adverb form of the word *forlorn*, which came into English more than 800 years ago. It is a derivative of the word *forlēosan*, which means "to lose." (Also note that *forlornly* contains the *-ly* suffix, which in this word means "in the manner of being.")

fortify (for´ tə fī´) *v.* To make stronger; to build a stronghold.
foundry (foun´ drē) *n.* A place where metal is melted and formed.
frantically (fran´ ti klē) *adv.* Quickly in a worried way.
frigid (fri´ jəd) *adj.* Very cold.
fume (fyōōm) *v.* To mumble something in an angry or irritated way.
furrow (fûr´ ō) *n.* A trench cut by a plow.
fuse (fyōōz) *v.* To join together by melting.

G
---

gable (gā´ bəl) *n.* A part of a wall that is enclosed by sloping sides of a roof, making a triangle-shaped section on a building.
gallinipper (gal´ ə nip´ ər) *n. informal.* Any of several insects that sting or bite.

gangly (gang´ glē) *adj.* Gangling; loose and awkward.
gaunt (gônt) *adj.* Very thin; bony.
geyser (gī´ zər) *n.* A hot-water fountain; a jet of hot water that shoots from the ground.

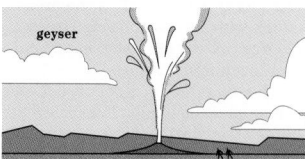
geyser

gingerly (jin´ jər lē) *adv.* Cautiously; warily.
gizzard (gi´ zərd) *n.* Intestine.
gore (gor) *v.* To pierce with an animal's horn or tusk.
gourd (gord) *n.* A melon-shaped fruit that can be dried and used as a bowl.
groschen (grō´ shən) *n.* A form of money worth $1/100$ of a schilling. (A schilling is worth about $7 1/2$¢.)
grozing iron (grō´ zing ī´ ərn) *n.* A steel tool for cutting glass.

H
---

haberdasher (ha´ bər da´ shər) *n. chiefly British.* One who sells men's clothing.
haggard (hag´ ərd) *adj.* Exhausted looking; gaunt.
hallow (hal´ ō) *v.* To make holy.
hamlet (ham´ lit) *n.* A small village.
haughtily (hô´ təl ē) *adv.* In an overly proud way.
heirloom (âr´ lōōm´) *n.* An object handed down in a family.

high-falutin' (hī´ fə lōō´ tn) *adj.* Appealing to a higher class of people; fancy; showy.
hogan (hō´ gôn) *n.* A Navaho dwelling.
homespun (hōm´ spən) *adj.* Made at home.
homestead (hōm´ sted) *n.* A home and land surrounding it that belonged to one's family or ancestors.
hone (hōn) *v.* To sharpen.
honeycomb (hun´ ē kōm´) *v.* To make full of holes like a bee's honeycomb.
hover (huv´ ər) *v.* To hang in the air.

Word History

Hover came from an older English word, *hoven*, which may have come into use as many as 800 years ago. Since the earliest records of this word, it has always had the same meaning.

hue (hyōō) *n.* A tint; a shade of color.
humiliate (hyōō mil´ ē āt´) *v.* To shame.

Word Derivations

Below are some words related to *humiliate*.
humiliated humiliating humility
humiliates humiliation

hypnotic (hip not´ ik) *adj.* Causing sleep.
hypotenuse (hī pä´ tə nōōs´) *n.* In a right triangle, the side opposite the right angle.

I
---

illuminate (i lōō´ mə nāt´) *v.* 1. To throw light upon; to shine upon. 2. To make understandable; to clarify.
immortality (im´ or tal´ i tē) *n.* The state of living forever; enduring fame.

impassable (im pas´ ə bəl) *adj.* Blocked.
impassioned (im pash´ ənd) *adj.* With great feeling.
impenetrable (im pen´ i trə bəl) *adj.* Impossible to get through.
inalienable (in āl´ yə nə bəl) *adj.* Not able to be sold or given away.
inauguration (in ô´ gyə rā´ shən) *n.* The ceremony in which a president takes office.
indenture (in den´ chər) *n.* A person bound by a contract to work for someone else.
indescribable (in´ di skrī´ bə bəl) *adj.* So extraordinary that it cannot be described.
indifferent (in dif´ ər ənt) *adj.* Not interested; not concerned.
inevitable (in ev´ i tə bəl) *adj.* Certain; sure.
inexorable (in ek´ sər ə bəl) *adj.* Absolute; unyielding.
inferno (in fûr´ nō) *n.* A place of extreme, almost unbearable, heat.
infrared (in´ fra red´) *adj.* Having to do with the invisible rays that are closest to the red end of the visible light spectrum. See illustration of **ultraviolet.**
ingenious (in jēn´ yəs) *adj.* Clever; skillful.
ingot (ing´ gət) *n.* A piece of metal in the shape of a bar or a block.

ingratiate (in grā´ shē āt´) *v.* To put oneself in the good graces of others.
innovation (in´ ə vā´ shən) *n.* The act of creating something new or original.
inquisitive (in kwiz´ i tiv) *adj.* Curious.
insurrection (in´ sə rek´ shən) *n.* A revolt; a rebellion.
intelligible (in tel´ i jə bəl) *adj.* Clear; understandable.
intensify (in ten´ sə fī´) *v.* To increase; to strengthen.
intensity (in ten´ si tē) *n.* Great strength.
interstellar (in´ tər stel´ ər) *adj.* Between the stars. **interstellar space:** the part of outer space that is beyond our solar system.
interval (in´ tər val) *n.* A time when action stops for a while; a pause.
intimacy (in´ tə mə sē) *n.* A closeness.
intricate (in´ tri kit) *adj.* Tangled; complicated.

Word History

Ingenious came into English about 500 years ago. It comes from the Latin word *ingenium*, which means "natural capacity." Some meanings of the word *capacity* are "the amount that can be held in a space" and "ability or power." (Also note that *ingenious* contains the *in-* prefix, which in this word means "within," and the *-ous* suffix, which in this word means "having" or "possessing.")

J
---

journeyman (jûr´ nē mən) *n.* A person who has completed an apprenticeship and can now work in a trade under another person.
juniper (jōō´ nə pər) *n.* An evergreen shrub with purple berries.

K
---

kaleidoscope (kə lī´ də skōp´) *n.* A constantly changing pattern.
kasha (kä´ shə) *n.* A soft food made from a grain, usually buckwheat.
kayak (kī´ ak) *n.* A light Eskimo canoe having a wooden or bone framework and covered with skins.

kayak

keelboat (kēl´ bōt) *n.* A shallow boat built with a keel, or long beam, on the bottom.
kiln (kil) *n.* An oven for firing glass, or heating it at very high temperatures, in order to make the color permanent.
knoll (nōl) *n.* A low, rounded hill; a mound.

L
---

lambent (lam´ bənt) *adj.* Glowing softly.
lance (lans) *n.* A long-shafted spear.
lariat (lâr´ ē ət) *n.* A rope tied with a movable loop at one end, used to catch cows and horses; a lasso.
learned (lûrnd) *v.* Past tense of **learn:** To gain new knowledge or skill. —*adj.* (lûr´ nid) Educated.
legendary (lej´ ən der´ ē) *adj.* From a story that has been passed down from a people's earlier times.

leisurely (lē´ zhər lē) *adv.* In a deliberate way; without hurry.
levity (le´ və tē) *n.* A lighthearted attitude.
limb (lim) *n.* An arm or leg.
lubricant (lōō´ bri kənt) *n.* A substance such as oil or grease that makes machine parts slippery, thus making the parts move easily.
lull (lul) *n.* A period of reduced noise or violence.
luxurious (lug zhŏŏr´ ē əs) *adj.* Grand; rich; elegant.
lynx (lingks) *n.* A wildcat; a bobcat.

M
---

magnification (mag´ nə fi kā´ shən) *n.* The amount of enlargement possible; the amount something is enlarged.
manacled (man´ ə kəld) *adj.* Handcuffed.

Word History

Manacled (which is a *manacle* with the inflectional *-ed* ending) came into English about 600 years ago. It came from the French word *manicle*, which came from a derivation of the Latin word *manus*, meaning "hand."

maneuver (mə nōō´ vər) *n.* A movement that calls for planning and skill.

Word Derivations

Below are some words related to *maneuver*.
maneuverable maneuverer
maneuverability maneuvering
maneuvered maneuvers

maneuvering (mə nōō´ vər ing) *n.* Planning and then acting according to plans.

manic (man´ ik) *adj.* Overly excited.

marrow (mar´ ō) *n.* 1. The soft substance in the hollow parts of bones. 2. The center; the core.

masculine (mas´ kyə lin) *adj.* Male; having to do with men.

Mass (mas) *n.* The chief service of the Roman Catholic Church.

mast (mast) *n.* A pole that supports the sails of a ship or boat. See illustration of **bow.**

Maya or **Mayan** (mä´ yə) or (mä´ yən) *n.* A member of a people who built an ancient civilization in Mexico and Central America. **Mayan** *adj.* Having to do with the civilization of the Mayas.

meditate (med´ i tāt´) *v.* To think deeply; to contemplate.

> ### Word History
> **Meditate** came into English in the year 1560. It was derived from *meditari*, a verb form of the Latin word *medēri*, which means "to remedy." (Also note that the word *meditate* contains the *-ate* suffix, which in this word means "to cause to be affected by.")

medley (med´ lē) *n.* A mixture; a jumble.

melodrama (mel´ ə drä´ mə) *n.* A play that exaggerates emotions

and encourages the audience to be sympathetic.

menial (mē´ nē əl) *adj.* Humble; lowly; boring; tedious.

merciful (mûr´ si fəl) *adj.* Forgiving.

mesa (mā´ sə) *n.* A small, high plateau that stands alone, like a mountain with a flat top.

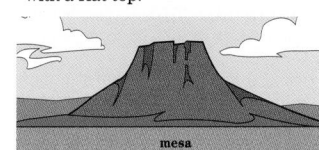
mesa

mesquite (me skēt´) *n.* A spiny shrub or tree in the legume, or pea and bean, family.

miaow (mē ou´) *n.* Meow; the sound a cat makes. —*v.* To meow; to make the sound a cat makes.

mill (mil) *n.* A factory.

miniature (min´ ē ə chər) *adj.* A small-sized model of something.

minute (mī nōōt´) *adj.* Detailed; careful.

mischievous (mis´ chə vəs) *adj.* Causing trouble in a playful way.

mobilize (mō´ bə līz´) *v.* To put into action.

monarch (mon´ ərk) *n.* A ruler; a king or a queen.

morale (mə ral´) *n.* The level of one's confidence.

morose (mə rōs´) *adj.* Sullen; gloomy.

mossback (môs´ bak) *n.* A wild bull or cow.

mother-of-pearl (muth´ ər uv pûrl´) *n.* A hard, shiny, multicolored substance found inside some mollusk shells.

736

move (mōōv) *v.* To make a motion or a suggestion to act on something in a meeting.

muck (muk) *v.* To clean out.

muff (muf) *v.* To do an action poorly; to miss; to mess up.

muster (mus´ tər) *v.* To work up; to gather.

mutilated (myōōt´ l āt´ əd) *adj.* Cut up; slashed.

myriad (mir´ ē əd) *n.* An immense number; many.

mystified (mis´ tə fīd) *adj.* Bewildered; baffled; puzzled.

mythology (mi thol´ ə jē) *n.* A collection of legends or fables.

N

netherworld (neth´ ər wûrld´) *n.* The region below the ground; hell.

nimbly (nim´ blē) *adv.* With quick, light movements.

nobly (nō´ blē) *adv.* In an honorable way.

nomination (no´ mə nā´ shən) *n.* A proposal that someone could hold a government position or office.

> ### Word History
> **Nomination** is a derivative of the word *nominate*, which came into English about 500 years ago. It came from a derivation of the Latin word *nomen*, which means "name." (Also note that the word *nomination* contains the *-ation* suffix, which means "connected to the process of.")

noncombatant (non´ kəm bat´ nt) *n.* A person who is not a part of the fighting during wartime.

novelty (no´ vəl tē) *n.* Something new or different.

nuclear reaction (nōō´ klē ər rē ak´ shən) *n.* A process in which the centers or cores of atoms are changed.

O

obliterate (ə blit´ ə rāt´) *v.* To destroy completely; to rub out; to erase.

> ### Word Derivations
> Below are some words related to *obliterate.*
>
> | | | |
> |---|---|---|
> | obliterated | obliterating | obliterative |
> | obliterates | obliteration | obliterator |

oblong (ob´ lông) *adj.* Being longer than it is wide.

obscure (əb skyōor´) *adj.* Not well known. —*v.* To hide; to cover up.

observatory (əb zûr´ və tor´ē) *n.* A place that is designed for astronomers to study the stars.

observatory

optical (op´ ti kəl) *adj.* Having to do with sight.

optimism (op´ tə miz´ əm) *n.* The belief that everything will happen for the best.

organic (or gan´ ik) *adj.* Produced by living things; was once alive.

737

orientation (or´ ē ən tā´ shən) *n.* A person's or object's position in relation to something else.

ornery (or´ nə rē) *adj.* Mean; grouchy; irritable.

oval (ō´ vəl) *adj.* Egg-shaped.

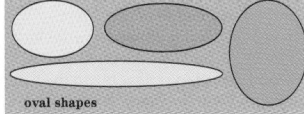
oval shapes

overseer (ō´ vər sē´ ər) *n.* A supervisor; a manager.

oxlip (oks´ lip) *n.* A flowering herb with pale-colored flowers.

P

pantaloons (pan´ tl ōōnz´) *n.* Trousers.

parch (pärch) *v.* To become very dry.

parliamentary procedure (pär´ lə men´ trē prə sē´ jər) *n.* A formal way to hold or conduct a meeting, following certain rules.

passion (pash´ ən) *n.* A strong liking or enthusiasm for something.

peculiarity (pi kyōō´ lē ar´ i tē) *n.* A strange or unusual feature.

peevishly (pē´ vish lē) *adv.* With irritation or lack of patience.

perimeter (pə rim´ i tər) *n.* The distance around the boundary of something.

persecute (pûr´ si kyōōt´) *v.* To torment; to oppress; to treat badly.

persist (pər sist´) *v.* To continue trying something; to refuse to give up or quit.

perspective (pər spek´ tiv) *n.* A way of looking at things in relation to each other.

> ### Word History
> **Perspective** came into English about 600 years ago. It came from the Latin word *perspectivus*, meaning "of sight" or "optical." This Latin word came from a derivation of *perspicere*, which can be broken into the word parts *per-*, meaning "through," and *specere*, meaning "to look." (Also note that the word *perspective* contains the *-ive* suffix, which means "performs the action of.")

persuade (pər swād´) *v.* To get others to think as you do about a subject or topic.

> ### Word Derivations
> Below are some words related to *persuade.*
>
> | | | |
> |---|---|---|
> | persuaded | persuading | persuasively |
> | persuader | persuasion | persuasiveness |
> | persuades | persuasive | |

pester (pes´ tər) *v.* To bother; to annoy.

peyote (pā ō´ tē) *n.* A cactus plant.

phenomenal (fi nom´ ə nl) *adj.* Remarkable.

pickerel (pik´ ər əl) *n.* A freshwater fish that is in the pike family.

piñon (pin´ yən) *n.* A kind of pine tree with edible seeds.

738

plateau (pla tō´) *n.* A tract of high, flat land; a tableland.

plead (plēd) *v.* To beg.

plumb (plum) *adv.* Completely.

pogrom (pə grum´) *n.* An organized attack on Jews in Russia in the late 1800s. Pogroms were encouraged by the Russian government at that time.

ponder (pon´ dər) *v.* To think about.

popular sovereignty (pop´ yə lər sov´ rin tē) *n.* A policy that said each state could decide whether to have slavery within its borders.

portage (pôr tázh´) *n.* The act of carrying boats and supplies from one waterway to another.

portage

portal (por´ tl) *n.* An entryway.

poultice (pōl´ tis) *n.* A wad of something soft and moist that is placed over a wound to heal it.

prankster (prangk´ stər) *n.* A person who plays tricks on people for fun.

precarious (pri kâr´ ē əs) *adj.* Uncertain; doubtful.

precaution (pri kô´ shən) *n.* Care taken beforehand.

pressure (pre´ shər) *v.* To force.

prevail (pri vāl´) *v.* To persuade.

primary (prī´ mer ē) *adj.* Main.

prime (prīm) *n.* The most successful or important period of time.

procedure (prə sē´ jər) *n.* The steps to follow in carrying out a routine or method.

proclaim (prō klām´) *v.* To announce publicly.

profound (prə found´) *adj.* Deep.

prominence (prom´ ə nəns) *n.* Fame; importance.

prominent (prom´ ə nənt) *adj.* Famous; well-known.

prophet (prof´ it) *n.* A person who tells events before they happen.

proposition (prop´ ə zish´ ən) *n.* An idea that is presented; a principle.

prosper (pros´ pər) *v.* To succeed; to thrive.

> ### Word History
> **Prosper** came into English about 600 years ago. It came from the French word *prosperer*, the origins of which are in the Latin words *prosperare*, meaning "to cause to succeed," and *prosperus*, meaning "favorable."

provisions (prə vizh´ ənz) *n. pl.* Supplies, especially food or tools.

ptarmigan (tär´ mi gən) *n.* A bird also known as a grouse.

pun (pun) *n.* A joke made by using words that sound almost the same but have different meanings.

pungent (pun´ jənt) *adj.* Sharp or strong smelling or tasting.

Q

quail (kwāl) *v.* To shrink back in fear.

quiver (kwi´ vər) *v.* To shake slightly.

quota (kwō´ tə) *n.* The amount one expects to receive.

739

369

R

racquetball (raˈkət bôlˈ) *n.* A sport played with a racket and small rubber ball in an enclosed room.

rampart (ramˈ pärt) *n.* A wall used as a defense for a city.

ramshackle (ramˈ shak əl) *adj.* Tumbledown; shaky.

rancid (ranˈ sid) *adj.* Stale; unpleasant.

rapscallion (rap skalˈ yən) *n.* A rascal; a scamp.

ration (rashˈ ən) *n.* A limited share of food.

ravage (raˈ vij) *v.* To damage heavily.

ravine (rə vēnˈ) *n.* A narrow, steep-sided valley worn into the earth by running water.

ravishing (ravˈ i shing) *adj.* Very beautiful.

recede (ri sēdˈ) *v.* To go backward; to back away.

Word Derivations

Below are some words related to *recede*.
receded	recession	recessionary
receding	recessional	recessive
recess		

recoil (ri koilˈ) *v.* To spring back from.

recrimination (ri krimˈ ə nāˈ shən) *n.* An accusation made in return for another accusation; blame given in return.

recruit (ri krōōtˈ) *v.* To get new members.

recruitment (ri krōōtˈ mənt) *n.* Signing up new soldiers.

refracting (ri frakˈ ting) *adj.* Passing through an object and changing direction, as a light ray passing into a lens at one angle and coming out at a different angle.

refuge (refˈ yōōj) *n.* A place of safety.

regiment (rejˈ ə mənt) *n.* A large body of soldiers.

remote (ri mōtˈ) *adj.* Far away and separate from others.

render (renˈ dər) *v.* To make.

renounce (ri nounsˈ) *v.* To give up; to reject.

repetitive (ri petˈ i tiv) *adj.* Repeated.

repulse (ri pulsˈ) *v.* To push back.

resonance (rezˈ ə nəns) *n.* Richness of sound; echoing.

reveille (revˈ ə lē) *n.* The playing of a bugle to awaken soldiers.

Word History

Reveille came into English in the year 1644. It comes from a derivation of the French word *eveillar*, meaning "to awaken," which is assumed to be derived from the Latin word *exvigilare*, meaning "to keep watch" or "to stay awake."

reverie (revˈ ə rē) *n.* A daydream.

rigid (rijˈ id) *adj.* Stiff; unbending.

ritual (richˈ ōō əl) *n.* A ceremony of worship; an act always performed on certain occasions.

rivulet (rivˈ yə let) *n.* A small stream of water.

---

rotate (rōˈ tāt) *v.* To revolve; to turn around; to spin.

Word Derivations

Below are some words related to *rotate*.
rotated	rotation	rotatory
rotating	rotator	

roust (roust) *v.* To decisively defeat and chase someone out of a place; to rout.

rowdy (rouˈ dē) *adj.* Rough; disorderly.

rudder (rudˈ ər) *n.* A broad, flat blade at the rear of a ship used to steer. See illustration of **bow**.

rutting (rutˈ ing) *n.* Mating.

S

saber (sāˈ bər) *n.* A heavy sword with a curved blade.

sabotage (sabˈ ə täzhˈ) *v.* To damage purposely.

salutation (salˈ yə tāˈ shən) *n.* Greeting.

samovar (samˈ ə värˈ) *n.* A decorative metal container with a spigot, or faucet, often used in Russia to heat water for tea.

Word History

Samovar came into English in the year 1830. It is a Russian word formed by joining the word parts *samo-*, meaning "self," and *varit'*, which means "to boil."

schooner (skōōˈ nər) *n.* A large sailing vessel.

scythe (sīthˈ) *n.* A tool with a long, curved blade for cutting grass or grain by hand.

scythe

sear (sēr) *v.* To roast; to burn.

seclude (si klōōdˈ) *v.* To keep away from others.

second (seˈ kənd) *v.* To verbally agree with a motion or suggestion to do something in a meeting.

sensor (senˈ sor) *n.* A device that can identify such things as light, sound, or temperature and send a signal telling what has been identified.

sentinel (senˈ tə nl) *n.* A person who stands watch; a guard.

shamefaced (shāmˈ fāst) *adj.* Embarrassed.

sharecropper (shârˈ kropˈ ər) *n.* A farmer who gives part of his or her crop as rent to the owner of the land.

shlemiel (shlə mēlˈ) *n. slang.* A fool who is both awkward and unlucky.

shmendrick (shmenˈ drik) *n. slang.* A nincompoop; a nobody.

shrill (shril) *adj.* High-pitched; piercing.

shroud (shroud) *n.* A covering for a dead body.

siege (sēj) *n.* An army's attempt to force surrender by surrounding the enemy's position, keeping out food and supplies.

---

simultaneously (sīˈ məl tāˈ nē əs lē) *adv.* At exactly the same time.

singe (sinj) *v.* To burn the surface of something.

sinister (sinˈ ə stər) *adj.* Harmful; threatening.

skedaddle (ski dadˈ l) *v. informal.* To run quickly away.

skeeter (skēˈ tər) *n. informal.* A mosquito.

skeletal (skelˈ i tl) *adj.* Like a skeleton; so thin that the shapes of bones show.

skirmish (skûrˈ mish) *n.* A fight between small forces.

skulk (skulk) *v.* To sneak.

slew (slōō) *n.* Many.

slump (slump) *v.* To sit with drooping shoulders.

Word History

Slump came into English in the year 1887. Its origins are probably in the Scandinavian languages. It is related to the Norwegian word *slumpa*, which means "to fall."

smithy (smithˈ ē) *n.* A blacksmith's shop; a place where horseshoes are made.

solace (solˈ is) *n.* Comfort.

solar system (sōˈ lər sisˈ təm) *n.* The sun and all the planets and other bodies that revolve around it.

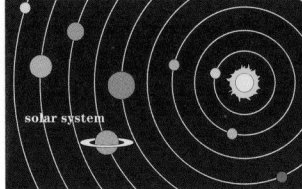

solar system

solder (sodˈ ər) *v.* To join metal pieces together by using a highly heated liquid metal at a joint without heating the pieces themselves.

solemnly (soˈ ləm lē) *adv.* In a very serious manner.

solitary (solˈ i ter ē) *adj.* Alone; single.

solstice (solˈ stis) *n.* The day of the year when the sun appears the farthest north and the day when it appears the farthest south in the sky.

soul-harrowing (sōlˈ harˈ ō ing) *adj.* Causing suffering to a person's innermost self.

span (span) *v.* To stretch across.

spasm (spazˈ əm) *n.* A seizure; a fit.

spawn (spôn) *v.* To lay eggs and deposit them in water.

speculation (spekˈ yə lāˈ shən) *n.* Thinking about a subject; pondering.

spew (spyōō) *v.* To pour out; to squirt out.

---

sphere (sfēr) *n.* A ball; a globe.

sphere

Word Derivations

Below are some words related to *sphere*.
sphered	sphering	spherule
spheric	spheroid	sphery
spherical	spherometer	

spike (spīk) *v.* To forcefully hit a volleyball down the other side of the net.

spire (spīr) *n.* A tall, pointed cone built on top of a tower; a steeple.

spirits (spirˈ its) *n.* A liquid containing alcohol.

stabilization (stāˈ bə lə zāˈ shən) *n.* The act of making something hold steady.

stance (stans) *n.* A person's mental position on a subject.

staple (stāˈ pəl) *n.* A basic, or necessary, food.

stockyard (stokˈ yärdˈ) *n.* A place where livestock such as cattle, sheep, horses, and pigs that are to be bought or sold, slaughtered, or shipped are held.

Stonehenge

Stonehenge (stōnˈ henj) *n.* A group of large stones in England placed in circular formations around 3,500 years ago, possibly as an astronomical calendar.

straddle (straˈ dəl) *v.* To sit with one's legs on each side of an object.

stroke (strōk) *n.* A sudden attack of illness caused by a blocked or broken blood vessel in or leading to the brain.

stygian (stijˈ ē ən) *adj.* Dark; gloomy.

succession (sək seshˈ ən) *n.* One thing happening right after another.

succulent (sukˈ yə lənt) *adj.* Juicy; tasty.

sufficient (sə fishˈ ənt) *adj.* Enough.

suffocate (sufˈ ə kātˈ) *v.* To smother; to choke.

sull (sul) *v.* To balk; to stop suddenly and refuse to move.

supple (supˈ əl) *adj.* Easily bent; not stiff.

suppress (sə presˈ) *v.* To stop; to put down.

supremacy (sə premˈ ə sē) *n.* A position of the highest power.

surpass (sər pasˈ) *v.* To go beyond.

sway (swā) *v.* To influence.

swivet (swivˈ it) *n.* A state of worry or fear.

synchronize (singˈ krə nīzˈ) *v.* To move together at the same rate.

Pronunciation Key: at; lāte; câre; fäther; set; mē; it; kīte; ox; rōse; ô in bought; coin; bŏŏk; tōō; form; out; up; ūse; tûrn; ə sound in about, chicken, pencil, cannon, circus; chair; hw in which; ring; shop; thin; thͤere; zh in treasure.

T

tan (tan) *v.* To turn animal hides into leather.

Word History

Tan came into English about 600 years ago, from the French word *tanner*, a derivation of the Latin word *tanum* or *tannum*. The Latin word means "tanbark," a type of bark that contains an astringent, or drying, substance used in the making of leather.

tangible (tan´ jə bəl) *adj.* Real; actual.
taper (tā´ pər) *v.* To stop slowly; to wind down.
teeming (tē´ ming) *adj.* Overflowing; swarming.
terminal (tûr´ mə nəl) *adj.* Eventually ending in death.
tethered (tethͤ´ ərd) *adj.* Tied by rope to a fixed object.
thresh (thresh) *v.* To separate grain from the stalk by beating it.
tidal flat (tī´ dəl flat) *n.* A flat area of land that is sometimes covered by tidal waters.
till (til) *v.* To turn over soil; to plow.
timpani (tim´ pə nē) *n.* A type of drum.

tipi (tē´ pē) *n.* A tent of the Native Americans of the Plains; a tepee.

Word History

Tipi, or **tepee**, came into English in the year 1743. It is a Native American word, meaning "to dwell," that originated with the Dakota tribe.

toboggan (tə bog´ ən) *n.* A long, narrow sled.
tome (tōm) *n.* One volume of a set of books.
tract (trakt) *n.* A large area of land.
transcribe (trans skrīb´) *v.* To change from one recorded form to another; to translate.
translucent (trans lōō´ sənt) *adj.* Hard to see through. Light is visible, but objects cannot be seen clearly.
transmit (trans mit´) *v.* To send; to communicate; to pass something.

Word Derivations

Below are some words related to *transmit*.
transmittable   transmittance   transmitter
transmittal   transmitted   transmitting

transmitter (trans mit´ ər) *n.* A device that sends out television or radio signals.
treason (trē´ zən) *n.* The act of betraying someone's trust.
trench (trench) *n.* A ditch; a long, narrow channel cut in the earth.
tributary (trib´ yə ter´ ē) *n.* A stream or river that flows into a larger one.
tribute (trib´ yōōt) *n.* Praise, honor, or gifts given to show respect or to show thanks.

744

trifling (trī´ fling) *adj.* Small and unimportant.
trilling r's (tril´ ing ärz) *n.* R's that are pronounced by rolling the tongue against the roof of the mouth.
trinket (tring´ kit) *n.* A small or cheap piece of jewelry.
tripod (trī´ pod) *n.* A three-legged table or stand.

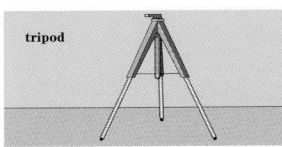
tripod

tsar (zär) *n.* An emperor of Russia before 1918.
tsarina (zä rē´ nə) *n.* An empress of Russia before 1918.
tumult (tōō´ mult) *n.* A great disorder; an uproar.
tundra (tun´ drə) *n.* A large, treeless plain in the arctic regions.
tunic (tōō´ nik) *n.* A short coat.
turbulent (tûr´ byə lənt) *adj.* Fierce; violent; wild.

Word History

Turbulent came into English in the year 1538. It came from a derivative of the Latin word *turba*, which means "confusion" or "crowd." (Also note that the word *turbulent* contains the *-ent* suffix, which means "the state of" or "the quality of.")

U

ultraviolet (ul´ trə vī´ ə lit) *adj.* Having to do with an invisible form of light. Ultraviolet rays are found just beyond the violet end of the visible light spectrum.

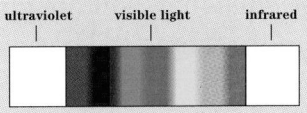
ultraviolet   visible light   infrared

unaccountably (un´ ə koun´ tə blē) *adv.* In a way that cannot be explained.
unanimously (yōō nan´ ə məs lē) *adv.* With the agreement of everyone.
undermine (un´ dər mīn´) *v.* To weaken.
unfurl (un fûrl´) *v.* To open out; to unroll.
unison (yōō´ nə sən) *n.* Behaving the same way at the same time. **in unison** *idiom.* Two or more people saying or doing the same thing at the same time.
unquenchably (un kwench´ ə blē) *adv.* Endlessly; in a persistent way.
upturned sentence (up´ tərnd sen´ təns) *n.* Higher inflection used at the end of a sentence, such as is used for a question.

V

vacuum (vak´ yōōm) *n.* A space with no air. A perfect vacuum is not possible; even in outer space there are some atoms and molecules of gas and radiation, although they are thinly scattered.

745

Pronunciation Key: at; lāte; câre; fäther; set; mē; it; kīte; ox; rōse; ô in bought; coin; bŏŏk; tōō; form; out; up; ūse; tûrn; ə sound in about, chicken, pencil, cannon, circus; chair; hw in which; ring; shop; thin; thͤere; zh in treasure.

vagabond (va´ gə bond´) *n.* One who wanders from place to place.
valiant (val´ yənt) *adj.* Brave; fearless.
velocity (və los´ i tē) *n.* Speed.

Word History

Velocity came into English around the year 1550. It came from the Latin word *velocitas*, a derivative of the word *velox*, meaning "quick." It may also be related to the Latin word *vegēre*, which means "to enliven." (Also note that the word *velocity* contains the *-ity* suffix, which can mean "quality," "state," or "degree.")

verify (ver´ ə fī´) *v.* To prove the truth.

Word Derivations

Below are some words related to *verify*.
verifiability   verification   verifier
verifiable   verified   verifying
verifiableness

vermilion (vər mil´ yən) *adj.* Bright red.
vindicate (vin´ di kāt´) *v.* To prove innocent.
vintage (vin´ tij) *n.* The grapes or wine produced in a vineyard in one year.
vintner (vint´ nər) *n.* A person who makes wine for a living.
vital (vīt´ l) *adj.* Very important; necessary.
vocation (vō kā´ shən) *n.* An occupation; a profession.

W

water buffalo (wô´ tər buf´ ə lō´) *n.* A kind of oxen with large curved horns and a bluish-black hide. Water buffaloes are trained to work in rice fields in Asia.

water buffalo

whopper (hwop´ ər) *n. informal.* A big lie.
wince (wins) *v.* To flinch; to start back from.
windlass (wind´ ləs) *n.* A roller turned with a handle used for lifting heavy weights.

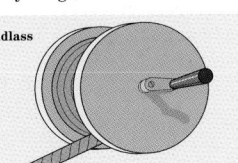
windlass

winnow (win´ ō) *v.* To remove the chaff, or husks, from grain.
wrath (rath) *n.* Anger; rage.

746

Y

yield (yēld) *v.* To give in; to stop arguing.
YWCA Young Women's Christian Association.

Z

Zulu (zōō´ lōō) *n.* A person from KwaZulu Natal in South Africa.

747

371

Internet Theme Resources

This list includes Internet resource suggestions that provide further insight into the unit themes at this level. Teacher discretion is advised. Some of these sites may contain content and images that may be inappropriate for student use. For more theme links visit http://www.sra4kids.com.

Back Through the Stars

Student Resources

Student Guide to the Johnson Space Center
http://www.jsc.nasa.gov/pao/students

Johnson Space Center at NASA sponsors this Web site in which students can learn about the space shuttle, the international space station, astronauts, the search for life on Mars, and much more.

Exploring the Planets Online/ National Air and Space Museum
http://ceps.nasm.edu/ceps/ETP

The National Air and Space Museum site provides background information on many topics in the history of space exploration, from ancient times to the latest discovery of the details on Jupiter's rings.

Teacher Resources

The Nine Planets
http://www.seds.org/billa/tnp

The Nine Planets Web site is an overview of the history, mythology, and current scientific knowledge of each of the planets and moons in our solar system.

Maya Astronomy
http://www.astro.uva.nl/~michielb/maya/astronom.html

This Web site features a detailed look into Mayan Astronomy with sections on **The Sun, The Moon, Political aspects of their cosmology,** and more.

Heritage

Student Resources

Life Stories
http://www.storypreservation.com/home.html

The **Center for Life Stories Preservation** provides for those who wish to record their life, family, and military stories and also information about how to conduct an interview, interview questions and genealogical links.

Eskimos in Alaska
http://tqjunior.advanced.org/3877/Index.htm

ThinkQuest Junior sponsors this site that offers background information about three Native Alaskan groups, **Inupiat, Siberian Yupik**, and **Yupik.**

Teacher Resources

Chinese Historical and Cultural Project
http://www.chcp.org/Pvirtual.html

The Chinese Historical and Cultural Project is a non-profit organization that provides a virtual museum and library with comprehensive information on the music, festivals, customs, and art of China.

Welcome to Puerto Rico!
http://welcome.topuertorico.org/culture/

Welcome to Puerto Rico! is an overview of the island of Puerto Rico with links to information about the architecture, arts, music, cuisine, folklore, and literature of Puerto Rico.

The Civil War

Student Resources

Selected Civil War Photographs
http://lcweb2.loc.gov/ammem/cwphome.html

This Web site is sponsored by the Library of Congress American Memories Collection and contains more than 1000 photographs of the Civil War, most photographed by famed photographer, Matthew Brady.

Music of the Civil War
http://www.geocities.com/SouthBeach/Boardwalk/2575/civil.html

This engaging site contains dozens of Civil War songs and lyrics. In addition to the songs, the site offers links to other Civil War sites.

The Underground Railroad Table of Contents
http://education.ucdavis.edu/NEW/STC/lesson/socstud/railroad/contents.htm

This site is sponsored by the UC Davis Division of Education and contains comprehensive information on the Underground Railroad.

Teacher Resources

CJ's Civil War Home Page
http://www.angelfire.com/ca/easylife/index.html

CJ's Civil War Home Page features maps, indexes of soldiers, pictures of flags, lists of battles, photographs, and more.

Black Soldiers in the Civil War
http://www.nara.gov/education/teaching/usct/home.html

This site contains excellent background information with embedded links to photographs and historical documents with brief explanations.

Poetry and Music of the War Between the States
http://www.erols.com/kfraser/

This site offers dozens of songs and lyrics that were created during the Civil War era. In addition, short biographies of songwriters and poets are also accessible by clicking highlighted names.

New Frontiers

Student Resources

Luxton Museum Indians of the Plains
http://www.schoolnet.ca/collections/luxton/index.htm?31,3

The Buffalo Nations Cultural Society presents the extraordinary history of the Indians of the Northern Plains and Canadian Rockies.

Museum of Westward Expansion
http://www.nps.gov/jeff/mus-tour.htm

Learn about explorers, Native Americans, mountain men and much, much more.

Teacher Resources

WestWeb
http://www.library.csi.cuny.edu/westweb/

From women artists of the West, to the great Native American cultures of the Southwest, this site offers comprehensive information and graphics from the West.

The West
http://www.pbs.org/weta/thewest/

This well-organized site, taken from the PBS documentary series, includes an interactive timeline, descriptions of historical events, and a resource of biographies, as well as journals, photos, and letters.

Journeys and Quests

Student Resources

The Columbus Navigation Home Page
http://www1.minn.net/~keithp/

Find information on Columbus's crew, his ships, how he navigated, and a timeline of his various journeys.

Lewis and Clark Trail
http://www.lewisandclark.org/

Follow Lewis and Clark on the epic journey of discovery. Although this site may be a bit challenging for students, teachers will find it very helpful.

Teacher Resources

The Wanderings of Odysseus A Study Guide for the Odyssey
http://www.xula.edu/Administrative/cat/baldwin/frameset.htm

This study guide will help you understand the Odyssey as well as provide you with pertinent definitions and historical background.

Program Appendix

The Program Appendix includes a step-by-step explanation of procedures for research-based effective practices in reading instruction that are repeatedly used throughout *SRA/Open Court Reading*. These practices may also be used in other instructional situations as well.

Table of Contents

Effective Teaching Practices

Teacher References

Reading Materials and Techniques

Different reading materials and techniques are appropriate at different stages of reading development. The purpose of this section is to discuss different types of reading materials and how they may be used most effectively.

Reading Big Books

Purpose

Many children come from homes where they are read to often, but a significant number of other children have not had this valuable experience. Big Books (Levels K and 1) offer all children crucial opportunities to confirm and expand their knowledge about print and reading. They are especially useful for shared reading experiences in the early grades.

The benefits of reading Big Books include engaging even nonreaders in:

- unlocking the books' messages.
- developing print awareness.
- participating in good reading behaviors.
- observing what a good reader does: remarking on the illustrations and the title, asking questions about the content and what might happen, making predictions, and clarifying words and ideas.
- promoting the insight that a given word is spelled the same way every time it occurs as high-frequency words are pointed out.
- reinforcing the correspondence between spoken and written words and spelling patterns.
- enjoying the illustrations and connecting them to the text to help students learn to explore books for enjoyment and information.
- interpreting and responding to literature and expository text before they can read themselves.

Procedure for Reading Big Books

During the first reading of the Big Books, you will model reading behaviors and comprehension strategies similar to those that will later be taught formally. During the second reading, you will address print awareness and teach comprehension skills such as categorizing and sequencing that help the reader organize information. In addition, you will teach skills such as inferencing and drawing conclusions that help the reader focus on the deeper meaning of the text. At first, teachers should expect to do all of the reading but should not prevent children from trying to read on their own or from reading words they already know.

- **Activate Prior Knowledge.** Read the title of the selection and the author's and illustrator's names. At the beginning of each Big Book, read the title of the book and discuss what the whole book is about before going on to reading the first selection.
- **Discuss Prior Knowledge.** Initiate a brief discussion of any prior knowledge the students have that might help them understand the selection.
- **Browse the Selection.** Ask children to tell what they think the story might be about just from looking at the illustrations. This conversation should be brief so that the children can move on to a prereading discussion of print awareness.

> *Big Books offer all children crucial opportunities to confirm and expand their knowledge about print and reading.*

- **Develop Print Awareness.** The focus of browsing the Big Books is to develop awareness of print. Urge children to tell what words or letters they recognize rather than what they expect the selection to be about.

    To develop print awareness, have children look through the selection page by page and comment on whatever they notice in the text. Some children may know some of the words, while others may only recognize specific letters or sounds. The key is to get the children to look at the print separately from the illustrations even before they have heard the actual text content. This process isolates print awareness so that it is not influenced by content. It also gives you a clearer idea of what your students do or do not know about print.
- **Read Aloud.** Read the selection aloud expressively. The reading enables the children simply to hear and enjoy the text as it is read through once. With this reading, you will be modeling behaviors and comprehension strategies that all children will need to develop to become successful readers—for example, asking questions, clarifying unfamiliar words, first by using the pictures and later by using context, or predicting what might happen next.
- **Reread.** Read the selection expressively again. During the second reading of the stories, you will focus on teaching comprehension skills. Also, to develop print awareness, point to each word as it is read, thus demonstrating that text proceeds from left to right and from top to bottom and helping advance the idea that words are individual spoken and written units. Invite the children to identify the rhyming words in a poem or chime in on repetitive parts of text as you point to the words. Or children can read with you on this second reading, depending on the text.
- **Discuss Print.** Return to print awareness by encouraging discussion of anything the children noticed about the words. Young children should begin to realize that you are reading separate words that are separated by spaces. Later, children will begin to see that each word is made up of a group of letters. The children should be encouraged to discuss anything related to the print. For example, you might ask children to point to a word or count the number of words on a line. Or you might connect the words to the illustrations by pointing to a word and saying it and then asking the children to find a picture of that word.
- **Responding.** Responding to a selection is a way of insuring comprehension. Invite the children to tell about the story by asking the children what they like about the poem or story or calling on a child to explain in his or her own words what the poem or story tells about. Call on others to add to the telling as needed. For nonfiction selections, this discussion might include asking children what they learned about the topic and what they thought was most interesting.

Tips for Using Big Books

- Make sure the entire group is able to see the book clearly while you are reading.
- If some students are able to read or predict words, encourage them to do so during the rereading.
- Encourage students to present and use their knowledge of print.
- Allow children to look at the Big Books whenever they wish.
- Provide small versions of the Big Books for children to browse through and try to read at their leisure.
- The reader of the Big Book should try to be part of the collaborative group of learners rather than the leader.

Reading Decodables and Building Fluency

Purpose

The most urgent task of early reading instruction is to make written thoughts intelligible to students. This requires a balanced approach that includes systematic instruction in phonics as well as experiences with authentic literature. Thus, from the very beginning, *Open Court Reading* includes the reading of literature. At the beginning of first grade, when children are learning phonics and blending as a tool to access words, the teacher reads aloud. During this time students are working on using comprehension strategies and skills and discussing stories. As children learn the code and blend words, recognize critical sight words, and develop some level of fluency, they take more responsibility for the actual reading of the text.

This program has a systematic instruction in phonics that allows the students to begin reading independently. This instruction is supported by *Open Court Reading* Decodables.

Practice

The *Open Court Reading* Decodables are designed to help the students apply, review, and reinforce their expanding knowledge of sound/spelling correspondences. Each story supports instruction in new phonic elements and incorporates elements and words that have been learned earlier. The children will use *Open Court Reading* Decodables of two different lengths in **Set 1**—eight pages and sixteen pages. The eight-page books focus on the new element introduced in the lesson, while the sixteen-page books review and reinforce the elements that have been taught since the last sixteen-page book. **Set 2 Decodable** books are all 16-page books. They review sounds from several lessons and provide additional reading practice. The primary purpose is to provide practice reading the words. It is important that the children also attach meaning to what they are reading. Questions are often included in the Teacher's Edition to check both understanding and attention to words.

Fluency

Fluency is the effortless ability to read or access words with seemingly little attention to decoding. It also involves grouping words into meaningful units and using expression appropriately. Fluency is critical but not sufficient for comprehension.

To become proficient readers who fully understand what they read, the whole process of decoding must become as automatic as possible. The children need to be so familiar with the sound/spellings and with the most common nondecodable sight words that they automatically process the letters or spellings and expend most of their energy on comprehending the meaning of the text.

While fluency begins in first grade, many students will continue to need practice in building fluency in second and third grades. Initially, students can use the *Open Court Reading* **Decodables** in grades 2 and 3, but fluency practice should include using materials from actual literature the students are reading. Fluent second graders read between 82 and 124 words per minute with accuracy and understanding, depending on the time of the year (fall/spring).

Fluent third graders can be expected to read between 107 and 142 words per minute; fourth (125/145); fifth (126/151); sixth (127/153).

Procedure

Preparing to Read

- Introduce and write on the board any high-frequency words introduced or reviewed in the story. Tell the students how to pronounce any newly introduced high-frequency words. Then point to each new word and have the children say it. Have them read any previously introduced sight word last. All of the *Open Court Reading* Decodables contain high-frequency words that may not be decodable. For example, the word *the* is a very common high-frequency word that is not decodable. Including words like *the* makes the language of the story flow smoothly and naturally. The children need to be able to recognize these words quickly and smoothly.

- Read the title. At the beginning of the year, you may need to read the title of the book to the

> *In order for them to become proficient readers who fully understand what they read, the whole process of decoding must become as automatic as possible.*

children, but as the year goes on, you should have a student read it whenever possible. The sixteen-page *Open Court Reading* **Decodables** contain two related chapters, each using the same sounds and spellings. In such cases, read the title of the **Decodable** book, then point out the two individual story titles. Have volunteers read the title of the story you are about to read.

- Browse the story. Have the children look through the story, commenting on whatever they notice in text or illustrations and telling what they think the story will tell them.

Reading the Story

After this browsing, the children will read the story a page at a time. Again, these books are designed to support the learning of sounds and spellings. The focus should not be on comprehension. Children should understand what they are reading, and they should feel free to discuss anything in the story that interests them. Any areas of confusion are discussed and clarified as they arise, as described below.

- Have the children read a page to themselves. Then call on one child to read the page aloud, or have the whole group read it aloud.

- If a child has difficulty with a word that can be blended, help her or him blend the word. Remind the child to check the **Sound/Spelling Cards** for help. If a word cannot be blended using the sound/spellings learned so far, pronounce the word for the child.

- If a child has trouble with a word or sentence, have the reader call on a classmate for help and then continue reading after the word or sentence has been clarified. After something on a page has been clarified or discussed, have that page reread by a different child before moving on to the next page.

- Repeat this procedure for each page.

- Reread the story twice more, calling on different children to read or read it in unison. These readings should go more quickly, with fewer stops for clarification.

Responding to the Story

Once the story has been read aloud a few times, have the children respond as follows:

- Ask the children what hard words they found in the story and how they figured them out. They may mention high-frequency words they didn't recognize, words they had to blend, and words whose meaning they did not know.

- Invite the children to tell about the story, retelling it in their own words, telling what they liked about it, or telling what they found interesting or surprising. Specific suggestions to use are listed in the Teacher's Edition.

- Questions are provided in the Teacher's Edition. They are designed to focus the children's attention on the words and not just the pictures. The questions require answers that cannot be guessed by looking at the pictures alone, such as a name, a bit of dialogue, or an action or object that is not pictured. Have the children point to the words, phrases, or sentences that answer the questions.

Building Fluency

Buiding fluency is essential to gaining strong comprehension. The more fluent the children become, the more they can attend to the critical business of understanding the text. Opportunities for children to build fluency may include:

- Have students "partner read" the most recent *Open Court Reading* Decodable twice, taking turns reading a page at a time. The partners should switch the second time through so they are reading different pages from the ones they read the first time. If there is time left, the partners should choose any of the previously read stories to read together. Use this time for diagnosis, having one child at a time read with you.

- Make sure that the *Open Court Reading* **Decodables** are readily available.

- Read **Decodables** with as many children as possible one at a time.

- Remind the children that they may read with partners during Independent Work Time.

The only way the children can become fluent readers is to read as much and as often as possible.

Purpose

Reading is a complex process that requires children not only to decode what they read but also to understand and respond to it. The purpose of this section is to help you identify various reading behaviors used by good readers and to encourage those behaviors in your students.

Reading Behaviors and Comprehension Strategies

There are four basic behaviors that good readers engage in during reading. These behaviors include the application of certain comprehension strategies, which are modeled while reading the Student Anthology (Levels 1–6).

Setting Reading Goals and Expectations

Good readers set reading goals and expectations before they begin reading. This behavior involves a variety of strategies that will help children prepare to read the text.

- **Activate prior knowledge.** When good readers approach a new text, they consider what they already know about the subject or what their experiences have been in reading similar material.
- **Browse the text.** To get an idea of what to expect from a text, good readers look at the title and the illustrations. They may look for potential problems, such as difficult words. When browsing a unit, have children glance quickly at each selection, looking briefly at the illustrations and the print. Have them tell what they think they might be learning about as they read the unit.
- **Decide what they expect from the text.** When reading for pleasure, good readers anticipate enjoying the story or the language. When reading to learn something, they ask themselves what they expect to find out.

Responding to Text

Good readers are active readers. They interact with text by using the following strategies:

- **Making connections.** Good readers make connections between what they read and what they already know. They pay attention to elements in the text that remind them of their own experiences.
- **Visualizing, or picturing.** Good readers visualize what is happening in the text. They form mental images as they read. They picture the setting, the characters, and the action in a story. When reading expository text, good readers picture the objects, processes or events described. Visualizing helps readers understand descriptions of complex activities or processes.

- **Asking questions.** Good readers ask questions that may prepare them for what they will learn. If their questions are not answered in the text, they may try to find answers elsewhere and thus add even more to their store of knowledge.
- **Predicting.** Good readers predict what will happen next. When reading fiction, they make predictions about what they are reading and then confirm or revise those predictions as they go.
- **Thinking about how the text makes you feel.** Well-written fiction touches readers' emotions; it sparks ideas.

Checking Understanding

One of the most important behaviors good readers exhibit is the refusal to continue reading when something fails to make sense. Good readers continually assess their understanding of the text with strategies such as:

- **Interpreting.** As they read, good readers make inferences that help them understand and appreciate what they are reading.

> *One of the most important behaviors good readers exhibit is the refusal to continue reading when something fails to make sense. Good readers continually assess their understanding of the text.*

- **Summing up.** Good readers sum up to check their understanding as they read. Sometimes they reread to fill in gaps in their understanding.

Clarifying Unfamiliar Words and Passages

Good readers pause often while reading to clarify unfamiliar words and passages. This behavior should become a natural response. Children can use a variety of clarifying strategies.

- **Apply decoding skills** to sound out unknown words.
- **Determine what is unclear** to find the source of the confusion.
- **Check a dictionary or the Glossary** to understand the meanings of words. As they read, good readers make inferences that help them understand and appreciate what they are reading.
- **Apply context clues** in text and illustrations to help them figure out the meanings of words or passages.
- **Reread the passage** to make sure the passage makes sense.

Procedures

Modeling and Thinking Aloud

Modeling and encouraging children to think aloud as they attempt to understand text can demonstrate for everyone how reading behaviors are put into practice. The most effective models will be those that come from your own reading. Using questions such as the following as well as your students' questions and comments will make both the text and the strategic reading process more meaningful to children.

- What kinds of things did you wonder about?
- What kinds of things surprised you?
- What new information did you learn?
- What was confusing until you reread or read further?

Model comprehension strategies in a natural way and choose questions and comments that fit the text you are reading, but try to present a variety of ways to respond to text.

- Pose questions that you really do wonder about.
- Identify with characters by comparing them with yourself.
- React emotionally by showing joy, sadness, amusement, or surprise.
- Show empathy with or sympathy for characters.
- Relate the text to something that has happened to you or to something you already know.
- Show interest in the text ideas.
- Question the meaning or clarity of the author's words and ideas.

Encouraging Children's Responses and Use of Strategies

Most children will typically remain silent as they try to figure out an unfamiliar word or a confusing passage. Encourage children to identify specifically what they are having difficulty with. Once the problem has been identified, ask the children to suggest a strategy for dealing with the problem. Remind children to:

- Treat problems encountered in text as interesting learning opportunities.
- Think out loud about text challenges.
- Help each other build meaning. Rather than tell what a word is, children should tell how they figured out the meanings of challenging words and passages.
- Consider reading a selection again with a partner after reading it once alone. Partner reading provides valuable practice in reading for fluency.
- Make as many connections as they can between what they are reading and what they already know.
- Visualize to clarify meanings or enjoy descriptions.
- Ask questions freely about what they are reading.
- Notice how the text makes them feel.

Reading Aloud

Purpose

Adults read a variety of materials aloud to children. These include Big Books, picture books, and novels. Research has shown that children who are read to are more likely to develop the skills they need to read successfully on their own.

Reading aloud at any age serves multiple purposes. Reading aloud:

- Provokes children's curiosity about text.
- Conveys an awareness that text has meaning.
- Demonstrates the various reasons for reading text (for example, to find out about the world around them, to learn useful new information and new skills, or simply for pleasure).
- Exposes children to the "language of literature," which is more complex than the language they ordinarily use and hear.
- Provides an opportunity to teach the problem-solving strategies that good readers employ. As the children observe you interacting with the text, expressing your own enthusiasm, and modeling your thinking aloud, they perceive these as valid responses and begin to respond to text in similar ways.
- Models adults' interest in and enjoyment of reading.

Procedures

The following set of general procedures for reading aloud is designed to help you maximize the effectiveness of Read-Aloud sessions.

- **Read-aloud sessions.** Set aside time each day to read aloud.
- **Introduce the story.** Tell the children that you are going to read a story aloud to them. Tell its title and briefly comment on the topic. To allow the children to anticipate what will happen in the story, be careful not to summarize.
- **Activate prior knowledge.** Ask whether anyone has already heard the story. If so, ask them to see if this version is the same as the one they have heard. If not, activate prior knowledge by saying, "First, let's talk a little about _____." If the story is being read in two (or more) parts, before reading the second part, ask the children to recall the first part.
- **Before reading.** Invite children to interrupt your reading if there are any words they do not understand or ideas they find puzzling. Throughout the reading, encourage them to do this.
- **Read the story expressively.** Occasionally react verbally to events or other aspects of the story. These responses might include showing surprise, asking questions, giving an opinion, expressing pleasure, or predicting events. Think-aloud suggestions are outlined in the next column.
- **Use Comprehension Strategies.** While reading aloud to the children model the use of comprehension strategies in a natural, authentic way. Remember to try to present a variety of ways to respond to text. These include visualizing, asking questions, predicting, making connections, clarifying, and summarizing.
- **Retell.** When you have finished reading the story, call on volunteers to retell it.
- **Discuss.** After reading, discuss with the children their own reactions: how the story reminded them of things that have happened to them, what they thought of the story, and what they liked best about the story.
- **Reread.** You may wish to reread the selection on subsequent occasions focusing the discussion on the unit theme.

> *Research has shown that children who are read to are more likely to develop the skills they need to read successfully on their own.*

Think-Aloud Responses

The following options for modeling thinking aloud will be useful for reading any story aloud. Choose responses that are most appropriate for the selection you are reading.

- **React emotionally** by showing joy, sadness, amusement, or surprise.
- **Ask questions** about ideas in the text. This should be done when there are points or ideas that you really do wonder about.
- **Identify with characters** by comparing them to yourself.
- **Show empathy with or sympathy for** characters.
- **Relate the text to something** that has happened to you or to something you already know.
- **Show interest** in the text ideas.
- **Question the meaning and/or clarity** of the author's words and ideas.

Questions to Help the Children Respond

At reasonable stopping points in reading, ask the children general questions in order to get them to express their own ideas and to focus their attention on the text.

- What do you already know about this?
- What seems really important here? Why do you think so?
- Was there anything that you didn't understand? What?
- What did you like best about this?
- What new ideas did you learn from this?
- What does this make you wonder about?

Reading Roundtable

Purpose

Adult readers discuss their reading, give opinions on it, and recommend books to each other. Reading Roundtable, an activity students may choose to participate in during **Independent Work Time**, provides the same opportunity for students in the classroom. Sessions can be small or large, and may be held in the classroom reading center. During Reading Roundtable, students share with their classmates reading they do on their own. They can discuss a book they have all read or one person can review a book for the others and then entertain questions from the group.

During Reading Roundtable, students can discuss and review a variety of books:

- Full-length versions of Anthology selections.
- Classroom Library selections.
- Books that children learn about when discussing authors and illustrators.
- Books related to the research or exploration of unit concepts can be shared with others who might want to read them for pleasure or for information.
- Interesting articles from magazines, newspapers, and other sources.

Procedures

Encouraging Reading

- Read aloud to your students regularly. You can read Classroom Library selections or full-length versions of Student Anthology selections.
- Provide a time each day for children to read silently. This time can be as short as ten or fifteen minutes, but it should be strictly observed. You yourself should stop what you are doing and read. Students should be allowed to choose their own reading materials during this time and to record reactions to their reading in their response journals.
- Establish a classroom library and reading center with books from the school or local library or ask for donations of books from students, parents, and community members.
- Take your students to the school library or to the public library.

Conducting a Reading Roundtable

- When several students read the same book and then discuss it during Reading Roundtable, they can use discussion starters. If the book is from a unit bibliography, they can discuss also how the book is related to the unit concepts.
- When a student reviews a book others have not read, he or she can use some of the sentence starters to tell about the book. These may include, "This book is about . . ., I chose this book because. . .,What I really like/don't like about this book is . . ." and so on.

Introducing Sounds and Letters

Purpose

In *SRA/Open Court Reading*, children learn to relate sounds to letters in Kindergarten through the use of thirty-one **Alphabet Sound Cards** (Level K). In the upper grade levels, **Sound/Spelling Cards** (Levels 1–6) are used to relate sounds and spellings. The purpose of the **Alphabet Sound Cards** is to remind the children of the sounds of the English language and their letter correspondences. These cards are a resource for the children to use to remember sound-letter associations for both reading and writing.

Each card contains the capital and small letter, and a picture that shows the sound being produced. For instance, the **Monkey** card introduces the /m/ sound and shows a monkey looking at bananas and saying /m/ /m/ /m/. The name of the picture on each card contains the target sound at the beginning of the word for the consonants, and in the middle for most of the vowels. Vowel letters are printed in red and consonants are printed in black. In addition, the picture associates a sound with an action. This action-sound association is introduced through a short, interactive poem found in the Teacher's Edition in which the pictured object or character "makes" the sound of the letter. Long vowels are represented by a tall—or "long"—picture of the letters themselves, rather than by a picture for action-sound association.

Procedures

- Display the cards 1–26 with the picture sides to the wall. Initially post the first twenty-six cards in alphabetical order so that only the alphabet letters show. The short vowel cards may be posted as they are introduced later. As you introduce the letter sound, you will turn the card to show the picture and the letter on the other side. Once the cards are posted, do not change their positions so that the children can locate the cards quickly.
- Before turning a card, point to the letter. Ask children to tell what they know about the letter. For example, they are likely to know its name and possibly its sound if the letter is one they have already worked with.

- Turn the card and show the picture. Tell the children the name of the card and explain that it will help them to remember the sound the letter makes.
- Read the poem that goes with the letter. Read it expressively, emphasizing the words with the target sound and the isolated sound when it occurs. Have the children join in to produce the sound.
- Repeat the poem a few times, encouraging all children to say the sound along with you.
- Follow the poem with the cards for the target sound. (These are listed within the lessons.)
- Name each picture and have children listen for the target sound at the beginning of the word. Ask children to repeat the words and the sound.
- For every letter sound, a listening activity follows the introduction of the cards. Lead the children in the "Listening for the Sound" activity to reinforce the letter sound.
- To link the sound and the letter, demonstrate how to form the capital and small letter by writing on the chalkboard or on an overhead transparency. The children practice forming the letter and saying the sound as they write.

Alphabet Sound Cards

The pictures and letters on the **Alphabet Sound Cards** also appear on the small sets of **Alphabet Sound Cards**. The Teacher's Edition specifically suggests that you use the **Individual Alphabet Sound Cards** for some activities. You may also use the small cards for review and for small-group reteaching and practice sessions. Have sets of the cards available for the children to use during **Independent Work Time** either alone or with partners. Add each small card to the Activity Center after you have taught the lesson in which the corresponding **Alphabet Sound Card** is introduced. Here are some suggestions for activities using the **Alphabet Sound Cards**:

1. **Saying sounds from pictures.** The leader flashes pictures as the others say the sound each picture represents.
2. **Saying sounds.** The leader flashes the letters on the cards as the others say the sound that the letters represent.

3. **Naming words from pictures.** The leader flashes pictures. The others say the sound, and then say a word beginning with that sound.
4. **Writing letters from the pictures.** Working alone, a child looks at a picture and then writes the letter for the sound that picture represents.

Tips

- Throughout the beginning lessons, help students remember that vowels are special by reminding them that vowels sometimes say their names in words. For example, the picture of the *a* on the long *a* **Alphabet Sound Card** is long because the long *a* says its name. The short *a* **Alphabet Sound Card** pictures the lamb, because the lamb makes the short *a* sound, and you can hear the sound in the word, *lamb*. In the later lessons, children will use both sets of cards to help them remember that the vowels have both a short and a long sound.
- From the very beginning, encourage children to use the **Alphabet Sound Cards** as a resource to help them with their work.
- Mastery of letter recognition is the goal children should reach so that they will be prepared to link each letter with its associated sound. If children have not yet mastered the names of the letters, it is important to work with them individually in **Independent Work Time**, or at other times during the day.
- The *Kk* card is a little tricky. A camera makes the /k/ sound when it clicks and the word *camera* begins with the /k/ sound. However, the word *camera* is not spelled with a *k*. While you need not dwell on this, be aware that some children may be confused by the fact that the *Cc* and *Kk* cards have the same picture.
- The picture on the *Qq* card depicts ducks, *quacking ducks*. Make sure that the children consistently call them *quacking ducks*, not *ducks*, and that they focus on the /kw/ sound.

The Alphabetic Principle: How the Alphabet Works

The Alphabetic Principle

Purpose

A major emphasis in the Kindergarten program is on letter recognition and attending to sounds. Children need to learn the alphabetic principle: that letters work together in a systematic way to connect spoken language to written words. This understanding is the foundation for reading. Children are not expected to master letter/sound correspondence in kindergarten, nor are they expected to blend sounds into words themselves. They are only expected to become an "expert" on their Special Letter as they learn how the alphabet works. Through this introduction to the alphabetic principle, the children will have the basic understanding required to work through the alphabet letter by letter, attaching sounds to each.

Key concepts of the Alphabetic Principle include:

- A limited number of letters combine in different ways to make many different words.
- Words are composed of sounds and letters represent those sounds.
- Anything that can be pronounced can be spelled.
- Letters and sounds can be used to identify words.
- Meaning can be obtained by using letters and sounds to figure out words.

Procedures for Kindergarten

The following steps can be used for introducing letters and sounds in Kindergarten. These steps may be adapted for students at other grades if they do not understand the alphabetic principle. The tone of these activities should be informal, fun, and fast-paced. The purpose of these activities is to familiarize the children with how the alphabet works by having them participate in group play with letters and sounds.

Introducing Letters

- Reinforce the idea that anything that can be pronounced can be spelled with the letters of the alphabet.
- Tell the children that you can spell any word. Have them give you words to spell.
- Write the words on the chalkboard and show them that the words contain the letters displayed on the **Alphabet Sound Cards**.
- Have the children help you spell the words by pointing to letters as you say them and then write them.
- Encourage the children to spell each word letter by letter.

Letter Expert Groups

- Have **Letter Cards** (Levels K and 1) available for the following set of letters: *b, d, f, h, l, m, n, p, s, t*. You will need two or three cards for each letter. (You will not need the **Alphabet Sound Cards** until later.)
- You will be the letter expert for the vowels.
- Divide the class into groups of two or three and assign each group a letter. Give each child the appropriate **Letter Card**.
- Tell the children that they are now in their Letter Expert groups and that they are going to become experts on their Special Letter's name, shape, and sound.

> *Children need to learn the alphabetic principle: that letters work together in a systematic way to connect spoken language to written words. This understanding is the foundation for reading.*

Making Words

- Begin each lesson with a rehearsal of each group's letter name.
- Demonstrate how letters work by writing a word in large letters on the chalkboard.
- Tell the children the experts for each letter in the word should hold up their **Letter Cards** and name the letter. One member of the group should stand in front of their letter on the chalkboard.
- Continue until all letters in the word are accounted for. Remember that you are responsible for the vowels.
- Demonstrate that you can make different words by changing a letter or by changing the letter order.

Identifying Sounds in Words

- Use the **Alphabet Sound Cards** to demonstrate that every letter has at least one sound.
- Give each child the **Alphabet Sound Card** for his or her Special Letter.
- Point out the pictures on the cards. Explain that each card has a picture of something that makes the letter's sound. The picture will help them remember the sound.
- Tell each group the sound for its letter. (Remember, you are the expert for the vowels.)
- Quickly have each group rehearse its letter's name and sound.
- Write a word on the chalkboard in large letters. Say the word first sound-by-sound and then blend the word.

- For each letter/sound in the word have one child from each Letter Expert group come forward and stand in front of their appropriate letter holding their cards. Although only one member of the group may come forward with the **Letter Card** or **Alphabet Sound Card**, all the children in a Special Letter group should say the name and/or sound of their letter when it occurs in words.
- Say the word again, pointing to the **Alphabet Sound Cards**.
- Ask children who are not already standing to help you hold the vowel cards.
- Vary the activity by changing one letter sound and having an expert for that letter come forward.
- End the activity for each word by saying the sounds in the words one by one and then saying the entire word. Encourage the children to participate.

Tips

- Remind the children to use the picture on the **Alphabet Sound Card** for their Special Letter to help them remember the letter's sound. The children are expected only to "master" their own Special Letter and share the information with their classmates. They are not expected to blend and read the words by themselves. These are group activities in which you work with the children to help them gain insight into the alphabet.
- Have children note that what they learn about the letters and words applies to the words they work with in Big Book selections.
- Occasionally, have children find their special letters in a Big Book selection. Play some of the letter replacement and rearrangement games with words encountered in the Big Books.

Developing the Alphabetic Principle

Purpose

The following activities are extended to provide kindergarten students with a more thorough understanding of how sounds "work" in words. In this group of exercises the children are introduced to specific letter/sound correspondences, consonants and short vowels. The children have previously been introduced to vowels and their special characteristics. This understanding is extended by introducing children to the convention that a vowel has a short sound in addition to its long sound. With this information and a carefully structured set of activities, the children can begin to explore and understand the alphabetic principle in a straightforward and thorough manner. The children not only listen for sounds in specified positions in words, they also link sounds to their corresponding letters. The activities in this group of lessons lay the groundwork for the children to work their way through the entire alphabet, learning letter-sound associations, and to understand the purpose and the value of this learning.

Move the children quickly through these activities. Do not wait for all the children to master each letter/sound correspondence before going on. The children will have more opportunities to achieve mastery. The goal of these activities is for the children to obtain a basic understanding of the alphabetic principle.

Procedures

Introducing Consonant Letters and Sounds

- Point to the **Alphabet Sound Card** and name the letter.
- Point to the picture. Tell the children the sound of the letter and how the picture helps them to remember the sound. Repeat the sound several times.
- Tell the children you will read them a short poem or an alliterative sentence to help them remember the sound of the letter. Read the poem several times, emphasizing the words with the target sound. Have the children join in and say the sound.
- After introducing and reviewing a letter/sound correspondence, summarize the information on the **Alphabet Sound Card**.

Generating Words with the Target Sound

- Brainstorm to create a list of words that begin with the target sound. Write the words on the chalkboard or on a chart. Include any of the children's names that begin with the target sound.
- Play the *I'm Thinking of Something That Starts With* game. Begin with the target sound and add clues until the children guess the word. If the children guess a word that does not begin with the target sound, emphasize the beginning sound and ask if the word begins with the target sound.
- Silly Sentences. Make silly sentences with the children that include many words with the target sound. Encourage the children to participate by extending the sentences: *Mary mopes. Mary mopes on Monday. Mary and Michael mope on Monday in Miami.*

Listening For Initial Sound

- Give each child a **Letter Card** for the target sound, /s/.
- Point to the picture on the **Alphabet Sound Card**, and have the children give the sound, /s/.
- Tell the children to listen for the first sound in each word you say. If it is /s/ they should hold up their *s* cards. Establish a signal so that the children know when to respond.
- Read a list of words, some beginning with /s/, some beginning with other sounds.

Listening for Final Sound

The procedure for listening for the final sound of a word is the same as that for listening for the initial sound. The children may need to be reminded throughout the activity to pay attention to the *final* sound /s/.

- Read a list of words, some ending with the target sound, some ending with other sounds. Avoid words that begin with the target sound.

Linking the Sound to the Letter

- **Word Pairs (initial sounds).** Write pairs of words on the chalkboard, one of each pair beginning with the target sound. Say the word beginning with the target sound and ask the children to identify it. Remind them to listen for the target sound at the beginning of the word, to think about which letter makes that sound, and to find the word that begins with that letter. For example,
Target sound: /s/
Word pair: *fit sit*
Which word is *sit*?

- **Word Pairs (final sounds).** Follow the same procedure used for initial sounds, this time directing the children to think about the sound that they hear at the end of the word. Since it is often more difficult for the children to attend to the ending sound, you may need to lead them through several pairs of words. Remind the children to listen for the target sound and to think about which letter makes that sound.

- **Writing Letters.** Using either the handwriting system outlined in the Appendix of Levels K and 1 of *SRA/Open Court Reading*, or the system in use at your school, have children practice writing capital and small letters. Remind the children of the letter sound and have them repeat it.

Comparing Initial Consonant Sounds

This activity is exactly like **listening for initial sounds** except that the children must discriminate between two sounds. They are given **Letter Cards** for both sounds and must hold up the appropriate card when they hear the sound.

Comparing Final Consonant Sounds

This activity is exactly like listening for final sounds except that the children must discriminate between two sounds. They are given **Letter Cards** for both sounds and must hold up the appropriate card when they hear the sound.

Linking the Consonant Sound to the Letter

In this activity to help children link sounds and letters, the children will make words either by adding initial consonants to selected word parts or by adding a different final consonant to a consonant-vowel-consonant combination.

Introducing Short Vowel Sounds

- Remind the children that the vowels are printed in red to remind them that they are special letters. (They are not special because they are printed in red.) They are special because they have more than one sound and every word must have a vowel sound.
- Point to the long *Aa* **Alphabet Sound Card** and remind the children that this letter is called a *vowel*. Vowels sometimes say their names in words, for example, *say, day, tray*. This vowel sound is called long *a*.
- Have the children repeat the sound.
- Sometimes vowels say different sounds. Point to the picture of the lamb on the short *Aa* card and tell them that *a* also makes the sound heard in the middle of *lamb*. This is the short *a*. Read the short vowel poem to help the children remember the short *a*.
- Have all the children join in saying /a/ /a/ /a/.

Listening for Short Vowel Sounds Versus Long Vowel Sounds

- Tell the children that you will read words with long *a* and short *a*. Review the two sounds.
- Give the children a signal to indicate when they hear the vowel sound. You may want one signal for short *a*, such as scrunching down, and another for long *a*, such as stretching up tall.
- Continue with lists of words such as: *add, back, aid, tan, bake, tame*.

Linking the Vowel Sound to the Letter

- Writing Letters. Have children practice writing the letter and review the sound of the letter.
- In this activity to help children link sounds and letters, the children will make words either by adding initial consonants to selected word parts or by adding a different final consonant to a consonant-vowel-consonant combination. Change the beginning of the word or the word ending, but retain the vowel sound to make new words, for example,

at	*hat*	*mat*	*pat*
ap	*map*	*tap*	*sap*
am	*Sam*	*Pam*	*ham*

Comparing Short Vowel Sounds

This activity requires children to discriminate between short vowel sounds in the middle of words. Review the vowel sounds.

- Say a word and have the children repeat it. Establish a signal to indicate whether they hear short *a* or short *o* in the middle of the word. For example, they can hold up the appropriate **Letter Card** when they hear a sound. Sample words: *cap, cot, rat, rot, rack, rock*.
- The way in which vowel sounds—in the initial, medial, and final position—combine to make words can be observed in a large set of words that does not contain silent letters or other special spelling conventions.

Linking the Sound to the Letter

- In this activity write a word on the chalkboard and help the children say it.
- Change the word by changing the vowel. Help the children say the new word, for example, *map, mop, hot, hat, pot, pat*.
- For a variation of this activity, write the pairs of words and simply have the children say which word is the target word; for example, the children see *tap* and *top*. Ask which word is *top*, directing the children's attention to the vowel.

Tips

- Lead and model the exercises as necessary until the children begin to catch on and can participate with confidence.
- To keep the children focused on the various activities, have them tell you the task for each activity; for example, after telling the children to listen for final sounds, ask the children what they will be listening for.
- Actively involve the students by giving them opportunities to tell what they know rather than supplying the information for them; for example, Do they know the letter name? Do they know the sound? Can they think of words that begin with the sound?
- Keeping the children focused on the idea that they are learning about sounds and letters so they can read these books themselves makes the lessons more relevant for the children.

Phonemic Awareness

The basic purpose of providing structured practice in phonemic awareness is to help the children hear and understand the sounds from which words are made. Before children can be expected to understand the sound/symbol correspondence that forms the base of written English, they need to have a strong working knowledge of the sound relationships that make up the spoken language. This understanding of spoken language lays the foundation for the transition to written language.

Phonemic awareness activities provide the children with easy practice in discriminating the sounds that make up words. Phonemic awareness consists of quick, gamelike activities designed to help children understand that speech is made up of distinct, identifiable sounds. The playful nature of the activities makes them appealing and engaging, while giving the children practice and support for learning about language. Once the children begin reading and writing, this experience with manipulating sounds will help them use what they know about sounds and letters to sound out and spell unfamiliar words when they read and write.

The two main formats for teaching phonemic awareness are oral blending and segmentation. These are supported by occasional discrimination activities and general wordplay. Oral blending encourages students to combine sounds to make words. Segmentation, conversely, requires them to isolate sounds from words. Other activities support discrimination, or recognition, of particular sounds. Sometimes simple songs, rhymes, or games engage students in wordplay. In these, the children manipulate words in a variety of ways. From these playful activities, the children derive serious knowledge about language.

As the children progress through different phonemic awareness activities, they will become proficient at listening for and reproducing the sounds they hear. It is essential for their progression to phonics and reading that they are able to hear the sounds and the patterns used to make up recognizable words. The phonemic awareness activities support the phonics instruction, but the activities are oral, and do not focus on sound/spelling correspondences. Because the children are not expected to read the words they are experimenting with, any consonant and vowel sounds may be used, even if the children have not been formally taught the sound and its spellings.

Oral Blending

Purpose

In oral blending, the children are led through a progression of activities designed to help them hear how sounds are put together to make words.

Until children develop an awareness of the component parts of words, they have no tools with which to decode words or put letters together to form words. Oral blending helps children master these component parts of words, from syllables down to single sounds, or phonemes. Oral blending is not to be confused with the formal blending of specific sounds whose spellings the children will be taught through phonics instruction. Oral blending does not depend on the recognition of written words; it focuses instead on hearing the sounds.

Oral blending focuses on hearing sounds through a sequence that introduces the most easily distinguished word parts then systematically moves to sound blending that contains all the challenges of phonic decoding (except letter recognition). This sequence provides support for the least-prepared child— one who comes to first grade with no concept of words or sounds within words. At the same time,

the lively pace and playful nature of oral blending activities hold the interest of children who already have some familiarity with words and letters.

Oral blending prepares children for phonics instruction by developing an awareness of the separate sounds that make up speech. Oral blending activities then continue in concert with phonics instruction to reinforce and extend new learning. And, because these activities involve simply listening to and reproducing sounds, oral blending need not be restricted to the sounds children have been or will be taught in phonics.

The tone of the activities should be playful and informal and should move quickly. Although these activities will provide information about student progress, they are not diagnostic tools. Do not expect mastery. Those children who have not caught on will be helped more by varied experiences than by more drilling on the same activity.

Procedures

Following is a description of the progression of oral blending activities.

Syllable Blending

Syllables are easier to distinguish than individual sounds (phonemes), so children can quickly experience success in forming meaningful

words. Tell the children that you are going to say some words in two parts. Tell them to listen carefully so that they can discover what the words are. Read each word, pronouncing each part distinctly with a definite pause between syllables broken by . . . . The lists of words that follow are arranged in sequence from easy to harder. They cover different types of cues. At any point where they fit in the sequence, include multisyllable names of children in the class.

Model

TEACHER: *dino . . . saur. What's the word?*

CHILDREN: *dinosaur*

Example Words

- First part of the word cues the whole word:
  vita . . . min   vaca . . . tion
  hippopot . . . amus   ambu . . . lance
- Two distinct words easily combined:
  butter. . . fly   straw. . . berry
  surf . . . board   basket . . . ball
- Two distinct words, but first word could cue the wrong ending:
  tooth . . . ache   tooth . . . paste
  water . . . fall   water . . . melon
- First part, consonant + vowel, not enough to guess whole word:
  re . . . member   re . . . frigerator
  bi . . . cycle   bi . . . ology

- Identifying clues in second part:
  light . . . ning   sub . . . ject
  in . . . sect
- Last part, consonant + vowel sound, carries essential information:
  yester . . . day   rain . . . bow
  noi . . . sy   pota . . . to
- Changing the final part changes the word:
  start . . . ing   start . . . er   start. . . ed

Initial Consonant Sounds

Initial consonant blending prepares students for consonant replacement activities that will come later. Tell the children that you will ask them to put some sounds together to make words. Pronounce each word part distinctly and make a definite pause at the breaks indicated. When a letter is surrounded by slash marks, pronounce the letter's sound, not its name. When you see /s/, for example, you will say ssss, not ess. The words that follow are arranged from easy to harder. At any point where they fit in the sequence, include names of children in the class.

Model
TEACHER: /t/ . . . iger. What's the word?
CHILDREN: tiger

Example Words
- Separated consonant blend, with rest of word giving strong cue to word identity:
  /b/ . . . roccoli   /k/ . . . racker
  /f/ . . . lashlight   /k/ . . . reature
- Held consonant that is easy for children to hear, with rest of word giving strong cue:
  /s/ . . . innamon   /l/ . . . adybug
  /s/ . . . eventeen   /n/ . . . ewspaper
- Stop consonant that is harder for children to hear preceding vowel, with rest of word giving strong cue:
  /t/ . . . adpole   /p/ . . . iggybank
  /d/ . . . ragonfly   /b/ . . . arbecue
- Single-syllable words and words in which the second part gives a weaker cue:
  /s/ . . . ing   /l/ . . . augh   /v/ . . . ase

Final Consonant Sounds

In this phase of oral blending, the last sound in the word is separated.

Model
TEACHER: cabba . . . /j/. What's the word?
CHILDREN: cabbage

Example Words
- Words that are easily recognized even before the final consonant is pronounced:
  bubblegu . . . /m/   Columbu . . . /s/
  crocodi . . . /l/   submari . . . /n/
- Multisyllable words that need the final consonant for recognition:
  colle . . . /j/ (college)   came . . . /l/ (camel)
- Single-syllable words:
  sa . . . /d/   gra . . . /s/   snai . . . /l/

Initial Consonant Sound Replacement

This level of oral blending further develops awareness of initial consonant sounds. The activity begins with a common word, then quickly changes its initial consonant sound. Most of the words produced are nonsense words, which helps keep the focus on the sounds in the word. Note that the words are written on the chalkboard, but the children are not expected to read them. The writing is to help the children see that when the sounds change, the letters change, and vice versa.

Model
TEACHER: [Writes word on board.] This word is *magazine*. What is it?
CHILDREN: *magazine*
TEACHER: Now I'm going to change it. [Erases initial consonant.] Now it doesn't start with /m/, it's going to start with /b/. What's the new word?
CHILDREN: *bagazine*
TEACHER: That's right . . . [Writes b where m had been.] It's *bagazine*. Now I'm going to change it again. . . .

Repeat with different consonant sounds. Then do the same with other words, such as: *remember, Saturday, tomorrow, lotion, million*. Continue with single-syllable words, such as: *take, big, boot, cot, seat, look, tap, ride, late*. There are two stages in using written letters:

- The replacement letter is not written until *after* the new "word" has been identified.
- Later, the replacement letter is written *at the same time* the change in the initial phoneme is announced. For example, the teacher erases *d* and writes *m* while saying, "Now it doesn't start with /d/, it starts with /m/."

Before children can be expected to understand the sound/symbol correspondence that forms the base of written English, they need to have a strong working knowledge of the sound relationships that make up the spoken language.

You may wish to alter the procedure when the consonants used have already been introduced in phonics by writing the replacement letter and having children sound out the new word. Feel free to switch between the two procedures within a single exercise. If the children are not responding orally to written spellings that have been introduced in phonics, don't force it. Proceed by saying the word before writing the letter, and wait until another time to move on to writing before pronouncing.

One-Syllable Words

The children now begin blending individual phonemes to form words. This important step can be continued well into the year. Continued repetitions of this activity will help the children realize how they can use the sound/spellings they are learning to read and write real words.

At first, the blended words are presented in a story context that helps the children identify the words. They soon recognize that they are actually decoding meaningful words. However, the context must not be so strong that the children can guess the word without listening to the phonemic cues. Any vowel sounds and irregularly spelled words may be used, since there is no writing involved.

Model
TEACHER: *When I looked out the window, I saw a /l/ /ī/ /t/. What did I see?*
CHILDREN: *A light.*
TEACHER: *Yes, I saw a light. At first I thought it was the /m/ /ōō/ /n/. What did I think it was?*
CHILDREN: *The moon.*
TEACHER: *But it didn't really look like the moon. Suddenly I thought, maybe it's a space /sh/ /i/ /p/. What did I think it might be?*
CHILDREN: *A spaceship!*

Once the children are familiar with this phase of oral blending, they can move to blending one-syllable words without the story context.

Example Words
- CVC (consonant/vowel/consonant) words beginning with easily blended consonant sounds (/sh/, /h/, /r/, /v/, /s/, /n/, /z/, /f/, /l/, /m/):
  nip   nap
- CVC words beginning with any consonant:
  ten   bug   lip
- Add CCVC words:
  flap   step
- Add CVCC words:
  most   band   went
- Add CCVCC words:
  stamp   grand   scuffs

Final Consonant Sound Replacement

Final consonant sounds are typically more difficult for children to use than initial consonants.

- Begin with multisyllabic words and move to one-syllable words.
- As with initial consonants, first write the changed consonant after students have pronounced the new word.
- Then write the consonant as they pronounce it.
- Then for sound/spellings that have been introduced in phonics instruction, write the new consonant spelling and have students identify and pronounce it.

Model
TEACHER: *[Writes word on board.] This word is* teapot. *What is it?*
CHILDREN: *teapot*
TEACHER: *Now I'm going to change it.* [Erases final consonant.] *Now it doesn't end with /t/, it ends with /p/. What's the word now?*
CHILDREN: *teapop*
TEACHER: *That's right . . .* [Writes *p* where *t* had been.] *It's* teapop. *Now I'm going to change it again. . . .*

Example Words
- Words that are easily recognized even before the final consonant is pronounced:
  picnic   picnit   picnis   picnil   picnid
  airplane   airplate   airplabe   airplafe

- Multisyllabic words that need the final consonant for recognition:

  muffin   muffil   muffim   muffip   muffit
  amaze   amate   amake   amale   amade

- Single-syllable words:

  neat nean neap neam neaj nead neaf
  broom broot brood broof broop broon

Initial Vowel Replacement

Up to now, oral blending has concentrated on consonant sounds because they are easier to hear than vowels. As you move to vowel play, remember that the focus is still on the sounds, not the spellings. Use any vowel sounds.

Model

TEACHER: [Writes word on board.] *This word is elephant. What is it?*

CHILDREN: *elephant*

TEACHER: *Now I'm going to change it.* [Erases initial vowel.] *Now it doesn't start with /e/, it starts with /a/. What's the word now?*

CHILDREN: *alephant*

TEACHER: *That's right . . .* [Writes *a* where *e* had been.] *It's alephant. Now I'm going to change it again. . . .*

Example Words

- Multisyllable words:

  angry ingry oongry ungry engry
  ivy   avy   oovy   evy   ovy   oivy

- One-syllable words:

  ink ank oonk unk onk oink
  add odd idd   oudd edd udd

Segmentation

Purpose

Segmentation and oral blending complement each other: Oral blending puts sounds together to make words, while segmentation separates words into sounds. Oral blending will provide valuable support for decoding when students begin reading independently.

Procedure

Syllables

The earliest segmentation activities focus on syllables, which are easier to distinguish than individual sounds, or phonemes. Start with children's names, then use other words. As with the oral blending activities, remember to move quickly through these activities. Do not hold the class back waiting for all children to catch on. Individual progress will vary, but drilling on one activity is less helpful than going on to others. Return to the same activity often. Frequent repetition is very beneficial and allows children additional opportunities to catch on.

- Say, for example, "Let's clap out Amanda's name. A-man-da."
- Have the children clap and say the syllables along with you. Count the claps.
- Tell the children that these word parts are called *syllables*. Don't try to explain; the idea will develop with practice. Once you have provided the term, simply say, "How many syllables?" after the children clap and count.
- Mix one-syllable and multisyllable words:

  fantastic   tambourine   good
  imaginary   stand   afraid

Comparative Length of Words

Unlike most phonemic awareness activities, this one involves writing on the chalkboard or on an overhead transparency. Remember, though, that the children are not expected to read what is written. They are merely noticing that words that take longer to say generally look longer when written.

- Start with students' names. Choose two names, one short and one long, with the same first initial (for example, Joe and Jonathan).
- Write the two names on the board one above the other so that the difference is obvious.
- Tell the children that one name is Jonathan and one is Joe. Have them pronounce and clap each name. Then, have them tell which written word they think says *Joe*.
- Move your finger under each name as they clap and say it, syllable by syllable.
- Repeat with other pairs of names and words, such as: *tea/telephone, cat/caterpillar, butterfly/bug.* Be sure not to give false clues. For example, sometimes write the longer word

on top, sometimes the shorter one; sometimes ask for the shorter word, sometimes the longer; sometimes ask for the top word, sometimes the bottom; sometimes point to a word and ask the children to name it, sometimes name the word and ask the children to point to it.

Listen for Individual Sounds

Activities using a puppet help the children listen for individual sounds in words. Use any puppet you have on hand. When you introduce the puppet, tell the children that it likes to play word games. Each new activity begins with the teacher speaking to and for the puppet until the children determine the pattern. Next, students either speak for the puppet or correct the puppet. To make sure all the children are participating, alternate randomly between having the whole group or individuals respond. The activities focus on particular parts of words, according to the following sequence:

1. **Repeating last part of word.** Use words beginning with easy-to-hear consonants, such as *f, l, m, n, r, s,* and *z.* The puppet repeats only the rime, the part of the syllable after the initial consonant.

Model

TEACHER: *farm*

PUPPET: *arm*

Once the pattern is established, the children respond for the puppet.

TEACHER: *rope*

CHILDREN: *ope*

Example Words

Use words such as the following: *mine . . . ine soup . . . oup   feet . . . eet*

2. **Restoring initial phonemes.** Now the children correct the puppet. Be sure to acknowledge the correction.

Model

TEACHER: *lake*

PUPPET: *ake*

TEACHER: *No, llllake. You forgot the /l/.*

TEACHER: *real*

PUPPET: *eal*

TEACHER: *What did the puppet leave off?*

CHILDREN: */r/. It's supposed to be real.*

TEACHER: *That's right. The word is real.*

Example Words

Use words such as the following:

look . . . ook   mouse . . . ouse sand . . . and

3. **Segmenting initial consonants.** The puppet pronounces only the initial consonant.

Model

TEACHER: *pay*

PUPPET: */p/*

Example Words

Use words such as the following:

moon . . . /m/   nose . . . /n/   bell . . . /b/

4. Restoring final consonants. The children correct the puppet. Prompt if necessary: *"What's the word? What did the puppet leave off?"*

Model

TEACHER: *run*

PUPPET: *ru*

CHILDREN: *It's run! You left off the /n/.*

TEACHER: *That's right. The word is run.*

Example Words

Use words such as the following:

meet. . . mee   cool . . . coo   boot. . . boo

5. Isolating final consonants. The puppet pronounces only the final consonant.

Model

TEACHER: *green*

PUPPET: */n/*

Example Words

Use words such as the following:

glass . . . /s/   boom . . . /m/   mice . . . /s/

6. Segmenting initial consonant blends. The sounds in blends are emphasized.

Model

TEACHER: *clap*

PUPPET: *lap*

Next have students correct the puppet.

TEACHER: *stain*

PUPPET: *tain*

CHILDREN: *It's stain! You left off the /s/.*

TEACHER: *That's right. The word is stain.*

Example Words

Use words such as the following:

blaze . . . laze   draw. . . raw   proud . . . roud

Discrimination

Purpose

Discrimination activities help children focus on particular sounds in words.

Listening for long vowel sounds is the earliest discrimination activity. Vowel sounds are necessary for decoding, but young children do not hear them easily. This is evident in children's invented spellings, where vowels are often omitted. Early in the year, the children listen for long vowel sounds, which are more easily distinguished than short vowel sounds:

- Explain to the children that vowels are special, because sometimes they say their names in words.
- Tell the children which vowel sound to listen for.
- Have them repeat the sound when they hear it in a word. For example, if the target vowel sound is long e, the children will say long e when you say *leaf* but they should not respond when you say *loaf*.
- Initially the children should listen for one long vowel sound at a time. Later they can listen for two vowel sounds. All **Example Words**, however, should contain one of the target vowels.

Procedure

Listening for short vowel sounds discrimination activities should be done once the short vowels /a/ and /i/ have been introduced. Short vowels are very useful in reading. They are generally more regular in spelling than long vowels, and they appear in many short, simple words. However, their sounds are less easily distinguished than those of long vowels. Thus, the activities focus only on /a/ and /i/. All the words provided have one or the other of these sounds. Either have the children repeat the sound of a specified vowel, or vary the activity as follows: Write an *a* on one side of the chalkboard and an *i* on the other. Ask the children to point to the *a* when they hear a word with the /a/ sound and point to the *i* when they hear a word with the /i/ sound. Use words such as the following:

bat	*mat*	*sat*	*sit*	*spit*
pit	*pat*	*pan*	*pin*	*spin*

Consonant sounds in multisyllable words. Discriminating these sounds helps children attend to consonant sounds in the middle of words.

- Say the word *rib* and have the children repeat it. Ask where they hear the /b/ in *rib*.
- Then say *ribbon* and ask the children where they hear the /b/ in *ribbon*.
- Tell the children that you will say some words and they will repeat each word.
- After they repeat each word, ask what consonant sound they hear in the middle of that word. Use words such as the following:

famous	*message*	*picky*
jogger	*flavor*	*zipper*

Phonemic Play

Purpose

Wordplay activities help the children focus on and manipulate sounds, thus supporting the idea that words are made of specific sounds that can be taken apart, put together, or changed to make new words. Through wordplay, children gain important knowledge about language.

Procedure

Producing rhymes. Many phonemic play activities focus on producing rhymes. A familiar or easily learned rhyme or song is introduced, and the children are encouraged to substitute words or sounds. An example is *"Willaby Wallaby Woo,"* in which children change the rhyming words in the couplet *"Willaby Wallaby Woo/An elephant sat on you"* so that the second line ends with a student's name and the first line ends with a rhyme beginning with W (for example, *"Willaby Wallaby Wissy/An elephant sat on Missy"*).

Generate alliterative words. Children can also say as many words as they can think of that begin with a given consonant sound. This is a valuable complement to discrimination activities in which the teacher produces the words and the children identify them.

Explicit, Systematic Phonics

The purpose of phonics instruction is to teach students the association between the sounds of the language and the written symbols—spellings—that have been chosen to represent those sounds.

As with all alphabetic languages, English has a limited number of symbols—twenty-six—that are combined and recombined to make the written language. These written symbols are a visual representation of the speech sounds we use to communicate. This is simply a code. The faster the children learn the code and how it works, the faster the whole world of reading opens to them.

Students are introduced to the sounds and spellings of English in a very systematic, sequential manner. This allows them to continually build on what they learned the day before. As each sound/symbol relationship is introduced, students are introduced to and practice with words containing the target sound/spelling and then reinforce their learning through the use of engaging text specifically written for this purpose.

It can be very difficult for children to hear the individual sounds, or phonemes, that make up words. When phonics instruction is explicit—students are told the sounds associated with the different written symbols—there is no guesswork involved. They know that this sound /b/ is spelled *b*. Therefore, students in an ***SRA/Open Court Reading*** classroom spend time learning to discriminate individual speech sounds and then they learn the spellings of those sounds. This systematic explicit approach affords students the very best chance for early and continuing success.

Introducing the Sounds and Using the Sound/Spelling Cards

Purpose

The purpose of the **Sound/Spelling Cards** (Levels 1–6) is to remind the children of the sounds of English and their spellings. The name of the picture on each card contains the target sound at the beginning for the consonants and in the middle for most vowels. In addition, the picture associates a sound with an action. This association is introduced through an interactive story in which the pictured object or character "makes" the sound. These cards are a resource for the children to use to remember sound/spelling associations for both reading and writing.

Procedure

Posting the Cards

Initially, post the first twenty-six cards face to the wall so that only the alphabet letters on the backs show. As you introduce each card, you will turn it to show the picture and the spellings on the front of the card. If, however, most of your students already have some knowledge of the letters—this is a second or third grade classroom and students are reviewing what they learned the year before—you may want to go ahead and place the cards with the picture and the spellings facing forward to provide support as they begin writing.

Make sure that the cards are positioned so that you can touch them with your hand or with a pointer when you refer to them and so that all of the children can see them easily. The cards should be placed where the children can readily see them during reading and writing.

Special Devices

- Vowel spellings are printed in red to draw attention to them. Consonants are printed in black. The blank line in a spelling indicates that a letter will take the place of the blank in a word. For example, the replacement of the blank with *t* in the spelling *a_ e*, makes the word *ate*. The blank lines may also indicate the position of a spelling in a word or a syllable. The blank in *h_* for example, means that the spelling occurs at the beginning of a word or a syllable.

- The blanks in *_ie_* indicate that the *ie* spelling comes in the middle of a word or a syllable, while the blank in *_oy* shows that the *oy* spelling comes at the end of a word or a syllable. Uses of blanks in specific spellings are in the lessons. Please note now, however, that when you write a spelling of a sound on the chalkboard or an overhead transparency, you should include the blanks.

- The color of the background behind the spellings also has a meaning. Consonants have a white background. The colors behind vowel spellings are pronunciation clues. Short vowel spellings have a green background, which corresponds to the green box that appears before some consonant spellings. Thus, before *_ck* or *x* you will see a green box, which indicates that a short vowel always precedes that spelling. Long vowel spellings have a yellow background; other vowel spellings, such as r-controlled vowels and diphthongs, have a blue background. The color code reinforces the idea that vowels are special and have different pronunciations.

Introducing the Sound/Spelling Cards

In first grade, each sound and spelling is introduced by using a see/hear/say/write sequence. In grades two and three the same sequence is used in the review of the cards.

1. **See:** Students see the spelling or spellings on the **Sound/Spelling Card** and the chalkboard or an overhead transparency.
2. **Hear:** Students hear the sound used in words and in isolation in the story. The sound is, of course, related to the picture (and the action) shown on the Sound/Spelling Card.
3. **Say:** Students say the sound.
4. **Write:** Students write the spelling(s) for the sound.

There are a number of important points to remember about this technique.

- The first item written on the chalkboard or an overhead transparency is the spelling of the sound being introduced. This gives the spelling a special emphasis in the mind of the child. It is the "see" part of the sequence.

- One of the causes of blending failure is the failure to teach sounds thoroughly during introduction of the **Sound/Spelling Card** and during initial sounding and blending. To help ensure success for all children, make certain that every child is able to see the board or screen.

- After you present the sound and spelling, have several students go to the board to write the spelling. Have them say the sound as they write the spelling. After they have written the spelling of the sound, give them a chance to proofread their own work. Then give the other students the opportunity to help with proofreading by noting what is good about the spelling and then suggesting how to make it better.

Sample Lesson, Using the Letter *m* and the Sound /m/

- Point to the **Sound/Spelling Card** and have students tell you whether it is a vowel or a consonant. Have them tell the name of the card. If they do not know it tell them it is Monkey. Point to the *monkey* in the picture and say the word monkey, emphasizing the initial consonant sound—*mmmonkey*.
- Point to the spelling *m*. Tell students that /m/ is spelled *m*.
- If you wish make up an alliterative sentence about the Monkey or use the alliterative story that accompanies the card. (In first grade this story is printed on the page on which the card is introduced. In grades two and three, the cards are printed in the Appendix of the Teacher's Edition.) For example, *When Muzzie the monkey munches bananas, the sound she makes is /mmmmmm/.*
- If students had ***SRA/Open Court Reading*** before, you can ask them if they learned an action such as rubbing their tummies to help them remember the sound. If your students don't have an action they associate with the cards already, make some up with your students. They will have fun and it will be another way for them to remember the sound/spelling relationships.
- Write *m* on the chalkboard or on an overhead transparency and say the sound. Write the letter again and ask the children to say the sound with you as they write the letter on slates, on paper, or with their index finger on a surface. Repeat this activity several times.

- Have the children listen for words beginning with /m/, indicating by some signal, such as thumbs-up or thumbs-down, whether they hear the /m/ sound and saying /m/ when they hear it in a word. Repeat with the sound in various positions in words. Encourage students to tell you and the class words with /m/ at the beginning and end as well as in the middle of words.
- Check students' learning by pointing to the card. Have students identify the sound, name the spelling, and discuss how the card can help them remember the sound.

Individual Sound/Spelling Cards

Use the **Individual Sound/Spelling Cards** for review and for small-group reteaching and practice sessions. Students can use them alone or

> *The faster the children learn the code and how it works, the faster the whole world of reading opens to them.*

with partners. Here are some suggestions for activities using the **Individual Sound/Spelling Cards**:

1. **Saying sounds from pictures.** The leader flashes pictures as the others say the sound each picture represents.
2. **Saying sounds.** The leader flashes the spellings on the cards as the others say the sound that the spellings represent.
3. **Naming spellings from pictures.** The leader flashes pictures. The others name the card, say the sound, and then name as many spellings as they can.
4. **Writing spellings from the pictures.** Working alone, a child looks at a picture and then writes as many spellings for that **Sound/Spelling Card** as he or she can remember.
5. **Saying words from pictures.** The leader presents a series of pictures. The others form words by blending the sounds represented.

Purpose

The purpose of blending is to teach the children a strategy for figuring out unfamiliar words. Initially, children will be blending sound by sound. Ultimately, the children will sound and blend only those words that they cannot read. Eventually, the blending process will become quick and comfortable for them.

Procedure

Learning the sounds and their spellings is only the first step in learning to read and write. The second step is learning to blend the sounds into words.

Blending Techniques

Blending lines are written on the chalkboard or an overhead transparency as the children watch and participate. The lines and sentences should not be written out before class begins. It is through the sound-by-sound blending of the words and the sentences that the children learn the blending process.

Sound-by-Sound Blending

- Write the spelling of the first sound in the word. Point to the spelling, and say the sound.
- Have the children say the sound with you as you say the sound again. Write the spelling of the next sound. Point to the spelling, and say the sound. Have the children say the sound with you as you say the sound again. After you have written the vowel spelling, blend through the vowel (unless the vowel is the first letter of the word), making the blending motion—a smooth sweeping of the hand beneath the sounds, linking them from left to right, for example, *ba*. As you make the blending motion, make sure that your hand is under the letter that corresponds to the sound you are saying at the moment.
- Have the children blend through the vowel. Write the spelling of the next sound. Point to the spelling and say the sound. Have the children say the sound with you as you touch the letter and say the sound again.
- Continue as described above through the word. After pronouncing the final sound in the word, make the blending motion from left to right under the word as you blend the sounds. Then have the children blend the word. Let them be the first to pronounce the word normally.
- Ask a child to read the word again and use it in a sentence. Ask another child to extend the sentence—that is, make it longer by giving more information. Help the child by asking an appropriate question about the sentence, using, for example, *How? When? Where? or Why?* Continue blending the rest of the words.

Whole-Word Blending

Once students are comfortable with sound-by-sound blending, they are ready for whole-word blending.

- Write the whole word to be blended on the chalkboard or an overhead transparency.
- Ask the children to blend the sounds as you point to them.
- Then have the children say the whole word.
- Ask the children to use the word in a sentence and then to extend the sentence.
- When all of the words have been blended, point to words randomly and ask individuals to read them.

Blending Syllables

In reading the Anthologies, students will often encounter multisyllabic words. Some students are intimidated by long words, yet many multisyllabic words are easily read by reading and blending the syllables rather than the individual sounds. Following a set of rules for syllables is difficult since so many of the rules have exceptions. Students need to remember that each syllable in a word contains one vowel sound.

- Have students identify the vowel sounds in the word.
- Have students blend the first syllable sound by sound if necessary or read the first syllable.
- Handle the remaining syllables the same way.
- Have students blend the syllables together to read.

Blending Sentences

Blending sentences is the logical extension of blending words. Blending sentences helps students develop fluency, which is critical to comprehension. Encourage students to reread sentences with phrasing and natural intonation.

- Write the sentence on the chalkboard or on a transparency, underlining any high-frequency sight words—words that the children cannot decode either because they are irregular or because they contain sounds or spellings that the children have not yet learned or reviewed. If the children have not read these words before, write the words on the board or an overhead transparency and introduce them before writing the sentence. These words should not be blended but read as whole words.

Building for Success

A primary cause of children's blending failure is their failure to understand how to use the **Sound/Spelling Cards**. Students need to practice sounds and spellings when the **Sound/Spelling Cards** are introduced and during initial blending. They also need to understand that if they are not sure of how to pronounce a spelling, they can check the cards.

Early blending may be frustrating. You must lead the group almost constantly. Soon, however, leaders in the group will take over. Watch to see whether any children are having trouble during the blending. Include them in small-group instruction sessions. At that time you may want to use the vowel-first procedure described below to reteach blending lines.

Extra Help

In working with small groups during **Independent Work Time**, you may want to use some of the following suggestions to support students who need help with blending.

Vowel-First Blending

Vowel-first blending is an alternative to sound-by-sound and whole-word blending for children who need special help. Used in small-group sessions, this technique helps children who have difficulty with the other two types of blending focus on the most important part of each word, the vowels, and do only one thing at a time. These children are not expected to say a sound and blend it with another at virtually the same time. The steps to use in vowel-first blending follow:

1. Across the board or on an overhead transparency, write the vowel spelling in each of the words in the line. For a short vowel, the line may look like this:
   a   a   a
   For a long vowel, the line may look like this:
   ee ea ea
2. Point to the spelling as the children say the sound for the spelling.

> *Blending is the heart and soul of phonics instruction and the key strategy children must learn to open the world of written language.*

3. Begin blending around the vowels. In front of the first vowel spelling, add the spelling for the beginning sound of the word. Make the blending motion and have the children blend through the vowel, adding a blank to indicate that the word is still incomplete. Repeat this procedure for each partial word in the line until the line looks like this:
   ma__ sa__ pa__
   see__ mea__ tea__
4. Have the children blend the partial word again as you make the blending motion and then add the spelling for the ending sound.
5. Make the blending motion and have the children blend the completed word—for example, *mat* or *seed*.
6. Ask a child to repeat the word and use it in a sentence. Then have another child extend the sentence.

7. Repeat steps 4, 5, and 6 for each word in the line, which might look like this:
   mat   sad   pan
   or
   seed meat team

Tips

- In the early lessons, do blending with as much direction and dialogue as is necessary for success. Reduce your directions to a minimum as soon as possible. You have made good progress when you no longer have to say, "Sound—Sound—Blend," because the children automatically sound and blend as you write.
- Unless the line is used to introduce or to reinforce a spelling pattern, always ask a student to use a word in a sentence and then to extend the sentence immediately after you've developed the word. If the line is used to introduce or to reinforce a spelling pattern, however, ask the children to give sentences at the end of the line. Students will naturally extend sentences by adding phrases to the ends of the sentences. Encourage them to add phrases at the beginning or in the middle of the sentence.
- Use the vowel-first procedure in small group preteaching or reteaching sessions with students who are having a lot of trouble with blending. Remember that you must adapt the blending lines in the lessons to the vowel-first method.
- The sight words in the sentences cannot be blended. The children must approach them as sight words to be memorized. If children are having problems reading sight words, tell them the words. Cue marks written over the vowels may help students.
   - ✓ Straight line cue for long vowels
     EXAMPLES: *āpe, mē, fīne, sō, ūse*
   - ✓ Curved line cue for short vowels
     EXAMPLES: *că̆t, pĕt, wĭn, hŏt, tŭg*
   - ✓ Tent cue for variations of a and o
     EXAMPLES: *âll, ôff*
   - ✓ Dot cue for schwa sound with multiple-syllable words
     EXAMPLES: *saläd, planët, pencïl, wagön*

Dictation and Spelling

Purpose

The purpose of dictation is to teach the children to spell words based on the sounds and spellings. In addition, learning dictation gives students a new strategy for reflecting on the sounds they hear in words to help them with their own writing.

As the children learn that sounds and spellings are connected to form words and that words form sentences, they begin to learn the standard spellings that will enable others to read their writing. As children learn to encode correctly, they develop their visual memory for words (spelling ability) and hence increase their writing fluency. Reinforcing the association between sounds and spellings and words through dictation gives children a spelling strategy that provides support and reassurance for writing independently. Reflecting on the sounds they hear in words will help students develop writing fluency as they apply the strategy to writing unfamiliar words.

A dictation activity is a learning experience; it is not a test. The children should be encouraged to ask for as much help as they need. The proofreading techniques are an integral part of dictation. Children's errors lead to self-correction and, if need be, to reteaching. The dictation activities must not become a frustrating ordeal. The children should receive reinforcement and feedback.

There are two kinds of dictation: Sounds-in-Sequence Dictation and Whole-Word Dictation. The two types differ mainly in the amount of help they give the children in spelling the words. The instructions vary for each type.

Procedure

Sounds-in-Sequence Dictation

Sounds-in-Sequence Dictation gives the children the opportunity to spell words sound by sound, left to right, checking the spelling of each sound as they write. (Many children write words as they think they hear and say the words, not as the words are actually pronounced or written.)

- Pronounce the first word to be spelled. Use the word in a sentence and say the word again (word/sentence/word). Have students say the word.
- Tell students to think about the sounds they hear in the word. Ask, "What's the first sound in the word?"
- Have students say the sound.
- Point to the **Sound/Spelling Card**, and direct the children to check the card. Ask what the spelling is. The children should say the spelling and then write it.
- Proceed in this manner until the word is complete.
- Proofread. You can write the word on the chalkboard as a model or have a child do it. Check the work by referring to the

> *Dictation of words and sentences helps the children both develop a spelling strategy and integrate reading and writing. It introduces proofreading in a purposeful way.*

Sound/Spelling Cards. If a word is misspelled, have the children circle the word and write it correctly, either above the word or next to it.

Whole-Word Dictation

Whole-Word Dictation gives the children the opportunity to practice this spelling strategy with less help from the teacher.

- Pronounce the word, use the word in a sentence, and then repeat the word (word/sentence/word). Have the children repeat the word. Tell the children to think about the word. Remind the children to check the **Sound/Spelling Cards** for spellings and to write the word.
- Proofread. Write or have a volunteer write the word on the chalkboard as a model. Check the word by referring to the **Sound/Spelling Cards**.

Sentence Dictation

Writing dictated sentences. Help students apply this spelling strategy to writing sentences. Dictation supports the development of fluent and independent writing. Dictation of a sentence will also help the children apply conventions of written language, such as capitalization and punctuation.

- Say the complete sentence aloud.
- Dictate one word at a time following the procedure for Sounds-in-Sequence Dictation.

  Continue this procedure for the rest of the words in the sentence. Remind the children to put a period at the end. Then proofread the sentence, sound by sound, or word by word. When sentences contain sight words, the sight words should be dictated as whole words, not sound by sound. As the children learn to write more independently, the whole sentence can be dictated word by word.

Proofreading

Whenever the children write, whether at the board or on paper, they should proofread their work. Proofreading is an important technique because it allows the children to learn by self-correction and it gives them an immediate second chance for success. It is the same skill students will use as they proofread their writing. Students should proofread by circling—not by erasing—each error. After they circle an error, they should write the correction beside the circle. This type of correction allows you and the students to see the error as well as the correct form. Children also can see what needs to be changed and how they have made their own work better.

You may want to have students use a colored pencil to circle and write in the correction. This will make it easier for them to see the changes.

Procedure for Proofreading

- Have a child write the word or sentence on the board or on an overhead transparency as a model.
- Have children tell what is good.
- Have students identify anything that can be made better.
- If there is a mistake, have the student circle it and write it correctly.
- Have the rest of the class proofread their own work.

The Word Building Game

The major reason for developing writing alongside reading is that reading and writing are complementary communicative processes. Decoding requires that children blend the phonemes together into familiar cohesive words. Spelling requires that children segment familiar cohesive words into their separate phonemes. Thus, both help the children develop a fundamental understanding of how the alphabetic principle works.

The Word Building Game gives the children a chance to exercise their segmentation abilities and to practice using the sounds and spellings they are learning. The game is a fast-paced activity in which the children spell related sets of words with the teacher's guidance. (Each successive word in the list differs from the previous one by one sound.)

For the Word Building Game, the children use their *Individual Letter Cards* (Levels K and 1) to build the words. (As an alternative they can use pencil and paper.) You will be writing at the chalkboard.

Give the children the appropriate *Letter Cards.* For example, if the list for the Word Building Game is *am, at, mat,* they will need their *a, m,* and *t* **Letter Cards.**

- Say the first word, such as *am.* (Use it in a sentence if you wish.) Have the children repeat the word. Say the word slowly, sound by sound. Tell the children to look at the *Sound/Spelling Cards* to find the letters that spell the sounds. Touch the first sound's card, in this case the Lamb card, and have the children say the sound. Continue the process with the second sound. Write the word on the board while the children use their *Letter Cards* to spell it. Have the children compare their words with your word and make changes as needed. Have the children blend and read the word with you.
- The children will then change the first word to make a different word. Say the next word in the list, *(at).* Segment the sounds of the word and have the children find the *Sound/Spelling Cards* that correspond. Write the new word *(at)* under the first word *(am)* on the chalkboard and have the children change their cards to spell the new word. Have them compare their words to yours and make changes as needed. Blend and read the word with the children. Continue in a like manner through the word list.

Reading Comprehension

Everything the students learn about phonemic awareness, phonics, and decoding has one primary goal—to help them understand what they are reading. Without comprehension, there is no reading.

Reading Comprehension Strategies

Purpose

The primary aim of reading is comprehension. Without comprehension, neither intellectual nor emotional responses to reading are possible—other than the response of frustration. Good readers are problem solvers. They bring their critical faculties to bear on everything they read. Experienced readers generally understand most of what they read, but just as importantly, they recognize when they do not understand and they have at their command an assortment of strategies for monitoring and furthering their understanding.

The goal of comprehension strategy instruction is to turn responsibility for using strategies over to the students as soon as possible. Research has shown that children's comprehension and learning problems are not a matter of mental capacity but rather their inability to use strategies to help them learn. Good readers use a variety of strategies to help them make sense of the text and get the most out of what they read. Trained to use a variety of comprehension strategies, children dramatically improve their learning performance. In order to do this, the teacher models strategy use and gradually incorporates different kinds of prompts and possible student think-alouds as examples of the types of thinking students might do as they read to comprehend what they are reading.

Comprehension Strategies

Descriptions of the strategies good readers use to comprehend text follow.

Setting Reading Goals

Good readers set reading goals and expectations before they begin reading. Readers who have set their own reading goals and have definite expectations about the text they are about to read are more engaged in their reading and notice more in what they read. Having determined a purpose for reading, they are better able to evaluate a text and determine whether it meets their needs. Even when the reading is assigned, the reader's engagement is enhanced when he or she has determined ahead of time what information might be gathered from the selection or how the selection might interest him or her.

Summarizing

Good readers sum up to check their understanding as they read. Sometimes they reread to fill in gaps in their understanding. Good readers use the strategy of summarizing to keep track of what they are reading and to focus their minds on important information. The process of putting the information in one's own words not only helps good readers remember what they have read, but also prompts them to evaluate how well they understand the information. Sometimes the summary reveals that one's understanding is incomplete, in which case it might be appropriate to reread the previous section to fill in the gaps. Good readers usually find that the strategy of summarizing is particularly helpful when they are reading long or complicated text.

Clarifying

Good readers use the clarifying strategy to help them understand the meaning of words and difficult ideas or passages. Clarifying the meaning of words involves using context, structural analysis, apposition, and resources outside the text such as a glossary or dictionary. Clarifying difficult ideas or passages involves recognizing that some part or some paragraph doesn't make sense, rereading for missed key points, reading on to see if the author clarifies the idea, using charts or other graphic organizers, using other strategies, and asking someone for help.

Asking Questions

Good readers ask questions that may prepare them for what they will learn. If their questions are not answered in the text, they may try to find answers elsewhere and thus add even more to their store of knowledge. Certain kinds of questions occur naturally to a reader, such as clearing up confusion or wondering why something in the text is as it is. Intentional readers take this somewhat informal questioning one step further by formulating questions with the specific intent of checking their understanding. They literally test themselves by thinking of questions a teacher might ask and then by determining answers to those questions.

Predicting

Good readers predict what will happen next. When reading fiction, they make predictions about what they are reading and then confirm or revise those predictions as they go.

Making Connections

Good readers make connections between what they are reading and what they already know from past experience or previous reading.

Visualizing

Good readers visualize what is happening in the text. They form mental images as they read. They picture the setting, the characters, and the action in a story. Visualizing helps readers understand descriptions of complex activities or processes. Visualizing can also be helpful when reading expository text. When a complex process or an event is being described, the reader can follow the process or the event better by visualizing each step or episode. Sometimes an author or an editor helps the reader by providing illustrations, diagrams, or maps. If no visual aids have been provided, it may help the reader to create one.

Procedures

Modeling and Thinking Aloud

One of the most effective ways to help students use and understand the strategies good readers use is to make strategic thinking public. Modeling these behaviors and encouraging students to think aloud as they attempt to understand text can demonstrate for everyone in a class how these behaviors are put into practice. Suggestions for think-alouds are provided throughout the teacher's guide.

The most effective models you can offer will be those that come from your own reading experiences. What kinds of questions did you ask yourself? What kinds of things surprised you the first time you read a story? What kinds of new information did you learn? What kinds of things were confusing until you reread or read further? Drawing on these questions and on your students' questions and comments as they read will make the strategic reading process more meaningful to the students. Below are suggestions for modeling each of the comprehension strategies.

- **Modeling Setting Reading Goals.** To model setting reading goals engage students in the following:

  - **Activate prior knowledge.** As you approach a new text, consider aloud what you already know about the subject or what your experiences have been in reading similar material.

  - **Browse the text.** To get an idea of what to expect from a text, look at the title and the illustrations. Look for potential problems, such as difficult words. Have students glance quickly at each selection, looking briefly at the illustrations and the print. Have them tell what they think they might be learning about as they read the unit.

  - **Decide what to expect from the text.** Anticipate enjoying the story or the language of the text or if reading to learn something, ask what you expect to find out.

- **Modeling Summarizing.** Just as the strategy of summarizing the plot and then predicting what will happen next can enhance a student's reading of fiction, so too can the same procedure be used to the student's advantage in reading nonfiction. In expository text, it is particularly logical to stop and summarize at the end of a chapter or section before going on to the next. One way to model the valuable exercise of making predictions and at the same time expand knowledge is to summarize information learned from a piece of expository writing and then predict what the next step or category will be. Appropriate times to stop and summarize include the following:

  - when a narrative text has covered a long period of time or a number of events
  - when many facts have been presented
  - when an especially critical scene has occurred
  - when a complex process has been described

- any time there is the potential for confusion about what has happened or what has been presented in the text
- when returning to a selection

Good readers use a variety of strategies to help them make sense of the text and get the most out of what they read.

- **Modeling Clarifying.** To model clarifying, share with students the methods that they can use to help them understand the meaning of words, difficult ideas, or passages. When an unfamiliar word or idea appears in the text, demonstrate how to stop often and apply one of the following clarifying approaches:

- While reading a difficult word, stop and say, "I don't understand what this means. I'm going to reread the passage and see if context clues help me get more information about the meaning of the word." If this does not work, explain that you look for structural clues that include the meaning of different parts of the word. Point out to students that the author sometimes provides the definition of words by using apposition. Encourage students to use a dictionary or glossary to find the meaning of a word or, if necessary, to ask someone else who may know the meaning of the word.

- While reading a difficult passage, again stop and say, "I don't understand what this means. I'm going to reread the passage to see if I missed a key point." If this does not work, explain that you will read on to see if the author clarifies the idea. Also, use visual clues such as photographs, charts, graphs, or other graphic organizers that may present the text in a different way. If none of these methods work, encourage students to ask someone for help.

Sharing your thinking aloud will help students hear how good readers use clarifying to gain better understanding of unfamiliar words and difficult passages.

- **Modeling Asking Questions.** Learning to ask productive questions is not an easy task. Students' earliest experiences with this strategy take the form of answering teacher-generated questions. However, students should be able to move fairly quickly to asking questions like those a teacher might ask. Questions that can be answered with a simple yes or no are not typically very useful for helping them remember and understand what they have read. Many students find it helpful to ask questions beginning with *Who? What? When? Where? How?* or *Why?* As students become more accustomed to asking and answering questions, they will naturally become more adept at phrasing their questions. As their question asking becomes more sophisticated, they progress from simple questions that can be answered with explicit information in the text to questions that require making inferences based on the text.

- **Modeling Predicting.** Predicting can be appropriate at the beginning of a selection—on the basis of the titles and the illustrations—or at any point while reading a selection. At first, your modeling will take the form of speculation about what might happen next, but tell students from the start what clues in the text or illustrations helped you predict, in order to make it clear that predicting is not just guessing. When a student makes a prediction—especially a far-fetched one—ask what in the selection or in his or her own experience the prediction is based on. If the student can back up the prediction, let the prediction stand; otherwise, suggest that the student make another prediction on the basis of what he of she already knows. Often it is appropriate to sum up before making a prediction. This will help students consider what has come before as they make their predictions about what will happen next. When reading aloud, stop whenever a student's prediction has been confirmed or contradicted. Have students tell whether the prediction was correct. If students seem comfortable with the idea of making predictions but rarely do so on their own, encourage them to discuss how to find clues in the text that will help them.

- **Modeling Making Connections.** To model making connections, share with students any thoughts or memories that come to mind as you read the selection. Perhaps a character in a story reminds you of a childhood friend, allowing you to better identify with interactions between characters. Perhaps information in an article on Native-American life in the Old West reminds you of an article that you have read on the importance of the bison to Native Americans. Sharing your connections will help students become aware of the dynamic nature of reading and show them another way of being intentional, active learners.

- **Modeling Visualizing.** Model visualizing by describing the mental images that occur to you as you read. A well-described scene is relatively easy to visualize, and if no one does so voluntarily, you may want to prompt students to express their own visualizations. If the author has not provided a description of a scene, but a picture of the scene would make the story more interesting or comprehensible, you might want to model visualizing as follows: "Let's see. The author says that the street was busy, and we know that this story is set during the colonial period. From what I already know about those times, there were no cars, and the roads were different from the roads of today. The street may have been paved with cobblestones. Horses would have been pulling carriages or wagons. I can almost hear the horses' hoofs going clip-clop over the stones." Remind students that different readers may picture the same scene quite differently, which is fine. Every reader responds to a story in her or his own way.

Reading Aloud

At the beginning of the year, students should be encouraged to read selections aloud. This practice will help you and them understand some of the challenges posed by the text and how different students approach these challenges. Make sure that you set aside time to hear each student read during the first few days of class—the days devoted to Getting Started are perfect for this—so that you can determine students' abilities and needs. **Independent Work Time** is also a good time to listen to any students who do not get to read aloud while the class is reading the selection together.

If your students have not previously engaged in the sort of strategic thinking aloud that is promoted throughout the **SRA/Open Court Reading** program, you will have to do all or most of the modeling at first, but encourage the children to participate as soon as possible.

As the year progresses, students should continue reading aloud often, especially with particularly challenging text. Model your own use of strategies not only to help students better understand how to use strategies but also to help them understand that actively using strategies is something that good, mature readers do constantly.

Most students are unaccustomed to thinking out loud. They will typically stand mute as they try to figure out an unfamiliar word or deal with a confusing passage. When this happens, students should be encouraged to identify specifically what they are having difficulty with. A student might identify a particular word, or he or she may note that the individual words are familiar but the meaning of the passage is unclear.

Active Response

Not only are good readers active in their reading when they encounter problems, but they respond constantly to whatever they read. In this way they make the text their own. As students read they should be encouraged to:

- Make as many connections as they can between what they are reading and what they already know.
- Visualize passages to help clarify their meanings or simply to picture appealing descriptions.
- Ask questions about what they are reading. The questions that go through their minds during reading will help them to examine, and thus better understand, the text. Doing so may also interest them in pursuing their own investigations. The questions may also provide a direction for students' research or exploration.
- Summarize and make predictions as a check on how well they understand what they are reading.

Tips

- Remember that the goal of all reading strategies is comprehension. If a story or article does not make sense, the reader needs to choose whatever strategies will help make sense of it. If one strategy does not work, the reader should try another.
- Always treat problems encountered in text as interesting learning opportunities rather than something to be avoided or dreaded.
- Encourage students to think out loud about text challenges.
- Encourage students to help each other build meaning from text. Rather than telling each other what a word is or what a passage means, students should tell each other how they figured out the meanings of challenging words and passages.
- Encourage students to freely share strategies they have devised on their own. You might want to write these on a large sheet of paper and tape them to the board.
- Assure students that these are not the only strategies that can be used while reading. Any strategy that they find helpful in understanding text is a good useful strategy.

- An absence of questions does not necessarily indicate that students understand what they are reading. Be especially alert to children who never seem to ask questions. Be sure to spend tutorial time with these students occasionally and encourage them to discuss specific selections in the context of difficulties they might have encountered and how they solved them as well as their thoughts about unit concepts.
- Observing students' responses to text will enable you to ascertain not only how well they understand a particular selection but also their facility in choosing and applying appropriate strategies. Take note of the following:
  ✓ Whether the strategies a student uses are effective in the particular situation.
  ✓ Whether the student chooses from a variety of appropriate strategies or uses the same few over and over.
  ✓ Whether the student can explain to classmates which strategies to use in a particular situation and why.
  ✓ Whether the student can identify alternative resources to pursue when the strategies she or he has tried are not effective.
  ✓ Whether students' application of a given strategy is becoming more effective over a period of time.

Becoming familiar and comfortable with these self-monitoring techniques gives readers the confidence to tackle material that is progressively more difficult. A good, mature reader knows that he or she will know when understanding what he or she is reading is becoming a problem and can take steps to correct the situation.

Reading Comprehension Skills

Purpose

An important purpose of writing is to communicate thoughts from one person to another. The goal of instruction in reading comprehension skills is to make students aware of the logic behind the structure of a written piece. The reader will then gain an understanding of both the facts and the intent of what they are reading. By keeping the organization of a piece in mind and considering the author's purpose for writing, the reader can make inferences or draw conclusions based on what was read. These are the "between the lines" skills that strong, mature readers utilize to get a complete picture of what the writer is not only saying, but what the writer is trying to say.

Effective comprehension skills include:

Author's Point of View

Author's point of view involves identifying who is telling the story. If a character in the story is telling the story, that one character describes the action and tells what the other characters are like. This is first-person point of view. In such a story, one character does the talking and uses the pronouns *I, my, me*. All other characters' thoughts, feelings, and emotions are reported through this one character.

If the story is told in third-person point of view, someone outside the story who is aware of all of the characters' thoughts and feelings and actions is relating them to the reader. All of the characters are referred to by their names or the pronouns *he/she, him/her, it*.

Sequence

The reader can't make any decisions about relationships or events if he or she has no idea in which order the events take place. The reader needs to pay attention to how the writer conveys the sequence. Does he or she simply state first this happened and then that happened? Does the writer first present the end of the story and then go back and let the reader know the sequence of events? Knowing what the sequence is and how the writer presents it helps the reader follow the writer's line of thought.

Fact and Opinion

Learning to distinguish fact from opinion is essential to critical reading and thinking. Students learn what factors need to be present in order for a statement to be provable. They also learn that an opinion, while not provable itself, should be based on fact. Readers use this knowledge to determine for themselves the validity of the ideas presented in their reading.

Main Idea and Details

A writer shouldn't be writing if he or she doesn't have something specific to say to his or her reader. The writer may state this main idea in different ways but the reader should always be able to tell you what the writing is about.

To strengthen the main point or main idea of a piece, the writer provides details to help the reader understand. The writer may use comparison and contrast to make a point, provide examples, provide facts, give opinions, give descriptions, give reasons or causes, or give definitions.

Compare and Contrast

Using comparison and contrast is one of the most common and easiest ways a writer uses to get his or her reader to understand a subject. Comparing and contrasting unfamiliar thoughts, ideas, or things with familiar thoughts, ideas and things gives the reader something within his or her own experience base to use in understanding.

> *A good writer thinks carefully about the message he or she wants to deliver and provides a logical structure that the reader can use to help understand the message.*

Cause and Effect

What made this happen? Why did this character act the way he or she did? Knowing the causes of events helps the reader to see the whole story. Being able to use available information to help to identify the probable outcomes (effects) of events or actions will help the reader to logically anticipate the story or article.

Classify and Categorize

The relationships of actions, events, characters, outcomes, and such in a selection should be clear enough for the reader to see the relationships. Putting like things or ideas together can help the reader understand the relationships set up by the writer.

Author's Purpose

Everything that is written is written for a purpose. That purpose may be to entertain, to persuade, or to inform. Knowing why a piece is written gives the reader an idea of what to expect and perhaps some prior idea of what the author is going to say.

If a writer is writing to entertain, then the reader can generally just relax and let the writer carry him or her away. If on the other hand, the purpose is to persuade, it will help the reader understand and keep perspective if he or she knows that purpose.

Drawing Conclusions

Often, writers do not directly state everything—they take for granted their audience's ability to "read between the lines." Readers draw conclusions when they take from the text small pieces of information about a character or event and use this information to make a statement about that character or event.

Making Inferences

Readers make inferences about characters and events to understand the total picture in a story. When making inferences, readers use information from the text, along with personal experience or knowledge, to gain a deeper understanding of a story event and its implications.

Procedure

Read the Selection

First have students read the selection using whatever strategies help them make sense of the selection. After this reading, carry on a discussion about the selection that will assure you and students that they did, indeed understand what they read. Discuss any confusion they may have and make whatever clarifications are necessary.

Reread

Revisiting or rereading a selection allows the reader to attend to the specific techniques and tools that authors use to organize and present information in narratives and expository genres. Once you are sure students have a basic understanding of the piece, have students reread it in whole or in part, concentrating on selected skills. Pick out examples of how the writer organized the piece to help the reader understand it.

Limit this concentration on specific comprehension/writing skills to one or two that can be clearly identified in the piece. If a piece has many good examples of several different aspects, then go back to the piece several times over a span of days.

Write

Solidify this connection between how a writer writes and reading by encouraging students to incorporate these different devices into their own writing. As they attempt to use specific organizational devices in their writing, they will get a clearer understanding of how to identify them when they are reading.

Writing

The ability to write with clarity and coherence is essential to students' success in school as well as in life. Communicating through writing is becoming more and more important in this age of computers and the information superhighway.

Purpose

Many adult writers believe that writing helps them think. For them, writing is a way of transforming knowledge into something more personal, something more useful. Most children have little experience with writing as a self-initiated, enjoyable activity that helps them think. The challenge in teaching writing is to show children how it is used by those who cherish it and use it with profit. Traditionally, students practice skills and demonstrate knowledge when they write in the classroom. In this context, students have little chance to use writing as a tool for expanding their understanding.

An environment with an emphasis on writing provides a multifaceted context for the development of higher-order thinking. Students learn to plan, which allows them to work out ideas in their heads; to set goals, which promotes interest and the ability to monitor progress; and to revise content, which engages them in the reworking and rethinking activities that elevate writing from a craft to a tool for discovery.

Reading is the ultimate source of good models for writing. Learning to read critically can dramatically expand a writer's repertoire and skills. In class discussions and in their Reading and Writing Workbook, students find and discuss exemplary writing techniques and conventions used by authors. Students are always asked to link to their own writing what they learn from writing lessons.

The Writing Process

Providing a routine or process for students to follow will help them to learn a systematic approach to writing. By following the steps of the writing process, students will learn to approach everything they write with purpose and thought. They learn that although writing takes time and thought, there are steps they can take to make their writing clear, coherent, and appealing to their audience.

Prewriting

Purpose

Prewriting is that phase of the writing process when students think through an idea they want to write about. To improve their writing, students should think about their ideas, discuss them, and plan how they want readers to respond. It is important for students to take time before writing to plan ahead so that they can proceed from one phase of the writing process to another without spending unnecessary time making decisions that

should have been made earlier. Prewriting is the most time-consuming phase of the writing process, but it may be the most important.

Procedure

Noting Writing Ideas

Students can make notes of writing ideas at any time, with a special time being set aside following the discussion of each reading selection. The writing ideas students get from a discussion might be concerned with the topic of the selection they just read or with an aspect of the author's style. You should keep such a list of writing ideas also, and think aloud occasionally as you make writing idea notes.

> *Deciding what to write about is probably the one thing students find most difficult about the writing process.*

Developing Writing Ideas

When students are ready to start a new writing piece, they should:

✓ look through the Writing Ideas section of their Writing Journal for an idea.

✓ decide how to use this idea in a writing piece.

✓ think about the intended audience and how they want that audience to feel when they read the piece.

✓ talk to others about this writing idea. Write a brief statement of what they hope to accomplish in the writing piece.

Students must make many decisions during the prewriting phase of the writing process. Most students can benefit from talking with a partner or a small group of classmates about these decisions. They may want to discuss some of the following points.

Genre or format of each writing piece. Having decided to use a writing idea such as "a misunderstanding on the first day of school," the student must decide how to use it—for example, as a personal narrative, a realistic fiction story, a poem, a fantasy story, a play, a letter, or whatever.

Audience. Although students' writing pieces will be shared with classmates and with you, some may ultimately be intended for other audiences.

Writing Purpose. Each student should write a sentence that tells the purpose of the piece he or she plans to write. The purpose statement should name the intended audience and the effect the

writer hopes to have on that audience. For example, a writer may want to describe her first day in school. The intended audience is kindergarten children, and she intends her story to be humorous. Her purpose statement would read, "I want to write a funny story for little children about my first day in kindergarten."

Planning Writing. Students should make notes on what to include in their writing pieces. Tell students that this list does not need to make sense to anyone but them. They should list key words or phrases to remind them of how they want to develop their ideas. For example, the writer's notes for "My First Day in School" might read:

my dream (night before)

clothes I wore

too many children no desks

Last person I talked to

1st impressions of teacher

decided to go home

what my mother said

Some writers may find it helpful to brainstorm with a partner or small group to list words and phrases they might use in a piece of writing. Sometimes this list can be organized into webs of related ideas or details. This kind of prewriting activity might be particularly useful for planning a descriptive piece. For planning a comparison/contrast piece, a writer might use another kind of visual organizer, such as a Venn diagram. Students planning fiction pieces might use a story frame or plot line.

Tips

■ Circulate as students make notes on writing ideas or work in small groups on prewriting activities.

■ Notice which students are having difficulty coming up with writing ideas. It may help to pair these students with students who have many ideas.

■ Do not worry if this phase of the process seems noisy and somewhat chaotic. Students must be allowed to let their imaginations roam in free association and to play around with words and ideas until they hit on something that seems right. They must be permitted to share ideas and help each other.

■ Do not worry if, in the early sessions, the class as a whole seems to have few ideas. Through the reading and discussion of selections in the reading anthology, most students will soon have more writing ideas than they can use.

Drafting

Purpose

During the drafting phase of the writing process students shape their planning notes into main ideas and details. They devote their time and effort to getting words down on paper. Whether students are drafting on scrap paper or on computer screens, your role is to encourage each writer to "get it all down." You must also provide a suitable writing environment.

Procedure

Points to Share

Here are some points to share with students before they begin drafting:

- Drafting is putting your ideas down on paper for your own use. Drafts are "sloppy copies."
- Don't worry about spelling. When you don't know how to spell a word, guess at the first letter and leave a space. The context will help you remember the word you want to write here later, when you have time to check the spelling in a dictionary.
- Use abbreviations to help you write faster.
- Crossing out is acceptable. It's fast and won't interrupt your thoughts the way erasing will.
- When you cannot think of a word or do not know what to say at a certain point, leave a space. You can go back later and fill in the gaps.
- Write on every other line so that you will have room to make revisions.
- Write on only one side of a page so that when you revise you can see all of your draft at once.
- As you draft, keep in mind your purpose for writing this piece and your intended audience.

Modeling Drafting

Using a chalkboard, a large chart, or an overhead transparency, model drafting for students by turning your own prewriting notes into sentences and paragraphs. Think aloud as you put your ideas into words. Work as fast as you can. Stress that you are not concerned with handwriting or spelling and that you do not want to be interrupted as you work. As you model, try to do the following:

- Leave a blank space in a sentence to show that you are having difficulty thinking of the best word.
- Put parentheses around a word you intend to change.

- Use abbreviations and invented spellings.
- Cross out words and sentences, or draw arrows to indicate that they should be moved to a different place in your piece.
- Use a caret to insert new words or a new sentence in the text.

> *The purpose of drafting is to let words pour out on paper and to express ideas quickly.*

Turning Notes into Sentences

Adding Details As students begin to write from their notes, they must think about the kinds of details they want to add and write sentences about them. Depending on the kind of piece students are writing, they may want to organize certain kinds of details in a particular manner:

- A personal narrative is probably best ordered as a straightforward chronological retelling of events. Dialogue may help to tell the story.
- A process description should be told in a step-by-step order. The draft should include as much information as possible; each step must be clear. If the piece needs cutting, the student can always do it later.
- A persuasive piece appeals to feelings. It requires facts as well as expert opinions.
- An interview could be written as a series of questions and answers.
- The order of details in a descriptive piece must be easy to follow—from left to right, top to bottom, or whatever order makes sense.
- A fictional story must include details describing characters, setting, and the characters' actions. Dialogue also helps to tell the story.

Using Word Processors for Drafting

Many students enjoy drafting on the screen of a computer more than drafting on paper. Once they have mastered the keyboard, they may find it easier to think as they write. Their first attempts look less sloppy, and they are often more willing to make changes and experiment as they draft. They will certainly find it neater to use the delete key on the word processor than to correct their mistakes by crossing out. Remind students who are drafting on computers to use these features of their word processing programs:

- cut and paste—as they compose, students can move phrases, sentences, and paragraphs from one place to another by cutting and pasting.
- split-screen—if they have made prewriting notes on a computer file, students can see their notes on one part of the screen as they type their drafts on the other part of the screen. They can even copy parts of their notes and "paste" them in their drafts. This feature would be especially helpful to students who are drafting research papers. A writer could copy notes from several different files to draft the research paper.
- saving—students should take care to save their documents as they compose on the computer. Make sure students understand how to avoid losing or erasing their draft.

Tips

Sometimes the hardest part of drafting is getting the first sentence down on paper. It may help a student who feels stuck even before she or he starts writing to begin a story in the middle or to write the word *Draft* in big letters at the top of the paper.

- If a student feels stuck during drafting, he or she may need to go back and try a different prewriting technique.
- After an initial fifteen or twenty minutes of imposed silence, some children may work better and come up with more ideas if they share as they write.
- You may find that it is difficult to get students to "loosen up" as they draft. Remember, most students have been encouraged to be neat and to erase mistakes when they write. It may help to share some of your own marked-up manuscripts with children.

Revising

Purpose

The purpose of revising is to make sure that a piece of writing expresses the writer's ideas clearly and completely. When writers revise, they work on focus, on telling enough, on clarity, and on order. They add or change information. They may experiment with new beginnings and endings. Writers revise by stepping back and reexamining their work. They reevaluate the content and ideas in their work. They ask: *Does it make sense? How can I make it clearer? What can I get rid of? Is this appropriate for my audience?* All of this helps them to become more thoughtful writers and better communicators.

Procedure

Modeling Revising

Students understand and learn best when they have good models to follow. Use the rough draft that you modeled when introducing the drafting phase and model revising it for students. The Teacher's Edition includes suggestions for introducing revising in an early lesson in unit one of each grade level. Model the process in this way:

- On an overhead transparency, show your rough draft. Be sure to include unclear and misplaced passages and incorrect word choices.

- Work quickly through your rough draft, thinking aloud as you revise. For example, "I think I should move this to the end. I need a better word here. This is good. I'll keep it as it is. I should say more about this. I'll add more details to describe this. Now this idea doesn't fit. I'll cross it out."

- Demonstrate some shortcuts for revising. Make arrows to show how you want to move words or sentences. Use an asterisk or a number to indicate an insertion. Cross out words or sentences. Tell students you will worry about neatness and correctness later.

- Elicit and discuss suggestions from students for further revisions. If you agree, make additional changes based on their suggestions. Remind students that during the revision phase of the writing process it is important to get feedback from others.

- Explain that they may revise this draft more than once; writing is a recursive process.

This brief demonstration of revising will not suffice, however, to turn your students into thoughtful revisers of their own writing. If students need help with revising at any time throughout the year, encourage them to refer to the Writer's Handbook in the back of their anthologies. Conduct minilessons on revising whenever necessary. Most important, continue to model revising as the year progresses.

> *Revising is a difficult concept for students to understand, let alone do. Much modeling, much work in Writing Seminar, and much practice are necessary before they become good at it.*

Model asking questions like the following when revising various kinds of writing:

- About a narrative:
  - ✓ Does my first sentence get my readers' attention?
  - ✓ Are events in the story told in an order that makes sense?
  - ✓ Have I included dialogue to help move the story along?
  - ✓ Does the story have a clear focus?
- About a description:
  - ✓ Have I used details that appeal to the senses?
- About a comparison/contrast piece:
  - ✓ Have I made a separate paragraph for each subject discussed?
- About an explanation:
  - ✓ Will readers understand what I am saying?
  - ✓ Are the steps of the explanation in a clear order?
  - ✓ Have I made effective use of signal words?
  - ✓ Have I included enough information?
- About fiction:
  - ✓ Have I described my characters and setting?
  - ✓ Does the plot include a problem, build to a climax, and then describe the resolution of the problem?
- About persuasive writing:
  - ✓ Have I made my position clear?
  - ✓ Does my evidence support my position?
  - ✓ Have I used opinions as well as facts, and have I said whose opinions I used?
  - ✓ Have I directed my writing to my audience?

Help students understand the value of asking questions like the following as they revise:

- About each paragraph:
  - ✓ Does each sentence belong in it?
  - ✓ Does each sentence connect smoothly with the next?
  - ✓ Does each sentence say something about the main idea?
- About each sentence:
  - ✓ Do the sentences read smoothly?
  - ✓ Have I combined sentences that were too short?
  - ✓ Have I broken sentences that were too long into two shorter sentences?
  - ✓ Have I varied the beginnings of the sentences?
- About the words:
  - ✓ Have I changed words that were repeated too often?
  - ✓ Do transition words connect ideas?

Evaluating Student Progress

Use students' writing folders to review their progress. Check first drafts against revised versions to see how each student is able to apply revision strategies. You may find that some students are reluctant to revise. You might then try the following:

- If a student doesn't see anything that needs to be changed or doesn't want to change anything, get him or her to do something to the paper—number the details in a description or the steps in a process, circle exact words, underline the best parts of the paper.

- Once a paper is marked, the student may not be so reluctant to change it. One reason many children do not like to revise is that they think they must recopy everything. This is not always necessary.

- Sometimes writers can cut and paste sections that they want to move. Or they can use carets and deletion marks to show additions and subtractions from a piece.

- Give an especially reluctant student a deadline by which she or he must revise a piece or lose the chance to publish it.

Students will hopefully be writing in other classes and on a variety of topics. Revision techniques can be used to improve writing in any curriculum area. Stress to students the importance of focusing on their intended audience as they revise.

Proofreading

Purpose

Writing that is free of grammatical, spelling, and technical mistakes is clearer and easier for readers to understand. By proofreading their pieces, students will also notice which errors they make repeatedly and will learn not to make them in the future.

After a piece of writing has been revised for content and style, students must read it carefully line by line to make sure that it contains no errors. This activity, the fourth phase of the writing process, is called proofreading and is a critical step that must occur before a piece of writing can be published. Students can begin proofreading a piece when they feel that it has been sufficiently revised.

Procedure

Using What They Have Learned

Students should be expected to proofread at a level appropriate to their grade. Young authors should not be held responsible for skills they have not yet learned. Older students will be able to check for a greater variety of errors than younger students and should be expected to take greater responsibility for their proofreading. For example, students in second grade can be expected to check for and correct omitted capital letters at the beginning of sentences, but they should not necessarily be expected to understand and correct capital letters in proper nouns or in names of organizations. Older students will have mastered many more grammatical, mechanical, usage, and spelling skills and can be expected to perform accordingly. When you spot an error related to a skill beyond a student's level, make clear to the student that you do not expect her or him to be responsible for the mistake, but do explain that the error still needs to be corrected. The following suggestions may be useful as you introduce proofreading to the children and help them develop their proofreading skills.

Proofreading Checklist

Have students use a proofreading checklist similar to the one shown here to help them remember the steps for effective proofreading. This checklist is on the Writing Folder provided with **SRA/Open Court Reading**. If your class does not have this writing folder, you might copy this checklist onto a piece of chart paper and place it in the writing center or on a bulletin board for students to refer to when they proofread.

Read each sentence.

✓ Does each sentence begin with a capital letter and end with correct punctuation?

✓ Do you notice any sentence fragments or run-on sentences?

✓ Are words missing from the sentence?

✓ Is any punctuation or capitalization missing from within the sentence?

✓ Do you notice any incorrect grammar or incorrect word usage in the sentence?

✓ Do you notice any misspelled words?

Look at the paragraphs.

✓ Are the paragraphs indented?

✓ Can very long paragraphs be broken into two paragraphs?

✓ Can very short paragraphs be combined into one paragraph?

Proofreader's Marks

Children should use standard proofreader's marks to indicate the changes they wish to make. Explain to students that these marks are a kind of code used to show which alterations to make without a long explanation. Students may also be interested to know that professional writers, editors, and proofreaders use these same marks.

You may want to review these marks one by one, illustrating on the chalkboard how to use them. For example, they may insert a word or a phrase by using a caret (^). If students wish to insert more text than will fit above the line, they may write in the margin or attach another sheet of paper. It may be a good idea, when such extensive corrections are made, for students to proofread their final copy carefully to make sure they have included all their alterations.

> *Proofreading their work helps students to communicate their ideas more effectively.*

Teacher Modeling

Model good proofreading skills for students by proofreading a piece of your own writing. You may want to be sure to include specific errors (misspelled words, incorrect capitalization, repeated words, incorrect paragraph indentation, etc.) so that you will use all the proofreader's marks as you model proofreading. Copy your draft onto an overhead transparency and proofread the piece together.

Sentence Lifting

Sentence lifting is a very effective method of showing students how to effectively proofread their own work.

■ Choose several pieces of student writing and look for common errors.

■ On an overhead, write several sentences. Include at least one sentence that has no errors.

■ Tell students that you are going to concentrate on one type of error at a time. For example, first you will concentrate on spelling.

■ Ask students to read the first sentence and point out any words they feel are spelled incorrectly. Do not erase errors. Cross them out and write the correctly spelled word above the crossed out word.

       quickly   basement
Margie ran ~~quidly~~ through the ~~basment~~

■ Next move to a different type of error. Ask students to check for capitalization and punctuation.

       quickly   basement
Margie ran ~~quidly~~ through the ~~basment~~ ⊙

■ Continue in this way, correcting errors as you go through the sample sentences.

Because students are working on their own sentences, they will be more inclined to both pay attention to what is going on and better understand the corrections that are made.

Using a Word Processor

If the children are using a word processor to write their pieces, they may wish to run a spell check on their document.

Caution them, however, that even the most sophisticated computer cannot catch every spelling error. Misuse of homophones and other words will not be caught by the computer if the misused words appear in the computer's dictionary. For example, if a student types *form* instead of *from*, the computer will not register a mistake because form is also a word.

Preparing the Final Copy

When students feel that they have thoroughly proofread their pieces, they should copy the work onto another sheet of paper, using their best handwriting, or type the work on a computer or typewriter. They should then check this copy against the proofread copy to make sure that they made all the changes correctly and did not introduce any new errors. You may need to proofread and correct students' papers one final time before publishing to make sure that they have caught all errors.

Tips

■ The publishing conference is a good time to assess students' proofreading abilities. Notice their proofreading skills, including comprehension of the concept, ability to use proofreader's marks correctly, and corrections from you and other students. Also note any improvement in writing based upon proofreading corrections. For example, does a student no longer omit end punctuation because he or she noticed this error repeatedly during proofreading?

■ You may also wish to circulate as children are proofreading on their own or in pairs.

✓ Are students able to check references when they are unsure of a spelling or usage?

✓ Are students criticizing each other's work constructively?

✓ Note students who are having difficulty. You may wish to address these difficulties during individual conferences.

Publishing

Publishing is the process of bringing private writing to the reading public.

Purpose

The purpose of writing is to communicate. Unless students are writing in a journal, they will want to present their writing to the public. Such sharing helps children to learn about themselves and others, provides an opportunity for them to take pride in their hard work, and thus motivates them to further writing.

Publishing their work helps motivate children to improve such skills as spelling, grammar, and handwriting. Publishing can be as simple as displaying papers on a bulletin board or as elaborate as creating a class newspaper. Publishing will not—indeed should not—always require large blocks of class time. Students will wish to spend more time elaborately presenting their favorite pieces and less time on other works. If students take an inordinate amount of time to publish their work, you may want to coach them on how to speed up the process.

Procedure

Publishing Conference

An individual publishing conference may be useful to students who have finished proofreading and correcting a piece of writing. In the conference, each student will discuss:

- what he or she would like to publish.
- how to prepare the piece for publication.
- what form the published work should take.

You will read through the piece, and tell the student if any corrections still need to be made. You may also make some suggestions about the best way to publish a piece if a student has trouble coming up with an idea. Make suggestions and give criticism as needed, but remember that students must retain ownership of their publishing. Leave final decisions about form and design of their work up to individual students.

Students should think about whether they want to illustrate their writing.

- Photographs might illustrate a personal narrative or biography.
- Drawings might illustrate a piece of fiction.
- A chart or graph might illustrate an article.
- Remind the children to provide captions if necessary.

Help students plan each page of their publication. They will need to decide where to place text in relation to any art they are using. Remind students to think about their intended audience when they are deciding on the form for their published piece. Will the form they have selected present their ideas effectively to the people they want to reach?

Publishing Checklist

The following checklist will help students when they are publishing their work. (Not every question applies to every form of publishing.)

✓ Have I chosen my best piece?
✓ Have I revised it to make it better?
✓ Have I proofread it carefully?
✓ Have I decided upon my illustrations?
✓ Have I recopied my piece carefully and illustrated it?
✓ Have I numbered the pages?
✓ Have I made a cover that tells the title and my name?

You may wish to copy this checklist and post it in the publishing center or in some other prominent place in the classroom.

Writing Seminar

Purpose

The purpose of Writing Seminar (Levels K–6) is for students to discuss their work in progress and to share ideas for improving it.

Writing Seminar is one of the activities in which students may choose to participate during **Independent Work Time**. Students will meet in small groups to read and discuss one another's writing. One student reads a piece in progress. Other students comment on the writing and ask questions about the ideas behind the writing. The student whose work is being critiqued writes down the comments made by his or her classmates and decides how to use these comments to make the writing better.

Procedure

Early Writing Seminar

To begin the conference, have one student writer read his or her revised draft as other students listen carefully. When the student has finished, invite other children to retell the story in their own words. If they have trouble retelling the story, the writer knows that he or she must make some ideas clearer.

Then have listeners who wish to comment raise their hands. The writer calls on each in turn. The listeners ask questions or make comments about the writing, telling, for example, what they like about it or what they might change to make it better. After several comments have been made, the writer notes any information that she or he might use. Another student then reads his or her piece.

Guidelines for Peer Conferencing

In an early session, work with students to establish guidelines for peer conferencing. You might suggest rules such as the following:

- Listen quietly while someone else is speaking.
- Think carefully before you comment on another person's work.
- Make your comments specific.
- Comment on something that you like about the piece before you comment on something that needs to be improved.
- Discuss your work quietly so as not to disturb the rest of the class.

Modeling Conference Behavior

You may need to model meaningful comments and questions. Examples of questions and sentence starters follow:

- What was your favorite part?
- I like the part where (or when) . . . .
- I like the way you describe . . . .
- What happened after . . . ?
- I'd like to know more about . . . .
- Why did _____ happen?
- What do you think is the most important part?

Teacher Conferencing

During Writing Seminar, you will want to schedule individual conferences with students to help them evaluate their writing so that they can recognize problems and find ways to solve them. Teacher conferences are useful during all phases of the writing process, but they are crucial during the revising phase. Writing conferences give you an opportunity to observe the children as they evaluate their writing, solve problems, make decisions about their work, and take responsibility for the development and completion of their work. The basic procedure for teacher conferences is as follows:

- Have the student read his or her first draft aloud. Offer a specific comment.
- Encourage the student to review feedback received on his or her draft during peer conferencing and to think aloud about possible changes.
- Ask questions that will help the student clarify her or his thinking about how to revise. (Try not to lead the student with content questions. You want to teach how to revise, not what to write.)
- Review strategies and references that the student could use to improve her or his work.
- Conclude the conference by having the student state his or her plan or goal for continuing work on the piece.

During teacher conferences, you might use the following responses to student writing.

- To open communication with the writer:
  - ✓ How is the writing going?
  - ✓ Tell me about your piece.
  - ✓ How did you get your ideas?
- To validate the writer's work and give encouragement:
  - ✓ I like the part where . . . .
  - ✓ I like the way you open your piece by . . . .
  - ✓ I like your description of . . . .
- To get the writer to think about clarity of meaning:
  - ✓ I wonder about . . . .
  - ✓ What happened after . . . .
  - ✓ Why did . . . ?
- To get the writer to think about direction and about writing strategies:
  - ✓ What do you plan to do with your piece?
  - ✓ How will you go about doing that?
  - ✓ What could I do to help you?

Concentrate on one phase of the writing process at a time. You might pay particular attention to revising content, proofreading content, or publishing. Remember to keep conferences brief and to the point. If you are calling the conference, prepare your comments in advance. Usually, a student will request a conference with you, but be sure that you confer regularly with every student if only to check that each one is continuing to write, revise, and publish. The following are some questions to ask yourself as you consider a student's first draft:

- Does the beginning capture my attention?
- Is this a good topic sentence?
- Is the ending conclusive?
- Is this information related to the topic?
- Does the sentence structure need to be varied by combining or shortening sentences?
- Is there a better word to express this idea?

As you confer with students, also recognize growth—evidence in the text that a student has applied what he or she learned in earlier conferences to another piece of writing. Some cues to look for when evaluating a student's growth as a writer include the following:

- The writer identifies problems.
- The writer thinks of solutions to a problem and understands why some solutions will work and some will not.
- The writer recognizes when and how the text needs to be reorganized.
- The writer identifies ideas in the text that need elaboration.
- The writer makes thoughtful changes and pays attention to detail.
- The writer takes advantage of peer and teacher conferences, books, and other resources to improve his or her writing.

Tips

- Completed pieces as well as works in progress can be shared during Writing Seminar. In the upper grades, as pieces become longer, a student may read only part of a piece—a favorite part, a part where she or he is having problems, one that has been revised, and so on.
- When a student requests a conference with you, focus first on the student's stated problem. Determine whether a problem really exists or whether you can simply assure the student that everything is fine. If there is no problem, you may end the conference with your reassurance. If there is a problem, continue the conference. Students who do not want to share their work may lack confidence in their writing abilities. Work with these students individually until they become acquainted with the process.

Classroom Discussion

The more students are able to discuss what they are learning, voice their confusions, and compare perceptions of what they are learning, the deeper and more meaningful their learning becomes.

Purpose

It is in discussions that students are exposed to points of view different from their own, and it is through discussion that they learn how to express their thoughts and opinions coherently. Through discussion, students add to their own knowledge that of their classmates and learn to explain themselves coherently and to ask insightful questions that help them better understand what they have read and all that they are learning through their inquiry/research and explorations. The purpose of Classroom Discussion is to provide a sequence through which discussion can proceed.

Procedure

Reflecting on the Selection

After students have finished reading a selection, provide an opportunity for them to engage in **whole-group** discussion about the selection. Students should:

- Check to see whether the questions they asked before reading have been answered. Encourage them to discuss whether any unanswered questions should still be answered and if so have them add those questions to the Concept and Question Board.

- Discuss any new questions that have arisen because of the reading. Encourage students to decide which of these questions should go on the Concept and Question Board.

- Share what they expected to learn from reading the selection and tell whether expectations were met.

- Talk about whatever has come to mind while reading the selection. This discussion should be an informal sharing of impressions of, or opinions about, the selection; it should never take on the aspects of a question-and-answer session about the selection.

- Give students ample opportunity to ask questions or to share their thoughts about the selection. Participate as an active member of the group, making your own observations about information in a selection or modeling your own appreciation of a story. Be especially aware of unusual and interesting insights suggested by students so that these insights can be recognized and discussed. To help students learn to keep the discussion student-centered, have each student choose the next speaker instead of handing the discussion back to you.

Recording Ideas

As students finish discussions about their reactions to a selection, they should be encouraged to record their thoughts, feelings, reactions, and ideas about the selection or the subject of the selection in their Writing Journals. This will not only help keep the selections fresh in students' minds, it will strengthen their writing abilities and help them learn how to write about their thoughts and feelings.

Students may find that the selection gave them ideas for their own writing, or it could have reminded them of some person or incident in their own lives. Perhaps the selection answered a question that has been on their minds or raised a question they had never thought of before. Good, mature writers—especially professional writers—learn the value of recording such thoughts and impressions quickly before they fade. Students should be encouraged to do this also.

Handing Off

Handing off (Levels 1–6) is a method of turning over to students the primary responsibility for controlling discussion. Often, students who are taking responsibility for controlling a discussion tend to have all "turns" go through the teacher. The teacher is the one to whom attention is transferred when a speaker finishes, and the teacher is the one who is expected to call on the next speaker, the result being that the teacher remains the pivotal figure in the discussion.

Having the children "hand off" the discussion to other students instead of the teacher encourages them to retain complete control of the discussion and to become more actively involved in the learning process. When a student finishes his or her comments, that student should choose (hand the discussion off to) the next speaker. In this way, students maintain a discussion without relying on the teacher to decide who speaks.

When handing off is in place, the teacher's main roles are to occasionally remind students to hand off and to monitor the discussion to ensure that everyone gets a chance to contribute. The teacher may say, for example, "Remember, not just boys (or girls)," or "Try to choose someone who has not had a chance to talk yet."

In order for handing off to work effectively, a seating arrangement that allows students to see one another is essential. A circle or a semicircle is effective. In addition, all of the students need to have copies of the materials being discussed.

Actively encourage this handing-off process by letting students know that they, not you, are in control of the discussion.

If students want to remember thoughts about, or reactions to, a selection, suggest that they record these in the Writing Journal. Encourage students to record the thoughts, feelings, or reactions that are elicited by any reading they do.

Exploring Concepts within the Selection

To provide an opportunity for collaborative learning and to focus on the concepts, have students form small groups and spend time discussing what they have learned about the concepts from this selection. Topics may include new information that they have acquired or new ideas that they have had.

Students should always base their discussions on postings from the Concept and Question Board as well as on previous discussions of the concept. The small-group discussions should be ongoing throughout the unit; during this time students should continue to compare and contrast any new information with their previous ideas, opinions, and impressions about the concepts. Does this selection help confirm their ideas? Does it contradict their thinking? Has it changed their outlook?

As students discuss the concepts in small groups, circulate around the room to make sure that each group stays focused upon the selection and the concepts. After students have had some time to discuss the information and the ideas in the selection, encourage each group to formulate some statements about the concept that apply to the selection.

Sharing Ideas about Concepts

Have a representative from each group report and explain the group's ideas to the rest of the class. Then have the class formulate one or more general statements related to the unit concepts and write these statements on the Concept and Question Board. As students progress through the unit, they will gain more and more confidence in suggesting additions to the Concept and Question Board.

Visual Aids During this part of the discussion, you may find it helpful to use visual aids to help students as they build the connections to the unit concepts. Not all units or concepts will lend themselves to this type of treatment; however, aids such as time lines, charts, graphs, or pictographs may help students see how each new selection adds to their growing knowledge of the concepts.

Encourage students to ask questions about the concepts that the selection may have raised. Have students list on the Concept and Question Board those questions that cannot be answered immediately and that they want to explore further.

Exploring Concepts across Selections

As each new selection is read, encourage students to discuss its connection with the other selections and with the unit concepts. Also encourage students to think about selections that they have read from other units and how they relate to the concepts for this unit.

Ultimately, it is this ability to make connections between past knowledge and new knowledge that allows any learner to gain insights into what is being studied. The goal of the work with concepts and the discussions is to help students to start thinking in terms of connections—how is this like what I have learned before? Does this information confirm, contradict, or add a completely different layer to that which I already know about this concept? How can the others in the class have such different ideas than I do when we just read the same selection? Why is so much written about this subject?

Learning to make connections and to delve deeper through self-generated questions gives students the tools they need to become effective, efficient, lifelong learners.

Tips

- Discussions offer a prime opportunity for you to introduce, or seed, new ideas about the concepts. New ideas can come from a variety of sources: students may draw on their own experiences or on the books or videos they are studying; you may introduce new ideas into the discussion; or you may, at times, invite experts to speak to the class.

- If students do not mention an important idea that is necessary to the understanding of some larger issue, you may "drop" that idea into the conversation and, indeed, repeat it several times to make sure that it does get picked up. This seeding may be subtle ("I think that might be important here") or quite direct ("This is a big idea, one that we will definitely need to understand and one that we will return to regularly").

Discussion is an integral part of learning.

- In order to facilitate this process for each unit, you must be aware of the unit concepts and be able to recognize and reinforce them when they arise spontaneously in discussions. If central unit concepts do not arise naturally, then, and only then, will you seed these ideas by direct

modeling. The more you turn discussions over to students, the more involved they will become, and the more responsibility they will take for their own learning. Make it your goal to become a participant in, rather than the leader of, class discussions.

- Help students to see that they are responsible for carrying on the discussion. After a question is asked always wait instead of jumping in with a comment or an explanation. Although this wait time may be uncomfortable at first, students will come to understand that the discussion is their responsibility and that you will not jump in every time there is a hesitation.

- As the year progresses, students will become more and more adept at conducting and participating in meaningful discussions about what they have read. These discussions will greatly enhance students' understanding of the concepts that they are exploring.

Discussion Starters

- I didn't know that . . . .
- Does anyone know . . . .
- I figured out that . . . .
- I liked the part where . . . .
- I'm still confused about . . . .
- This made me think . . . .
- I agree with _____ because . . . .
- I disagree with _____ because . . . .
- The reason I think . . . .

Inquiry/Research and Exploration

Research and Exploration form the heart of the *SRA/Open Court Reading* program. In order to encourage students to understand how reading can enhance their lives and help them to become mature, educated adults, they are asked in each unit to use what they are learning in the unit as the basis for further exploration and research. The unit information is simply the base for their explorations.

There are two types of units in the *SRA/Open Court Reading* program—units based on universal topics of interest such as Friendship, Perseverance, and Courage and research units that provide students a very solid base of information upon which they can base their own inquiry and research. Units delving into such areas as fossils, astronomy, and medicine invite students to become true researchers by choosing definite areas of interest—problems or questions to research in small cooperative groups and then present to their classmates. In this way, students gain much more knowledge of the subject than they would have simply by reading the selections in the unit.

The selections in the units are organized so that each selection will add more information or a different perspective to students' growing bodies of knowledge.

Exploring through Reflective Activities

Purpose

The units in *SRA/Open Court Reading* that deal with universal topics will be explored through reflective activities. These units— such as Courage, Friendship, and Risks and Consequences—are organized to help students expand their perspectives in familiar areas. As they explore and discuss the unit concepts related to each topic, students are involved in activities that extend their experiences and offer opportunities for reflection. Such activities include writing, drama, art, interviews, debates, and panel discussions. Throughout each unit, students may be involved in a single ongoing exploratory activity, or they may participate in a number of different activities. They may choose to produce a final written project or a visual aid to share with the rest of the class the new knowledge that they have gained from their reflective activities. During **Independent Work Time** students will work individually or in collaborative groups on their exploration and/or projects.

The reflective activities will be activities of students' own choosing that allow them to explore the unit concepts more fully. They are free, of course, to make other choices or to devise activities of their own.

Procedure

Choosing an Area to Explore

Students may work on the reflective activities alone, in pairs, or in small groups. They have the option of writing about or presenting their findings to the whole group upon completion. Before choosing a reflective activity, students should decide what concept-related question or problem they wish to explore. Generally, it is better for students to generate questions or problems after they have engaged in some discussion but before they have had a chance to consult source materials. This approach is more likely to bring forth ideas that students actually wonder about or wish to understand. Students may also look at the questions posted on the Concept and Question Board or introduce fresh ideas inspired by material they have just finished reading. Students who are working in pairs or in small groups should confer with one another before making a decision about what to explore. Some of the students may need your assistance in deciding upon, or narrowing down, a question or a problem so that it can be explored more easily. A good way to model this process for students is to make webs for a few of your own ideas on the chalkboard and to narrow these ideas down to a workable question or problem.

Organizing the Group

After a question or a problem has been chosen, the children may choose an activity that will help them to explore that problem or question. The students' next responsibility is to decide who is going to explore which facet of the question or the problem (when they are conducting a literature search, for example) or who is going to perform which task related to the particular reflective activity (when they are writing and performing an original playlet or puppet show, for example). Lastly, students need to decide how, or if, they want to present their findings. For instance, after conducting a literature search, some students may want to read and discuss passages from a book with a plot or theme that relates to a unit concept. Other students may prefer acting out and discussing scenes from the book.

Deciding How to Explore

The following suggestions may help you and your students choose ways in which to pursue their explorations. You may want to post this list in the classroom so that groups have access to it as they decide what they want to explore and how they want to proceed.

Exploration Activities

- Conduct a literature search to pursue a question or a problem. Discussion or writing may follow.
- Write and produce an original playlet or puppet show based on situations related to the concepts.
- Play a role-playing game to work out a problem related to the concepts.
- Stage a panel discussion with audience participation on a question or problem.
- Hold a debate on an issue related to the concept.
- Write an advice column dealing with problems related to the concepts.
- Write a personal-experience story related to the concepts.
- Invite experts to class. Formulate questions to ask.
- Conduct an interview with someone on a subject related to the concepts.
- Produce and carry out a survey on an issue or question related to the concept.
- Produce a picture or photo essay about the concept.

EXAMPLE: In the Heritage unit in grade 5 of **SRA/Open Court Reading,** students read "In Two Worlds: A Yup'ik Eskimo Family." This selection is about how three generations of Eskimos living in Alaska near the Arctic strive to adopt the best of modern ways without abandoning their traditional values. During the class discussion, some students may note that Alice and Billy Rivers want their children to learn both the new and the old ways of living. As the discussion continues, many students may conclude from the story that the older generations hope that future generations will continue to value their roots and their cultural traditions. Students then relate this story to their own heritage. Some students may share information about their customs or traditions.

Students choose some reflective activities that will help them learn more about heritage and that will answer some of their questions about the unit concepts. Some students may be interested in interviewing family members or close friends about their cultural traditions and heritages. These students review what they know about interviewing. They proceed by:

- Contacting in advance the person(s) they want to interview.
- Preparing a list of questions to ask.
- Preparing a list of subjects to discuss, deciding how to record the interview (by audiotape, videotape, or taking notes).
- Deciding whether to photograph the person and, if so, getting permission to do so in advance—collecting the equipment necessary for conducting the interview.

After they conduct the interviews, students decide how they wish to present the information that they have collected.

> *Exploring through reflective activities allows students to gain a wider perspective on a concept by relating it to their own experiences. Students quickly become aware that it is their responsibility to learn and to help their peers learn more about the unit concepts.*

EXAMPLE: Another group of students in the same fifth-grade class may be more interested in planning a photo essay about one family or about a neighborhood with many families belonging to a particular culture. These students may decide to reexamine "In Two Worlds" to notice how the text and the photographs complement each other and what information is conveyed in each photograph. They may also decide to examine some photo essays listed in the unit bibliography. These students will need to make some advance preparations as well. They proceed by:

- Determining which neighborhood and which family or families to photograph.
- Contacting in advance the persons to be interviewed and photographed.
- Touring the neighborhood in advance of the photo shoot.
- Making a list of questions to ask the family or families about their heritage or about their neighborhood.

- Thinking about what information to include in their essay so that they can determine what photographs to take.
- Collecting the equipment necessary for conducting interviews and photographing subjects.

After students collect the information and take photographs, they may write and organize the photo essay and present it to the class. The teacher should remind students of the phases of the writing process and encourage them to proofread and revise their work until they are completely pleased with it. Students can continue discussing heritage and raising any new questions that they wish to explore. The teacher should remind them that as they read further, they may think of a variety of ways to explore the unit concepts. The teacher should then ask students to post on the Concept and Question Board any new questions they have about heritage. Students should sign or initial their questions so that they can identify classmates with similar interests and exchange ideas with them. The teacher should encourage students to feel free to write an answer or a note on someone else's question or to consult the board for ideas for their own explorations. From time to time, the teacher should post his or her own questions on the Concept and Question Board.

Tips

- The bibliographies located at the end of each unit in the student anthology and the Classroom Library contain books related to the unit concepts. Remind students that these are good sources of information and that they should consult them regularly— especially when they are exploring concept-related ideas and questions.
- Some students work better within a specified time frame. Whenever they are beginning a new activity, discuss with the children a reasonable period of time within which they will be expected to complete their explorations. Post the completion date somewhere in the classroom so that students can refer to it and pace themselves accordingly. At first, you may have to help them determine a suitable deadline, but eventually they should be able to make this judgment on their own.

Exploring through Research

Purpose

Students come to school with a wealth of fascinating questions. Educators need to capitalize on this excitement for learning and natural curiosity. A classroom in which only correct answers are accepted and students are not allowed to make errors and consider alternative possibilities to questions can quickly deaden this natural curiosity and enthusiasm. The purpose of the research aspect of this program is to capitalize on students' questions and natural curiosity by using a proven structure. This structure helps students to not get lost or bogged down but at the same time to preserve the open-ended character of real research, which can lead to unexpected findings and to questions that were not originally considered.

There is a conventional approach to school research papers that can be found, with minor variations, in countless textbooks. It consists of a series of steps such as the following: select a topic, narrow the topic, collect materials, take notes, outline, and write. By following these steps a student may produce a presentable paper, but the procedure does not constitute research in a meaningful sense and indeed gives students a distorted notion of what research is about. We see students in universities and even in graduate schools still following this procedure when they do library research papers or literature reviews; we see their dismay when their professors regard such work as mere cutting and pasting and ask them where their original contribution is.

Even elementary school students can produce works of genuine research—research that seeks answers to real questions or solutions to real problems. This skill in collecting and analyzing information is a valuable tool in the adult world in which adults, as consumers, are constantly analyzing new information and making informed decisions on the basis of this information. Preparing students for the analytic demands of adult life and teaching them how to find answers to their questions are goals of education.

Procedure

In order to make the Research productive, the following important principles are embodied in this approach:

1. Research is focused on problems, not topics.
2. Conjectures—opinions based on less than complete evidence or proof—guide the research; the research does not simply produce conjectures.
3. New information is gathered to test and revise conjectures.
4. Discussion, ongoing feedback, and constructive criticism are important in all phases of the research but especially in the revising of problems and conjectures.
5. The cycle of true research is essentially endless, although presentations of findings are made from time to time; new findings give rise to new problems and conjectures and thus to new cycles of research.

Following a Process

While working with the research units, students are encouraged to follow a set pattern or cycle in order to keep their research activities focused and on track. Students may go through these steps many times before they come to the end of their research. Certainly for adult researchers, this cycle of question, conjecture, research, and reevaluate can go on for years and in some cases lifetimes.

This cycle includes:

1. **Decide on a problem or question to research.** Students should identify a question or problem that they truly wonder about or wish to understand and then form research groups with other students who have the same interests.
   - My problem or question is _____.

2. **Formulate an idea or conjecture about the research problem.** Students should think about and discuss with classmates possible answers to their research problems or questions and meet with their research groups to discuss and record their ideas or conjectures.
   - My idea/conjecture/theory about this question or problem is _____.

3. **Identify needs and make plans.** Students should identify knowledge needs related to their conjectures and meet with their research groups to determine which resources to consult and to make individual job assignments. Students should also meet periodically with the teacher, other classmates, and research groups to present preliminary findings and make revisions to their problems and conjectures on the basis of these findings.
   - I need to find out _____.
   - To do this, I will need these resources: _____.
   - My role in the group is _____.
   - This is what I have learned so far: _____.
   - This is what happened when we presented our findings: _____.

4. **Reevaluate the problem or question based on what we have learned so far and the feedback we have received.**
   - My revised problem or question is _____.

5. **Revise the idea or conjecture.**
   - My new conjecture about this problem is _____.

6. **Identify new needs and make new plans.**
   - Based on what I found out, I still need to know _____.
   - To do this, I will need these resources: _____.
   - This is what I have learned: _____.
   - This is what happened when we presented our new findings: _____.

Procedure for Choosing a Problem to Research

1. Discuss with students the nature of the unit. Explain to students that the unit they are reading is a research unit and that they will produce and publish in some way the results of their explorations. They are free to decide what problems or questions they wish to explore, whom they want to work with, and how they want to present their finished products. They may publish a piece of writing, produce a poster, write and perform a play, or use any other means to present the results of their explorations and research. They may work with partners or in small groups.

2. Discuss with students the schedule you have planned for research projects: how long the project is expected to take, how much time will be available for research, when the first presentation will be due. This schedule will partly determine the nature of the problems that students should be encouraged to work on and the depth of the inquiry students will be encouraged to pursue.

3. Have students talk about things they wonder about that are related to the unit subject. For example, in the grade 3 unit, Money, students might wonder where money in the money machine comes from or how prices are determined. Conduct a free-floating discussion of questions about the unit subject.

4. Brainstorm possible questions for students to think about. It is essential that the children's own ideas and questions be the starting point of all inquiry. *Helpful hint:* For the first research unit, you might wish to generate a list of your own ideas, having students add to this list and having them choose from it.

5. Using their wonderings, model for the children the difference between a research topic and a research problem or question by providing several examples. For example, have them consider the difference between the topic California and the problem, *Why do so many people move to California?* Explain to them that if they choose to research the topic California, everything they look up under the subject heading or index entry California will be related in some way to their topic. Therefore, it will be quite difficult to choose which information to record. This excess of information also creates problems in organizing their research. Clearly, then, this topic is too broad and general. Choosing a specific question or problem, one that particularly interests them, helps them narrow their exploration and advance their understanding. Some possible ideas for questions can be found in the unit introduction. Ideas can also be generated as you and your students create a web of their questions or problems related to the unit subject. For example, questions related to the subject California might include the following:

- Why do so many people move to California?
- How have the different groups of people living in California affected the state?

6. A good research problem or question not only requires students to consult a variety of sources but is engaging and adds to the groups' knowledge of the concepts. Furthermore, good problems generate more questions. Help students understand that the question, *Why do so many people move to California?* is an easy one to research. Many sources will contribute to an answer to the question, and all information located can be easily evaluated in terms of usefulness in answering the question. Helpful hint: Students' initial responses may indeed be topics instead of problems or questions. If so, the following questions might be helpful:
   - What aspect of the topic really interests you?
   - Can you turn that idea into a question?

7. Remember that this initial problem or question serves only as a guide for research. As students begin collecting information and collaborating with classmates, their ideas will change, and they can revise their research problem or question. Frequently, students do not sufficiently revise their problems until after they have had time to consider their conjectures and collect information.

8. As students begin formulating their research problems, have them elaborate on their reasons for wanting to research their stated problems. They should go beyond simple expressions of interest or liking and indicate what is puzzling, important, or potentially informative, and so forth, about the problems they have chosen.

9. At this stage, students' ideas will be of a very vague and limited sort. The important thing is to start them thinking about what really interests them and what value it has to them and the class.

10. Have students present their proposed problems or questions, along with reasons for their choices, and have an open discussion of how promising proposed problems are. As students present their proposed problems, ask them what new things they think they will be learning from their exploration and how that will add to the group's growing knowledge of the concepts. This constant emphasis on group knowledge building will help set a clear purpose for students' research.

Even elementary school students can produce works of genuine research—research that seeks answers to real questions or solutions to real problems.

11. Form research groups. To make it easier for students to form groups, they may record their problems on the chalkboard or on self-sticking notes. Final groups should be constituted in the way you find best for your class—by self-selection, by assignment on the basis of common interests, or by some combination of methods. Students can then meet during **Independent Work Time** to agree on a precise statement of their research problem, the nature of their expected research contributions, and lists of related questions that may help later in assigning individual roles. They should also record any scheduling information that can be added to the planning calendar.

Using Technology

The **Research CD-ROM** (Levels 1–6), an interactive software program supports student research by helping them organize and conduct their research. In addition, SRA's Home Page on the World Wide Web directs students to resources they can use in their research. Also, a Student Bulletin Board supports communication and collaboration with students across the country. Just click on **www.sra4kids.com/student.**

Students using **SRA/Open Court Reading** have the opportunity and the wherewithal to expand their research groups nationwide and find out what other **SRA/Open Court Reading** students are doing with their unit explorations.

Tips

- If students are careful about the problems or questions they choose to research, they should have few problems in following through with the research. If the problem is too broad or too narrow, they will have problems.

- Have students take sufficient time in assessing their needs—both knowledge needs and physical needs in relation to their research. Careful preplanning can help the research progress smoothly with great results.

- Encourage students to reevaluate their needs often so they are not wasting time finding things they already have or ignoring needs that they haven't noticed.

- Interim presentations of material are every bit as important, if not more so, than final presentations. It is during interim presentations that students have the opportunity to rethink and reevaluate their work and change direction or decide to carry on with their planned research.

Independent Work Time

Every teacher and every student needs time during the day to organize, take stock of work that is done, make plans for work that needs doing, and finish up incomplete projects. In addition, time is needed for individualization and for peer conferencing.

Purpose

Independent Work Time is the period of time each day in which students work independently or collaboratively to practice and review material taught in the lessons.

A variety of activities may occur during this time. Students may work on a specific daily assignment, complete an ongoing project, work on unit exploration activities, focus on writing, or choose from among a wide range of possibilities. With lots of guidance and encouragement, students gradually learn to make decisions about their use of time and materials and to collaborate with their peers.

A goal of **Independent Work Time** is to get students to work independently. This is essential since **Independent Work Time** is also the time during which the teacher can work with individuals or groups of children to reinforce learning, to provide extra help for those having difficulties, to extend learning, or to assess the progress of the class or of individuals.

Procedure

Initially, for many students, you will need to structure **Independent Work Time** carefully. Eventually, students will automatically go to the appropriate areas, take up ongoing projects, and get the materials they will need. **Independent Work Time** will evolve slowly from a very structured period to a time when children make choices and move freely from one activity to the next.

Adhere firmly to **Independent Work Time** guidelines. By the time the children have completed the first few weeks of school, they should feel confident during **Independent Work Time**. If not, continue to structure the time and limit options. For young children, early periods of **Independent Work Time** may run no more than five to eight minutes. The time can gradually increase to fifteen minutes or longer as the children gain independence. Older students may be able to work longer and independently from the very beginning of the school year.

Introducing Independent Work Time

Introduce **Independent Work Time** to the children by telling them that every day there will be a time when they are expected to work on activities on their own or in small groups. For young children in the beginning, you will assign the **Independent Work Time** activities to help

the children learn to work on their own. Point out the shelf or area of the classroom where **Independent Work Time** materials are stored. Tell the children that when they finish working with the materials for one activity, they are to choose something else from the **Independent Work Time** shelf. New activity materials will be added to the shelf from time to time. Make sure that the children know that they may always look at books during **Independent Work Time**. If children have writing journals, you may want to make these available at the **Independent Work Time** as well.

Tell older students that they will have an opportunity each day to work on their unit explorations, their writing and other projects. Students will be working independently and collaboratively during this time.

Guidelines

- Make sure each child knows what he or she needs to do during **Independent Work Time**.
- Demonstrate for the whole group any activity assigned for **Independent Work Time**; for example, teaching the children a new game, introducing new materials or projects, or explaining different areas.
- For young children, it is essential to introduce and demonstrate different activities and games before the children do them on their own. With games, you may want to have several children play while the others watch. Make sure that all the children know exactly what is expected of them.
- In the beginning, plan to circulate among the children providing encouragement and help as necessary.
- Once students are engaged in appropriate activities and can work independently, meet with those children who need your particular attention. This may include individual students or small groups.
- Let the children know that they need to ask questions and clarify assignments during **Independent Work Time** introduction, so that you are free to work with small groups.
- Be sure that students know what they are to do when they have finished an activity and where to put their finished work.

Establish and discuss rules for **Independent Work Time** with the children. Keep them simple and straightforward. You may want to write the finalized rules on the chalkboard or on a poster. You may want to review these rules each day at

the beginning of **Independent Work Time** for the first few lessons or so. You may also wish to revisit and revise the rules from time to time. Suggested rules include:

✓ Be polite.
✓ Share.
✓ Whisper.
✓ Take only the materials you need.
✓ Return materials.

Setting Up Your Classroom for Independent Work Time

Carefully setting up your classroom to accommodate different **Independent Work Time** activities will help assure that the **Independent Work Time** period progresses smoothly and effectively. While setting up your classroom, keep the primary **Independent Work Time** activities in mind. During **Independent Work Time** the children will be doing independent and collaborative activities. In kindergarten and first grade, these activities may include letter recognition and phonemic awareness activities and writing or illustrating stories or projects. In addition, they will be working on individual or small group projects.

Many classrooms have centers that the children visit on a regular or rotating basis. Center time can be easily and efficiently incorporated into the **Independent Work Time** concept. For example, the activities suggested during **Independent Work Time** can be incorporated into reading and writing centers. Other typical classroom centers include an art center, math center, science table, play area, etc.

The following are suggestions for space and materials for use during **Independent Work Time**:

1. **Literacy or Reading Center** supplied with books and magazines. The materials in the Literacy Center should be dynamic—changing with students' abilities and reflecting unit themes they are reading. You may wish to add books suggested in unit bibliographies and books from the literature collections available with each unit.

2. **Writing Center** stocked with various types and sizes of lined and unlined paper, pencils, erasers, markers, crayons, small slates, and chalk. The area should also have various **Letter Cards**, other handwriting models, and worksheets for those students who want to practice letter formation or handwriting.

Students should know that this is where they come for writing supplies. In addition to the supplies described above, the Writing Center can also have supplies to encourage the children to create and write on their own:

✓ magazines and catalogs to cut up for pictures; stickers, paint, glue, glitter, etc. to decorate books and book covers; precut and stapled blank books for the children to write in. (Some can be plain and some cut in special shapes.)

✓ cardboard, tag board, construction paper, etc., for making book covers. (Provide some samples.)

✓ tape, scissors, yarn, hole punches for binding books.

✓ picture dictionaries, dictionaries, thesaurus, word lists, and other materials that may encourage independence.

3. **Listening Center** supplied with tape recorder, optional headphones, and tapes of stories, poems, and songs for the children to listen to and react to. You might also want to provide blank tapes and encourage the children to retell and record their favorite stories or make up and tell stories for their classmates to listen to on tape. You may also want to make available the audiocassettes that are available with the program.

4. **Independent Work Time Activity Center** supplied with daily Alphabet Flash Cards, individual Alphabet-Sound Card sets (Kindergarten), **Individual Sound/Spelling Cards** and **High-Frequency Word Flash Cards** (Grades 1-3), and other materials that enhance what the children are learning. Other commonly used classroom materials that enhance literacy can be included (for example, plastic letters, puzzles, workbooks).

Since students will be working on their inquiry/research projects during **Independent Work Time**, make sure there are adequate supplies to help them with their research. These might include dictionaries, encyclopedias, magazines, newspapers, and computers— preferably with Internet capability.

5. **Game Corner** with the games introduced during **Independent Work Time**, along with any other educational games you normally use.

Students thrive in an environment that provides structure, repetition, and routine. Within a sound structure, the children will gain confidence and independence. This setting also provides opportunities for flexibility and individual choice that allow the children to develop their strengths, abilities, and talents to the fullest.

Suggestions for English as a Second Language Learners

Independent Work Time affords students who are English as a Second Language Learners a wealth of opportunities for gaining proficiency in English. It also encourages them to share their special backgrounds with their peers. Since you will be working with all students individually and in small groups regardless of their reading ability, those students who need special help with language will not feel self-conscious about working with you. In addition, working in small groups made up of students with the same interests rather than the same abilities will provide them with the opportunity to learn about language from their peers during the regular course of **Independent Work Time** activities.

Some suggestions for meeting the special needs of children with diverse backgrounds follow:

■ Preread a selection with English as a Second Language Learners to help them to identify words and ideas they wish to talk about. This will prepare them for discussions with the whole group.

■ Preteach vocabulary and develop selection concepts that may be a challenge for students.

■ Negotiate the meaning of selections by asking questions, checking for comprehension, and speaking with English as a Second Language Learners as much as possible.

> *Independent Work Time is the period of time each day in which students work independently or collaboratively to practice and review material taught in the lessons.*

■ Draw English as a Second Language Learners into small group discussions to give them a sense that their ideas are valid and worth attention.

■ Pair English as a Second Language Learners with native English speakers to share their experiences and provide new knowledge to other children.

■ Have English as a Second Language Learners draw or dictate to you or another student a description of a new idea they may have during **Independent Work Time** activities.

Tips

■ **Establish clear, easily articulated guidelines** for the children to follow during **Independent Work Time**. Make sure the children know what is expected of them. Have children tell you what they will be doing during **Independent Work Time**, including how to play games and complete Activity Sheets.

■ **Encourage responsibility and independence** by reminding the children to follow the rules set up for **Independent Work Time**—showing respect for each other and the materials that are provided.

■ **Encourage cooperation and collaboration** by providing the children with opportunities to engage in age-appropriate group activities. Games are an ideal group endeavor for young children, as are simple plays and art projects.

■ **Encourage respect for individual differences** and talents by providing a wide range of activities and projects. There should be some activity to showcase every child's unique abilities.

■ **Establish areas and times for** the children to display and present their work to you and each other.

■ **Encourage group projects** that help develop each student's ability to work cooperatively.

■ **Look for special talents and abilities** in each student and provide opportunities for students to display these special talents.

■ **Encourage children to try new things.** Provide opportunities for the children to expand their horizons. For example, have children work with a new partner or a small group to try out a new activity. Or have a "grab bag of activities" day in which children pick a card delineating their assignment for the day.

Assessment

Assessment can be one of your most effective teaching tools if it is used with the purpose of informing instruction and highlighting areas that need special attention.

Purpose

Assessment is a tool the teacher uses to monitor students' progress and to detect students' strengths and weaknesses. Evaluation of student learning is addressed in two ways: Informal Assessment and Formal Assessment. Informal, observational assessment, or a quick check of students' written work is presented in the Teacher's Edition in the form of assessment suggestions. Formal Assessment consists of performance assessment (both reading and writing) and objective tests (multiple choice and open response).

Procedure

Informal Assessment

Observation

Observing students as they go about their regular classwork is probably the single most effective way to learn in depth your students' strengths and areas of need. The more students become accustomed to you jotting down informal notes about their work, the more it will become just another part of classroom life that they accept and take little note of. This gives you the opportunity to assess their progress constantly without the interference and possible drawback of formal testing situations.

In order to make informal assessment of student progress a part of your everyday classroom routine, you might want to start by preparing the materials you will need on hand.

- Enter students' names in the Teacher's Observation Log.
- Before each day's lesson begins, decide which students you will observe.
- Keep the Teacher's Observation Log available so that you can easily record your observations.
- Decide what aspect of the children's learning you wish to monitor.
- During each lesson, observe this aspect in the performances of several children.
- Record your observations.
- It may take four to five days to make sure you have observed and recorded the performance of each student. If you need more information about performance in a particular area for some of your students, you may want to observe them more than once.

Written Work

Students are writing one thing or another all day long. Each of these pieces of writing can provide you with valuable information about your students. Two very helpful resources that students will work in daily are the *Reading and Writing Workbook* (Levels K–6) and the *Inquiry Journal* (Levels 2–6).

- The *Reading and Writing Workbook* includes skills practice lessons that act as practice and reinforcement for the skills lessons taught during the reading of the lesson or in conjunction with the lesson. These skill pages give you a clear picture of students' understanding of the skills taught. Use them as a daily assessment of student progress in the particular skills taught through the program. In the Reading and Writing Workbook, students practice each of the skills taught in the program.
- The *Inquiry Journal* can give you invaluable information on how students are progressing in many different areas. In the *Inquiry Journal*, students
  - ✓ Record what they know about the concepts and what they learn. You will be able to monitor their growing ability to make connections and use their prior knowledge to help them understand new concepts.
  - ✓ Keep a record of their research: what resources they need, what they have used, where they have looked, and what they have found. You can keep track of students' growing ability to find the resources and knowledge base they need to answer the questions they pose.
  - ✓ Keep track of their work with their collaborative groups. This will give you a good idea of students' growing ability to work with peers for a common goal—the acquisition of new knowledge.
  - ✓ Practice study and research skills that will help them in all of their schooling. You can easily keep track of how well they are learning to use such things as library resources, reference books, visual organizers, and much, much more.

Dictation

In grades 1–3, students use dictation to practice the sound/spelling associations they are learning and/or reviewing. Collect the dictation papers and look through them to see how the children are doing with writing and with proofreading their words. Record notes on the papers and keep them in the student portfolios.

Portfolios

Portfolios are more than just a collection bin or gathering place for student projects and records. They add balance to an assessment program by providing unique benefits to teachers, students, and families.

- Portfolios help build self-confidence and increase self-esteem as students come to appreciate the value of their work. More importantly, portfolios allow students to reflect on what they know and what they need to learn. At the end of the school year, each student will be able to go through their portfolios and write about their progress.
- Portfolios provide the teacher with an authentic record of what students can do. Just as important, portfolios give students a concrete example of their own progress and development. Thus, portfolios become a valuable source of information for making instructional decisions.
- Portfolios allow families to judge student performance directly. Portfolios are an ideal starting point for discussions about a student's achievements and future goals during teacher/family conferences.

You will find that there are many opportunities to add to students' portfolios.

Reading

- During partner reading, during **Independent Work Time**, or at other times of the day, invite students, one at a time, to sit with you and read a story from an appropriate Decodable (Levels 1–3) or from the Anthology.
- As each student reads to you, follow along and make note of any recurring problems the student has while reading. Note students' ability to decode unknown words as well as any attempt—successful or not—to use strategies to clarify or otherwise make sense of what they are reading. From time to time, check students' fluency by timing their reading and noting how well they are able to sustain the oral reading without faltering.
- If the student has trouble reading a particular Decodable story, encourage the student to read the story a few times on her or his own before reading it aloud to you. If the Decodable has two stories, use the alternate story to reassess the student a day or two later.
- If after practicing with a particular Decodable and reading it on his or her own a few times, a student is still experiencing difficulty, try the following:
  - Drop back two Decodables. (Continue to drop back until the student is able to read a story with no trouble.) If the student can read that book without problems, move up one book.
  - Continue the process until the student is able to read the current Decodable.

Standardized Tests

Throughout their school careers, the students will be expected to show their achievement through the use of standardized tests. A standardized test is simply a test of specific tasks and procedures that can be compared across geographical areas. These are the national and state achievement tests that many students take yearly. These are generally the tests that are used for accountability purposes.

Standardized tests are generally a combination of easily scored items such as multiple choice, true or false, fill-the-in-blank, or very short completion tasks. In order to be sure that you are testing the students' knowledge of what is being taught, you need to be sure that the students are familiar with the type of test you are giving and know how to produce the answers. Many students have had difficulty with such tests simply because they did not understand the test format and, although thoroughly familiar with subject content, they could not exhibit their knowledge because of confusion with the test itself.

Each of the Formal Assessment Components in **SRA/Open Court Reading** discussed below, contains standardized-test-format questions as well as performance assessment items. As students progress through the grades, they will become very familiar with these different test formats assuring that they will be able to easily adjust to whatever test format they are required to use.

Preparing for Formal Assessment

Written Tests

- Have the children clear their desks.
- Make sure the children can hear and see clearly.
- Explain the instructions and complete one or two examples with students before each test to make sure they understand what to do.
- Give students ample time to finish each test.

> *Observing students as they go about their regular classwork is probably the single most effective way to learn in depth your students' strengths and areas of need.*

Selection Tests

Students reading **SRA/Open Court Reading** in Grades 1–6 are given the opportunity after reading and discussing each selection to exhibit what they have learned and practice their test-taking skills by completing the comprehension assessment found in the Comprehension and Writing Assessment Book.

Each of these tests contains multiple choice items that are primarily concerned with simple recall and literal comprehension. In addition, students are asked to complete short-answer items that require them to make connections to other stories in the unit and give a written account of what they read. The combination of multiple choice and written response gives you the best view of what students understand and how well they are able to connect their new knowledge to what they already know.

End-of-Unit Tests At the conclusion of each unit, students are given a fairly extensive test that requires them to transfer what they have learned to new selections on the same concept as the selection in the student anthology. In addition to simply reading the new selections and answering questions, students must explain how the new piece adds to the pieces they read in the unit and what new learning they have gleaned from the piece.

In addition, students are asked to write short pieces on specific subjects related to the unit concepts. Through this writing, they must exhibit their growing ability to organize their writing and produce finished pieces that are not only coherent but also structurally and technically correct. Spelling, punctuation, sentence structure, and such are formally assessed through these writing pieces. Scoring rubrics are provided to help guide you through students' writing.

Tips

- When observing students, do not pull them aside; rather, observe students as part of the regular lesson, either with the whole class or in small groups.
- Encourage students to express any confusion they may be experiencing. The questions students ask can give you valuable insight into their progress and development.
- The more comfortable students become with standardized-test formats—usually multiple choice—the more confident you and they will be in the fact that the test is testing their knowledge of a subject rather than their test-taking skills.
- Make sure students know that the ultimate purpose of assessment is to keep track of their progress and to help them continue to do better.

Audiovisual and Technology Resource Directory

This directory is provided for the convenience of ordering the Technology Resources listed on the Technology pages in each Unit Overview.

Clearvue/eav

6465 North Avondale Avenue
Chicago, IL 60631-1996
800-CLEARVU (253-2788)
Fax: 800-444-9855

Coronet/MTI

108 Wilmot Road
Deerfield, IL 60015
800-777-8100

Entrex

PO Box 30029
Victoria BC V8X5E1

Forest Technologies/ Discovery Channel

7700 Wisconsin Ave.
Bethesda, Maryland 20814
888-404-5969
www.discovery.com

The Learning Company, Inc.

6493 Kaiser Drive
Fremont, CA 94555
510-792-2101
Fax: 510-713-6072
www.learningco.com

Macmillan/McGraw-Hill School Division

220 East Danieldale Road
De Soto, TX 75115
800-442-9685

Orange Cherry New Media

P.O. Box 505
Pound Ridge, NY 10576
914-764-4104
Fax: 914-764-0104
Email: nmsh@cloud9.net

Pyramid Film & Video

P.O. Box 1048/WEB
Santa Monica, CA 90406
800-421-2304
Fax: 310-453-9083
www.pyramidmedia.com

Queue, Inc.

338 Commerce Drive
Fairfield, CT 06432
800-232-2224
Fax: 203-336-2481
QUEUEINC@aol.com

Rabbit Ears Video

6493 Kaiser Drive
Fremont, CA 94555
510-792-2101
Fax: 510-713-6072
www.mecc.com

SRA/McGraw-Hill

220 East Danieldale Road
De Soto, TX 75115-9960
888-SRA-4543
www.sra4kids.com

Open Court Reading
Glossary of Reading Terms

This glossary includes linguistic, grammatical, comprehension, and literary terms that may be helpful in understanding reading instruction.

acronym a word formed from the initial letter of words in a phrase, **scuba (self-contained underwater breathing apparatus)**.

acrostic a kind of puzzle in which lines of a poem are arranged so that words or phrases are formed when certain letters from each line are used in a sequence.

adjective a word or group of words that modifies a noun.

adventure story a narrative that features the unknown or unexpected with elements of excitement, danger, and risk.

adverb a word or group of words that modifies a verb, adjective, or other adverb.

affective domain the psychological field of emotional activity.

affix a word part, either a prefix or a suffix, that changes the meaning or function of a word root or stem.

affricate a speech sound that starts as a stop but ends as a fricative, the /ch/ in **catch**.

agreement the correspondence of syntactically related words; subjects and predicates are in agreement when both are singular or plural.

alliteration the repetition of the initial sounds in neighboring words or stressed syllables.

alphabet the complete set of letters representing speech sounds used in writing a language.

alphabet book a book for helping young children learn the alphabet by pairing letters with pictures whose sounds they represent.

alphabetic principle the principle that there is an association between sounds and the letters that represent them in alphabetic writing systems.

alveolar a consonant speech sound made when the tongue and the ridge of the upper and lower jaw stop to constrict the air flow, as /t/.

anagram a word or phrase whose letters form other words or phrases when rearranged, for example, **add** and **dad**.

analogy a likeness or similarity.

analytic phonics also deductive phonics, a whole-to-part approach to phonics in which a student is taught a number of sight words and then phonetic generalizations that can be applied to other words.

antonym a word that is opposite in meaning to another word.

appositive a word that restates or modifies a preceding noun. For example, **my daughter, Charlotte**.

aspirate an unvoiced speech sound produced by a puff of air, as /h/ in **heart**.

aspirated stop a stop consonant sound released with a puff of air, as /k/, /p/, and /t/.

auditory discrimination the ability to hear phonetic likenesses and differences in phonemes and words.

author's purpose the motive or reason for which an author writes, includes to entertain, inform, persuade, and explain how.

automaticity fluent processing of information, requiring little effort or attention.

auxiliary verb a verb that precedes another verb to express time, mood, or voice, includes verbs such as **has, is, will**.

ballad a narrative poem, composed of short verses to be sung or recited, usually containing elements of drama and often tragic in tone.

base word a word to which affixes may be added to create related words.

blank verse unrhymed verse, especially unrhymed iambic pentameter.

blend the joining of the sounds of two or more letters with little change in those sounds, for example /spr/ in **spring**, also **consonant blend** or **consonant cluster**.

blending to combine the sounds represented by letters to sound out or pronounce a word, contrast with **oral blending**.

breve the symbol placed above a vowel to indicate that it is a short vowel.

browse to skim through or look over in search of something of interest.

canon in literature, the body of major works that a culture considers important at a given time.

case a grammatical category that indicates the syntactic/semantic role of a noun phrase in a sentence.

cause-effect relationship a stated or implied association between an outcome and the conditions that brought it about, also the comprehension skill associated with recognizing this type of relationship as an organizing principle in text.

chapter book a book long enough to be divided into chapters, but not long or complex enough to be considered a novel.

characterization the way in which an author presents a character in a story, including describing words, actions, thoughts, and impressions of that character.

choral reading oral group reading to develop oral fluency by modeling.

cinquain a stanza of five lines, specifically one that has successive lines of two, four, six, eight, and two syllables.

cipher a system for writing in code.

clarifying a comprehension strategy in which the reader rereads text, uses a dictionary, uses decoding skills, or uses context clues to comprehend something that is unclear.

clause a group of words with a subject and a predicate used to form a part of or a whole sentence, a dependent clause modifies an independent clause, which can stand alone as a complete sentence.

collaborative learning learning by working together in small groups.

command a sentence that asks for action and usually ends with a period.

common noun in contrast to **proper noun**, a noun that denotes a class rather than a unique or specific thing.

comprehension the understanding of what is written or said.

comprehension skill a skill that aids in understanding text, including identifying **author's purpose**, **comprehending cause and effect relationships**, **comparing and contrasting** items and events, **drawing conclusions**, distinguishing **fact from opinion**, identifying **main ideas**, making **inferences**, distinguishing **reality from fantasy**, and understanding **sequence**.

comprehension strategy a sequence of steps for understanding text, includes asking questions, clarifying, making connections, predicting, summarizing, and visualizing.

conjugation the complete set of all possible inflected forms of a verb.

conjunction a part of speech used to connect words, phrases, clauses, or sentences, including the words **and, but, or**.

consonant a speech sound, and the alphabet letter that represents that sound, made by partial or complete closure of part of the vocal tract, which obstructs air flow and causes audible friction.

context clue information from the immediate text that helps identify a word.

contraction a short version of a written or spoken expression in which letters are omitted, for example, **can't**.

convention an accepted practice in spoken or written language, usually referring to spelling, mechanics, or grammar rules.

cooperative learning a classroom organization that allows students to work together to achieve their individual goals.

creative writing prose and poetic forms of writing that express the writer's thoughts and feelings imaginatively.

cuing system any of the various sources of information that help to identify an unrecognizable word in reading, including phonetic, semantic, and syntactical information.

Glossary of Reading Terms (continued)

cumulative tale a story, such as The Gingerbread Man, in which details are repeated until the climax.

dangling modifier usually a participle that because of its placement in a sentence modifies the wrong object.

decodable text text materials controlled to include a majority of words whose sound/spelling relationships are known by the reader.

decode to analyze spoken or graphic symbols for meaning.

diacritical mark a mark, such as a breve or macron, added to a letter or graphic character, to indicate a specific pronunciation.

dialect a regional variety of a particular language with phonological, grammatical, and lexical patterns that distinguish it from other varieties.

dialogue a piece of writing written as conversation, usually punctuated by quotation marks.

digraph two letters that represent one speech sound, for example /sh/ or /ch/.

diphthong a vowel sound produced when the tongue glides from one vowel sound toward another in the same syllable, for example /oi/ or /ou/.

direct object the person or thing that receives the action of a verb in a sentence, for example, the word **cake** in this sentence: **Madeline baked a cake**.

drafting the process of writing ideas in rough form to record them.

drama a story in the form of a play, written to be performed.

edit in the writing process, to revise or correct a manuscript.

emergent literacy the development of the association of meaning and print that continues until a child reaches the stage of conventional reading and writing.

emergent reading a child's early interaction with books and print before the ability to decode text.

encode to change a message into symbols, for example, to change speech into writing.

epic a long narrative poem, usually about a hero.

exclamatory sentence a sentence that shows strong emotion and ends with an exclamation mark.

expository writing or **exposition** a composition in writing that explains an event or process.

fable a short tale that teaches a moral.

fantasy a highly imaginative story about characters, places, and events that do not exist.

fiction imaginative narrative designed to entertain rather than to explain, persuade, or describe.

figure of speech the expressive, nonliteral use of language usually through metaphor, simile, or personification.

fluency freedom from word-identification problems that hinder comprehension in reading.

folktale a narrative form of genre such as an epic, myth, or fable that is well-known through repeated storytellings.

foreshadowing giving clues to upcoming events in a story.

free verse verse with irregular metrical pattern.

freewriting writing that is not limited in form, style, content, or purpose, designed to encourage students to write.

genre a classification of literary works, including tragedy, comedy, novel, essay, short story, mystery, realistic fiction, poetry.

grammar the study of the classes of words, their inflections, and their functions and relations in sentences; includes phonological, morphological, syntactic, and semantic descriptions of a language.

grapheme a written or printed representation of a phoneme, such as **c** for /k/.

guided reading reading instruction in which the teacher provides the structure and purpose for reading and responding to the material read.

handing off a method of turning over to the students the primary responsibility for controlling discussion.

indirect object in a sentence, the person or thing to or for whom an action is done, for example, the word **dog** in this sentence: **Madeline gave the dog a treat**.

inference a conclusion based on facts, data, or evidence.

infinitive the base form of a verb, usually with the infinitive marker, for example, **to go**.

inflectional ending an ending that expresses a plural or possessive form of a noun, the tense of a verb, or the comparative or superlative form of an adjective or adverb.

interrogative word a word that marks a clause or sentence as a question, including **interrogative pronouns who**, **what**, **which**, **where**.

intervention a strategy or program designed to supplement or substitute instruction, especially for those students who fall behind.

invented spelling the result of an attempt to spell a word based on the writer's knowledge of the spelling system and how it works, often with overemphasis on sound/symbol relationships.

irony a figure of speech in which the literal meaning of the words is the opposite of their intended meaning.

journal a written record of daily events or responses.

juvenile book a book written for children or adolescents.

legend a traditional tale handed down from generation to generation.

leitmotif a repeated expression, event, or idea used to unify a work of art such as writing.

letter one of a set of graphic symbols that forms an alphabet and used alone or in combination to represent a phoneme, also **grapheme**.

linguistics the study of the nature and structure of language and communication.

literary elements the elements of a story such as **setting**, **plot**, and **characterization** that create the structure of a narrative.

macron a diacritical mark placed above a vowel to indicate a long vowel sound.

main idea the central thought or chief topic of a passage.

mechanics the conventions of capitalization and punctuation.

metacognition awareness and knowledge of one's mental processes or thinking about what one is thinking about.

metaphor a figure of speech in which a comparison is implied but not stated, for example, **She is a jewel**.

miscue a deviation from text during oral reading in an attempt to make sense of the text.

modeling an instructional technique in which the teacher serves as an example of behavior.

mood the literary element that conveys the emotional atmosphere of a story.

morpheme a meaningful linguistic unit that cannot be divided into smaller units, for example, **word**; **a bound morpheme** is a morpheme that cannot stand alone as an independent word, for example, the prefix **re-**; a **free morpheme** can stand alone, for example, **dog**.

myth a story designed to explain the mysteries of life.

narrative writing or **narration** a composition in writing that tells a story or gives an account of an event.

nonfiction prose designed to explain, argue, or describe rather than to entertain with a factual emphasis, includes biography and autobiography.

noun a part of speech that denotes persons, places, things, qualities, or acts.

novel an extended fictional prose narration.

onomatopoeia the use of a word whose sound suggests its meaning, for example, **purr**.

oral blending the ability to fuse discrete phonemes into recognizable words; oral blending puts sounds together to make a word, **see also segmentation**.

orthography correct or standardized spelling according to established usage in a language.

oxymoron a figure of speech in which contrasting or contradictory words are brought together for emphasis.

paragraph a subdivision of a written composition that consists of one or more sentences, deals with one point, or gives the words of one speaker, usually beginning with an indented line.

participle a verb form used as an adjective, for example, **the skating party**.

personification a figure of speech in which animals, ideas, or things take on human characteristics.

persuasive writing a composition intended to persuade the reader to adopt the writer's point of view.

phoneme the smallest sound unit of speech, for example, the /k/ in **book**.

phonemic awareness the ability to recognize that spoken words are made up of discrete sounds and that those sounds can be manipulated.

phonetic spelling the respelling of entry words in a dictionary according to a pronunciation key.

phonetics the study of speech sounds.

phonics a way of teaching reading that addresses sound/symbol relationships, especially in beginning instruction.

phonogram a letter or symbol that represents a phonetic sound.

plot the literary element that provides the structure of the action of a story, which may include rising action, climax, and falling action leading to a resolution or denouement.

plural a grammatical form of a word that refers to more than one in number; an **irregular plural** is one that does not follow normal patterns for inflectional endings.

poetic license the liberty taken by writers to ignore conventions.

poetry a metrical form of composition in which language is chosen and arranged to create a powerful response through meaning, sound, or rhythm.

possessive showing ownership either through the use of an adjective, an adjectival pronoun, or the possessive form of a noun.

predicate the part of the sentence that expresses something about the subject and includes the verb phrase; a **complete predicate** includes the principal verb in a sentence and all its modifiers or subordinate parts.

predicting a comprehension strategy in which the reader attempts to figure out what will happen and then confirms predictions as the text is read.

prefix an affix attached before a base word that changes the meaning of the word.

preposition a part of speech in the class of function words, such as **of**, **on**, **at**, that precede noun phrases to create prepositional phrases.

prewriting the planning stage of the writing process in which the writer formulates ideas, gathers information, and considers ways to organize them.

print awareness in emergent literacy, a child's growing recognition of conventions and characteristics of written language, including reading from left to right and top to bottom in English, and that words are separated by spaces.

pronoun a part of speech used as a substitute for a noun or noun phrase.

proofreading the act of reading with the intent to correct, clarify, or improve text.

pseudonym an assumed name used by an author, a pen name or nom de plume.

publishing the process of preparing written material for presentation.

punctuation graphic marks such as comma, period, quotation marks, and brackets used to clarify meaning and give speech characteristics to written language.

question an interrogative sentence that asks a question and ends with a question mark.

realistic fiction a story that attempts to portray characters and events as they actually are.

rebus the use of a picture or symbol to suggest a word or syllable.

revise in the writing process, to change or correct a manuscript to make its message more clear.

rhyme identical or very similar recurring final sounds in words, often at the ends of lines of poetry.

rime a vowel and any following consonants of a syllable.

segmentation the ability to break words into individual sounds; **see also oral blending**.

semantic mapping a graphic display of a group of words that are meaningfully related to support vocabulary instruction.

semantics the study of meaning in language, including the meanings of words, phrases, sentences, and texts.

sentence a grammatical unit that expresses a statement, question, or command; a **simple sentence** is a sentence with one subject and one predicate; a **compound sentence** is a sentence with two or more independent clauses usually separated by a comma and conjunction, but no dependent clause; a **complex sentence** is a sentence with one independent and one or more dependent clauses.

sentence combining a teaching technique in which complex sentence chunks and paragraphs are built from basic sentences.

sentence lifting the process of using sentences from children's writing to illustrate what is wrong or right to develop children's editing and proofreading skills.

sequence the order of elements or events.

setting the literary element that includes the time, place, and physical and psychological background in which a story takes place.

sight word a word that is taught to be read as a whole word, usually words that are phonetically irregular.

simile a figure of speech in which a comparison of two things that are unlike is directly stated usually with the words **like** or **as**, for example, **She is like a jewel**.

spelling the process of representing language by means of a writing system.

statement a sentence that tells something and ends with a period.

study skills a general term for the techniques and strategies that help readers comprehend text with the intent to remember, includes following directions, organizing, locating, and using graphic aids.

style the characteristics of a work that reflect the author's particular way of writing.

subject the main topic of a sentence to which a predicate refers, including the principal noun; a **complete subject** includes the principal noun in a sentence and all its modifiers..

suffix an affix attached at the end of a base word that changes the meaning of the word.

summarizing a comprehension strategy in which the reader constructs a brief statement that contains the essential ideas of a passage.

syllable a minimal unit of sequential speech sounds comprised of a vowel sound or a vowel-sound combination.

symbolism the use of one thing to represent something else in order to represent an idea in a concrete way.

synonym a word that means the same as another word.

syntax the grammatical pattern or structure of word order in sentences, clauses, and phrases.

tense the way in which verbs indicate past, present, and future time of action.

text structure the various patterns of ideas that are built into the organization of a written work.

theme a major idea or proposition that provides an organizing concept through which by study, students gain depth of understanding.

topic sentence a sentence intended to express the main idea of a paragraph or passage.

tragedy a literary work, often a play, in which the main character suffers conflicts and which presents a serious theme and has an unfortunate ending.

usage the way in which a native language or dialect is used by the members of the community.

verb a word that expresses an action or state that occurs in a predicate of a sentence; an **irregular verb** is a verb that does not follow normal patterns of inflectional endings that reflect past, present, or future verb tense.

visualizing a comprehension strategy in which the reader constructs a mental picture of a character, setting, or process.

vowel a voiced speech sound and the alphabet letter that represents that sound, made without stoppage or friction of the air flow as it passes through the vocal tract.

vowel digraph a spelling pattern in which two or more letters represent a single vowel sound.

word calling proficiency in decoding with little or no attention to word meaning.

writing also **composition** the process or result of organizing ideas in writing to form a clear message, includes persuasive, expository, narrative, and descriptive forms.

writing process the many aspects of the complex act of producing a piece of writing, including prewriting, drafting, revising, proofreading, and publishing.

Scope and Sequence

Reading

Level	K-A	K-B	K-C	K-D	K-E	1-A	1-B	1-C	1-1	1-2	2-1	2-2	3-1	3-2	4	5	6
Print/Book Awareness (Recognize and understand the conventions of print and books)																	
Capitalization			✔		✔	✔	✔	✔	✔								
Constancy of Words																	
End Punctuation			✔			✔	✔	✔	✔								
Follow Left-to-right, Top-to-bottom																	
Letter Recognition and Formation	✔				✔	✔	✔	✔	✔	✔							
Page Numbering																	
Picture/Text Relationship			✔	✔													
Quotation Marks																	
Relationship Between Spoken and Printed Language																	
Sentence Recognition																	
Table of Contents																	
Word Length																	
Word Boundaries																	
Phonemic Awareness (Recognize discrete sounds in words)																	
Oral Blending: Words/Word Parts				✔			✔										
Oral Blending: Initial Consonants/Blends					✔		✔										
Oral Blending: Final Consonants			✔		✔		✔										
Oral Blending: Initial Vowels																	
Oral Blending: Syllables								✔		✔							
Oral Blending: Vowel Replacement																	
Segmentation: Initial Consonants/Blends																	
Segmentation: Final Consonants																	
Segmentation: Initial Vowels						✔	✔										
Segmentation: Words/Word Parts																	
Rhyming						✔											
How the Alphabet Works																	
Letter Knowledge						✔											
Letter Order	✔					✔	✔										
Sounds in Words						✔	✔	✔	✔	✔							
Letter Sounds					✔	✔	✔										
Phonics (Associate sounds and spellings to read words)																	
Blending Sounds into Words							✔										
Consonant Clusters									✔	✔							
Consonant Digraphs							✔						✔				
Consonant Sounds and Spellings						✔											
Phonograms							✔										
Syllables										✔							
Vowel Diphthongs								✔	✔	✔							
Vowels: Long Sounds and Spellings					✔			✔	✔	✔							
Vowels: *r*-controlled							✔		✔								
Vowels: Short Sounds and Spellings						✔	✔	✔	✔	✔							

  Skills, strategies, and other teaching opportunities
✔ Formal or informal testing opportunities

Reading (continued)

Level	K-A	K-B	K-C	K-D	K-E	1-A	1-B	1-C	1-1	1-2	2-1	2-2	3-1	3-2	4	5	6
Comprehension Strategies (Self-monitoring techniques)																	
Asking Questions/Answering Questions																	
Clarifying																	
Predicting/Confirming Predictions																	
Making Connections																	
Summarizing																	
Visualizing																	
Comprehension Skills (Deciphering the meaning of text)																	
Author's Point of View											✔	✔	✔	✔	✔	✔	✔
Author's Purpose											✔	✔	✔	✔	✔	✔	✔
Cause/Effect				✔				✔			✔	✔	✔	✔	✔	✔	✔
Classify/Categorize				✔			✔				✔	✔	✔	✔	✔	✔	✔
Compare and Contrast			✔			✔						✔	✔	✔	✔	✔	
Draw Conclusions			✔			✔						✔	✔	✔	✔		✔
Fact/Opinion											✔	✔	✔	✔	✔	✔	✔
Main Idea and Details											✔	✔	✔	✔	✔	✔	✔
Making Inferences											✔	✔	✔	✔	✔	✔	✔
Reality/Fantasy											✔						
Sequencing								✔							✔	✔	✔
Vocabulary																	
Antonyms					✔	✔					✔	✔			✔	✔	
Comparatives/Superlatives										✔	✔				✔	✔	
Compound Words								✔			✔	✔			✔	✔	✔
Connecting Words																	
Context Clues											✔	✔	✔	✔	✔	✔	✔
Contractions																	
High-Frequency Words	✔				✔			✔			✔						
Homophones/Homonyms												✔		✔	✔	✔	✔
Idioms																	
Inflectional Endings								✔	✔				✔		✔		
Irregular Plurals								✔		✔	✔		✔		✔	✔	✔
Multiple Meaning Words															✔	✔	✔
Multisyllabic Words																	
Position Words				✔	✔												
Prefixes										✔	✔		✔		✔	✔	✔
Question Words																	
Root Words															✔	✔	✔
Selection Vocabulary	✔	✔	✔	✔	✔	✔	✔	✔	✔	✔	✔	✔	✔	✔	✔	✔	✔
Suffixes								✔	✔	✔	✔		✔		✔	✔	✔
Synonyms		✔					✔						✔		✔	✔	✔
Time and Order Words (Creating Sequence)				✔				✔			✔						
Utility Words (Body Parts, Colors, Common Classroom Objects, Days of the Week, Time of Day, Weather Words)			✔						✔	✔							
Word Families															✔	✔	✔

Scope and Sequence

Writing/Composition

Level	K-A	K-B	K-C	K-D	K-E	1-A	1-B	1-C	1-1	1-2	2-1	2-2	3-1	3-2	4	5	6
Approaches																	
Collaborative Writing																	
Group Writing																	
Process																	
Prewriting																	
Drafting																	
Revising																	
Proofreading																	✔
Publishing																	
Forms																	
Biography/Autobiography															✔	✔	✔
Describe a Process											✔			✔	✔	✔	✔
Descriptive Writing																	
Expository															✔	✔	✔
Folklore (Folktales, Fairy Tales, Tall Tales, Legends, Myths)															✔	✔	✔
Historical Fiction															✔	✔	✔
Informational Text															✔	✔	✔
Journal Writing																	
Letter Writing																	
Narrative																	
Personal Narrative																	
Persuasive Writing															✔	✔	✔
Play/Dramatization																	
Poetry																	

Skills, strategies, and other teaching opportunities

✔ Formal or informal testing opportunities

Writing/Composition (continued)

Level	K-A	K-B	K-C	K-D	K-E	1-A	1-B	1-C	1-1	1-2	2-1	2-2	3-1	3-2	4	5	6
Writer's Craft																	
Characterization			✔				✔	✔				✔		✔	✔	✔	✔
Descriptive Writing											✔	✔	✔	✔	✔	✔	✔
Dialogue																	✔
Effective Beginnings											✔	✔		✔	✔	✔	✔
Effective Endings																	
Event Sequence																	✔
Figurative Language							✔				✔			✔	✔	✔	✔
Identifying Thoughts and Feelings																	
Mood and Tone																	
Plot (Problem/Solutions)				✔				✔			✔			✔	✔	✔	✔
Point of View																	✔
Rhyme	✔					✔					✔						
Setting			✔					✔			✔		✔		✔	✔	✔
Suspense and Surprise																	
Topic Sentences											✔	✔	✔	✔	✔	✔	✔
Using Comparisons																	
Purposes																	
Determining Purposes for Writing																	✔

Scope and Sequence

Integrated Language Arts

Level	K-A	K-B	K-C	K-D	K-E	1-A	1-B	1-C	1-1	1-2	2-1	2-2	3-1	3-2	4	5	6
Grammar																	
Parts of Speech																	
Adjectives			✔							✔	✔	✔			✔		✔
Adverbs															✔		✔
Conjunctions											✔				✔	✔	✔
Nouns					✔			✔		✔	✔		✔	✔	✔	✔	✔
Prepositions					✔										✔		
Pronouns								✔		✔	✔		✔	✔	✔	✔	✔
Verbs		✔								✔		✔			✔	✔	✔
Sentences																	
Parts (Subjects/Predicates)											✔		✔	✔	✔	✔	✔
Structure (Simple, Compound, Complex)							✔					✔			✔	✔	✔
Types (Declarative, Interrogative, Exclamatory, Imperative)					✔		✔				✔		✔	✔	✔	✔	✔
Verb Tenses										✔			✔	✔	✔	✔	✔
Verbs (Action, Helping, Linking, Regular/Irregular)												✔			✔		
Usage																	
Adjectives			✔										✔	✔	✔	✔	✔
Adverbs													✔	✔	✔	✔	✔
Nouns					✔			✔					✔	✔	✔	✔	✔
Pronouns								✔					✔	✔	✔	✔	✔
Verbs		✔			✔			✔			✔	✔	✔	✔	✔	✔	✔
Mechanics																	
Capitalization (Sentence, Proper Nouns, Titles, Direct Address, Pronoun *I*)			✔		✔			✔							✔	✔	✔
Punctuation (End punctuation, comma use, quotation marks, apostrophe, colon, semicolon, hyphen, parentheses)			✔					✔	✔		✔				✔	✔	✔
Spelling																	
Contractions								✔					✔	✔			✔
Inflectional Endings								✔				✔	✔	✔		✔	
Irregular Plurals								✔				✔			✔	✔	✔
Long Vowel Patterns								✔			✔					✔	✔
Multisyllabic Words																	
Phonograms																	
r-controlled Vowel Spellings							✔				✔						
Short Vowel Spellings																	
Sound/Letter Relationships						✔	✔	✔	✔	✔							
Special Spelling Patterns (*-ough, -augh, -all, -al, -alk, -ion, -sion, -tion*)																	
Listening/Speaking/Viewing																	
Listening/Speaking																	
Analyze and evaluate intent and content of Speaker's Message																	
Answer Questions																	
Compare Language and Oral Traditions																	

☐ Skills, strategies, and other teaching opportunities
✔ Formal or informal testing opportunities

Integrated Language Arts (continued)

Level	K-A	K-B	K-C	K-D	K-E	1-A	1-B	1-C	1-1	1-2	2-1	2-2	3-1	3-2	4	5	6
Listening/Speaking (continued)																	
Determine Purposes for Listening																	
Follow Directions																	
Learn about Different Cultures through Discussion																	
Listen for Poetic Language (Rhythm/Rhyme)																	
Participate in Group Discussions																	
Respond to Speaker																	
Speaking																	
Compare Language and Oral Traditions																	
Conduct Interviews/Surveys																	
Describe Ideas and Feelings																	
Give Directions																	
Learn about Different Cultures through Discussion																	
Participate in Group Discussions																	
Present Oral Reports																	
Read Fluently with Expression, Phrasing and Intonation																	
Read Orally																	
Share Information																	
Summarize/Retell Stories																	
Use Appropriate Vocabulary for Audience																	
Viewing																	
Appreciate/Interpret Artists' Techniques																	
Compare Visual and Written Material on the Same Subject																	
Gather Information from Visual Images																	
View Critically																	
View Culturally Rich Materials																	
Inquiry & Research/Study Skills																	
Charts, Graphs, and Diagrams/Visual Aids										✔		✔	✔	✔	✔	✔	✔
Compile Notes																	
Follow Directions																	
Formulate Questions for Inquiry and Research																	
Give Reports																	
Make Outlines																	
Maps and Globes												✔	✔	✔	✔	✔	✔
Note Taking											✔		✔	✔	✔	✔	✔
Parts of a Book											✔		✔				
Summarize and Organize Information																	
Time Lines												✔	✔	✔	✔	✔	✔
Use Appropriate Resources (Media Source, Reference Books, Experts, Internet)											✔		✔	✔	✔	✔	✔
Using a Dictionary/Glossary												✔			✔	✔	✔
Using a Media Center/Library										✔	✔			✔	✔	✔	✔
Using an Encyclopedia										✔				✔	✔	✔	✔
Using Newspapers and Magazines																	
Using Visual Aids																	

Level 5 Index

Level 5 Index (continued)

Program Appendix

Program Appendix

Program Appendix

Level 5 Index (continued)

H

I

Program Appendix

Program Appendix

Program Appendix

Level 5 Index (continued)

Level 5 Index (continued)

Classroom Library Acknowledgments (*continued*)

Notes

Use this page to record lessons or elements that work well
or need to be adjusted for future reference.

Lessons that work well.

Lessons that need adjustments.

Open Court Reading

Program Evaluation

As part of SRA's interest in updating and improving our curricula, we ask that you take a few moments to complete this questionnaire and return it to us.

You can tear this page out, fold and seal it with the address showing, or you may feel free to add additional comments, using another piece of paper and your own envelope.

We look forward to your comments and suggestions.

Sincerely,
SRA/McGraw-Hill

Your name _____ **Grade Level Reviewed** _____

Your title _____ **Date** _____

School _____

Address _____

City _____ **State** _____ **Zip** _____

1. How long have you been teaching *Open Court Reading?* _____

2. What do you consider to be *Open Court Reading's* strongest features? _____
_____
_____

3. What do you consider to be *Open Court Reading's* weakest features? _____
_____
_____

4. Do the lessons provide appropriate information for teaching each literature selection? _____

5. Is the phonics lesson material clear and helpful? _____

6. Is the instruction for comprehension skills and strategies clear and helpful? _____

7. Are the language arts skills materials clear and helpful? _____

8. Are the unit themes and activities appropriate and useful? _____

9. Are you satisfied with the achievement of your class using *Open Court Reading?* _____

10. What specific changes, if any, would you like to see in the next edition of *Open Court Reading?* _____
_____
_____

11. Is the pacing of each lesson appropriate? _____
_____
_____

12. How would you compare *Open Court Reading* with other reading programs you have taught? _____
_____
_____
_____

Additional comments

_____
_____
_____
_____

BUSINESS REPLY MAIL
FIRST-CLASS MAIL   PERMIT NO 4168   COLUMBUS OH

POSTAGE WILL BE PAID BY ADDRESSEE

SRA MCGRAW HILL
8787 ORION PL
COLUMBUS OH 43240 - 9915